1 MONTH OF
FREE
READING

at

www.ForgottenBooks.com

By purchasing this book you are eligible for one month membership to ForgottenBooks.com, giving you unlimited access to our entire collection of over 1,000,000 titles via our web site and mobile apps.

To claim your free month visit:

www.forgottenbooks.com/free1202468

ISBN 978-0-331-50639-6
PIBN 11202468

THE CANADIAN
ANNUAL REVIEW

OF

PUBLIC AFFAIRS

BY

J. CASTELL HOPKINS, F.S.S., F.R.G.S.

1919

NINETEENTH YEAR OF ISSUE

ILLUSTRATED

TORONTO:

THE CANADIAN ANNUAL REVIEW, LIMITED

1920

Warwick Bros. & Rutter, Limited
Printers and Bookbinders
Toronto

WITH RESPECT AND ESTEEM

THIS VOLUME

IS

INSCRIBED

TO

SIR FREDERICK WILLIAMS-TAYLOR, D.C.L.

A Banker whose keen vision, financial knowledge, and an experience gained in the capital of the Empire as well as in the
commercial metropolis of Canada has enabled him to embody
the highest traditions of his institution and his profession; a Canadian whose financial position and
personal patriotism were substantial elements
in conserving, developing and utilizing the
national wealth of Canada for
service in the great cause of
Empire and Liberty in the
World War.

BY

THE AUTHOR.

PREFACE

This issue of THE CANADIAN ANNUAL REVIEW deals with developments of a constitutional and international character which make the facts narrated the most important to Canada of any in its nineteen years of publication. Hence the consideration given in its pages to such subjects as the Peace Conference, International Labour, League of Nations, Empire conditions and Foreign relations. Ever since the REVIEW was started in 1901 I have felt that Canada had entered the 20th Century with a pending and inevitable evolution into Empire and world politics, and each of these 19 volumes has had a specific space allotted to this development; to-day Canada is one of a group of British nations belting the world with a power for peace and progress which will be effective in just the degree which their spirit of Imperial Co-operation warrants and as it makes for permanence.

Locally, the growth of the Farmers' movement, the developments in Labour, Industry and Education, and the visit of the Prince of Wales, made the year a vital one to the interests of the individual Canadian. The bulk of the book is great and the effort involved in its preparation too heavy to indicate here; the value of the work can, perhaps, be tested by the feelings of Canadian Archivists, of the many historical specialists delving into the past under Government supervision, of the speakers, students and journalists of to-day, if they suddenly came across the 19 volumes of a similar work for the years 1800-1819!

J. CASTELL HOPKINS.

An Official Map of the Western Front when the Hindenburg Line was broken through by the British and Canadian Forces—by Courtesy of Field Marshal Lord Haig to the Author. The point where troops are thickest on both sides is the British-German front.

A Belgian Army.
B British Army.
C French Army.
D American Army.
E German Army.

TABLE OF CONTENTS

CANADIAN ECHOES OF THE WORLD WAR

	PAGE
International War Conditions, Statistics and Summaries	17
International Casualties of the War	18
British Shipping and Other Statistics	20
Canadian Military Incidents and War Memories	20
Canada's 70 Generals in the War	21
Canadian War Work and Military Strength	23
Canadian Enlistments, Defaulters and Exemptions	24
The McAvity Case in New Brunswick	26
Canadian Victoria Cross Winners	27
Special War Services and Honours	28
War Incidents and Events of the Year	30
Safeguarding the Graves of Canada's Dead	31
General Sir Arthur Currie; His Return to Canada and Public Reception.	33
Attack by Sir Sam Hughes; Replies by Officers	34
The General in England; Reviews and Incidents	36
General Currie's Speeches in England	37
Parliamentary Recognition; Speeches and a Resolution	38
Canadians and the Victory Parade in London	39
The General's Reception and Speeches in Canada	41
Return of the Troops; Disturbances in England; Canadians in Russia. .	45
Troubles of the Waiting Troops—Kinmel, Epsom, Witley	46
Canada's Welcome to its Soldiers	49
Canadians in Russia; Services and Quick Return	52
Military Charges and Complaints	54
Argyll House and the Minister's Report	56
War Organizations; War Memorial Proposals; War-Time Incidents of 1919	57
The Canadian Red Cross Society	58
The Canadian Patriotic Fund	60
War Memorials and Canadian Archives	61
Military Incidents of the Year	62
Who Won the War? An Important Discussion of the Year	63
American Battles in the War	64
Comparative Costs in the War	66
Comparison as to Men, Casualties and Naval Power	67
The Dominant Fact in Victory	68

CANADIAN RELATIONS WITH FOREIGN COUNTRIES

The Making of Peace; Canada's Share in a Great Event	70
The British Dominions and the Versailles Conference	70
Preliminary Constitutional Discussion	71
Meeting of the World Peace Conference	73

PAGE

President Wilson and Mr. Lloyd George 74
The Canadian Premier's Part in the Conference 76
Discussions regarding German Colonies 77
The Dominions to Sign the Treaty 78
The Canadian Premier returns Home 80
Terms and Signatories of the Treaty of Versailles 82
The Treaties with Austria and Bulgaria 85
The League of Nations; Position of Canada and the Dominions 87
Presentation and Discussion of the Plan 87
The Covenant of the League 88
Representation of the British Dominions 92
Rejection of the League by the U.S. Senate 95
The Peace Treaty and the World's Labour Interests 98
Parliamentary Approval of the Treaty and the League of Nations 99
The Constitutional Issue of Ratification at Ottawa 100
Canada and the Making of the Treaty 101
The National Status of Canada Discussed 104
Relations of Canada and Great Britain with the United States 109
American Influence in Canada 111
British and American Relations 111
The Pan-American Union and Canada 113
Fisheries Treaty between Canada and United States 114
Canadian Representation at Washington 115
United States Visitors; Reciprocity and Other Incidents 115
International Waterway and Power Questions 118
The Canadian Deep Waterways and Power Association 120
The International Joint Commission 122
International Incidents of the Year 122
United States Control of British Cables and Press News 123

CANADIAN RELATIONS WITH THE EMPIRE

The British Empire in 1919; Its Unity and Problems 127
Princess Patricia's Wedding 131
The King's Representative in Canada 132
Lord Milner and the Dominions 135
Discussion of Canada's National Status 137
Judicial Committee of the Privy Council 140
Empire Incidents of the Year 143
Eminent British Visitors to Canada 148
The Imperial Preference Question and British Action 149
The New British Policy of 1919 150
Opposition of British Free Trade Liberals 151
Empire Opinion of the Policy 153
New Regulations and Empire Trade Support 155
Titles in Canada; Government Policy and Parliamentary Action 157
Hereditary Titles in Canada 157
Knighthood in Principle and Practice 158
Character of the Movement against Titles 160

CONTENTS

PAGE

Parliamentary Discussion; Titles and Democracy 160
The Press and the Titles Discussion 164
Discussion and Conclusions of the Titles Committee 164
Debate in Parliament on Address to the King 166
Further Comments of the Press 170
British Honours and Canadian Incidents 171
Foreign Decorations of the Year 172
Questions of Independence or Separation from the Empire 173
Naval Problems and Conditions; The Navy League of Canada 178
United States Naval Plans 180
The Canadian Government's Naval Policy 181
Canadian Merchant Shipping and Marine 183
The Work of the Navy League of Canada in 1919 186
Canadian Visit and Speeches of Admiral, Lord Jellicoe 192
Lord Jellicoe's Report on his Naval Mission to Canada 199
The Naval Requirements of Canada 200
Administration of Naval Services 201
Proposed Personnel of the Royal Canadian Navy 203
The Question of Discipline 204
Britain in 1919: After-War Reconstruction and Recovery 204
The British Financial Situation in 1919 205
The British Commercial Situation in 1919 207
British Political Matters of Empire Import 208
Mr. Asquith and British Liberal Policy 211
British Incidents of the Year 213
Ireland: Dissensions and Disorders of 1919 213
The General Condition of Ireland in 1919 214
Progress of the Sinn Fein Movement 217
The Church and the People of Ireland 221
American-Irish Envoys in Ireland 222
The Irish Problem and the United States 224
Ireland and the Viewpoint of Ulster 229
British Policy and Proposals for Ireland 231
Canadian-Irish Opinions and Action 236
India in 1919; Constitutional Reform and Nationalism 238
Disorder, Agitations, and Conflicts of 1919 240
Mr. Montagu's Constitutional Act 242
South Africa in 1919; The Separationist Campaign 244
General Smuts and the League of Nations 245
The Nationalist Movement in South Africa 246
Government Changes and Political Issues 249
Australian Conditions and Elections of 1919 252
The Government and Policy of W. M. Hughes 253
The General Elections of 1919 256
Australian Conditions and Statistics 257
Australian Incidents of the Year 258
Relations with or Conditions in, Other Empire Countries 258
Politics and Changes of Government in Newfoundland 259

PAGE

Resources and Progress of Newfoundland 261
Newfoundland Incidents of the Year 262
New Zealand Leaders at Versailles and in Canada 263
Political Changes and Elections in New Zealand 264
New Zealand Incidents of the Year 265
Importance of the West Indies to Canada 266

THE PRINCE OF WALES IN CANADA

The Prince's Tour of Canada; His Welcome, Personality and Speeches... 272
Preliminaries of the Royal Visit 273
Arrival of the Prince; Welcome to Canadian Shores 276
The Royal Reception at Quebec 280
The Prince of Wales in Toronto 282
National Reception at Ottawa; Welcome at Montreal 285
Northern Ontario and the Gateway of the West 290
The Prince on the Prairies: A Western Welcome 293
The Prince on the Pacific Coast 297
From the Rocky Mountains to Winnipeg 300
Ontario Tour of the Prince 303
The Royal Visit to Montreal 307
Farewell Visit and Speech in Toronto 311
Farewell Speech at Ottawa 313
The Prince of Wales in the United States 314
Arrival at Halifax; Farewell to Canada 318

AGRICULTURE: THE ORGANIZED FARMERS

Agricultural Conditions: Wheat and Dairying, Prices and the Farmer.. 321
The Canadian Farmer as a Class 323
The Government and the Canadian Farmer 327
The Farmer and Government Price Policy 333
The Farmer and the Rise in Prices 337
Relation of the Farmer and the Consumer 340
General Interests of the Canadian Farmer in 1919 349
The Organized Farmer: Origin and History of the Western Movement.. 354
Organization in Saskatchewan, Manitoba, Alberta 354
Founding of The Grain Growers' Guide 357
Organization of the Grain Growers' Grain Co., Ltd. 358
Co-operative Organization in Saskatchewan and Alberta 360
The United Grain Growers Ltd. 362
The Canadian Council of Agriculture 364
The Women's Farm Organizations 370
The Pioneer Farmers' Organization—The Grange 373
The Patrons of Industry in Ontario 375
The Non-Partisan League in Canada and the States 377
Formation of the United Farmers of Ontario 380
The Grain Growers Enter Politics 382

PAGE

THE 1919 RECORD OF FARMERS' ORGANIZATIONS

The Canadian Council of Agriculture 389
The Saskatchewan Grain Growers' Association 390
The United Farmers of Alberta 392
The Manitoba Grain Growers' Association 395
The United Grain Growers Limited 397
United Farmers in Other Provinces 397
The United Farmers of Ontario 398
The United Farm Women of Ontario 402
The United Farmers' Co-operative Co., Ltd. 402

INDUSTRY: THE ORGANIZED MANUFACTURERS

The Industrial Situation: Manufacturers and the Country 404
Progress of the Greater Manufacturing Industries 410
Manufacturers and the 1919 Problems of Prices and Values 422
    The Cost of Living Commissioner and the Manufacturer 424
    The Parliamentary Enquiry and the Manufacturers 426
    Manufacturers, Retailers and the Board of Commerce 427
Scientific Research: Its Influence upon Canadian Industry 430
The Canadian Manufacturers' Association in 1919 435
The Tariff: Attitude of the Organized Manufacturers 440
    The Canadian Reconstruction Association 443
Proceedings of the Alberta Industrial Congress 444

LABOUR: THE ORGANIZED WORKMEN

Socialism and Labour: The I.W.W., Bolshevism and the O.B.U. 447
    Socialism in the United States and Canada 447
    The I.W.W. in the United States 449
    Bolshevism in its 1919 Developments 451
    The One Big Union in Canada 456
    The Winnipeg Strike: The O.B.U. Defeated 460
    Echoes of the Strike: The Sedition Trial 477
    Echoes of the Strike: In Winnipeg 484
    Echoes of the Winnipeg Strike: Trouble Elsewhere 486
    After the Winnipeg Strike: The O.B.U. 491
Organizations in Canada: The Trades and Labour Congress 495
    Policy of the Trades and Labour Congress 495
    The United Mine Workers of America 500
    The Canadian Federation of Labour and Other Organizations 501
The Government and Labour: The Royal Commission and Industrial
    Conference 503
    The Royal Commission on Industrial Relations 506
    The National Industrial Conference 509
Canada and International Labour Conferences of 1919 514
    The United States Industrial Conference 514
    International Labour Conference at Washington 515

PAGE

EDUCATIONAL INTERESTS AND INSTITUTIONS

Educational Problems and Conditions: Education in the Provinces 520
   The General Educational Situation 520
   Educational Problems of the 'Day 521
   Separate Schools in Canada 523
   The National Conference on Education 526
   Technical Education in Canada 530
   Educational Issues and Conditions in Ontario 531
   Quebec and Compulsory Education 539
   Schools in the Maritime Provinces 544
   Education in Manitoba During 1919 547
   Educational Conditions in Saskatchewan 549
   Educational Conditions in Alberta 554
   Education in British Columbia During 1919 558
The Universities and Colleges of Canada in 1919 558
   The University of Toronto in 1919 563
   McGill University, Montreal, in 1919 565
   Queen's University, Kingston, in 1919 567
   Laval University—The University of Montreal 569
   The Four Western Universities 571
   Dalhousie and the Maritime Universities 575
   Other Canadian Universities and Colleges 576

DOMINION GOVERNMENT AND POLITICS

Sir Robert Borden as Prime Minister in 1919 578
Changes in the Government; Incidents of Administration 581
The Militia Department and General Mewburn's Policy 592
Reconstruction Plans; Pensions and Land Settlements 595
Political Conditions in 1919: Position of the Liberal Party 600
The Liberal Convention of 1919: Mackenzie King as Party Leader..... 603
Dominion Parliament and Legislation; Bye-Elections of the Year 610
Political Affairs and Incidents: The G.W.V.A. and I.O.D.E. 617
   The Great War Veterans and Other Military Bodies 618
   The Imperial Order, Daughters of the Empire 622
Canadian Railway Policy and Conditions in 1919 625

THE PROVINCE OF ONTARIO IN 1919

The Hearst Government: The Legislature and Political Affairs 631
   Departmental Reports and Statistical Detail 632
   The 1919 Session of the Legislature 637
   Prohibition and Mr. McGarry's Budget 642
   Opposition Policy and Government Appointments 644
General Elections in Ontario: Defeat of the Hearst Government 647
   The Government Policy in the Campaign 648
   The Liberal Policy in the Campaign 651
   The Farmers and the Campaign 655
   The Labour Party in the Campaign 657

Prohibition, Soldiers, Women, in the Election 659
Result of the Elections 661
Formation and Policy of the Drury Government 666
The Hydro-Electric Situation and Radial Railway Policy ...:......... 670
Ontario Incidents of 1919 676

QUEBEC AND THE MARITIME PROVINCES

General Conditions in Quebec: Politics and Legislation in 1919 677
    The 1st Legislative Session of 1919 681
    The Quebec Prohibition Bill of 1919 686
The Gouin Government and the Electoral Victory of 1919........... 689
    The Meeting of the New Legislature 694
Progress and Politics in Nova Scotia during 1919 695
    The Government and Departmental Reports 697
    The Meeting of the Nova Scotia Legislature 699
    Nova Scotian Incidents of the Year 704
Development and Public Affairs in New Brunswick during 1919 ...).. 705
    The Foster Government and Provincial Policy 707
    The New Brunswick Legislature in 1919 712
    Prohibition, Finances, Politics in New Brunswick 714
Conditions and Affairs in P. E. Island; The Provincial Elections 722
    Government and Legislation in the Island ...:................. 723
    The General Elections of 1919 725

THE WESTERN PROVINCES AND BRITISH COLUMBIA

Manitoba: Its Progress, Government, Politics and Legislation in 1919.. 728
    Provincial, Administrative and Departmental Affairs 730
    The 1919 Session of Legislature 738
    Other Affairs and Incidents of the Year 744
Alberta: Progress, Government, Politics and Legislation in 1919 746
    The Stewart Government and Policy in 1919 752
    The 1919 Session of the Legislature 761
    Prohibition, Railways and Other Alberta Questions 766
Saskatchewan: Its Progress, Administration, Legislation and Affairs.. 772
    Agricultural Conditions and the Department of Agriculture 772
    The Martin Government and Political Conditions 777
    Meeting and Enactments of the Legislature 783
British Columbia: Progress, Government and Legislation 787
The North-West Territories 797
The Territory of the Yukon 797
Canadian Obituary for 1919 798
Index to Names 933
Index of Affairs 943

SPECIAL SUPPLEMENT

A Great Canadian Institution; The Canadian Pacific Railway in 1919: Annual Reports and the First Addresses of E. W. Beatty, K.C., LL.D., as President of the Company 805

Canada's Financial Position in 1919; Annual Addresses of Sir Edmund Walker and Sir John Aird; Reports of the Canadian Bank of Commerce 816

Canada's Position after the War; Addresses by Sir Frederick Williams-Taylor and Sir Vincent Meredith; Reports of the Bank of Montreal 827

Canadian Conditions and Progress; Addresses of C. E. Neill, Sir Herbert Holt and E. L. Pease; Annual Report of the Royal Bank of Canada 842

An Important Banking Institution; Addresses by Sir Montagu Allan and D. C. Mararow; Annual Reports of the Merchants Bank of Canada 856

A Record of Great Progress. Addresses by Clarence A. Bogert and Sir Edmund Osler; Annual Reports of the Dominion Bank 866

A Great Insurance Institution. Address of Herbert C. Cox and Annual Reports of the Canada Life Assurance Company 876

A Remarkable Insurance Record. Annual Report and Statements of the Sun Life Assurance Company of Canada 887

A Prosperous Canadian Institution. Addresses by H. J. Daly and J. Cooper Mason; Annual Reports of the Home Bank of Canada ....., 891

A Leading Canadian Institution. Addresses by Featherstone Osler and A. D. Langmuir; Annual Reports of the Toronto General Trusts' Corporation 898

Canada as a Producer of Motor Cars; Enterprise Reflected at the Overland Factories, Toronto 905

ADVERTISEMENTS

NEWFOUNDLAND: THE NORWAY OF THE NEW WORLD....... 908

THE NATIONAL PARK BANK OF NEW YORK 909

GUTTA PERCHA & RUBBER, LIMITED, Toronto 910

CONFEDERATION LIFE ASSOCIATION 911

WOOD, GUNDY & COMPANY, Toronto ..,........................ 912

A. E. AMES & CO., Toronto 913

LONDON GUARANTEE & ACCIDENT COMPANY, LIMITED....... 914

CANADA PERMANENT MORTGAGE CORPORATION 914

THE NATIONAL CITY COMPANY, LIMITED, Montreal and Toronto 915

WESTERN ASSURANCE COMPANY & BRITISH AMERICA ASSUR-

    ANCE COMPANY 916

THE R. S. WILLIAMS & SONS CO., LIMITED, Toronto 917

CANADIAN GENERAL ELECTRIC CO., LIMITED, Toronto 918

CANADIAN ALLIS-CHALMERS, LIMITED, Toronto 918

DOMINION SECURITIES CORPORATION LIMITED, Toronto 919

CENTRAL CANADA LOAN AND SAVNGS COMPANY, Toronto 919

DOMINION TEXTILE COMPANY, LIMITED, Montreal 920

THOMAS ALLEN, PUBLISHER, Toronto 921

S. B. GUNDY, Toronto 922

THOMAS NELSON & SONS, LIMITED 923

McCLELLAND & STEWART, LIMITED, Toronto 924

THE RYERSON PRESS, Toronto 925

THE GEO. M. HENDRY CO., LTD., Toronto 926

WARWICK BROS. & RUTTER, LIMITED, Toronto 927

CANADA STEAMSHIP LINES, LIMITED, Montreal 928

CANADA STEAMSHIP LINES, LIMITED, Toronto 929

THE CANADIAN PACIFIC RAILWAY—BANFF SPRINGS HOTEL 930

CANADIAN NATIONAL RAILWAYS 931

CANADIAN NATIONAL—GRAND TRUNK RAILWAYS 932

ILLUSTRATIONS

H.R.H. THE PRINCE OF WALES, K.G. M.C., While on His Canadian Tour
of 1919 ....*Frontispiece*

AN OFFICIAL MAP OF THE WESTERN FRONT When the Hindenburg Line
was broken through by the British and Canadian Forces—by Courtesy
of Field Marshal Lord Haig to the Author. The point where troops
are thickest on both sides is the British-German Front 4

FIELD MARSHAL THE EARL HAIG OF BEMERSYDE, K.T., O.M., G.C.V.O.,
Appointed Commander of the British Armies at home in 1919...... 16

RANCHING SCENE near Prince Albert, Sask. 48

SULPHIDE PLANT at Smooth Rock Falls in Northern Ontario 112

FRUIT FARM AND VINEYARD near Fruitland, Niagara District, Ontario.. 160

A WESTERN CANADA OATFIELD—Pilot Mound, Manitoba 208

H. R. H. THE PRINCE OF WALES at Lethbridge, Alberta, 1919 272

H. R. H. THE PRINCE OF WALES Reviewing Kilties, Victoria, B.C., Sept.
24, 1919 272

H. R. H. THE PRINCE OF WALES at Guelph College 304

IRRIGATION SCENE IN SOUTHERN ALBERTA—A part of the great C.P.R.
undertaking in that Province 336

R. W. E. BURNABY, President of the United Farmers' Co-Operative Society of Ontario; Elected in 1919 President of the United Farmers of
Ontario 368

H. W. WOOD, President United Farmers of Alberta and of the Canadian
Council of Agriculture 368

PROFESSOR J. C. McLENNAN, O.B.E., LL.D., Ph.D., D.Sc., F.R.S., University
of Toronto; a Distinguished Canadian Scientist 432

J. MURRAY CLARK, M.A., K.C., LL.D., President of The Royal Canadian
Institute, 1919; a Leader in the Scientific Research Movement and
in that for a United Empire 432

FACTORIES OF GUTTA PERCHA & RUBBER, LIMITED, Toronto, Canada 464

THE VERY REV. WM. R. HARRIS, D.D., LL.D., D.LITT. 528

THE REV. JAMES B. DOLLARD, D.LITT. 528

THE HON. WM. LYON MACKENZIE KING, C.M.G., M.A., M.P., Elected Leader
of the Liberal Party of Canada in 1919 560

THE HON. SIR HENRY LUMLEY DRAYTON, K.C.M.G., M.P., Appointed
Dominion Minister of Finance, 1919 560

PAPER MILL OF THE SPANISH RIVER PULP AND PAPER CO., LTD., at
Espanola in Northern Ontario 624

THE HON. ERNEST CHARLES DRURY, M.L.A., Appointed Prime Minister of
Ontario in 1919 656

THE HON. MANNING WILLIAM DOHERTY, M.L.A., Appointed Minister of
Agriculture for Ontario in 1919 672

THE HON. ROBERT HENRY GRANT, M.L.A., Appointed Minister of Education
for Ontario in 1919 672

THE HON. HONORÉ MERCIER, K.C., M.L.A., Appointed Minister of Lands and Forests for the Province of Quebec in 1919 688

THE HON. WILLIAM EDGAR RANEY, K.C., M.L.A., Appointed Attorney-General of Ontario in 1919 752

ROBERT HENRY HALBERT, President United Farmers of Ontario and elected M.P. for North Ontario, 1919 752

MRS. J. S. WOOD, President of the Women's Section Grain Growers' Association of Manitoba 784

MRS. JOHN MCNAUGHTAN, Four years President Women's Section Saskatchewan Grain Growers' Association 784

MRS. G. A. BRODIE, President of The United Farm Women of Ontario in 1919 784

MRS. WALTER PARLBY, President United Farm Women of Alberta, 1919. 784

WINDSOR STATION AND HEAD OFFICE OF THE CANADIAN PACIFIC RAILWAY, Montreal 805

SIR H. VINCENT MEREDITH, BART., President The Bank of Montreal 826

SIR F. WILLIAMS-TAYLOR, D.C.L., General Manager The Bank of Montreal 826

D. C. MACAROW, General Manager Merchants Bank of Canada 856

THE DOMINION BANK, Toronto 866

MR. H. J. DALY, President of The Home Bank of Canada 892

MR. A. D. LANGMUIR, General Manager of The Toronto General Trusts Corporation 898

THE HANOVER NATIONAL BANK of the City of New York 910

CANADIAN BOOKS IN 1919

HISTORY, POLITICS, BIOGRAPHY, ECONOMICS

British Supremacy and Canadian
　Self Government ....J. L. Morrison, M.A., D.Litt.Toronto:　Oxford Press.
The Constitution of Canada ....Hon. Wm. Renwick Riddell.Toronto:　Oxford Press.
The Unsolved Riddle of Social Jus-
　tice ....Stephen Leacock ....Toronto:　Oxford.
Louisbourg from its Foundation to
　its Fall ....Hon. J. S. McLennan ....Toronto:　Macmillan.
Reconstruction and National Life..C. F. Lavell ....Toronto:　Macmillan.
The State in Peace and War ....Prof. John Watson ....Toronto:　Macmillan.
Canadians in France 1915-18 .....Capt. Harwood Steele ....Toronto:　Copp-Clark.
Politics and the C.A.M.C. ....Dr. Herbert A. Bruce ....Toronto:　Ryerson.
My Three Years in a German
　Prison ....Hon. Henri S. Béland, M.D..Toronto:　Ryerson.
Papers and Records ....Ontario Historical Society..Toronto:　Society.
The Maple Leaf's Red Cross ......Mary Macleod Moore ......London:　Skiffington.
Wake Up, England! ....G. C. Cunningham ......London:　P. S. King.
Cyclopædia of Canadian Biography.(Edited)　Hector　Charles-
　　　　　　　　worth ....Toronto:　Hunter-Rose.
A Labrador Doctor ....W. F. Grenfell, C.M.G. ....London:　Houghton.
Canada's Sons and Great Britain inLieut.-Col. G. C. Nasmith,
　the World War ...............C.M.G. ....Toronto:　Allen.
Reminiscences: Political and Per-
　sonal ....Sir John Willison ....Toronto:　McClelland.
When Canada was New France ....Dr. George H. Locke .....Toronto:　Dent & Sons.
Before the Bar, Prohibition Pro
　and Con ....J. A. Stevenson ....Toronto:　Dent & Sons.
The Birthright ....Arthur Hawkes ....Toronto:　Dent & Sons.
Bridging the Chasm: A Study of
　the Ontario-Quebec Question..P. F. Morley ....Toronto:　Dent & Sons.
Production and Taxation in Canada.W. C. Good ....Toronto:　Dent & Sons.
Labour in the Changing World...R. M. MacIver ....Toronto:　Dent & Sons.
Over the Canadian Battlefields ...John W. Dafoe ....Toronto:　Allen.
The Spider Web: The Romance of
　a Flying-boat ....Major Douglas Hallam ....
Canadian Folk Lore ....A Reprint ....New York:　Am. Folk Lore.
Three Times and Out: An Escape
　from Germany ....Nellie L. McClung ....Toronto:　Allen.
La Drait Paroissial Province du
　Quebec ....Jean F. Pouliot ....Fraserville:　St. Laurent.
Impressions of War ....Hon. Frank Carrel ......Quebec:　Telegraph.
Vanguards of Canada ....Rev. Dr. John Maclean ....Toronto:　Ryerson.
The Official War Story of the C.A.
　M.C. ....Col. J. G. Adami, M.D., F.R.S.Toronto:　Musson.
Industry and Humanity ....Hon. W. L. Mackenzie King.Toronto:　Allen.
The Secret of Heroism ....Hon. W. L. Mackenzie King.Toronto:　Musson.
Sir Wilfrid Laurier ....Peter McArthur ....Toronto:　Dent & Sons.
Pen Pictures from the Trenches...Lieut. Stanley Rutledge ....Toronto:　Ryerson.
Les Petites Choses de Notre His-
　toire ....Pierre Georges Roy ......Lévis:　................
Montréal Sous le Régime Francois..E.-Z. Massicotte ....Montreal:　Ducharme.
Obeservations　sur　L'Histoire　de
　l'Acadie　Francoise　de　M.
　Moreau ....L'Abbé a Couillard-Després.Montreal:
A History of the Military and NavalEdited by the Historical Sec-
　Forces in Canada: Vol. I. The　tion of the General Staff
　Local Forces of New France..　of Canada ....Ottawa:　Government.
The Grey Nuns in the Far North.Father P. Duchaussois, O.M.I.Toronto:　McClelland.
Aviation in Canada, 1917-18 ....Lieut. Alan Sullivan .....Toronto:　Rous and Mann.
Cours d'histoire du Canada, Vol. I.Thomas Chapais ....Quebec:　Garneau.
Histoire du Canada ....L'Abbe Adelard Desrosiers.Montreal:　Beauchemin.
The Canadian Dominion ....Prof. Oscar D. Skelton ...New York:　Glasgow.
Etudes et Appréciations ....Mgr. L. A. Paquet ......Quebec:　Franciscana.
La Mutualité ....Avila Bourbonnière ....Montreal:　Ducharme.
Papers and Records ....Wentworth History Society..Hamilton:　Society.
Conférences, Discours, Lettres ...Cynlle-F. Délage ......Quebec:　Privately Printed.
Handbook for New Canadians ....Alfred Fitzpatrick ....Toronto:　Ryerson.
Andrew Hunter Dunn, 5th Bishop
　of Quebec ....Percival Jolliffe ....London:　S.P.C.K.
Prohibition in Canada: A History
　of the Temperance Movement..Miss R. E. Spence ....Toronto:　The Pioneer.
The Great War in Verse and Prose.(Edited)　J. E. Wetherell.Toronto:　Dept. of Education.

[12]

Melanges Historiques: Etudes,
    éparses et Médites de Benj.
    Sulte, Vols. III.............Geores Machelosse ....Montreal: Ducharme.
Le Sieur de Vincermies and IV...Pierre-Georges Roy ......Quebec: Charrier and Dugal.
The Maseres Lettres 1766-1768 ..(Edited) W. Stewart Wal-
    lace ....Toronto: Oxford Press.
Laurier: Sa vie; Ses œuvres .....Hon. L. O. David ....Beauceville: L'Eclaireur.
Canada at War: A Record of Hero-
    ism and Achievement ....J. Castell Hopkins ......Toronto: Annual Review.
Report of the Ministry: Overseas
    Military Forces of Canada ....Sir Edward Kemp, Minister.Ottawa: Government.
Flag and Fleet: How the British
    Navy won the Freedom of the
    Seas ....William Wood ....Toronto: Macmillan.
Transactions of the London and
    Middlesex Historical Society......................London: Society.
Wake Up, Canada! Reflections on
    Vital National Issues ....C. W. Peterson ....Toronto: Macmillan.
Canada's Hundred Days: With the
    Canadian Corps from Amiens
    to Mons ....J. F. B. Livesay ....Toronto: Allen.
The Canadian Annual Review of
    Public Affairs ....J. Castell Hopkins ....Toronto: Annual Review.
Papers and Records ....Lennox and Addington His-
    torical Society ......Napanee: Society.
Papers and Records ....Kent Historical Society ....Chatham: Society.
Report of the Bureau of Archives,
    Ontario ....(Edited) Dr. Alex. Fraser.Toronto: King's Printer.
National Conference on Education..Report of Proceedings .....Winnipeg: Conference.

FICTION AND NOVELS

Wild Youth and Another ....Sir Gilbert Parker ....Toronto: Copp-Clark.
The Sky Pilot of No Man's Land..Ralph Connor (Rev. Dr. C.
    W. Gordon) ....London: Hodder.
The Man Who Couldn't Sleep....Arthur J. Stringer ....Indianapolis:Bobbs-Merrill.
Drums Afar ....J. Murray Gibbon ....Toronto: John Lane.
Mist of Morning ....Isabel E. MacKay ....Toronto: McClelland.
The River's End ....James Oliver Curwood ....New York: Cosmopolitan.
Embers ....Jeffrey Deprend ....Toronto: Musson.
Love in the Wild ....A. P. McKishnie ....Toronto: Allen.
Janet of Kootenay ....Evah McKowan ....Toronto: McClelland.
Rainbow Valley ....L. M. Montgomery ......Toronto: McClelland.
Joan at Halfway ....Grace McLeod Rogers ....Toronto: McClelland.
Wooden Spoil ....Victor Rosseau ....New York: Doran.
Polly Masson: A Political Novel..William Henry Moore ....Toronto: Dent & Sons.
The Rapids ....Alan Sullivan ....Toronto: Copp-Clark.
The Night Operator ....Frank L. Packard ....Toronto: Copp-Clark.
From Now On ....Frank L. Packard ....Toronto: McClelland.
Bull Dog Carney ....W. A. Fraser ....Toronto: McClelland.
The Touch of Abner ....H. A. Cody ....Toronto: McClelland.
From the Life ....Harvey J. O'Higgins ....New York: Harpers.
The Unknown Wrestler ....H. A. Cody ....Toronto: McClelland.
The Heart of Cherry McBain ....Douglas Durkin ....Toronto: Musson.
Canadian Stories ....George Iles ....Montreal: Witness Press.
The Girl of O.K. Valley ....Robert Watson ....Toronto: McClelland.
Golden Dicky ....Marshall Saunders ......Toronto: McClelland.
Going West ....Basil King ....Toronto: Musson.

POETRY

Vimy Ridge and Other Poems ....Alfred Gordon ....Toronto: Dent & Sons.
Odes to Trifles and Other Rhymes.R. M. Essie ....Toronto: Dent & Sons.
The Ballad of Tsoquiem ....Lionel Hawais ....Vancouver: Citizen Co.
Canadian Poems of the Great War:
    An Anthology ....(Edited) John W. Garvin..Toronto: McClelland.
In Flanders Fields and Other
    Poems ....Lieut.-Col. John McCrae ..New York: Putnam.
Flowers of the Wind ....G. Murray Atkin ......New York: Kennertey.
Leaves of Empire ....W. E. Grant ....Toronto: Ryerson.
Childhood's Paradise ....James L. Hughes, LL.D. ..Toronto: Ryerson.
The Song of the Prairie Land ...Wilson McDonald ....Toronto: McClelland.
The Fighting Men of Canada ....Douglas L. Durkin ......Toronto: McClelland.
Songs of an Airman and Other
    Poems ....Hartley M. Thomas .....Toronto: McClelland.
The Little Marshal ....Owen E. McGillicuddy ...Toronto: Goodchild.
Spun Yarn and Spindrift ....Norah Holland ....Toronto: Dent & Sons.
Irish Poems ....Arthur Stringer ....Toronto: Dent & Sons.
Book of Poems ....Lloyd Roberts ....Toronto: Goodchild.
Leaves in the Wind ....Rev. D. A. Casey ....Toronto: McClelland.
War Poems, Songs and Other Verse.Ebeneser Bain ....Montreal: Privately Printed.
Sitka Spruce: Songs of Queen
    Charlotte Islands ....D. E. Hatt ....

MONOGRAPHS AND PAMPHLETS

Young Man's Parliamentary Guide."M.P." ....Toronto: Macmillan.
The Archievements of a Modest Old
    Gentleman ....F. D. L. Smith ....Toronto: Macmillan.
Service in Banking ....Home Bank of Canada ....Toronto: Privately Printed.
War Loans, Resources and Progress
    of Canada ....A. E. Ames & Co. ....Toronto: Privately Printed.
Canada: Victory Souvenir ....An Illustrated Symposium..London: Canada Co.
Canada: Victory Number ....An Illustrated Symposium..London: Canada Co.
Canada's Share in War, Victory
    and Peace ....An Illustrated Symposium..Quebec: Chronicle.
City Government, Ottawa ....Dr. J. H. Putnam ....Ottawa: Hope.
Women of To-day and To-morrow..Marjory MacMurchy .....Toronto: Reconstruction Ass'n.
The 1st Canadian Division in 1918Capt. J. D. Craig ....London: Barr.
The Centenary Celebration of theLundy's Lane Historical
    Battle of Lundy's Lane ..... Society ....Niagara Falls: Society.
Compulsory Education ....C. J. Magnan ....Quebec: L'Action Sociale.
Robert Randall and the Le. Breton
    Flats ....Hamnett Hill ....Ottawa: Hope & Sons.
The Employment Service of Canada
Mgr. Paul Bruchési, Archevêque deBryce M. Stewart ....Kingston: University.
    Montreal ....Hon. L. O. David ....
Afterthoughts of Armageddon ....Lieut.-Col. L. Moore Cos-
                                 grave ....Toronto: S. B. Gundy.
The Future of Canada: Canadian-
    ism or Imperialism ....John Boyd ....Montreal: Beauchemin.
A Successful Experiment in Inter-
    national Relations ....An Address ....Ottawa: King's Printer.
L'Epopée du Vingt-Deuxième .....Claudius Corneloup .....Montreal: Beauchemin.

RELIGIOUS AND MISCELLANEOUS

Canadian Singers and Their Songs.Edward S. Carswell ......Toronto: McClelland.
The Quest of the Ballad ....W. Roy Mackenzie ......Princeton: University Press.
The Book of the Machine Gun ...Maj. F. V. Longstaff ....London: Rees.
The Red Cow: Rural Sketches....Peter McArthur ....Toronto: Dent & Sons.
Essays on Occultism, Spiritism andDean W. R. Harris, D.D.,
    Demonology .... LL.D. ....Toronto: McClelland.
The Hohenzollerns in America ...Stephen Leacock ....Toronto: S. B. Gundy.
Guide to Artistic Skating ......C. A. Meagher ....Toronto: Nelson & Sons.
Spiritual Voices in Modern Litera-
    ture ....Rev. Trevor H. Davies ...Toronto: Ryerson.
The Young Christian ....A Symposium ....Toronto: Ryerson.
Three Comrades of Jesus ....Dr. Albert D. Watson ...Toronto: Ryerson.
The Battle Nobody Saw ....Byron H. Stauffer ......Toronto: Ryerson.
Mainly for Mother ....Lieut. Arnine Norris ....Toronto: Ryerson.
Canada in Khaki ....A Symposium ....London: Memorials Fund.
The Lamps ....An Arts and Letters Club
                                 Symposium ....Toronto: The Club.
Leaders of the Canadian Church..Rev. W. Bertal Heeney, B.D.Toronto: Musson's.
Birds of Peasmarsh ....E. L. Marsh ....Toronto: Musson's.
The Vocational Educational of
    Girls ....Arthur H. Leake ....Toronto: Macmillan.
The Twentieth Plane: A Psychic
    Revelation ....Albert D. Watson, M.D. ....Toronto: McClelland.
The New Opportunity of the
    Church ....Rev. Dr. Robert E. Speer..Toronto: Macmillan.
The Almosts: A Study of the Fee-
    ble-Minded ....Helen MacMurchy ......Toronto: Allen.
The Canadian Girl at Work .....Marjory MacMurchy ......Toronto: Depart. of Education.
Why We Fail as Christians .....Robert Hunter ....Toronto: Macmillan.
Optimism and Other Sermons ...Rev. Dr. Robert Law ....Toronto: McClelland.
Building the North ....J. B. MacDougall ......Toronto: McClelland.
The Boy Scout Handbook ....(Edited) Gerald H. Brown..Ottawa: Association.
The Girl of the New Day ......Ellen B. Knox ....Toronto: McClelland.
Through St. Dunstan's to Light..Pte J. H. Rawlinson .....Toronto: Allen.
Our Little Quebec Cousin ....Mary Saxe ....Boston: Page.
Essays on Wheat ....A. H. Reginald Buller ...Toronto: Macmillan.
Forests and Trees ....B. J. Hales ....Toronto: Macmillan.

BOOKS OF REFERENCE

The Canadian Annual Review ofJ. Castell Hopkins, F.S.S.,
    Public Affairs .... F.R.G.S. ....Toronto: Annual Review.
The Canadian Almanac ....(Edited) Arnold W. Thomas.Toronto: Copp-Clark.
Heaton's Annual and Commercial
    Handbook ....(Edited) Ernest Heaton...Toronto: Heaton.
The Canadian Year Book ....(Edited) Ernest H. Godfrey.Ottawa: King's Printer.
The Canadian Newspaper Directory.A. McKim, Limited .....Montreal: McKim.
Who's Who and Why, 1919-20....(Edited) B. M. Greene ....Toronto: International Press.

Review of Historical Publications (Edited) G. M. Wrong.
   Relating to Canada .... H. H. Langton
                                    W. S. Wallace Toronto: University.
Statistical Year Book of Quebec...(Edited) G. E. Marquis ...Quebec: King's Printer.
Canadian Bank of Commerce ....Annual Report ....Toronto: Privately Printed.
The Royal Bank of Canada ......Annual Report ....Montreal: Privately Printed.
The Monetary Times Annual..... (Edited) W. A. McKagne..Toronto: *Monetary Times.*

FIELD MARSHAL THE EARL HAIG OF BEMERSYDE, K.T., O.M., G.C.V.O.
Appointed Commander of the British Armies at home in 1919

THE
CANADIAN ANNUAL REVIEW
OF
PUBLIC AFFAIRS

ECHOES OF THE WORLD WAR

International War Conditions, Statistics and Summaries.
During 1919 the profound and varied influences of the War were felt in every corner of the world, Technically and provisionally it had ceased in the Armistice of Nov. 11, 1918; practically there was little peace for mind or body, nation or institution, in the greater portion of humanity. The overthrow of historic governments, the destruction of great organized national communities, the attacks upon all existing systems of rule or fabrics of nationality, the unrest of classes and masses, the accentuated distrust of mixed racial units, the exaggerated ideals and hopes of nationalist agitators anxious to build a roof before the cellars were laid, the starvation of whole communities, the suffering and privation of entire nations, the degradation, robbery and oppression of the rich and well-born in the greater part of Europe and the elevation to power or influence of robbers, riff-raff or grossly ignorant persons in the great centres of population, the reign of pillage and poverty, license and crime, covered by the operations of Bela Kun in Hungary, the Socialists in Austria, the Spartacans in Berlin and Bavaria, the Bolsheviki in Russia—all these things left an irreparable stain and permanent stamp upon the mind, as well as the map, of the world.

War, in fact, remained long after preliminary peace was declared and its final terms discussed and settled. In the Baltic regions Letts and Esthonians, German-led Russians and the Bolsheviki, fought for months; south of Petrograd General Yudenitch struggled unsuccessfully to capture the capital from the Bolsheviki; on the far north Russian front the anti-Bolshevist Archangel Government fought on despite the British withdrawal of troops while in eastern Russia Kolchak's army struggled in alternative success and failure; in southern Russia General Denekine fought steadily but, unsuccessfully in the end, against the ''Reds'' and the Ukrainians while the latter, under Petlura, fought the Bolshevists and the

Poles; Polish and Bolshevist war, or temporary armed peace, continued and Hungary was overwhelmed for a time by Bolshevist action, over-run and occupied by the Roumanians, though it finally settled down to develop stable government; on the Adriatic D'Annunzio at Fiume kept Italy and the Jugo-Slavs on tender-hooks, in Albania all kinds of races fought for supremacy and in Asia Minor Turkish forces for a time defied the Allies; in Bessarabia there was fighting between Ukrainians, Bolsheviki and Roumanians while in Western Hungary local Soviet or Red troops were fighting Czecho-Slovaks; Jugo-Slavs and German Austrians in Carinthia, Serbians and Montenegrins in Montenegro, Italians and Jugo-Slavs in the Alpine regions, Poles and Ruthenians in Eastern Galicia, were fighting from time to time. There was strife between the Finns and the Bolsheviki and war between the Afghans and the British with irresponsible and irrepressible conflicts between Greek and Turk, Bulgarian Reds and Royalists, Mexican bandits and Carranza rule.

There was, of course, a bright side to the conditions of 1919 which could not exist during a state of world war. Chaotic opinions might and did exist but there was opportunity for stable, thoughtful, public opinion to assert itself and for individual leadership of the higher type to exercise its proper influence. Storms were inevitable but the aftermath was more and more encouraging; the financial shock of peace in 1919—which was as great as that of the shock of war in 1914—was met with courage and skill; the menace of increasing prices and wages was faced with an endurance which promised well for future stability; the welter of war and revolution and misery in Central Europe and Russia was in some degree counteracted by the unexpected recovery of Great Britain, the tremendous prosperity of the United States and Canada, the rapid recovery of South American countries, the war-gathered wealth of neutral countries in Europe; the varied Labour troubles of the year lessened and the horizon brightened as the first year of international trial in peace followed the brief period of triumph in war. In a broad, general way the future rights of the small nations of Europe were safe-guarded; Palestine and Mesopotamia and Armenia were released from the cruel rule of the Turk and regions along the Euphrates and Tigris began to reach out under British guardianship to conditions which promised to make them blossom like an oriental flower; Jerusalem became the free headquarters of the Hebrew race and the Christian world rejoiced in the progress and liberty enthroned at the seat of its ancient faith; Britain and the United States were given an opportunity—which was not wholly grasped by the latter—to bridge the chasm of a century, and to unite in friendly rivalry for the practical rule of a more peaceful world.

International Casualties of the War. Gradually, during the year, figures and facts regarding the tremendous conflict were made public, statistics were more fully summarized and the basis laid

for a ripened historical view of conditions. Upon the whole
they corroborated the estimates given from year to year in *The
Canadian Annual Review* but they, naturally, were more complete.
It is probable that the careful estimate of total deaths or fatal
casualties in the struggle, as finally compiled by Prof. E. L. Bogart
of the University of Illinois,* and stated at 9,998.771 were approximately correct. He placed the total of seriously wounded at
6,295,512, the otherwise wounded at 14,002,039, the prisoners or
missing as 5,983,600; the total direct costs were estimated at $186,-
333,637,097 and the indirect costs, including capitalized value
of human life, property losses on sea and land, loss of production, etc., at $151,612,542,560. Of the men engaged in
the war, or in military service apart from the actual fighting,
and including the new levies called up from time to time
in all parts of the world, available estimates put the total at 50,-
000,000—all of whom were withdrawn from production and civil
life and 36,000,000 of whom were either killed or wounded, maimed,
weakened by captivity, or lost in the sad column of missing. At the
best these figures are estimates though they are well within the
mark; no statistics can cover the loss of vitality and health and
strength in whole nations, or the injury done to property, or soil,
as in the churned up, riddled and poisoned lands of the Western
and Eastern fronts which might never again be productive; no
values can be placed upon the priceless heir-looms destroyed in the
invaded countries or in the centuries-old national and individual
collections of statuary and paintings, tapestry and furniture and
antiques, in Bolshevised Russia and Hungary or starving Austria;
nor can figures indicate fully the passing of European treasures
of art and history from the impoverished or pillaged classes into
the hands of rich Americans.

Canada's war-toll was stated by the Department of Militia on
Aug. 12, 1919 as follows: Killed in action or died of wounds—
officers, 2,536 and other ranks 48,333; died—officers, 234 and other
ranks, 3,706; missing—officers, 352 and other ranks, 7,767; prisoners of war—officers, 130 and other ranks, 2,688; wounded—officers,
6,344 and other ranks 143,365. The total casualties, therefore, were 215,455. Those of the United States were made
public by the War Department at Washington, on the same date, as
follows: Killed in action or died of wounds 49,498, wounded 205,690
and prisoners 4,480—a total of 259,668. The total British Empire
losses were stated officially by Mr. Bonar Law (*Times*, Feb. 28) as
follows: Killed, died of wounds and finally missing, 835,743 and
of these 176,305 were from the Dominions and India; wounded
2,047,211 of whom 438,527 were from the external Empire. There
were, also, 22,258 killed in the Royal Navy and 4,894 wounded with
6,106 fatalities in the Aviation Force and 10,373 wounded—making the total of all British Empire casualties as 2,926,585.

The official German figures as announced on Apl. 13, showed

---

*Note.—"Direct and Indirect Causes of the World War" published in *The Annals*
issued at Philadelphia, by the American Academy of Political Science.

1,486,952 killed or died of wounds and 24,329 of sickness; the deaths of civilians from sickness or, as Dr. Rubner, Privy Councillor of Prussia, put it "from the Blocade" were 88,208 in the first year of War, 121,174 in the second year, 259,627 in the third and 293,700 in the fourth. The deaths in the famous Ypres salient which holds so large a place in the Canadian annals of the War were stated by Mr. Winston Churchill in Parliament on Mch. 5 for the period of July 31-Nov. 18, 1917 as follows: British, 10,795 officers and 207,838 of other ranks; Canadians, 496 officers and 11,917 of other ranks; Australians, 1,289 officers and 26,502 of other ranks.

British Shipping and Other Statistics. British shipping, including merchant vessels and 675 fishing vessels of small tonnage, totalled a loss of 3,154 vessels with a gross tonnage of 9,830,855 and 15,313 lives lost; the damaged vessels numbered 1,885 with a tonnage of 8,007,967; the tonnage destroyed by submarines comprised the bulk of losses and totalled 6,692,642 with a similar proportion damaged totalling 7,335,827.[*] The entire Allied shipping loss in the War was officially stated in the British Parliament up to Apl. 30, 1919 as 5,538,918 tons of which the United States share was 341,512 tons. It may be added that, according to an official statement by Mr. Winston Churchill in Parliament on June 6, the total strength of the Allies on the various fronts at the time of the Armistice was as follows:

	Total rationed on Western Front.	Elsewhere	Mobilized Strength.
British Empire	1,932,000	2,091,442	5,680,247
France	2,563,000	not known	5,075,000
United States of America	1,903,000	10,000	3,707,132

Canadian Military Incidents and War Memories. The facts of Canada's War record became better known during 1919; in the years to follow they were certain to be greatly amplified and glorified. The outstanding events of the Canadian campaigns throughout four years of terrific fighting, trench privations and gallant achievement were impressed on the public mind; yet the people as a whole were too near the scene and too close to the individual influences of the struggle, to grasp it as a great historical picture of national action. The share of this or that Division, Brigade or Battalion was known locally, and in part, but was not yet recorded in detail or recognized in any consecutive or organized form as portions of a succession of great campaigns carried out over a term of years by tens of millions of international and Imperial soldiers.

As a matter of fact the achievements of the 1st Division at the 2nd Battle of Ypres which began on Apl. 22nd, 1915; the intense fighting of the 2nd Division in April 1916 around the blood-stained craters of St. Eloi and that of the 3rd Division in June 1916 at Sanctuary Wood; the struggle at Courcelette (Sept. 15, 1916) of the 2nd Division with the brilliant part taken by the French-

---

*Note.—British White Paper No. 199 issued Oct. 16, 1919.

Canadians and the Regina Trench fighting of October and November in which the 4th Division took a signal share; the action of the entire Canadian Corps in the Battle of Vimy Ridge during April 1917 and the succeeding struggles around Arleux and Fresnoy in which the 1st and 2nd Divisions were chiefly concerned; the conflicts at Hill 70 and around Lens in August and September, 1917 in which the whole Corps was involved and the ensuing victories at Passchendaele and Bellevue Spur in October and November of that year; the last hundred days of August-November, 1918 in which the Canadian Corps under General Currie won battles in the Amiens, Arras and Cambrai campaigns—notably at Drocourt-Quéant, the Canal du Nord, Douai, Valenciennes and Denain—which rank amongst the brilliant actions of the greatest struggle in all history; these were landmarks in Canada's record which were bound to grow larger upon the canvas of national history as the months and years passed.

Canada's 70 Generals in the War. Of the men who led this Army of 100,000 men (more or less and from time to time) the outstanding figures were, of course, the Corps Commanders—Lieut.-General Sir E. A. H. Alderson, K.C.B. from Sept. 13, 1915 to May 28, 1916; Lieut.-General the Hon. Sir J. H. G. Byng, K.C.B., K.C.M.G., M.V.O., (afterwards Lord Byng of Vimy) from the latter date to June 9th, 1917: General Sir Arthur W. Currie from this last date to the end of the War. Under these successive Commanders in the Field or those at Headquarters in England were nearly 70 General Officers of the Overseas Military Forces of Canada whose names will have a place in National and Imperial history and of whom an official list follows:

In The Field Command	Name	Date of Service
1st Division	Lieut.-Gen. Sir E. A. H. Alderson, K.C.B.	22.9.14 to 13.9.15
" "	Maj.-Gen. Sir A. W. Currie. K.C.M.G., C.B.	13.9.15 to 9.6.17
" "	Maj.-Gen. Sir A. C. Macdonell, K.C.B., C.M.G., D.S.O.	9.6.17 to Armistice
2nd Division	Maj.-Gen. Sir S. B. Steele, K.C.M.G., C.B., M.V.O.	25.5.15 to 6.6.15
" "	Maj.-Gen. Sir R. E. W. Turner. V.C., K.C.M.G., C.B., D.S.O.	17.8.15 to 5.12.16
" "	Maj.-Gen. Sir H. E. Burstall, K.C.B.	15.12.16 to Armistice
3rd Division	Maj.-Gen. M. S. Mercer, C.B.	20.11.15 to 3.8.16
" "	Maj.-Gen. L. J. Lipsett, C.B., C.M.G.	16.6.16 to 13.9.18
" "	Maj.-Gen. Sir F. O. W. Loomis. K.C.B., C.M.G., D.S.O.	13.9.18 to Armistice
4th Division	Brig.-Gen. Lord Brooke, C M.G.	19.11.15 to 11.5.16
" "	Maj.-Gen. Sir David Watson, K.C.B.	25.4.16 to Armistice
1st Infantry Brigade	Brig.-Gen. M. S. Mercer, C.B.	22.9.14 to 20.11.15
" " "	Brig.-Gen. G. B. Hughes, C.M.G., D.S.O.	26.11.15 to 13.2.17
" " "	Brig.-Gen. W. A. Griesbach, M.P., C.M.G., D.S.O.	14.2.17 to 15.2.19
" " "	Brig.-Gen. G. E. McCuaig, C.M G.	27.2.19 to Armistice
2nd Infantry Brigade	Brig.-Gen. A. W. Currie, C.B.	22.9.14 to 13.9.15
" " "	Brig.-Gen. L. J. Lipsett, C.M.G.	13.9.15 to 16.6.16
" " "	Brig.-Gen. F. O. W. Loomis, C.M.G.	2.7.16 to 7.12.17
" " "	Brig.-Gen. J. F. L. Embury, C.M.G.	1.1.18 to 16.3.18
" " "	Brig.-Gen. F. O. W. Loomis, D.S.O.	16.3.18 to 13.9.18
" " "	Brig.-Gen. R. P. Clark, D.S.O., M.C.	6.10.18 to Armistice
3rd Infantry Brigade	Brig.-Gen. R. E. W. Turner. V.C., C.B., D.S.O.	22.9.14 to 13.8.15
" " "	Brig.-Gen. R. G. E. Leckie, C.M.G.	13.8.15 to 13.2.16

In The Field Command	Name	Date of Service
3rd Infantry Brigade	Brig.-Gen. F. O. W. Loomis, D.S.O.	9.3.16 to 14.8.16
" " "	Brig.-Gen. G. S. Tuxford, C.B., C.M.G.	12.8.16 to Armistice
4th Infantry Brigade	Brig.-Gen. Lord Brooke, C.M.G.	25.6.15 to 17.11.15
" " "	Brig.-Gen. R. Rennie, C.B., C.M.G., M.V.O., D.S.O.	10.11.15 to 18.9.16, 27.2.19 to Armistice
" " "	Brig.-Gen. G. E. McCuaig, C.M.G., D.S.O.	14.9.18 to 27.2.19.
5th Infantry Brigade	Brig.-Gen. J. P. Landry	20.5.15 to 30.8.15
" " "	Brig.-Gen. D. Watson, C.B.	30.8.15 to 25.4.16
" " "	Brig.-Gen. A. H. Macdonell, C.M.G.	22.4.16 to 23.7.17
" " "	Brig.-Gen. J. M. Ross, D.S.O.	23.7.17 to 10.8.18
" " "	Brig.-Gen. T. L. Tremblay, C.M.G.	10.8.16 to Armistice
6th Infantry Brigade	Brig.-Gen. H. D B Ketchen, C.M.G.	25.6.15 to 18.6.16
" " "	Brig.-Gen. A. H. Bell, C.M.G., D.S.O.	27.11.16 to 8.10.18
" " "	Brig.-Gen. A. Ross, C.M.G., D.S.O.	8.10.18 to Armistice
7th Infantry Brigade	Brig.-Gen. A. C. Macdonell, C.B., C.M.G., D.S.O.	23.12.15 to 9.6.17
" " "	Brig.-Gen. H. M. Dyer, C.M.G., D.S.O.	9.6.17 to 12.9.18
" " "	Brig.-Gen. J. A. Clark, D.S.O.	12.9.18 to Armistice
8th Infantry Brigade	Brig.-Gen. V. A. S. Williams	23.12.15 to 3.6.16
" " "	Brig.-Gen. J. H. Elmsley, C.M.G.	19.6.16 to 25.5.18
" " "	Brig.-Gen. D. C. Draper, C.M.G.	27.6.18 to Armistice
9th Infantry Brigade	Brig.-Gen. F. W. Hill, C.M.G., D.S.O.	9.1.16 to 21.7.18
" " "	Brig.-Gen. D. M. Ormond, C.M.G.	21.7.18 to 21.2.19
10th Infantry Brigade	Brig.-Gen. G. S. Tuxford, C.M.G.	11.1.16 to 11.8.16
" " "	Brig.-Gen. F. S. Meighen	14.4.16 to 16.7.16
" " "	Brig.-Gen. W. St. P. Hughes, D.S.O.	16.7.16 to 18.1.18
" " "	Brig.-Gen. E. Hilliam, C.M.G., D.S.O.	18.1.17 to 12.11.17
" " "	Brig.-Gen. R. J. F. Hayter, C.M.G.	19.12.17 to 28.10.18
" " "	Brig.-Gen. J. M. Ross, C.M.G.	28.10.18 to Armistice
11th Infantry Brigade	Brig.-Gen. F. O. W. Loomis, D.S.O.	16.5.16 to 2.7.16
" " "	Brig.Gen. V. W. Odlum, C.B., C.M.G., D.S.O.	19.7.16 to Armistice
12th Infantry Brigade	Brig.-Gen. F. O. W. Loomis, D.S.O.	5.1.16 to 9.3.16
" " "	Brig.-Gen. Lord Brooke, C.M.G., M.V.O.	11.5.16 to 15.9.16
" " "	Brig.-Gen. J. H. MacBrien, C.M.G., D.S.O.	20.9.16 to 13.12.18
" " "	Brig.-Gen. J. Kirkcaldy, D.S.O.	13.12.18 to Armistice
Corps Artillery	Brig.-Gen. H. E. Burstall, C.B.	18.9.15 to 15.12.16
"	Maj.-Gen. E. W. B. Morrison, K.C.B., C.M.G., D.S.O.	12.12.16 to Armistice
1st Divisional Artillery	Brig.-Gen. H. E. Burstall, C.B.	22.9.14 to 18.9.15
" " "	Brig.-Gen. E. W. B. Morrison.	18.9.15 to 27.9.15
" " "	Brig.-Gen. H. C. Thacker, C.M.G., D.S.O.	27.9.15 to Armistice
2nd Divisional Artillery	Brig.-Gen. H. C. Thacker, C.M.G.	7.6.15 to 25.6.15
" " "	Brig.-Gen. E. W. B. Morrison,	25.6.15 to 18.12.16
" " "	Brig.-Gen. H. A. Panet, C.M.G., D.S.O.	18.12.16 to Armistice
3rd Divisional Artillery	Brig.-Gen. W. O. H. Dodds, C.M.G.	11.8.16 to 20.6.16
" " "	Brig.-Gen. J. F. Mitchell, D.S.O.	20.6.16 to 9.12.17
" " "	Brig.-Gen. J. S. Stewart, D.S.O.	9.12.17 to Armistice
4th Divisional Artillery	Brig.-Gen. W. O. H. Dodds, C.M.G.	2.10.16 to 3.2.17
" " "	Brig.-Gen. C. H. MacLaren, D.S.O.	20.6.17 to 3.11.17
" " "	Brig.-Gen. W. B. M. King, C.M.G.	27.11.17 to Armistice
5th Divisional Artillery	Brig.-Gen. W. O. H. Dodds, C.M.G.	8.2.18 to 9.1.19
" " "	Brig.-Gen. G. H. Ralston, D.S.O.	9.1.19 to Armistice
Garrison Artillery	Brig.-Gen. A. G. L. McNaughton, D.S.O.	10.11.18 to Armistice
Cavalry Brigade	Brig.-Gen. Rt. Hon. J. E. B. Seely, C.B., D.S.O.	12.14 to 20.5.18
"	Brig.-Gen. R. W. Paterson, D.S.O.	20.5.18 to Armistice
Corps of Canadian Engineers	Brig.-Gen. C. J. Armstrong.	18.9.15 to 7.8.16
" " "	Maj.-Gen. W. B. Lindsay, C.M.G.	7.8.16 to Armistice
Canadian Machine Gun Corps	Brig.-Gen. R. Brutinel, C.M.G., D.S.O.	28.10.16 to Armistice
Corps of Canadian Railway Troops	Maj.-Gen. J. W. Stewart, C.B., C.M.G.	1.1.17 to Armistice
Canadian Forestry Corps	Brig.-Gen J B White, D.S.O.	18.3.17 to 30.11.18
Canadian Representative at G.H.Q.	Brig.-Gen. R. Manley Sims	12.12.16 to 6.6.18
Canadian Section, G.H.Q. 1st Echelon	Brig.-Gen. J. F. L. Embury	1.10.16 to Armistice
Canadian Army Medical Corps (Director-General of Medical Services)	Maj.-Gen. G. la F. Foster, C.B.	16.7.18 to Armistice
Director of Medical Services	Surg.-Gen. G. C. Jones, C.M.G.	22.9.14 to 9.2.17
" " "	Surg.-Gen. G. la F. Foster, C.B.	9.2.17 to 16.7.18
" " "	Surg.-Gen. J. T. Fotheringham.	17.3.17 to 4.4.18

In The Field Command	Name	Date of Service
Director of Medical Services (France)	Brig.-Gen. A. E Ross, C.B., C.M.G.	16.7.18 to Armistice
Headquarters, O.M.F.C.		
Chief of General Staff	Lt.-Gen. Sir R. E. W. Turner, V.C., K.C.B., K.C.M.G., D.S.O.	18.5.18 to Armistice
G.O.C., Canadian Troops,	Lt-Gen. Sir R. E. W. Turner, V.C.,	
British Isles	K.C.B., K.C.M.G., D.S.O.	5.12.16 to 18.5.18
General Staff Officer, 1st	Brig.-Gen. H. F. McDonald, C.M.G.,	
Grade	D.S.O.	19.12.16 to 30.12.18
Adjutant-General	Maj.-Gen. P. E. Thacker, C.B., C.M.G.	5.12.16 to Armistice
Quartermaster-General	Brig.-Gen. A. D. McRae, C.B.	5.12.16 to 18.3.18
" "	Brig.-Gen. D. M. Hogarth, C.M.G., D.S.O.	19.3.18 to Armistice
Canadian Forestry Corps ..	Maj.-Gen. A. McDougall, C.B.	6.9.16 to Armistice
Director of Veterinary Services and Remounts	Brig.-Gen. W. J. Neill	16.7.15 to 12.3.18
Director-General of Engineer Services	Brig.-Gen. G S., Maunsell	1.4.16 to 5.3.17
Canadian Army Pay Corps	Brig.-Gen. J. G. Ross, C.M.G.	19.8.15 to Armistice
Canadian Concentration Camps, Witley and Bramshott	Brig.-Gen. A. H. Bell, C.M.G., D.S.O.	1.4.19 to Armistice
Canadian Training Division, Ripon	Brig.-Gen. D. M. Ormond, C.M.G., D.S.O.	26.2.19 to Armistice
Canadian Training Division, Bramshott	Brig.-Gen. F. S. Meighen, C.M.G.	16.7.16 to 19.6.18
" " "	Brig.-Gen. J. H. Elmsley, C.B., C.M.G., D.S.O.	27.6.18 to 16.8.18
" " "	Brig.-Gen. R. Rennie, C.B., C.M.G., D.S.O., M.V.O.	18.9.18 to 21.2.19
Canadian Training Division, Witley	Brig.-Gen. R. G. E. Leckie, C.M.G.	16.12.16 to 13.2.17
" " "	Maj.-Gen. G. B. Hughes, C.M.G.	18.2.17 to 22.7.18
" " "	Brig-Gen. F. W. Hill, C.B., C.M.G., D.S.O.	27.7.18 to 31.3.19
Canadian Training Division, Shoreham and Seaford ..	Brig.-Gen. H. M. Dyer, C.M.G., D.S.O.	12.9.18 to 25.3.19
Canadian Training Division, Borden	Brig.-Gen. C. H. Maclaren, C.M.G., D.S.O.	4.11.18 to 13.3.19
Canadian Training Division, Shorncliffe	Maj.-Gen. Sir S. B. Steele, K.C.M.G., C.B., M.V.O.	5.8.15
Canadian Training Division, Crowborough	Brig.-Gen. W. St. P. Hughes, D.S.O.	1.5.17 to 31.7.17
Canadian Training Division, Brighton	Maj.-Gen. J. C. McDougall	7.11.16 to 21.12.16
" "	Brig.-Gen. J. P. Landry	21.12.16 to 2.1.17

Canadian War Work and Military Strength. During the year many statistics of Canadian War action were summarized and made public. It was found that 500 Canadian factories from Halifax to Vancouver had sent overseas 62,000,000 shells worth over 1,000 million dollars; that $65,000,000 had been spent upon the rapid construction of vessels which included steamers, freighters, submarines, armed trawlers and drifters, patrol boats, etc.; that between 1914-15 and 1917-18 $1,700,000,000 worth of food supplies had been shipped abroad—chiefly to Britain; that over $2,000,000,000 had been borrowed by the Government from the Canadian people in 1915-19 and at least half of this utilized for credits to Great Britain; that the Registration of the people in June 22nd, 1918 had shown a final total of 5,245,606 men and women 16 years of age and over and afforded tabulated information as to availability of workers, ages and capacity for work, fitness for active service, etc.; that 50,000 Canadian soldiers, who had left their country for active service between 1914 and 1916 had married English, Irish or Scotch girls; that in the Canadian Expeditionary Force 465,984 had enlisted under the voluntary system and 83,355 under the Military Service Act together with, in the latter case, 24,933 on leave or discharged as compassionate cases and 16,300 struck off strength as liable only to noncombatant service; that out of 515,456 soldiers 228,751 were British-born (United Kingdom) and 286,705 Canadian-born.* The figures by Provinces were as follows:†

Province	Volunteers	Draftees
Ontario	205,808	27,087
Quebec	52,993	19,050
New Brunswick	18,935	5,157
Nova Scotia and P. E. I.	24,456	5,442
Manitoba	54,756	6,787
Alberta	36,013	5,987
Saskatchewan	27,044	8,204
British Columbia and Yukon	43,652	5,641

Canadian Enlistments, Defaulters and Exemptions. Of the 72,000 Quebec enlistments *L'Evenement* of Quebec (Apl. 14) claimed that 36,000 were French-Canadians from that Province and that out of the Dominion total there were at least 14,000 more or 50,000 from all the Provinces. Of the drafted men throughout Canada 47,509 went overseas and, on Oct. 31, 1918 within two weeks of the Armistice, there were available in Canada for re-inforcements 35,000 men of whom 25,000 were Infantry. In this connection it may be added that defaulters, or absentees under the Military Service Act, were not relieved of their penalties until late in the year and searches or prosecutions were carried on throughout Canada with varying degrees of activity or efficiency and with widely-different penalties. In Quebec a system of small fines was pursued by local Courts and to this objection was taken in Ontario, and elsewhere, and in Parliament it was both criticized and defended.

A despatch from Quebec City in the Toronto *Globe* of Feb. 7th stated that "practically all the absentees from the parish of Pont Rouge, in the county of Portneuf, that have kept away from town since the calling of their class, rode to town to-day under the guidance of Father Maurice Tessier, vicar of the parish. A large batch from the parish junction also appeared in court under the guidance of Rev. Father R. Guay, pastor of the parish." These men pleaded guilty and were released on payment of nominal fines, by the Hon. C. Langelier, Judge of the Court of Sessions. Speaking in Court on Feb. 9th Judge Langelier referred to criticisms as to this procedure and said:‡ "It seems that in Ontario the sentiment would require that all absentees be sent to the penitentiary. We do not feel that way. We judge each individual case according to its own particular merits, and according to our own conscience."

The Hon. Mr. Meighen, acting-Minister of Justice at Ottawa, stated that this was not according to instructions from his Department and on the 11th the Department wired the Deputy Attorney-

---

*Note.—Maj.-Gen. S. C. Mewburn, Minister of Militia in Parliament on Mch. 19, 1919.

†Note.—Official Memorandum tabled in Parliament on Apl. 11th.

‡Note.—Montreal *Star* despatch Feb. 10, 1919.

General at Quebec declaring that minimum fines of $5.00 under the circumstances were not appropriate and in fact, were illegal. Judge Langelier, in reply, declared that his maximum fines went as high as $75.00 and that his fine of $5.00 as a minimum was in cases where the men had been misled by advisers or were too poor to pay a larger amount; he did not believe gaol a wise or fitting punishment in these cases—branding the young men as defaulters was, he thought, a sufficient punishment. The instructions as to leniency which the Judge believed he had received from the Federal Department of Justice were later on admitted to have been given but by a subordinate official and "erroneously." Judge H. Lanctot of Montreal on Feb. 26th, dealt with similar absentee cases and sentenced four of them to six hours in gaol and others to fines running from $10 to $25.

Meanwhile, on Feb. 24th, an Order-in-Council was passed at Ottawa imposing a minimum fine of $250 and a maximum of $5,000, with alternatives of imprisonment, in place of the single summary punishment running up to two years in prison. In Parliament the subject was referred to from time to time with F. J. Pelletier, J. Demers, G. W. Parent and J. W. Edwards amongst those who urged milder treatment of these men. On Apl. 9th a stormy debate took place on this and kindred subjects, such as slackness in recruiting etc., and General Mewburn, Minister of Militia, declared that defaulters should be disfranchised and deprived of civil rights for a term of years. On May 19th, Hon. Mr. Meighen reported the names of 7 men from Kent County, New Brunswick, who had been fined $250 or $300 costs with the alternative of a year's imprisonment. At the close of the year (Dec. 22) when a Royal Proclamation of Amnesty was finally issued for offenders of any Military nature under the Act the number still at large was estimated at 15,000 with about the same number confined in prisons. Final figures were published during the year as to the whole complicated action and results of the Military Service Act. On Feb. 27th it was officially stated that Mr. Justice L. P. Duff as a Central Appeal Court had heard 50,467 appeals; that these constituted 50% of the cases coming before the local authorities; that of this total 23,172 were refused exemption and 19,471 granted conditional exemption and the balance deferred for future consideration. On Apl. 3rd, 1919, Mr. Meighen, for the Department of Justice, gave the following general statistics of M.S.A. results:

Province	Registered and applied for exemption.	Applications granted.	Applications refused.	Applications pending at Armistice.	Ordered to report for service.	Reported for service by Nov. 11, 1918.
Alberta	25,389	17,934	7,306	149	9,310	7,870
British Columbia	15,075	8,473	6,414	188	7,162	6,417
Manitoba	20,124	10,102	9,872	650	9,470	9,044
New Brunswick	15,553	8,225	7,092	236	6,661	6,069
Nova Scotia	23,556	14,689	8,210	657	7,977	6,648
Ontario	116,092	65,089	42,866	8,637	44,796	40,687
P. E. Island	4,231	2,631	1,572	28	1,121	1,082
Quebec	113,291	58,644	51,856	2,791	46,104	27,277
Saskatchewan	43,318	30,440	12,450	428	11,079	10,016

The McAvity Case in New Brunswick.   An interesting local trial of a military nature, and with excessively severe results, was that of Lieut.-Col. James L. McAvity of St. John who had raised and commanded the distinguished 26th New Brunswick Battalion. In the Court Martial, which opened at St. John on May 8th with Brig.-Gen. V. A. S. Williams presiding the others associated with Colonel McAvity in the charges dealt with were Major F. H. Rowe, Capt. G. Earle Logan, Capt. R. Ingleton, Lieutenants Stockwell Simms and J. H. Belyea and Sergt.-Maj. J. W. Rawlings. Colonel McAvity was a well-known and respected citizen and officer; all the defendants were men of good standing; eminent Counsel such as Dr. J. B. M. Baxter, K.C., H. A. Powell, K.C. and F. J. G. Knowlton were retained. The charges dealt with the New Brunswick Depôt battalion at Camp Sussex and involved an alleged conspiracy on the part of these officers to defraud the Battalion of specific sums of money.

Passing over technicalities, Colonel McAvity in his defence (May 14) stated that of necessity he had left the management of the canteen in the hands of Lieut. Belyea, being over-busy himself with other matters; that as soon as he was told that there was a deficit he expressed his willingness to make it good and he did so. He earnestly denied that he ever intended, or had been guilty of, the slightest dishonesty in connection with the matter. He had felt responsible for the Fund and had so acted. He had every confidence in Lieut. Belyea until he found things were not going right and he then dismissed him. The special fund in question was intended to pay expenses in connection with the Battalion for which there was no Government allowance and was kept in his name as the responsible head. He had paid out of his own pocket large sums of money from the time he raised the 26th Battalion right through to the time of this Enquiry.

It appeared that the Canteen liabilities had been $15,000 with goods in hand worth $8,000 and $7,000 deposited by Colonel McAvity to meet the deficit; that the Fund was kept and managed as a private one and that the Colonel had from time to time checked out small sums for personal use. Brig.-Gen. A. H. Macdonell, C.M.G., D.S.O., commanding the District testified as to the high character of the accused and his reputation as a man of honour and declared his belief that the whole trouble was due to the carelessness of the Canteen Secretary. On the 28th Ingleton and Simms were declared not guilty and the other cases forwarded to Ottawa for final adjudication. On June 10th Colonel McAvity was cashiered, Capt. Logan dismissed the Service, Lieut. Belyea cashiered with six months imprisonment, Major Rowe severely reprimanded and Rawlings reduced to the ranks.

Canadian Journalists in the War. It is interesting to note that there were many Canadian journalists in the Forces which went Overseas—the author knows of about 240 and of these one-sixth were killed and many more wounded or gassed. Some of the best known were Major Olivar Asselin, Montreal *Nationalist* and Lieut.-Col. Hercule Barré, *La Patrie*, Montreal; Major R. J. Burde, M.C., Alberni, (B.C.) *News;* Capt. Gregory Clark, M.C., and Capt. J. W. G. Clark, D.F.C. Toronto *Star;* Capt. E. E. Cinq-Mars, *La Presse*, Montreal and Lieut. H. C. Crowell, Halifax *Chronicle;* Lieut.-Col. J. A. Cooper, *Canadian Courier*, Toronto, and Major Henri Chassé, D.S.O., M.C., Quebec *L'Evenement;* Lieut. E. E. Dennis, M.C., Halifax *Herald;* Major John S. Lewis, *Montreal Star* and Pte. J. D. Logan, M.A., PH.D., Toronto *News;* Lieut.-Col. C. D. McPherson, M.L.A., Portage (Man.) *Graphic* and Major Sir Andrew Macphail, M.D., *University Magazine*, Montreal; Major James McAra, Indian Head *Vidette*, and Major-General Sir E. W. B. Morreson, K.C.B., C.M.G., D.S.O., Ottawa *Citizen;* Brig.-Gen. Victor W. Odlum, C.B., C.M.G., D.S.O., *Vancouver* World, and Major-Gen. Sir David Watson, K.C.B., C.M.G., Quebec *Chronicle;* Lieut. G. G. Nash, M.C., and Major C. Beresford Topp, D.S.O., M.C., and Bar, Toronto *Mail and Empire;* Major Gordon Southam, Hamilton *Spectator* and Fl.-Com. A. H. Sandwell, Montreal *Star;* Pte. Harris Turner, M.L.A., Saskatoon *Star* and Capt. W. Wallace, M.C., Toronto *Star;* Lieut. E. C. Whitehead, Brandon *Sun* and Capt. S. G. Webb, M.B.E., M.S.M., Winnipeg *Tribune;* Lieut. Jaffray Eaton, Toronto *Globe* and Lieut.-Col. W. F. Edgecombe, Toronto *News.*

Canadian Victoria Cross Winners. There were 64 Victoria Cross winners in the Canadian Corps of whom 27 were killed and of whom about half were born in the Dominion. The official list published in England on July 31, 1919 was as follows:

Name	Unit	Action	Date
Lieut. W. L. Algie	20th Bn.	Cambrai	11.10.18
Lieut.-Col. W. G. Barker, D.S.O., M.C.	R. F. A.	Foret de Mormel	27.10.18
Capt. E. D. Bellew	7th Bn.	Ypres	24.4.14
Corp. C. Barron	3rd Bn.	Passchendaele Ridge	6.11.17
Lieut.-Col. W. A. Bishop, D.S.O., M.C., D.F.C.	R. F. C.	Near Cambrai	
Cpl. A. Brereton	8th Bn.	E. of Amiens	9.8.18
Lieut. J. Brillant, M.C.	22nd Bn.	E. of Mehari Court	8.9.8.18
Pte H. Brown	10th Bn.	Hill 70, near Loos	16.8.17
Sergt. Hugh Cairns, D.C.M.	46th Bn.	Valenciennes	1.11.18
Cpl. Leo Clarke	2nd Bn.	Near Posieres	9.9.16
Lieut. R. G. Combe	27th Bn.	S. of Acheville	3.5.17
Lieut.-Col. W. H. Clark-Kennedy, C.M.G., D.S.O.	24th Bn.	Arras	27,28.8.18
Lieut. F. W. Campbell	1st Bn.	Givenchy	15.6.15
Cpl. F. G. Coppins	8th Bn.	Hackett Woods	9.8.18
Pte. J. B. Croak	13th Bn.	Amiens	8.8.18
Pte. T. Dinesen	42nd Bn.	Parvillers	12.8.18
Cpl. F. Fisher	13th Bn.	St. Julien	23.4.15
Lieut. G. M. Flowerdew	Strathcona's Horse	N.E. Bois de Moreuil	30.3.18
Cpl. H. J. Good	13th Bn.	Hanguard Wood	8.8.18
Lieut. P. M. Gregg, M.C.	R. C. R.	Cambrai	1.10.18
Lieut. S. L. Honey, D.C.M., M.M.	78th Bn.	Bourlon Wood	2.10.18
Sergt. R. Hanna	29th Bn.	Lens	21.8.17
Cpl. B. S. Hutheson	75th Bn.	Line	2.9.18
Lieut. F. M. W. Harvey	Strathcona's Horse	Guyencourt	27.3.17
Sgt. F. Hobson	20th Bn.	N.W. Lens	15.8.17
Pte. T. W. Holmes	4th C. M. R.	Near Passchendaele	26.10.17
Cpl. J. Kaeble, M.M.	22nd Bn.	Neuville-Vitasse	8,9.6.18
Lieut. F. G. Kerr, M.C., M.M.	3rd Bn.	Bourlon Wood	27.9.18
Pte. J. C. Kerr	49th Bn.	Courcellette	16.9.16
Pte. C. J. Kinross	49th Bn.	Passchendaele Ridge	28,29,31.10.17
Sgt. A. G. Knight	10th Bn.	Villers-les-Cagnicourt	2.9.18

Name	Unit	Action	Date
Cpl. F. Konowal ....47th Bn.		......Lens	.......22,24.8.17
Major O. M. Learmonth,			
M.C. ....2nd Bn.		......E. of Loos 18.8.17	
Lieut. G. T. Lyall ....102nd Bn.		.....Bourlon Wood 2.9.18	
Major T. W. MacDowell,			
D.S.O. ....38th Bn.		......Vimy Ridge 9,13.4.17	
Capt. John MacGregor, M.C.,			
D.C.M. ....2nd C. M. R.		...Cambrai 3.10.18	
Lieut. G. B. McKean, M.M..14th Bn.		......Gavrelle Sector 27,28.4.18	
Lieut. H. McKenzie, D.C.M.7th Can. M.		G.Meetcheele Spur 30.11.17	
Co.			
Lieut. Alan A. McLeod ... R. A. F.		.....Gazetted 1.5.18	
Cpl. W. H. Metcalfe, M.M..16th Bn.		.....Arras 2.9.18	
Pte. W. J. Milne ....16th Bn.		.....Near Thelus 9.4.17	
Capt. C. N. Mitchell, M.C. ..		Caralde Escaut 8.10.18	
Sgt. William Merrifield.....4th Bn.		.....Abancourt 1.10.18	
Cpl. H. G. B. Miner .....58th Bn.		.....Demuin 8.8.18	
Sgt. G. H. Mullin, M.M ...		Passchendaele 30.10.17	
Pte. Claude J. P. Nunney,			
D.O.M., M.M. ....88th Bn.		.....Drocourt-Queant 2.9.18	
Capt. C. P. J. O'Kelly, M.C.52nd Bn.		.....S.W. Passchendaele 26.10.17	
Pte. M. J. O'Rourke ......7th Bn.		.......Hill 60, near Lens ...15,17,8.17	
Pte. J. G. Pattison ......50th Bn.		.....Vimy Ridge 10.4.17	
Major G. R. Pearkes, D.S.O.,			
M.C. ....5th C. M. R.		...Near Passchendaele 30,31.10.17	
Lieut.-Col. C. W. Peck,			
D.S.O. ....16th Bn.		.....Cagnicourt 2.9.18	
Piper J. Richardson ......16th Bn.		.....Regina Trench 8.10.16	
Pte. J. P. Robertson ......27th Bn.		.....Passchendaele 6.11.17	
Lieut. C. S. Rutherford,			
M.C., M.M ....6th C. M. R. Bn.Monchy		..............26.8.18	
Pte. Walter L. Rayfield ....7th Bn.		......Arras 2.9.18	
Capt. F. A. C. Scrimger,			
M.C. ....14th Bn.		.....Near Ypres 25.4.15	
Lieut. R. Shankland ......43rd Bn.		.....Passchendaele 26.10.17	
L. Sgt. E. W. Sifton .....18th Bn.		.....Neuville-St. Vaast 9.4.17	
Sgt. R. Spall ....P. P. C. L. I...Near Parvillers 12,13.8.18			
Lieut. H. Strachan, M.C. ..Ft. Garry Horse.Masnieres 20.11.17			
Lieut. J. E. Tait, M.C. ....78th Bn.		.....Amiens 8,12.8.18	
Pte. John F. Young ....87th Bn.		.....Arras 2.9.18	
Sgt. R. L. Zengel, M.M. ...33rd Bn.		.....E. Warvillers 9.8.18	

Though the above list is official Capt. Coulson Norman Mitchell, M.C., of the 4th Batt., Canadian Engineers, who won his V.C. on October 8-9, 1914 is omitted; so is Lieut. Ronald Neil Stuart, R.N. of Charlottetown who won the V.C. and D.S.O. and, in 1919, the Navy Cross, and the late Lieut. Edmund de Windt who served from Calgary in the 31st Canadian Battalion, joined the Royal Irish Rifles and won his honour on Mch. 21, 1918. Another Canadian serving with H.M. Submarine, E.-14, was Lieut. Com. Geoffrey Saxton-White of Duncan, B.C. who obtained the V.C. for a deed, followed by his death, on Jan. 28, 1918. Of the winners of the Victoria Cross in the Canadian Forces, Rayfield, Millin, Zengel, Hutcheson, Metcalf and Miner had been born in the United States and the press of that country soon found out this interesting fact; fully one-half of the remainder were born in the United Kingdom. The number of V.C's won by Canada was large in proportion to a total of 578 awarded during the War but the British allotment to the Dominion was probably a generous one.

Special War Services and Honours. Ten men in the armies of the Empire probably deserved the Cross to every one who received it; hence the large number of D.S.O's and Bars and, though the total of 254,158 Honours awarded during the years of war to all British and Empire troops seems large it was not really so when apportioned amongst 6,000,000 soldiers and in battles of which every phase was a testing time for courage, coolness and skill. Canada's total Honours were 17,000. Reference must be made here to the 2nd bars of the D.S.O. which, in 1919, were granted to some distinguished Canadian officers. To win the D.S.O. once was an illustration of bravery, to win it twice was a proof of continuous courage, to win it a third time indicated a gallantry and skill equal to and perhaps excelling those of a V.C. winner. The recipients of a 2nd Bar in 1919 were Lieut.-Col. R. D. Davies, D.S.O., 44th Batt., Lieut.-Col. J. P. MacKenzie, D.S.O., Engineers, Lieut.-Col. C. M. Edwards, D.S.O., 38th Batt., Lieut.-Col. W. F. Gibson, D.S.O., 7th Batt., Lieut.-Col. E. W. MacDonald, D.S.O., M.C., 10th Batt., Lieut.-Col. L. T. McLaughlin, D.S.O., 2nd Batt., Lieut.-Col. A. W. Sparling, D.S.O., 1st Batt., Lieut.-Col. J. A. Clark, D.S.O., 72nd Batt., Lieut.-Col. W. W. Foster, D.S.O., 52nd Batt., Lieut.-Col. James Kirkcaldy, C.M.G., D.S.O., 78th Batt., Lieut.-Col. W. S. Latta, D.S.O., 29th Batt., Lieut.-Col. L. F. Page, D.S.O., 50th Batt., Lieut.-Col. R. A. Macfarlane, D.S.O., 58th Batt., Lieut.-Col. H. J. Riley, D.S.O., 27th Batt.

As indicating the wide-spread nature of Canadian services in the War it may be mentioned that Lieut.-Col. Joseph Whiteside Boyle was awarded the Roumanian Orders of the Crown, the Star and Regina Maria for services in that country and a D.S.O. for services in eastern Russia; that Major Hector Read was given the O.B.E. for services in West Africa and Lieut.-Col. C. H. L. Sharman, O.B.E., the C.M.G. for Military operations in northern Russia; that Lieut.-Gen. Sir W. R. Marshall drew special attention to the work of Lieut.-Col. J. W. Warden, D.S.O., in Mesopotamia; that Lieut.-Col. C. H. Mitchell, C.B., C.M.G., D.S.O., received the Order of the Crown of Italy for the Allied campaign in that country. It may be added that H.M. the King personally decorated Major W. G. Barker with the V.C., D.S.O. and Bar and M.C. and two Bars on Mch. 1st; that Lieut.-Col. W. H. Clark-Kennedy of Montreal was similarly invested with the Victoria Cross, C.M.G., D.S.O. and Bar on the same day; that Major Clarence R. Young of Guelph was decorated on Mch. 15 by His Majesty with the D.S.O., M.C. and two Bars.

On Mch. 26th the Municipal Council of Mons gave an official farewell to Major-Gen. Sir F. O. W. Loomis, K.C.B., C.M.G., D.S.O., in command of the 3rd Canadian Division which, as a part of the 1st British Army, liberated that famous town on Nov. 11, 1918. The General was presented with a beautiful flag, on which, in addition to symbols associated with the Canadian Corps, were inscribed the names of famous towns where Canadian soldiers had particularly distinguished themselves. At the same time General Loomis received from the Belgian King the Order of Leopold. On Apl. 2nd a Bar to the D.S.O. was gazetted to this officer and to Brig.-Gen. W. A. Griesbach, C.B., C.M.G., D.S.O., for "great gallantry and brilliant leadership." The 4th Canadian Brigade of the Mons Command was, it may be added, led by Brig.-Gen. G. Eric McCuaig,

c.m.g., d.s.o., and Bar who, at 32, was said to be the youngest of
that rank in the Canadian Army.

Of regular Army Medals awarded to British Empire forces
in the War there was (1) the British War Medal given to all soldiers who left their native land, in any part of the British Empire,
and whether they eventually entered a theatre of war or not; (2)
the Inter-Allied Victory Medal was for all who actually entered a
theatre of war; (3) the Mercantile Marine War Medal was for
men of the Merchant Service who entered certain danger zones.
The Canadian Government undertook a record of the War Services
of all Canadian officers who were engaged in any of the 34 specified theatres of war; on Oct. 28th Maj.-Gen. Mewburn, Minister
of Militia, announced at Victoria, B.C. that a Silver Cross, hung
from a purple ribbon, would be given to every mother who had lost
a boy at the Front.

War Incidents of the Year included a statement that the Dominion Board of Censors had refused transmission during the War
to 3,600 messages at the Hazel Hill and Canso, N.S., stations and
had enquired into 30,000 other messages before they were passed
while drawing the attention of United Kingdom Censors to another 18,000; the appointment by the Government of a Committee
composed of Hon. A. K. Maclean, Sir George Foster, General S. C.
Mewburn, Hon. C. C. Ballantyne, Sir H. Laporte of the War Purchasing Committee and J. W. McConnell of the War Trade Board
to report on the disposition of the millions of dollars worth of war
supplies in steel, leather and woollen goods, arms and ammunition,
etc., owned by the Government; the cutting of the War appropriation of $500,000,000 in 1918 to $350,000,000 for 1919 by Sir Thomas
White, Minister of Finance; the announcement that the British
Remount Commission in Canada of which, latterly, Brig.-Gen. Sir
C. V. Gunning was O.C., had purchased in Canada 31,402 horses;
the decision of the Supreme Court of Canada (May 21) that both
the *Imo* and *Mont Blanc* were responsible for the terrific explosion
of 1918 in Halifax harbour which caused so much destruction and
loss of life—Justices F. A. Anglin, L. P. Brodeur and P. B. Mignault being the majority and Chief Justice Sir Louis Davies and
Hon. J. Idington dissenting with the declaration that the *Imo* was
solely to blame.

On Jan. 4th, Sir Robert Borden opened in London an exhibition of nearly 400 Canadian War Memorial paintings by British
and Canadian artists including a huge picture of the Canadians
opposite Lens by Major Augustus John; paintings of the Vimy
Ridge battle and that of Ypres (2nd) by Major Richard Jack; a
picture of Courcelette by Capt. Louis Welter and of the Fleet of
transports, which carried over the 1st Division, by Norman Wilkinson; a painting called "Sacrifice" by Charles Sims, R.A., which
vividly illustrated the much-discussed crucifixion of a Canadian
soldier; a picture called "The Gunpit" by Windham Lewis together
with the portraits of many Canadian Generals—Currie, Lipsett,

Burstall, Watson, Macdonell and Loomis—by Major Sir William Orpen, R.A.

Safeguarding the Graves of Canada's Dead. During the year the work of safeguarding the graves of Canadian dead was actively carried on by the Imperial War Graves Commission, appointed in 1917, with H.R.H., the Prince of Wales as Chairman, the Dominions High Commissioners as members together with the Secretaries of State for War, the Colonies and India—and Sir George Perley as the Canadian representative. Each part of the Empire contributed to the expense a share proportionate to the number of its dead. The work of the Commission commenced where the labours of the War Office ceased. The Army had been responsible for the registration and temporary marking of all war graves in the various theatres of war and for the temporary fencing, tidying and surveying of all war cemeteries. It was also responsible for the exhuming and bringing into permanent cemeteries of all bodies buried in isolated graves. That done, the War Graves Commission continued the work. It took over each cemetery when completed by the Army and, after carrying out in it such permanent construction work as might be decided upon, made the necessary arrangement for its maintenance in perpetuity. The graves of officers and men bore headstones of uniform dimensions with rank, name, regiment and date of death; friends or relatives could at their own expense add a short inscription; in every cemetery there was a great memorial stone on broad steps and elsewhere a memorial cross; the cemeteries were carefully laid out, planted with flowers or shrubs and surrounded with a final enclosure of low walls.

Various War Events of 1919. Speaking upon a moot point in the Commons on May 27th Sir Edward Kemp, Overseas Minister of Militia, stated as to the alleged crucifixion of a Canadian soldier that: "We succeeded in getting the affidavits of two Canadian soldiers who witnessed the scene. One wore the Victoria Cross and the father of one of them was employed in a position of importance in London. I do not think there can be any doubt but that the Germans were guilty of this atrocity." Other incidents included the announcement that Canadians during the War were supposed to pay a royalty for the use of German patents and that $30,000 had been so paid but that a large number of German trade marks and patents had been illegally used and many inferior articles—chiefly drugs—sold; the appointment in London during July of General the Hon. Sir Julian Byng as Chairman of the Board of Management of a United Service Fund to deal with the Canteen profits which had accumulated during the War to a total of $35,000,000 and of which Canada's share was transferred to Ottawa in December—the British moneys being utilized for (1) the benefit of widows, children and orphans of deceased officers and men, (2) the benefit of disabled and discharged officers and men, (3) the provision of social and

recreation benefit for the serving officers and men; the sentence by
Mr. Justice Barry at Fredericton, N.B. on Oct. 31st of Werner
Horn, the German-American who, on Feb. 2nd, 1915 had tried to
blow up the St. Croix Bridge with dynamite, to ten years in the
Dorchester Penitentiary; the Report in October of the Special
Committee of Enquiry (Lords Sumner, Inchcape and Colwyn)
exhonerating the British Cellulose and Chemical Manufacturing
Co., Ltd., in which Lieut.-Col. W. Grant Morden, M.P., and others
were interested, from the charges of Government favouritism,
profiteering, etc., made in the press and elsewhere during 1918.

On Nov. 11th, 1919 at the suggestion of His Majesty the King,
Canada, with all the countries of the Empire, observed the anniversary of the Armistice by maintaining silence of action and work
for the space of two minutes at 11 o'clock in the morning—incidentally the day was celebrated throughout the country by school
exercises, flag presentations, parades, speeches, etc.   An interesting
matter which must be referred to was the public recognition given
during the year by Roumania to the War services of Lieut.-Col.
Joseph W. Boyle, D.S.O. of Yukon fame.   To his father, Charles
Boyle of Woodstock there came a letter from Queen Marie of
Roumania, dated at Bucharest on Dec. 6th, 1918, in these terms:
"I want to tell you that your son is quite well and working as only
he can work, with all his soul and all his ability.   He came into our
life when I and my country were sorely tried, and he has set about
helping me and my people with the unselfish completeness you
probably know of him.   At a time when Roumania was completely
abandoned by her Allies, because her situation was so desperate,
your son did not forsake our cause and since then at every emergency he has been faithfully at my side."   In a message to the Canadian people given (Mch. 30, 1919) on leaving London the Queen
paid further tribute to his services while national Orders and, it
was said, a national title were conferred upon this Canadian
whose romantic war-career had included the Western front, Russia,
Roumania and other regions of the near East with a record worthy
of the pen of the most brilliant novelist.

Meanwhile, on Jan. 11th the regulations affecting unlawful
societies, publications, etc., had been amended so that "no conviction for such offence should be had unless the prosecution is assented
to or approved by the Attorney-General of the Province in which
the offence was alleged to have been committed."   On Jan. 23 a
sweeping withdrawal of war-time restrictions on trade was announced and on Mch. 21st Canadian claims against persons in enemy
countries and against enemy Governments were reported to the
Enemy Debts Committee at Ottawa as $31,525,000.   This comprised
debts owing by individuals and corporations in Germany, Austria
and lands allied with them, to Canadians, to the amount of $775,-
000, claims for property of Canadians in enemy countries aggregating $750,000, and demands for compensation for damages due to
illegal methods of warfare to the extent of $30,000,000.   Set off

against these claims were debts owed by Canadians to enemy nationals of $1,660,000 and enemy property in Canada worth, according to a conservative estimate, $38,000,000. It may be added that, though addresses of farewell were issued by Commanders to various Military bodies few of these were published in Canada—those of Generals Macdonell and Loomis received some slight attention during the year. That of Lieut.-Col. A. Hamilton Gault, D.S.O., to the famous Princess Patricias, at demobilization, deserves a special place here:

During the past 4½ years of war the Battalion has ever carried out its duty faithfully; in defence, invincible; in attack supreme; it never lost a position during the early days of the overwhelming German offensives, and when the time came to attack and the initiative passed into our hands, it never failed to capture the objectives allotted to it. The Battalion's record has been a proud and glorious one; on its colours will be emblazoned the names of hard-fought battles and stubborn fights, including those of St. Eloi and Ypres, 1915; Sanctuary Wood and the Somme, 1916; Vimy and Passchendaele, 1917; Amiens, Arras and Cambrai, 1918; and to you, my comrades is all the credit due, for by giving the best that was in you, by always playing the game, you have proved your loyalty to the colours and have made the Battalion what it is to-day.

General Sir Arthur Currie; His Return to Canada and Public Reception.
The year opened with the Canadian Commander, then only 43 years of age, at the height of his reputation; with the insignia of G.C.M.G. added by his Sovereign to the K.C.B. which he already held; with the suggestion in a number of British and Canadian papers that he was fitted for active service in the field of politics; with a distinguished and indisputable place in history as the head of a Corps which had performed great deeds and occupied a permanent niche in the valhalla of the world-war. Yet there was unpleasant and irresponsible gossip regarding the General amongst a section of returned men; an inevitable result of four years of war in which one man had forged ahead of all others in an organized group of 100,000 men with another hundred thousand passing through and out of its ranks. What it was about no one seemed really to know but the loose talk had an influence upon public opinion which the later and personal denunciations of Sir Sam Hughes increased. The only charge which took any formal shape was that of undue sacrifice of men to win victories—an allegation which has been made against every great commander and is easy to prove superficially and difficult to disprove thoroughly. General Currie seemed to anticipate this attack when he wrote from London on Feb. 6th to Charles Nelson, a friend in Vancouver, as follows:

I regret the casualties, yet when one considers the scope of the operations, I am quite sure history will say that the casualties in the Corps were not excessive. The most of our casualties in recent operations were sustained between Aug. 8 and Oct. 2nd. In that time the Canadian Corps, consisting of four Divisions met and defeated 47 German Divisions, of which 15 have never since been heard from. On the Western Front on Aug. 8th there were 184 German Divisions, which were opposed by the American Army, the

French Army, the Belgian Army and the British Army of which we formed
a part. To defeat one-quarter of that German Army was certainly doing
more than our share, and you cannot accomplish that without casualties.
Had things been taken easier the casualties would have been less but we
would probably to-night have been somewhat west of Valenciennes, with
another Winter's campaign staring us in the face, and a big battle to be
fought in the Spring..........We are very proud that we finished up the
War on the old battle-field of Mons, the recapture of which meant much
to the British Army and the French nation.

To the first issue of *Back to Mufti,* a journal published by the
Department of Soldiers Civil Re-establishment at Ottawa (Feb.
22), Sir Arthur Currie contributed a message for the Canadian
people in which he paid the most glowing tribute to his soldiers:
"By their unfaltering devotion, generous sacrifice, and splendid
bravery these khaki-clad men have made permanently secure the
freedom and prosperity of the country. They have written
'Canada' in bold outstanding letters in the world's roll of honour.
They have secured for Canada the right to speak as a nation admired and respected in the concert of nations. The meaning of
their victory can be gained only by the survey of all we stood to
lose in the moral, political and material fields in case of defeat."
He urged national care of these men, consideration and co-operation,
education and encouragement.

Attack by Sir Sam Hughes; Replies by Officers. In Parliament on Mch. 4th General Sir Sam Hughes promulgated charges
against General Currie which evoked swift answers from competent
sources but, unfortunately, both criticisms and replies were more or
less technical and only a painful atmosphere of unpleasantness remained for the civilian mind to absorb. As usual General Hughes
spoke without mincing words or statements and with supreme confidence in his own opinions and judgments. He quoted from a letter
which he had written to Sir Robert Borden on Oct. 1, 1918 describing "the useless massacre" of Canadian boys at Cambrai, referring
to "massacres at Lens, Passchendaele, etc., where the only apparent object was to glorify the General in command, and make it impossible, through butchery, to have a Fifth and Sixth Division and
two Army Corps!" As to the rest, one other quotation from a
characteristic speech may be given: "I have just this to say about
Mons. Were I in authority, the officer who, four hours before the
Armistice was signed, although he had been notified beforehand
that the Armistice was to begin at eleven o'clock, ordered the
attack on Mons, thus needlessly sacrificing the lives of Canadian
soldiers, would be tried summarily by court martial and punished
so far as the law would allow."

Wide and glaring attention was given to this speech in the
press though, by a curious coincidence, the Mons charge was met
by a letter received and published in Victoria from General Currie
on the day following: "We regarded it as an especial privilege that
we were able to drive the Boche from the historic city and battle
field of Mons before we knew the Armistice was coming into effect.

I received the news of the taking of Mons before I received the wire from General Headquarters to the effect that at 11 o'clock hostilities would cease." Indirectly, the allegation of wilful sacrifice of soldiers for personal ambition, was also answered by a letter written on Feb. 5th—a month before this charge was laid—and published in the Vancouver *World* with this phrase included: "I do not know what I shall do when I return to Canada. I thank God that I am alive, and the first thought that comes to one's mind is to devote the rest of one's life toward bettering the condition of all those who served in France—their wives, families or any other dependents. I believe the survivors have not been permitted to survive for nothing."

Meantime, Lieut.-Col. Cyrus W. Peck, V.C., D.S.O., had, on Mch. 6th, come to the defence of his leader and the British generals in a press interview in which he said: "General Currie needs no defence as to military ability or the care he took in all engagements to conserve the lives of the soldiers under him, but such wild charges as Sir Sam Hughes made in the House of Commons must be answered. I was aghast when the former Minister of Militia made his statements. General Currie, in my opinion, and in the opinion of most of the soldiers I have come in contact with, is one of the finest leaders in the War, and the care and safety of his men always took first place in his mind." The Toronto *Globe* (Mch. 6) editorially condemned the attack upon the General and reviewed conditions at the various battles dealt with: "At Hill 70 the outstanding quality of the Canadian leadership was caution and thorough preparation. Instead of attempting a frontal assault on Lens, infinite pains were taken to outflank the city's defences from the north. Of Passchendaele, the story is easily told. General Currie was acting there strictly under the orders of British General Headquarters. · . . . His men had to fight in the open, as the British and Australians had fought before them, and upon ground that looked like a stage setting for Danté's Inferno. . . . But it is in his references to the fighting about Cambrai that Sir Sam Hughes in his letter of Oct. 1st shows not only his bitter hatred of the men who were handling the Canadian Corps in the field, but his utter ignorance of the nature of the operations then in progress." Many proofs followed to indicate the alleged impossibility and ignorance of General Hughes' statements. To the Canadian Club, Toronto, on Apl. 14th Brig.-General W. A. Griesbach, C.B., C.M.G., D.S.O., paid a great tribute to his late Commander:

In my judgment the leadership of the Canadian Corps was scientific, skillful and courageous throughout the whole of the major operations, and in no single case coming under my observation has any Canadian soldier been sacrificed, nor has he died in vain. The leadership of the Canadian forces was skilled, honest and conscientious. There always was careful appreciation of the local situation, always carefully prepared plans, and every move was actuated by a desire to get results at the smallest possible cost. For its size and numbers, the Canadian Army was the most powerful fighting machine on earth. Knowing these things, to have to come home and listen to stories of needless sacrifice of men is to me a terrible and a scandalous thing. Something has been said about Sir Arthur Currie—I can only say that he is a great Canadian and a great general. A man with a big heart, a fine soldier, a sound strategist, an honest, kindly courageous man. He may have offended some people, but under his leadership the Canadian forces were always successful, and never once failed. As a result of this the Canadians were looked upon by the British, the French and the United States armies as a great fighting organization. General Currie had to sit in council with other big men and he was not the least among them.

At Victoria, B.C., Lieut.-Col. W. W. Foster, D.S.O., M.C., on Apl. 24th told *The Colonist*, in this connection, that: "It is only voicing the opinion of every officer in France, I am sure, when I say that in Sir Arthur Currie the Canadian Corps had the most competent Commander that any Corps could possibly have had and one whose energies were devoted to accomplishing his task with the least possible loss of life. For this Sir Arthur was noted throughout."

The General in England; Reviews and Incidents.   About this time Sir Arthur Currie was made a member in England of the Military Council of the Minister of Canadian Overseas Forces and, on May 3rd, he led 5,000 Canadian troops in a triumphal march through London from Grosvenor Gate to the Marble Arch, followed by 6,000 Australians, New Zealanders, South Africans and Newfoundlanders under Lieut.-Gen. Sir H. G. Chauvel, Brig.-General R. Young, Lieut.-Col. E. F. Thackaray and Lieut.-Col. A. E. Bernard, M.C., respectively. General Currie's staff included Maj.-Gen. E. W. B. Morrison and Brig.-Generals R. J. F. Hayter, R. Brutinel, C. J. Armstrong, N. W. Webber, G. J. Farmer, E. de B. Panet with H.R.H. Prince Arthur of Connaught, who had served as G.S.O. with the Canadians in France, and Brig.-General J. E. B. Seely, M.P., who had commanded the Canadian Cavalry Brigade.

The troops were commanded in their detachments by Brig.-General R. W. Paterson, D.S.O., Major-Gen. Sir Henry Burstall, Major-General Sir David Watson, Brig.-Generals R. Rennie, H. A. Panet, T. L. Tremblay, Alex. Ross, W. B. M. King, J. M. Ross, V. W. Odlum, J. Kirkcaldy and Lieut.-Colonels S. H. Osler, C.M.G., D.S.O., J. G. Weir, D.S.O., R.H.M. Hardisty, M.C., H. T. Hughes, C.M.G., D.S.O., M. A. Scott, D.S.O., and W. K. M. Anderson, D.S.O., Overhead flew an aerial escort of 14 Aeroplanes from the Canadian Air Force manned, amongst others, by Major R. Leckie, D.S.O., D.S.C., D.F.C., Major S. T. Hozell, D.S.O., M.C., and Bar, D.F.C. and Major A. E. McKeever, D.S.O., M.C. and Bar.   The streets were crowded with cheering people, and flags and banners flaunted gaily in the air, as this Empire parade passed through the great metropolis.   At the reviewing point outside Buckingham Palace stood the King and Queen accompanied by Queen Alexander, the Prince of Wales, the Princess Mary and the Duke of Connaught.   Field Marshal Haig with Generals Plumer, Birdwood, Byng and Horne were in attendance and Sir Edward Kemp, with his Council, and Sir George Perley were also present.   As the Canadian Contingent passed the King, General Currie saluted and took his place on the dais; so with the

Commanders of the other Empire Divisions. The King addressed the troops briefly and each soldier received a facsimile of his speech.

Following this event Sir Arthur Currie took part in various public affairs in England and, on May 6th, a private letter was partially published at Ottawa saying that he hoped to be home in June and that he had no intention of entering politics, although several seats had been offered him: "I am altogether out of touch with home problems and affairs and it would, therefore, be useless for me to enter politics, even if I had the inclination. I know several factions are hardly playing the game with me, but I am a soldier first and last and, while a member of the C.E.F., I will respect discipline and not attempt to answer them even though my friends are urging me to do so."

General Currie's Speeches in England. On May 20th a Dinner was tendered the General by the Canada Club, a 100-year-old organization of London, with the Duke of Connaught in the chair and General Byng amongst those present. The Prince of Wales spoke and made his first announcement of a coming visit to Canada. The Royal chairman, after a tribute to the Canadian Corps, added: "Their Commander proved himself to be a thorough soldier; he imbued his men with military ardour, he maintained a proper discipline; he had the warm support of the Divisional Commanders, and was on the best relations with all the different Corps Commanders of the British Army." Sir Arthur, in his reply, spoke warmly of Generals Rawlinson and Horne under whom, as Army leaders, the Corps had long fought and declared that: "We are going home filled with a deeper appreciation of the might, the majesty and the power of our Empire, more than ever convinced that Britain never unfurls her colours except in the cause of justice and right; we are going back to a wonderful land of promise and hope, the cherished land of freedom and a new chance, with a broader outlook, a more kindly humanity, and a truer conception of the things really worth while."

On May 21st there was a last foregathering in England, at the Savoy Hotel, of the officers of the 4th Division with speeches from Generals Watson, Turner and J. H. MacBrien. Sir Arthur Currie followed and compared Vimy with the three great final battles of the Corps: "At Vimy Canadians attacked on a front of 7,000 yards and made a penetration of 10,000 yards. They captured 67 guns and 7,000 prisoners, and suffered over 20,000 casualties. At Amiens their penetration was 24,000 yards. They fought 16 German divisions, captured 196 guns and about 10,000 prisoners, and their casualties in the effort were 11,000. . . . Beginning on Aug. 26th, by Sept. 3rd the Canadians had taken the outlying system of trenches—the Quéant-Drocourt Switch—and broken the Hindenburg Line. They made a penetration of 20,000 yards and took 100 guns and 11,000 prisoners. . . . At Cambrai they fought 13 German divisions, and 13 machine-gun battalions and captured 207 guns and 10,000 prisoners.'' At the Mansion House, on May 26th, the General was entertained by the Lord Mayor with six Cabinet Ministers present, Earl Reading, just back from Washington, the Duke of Connaught, General Byng and many representative Canadians.

The Lord Mayor in his speech declared that ''high military authorities consider that Sir Arthur Currie's conduct of the pursuit of the enemy in the last phase of the war was a masterpiece of tactics.'' In his reply the General paid generous tribute to the London Divisions in the War and, especially, to the brilliant achievements of the Guards and went on, in language which the London press described as that of a statesman, to deal with the lessons of the War and world conditions resulting from it. He declared the British Empire to be breaking the trail for human progress: ''The British Empire is the workshop where the ideas of practical democracy are forged, welded and made workable. The improvement of the method of governing the British Empire must of necessity react upon and influence the League of Nations and it is our plain duty that, having done so much to secure the world against German hegemony we leave nothing undone that will tend to perfect the body politic. . . . The national spirit of the Dominions has been matured by the War, but the ties which bind the Empire together have by no means been weakened. On the contrary, I believe there is now a strong feeling that machinery should be erected which will make out of the British Empire a constellation of free nations, equal, united by common goodwill, common ideals, reciprocal confidence, all under one flag and one King.''

A Dominion Day dinner in London, with Sir George Perley in the chair, and speeches from Lieut.-Col. L. C. M. S. Amery, M.P., Under-Secretary for the Colonies, Hon. C. J. Doherty and Hon. A. L. Sifton for Canada, Sir Hamar Greenwood, K.C., M.P., as Under-Secretary for the Home Office and Gen. Sir Richard Turner, was also addressed by General Currie who declared there now was a new war to win: ''The policy of drift cannot be tolerated, and that of dilly-dally cannot be excused. If Bolshevism rears its ugly head, shoot it up. If any wrong influence is active, it must be actively countered. Training is merely education; discipline only self-control. . . . Canada must be prepared to take her part in the responsibilities as well as the privileges of our Empire.''

Parliamentary Recognition; Speeches and a Resolution. In Canada, on July 7th, Parliament took up the question of its Army's services and its Commander's work. It was just before prorogation and there had been rumours that the Dominion would follow the British example by amply recognizing and generously rewarding the achievements of its war leaders. A recognition of the services of the soldiers was given but no spectacular reward, such as the Earldoms granted to Haig and Beatty or the money grants of $500,000 accorded to each of them was even considered nor was it practicable in a democracy of the form which Canada was developing. In a few brief words Sir Robert Borden presented to Parliament a Resolution of thanks to the Canadian forces in which, however, no personal reference was made to the Officer Commanding the Corps. The Premier spoke briefly of the General in his speech:

There has been a whisper of criticism that he was not sufficiently mindful of his duty to safeguard the lives of those under his command. In my judgment no criticism could be more unjust. Indeed, I know that on more than one occasion, and especially on one notable occasion, he took a stand in defiance of military precedents. That stand he took for one reason and one reason alone; his duty to avoid any needless sacrifice of the troops under his command. No General at the front more fully realized that solemn duty; and during the last 18 months of the War there was no General whose judgment was more respected, none whose ability and thoroughness were more relied upon, than he who then commanded the Canadian Corps.

A short but eloquent eulogy of the achievements of the Corps followed and the Resolution was then seconded by D. D. McKenzie, Opposition leader and supported by Hon. R. Lemieux. To General Currie, Mr. McKenzie referred as a great Canadian: "In the United States it has been a matter of pride for the American veteran to say: 'I was with Grant.' The day will come when the gallant veterans of the Grand Army of Canada will be proud to tell their children: 'I was with Currie.'" Mr. Lemieux declared that the War was one of the common soldier and not of generals and officers. The Resolution was unanimously passed as follows:

That the thanks of this House be given to the General Officer Commanding, to the officers, non-commissioned officers and men of the Canadian Army Corps and to the other Canadian military forces, and also to the women in the Canadian medical services and other services auxiliary thereto, for the unflinching courage, the steadfastness, and the skill with which throughout the War they served the cause of their country and Empire in circumstances of unexampled hardship, and for their splendid contribution to the final victory of right and liberty.

That the thanks of this House be given to the officers, petty officers and men of the Royal Canadian Naval Service and the Royal Canadian Naval Air Service for their services in guarding the shores of Canada and in preserving the sea communications upon which the commerce of the Dominion and the maintenance of the forces in the field depended.

That the thanks of this House be accorded to those Canadians who served in other than Canadian units, whether in the British naval, military or air forces, or elsewhere, for the determination and fortitude with which they thus upheld their Empire's cause with such credit to their country's name.

That this House doth acknowledge with deep gratitude the valour and devotion of those who laid down their lives in the service of their country and Empire, and offers its sympathy to their relatives and friends in the sorrows they have sustained.

Canadians and the Victory Parade in London. Following this incident in Canada came the rather curious one in London associated with the splendid and variously termed Peace or Victory Parade of Allied national troops, Empire soldiers, sailors of the British Navy and the British-Canadian masters of the air, through

London on July 19th. It was, perhaps, the greatest demonstration
in the whole vivid drama of London's history; it was the concentrated exhibition of war colour in a triumph which involved all
nations and the whole world.   By the merest accident of a last
moment's effort Canada was represented with all the other Empire
dominions and nations and Allied troops from everywhere—the
United States and France, Belgium and Roumania, Czecho-Slovakia and Italy, Japan and Poland, Siam and Serbia.   Why this
hesitation and hurried participation it is hard to say.

On July 9th a despatch from London in the Montreal-*Star*
drew attention to the fact that no Canadian troops were to take part
in the great Parade although, it was added, there were 28,000
Canadian troops still overseas awaiting transportation to Canada.
On the 18th General Currie took the unusual step of giving a press
interview as to a situation which was arousing interest and wide
criticism in London and stated that: "The decision for the Canadians not to participate was arrived at without consultation with
myself and I, personally, regret such a decision exceedingly.   It is
likely to create a most unfavourable impression both in Canada
and in England; there are at least a thousand Canadians in and
around London, many of them wounded on the Western front, who
can be assembled for the purpose; I have received many applications from officers and men who are anxious to participate."   The
official programme had stated that he, with other generals, would
ride with Field-Marshal Haig, but the absence of any other Canadians in the procession would create an awkward situation and, he
added, he had not decided to take the place assigned to him.   At
the same time Canadian Military Headquarters at Argyll House
issued a statement to the press declaring that:

It is a matter of deep regret that it has been found impossible to
accept the invitation extended by the War Office to the Canadian Forces to
take part in the Peace celebration procession.   Unfortunately, owing to
the Canadian scheme of demobilization, all organized units have already
been repatriated.   Canadian soldiers still remain in this country, but while
they individually represent a number of fighting units the circumstances
of departure prevent their being given a ceremonial formation.

Following this the evening press had all kinds of rumours as
to real or alleged reasons for this decision and Sir Arthur Currie's
statement.   Canadian theories and discussion were many-sided with
much gossip as to supposed differences between Headquarters
officers and the Corps Commander.   It was said in London that the
King sent a personal expression of his wish to Argyll House that
Canada should be represented, and some papers said that Sir
Robert Borden intervened; whatever may have happened 225 Canadians finally lead the forces of the external Empire in the Parade
with Generals Currie and Turner riding in front side by side.
The great throngs gave many expressions of pleasure at the fact
that some Canadians, at least, were there.   A few days later (July
23) the Canadian general stood upon the dais of Cambridge Uni-

versity with the King of the Belgians, the Prince of Wales, F. M. Sir Douglas Haig, Admirals Beatty, Sturdee and Wemyss of the Royal Navy, Generals Rawlinson, Birdwood, Wilson and Horne of the British Army, Monash of the Australian Forces and Pershing of the Americans and received one of England's highest compliments, the Honourary degree of LL.D. On the 19th he had shared with these and other Allied commanders the hospitality of the Prince of Wales at a formal banquet.

On Aug. 9th he sailed for Canada with a final word of thanks, through the Liverpool *Daily Post*, to those who had treated him and his gallant forces so well in England: "One thing which has struck me more than any other is that the Canadians and English understand each other better than they did before, and that surely tends for the solidarity of the Empire. Before the war we did not know each other well enough. I am an Imperialist. The sort of Imperialism I believe in justifies me in claiming the right to share in the traditions of this country. . . . We want a greater intimacy between the different parts of the Empire, a greater tolerance, a greater understanding, a closer study of each other's problems, and a more perfect co-operation." He added that Canadians had married 35,000 English or Scottish girls and expressed the wish that both in England and Canada children would be better instructed in respect for their parents. On Sir Arthur's departure *Canada*, a London journal, representing much Canadian sentiment in the Metropolis, described (Aug. 9) his speeches as indicating distinct promise of statesmanship, declared that he had won the "strong admiration and respect" of the Mother Country and hoped that his ability would be turned to the fullest account in Canada's day of peace. It was generally understood that a high position was open to him in the British Army but that he preferred to return home.

The General's Reception and Speeches in Canada. His reception was a worthy one in its formal presentation of public approval but it lacked the enthusiastic personal greetings given in England to Haig or Allenby and in the United States to Pershing. Canadians once more proved themselves an undemonstrative people,—a condition from which only Pretoria Day in 1902 or the personal magnetism of the Prince of Wales in 1919 had, in late years, been able to stir them. Halifax received the General as he landed from the *Caronia* on Sunday, Aug. 17th, with a Civic address presented by Mayor J. S. Parker which reviewed the responsibilities he had so bravely and skillfully borne and declared that: "The devotion with which you performed your duty, the thoroughness with which you completed your preparations, the spirit of hope with which you inspired the troops, and the extraordinary succession of victories that crowned your efforts, have won for you our deepest gratitude and a lasting name in the records of our country. As step by step you were promoted to positions of increasing responsibility you never lost sympathy and regard for the men in the ranks." His reply was brief and included a tribute to Colonels A. H. Borden and J. L. Ralston of Nova Scotia. At Ottawa on Aug. 18 he was welcomed home by a guard of honour from the ranks of his old soldiers, by crowds who lined the streets of the Capital, by a joint Federal and Civic reception on Parliament Hill.

The latter was marked by brief, informal, addresses from Sir George Foster, Acting-Premier and Mayor Harold Fisher, the reading of a letter from Sir Robert Borden referring to the General's "splendid record of distinguished service to Canada and the Empire," and by the presence of most of the Ministers and Generals Fiset, Watson, Loomis, Macdonell, Morrison, Williams, etc. A banquet at the County Club followed with General Mewburn, Minister of Militia as the host and his formal announcement that Lieut.-General Currie had been created a full General—the only one possessed by the Dominion—and appointed Inspector-General of Canada's Forces and Military Councillor. It was a most representative military function and, in his speech, the Minister stated that Sir Arthur Currie had risen by sheer ability, and that his appointment to the Canadian command was on recommendation of F. M. Sir Douglas Haig; that "at all times he had displayed great tact, judgment and skill in the handling of men and in the working out of the many difficult problems that had confronted him"; that he had shown a splendid grasp of the situation and had built up an Army in France composed of "the most magnificent soldiers the world had ever seen."

In his reply General Currie dwelt, as in various succeeding speeches throughout Canada, upon the last 100 days of the War and added: "I am glad to say that our citizen army fought against the greatest military machine the world has ever produced, yet never lost a gun in four years; that in the last two years they never failed to take an objective and that there were some of our Divisions which never allowed a hostile foot to enter their trenches. We never lost an inch of ground that we had once consolidated." On Aug. 26-7 the General was in Montreal where a parade shared in by a dozen generals and passing through great crowds of people was held, with an enthusiastic demonstration by veterans at the Khaki Club, which evoked this declaration: "The Canadian Corps was one big machine and it was the spirit of co-operation that won us success. If any problems are to be confronted in Canada or any difficulties are to be overcome, the only way to meet them is by standing together again, and if we stood by one another in the Field we can do the same in civil life. We are all comrades here as we were all comrades there. The rest of my life, as far as I am able, will be devoted, first, to helping the widows and orphans of those who are not coming back; and, next, to helping you boys who exposed your bodies as a living bulwark against dangers that threatened the world."

A great banquet followed at the Ritz-Carlton with a speech which surprised his audience of 250 military men and 150 civilians, for its strength and style; on the 27th a Luncheon of the Canadian Club brought together 900 prominent citizens and evoked generous tributes in speech and applause to the guest of the day. Major G. C. McDonald, the chairman, declared that: "We consider General Currie in a class by himself. He is our greatest Canadian. In every capacity in which he appears he has proved an honour to Canada and to himself. As a subordinate officer he has shown himself loyal and faithful to his superiors, and as Commander he has had the most fervent loyalty and admiration, as well as the affection of his followers. His messages to the troops were probably the most inspiring of any given on the field of modern battle. . . Aside from the faith that we would win the War the greatest factor in the success of the Canadian Corps was the confidence in its leadership. That this confidence was justified was proved by the consistent success of every operation undertaken by General Currie. . . . It is my greatest pride to have served under General Currie and I consider it the greatest privilege of my life to introduce him to-day." Sir Arthur's response was a sustained and vigourous eulogy of the services of the Canadian soldier in the War.

Toronto received the General—who, in this journey across Canada, was accompanied by his wife and children—on Aug. 29th with a preliminary welcome at the station by 500 singing school children and a Civic reception at which Mayor T. L. Church read an Address declaring that: "We are proud that a native son of our beloved Province possessed the natural gift of leadership and the courage and ability as a soldier to win for himself a place among the great generals of the War." At Massey Hall, a little later, thousands of people heard an address to a joint meeting of the Empire and Canadian Clubs, with R. A. Stapells in the chair, and were given a brief statement as to the allegations of Sir Sam Hughes regarding Mons—though his name was not mentioned: "The orders of the Commander-in-Chief of the Allied Forces were that there was to be no relaxation in the pressure on the enemy during the visit of the German plenipotentiaries to the Allied headquarters. It was 5 o'clock on the morning of Nov. 11 when the Germans agreed to the terms of the Armistice. Nobody knew before 5 o'clock whether they would accept the terms. We were ordered to continue the pressure. Before 5 o'clock that morning Mons was in our possession." The Provincial Command of the G.W.V.A. also tended a formal welcome and offered to Sir Arthur a life membership in that important organization of soldiers.

In the evening there was a banquet by the Originals Club at which the General expressed himself as follows: "This is my Imperialism. England is my England, although I have no English in me. Scotland is my Scotland and Ireland my Ireland. I have a little of both. All the traditions of Britain are the traditions of Canada too. We cannot be indifferent to England, Ireland, or Scotland nor they to us. Canada must go to war if Britain does. If we don't want to go then we must tell Britain we don't want to belong to the British Empire." As to local affairs: "We must have a Militia. . I believe we can create an organization which will give the people their money's worth, which will give them a training that will prepare them for any contingencies of the future."

Following his first day's reception—he stayed during his visit with Sir Henry Pellatt at Casa Loma—General Currie addressed an Exhibition luncheon on the 30th and urged upon business men and Governments, alike, the claims of the returned men to consideration, positions and aid wherever required. The Toronto branch of · the Girl Guides of Canada was also addressed by the General and on Sept. 1st he was at his old home town of Strathroy where an enthusiastic reception was given. Here he stayed with members of his family until the 27th when he left for the West. A visit was paid during this period, however, to London, where the General opened the Western Fair on the 8th and told the Canadian Club that there was danger of Bolshevism, even in Canada; "I believe that there is still a German menace. Ninety per cent. of the heads of the Russian Soviet Government are Germans, and their agents are active everywhere. There are agents in London, Ont., whose names I know." He also repeated the remark, made in other speeches, that there was no real glamour about War: "It is simply butchery."

In Winnipeg, on Sept. 30th, Sir Arthur received a formal welcome from the City, the Lieut.-Governor and the Provincial Government. Mayor C. F. Gray presented an Address and to it the General replied: "I am not a believer in large standing armies. Those who went through the late war never want to see any further wars. But I think we will build up a Militia system which will be of service to the country and, if another war should come, will be the means of Canada supplying the necessary forces to take her proper share in it." He also spoke to large gatherings of the Canadian Club. At Regina on Oct. 2nd he was given a great reception when he passed through accompanied by Lady Currie and his two children and so at New Westminster and other points *en route*. Speaking to the Canadian Club, Vancouver, on Oct. 4th, after receiving the Civic welcome and Address with, also, a silver tea service for himself and a silver card-case for Lady Currie, he declared the situation of the returned men to be fairly satisfactory: "I do not mean to say that all are fully re-established, but of the great many hundreds to whom I have spoken since landing in Canada only a small percentage have been out of work or in grave trouble as a result of service."

At Victoria he was given a warm welcome with an Address from the Province presented by the Premier, Hon. John Oliver, together with a handsome silver tray. The Great War Veterans followed with an Address which declared that: "It was our privilege to serve with you, rendering service to the very limit of human courage and endurance; doing 'our bit' to ensure the success of your skilfully conceived plans." A banquet was tendered by the

British Campaigners' Association on Feb. 6th and the General was given an enthusiastic welcome; on the same day Sir Arthur and Lady Currie held a public reception in the Parliament Buildings. Other functions followed and on Nov. 28th the General in a Vancouver interview stated that: "Although the time is not at hand for the adoption of any scheme of compulsory training, it is bound to come later. It is the only fair and democratic way in which any extensive Militia scheme can properly be carried out."

This was on his way to take up official duties at Ottawa and, at Calgary on Dec. 2nd, a Civic reception and luncheon were tendered to him and to Brig.-Generals A. H. Bell, C.M.G. and H. F. McDonald, C.M.G., D.S.O. of that City. At Regina on Dec. 4th a banquet was tendered the Inspector-General with Brig.-Generals J. F. L. Embury, C.M.G., D.S.O., K.C. and Alex. Ross, C.M.G., D.S.O., K.C. joining in the welcome. On Dec. 11th, he reached Ottawa and took over his duties at the Militia Department. This review of an interesting event of the year may conclude with the comment of Brig.-General C. H. Mitchell, C.B., C.M.G., D.S.O. at Toronto on Aug. 28th: "There is one outstanding figure in the 2nd battle of Ypres. He is General Sir Arthur Currie. At that time he commanded the 2nd Infantry Brigade. . . . He developed from a business man to a real soldier—a tactician and strategist. I saw him in action from the very first and I know whereof I speak. . . . I consider, and I know that great military men will agree, that General Harrington of the British Army and General Currie, commanding the Canadians, were two of the greatest 'finds' of the whole war."

Return of the Troops; Disturbances in England; Canadians in Russia. Through all the early portion of the year troops streamed across the Atlantic for Canada as rapidly as the strained transport system of the United Kingdom and its great resources in ships could be utilized. Vast as was the shipping, however, still greater were the calls. Far-away Australia and South Africa demanded the quick return of their men, the United States, in strident tones, wanted its 2,000,000 men returned at once. Canada was hungry for its sons to come back, tens of thousands of women from Canada and still greater numbers from other countries, wanted to return with their men-folk; while the revival or re-organization of British export trade insistently demanded ships for its distribution abroad. Delays under such conditions were inevitable, impatience amongst the soldiers retained in England was equally certain, disturbances such as those of Kinmel Park and Witley were not unnatural though none-the-less regrettable.

The Overseas Minister, Sir Edward Kemp, and his Council did much to alleviate the discontents and discomforts of the waiting period but they could not meet all the demands of a soldiery sick of war and eager to return home with a small minority in the ranks ever ready for trouble and some, perhaps, seeking an opportunity to create it. There was a system of general training maintained at all the Camps—for purposes of preserving health, preparing the troops gradually for demobilization, and providing occupation for an otherwise idle period. Instruction of a special nature was supplied by the Khaki University in all areas, and sports and athletics were encouraged. The chief Camps and commanders were as follows:

Borden, under Brig.-General C. H. Maclaren,. C.M.G., D.S.O.
Bramshott, under Brig.-General Robert Rennie, C.B., C.M.G., D.S.O., M.V.O.
Seaford, under Brig.-General H. M. Dyer, C.M.G., D.S.O.
Whitley, under Brig.-General F. W. Hill, C.M.G., D.S.O.

A Concentration Camp was opened at Ripon in connection with the plans of the Khaki University and for the purpose of assembling soldiers and giving instruction in advanced educational work to suitable students. It proved popular and there was keen competition to gain admittance with, in March, between 750 and 800 students in attendance. The Battalion schools were organized for men seeking elementary education in agriculture and commercial arithmetic. Literature of a useful nature about Canada was distributed and money appropriated for expenses incurred in training Canadian athletic teams and supplying sporting equipment, etc. The Y.M.C.A. was at work in all areas with distribution of boxing gloves and footballs, etc., and preparations for an extensive athletic programme. In each area there were from four to six Y.M.C.A. huts supplied with concert parties, luxuries, cinemas, table games and free stationery. There were also canteens selling various goods such as cleaning kits, etc., at cheapest rates. Pamphlets on citizenship were distributed up to 50,000 copies.

Troubles of the Waiting Troops—Kinmel, Epsom, Witley. With it all, however, there was discontent and impatience, there were rumours of precedence in shipment to Canada being given soldiers of the M.S.A. draft over those of early contingents, there were evidences of the February programme of shipments having fallen short by fully one-third and there was a known cancellation of several sailings. On Mch. 7th exaggerated reports were published in England and cabled to Canada of disturbances at Kinmel Park, about five miles from Rhyl in Wales and not far from Liverpool, where about 15,000 Canadians, under Camp Commandant M. A. Colquhoun, C.M.G., D.S.O., awaited embarkation. It was said that 6,000 men were involved in the fighting with 27 persons killed and many wounded. As a matter of fact 3 rioters and 2 men on picket duty were killed and 21 injured. The trouble lasted during Mch. 4th and 5th when there was parading and rioting led by some soldiers of foreign extraction of whom one carried a red flag; there was considerable looting and disorder with bodies of men marching as far as a village called Abergele, four miles away, and some slight fighting with troops which stood their ground. A staff officer came from London by aeroplane and addressed the men, followed, a little later, by General Sir Richard Turner who spoke to detachments in a number of different parts of the Camp and explained the situation and supposed grievances.

The troubles subsided and a Court of Enquiry was at once convened of which Maj.-Gen. Sir H. E. Burstall, K.C.B., C.M.G. was presiding officer. In the Commons at Ottawa on Mch. 17th a despatch from Sir Edward Kemp was read stating that there had been unrest due to the natural homesickness of the men, to the unavoidable inaction of active spirits accustomed to strenuous war conditions, the monotony of a waiting period, the unavoidable fact of the Armistice having been followed by one of the most severe winters England had ever experienced and a consequent shortage of fuel, the unpleasant and everywhere prevalent Influenza, a general atmosphere of surrounding Labour unrest. Lieut.-Col. A. C. Pratt, M.L.A., who returned from England about this time laid the whole blame for the situation on the Canadian administration at Argyll House—in a Halifax interview of Mch. 19th in which he vehemently denounced General Turner, Sir Robert Borden and Sir George Perley.

Replying to questions in the Imperial Parliament and an insinuation that the trouble was due to wet canteens Mr. Winston Churchill stated on Mch. 19th that the Camp was entirely in the hands of the Canadian authorities and that: "Wet canteens were not, and never had been, provided for Canadian troops, except upon the decision of the Canadian authorities. He was informed that so far from their provision causing disturbances, it had quite a contrary effect." Following this the Court-Martial had proceeded at Liverpool with General Burstall as President and Colonels C. M. Nelles, C.M.G., H. H. Mathews, D.S.O., J. L. Ralston, D.S.O. and J. B. Donnelly, D.S.O., with 12 others, as members of the Court. After sitting from Apl. 16th till June 7th and trying 38 cases, involving 50 prisoners charged with mutiny and other offences, the Court acquitted 17 and convicted 27 of mutiny and 6 of minor charges. The sentences included various terms of imprisonment.

Unrest continued amongst the soldiers, however, based chiefly upon the continued postponement of sailings from time to time with, also, many of the conditions mentioned in connection with Rhyl. At Epsom on June 17th about 400 Canadians attacked the local police station in order to release some Canadian soldiers who were under arrest and who, it was afterwards stated, would shortly have been handed over to the Canadian authorities. Several British policemen were wounded—one so seriously that he died next morning. Five or six Canadians were also injured—one seriously. Some preceding friction had occurred between a local and rough race-track element and the Canadian troops—who also appeared quite ready for a "shindy." At the ensuing Surrey Assizes (July 23) five Canadian soldiers were found guilty of manslaughter and sentenced to 12 months' imprisonment. On June 19th, following similar delays in transportation, owing to the Labour dock-strikes at Liverpool, demonstrations took place at Witley Camp with its

16,000 men which ended in a small riot, the burning of several buildings and injury to three of the men. A few days before this at South Ripon Camp there had been trouble, with canteen looting as the chief offence. As to the prisoners in this and other connections Sir Edward Kemp stated in October that every case had been investigated and out of 274 only 46 men were still held and that their sentences expired in January, 1920. In the British Parliament on June 22nd Col. Leslie Wilson, of the Ministry of Shipping, said in reply to a question:

> I would like to inform the House that by the 30th of June no less than 87·2 per cent. of the Canadian troops will have embarked for Canada. I think it is only right for me to say, also, on behalf of the Ministry I represent, that we have carried out, not only what we said we would carry out in regard to the repatriation of Canadian troops, but more than that. Certainly with regard to the last two or three months we have carried more troops than the Canadian authorities suggested that we should carry. I think I may say that we have met practically every request that has been put forward. I am sure it is incorrect to say that the American troops are being repatriated at a greater rate than the Canadians. I know they are not being repatriated in British ships. We have repatriated 134,500 United States troops in British ships, whereas we shall have embarked by June 30, 238,000 Canadians—that is 87·2 per cent. of the total number to be repatriated. No British ships have been used during the last two months for the repatriation of American troops which the Canadians were willing to take.*

Meanwhile, the Canadian troops were receiving a warm welcome in their home towns as they gradually returned to Canada at the average rate of 3,400 a month between the Armistice and the end of June 1919. There was no apparent effort and, if there had been one, it would have been difficult to realize, to give them a reception in organized units of Brigades or Divisions. In the main, Battalions came together and, in the cases where they represented specific centres, a fitting welcome was organized. Before leaving England, and so far as demobilization conditions permitted, they were given suitable farewells—more would have been done in this respect if the Canadian command had encouraged it. At Witley Camp, for instance, on Apl. 24th the Duke of Connaught, accompanied by Prince Arthur of Connaught, presented the King's Colours to the 18th West Ontario, the 20th Central Ontario and the 24th Montreal Battalions.

Addressing the assembled troops, after the stately ceremony, the Duke expressed his pleasure in handing to their charge Colours emblematic of loyalty to King and country and added: "My son, who is here with me to-day, saw the 2nd Division going into action at Vimy Ridge, and he says that he will never forget it as long as he lives. I do not suppose I shall ever have the pleasure of seeing you again—certainly not in the Old Country. . . . May you meet in the great Dominion with the gratitude and respect of your fellow-countrymen, as you leave England carrying with you the

---

*Note.—According to the Report of the U. S. Secretary of the Navy for 1918-9 by the end of July, 1919, 1,770,484 U. S. troops had been returned of whom 1,518,149 were in U. S. transports.

Ranching Scene near Prince Albert, Sask.

affection and respect of the whole British Army and of the whole British nation." The enthusiastic reception given the troops who shared in the Empire parade through London and by the massed millions who saw the tiny Contingent in the Peace Day parade could never be forgotten by those who were present.

Canada's Welcome to its Soldiers. On Mch.9th the Royal Canadian Regiment with detachments of the 42nd and 49th Battalions of Nova Scotia were welcomed home by the people of Halifax and a local journal declared that "for once the latter forgot to be apathetic and went quite mad with enthusiasm." A formal reception by the Lieut.-Governor and Government, and the Mayor of the City, followed; the streets contained 6 triumphal arches and were gaily decorated while the city was illuminated at night and a great banquet concluded the reception. Lieut.-Colonels C. R. E. Willetts, D.S.O., and Claude H. Hill, D.S.O., were in command of the R.C.R's. On Mch. 11th the famous 42nd Highlanders of Montreal who fought in most of the Canadian battles of the Western Front under (1) Lieut.-Col. G. S. Cantlie, D.S.O., (2) the late Lieut.-Col. Bartlett McLennan, D.S.O., and (3) Lieut.-Col. Royal L. H. Ewing, M.C., D.S.O., were welcomed by massed crowds in Montreal. The still more famous P.P.C.L.I., the Princess Pats of popular parlance, were cheered all along the line from Halifax until they arrived at Ottawa on Mch. 19th and marched in full fighting dress with rifles and bayonets, through two miles of cheering people, until they reached Parliament Hill where, on a special dais, the Governor-General extended to them a national welcome; described them as taking "a place alongside the historic regiments of the Old Country in the splendid armies of the Empire," and proving their military efficiency, courage and devotion; congratulated them on being made, as a Regiment, part of the permanent military forces of Canada. They were under command of Lieut.-Col. A. Hamilton Gault, D.S.O. and with him was Lieut.-Col. A. A. M. Adamson, D.S.O. his predecessor in command; their memorable record included these battlefields:

    1915 St. Eloi, Polygon Wood, Ypres.
    1916 Zillebeke, Somme, Regina Trench, Courcelette.
    1917 Vimy Ridge, Hill 70, Passchendaele.
    1918 Amiens, Monchy, Jigsaw Wood, Valenciennes, Mons.

At this time the 49th Battalion and the 4th and 5th Canadian Mounted Rifles were *en route* from Halifax to Montreal. Every town, village and platform on the line which the train passed through from Moncton, N.B. was decorated with flags and bunting while banners were flying from almost every house on the route. The 5th C.M.R. was enthusiastically welcomed at Sherbrooke where it had been mobilized under its late Commander, Lieut.-Col. G. H. Baker, M.P. and, a day later, Mch. 18, at Montreal where a night reception was given which showed the Canadian metropolis ablaze with lights and fireworks and torches and included a parade through streets so crowded that the soldiers, who were under command

3

of Lieut.-Col. R. W. Rhoades, D.S.O., M.C., had to march single file accompanied by a continuous detonation of bombs; it was followed by a dance of the Victoria Rifles in the Armouries and a Civic welcome by Mayor Martin.

The 4th C.M.R. were enthusiastically welcomed in Toronto on Mch. 19th when, in a two mile route, the men were almost swept off their feet by dense masses of cheering men, women and children. At the Parliament Buildings they were reviewed by electric light, with searchlights and torches making the scene as bright as noonday and spectacular blackness in the background; cheering crowds were everywhere. The salute was taken by Brig.-Gen. J. A. Gunn, C.M.G., D.S.O. and the Regiment was commanded by Lieut.-Col. W. R. Patterson, D.S.O., and Major Victor Sifton, D.S.O., 2nd in command. Edmonton, on Mch. 22nd, gave an historic reception to the 49th Battalion as it marched through streets lined with practically the whole of the population to the Parliament Buildings where Lieut.-Governor R. G. Brett and Premier the Hon. C. Stewart, gave a formal welcome and Mayor Clarke presented an Address to Lieut.-Col. R. H. Palmer, D.S.O., for his Battalion—originally raised and commanded by Brig.-Gen. W. A. Griesbach, C.M.G., D.S.O., M.P.

So at Winnipeg, on Mch. 23rd, when the whole City turned out to welcome the 43rd (Cameron) Highlanders under Lieut.-Col. W. K. Chandler, D.S.O. and the 10th Field Ambulance Corps under Lieut.-Col. T. M. Leask, D.S.O., and Bar. Of the original officers of the 43rd only Col. Chandler remained, the regiment had fought in nearly all the Canadian battles of the War, its commanders had included the late Lieut.-Col. R. M. Thomson and Colonels H. M. Urquhart, M.C., D.S.O. with Bar, and Wm. Grassie, D.S.O., one of its distinguished officers was Capt. Robert Shankland, V.C., D.C.M. The Civic address presented by Mayor C. F. Gray was an eloquent eulogy of the Battalion's services and of the country to which they were returning as citizens. On the same day Toronto was welcoming the 58th Battalion commanded by Lieut.-Col. G. F. McFarland with Major D. Carmichael, D.S.O. and Bar, M.C. and Bar, as second in command and the 2nd C.M.R. The Address presented by Mayor T. L. Church was eloquent in terms: "We welcome you for the glorious victories you have won, for the glory you have brought to Canada, for the sacrifices you have made for our safety and the welfare of the world, for the blood you shed and the dead you left on those far away fields. . . . Your glorious deeds in defence of the civilization of the world will be an inspiration and pride to Canadians forever."

Calgary gave a hearty welcome to the 8th Field Ambulance on Mch. 21st. Montreal on Apl. 20th gave a royal reception to the 13th and 14th Battalions of whose 2,000 and more men less than 100 "originals" were with the marching troops while 10,000 more had passed through their ranks and lay beneath the crosses of the Western Front. A riot of colour and decorations met their eyes while great crowds cheered with fervour and spirit; Major-General

E. W. Wilson, C.M.G. with a group of distinguished war officers reviewed the march past; Major Sinclair was in command of the 13th and Lieut.-Col. Richard Worrall, M.C., D.S.O., of the 14th. The "Terrible Tenth" which had fought through the War from Valcartier and through the last great hundred days, whose great ranks had included 14,000 men in the years of war and whose commander, Lieut.-Col. E. W. Macdonald, M.C., D.S.O., in his 27th year, was the youngest C.O. in the Canadian Corps, received a great welcome through the towns of Alberta and at Edmonton on Apl. 22-23. So with the "Fighting Fifth" of Saskatchewan, about the same time, on its return to that Province with a record of one C.B. and 3 C.M.G.'s; 7 bars to the D.S.O. and 16 D.S.O.'s; 7 bars to the M.M., and 181 M.M.'s. It was proud of having given Brig.-Generals G. S. Tuxford, H. M. Dyer and E. Hilliam to the Army. Its Commander was Lieut.-Col. L. P. O. Tudor, D.S.O., who had succeeded Generals Tuxford and Dyer.

Toronto, on Apl. 23rd welcomed its 3rd Battalion led by Lieut.-Col. J. B. Rogers, D.S.O., M.C., its 4th led by Lieut.-Col. C. M. Nelles and a part of its 1st Battalion; Winnipeg, on May 6th cheered its 16th (Canadian Scottish) Battalion and the 8th or "Little Black Devils," commanded by Lieut.-Col. A. L. Sanders, D.S.O., M.C. and Bar who had enlisted as a private; Quebec and Montreal on May 18-19 gave a fitting reception to the famous 22nd (French-Canadian) Battalion which had so distinguished itself at Courcelette and elsewhere. Quebec City opened its heart to this Regiment in a parade through decorated streets; it was given an official reception by the Provincial Government and City officials and the officers a luncheon at the Garrison Club and a dinner at the Chateau Frontenac. In Montreal, St. Catherine and other streets showed a blaze of colour, flags and decorations were everywhere, and a mass of cheering, singing people filled the streets as the Battalion swung through under Lieut.-Col. L. R. Laflèche; so with the 24th Batt. on the preceding day under command of Lieut.-Col. C. F. Ritchie, D.S.O., M.C. Halifax, on May 16, acclaimed its own 25th Nova Scotia Battalion and St. John on the 17th enthusiastically welcomed the "Fighting 26th" of New Brunswick under command of Lieut.-Col. W. R. Brown, D.S.O. and Bar—in succession to Lieut.-Colonels J. L. McAvity, A. E. G. McKenzie, D.S.O., and C. G. Porter, D.S.O.

Montreal, again, on June 8th acclaimed a returning Battalion, the 87th and crowded, decorated streets once more cheered the march of the men under Lieut.-Col. R. Bickerdike, D.S.O.; Toronto on the same day gave a great reception to the 75th and 102nd Battalions as, under the respective commands of Lieut.-Col. C. C. Harbottle, D.S.O., and Lieut.-Col. F. Lister, C.M.G., D.S.O., M.C., they marched through huge crowds to the Parliament Buildings where the salute was taken by Brig.-Gen. J. A. Gunn; in Winnipeg, on June 12th cheering crowds welcomed the 78th Battalion under command of Lieut.-Col. J. N. Semmens, D.S.O., and the 12th Field Ambulance; cordial welcomes were given at Edmonton to the Alberta

31st Battalion, at Vancouver to the splendid 7th B.C. Battalion which had lost 1,400 officers and men and suffered 7,000 other casualties; so with a great number of Batteries and Battalions of all kinds and degrees of fame as they returned in small òr large units, or scattered elements, to hundreds of Canadian centres. At Montreal, on Sept. 27th, an eminent but sometimes over-looked branch of the Military forces was honoured by a banquet to the Laval and St. Cloud Hospital Units—commanded respectively by Lieut.-Col. George Beauchamp and Lieut.-Col. Arthur Mignault—at which Maj.-Gen. J. T. Fotheringham, c.m.g. stated that out of 750,000 cases handled by Canadian hospitals in the War less than 3 per cent. had died. Returned soldiers and civilians all over Canada joined in celebrating Peace Day on July 19th—chiefly with flags, and parades and holiday observances and many "Peace" sermons on the following day (Sunday). A moot point as to the actual date of peace, in a technical sense, was dealt with by Sir Allen Aylesworth, k.c., Toronto, in an authoritative opinion made public on July 22nd and concluding as follows:

In my opinion the War ends when the King so declares. Such declaration will be announced by a Royal proclamation to be issued in England just as the existence of the state of war was announced in 1914. Under the British Constitution it is the King who makes war or makes peace and he so announces to all his liege subjects—not those in Great Britain alone, but equally and by the same proclamation to those in Ireland and in his Dominions beyond the seas as well. The method by which the existence of the state of war was officially made known to Canadians demonstrates the correct constitutional course followed.

There was an official proclamation made in England and thereupon the whole British Empire—the King's Dominions everywhere throughout the world—at once were at war. And the War was between "His Majesty" and his enemies—so the Canadian official proclamations describe it—and it needed no proclamation from Ottawa to create the state of war for Canada. The Canadian proclamations were merely to make the fact better known to the people of this country but the Canadian Parliament fully recognized and authoritatively stated what the fact was in the statute referred to (5 Geo. V. C. 2) which declares in Sec. 5 that War has continuously existed since the fourth of August, 1914 though the Canadian proclamation to that effect was not issued till 19th August, 1914.

Canadians in Russia; Services and Quick Return. Meanwhile, though the War was over on the Western Front Canada was still at War, in a technically irregular but very necessary way, in far-away Russia. The Dominion Government in this connection stood by the policy of the Empire and its Allies for some months and in March 1919 there were 369,000 Allied troops* on the northern Russian fronts together with about 500,000 others—British, French, Roumanian, Italian, Serbian and Greeks—in the Balkans, Asia Minor, Southern Russia, etc. They were all there because of Russian conditions. The Archangel Front at this time included the following troops: British, 13,100; United States, 4,920; French, 2,345; Italians, 1,340; Serbians, 1,290; Russians, 11,770; total, 34,765. The Siberian Front included British,

*Note.—Statement of Stephen Pichon, French Foreign Minister, Paris, Mch. 26th.

1,600; Canadian, 4,000; United States, 7,500; French, 7,600; Italian, 2,000; Serbians, 4,000; Russians, 210,000; Poles, 12,000; Roumanians, 4,000; Japanese, 27,000; Czecho-Slovaks, 55,000; total, 334,700. The Canadian Commander of the forces at Vladivostock was Maj.-Gen. J. H. Elmsley, C.M.G., D.S.O., with Brig.-General H. C. Bickford, C.M.G., as 2nd in Command.

The action of the Government in sending these troops to Russia was much discussed and opposition was expressed by organized Labour as it was in England and the United States. The Hon. N. W. Rowell explained and defended the original policy of intervention at length, in Parliament on Apl. 1st, as one of (1) checking the German expansion and influence in Russia; (2) helping the Czecho-Slovak forces of 300,000 men to get back to their country; (3) taking part in an expedition which all the Allies had agreed to support. Nothing was said about fighting the Bolsheviki: "The question arose as to how the Contingent that would represent the British Empire should be composed. Great Britain herself had thrown every man she could spare into the line on the Western front. Australia, New Zealand, South Africa and Great Britain had each, in proportion to population, put more men into the battle line than Canada; and when it came to a question of how the British Commonwealth contingent should be made up we felt that it was only right that, as we could not comply with the request of the War Office to send another Contingent to France, we should at least be prepared to provide a brigade for Siberia."

The troops reached Vladivostock too late to serve the purposes mentioned; in the main they did garrison duty though the Minister of Militia in answering a question in the Commons on Apl. 7th admitted they, also, were fighting against the Bolsheviki; in June they returned to Canada. On Nov. 13th Mr. Lloyd George announced that the British troops in Russia would also be recalled and said of the Russians who were opposing the Bolshevist terror-rule: "We have already given real proof of our sympathy; we have sent a hundred million pounds worth of material, and of support in every form and not a penny of it do I regret, in spite of the heavy burdens which are cast upon us. It was a debt of honour that we had to discharge. We have given them the opportunity, if Russia wished to be liberated, of equipping her sons in order to free themselves."

Though not specified above there was the 16th Brigade of Canadian Field Artillery under Col. C. H. L. Sharman, C.M.G., O.B.E., which reached Archangel in September, 1918 and was immediately sent down 200 miles south to help the British hold a point at the junction of the Vaga and Dwina Rivers. Here, from January to May, they fought one long rear-guard artillery action against large numbers of the Bolsheviki, until, eventually, the Allied Russians went over to the enemy and only through getting into touch with the British fleet and the splendid work of the artillery itself was the Force eventually saved. There was, also, in the Murmansk Sector a so-called "Syren Force" of Canadians under Lieut.-Col. J. E. Leckie, C.M.G., D.S.O., of Vancouver and Lieut.-Col. L. H. Mackenzie, D.S.O. of New Glasgow which distinguished itself in handling the transportation work of the British troops sent from the Murmansk front to Archangel. With other small Canadian parties scattered through this region they shared in much isolated but strenuous fighting. Another Canadian element, far-away in Southern Russia, was a squadron of Aviators under Lieut.-Col. Raymond Collishaw, D.S.O., D.S.C., D.F.C., which helped the Denekine armies and did gallant service.

Military Charges and Complaints. It was inevitable that the return of 300,000 officers and men from the front or from England should result in the formulation of certain complaints, the presentation of charges against those in authority, an interchange of military and civilian personalties, the exploitation of a few individual animosities. Allegations were made as to maladministration on the part of Canadian headquarters in London (Argyll House), as to supposed jealousies amongst superior officers there and in France, as to strained relations between Argyll House and General Currie, as to unfair advice to the Crown in the distribution of Honours. Much was made of these charges in the press with a minimum of attention to the replies given or to the obvious and unavoidable difficulties of those in authority under war conditions.

Brig.-Gen. C. A. Smart, C.M.G., M.L.A., raised certain issues very strongly in the Quebec Legislature on Mch. 14th which may be summarized in the following extract: "I feel it is up to me to tell the people of Canada how the Canadian Medical Service blundered overseas; how patronage, influence, pull went to paralyze the good work of the medical service. The whole trouble is to be traced to Argyll House. And may I add that personally, after seeing all that I have seen, I have not the slightest confidence in those who administer Canadian affairs in England." On Apl. 1st he issued a statement describing a letter alleged to have been written by General Currie to Sir Thomas White in November, 1918, which "protested against the dastardly and outrageous statements that are being circulated in England by a very senior officer, statements prejudicial to good order and military discipline and likely to create unrest." He urged an official enquiry: "Such a Commission should have wide powers and be authorized to investigate fully: (1) The Colonel Bruce report and recommendations; (2) the report of the Baptie Commission; (3) Colonel Bruce's reply to the Baptie Report; (4) the Taplow Hospital Scandal; (5) the report of Lieut.-Col. J. S. Jenkins, submitted to the Overseas Minister of Militia in November, 1918."

These charges were brought up in Parliament by Hon. R. Lemieux on Apl. 15th and replied to by Major-Gen. S. C. Mewburn and Sir Thomas White. The latter asked if the administration of the Medical Services was so bad how could the fruition and result be so good! "When I was overseas in 1916, I visited many Canadian and Imperial hospitals and talked with scores of officers at the front and in England and I had an opportunity of consulting with medical men of the highest standing in London. I have, on numerous occasions, discussed all phases of the war with returned officers and men, and if there is one thing I have heard more than another in connection with the conduct of the war it is that the Canadian Army Medical Service is almost in a class by itself for excellence. I do not believe that any army in history has had the care that the Canadian army has enjoyed with respect to its sick and wounded." A long letter from Prof. Sir Andrew Macphail, M.D., was read denouncing, and replying to, Colonel Smart's charges and speaking of his personal experiences in the C.A.M.C.

Following this interchange, Lieut.-Col. A. C. Pratt, M.L.A. of Ontario, one-time C.O. of the 133rd Battalion, gave an interview to the press immediately upon landing at Halifax on Mch. 19th in which he declared the Rhyl troubles to be directly due to Argyll House mismanagement, claimed that in his own visits there he had encountered nothing but "bungling, incompetent, discourteous men" and criticized Sir George Perley and Sir Edward Kemp. In the Legislature on Mch. 27th he made another vehement attack upon the Canadian administration of the Forces in London. He excepted General Sir R. E. W. Turner, whom he characterized as most efficient and with the welfare of the soldiers at heart and also commended Colonel Thomas Gibson and Colonel M. A. Colquhoun; he told various stories and alleged incidents reflecting upon the Canadian Headquarters Staff and said that the reason for the Rhyl riots was that the men had not been treated properly which, he declared, was proved by subsequent events as the men were afterwards given their pay and 20,000 were sent home within a week. He charged that members of the Royal Air Force who could not get home, because of alleged lack of shipping accommodation, found that by "salving" the hand of a ticket-seller they could get a berth and passage to Canada. These ticket sellers made at times £75 a week.

The response to these and other attacks were varied. The Toronto *Globe* demanded a Parliamentary enquiry; the Toronto News declared that the trouble was due to Colonel Pratt's opinions not being acceptable to Argyll House and pointed out that 73% of the officers there on June 11 had seen active service and that after July 7th every officer on the staff was in that category; Headquarters officials described them as due to personal animosities, and high authorities (anonymously) denied the R.A.F. allegations absolutely; the Toronto *Star* and St. John *Telegraph* were inclined to think that the charges simply embodied under-currents of unpublished knowledge; the Vancouver *Journal* said that the minor specific charges might all be true and yet the general charge of Departmental incompetency quite untrue; the Ottawa *Journal* described them as irresponsible, vague and sensational.

Argyll House and the Minister's Report. Many returning officers spoke of conditions as very different from those described by General Smart or Colonel Pratt. Colonel, the Hon. Angus Macdonell, C.M.G., 2nd in command of the Canadian Railway Troops, spoke at Ottawa on Apl. 29th of what he personally knew; "The efficiency, promptness and absolute fairness with which the Overseas Minister, Sir Edward Kemp, and Sir Richard Turner and their representatives both in England and France handled all matters relative to the C.R.T. referred to them, could only have been forthcoming from an organization whose one object was to help in every way the Canadian troops in France." To *The Canadian Gazette* in London (May 1), just before sailing for Canada, Sir Edward Kemp dealt with this issue in a general way:

> I can only say that the story of Canadian Headquarters in London is one of the finest stories of war-work that I know. When the war began we had no such organization at all. We had to begin at the bottom and build up. Sir George Perley was, after a time appointed Overseas Minister and, later, I succeeded him. The work is stupendous but the staff have stuck to it splendidly. I consider it is the finest organization possessed by Canada and one of which she may be justly proud. The men composing the staff are individually most conscientious and most capable. Indeed they are men who, if they were in politics, would make a first-rate Government. There never was a time when they stuck more loyally to their jobs than now. And it must be remembered that they are all anxious to get home to their work and that it is at a sacrifice, on their part, that they are here. There has never been a breath of scandal. Even in the matter of repatriating the troops we are doing much better than anyone anticipated. The work done by Headquarters at Argyll House is wearing work, but it is done willingly and strenuously; and people who know appreciate it. Generals of Canadian Divisions have spoken in the highest terms of it, and so have English officers. I am quite ready to tell the House that Canada has every reason to be proud of Canadian Headquarters in London.

As Minister of Overseas Forces Sir Edward's Military Council at this stage was composed of Lieut.-Col. T. Gibson, D.S.O., Assistant Deputy Minister, Colonel G. S. Harrington (Deputy Minister) who acted as Vice-Chairman, Lieut.-General Sir R. E. W. Turner V.C., Chief of the General Staff, Major-General P. E. Thacker, C.B., Adjutant General, Brig.-General D. M. Hogarth, C.M.G., D.S.O., Quarter-Master-General, Col. W. R. Ward, C.B.E., Accountant-General, Maj.-General G. L. Foster, C.B., Director General of the Medical Services and Brig.-General J. G. Ross, C.M.G., Paymaster-General. The Minister was in Ottawa on May 12th and submitted to Parliament an elaborate and able review of the whole work of the Canadian Corps and record of the Canadian administration of War affairs in England. It was published in book form* as the Report of the Ministry of Overseas Forces of Canada, for 1918.

It described in succinct form the composition and control of the forces in England and France; it reviewed the nature and duties of the General Staff and the Adjutant General's and Quartermaster-General's branches; it analyzed the operations of the

---

*Note.—See also pages 347-54 in *The Canadian Annual Review* for 1918. Colonel Thomas Gibson had much to do with the preparation of this valuable statement.

Canadian Corps in 1918 and gave an historical statement regarding the Cavalry, R.A.F., Railway Troops, Forestry Corps, the Tank Battalion, C.A.M.C., C.A.D.C., Chaplain Services, Army Pay Corps, Accountant and Auditors' Work, Record Office and Estate Branches, Purchasing Committee, Military Funds, War Records, Red Cross, Y.M.C.A., etc.; it reviewed the organization, administration and functions of the Canadian Corps. In the Commons on May 27th Sir Edward Kemp spoke at great length in this connection and reviewed his work in England since going over as Minister in November 1917; stated that the Report submitted as above was written under the direction of General Sir Arthur Currie; reviewed the conditions and statistics of the various services and described the demobilization plans and policy; dealt with Aviation and the war record of the various divisions of the Forces. He did not deal directly with the charges or allegations mentioned above excepting those referred to in the Bruce Report of 1916.

Meantime, Dr. Herbert A. Bruce had thrown further fuel into the medical part of the fire by publication of his book entitled *Politics in the Canadian Army Medical Corps*. It was an elaboration of the allegations and conclusions of his famous Report and included publication of the investigating Report of Sir William Babtie's Commission as well as other documents and data illustrating his sub-title; "A history of intrigue containing many facts omitted from the official records and showing how efforts at retaliation have been baulked." General Smart on July 7th returned to the attack in a speech at Montreal and fiercely criticized Sir William Babtie, Sir George Perley and Sir Edward Kemp. It may be added that the Overseas Ministry in London was closed during October when Sir Edward returned, finally, to Canada.

War Organizations; War Memorial Proposals; War-Time Incidents of 1919. The Canadian Red Cross Society had much work to do in 1919 even though the War was over; in fact its services in such epidemic sicknesses as the Influenza were conspicuous. As it had existed for many years before the War so it also decided in this year to maintain its position and an application to Parliament was arranged for an amendment to its charter permitting the extension of its activities to the civilian population during peace times and for the alleviation of pain and suffering wherever they might be found—an amendment readily accorded by Parliament. Sir R. S. Lake, Lieut.-Governor of Saskatchewan, in moving this Resolution at the annual meeting in Toronto, on Feb. 27th, stated that the British Red Cross was taking similar action and H. E. the Duke of Devonshire in his address urged the necessity of perpetuating the work of the War period. "That accumulation of work," he said, "would form one of the greatest heritages that could be handed down to posterity." He pointed out that in the first year of the War the Canadian Red Cross Society had raised a little over one million dollars, while during the past year the receipts had totalled well over five millions.

The Canadian Red Cross Society. Lieut.-Col. Noel Marshall presided and his Report as Chairman of the Central Council showed that during 1918 the following articles were sent overseas: 1,608,214 socks, 370,000 pyjamas, 223,000 shirts, 327,000 personal property bags, 79,000 dressing gowns and 680,000 towels. There were 46,768 cases of supplies purchased in England. The Canadian Ambulances in France carried 316,433 men during 1917 and 1918. The Report of the Hon. Treasurer, F. Gordon Osler, showed that the total revenue, including a balance on hand at the first of the year of $381,319, amounted to $5,066,388. This was made up of receipts totalling $4,632,112, interest on deposits, $49,916 and customs taxes refunded $3,039. The chief expenditures, which totalled $3,071,339, included ambulances $40,464; St. John's Hospital Brigade, $75,000; special objects $530,188, administration expenses, $47,190 and various supplies. The Officers elected for 1919 were as follows:

President	H. E The Duchess of Devonshire	Ottawa
Hon. President	The Hon. S. C. Mewburn, C.M.G., M.P.,	"
Hon. Vice-President	General Sir Arthur Currie, G.C.M.G., K.C.B.	Vancouver
Vice-President	Rt. Rev. T. J. McNally, Bishop of Calgary	Calgary
" "	Hon. Charles Stewart, M.L.A.	Edmonton
" "	Sir Charles Hibbert Tupper, K.C.M.G., K.C.	Vancouver
" "	George F. Galt	Winnipeg
" "	Lieut.-Col. T. G. Loggie	Fredericton
" "	Lady Tilley	St. John
" "	Mrs. Wm. Dennis	Halifax
" "	Brig.-Gen. Sir John S. Hendrie	Hamilton
" "	Brig.-Gen. Sir Henry Pellatt	Toronto
" "	Hon. F. L. Hassard	Charlottetown
" "	Rt. Hon. Sir Charles Fitzpatrick	Quebec
" "	Huntley R. Drummond	Montreal
" "	Sir Richard S. Lake	Regina
" "	Commissioner A. B. Perry, C.M.G.	Regina
Chairman Central Council	Lieut.-Col. Noel Marshall	Toronto
Hon. Corresponding Secretary	Mrs. H. P. Plumptre	Toronto
Hon. Recording Secretary	B. S. McInnes	Toronto
Hon. Treasurer	F. Gordon Osler	Toronto

In London on June 25th it was announced that the Canadian Red Cross had donated the Bushey Park Hospital buildings to the King for such public use as he deemed best and that His Majesty had decided to dedicate the property, valued at $120,000, as a Camp centre for delicate children of whom, it was stated, 3,000 could be accommodated. At Toronto on Sept. 3rd a Conference of Red Cross supporters was held with Colonel Marshall in the chair for the purpose of organizing an Ontario Provincial branch.   Mrs. H. P. Plumptre, in explaining this step as necessary at this time, though not so during the War, stated that the health of the people at home would now be the chief mission of the Red Cross and, as the B.N.A. Act gave each Province control of its Health laws, Provincial organization had become necessary: "In organizing the work for peace, there would be no competition with other organizations, but rather co-operation. Infant life—to make Canada safe for infancy—would be one of the first cares. Then provision should be made for emergencies such as the disaster at Halifax and the Influenza epidemic. Emergencies of time and place should be provided for. There were places, even in Ontario, where medical help and nurses could not be procured and this meant sacrifices at times, of a new-born babe, and sometimes of the mother, too. In Ontario the death rate of babies was one in every ten.'' The new Branch was fully organized on Dec. 5th with Mrs. Plumptre as President and Colonel Marshall as Hon. Treasurer. The other Provincial Branches met during the year and warmly approved the new Peace programme of the Society—especially those of Quebec and Nova Scotia which re-elected W. R. Miller and Mrs. William Dennis President, respectively. The following suggestions for future use, presented by the Saskatchewan body, were approved by Dominion Headquarters:

1. That the Red Cross Society co-operate with the Departments of Public Health, whether Dominion, Provincial or Municipal in all measures having in view the improvement of health, the prevention of disease and the mitigation of suffering.

2. That the Society establish a Red Cross medical and nursing service which will be available in all cases of public disaster or calamity.

3. That the Society encourage doctors and nurses to establish themselves and carry on their profession in the more sparsely settled portions of the Dominion; that it assist in providing adequate hospital accomodation in such districts, and in the maintenance of the same.

4. That the Society co-operate in the dissemination of a better knowledge of sanitation and health problems throughout all classes of the community, and encourage a larger number of persons to enter the medical and nursing professions.

5. That those who have performed naval and military service in time of war should, with their dependents, be considered to have a special claim upon the peace-time activities provided for by the amended charter of the Canadian Red Cross Society.

Provincial home rule in control and local policy was fully established. Up to July 31, 1919 and following the Armistice the work of the Society was largely associated with demobilization, and a detailed report of the seven months prepared by Lieut.-Col. H. W. Blaylock, C.B.E., Chief Commissioner overseas, showed that on Jan. 1 there were 40,247 cases of Red Cross supplies on hand, and that since then 36,973 cases had been received from Canada. By July 31st 65,680 cases had been shipped out, and the balance of 11,540 were allocated and in course of distribution. The hospital ships leaving for Canada had been individually visited, and everything possible done to assist the Medical Service in getting the sick and wounded home in comfort. The last unit in France to close its doors was the Hotel du Nord, which had to its credit the proud record of having fed and housed nearly 10,000 nursing sisters in less than 15 months.

The demobilization work of the Society included the care of Canadians who had been Prisoners of War on German soil, during the period of demobilization, transport, home-coming and repatriation to Canada; care of sick and wounded Canadian soldiers in Hospitals, Convalescent Homes, etc., in England and France during this period and in transit to Canada and in hospitals and convalescent homes in Canada; maintenance of complete Red Cross establishments in Siberia under the direction of Lieut.-Col. J. S. Dennis and with the Canadian forces of occupation in Germany while it remained there. At the close of the year Colonel Marshall was in London and stated to *Canada* on Nov. 22nd that "during the five years, 1914-1919, the Society had handled about 30 million dollars in cash and supplies and that, in view of the number of Canadian relatives of dead soldiers who would visit the graves in the battle areas next year, it had been decided to maintain a hostel and information bureau in London for their comfort and assistance at 20, Prince's Gardens, South Kensington, to be in charge of Mrs. David Fraser, who was at the head of one of the principal departments of the Society's work during the war." On Dec. 4th he was given a Dinner with Sir George Perley in the chair and a number of representative Canadians present. Later figures, up to the close of 1919, showed that during 5½ years the Society had handled $11,000,000 in cash, collected $5,500,000 for the British Red Cross and shipped overseas goods and supplies to the value of $30,000,000; during the war period 1,400 branches had been established in Canada and 10,000 auxiliary branches formed. The Receipts for 1919 were $2,791,998 of which $1,995,311 was from balance brought forward and Customs refunds.

The Canadian Patriotic Fund held an Executive meeting at Ottawa on Apl. 9th which was largely attended with every Province represented. H. E. the Duke of Devonshire presided and the total contributions up to Mch. 31st, 1919 were stated as $47,115,261 and the balance on hand as $8,662,941 with $300,000 more of collectible subscriptions and current monthly requirements of about $800,000. It was finally decided that the Branches should be asked to continue their relief work along present lines for another year, at the end of which period the extent, if any, of the Fund's continuing obligation would be apparent. In Parliament on June 19th Sir Herbert Ames, so long Hon. Secretary of the Fund, explained an amendment to its Incorporation Act which, eventually, was approved. He stated that demobilization had been so rapid that the officials found themselves with a large surplus in hand and they asked permission "to continue their work for the families of discharged sailors and soldiers while their funds lasted, feeling that this would be in conformity with the wishes of the subscribers." At an Executive meeting on Sept. 3rd Sir Herbert Ames resigned his position and was succeeded by W. F. Nickle, K.C., M.P.; Sir Thomas White also resigned as Treasurer and was replaced by Sir Henry Drayton, the new Minister of Finance. The balance then in hand was stated as about $6,000,000 and the future administration of the Fund was relegated largely to Provincial headquarters.

In Alberta a movement developed in favour of transferring local moneys to the Red Cross but was strongly opposed by the Patriotic Fund leaders of that Province; at the same time it was announced that the Federal Government intended to use the machinery of the Fund for distributing demobilization relief. Writing to Mr. Nickle, in a letter made public on Dec. 22nd, Sir Robert Borden expressed satisfaction that "the Canadian Patriotic

Fund has agreed to undertake the administration of the appropriation provided by Parliament for the relief of ex-members of the Forces, who, through no fault of their own, are unable to secure employment during the coming winter.'' It may be added that the final Report of the Toronto and County of York Patriotic Association showed the following financial facts: Total raised in four campaigns, $9,820,550; amount still outstanding, $549,238; City subscription still owing to Fund, $300,000 and County of York, $30,000; paid to soldiers' dependents, $6,462,237; and to Red Cross, $1,294,152.

War Memorials and Canadian Archives. During March it was announced that the French Government had presented to that of Canada, a section of the Vimy Ridge for Memorial purposes and that the Belgian Government had also stated its desire to award a grant of land at Ypres for a Canadian Memorial museum and shrine. In September it was stated that these offers had been accepted by General Currie and the Canadian Government with gratification and that the memorials to be erected on the Vimy Ridge and at Ypres would take the form of Canadian Halls of Record, dedicated to the Canadian dead and for the benefit of the world's future pilgrims to the famous Battlefields. At this time, also, a Committee of officers representing the British Expeditionary Force, the Dominions and India, was constituted in London with Lieut.-General Sir G. M. W. Macdonogh, K.C.M.G., C.B. as Chairman, to consider claims made by units for the erection of permanent memorials on specific battlefields. Lieut.-Colonel H. T. Hughes, C.M.G. represented Canada on what was finally called the Battle Exploits Memorials Committee with headquarters at the War Office. The Canadian Government submitted detailed plans to this Committee and the following sites were eventually accepted with a preliminary vote of $500,000, and the promised co-operation of the French and Belgian Governments:

1. St. Julien
2. Courcelette
3. Observatory Ridge (Sanctuary Wood)
4. Vimy (Hill 145)
5. Passchendaele
6. Caix (Between Caix and Le Quesnel)
7. Dury (Drocourt-Quéant Line)
8. Bourlion Wood

Memorials in Canada were projected during the year at Edmonton in the form of a Soldiers' Memorial Hall, to cost $200,000; at Ottawa for the new Parliament Buildings in honour of the late Colonel George Harold Baker, M.P., who was killed in battle; at Acadia University in the form of a gymnasium and in honour of the 600 students who went on active service; at Brantford in the form of an obelisk with arches and special buildings around the sides; at Regina as a Provincial War Museum; at Carman, Manitoba, a Dufferin-Carman Memorial Hall, in memory of the soldiers of the district who died in the War. Brig.-General V. W. Odlum suggested a Vancouver square based upon that of Trafalgar in London with a Memorial erected in the centre to the men of the

City who had fallen. On Sept. 30 the Lieut.-Governor of New Brunswick unveiled at St. John a granite and bronze soldiers' Memorial, in Ferndale Cemetery, erected by the local Daughters of the Empire chapters—apparently the first in Canada. At Amiens Cathedral, France, on Apl. 12th a Memorial tablet was unveiled by the Archbishop of Amiens in the presence of many well-known Canadians and in honour of the officers and men of the Royal Canadian Dragoons who had fallen in the War. At Mons in August the two guns of the Canadian Artillery which fired the last shots in the world war were presented to the City on behalf of the Canadian authorities.

Another kind of war memorial was the great collection of trophies, records, pictures and historical papers which Dr. A. G. Doughty, Dominion Archivist, had got together during the struggle. Various Governments, institutions, Battalions and individuals contributed to the collection which included the following: 20 aeroplanes, 5,000 rifles, 1,000 machine-guns, shells of all calibres ranging between 9½ inches in diameter to a giant projectile 12 ft. high, 600 tons of war records which Maj.-Gen. Mewburn stated in Parliament to have a value beyond estimate. A Committee consisting of Sir Edmund Walker, Toronto, Brig.-Gen. E. A. Cruikshank, Ottawa and Dr. Doughty was appointed to deal with the matter of a suitable building to house the collection which, in detail, included such interesting items as Prinz Eitel Friedrich's helmet, Marshal Von Hindenburg's sword and the telephone used by General Ludendorff at Spa.

The Records included newspaper clippings and published books; the official gazettes of the United Kingdom, Canada and France; regimental publications, trench papers, etc., official communiques and press reports; Canadian military badges; replicas of regimental colours; reports of the history of the organization of each unit of the C.E.F.; other historical papers as to such units, general and routine orders, lists of Honours and awards to Canadians with statements of the services for which each was granted and photographs of the recipients; maps of all areas and actions in which the Canadians served; narratives of events at the front by actual participants; copies of official documental maps and photographs, having special historical value; a complete photographic record of the Canadians in the field; sketches and paintings of historical scenes.

Military Incidents of the Year included the presentation at Winnipeg to Sir John Eaton (Sept. 26) by returned soldiers in his Toronto and Winnipeg establishments of the famous painting "The Surrender of the German Fleet" by W. L. Wylie, R.A.; the succession of great banquets early in the year given in the Toronto Armouries to returned soldiers by a Committee of which Brig.-Gen. John A. Gunn, C.M.G., D.S.O. was the head; the taking over for a time of General Turner's duties in England by Brig.-Gen. J. H. MacBrien, C.B., C.M.G., D.S.O., and the retirement of Brig.-Gen. R. J. F. Hayter, C.B., C.M.G., D.S.O., after eight years' services with the

Canadian Militia or Army to return to his old Imperial unit the Cheshire Regiment; the claim in the House of Commons on Oct. 6th by Lieut.-Gen. Sir Sam Hughes, that he had initiated or originated, or first urged, the use of the Trench plan in defence warfare, the use of shield shovels or preliminary steel plates in the trenches, the system of hidden machine gun positions in the rear, the use of cotton hose filled with explosive for destroying parapets and wire entanglements and, also, that of iron pipes filled with explosive, the invention of a trench mortar of which 100,000 were used and the recommendation and preparation of a direct-fire gun in October, 1914. The following were the chief appointments of returned officers to military and civilian posts during the year.

Position	Name	Address
Canadian Trade Commissioner at Paris	Lieut.-Col. Hercule Barré	Montreal
O. C. Military District, No. 11	Maj.-Gen. J. H. Elmsley, C.B., C.M.G., D.S.O.	Toronto
Deputy Minister of Health	Lieut.-Col. John A. Amyot, C.M.G., M.D.	Toronto
Director, Department of Physics, McGill University	Lieut.-Col. A. S. Eve, C.B.E., F.R.S.	Montreal
Hon. A. D. C. to H. E. the Governor-General	Col. J. L. R. Parsons, C.M.G., D.S.O. and Bar	Regina
Civil Service Commissioner for Montreal	Lieut.-Col. F. M. Gaudet, C.M.G.	Montreal
Commandant, Royal Military College	Maj.-Gen. Sir A. C. Macdonell K.C.B., C.M.G., D.S.O.	Kingston
Dean of Applied Science, Toronto University	Brig.-Gen. C. H. Mitchell, C.B., C.M.G., D.S.O.	Toronto
O. C. Military District, No.1	Brig.-Gen. Henri A. Panet, C.B., C.M.G., D.S.O.	Ottawa
O. C. Alberta Military District	Brig.-Gen. A. H. Bell, C.M.G., D.S.O.	Calgary
Collector of Customs, Vancouver	Lieut.-Col. Alfred B. Carey, C.M.G., D.S.O.	Vancouver
Chief of Manitoba Law Enforcement Department	Colonel J. G. Rattray, C.M.G., D.S.O.	Winnipeg

Who Won the War? An Important Discussion of the Year. In this discussion—which was not initiated by Great Britain or Canada—all the Dominions of the British Empire were, as a matter of sentiment, of historical values and of the traditions of youthful nations in the making, greatly interested. They had made tremendous sacrifices and had played the hard game of war bravely and well from the beginning; they were vitally concerned in the place held by the United Kingdom and the Empire in the final stages of the conflict. The claim put forward in the United States, with more or less authority and with some force upon occasion, was that in the Spring of 1918 the Allies were exhausted, their armies on the Western front at one stage either in retreat or with their backs to the wall and with their numbers less than the available armies of the enemy; that it was the knowledge and development of the fresh resources and immense armies of the United States which revived the spirits, strengthened the stamina, gradually increased the numbers of the Allies and enabled them to strike the final blow with energy and despatch; that it was American money and munitions which all through the war proved the backbone of Allied military power and American soldiers who won some of the greatest victories in the last stages. There is enough truth in certain of these statements to make a case of which Americans could well be proud; there was a side to it, however, of which the average American had never heard, though it was well understood by those in authority, or those with experience of the war, and by the best informed section of the press.

The claim of winning the war was not official except, perhaps, in the case of the Secretary of the Navy and certain Senators, or in such instances of speech as President Wilson's 1918 reference to the splendid transportation of 2,000,000 American troops to Europe with only a slighting reference to the share taken by the British Navy! But it was part of a persistent, underground, and continuous propaganda in the Republic against Great Britain, against the League of Nations and the Peace Treaty, against the Dominions' new place in Foreign affairs, against a British Empire which included India and Egypt and Ireland, against the possibility of closer relations or of real friendship with Great Britain, or any indirect alliance between the United States and the British Empire. This propaganda was backed by all the influences which originally opposed the entrance of the United States into the War and it promised, unless checked, to form a new school of history, a new inflation of a patriotism which was not desirable as an element of international relations. As the Detroit *Free Press* put it early in February, 1919 so also many millions of Americans asserted: "A flood of American manhood set in the direction of the European battlefields and, beginning with that little brush along the Meuse, filled and swelled until it overwhelmed the enemy that had successfully resisted the combined military strength of half a dozen European nations!"

American Battles in the War. It was not unfair to claim Chateau Thierry or the Meuse-Argonne advance as important battles of the War; but they did not begin to rank in vital or world importance with those of Mons or the 1st Marne, with those of the 1st and 2nd Ypres, or with the terrific conflict of Verdun, or with the enemy's victories at Tannenberg or Caporetto, or with the British-Canadian breaking of the Hindenburg Line. It was Marshal Foch's counter offensive, beginning on July 18, 1918, which, in a military sense, won the war; back of this was the persistent aggressive fighting of 1916-17 which weakened the enemy; everywhere was the influence of quiet, steady naval support to the Allies or pressure upon the enemy. In the counter-offensive of 1918 the Americans shared but with a much smaller proportion of troops actively engaged than any of the Allies except Belgium. In a despatch from Paris on June 14th, 1919 F. H. Simonds, the not too-British correspondent of the New York *Tribune,* dealt as follows with the Chateau Thierry legend, which had grown by that time to formidable dimensions—though no one man could then destroy, or can now greatly weaken, its influence in the United States:

When the 2nd and 3rd United States Divisions arrived on June 1st the great German advance was almost at an end. The victorious Germans had been advancing for six days. They had outrun their artillery and their supplies. The best proof that the advance was about at an end is found in the fact that the Americans were never attacked on the lines they took up, save as the 3rd Division participated in the general German offensive six weeks later. It is, therefore, inaccurate to assert that the intervention of the 2nd Division on the Chateau Thierry road or the 3rd Division south of Chateau Thierry, saved Paris, stopped the great German drive, or did more at the moment than to support and to relieve the exhausted French divisions and conceivably halt the Germans a mile or two short of the position they might have reached before they were compelled to abandon their advance.

General Pershing in his official Report, made public on Dec. 14, 1919, declared that the Allied troops were exhausted at the time of the last German offensive. There was no doubt of that but they, none-the-less, continued to hold the lines of Paris and the Coast subject to strategic retreats and defeats which kept the situation serious—as it had been at intervals during four years of savage struggle; but the German troops and resources were still more exhausted and this last advance only needed to be checked in order to make the end assured. In this checking process the fresh American troops shared at Chateau Thierry; they shared also in the succeeding counter offensive but their fighting at St. Mihiel and advance on Sedan were no more conspicuous in fighting qualities than the British campaign on the Soissons-Rheims front, the British advance on Cambrai, the Canadian attack on the Hindenburg Line at Drocourt-Queant, the French advance on Laon, Lille and Douai—all with troops war-weary and exhausted. Nor was their fighting as strategically important as several of these other Allied victories.

The American troops took a gallant and memorable part in the final struggles of the War but they did not win the campaign as a whole or even its greatest battles, they contributed their share to an inevitable end which would have come a little later without them but was as certain to come as was the fact of British tenacity, or French pluck, or the capacity of the Allies to endure to the end. General Peyton C. March, U.S. Chief of Staff, in his Report of June 30, 1919, practically admitted this when he said: ''After a study of the entire situation I came to the conclusion that the War might be brought to an end in 1919, provided we were able to land in France by June 30 of that year 80 American divisions of a strength of 3,360,000 men.'' As a matter of fact less than 50 Divisions and only 2,000,000 men had been landed in France by the close of the War. It is, therefore, clear, according to General March's own official statement that 1,360,000 more men than were actually sent over were required to ''Win the War''—and even this estimate of victory was for a year later than proved to be the case!

An excellent test of the share taken by troops in a campaign is that of captured prisoners and guns. As to this General Pershing in his Report stated the total of captures by the 1st and chief

American Army, between Sept. 26th and Nov. 11th, 1918, at 26,000 prisoners and 847 guns; the Canadian Army of 100,000 men, alone, between Aug. 8th and Oct. 3rd took 28,000 prisoners and 500 guns. Official figures of the prisoners and guns taken from July 18th to Nov. 11—inclusive of the Italian and Eastern fronts—showed the following figures: British, 350,000 prisoners and 4,000 guns; French, 175,000 prisoners and 2,250 guns; Americans, 43,500 prisoners and 1,450 guns; Italians, 225,000 prisoners and 2,000 guns; Belgians, 14,500 prisoners and 474 guns—a total of 765,000 prisoners and 8,724 guns for all the Allies compared with 43,500 prisoners and 1,450 guns for the Americans.*

At this time, also, it must be remembered, the British campaign in Palestine and Mesopotamia was defeating the Turk while the Allied forces at Salonika (chiefly British) kept Bulgaria at bay, finally took that country and Turkey out of the War, and thus compelled Austria, already weakened by Italian and Russian blows, to also withdraw. Comparisons are always ungracious but they are, from an historical standpoint sometimes necessary. What of the nations behind the soldiers? France endured and fought while Britain and the British Empire fought and paid, made munitions and provided seas safe for transportation—despite the damages of the Submarine and two years and a half of continuous preceding protest from the United States. The latter country, for 2½ years, provided some money and many munitions while accumulating much gold and wealth; eventually she organized and sent abroad a splendid army of 2,000,000 men of whom a part shared in the last stages of the war.

Comparative Costs in the War. How did the nations compare as to war costs? Approximately the United States,† with an estimated national wealth of $225,000,000,000, spent $32,080,000,-000 of which $9,455,000,000 was in well-secured loans to the Allies; the British Empire, with a national wealth of about $160,000,000,-000, spent $48,522,000,000 of which the United Kingdom had lent to its Allies $8,695,000,000—part of it lost in the Russian upheaval; France and Italy, with a combined national wealth of about $100,-000,000,000, had together expended $38,200,000,000. Financially, therefore, the British Empire, with a much smaller white population, had borne a far greater burden than the United States or any other Power. Moreover, Great Britain, in its vast credit system, its financial policy and absolute assurance, its resources and continued trade, had sustained the whole fabric of the world's finance from the 4th of August, 1914 onwards; it was not New York which stayed the collapse of the world's financial structure at the beginning of the war, it was London; it was not the United States which held the Allied nations together during four years of desperate struggle, it was the United Kingdom.

---

*Note.—British War Office Statement.

†Note.—E. L. Bogart, Professor of Economics in the University of Wisconsin.

As to the $9,400,000,000 which the United States had lent the Allies—part of it to Britain—and about which so much was said by American speakers and writers, Great Britain lent her Allies an almost equal sum while carrying her own enormous burdens and with only a casual reference to the total amount in her annual Budget speeches. At the close of the War Britain was spending $1,750,000,000 a year upon the Navy which had guarded American troops across the seas and the merchantile marine which had transported 48% of them*—the British bill to the United States for carrying 1,000,000 of these troops was $82,000,000.

Comparison as to Men, Casualties and Naval Power. What about man-power? The United States mobilized 3,800,000 men or 4% of its population; Great Britain mobilized 5,704,000 men or 12% of its population, and the British Empire, exclusive of India, 7,130,000 or 24% of its total white population—with India the total enlistment was 8,654,000. France, whose soil was invaded, mobilized 9,717,000 men or 20% of its population and Italy 5,250,000 or 15%. As General Pershing put it in a message (Dec. 7, 1918) to Alton B. Parker of New York, written a year before his official Report appeared: "The achievements of the British Empire for humanity are too manifold to enumerate in a short message. Steadfast or in adversity, wounded with a thousand wounds, Britain's hammer blows have never weakened nor faltered. But for the tenacity of her people the war would have been lost." There was, indeed, no more than equality in the fighting strength of the British and United States forces after the steady flow of new and untried men from the United States had been going on for 12 months as the following figures show:

Dates 1918	British Army in France		American Army in France	
	Ration Strength	Combatant Strength	Ration Strength	Combatant Strength
March 11	1,828,000	1,293,000	245,000	123,000
April 1	1,687,701	1,151,000	319,000	214,000
Sept. 23	1,752,829	1,200,000	1,641,000	1,195,00C
Nov. 11	1,731,578	1,164,000	1,924,000	1,160,000

What about casualties? The United States had a total force at the front in November of 2,040,000 and its casualties were approximately 264,000 or 13% with about 58,000 of these killed; the United Kingdom had 5,700,000 on the various fronts at different periods with total casualties of 2,453,266 or over 40% and of these about 550,000 were killed; for the British Empire the casualties were 3,038,000 with a total of 712,800 killed and Canada's figures of over 200,000 casualties, alone, nearly equal to those of the United States; the total casualties of France and Italy combined were 6,200,000.†

What about munitions, trade and transport, the Navy—in a word, sea-power? It was Britain's Navy which kept the wheels of the world's industry running in 1914-18 as a vital force in War action; it was the British Navy which enabled British and Canadian and American factories to produce, in certainty of reaching their markets, the enormous amount of munitions and war supplies needed by the Allies to catch up to and pass Germany's preparation and production of years; it was the British Navy which prevented Germany from keeping its trade, from interchanging securities and from obtaining help, while first holding up and then subduing the Submarine menace; it was the British Navy which turned the seas into a transportation highway for Allied products, munitions, armies and trade. Admirals Sims and Rodman saw this clearly and have so stated.*

The Dominant Factor in Victory. The slogans of "We won the war" and "After England failed"—the latter as a parody on the initials of the American Expeditionary Forces—which were so popular in the United States during 1919 were not regarded with approval by thinking men and intellectual leaders, by journals such as the New York *Tribune* and the New York *Times*, by politicians such as Roosevelt or Root, or by American correspondents such as F. H. Simonds. Speaking in Toronto on June 5th President Grier Hibben of Princeton University presented his view as follows: "I want to make it very clear that I deplore a certain vainglorying thought expressed by some United States newspapers—not newspapers of repute I am glad to say—in regard to the part that the United States played in the War. It is very easy to say that the Allies were only waiting for the United States to come into the conflict and that then the War was won; but what happened in the years prior to the entry of the United States. What of the front line that swayed backward and forward and never broke, that held the enemy and gradually reduced his power? What was our security? It was that Line and the British Navy."

The British leaders did little boasting about the War and made no comparative statements but Sir Douglas Haig in his Despatch of Dec. 21, 1918, did make the following comment after a brief reference to the prisoners and guns taken in the last months of the struggle: "These results were achieved by 59 fighting British divisions which in the course of three months of battle engaged and defeated 99 separate German Divisions. This record is a proof of the overwhelmingly decisive part played by the British armies on the western front in bringing the enemy to his final defeat." He added that throughout practically the whole of the long succession of battles which ended in the complete destruction of the German powers of resistance the attacking British troops were numerically inferior to the German forces they defeated. The British Commander in his final despatch of Mch. 21, 1919, indicated what, in his view, was the basic cause of victory: "So far as the military situation is concerned, in spite of the great accession of strength which Germany received as the result of the defection of Russia, the battles of 1916 and 1917 had so far weak-

*Note.—See *The Canadian Annual Review* for 1919, pages 249-52.

ened her armies that the effort they made in 1918 was insufficient to secure victory. Moreover, the effect of the battles of 1916 and 1917 was not confined to loss of German man power. The moral effects of those battles were enormous, both in the German Army and in Germany. By their means our soldiers established over the German soldier a moral superiority which they held in an ever-increasing degree until the end of the war—even in the difficult days of March and April, 1918.'' Early in July General Botha left England for South Africa and issued a farewell statement—destined unfortunately to be a final one—in which he clearly indicated his view of this subject.

I carry away with me the conviction that of all the peoples in the Alliance the peoples of the British Empire have played a greater part than any. This war was in my judgment primarily a French war. It was not a British war essentially. Nevertheless the British people made the war their own and so saved not only France but also civilization itself. To me as an observer coming from a great way off, and for certain reasons perhaps able to survey and estimate the varied and conflicting elements in this vast struggle with more detachment than some of my fellow-delegates at the Peace Conference, the part played by Great Britain from the day war was declared until this hour is one that places her first amongst the nations of the earth. We have her, primarily, to thank for the overthrow of Prussianism and the saving of the world, and she has come out of the terrible ordeal of sacrifice, with her *prestige* higher than ever it has been.

Much was said as to American industrial efforts for War purposes and the help thus rendered the Allied cause— for a heavy financial consideration. But during this war period British industrial organization, also, was marvellous with, in 1918, over 4,000,000 men and women working at munitions; more than 5,000 privately-owned factories and works taken over and under Government control with, at the same time, every nerve of the nation strained to send men to the Front. British clothing and boot factories supplied the greater proportion of equipment for the Belgian, French, Italian and, prior to the Soviet Revolution, Russian armies and 2,000 miles of railway track, 1,000 locomotives and tens of thousands of railway cars were shipped abroad. British women were, in 1918, doing 1,700 different kinds of work which, previously, had been done by men and including over 1,000,000 directly employed in Munition-producing plants; over 500,000 employed in Engineering and Chemical works; 300,000 working as farm labourers. The British output of shells during the War was 200,000,000 rounds, and the production of big guns 250,000.

At the close of the War American and Dominion armies were demobilized and the United States declined to undertake a Mandate for, or any responsibility in respect to, the ''white man's burden'' in Asia and Africa or in the maintenance of the peace so hardly won in war-tossed Europe. Great Britain, without discussion or serious hesitancy, assumed or continued her great Imperial work in Palestine and Mesopotamia, in South-West and East Africa, and in the Pacific, while arranging for military forces abroad which, at the close of demobilization, totalled 859,000 men.

CANADIAN RELATIONS WITH FOREIGN COUNTRIES

The Making of Peace; Canada's Share in a Great Event. The issues involved in the Peace Congress at Versailles in 1919 seemed almost too great and varied and complicated for any body of men to determine; some of them were too full of the fire and passion of war even to discuss amicably. Into this cauldron of European and Eastern controversy, geographical, racial, national and even religious feeling was interjected, for the first time, the fresh viewpoint of Western thought and summary action. The value of detached minds—if impartial—was at such a juncture very great; the danger was in a possible ignorance of conditions which was fundamental and not superficial. President Wilson represented a school of thought which, in the United States, had rather despised European institutions, traditions, problems, and he came to an attempted solution of the most complex issues ever discussed with only a book knowledge and with advisers who knew something of men but little of a thousand years in Europe and the Orient. Much, therefore depended upon the President's personality and breadth of thought so far as this new factor was concerned.

The British Dominions and the Conference. The representatives of the Dominions, on the other hand, went to Versailles with an inherited knowledge of conditions abroad, a certain traditional share in them as parts of a world Empire and its long record of war and diplomacy, a certain preceding co-operation with the makers of history in this period through membership of the Imperial War Cabinet and Imperial Conferences. At the same time they were quite detached from the passionate territorial disputes of Jugo Slavs and Italians, Poles and Galicians, Greeks and Turks, Serbs and Bulgars, except where the war had brought them to the fringes of such feelings; they had, also, a strong desire to keep their new nations before the eyes of the world as dignified and influential entities in a great gathering.

It would be well at this point in the narrative of the first real share of Canada, Australia, South Africa and India in the foreign politics of the nations, to say that the influence which they wielded and the part they took was not based upon their own power or even their own share in the war—vital and valuable as the latter might seem to be and really was to the British Empire as such. As nations apart from the Empire they were small and far-away, they ranked as yet, perhaps unfairly, with the lesser South American countries and the smaller States of Europe; the 100,000 men whom Canada kept in the field, with all their gallantry and their achievements, could not have obtained a successful hearing in the Conference against the representatives of millions of other combatants if their Delegates had not been backed by, and come from a part of, the British Empire. It was this great power behind them which compelled representation at the Congress for Dominions which had no technical place in that body; which placed their representatives on vital Committees and made their advice and opinions factors in the settlement of world issues; which compelled the United States delegates to give way and accept their membership in the Conference and in the League of Nations.

Borden, Hughes, Botha, Smuts, Lord Sinha and Massey were able men but so were Venizelos of Greece, Pessoa of Brazil, Pashitch of Serbia, Vesnitch of Croatia, Chinda of Japan, Bratiano of Roumania, and many more who took little share in the discussions or decisions. But the men of the Dominions represented a great Empire as well as their own countries and a power and prestige were theirs much greater than the press of the day in Canada indicated. When, as in the case of Sir Robert Borden, this condition was accompanied by a calm and judicial mind, a sane and careful outlook, a judgment which the British leaders of the Congress understood and respected, the influence wielded was far out of proportion to the population and actual power of the country represented. Even the above title of "Foreign Relations of Canada" would be an absurdity and an anchronism if it were not for the peculiar British Empire system which in 1919 permitted of new constitutional developments and by its own inherent power compelled other nations to respect and accept them.

The British Dominions had won, it is true, a position in the War but to Europe it was still a rather vague one; it was a part of the canvas of British colouring and an element of British preponderance in action on sea and land; their place in the British Empire was still more vague and intangible so far as constitutional conditions and national powers were concerned; the fact that the population of the four Dominions was as great as that of Greece, Norway, Serbia, Sweden, Bulgaria and Denmark or nearly as large as that of Portugal, Roumania, Belgium and Sweden combined was not thought of or appreciated. To Canada and the others this was the crux of the situation from a purely local standpoint and it was the evolution of national representation and position at the Conference, held with and backed by Empire strength and influence, that proved the testing point of Dominion statecraft and the strength of Mr. Lloyd George's support. As the latter said in Parliament on Feb. 11th "it took time to settle this difficult question."

Preliminary Constitutional Discussion. Sir Robert Borden's position and the attitude of Canada toward the Conference were detailed in correspondence made public in a Parliamentary speech by Hon. N. W. Rowell on Sept. 10, 1919 and in a Government return brought down early in October. On Oct. 27th, 1918 the British Prime Minister had cabled Sir Robert that: "I think that you ought to be prepared to start without delay for Europe, if the

Germans accept the terms of the Armistice which we shall propose
after our meeting at Versailles this week, as the Peace Conference
will in that event probably open within a few weeks, and this will
have to be preceded by Inter-Allied Conferences of at least equal
importance. It is, I think very important that you should be here
in order to participate in the deliberations which will determine the
line to be taken at these Conferences by the British delegates.''
This was practically a re-convening of the Imperial War Cabinet
and the Canadian Prime Minister at once asked Mr. Lloyd George
for something wider and more defined and, in a cable of Oct.
29th, said:

There is need of serious consideration as to representation of the
Dominion in the Peace negotiations. The press and people of this country
take it for granted that Canada will be represented at the Peace Conference.
I appreciate possible difficulties as to representation of the Dominions; but
I hope you will keep in mind that certainly a very unfortunate impression
would be created and possibly a dangerous feeling might be aroused if
these difficulties are not overcome by some solution which will meet the
national spirit of the Canadian people. We discussed the subject today in
Council and I found among my colleagues a striking insistence which doubtless is indicative of the general opinion entertained in this country. In a
word they feel that new conditions must be met by new precedents.

In reply (Nov. 3) Sir Robert was urged to come at once to Lon-
don and help in solving this and other problems of the moment.
The Canadian Premier, accompanied by Messrs. Foster, Sifton, and
Doherty then sailed for England,* and on Dec. 4th Sir Thomas
White, Acting Prime Minister cabled a secret statement to Sir
Robert Borden: ''Council to-day further considered Canadian representation at Peace Conference and is even more strongly of
opinion than when you left, that Canada should be represented.
Council is of the opinion that, in view of the war efforts of Dominions, other nations entitled to representation at Conference should
recognize unique character of British Commonwealth composed of
a group of free nations under one Sovereign and that provision
should be made for special representation of these nations at Conference.'' On Jan. 2nd, 1919 Sir Robert cabled that he had taken
up this question in the Imperial War Cabinet and spoken frankly
and firmly as to Canada's attitude; he also pointed out that Canada
had no special interest such as the other Dominions in the arrangement of territorial matters; he urged that the British Empire had
the right to define constitutional relations between the nations
which composed it and a consequent right to distinctive representation. His proposal, as follows, was accepted:

First. Canada and the other Dominions shall each have the same representation as Belgium and other small allied nations at the Peace Conference.
Second. As it is proposed to admit representatives of Belgium and
other small nations only when their special interests are under consideration, I urged that some of the representatives of British Empire should
be drawn from a panel on which each Dominion Prime Minister shall have
a place.

*Note.—See *The Canadian Annual Review* for 1918, page 165.

Meeting of the World Peace Conference. On Jan. 18th, 1919, the greatest diplomatic and deliberative body—representing the widest area and largest population—in the history of international relationships met at the Quai d'Orsay, Paris. On the outside of a table, shaped in horseshoe fashion, sat the French and British and American and Italian, Belgian and Brazilian and Japanese delegates; with the British Empire representatives were those of Canada, Australia, South Africa, New Zealand, Newfoundland and India; inside the ring of the tables sat the delegates from the smaller nations of the world and China. M. Clemenceau, Premier of France, was elected President and after some speeches of lofty principle and high thought the Conference settled down to arrangements as to membership and organization along the following defined lines:

The belligerent Powers with general interests—the United States of America, the British Empire, France, Italy, and Japan—shall take part in all meetings and Commissions. The belligerent Powers with particular interests—Belgium, Brazil, the British Dominions and India, China, Cuba, Greece, Guatemala, Haiti, Hedjaz, Honduras, Liberia, Nicaragua, Panama, Poland, Portugal, Roumania, Serbia, Siam, and the Czecho-Slovak Republic—shall take part in the sittings at which questions concerning them are discussed. The Powers in a state of diplomatic rupture with the enemy powers—Bolivia, Ecuador, Peru, and Uruguay—shall take part in the sittings at which questions concerning them are discussed. The neutral Powers and States in process of formation may be heard either orally or in writing when summoned by the Powers with general interests, at sittings devoted especially to the examination of questions directly concerning them, but only so far as these questions are concerned.

The question of Representation was settled without serious discussion except in the case of the British Dominions. Here the opposition of the United States was registered and had not the British Government been united with its Dominions, in pressing the matter through, continental jealousies and rivalries would have made the United States all powerful. But the British Empire was too strong for critics or opponents and the arrangements were made as follows: Five representatives each for the United States of America, the British Empire, France, Italy, and Japan; three each for Belgium, Brazil, and Serbia; two each for China, Greece, the King of Hedjaz, Poland, Portugal, Roumania, Siam and the Czecho-Slovak Republic; one each for Cuba, Guatemala, Haiti, Honduras, Liberia, Nicaragua, and Panama; one for Bolivia, Ecuador, Peru and Uruguay. The British Dominions and India were each represented as follows: Two delegates each for Australia, Canada, South Africa, and India, including the native States; one delegate for New Zealand. Although the number of delegates were not to exceed the figures above mentioned, each delegation had the right to avail itself of the panel system. In the final membership five great Powers, 21 small nations, 5 British Dominions, and China were represented and the British Empire Delegation was constituted as follows:

United Kingdom	...Rt. Hon.	D. Lloyd George	.... Prime Minister
" "	... "	A. J. Balfour	...... Foreign Minister
" "	... "	A. Bonar Law	...... Lord Privy Seal
" "	... "	George N. Barnes	... Minister without Portfolio
" "	... "	Lord Reading	..... Lord Chief Justice
*Canada	.... "	Sir Robert Borden	.. Prime Minister
"	..........Hon. Arthur L. Sifton	.... Minister of Customs
"	..........Rt. Hon. Sir George E. Foster	Minister of Trade and Commerce
"	..........Hon. Charles J. Doherty	..... Minister of Justice
Australia	... ...Rt. Hon. William M. Hughes	.. Prime Minister
" "	.... "	Sir Joseph Cook	.... Minister of the Navy
South Africa	......Gen. The Rt. Hon. Louis Botha	Prime Minister
" "	...... " The Rt. Hon. J. C. Smuts	Imperial War Cabinet
New Zealand	......Rt. Hon.	William N. Massey	.. Prime Minister
" "	"	Sir J. G. Ward	... Minister of Finance
India	.... "	E. S. Montagu	.. Secretary of State for India
"	"	The Lord Sinha	.... Under Secretary for India
"	............H. H.	The Maharajah of	
	Bikanir	.... Indian Ruler	

President Wilson and Mr. Lloyd George.   It is impossible here
to deal with the proceedings and discussions and problems of the
gathering in detail. In a general sense the cables to this continent
made President Wilson dominate the entire Conference and, as
one journal put it, "wield the greatest powers in history"; his
League of Nations plan appeared to over-shadow every other issue;
his attitude on the Fiume controversy loomed large in an importance
far beyond that of any other problem. As Frederick Moore, a New
York *Tribune* special correspondent at Paris, put it on Feb. 11th:
"He sits at the Villa Murat, now known to the Americans here as
the White House, summons the Premiers to come before him and
tells them, in effect, that military force cannot be employed against
Russia, that Italy can have but a certain share of Dalmatia, that
the frontier of Poland and Czecho-Slovakia shall be such and such
and that the Pacific Islands lying between Japan and Australia
shall be opened or closed to immigration!"

This is an illustration of the general information given the
people of the United States and, through the same cable system, to
the people of Canada, during the sittings of the Conference. These
were great and important matters but, in reality, the constructive,
placative, diplomatic, statesmanlike centre of the whole Conference
was David Lloyd George while, in knowledge of the great game of
diplomacy, whether secret or public, and of all the essential elements of the problems involved, Arthur J. Balfour was the power
behind the scenes. The trouble with the open diplomacy favoured
by President Wilson and displayed in his speeches, but not practised
by the Conference, was that the Europe of a myriad races—to say
nothing of Asia—mistook patriotic oratory and theoretical principles of great beauty for practical intentions and international
policy and were increasingly difficult to placate when the time of
inevitable compromise and restriction of conflicting ambitions came.

The use of the phrase "self-determination," excellent as it
was in application to nations in the making such as Czecho-Slovakia
or Poland was easily distorted to apply to the promoting of rebellion in Egypt, or India, or Ireland, or to the projected evolution of

---

*Note.—These four Delegates sat alternatively—only two Canadians being entitled
to membership at the same time; so with the two from New Zealand.

a multitude of tiny States which had no real place and no chance of permanent life. So with intellectual appeals to a selfless, generous-spirited, thoughtful democracy which did not exist in turbulent, war-worn and passion-torn Europe or in the semi-barbarism and chaos of a Russia without a soul. So, also, with his attacks upon a secret diplomacy of the past which had averted more wars than its mistakes ever could have caused and which was absolutely suited to the Europe and Asia of the past and to periods when there was practically no press and little inter-communication between nations —sometimes indeed to these later days when publicity so often means passion and discussion means the promotion of prejudice. But Mr. Wilson was a man of great ability, his speeches had and will carry to the pages of history a ring of authority and personal force, his nation had done great service in the War and he deserved a high place in the Councils of Peace.

The final developments of the Conference gave a structure not dissimilar to that of the Big Four who had controlled the Supreme War Council—Wilson, Lloyd George, Clemenceau and Orlando. It was at first intended to have an Inner Council of 25 composed of the representatives of the five Great Powers which, under the Panel system, would have included one Dominion representative, under rotation, as part of the British Empire delegation; in practice, however, this was changed into a Council of Ten composed of the Prime Ministers and Foreign Secretaries of these five Powers—President Wilson ranking as both a ruler and Prime Minister. Gradually this Council of Ten became, for purposes of quick decision and the expediting of negotiations, a Council of Four. This powerful body finally decided all matters of disputed policy and in it Great Britain was easily the dominant influence while President Wilson remained the conspicuous figure.

Not that Great Britain got everything that she wanted or that Mr. Lloyd George had all things go as he desired but his knowledge of statecraft, of the War and its issues, of Europe and its conditions, with a certain fundamental knowledge of human nature, gave him a personal supremacy which the tremendous reserve power and war services of the British Empire further strengthened—the fact of 14 delegates out of 70 also adding an influence of its own. The British experts in attendance were many with 28 from the War Office, 22 from the Admiralty, 13 from the Air Department and 26 representing Economic trade and shipping interests, while India and the Dominions had 75. A Paris correspondent (H. N. Moore) of the Montreal *Star* put this very well on Apl. 28th: "Here, close to the proceedings, as each day passes, one realizes more and more what a great part the British Empire is taking in the making of the peace. Gradually, almost imperceptibly, she seems to impose her will on the other Powers, gaining a point here, winning over some reactionary delegation there, doing her best to bring about a peace that will stand."

The Canadian Premier's Part in the Conference. Sir Robert Borden left London for Paris on Jan. 11th after conference with various British ministers and with Sir Edward Kemp, and Sir George Perley, and General Currie who had come over from France. Sir George Foster, Hon. A. L. Sifton and Hon. C. J. Doherty left a little later. The Canadian Premier had been offered the 5th place in the British Delegation at the opening but he stood aside, on this occasion, in favour of Sir W. Lloyd of Newfoundland. The first great problem with which Sir Robert was identified was that of Russia. He was understood to have suggested in the Imperial War Cabinet, late in 1918,* that all sections of Russian rule, or attempted rule, should be asked to send representatives to appear before the Conference with a view to adjusting their difficulties; this was modified to a proposed meeting at Prinkipo, in the Sea of Marmora, between delegates from Bolsheviki and other Russian Governments and representatives of the Peace Conference; at the end of January Sir Robert was asked to head the British delegation at the meeting which, however, circumstances finally prevented.

Early in February there were several lengthy consultations between the Canadian Premier and President Wilson while Sir George Foster and Mr. Doherty held conference with members of the French Government and representatives of Roumania; Sir Robert also spoke at a dinner given in honour of the British Dominions delegation by the Franco-Anglo-American Commission; on Feb. 5th it was announced that the Canadian Premier had accepted place as a British member upon the important Commission appointed to deal with the claims for a larger Greece which should include Epirus, the West Coast of Asia Minor and islands in the eastern Mediterranean. Sir Eyre Crowe of the British Foreign Office was his colleague, together with two representatives each from the United States, France and Italy. Sir Robert Borden became Vice-Chairman and, eventually, this Committee on Greek Boundaries was recognized as one of the most efficient acting under the Conference. In this general connection he registered a serious protest against prolonged delays in the Conference—due very largely to the League of Nations' question being given precedence, under President Wilson's pressure, of other complicated problems.

The occasion was a Canadian Y.M.C.A. soldiers' gathering in Paris on Feb. 15th when Sir Robert said: "More than three months have elapsed since the Armistice was declared and let us not flatter ourselves that our soldiers believe no time has been wasted. They are amazed at the extremely deliberate methods employed and at some of the subjects upon which time has been spent. They know, and before God, they have a right to know and know without one moment's unnecessary delay, whether there is to be further fighting and if so, for what cause, for what purpose." On Feb. 19 Canada was directly represented, for the first time, on the Council of Ten

*Note.—J. W. Dafoe, of the Winnipeg *Free Press*, in special correspondence to Canadian papers, Jan. 24, 1919.

with Mr. Balfour and Sir Robert Borden present to discuss the position of Serbia and the Jugo-Slavs. At this period Sir Robert's position was distinctly one of influence and the New York *Herald* correspondent on Feb. 3rd, described him in a cable as "one of the great leaders of the Peace Conference" and quoted him as opposed to secret treaties and as saying that: "It is perfectly true that negotiations must frequently be conducted under the seal of confidence, as otherwise they would be ineffective, but this is entirely consistent with the principle that the conclusions reached through such negotiations, must be publicly announced." The further comment was made that "once or twice it was Sir Robert Borden who intervened to keep the consideration of Far Eastern matters along safe, smooth and satisfactory channels. He has a remarkably complete knowledge of many details that are not understood by all our own (U.S.) delegates."

Sir Robert Borden took an influential part in the League of Nations' discussion and the framing of its clauses; on Apl. 11th and other days there were renewed conferences between the British Prime Minister and the Prime Ministers of the Dominions, to whom Mr. Lloyd George gave full reports of the proposals under consideration by the Council of Four; their advice and assistance was sought on questions of serious importance and, in this way, the Canadian Premier was kept closely in touch with the proceedings and was able to present his views on all matters affecting Canadian interests. On Apl. 25th Sir Robert met the Inner Council of the Conference and discussed subjects of importance; during the same week he presided several times at meetings of the British Empire Delegation.

Discussions regarding German Colonies. The Canadian Premier shared in the issues raised about and around the German Colonies and on Jan. 24th appeared before the Council of Ten with Mr. Hughes of Australia, General Smuts of South Africa and Mr. Massey of New Zealand to discuss the question of their disposition —complicated by the war-time Treaties between Great Britain and France, and Great Britain and the King of the Hedjaz, regarding British and French spheres of power in Palestine, Syria, etc. President Wilson's general idea was a sort of internationalization of the German and Turkish and Austrian possessions which involved semi-civilized races or did not come under the self-determination policy. As finally developed by discussion it took the form of Mandatory administration of Colonial German areas by the Powers interested with responsibility to the League of Nations. Canada was not directly concerned but the Union of South Africa definitely claimed German Southwest Africa; in the Pacific, Australia claimed New Guinea and the Bismarck Archipelago; New Zealand wanted Samoa and Japan desired the Marshall Islands and the Carolines. Japan also suggested an equatorial delimitation between British and Japanese spheres of influence in the Pacific.

The Canadian Premier sympathized with the aspirations of his Dominion colleagues; incidentally the arrangement come to on Jan. 30th for a system of Mandates brought the Dominions and the United States into sharp antagonism. Mr. Hughes insisted on the complete annexation of New Guinea to Australia and Samoa to New Zealand which Mr. Wilson opposed; the mandatory compromise was eventually accepted and in these cases the mandate was modified by a practically complete delegation of administrative authority to the State concerned. The problems which then had to be settled were: (1) who was to pay for the development of the territory; (2) what rules regarding tariffs were to be observed and, (3) were the mandatories to be allowed to exclude people or capital they did not wish to enter. As to these the Dominions of Australia, New Zealand and South Africa submitted a scheme of administration but in their proposals Canada did not participate. Mr. Premier Hughes expressed himself in an interview on Feb. 6th as follows: "We prefer not to accept the Mandate principle, but if compelled to do so it is imperative that we must make the same laws and have over the new territories the same power as we exercise over Australia." He wanted the northern Pacific Islands as well as those of the South but only the latter were allotted to Australasia and Japan, in accordance with its war-time Treaty, got the Marshall and Caroline Islands—under mandate.

One of the matters which Sir Robert Borden pressed upon the British Committee and the Conference was that of Canadian war damages and claims upon the enemy. A Commission in Canada composed of Hon. Martin Burrell (Chairman) Thomas Mulvey, K.C., of the State Department, C. C. Robinson for that of Justice and J. R. Forsyth of the Finance Department, had been investigating conditions and classifying claims since the first of the year. These claims ran from Brazeau Collieries' shares of which a million were held in Germany and lands supposed (very doubtfully) to be held in British Columbia for the German Kaiser, to large blocks of C.P.R. stock (about $10,000,000) held by Germans and a number of ships and vessels sunk by Submarines. So many other countries had similar or immensely larger claims and the resources of Germany were limited so obviously that the question was one of extreme delicacy and difficulty.

The Dominions to Sign the Treaty. Another important matter which Sir Robert had to deal with before the Conference was over, and the terms of the Treaty settled for German acceptance, was the question of signatures to the Treaty itself. Under date of Mch. 12th, 1919 the Canadian Premier circulated at the Conference a Memorandum prepared on behalf of the Dominion Prime Ministers and declaring that they had reached the conclusion that all the treaties and conventions resulting from the Peace Conference should be so drafted as to enable the Dominions to become Parties and Signatories, thereto, in order to give suitable recognition to the part played at the Peace Table by the British Delegation as a whole and to record the status thus attained by the Dominions. The document then proceeded:

The procedure is in consonance with the principles of constitutional government that obtain throughout the Empire. The Crown is the supreme executive in the United Kingdom and in all the Dominions, but it acts on the advice of different Ministries within different constitutional units; and under Resolution IX of the Imperial War Conference, 1917, the organization of the Empire is to be based upon equality of nationhood. Having regard to the high objects of the Peace Conference, it is also desirable that the settlements reached should be presented at once to the world in the character of universally accepted agreements, so far as this is consistent with the constitution of each State represented.

On the constitutional point, it is assumed that each Treaty or Convention will include clauses providing for ratification similar to those in the Hague Convention, 1907. Such clauses will, under the procedure proposed, have the effect of reserving to the Dominion Governments and Legislatures the same power of review as is provided in the case of other contracting parties. It is conceived that this proposal can be carried out with but slight alterations of previous treaty forms. Thus:

(a) The usual recital of Heads of State in the Preamble needs no alteration whatever, since the Dominions are adequately included in the present formal description of the King, namely, His Majesty the King of the United Kingdom of Great Britain and Ireland and of the British Dominions beyond the Seas, Emperor of India.

(b) The recital in the Preamble of the names of the Plenipotentiaries appointed by the High Contracting Parties for the purpose of concluding the Treaty would include the names of the Dominion Plenipotentiaries immediately after the names of the Plenipotentiaries appointed by the United Kingdom. Under the General heading 'The British Empire' the sub-headings The United Kingdom, The Dominion of Canada, The Commonwealth of Australia, The Union of South Africa, etc., would be used as headings to distinguish the various Plenipotentiaries.

(c) It would then follow that the Dominion Plenipotentiaries would sign according to the same scheme.

This policy was accepted by the British Delegation and acted upon by the Conference—the only serious objection coming from the German delegates who, on May 7th, when handed the Treaty for consideration questioned the right and credentials of British Dominions as expressed in the document. A Canadian Order-in-Council followed the acceptance of this proposal and, on Apl. 10th, requested His Majesty the King "to issue letters patent to the Right Hon. Sir Robert Laird Borden, the Right Hon. Sir George Eulas Foster, the Hon. Arthur Lewis Sifton and the Hon. Charles Joseph Doherty, as Commissioners and Plenipotentiaries in respect of the Dominion of Canada with full power and authority to sign any treaties concluded at the Peace Congress." The request was granted and the Royal authority duly accorded. It may be added here that the Canadian Ministers accompanying Sir Robert Borden took their full share in the work of the Conference and its Committees and the British Delegations.

Sir Robert, early in March, was appointed a member of the British Economic Committee which was to suggest policies and formulate machinery for the Supreme Economic Council of the

Conference. A little later Sir George Foster became a member of this Council whose duties were of the first importance. It controlled, for the period of the Armistice, shipping, the extent and character of the blockade, the distribution of food to all the European countries, and the allocation of raw materials and rebuilding supplies; and was finally charged with determining to what degree this control should be continued during the reconstruction period following the signing of peace. Early in May this body requested the appointment of a Canadian Director of Food Supplies and Dr. J. W. Robertson, C.M.G. of Ottawa was selected by the Canadian Government. Mr. Doherty was Chairman of a British delegation dealing with economic settlements and pre-war contracts and also dealt, on behalf of Canada, with the question of credits to Italy, Greece and Belgium. He was member of a British Sub-Committee on the League of Nations and was legal adviser to the Canadian delegation on many vital issues. Mr. Sifton was the chief British delegate on the Committee appointed by the Conference to report upon international claims as to Ports, Rivers and Railways—the Fiume controversy between Italy, the Jugo-Slavs and the United States coming, no doubt, within his purview. Sir George Foster took an active part in many meetings and consultations.

The Canadian Premier returns Home. Meantime, there had been continued calls from Canada for Sir Robert Borden to return home —calls which seemed to deprecate the Dominion taking any large part in these international and Imperial issues. The position was not dissimilar, in some respects, to the Republican attitude in the United States toward President Wilson and was defined by the Toronto *Globe* as follows on Feb. 1st: "Is there any reason why the Premier of Canada should remain in Paris in what is manifestly a subordinate capacity until the boundaries of Czecho-Slovakia and Poland are arranged, the tangled mess of Balkan intrigue is sorted out, and the last comma is inserted in the Peace Treaty? Canada's work must be done on this continent. It is a great work, worthy of the best that is in the Canadian people." As to diplomacy it was said to fascinate the Premier: "In 1917-1918, and now in 1919, he has found it necessary to answer calls to take part in the larger affairs of the Empire in London or in Paris. His presence on each occasion for a short time was probably necessary, but in the last analysis Canada must be governed by Canadians for Canadians. The proper seat of such a Government is Ottawa." To this and similar utterances a reply came from J. W. Dafoe in a *Globe* despatch written from Ottawa on Mch. 23: "Those who take this view are willing, apparently, to contract Canada out of the Society of Nations, so far as having anything to say about the future international order of the world is concerned." Yet, he pointed out, the old international system, which was being reconstructed, had cost Canada 60,000 lives and a billion and a half dollars.

It is suggested in Canada that our delegates have no real power in Paris, and they are there only for the look of the thing. This is not correct. The limitation of the governing body of the Conference from 25, as originally decided upon, to 10, constituted an undoubted grievance to the British Dominions, but these Dominions have, nevertheless, a real influence in the secret conclave of a controlling body which none of the secondary powers—not even Belgium or Serbia or Roumania—enjoys. British policy in the Council of Ten is the subject of constant consideration by the Empire delegations, which meet in conference two or three times a week, and sometimes daily. It would be quite accurate to say that in these meetings Sir Robert Borden, General Botha and Mr. Hughes meet British Ministers on terms of entire equality and their views receive respectful consideration. The British representation on the Council of Ten changes its personnel: Sir Robert Borden has served upon it, upon occasion, as one of the British representatives.

The influence of the British Delegation upon the ruling Council of the Conference was, as a matter of fact, very great—frequently it was dominating in its power. The question of Sir Robert's return came up in other forms, however, and despite an urgent request from Mr. Lloyd George to remain for the signing of the Treaty, the Canadian Premier in the middle of May decided to return home, together with Mr. Sifton, leaving Sir G. Foster as head of the delegation. According to a Paris despatch in the London *Daily Telegraph* there was deep regret at the Canadian Premier's departure: "His position as leader and senior Dominion representative in Paris caused him to be watched with intense interest by the other delegates. His work and his criticisms have been valuable, both in Committee and at the Councils, and it would be unjust not to express to Canada deep appreciation of his steady and consistent work in furtherance of the interests of his own country, of the Empire and of the new world which is being slowly brought to birth."

Sir Robert was in London on May 15 and was received by the King and the Prince of Wales. On the 16th he was the guest at luncheon of the Empire Parliamentary Association with Mr. Bonar Law in the chair and received high tribute for his work in both Empire and world conference: "In all the negotiations during the war and in connection with Peace, there is no one on whose sound judgment and far-sighted wisdom we have had more reason to rely than upon our guest of to-day." The Canadian Premier in a careful speech pointed out that he had been in England or France for 9½ months out of the past twelve engaged in matters of either war or peace-making; he did not think the 4 months spent on the Treaty had been excessive. After pointing out that the completed document had been met with varied criticism, with some doubt and hesitation by those most concerned, he added: "Without concessions, without infinite patience, and without the most remarkable effort it would have been impossible to have any peace at all, or to have the Allied nations united in the terms of peace which should be presented to Germany. The miracle is not that there was reluctance or, perhaps, hesitation on the part of the representatives of some of the nations to adopt and accept the terms which eventually were made

4

public. The miracle is that you should get the representatives of 32 nations such as I have described united to present to the Germans a treaty of peace such as has been presented as their unanimous decision.'' The Premier and Mr. Sifton arrived at Halifax on May 25 and the former issued a statement in which he mentioned that this was his 8th voyage across the Atlantic since the War began, spoke of his 7 months' continuous absence and the necessity of giving immediate attention to urgent matters at Ottawa, excused himself, therefore, from the public reception tendered by Halifax.

Terms and Signatories of the Treaty of Versailles. Mr. Sifton, shortly after this, returned to Paris and was present at the signing of the Treaty which was done amid scenes of historical splendour at Versailles but with forms of simple dignity. The document had, since May 7th been in the hands of the Germans, had been the subject of vigourous protests and almost pathetic appeals, of keen discussion and characteristic strength of language, of some not very important modifications. On June 28th the accredited representatives of Germany—in these negotiations none of the well-known men, whose names had been the property of the world for years, appeared—attended at Versailles to put their names to a document which had been prepared by the victors in the world-war. The Treaty was signed in the following order:

United States*	Hon. Woodrow Wilson, Hon. Robert Lansing, Hon. Henry White, Hon. Edward M. House, General Tasker H. Bliss.
British Empire†	Rt. Hon. David Lloyd George, Rt. Hon. A. Bonar Law, Rt. Hon. The Viscount Milner, Rt. Hon. A. J. Balfour, Rt. Hon. G. N. Barnes.
Canada	Rt. Hon. Sir George E. Foster, Hon. C. J. Doherty.
Australia	Rt. Hon. W. M. Hughes, Rt. Hon. Sir Joseph Cook.
South Africa	Rt. Hon. Louis Botha, Lieut.-Gen. The Rt. Hon. J. C. Smuts.
New Zealand	Rt. Hon. W. F. Massey.
India	Rt. Hon. E. S. Montagu, Maj.-Gen. H. E. The Maharajah of Bikanir.
France	Georges Clémenceau, M. Pichon, L. L. Klots, André Tardieu, Jules Cambon.
Italy	V. E. Orlando, Baron S. Sonnino, S. Crespi, Marquis G. Imperiali, S. Barsilai.
Japan	Marquis Saionsi, Baron Makino, Viscount Chinda, H. Matsui, H. Ijuin.

Belgium, Bolivia, Brazil, China, Cuba, Ecuador, Greece, Guatemala, Haiti, Hedjaz, Honduras, Liberia, Nicaragua, Panama, Peru, Poland, Portugal, Roumania, Jugo-Slavia, Siam, Czecho-Slovakia, Uruguay and Germany also signed in the above order. Herr Adolph Müller, Foreign Minister in the Bauer Government, and Johannes Bell, Minister of Colonies, signed for the original German delegates who had refused to do so. It is impossible to reprint the Treaty here in full; it would occupy at least 160 pages of *The Canadian Annual Review*. Its chief divisions were the Covenant of the League of Nations; the Boundaries of the new

*Note.—The United States of America came first in the Conference and signed first in the Treaty because it was personally represented by its ruler—the President of the Republic and because it came first alphabetically—America.

†Note.—The appointed Plenipotentiaries of the United Kingdom and the Dominions signed for H.M. the King.

Germany; the political clauses relating to territories and boundaries throughout Europe—Belgium, the left bank of the Rhine, the Sarre Basin, Czecho-Slovakia and the new Poland, East Prussia, and Memel, Dantzig and Schleswig, Heligoland and the Russian States; German rights and interests outside of Germany—which included renunciation of all overseas possessions in favour of the Allied Powers and dealt with interests in China, Siam, Liberia, Morocco, Egypt, Turkey and Bulgaria and Shantung; Military, Naval and Aerial clauses including regulations as to armament, munitions and war material, recruiting and military training, fortifications, Naval forces, etc.; Prisoners of War and Graves, Penalties, Reparation, Guarantees; Financial and Economic clauses; Aerial Navigation, Ports, Waterways and Railways, Navigation; Clauses relating to the Elbe, the Oder, the Mennen, and the Danube and making these rivers in part international; clauses relating to the Rhine and the Moselle; International Transport and Labour. The details of the Treaty may be summarized here as briefly as possible for purposes of reference and record:

Limitation of German Powers: Conscription to be abolished in Germany and Army limited to 100,000 men; enlistment to be voluntary and only for long service; no trained Army reserves allowed and supply of guns and shells rationed; Government Arsenals abolished and German Navy not to exceed 6 Battleships, 6 Light Cruisers, 12 Torpedo Boats, 12 Destroyers; no Submarines, Aeroplanes or Airships allowed, Heligoland forts to be destroyed and Kiel Canal opened to ships of all Nations; Holland to be asked to surrender Wilhelm II to the Allies; and his trial provided for by Special Tribunal of the Five Great Powers; German War criminals to be tried by Military Tribunal and Germany to deliver them up as required.

Indemnities to be Paid: Germany to accept responsibility for all War loss and damage. To pay Belgium's debt to the Allies and the cost of Armies of Occupation; to pay on account £1,000,000,000 within two years, £2,000,000,000 between 1921-6 and £2,000,000,000 later; these amounts to be used for civilians injured by war acts, by air raids, by cruelties, or by "U" Boat campaign, for prisoners maltreated, for pensions and separation allowances, for property damaged or damage done to civilians by forced labour and in repayment of levies and fines; Germany to be told the total sum required for above purposes by May 1, 1921 and time limit for full settlement by Germany of indemnity to be 30 years.

Payment of Indemnities in Kind: On account of losses caused by "U" Boats and mines the Allies to have right of replacing merchant ships, ton for ton and class for class, and Germany therefore to surrender all ships of 1,600 tons and over with one-half of her ships between 1,600 and 1,000 tons and a quarter of her steam trawlers and fishing boats; also Germany to build for the Allies every year for five years 200,000 tons of shipping. For destroying French and Belgian mines Germany to give control of rich Saar coalfield to France for at least 15 years and to send specified quantities of coal for ten years to Belgium, France and Italy. For looting and destruction of industrial and agricultural machinery in France and Belgium, Germany to replace cattle and live-stock looted and machinery destroyed; to devote her resources to restoration of invaded areas and to protect Allied trade against unfair competition; to give Allied shipping most-favoured-nation-treatment for five years at least.

Payment of Indemnity in Territory: German Colonies to be surrendered to the Allies and natives freed from German cruelty; Germany to restore

Alsace-Lorraine to France free of debt and the French frontier to be as in 1870 before German attack on France in that year; Belgium to have Moresnet, Eupen, and Malmedy; Districts of Posen and West Prussia seized by Prussia when Kingdom of Poland was divided to be restored to Poland together with Upper Silesia; the frontier of East Prussia to be fixed by popular vote and Dantzig to be a free city and the sea-port for Poland; the people of Schleswig by popular vote to decide whether they shall remain German or be Danes; German influence in Luxemburg to be abolished; the Brest-Litovsk Treaty with Russian Bolshevists cancelled and Germany to give up her gains under that treaty and to recognize full independence of all territories formerly part of Russian Empire; Treaty of Bucharest cancelled. Germany's control of Roumanian oilfields and produce to end; and her Allies' seizure of Roumanian territory to be cancelled; British Protectorate of Egypt to be recognized by Germany and Germany to lose her concessions and property in China, Siam, Liberia and Morocco.

Guarantees of the Treaty: To make sure that Germany shall observe the Terms of Peace that country shall be occupied in part by the Allies as long as necessary; the League of Nations established by the Treaty to be responsible for seeing that many of the provisions are carried out by Germany; an agreement proposed between Great Britain and the United States to come to the aid of France should Germany attack her in any unprovoked way.

There was jubilation in many British centres over the signing of the Treaty; the King issued a Message of congratulation to the Empire on the termination of the War; Clémenceau, Lloyd George and President Wilson were given ovations at Versailles and Paris; Lloyd George received a tremendous welcome in Parliament. Canadian feelings were very quietly expressed—the most conspicuous feature being sermons in many pulpits on the succeeding Sunday. In the British Commons, on July 3rd Mr. Lloyd George paid tribute to his Empire colleagues as follows: "I should like also to be able to say how much we owe to the Prime Ministers and other members of the great Dominion Governments for the assistance which they gave—Sir Robert Borden, Mr. Hughes, Mr. Massey, and General Botha. They took part in some of the most difficult Commissions, notably the Territorial Commissions, for the adjustment of the extraordinarily delicate and complex ethnical, economic and strategic questions which arose between the various States throughout Europe. They, in the main, represented the British Empire on many of these most difficult Commissions, and we owe a great deal to the ability and judgment with which they discharged their func-tions." In concluding this general reference to the Conference and Canada's share in its proceedings a quotation of May 24 may be given from *Saturday Night,* an able Toronto journal, not usually eulogistic of the Dominion Government and its works:

Honour is due to Sir Robert Borden in the matter of the Peace Conference to an extent that few Canadians realize. His work has been done unobtrusively, and he has not, like President Wilson, had the advantage, or disadvantage, of a vast corps of newspaper correspondents to keep him in the limelight. Yet even those political opponents of Sir Robert, who have gleaned actual knowledge of events in Paris, have come to the conclusion that the 'Big Four' have had no more industrious and astute aide than Sir Robert. The vast preparatory work to be done in connection with the innumerable settlements and clauses of the Peace Treaty was of a kind to bring out the best elements in Sir Robert—the unquestionable distinction of his legal mind, and the justice and sobriety of his temperament. There is the best of reason to believe that the statesmen of other nations learned to place much reliance . on his judgment, and that more and more the Prime Minister of Great Britain availed himself of Sir Robert's ability and foresight.

The Treaties with Austria and Bulgaria. Associated with the German Peace Treaty and coming into operation and effect at the same time, were the Treaty with Poland and the Rhine Valley and Saar Basin arrangements; the Franco-Anglo-American Treaty was signed by French, British and American plenipotentiaries but rendered nugatory by the action of the United States Senate. The Treaty with Austria was subsidiary to the other and without serious complications; the old Empire, powerful in its unity but now shattered and ruined, was not strong enough to refuse any document promulgated by the Allied Powers. Less than one-third of the Austro-Hungarian realm remained and its Government was too feeble and uncertain and diplomatically ignorant to do more than protest. The Treaty was signed at St. Germain on Sept. 10 and ratified by the Austrian Assembly on Oct. 17. It consisted of 381 Articles or clauses and followed, in a general way, the lines of the German agreement. Part I was the League of Nations Covenant which Austria accepted though it was only to be a member on the vote of the other members of the League; Part II detailed the new boundaries of Austria and dealt with the cession of great slices of territory to Italy, Poland, Czecho-Slovakia and Jugo-Slavia—recognizing, also, the national independence of the four later countries; Part III dealt with the political conditions of the new nations and Italian acquired territories, with renunciation of all rights or interests in Morocco, Egypt, Siam and China.

Under this Section Austria recognized the British protectorate of Egypt and accepted a limitation of its Army to 30,000 men and its Navy to 3 Patrol boats on the Danube. Other divisions of the Treaty covered the matter of Reparations and created a Commission to deal with the conditions and allot payments; compelled the return to Italy of Tuscan Crown jewels and heirlooms of the historic Houses of Medici and Lorraine looted from their countries in other centuries; enforced the return, also, of various famous paintings and works of Art taken at different periods from Italy, Belgium, Poland and Bohemia; enacted unusual if not actually unique, protection for Minorities. This Article 66 was as follows and in it the influence of Lloyd George and British Empire opinions were clearly visible:

All Austrian nationals shall be equal before the law and shall enjoy the same civil and political rights without distinction as to race, language, or religion. Differences of religion, creed, or confession shall not prejudice any Austrian national in matters relating to the enjoyment of civil or political rights—as for instance admission to public employments, functions, and honours, or the exercise of professions and industries.

No restriction shall be imposed on the free use by any Austrian national of any language in private intercourse, in commerce, in religion, in the

press, or in publications of any kind, or at public meetings. Notwithstanding
any establishment by the Austrian Government of an official language,
adequate facilities shall be given to Austrian nationals of non-German
speech for the use of their language, either orally or in writing, before
the Courts.

The Treaty was signed by Hon. F. L. Polk, Hon. Henry White
and Gen. Tasker H. Bliss for the President of the United States of
America; by Rt. Hon. A. J. Balfour, Rt. Hon. A. Bonar Law, Lord
Milner and Rt. Hon. G. N. Barnes for His Majesty the King and
for Canada by Sir A. E. Kemp, Minister of the Overseas Forces, for
Australia by Hon. G. F. Pearce, Minister of Defence, for South
Africa by Lord Milner, Secretary for the Colonies, for New
Zealand by Sir Thomas Mackenzie, High Commissioner, and for
India by Lord Sinha; by Charles Renner, Chancellor, for the Re-
public of Austria and by representatives of France, Italy, Japan,
Belgium, China, Cuba, Greece, Nicaragua, Panama, Poland, Portu-
gal, Roumania, Jugo-Slavia, Siam and Czecho-Slovakia. The
Treaty with Bulgaria was signed at Paris on Nov. 27 and under its
terms the clauses of the German Treaty as to League of Nations,
Labour, Aerial Navigation, Penalties, etc., were practically included
and accepted; Western Thrace was ceded to the Allied Powers for
their disposition, and the independence of the Serb-Croat-Slovene
State (Serbia with Austrian additions) was recognized; drastic but
necessary clauses for protection of minorities were included and the
Roumanian and Greek frontiers restored to pre-war conditions; the
Army was reduced to 20,000 men, universal military service was
abolished, only one factory for war material permitted and all war-
vessels surrendered to the Allies; Reparation was placed at $445,-
000,000 to be paid in half-yearly payments.

The Austrian Treaty was discussed in the Canadian House of
Commons on Oct. 14 when Mr. Doherty, Minister of Justice, stated
that it was, upon the whole, drawn on lines and based upon principles similar to those of the German Treaty and intimated that an
authentic copy of the Treaty had not yet arrived though the Government had a copy as originally prepared and in which only im-
material changes had been made. The Government was, therefore,
prepared to advise the ratification of the Treaty without Parliamentary approval but if the exact text arrived in time it would be
duly submitted. A. R. McMaster, D. D. McKenzie, Hon. W. S.
Fielding, from different standpoints, thought that Parliament
should have an opportunity of considering the Treaty. Mr. Fielding observed that approval of the German Treaty was deemed by
the Government essential; that of the Austrian, which was similar
in terms, was declared unnecessary! Upon Mr. Doherty's motion
the House accepted a Senate amendment to the German Treaty Bill
empowering the Government to carry that Treaty into effect, voting
the necessary funds and applying this clause, by anticipation, to
the Austrian Treaty.

On Oct. 24 Mr. Doherty was able to submit the latter Treaty and moved accordingly that "Parliament do approve of the Treaty of Peace between the Allied and Associated Powers and Austria signed at St. Germain on Sept. 10, 1919, and signed on behalf of His Majesty, acting for Canada, by the Plenipotentiary therein named." In his succeeding speech he made a claim of wide constitutional import: "Before that power (to give effect to the Treaty) could come to be exercised at all, the Treaty would have to become binding upon Canada, and it would only have become so binding by reason of the ratification of His Majesty on the advice of the Government of Canada." Mr. McKenzie claimed that this approval was an empty form because (1) the King could, in any case, ratify the Treaty and (2) because of the preceding authority given by Parliament to carry out its terms; several brief speeches followed and the Resolution was carried without division.

The League of Nations; Position of Canada and the Dominions. This great compact was a part of the German Treaty of Peace and of succeeding Treaties with Austria and Bulgaria; it was pressed upon the Conference by President Wilson as vital to the success and enforcement of the whole Agreement; it was dealt with at the cost of serious delay in urgent and almost paralyzing conditions in Central Europe; its clauses were greatly aided, its principles largely evolved, its practical side built up and developed by British expert aid and the constructive statecraft of Lord Robert Cecil, Mr. Balfour and General Smuts; it was approved in the main by the representatives of the British Dominions except as to the Colonial mandatory clause; under its terms the German Colonies were allotted to the care and control of the Great Powers and the British Dominions though the United States refused to accept any responsibility for Constantinople, Armenia, Syria, Palestine, Mesopotamia or Arabia which the other Powers would have agreed in part, at least, to place under its mandate; it finally obtained unanimous approval from the Conference.

Presentation and Discussion of the Plan. President Wilson and Mr. Lloyd George presented the initial plan and proposals to a Plenary meeting of the Conference on Jan. 25 in speeches marked by brevity and careful language. The President claimed to be speaking for the people of many countries still under the lash of the war scourge: "We are bidden by these people to make a peace which will make them secure. We are bidden by these people to see to it that this strain does not come upon them again. It is a solemn obligation on our part, therefore, to make permanent arrangements that justice shall be rendered and peace maintained. This is the central object of our meeting. Settlements may be temporary, but the action of the nations in the interest of peace and justice must be permanent. We can set up permanent processes. We may not be able to set up a permanent decision." His definition of the proposed League was "continuous superintendence of the peace of the world by the associated nations of the world."

The British Prime Minister declared the people of the British Empire to be behind the plan, described the late war as "organized savagery" and the time as near for some better method of settling disputes: "I don't know whether this will succeed. But if we attempt it, the attempt will be a success, and for that reason I second the proposal." Other speakers followed and the Resolution appointing a Committee to evolve details as to the constitution and functions of a League of Nations was passed unanimously upon the following basis:

It is essential to the maintenance of the world settlement which the associated nations are now met to establish that a League of Nations be created to promote international obligations and to provide safeguards against war. This League should be created as an integral part of the general Treaty of Peace and should be open to every civilized nation which can be relied on to promote its objects. The members of the League should periodically meet in international Conference and should have a permanent organization and secretaries to carry on the business of the League in intervals between the Conferences.

This Committee, when appointed, included for the United States President Wilson and Colonel House; for the British Empire Lord R. Cecil and General Smuts; for France Léon Bourgeois and F. Larnaude; for Italy V. E. Orlando and for Japan Baron Chinda; together with delegates from Belgium, Serbia, Brazil, Portugal and China. Beginning on Feb. 4 it held daily sessions and made steady progress—the most vital point of difference being the amount of power to be delegated to the League for enforcement of its decisions. As to this the British and American delegates were at one in desiring a moderate form; the French representatives stood for a League with power to enforce its decrees by arms. So acute did the debate become that on Feb. 9th M. Clémenceau issued what was practically an appeal to the American people and was vigourously approved by the French press. In it, after depicting a possible revival of German war fever, he summed up the French hope of the future: "Of course, a Society of Nations in which America and France enter must be supported profoundly by the conviction of their peoples and by a determination of each nation entering into the agreement to þe willing to renounce its traditional aloofness from other peoples and willing to employ the national strength outside its own country in time of peace as well as under the pressure of war."

The Covenant of the League. This helped to clear the air and on Feb. 14 President Wilson presented a compromise and unanimous report to the Supreme Council of the Conference—only the French and Czecko-Slovaks having voted for an Inter-Allied Military force—which was finally accepted. The Preamble and basis of the League constitution read as follows: "The High Contracting parties, in order to promote international co-operation and to achieve international peace and security by the acceptance of obligations not to resort to war, by the prescription of open, just and honourable relations between nations, by the firm establishment of the understandings of international law as the actual rule of conduct among Governments, and by the maintenance of justice and a scrupulous respect for all treaty obligations in the dealings of organized peoples with one another, agree to this Covenant of the League of Nations.''

Article I stated that the original members of the League would be the 32 signatories to the Treaty, 13 countries specified in the Annex who would be invited to join, and any other self-governing State, Dominion or Colony not named therein but which was accepted by a two-thirds vote of the Assembly and agreed to carry out the same obligations and principles. Any member of the League could withdraw after 2 years' notice and the fulfilment of all its international obligations under the compact. The League was to be governed and its policy carried out through (1) an Assembly composed of representatives of the nations of the League and (2) a Council consisting of representatives of the five principal Allied and Associated Powers, together with representatives of four other members of the League: ''The Assembly (and also the Council) shall meet at stated intervals and from time to time, as occasion may require, at the seat of the League or at such other place as may be decided upon. The Assembly (and also the Council) may deal at its meetings with any matter within the sphere of action of the League or affecting the peace of the. world. At meetings of the Assembly each member of the League shall have one vote, and may have not more than three representatives.''

The Council was to be permanently composed of one representative each of the five Great Powers—The British Empire, United States, France, Italy and Japan and 4 other members to be elected from time to time by the Assembly: ''With the approval of the majority of the Assembly the Council may name additional members of the League whose representatives shall always be members of the Council; the Council with like approval may increase the number of members of the League to be selected by the Assembly for representation on the Council. Any member of the League not represented on the Council shall be invited to send a representative to sit as a member at any meeting of the Council during the consideration of matters specially affecting the interests of that member of the League. At meetings of the Council, each member of the League represented on the Council shall have one vote, and may have not more than one representative.'' Article V provided that, except where otherwise expressly provided in the Covenant or by the terms of the Peace Treaty, decisions at any meeting of the Assembly or of the Council would require the agreement of all the members of the League represented at the meeting. The first meeting of the League was to be called by the President of the United States, the seat of the League was to be at Geneva and the first Secretary-General was to be the Hon. Sir Eric Drummond, all appointments and positions were to be equally open to men and women, the expenses of the meetings were to be apportioned amongst the member-nations. The following were the most important clauses of the Covenant:

Art. IX. The members of the League recognize that the maintenance of peace requires the reduction of national armaments to the lowest point consistent with national safety and the enforcement by common action of international obligations. The Council, taking account of the geographical situation and circumstances of each State, shall formulate plans for such reduction for the consideration and action of the several Governments. Such plans shall be subject to reconsideration and revision at least every ten years. After these plans have been adopted by the several Governments, the limits of armaments therein fixed shall not be exceeded without the concurrence of the Council.

The members of the League undertake to inter-change full and frank information as to the scale of their armaments, their military and naval programmes and the condition of such of their industries as are adaptable to warlike purposes.

Art. X. The members of the League undertake to respect and preserve as against external aggression the territorial integrity and existing political independence of all members of the League. In case of any such aggression or in case of any threat or danger of such aggression the Council shall advise upon the means by which this obligation shall be fulfilled.

Art. XI. Any war or threat of war, whether immediately affecting any of the members of the League or not, is hereby declared a matter of concern to the whole League, and the League shall take any action that may be deemed wise and effectual to safeguard the peace of nations. . . . It is also declared to be the friendly right of each member of the League to bring to the attention of the Assembly or of the Council any circumstance whatever affecting international relations which threatens to disturb international peace or the good understanding between nations upon which peace depends.

Art. XII. The members of the League agree that if there should arise between them any dispute likely to lead to a rupture, they will submit the matter either to arbitration or to enquiry by the Council, and they agree in no case to resort to war until three months after the Award by the arbitrators or the Report by the Council.

Art. XIII. The members of the League agree that whenever any dispute shall arise between them which they recognize to be suitable for submission to arbitration and which cannot be satisfactorily settled by diplomacy, they will submit the whole subject-matter to arbitration.

Disputes as to the interpretation of a treaty, as to any question of international law, as to the existence of any fact which, if established, would constitute a breach of any international obligation, or as to the extent and nature of the reparation to be made for any such breach, are declared to be among those which are generally suitable for submission to arbitration.

For the consideration of any such dispute the Court of Arbitration to which the case is referred shall be the Court agreed on by the parties to the dispute or stipulated in any Convention existing between them.

The members of the League agree that they will carry out in full good faith any award that may be rendered, and that they will not resort to war against a member of the League which complies therewith. In the event of any failure to carry out such an award, the Council shall propose what steps should be taken to give effect thereto.

Art. XIV. The Council shall formulate and submit to the members of the League for adoption plans for the establishment of a Permanent Court of International Justice. The Court shall be competent to hear and determine any dispute of an international character which the parties thereto submit to it. The Court may also give an advisory opinion upon any dispute or question proffered to it by the Council or by the Assembly.

Art. XVI. Should any member of the League resort to war in disregard of its Covenants it shall *ipso facto* be deemed to have committed an act of war against all other members of the League, which hereby undertake immediately to subject it to the severance of all trade or financial relations, the prohibition of all intercourse between their nationals and the nationals of the covenant-breaking State, and the prevention of all financial, commercial, or personal intercourse between the nationals of the covenant-breaking State and the nationals of any other State, whether a member of the League or not.

It shall be the duty of the Council in such case to recommend to the several Governments concerned what effective military, naval or air force the members of the League shall severally contribute to the armed forces to be used to protect the covenants of the League. The members of the League agree, further, that they will mutually support one another in the financial and economic measures which are taken under this Article, in order to minimize the loss, and inconvenience resulting from the above measures, and that they will mutually support one another in resisting any special measures aimed at one of their number by the covenant-breaking State, and that they will take the necessary steps to afford passage through their territory to the forces of any of the members of the League which are co-operating to protect the covenants of the League.

Art. XVIII. Every treaty or international engagement entered into hereafter by any member of the League shall be forthwith registered with the Secretariat and shall as soon as possible be published by it. No such treaty or international engagement shall be binding until so registered.

Art. XIX. Nothing in this Covenant shall be deemed to affect the validity of international engagements, such as treaties of arbitration or regional understandings like the Monroe Doctrine, for securing the maintenance of peace.

Articles followed defining the Mandatory principles of the Peace Treaty and methods of application to German Colonies, pledging protection and advancement of the interests of Labour in all countries, undertaking supervision over illegal international traffic and improper trade in ammunitions, etc., promising steps for control and prevention of disease and the encouragement of Red Cross activities. The Mandatory clause dealing with German Colonies and Eastern possessions of the Turkish Empire was long and elaborate. As Article XIX it declared that the well-being and development of these peoples was a "sacred trust of civilization," that securities for the performance of this trust should be embodied in the constitution of the League, that the character of the Mandate must differ according to the state of development reached by the people concerned,—their geographical situation or economic conditions. It was pointed out that in some cases, as in the Near East, the stage reached warranted a provisional independence with, chiefly, advice and assistance from the mandatory Power; that in regions such as Central Africa the mandate would involve responsibility for administration subject only to freedom of religion and the maintenance of public order and morals; that in territories such as South-West Africa and certain Southern Pacific islands the Mandate would involve practical incorporation as integral parts of the Mandatory States. In all cases where the Mandate was given and accepted there should be an annual statement to the League; wherever "the degree of authority, control or administration to be exercised by the Mandatory State" was not previously agreed upon by the High Contracting Parties it should be explicitly defined by the Executive Committee of the League in a special Act or Charter; in this general connection a Mandatory Commission was to be established at the seat of the League.

Following the acceptance of the League Constitution President Wilson on Feb. 15 sailed for the United States in order to confer with Congressional Committees and leading public men and to present to the nation generally the principles underlying the admittedly great ideal which he had hoped to develop.* At Boston on the 24th he was welcomed by 200,000 people and at New York on Mch. 4 he analyzed the need of Europe for such an agreement, for such a controlling, overhead force as this proposed League would establish. As in all his speeches he was very sweeping in general assertions and conclusions; the statement that "Europe sees that its statesmen have had no vision" is an illustration. He was very emphatic as to the disgrace of the United States if it failed to support the League, the imperative appeal of Europe to its heart and humanity, its great responsibility as being "the most famous and the most powerful nation in the world!" The President then returned to Paris and the movement in the United States against the League grew steadily in volume and effect; against him as representing a minority party in Senate and Congress and, it was claimed, not the country as a whole; against the proposed combination of nations as one in which a "coloured majority" would control the world; against the alleged excessive power of Great Britain in its decisions through the admission of British Dominions to its Councils; against the reversal of Washington's policy of non-intervention in European policies and wars, and against some alleged danger to the Monroe Doctrine.

Representation of the British Dominions. Meantime, one of the problems most important to Canada and the other Dominions had developed and been warmly discussed—the national recognition of these British countries in the proposed League. Full recognition had been obtained in the Conference, itself, thanks to the effective pressure of Mr. Lloyd George and the powerful initiative of what was termed the British League of Nations. Sir Robert Borden on Jan. 21 issued a statement as to the stand taken by the Dominions and described it as based, primarily and fundamentally, upon a Resolution moved by himself at the Imperial War Council of 1917 which was accepted by the United Kingdom and the other Dominions, and which declared that the readjustment of the constitutional relations of the component parts of the British Empire should be based on the full recognition of the Dominions as autonomous nations of an Imperial Commonwealth. This principle, he pointed out, had been illustrated and carried into effect by the Peace Conference itself in the representation accorded to the Dominions: "The ideal of equal nationhood has impressed itself very powerfully upon the imagination of the people of the Domin-

---

*Note.—For origin of League proposal see *The Canadian Annual Review* for 1918, pages 108-11.

ions during the present War, and they are satisfied of like recognition in the greater League of Nations, to establish which the Peace Congress will forthwith bend its energies.'' Mr. Premier Hughes of Australia approved this general position in an interview of the same date.

Formal action had not yet been taken but it was assumed from these statements that the British Dominions intended to ask that the precedent established by the Peace Conference should also apply with respect to the League of Nations and that the Dominions be given representation as national entities and also as partners in the British family of nations known as the British Empire.   On Jan. 25 the League of Nations formed the chief subject at a Plenary session of the Conference when Sir R. Borden and Sir G. Foster were present as direct Canadian representatives and Mr. Doherty as one of the United Kingdom delegation. In the course of the discussion Sir Robert Borden said: ''I have a great deal of sympathy with the point of view of the smaller nations because, possibly, the constitution of the League affects them even more closely than it does the status of the Great Powers of the world.'' He followed with what M. Clémenceau described as a ''gentle reproach'' for the self-constitution of the Committee of Ten of the Conference into a permanent Supreme Council similar to that which had latterly carried on the War. Speaking to a Y.M.C.A. meeting at Paris on Feb. 15 the Canadian Premier was clear but emphatic in his words:

The proposed constitution of the League of Nations has been laid before the Peace Conference by the Committee appointed for that purpose; it affords a sound working basis for that discussion and consideration which it will receive in due course. A formal organization is necessary, because it gives to the public conscience of the peoples of the world an opportunity of expressing in unity and co-operation their strong desire and firm purpose to maintain the world's peace. But the machinery itself will count for little unless the conscience and will of the people give it essential vitality and strength to assert, and if necessary to enforce, that supreme purpose.

Mr. Doherty presented to the Conference a personal plan for the League which looked to the election of its governing body by some international system of popular vote. Various and vital discussions of the League document and its constitutional and international details followed in Conference and in Committees and in the British Empire delegation. On Mch. 24 Sir Robert Borden issued a Memorandum for consideration in which objection was taken to many points in the proposed arrangement. To Article X reading as follows, strong exception was taken: ''The High Contracting Parties (which included Canada) undertake to respect and preserve as against external aggression the territorial integrity and the political independence of all States members of the League.'' Sir Robert urged that this clause should be amended so as to allow signatory Powers to withdraw from the League under certain conditions*; this view found, later on, much support in the United States and in the Canadian Parliament. The Memorandum was not made public but according to the *Morning Post* correspondent at Paris its aim was to remove ambiguities from the Covenant and to emphasize the fact that the British Dominions did not feel it would be incumbent on them to take the responsibility of entering and deciding on differences that might arise between European nations in cases where the British Empire was not directly involved. Col. E. M. House of the United States delegation stated in an interview on Mch. 24 that some modification in Article X might be desirable.

The ensuing discussion of the League in the United States was long, acrimonious and partisan; at the same time it was conducted with great ability and much argument of a high character; the controversy involved several points of specific interest to Canada and other British Dominions. In presenting the Treaty and the League Covenant to Congress on July 10 President Wilson declared that they constituted a world settlement. He defined the theory and principles of the Treaty but did not go into details; so with the League Covenant which he described as a means of guarding the structure of peace and the special Treaty with France which he declared was a means for the temporary protection of that country. As a matter of fact the latter was a compromise with Clémenceau's insistence upon a compulsory enforcement clause in the League of Nations. The opposition to both the Treaty and the Covenant was led by Senator Cabot Lodge, Senators W. E. Borah and A. B. Cummins, Charles E. Hughes, Senator P. C. Knox and Elihu Root; it took the form of proposed reservations which would have nullified or weakened various clauses in either document or, taken together, would practically have read the United States out of the compact.

The specific points of most importance were (1) a demand for unconditional right of withdrawal from the League of Nations; (2) absolute freedom for United States to oppose acquisition of territory by any non-American power in the Western hemisphere; (3) refusal to assume under Article X, or any other Article, any obligation to preserve the territorial integrity or political independence of any other country or to interfere in controversies between other nations, or to employ the military or naval forces of the United States in such controversies, or to adopt economic measures for the protection of any other country against external aggression, or for the purpose of coercing any other country, or for the purpose of intervention in the internal conflicts or other controversies which might arise in any other country; (4) refusal to submit for arbitration or enquiry by the Assembly or the Council of the League of Nations, any questions which, in the judgment of the United States, depended upon or related to the Monroe Doctrine; (5) protests against the representation of British Domin-

---

*Note.—The authority for this statement is "Windermere," the usually well-informed and careful correspondent of the Montreal *Star*.

ions in the Council or Assembly of the League as giving the British Empire too great an influence. This latter point was keenly followed in Canada. In a letter to Hon. A. L. Sifton on May 6 signed by M. Clémenceau, President Wilson and Mr. Lloyd George, the "Big Three" had defined the situation in the following terms:

The question having been raised as to the meaning of Article IV of the League of Nations covenant (which provides that any member of the League may be elected to the Council by a majority vote of the Assembly), we have been requested by Sir Robert Borden to state whether we concur in his view that upon the true construction of the first and second paragraphs of that article representatives of the self-governing Dominions of the British Empire may be selected or named as members of the Council. We have no hesitation in expressing our entire concurrence in this view. If there were any doubt it would be entirely removed by the fact that the Articles are not subject to a narrow or technical construction.

W. H. Taft, one-time President of the United States, in supporting the League took exception to this condition but did not think it important as the decisions of the Council had to be unanimous; later on, as the discussion continued, he suggested modifications which would have compelled the exclusion of British Dominions from the League Council. Writing from Quebec on July 20 to W. H. Hays, Republican National Chairman, Mr. Taft urged six reservations to meet the objections of many who favoured the Treaty and the League and one of them was that self-governing Colonies and Dominions could not be represented on the League Council at the same time with the Mother Government, or be included in any of those clauses where the parties to the dispute were excluded from its settlement. To this Mr. Doherty, Canada's Minister of Justice, responded on July 25 with the statement that the right of Canada as a member of the League to be eligible for representation on the Council, under the provisions of the Covenant, was insisted upon by her representatives, and that those provisions conferred upon her that right was clearly understood and unequivocally recognized by all concerned. In his conference with the U.S. Senate Committee which began on Aug. 20, President Wilson dealt with this voting issue by declaring that in the League Assembly while each of the 4 British Dominions and India would have a vote and the United Kingdom one, or six, altogether, they would in matters affecting the British Empire have but one vote.

Rejection of the League by the U. S. Senate. The President at this stage in the controversy made a speaking tour of the United States (Sept. 3-26) which only ended with his sudden seizure of illness. These addresses were calculated to appeal to the popular view of things so far as Mr. Wilson could do it; they described the War and the Treaty and the League as a triumph of democracy; they attributed all the evils of the past, the menaces of war and peace, the desperate struggle now over, to the faults of European statesmen and the evils of non-democratic rule; they paid few compliments or none to the Great Powers whom the United States had joined in the recent struggle; they laid much stress upon Mr. Wilson's view of European problems and as to the relationship of the proposed solution to "American ideals." Arrangements such as the Treaty of London, which in 1916 promised Italy certain territory in Dalmatia, etc., which was necessarily secret in a time of war and by its provisions brought Italy as an ally into the struggle, was stigmatized (for instance) in a speech on Sept. 9 as follows: "One of the difficulties in framing this Treaty was the fact that after we got over there private, secret, treaties were springing up on all sides like a noxious growth. You had to guard your breathing apparatus against the miasma that arose from them!" On Sept. 10 the Majority Report of the Foreign Relations Committee of the Senate presented for adoption four Reservations to the Treaty and 45 amendments. Its reference to the British Empire vote and the League was as follows:

The first amendment offered by the Committee relates to the League. It is proposed so to amend the text as to secure for the United States a vote in the Assembly of the League equal to that of any other Power. Great Britain now has, under the name of the British Empire, one vote in the Council of the League. She has four additional votes in the Assembly of the League for her self-governing Dominions and Colonies which are, most properly, members of the League and signatories to the Treaty. She also has the vote of India, which is neither a self-governing Dominion nor a Colony, but merely a part of the Empire and which, apparently, was simply put in as a signatory and member of the League by the Peace Conference because Great Britain desired it. Great Britain also will control the votes of the Kingdom of Hedjaz and of Persia. With these last two votes, of course, we have nothing to do. But if Great Britain has six votes in the League Assembly, no reason has occurred to the Committee and no argument has been made to show why the United States should not have an equal number.

To this contention and proposal the President replied in a statement issued at San Francisco on Sept. 18: "The consideration which led to assigning six votes to self-governing portions of the British Empire was, that they have in effect, in all but Foreign policies, become autonomous self-governing states, their policy in all but Foreign affairs, being independent of the control of the British Government, and in many respects dissimilar from it. But it is not true that the British Empire can outvote us in the League of Nations, and therefore control the action of the League, because in every matter, except the admission of new members in the League, no action can be taken without the concurrence by a unanimous vote of the representatives of the States which are members of the Council, so that in all matters of action, the vote of the United States is necessary and equivalent to the united vote of the representatives of the several parts of the British Empire." An interesting comment upon this controversy was the statement of M. Pichon, French Minister of Foreign Affairs (Sept. 24) that the British Dominions must have their place in the League; they had, during the War, raised nearly 3,000,000 men and therefore had earned it.

Meantime the Senate which controlled the Treaty and the League so far as the United States was concerned,—through its power of ratification or rejection of all treaties—had been discussing the question at great length and continued to do so for a couple of months with the Republican opponents of the President in a majority. On Oct. 22-3 the Foreign Relations Committee submitted a revised and enlarged series of Reservations from those of Oct. 10 totalling 15 in all and including an amendment by Senator H. W. Johnson of California which provided that: "When any member of the League has or possesses self-governing Dominions or Colonies or parts of Empire, which are members of the League, the United States shall have votes in the Assembly or Council of the League numerically equal to the aggregate vote of such member of the League and its self-governing Dominions and Colonies and parts of Empire in the Council or Assembly of the League." It was rejected by 40 to 38 as were similar ones by Senators J. K. Shields of Tennessee and G. H. Moses of New Hampshire.

Finally, on Nov. 19, the question of ratifying or rejecting the Treaty and the League of Nations came up and the Resolution of Senator Lodge, containing many of the Reservations mentioned above, was voted down by 55 to 39 after the President had written Senator G. M. Hitchcock that the Resolution did not provide for ratification but rather for nullification. A motion for "unconditional ratification" was then defeated by 53 to 38. Alone of the Great Powers, after four months of bitter debate, the United States had rejected the Treaty negotiated by its President and Secretary of State together with the League of Nations which its Chief Executive had flung into the arena of nations as the chief end and aim of the prolonged Peace Conference. A perhaps unexpected result of United States action was to leave the British Empire absolutely dominant in the Supreme Council of the Allies and in the partly formed League of Nations.

Ratification of the Treaty and the League was prompt in the other countries concerned. In his Parliamentary address of July 3 Mr. Lloyd George commended the League—though with studied moderation. After a reference to the little quarrels which might in the end be settled by a great flame of war, he said: "This League of Nations is an attempt to do it by some less barbarous methods than war. Let us try it. I beg this country to try it seriously, and try it in earnest. It is due to mankind that we should try it—anything rather than the horror of the last $4\frac{1}{2}$ years. I believe it will succeed in stopping something. It may not stop everything. The world has gone from war to war until at last we have despaired of stopping it. But society, with all its organizations, has not stopped every crime. It makes crime difficult and it makes crime unsuccessful, and that is what the League of Nations will do." The Treaty and the League were ratified by the King of Italy on Oct. 7th, following, by King George for the British Empire on Oct. 10 and by France on Oct. 21. Geneva was the seat of government of the League and on Aug. 12 it was announced that Sir Herbert B. Ames, M.P., of Canada, would be Financial Director in the Secretariat of the League; Sir Eric Drummond, Private Secretary to Mr.

Balfour, had, already, been appointed Secretary of the League. An interesting point raised at the close of the year was that out of the 32 initial member-nations of the League 17 were Roman Catholic, 11 Protestant and 4 non-Christian. If all the other 13 States invited to join were to accept the League would stand 16 Protestant, 24 Catholic and 5 non-Christian.

The Peace Treaty and the World's Labour Interests. At a time when social unrest and every kind of national disorder were rampant in Europe and, indeed, everywhere, no issue was more vital than this one of Labour conditions in the new Era of peace and progress which, it was hoped—not always with good bases—would develop after the War. For the first time in history it was decided to deal with this subject in connection with a Treaty of Peace and in its treatment Canada felt a specific interest and its Prime Minister had a prominent part. The policy was a natural outcome of the League of Nations' plan and its development was placed by the Conference in the hands of a Commission composed of two representatives of each of the five Great Powers and five others representing the smaller nations.

The Rt. Hon. G. N. Barnes and Sir Malcolm Delavigne were the British delegates and Sir Robert Borden represented Canada at the earlier meetings of the Commission; at the first meeting on Feb. 1st, Samuel Gompers of the United States delegation, was appointed Chairman. During the ensuing month 20 meetings were held and a draft Convention prepared for submission to the Conference. In its work of construction the Commission was greatly aided by a British Committee which included six prominent Labour leaders of whom Arthur Henderson, J. H. Thomas, and C. W. Bowerman were the best known. The recommendations of this Committee went before the British Empire Delegation at the Peace Conference of which Sir R. Borden was an active member and, after receiving its approval, passed to the Commission, where they were in the main accepted. In these discussions P. M. Draper, Secretary of the Canadian Trades and Labour Congress, had a personal voice and influence.

As finally approved by the Peace Conference and duly incorporated in the Treaty, it was decided that as the League of Nations had for its object the establishment of universal peace and as such a peace could only be established if based upon social justice, there should be (1) an International Conference held annually to propose Labour reforms for adoption by the States comprising the League of Nations; (2) an Executive body for this Conference to prepare the agenda for consideration and an International Labour Office for the collection and distribution of information; (3) four representatives from each State in the Conference—two for the State and one each for employers and employed; (4) the Conference to have power to adopt by a two-third majority recommendations or draft conventions on Labour matters which must then be brought by each State before the authority or authorities within whose competence the matter lay for the enactment of legislation or other action—with obligation to ratify and carry on such Convention and penalties for failure which could involve economic action by the League of Nations; (5) the 1st meeting to be held at Washington and to discuss the 8-hour day question, the problem of unemployment and the employment of women and children.

In the plenary Peace Conference of Apr. 14th, the Convention was discussed and Sir Robert Borden asked that it be made clear that the British Dominions had the same representation and recognition as in the League of Nations and the clause which was accepted declared that: "The original members of the League of Nations (of whom Canada was one) shall be the original members of this organization and hereafter membership of the League of Nations shall carry with it membership of the said organization." At one stage of the discussion Sir Robert was charged with the duty of bringing together representatives of the more important industrial Powers and of endeavouring to reconcile certain divergencies of view in respect to the affirmation of general principles. On Apr. 28th, following, in plenary Conference, again, Sir R. Borden moved and the Conference accepted the following clauses for insertion in the Treaty as the general principles of the Labour Conference and with the introductory declaration that "Labour must not be considered an article of commerce:"

1. The guiding principle above enunciated that Labour should not be regarded merely as a commodity or article of commerce.

2. The right of association for all lawful purposes by the employed as well as by the employers.

3. The payment to the employed of a wage adequate to maintain a reasonable state of life as this is understood in their time and country.

4. The adoption of an eight-hour day or a 48-hour week, as the standard to be aimed at where it has not already been obtained.

5. The adoption of a weekly rest day of at least 24 hours, which should include Sunday whenever practicable.

6. The abolition of child labour and the imposition of such limitations on the labour of young persons as shall permit the continuation of their education and assure their proper physical development.

7. The principle that men and women should receive equal remuneration for work of equal value.

8. The standard set by law in each country with respect to the condition of Labour should have due regard to the equitable economic treatment of all workers lawfully resident therein.

9. Each State should make provision for a system of inspection in which women should take part in order to insure the enforcement of the laws and regulations for the protection of the employed.

Parliamentary Approval of the Treaty and the League of Nations. Despite all the enormous difficulties of negotiation, the complex processes of settlement, the innumerable problems of racial and international divergence, the opposing points-of-view amongst the negotiators, the Treaty and the League of Nations finally reached Ottawa for approval by Parliament before its formal ratification by the King for the whole British Empire. Technically and constitutionally, this approval was not necessary;

practically, under the loose yet strong system of Empire rule, all Treaties had in recent years (since 1878) been submitted to the Dominion Governments before becoming operative as to the Dominions. Under this system a number of British Commercial treaties had not been acceded to by Canada; Sir John A. Macdonald had also helped to negotiate, had signed and passed through the Dominion Parliament, the Treaty of Washington in 1871; Sir Charles Tupper had been appointed a British Plenipotentiary with Lord Dufferin to negotiate the French Treaty of 1893 which he signed and which Parliament approved.

The Constitutional Issue of Ratification. The question came up in a new form in connection with a Treaty which was world-wide in its scope and in which British Empire members of a World Conference had asserted a national status for British Dominions in addition to and as part of their Imperial status. The Delegates of Canada and other Dominions had shared representation on an equal constitutional footing with those of the United Kingdom, they had signed the Treaty as Plenipotentiaries of the King for their respective Dominions, they were to be members of the League of Nations and the International Labour Conference, and of their governing bodies, upon an equal footing with the United Kingdom, they had claimed the right to ratify the Treaty by their Dominion Parliaments prior to the King's signature—a right not inherent in the British Parliament itself. On July 4th, 1919, Lord Milner, Secretary of State for the Colonies, cabled to Canada as follows: "It is hoped that the German Treaty may be ratified by three of the principal Allied and Associated Powers and by Germany before the end of July." Under date of July 9th Sir Robert Borden replied that: "No copy of the Treaty has yet arrived, and Parliament has been prorogued. Kindly advise how you expect to accomplish the ratification on behalf of the whole Empire before the end of July." Lord Milner replied in a state document of some importance:

I have now consulted with the Prime Minister in regard to your most secret telegram of July 9th. Our view is that an early ratification, especially now that Germany has ratified, is of the highest importance. In the British constitution there is nothing which makes it necessary for the King to obtain the consent of Parliament before ratifying the Treaty. With perfect constitutional propriety the King can ratify on the advice of his Ministers. For a Treaty of this far-reaching importance, and one embracing the whole Empire, the King has only to act at the instance of his constitutional advisers, the Dominion Ministries as well as that of the United Kingdom. But, inasmuch as the Dominion Ministers participated in the Peace negotiations, and side by side with the Ministers of the United Kingdom signed the preliminaries of the Treaty, we hold that His Majesty, if he now ratified the Treaty for the whole Empire, would have the same constitutional justification in doing so in respect of the Dominions as he has in respect of the United Kingdom.

The King by a single act, would bind the Empire as it is right that he should do so, but that act would represent the considered judgment of his constitutional advisers in all the self-governing States of the Empire because it would be merely giving effect to an international pact which they

had all agreed to. We realize at the same time the difficulty in which you
are placed by your pledge to Parliament. We are willing, in order to meet
this difficulty, to delay ratification (which, if we alone were concerned, we
should desire to effect immediately) as long as we possibly can in order to
give you time to lay the Treaty before your Parliament. I am communicating
with the Governments of South Africa and New Zealand and Australia, explaining the urgency, and begging them to submit the Treaty to their Parliaments without delay, if they feel bound to do so before assenting to its
ratification.

Sir Robert replied on July 29th and emphasized the opinion
that "there is considerable doubt whether under modern constitutional practices the King should ratify without first obtaining the
approval of Parliament." He felt this to be especially so in the
case of a treaty imposing burdens or involving changes in the laws
of a people or affecting territorial rights. He specifically differed
from the view that the signature of the Dominions Ministers to the
Treaty was equivalent to advice to ratify, asking the pertinent
question: "Do you regard this as holding good in the case of the
signature of the United Kingdom plenipotentiaries?" He promised
consideration by Parliament in September and, on Aug. 2nd, Lord
Milner again cabled a statement of the severe pressure from public
opinion for early ratification and declaring it impossible to promise
that ratification should be kept back after Sept. 11th. On Aug. 4th
the Canadian Premier cabled that Parliament was called for Sept.
1st and added: "I cannot emphasize too strongly the unfortunate
results which would certainly ensue from ratification before the
Canadian Parliament has had an opportunity of considering the
Treaty."

Parliament met in special Session on Sept. 1st and the Speech
from the Throne, read by H.E. the Duke of Devonshire, referred
briefly to the urgency of immediately considering the Treaty and
stated that "my advisers are of the opinion that this Treaty ought
not to be ratified on behalf of Canada without the approval of
Parliament." Sir Robert Borden then presented authenticated
copies in French and English of (1) the Treaty of Versailles signed
on June 28th, 1919; (2) the Protocol supplementary to the Treaty
signed on the same day; (3) the Agreement between the United
States, Belgium, the British Empire and France and Germany as to
military occupation of the Rhine Provinces, of the same date; (4)
the Declaration by the Governments of the United States, Great
Britain and France as to the occupation of the Rhine Provinces,
June 16th, 1919; (5) Reply of the Allied and Associated Powers to
the Observations of the German delegation on the conditions of
Peace, June 16th, 1919, and (6) the Treaty of Peace between the
United States, the British Empire, France, Italy and Japan on the
one side, and Poland on the other, signed on June 28th.

Canada and the Making of the Treaty. On Sept. 2nd the Prime
Minister moved a Resolution declaring that "it is expedient that
Parliament do approve of the Treaty of Peace between the Allied
and Associated Powers and Germany (and the Protocol annexed

thereto), which was signed at Versailles on the 28th day of June, 1919, a copy of which has been laid before Parliament, and which was signed on behalf of His Majesty, acting for Canada, by the plenipotentiaries therein named, and that this House do approve of the same." In his carefully-worded speech, Sir Robert referred to the 32 nations (including the British Dominions and India), which had met in secret Plenary Session on May 6th and finally and unanimously adopted the terms of this complicated and vitally important document; to the fact that all these nations of varying and sometimes conflicting ideals and aspirations, widely divergent in status, in power, and in political development, and separated sometimes by ancient antagonisms and long-standing jealousies, did finally give their undivided assent to a Treaty which, whatever its imperfections might be, was designed in all sincerity to assure the future peace of the world.

After a statement of the urgency of action and the necessity of submitting the Treaty to Parliament, he described its terms as severe and even stern, but when the devastation of France and Belgium was compared with the smiling and untouched country-side of Germany, the converse seemed true. A summary of the chief provisions of the Treaty followed with a review of the League of Nations Covenant and the Labour policy of the Conference. He then dealt with the status of Canada in connection with these great international developments and, incidentally, indicated the vital part taken by himself, personally, in the constitutional problems of the time. In June, 1918, at his instigation, the Imperial War Cabinet had appointed a Committee composed of the Prime Ministers of the Empire, aided by the highest British military experts, to go into the whole question of how, when and where to make a supreme effort to win the War; an elaborate Report was prepared when what he described as "the rapid and wholly unexpected march of events," ending in the Armistice, occurred. Shortly after that the British Prime Minister urged him to come to London where, in November, 1918, the status of the Dominions at the coming Conference became at once a vital question:

Various methods, which it is not necessary to explain, were suggested. In the end I proposed that there should be a distinctive representation for each Dominion similar to that accorded to the smaller Allied powers, and in addition that the British Empire representation of five delegates should be selected from day to day from a panel made up of representatives of the United Kingdom and the Dominions. This proposal was adopted by the Imperial War Cabinet. Early in December preliminary conversations on the making of peace took place in London between representatives of the British Empire, of France and of Italy, and the proposal which I had already put forward was accepted in principle. The preliminary Peace Conference began at Paris on Jan. 12th, 1919, and the question of procedure, including that of representation, was immediately taken up by the representatives of the principal Allied and Associated Powers, afterwards commonly known as the Council of Ten. At first strong objection was made to the proposed representation of the British Dominions. Subsequently there was a full discussion in the British Empire delegation, at which a firm protest was made against any recession from the proposal adopted in London. In the end that proposal was accepted.

Sir Robert pointed out the effective position which the panel system gave to Canada and the other Dominions: "At Plenary Sessions there were sometimes three Canadian Plenipotentiary delegates, two as representatives of Canada and one as representative of the Empire. Moreover, throughout the proceedings of the Conference the Dominion delegates, as members of the British Empire delegation, were thoroughly in touch with all the proceedings of the Conference and had access to all the papers recording its proceedings. Dominion Ministers were nominated to and acted for the British Empire on the principal Allied Commissions appointed by the Conference from time to time to consider and report upon special aspects of the conditions of peace." On several occasions he, himself, was charged with the duty of attending as one of the British Empire representatives on the Council of Five; he was asked by Mr. Lloyd George to present the case in respect to the Treaty clauses on Economic questions, on the International control of Ports, Waterways and Railways and on Submarine Cables; during the last month of his stay in Paris he acted regularly as Chairman of the British Empire Delegation during the absence of the Prime Minister of the United Kingdom in attendance at the, then, Council of Four.

The Canadian Premier led the Dominions in respect to the new Imperial method of assenting to the Treaties concerned: "I proposed that the assent of the King as High Contracting Party to the various Treaties should, in respect of the Dominions, be signified by the signature of the Dominion plenipotentiaries, and that the preamble and other formal parts of the Treaties should be drafted accordingly. This proposal was adopted in the form of a memorandum by all the Dominion Prime Ministers at a meeting which I summoned, and was put forward by me on their behalf to the British Empire delegation, by whom it was accepted. The proposal was subsequently adopted by the Conference." In the League of Nations, also, and the International Labour Conference the position of the Dominions was secured so as to give them the rights of all small nations *plus* the representation and prestige of the British Empire as the greatest of the Great Powers. Sir Robert concluded these references with a significant statement:

I hope the House will realize that the recognition and status accorded to the British Dominions at the Peace Conference were not won without constant effort and firm insistence. In all these efforts the Dominions had the strong and unwavering support of the British Prime Minister and his colleagues. The constitutional structure of the British Empire is imperfectly understood by other nations, even by a nation so closely allied in kinship, in language and in character of its institutions as the United States of America. Such lack of comprehension need excite no surprise because the association between the Mother Country and the great self-governing Dominions has been for years in a condition of development and that development is not yet complete. The future relationship of the nations of the Empire must be determined in accordance with the will of the Mother Country and of each Dominion in a constitutional Conference to be summoned in the not distant future. Undoubtedly it will be based upon equality of nationhood.

To his British colleagues at the Peace Conference, Sir Robert paid high tribute: "The immense labours and responsibilities which devolved upon the British Plenipotentiaries, and especially upon Mr. Lloyd George and Mr. Balfour, can only be realized by those who were intimately associated with them in the labours of the Conference. When the time comes for a fuller history of the events at Paris between the middle of January and the end of June, there will be an even warmer appreciation and recognition of their service to the Empire and to the world." Appreciation for valuable assistance was also expressed to various Canadians associated with the Conference under the Canadian Plenipotentiaries—Lloyd Harris, Frank P. Jones, Dr. J. W. Robertson, P. M. Draper, O. M. Biggar, K.C., and L. C. Christie. In reply to an enquiry the Premier stated that if the Treaty were not ratified by Parliament it would, of course, involve the fate of the Government which presented it to Parliament for ratification.

The National Status of Canada Discussed. In the debate which followed and lasted until Sept. 11th, a number of speakers took part and the speeches turned very largely upon the new national position claimed for Canada and eulogized, minimized, criticized, or denied it as the case might be. On Sept. 8th D. D. McKenzie, Parliamentary Liberal leader, followed the Premier in the adjourned discussion and very frankly doubted the ability of the majority of members to discuss this great question from the standpoint of knowledge in the history of treaties, in universal world history, or in diplomatic negotiation. He proceeded to deprecate the talk of nationality: "We are not a nation in the true sense of the term. We are part of a great Empire of which we are proud, and we are nothing else. I maintain that it is not a strength but a weakness for us to put ourselves to one side, to separate ourselves from the rest of the Empire, and attempt to become a separate nation, or a separate part of the Empire as far as these (Treaty) obligations are concerned."

He contended that this Dominion was not a nation, that Canadian legislation could still legally be vetoed by the King, or by the King-in-Council, and that the constitution of Canada was a product of the British Parliament and could only be revised with its approval; he opposed the mixing up of Canada in the petty quarrels of smaller European or American States and Asiatic countries; he argued that the Treaty was absolutely obligatory upon Canada as part of the Empire and that the Canadian Plenipotentiaries were appointed by the King and represented the Empire and not Canada; he contended that this Canadian Bill, like that of the United Kingdom, was simply an enabling Act and not a ratification at all. The Hon. A. L. Sifton, in reply, pointed out that the powers that were given by the King to the Plenipotentiaries were not powers to act for the British Empire as a whole, but powers to sign treaties for the Dominion of Canada. As to the rest: "The Government take the position that the Dominion has up to date done everything it could for the purpose of assisting and keeping within the British Commonwealth, and we have no desire to raise any question of that kind at this stage of our history."

The Hon. H. S. Béland (Lib.), took the ground that not being a Sovereign State, Canada could very well have left it to the representatives of Great Britain to enter the League of Nations. In such an event, *ipso facto* Canada, as an integral part of the British Empire, would have been a member of the League and would have shared in its benefits without being exposed to most difficult and dangerous situations politically and militarily. He claimed that by joining the League, Canada had tied its hands and surrendered to a Council of nine men sitting in Geneva the right to dispose of Canadian troops to quell disorder in any of the five continents, or to carry on war, great or small, on the surface of the earth.

Brig.-Gen. W. A. Griesbach (Cons.), claimed that Canada had entered the League as a Sovereign State: "It is true that many of the incidents and attributes of sovereignty are absent from our status. That is so because of the peculiar relations which exist between ourselves and the rest of the Empire. The League of Nations and the world must take us as they find us; they must have regard for the conditions under which we live. They must accept us and realize that we are a nation and a company of nations with a common Sovereign and a common flag." H. M. Mowat (Lib.-Unionist), declined to take a strict legal view of the situation: "We are beyond the ordinary international law, or constitutional law, as it is generally understood in Europe. We cannot be circumscribed by it. The British constitution is an extraordinary erection in that it has come on bit by bit, liberty upon liberty, line upon line. We govern well and satisfy the people of the British Empire because of the elasticity of our Constitution, and we hope nothing will be done to restrict it or make it less elastic." L. T. Pacaud (Lib.), especially deprecated Article X: "By the adoption of Article X we are stripping this Parliament of its most valued prerogative; we are placing the Canadian people at the beck and call of a Council not responsible to the nation for its actions. By one stroke of the pen we are mortgaging our freedom, receiving practically nothing in return."

A logical and eloquent speech was delivered by Ernest Lapointe, one of the Liberal leaders, on Sept. 9th. His constitutional contention was similar to that of Lord Milner and he quoted Todd, Anson, and others, to prove that in the British Empire the Sovereign power of treaty-making was vested in the Crown acting upon the advice of responsible Ministers. "Has," he asked, "the Canadian Parliament more power with regard to the ratifying of treaties than the Parliament of the Mother Country"? He declared that Canada had "absolutely no right to change, alter, or modify" the Treaty in any way. "We cannot change one line of it." The number of Powers signing the Treaty was 27, not 32, and the five Dominions were there simply as portions of the British Empire: "The Treaty is made between the British Empire and the other powers, and whether we approve of it or not, it binds the whole of the British Empire, including the Dominion of Canada." Refusal to accept the Treaty would be tantamount to a declaration of independence and a formal separation from the Empire.

Mr. Lapointe then asked the rather fundamental question: "If we are for all purposes separate and distinct members of the League, what would be our position in case of a conflict between Great Britain and another member of the League, in which the Executive of the League should decide against Great Britain and a war ensue?" In that event Canada would have to keep its pledge, redeem its obligations, and side with the other members of the League against Great Britain, and thereby withdraw from the Empire, or else it would disregard and break its pledges under the Treaty and take sides with Great Britain. He contended that militarism threatened to have a new growth in the United States, Great Britain, and even in Canada and, incidentally, deprecated Admiral Lord Jellicoe offering his naval advice to the Dominions; he suggested a Reservation clearly stating that approval of the Treaty must not impair the rights of the Parliament of Canada.

Apart from the Premier's careful statement the chief Government speech of the debate was that of Hon. N. W. Rowell, who followed Mr. Lapointe and commented on the divergence of viewpoint between his remarks and those of Mr. McKenzie. Constitutionally, he claimed, the British Act of Parliament as to the Treaty was one of approval, so was the proposed Canadian Act; only the King could actually ratify the Treaty. There were, he said, three stages —the Executive act of signing which settled the terms of the Treaty, the Parliamentary act of approval and the Executive act of ratification by the King in person, which gave it legal effect. After dealing with the strength of the British Empire as resting upon the constitutional rights granted to its different portions, he declared that Canada's position was no longer "anomalous or abnormal" as Mr. Lapointe had contended. By Order-in-Council of Apr. 10th, 1919, H.M. the King, through the Governor-General of Canada, had been asked to issue letters-patent to each of the Canadian Ministers at Paris to act as "Commissioner and Plenipotentiary in respect to the Dominion of Canada with full power and authority" in respect to the Peace Conference. This had been done upon recommendation of the Governor-General-in-Council in Canada under date of Jan. 1st, 1919 and in the authority thus issued, H.M. the King declared, as to the succeeding action of his Canadian plenipotentiaries, that "We will never suffer either in the whole or in part, any person whatsoever to infringe the same or act contrary thereto as far as it lies in Our power."

Mr. Rowell spoke at length as to the League of Nations Covenant which he described as a splendid effort to promote and enforce arbitration; to provide guarantees and safeguards against war and to establish a sort of national and international insurance of peace. Under Art. X the Council of the League would act in an advisory capacity and any military action suggested for Canada, as an illustration, would have to be sanctioned by its Parliament; in the event of any recommendation being made as to Canadian action of any kind, Canada would at once become entitled to full and direct representation on the Council itself; as the decisions of that body would have to be unanimous in order to become operative no action could follow regarding Canada without that country's approval. As Mr. Rowell put it "She cannot be compelled to take action unless she agrees to it"; he added that this was also the official explanation and interpretation of the British Government as to this subject.

Lucien Cannon (Liberal), followed and was inclined to deprecate the terms of the Treaty as too severe upon Germany; he doubted the wisdom of a public trial of Wilhelm II and hoped to see Germany soon represented on the League of Nations; he criticized the Shantung grant to Japan and the omission of any reference to Canadian indemnity; he would like to have seen the Treaty give Ireland "the right of self-determination" and compared the Irish problem in this respect to that of Bohemia. He asked a rather interesting question as to why Mexico had not been invited to join the League and wondered whether it was because the United States had designs upon that country; he thought the League was, in some respects, dangerous to Canadian autonomy and that there should be a reservation safeguarding such rights.

W. F. Maclean (Ind. Cons.), took a remarkable view of Canada's foreign relations. The Dominion was "a great State of the North American Continent" and, in settling the future of Canada, "we must have even more regard for this Continent than for our European connections and alliances. It is the democracy of America, as exemplified by the United States and Canada, that is the saving grace of the world to-day." The Hon. Rodolphe Lemieux (Lib.) dealt at length with Art. X and Canadian liability in the premises. This clause was "the teeth of the Covenant" and he claimed that it involved the surrender of control by Canada over the military forces and defences of the Dominion. He totally denied the "national" position of Canada and urged as a slogan for its people: "Let well enough alone; let us not be involved in the domestic affairs of the United Kingdom or in its Foreign policy."

W. F. Cockshutt (Cons.) criticized the League along lines recently stated by the Duke of Northumberland: "As a matter of fact, this policy is indistinguishable from that of the balance of power; both are based on the principle of combination against an aggressor. The only difference is that one is reasonably effective; the other is not." He also thought the German indemnity too small and deprecated the proposed trial of the Kaiser in London. The succeeding speech of Hon. W. S. Fielding (Sept. 11th) was notable for its agreement in many respects with the constitutional point-of-view expressed by Mr. McKenzie. While he regarded the Treaty as in the main a good one and a great document in human history, he also declared his emphatic judgment that: "The whole policy of the Government in relation to the Peace Conference and in regard to the proceedings which they are now asking us to engage in is a colossal humbug, designed to impose upon an innocent Parliament and to bamboozle a too-credulous people. It is my judgment that it was not necessary for our representatives to go to Paris under the terms and conditions which took them there. It is my judgment that the present procedure for ratifying, or approving, if the word is preferred, this Treaty, is entirely unnecessary."

He objected to any representation at Geneva "separate and apart from the British Empire." He feared that it would give the United States an opportunity to enter a wedge of separation: "We are a part of the British Empire, and I desire that we shall always remain so, and I therefore regret the policy of Hon. gentlemen in pleading for separate recognition apart from the British Empire. By their demand for separate recognition apart from the British Empire they are beginning—they may not have meant it so—to break up the British Empire." As to the rest: "Any attempt to call Canada a nation in the world sense, in the sense of international law or international negotiations, is simply an attempt to lift oneself by pulling at one's boot straps." Mr. Fielding moved the following Resolution, seconded by Mr. Lapointe:

That in giving such approval this House in no way assents to any impairment of the existing autonomous authority of the Dominion, but declares that the question of what part, if any, the forces of Canada shall take in any war, actual or threatened, is one to be determined at all times, as occasion may require, by the people of Canada through their representatives in Parliament.

The Hon. C. J. Doherty in reply to various speakers, dealt at length with the autonomous position of Canada within the British Empire as being one in a group of nations. He agreed, as Minister of Justice, in Mr. Rowell's contention as to representation in the Council of the League of Nations; he argued that the United Kingdom was not a distinctive member of the League though the British Empire was and that the four British Dominions and India were distinctive members. Obviously, therefore, if a question came up involving the interests of the Empire there would be six British votes involved; there could be no vital disagreement because any conclusion in the Council had to be unanimous. Canada, as a distinct member, would have the right to withdraw from the League and still remain a part of the British Empire. L. J. Gauthier, who followed, made the interesting point that if Canada left the League it would not be a member though as part of the Empire it would still have representation! He also contended that the Dominion could not remain a part of the Empire and also be a nation. Speeches followed by E. B. Devlin (Lib.), Col. Cyrus W. Peck, v.c., A. R. McMaster, C. G. Power, G. W. Parent, O. Turgeon, J. J. Denis, M. E. d'Anjou—all Liberals—and then the vote was taken on Mr. Fielding's amendment which was negatived by 102 to 70; Sir Robert Borden's motion for approval of the Treaty was carried without division. The Bill enacted, in accordance with the Resolution, had its second reading on Sept. 23rd under Mr. Doherty's guidance and was explained as an enabling Act to give effect to the provisions of the Treaty. It was passed with little further discussion. Similar Resolutions and legislation were passed as to the Polish Treaty and the Rhine Agreement.

In the Senate these Resolutions were moved by Sir James Lougheed and approved on Sept. 4th and the legislation passed in due course. During the debate Senator Lougheed made a notable speech and declared that if Canada failed to assume its proper responsibility under and within the League of Nations, it would act the part of a poltroon; the Hon. G. D. Robertson, Minister of Labour, paid high tribute to Sir Robert Borden's part in the Peace Conference and especially as to the Labour clauses which he described as largely the result of Sir Robert's diplomacy; Hon. R. Dandurand suggested that Canada reserve her decision until the United States and other Powers had taken action; Hon. Wm. Roche, Hon. L. O. David and Hon. F. L. Beique laid stress upon the possibility of Canada finding herself some day in conflict with Great Britain and other countries through its place in the League; the Hon. G. W. Fowler declared that in case of Great Britain being involved in a League controversy, Canada would follow the Motherland; Hon. Hewitt Bostock, Liberal Leader, moved that discussion be postponed for purposes of study until Sept. 16th but the motion was "lost on division."

Meantime, the Parliaments of New Zealand (Sept. 2nd) and South Africa (Assembly, Sept. 10th and Senate, Sept. 12th) had approved the Treaty and a little later that of Australia did so— House of Representatives Sept. 19th and Senate Oct. 2nd; India came under the more direct authority of Great Britain and had no Parliament to take such action. On Oct. 10th H.M. the King formally ratified the Treaties with Germany and Poland and the Rhine Agreement. The King of Italy had already done so on Oct. 7th and Germany on the 9th; Belgium followed on the 13th, France on the 21st and Japan on the 30th.

Relations of Canada and Great Britain with the United States. The interests of Canada and Great Britain in respect to the United States were, in 1919, so largely interlaced that it was often hard to differentiate them. American power on the sea, whether evolved in a spirit of friendship and alliance with the great naval power of Britain, or in one of competition and rivalry, was equally important to Canada; the peace along the Dominion's 3,000 miles of United States border-line was as vital to the Foreign policy of the Empire, pledged to protect that peace and that border, as it was to Canada and its people; freer or more restricted trade relations between Canada and the United States, or the United States and Great Britain, met a thousand interests and touched many vital points in British-Canadian conditions; financial interests were closely inter-related as the fall of exchange and the conditions of currency illustrated; any anti-British propaganda in the United States affected Canadian interests and policy while friendly feelings in the United States toward Canada helped though, not in quite the same degree, British diplomacy and action in the States.

During the Peace Conference a Treaty was made between the United States and the French Republic and a similar one between Great Britain and the French Republic—signed in the former case by President Wilson and Mr. Secretary Lansing—which declared that if the stipulations of the Versailles Treaty concerning the left bank of the Rhine were not observed by Germany or should not "assure immediately to France appropriate security and protection" the United States (and Great Britain) "shall be bound to come immediately to her aid in case of any unprovoked act of aggression directed against her by Germany." This Treaty and the British one were signed on June 28th at the same time as that of Versailles; they were both subject to approval by the Council of the League of Nations and that of the United States to acceptance by the American Senate. The British Treaty was duly ratified; that of the United States was suspended by the Senate's failure to approve its terms. But this agreement and that of Poland, in addition to the Peace Treaty and the League of Nations plan, definitely plunged the United States into the political world arena; incidentally it enhanced the importance to Canada of its place in the British Empire as a safeguard against a great neighbour's ambitious policies of the future. If the United States should finally withdraw from all these obligations and Treaties, then Canada lost much of the protection it might have had from the League of Nations, in addition to that already afforded by the power of the Empire.

Sir Robert Borden believed and hoped that the creation of the League and the events of the year would bring about very intimate British-American relations and, in reply to a request from the New York *Sun* for his opinion on this point he wrote on June 9 that: "Not only is a League of Nations established, but there has been formed a virtual alliance between the two great English-speaking nations, the United States of America and the British Empire, in their determination to keep the peace of the world. That, I believe, is a great step; for I do believe, and I think you will believe, that these two nations have it within their power, if they are connected in purpose and in effort, to keep the peace of the world at all times in the future. They could have done that thing in the last weeks of July, 1914, and spared the world all the sacrifice and sorrow that it has since endured. Here are two nations, or rather two Commonwealths, committed to the same ideals of democracy, connected by like traditions, speaking the same language, having the same literature, the same customs and habits of life; and if these two

Commonwealths cannot stand together to maintain the Peace of the world, then I do not think there is much hope for humanity in the years to come.'' The defeat of the League in Congress was a blow to many who shared the belief of Canada's Premier.

American Influence in Canada. Meantime, United States financial and industrial interests in Canada were steadily growing and at this stage $1,272,000,000 of American money was invested in the Dominion* of which $713,000,000 was in bonds, $315,000,000 in lumber and industrial enterprises and $94,000,000 in Insurance Companies. This financial interest, represented by 500 firms which were branches of United States concerns and were steadily increasing in number; the steady and now increasing migration of American farmers into Western Canada; the tendency there, in great degree, and elsewhere in lesser measure, to experiment in United States political movements and policies—such as the Referendum, the open diplomacy idea, hostility to Oriental races and the colour prejudice; organizations such as the Non-Partisan League, the United Mine Workers of America, the I.W.W. and countless Fraternal bodies; all had their influence on Canadian conditions as had the ever-present Americanized cable service of the press from London, the United States theatrical syndicates throughout Canada and the United States patriotism of the moving picture shows. On the other hand Canadians continued to believe in their own form of government and to declare that no such fiasco as the defeat of the Peace Treaty and the League of Nations could occur in Canada nor would the close relation between Canadian Executive and Legislative government permit of such facts as the closing of Congress in March, 1919, with Army and Navy, Agriculture and Shipping, Railway and other appropriations for over $4,000,000,000 held up indefinitely.

British and American Relations. Great Britain did all that was possible in 1919 to develop and increase friendly relations with the United States and in this was, of course, working for Canadian interests as well as her own. The reception of President Wilson in London and elsewhere during January, from King and people alike, was of the most cordial and even enthusiastic character; while the death of Mr. Roosevelt, on Jan. 6th, evoked an almost national expression of regret for the man who had done so much for the Allied cause. In the Peace Conference Great Britain supported President Wilson in his League of Nations policy and helped him to frame its constitution and organize its practical application; acted as a mediator in the Italian-Fiume dispute and gave Mr. Wilson partial support of a compromise nature; accepted eventually the Mandate plan of the United States for German Colonies though not in the detail originally proposed; gave the Republic first place at the Conference and in signature of Treaties—nominally because of its representation by the ruler of the nation or because the word

*Note.—*Monetary Times* Annual, Jan. 3, 1919.

"America" gave it precedence; recognized and supported the Monroe Doctrine as an international understanding consistent with the principles of the League Covenant. The British people gave an enthusiastic reception in London to the parades of American troops and the Government placed them at the head of the procession in the Victory celebrations.

On the other hand, the United States at the Conference stood by Great Britain and the Empire in refusing to receive the "Nationalist" or Separationist delegates from Ireland, South Africa and Egypt or to recognize the "self-determination" policy as applicable to countries within the British Empire or as aids to revolution within its boundaries. It supported recognition of the British protectorate of Egypt and, after preliminary opposition, agreed to the admission of the British Dominions and India upon an equal footing with other small nations; abandoned the Freedom of the Seas contention as against Great Britain; in many and most important details of the Treaty-making American delegates supported, or were led by, British opinion and experience. To aid in completing the Peace edifice which the Conference constructed, Viscount Grey of Falloden, K.G., came to the United States as Special Ambassador on Sept. 27th; but the negative action of the United States Senate as to the Treaty nullified in great measure the value of his brief mission.

Similarly, the English-Speaking Union which had been formed on July 4th, 1918, to increase mutual knowledge amongst the peoples of the Empire and the Republic and of which Rt. Hon. A. J. Balfour, O.M., was President for England and Hon. W. H. Taft for the United States, did what was possible to meet anti-British propaganda in the United States and anti-American ideas in Great Britain. This and other matters found a place in Mr. Balfour's reference on Dec. 11th, 1919 to the United States and the Peace Treaty: "It is to me a feeling of deepest regret that so much of the common work between the two countries should come to an end before its full fruition could be enjoyed by the world at large." An interesting event in this general connection was the purchase by a British syndicate of the ships and assets of the International Merchantile Marine Co.; it involved 750,000 tons of shipping valued at $135,000,000 and was approved by the Board of the Company on May 20th. Another was the order of President Wilson, announced on Dec. 26th, that the seven German liners used to bring back American troops and since held in New York harbour for settlement of disputed points should be handed over to Great Britain.

An American Society with a growing influence upon Peace and friendly international relations—through the medium of a judicious and able series of publications upon international issues and conditions—was the Carnegie Endowment for International Peace, founded in 1910 by the late Andrew Carnegie with Elihu Root as President in 1919, George Gray, Vice-President and James Brown Scott, Secretary. The Executive or Board of Trus-

Sulphide Plant at Smooth Rock Falls in Northern Ontario

tees included such names as Nicholas Murray Butler, David Jayne Hill, George W. Perkins, Oscar S. Straus, John Sharp Williams, H. S. Pritchett, with headquarters at Washington; and the publications at this time totalled 16 under the auspices of the Division of Intercourse and Education, 9 in that of Economics and History, 27 in that of International Law, a number of Classics of International Law translated and re-published, 25 Economic Studies of the War, and 31 pamphlets upon all manner of international subjects. It was a great work, well done, with, however, the omission of many British state documents of international importance and value. The following were the announced objects:

1. To promote a thorough and scientific investigation and study of the causes of war and of the practical methods to prevent and avoid it.
2. To aid in the development of international law, and a general agreement on the rules thereof, and the acceptance of the same among nations.
3. To diffuse information, and to educate public opinion regarding the causes, nature, and effects of war, and means for its prevention and avoidance.
4. To establish a better understanding of international rights and duties and a more perfect sense of international justice among the inhabitants of civilized countries.
5. To cultivate friendly feelings between the inhabitants of different countries, and to increase the knowledge and understanding of each other by the several nations.
6. To promote a general acceptance of peaceable methods in the settlement of international disputes.
7. To maintain, promote, and assist such establishments, organizations, associations, and agencies as shall be deemed necessary or useful in the accomplishment of the purposes of the Corporation, or any of them.

The Pan-American Union and Canada. As touching upon Canada's place in foreign affairs, its interest in British concerns and United States dominance in the Western hemisphere, reference should be made to the growing strength in 1919 of the Pan-American Union which comprised the United States and 20 South American republics. This Union submitted a Memorandum to the Peace Conference which described itself as a powerful and actual American League of Nations and declared its policy to be a strengthening of the Supreme Council of the Union for the Western Hemisphere, the firm establishment of Pan-American solidarity and the Monroe Doctrine, the promotion of Pan- American commerce and intercourse. The document was, in effect though not in words, a challenge to the other Leagues of Nations— that of Versailles and that of the British Empire. This League already had headquarters in a handsome building at Washington with a Governors' Board composed of the Secretary of the United States and the diplomatic representatives in Washington of the other Republics. It was administered by a Director-General, one of the Ambassadors at Washington chosen by the Board, and assisted by a staff of international experts, statisticians, editors, compilers, translators and librarians. An incident of the war period in this connection was the passage of many South American securities from British to United States hands; a development of

5

1919, however, was the surprisingly great increase of trade between Great Britain and these republics; a suggestion of the *Canada-West India Magazine* of June was that Canada might also obtain a share in this trade if she secured from Great Britain such South American securities as were still held in London as exchange for imports from the Dominion.

Fisheries Treaty between Canada and United States.   On Sept. 2nd, 1919, a complicated question of many years was settled by the signing at Washington of a Treaty between the United States and Great Britain for the protection of the Sockeye salmon of the Fraser River system in British Columbia and the lower portion of the Gulf of Georgia and Juan de Fuca Strait in the State of Washington.   The Hon. R. Lansing, Secretary of State, signed for the United States and the Hon. R. C. Lindsay, Charge d'Affaires of the British Embassy with Sir John Douglas Hazen, Chief Justice of New Brunswick, signed for Canada.   The Treaty had been negotiated and its terms settled by the American-Canadian Fisheries Commission, appointed in 1918 for the purpose of considering questions involving the fisheries of the United States and Canada, and of reaching a basis for settlement.

The United States Commissioners were: Hon. William C. Redfield, Secretary of Commerce and Dr. Hugh M. Smith, Commissioner of Fisheries; those for Canada were Chief Justice Sir J. Douglas Hazen, G. J. Desbarats and William A. Found.   The Conference held hearings at Boston and Gloucester, Mass.; St. John's, Newfoundland; Seattle, Wash.; Prince Rupert, B.C.; Ketchikan, Alaska; Vancouver, B.C.; New Westminster, B.C., and at Ottawa.   As a result of their deliberations and of recommendations made the Treaty was finally negotiated and, under its terms, an International Fisheries Commission of four members was created to conduct investigations into the life history of the salmon, hatcheries, methods, spawning ground conditions, etc.   In an appendix to the Treaty regulations for the protection of sockeye salmon were set out and the Commission recommended modifications or additions to the regulations, or the extension of the regulations, to cover other varieties of salmon.   They were to continue in effect for eight years and thereafter until one year from the time either signatory gave notice of a desire for revision. The Convention was to remain in effect for 15 years and thereafter until two years from the date either party might give notice of a desire to terminate it.

The regulations provided that all salmon fishers in the Treaty-waters of either country should be licensed in the United States by the State of Washington, and in Canada under the provisions of the Fisheries Act.   Licenses issued in the United States should not exceed those issued in 1918, and the number of gill-nets licensed in Canada in any year should not exceed 1,800.   The use of nets other than drift nets, purse seines and trap nets for sockeye salmon was prohibited.   During the years 1920 to 1927, inclusive, salmon fishing, except for scientific purposes, was prohibited from July 20 to July 31. All salmon trap nets were limited in length to 2,500 feet, and no more than two-thirds of any passageway could be closed by trap nets. Purse seines were limited to 1,900 feet, and drift nets to 900 feet.

Canadian Representation at Washington. A question which came up in this year was that of the appointment of a Canadian representative at Washington. It arose, naturally, out of the work done by the Canadian War Mission at the U. S. capital under Lloyd Harris and in co-operation with the British War Mission. Mr. Rowell, President of the Privy Council, told Parliament on May 5th that the Mission was to be closed but not until permanent representation of some kind had been arranged. Between February, 1918, and the Armistice, it had secured for Canadian industries contracts totalling $231,045,544. As to the future, the Minister said: "While the several British Ambassadors at Washington have rendered admirable service to Canada, our business with the United States is now on so large a scale that the Government is convinced that our interests can only be adequately protected by a Canadian representative resident in Washington. Therefore, it has been decided to continue the War Mission until permanent representation is arranged for." He added these rather significant words:

If this representative is to be truly a Canadian representative, his functions must have a wider scope than that of merely dealing with matters of trade. The condition creates the need; the need undoubtedly will be met when the arrangements are completed. Moreover, Canada has a unique opportunity of being the means of keeping more closely together than they have been in the past, the Mother Country and our sister nation to the south. We understand the Americans better than the Old Country people do, and we understand the Old Country people better than the Americans do: we may be interpreter between the two. I am sure, therefore, that the appointment of a Canadian representative at Washington is in the interests of the Empire as a whole as well as of Canada.

In the ensuing discussion the Hon. R. Lemieux strongly supported the proposal, spoke of the future close alliance between the United States and Canada and urged the appointment of Sir Charles Gordon of Montreal to the post. Journals such as the Toronto *Star* and Winnipeg *Free Press* vigourously endorsed the plan and it was pointed out that the trade of Canada and the United States in 1913 was $608,251,944 and in 1919, under war conditions, $1,224,666,313.

United States Visitors; Reciprocity and Other Incidents. An international incident of the year was the visit to Western Canada in August of 200 American Editors, members of the U.S. National Editorial Association, on their way to a Convention in Victoria, B.C. Hon. Guy W. Hardy, Member of Congress, was President and at Winnipeg on July 28th responded to the formal welcome tendered by J. Bruce Walker of the Immigration Department. They were the guests of the City at a luncheon and were banquetted by the Board of Trade during their stay. In the next few days they were entertained at Portage La Prairie, Saskatoon, Battleford and Wainwright; on Aug. 2nd, they were dined and otherwise publicly welcomed at Edmonton with addresses from the Lieut.-Governor, for the Province, and M. R. Jennings, for the newspapers of Alberta; at the splendid Jasper Park on the 3rd they were the guests of the Dominion Government and then spent three days in the mountains; at Vancouver on the 7th they were entertained by the City Council and Board of Trade.

After a visit to Seattle and Portland, U.S., their Convention opened at Victoria on Aug. 18th. On the return trip the party were cordially welcomed at Banff, Red Deer, Calgary, Lethbridge, Medicine Hat, Moose Jaw, Regina and Brandon, arriving at Winnipeg again on Aug. 25th, after an 8,000-mile tour. The Regina visit on Aug. 25th was notable for a banquet at which Mr. Bruce Walker, who had officially accompanied the party, was given a presentation and by an address from R. J. C. Stead, author and poet, and Dominion Publicity Director, who said, amongst other good things, that: "It is not a nation's natural resources that make it great, else Russia would be the greatest amongst nations; nor is it numbers of people, or China would be the greatest. . . . Without journalism, there can be no literature; without literature, no idealism; without idealism, no vision; and without vision the people perish."

About a year after he had told Congress (Dec. 31st, 1918) that the United States should have "incomparably the greatest Navy in the world," Josephus Daniels, U.S. Secretary of the Navy, was 'dined by the Canadian Club at Victoria, (Sept. 11) and told its members that: "Together, Canada and the United States have pioneered for freedom and the highest principles of democracy. Together, they must pioneer for peace and the safety of the world." Admiral Rodman, who had commanded the 6th U.S. battle squadron in European waters, spoke of his pleasure in serving under Admiral Beatty and described the great work of the British Navy in the War as he had already described it in his own country. In September it was announced that reciprocal arrangements between the United States and Canada, through the Department of Soldiers' Civil Re-Establishment, had been completed whereby each country undertook, when occasion should arise, the after-care of dependents of the other country found within its own borders. It was estimated at this time that 33,355 recruits for the Canadian Forces had come from or through New York and that 8,000 Americans enlisted in Canada; that 13,853 recruits joined the British Forces from or through New York with about 5,000 British reservists. On Oct. 9th Congress repealed, with a slight and perfunctory debate and no opposition, the famous Reciprocity compact, or Canadian Reciprocity Act, of 1911 which had been the spectacular theme of a general election in Canada and had caused the defeat of the Laurier

Government. The chief speech of the occasion was by Hon. G. M. Young of North Dakota, who declared that:

There is little fear of Canada ever passing a law to accept or put in operation the Reciprocity law now on our statute books. Why should she? Canada was made a present in the Underwood tariff law of practically all she was trading for in the proposed Reciprocity arrangements. While it was a one-sided agreement, still Canada did give a certain degree of preference to United States' manufacturers. Why should Canada agree to do this now, when practically all she asked for was given her by the Underwood Law? The only reason that the Laurier Government ever thought of signing such an agreement was to secure free access to our markets for her agricultural produce.

In the *University Magazine* for November, Sir Andrew Macphail made an original contribution to international issues by declaring that the Ashburton Treaty should be revised and that the time had come for a new boundary line which would give to Canada a large part of the State of Maine and thereby afford an all-the-year Canadian outlet to the sea. He contended that such an arrangement was essential to the future national development of Canada and pointed out that when the Dominion was at war and the United States a neutral nation, the Canadian Pacific could not be used to transport soldiers to the port of St. John because it ran through United States territory. He thought the subject should come before the League of Nations under a section of Art. XIX: "The Assembly may from time to time advise the reconsideration by members of the League of treaties which have become inapplicable and the consideration of international conditions whose continuance might endanger the peace of the world." The suggestion was discussed here and there and the Boston *Transcript* expressed doubt as to whether the writer were satirical or serious.

Another incident, typical of certain troubles arising from time to time, was the enforced resignation on Dec. 4th of the Hon. Annie A. Aitken, Superintendent of Rutland Hospital, and a sister of Lord Beaverbrook, followed by an investigation through agents of the U.S. Justice Department with final instructions to Miss Aitken to either publicly apologize for an alleged insult to the American flag or else to leave the country within 48 hours under penalty of arrest if she did not do one or the other. She returned to New Brunswick. The trouble arose over a contemptuous remark about the flag by Miss McLane, another Canadian nurse, a demand from the Hospital nurses in general that she be compelled by the Superintendent to apologize and salute the flag, and the refusal of Miss Aitken to act in the matter.

Another flag incident occurred in the experience of Controller H. J. Halford of Hamilton, Vice-President of the International Journeymen Barbers' Union, who early in September, attended the sessions of his organization at Buffalo, U.S. A delegate from New England during his speech referred to the British flag as one of "oppression." Mr. Halford followed and rebuked the speaker: "That uncalled-for reference is an insult to the Canadian delegates and we won't stand for it. The Canadian delegates are proud of the British flag, and I wish to emphasize the fact that out of Canada's 8,000,000 population, 500,000 of her gallant sons donned khaki, not only to fight for freedom and democracy, but to defend the British flag." A retraction and apology were freely given.

International Waterway and Power Questions. One of the international questions of this period was that of the uses, diversion and allotment of St. Lawrence water-power and the applications to and decisions of the International Waterways Commission in this connection. The estimated 24-hour low-water power of the River was 2,395,000 h.p., that of the international part of the waterway was about 800,000 h.p., and Canada's share about 400,000 h.p. The use of these powers was a matter of controversy (1) as to corporate or government control; (2) as to the grant of rights on the Canadian side and in Canadian power facilities to United States corporations; (3) as to the development of unpleasant relations and international friction out of too hard and fast rules in this connection and at Niagara, also, with a fear expressed in some quarters of United States retaliation in respect to Canadian coal supplies; (4) as to the ambition of the Ontario Hydro-Electric Commission to see the waterpowers of Canada conserved for Canadian use alone. A question of much discussion in 1917-19 and dating, in its origin, more than 10 years before that, was the application of the St. Lawrence River Power Co.—a subsidiary corporation, together with the Long Sault Development Co., of the Aluminum Company of America which was already developing power from the St. Lawrence at Massena Springs, N.Y.—for the right to construct a dam or weir between the lower or eastern end of Long Sault Island in the St. Lawrence and the United States shore, connecting with its canal, and for the purpose of increasing the flow of water to its power plant at Massena which, latterly, was assisting in aluminum production.

In this general connection and in a diplomatic Note to the United States Government on Feb. 27th, 1906, Sir Mortimer Durand, then British Ambassador, stated that it had been represented to the Canadian Government that the Massena Water Power Co. had made application to the Government of the United States for permission to dam the south channel of the St. Lawrence River at Long Sault Island. The Ambassador pointed out that the favourable consideration of the application would appear to involve a contravention of the Ashburton Treaty of 1842 between the United States and Great Britain, which stipulated that "the channels in the River St. Lawrence, on both sides of Long Sault Island and of Barnhardt Island, shall be equally free and open to the ships, vessels and boats of both parties." He also drew attention to Article III of the Treaty between the United States and Great Britain relating to Boundary waters:

It is agreed that, in addition to the uses, obstructions and diversions heretofore permitted or hereafter provided for by special agreement between the parties hereto, no further or other uses or obstructions or diversions, whether temporary or permanent, of boundary waters on either side of the line affecting the natural level or flow of boundary waters on the other side of the line shall be made, except by authority of the United States or the Dominion of Canada within their respective jurisdictions and with the approval, as hereinafter provided, of a joint Commission to be known as the International Joint Commission.

When the matter came before this International Commission in 1918 as a War measure associated with the supply of aluminum for British war requirements, that body in response to an urgent communication from the U.S. Secretary of War (Aug. 23rd, 1918) granted an Order stating that "as an interim measure the construction of the said weir and its maintenance until the expiration of the term of five years from the date hereof, or until the termination of the present war, is hereby approved." Certain conditions were attached and it was declared that "in the foregoing Order the Commission shall not be deemed to have considered nor passed upon any question pertaining to the rights of the applicant to divert water from the St. Lawrence River." The Dominion Government, through Hon. Hugh Guthrie, Attorney-General, had opposed this decision and had sent Messrs. Meighen and Sifton to Washington to affect some arrangement which should avoid any grant of rights to a private corporation.

A good deal of criticism followed in the Canadian press which, apparently, feared the influence of a large United States corporation upon an international highway. The International Waterways Commission, which included C. A. Magrath (Chairman for Canada), with P. B. Mignault, K.C., afterwards appointed to the Supreme Court of Canada and H. A. Powell, K.C., as the Canadian members and Obadiah Gardner (Chairman for the United States) with R. B. Glenn and Clarence D. Clark as the American members, issued in November a learned statement by Mr. Mignault explaining and defending the judgment. The Commission was described as a Court with final powers in these matters and, it was declared, its decisions were as carefully given as those of any Canadian Court with the added importance of being international in effect. Other efforts were made to obtain power rights on the St. Lawrence and notably that of the New York and Ontario Power Co., in which capital from both countries was interested, for additional privileges at the Long Sault Rapids in connection with its plant at Waddington, N.Y. The Dominion Government opposed the application on the grounds that:

(1) It will interfere with the full and economic development of the St. Lawrence system as regards the navigation thereof and the power potentialities therein, which are common to both bordering countries and of equal advantage to each country; (2) it will interfere with the complete regulation, by a dam at Canada Island, of the level and outflow of Lake Ontario; (3) the future development of the river will necessitate the acquisition of any rights the applicant may have in the river, and the Government of Canada considers it inadvisable to create more; (4) the St. Lawrence River has enormous potentialities that should be developed in the most efficient and economical manner for future generations. Such a piecemeal policy as proposed is not in conformity with this doctrine.

The Government took up the question with the United States along these lines and in a broad spirit, looking to large development of these waterways and their power; at the same time the Commission was studying various projects with a view to special development in the 113 miles of river between Canada and the United States, running from Lake Ontario to Cornwall, and in which it was estimated that there was 1,000,000 h.p. capable of use; in this part of the project Sir Adam Beck and the Hydro Commission of Ontario were vitally interested. It was understood in September, 1919, that the Governments concerned were discussing a combined scheme of waterway development so that the St. Lawrence should be made navigable for ocean vessels from the sea up into Lake Ontario at the same time that its power potentialities were being developed. With the completion of the Welland Ship Canal it would thus become possible for ocean vessels to proceed 2,100 miles inland.

The Canadian Deep Waterways and Power Association. To discuss this project a Great Waterways Conference was held at Windsor, Ont., on Nov. 18-19 with 23 cities and towns represented —including Ottawa, Toronto, London, St. Thomas, Washington, New Orleans, Duluth, Detroit and New York. A number of prominent delegates were present of whom F. H. Keefer, K.C., M.P., Sir Adam Beck, E. L. Cousins, Toronto, W. B. Burgoyne, St. Catharines, W. M. German, K.C., Welland, W. H. Breithaupt, Kitchener, O. E. Fleming, K.C. and W. C. Kennedy, M.P., Windsor, G. A. Graham, Fort William, W. S. Bowden, Goderich, Hon. Sidney Story, New Orleans, C. P. Craig, Duluth and W. H. Adams, Detroit may be mentioned. The chair was occupied by F. A. Nancekivell of Windsor who in his speech laid down these bases for action: "The world's markets are being re-aligned; and if we are to have prosperity, we must reach out for foreign trade both in our natural and manufactured products. And, if we are to compete with other countries for world-trade, we must keep down our costs of production and delivery. Transportation charges on raw material and finished products constitute quite a large percentage of the cost to the ultimate consumer. Therefore, any saving effected in such charges will yield big results in both foreign and domestic trade. Water Transportation, as every one knows, is much cheaper than rail transportation; and, when we consider what a wonderful natural system of inland waterways is the joint heritage of Canada and the United States, and how comparatively little is necessary to be done in addition to that already done, to give us a deep waterway from the Atlantic Tidewater to the head of the Great Lakes, then, surely now is the time to get behind the project and push it through."

C. P. Craig, known as the Father of the Deep Waterways movement in the United States, made the following points: "It is a great thought to create on this Continent an American Mediterranean which will be to this wonderful country what the Mediterranean has been to Europe; but it is just as great a thought and one just as inspiring to think of two great nations joining together to do this common thing for a common good." The way to the sea, opening our front door to the sea, was his answer to the problem of higher freight rates. The electric power of the St. Lawrence, if properly utilized, would, he declared, save 36,000,000 tons of coal a year. Other speakers were R. J. Maclean, Detroit, and F. H. Keefer, who strongly supported the scheme and described the Power section of it as the greatest ever proposed; O. E. Fleming, K.C., W. H. Adams, Hon. S. Story, W. E. Gundy, W. M. German, Col. J. A. Aikin of New York and Sir Adam Beck.

The latter stated that by deepening the Welland Canal from 25 to 30 feet and the St. Lawrence at one or two points, 90 per cent. of all ocean-going vessels in the world would be able to traverse the Great Lakes freely: "The Power possibilities of the St. Lawrence are unexceeded anywhere. For four years, the Hydro-Power Commission has had a skilled staff of engineers and investigators, in constant research and investigation, collecting information and data regarding the possibilities of this development. At Cedar Rapids from 160,000 to 180,000 horse-power can be developed. It is advisable to deepen the St. Lawrence at this point, or the Power development will be imperilled. At Morrisburg and the Long Sault Rapids, perhaps, a million horse-power can be developed. Two million horse-power can be developed from the waters of Lake Ontario, and probably two million more between the borders of Ontario and Montreal." He estimated $100,000,000 as the cost of the Great Lakes and St. Lawrence development and the coal saved in the Power part of the scheme as 100,000,000 tons. An organization was then formed called the Canadian Deep Waterways and Power Association with W. M. German, K.C., Welland as Hon. President, Sir Adam Beck and Mayor T. L. Church, Toronto, as Hon. Vice-Presidents, O. E. Fleming, K.C. as President, F. Maclure Sclanders, F.R. G.S., Windsor, as Hon. Secretary-Treasurer. Resolutions were unanimously passed as follows:

I. That one of the objects of this Association shall be to act in conjunction with and co-operate with the Great Lakes-St. Lawrence Tide-Water Association and any other like organization having similar objects in carrying on the work that we deem urgent and most essential to this country—the opening up of the natural waterways from their head to the tide waters on the St. Lawrence River; and to facilitate and cheapen transportation and power development.

II. That this Association is of the opinion that the work to be undertaken in the deepening of the Natural Watercourse for ocean-going shipping should be undertaken by the Governments of the United States and Canada jointly, and that it should be operated as a joint undertaking, so far as the Watercourses may be International; that the water-powers of the St. Lawrence should be developed to their fullest extent for the purpose of producing a revenue—such revenue to be used to provide a sinking fund for the retirement of the capital expenditure, payment or interest and maintenance and operation of the Canal system and Hydro-electric operation; and that in this way, in our opinion, the project should be made self-supporting.

This movement and the desire of the Ontario Hydro Commission for right to develop some of the St. Lawrence water-powers in order to electrify railways and help the industries of Ontario were not exactly popular in Quebec and the project was claimed to involve large sums of money for the purchase or possible elimination of already established Power interests in the St. Lawrence. The Dominion Government believed that the problem, being international and inter-Provincial, would require Federal control; that a deepened waterway would have to be constructed as well as the power development, because the friends of the project in the United States wanted their chief Lake cities to become ocean ports. The plan decided upon was to refer the subject to the International Joint Commission for study and report, following upon certain technical details which had been officially looked into by United States and Canadian experts, and were reported upon at the close of the year.

The International Joint Commission. Meanwhile, this Commission had been doing good work along general lines. In the boundary waters, which its decisions affected, there were 2,500 miles of water front with more navigation, it was said, on the Great Lakes than entered the ports of Boston and New York, Liverpool and London, during a year; with 7,000,000 people living on those boundary waters and 6,000,000 h.p. under development. One of the problems was that of improving polluted waterways and controlling drainage canals and plants and other matters connected with sanitary conditions. The Commission had been making exhaustive enquiries along this line since Jan. 11, 1909, when the United States and Canada Waterways Treaty of that date ordered an investigation; elaborate reports had been published from time to time with various recommendations.

By a Dominion Order-in-Council early in 1919, the Government accepted the Reports and especially the recommendation which had been agreed to by the United States authorities that, in order to remedy or prevent the pollution of boundary waters, and to render them sanitary and suitable for domestic purposes and other uses, and to secure adequate protection and development of all interests involved on both sides of the boundary, it was advisable to confer upon the International Joint Commission "some additional jurisdiction to make rules and regulations, directions and orders, as in its judgment may be deemed necessary to regulate and prohibit the pollution of the boundary waters and waters crossing the boundary."

International Incidents of the Year. Incidents of the year, in connection with international relations, was the apparently justified rumour that Sir Robert Borden could have become British Ambassador to the United States had he desired; the address by Mr. Daniels, U.S. Secretary of the Navy, (elsewhere referred to) at Victoria and that of Hon. Newton D. Baker, U.S. Secretary of War, to the Canadian Club, Ottawa, on Jan. 11th, together with a notable

speech by Sir John Willison of Toronto at Bridgeport, Conn., on
Feb. 27th; the recommendation to Congress by Mr. Daniels and the
Navy Department on May 28th of provision in the 1920 Appropriation Bill for a Navy of 250,000 men or 23,000 less than were now in
the service, to be utilized as a "temporary force"; the Conference
between the Secretary for War, General P. C. March, U.S. Chief of
Staff and the Military Committee of Congress on Jan. 16th resulting in postponing to a new Congress the War Department's Bill for
a 500,000 army costing $1,185,000,000 a year; the agitation in
Canada to control or modify the United States' flag-waving tendency of picture shows and vaudeville performances; the appointment of Lieut.-Col. John A. Cooper of Toronto as Director of a
Canadian Publicity Bureau with headquarters in New York and a
staff to assist in making Canada, its policy and progress, better
known in the States; the useful tour in the Republic of the Canadian War Memorial Exhibition and consequent extension of knowledge as to Canada and its part in the war.

Other international matters included the unpleasant experience
of Hon. Walter Scott, lately Premier of Saskatchewan, who at Pembina, N.D., while *en route* from Victoria, B.C., to a point in Minnesota, was on July 28th arrested and sent to gaol (from which he
escaped) by a U.S. Immigration official, because he did not have a
passport; the remarkable ovation given at Boston on Sept. 1st to a
parade of American Veterans in the Canadian Army and the rather
extraordinary statement by its commander, Lieut.-Col. P. A.
Guthrie (lately of Fredericton) that 110,000 Americans volunteered
for the Canadian service; the international exchange situation
caused by war conditions and trade balances against Great Britain
and Canada which caused sterling to go down to very low figures—
though not the lowest to be reached—by the end of the year with,
amongst other consequences, a discount on Canadian currency in
the United States of 10 per cent., and a refusal in many American
centres and institutions to accept it at all; urgent pressure by the
Canadian Government at Washington for prompt return of 25,000
Canadian box-cars held by United States railways and the official
statement on Nov. 11th that, since the first of the year, the average
number of Canadian cars in the United States was 45,067, while the
average number of United States cars in Canada was 19,926 and
the inference drawn by the Canadian Railway War Board that
Canadian cars were being used for local service in the United
States.

United
States
Control of
British
Cables and
Press News.

Canadians did not at this time understand the
Cable service or the News system which provided
their newspapers with world "information," and
themselves with impressions which, day by day,
trained their minds imperceptibly but surely. The
British were the Cable pioneers of the Atlantic
through F. N. Gisborne, who in 1852 laid the first ocean
cable in America between P.E. Island and New Brunswick, and

in 1853 interested Cyrus W. Field of New York in the project of an Atlantic Cable. British capital and British business ability made the Cable system a success and laid all the cables to and from points on British soil—with the exception of some American coasting lines.

It was in 1909 that the Anglo-American Telegraph Company and the Direct United States Cable Co., representing $50,000,000 of British capitalization and controlling six Atlantic cables, approached the Western Union Telegraph Co., lessees of two American-owned cables, with the object of obtaining a working arrangement for the 8 Companies under one Traffic manager. This was agreed to and the experienced British manager took charge. A little later, however, the Americans insisted upon complete control of the whole system, threatened to cut off their land communication if consent were not given, laid a heavy conductor cable from Cornwall to Newfoundland and a new heavy line from Newfoundland to Coney Island, U.S. Finally, the pressure was successful and the British Companies agreed (1912) to lease their property to the Americans for 99 years at a rate of 6 per cent. on capitalization.

By the year 1919 the United States had obtained absolute control over 16 cables on the Atlantic while the British held one and the French three; the Americans had made great war profits on their transmission of news and messages and were preparing to utilize instruments enabling their operators to speak direct from New York to London; the bulk of business carried was American and the situation, in case of conflicts of opinion or policy between the United States and the British Empire, had become unpleasantly clear to those who understood the situation. Landing on British soil did not mean much, when diversion to Spain or Portugal on the other side and connecting up the Atlantic cables on this side with the Coastal cables at New York would cut the former out of Nova Scotia and Newfoundland entirely. Controversy did in fact develop over the U.S. Postmaster-General's Cable action in 1918. At this time, also, the Americans (Western Union) were extending their service to South and Central America and the West Indies, with obvious influence over trade development, while a lawsuit stood in the British Courts concerning the lease mentioned above.

The Empire Cable across the Pacific was of priceless service in the War and in 1919 a movement began for a duplicate cable from Vancouver to Australia while the Marconi interests at the same time offered to send to Australia a British News service on a ten years' contract at 50 cents a word; the United States also proposed a second American cable from San Francisco across the Pacific while Japan stated an intention of laying one to the United States. In September it was announced that the American project was held up until a substitute for gutta percha could be discovered or British interests furnish the material from British-owned trees in the Philippines.

Meanwhile, the Americans had obtained, quite naturally, control of the cabled News Service to this continent as well as of the Cables. The newspapers of the United States had to have European news and that news was given them by the American Associated Press which had become a huge corporation with agents and correspondents everywhere and unequalled facilities in London particularly. The news had to appeal to the feelings, policy, beliefs, or prejudices in international affairs, of at least the majority of United States papers; those opinions were, during many decades not too friendly to Britain, not particularly anxious to obtain both sides in British controversies, not averse to any sensational utterances or descriptions which would interest their readers, not anxious for the best view of British conditions, not desirous of seeking elements of unity amongst British countries. As was wholly natural, the viewpoint of British affairs was that of a Foreign country—coloured in this case by the prejudices unavoidable under divergent institutions and traditional hostilities which, though gradually dying out, were still effective during much of this period. The idea and ideals of Britain, as it lay on the verge of Europe, and those of the United States 3,000 miles away in space and 100 years in feeling from the European continent, were also vastly different as to nearly all international conditions and policies. Inevitably, therefore, the Cable News service was Americanized—written by Americans in London, and edited by Americans in New York for the perusal of Americans in the United States.

Into this system came the papers of Canada. It was cheaper, easier and, at first, inevitable that they should share with American journals in the distribution of this news. In earlier years Canadians were quite unable to afford a separate service; in later years costs increased and war difficulties supervened; at the present time many decades of education in American news has made them fearful and suspicious of any British suggestions for an all-British service. They fear British propaganda and forget the American propaganda which has been imperceptibly operative during years which run back and beyond the life of the present generation. Under this condition of affairs the Cable news to the United States and Canada has always been inclined to enlarge upon British difficulties and problems and to minimize or ignore British successes in commerce, finance, politics, government, Empire and war; it has made the most of Irish or Labour unrest or Radical discontents; in days when a British Conservative Government might have just won an election with a hundred majority or a Coalition have swept the country as did Lloyd George in 1918, the extreme views of the hostile London *Daily News* or Manchester *Guardian* would be cabled out until those organs of a small minority were better known in the United States (and Canada) than others which really led public opinion.

When questions between Great Britain and the United States (involving Canada) were at issue practically all Canadian news came through American channels; a notable instance was the

Alaska Boundary matter where a Canadian opinion hostile to Great Britain was formed by the American cable service, combined with "despatches from Washington," which filled Canadian papers. During 1919 an absolutely impossible proposal by an irresponsible person that the West Indies should be sold to the United States was made into a continental issue and became the subject of many Canadian editorials; under this system the Irish Rebellion of 1916 was made to appear much more important to the Canadian people than the Battle of Jutland which decided the naval issue of a world war.

During 1919 efforts were made to find a way out of the situation. The Canadian Press Ltd., as an organization, had recently obtained control of the local collection and distribution of news to Canadian papers and it had made an arrangement with the American Associated Press for the use and control of its British and world news in the Dominion; by a process of elimination and selection a change for the better was noticeable but it was at the best negative and not constructive. Cheaper cable rates, or in other words, substantial Government assistance, would have helped, but it was not forthcoming from Canada and the Empire Press Union in London could arrive at no satisfactory conclusion as to replacing or reforming the existing News Agencies there. Its Cable News Committee in August made some suggestions of which the chief ones follow:

1. That immediate steps be taken to improve the existing cable services by reducing the wordage of Government messages.
2. That an adequate system of Wireless should be established as soon as possible.
3. That a second Cable should be laid without delay, as a part of the All-Red scheme, from Bamfield to Norfolk Island, and certainly, in the first instance, from Bamfield to Fanning Island.
4. That better use should be made of the ex-German Atlantic cable.
5. That subventions should be granted with a view to reducing cable and wireless rates, in order to encourage inter-communication between all parts of the Empire.
6. That the deferred Press tariff should be resumed, and extended as soon as possible to South Africa and to India.

Unfortunately, the first clause referred to the only method by which certain vital British Government views could be seen or known by the people of Canada as a whole. Reuters had, meanwhile, been subsidized to a limited extent for this and similar purposes during the War and this was continued up to Dec. 31, 1919, but the British Government would not undertake to go on with it without Dominion co-operation. At its Annual meeting in Toronto on Nov. 26, the Canadian Press, Ltd., took up this question and discussed a Canadian Service in London supplementary to the American Associated Press and dealing chiefly with British Empire news. F. R. Martin, Assistant General-Manager of the A.A.P., was present and it was finally stated that a general system of closer co-operation with the American system had been arranged.

CANADIAN RELATIONS WITH THE EMPIRE

The British Empire in 1919; Its Unity and Problems. The problems of the Empire at this time were many, and in all its countries or new nations they were more or less inter-acting and of mutual interest. Labour, reconstruction, Finance, Industry, Production and national powers had many similar developments in all the Dominions while the influence of British policy and conditions was everywhere felt. The Empire itself was in a melting-pot of new thoughts and relations; its countries outside of the United Kingdom had suddenly been plunged into the League of Nations with new functions, duties and an enlarged status; they had become national Dominions with foreign interests and relations never before dreamt of and responsibilities greater than their peoples altogether realized; they claimed, through Sir Robert Borden and through speeches by various British Ministers, to be members of a British League, or Commonwealth, of Nations.

The United Kingdom was still the heart of the Empire's power and had added to its area of control Egypt, with 350,000 square miles of territory, historic greatness, fertility of soil and the world's route to the Orient; Cyprus, small but rich and prosperous and which had hitherto been considered, technically, a Turkish possession; German South-West Africa with its mineral and other resources and area of 322,450 square miles; German East Africa with 384,180 square miles and great possibilities of development—making safe, with other territories, the red line of British soil and British railways from the Cape to Cairo; part of Togoland and the Cameroons in Africa, say 112,000 square miles; Samoa and German New Guinea and the Pacific Islands which were so vital to Australia and New Zealand and now rounded off and completed British power in the Pacific, with an area of 91,000 square miles; Palestine and Mesopotamia with about 150,000 square miles of the most historic treasure-house of the world and, in the latter case, immense wealth of fertility and possibility. Of course this vast accretion of territory was not deliberate or even technical annexation; much of it was under mandates from the League of Nations and because of imperative demands from the Union of South Africa, the Dominion of New Zealand, the Commonwealth of Australia, and, as a supporting partner, the Dominion of Canada. The exact mandatory results of the Treaty of Versailles—and under the conditions specified they involved practical though not nominal sovereignty—were as follows:

Territory	Recognised Mandatory
Togoland and The Cameroons	Great Britain and France
South-West Africa	Union of South Africa
South-East Africa	Great Britain
Samoan Islands	Dominion of New Zealand
Nauru Island, in Pacific	British Empire
Bismarck and Solomon Islands; Kaiser Wilhelm's Land	Commonwealth of Australia

For the first time in history, the British Empire had taken part in a great war as a unit in action; for the first time, also, its Dominions participated in a world-peace as national units yet constitutional partners. To the War it had sent 8,654,467 fighting men and nearly 1½ million non-combatant helpers. Of the former, 5,399,563 were available at one time or another for fighting in France; 145,764 were sent to help Italy, 404,207 British soldiers were, from first to last, at Salonika while the Dardanelles employed 467,987 more and gave undying fame also to Australia and Newfoundland; Mesopotamia took 889,702 and Egypt and Palestine 1,192,511 while others fought in widely separated African areas. British Empire casualties totalled 2,724,203 in France and Belgium, 119,578 at the Dardanelles, 28,092 in the Balkans, 111,549 in Mesopotamia, 59,996 in Egypt and Palestine, 19,572 in East Africa; the percentage of troops on active service to white male population was 25:36 in the United Kingdom, 13·48 in Canada, 13:43 in Australia, 19·35 in New Zealand and 11·12 in South Africa while that of casualties to white male population was 10·91 in the United Kingdom, 6:04 in Canada, 8·50 in Australia and 9:80 in New Zealand; the cost of the War to the Empire, up to the close of 1918 was, approximately, $35,000,000,000, in which the chief share, of course, fell upon the United Kingdom with about 2,000 millions for Canada, 1,500 millions for Australia, 650 millions for India, 400 millions for New Zealand, 160 millions for South Africa, $10,000,-000 for Newfoundland and a total for the lesser Colonies and Protectorates of $200,000,000.

Given stability of institutions, reasonable willingness to work in the individual and reasonable unity of feeling and action amongst its nations and people, the British Empire came out of the War as the greatest and most powerful nation or community of nations, on earth.   It still possessed the largest merchantile fleet and naval forces in the world with more strategic harbours, coaling stations and trade positions than it had even in its days of pre-war supremacy; it possessed the greatest gold, silver, precious stones, coal and iron resources of the world with the largest grain-growing, cotton-producing and food-raising resources of the world; it had more than a quarter of the world's population under its flag and a quarter of its area; the total pre-war wealth of the Empire was estimated at $175,000,000,000, its total trade was over $10,000,-000,000, the yearly income of its peoples was $15,000,000,000 and the revenues of its various countries totalled $2,000,000,000.*   In 1919 these figures were greatly enlarged by increased and growing values.   The Empire as a whole had, during the War, vitally improved its machinery for production and industry, its facilities for the construction of shipping, its markets for coal and manufactured goods, its financial knowledge and confidence and banking facilities, the position of London as the nerve centre of the world's greatest interests.

*Note.—Sir Robert Giffen: *Hazell's Annual*, which is officially recognised in Great Britain; *The Canadian Annual Review* for 1914.

The King and the Empire. Of Imperial unity the Crown remained the chief and most conspicuous link. The King continued, during this year, to take and express a personal and profound interest in the developments and affairs of the external Empire. Engrossing as were his calls from international affairs and the gigantic war-burdened problems of the United Kingdom, he never lost an opportunity to show personal concern in Empire incidents and conditions—from the bestowal of Honours upon gallant soldiers of the Dominions to the formal recognition of their services in the Speech from the Throne on Feb. 11th: "For the last few months the Imperial War Cabinet has been in continuous session, and my counsels in regard to the War and external affairs have been both strengthened and enlightened by the presence of the leading Ministers of my self-governing Dominions, and of representatives of my Indian Empire. The inspiring sacrifice and the invaluable service which have been rendered by the Peoples of the Dominions and of India during the War have won for them an important place in the counsels of the world, and it has been a source of especial satisfaction to me that their title to representation has been fully recognized in the Paris Conference."

His Majesty delivered a good many more speeches in 1919 than was usual with him and they included a notable one on the Housing problem addressed to a large delegation on Apr. 11th, with a declaration that, in an adequate solution of this question, lay "the foundations of all social progress"; a quite elaborate address on Education (July 30th) to another delegation at Buckingham Palace in which he said that only in this way could the best in physical, mental and spiritual conditions be developed; one on general conditions, in reply to a London Corporation address (July 29th), in which he urged the development of trade, the re-creation of the Merchant Marine, the development of ports, the enlargement and modernization of dock facilities, the deepening of river channels, the cultivation of individual industry and thrift, the greatest possible production of necessary commodities.

During the War the King had been unwearied in visiting the British and Empire troops at the front and in seeing them in trench and in camp, in hospital and in recreation huts; on May 3rd, 1919, he inspected an Empire parade through London of 11,000 men, took the salute at the foot of Constitution Hill and issued a Message to the Overseas troops in which he declared that: "We and future generations will never forget the part played by the Canadians in the second battle of Ypres and on the Vimy Ridge; by the Australians and New Zealanders at Gallipoli, and in the advance in France in the spring of 1917; by the troops of all three Dominions in the breaking of the Hindenburg line last year; by the South African Brigade in Delville Wood; by the Royal Newfoundland Regiment at Monchy le Preux."

On Empire Day he was present with the Queen at a service in Westminster Abbey in memory of the officers and men who had

fallen in the War and as a thanksgiving for its victorious conclusion. On May 5th His Majesty wrote expressing pleasure that the
Empire Parliamentary Association had placed special apartments in
Westminster Palace at the disposition of visiting members of Parliament from the Dominions: "I feel confident that this Parliamentary comradeship within the Empire will make the members
of all the Parliaments better acquainted with each other, and with
each other's problems, and so realize more and more their great
common interests in those long traditions of Parliamentary government which they have inherited." On June 3rd there were many
newspaper tributes to the King and amongst them none were more
to the point than that of the Montreal *Star*:

> Probably no single individual among all his millions of subjects has
> played a more ardous part, has worked longer hours, has born a more
> crushing load of worry and responsibility than King George the Fifth during
> the last five terrible years. These duties and these responsibilities reached
> their climax during the years of the War and have not relaxed their
> severity since the Armistice. Anarchy has spread its bloody wings over many
> a fair land and the institution of kingship has in three great countries,
> where it seemed most firmly established, failed to weather the gale. Surely
> it is not by mere chance that our King has come through the tempest more
> firmly enthroned in his peoples' affections than ever before. Surely the
> Man has had something to do with making still more firm the loyalty of
> the nations to the King. Patient, tactful, wise, labourious, self-effacing as
> his high position will permit, kind and faithful to the best traditions of
> his people and his station, George the Fifth deserves that wherever his loyal
> peoples are gathered together the prayer that should arise for him should come
> straight from their hearts.

A visit was paid by the King and Queen to the Orpington (Ontario) Hospital on May 29th; on June 28th after the first signatures
to the Peace Treaty, King George issued a Message declaring that
it "manifests the victory of ideals, of freedom and of liberty for
which we have made untold sacrifices"; to the President of the
United States he sent a Message of congratulation and hope that
"the American and British people, brothers in arms, will continue
forever to be brothers in peace." His Majesty unveiled on Sept.
6th a statue of Sir George E. Cartier at Montreal, by pressing an
electric button in Balmoral Castle, Scotland, while a message was
read, also, by H.E. the Duke of Devonshire. On Nov. 6th the King
issued a Message to the peoples of the Empire which, after expressing the belief that they would all like to mark, on Nov. 11th, the
first anniversary of the Armistice, added:

> To afford an opportunity for the universal expression of this feeling,
> it is my desire and hope that at the hour when the Armistice came into
> force, the 11th hour of the 11th day of the 11th month, there may be for the
> brief space of two minutes, a complete suspension of all our normal activities.
> During that time, except in the rare cases where this may be impractic-
> able, all work, all sound and all locomotion should cease, so that in perfect
> stillness the thoughts of everyone may be concentrated on reverent remem-
> brance of the glorious dead.

As a result of this command all over Canada, and all around
the world's British belt of land and sea, a stoppage of trains took

place on land and of ships on the waters, cessation of traffic on the streets, while silence was observed in schools, shops, mines, factories, and homes. In Canada Sir George Foster, Acting Prime Minister, urgently requested the people to observe the wishes of the King. On Nov. 19th His Majesty thanked by Message the Overseas workmen who had volunteered their services for the production of ships and munitions during the War and who were now repatriated to their homes; to Canada, in the closing months of the year, he sent H.R.H. the Prince of Wales for what became a memorable visit; in the Commons on Dec. 23rd, the King's speech stated that the Prince would visit India to inaugurate the new constitution of that great Empire. An interesting incident of the year was the appearance in the *Quarterly Review* (August) of an article in which Prof. A. S. Rait made public certain letters of the late Queen Victoria to her daughter, the Crown Princess Victoria, wife of the Emperor Frederick, and mother of Wilhelm II, in which she indicated clearly her distrust of Prince Bismarck and the German militarists. Two quotations may be given as contra to certain statements current in Canada during the War:

I. Extract from Diary of May 6th, 1875: Saw Mr. Disraeli and talked about the very alarming rumours from Germany as to war. This began by dictatorial and offensive language to Belgium, then by reports of the Germans saying they must attack the French, as these threatened to attack them, and a war of revenge was imminent in consequence, which the increase of French armaments proved. I said this was intolerable, that France could not for years make war, and that I thought we ought, in concert with the other Powers, to hold the strongest language to both countries, declaring they must not fight, for that Europe would not stand another war.

II. Letter to Crown Princess, June 8th, 1875: I am not worked upon by anyone; but Bismarck is a terrible man, and he makes Germany greatly disliked—indeed no one will stand the over-bearing, insolent way in which he acts and treats other nations—Belgium, for instance. You know that the Prussians are not popular, unfortunately, and no one will tolerate any Power wishing to dictate to all Europe. This country, with the greatest wish to go hand in hand with Germany, cannot and will not stand it.

Princess Patricia's Wedding. The popularity of "Princess Pat" as she was everywhere called in Canada, was much in evidence after the announcement of her coming marriage to Commander the Hon. Alex. R. M. Ramsay, D.S.O., of H.M.S. *King George V*, and brother of the Earl of Dalhousie, which was fixed for Feb. 27th, 1919. Many personal and public gifts followed from Canada —a few of the donours being Lady Allan, Sir Robert Borden, General Burstall, Officers of the 1st Canadian Division, Canada Club, London, Daughters of the Empire, Lady Drummond, Sir George and Lady Foster, Mrs. Hamilton Gault, Lord Mount Stephen (cheque), Sir Edward and Lady Kemp, Lady Strathcona, Sir George and Lady Perley, Princess Patricia's Canadian Light Infantry, Commander and Mrs. J. K. L. Ross, Lord and Lady Shaughnessy; many soldier memories went back to the days at Orpington when the serious-eyed, quietly-dressed Princess gave so much of her time to caring for wounded Canadians; many newspaper editorials of a pleasant nature were written as to the charming Princess who had given her name and heart to one of the most famous Battalions in the War and one of which Canada was very proud.

Lady Borden, wife of the Prime Minister, wrote early in January to the wives of the Lieut.-Governors suggesting voluntary contributions for a national gift—preferably furs or something else distinctly Canadian. In the letter it was stated that during her residence in Canada Her Royal Highness by charm of manner and kindly and unaffected interest in their welfare, became greatly endeared to Canadians. Eventually $7,000 was collected and invested for the Princess in Canadian Victory bonds enclosed in a silver casket. On Feb. 24th, at Bramshott, the Princess reviewed her war-worn Battalion, as Colonel-in-Chief, for the last time and made a ringing little speech of admiration and regard for the Regiment and of special recognition of the splendid service "rendered to the Empire" by its founder and Commanding Officer, Lieut.-Col. Hamilton Gault, D.S.O.; to its Regimental Colours the Princess affixed a bronze laurel wreath in recognition of "heroic services in the Great War."

The wedding ceremony in Westminster Abbey on Feb. 27th was a national incident with an Imperial setting; the King and Queen and Queen Alexandra, with practically all the Royal family were present; the Duke of Connaught gave away his daughter who by her own expressed wish and with the King's authority, had relinquished her royal designation and the title of Princess and now became the Lady Patricia Ramsay. There were immense, cheering, crowds along the line of the Royal procession. Shortly afterwards it was announced that Commander Ramsay had been appointed Naval Attaché at Paris. Royal incidents of the year included the service in its early months of H.R.H. Prince Albert with the Headquarters Staff of the Canadians at Bonn, Germany; the death of Prince John, the delicate youngest son of their Majesties, at Sandringham on Jan. 18th, in his 14th year; the removal by the King's order of the Dukes of Albany and Cumberland from place and rank as Peers and Royal dukes of Great Britain because of military service with the German armies in the late War.

The King's Representative in Canada. The Duke of Devonshire as Governor-General in Canada, Sir Ronald C. Munro-Ferguson in Australia, the Earl of Liverpool in New Zealand, Lord Buxton in South Africa, remained during 1919 as the King's representatives in those Dominions. In Canada the Duke took a quiet but continuous interest in Canadian affairs, performed his conventional duties with dignity and his public work with personal interest and close attention. His speeches were straight-forward and to the point. To the Quebec Canadian Club on Jan. 28th he gave an explicit warning against Bolshevism "which requires dark and hidden places in which to flourish but, if taken in time and dealt with in the proper manner, can be uprooted." Elimination of slums was one means of meeting such evils. At Montreal on Feb. 10th His Excellency opened an Exhibition of British Naval Photographs and pointed out a war-fact which was often overlooked: "We have seen the magnificent response made when the call came. But splendid as that response was it would have been of no avail but for the might of the British Navy, which kept the seas open, and made it possible for these ships with their soldiers, munitions and supplies to safely reach their destination."

At a great banquet (Feb. 26th) in the Toronto Armouries given to 3,000 returned soldiers and their friends, the Governor-General was present, together with General Pau, one of the French heroes of the War. The key-note of his speech was: "We accomplished much during the time of war. We must do more in times of peace." On Mch. 7th the Duke was again in Montreal inspecting the General Hospital, the Knights of Columbus Hut, the University Settlement and the Montreal Association for the Blind; later he attended a dinner of the Mining Institute with the President, D. H. McDougall, in the chair and in his speech urged more attention to Research work and the development of Canada's natural resources. As to the rest: "I am an optimist. I have implicit faith in the inherent, sound common-sense of the citizens of the British Empire. We may do odd things sometimes; we may do the right thing in a very odd manner but we generally arrive at the right result."

Parliament had been opened, meanwhile, on Feb. 20th and on Mch. 30th the Women's Canadian Club at Ottawa was addressed at some length; in Montreal on May 2-3 His Excellency opened a new Khaki Club organized by the Khaki League of which G. F. Benson was President and with the simple, accurate statement that: "The returned soldier is a man and wants to be treated as such. He does not want to be petted, patronized or ordered. He wants to settle down once more as a citizen, doing his duty in that capacity as he did when a soldier." On May 13th the Duke was in Toronto attending a Red Cross meeting and for the purpose of conferring certain War decorations. Following the Summer season came a visit to the West. He was in Winnipeg on Sept. 11th and on the 12th visited Selkirk with a tribute in his speech to the Peace Treaty and the work of Canadian statesmen at the Conference: "Their participation in the arranging of the Peace terms means that Canada is recognized as a nation in herself. This does not involve any abrogation of the duties of Canada as a self-governing Dominion of the Crown. Canada has a duty to fulfill toward the Empire in taking part in great Imperial questions though with a complete and absolute control over her own affairs."

The Duke, who was accompanied by the Duchess with Lady Dorothy Cavendish and suite, was welcomed at Swan River, Man., on the 13th and visited, by motor-car, the wheat fields of the district; later he went to The Pas, in the newly-developed North of the Province; on the 16th, after calling at other places, he was given a public reception at Prince Albert, Sask., and on the following day was in Saskatoon where he visited the University and other institutions. At Edmonton on Sept. 19th a long and varied programme was provided and a rousing welcome given; New Westminster, B.C., was reached on Sept. 30th after some intervening points had been visited, and Victoria on Oct. 1st. Many functions were attended and institutions visited in this capital with an address to the Canadian Club on the 2nd. On this occasion His Excellency made the following statement: "Canadians must not forget that the Act of Confederation, which made Canada one and united, is the foundation upon which every self-governing Dominion of the Crown has been built up. The laws of South Africa, Australia and other dependencies may differ in many details, but in fundamental principles the Act of Confederation is the foundation of the Empire as we know it to-day."

Following this came a visit to the Courtenay Soldiers' Settlement, to Duncan and Nanaimo—all on Vancouver Island—and with all kinds of addresses from various public organizations. The Fruit-growing region of the Mainland was then visited with a warm welcome at Vernon and other points. The Vice-regal party was at Calgary on Oct. 22nd and the Duke addressed the Canadian Club and the Women's Canadian Club at Luncheon and told them, amidst applause, that "the strongest institution of our Empire is the British throne"—illustrated by the Prince of Wales' tour. Incidentally, after an investiture of soldiers at the Armouries, the Duke presented to Miss Dolores Von Apalup the gold medals of the Royal College of Music and the Royal Academy of Music—said to be the first Canadian student to pass this double examination of two famous British Institutions. As at many other places during the tour the Duchess of Devonshire held a reception and was specially entertained in other ways.

Regina was reached on the 24th and the donation by His Excellency announced of 27 bronze medals for competition in the schools of Saskatchewan; many duties were performed and formal visits and receptions were attended and what had become the usual Canadian Club speech delivered. A strong point was made as follows: "The British is a non-military nation and the policy of 'peaceful penetration' has been the dominant factor determining the spread of Empire to the remotest corners of the globe. In pursuing this policy the British have always taken with them the great traditions of British liberty and justice, and it is largely a result of this policy that, when other dynasties are crashing to the ground, British loyalty is being more firmly entrenched in every portion of the Empire." He urged greater attention in popular and legislative ways to Public Health and, as in other addresses, dealt with the importance of the Victory Loan and its success. Back at Ottawa, on Oct. 27th, the Duke subscribed to $10,000 worth of bonds.

A Red Cross branch was opened in Toronto by His Excellency on Nov. 11th, on the 12th he was the guest of the local Canadian

Club and a little later presented Toronto with a Prince of Wales Honour Flag for reaching its Victory Loan objective of $90,000,-000; he was at Halifax on the 24th to bid farewell to the Prince of Wales. Meanwhile, some personal incidents had included the sale in London of the famous Picadilly residence of his family—Devonshire House—at a price said to be $3,750,000; the marriage of Lady Blanche Cavendish on Apr. 30th, in London, to Capt. J. M. Cobbold of the Scots Guards; the return to Canada in June of the Duchess, after some months spent in England.

Lord Milner and the Dominions. It was, perhaps, characteristic of the broad-mindedness of British public life that in the British elections at the close of 1917 so many Colonial-born candidates were elected to Parliament. Canada was particularly well represented in Rt. Hon. A. Bonar Law, the Conservative leader, and Lawrence Lyon, Coalition-Unionist, who was elected for Hastings by 7,000 majority; Lieut.-Col. W. Grant Morden, Coalition-Unionist, elected for Brentford by 9,677 to 2,620 and Donald Macmaster, K.C., (C.U.) in Chertsey by over 9,000 majority; Dr. T. J. Macnamara and Ian Malcolm, both well-known politicians; Major J. E. Molson in Gainsborough (C.U.) by 2,000 majority and Sir Hamar Greenwood, K.C., Coalition-Liberal, in Sunderland by 27,-646 to 9,678; Lieut.-Col. C. W. Weldon McLean, C.M.G., D.S.O. and 2 Bars as Member for Lincolnshire. Australia was represented by four members including Sir Newton Moore, an ex-State Premier and Agent-General.

This uncriticized admission to Parliament of Overseas members was a part of the point of view which never seemed to fear interference with a self-government too deeply rooted in past freedom to be affected by any extraneous influences. Such incidents as the permanent representation of South Africa in the War Cabinet through General Smuts and his speeches leading Britain along certain lines of League of Nations policy, or the free hand given Mr. Premier Hughes of Australia in advocating Protective duties and Imperial preference, also illustrated this condition of thought. In July Sir Hamar Greenwood, who had won his spurs in English public life, was appointed an Under-Secretary for Foreign Affairs and additional Parliamentary Secretary to the Board of Trade with charge of the new Department of Overseas Trade.

The latter appointment was, no doubt, due to Lord Milner, who had for some months previously been Secretary of State for the Colonies. He made some notable speeches during this year and continued to hold one of the high places in British public life. Curiously enough he had a reputation in Canada, amongst those who believed in closer Imperial relations as perhaps the most sane, moderate and constructive of the advocates of that policy; the opposing section in Canada criticized him as the ablest of the reactionary forces. His opinions were expressed, in part, to the *Sunday Express* of London on Mch. 30th with the declaration that: "In every administrative act we must think of the Dominions as friends and relations. The British Empire is not a Delian League. We are free and equal members of the community, and while we have no hostility to friendly and foreign nations, still we will give the preference in all things to our own family." He welcomed the initiation of Preference in tariff matters and thought the principle should be extended to Emigration, Shipping, Cables, Wireless systems and Finance.

A Committee of the British Cabinet should, he added, be created to deal specially with Imperial issues and the Foreign policy of the Empire and be open to statesmen of the Dominions as had been the Imperial War Cabinet. When the Prime Ministers could not be present they might send prominent members of their own Governments to act for them. In an address on July 9th to a group of Overseas representatives he stated that: "The only possibility of a continuance of the British Empire is on a basis of absolute out-and-out equal partnership between the United Kingdom and the Dominions. I say that without any kind of reservation whatsoever. It is very easy to say that; but undoubtedly the working out of it in practice without bringing about the severance of relations between us and the Dominions will be one of the most complicated tasks which statesmanship has ever had to face." The Dominions would have to be represented in Foreign Conferences but they would, he pointed out, be always more or less up against the same opposition as was presented by Foreign leaders at Versailles: "Well, how do we stand? What are you? If these Dominions are independent nations, well and good. But you ask us to welcome them as British Dominions. They are part and parcel of you. If they are to be separately represented, that is merely a dodge of yours, for doubling, trebling, and quadrupling your own representation!"

It is quite certain that in the future the British Dominions will be independently represented in international affairs, and it is also quite certain—at least, I hope so—that inasmuch as they regard themselves as closely allied with us as members of a permanent political alliance which we call the British Empire, nothing that foreign nations can say or any criticisms they can offer can alter that. It is certain, I think, that if in International Conference treaties of the future the British Dominions appear as separate members, foreign countries will have to accept the position that that does not prevent them from remaining in a separate, distinct, and intimate relationship of their own with the United Kingdom. We have to realize the two things, that they may be members of the League of Nations side by side with the United Kingdom, and at the same time that they have a right to be, as they intend to be, members of a British League of Nations inside the Empire.

Writing on Sept. 15th to *The Future*, an official London publication, Lord Milner emphasized a preceding point: "The United Kingdom and the Dominions are partner nations, not yet, indeed, of equal power, but for good and all of equal status. It is the paramount duty of British statesmanship to see that the free union between them and us which has been so gloriously maintained during the War shall be continued and strengthened in the years to come." At Toronto on Sept. 18th Lord Finlay of Nairn, formerly Lord

Chancellor, doubted the possibility of an Imperial Parliament and rather supported the suggestion of Lord Milner: "I feel that we should rather seek to draw the bonds tighter by developing the functions of the Imperial Cabinet which played so important a rôle during the War. An Imperial Cabinet is admirably adapted for the consideration of the problems which affect the Empire as a whole or in part."

Speaking to the Empire Parliamentary Association on Dec. 15th the Rt. Hon. A. J. Balfour referred to the glorious memories and common partnership of the War and to the inevitable reactions following such a prodigious strain: "The difficulty which has constantly been present to the statesmen both in the Dominions and at home for a generation or more is still with us—the difficulty of finding some organization which shall increase unity of action and unity of sentiment and shall not interfere with the absolute autonomy of the great constitutional elements of this community of nations." Incident to this free recognition of the Dominions and readiness to admit them to National equality in the Empire was the appointment of their representatives on the Committees of the Peace Conference—positions highly prized and greatly desired by many British public servants well fitted for the duties. Amongst them were the following:

Commission on Responsibility of the Authors of the War	Rt. Hon. W. F. Massey	New Zealand
Committee on Reparation	Rt. Hon. W. M. Hughes	Australia
Commission on Polish Affairs	Rt. Hon. Louis Botha	South Africa
International Economic Commission	Rt.-Hon. Sir Geo. E. Foster	Canada
International Control of Ports, Waterways and Railways	Hon. A. L. Sifton	Canada
Sub-Committee on Pre-War Contracts	Hon. C. J. Doherty	Canada
Commission on Boundaries of Greece	Rt. Hon. Sir Robert Borden	Canada

Discussion of Canada's National Status. This problem was widely discussed during the year and notably so in respect to the Peace Conference and League of Nations; Sir Robert Borden and various leaders in the external Empire, with Lord Milner and many British leaders, took the view that nationality and Empire were quite compatible; Nationalists who wanted separation rejoiced in the idea that nations within an Empire must soon disintegrate, just as in earlier days Dr. Goldwin Smith and his colleagues in thought had everywhere agreed that Colonies became like ripened fruit which must inevitably drop from the parent stem; rival nations, or foreign critics, or enemies of the Empire, hoped to enter all kinds of diplomatic wedges and to encourage jealousies or rivalries amongst the Dominions and the United Kingdom at Versailles and elsewhere; President Wilson's "self-determination" for small nations promised to such interests the creation of serious trouble in India, Egypt, Ireland and South Africa but, as with some of the expectations of the Kaiser, many were doomed to disappointment.

A possibility of continued diplomatic friction under League of Nations' action was premised in certain United States interpretations of the League and notably, perhaps, in the President's address to his people on June 28th when he described it as creating a new order: "Under it backward nations—populations which have not yet come to political consciousness and peoples who are ready for independence but not quite prepared to dispense with protection and guidance—shall no more be subjected to the domination and exploitation of a stronger nation, but shall be put under the friendly direction and afforded the helpful assistance of Governments which undertake to be responsible to the opinion of mankind in the execution of their task by accepting the direction of the League of Nations." If the League of Nations should really undertake to adjudicate upon the rights and readiness of peoples to repudiate their allegiance or national associations or to deal, as this document intimated, with "the rights of minorities and the sanctity of religious beliefs and practices" there was no limit to the possibilities of trouble. But the British and Dominion leaders did not seem to fear these conditions and they hoped to make the League a sane organ of international peace and not an instrument of disorder, disintegration and conflict. In any case, as W. M. Hughes of Australia, put it at Melbourne on Sept. 9th: "Whatever becomes of the League of Nations, the League of the British Empire will never perish."

The Canadian Premier's views of Canada's position at Versailles and after, has been treated elsewhere and he stated in Parliament on Sept. 2nd that the situation would be further dealt with in a great Imperial Conference: "The future relationship of the nations of the Empire must be determined in accordance with the will of the Mother Country and of each Dominion at a constitutional Conference to be summoned in the not distant future. Undoubtedly it will be based upon equality of nationhood. Each nation must preserve unimpaired its absolute autonomy, but it must likewise have its voice as to those external relations which involve the issue of peace or of war." Like Lord Milner, L. S. Amery, M.P., an Under-Secretary for the Colonies, fully recognized this condition and at a Canadian dinner in London on July 1st said: "Canada has now entered upon her future as a nation, with her national status clear to all the world. She has also entered, as a co-partner with Britain, in the great responsibility of Empire. She shares our responsibility for the maintenance of that sea power without which the Empire can not exist for a moment. In all things necessary Canada is now prepared to take up her share to fit herself for the true partnership of Empire."

In the Canadian Parliament on Sept. 9th the Hon. N. W. Rowell dealt with the Empire part of the problem as follows: "I say the position of Canada is wonderfully advanced over the old position. We are recognized now as a nation of equal status with the Mother Country and other Dominions. The Constitutional Conference must work out the details. They are not easy to work out and will be fraught with the greatest difficulty. No one should minimize the difficulties of the situation. There is no parallel for an Empire like this of self-governing nations seeking to work together. It is the greatest experiment in democratic Government that the world has ever seen. But I believe a solution will be found." The Hon. C. J. Doherty on the 11th dealt with the subject from a constitutional standpoint: "The British Empire is composed of different countries living together under one King and all these countries have unanimously and repeatedly recognized the fact that they—I am speaking now of the self-governing Dominions of the United Kingdom—constitute a group of nations which group of nations is the British Empire."

In other directions the discussion proceeded from various standpoints. There was now no party Government in Dominion affairs but the Conservatives in tradition, speech and platform, were usually looked upon as identified more or less with policies of Imperial union—though the Liberals had put into effect such practical proposals as the Laurier preferential tariff. The former party up to 1919 had never had a Convention of the kind which the Liberals called in this year and which took straight issue (on Aug. 6th) against what Imperialism was said to be in the following Resolution: "We are strongly opposed to any attempt to centralized Imperial control and are of the opinion that no organic change in the Canadian constitution in regard to the relation of Canada to the Empire ought to come into effect until after being passed by Parliament, and after it has been ratified by vote of the Canadian people in a Referendum." The Farmers' platform as published by the Canadian Council of Agriculture earlier in the year included the following reference to this subject:

We believe that the further development of the British Empire should be sought along the lines of partnership between nations free and equal, under the present governmental system of British constitutional authority. We are strongly opposed to any attempt to centralize Imperial control. Any attempt to set up an independent authority with power to bind the Dominions, whether this authority be termed Parliament, Council or Cabinet, would hamper the growth of responsible and informed democracy in the Dominions.

Outside of these specific organizations, public opinion did not express itself very coherently on these issues except that all the larger societies in English-speaking Canada—the I.O.D.E., the Orange Order, the Navy League, for instance—had a tendency to advocate closer Imperial unity. The press was British in its general desire to retain the Imperial connection; it was not as a rule constructively Imperialistic. A few journals were actively opposed to any policy of an Empire nature and like Sinn Fein, wanted "ourselves alone." Mixing and merging with these aspirations and shades or divergencies of feeling and view was the often dormant but at times irrepressible, element of sentiment. It had carried an Election in 1891, it sprang into being again in 1899, it struck fire into the people in 1914. Perhaps an interchange of thought with General Botha, described by Mr. Premier Hughes of Australia in a speech at Brisbane—*Daily Mail,* Oct. 26th—indicated most fully what is meant. General Botha was stated to have said to Mr. Hughes in conversation: "If you call to us across the ocean, we shall come to you. We look upon you as the outpost of the Empire. You stand between us and that outer world of thousands of millions which hems us about. If you fall, we fall; if we call you, we know you will come." To this the Australian Premier replied amidst tremendous cheers from his audience: "So it is with New Zealand and Australia. Those who touch us, touch Canada. Those who touch Britain, touch us." As a keen analysis of the new status attained by Canada in this year, and which was not always clearly understood by its own people, the following from a pamphlet by an American publicist, Dr. George Burton Adams, may be quoted:

> It must be carefully observed that the independence of a sovereign state is not proposed for the members of the British Empire. It is not necessary that they should have the power to make treaties opposed to the rest of the Empire or to make separate war and peace. All that is implied is independ- ence within the Commonwealth, which means no more for each than a posi- tion of exact equality in such questions with every other member of the Commonwealth. Two things appear indispensable to such an independence: One is an equal share, an effective voice and proportional determining in- fluence in all decisions which settle the policy of the Commonwealth; the other is security that when treaties and other relations with foreign states concern one member, exclusively, that member shall have the final voice, not of course in disregard of the other members but as the judge of last resort. So much independence as this last has already been practically con- ceded in some cases, as between Canada and the United States for example, but it should be made universal and constitutional. This is the kind of independence which already exists in regard to internal questions, and no revolutionary change is demanded to put the Empire as it now exists upon this basis in foreign affairs.

Judicial Committee of the Privy Council. There had for years been a small body of determined opinion in Canada against the continuance of Appeals to the Privy Council; they were aggres- sive and their antagonism was shown whenever questions of British relationship were under discussion; the great body of public opin- ion, as usual in such cases, was inert though not favourable to any action in the premises. There were several large issues involved— one was the advantage to the Provinces in cases of inter-Provincial dispute, or questions of constitutional interpretation or contro- versies with the Dominion, of having an absolutely impartial, able and respected body of jurists to deal with this subject; another, in large financial or corporate matters, was the value of an extraneous and eminently learned opinion upon points which might easily in- volve local prejudices; still another was the impartial or aloof attitude of mind essential to the proper construction of Canada's constitution or British North America Act. There was involved, also, the fundamental right of British subjects everywhere to go to the foot of the Throne, to appeal to the King as a last resort; and the Judicial Committee formulated its judgments as laid before and approved by the King. The Members of the Committee usually attending Sessions were the Lord Chancellor, the Lords of

Appeal and such members of the King's Privy Council as had held judicial office. The Lord President of the Council was *ex officio* a member with preceding holders of that office but did not usually sit; in appeals from Dominion Courts four Judges were a quorum. The members, or available members in 1919, were as follows:

Lord Birkenhead	Lord High Chancellor
Lord Atkinson	Lord of Appeal
Lord Wrensbury	Lord of Appeal
Lord Shaw	Lord of Appeal
Lord Dunedin	Lord of Appeal
Lord Moulton	Lord of Appeal
Lord Sumner	Lord of Appeal
The Earl of Halsbury	Ex-Lord Chancellor
Viscount Haldane, O.M.	Ex-Lord Chancellor
Lord Buckmaster	Ex-Lord Chancellor
Viscount Finlay of Nairn	Ex-Lord Chancellor
The Earl of Loreburn	Ex-Lord Chancellor
Lord Kinnear; Lord O'Brien	Great Britain
Viscount Mersey; Lord Parmoor	Great Britain
Rt. Hon. Sir Samuel J. Way	Australia
Rt. Hon. Sir S. W. Griffith	Australia
Rt. Hon. Sir Edmund Barton	Australia
Rt. Hon. Syed Ameer Ali	India
Rt. Hon. Sir John Edge	India
Rt. Hon. Sir L. H. Jenkins	India
Rt. Hon. Sir J. Rose-Innes	South Africa
Rt. Hon. Sir Charles Fitzpatrick	Canada
Lord Strathclyde	Scotch Court of Session

As with the Panels of the Peace Conference, the Judges did not all sit together at any one time but they constituted a Court of the greatest legal minds and jurists of the Empire and all were available from time to time. As a rule Canadian Judges were not hostile to the continuance of this Appeal and they recognized in their judgments the value of the reference. An exception in 1919 was the Hon. Archer Martin of the British Columbia Court of Appeal who, on May 5th, stated in a legal decision that: "When our sons have shown that Canada is fit to cope with any nation in the world on the field of war, certainly the fathers of these sons who have been at the front ought to, at least, be able to cope with all competitors in the field of jurisprudence. Surely our intellectual development has not been arrested. We ought to be able to dispose of these matters." J. S. Ewart, K.C., an able lawyer and advocate of separated Nationalism for Canada, never lost an opportunity of advocacy along similar lines; the Manitoba *Free Press* (Sept. 24th) while admitting the services rendered to Canada in a long series of past constitutional cases, urged abolition of the appeal on the ground of (1) interference with national status; (2) weakening the position of the Supreme Court of Canada; (3) distrust of its competency to interpret Canadian-made commercial and corporation law.

To such contentions *Canada*, a London journal, had on Aug. 30th replied as follows: "The Common Law in Canada is imported from the Old Country, and when their own Judges differ in their interpretation surely the obvious and sensible thing is to go for the final interpretation to the highest and most respected Court of Appeal in the world, which is that of the Privy Council? Moreover the cost of the maintenance of this most learned and impartial tribunal is borne entirely by the Mother Country, where British law originated.'' When Lord Finlay of Nairn was in Toronto on Sept. 18th he spoke at length on this subject:

We have in the Privy Council Appeal an institution which is, I believe, valued greatly by the mercantile community as well as by many others in Canada. And in retaining it, you have the satisfaction of knowing that there is brought to bear on the adjudication of your cases a knowledge and experience which is accumulated through the settlement of analogous cases from all parts of the Empire. There is thus a breadth of view acquired by the Judicial Committee of the Privy Council which ensures most thorough efficiency for the tribunal. I, however, believe that its efficiency might still be improved and I should welcome the presence of Canadian Judges on the spot, who have special knowledge and experience of their own affairs. The independence of the Privy Council has been authoritatively asserted in the numerous prize cases which have been brought before it during the War, and the independence displayed in these cases is characteristic of its detached attitude in all cases. The Privy Council is not the tool of any party in power and is not subject to the dictation or influence of the Executive as is the case with the Supreme Courts in some other countries.

During 1919 a large number of important cases went from Canada as well as from other parts of the Empire—illustrated by the 21 appeals from India before the Judicial Committee in November. The Initiative and Referendum Act of Manitoba was on July 3rd declared *ultra vires* and unconstitutional and, in a London *Times* review of this decision as to legislation which might, in itself, be good or bad but which undoubtedly took away powers from the Provincial Legislature which had been granted by the B.N.A. Act that journal drew attention to the fact that the Act purported to give the electorate authority to initiate and sanction legislation without reference to the Legislature or to the Lieut.-Governor, the King's representative in the Province, and then proceeded as follows: ''It did this by ignoring the Lieut.-Governor's right of veto, and through him the right of veto of the King. That, the Judicial Committee has now decided, is unconstitutional, because the Act of 1867 embodies the normal British practice of requiring assent, both of Sovereign and of Legislature, before an Act can become law of the land.''

Both in this appeal and in another as to Divorce the Judicial Committee expressed regret that the appeals had not been first argued before the Supreme Court of Canada. It was, their Lordships stated, desirable that subjects affecting the constitution of Canada should go to Ottawa before appeal to London; they attached much importance to the experience and learning of the Judges in that Court. The judgment as to Divorce (Walker *vs.* Walker) decided that the English Act of 1857, in this respect, was part of the substantive law of Manitoba and that the Province could therefore establish a Divorce Court if it wished. Another important judgment was that affecting the Ontario Separate School question and discussing the appeal from a judgment of the Appeal Court of Ontario. The following table, though not complete, illustrates the varied nature and importance of the 1919 Canadian cases before this Empire Court:

Cause	Subject
Montreal Tramways Company vs. Robinson	Action for damages in respect of the death of the Respondent's husband.
Quebec Railway, Light, Heat and Power Co., Ltd, vs. Vandry and others	Claims in respect of damage by fire alleged to have been caused through defective plant.
Montreal Tramways Co. vs. Savignac	Personal injuries; Workmen's Compensation Act.
Toronto Railway Co. vs. The Corporation of the City of Toronto	Liability of Appelants to contribute to cost of high level bridge; powers of Railway Board; competency of Railway Act, 1903.
Toronto Railway Co. vs. The Corporation of the City of Toronto	Questions of liability for the cost of removing snow.
Taylor vs. Davies and others	Alleged fraudulent conveyance.
Toronto Railway Co. vs. The Corporation of the City of Toronto	Inadequate service of street cars; imposition of penalty by Ontario Railway and Municipal Board.
Emerson-Brantingham Implement Company vs. Schofield	Sale of a gas traction engine; alleged breach of warranty.
Montreal Tramways Company vs. McAllister	Personal injury.
Canadian Pacific Railway Company, owners of Princess Sophia vs. Relatives of crew lost in foundering of the Steamer	Claimed that B.C. Workmen's Compensation Board had no jurisdiction as disaster was in Foreign waters; claimed that Merchant Shipping Act should rule terms of compensation.

Empire Incidents of the Year. Events and conditions of importance to Canada—sometimes indirectly so and sometimes so because of their bearing on the future—were many in Great Britain during 1919. One was the appointment of a Federal Devolution Commission to deal with the proposed establishment of separate Legislatures in the United Kingdom or, as it was officially called "a Scheme of Legislative and Administrative Devolution." The Speaker of the Commons—Rt. Hon. J. W. Lowther—was Chairman with 16 other members of that House and 16 Peers as members of the Commission. The former did not include any of the party leaders and was evidently intended to be a working body—Donald Macmaster, K.C., lately of Canada, was one of the list. The Peers were in many cases very well known and included Lord Charnwood, Lord Faringdon, Lord Gladstone, Lord Inchcape and Lord Harcourt. The terms of reference stipulated that the Commission should have regard to:

1. The need of reserving to the Imperial Parliament the exclusive consideration of (a) Foreign and Imperial affairs; and (b) subjects affecting the United Kingdom as a whole.

2. The allocation of financial powers as between the Imperial Parliament and the subordinate Legislatures, special consideration being given to the need of providing for the effective administration of the allocated powers.

3. The special needs and characteristics of the component portions of the United Kingdom in which subordinate Legislatures are set up.

The participation of Lord Beaverbrook in public affairs continued in 1919 to be a factor though not in the wider spheres of Imperial administration. His energy seemed to be only limited by health conditions and his movements were generally of a nature interesting to the Canada of his early fortunes. After spending the first months of the year at Paris and on the Continent, he was in Montreal, in the middle of June, when the *Financial Times* published a record of his financial exploits in Canada as W. Max Aitken when founding the Royal Securities Corporation at Halifax— which he afterwards removed to Montreal: "With the removal to Montreal, and the subsequent bringing into the group of a number of industrial leaders of this Province and Ontario, the field was much expanded and the Corporation undertook some of the most spectacular, and as the event has proved, well-conceived of the big industrial combinations of the period. Among these was one which, with the exception of the Laurentide enterprise, was the first public Pulp and Paper flotation in Canada, namely Price Bros. & Company, Limited."

The various Beaverbrook corporations organized in Canada during this period were, in 1919, employing tens of thousands of men and paying out millions of dollars in wages. A considerable proportion of the securities thus issued were sold in England, and had, practically without exception, earned good returns for their purchasers and won financial reputation for Canada abroad. Besides the Price Company these concerns included the Canadian Car and Foundry, the Steel Company of Canada and the Canada Cement—a combination whose assets were valued at 141 millions. It was Lord Beaverbrook's success in these financial matters that paved the way for his success in England. During his 1919 visit to Canada he was in New Brunswick for a time and announced a gift of 5 Scholarships for his native Province, to be available at any Canadian University, in Arts, Theology, Law, Medicine or Civil Engineering—with a deposit of $25,000 in the Montreal Trust Company for the purpose. At the village of Beaver Brook, from which he had taken his title, a handsome school was erected during the year by Lord Beaverbrook.

In London on Aug. 6th as organizer of the successful and most valuable Canadian War Records Department, he gave a farewell dinner to the Staff with Sir Edward Kemp, Sir H. Greenwood, Percy Hurd and other guests present. Mr. Hurd and others spoke of the host's tireless leadership in the work of providing cinematograph photographs, paintings and permanent memorials of Canada's share in the War. In November it was announced that Lord Beaverbrook had joined the Board of the Provincial Cinema Theatres Co., and the *Daily Sketch* stated that this also involved the purchase of its ordinary stock shares for $2,000,000 with control of 35 theatres and the largest single film business in the country.

In this connection Lord Beaverbrook was responsible for a bit of patriotic policy. He had become, in 1917, Chairman of the War Office Cinematograph Committee with Sir Reginald Brade representing the War Office and Sir William Jury providing the technical knowledge and experience. They obtained films on the different War fronts of inestimable historic value and those relating to the Canadian Corps were transferred to the Dominion Government; the others were shown throughout England and realized profits in the second year (1919) of $350,000 which were distributed amongst British War charities, with $50,000 to Canada and $25,000 each to the other Dominions and India.

A personal development, interesting to Canadians in another way, was the talk of 1918 in New York, which was transferred to Canada, regarding the Marquess and Marchioness of Aberdeen. The position of the former as a popular one-time Governor-General and of the Marchioness as Advisory President of the National Council of Women, made the subject important. For some years they had been collecting money in the United States for certain Irish charities, travelling at their own expense and turning over a total of over $100,000 to the Funds concerned. It would appear that Lady Aberdeen offended certain interests by refusing to appear on a charity performance platform with the notorious Evelyn Thaw while the extreme Irish element in New York also found that they could not use the Aberdeens for their purposes. Charges of irregularity in respect to Irish charity moneys were laid against them by the District Attorney's office and it was not until Jan. 9th, 1919, that a statement of complete exoneration was issued. A little later it was announced that Lord Aberdeen had sold the greater part (about 50,000 acres) of his famous estates in Aberdeenshire with a sale condition attached which ensured opportunity to the tenants to become owners of holdings numbering 660 with a gross rental of $140,000. Lord Aberdeen retained Haddo House and 13,000 acres; in British Columbia his fruit farms were also disposed of under special conditions.

Other incidents of the year included the continued prosperity of the Royal Colonial Institute—which for 50 years had greatly aided in making Canada and other British countries known in Britain and abroad—with the announcement of 13,733 members and a most successful year under the presidency of the Duke of Connaught; the celebration of Dominion Day in London by an impressive ceremony in dedication of a Memorial window at Westminster Abbey to the late Lord Strathcona and Mount Royal who was described in the tablet underneath as "a great Canadian Imperialist and Philanthropist"—the Committee in charge of funds, etc., including H. H. Asquith, A. Bonar Law, Lord Northcliffe, Lord Aberdeen and Lord Pirrie, with J. G. Colmer, C.M.G., as Hon. Secretary; the plan proposed on behalf of the Australian Government by Hon. W. A. Watt, Treasurer and Acting Prime Minister, for the administration, conversion and extinction of the War debts of the British Empire—estimated at £7,350,000,000—by a principle

6

of pooling the strength of the various States with joint management and liquidation through a Joint Commission of Experts.

An important appointment was that of Sir George E. Foster to represent Canada on the Imperial Investigation Board created by the Crown, upon recommendation of the Imperial War Conference, for the purpose of reviewing questions relating to maritime transport and to the development of the sea communications of the Empire and, with one representative each, from the Colonial Office, India Office, Board of Trade, Canada, Australia, New Zealand, South Africa and Newfoundland. On Sept. 17th the British Overseas Bank was opened in London with £2,000,000 paid-up capital and 8 Banks represented in its formation covering England, Canada, Scotland, Ireland, South America and the East, with $900,000,000 of Assets, as follows: Union Bank of Scotland Ltd., Wm. Deacon's Bank Ltd., Anglo-South American Bank Ltd., Glyn, Mills, Currie & Co., Northern Banking Co. Ltd., Belfast, Imperial Ottoman Bank, Hoare's Bank and The Dominion Bank, Canada. Viscount Churchill, G.C.V.O. was Governor and S. L. Jones, London Manager of the Dominion Bank, was on the Governing Council. Mr. Jones, in an interview on this date, described the new organization as, in part, a corollary to the British bank amalgamations which had produced out of a number of small banks, some of them centuries old, five gigantic corporations, each with enormous resources and headquarters in the City of London.

Following the Conference of 1918 an Imperial Mineral Resources Bureau was organized in 1919 to (1) collect, co-ordinate, and disseminate information about resources, production, treatment, consumption, and requirements of every mineral and metal of economic value within the Empire; (2) to ascertain the scope of the existing agencies, with a view ultimately to avoid any unnecessary overlapping which might prevail; (3) to devise improvement in methods of these agencies and to supplement their work so as to obtain additional information; (4) to advise on the development of the Mineral resources of the Empire, or of particular parts of it so that such resources might be made available for Imperial defence or industry. A Royal Charter of Incorporation was arranged with the Lord President of the Council as President and Sir Richard Redmayne, K.C.B., as Chairman. The following nominations for membership were made:

The Canadian Government ....Dr. Willet G. Miller
Commonwealth of Australia ....W. S. Robins
Dominion of New Zealand ....Thomas Hutchinson Hamer
Union of South Africa ....Rt. Hon. W. P. Schreiner, C.M.G.
Dominion of Newfoundland ....Rt. Hon. Lord Morris, K.C.M.G.
Empire of India ....R. D. Oldham, F.R.S.
The Secretary for the Colonies ......J. Evans, D.SC.
The British Minister of ReconstructionW. Forster Brown
    "   "   Prof. H. C. H. Carpenter
    "   "   Dr. F. H. Hatch
    "   "   Sir Lionel Phillips
    "   "   Edgar Taylor
The British Minister of Reconstruction Wallace Thorneycroft

Meanwhile, several military Committees were sitting in London. One, on Internal re-organization of the Army and Empire Forces and on which Maj.-Gen. J. H. McBrien represented Canada, dealt with conditions generally and, it was understood, favoured the Canadian plans as to Engineer organization, also a Divisional war strength of 12 Battalions with any future Dominion war contributions, if given, to be along the lines of completeness shown by the Canadian Corps organization in the late War. Another Committee was studying the wider problems of Imperial Defence as applied to future War conditions and a third one considered the question of exchanging officers between the Mother Country and the Dominions upon a larger scale than that already in operation as to India and Australia. In Canada, an interesting incident was the slow but sure development of hostility to the American films displayed in Picture Theatres all over the country which showed Americanized views of the War, of patriotism, of social and moral issues, with continuous presentation of the United States' flag and a complete indifference to the divergent opinions of Canada upon many matters treated.

Early in the year Messrs. J. and J. J. Allen, who controlled 25 of these theatres in Canada and had 6 more under construction and who had made vigourous efforts during the War to meet Canadian sentiment along these lines, announced the formation of a Company called British Films, Ltd., and issued a public statement that the concerns controlled by them would immediately curtail their importation of United States films from 20 to 30 per cent. in favour of British films which, it was said, could be laid down in Canada at one-third the cost of American films with, also, a 10 per cent. tariff advantage. It was said at this time, with truth, that the average Canadian was interested in the War in about this order: (1) Canada; (2) Britain; (3) other British countries; (4) Belgium; (5) France; (6) United States; (7) Italy, Japan, etc.; while the Films reaching the Canadians were in about this order: (1), (2), (3), (4), United States; (5) France; (6), Britain, (7) Italy, Japan, Canada, etc. Other corporations followed the lead of the Allens and a considerable change in the situation was expected.

A word must be added here as to some large figures in Empire life who were lost during the year and including the Rt. Hon. W. P. Schreiner, C.M.G., K.C., High Commissioner for South Africa in London and ex-Premier of Cape Colony who died on June 28th; the Rt. Hon. Sir John McCall, K.C.M.G., M.D., 10 years Agent-General for Tasmania in London, on June 28th; Lord Rayleigh, P.C., O.M., F.R.S., D.C.L., LL.D., the great physicist, on June 30th; the Rt. Hon. Sir William Macgregor, G.C.M.G., Governor, in turn, of Fiji, British New Guinea, Lagos, Newfoundland and Queensland, on July 3rd; Sir Edward H. Holden, Bart, M.P., Chairman of the London Joint City and Midland Bank, and a great financier, on July 23; Admiral Lord Beresford of Metemmeh, G.C.B., G.C.V.O., on Sept. 8th; Field Marshal Sir Evelyn Wood, G.C.B., G.C.M.G., V.C., on Dec. 2nd.

Eminent British Visitors to Canada. During 1919 there were a good many prominent visitors in the Dominion from the United Kingdom and other parts of the Empire who, in newspaper interviews, Canadian Club and other addresses, and in various informal ways, contributed to the growth of good feeling and knowledge. The Prince of Wales was, of course, first and foremost. Sir Arthur Pearson, the noted English publisher and blind philanthropist who, at St. Dunstan's, had built up an important institution for the blind, was in Toronto on Jan. 6th, at Montreal on the 10th, and at other centres. Viscount Finlay of Nairn, one-time Lord Chancellor, addressed the Canadian Bar Association at Winnipeg on Aug. 29 upon "Retaliation and the Indirect Blocade" and paid a special tribute to Lord Robert Cecil as Minister of Blocade and directing influence of this great force for victory; in Toronto he was accorded a Civic reception and addressed the Empire Club on Sept. 18; at Montreal he was banquetted by the local Bar Association on Sept. 25, addressed the Canadian Club on the 26th and later was entertained at Ottawa. Maj.-Gen. Sir R. S. S. Baden-Powell was another visitor in May with greetings from the Boy Scouts of Britain to those of Canada and congratulations on the winning of the War; he was entertained at Halifax and St. John.

Viscountess Rhondda, the brilliant daughter, heiress and business assistant of the late British Food Administrator, was in Toronto on Aug. 28th and then left for Winnipeg and a visit to the Peace River where she had inherited large interests and investments. Capt. Sir Bertram Hayes, K.B.E., D.S.O., of the *Olympic,* who had distinguished himself as a marine officer in the War was welcomed at Halifax and St. John and was given a cordial reception in Toronto on Oct. 8 and presented with a loving-cup in appreciation of 35,000 Toronto soldiers who had been carried across the Atlantic on board his famous Liner. Other visitors were Beckles Willson, Canadian writer in London who was in charge of a collection of Canadian Trophies for the future War Museum at Ottawa; Sir Harry Lauder, who toured Canada professionally, and was welcomed personally in many places and told a Montreal gathering on Jan. 9 that "the War was not won by the slackers or the shirkers, or the pacifists, or those whose religion wouldn't allow them to fight, but by plain men, real men—men who were men;" Sir Arthur Whitton Brown, the Atlantic flyer, who was at Montreal and Toronto in October, and Sir Harry Brittain, K.B.E., M.P., who was in Canada in November arranging for a 1920 Imperial Press Conference.

Maj.-Gen. Sir Frederick Robb, K.C.B., K.C.V.O., Military Secretary to the late Lord Kitchener; Sir Charles Eliot, lately British Commissioner in Siberia and Sir George Hunter, Chairman of the famous Swan-Hunter firm of Wallsend-on-Tyne; the Marquess of Anglesey, who visited his ranches at Walhachin, B.C. and Maj.-Gen. Sir P. G. and Lady Twining; Maj.-Gen. Sir Percy Girouard, K.C.M.G., D.S.O., who returned for a brief visit after many years' service in many British countries and Lieut.-Col. Sir Campbell Stuart, a Canadian who had recently been elected a Director of the London *Times;* Sir Alan Sykes, M.P., a one-time farmer of 20,000 acres in Saskatchewan and now a leading English financier; Lord Ashley, son and heir to the Earl of Shaftesbury, were other visitors of the year.

Sir Thomas Lipton paid Toronto a passing visit on May 23 and Maj.-Gen. Sir F. B. Maurice, K.C.B., lately Director-General of Military Operations, spoke in Toronto on Apr. 10. Lieut.-Gen. Sir Percy Lake, K.C.B., K.C.M.G., one-time Commander of the Canadian Militia and latterly of the British forces in Mesopotamia; Commander the Earl of Glasgow D.S.O., of the Royal Navy and Sir John Eardley-Wilmot, Bart.; Donald Macmaster, K.C., M.P., on a visit to his old home in Montreal and the Rt. Hon. J. H. Thomas, M.P., the British Labour leader, were also in parts of Canada. Another labour type (Ben. Tillett, M.P.) came during September and made several elaborate speeches of a bitterly pessimistic nature—notably at Hamilton on the 25th where he spoke as fraternal delegate from the British Trades Union Congress to that of Canada and in Toronto on Oct 23rd when he declared that: "During this war Capital has increased by leaps and bounds. It has watered its stock so that it contains more power than Niagara itself, and Labour must pay for this watered stock in tears and blood."

Dr. C. W. Saleeby, the English Sociologist, and Lord Leverhulme, the English capitalist and advocate of a six-hour day in two shifts; the Duke of Sutherland who had large interests in Alberta and British Columbia, and Percy Hurd, M.P., a well-known British journalist; F. A. McKenzie, a British war-correspondent and Sir James Ball, British Timber Controller; Thomas Naylor of the London *Daily Chronicle,* and Sir Charles Hanson, M.P., ex-Lord Mayor of London; Sir T. W. Grattan-Esmonde, Bart, ex-M.P., Sir Alfred Davies, K.B.E., C.B., Secretary of the Welsh Department of the Board of Education and Sir Arthur Newsholme, K.C.B., M.D., were other tourists of the time. An intended visitor, A. G. Gardiner, Editor of the Pacifist, anti-war and alleged pro-German London *Daily News,* was bitterly criticized by the Toronto *Telegram,* on Nov. 29—and the local Canadian Club, also, for inviting Mr. Gardiner to address it. He did not cross the border. Lord Jellicoe's important visit is referred to elsewhere.

The Imperial Preference Question and British Action. Sixteen years after Joseph Chamberlain initiated his campaign for an Imperial Preference Tariff in the United Kingdom it became, in part, a reality with his son as Chancellor of the Exchequer and a combination of parties to put it into operation. So far as the initiation of the principle was concerned, however, Canada under Sir Wilfrid Laurier had led the way, other British countries had followed and in 1919, when the British Government finally took action, the Tariffs of the Empire were as follows:

1. Commonwealth of Australia—The Tariffs Act No. 7 of 1908, as amended by Acts No. 39 of 1910, and of 1911, and by Resolution of the Commonwealth Parliament on Dec. 3, 1914, provided for preferential rates of duty on British goods, 5 to 10 per cent, *ad valorem* lower than the general rates of duty.

2. Dominion of New Zealand—Preferential treatment was accorded produce and manufactures of the British Empire under the Tariff Act No. 35 of 1908, as amended in 1915 by the imposition of additional duties of 10 per cent. *ad valorem* on certain goods not the produce or manufacture of some part of the British Dominions.

3. Union of South Africa—Preferential treatment was accorded under the Tariff Act No. 26 of 1914, as amended by Act 22 of 1915, by means of a rebate of import duty on certain British goods to the extent of 3 per cent, *ad valorem*, and in some instances rebates equivalent to one-fifth of the duty.

4. Rhodesia—Provision was made in the Customs Tariffs of Southern and Northern Rhodesia for the preferential treatment of British goods by according a rebate of duty upon certain articles the produce or manufacture of the United Kingdom.

5. Dominion of Canada—The Customs Act No. 11 of 1907 contained a British Preferential Tariff providing for special rates of duty on British goods, 5, 7½, 10 per cent. *ad valorem* lower than the general rates of duty. It was based upon the Act of June 13, 1898 under which a Preference was granted the United Kingdom of ¼ of the ordinary Tariff and raised to ⅓ by amendments of July 7, 1900.

6. Barbados, British Guiana, St. Lucia, Saint Vincent, Grenada, Leeward Islands, Trinidad and Tobago—Under the Canadian-West Indian Reciprocity Agreement of 1912, certain goods, the growth, produce, or manufacture of the United Kingdom, the Dominion of Canada and Newfoundland, were accorded preferential rates of duty when imported into the Colonies indicated, equivalent to a rebate of one-fifth of the general rates of duty.

The New British Policy of 1919. Several Imperial Conferences had expressed themselves favourable to this principle but in a rather academic way and so had various Empire Chambers of Commerce Congresses in much stronger terms; Mr. Chamberlain had staked his political life upon the principle and had, for the time being, lost.* It remained for the War to force tariffs upon the British mind as a necessity of revenue and a safeguard of national production, to remove something of the sacred aspect from Free-trade principles and to make them a matter of expediency rather than immutable law. The Imperial War Cabinet and the Imperial War Conference of 1917 decided that the time had come to initiate some kind of public action; Reports of Commissions containing Free traders and Protectionists agreed as to the necessity; Mr. Austen Chamberlain on Apr. 30, 1919, in presenting his Budget, outlined the Government's policy:

The range of our present Customs Duties is not wide, though it covers more articles than people are apt to suppose. Only three Colonial or British overseas products fall into the categories subject to duty at the present time or in any large quantity—namely, tea, cocoa, and rum; but there are many other dutiable articles which appear in our Customs returns from His Majesty's possessions overseas. I need name only such articles as coffee, sugar, tobacco, and wine. Though the beginning may be small, the measure of what I am inviting the Committee to do is not the amount of

*Note.—For particulars of the Joseph Chamberlain campaign see *The Canadian Annual Review* for 1903; for later details see the volumes of 1917-18.

British Imperial trade which secures preference at this moment, but the opportunities for the development of that trade, which I invite the Committees to open out. There is room for vast extension.

There never was a time when it was more important to the Empire as a whole, or to us in particular, that development should take place. From the small beginnings of to-day I hope that many Members of this House will live to see a really wide structure of inter-Imperial trade develop. In deciding on the form which Preference is to take I have had four main considerations before me. In the first place the Preference should be substantial in amount. In the next place the rates should as far as possible be few and simple. Thirdly, where there is an existing Excise duty corresponding to the Customs duty which is affected, the Excise duty must be proportionately altered. We cannot give preference at the expense of the home producer. Lastly, in carrying out this policy I have to remember the interests of our Allies and as far as practicable to avoid increasing duties on their products for the purpose of giving preference.

As to details there was to be (1) a preference of one-third on such manufactures as clocks, watches and parts, motor-cars and cycles, and pianos, phonographs and other musical instruments and parts; (2) a rate of one-sixth of the duty on consumable commodities, apart from alcohol, and including tea, cocoa, coffee, chicory, sugar, glucose, molasses, currants, dried fruits, tobacco and gasoline; (3) a rate of two-fifths on Moving Picture films and wine of 30 degrees proof, or under, with one-third on wine over 30 degrees proof: "The effect of the Preference proposal as a whole on revenue will be a reduction of about £2,500,000 in the current year, and something over £3,000,000 in the full year, and without allowing for any large increase in the imports of Colonial products. The great bulk will be in respect of the tea." Sept. 1st was the date set for the measure to be operative except as to tea which was fixed for June 2nd. Spirits were in a complicated situation: "For the purpose of the duties spirits are divided into five classes, all subject to Customs duty—rum, brandy, Geneva, and another spirit and home-made spirit, including whiskey. Over 80 per cent. of the rum comes from Empire sources. The imports from the Empire of other spirits are at present small, and, I think, likely to continue so, at any rate for a long time to come, though they are capable of some development. I propose to fix the rate of preference at 2s. 6d. per gallon, and to give this preference not by a reduction of the duty on Colonial spirits, but by an increase in the duty on Foreign spirits."

Opposition of British Free Trade Liberals. The attitude of the Liberal party—outside of Unionist ranks—was instantly antagonistic and Labour in the House was solidly opposed. Preferential duties were declared to be paving the way to Protection, they would ensure retaliation by foreign nations and notably Britain's Allies, they would result at once in United States capitalists setting up works in Canada to manufacture for the British market. In the Commons divisions were taken on the main points but defeated by majorities of over 200. At Newcastle-on-Tyne (May 17) Rt. Hon. H. H. Asquith gave four reasons for opposition: (1) It was an absolutely unjustifiable abandoqment of revenue; (2) it was absolutely illegitimate to use war taxes (which many of these duties had been) for the introduction of Preference; (3) the so-called Preference was a total sham as there was no advantage of any sort to the Dominions; (4) though trivial in themselves the proposals were intended as the pioneers of a fully planned system of Imperial Protection.

Mr. Asquith followed up this speech with a Free-trade campaign which commenced at Leeds on June 19 when he declared the time to be one of disquietude and the new policy merely a preliminary one which the utterances of Mr. Chamberlain, Sir Auckland Geddes and W. M. Hughes of Australia were taken to prove: "There never was a time when it more behooved Free Traders to be on their guard. First, because in the Budget, Preference—which means sooner or later, and which is intended to mean sooner rather than later, a Protectionist tariff—is stealthily making its way across the threshold of our fiscal citadel; secondly, because the impending reconsideration of the restrictions on our import trade will afford endless opportunities under various disguises and pretexts for the continuance in time of peace of a Protection which was undesigned, indirect, and avowedly temporary in time of war."

Much was said by Liberals as to the working of the old-time Preference in the protectionist days of 1840 when a Select Committee of Parliament reported conditions which make interesting reading, in their revived form, to any Canadian who may remember that the Annexationist movement and hard times of 1849 in British America were largely caused by the abrogation of the British Preferential duties. The Party literature summarized this 1840 Report as declaring (1) that the whole system of Preferenc was rotten to the core; (2) that it was a curse and a blight on the Colonies; (3) that it was an intolerable burden on the consumers and manufacturers in the United Kingdom; (4) that it imposed a ruinous restraint on British shipbuilding and shipping; (5) that it was a constant source of misunderstanding and disagreement between the different parts of the Empire. On the other hand, Sir Alfred Mond, a member of the Government and a keen Radical Free-trader of other days said on May 20: "As one who for many years was one of the leading protagonists in the fiscal controversy, and as one who has fought that battle without stint and with sincerity and strength, I am now charged with changing my faith because in the Finance Bill there is a movement for freer trade between us and the different parts of the Empire. How anyone can contend that a reduction of existing duties can be an infringement of the principle of Free trade quite passes my comprehension."

In Parliament on July 9 Wedgewood Benn (Lib.), moved to omit from the Finance Bill the Imperial Preference clause but was defeated by 273 to 56 and an amendment allowing the Government to extend the principle to Mandated States was approved. On July 23 the Liberals again opposed the third reading with an amendment declaring that the Government's policy "introduces Protection into the fiscal system of this country and initiates a system of Colonial Preference which must ultimately lead to the taxation of imports of food and raw material." It, also, was defeated by 221 to 50 after Mr. Chamberlain had stated that: "I believe the principle we establish that where there is a Duty there is to be Preference will be a permanent feature of our fiscal policy. I repeat what I said when I opened this debate: that if this Budget is referred to in the future with any words of praise or commendation, it will be because, for the first time, it established that principle by a legislative Act."

On Sept. 1st the War import restrictions were very largely suspended but a limited number of "unstable" key industries were scheduled for import prohibition except under license and payment of a license fee. They included dye-stuffs, synthetic drugs, optical glass, scientific instruments, certain fine chemicals and magnetos. This, also, was regarded by dissenting Liberals as a thin end of the Protection wedge. Sir Donald Maclean, the acting Leader, did not conceal his alarm and at Bradford on Nov. 14 said: "Speaking with all the sincerity I can summon, I say that those people who have deluded themselves into thinking that votes for a little Imperial Preference amounted to nothing have been giving away the principles of Free trade, and you have only got to watch the honest, out-spoken Tory Protectionists to know what has happened. They have won their first victory." So with the Anti-Dumping or Import Regulation Bill which constituted a Committee to regulate the importation of goods with a view to preventing dumping, safeguarding key industries and industries affected by the depreciation of a foreign currency, and assisting the revival of hop-growing; to regulate temporarily the exportation of certain goods, and to authorize the granting of credits and the undertaking of insurances for the purpose of re-establishing Overseas trade. Mr. Asquith described it at Birmingham on Nov. 28 as "a blow at the principle of Free-trade and at the freedom of trade in its largest and widest significance." This legislation was really all of a part; just so far as details or elements went in the direction of Protection it concerned the Empire as every item of Tariff extension was intended to involve a future preference to some Dominion or Imperial interest.

Empire Opinion of the Policy. Canadian readers of the newspapers found it difficult to follow this movement and as a rule despatches did not do very much to enlighten them. The general feeling was that a beneficial step had been made toward a real Preference but that the vital fiscal battle in Great Britain was still to come. The British Liberal fear of retaliation from Foreign countries was indirectly met by the Toronto *Globe* (Lib.) on Mch. 27: "Any effective preference granted British Dominions in the markets of the Motherland, involving free admission of goods, would probably bring about the adoption throughout the Empire of more effective return Tariff preferences than are now given to imports from Great Britain." The Montreal *Star* (Cons.) declared on Apr. 3rd that: "A preferential tariff throughout the Empire would be of great benefit to Canada. Many industries natural to this country would acquire a position of advantage in manufacturing for export to other British countries. This advantage would extend to raw materials required for British industries. Many branches of American factories have been established in Canada and the movement will be accentuated if an Imperial preferential system is established."

When the actual terms of the measure became known a good deal of satisfaction was expressed. Sir George Perley in London (May 3) thought it would give Canada an opportunity of supplying goods to Great Britain which had previously come from enemy countries; Mr. W. P. Schreiner, South African High Commissioner, declared that it would afford an opportunity for South African wines and spirits and would be productive of great mutual benefit and a strengthening of Empire relations. Sir Thomas Mackenzie, New Zealand High Commissioner, said that the policy was along the line of New Zealand aspirations and would enable the British people to negotiate with other nations on a more equitable basis. Rt. Hon. W. F. Massey, Premier of New Zealand, on May 7 described it as a modest but welcome installment and urged extension of the principle to inter-Empire communications and financial transactions. Sir George Foster, speaking at a dinner in London on May 5, expressed confidence that the British Parliament would accept this first step in a new business fraternity: "But it is not alone in tariffs, not perhaps in tariffs chiefly, that the spirit of Empire partnership can most forcibly be expressed." Co-ordination and co-operation were the watchwords of Empire trade.

Mr. Premier Hughes of Australia was not satisfied with the extent of the Preference and in several speeches during June presented a definite policy that would give all important Overseas industries a British preference and similar advantages to British manufacturing in Dominion markets. As to Mr. Massey's plea Mr. Chamberlain had on May 21 already clearly indicated his policy: "We intend to inform our whole policy by this principle of Preference, and where we have a control of Capital issues we have directed that a preference should be given to issues intended for the development of the Dominions and the overseas territories of His Majesty and, similarly, we have directed in contracts for purchases made outside the United Kingdom that a preference should be given to the products of His Majesty's Dominions." By the close of the year the Admiralty, Ministry of Munitions, War Office, India Office and Crown Agents for the Colonies had all stated their intention of considering Canadian tenders for all supplies purchased in future.

An evidence of this policy was shown by the Colonial Office award of a portion of an order for rolling stock for a Jamaica railway to a Canadian firm despite the protest of the Jamaican Government that the tender price was about $60,000 higher than that of the American competitors from whom the Government had proposed to obtain its requirements. The reply of Lord Milner to the representations of the Jamaican authorities was that it was desirable to promote trade within the Empire. A compromise was finally effected, with three locomotives and 30 cars bought from Canada, and the remainder from the United States. Lloyd Harris, Canadian Trade Commissioner, speaking in London on Oct. 17 pointed out that the British Empire possessed every natural resource which was known, and could produce everything which was wanted. Better than any other way could it be bound solidly and permanently by bonds of trade: "We must first ascertain what our requirements are and then secure them from wherever in the Empire they are to be found. But what has been the practice? When you have wanted raw materials, where have you gone for them? Anywhere but in the Empire." Britain had gone to Spain for iron ore when Newfoundland had the biggest deposits of iron ore in the world, and to Greece for magnesite when Canada contained all that was needed. He urged that the British peoples should get together and co-ordinate their trade, and that could best be accomplished, in his opinion, by the establishment of an Empire Trade Council.

New Regulations and Empire Trade Support. Before the Preference came into operation on Sept. 1st, regulations were issued by the British Board of Trade which (1) provided that goods should not be deemed, for the purposes of Section 8 of the Finance Act, 1919, to have been manufactured in the British Empire unless at least 25 per cent. of their total value was the result of labour within the British Empire; (2) that in calculating the proportion of value which was the result of labour within the British Empire there might be included under the head of labour the cost to the manufacturer of any materials of purely Empire origin entering into the composition of the article and including wages, proportion of fuel, supervision and other factory expenses, and the cost of the labour of packing for retail sale.

Meanwhile, early in March, the Federation of British Industries which included in its membership about 17,000 manufacturing and producing firms in Great Britain, had created an Overseas department and invited a number of Canadian officers who were then in England and had some business experience, to tour the chief manufacturing centres of the country, and see something of conditions, values and prices before returning home. The programme of this body included the appointment of Trade Commissioners in every part of the world who would be first-class men, versed in foreign customs and whose business it would be to constitute a "chain of commercial outposts throughout the world" and to put the special information they were able to collect at the service of British firms.

By June these informal commissioners had been appointed to Greece, which was formerly the centre of a group of markets under German economic dominance, Spain, Portugal, Northern Africa and the East Indies. Though not especially an Imperial organization, it was calculated to develop most quickly in British countries.

Another trade body of the year, of more explicit character, was the British Empire Producers' Organization which, after considerable preliminary work, had drawn to its standard the South African Federated Chamber of Industries, comprising 42 producing and manufacturing industries in South Africa; the Australian Sugar Producers' Association, with 1,300 growers; the New Zealand Farmers' Union; the British Sugar-Beet Growers' Association; the Indian Sugar Producers' Association; the National Sugar Association; the United Planters' Association of Southern India, with its 13 separate bodies; the Indigo Planters of the Empire; the Ceylon Association; and the Rubber Growers' Association, with its 489 companies which comprised almost a world-rubber monopoly. With it were affiliated the Associated Chambers of Manufacture of Australia; the Canadian Manufacturers' Association; the Chamber of Agriculture of Mauritius; and the West India Committee, which controlled the commercial destinies of the British West Indies. The objects were, in brief, the creation of a system of Empire trade, communication and combination and' were officially stated as follows:

Forming our conception of a Commonwealth of Britannic nations, each governing its own affairs but perceiving its deep interest in the progressive welfare of the rest of the Empire, the first proposition toward mutual self-help is that British materials should be developed primarily for British manufacture. In other words, the proper customers for our boundless stores of metals are the engineering and allied industries in the United Kingdom and other Dominions. The proper customers for such materials, again, as rubber, sugar, cereals, copra, palm kernels, cotton, wool, jute, and many other riches of our Empire, are the British factories and mills in which these products are refined or worked up for general consumption, or the British homes to which they are distributed direct. ' Conversely, the proper customers for British machinery and other manufacturers are the farming, planting and mining industries developing the vast natural resources of an Empire that is still largely unexplored virgin territory.

This organization was essentially a product of the Preference idea; it was further developed in the movement to promote Empire cotton-growing, to develop production in Egypt and India, British West Africa and the West Indies, and elsewhere, so as to relieve dependence upon the United States—from which country in 1916, 16,468,000 centals were taken out of a total import of 21,710,000. The British Chambers of Commerce, at their annual meeting on Apr. 15, urged upon the Government the importance of developing with the utmost expedition the growing of cotton in such portions of the Empire as were favourable to its production, since the inadequate supply of raw cotton was proving a grave menace to the staple industry of Lancashire.

Titles in
Canada;
Government
Policy and
Parliament-
ary Action. Anything affecting the rights or privileges of the Crown in Canada; anything which differentiated one Dominion from another or from the United Kingdom in public thought and practice; anything which eliminated a British custom from Canadian life, was at ' this time of importance and was an Empire question.

The conferring of British titles upon Canadians, in reward for services to the State, had been a custom and practice since the earliest days of Constitutional rule in Canada and had been, until recently, an unquestioned part of the British connection which Canadians were and are supposed to cherish. With a few exceptions the power had not been abused though it gradually passed, in practice, from the direct hands of the Sovereign to those of the Colonial Secretary and the Governor-General and, in ordinary practice though not in theory or stated principle, to those of the Dominion Prime Minister.

Hereditary Titles in Canada. In the days prior to Confederation few could object to the Baronetcies conferred upon Chief Justice Sir James Stuart of Lower Canada, Sir A. N. McNab, one-time Prime Minister of the Canadas, Sir L. H. Lafontaine, the hero of French-Canadian Liberal thought, or Sir John Beverly Robinson, the centre of Loyalist and Tory activities in Upper Canada for a generation and then Chief Justice of the Province; so in the time immediately following Confederation there was nothing in the same honour conferred upon Sir G. E. Cartier, Sir John Rose, Sir George Stephen and Sir Charles Tupper to arouse criticism even from opponents of these leaders.* Had the hereditary principle been confined in its application to a few carefully selected men in the highest and most clearly recognized rank of great public service, no serious agitation would have arisen in 1917-19 as to that branch of the title question. The Peerages conferred upon Lord Mount Stephen, Lord Strathcona, and Lord Shaughnessy were never seriously criticized; that given to Sir Hugh Graham as Lord Atholstan, although well merited and intended as an honour to the Press, did arouse some journalistic antipathy. It really seems, however, that difficulty did not arise until the honours were conferred with the approval of the Canadian Prime Minister; no Governor-General in the past decade would have recommended an hereditary or other honour against the advice of his Prime Minister; that conferred upon Mr. Flavelle was an Imperial recognition for services as head of an Imperial War organization in Canada. The question of principle or of the appropriateness of such titles in a democracy was another matter; the British democracy accepted the principle, that of the American did not. The Canadian movement of 1918-9 in this respect was either part of a large development which unconsciously preferred American forms to British or else it proposed to overthrow an institution of the Empire because in a

---

*Note.—Other and more recent recipients of this honour were Sir Edward Clouston and Sir Vincent Meredith, eminent financial men of Montreal, and Sir Joseph W. Flavelle.

psychological moment of intense unrest the unpopularity of one
or two recipients of honour was, for the moment, obvious.

Knighthood in Principle and Practice. As to the ordinary
non-hereditary title of Knighthood, the question was and is quite
different. It was intended to mark distinctive services to the State
in Canada, or to the Empire in Canada; it was valued by those
who understood the honour not so much because it conferred a
prefix to their names as because it was one of the few marks of
distinction in the world which was recognized everywhere, and
which carried with it in almost every country a stamp of acknowledged position and achievement. A European baron might be the
penniless younger son of the son of a baron, or the brother of another, and of no particular local standing or position; but a British
Knighthood meant and means to-day that the Australian or Canadian or South African holding it is a person of consequence in
his own country. In Canada, also, it stood for something definite
in recognized position; something apart from the everlasting question of money or wealth. The stamp of gold was replaced by another standard and it was the only other one upon the American
continent.

There was no agitation in this connection until about 1917; the
press usually, if somewhat perfunctorily, praised the yearly recipients of Honours; there was no apparent appreciation of this institution as a "danger to democracy" until some development of war
psychology suddenly flamed into feeling over the matter. Was this
feeling nurtured by the anti-British spirit which always has existed
and always will exist in a clever but not numerous portion of the
people? Was the genuine democracy of political leaders and the
public at large misled by a small section of Americanized thought
and republican feeling which refused to accept Great Britain as
what an American publicist* had called "the greatest political democracy in the world?" Was it based, in this small section of the
community, upon a desire to emphasize the fact of Canada being
an American and continental rather than British democracy?

Cable conditions referred to in the preceding pages of this
volume might indicate a basis for this latter supposition. The movement did not seem to be directed against any but British titles; no
part of the press or section of the speakers denounced the constant
use of the prefix "Honourable"—even when it was not technically
correct; no objection was taken to Judicial forms of dignity and
titles or to Church distinctions—from those of the Catholic Hierarchy to the Methodist Doctor of Divinity; no opposition was expressed to the hosts of Military honours awarded from day to day;
no word was said against the hundreds of honours awarded to
Canadian soldiers and civilians in connection with the War by the
Kings of Italy and Serbia and Greece and Roumania and the President of France.

---

*Note.—Dr. Theodore Marburg, Toronto, April 10, 1919.

Had the privilege been abused, or did Canadian Prime Ministers from time to time recommend, or approve, or permit the selection of, unsuitable names for the Governor-General's submission to the King *via* the Colonial Office? There was a tendency, and in this the Governor-General followed British precedents, to (1) recognize the holders of certain offices as specially eligible for the honour of Knighthood and to consider the Prime Ministers of the Dominion and the Provinces, Lieutenant-Governors and Chief Justices, as obviously persons of Canadian distinction and, *prima facie*, fitted for Imperial honours. The selections in this connection were practically never criticized. Amongst politicians not included in this category there were a few who had been recommended for reasons of party expediency or who were afterwards discredited by events in which they shared. But the number of the latter could be counted on the fingers of one hand.

Other selections were made to represent important classes in the community such as Sir James Grant or Sir William Hingston or Sir Thomas Roddick, for the profession of Medicine; Sir William Dawson, Sir Daniel Wilson, Sir William Peterson or Sir Robert Falconer, in the control of great educational institutions; Sir Hugh Graham or Sir J. S. Willison as representing the Press of the Dominion; Sir Joseph Hickson or Sir W. C. Van Horne or Sir William Mackenzie or Sir William Whyte as embodying the great railway work and progress of the community; Sir John Bourinot or Sir James Le Moine or Sir Clive Phillipps-Wolley as speaking for the Literature of the country; Sir Edmund Walker or Sir F. Williams-Taylor for the Banking interests of Canada; and Sir Casimir Gzowski, Sir Sandford Fleming and Sir C. Schrieber for some of the great engineering feats of the country; Sir Æmilius Irving and Sir A. B. Aylesworth as representing the Bar; Sir George Garneau, Sir George Gibbons or Sir Adam Beck for the public life of Canada apart from politics; Sir W. D. Otter or Sir A. W. Currie or Sir E. P. C. Girouard as illustrating the Military achievements of the people. It is safe to say that no serious exception has ever been taken to these names, or to those of 40 leaders in public life who might be mentioned, or as to 40 eminent judges who had a place in the lists of the last half-century.

As the C.B., C.M.G. and C.V.O. did not carry titles they came under another category; they could not create class or social distinction as they involved neither title nor monetary power; they constituted simply a phase of public recognition, through the Crown, of public service. They covered in their distribution every form of national work and activity; no public exception was ever taken to them and very little was said about them in the 1918-19 debates; if there was a concrete objection it was that they were British honours and this was only vaguely expressed. As the 250 recipients of the C.M.G., C.B. and C.V.O. in the 50 years since Confederation—with the addition of 500 recent winners of that badge of British courage, the D.S.O.—could hardly be described as forming a class or differentiating between democratic divisions of social life and as the 100 recipients of Knighthood in the same period of half-a-century, or an average of two creations a year, would have found it very difficult to establish an aristocratic society in the scattered centres of Canada if they had so desired, it is not easy to explain the heated Parliamentary discussion of this question in 1919.

Character of the Movement against Titles.   The issue developed slowly but steadily. The *Grain Growers' Guide* in 1918 had declared that "these tin-pot titles have no place in a democratic country;" the Manitoba Grain Growers' Convention and other similar bodies early in 1919 advocated the discontinuance of the conferment of titles upon Canadians; J. B. Musselman, a Saskatchewan leader in the Farmers' party, declared in the official journal on Feb. 5 that: "It is all wrong. First and foremost because titles are granted by the Imperial authorities." This vein of thought was echoed later in the year by Hon. R. Lemieux in the Commons (Sept. 10) when he said that "we have abolished all titles and I think that the cause of Imperialism will, because of the absence of titles, perish after a certain time;" despatches from the ultra Radical and anti-war Manchester *Guardian* (May 1) and London *Daily News* (May 5) declared (1) that titles tended to produce "a social tradition alien to the spirit of Canadian democracy" and (2) that "the title business in Canada is doomed;" to these organs of extreme thought was added a despatch from that journal of society "frills," *Truth*, describing the titles with which it filled its social columns as "tomfooleries;" the Toronto *Farmer's Sun* in the days before it became the organ of the United Farmers of Ontario, continued to refuse recognition to any British titles in Canada and to refer to "Mr. Borden" as it previously had done to "Mr. Laurier;" the criticisms as to conferment of titles in England made by those who wanted to curtail their political creation and restore the King's prorogative in this connection were cabled out as an aid to those who proposed to remove altogether the Royal prorogative in this respect so far as Canada was concerned; the Toronto *Globe* and *Star* and some other journals from time to time urged the abolition of any yearly distribution of distinctions.

A few speeches, not very many, were heard in favour of the abolition of titles; everywhere Military honours were excepted from the discussion. There was no organized movement, no party advocacy, no heated controversy throughout the country, no mass of petitions was presented to Parliament, no flood of telegrams despatched from the constituencies, no public meetings held; yet Parliament dealt with the subject in April, 1919 and was swept off its feet by a spirit of keen hostility shown to this hitherto inoffensive institution of the country amongst about 100 of its members.

Parliamentary Discussion; Titles and Democracy.   Following up his motion in the Commons during the 1918 Session* and the

---

*Note.—See *The Canadian Annual Review* for 1918, pages 563-6.

Fruit Farm and Vineyard near Fruitland, Niagara District, Ontario

Government's announcement of policy in the form of an Order-in-Council asking His Majesty to grant no more hereditary honours in Canada and no others except upon the advice of the Canadian Prime Minister, W. F. Nickle moved in Parliament on Apr. 14 an Address to the King praying that "Your Majesty hereafter may be graciously pleased to refrain from conferring any titles upon your subjects domiciled or living in Canada, it being always understood that this humble prayer has no reference to professional or vocational appellations conferred in respect to commissions issued by Your Majesty to persons in Military or Naval Services of Canada or to persons engaged in the administration of Justice of the Dominion.''

Mr. Nickle declared in his speech that public opinion was behind him in the proposed abolition of titular distinctions in Canada and that democracy would not stand "class distinction that pretends to give one man a better social position than another, not by virtue of abilities, but by virtue of influence.'' He reviewed the whole order of Knighthood in a most unflattering way and denounced the honours of the Order of the British Empire as being scattered broadcast and to a ridiculous extent; he brought together every humourous situation or mixing up of the mediæval and modern elements of all Monarchical honours in such a clever way as to cast a maximum of contempt upon the whole institution. R. L. Richardson followed with a typically radical speech directed against autocracy in general, against the very large conferment of Honours in England for services in a very large war, against the preceding distribution of titles in Canada, against the hereditary principle in particular, against any setting up of a "cheap, tinselled aristocracy in Canada,'' and, finally, moved an amendment to Mr. Nickle's motion with the additional request that measures be taken "to ensure the extinction of hereditary titles at present in existence in the Dominion at the death of the present possessors thereof.'' J. H. Burnham followed briefly and F. F. Pardee approved of all that had been said by Messrs. Nickle and Richardson.

Sir Thomas White, acting Prime Minister, then spoke as "having accepted the honour of Knighthood'' and preferring, therefore, not to defend titles as such; but he described the policy of the Government in the premises and put on record some interesting historic details. He pointed out that the question of these distinctions had never been a party one and then laid before the House a Dominion Order-in-Council of Feb. 19, 1902—during the Government of Sir Wilfrid Laurier—in which the then Prime Minister described the conferring of titles upon Canadians by H.M. the King, upon the advice only of British Ministers, as an invasion of local self-government and urged that in future such Honours should only be granted after recommendation by the Governor-General and upon the advice of the latter's responsible Ministers. No objection was expressed to titles *per se* and, on Apr. 23, Mr. Chamberlain, then Secretary of State for the Colonies, replied as follows: "In dealing with this subject I have been desirous of meeting the views of your Ministers so far as possible, but as the responsibility for making recommendations to the Sovereign in regard to appointments to an Imperial Order such as that of Saint Michael and Saint George rests with the Secretary of State and not with your Ministers it is his duty to obtain the best advice he can and he must be the sole judge of what is the best advice."

There the matter had rested until 1918 when Sir Robert Borden took up more advanced ground than his predecessor and, on Mch. 25, had passed an Order-in-Council urging the abolition of "the heritable quality or effect" of titles in Canada, declaring that "the hereditary peerage as an institution can find neither historic justification nor scope for usefulness in a state structure and system such as that which now exists in Canada." He admitted, however, that "honours conferred directly upon deserving recipients under appropriate conditions and by proper authority will be respected by the community." Recommendations were then officially made as recorded in *The Canadian Annual Review* for 1918 and these had been tentatively accepted in so far as the advice of the Canadian Prime Minister preceding the bestowal of future honours was concerned; action had remained in abeyance as to the request for abolition of existing hereditary titles in Canada after a prescribed period.

The Minister of Finance then outlined the policy of the Government in the premises. War honours had been conferred largely and with the approval of the Government; at its close the question of rewarding civilians for war-work became insistent. The Government last autumn, in connection with the New Year's list, decided that the granting of titular honours and decorations in respect of civilian services—the Red Cross, the Patriotic Fund, Munitions, etc.—should be suspended, with a view to having the whole question given the fullest consideration. A large list had been prepared and on this action had been suspended; on Jan. 3rd a cablegram came from the Premier, who was in London, stating that the suspension should be continued and that the whole question of civil honours for war services and of titles in general should be submitted to a Select Committee of the Commons. Sir Thomas stated that he would move an amendment to Mr. Nickle's motion proposing that "the subject matters of the said motion and amendment together with the questions of conferring honours, titular distinctions and decorations upon the subjects of His Majesty ordinarily resident in Canada, including those who have performed overseas, in Canada or elsewhere, naval, military or civilian services in connection with the War be referred for consideration and report to a Special Committee." He hoped that careful consideration would be given the matter and it would then be for the House to adopt, modify or reject the recommendations made. The attitude of the House would, without doubt "be of the utmost value for the guidance of the Government." The following Committee was appointed:

Conservatives	Liberals
W. F. Nickle, K.C.	W. A. Buchanan
R. F. Green	Michael Clark
Lieut.-Col. C. W. Peck, V.C.	Levi Thompson
W. D. Cowan	R. L. Richardson
Rev. Dr. H. P. Whidden	E. W. Nesbitt
W. S. Middlebro	F. F. Pardee, K.C.
W. F. Cockshutt	Hon. C. Murphy
Sir H. B. Ames	A. B. McCoig
S. R. Elkin	D. C. Ross
F. B. McCurdy	A. R. McMaster
Liberals	A. B. Copp
Hon. R. Lemieux	J. H. Sinclair
J. A. Robb	Hon. W. S. Fielding

Seven of the Liberals named were Unionists but most of them
were known to be antagonistic to titles while all the strongest critics
of the institution were included in the list; it was at once seen that
a majority were of this school while Mr. Nickle, the leading Conservative exponent of Radicalism in this connection became Chairman of the Committee. A. R. McMaster followed the Minister of
Finance in his speech and the burden of his comment was that
titles contravened the principles of democracy which he emphasized
as those of the French Revolution—"Liberty, fraternity and equality." Michael Clark took an opposite view and described Messrs.
Nickle and Richardson as "My democratic, radical, iconoclastic and,
I might almost say, Bolshevistic friends from Kingston and Springfield"; declared the ambition for distinction at the hands of one's
fellow-men, as represented by the Sovereign, not an evil thing in
itself; defended the traditions and work and hereditary position of
the British nobility and eulogized their splendid place in the War;
asked why there was no opposition to such designations as "Es-
quire" or "Honourable," to religious prefixes or War honours;
declared that autocracy did not lie in titles but in power and
referred to the United States as an autocracy of wealth.

W. F. Cockshutt, a veteran Conservative as Mr. Clark was an
old-time Liberal, took a somewhat similar position, approved of
titles properly earned and lived up to and declared the word "democracy" was being worked to death. He did not, however, enter into
any serious defence of the system. D. D. McKenzie, Liberal leader
in the House, thought the Government should deal with the matter
on its own responsibility, and declared that the workman was thinking far more of the price of meat and flour than of the question of
titles; "Let us show our democracy by going to the homes of the
poor, and seeing to it that there shall be an even distribution of
the great wealth of this country." Capt. R. J. Manion deprecated
any large distribution of war honours to civilian workers but did
not believe there was "any real open agitation in connection with
the question;" at the same time he was opposed to any Knighthoods
being granted in Canada. Ernest Lapointe declared that nobody
had "tried to defend the institution of titles" and after some other
very brief speeches the vote was taken on Sir Thomas White's

amendment with 71 in favour and 64 against and the unusual number of 24 pairs.

The Press and the Titles Discussion. There were various opinions expressed in the papers at this time but the discussion was not a really serious or fundamental one. Only a few journals seemed to feel strongly upon the subject and very few reached to the roots of it in their comments; as in the Commons the discussion was academic with, however, one obvious and clear line of thought —resentment at certain honours recently bestowed. One interesting suggestion by the Winnipeg *Free Press* (Lib.) on Apr. 15, at the same time, indicated one of the more or less concealed but very real bases of the movement: "A vigourous young nation like Canada should be able to devise its own honour titles without falling back on the dying aristocratic distinctions of the old world. If we must have civilian honours, cannot we devise them for ourselves?" The Halifax *Chronicle* (Lib.) of Apr. 16 declared that: "Titles of honour have few supporters and fewer advocates among the people of Canada. Yet this old world idea, so foreign to the spirit of our country, appears to be strongly entrenched in the Government at Ottawa." Much Conservative opinion was represented by the Montreal *Gazette* which declared that: "No one disputes that there are degrees of men, nor combats the proposition that merit deserves reward. . . . The distinction of knighthood by the Crown is sought and envied, a great mark of service every man may covet; and it is not the bestowal of the honour that is to be resented, but its too frequent bestowal. The cure is not to be sought in the extinction of titles, or any other prefix or suffix in vogue, but in the careful bestowal of the dignity so as to preserve its value." So with the Victoria *Colonist* (Apr. 15) which came out distinctly against the proposed changes:

To do away with the practice of giving honour where honour is due is a retrograde step. There are ranks in the Army which denote ability, and which show that men stand out above their fellows in military knowledge or prowess or leadership or strategy. It is the same in the Navy. Why men engaged in commerce or trade, in politics, on the bench or at the bar, in literature, in agriculture, or, in fact, in any useful walk of life, should not be honoured because they have served their country well, we are at a loss to know. People say the practice is not democratic, for all men are equal. That is a cant phrase of the age which will only become a truism when men and women are created of equal intelligence and possessed of equal ability to grasp all the opportunities that arise.

Discussion and Conclusions of the Titles Committee. The first meeting of the Committee was held on Apr. 25 and Mr. Nickle was elected Chairman. The reports of this and succeeding sessions in the press were very meagre and discursive but at the first meeting it was unanimously agreed, after 15 minutes' discussion, to recommend that hereditary titles in Canada should cease on the death of the present holders of such titles. The Hon. W. S. Fielding claimed that titles which follow a name did not appear to cause objections and that the elimination of such titles as "Sir" and

"Baron" would satisfy most people. No one; he thought, took exception to a man holding a C.M.G., or an I.S.O. Lieut.-Col. C. W. Peck, V.C., D.S.O., thought all fairly earned military titles should be bestowed before any restriction took place; Dr. Michael Clark declared that the situation could be met by a simple recommendation that in future distinctions should not be so generously bestowed. He considered the matter to be one between the King and his subjects and the present movement as a slur upon His Majesty. Rev. Dr. H. P. Whidden thought there was enough "social tomfoolery" in the country: "The objectionable feature of the practise arises not so much from the holders of titles as from their wives." References were made of a personal nature to existing Canadian holders of titles which the press was asked not to report.

According to a despatch in the Toronto *Globe* of May 1st, the Committee at its meeting of the preceding day heard Levi Thomson of Qu'Appelle, express the opinion of the majority when he declared that titles should be dealt with as one deals with a mad dog, "cutting the tail off behind the ear!" The members decided after a brief discussion, by 20 to 3, that the conferring of Knighthoods on Canadians residing in Canada should be discontinued. By the same vote it rejected an amendment by W. F. Cockshutt that titles should not be abolished immediately, but that His Majesty and his advisers be petitioned to use more discrimination in the future. The minority were Sir Herbert Ames, W. F. Cockshutt and Michael Clark.

During the debate Mr. Cockshutt declared that from amongst 8,000 working men in his constituency of Brantford there had not come a single objection to the granting of Knighthoods. He also argued that "nothing gives more dignity than a title. . . . . Gifts of money or lands are of no use to many men already wealthy. It is an inspiration to some people to have an ideal to live up to. We must all have a reason for working." Duncan C. Ross stated that his section was disgusted with the whole system and would be glad to see it cease. The Western members said that in the West there was a general objection to titles. Dr. Clark expressed the opinion that so far as the West was concerned anti-British sentiment amongst those coming from other than British countries might explain the attitude as to titles.

On May 7 Dr. Clark and Mr. Cockshutt sought to prove that the agitation was against British honours by moving that the prefix "Honourable" be abolished; only the mover and seconder voted for it. Messrs. Lemieux and McMaster then moved that the conferment of all lesser titles leading up to Knighthood such as C.M.G., C.B., etc., should be discontinued and this was carried by 10 to 2. General Griesbach made a strong appeal for military men and Sir H. B. Ames declared that the Order of the British Empire should be excepted. It was intended to honour civilians who had done meritorious work in the War as well as soldiers. He urged that the whole question of the bestowal of titles under this Order be submitted to the next Imperial Conference. Dr. W. D. Cowan of Regina proposed that to take the place of Knighthoods there should be a Canadian Academy of Merit, so that there should be something to which a man might aspire. Mr. Cockshutt and Dr. Clark then urged, as the Committee had decided to refuse all titles from the King, that they should also disallow all foreign titles; Mr. Thomson declared that they were dealing with the conferment of titles and not their acceptance but that he was opposed to the acceptance of any Foreign orders or titles. Mr. Cockshutt's view was approved by the Committee. A sub-Committee was appointed to draft a Report—Messrs. Nickle, Fielding, Whidden and Cockshutt. The Report was drafted and accepted by Committee on May 14 with an attendance of 13 members; it recommended an Address to H.M. the King in the following words with some succeeding comments:

We, Your Majesty's most dutiful and loyal subjects, the House of Commons of Canada in Parliament assembled, humbly approach Your Majesty, praying that your Majesty may be graciously pleased:—

(a) To refrain hereafter from conferring any title of honour or titular distinction upon any of your subjects domiciled or ordinarily resident in Canada, save such appellations as are of a professional or vocational character or which appertain to an office.

(b) To provide that appropriate action be taken by legislation or otherwise to ensure the extinction of an hereditary title of honour or titular distinction and of a dignity or title as a Peer of the realm, on the death of a person domiciled or ordinarily resident in Canada at present in enjoyment of an hereditary title of honour or titular distinction or dignity or tilt as a Peer of the realm, and that thereafter no such title of honour, titular distinction or dignity or title as a Peer of the realm shall be accepted, enjoyed or used by any person or be recognized.

All of which we humbly pray Your Majesty to take into your favourable and gracious consideration.

A suggestion was made that the titles of 'Right Honourable' and 'Honourable' be discontinued, but the suggestion did not meet with approval of the Committee. Your Committee, however, do not recommend the discontinuance of the practice of awarding military or naval decorations, such as the Victoria Cross, Military Medal, Military Cross, Conspicuous Service Cross,* and similar decorations to persons in Military or Naval services of Canada for exceptional valour and devotion to duty. Your Committee further recommends that appropriate action be taken by legislation or otherwise to provide that hereafter no person domiciled or ordinarily resident in Canada shall accept, enjoy or use any title of honour or titular distinction hereafter conferred by a Foreign ruler or Government.

Debate in Parliament on Address to the King. The Report was discussed by the Commons on May 22 and approved by a vote of 96 to 43; the debate evoked some extreme utterances and a continuous appeal to democracy as against aristocracy and autocracy with an incidental declaration by Dr. Michael Clark that the Sovereign should be left out of the discussion; there were various criticisms directed against the Canadian Ministers as really responsible for the recommendation and the distribution of titles in Canada. Mr. Nickle moved that the Report be adopted and his

*Note.—No doubt the Distinguished Service Cross—so re-constituted in 1915 but applicable only to Royal Navy services.

speech was first directed to an attack upon the British Government for not at once accepting the full demands of the Canadian Government as expressed in 1918. He declared once more that the conferring of titles created a class which was hostile to democracy, claimed that it caused corruption which was hostile to good government, proclaimed that virtue should be its own reward and stated that a title conferred by the Crown was an indignity and its acceptance a personal degradation!

D. D. McKenzie followed and declared himself in favour of the principle of the Resolution but not of bringing it directly to the attention of the King: "If there is anything to be reformed in connection with it, it is a domestic reform so far as Canada is concerned, and should be, and can be carried out without referring the matter to His Majesty." He did not attach a great deal of importance to the subject and only voted for the motion because he had nothing better to offer; he did not seem to think that it meant abolition of future distinctions: "Great care should be taken that no person is recommended for the honour except one who is highly worthy of it, and to whom the granting of a title would be recognized by the Canadian people as something that was eminently deserved."

Dr. Charles Sheard, Toronto, took strong exception to the form of the Address as not courteous to His Majesty; denied that there was any excitement or strong public opinion in the country upon the subject; declared that such feeling as did exist was caused by an impression from some recent honours that wealth was the chief consideration or condition; declared that in the premises any rebuke or censure was due, not to the head of the Empire or the institution itself, but to those who advised the honours. He made an earnest appeal for titular distinctions as a strong incentive to honest public work and devoted professional effort: "From the cradle to the grave the greatest incentive and the strongest inspiration to extra effort and extra endeavour on the part of the human being is appreciation. In the great school of life this principle still prevails, and I sincerely trust that Parliament will not put any stumbling-blocks in the way of the application or bestowment of such evidences of appreciation." Lord Lister, Sir James Simpson, Sir William Osler, Sir Joshua Reynolds, Sir William Herschell, were instanced, and the V.C. used as a military illustration. He concluded with a strong utterance:

I do not know, Mr. Speaker, if Canada ever hopes to attain a place, or maintain a position, amongst the civilized nations of the world. I do not know if this Parliament of Canada is ever hopeful to realise and recognise the proud stand of our soldiers who fought for liberty and for their King. But if Canada is to be relieved from the stigma of a transaction of this kind which can only be characterized as a farce, she must eradicate from her records that ridiculous resolution and recommendation of the report which I feel convinced will only be regarded as a laughing stock by the country.

A. R. McMaster followed and endorsed all Mr. Nickle's opinions. He denounced the "title factory" in England and Canada, declared

in reply to an interjection as to the French Revolution that
"everyone has got to endorse the Revolution" and urged the House
to "do away with a system which has no place in the free air of
North America." Dr. Clark, a Western Radical, was as keen in
his criticism of the Resolution as Dr. Sheard, an Eastern Conservative. As to the Report: "I should have been very sorry to concur,
because I cannot, the way my mind is trained, concur in anything
which is the embodiment at once of democratic cant and illogical
nonsense." He dealt with the Committee's refusal to abolish the
designation of "Honourable" and claimed that the result would
be the abolition only of titular distinctions conferred by the King
and not such as were conferred by the B.N.A. Act. J. H. Burnham
followed along the lines of Messrs. Nickle and McMaster and compared those who believed in the conferment of titles in Canada to
the Junkers of Germany and the aristocrats of Russia. General W.
A. Griesbach drew attention to the fact that, if this Resolution
passed, in any future war Canadians would be under a handicap:

Canadians serving in co-operation with Australians, South Africans,
New Zealanders or British troops, would be unable to accept such honours
and awards as might be bestowed on officers of equal rank in the other
forces. It may occur to some one, Mr. Speaker, as being a matter of very
small moment; but I assure you, as a soldier, that it is, on the contrary,
of considerable importance. A soldier does not ask very much; he does
not get very much. But he does wear with proper pride the ribbons and
the distinctions of the orders which he has gained. These distinctions cost
the soldier a great deal, and are earned with a labour that is inconceivable
to those who are not of his calling. It is almost futile to attempt to convey
to the civilian mind all that they do mean to him.

Capt. R. J. Manion thought that honours such as C.B. and
C.M.G. should not have been interfered with. G. B. Nicholson
declared that he represented a constituency in which 95 per cent.
of the adult manhood worked with their hands and the remaining 5
per cent. worked in some other way perhaps equally as hard. Yet
it was not until he heard some of the speeches in the House that he
had known the country was at all disturbed on this subject. He
asked if Roosevelt or Taft were not Democrats because they had
accepted University distinctions or Mr. Lemieux because he had
received the Legion of Honour or Sir W. Mulock because he had
accepted Knighthood! He moved an amendment seconded by Dr.
Sheard:

That the Report be not now concurred in, but that it be referred back
to the Special Committee with instructions to amend the same by striking
out paragraph (a) of the proposed Address to His Majesty, and by
striking out all the paragraphs after the said proposed address, and by adding
the following paragraph to the report of the said Special Committee:—
That in making recommendations to His Majesty for the conferring of
knighthoods or other titular distinctions upon persons domiciled or ordinarily resident in Canada the greatest care should be exercised in the selections of the persons recommended, and that special regard should be paid to
the personal merit and the distinguished services of the said person.

W. F. Cockshutt spoke openly along lines which had not yet
been definitely dealt with: "I see something beneath the surface in

the Resolution moved by the Hon. Member for Kingston (Mr. Nickle). I have said so in the Committee and I am not afraid to say so here. There are but very few ties between the Dominion of Canada and the Empire at the present time, and they have been described on more than one occasion as being lighter than air, but strong as iron. The conferring of titles by His Majesty is one slender thread that has been recognized ever since we become a Dominion, up to the present time, as one of the prerogatives of the Crown. Another is the appeal to the Privy Council, and it is rather strange to see that many of the same men who are at the present time bent upon destroying titles are also of opinion that in matters of litigation there should be no appeal beyond the High Courts of Canada. These same gentlemen, if one talks privately with many of them, state that the Governor-General of Canada is a figurehead and costs a great deal of money to the country and ought to go. Time and again I have heard that stated, and it cannot be disputed, although some of them have not the courage to get up and say so. What other ties remain? We have simply the Crown and King left to bind us to the Motherland, and three legs having gone it will not be hard to knock out the fourth.'' Mr. Cockshutt, added an objection to the King being insulted by ''such rubbish as is contained in this Report.''

Sir Thomas White stated that the motion did not involve a question upon which the Government had ''any pronounced policy'' and that the Committee chosen had the entire confidence of the House, expressed his agreement with much of what the Opposition leader (Mr. McKenzie) had said and deprecated the ''disproportionate importance'' given to the subject: ''My own view is that there is not and should not be objection to the principle of titular distinctions; but I do believe that the circumstances surrounding their bestowal are of the utmost importance. I think that in all the British-speaking countries the bestowal has been on altogether too generous a scale and has not proceeded upon the principle that it should have proceeded. I believe that if the question of bestowal had received more careful consideration in the past by all Governments in Canada, this question would not be before us to-night.'' He believed in the State being able to mark its appreciation of public work; he considered the Report of the Committee as too sweeping.

R. L. Richardson followed in support of abolition and J. W. Edwards asked why the appeal was not addressed to the Canadian Ministers who were responsible and not to the King who took their advice. He did not believe in going beyond the point of hereditary titles and did not think there was any general demand for action. With this view Hon. F. B. Carvell largely agreed though personally opposed to titles; Hon. N. W. Rowell declared that the country as a whole was opposed to any further titles being conferred; Hon. W. S. Fielding did not concur in the view that as a matter of principle there was anything wrong in the conferring of honours for public service; Hon. R. Lemieux declared that Sir Wilfrid Laurier had refused a Peerage and was not consulted about his knighthood but "on taking his seat at Windsor Castle, as one of His Majesty's Privy Councillors, he found his title in front of him." In concluding the debate Mr. Nickle read a telegram from the President of the Brantford Trades and Labour Council as to Mr. Cockshutt's statement that he had heard no protest from that city and declaring that 1,487 Labourites were opposed to the granting of "Imperial titles." Mr. Nicholson's amendment was then negatived by 96 to 43 and the Report adopted on division and ordered to be engrossed.

Further Comments of the Press. Comments upon this matter were made in accordance with the degrees of Radicalism professed by the journals concerned. The Toronto *Globe* and *Star* rejoiced over the success of Mr. Nickle's efforts; varied flings were had at titles and there holders by papers like the Toronto *Telegram* and *World*; Capt. J. W. Magwood presented in the Toronto Methodist Conference a motion, which was not approved, urging that no further degrees in Divinity be granted the Ministers of that Church; the Hamilton Methodist Conference (June 4) declared against any titles except those granted for services on the field of battle; the St. John *Standard* urged the dropping of all military designations and distinctions (July 9) and described their retention as dangerous to democracy. So it was in some other quarters.

On the other hand a number of Conservative papers stood by the principle of Honours as British and the democracy of Great Britain as being equally good and equally free with that of the United States. The Montreal *Star* was conspicuous in its comments and on May 16 observed that: "The whole thing is very petty. The majority of opinion in this country is undoubtedly opposed to hereditary distinctions; though logically, hereditary wealth has more dangerous possibilities. But we refuse to believe that Canadian common-sense resents awards of honour for honourable public service. For personal success in industry and commerce there are financial prizes which are impossible to men who give their lives to their country in science, in education, on the battle-field and in public service. Are we to rear the rising Canadian generations in no higher ambition than to be millionaires? Are the Goulds and Vanderbilts and Rockefellers of this continent to be their ideals? But, the title privilege has been grossly abused, is the complaint. Granted! If, however, we started abolishing every privilege that had been abused how much would be left? There have been many unworthy M.P's, but few people want to abolish Parliament."

The Ottawa *Journal* of May 10 pointed out that: "There are many men in Canada to-day giving of their ability, their time, and their means to the public welfare—giving services that could not be bought with or estimated in money. If the granting of Knighthoods to such men is an inducement to them and to others to devote themselves to public service, it would seem to be not unwise to distribute a few." A different angle was touched upon by Rev. Dr.

Hall of the Naval Institutes, at Montreal on June 8: "We who are home-born are to be less Britons in Canada than in any other part of the Empire, and the King is to be less a King in Canada than in any other part of his Dominions. The Resolution is an indignity to the King's Majesty, a blow at Imperial unity, and a Parliamentary recrudescence of that Bolshevik demon which is against all authority in the State and all dignity in public life."

British Honours and Canadian Incidents. Meantime, the order of the day in Great Britain was the reward of distinguished service during the War—at home or in the field. Mr. Lloyd George did not care for a Peerage as, like so many British leaders in the past, he could not afford to leave the House of Commons at this stage in his career but he was given by special exercise of the King's prerogative, the Order of Merit (O.M.) an honour confined to 24 men preeminent in some branch of public service—Government or Science, Army or Navy, Literature, Music or Art. Admiral Beatty was made Admiral of the Fleet—equivalent to the Military rank of Field Marshal and Field Marshal Haig was appointed to the head of the Armies at home while both leaders were given the Order of Merit. A few of the other Honours from the Crown or grants from Parliament were as follows:

Name	Parliamentary grant	Title
Admiral Sir David Beatty, G.C.B., O.M., G.C.V.O., D.S.O.	$500,000	Earl Beatty
F.M. Sir Douglas Haig, K.T., G.C.B., G.C.V.O.	500,000	Earl Haig of Bemersyde
F.M. Sir Edmund Allenby, G.C.B., K.C.M.G.	250,000	Viscount Allenby of Migiddo
F.M. Sir Herbert Plumer, G.C.B., G.C.M.G., G.C.V.O.	150,000	Lord Plumer of Messines
General Sir Henry Rawlinson, Bart., G.C.B. G.C.V.O.	150,000	Lord Rawlinson
General The Hon. Sir Julian Byng, K.C.B., K.C.M.G., M.V.O.	150,000	Lord Byng of Vimy
General Sir Henry Horne, K.C.B., K.C.M.G.	150,000	Lord Horne of Stirkoke
Admiral of the Fleet Viscount Jellicoe of Scapa	250,000	
F.M. Viscount French of Ypres	250,000	
General Sir William Birdwood, G.C.M.G., K.C.B.	50,000	Baronetcy
Rt. Hon. Sir Satyendra P. Sinha	India	Lord Sinha
Maj.-Gen. Sir J. W. McCay, K.C.M.G., C.B.	Australia	K.B.E.
General Sir Arthur Currie, K.C.B., K.C.M.G.	Canada	G.C.M.G.
Maj.-Gen. Sir N. R. House, V.C.	Australia	K.C.M.G.
Maj.-Gen. Sir John Monash, K.C.B.	Australia	G.C.M.G.
Lieut.-Gen. Sir H. G. Chauvel, K.C.B.	New Zealand	G.C.M.G.

Besides the large Parliamentary grants above mentioned, Admirals Madden, Keyes, Sturdee, de Robeck and Tyrwhitt, F. M. Sir H. H. Wilson, General Sir W. Robertson and Air Vice-Marshal Trenchard were voted $50,000 each. The Order of the British Empire had, meantime, been established for the purpose of recognizing and rewarding in a way which money could not do, of the State be warranted in doing, the services in the War of rich and poor, great and small, civilian and combatant. It was a most democratic Order and it was a curious fact that this policy of freely honouring all classes from the peer or his wife to the workman or his wife, through all the different grades of society, either caused or intensified an hostility felt in certain Canadian quarters to the

Order. The O.B.E. conferred for comparatively humble services and therefore very numerous, was ridiculed while the K.B.E. or Knighthood, necessarily given to few in number was denounced. Some ensuing incidents threw light upon certain phases of this discussion. At Washington, on Nov. 13, the Prince of Wales conferred various British Honours upon American leaders in the War which he had been practically debarred from giving in Canada to Canadians—including a G.C.M.G. to Admiral W. S. Benson, K.C. M.G. to Lieut.-Gen. Crowder and Rear Admiral A. P. Niblack and K.C.B. to Maj.-Gen. W. J. Snow and three others. These Orders, when conferred upon citizens of a foreign country, did not involve the ordinary prefix of Knighthood.

At a time when Canadians at home were unable to receive the honour of Knighthood a Canadian in Rio de Janeiro—Alex. Mackenzie for many years a member of the Toronto law firm of Blake, Lash and Cassels—was knighted for war services in Brazil. So in other parts of the Empire or Foreign countries. On Dec. 31 it was announced by the Halifax *Chronicle* that Hon. G. H. Murray, Premier of Nova Scotia, and Sir Lomer Gouin, Premier of Quebec, had been appointed Grand Officers of the Order of the Crown of Belgium by King Albert. The Halifax journal, which had opposed the further granting of British titles in Canada, declared that Mr. Murray's "countrymen will everywhere rejoice that he has been honoured for a signal service"—helping Belgian relief during the War. Shortly before this on Oct. 14 Sir George Garneau of Quebec was honoured by His Holiness the Pope, for generosity in the erection of a local church, with the rank of Knight of the Order of Gregory the Great and on Oct. 13 the ceremony of investiture was performed by H.E. Cardinal Bégin in the Archbishop's Palace. No one seemed to realize the incongruous character of these incidents and Parliamentary policy. For the first time in many years there were at the end of 1919 no announcement of Canadian New Year Honours. Meanwhile, during the year 8 Military Knighthoods had been conferred—Major-Gen. Sir E. W. B. Morrison being the last, 25 C.B's, 44 C.M.G's and 48 C.B.E's granted—all for military services—while F. Orr Lewis of Montreal and London was made a Baronet and G. McLaren Brown, European manager of the C.P.R., James W. Woods, Toronto, and Wm. E. Stavert, Montreal, were knighted for civilian services in Imperial War Missions. Chief Justice Sir L. H. Davies and Hon. L. P. Duff of Canada's Supreme Court were sworn of the Privy Council.

Foreign Decorations of the Year. Meanwhile hundreds of Foreign decorations had been conferred upon Canadians and the King's consent to their acceptance gazetted. A few only can be mentioned here as being illustrative of the wide range of war services rendered by Canadians and honoured by Foreign rulers: Grand Cordon of the Order of the Sacred Treasure, Japan, upon Lieut.-Gen. Sir G. M. Kirkpatrick, K.C.B., K.C.S.I.; Order of St.

Sava (4th class) Serbia, Col. H. W. Blaylock, C.B.E.; Order of Danilo (2nd class) Montenegro, Brig.-Gen. D. M. Hogarth, D.S.O. and Col. F. S. Morrison, D.S.O.; Order of the Crown of Italy, Lieut.-Col. C. H. Mitchell, C.B., C.M.G., D.S.O.; Order of the Crown of Belgium, Hon. Sir G. H. Perley, K.C.M.G.; Order of Leopold, Belgium (Chevalier) Lieut.-Col. D. S. Tamblyn, O.B.E., D.S.O.; the American Distinguished Service Medal, Gen. Sir A. W. Currie, G.C.M.G., K.C.B.; Orders of the Star of Roumania, Crown of Roumania and Regina Maria, Lieut.-Col. J. W. Boyle; Order of the White Eagle (5th Class) with swords, Serbia, Capt. J. K. Mossman, M.C.; Croix de Guerre and gold star and Ruban du Blessé de Guerre, France, Mrs. T. Charles Henshaw of Vancouver; Croix de Guerre and Palm, France, Maj.-Gen. Sir David Watson, K.C.B., C.M.G.; Croce di Guerra, Italy, Brig.-Gen. C. H. Mitchell, C.B., C.M.G., D.S.O. The French Legion of Honour was granted most generously to Canadians in 1919 with Lieut.-Col. L. H. Bodwell, O.M.G., D.S.O. of Vancouver; Brig-Gen. George N. Cory, C.B., D.S.O.,; Brig.-Gen. William F. Sweny, C.M.G., D.S.O. and Lieut.-Col. Noel Marshall of Toronto amongst those receiving the rank of Chevalier or Commander.

Questions of Independence or Separation from the Empire.   It was inevitable that a great war in which the Dominions took a great part should lead to wide discussion and to some changes in the relationship of the parent and daughter States of the Empire. Restlessness was in the air and in every phase of politics or government; change was the constant cry and, as usual in democracies, change and improvement were supposed to be synonymous terms. Whether some of the changes proposed in Canada had a separationist tendency or not was uncertain; there were undoubtedly some in Canada who hoped that such a result would follow; there were some, also, who urged specific steps such as the abolition of Titles and Privy Council appeals with that end obviously in view. There were not many in this latter category but those who did take the stand were well known with, usually, some ability and a capacity for aggressive leadership; they were, also, and naturally, opposed to any and all policies of closer union with the other countries of the Empire; they made much of the National status discussion of the year along lines certainly not intended by the Government or Parliamentary leaders; they continuously misrepresented British aims, policy, proposals and politics while supporting separationist activities in Ireland or India or Egypt or South Africa or any other country which happened to be British.

Though opposed to Imperial Federation or any Empire responsibilities they were usually quite willing to accept the new and infinitely greater responsibilities of the League of Nations. Publicists such as Henri Bourassa, J. S. Ewart and Lindsay Crawford, were opposed to the creation of an Imperial Cabinet, an Imperial Council or even the Imperial Conferences of the day and feared powers, which were always subject to the approval

of the governing bodies of the Dominions, because they might
involve Canada in war for the defence of an Empire which had
guaranteed to defend and was obviously able and willing to defend
Canada in return. Yet they were quite ready to approve the
clause in the League Constitution which bound Canada "to respect
and approve and preserve as against external aggression the
territorial integrity and existing political independence" of all
the 32 Nations in the League. So sane an organ of Imperial thought
as *The Round Table* dealt with this enactment (June, 1919) as
creating a great transformation in Canada's status: "By an act
done here and now in Paris, Canada and Australia could be committed to war by the movement, 20 years hence, of German armies
across the Rhine. This is but one possibility, and not the most
probable. The movement of hostile forces across any frontier in
Europe will commit them to war. The whole state of Europe becomes
their daily and hourly concern."

But the Canadian public had not yet grasped this fact and,
meanwhile, the new national status of Canada aided the hitherto loose and nebulous talk of Independence. It was not as yet
dangerous or disturbing; it was only serious as an educative influence on thoughtless minds or as a factor in eliminating minor
elements of existing unity. There was, however, an undoubted
confusion in current terms of discussion; a desire in some quarters
to combine the impossible and to have the great privileges, power
and *prestige* of British citizenship with certain minor "rights"
of small nations such as Mexico or Peru which were incompatible
with any existing or known system of Imperial union. For instance, a despatch from Washington in the Winnipeg *Free Press*
of Apr. 26—from a foreign country and with a foreign viewpoint
which had no love for the British Empire as such—declared it
imperative that Canada should be represented there by an Ambassador; in so representative and loyal a journal as the Montreal
Star on Aug. 7th it was stated that "Canada enters the League
of Nations recognized by the world as an independent Power;"
the Winnipeg *Free Press* took the line on Oct. 8, as to Lord Milner's technically correct claim that the King could bind the Empire
as well as the United Kingdom in his signature to a Treaty, that
"We should have been bound technically in law; but in fact we
should not have been bound at all;" the *Farmers' Sun* of Toronto
declared on Aug. 13, in discussing Empire conditions, that the
"time is at hand when, with us, it will be 'Canadians first, Canadians last, and Canadians all the time' just as across the line
it is 'America first'."

In all these and similar statements there was no direct advocacy of separation; it might be, as the Toronto *Globe* put it on
May 7th, that "Every additional measure of freedom granted the
overseas Dominions has been a new tie of sentiment and affection
between them and Britain." Yet this confusion of phrase
and thought was undoubtedly helpful to all who believed in
American republicanism as against British institutions, or disliked

for any reason the ties that bound Canada and Britain together. During 1919 *Le Devoir* and *Le Nationaliste,* under the control of Mr. Bourassa, formed a loose alliance with J. S. Ewart, K.C., and his monthly organ—*The Canadian Nation*—with interchangeable articles and attacks upon everything British. As the Toronto *Globe* of May 12th put it: "Mr. Ewart of Ottawa, objects to the description of him as a follower of Mr. Bourassa. At present, however, Mr. Ewart's views are not distinguishable from Mr. Bourassa's. Both advocate the separation of Canada from the British Empire." To those unfamiliar with the French Nationalist's opinion this extract from *The Problem of the Empire* by Henri Bourassa (page 42) may be quoted: "Before all we prefer national independence, neutrality and peace. When the approaching hour for making a decision has been reached we will begin by demanding Independence for Canada." During the year *Le Devoir* advocated Irish independence and outdid the keenest Sinn Feiner in its denunciation of the English; it *camouflaged* the "self determination" policy of the Peace Conference in connection with peoples and countries set free from the autocratic and alien rule of the German, Turkish or Austrian powers as applicable to the beneficially governed and gradually developing liberties of various small nations in the British Empire; it persisted in misrepresentation of Canada's status, policy and action in the World War as well as the position of Britain, herself.

Mr. Ewart's advocacy of Independence was carried on with the claim that "the British King," as he had put it in a Winnipeg address (Canadian Club, 1906) might still remain King in name. But he was to have no power and Canada was to be like Bolivia or Belgium, "self-existent, autonomous, sovereign." In an addendum to his *Kingdom Papers* (August, 1917), he illustrated his contention as follows: "Discontented with the political subordination of Canada; anxious that she should cease to be 'an adjunct even of the British Empire;' longing for her elevation to respectability, I have for some years, through the *Kingdom Papers,* urged our assumption of the status of an internationally recognized state, but with the retention of the present King of Canada." Following events, however, wrecked his hopes and, while Canadians were talking of their National status in the Empire and Canada was unconsciously preparing to take its place as a British nation in a League of Nations, Mr. Ewart announced that the alternative was between "deeper subordination" to Britain or complete separation: "Under such circumstances, we cannot hesitate to reply that we elect for self-respecting national life as the Republic of Canada." During the two years following this time, Mr. Ewart never lost an opportunity of attacking Great Britain's conduct of Empire or world affairs. In 1919 matters came to a head in the interchange arrangement between *The Canadian Nation* and *Le Devoir* with a constant contribution by him to a monthly journal in Toronto called *The Statesman,* edited by Lindsay Crawford, a clever Irishman who wanted an

Irish Republic, an independent South Africa, a separated Australia, a Home Rule India, a Canadian Republic.

Addressing a Labour meeting in Ottawa on Mch. 31 Mr. Ewart referred to the need of greater knowledge if Canada was to "rise to the status of an independent nation;" on Nov. 23rd he delivered an address at the Reform Club, Montreal, which evoked considerable discussion along lines which Victor E. Mitchell, K.C., dealt with in the Montreal *Star* of Dec. 6, as follows: "Mr. Ewart is an extreme Nationalist—one who favours separation from the British Empire. He is, like Mr. Bourassa, entitled to his views and to express them publicly, but there is no doubt that they are endorsed by none but Bolsheviks and others of that ilk." Lord Jellicoe's visit evoked indignation from Messrs. Ewart and Bourassa and a demand that his advice be not taken and no support be given Great Britain in Naval matters. Mr. Ewart took the line in his little journal that the British Navy did not protect Canada and that the Monroe Doctrine did and should. As he put it on Nov. 15: "I will add that if Canada had to depend upon either the United Kingdom or the United States, I should choose our neighbour—for the reason that community of interests secures fulfilment of expectations, whereas diversity produces disappointments." On Nov. 29 he put this "situation" in an even more interesting form: "I repeat that Canadians cannot be sure, in case of future trouble—with the Japanese or others—that the British Navy will not be fighting on the side of our opponents!" In *Le Devoir* of Dec. 2 these articles were republished with approval.

Meanwhile, Mr. Crawford and his Toronto journal had been doing their best along these lines. On Feb. 22 *The Statesman* declared that self-determination was not for Poland and Serbia only: "We shall recognize the fact that our lot is cast on these shores, and that in all our international relations our policies must be conditioned by the knowledge that our future lies on this Western hemisphere." There must be no paltering with Empire unity, or Imperial ideas of greatness; Canada must be a sovereign nation such as the little nations of Europe and South America. As Mr. Crawford put it before the Reform Club, Montreal, on Mch. 8: "There must be only one mentality in Canada, and that is the Canadian mentality. The English, Irish or inhabitants of other countries who arrive here ought to have a loyalty to only one country—that is, Canada." On July 12 *The Statesman* declared that "for Canada there can be no future as a nation so long as it is confined within the limits of Empire, nor can there be any guarantee that the freedom we enjoy will be preserved;" as for the War, it was stated on Oct. 18 that "our patriotism took the form of national suicide, and all in the interest not of Canada, but of England."

Mr. Crawford was at Springfield, Mass., on Nov. 9 addressing a meeting of Irishmen together with the well-known Sinn Feiner of New York, Judge D. F. Cohalan, who had been under suspicion as a pro-German during the War. The Canadian journalist was reported as follows: "What we must have before peace is declared is absolute liberty for all people. Freedom for Ireland, for Egypt, for Canada, liberty for Germany, whose peace and hope of future prospects are being destroyed by this Treaty, hope for Austria, which has been dismembered and thrown to the wolves. . . .   Where men think in Canada, there is a trend towards absolute independence, and the establishment of a Canadian Republic." Judge Cohalan followed with interesting remarks as to Great Britain being a "sea pirate" and the necessity of removing the British flag from the Western Hemisphere and the West Indies. At this stage Mr. Crawford joined the League of Oppressed Peoples in New York as a "sponsor" and was supported by a number of persons who had been conspicuous in the "interests of peace" during the late War—Rev. Dr. J. H. Holmes, B. W. Huebesch, Rev. Dr. J. L. Maques, Amos Pinchot, Rose Schneiderman, Mrs. Henry Villard and Oswald Garrison Villard —with a platform advertised in *The Statesman* which denounced "the armies of coercion, defying common law, resorting to extreme violence and cruelty in Ireland, Egypt, India!"

The subject was, incidentally, debated in the Commons during the Peace Treaty and League of Nations' discussion. On Sept. 9th W. F. Maclean declared that Canada's future lay on this continent and not with European countries; Lucien Cannon stated that "no more shall we be bound to go to war simply by the fact that England has declared war" and urged the abolition of Privy Council appeals and the right of the British Parliament to amend or in any way control the constitution of Canada; the Hon. N. W. Rowell, in reply, repudiated any idea of making Canada an independent nation and declared that "the people of this country are determined, on the one hand, to maintain their connection with the Motherland; they are determined, on the other hand, to exercise the powers of a nation within the Empire." Hon. W. S. Fielding on Sept. 11 endorsed this view and added: "I have no sympathy in the world with anybody who wants to make this an independent nation, separate and apart from Great Britain."

Hon. C. J. Doherty in referring to Canada's status under the Peace Treaty declared that: "We have grown up to nationhood, and it is ours. What came over there was the recognition of our nationhood." G. W. Parent approved Mr. Ewart's denunciation of Imperialism and A. R. McMaster declared that: "If we are to reach out for the position of a nation having equal status to that of Great Britain, then we must be given the right to name our own Ambassadors. I imagine that if we are to have this full sovereignty—and I wish it for my country—we should have the right to name our own Governor-General." L. J. Gauthier did not want separation: "We are not secessionists; we want to remain with Great Britain. And, may I be permitted to say, our only safeguards (Quebec) are His Majesty the King, the

7

Union Jack and the British authorities. I have confidence in no other.''

Naval Problems and Conditions; The Navy League of Canada. Great Britain had come out of the War with an immense Navy in both ships and *personnel* and sea-power; its silent forces had convoyed over 13,000,000 soldiers with only 2,700 lost through enemy action, 25,000,000 tons of explosives and 51,000,000 tons of fuel or fuel oil; its sea blockade of Germany had shortened the War and done much to directly compel the final surrender through German shortage of raw material for ordnance; its Merchantile Marine had incurred losses of 9,055,668 tons during the War or 10 times as much as France or Italy and 17 times as much as the United States while these gallant merchant seamen ensured the vital transport of supplies and men for all the Allies over the seas of the world. Because of British sea-power its Empire was the only nation originally in the War which conquered enemy territory and lost none of its own; within the British Empire, during the War, and over many seas, 140,000,000 tons of food and material were carried and, despite submarines, the number of vessels arriving and departing from United Kingdom ports increased from year to year as the War went on. Canada benefitted in the safe carriage of over 400,000 troops across the ocean, in the carriage of products overseas which increased $1,000,000,000 in value, and totalled 3,000 millions in the years of war. As President Poincaré of France put it in London on Nov. 10:

> While the British Army was giving so many proofs of valour and stubbornness on land, your Majesty's Fleet, constantly kept up and strengthened by the uninterrupted activity of new types of vessels, retained the mastery of the seas, immobilized the enemy's vessels in the North Sea and Baltic ports, little by little cleared the Channel and the Atlantic of the German submarines, assured in friendly accord with the French Navy the arrival of American munitions and provisions, and afterwards protected the regular transport of the troops which the United States in their turn sent to the defence of the civilized world. These marvellous efforts were not for one moment relaxed throughout the whole duration of hostilities, and they only ceased on the day when the vanquished enemy asked for mercy.

During the War nearly $1,500,000,000 was spent upon the Naval programme and 2,000,000 tons of shipping built for defence purposes; the Naval estimates for 1919-20, owing chiefly to high wages and prices, were more than the total during the last year of the War—$787,644,000. At the same time there was a reduction in *personnel* during 1919 from 407,000 to 280,000 officers and men. The Naval costs of the war period it may be added, were $1,028,667,985 in 1915-16, $1,049,386,090 in 1916-17, $1,136,-944,455 in 1917-18 and $1,625,000,000 in 1918-19 (estimated)—a total in round figures of 4,840 million dollars.

On. Apr. 7th the Grand Fleet was dispersed after an historic existence of 4 years and 8 months and Admiral Sir David Beatty on that day hauled down his flag as Commander-in-Chief. The enemy in the North Sea—for whom Naval concentration had so long existed, having ceased to threaten, the old-time divisions were resumed and there were once more Home and Atlantic Fleets, Mediterranean, West Atlantic, South America, China, Australia and Home Base Squadrons. Cruiser squadrons again were patrolling the Seven Seas; the time was said to be ripe for co-operation amongst the Dominions to strengthen the bases of this sea-power and to help the over-burdened Motherland in some part of a world policy which also served every section of the British Empire. Financial conditions had already made reductions necessary for Great Britain and Rt. Hon. W. H. Long, 1st Lord of the Admiralty, stated in July that when the Armistice was concluded there were 302 new warships and 806 auxiliaries under orders, while at the time of speaking there were only 84 warships and 110 auxiliaries under completion and these chiefly to replace old ships or meet the ravages of war.

Canada had a Naval part in the War though it was not a spectacular one such as that of the Australian Fleet and the great New Zealand battleship. In August, 1914, the most powerful fleet the world had ever seen was concentrated, with a few exceptions such as the Mediterranean squadron, in the North Sea; when the War ended there were, in addition to the magnificent Grand Fleet, British squadrons on the Atlantic convoying men and munitions, in Southern European waters and at various vital points elsewhere safe-guarding convoys for the eight fronts of British war. In November, 1918, British war-ships were aided by a number of small Canadian vessels; the former were patrolling the coast of Nova Scotia and New Brunswick while the latter were helping in the lookout for mines and submarines. Canadian-built drifters and trawlers were also patrolling the Mediterranean in the interests of the Allies; they were sweeping the coasts of Portugal and of Spain; they were operating off the coast of West Africa; they were helping to secure merchantmen through the danger zones; they were assisting in the protection of the American coast by operating off New York, Norfolk and Hampton Roads, Virginia. The Canadian Department of Naval Service had, from 1916 onwards, rushed the building or purchase of these vessels while the British Admiralty supplied trained men to teach the crews. The Admiralty had anticipated before the War that mines would be largely used in the next conflict at sea and there was a well-trained mine-sweeping establishment in full operation.

By 1918 a large number of Canadian trawlers and drifters were ready and in service; the trawlers' crews consisted in most cases entirely of Canadians enrolled with the Royal Naval Canadian Volunteer Reserve. On the drifters were numbers of men who had seen service on Imperial ships in foreign waters. The patrolling of the coasts and waters from Halifax up to Labrador was no easy task; the German U-boats known to be in the offing during the spring of this year were 16-knot vessels, equipped with highly efficient hydrophones, by which the approach of other vessels could be detected at long distances; the events of July, 1918, showed what could be done against and despite the most careful guardianship—though the sinkings of that period might have been much greater and vast quantities of mines sown by the enemy were, in fact, quietly swept up. · When the Armistice came demobilization was rapid and the fishermen returned from their deeds of war to the more commonplace perils of every-day life on the sea. Speaking at Halifax on Feb. 18 Admiral W. Oswald Story, in command of the British North Atlantic Squadron, spoke of Canada's Naval war-work as follows: "On this coast we have had over 100 vessels of the Navy operating, manned by between 4,000 and 5,000 Canadians. The service these men have rendered to Canada has been great. They have had to man small ships, and live a life to which they were not accustomed in any way. They have borne these hardships cheerfully, and there conduct throughout has been irreproachable."

United States Naval Plans. The Americans in 1919 showed no intention of any Naval demobilization or decrease such as Great Britain was carrying out. The direct opposite was the case and Mr. Daniels, Secretary of the Navy, who had declared in 1918 that if the League of Nations was not accepted by Congress and European armaments restricted the United States would equal in its fleets the greatest Naval power, explained his plans to the Naval Committee on Jan. 1st as including a Navy "fit and on its toes with two great fleets." One of these was to be based on the Pacific Coast and the other on the Atlantic Coast, with joint war manoeuvres as a part of the regular programme of training. This plan, he added, was approved by Admiral W. S. Benson, Chief of Naval Operations, and "an Admiral who can stay long enough to stir up ambition" would be placed in command of each fleet and all officers kept on their ships for two years at a time. The Fleets, it was expected, would be equal in their distribution of capital ships. The Submarine bases at San Diego, Key West, and New London, and the Air defence stations at San Diego and Pensacola, were to be retained. An increase in the permanent strength of the Marine Corps from 17,400 to 26,297 men was advised; all capital ships were in future to be electrically driven while the *New Mexico* dreadnaught had, already, developed 31,000 horse-power with a 25 per cent. saving in fuel; the Secretary asked the right to spend a $36,000,000 Aviation appropriation at once.

The Naval situation at this time, according to the U.S. *Navy Year-Book*, showed the value of all United States fighting craft, from dreadnoughts to gun-boats, as $500,000,000, while the actual fighting ships of the rival Powers were compared as follows: Great Britain, 702 ships with a tonnage of 2,415,962; the United States, 244 ships with a tonnage of 931,803; Japan, 136 ships and a tonnage of 599,801; France, 239 ships and a tonnage of 580,668; Germany, 276 ships, totalling 561,669 tons, and Italy, 228 ships with a tonnage of 287,065. The United States was described as far in the lead of other Powers in ships under way and projected—the total figures were 350 ships and 1,124,473 tons; for Great Britain the figures given were 210 ships and 475,796 tons; Japan had 54 ships under way but their tonnage was not known. At the close of the year the recommendations of the U.S. Navy Board for 1921 included 2 battleships, one battle-cruiser, ten scout cruisers, five destroyers and six submarines: "The Navy of the United States, ultimately, should be equal to the most powerful maintained by any other nation of the world," and this not later than 1925, said its Report—as it had done in preceding years.

The great difficulty of the American Navy at this stage in its expansion was a shortage in *personnel*—the fact of the Service being unpopular with American young men, a failure in recruiting, a growing tendency to desertion amongst the sailors, themselves. Meantime the question of an American Navy which might become stronger—at least on paper—than that of the British Empire was an important matter to Canada which, under such circumstances, would be face to face with both military and naval dominance by the United States on and around this continent. It would face the need of either supporting and strengthening the British Navy or leaning absolutely upon the consideration, generosity and good-will of a Foreign nation! To Canadian trade and shipping the British fleets, therefore, seemed to be vital at this juncture and sea-power essential; to the British Empire safe sea-routes were as necessary as safe railways to the United States.

The Canadian Government's Naval Policy.   The Department of Naval Service, of which Hon. C. C. Ballantyne was Minister, had under its control in 1919 the Royal Naval College, which was intended to impart a complete education in Naval Science, with 43 Cadets in attendance at Esquimalt, B.C., and a record of 51 graduates on active service during the War; the Royal Canadian Navy which included H.M.C.S. *Rainbow*, 2 submarines on the Pacific Coast, the British sloop *Shearwater*, H.M.C.S. *Niobe*, and 2 auxiliary Patrol vessels with 60 trawlers and 100 drifters; the 10,000 recruits for various Naval services obtained during the war with 700 officers and 4,768 men in active service at the close of 1918; the Canadian Radio-Telegraph Service with 200 stations afloat or ashore and the equipment of Naval ships and stores transport as part of its work; the Naval Intelligence Branch charged with the collection and distribution of information as to Naval and marine questions; the Canadian Atlantic Coast Patrol consisting of 123 vessels of different nature, Hydrographic Surveys and surveys of Tides and Currents, Naval Stores, Stefanson's Canadian Arctic Expedition, Fisheries Protection and 30 Life Saving Stations.

Much special work in these years had been thrown on the Department by co-operation with the Admiralty in examination at Halifax of neutral vessels, in the convoy of general shipping, in troops and store transportation, in supervision of exports totalling, during 1915-18, 11¼ million tons of freight, in refitting and repair work at Canadian dockyards, in the defensive armament of merchant shipping, in the preliminaries of a Royal Canadian Naval Air Service which had some slight development and in a construction of ships for the Allied Powers which reached the following figures* during the War:

For the Imperial Government	....	12 Submarines
" " "	....	60 Armed Trawlers
" " "	....	100 Armed Drifters
" · " "	....	550 Coastal Motor Patrol-boats
" " "	....	24 Steel Lighters (Mesopotamia)
For the French Government	....	6 Armed Trawlers
" " "	....	36 Coastal Motor Patrol-boats
For the Italian Government	....	6 Submarines.
For the Russian Government	....	1 Large Armed Icebreaker
" " "	....	Several Submarines

During the early part of the year, despite protests from various quarters, the demobilization of the Naval forces proceeded rapidly and by Apr. 15, 3,490 officers and men had been discharged. In the House on May 7 William Duff, Liberal member for Lunenburg, N.S., made a vigourous attack upon the Canadian Naval authorities in connection with the Submarine activities of 1918; the Minister replied at some length on May 26. A statement was issued by the Department on July 10 that Canadians who had served in the Imperial Naval Service during the War would receive a war badge, provided they fulfilled the conditions for the award of this badge to members of the Canadian Naval Service. During the visit of Mr. Premier Massey of New Zealand in July, he urged Canadian participation in creating a great British Pacific Naval force and at Victoria on July 17 said: "Our position as an Empire is so vastly different from that of any other nation that sea-power is absolutely necessary to us. If we are not afforded the means of protecting our sea routes, the Empire will fall to pieces. If there is one thing upon which the British Empire must insist, in and out of the Peace Conference, it is a strong Navy."

Meantime, the question of creating a Canadian Navy was under discussion with a powerful Canadian Navy League pressing for action. The British Government had, in its re-organization, offered battleships and other vessels for Canadian use and as the nucleus for a new defence system and, though little publicity was given the matter, the Toronto *Globe* of Apr. 16 declared that Canada should not hesitate to accept: "In the case of Australia it is understood that the 6 destroyers and 6 submarines accepted by that Commonwealth are vessels of the most up-to-date standards, replacing ships of the Australian Navy that have been considerably worn in service during the recent War." It was understood, however, that Government policy awaited Lord Jellicoe's visit and, on Nov. 19, Mr. Ballantyne, Minister of Naval Service, intimated in an interview that the Government would undertake in the very near future to formulate a Naval policy for Canada, and

*Note.—Naval Service Department Report for Mch. 31, 1919.

might be prepared to submit its proposals to Parliament at the next Session.

At the same time he announced the coming of Lord Jellicoe to Ottawa on the 27th and stated that the Admiral would give the Government, in an advisory capacity, the benefit of his experience and knowledge of Naval defence. It was pointed out, in a portion of the press, that Canada had the nucleus of an excellent Navy in the shape of 10,000 young men and boys who had undergone training in Canada during the War and served in patrol and other duties in home and European waters. With the creation of a Canadian Merchantile Marine such as Canada had begun, with 53 ships launched or under construction, the necessity also had arisen of providing some sort of Cadet system for the creation of an adequate supply of officers to man these ships. Then followed the visit of Lord Jellicoe, his consultation with the Government and his guarded speeches in the country; at the close of the year it was apparent that the Government hesitated over the question of expense with a tendency to let the matter stand over. *The Globe* of Dec. 5 dealt with the situation as follows:

The British Fleet is the largest and most powerful in the world, though it is greatly reduced in numbers of ships and *personnel* since hostilities ceased. The cry in Britain is not for more ships, but for decreased expenditures. That does not mean that she will not keep her Navy in efficient shape for the work that falls to it in peace time, and for any emergency that may arise. Canada can best help in this respect by training men for service afloat, maintaining a sufficient number of vessels of the requisite type for that purpose. Proposals that Canada should set about the acquiring of a big fleet, including capital ships, costing large sums for construction and running expenses, are not in keeping with the times and conditions. A few vessels of modern type would suffice for the training of the Canadian naval militia and aid in the protection of our commerce. They must be controlled by this country. That would not hinder their becoming part of the Empire fleet in time of war on the decision of the Canadian Parliament.

Canadian Merchant Shipping and Marine. All countries were interested in the shipping problem in 1919; trade and commerce were affected by the shortage, prices were influenced and United States ambitions had been aroused by the opportunity. The tonnage of Great Britain in 1914 was 18,892,000 and that of British Dominions 1,682,000; in June, 1919, the former had a tonnage of 16,545,000 and the latter 1,863,000. The United States in 1914 had 2,027,000 tons of sea-going ships and 2,260,000 on the Great Lakes; in 1919 the figures were 9,773,000 and 2,160,000 respectively. There was still a large British superiority but the competition of the United States was obvious; before the War the United Kingdom controlled 42 per cent. of the world's tonnage and the United States 4·46 per cent.; in 1919 the respective figures were 34 per cent. and 20 per cent. British conditions would, in the near future, be improved by the addition of a part of the 1,768 German ships which were to be distributed amongst the Allies. Changes in other countries were slight and the total of the world's tonnage in 1919 was 47,897,000 compared with 45,404,000 in 1914; the shortage in transport was due to the fact that there had been none of the normal and natural increase in yearly tonnage which would have made the total 55,000,000 tons—to say nothing of increased efficiency. The cessation of harbour construction during 4½ years, the restrictions on new dry-dock facilities, lack of plants for repairing ships and frequent delays in port, etc., added to the difficulties of the shortage.

Canada, during 1918, still showed a decrease in its registered shipping—the tonnage of vessels of Canadian registry, leaving home ports for overseas, being 1,531,311 and the freight carried only 837,516 as compared with 2,208,344 tons and 899,113 tons respectively, in 1917. Comparison with all vessels outward bound and carrying cargoes from Canadian ports showed a total of 13,206,682 tons and 9,922,647 tons of freight; the Canadian ship tonnage was therefore 11·60 per cent. and of freight carried 8·44 per cent. Before the War it was estimated that Canada was paying other nations $30,000,000 for sea-borne transportation; during the War the amount was much greater. The Government, however, had latterly undertaken a considerable ship-building programme and the output increased yearly; in 1917 the new tonnage was 24,954 valued at $4,398,570 and in 1918 53,912 tons. Although the aggregate tonnage built in 1918 was the largest in 33 years it was far below the output during any year in the "Seventies," when the wooden shipbuilding industry had been in operation with a product ranging from 103,581 tons in 1871 to 188,098 tons in 1879. In 1917-19 much of the material required for steel ship-building had to be imported from the United States—including plates, angles, beams, etc., to a total of over $12,000,000 in value.

The building operations of 1918-19 were carried out as a Government enterprise and in the middle of the latter year 45 ships were under construction with every shipyard busy—including Halifax, New Glasgow, Lévis, Three Rivers, Montreal, Kingston, Welland, Collingwood, Port Arthur, Prince Rupert, Vancouver and Victoria; the vessels of this Canadian Government Merchantile Marine were being built of three types—one, two and three deckers—and in 7 sizes. There were two vessels of 2,800 tons each; 4 of 3,400; 5 of 3,750; 8 of 4,300; 8 of 5,100; 16 of 8,100 and 2 of 10,500. The cost of the ships was placed at $52,000,000 and the total dead-weight tonnage was 265,000; 6 of them were delivered by July, 1919, with 30 more expected by the close of the year and the balance in 1920. New services were put in operation during the year—notably with the West Indies and Argentine and the ships, as they came into operation, passed under control of the Canadian National Railways to whose business they were to be contributory; R. B. Teake was appointed Manager of the Steamship Company under the name of the Canadian Government Merchant Marine, Ltd., with headquarters at Montreal—reporting directly, however, to D. B. Hanna and the Board of the National Railways at Toronto where R. G. Vaughan was appointed Superintendent. Speaking in the Commons on May 8,

Mr. Ballantyne, Minister of Marine and Fisheries and Naval
Service reviewed this policy and made the following statement:

There were three reasons why the Government adopted the policy of
building up a Merchantile Marine. The first for reasons arising out of the
conditions brought about by the War. The second was the desirability of
building up our export trade. At no time in our history have the prospects
been so favourable as at present for the building up and expanding of our
export trade. The third reason was that Canada has a vast railway system,
and it was proper that the Government, in order to complete the chain of
transportation and to place our Government railways on as favourable a footing
as possible, should supply those railways with the necessary steamship service. We hope to see our ships on the Atlantic and on the Pacific Oceans—
plying to England, to Australia, to New Zealand, to South Africa, to South
America and to all the ports with which Canada can carry on a foreign trade.

By the close of the year the total ships arranged for were
60 with a tonnage of about 350,000; 15 ships had been delivered
and there had been a number of sailings while vessels of the
Service had carried Canadian products to St. John's, Cuba, Jamaica, Barbados, Trinidad, Bordeaux, Demerara, Buenos Aires,
London, Liverpool, Havre and Bristol. In an interview at Montreal
on Dec. 4 Mr. Ballantyne declared that "the manufacturers of
Canada now possess, in the Canadian Government Merchant
Marine, the keys which will open to Canadian industry the ports
of the world. I believe that a wonderful opportunity has presented
itself to industrial Canada, and my message to the manufacturers is to advise them to take advantage of the facilities offered
by Canada's merchant marine without delay, and concentrate
their energies in doubling and redoubling the Canadian export
trade." Lord Jellicoe in his Canadian speeches urged the strengthening of the country's Merchantile Marine as essential to trade;
Lloyd's Register for June 30, 1919, stated that Canada then had
under construction 59 vessels of 155,542 tons of which 43 vessels
of 134,757 tons were of steel.

Toward the close of the year it was stated that the British
Government had agreed to the transfer of Canadian ships then
under British registry to Canadian registry but with the retention of certain Government rights. Under the British Shipping
Act of 1884, ocean-going vessels registered anywhere in the British
Empire were *de facto* under British registry. The British Registrar-
General of Shipping delegated his functions to representatives
in the principal ports of the Overseas Dominions, usually the
Collectors of Customs, and these officials accepted registry of
vessels and reported to the Registrar-General, who thereupon
inscribed the vessels as having been granted British registry.
No definite action was taken during the year. Efforts were also
made to obtain a similar transfer of registry by the Canadian
Pacific Ocean Services, Ltd., but no conclusion was reached.

Meantime, the United States had been making great efforts
at Merchantile Marine expansion and the Shipping Board announced its policy at Washington on June 12 as follows: (1) Completion
of some 13,000,000 dead-weight tons of Government shipping

at an additional cost of $673,000,000, and a total cost of $3,400,000-
000; (2) transference of the fleet to private ownership as rapidly
as the demand will permit, vessels to be operated in the meantime
by the Government.   Private ownership was urged for the following reasons: (1) To give the overseas trade the full benefit
of competitive service, (2) to leave steamship operators free to
render this competitive service, (3) to teach present and prospective steamship operators a confidence which they must feel
before they could be expected to invest their money in existing
ships and (4) to place the orders for new ships, without which
the outlook for the American shipbuilding industry would not be
encouraging.   Originally the U.S. Shipping Board had planned
to build 3,148 ships of 17,395,061 deadweight tonnage and the
Shipping Act of Sept. 7, 1916, called for acquisition of a Merchant
Marine ''adequate to the commerce of the United States.''   The
total proposed in 1919 had shrunk by 4 million tons but it was
still sufficient to make the British Empire understand the efforts
which were being made in the United States as to both Naval
power and marine extension.

The Work of the Navy League of Canada in 1919.   It cannot
be said that public opinion in Canada was greatly stirred up
over the Navy issue of the year; it is a question if the War had
not too greatly dulled the sensibilities of the people for much
activity in this respect.   Yet many did recognize that the need
for adequate protection of sea routes and commerce was as
great as ever—even though the United States and Japan were
the rivals of the future instead of Germany; the inter-dependence
of the countries of the Empire was as obvious as before the War
and co-operation in defence was still the cheapest and best course
of action; the strategic value of a defence machinery in which each
unit had its allotted task in case of emergency was as clear as
ever; the desirability of Dominion Navies being under local peace
administration and the fact of concentration in Imperial effort
and harmony in detail producing economy in expenditure and
efficiency in war result were equally obvious.   Hence the importance of the work undertaken by the Navy League of Canada
in 1917-18 under the Presidency of W. G. Ross, with headquarters
at Montreal, and continued in 1919, under the Presidency of
Æmilius Jarvis, with headquarters at Toronto.   The League grew
rapidly with, at the beginning of this year, 169 branches and
70,832 members and a platform formulated and adopted at its
Victoria meeting (Feb. 8, 1919), as follows:

Whereas the British Empire, 'A League of Free Nations,' was made
possible by the British Navy, has been developed under its protection, and
enjoys unity and security through its power to resist and overcome enemy
attack; and whereas during the Great War the unity so secured has proved
of inestimable advantage to all the British Dominions; and whereas uninterrupted freedom of intercourse between the various parts of the Empire
is essential to the well-being and existence of the British Empire, and whereas
the time has now come when Canada should join the other British Dominions
in relieving the overburdened British taxpayer of a portion of the immense

obligation which he now carries, and should assume her full and fair share of the cost and responsibility of maintaining a united naval defence; and whereas the naval policy of Canada and its administration, should be determined on broad lines and in co-operation with Great Britain and the Overseas Dominions.

Be it resolved that the Navy League of Canada is in favour of a naval policy for Canada which will have regard to the needs of the whole British Empire, and in deciding upon such policy political exigencies should be disregarded and the opinion of the most eminent naval strategists alone considered; and the fundamental idea shall be Empire Naval Defence, and that the Fleet units may be either acquired or built, that the Dominions shall retain control of their ships, that there shall be a complete standardisation of *personnel*, ships and equipment, and that the whole shall be of the best, and that in times of war all the fleets shall be under one supreme command.

The policy of the League included the following lines of work with emphasis on education of the public in Naval history, conditions and defence as the pivot of its operations: (1) To disseminate among the people of Canada a knowledge of the necessity and use of sea-power as the keystone of Empire and National defence and commercial prosperity; (2) the advocacy of a policy under which Canada shall assume her proper share of the cost and maintenance of protecting her own trade routes and coast defences; (3) the creation of a marine policy that will tend to build up our Merchantile tonnage and the establishment of a Naval Reserve Force composed of Canadian officers and men who have served either in the Imperial or Canadian Naval forces; (4) the support of all just claims of officers and men of the Royal Canadian Navy and its auxiliaries with regard to pay and pensions, and that merchant officers and men in times of war be put on an equal footing in this regard; (5) the support of Sailors' Institutes in Canadian ports so as to better the conditions of the Merchant seamen when ashore; (6) the application of steady pressure upon Parliament and the Government for the most efficient administration of the Department of Naval Service, and the abandonment of the present system of the portfolio of Marine, Fisheries and Naval Defence being under one Minister; (7) the application of steady pressure upon all citizens to see that public men and Members of Parliament should insist upon the administration of maritime policy being kept free from partisan action; (8) the encouragement and extension of Naval Colleges and of the Boys' Naval Brigade movement, and the establishment of proper training institutions so that all Canadian ships shall be manned by British-born sailors.

The League was governed by a Council composed of the Presidents of Provincial Divisions, or their authorized representatives, and on Feb. 6-8 the 2nd annual meeting was held at Victoria, B.C., with W. G. Ross in the chair and the following present: J. A. Irvine for Alberta, Arthur Coles, British Columbia; W. T. Kerby, Manitoba; C. B. Allen, New Brunswick; F. K. Warren, Nova Scotia; Chief Justice J. A. Mathieson, P.E. Island; James Carruthers, Quebec; Allan Sproatt, Saskatchewan; M. P. Fennell,

Jr. of Montreal, Hon. Secretary-Treasurer. President Ross in his address declared that "the War has opened our eyes and the people now realize that in future, without question, they must contribute to the Empire's naval defence in order that the freedom of the seas and our commerce will at all times be maintained. In the past our whole thought and energies have been fixed on the development of our own country, our outlook was too limited; but a great change has arisen out of the War, *viz.*, that not only must we keep on developing our own country, but we must also devote our minds and energies toward the larger ideals and a closer affinity to the Motherland, which means an adequate contribution to the Naval protection of the Empire and the expansion of our trade in order that we, who are charged with the care of the great heritage to which we have fallen heirs, may take our just share in the development of this great legacy and the protection of our shores and our commerce."

Particulars were given by Mr. Ross of the organization of the League and of the campaign for Funds which in 1918 produced a total of $1,781,577; details were given of propaganda work, the celebration of Nelson Day, the co-operation of the I.O.D.E. under Mrs. A. E. Gooderham, the operations of the Boys' Naval brigades and the Relief Work of the League. General regret was expressed and a Resolution passed as to the death of Sir Clive Phillipps-Wolley, Hon. President; the Government was advised as to the "absolute necessity" of maintaining Naval Colleges in Canada; a Memorial was adopted urging legal protection of "the honour and dignity" of the Union Jack and other ensigns and flags of the Empire and Canada by making it an offence to use such flags for any advertising purpose; a Navy Day was advocated by Resolution as a national holiday in honour of the Battle of Trafalgar and the German Fleet surrender; the Government was urged, in view of its policy of Merchantile Marine development, to "provide all proper facilities for the training of Canadians as merchant seamen;" the League's belief in the great educational importance of Moving Pictures was expressed and Governments were asked for a more rigid supervision—particularly in respect to the representations of foreign troops or navies as occupying a greater place in the World's War than those of the British Navy and Army.

Other Resolutions included an instruction to the President authorizing presentation to the Government at Ottawa of certain complaints and grievances which were current against the administration of the Naval Department; recommending that all men engaged in the Naval service of Canada during the War, and including the R.N.C.V.R., should be granted the privileges of the Soldiers' Settlement Act; setting aside the sum of $100,000 to aid in the erection of a Seamen's Memorial Institution adjacent to the Firth of Forth as "Canada's tribute to the seamen of the Empire;" appointing Æmilius Jarvis and Hon. James Craig as a Special Committee to deal with the matter of pensions and allowances by the League to seamen of the British or Canadian

Merchantile Marine; appropriating $200,000 as an endowment for the Seamen's and Firemen's Union Home at Limpsfield, England—an institution in which Peter Wright was greatly interested—and thanking the latter for his splendid speeches in a recent tour of Canada. Outgoing Presidents were, through special by-law, created Hon. Presidents of the League and *ex-officio* members of the Council. Commodore Æmilius Jarvis of Toronto was elected President, W. R. Allan, Winnipeg and Mrs. A. E. Gooderham, Toronto, Vice-Presidents and W. G. Ross, Montreal, Hon. President; the following grants, with many lesser ones, were approved by the Council:

Completion of Navy League Home for Sailors	*Halifax	$75,000
Erection of Navy League Home	Sydney, N.S.	25,000
Erection of Sailors' Institute in P.E. Island	Charlottetown	25,000
Endowment Fund for New Brunswick Sailors' Institute	St. John	50,000
Erection of Navy League Home for Sailors	Montreal	200,000
Establishment of a Sailors Institute	Vancouver	65,000
To assist the Port Arthur Sailors' Institute	Port Arthur	12,000
Relief of British and Canadian Merchant Seamen	England and Canada	100,000
To assist British and Foreign Sailors' Society	" "	32,500
St. John Sailors' Institution	St. John	55,000
To King George's Fund for British Merchant Seamen	England	500,000
To Overseas Relief Fund	"	120,000
To Navy League in England	"	10,000
To Educational Work in Canada	Toronto	25,000

The latter amount was appropriated for the work of a proposed Dominion Educational Committee—Commodore Jarvis stating in his address, upon election as President, that this, "the main feature of the League's work, has hardly been touched." On Feb. 26 Mr. Jarvis asked J. Castell Hopkins who had been Chairman of the Ontario Educational Committee for a few months, to assume charge of the new Committee which was duly constituted out of the Ontario Committee as follows: Sir R. A. Falconer, Hon. James Craig, Rev. Father A. E. Burke, H. G. Kelly, C. A. B. Brown, A. H. U. Colquhoun, LL.D., Deputy-Minister of Education, and F. D. L. Smith—all of Toronto—with Mr. Hopkins as Chairman. Later on additions from other Provinces were made including Léon-Mercier Gouin of Montreal, Prof. Archibald Mc-Meehan, Halifax, Percy Pope, Charlottetown and W. H. Atherton, Ph.D., Montreal. Meanwhile, the headquarters of the League had been moved to Toronto following Mr. Jarvis' election as President and, a little later in the year, Gordon B. Jackson, B.A., LL.B., a barrister and officer of the R.N.C.V.R. was appointed Secretary

---

*Note.—For this Home $100,000 had been voted in 1918 and Lord Furness had donated $25,000 for the site.

with D. A. Paine Treasurer. As a result of ensuing representations to the Re-establishment Parliamentary Committee at Ottawa many of the League's suggestions as to ex-Service men and Naval Forces were accepted by that body and recommendations made accordingly.

A special meeting of the Dominion Council was held at Ottawa on Nov. 28-9 with Mr. Jarvis in the chair. The chief incidents of the meeting were a visit by Admiral Lord Jellicoe and a brief address, and the waiting of the members, as a Delegation, upon Sir Robert Borden and Sir H. Drayton representing the Cabinet. President Jarvis presented to the Prime Minister an Address which expressed satisfaction with the Government's policy in establishing a National Merchantile Marine; urged a revision of present obsolete methods of manning merchant ships and asked for support to the League in its policy of training boys and establishing Naval brigades at Vancouver, Victoria, and Nanaimo, Saskatoon, Calgary, Nanton and Edmonton, Toronto, Windsor and Hamilton, Kingston, Galt, Welland and Cobalt, Belleville, Port Arthur, Sault Ste Marie, London, Montreal and Charlottetown; declared that the Government should assist the League in providing better accommodation for Canadian sailors when ashore at Canadian ports and pointed to an expenditure by the League of $800,000 in this respect—with Naval Institutes already established, or under way, in Montreal, Quebec, Halifax, Sydney, Charlottetown, St. John, Port Arthur, Vancouver, Victoria, Esquimalt, Nanaimo and Toronto; stated that since organization the Navy League had raised $3,250,000 and that it was anxious to assist any Canadian Government in the adoption of the adequate National Maritime policy which it deemed essential to the continued existence of the Empire and to its vital co-operation in time of war.

Sir Robert Borden in his reply intimated that Government policy was largely a matter of finding the money: "There is no doubt that a policy which will develop the sea-power of the nation is essential." Careful consideration was promised. At this meeting of the Council Mr. Castell Hopkins, as Chairman of the Dominion Educational Committee, also presented a report of work carried, out during the past eight months and including the issue of Colonel William Wood's *Flag and Fleet* as a Naval Reader for the schools, publication and circulation of a series of Leaflets regarding the history and achievements of the Royal Navy to a total of over 500,000; arrangements for the translation of some of these Leaflets into French and preliminary steps in the publication of 12 Booklets upon Naval history for the use of children under 12 years. Mr. Hopkins and Hon. James Craig, Chairman of the Relief Committee of the League, were appointed Honourary members of the Dominion Council.

During the year H.R.H. the Prince of Wales accepted the position of Patron of the League. Other incidents included the visit of Capt. A. F. B. Carpenter, v.c., who commanded the famous *Vindictive* in the Zeebrugge affair and who, during March, addressed various meetings in Canada under Navy League auspices—especially at Toronto, Winnipeg and Victoria; and the continued speech-making tour of Canadian centres by Peter Wright as the guest of the Navy League and representative of the British Seamen's Union with its 150,000 members. His rugged style, forceful expression, and embodiment of English Labour opinion along certain lines, made him a popular and interesting speaker. He addressed the Toronto branch of the Canadian Manufacturers' Association on Jan. 13, and in an interview on the 15th dealt in a typical way with Bolshevism as being the end of civilization: "It has for its creed the words 'high wages,' 'no work,' 'theft' and 'no taxation'." He was at Winnipeg on the 28th and addressed a citizens' meeting there; at Calgary on Feb. 23 he spoke to a Miners' Convention and described the futility of strikes; at Edmonton on the 25th he addressed the Dominion Labour party and afterwards the Rotary Club; he spoke to a large meeting at Regina on Mch. 3rd and at other points *en route* to the Coast. On Apr. 2 he was back in Toronto and addressed a great Soldiers' banquet at the Armouries and afterwards spoke at various other meetings; he was at Halifax on the 20th and in St. John on the 28th. Returning home he presented certain views of British sailors as to Germany at the Peace Conference in Paris and then spent a month in Norway and Sweden advocating a minimum wage for sailors in those countries. There and in France, Denmark and Holland, he afterwards stated, leading men declared that beyond doubt the British Navy had won the War. Later in the year Mr. Wright was back in Canada and spoke at Winnipeg on Oct. 12 and at a mass-meeting in Toronto on the 18th; he was in Winnipeg again on the 26th and in the next few days made several speeches upon Naval and other subjects. His work in Canada was both energetic and effective. It may be added that the chief Provincial officials of the League at the close of 1919 were as follows:

Division	President	Secretary	Headquarters
British Columbia	Arthur Coles	H. J. Davis	Victoria
Greater Vancouver	Sir C. H. Tupper	A. S. Conway	Vancouver
Alberta	Pat. Burns	J. A. Irvine	Calgary
Saskatchewan	George E. McCraney	Allan Sproatt	Saskatoon
Manitoba	W. B. Allan	B. Bingham	Winnipeg
Ontario	Æmilius Jarvis	E. Tunmer	Toronto
Quebec	R. Wilson Reford	R. T. Heneker	Montreal
New Brunswick	Lieut.-Col. E. T. Sturdee	C. B. Allan	St. John
Nova Scotia	F. K. Warren	R. H. Price	Halifax
P.E. Island	Hon. J. A. Mathieson	J. O. Hyndman	Charlottetown

Succeeding incidents in the League's work included a gift of the schooner *Pinto* from the League in England and its use as the training-ship for Toronto's Naval Brigade; the Resolution of the New Brunswick Division (Jan. 21) placing on record its unqualified appreciation of Britain's Grand Fleet, "whose eternal vigilance, unconquerable determination, splendid seamanship and bravery, exemplifying the best traditions of the British Navy, made this great triumph possible, and emphasized to the world

the vital importance of maintaining the naval supremacy of Great
Britain, not only for the protection of the Empire, itself, but
for the peace of the world at large;" a Resolution of the Victoria,
B.C., Branch (Jan. 29) demanding the immediate re-establishment of the Royal Navy Canadian Volunteer Reserve on a pre-
war basis; the requests of the British Columbia Division at its
annual meeting of Feb. 5 for (1) a local training ship for boys
on practical lines, (2) the non-employment of enemy aliens in
the Canadian Mercantile Marine, (3) the construction without
delay of a large Pacific Coast dry-dock, (4) the re-establishment
of the R.N.C.V.R. and retention of the Royal Naval College at
Esquimalt; the Educational report of Mrs. C. D. Neroutsos showing
active work in the British Columbia League along these lines
and especially in the schools of the Province.

The work of the Ontario Division included the up-keep of the
Boys' Naval Brigade with its 768 boys on the roll and the use
of two training ships; the development of educational work under
a Committee which was similar in composition to that of the
Dominion Committee so far as the Ontario membership was concerned and which made a specialty of moving pictures; the Relief Department which Hon. James Craig supervised and which
paid special attention to assisting sailors and dependents of the
Merchant Marine who needed help. In the Women's department
2,409 socks, 1,460 sweaters, 8,000 miscellaneous articles, 4,000
Christmas bags, were gathered. Work was carried on as in pre-
War days for shipwrecked sailors, or those in distress in the Sea
coast towns, etc.; 17 new branches were formed making a total of
125 and the Nelson Day campaign throughout the Province, under
the direction of A. M. Hobberlin, Chairman, proved an educational
factor and a financial success.

**Canadian
Visit and
Speeches of
Admiral,
Lord
Jellicoe.**
Viscount Jellicoe of Scapa, G.C.B., O.M., G.C.V.O.,
Admiral of the Fleet and victor of Jutland, toured
a portion of the Empire in 1919 as a consequence
of the request of the Imperial War Conference of
1918 and gave his advice as to Naval conditions
and requirements in Australia, New Zealand and
Canada. Early in the year Lord Jellicoe's book, *The Grand Fleet*,
had appeared and raised again the controversy as to conditions
connected with the Admiralty and the War, the Fleet and the
Battle of Jutland. The reviews took a wide range but, on the
whole, were complimentary to the Admiral—the London *Times*,
in referring to it and to past criticisms upon Lord Jellicoe, saying
on Feb. 14: "Lord Jellicoe is entitled to ample vindication. No
fair-minded man can study his book without feeling that at Jutland the traditions of the Royal Navy were brilliantly maintained,
and that, though mist and haze saved the enemy from complete
destruction, the High Sea Fleet was thenceforth practically in-
terned. From that moment the Grand Fleet so rapidly grew
in strength that at long last it became the embodiment of tremendous and overwhelming power."

While the world was discussing his book the Admiral was preparing for his Empire tour and in London, on Feb. 14, he was given a Dinner before departure on H.M.S. *New Zealand*. Sir Thomas Mackenzie, High Commissioner for New Zealand, presided and said to the guest of the day: "The sea has been our protection, and so long as Britain is true to herself, and sees to it that the Service is ready for any eventuality, so long will the sea be our great line of defence. When Britain ceases to control it, however, we shall become slaves of the ocean. Your voyage will be at once a demonstration of the power of Empire and an indication to our enemies that if an attack is made upon the old British lion the young whelps will rise and, to the extent of their ability, rally round him." The Tour started on Feb. 20, 1919 and was to end on May 11, 1920; it was arranged for the Admiral to go to India first, to Australia and New Zealand, then to Canada and, homeward, *via* South Africa. Wherever possible he was to co-ordinate the Services, plan co-operation of the various units, point out the shifting tendencies of trade to the South Pacific and Indian oceans, deal with the paramount importance of protecting trade routes and Imperial commerce. He was in India during March and April and reached Australia in May, paid a visit to New Zealand in the Autumn and left for Canada in October.

In the Admiral's speeches and reports at this time there was very little expression of hope for peace from, or dependence upon, the League of Nations; the preparations of the United States, Japan, France and Italy, like those of Great Britain herself, were obviously for national protection and power apart altogether from the League. This issue W. M. Hughes, Premier of Australia, put clearly in one of his 1919 speeches: "If we in Australia are attacked, to whom shall we call—the League of Nations or the British Empire? Unless there is an Imperial system of defence, unless every part of the Empire knows that between them and danger is the British Navy, this Empire is the fabric of a dream." While in Australia Lord Jellicoe was the guest of many banquets, addressed the Navy League and various organizations and conferred with Governments and public men. In his speeches he declared that there should be sufficient Empire ships to guard the long lines of communication between Britain and Australia; that it was to be hoped that sufficient provision would be made both by the Mother Country and the Overseas Dominions to insure the impossibility of defeat to the British Navy; that "the lesson I am trying to preach is preparation for war and that the British Empire depends now, more than ever, upon naval supremacy."

Lord Jellicoe's Australian Report was issued before his arrival in Canada but, despite the public interest in its terms, little was cabled about it and that little of the vaguest character; with, however, emphasis upon the cost of equipment and maintenance. Throughout this elaborate document, as officially published, the Admiral assumed that future danger to the Empire lay in the Pacific and the Far East; the other dominant note was insistence on the value of capital ships as the chief weapon at sea. His proposals were based upon the premise that (1) Australia was powerless against any great Naval Power without the British fleet and (2) that it was impossible to consider the naval requirements of Australia without taking account also of the naval requirements of the Pacific and Indian Oceans as a whole; (3) that there should be a strong Empire fleet in Far Eastern seas. The question was, fundamentally, he declared, one in which the safety of Australia, New Zealand, India and South Africa were bound up; the Far Eastern fleet should, therefore, be provided by these constituent parts of the Empire, including Great Britain, with the closest co-operation and unity of direction in war between the various squadrons composing the Fleet.

The Naval force which he proposed should include 8 Dreadnought battleships, 8 battle-cruisers, 10 light cruisers, 40 destroyers, 30 submarines and 28 lesser vessels; it might include, as a beginning, ships of the Royal Navy, the East Indies Squadron, the Royal Australian Navy, with any other vessels stationed in Far Eastern waters or which might be furnished by Canada, New Zealand and the Malay States. He estimated the initial cost at $45,000,000 and the annual cost at $100,000,000 of which he allotted $75,000,000 to Great Britain, $20,000,000 to Australia and $5,000,000 to New Zealand. India was considered separately, as paying for its own Military defence at a cost of $150,000,000 per annum, and its assessment was placed at $11,000,000 a year for the upkeep of harbours and the East Indies Squadron. As to Canada its share should, he thought, be what was necessary to provide and maintain a small force of light cruisers on her Pacific seaboard for the protection of her trade in those waters, as well as a Naval force on her Atlantic seaboard. Lord Jellicoe pointed out how greatly rival nations were developing naval construction, and gave certain statistics as follows:

Great Britain. Super-dreadnoughts over 30,000 tons, 1; Super-dreadnoughts under 30,000 tons, 28; Dreadnoughts, 10; with 4 second-class battle-cruisers.

United States. Super-dreadnoughts over 30,000 tons, 23; Super-dreadnoughts under 30,000 tons, 4; Dreadnoughts, 8.

Japan. Super-dreadnoughts over 30,000 tons, 8; Dreadnoughts, 5; with 3 powerful cruisers.

France. Super-dreadnoughts under 30,000 tons, 12; Dreadnoughts, 4.

Italy. Super-dreadnoughts over 30,000 tons, 4; Dreadnoughts, 5.

Many other branches of the question of defence were dealt with but these were the big and vital points. It was intimated that the Naval defence of the Empire under his plans would, as a whole, cost the United Kingdom 74·12 per cent., Australia 7·74 per cent., New Zealand 2·02 per cent., Canada 12·30 per cent and South Africa 3·82 per cent. For Canada this would include both the Atlantic and Pacific Coasts and the figures were based upon a medium between population and trade. The Australian Report was submitted to the Commonwealth Parliament on Oct. 22; that for New Zealand about the same time. In the latter case, after quoting the Admiralty memorandum to the Conference of ·1909 favouring a single Imperial Navy, it was stated that this ideal was not attainable, and he added: "Experience has shown abundantly that responsibilities in regard to Naval defence are far more cheerfully recognized and shouldered if the result of the effort is apparent to those making it—in other words, if the ships provided are self-made by the people paying for them and are manned by their own kith and kin." The general principle of the proposals was that New Zealand should co-operate by paying for, manning and maintaining, a certain proportion of the Far-Eastern fleet and all vessels required for the harbour defence of New Zealand, and by providing such portions of the *personnel* as practicable. The ships maintained would be, in all essentials, a portion of the Royal Navy under the suggested title of the New Zealand Division. The reasons given for this policy and details of operation were similar to the Australian statements.

On Nov. 8th Lord Jellicoe arrived at Victoria, B.C., and was officially welcomed and cordially entertained. In an interview the Admiral stated that he had been invited by the several Dominions to consult with them on the question of Naval defence, but it was far from his purpose to lay down any hard and fast rule whereby that end would be accomplished. Functions at Victoria included a visit to Esquimalt, a brilliant ball given by local Navy League at the Empress Hotel and an address to a great meeting of the Canadian Clubs. The vital point of this first speech on Canadian soil was the following: "To my mind the British Navy should not be kept short of Overseas squadrons. I believe that the Empire as a whole realizes the imperative necessity of maintaining ships-of-war not only in home waters, but in close proximity to the most distant Dominions. We must see to it that our overseas Naval forces are never again permitted to be as they were prior to the war. It is due those gallant souls that were given up for the Empire in its hour of peril that such a condition should not exist again." General Sir Arthur Currie spoke briefly, declared that our great menace before the War was unpreparedness and urged upon Canada the Naval motto of Duty and Service: "Let us see that Canada does as much as she possibly can for the Navy."

Vancouver accorded Lord Jellicoe a warm greeting on Nov. 15, a Civic address was presented and other functions shared in. To the local Canadian Club on the 19th he dealt, indirectly, with the objection to his mission voiced at Montreal on the 15th by A. R. McMaster, M.P., and pointed out, again, that it was purely one of advice and not dictation: "I am only putting before a gathering like this the reasons that make it imperative that the British Empire should maintain its command of the Sea. What was it that made it possible for the War to be won? It was sea-power. What was it that imperilled our safety at one

time and made it within the bounds of possibility for Great
Britain to lose the War? It was the loss, temporarily, of the
command of the sea owing to the Submarine warfare." At
Calgary the Navy League entertained Admiral and Lady Jellicoe
at a banquet attended by various Provincial leaders with a formal welcome to Alberta by the Lieut.-Governor (R. G. Brett)
and Mr. Premier Stewart. R. B. Bennett, K.C., presided and
Lord Jellicoe was explicit upon certain points: "It is my mission
in Canada to advise the Dominion Government, where my advice
is sought, and only where it is sought, in what manner, if they
so desire it, they can co-operate in maintaining the sea-power
of the British Empire. There is a feeling abroad that the Mil-
lenium is in sight, and that there will be no more wars. I
sincerely hope that the League of Nations will meet with the
best possible success, but events of the past few days have dis-
heartened those who had faith in an immediate result. Where
the existence of an Empire is the consideration, I cannot help
thinking that the people will want to be sure that they are absolutely secure under a League of Nations before they will consent to cutting down expenditure for Naval defence. Before
ducks and drakes are played with the Navy, let us be sure that
we cannot economize in personal expenditure when we have at
stake our whole national existence."

In Regina on Nov. 22 the Admiral was honoured with a reception in the Parliament Buildings under the auspices of the
Navy League; at Winnipeg on the 24th he was the guest at
luncheon of the local Navy League; the Mayor (C. F. Gray) had
previously asked all citizens to decorate their stores and homes
and to join in a popular democratic demonstration in recognition
of their guest's great services. A warm welcome was given and
to the Navy League's 500 guests Lord Jellicoe made an effective
speech. He declared that it was in the interests of Canada to
do its share: "Trade will not protect itself," and he pointed out
that in an unrestricted submarine warfare such as Germany
had carried on, even neutral carriers were not immune. Investigation had showed that $70,000,000 of yearly trade went out of
western Canadian ports and $265,000,000 worth out of its eastern
ports. It was difficult for people so far inland as Winnipeg to realize
the necessity for sea protection; still, their great stores of grain
should make Westerners think of the need of protection in order
that these might be safely transported. "Sea supremacy for
the British League of Nations" was defined as the object of his
mission.

Lord Jellicoe arrived at Ottawa on Nov. 27 and stayed at
Government House; press despatches from the capital during
preceding weeks had indicated a decided Government policy of
"going slow." The Admiral at once got into touch with Ministers and Departments and, especially, with the Minister of Naval
Defence and the Naval Sub-Committee of the Cabinet which
included Sir R. Borden, Sir H. Drayton, General Mewburn and

Mr. Ballantyne; there were for a time daily conferences in the Privy Council Chamber. On Nov. 30, with H.E. the Duke of Devonshire present Lord Jellicoe addressed the local Canadian Club and pointed out that of recent years, in pre-war days, the people of the Overseas Dominions did not see much of the British Navy. The reason was that "we were obliged to concentrate our forces in home waters because of the menace of growing German strength;" the world well understood now that it was British sea-power, thus concentrated, which enabled the British and Allied armies to carry out their tasks. Finally, he added these concise words: "The British League of Nations should ensure the safety of sea communications. People say the chances of war in the future are very remote. I am sure that every member of this great audience will say the same thing of the chance of fire in his own house. Notwithstanding that, I will venture the assertion that 90 per cent. of your houses are insured. Therefore, while I realize as well as others the necessity of economy, I would say, Do not forget what one single day of war cost during the years from 1914 to 1918."

The Admiral was in Toronto on Dec. 6 and in the evening addressed a great mass-meeting at Massey Hall with Æmilius Jarvis, President of the Navy League of Canada, in the chair. During his speech he paid high tribute to the war-work and gallantry of the British Merchantile Marine, with its loss of 15,000 officers and men, and declared that: "At the back of the whole allied Naval effort, and, indeed, at the back of the whole allied military effort lay the Grand Fleet. . . The Fleet at the commencement of the War comprised 650 vessels of all sorts. At the end of the War it comprised 5,000." With all possible reductions in Naval force and *personnel* the burden upon Great Britain, in view of the increased cost of everything, would be as great as before the War and not less than $250,000,000 a year—and sea communications would, even then, not be protected as they should be. The Toronto *Globe* in its comment upon this address (Dec. 8) and various proposed plans of defence, said: "Canada can await the definite emergence of these new ideals, but there will be no change in her determination to shape her own defence plans—an aim quite consistent with the homogeneity of all British Naval forces and with their co-operation in War." A Navy League banquet followed at night and once more the Admiral dealt with the achievements of the Navy. As to the rest: "Canada, just as much as other portions of the Empire, is interested in the question of sea communications for the Merchantile Marine, because Canada's produce cannot get to its markets except by means of ships belonging to the Marine. Canada's prosperity is bound up in the use of the sea." President Jarvis of the League and Hon. H. J. Cody also spoke. A Civic address was presented on the 8th with a typical reply from the Admiral; the Canadian and Empire Clubs were addressed in joint meeting and

2,500 women under the auspices of the Women's Canadian Club.

Montreal was visited on the following day, the Harbour and Port inspected, a Young Men's Canadian Club addressed with Bainbridge Colby of the U.S. Shipping Board present, a private dinner was given by Hon. C. C. Ballantyne. At the latter function Lord Jellicoe emphasized the importance, whatever its size, of a first-class up-to-date Navy: "One has to remember that it takes time to create a Navy. It takes nine years to make a lieutenant from the time he enters the Navy, until he is qualified to keep watch on one of His Majesty's ships-of-war. It takes the same time to take a boy and turn him into a petty officer or gun-layer—that is an efficient one." After a further period in Ottawa came a visit to St. John on Dec. 11 where he was the guest of a Civic banquet and speaker at a joint meeting of the local Navy League and Canadian Club. Lord Jellicoe reached Halifax on the 12th and was entertained at a banquet by the Nova Scotia Division of the Navy League with F. K. Warren in the chair and addresses from Lieut.-Governor Grant and Hon. G. H. Murray. An indirect reference to local Navies was made in speaking of Admiral Lord Fisher, who had in his day withdrawn the North American Squadron for the vital purposes of concentration to meet the German menace. "This," said the speaker, "could not have been done if that fleet had belonged to Canada."

There were many and varied comments upon these speeches. The Toronto *Star* looked for a purely Canadian Navy controlled by Canada; the Ottawa *Citizen* feared politics in such a force and wanted a combination of British and Canadian efforts; the St. John *Telegraph* urged a fleet of light cruisers and the Saskatoon *Star* deprecated any Naval expenditure at this time; *L'Evenement*, of Quebec, urged caution but recognized Canada's duty to aid the Empire and the Montreal *Gazette* considered Canada financially incapable of building an adequate Navy and favoured contribution of money or ships to the British Navy; the Toronto *Globe* wanted a number of training ships and a volunteer Naval contingent, while the Toronto *World* denounced the whole thing as Imperialism and opposed any action; the *Farmers' Sun* opposed any Naval policy at this juncture and the Montreal *Star* urged Canada's moral obligation to aid the Empire and help protect herself; *La Patrie*, of Montreal, opposed any Naval action for the present. Mr. Ballantyne, Minister of Naval Services, stated at a Montreal dinner on Dec. 15 that the Government was considering the advice of Lord Jellicoe. He thought the time had now come when Canada should provide her own Naval defence and referred to "the miserable apology for Naval defence we have to-day;" he stated that during the War enemy submarines had sunk a 7,000-ton merchant vessel only 700 miles from Halifax. Whatever policy the Government did propose, he was satisfied, if his colleagues agreed with him, that it would be an efficient one.

**Lord Jelli-
coe's Report
on his Naval
Mission to
Canada.**

This important document, though actually issued
early in 1920, was essentially a matter of the year
under review and was submitted to H.E. the Governor-General on Dec. 31, 1919. Lord Jellicoe first
stated the terms of his appointment by the Lords
of the Admiralty as follows: "To advise the Domin-
ion authorities whether, in the light of the experience of the War,
the scheme of naval organization which has been adopted, or may
be in contemplation, requires reconsideration; either from the
point of view of the efficiency of that organization for meeting
local needs, or from that of ensuring the greatest possible homo-
geiety and co-operation between all the naval forces of the Empire,
and, should the Dominion authorities desire to consider how far
it is possible for the Dominion to take a more effective share in
the naval defence of the Empire, to give assistance from the
naval point of view in drawing up a scheme for consideration."
The Canadian Government had added to these instructions a
series of questions as to methods of Defence, Naval bases, co-operation and administration, *personnel* required in a Royal Canadian
Navy of the future, wireless communication and various defensive measure—coastal or otherwise.

The Admiral stated that he had visited the following ports:
Esquimalt, Victoria, McNeill (Vancouver Island), Vancouver
City, Ottawa, Montreal, Quebec, Halifax and St. John; and, by
invitation, the cities of Calgary, Regina, Winnipeg and Toronto,
Members of his Staff had visited Alberni, Uchucklesit Harbour,
Bamfield Creek on Vancouver Island, Prince Rupert, Sydney,
Shelburne and Liverpool. Passing to the local situation Lord
Jellicoe first eulogized the work of the Navy League of Canada
and then pointed out that in August, 1911, H.M. the King had
approved of the naval force of Canada being styled the Royal
Canadian Navy and its ships designated as His Majesty's Canadian. Ships; he mentioned the heavy financial burden in recent
years placed upon the United Kingdom and the current reduction of ships and *personnel* in the British Fleet; he emphasized
the fact of this policy having increased the importance and value
of co-operation on the part of the overseas Dominions for the
protection of sea communications and general naval defence;
he pointed out that modern conditions of naval warfare greatly
increased the difficulty of preventing the escape of isolated
raiders from a blockaded area and it, therefore, became increasingly necessary to keep sufficient naval forces in various parts of
the world to protect trade, and to ensure the early capture or
destruction of such enemy vessels as might escape the main blockade with the object of interrupting overseas communications
by gunfire, torpedoes, mines, or aircraft; he stated that War
experience had also shown that submarines could operate successfully at immense distances from their bases, and that this fact
necessitated the provision of defence against this type of attack
in almost all parts of the Empire while the growing development

of aircraft produced another type of attack which must be met by local forces, even when the hostile nation was at a considerable distance.

In the course of his introductory comments the Admiral referred to the wide separation of Canada's two coasts and added "for safety under all conditions each of the Canadian coast lines requires certain local defences and, in addition, each requires a naval force to guard the trade and the coast." He pointed out that it was naturally more difficult to attain and maintain a high pitch of efficiency in a small naval force than in a large fleet: "The important element of competition is largely absent; there are fewer brains at work on improvements and innovations; and the officers, particularly those in the higher ranks, have insufficient experience in fleet work." These difficulties would be largely overcome if the officers in particular, as well as some of the men, of the Royal Canadian Navy, spent a proportion of their time in ships of the Royal Navy, with frequent meetings of Canadian vessels and those of the other Dominions or of the Royal Navy; fleet exercises should be carried out annually on a large scale and would give opportunities for acquiring experience, would produce interchange of ideas, and would promote competition. With small Naval forces in Canada it would be more economical to train officers and specialists in England than in local establishments and cheaper to train boys on shore than in training ships. The necessity for discipline was described as an axiom in all ages and in all armed forces; in a new Navy it should be instilled, if possible, in early youth and with great care, by skilled instructors and without undue severity.

The Naval Requirements of Canada. This was the first section of the Report proper and Lord Jellicoe's premise to its consideration was fundamental: "The late War has once again demonstrated the dependence of the British Empire on the safety of its sea communications. Sea Power has saved the Empire as on many occasions before, but in this case it has also saved the cause of the Allies and of Civilization. General recognition of this fact will surely lead to the maintenance of British sea supremacy in the future. A Navy of very considerable strength is still required for this purpose, although the menace of our late enemies has ceased to exist." The Admiral pointed out that Canada had an Overseas trade in the last pre-war year of $600,000,000 and that its merchant shipping was steadily increasing and then dealt with tentative plans for meeting the situation of local and trade defence and of Empire defence. The Naval force which he described as "adequate purely for the protection of Canada's trade and Canada's ports," under existing conditions, included 3 light cruisers, 1 flotilla leader, 12 torpedo craft, 8 submarines and 1 parent ship with certain auxiliary small craft.

If Canada desired to aid in Imperial defence in any proportionate manner the requirements would be different. At current and increasing rates of pay Lord Jellicoe did not think British yearly estimates could go below $277,000,000 or the annual cost of the Royal Australian Navy below $10,000,000; New Zealand had spent $10,000,000 upon a battle cruiser for the British Navy in 1909 and was preparing for current expenditures along Naval lines. The Admiral pointed out that at the above rates the United Kingdom was spending £1 4s. per head to protect Overseas trade or an insurance premium of 3·6 per cent.—upon Canadian as well as British trade though he did not say so. Details were gone into as to the value to the Empire of three different fleets at a maintenance cost of $25,000,000, $17,500,000 and $10,000,000 respectively. In the following table the cost of new vessels, of maintenance and of replacement, were included together with the first cost of construction in such cases as the ships might not be provided as a gift from the United Kingdom:

5 MILLION POUNDS (25 MILLION DOLLARS) FLEET	3½ MILLION POUNDS (17½ MILLION DOLLARS) FLEET	2 MILLION POUNDS (10 MILLION DOLLARS) FLEET	1 MILLION POUNDS (5 MILLION DOLLARS) FLEET
2 Battle Cruisers ..	1 Battle cruiser		————
7 Light Cruisers ..	5 Light Cruisers ...		————
1 Flotilla Leader ..	1 Flotilla Leader ...	2 Light Cruisers ...	————
12 Destroyers	6 Destroyers ......:.	1 Flotilla Leader ...	————
1 Destroyer Parent Ship	1 Destroyer Parent Ship		————
16 Submarines	8 Submarines	8 Submarines	8 Submarines
1 Submarine Parent Ship	1 Submarine Parent Ship	1 Submarine Parent Ship	————
2 Aircraft Carriers .	1 Aircraft Carrier ...		————
4 Fleet Minesweepers	2 Fleet Minesweepers.		————
4 Local Defence Destroyers	4 Local Defence Destroyers	4 Local Defence Destroyers	4 Local Defence Destroyers
8 "P" Boats	8 "P" Boats	8 "P" Boats	8 "P" Boats
4 Trawler Minesweepers	4 Trawler Minesweepers	4 Trawler Minesweepers	4 Trawler Minesweepers

The two last proposals were purely defensive: "In the case of the estimate of £2,000,000 per annum, defence of Canada's trade in the Pacific is given in addition, but there is little naval force which can be used offensively; in other words whilst Canada would be protecting her own interests defensively it would fall to the lot of the United Kingdom, with the assistance of the other Dominions, to endeavour to take such action as would be necessary to bring war to a conclusion." Either of the first forms would be a substantial aid to the Empire in time of war. Lord Jellicoe at this point was uncompromising in his advocacy of battle-cruisers, great line-of-battle ships, as essential to serious modern defence: "Millions of tons of cargo, and in time of war, of men and stores also, are carried in ships, and until some other means of carrying these millions of tons over or under the ocean have actually materialized it is imperative for the British Empire to retain the command of the surface of the sea. This need will continue until, if ever, surface men-of-war lose their métier, and are displaced by aircraft or submarines. The capital ship is the strongest form of engine of war which exists for operating on the seas."

Administration of Naval Services. Lord Jellicoe based his recommendations in this respect upon keeping the Naval Service out of party politics and stated, in passing, that the organization under which the Royal Navy was administered by a Board of Admiralty had stood the test of time and had, indeed, been followed in its general principles in the present organization of the British War Office; that recent war experience 'had also shown that the main basis of Admiralty organization was sound. This organization was described as based upon (1) the pre-eminence of final Civil control by Parliament which, in practice, covered only matters of policy and finance; (2) responsibility of the 1st Lord to Parliament; (3) presence on the Board of naval officers of high reputation and possessing sea experience, in whom the Service afloat had full confidence; (4) the allocation by the First Lord to each member of the Board of certain definite duties for the control of which they were responsible to the Board as a whole.

He pointed out that under Paragraph 10 of the Naval Service of Canada Act, the Governor-in-Council might appoint a Naval Board to advise the Minister on all matters relating to naval affairs which could be referred to the Board by the Minister; he recommended the creation of a Canadian Navy Board similar in some though not all, respects, to the Militia Council: "A wise interpretation by the Minister of his powers and functions, and the degree to which he shall fall in with his expert colleagues of the Board on technical questions is necessary for the success of the system." Some differences were inevitable and when they could not be adjusted, it was suggested that the Chief of the Naval Staff should be empowered to present to the Prime Minister a statement of the case as seen by the Naval Members of the Board. Many details of management, control, authority, *personnel* were suggested for consideration with much information as to the way certain phases and divisions of administration had worked in London under war conditions. As to communication between the Canadian Naval Board and the Admiralty, secrecy and rapidity were described as the two essentials in war. Summarized, his chief conclusions were as follows:

1. It is very desirable that there should be a Minister for the Navy responsible only for that Service.

2. In this event, it is suggested that all other seafaring affairs should be conducted by another Minister with perhaps the title of 'The Minister of Marine and Fisheries.'

3. It is proposed that a Shipping Committee comprising representatives of ship-owners, fishery firms, the Marine Department, and the Naval Staff, should meet periodically to consider questions of general development of marine resources. Their functions would be purely advisory in peace, but in war they would take control of shipping, their Chairman acting as Shipping Controller.

4. A member or branch of the Naval Staff should be concerned with trade and fishery questions and the war training and the constructional work involved.

5. On the outbreak of war, in addition to the Shipping Committee, possessing the same powers and functions as the Ministry of Shipping in England during the late War, the Naval Staff branch referred to in No. 4 should carry out the duties of the Mercantile Movements Division.

6. Arrangements concerning the strengthening of the hulls to take defensive armament in merchant ships and fishing vessels would be dealt with by this Shipping Committee.

7. It is desirable that a knowledge of Naval warfare should form part of the qualifications of Merchant Service officers for a certificate.

8. Designs of fishing craft should be encouraged along lines tending to efficient auxiliary vessels for naval use in war time, so far as is consistent with their ordinary work.

Proposed Personnel of the Royal Canadian Navy. The Admiral's premise in this connection was the great importance of the Royal Canadian Navy and the Royal Navy holding themselves in the very closest relationship. The ships should be of similar types, the *personnel* actuated by the same motives, trained on the same lines, imbued with the same traditions, governed by a practically common discipline and aiming at the same high standard of efficiency. In order to work together in war he thought it desirable that Canadian Staff Officers should receive their training at the Naval Staff College at Greenwich in conjunction with officers of the Royal Navy and of the other Dominions. The Canadian Navy should also have efficient representation on the Admiralty Naval Staff and, it was pointed out, for some years to come the larger portion of the officers and men of the Royal Canadian Navy would necessarily be lent from the Royal Navy; as their replacement by officers and men entered and trained in Canada, would take place gradually the old spirit of discipline and efficiency should be carried on without a break. The organization of the Royal Naval College of Canada was approved and it was recommended that officers of the military branch should continue to be entered as Cadets in this institution. The regulations governing entry and training up to the rank of Lieutenant should follow closely the lines already laid down by the Admiralty.

Until suitable training establishments were in existence in Canada, it was suggested that officers should be sent to England to undergo their necessary courses in gunnery, torpedo work, etc. A certain number of officers should be selected to specialize in gunnery, torpedoes, navigation, engineering, signals, and wireless telegraphy with such other specialist branches as might be developed in the future: "It is most important that the standard of qualifications in the various branches of the service should be the same as that for the Royal Navy." The Admiral laid stress upon the fact that in the case of a small Navy, from the very nature of things, it was not easy for an officer to maintain efficiency, and impossible for him to gain full experience; that it was essential, therefore, both for efficiency and for the future of the officers themselves, that means be found for providing such officers with opportunities: "The most certain method of obtaining this would be by placing all officers of the military branch of all the Navies of the Empire on one General List, from which they would be promoted to the ranks of Commander and Captain by selection, as is the case in the Royal Navy to-day. Under this arrangement officers of each Dominion Navy of the Empire would serve a proportion of their time in ships of the Royal Navy, thus standardizing their ideas, and gaining such experience as can only be obtained in a large fleet. At the same time officers of the Royal Navy would serve a proportion of their time in the various Dominion Navies, thus gaining that wider knowledge of the Empire which is so necessary in the scheme of Imperial Navy Defence.''

In dealing with possible objections it was pointed out that the promotion of officers on a General List would necessarily be made by the Board of Admiralty on their records of service, recommendations being forwarded from the Dominions in a manner similar to that now done by the respective Commanders-in-Chief on foreign stations. The establishment of the various ranks in the General List would need to be fixed from time to time by the Admiralty in conjunction with the Dominion Navy Boards. A necessary attribute to this scheme or system would be a close *liaison* between the Admiralty and the respective Navy Boards. If separate Lists were established, it was clear that certain qualifications for promotion should be laid down in order to ensure a uniform level of ability in the higher ranks of the Navies of the Empire and these were duly specified. The Pension question, training and appointment of Petty officers, seamen ratings and recruiting, together with Naval reserves—the latter including the creation of a Royal Canadian Naval Reserve based upon the Royal Naval Reserve of England—were dealt with in detail.

The Question of Discipline. This matter and its special application to a Canadian Service were treated at length based upon the conclusion (1) that lack of discipline was obviously incompatible with efficiency in war; (2) that lack of discipline was dangerous even in times of peace as producing indolence, indifference, slackness and inefficiency; (3) that lack of discipline on board ship led to personal unhappiness and discomfort—a point proved in wide experience. True discipline, Lord Jellicoe pointed out, was obtained by infusing the spirit of discipline in the mind of the young and thereafter maintaining the practice through (1) the habit of obédience learned by o s; (2) a realization of the importance and nobility of duty; (3) the taking of a real pride in the Service. The methods of maintenance were ''inflexible firmness tempered with reason,'' a strict regard to discipline in minor matters and a spirit of mutual confidence between officers and men. Such discipline produced calmness in emergency, firmness of character, personal confidence and self-respect. Varied details followed as to ship conditions, causes of complaint or irritation, with general comments on the principle and practice of discipline.

Britain in 1919: After-War Reconstruction and Recovery. One of the marvels of this year to the student of the future will be the buoyant development of the United Kingdom after its tremendous war experiences and burdens. It was not clearly visible to other nations at the moment; apart from their own internal difficulties they heard no boasting on the subject. As the Rev. Dr. S. D. Chown, the head of Canadian

Methodism, put it (July 10) : "The Briton has no self-advertising instinct. He will not tell you what he is going to do. He does great things by stealth, and lets them be found out by accident, and he does not care whether the accident happens or not. . . . We feel that probably his silence comes from the consciousness of a great background. He has come to manhood through centuries of growth punctuated by hard fighting, and long ago he put away childish things."

United States opinion, which always had great influence in Canada owing to press despatches and ever-present newspapers, was prone to overlook the rapidity and certainty of British recovery and the brighter side of British finance and trade. Robert Fleming, an English financial authority—eminent but not well-known to the public—was interviewed by the *New York Tribune* on Feb. 23 and declared that Englishmen had by no means sold all their American holdings and Securities; that when matters were adjusted it would be found that current British investments in the States were more than the total British indebtedness to that country. During the War Great Britain was in fact, as Kipling put it "the Bank of the Open Credit, the Power-house of the Line" and in this year of reconstruction she kept her head and renewed her reputation.

The British Financial Situation in 1919.   Before the War Great Britain was saving money and investing part of it abroad at a rate of many hundred millions a year with assumed capital investments of $85,000,000,000 which were really much larger; at the end of the War she had $40,000,000,000 to charge against her resources with at the same time a greatly increased valuation in many securities held; with a population of 45,000,000 her revenues in 1919 were equal to those of the United States with its 100,000,000 population—though her Debt per head was $890 to the American $200; in taxation her people were back again to the conditions following the Napoleonic wars but with infinitely wider resources, capabilities, and control over the money-producing areas of the world.   An American writer in *The Street*, a New York financial journal, at this time indicated with approximate accuracy the British conditions of 1816 and 1919—the years after Britain's greatest wars:

	1816	1919
Population	20,000,000	46,500,000
National Wealth	$12,500,000,000	$116,000,000,000
National Debt	4,475,000,000	37,890,990,000
National Income	1,500,000,000	17,500,000,000
National Debt Charges	165,000,000	1,814,780,000
Ratio of Debt to Wealth	35%	32%
Ratio of Debt Charges to Income	11%	10%

According to Edgar Crammond, F.S.S., an eminent statistician, the production of commodities and services for the feeding, clothing and maintenance of the nation which had, in 1907, given a surplus of 2,500 million dollars, in 1917 gave a similar surplus of 7,500 millions while the National income had similarly advanced from $10,500,000,000 to $16,500,000,000.* With an increase of 50 per cent. in productive power and in ,values he had no fear of the future: "Our assets must be measured in the same monetary values as our liabilities, that is to say, in 1919 money values, not in 1914 money values. In 1914 I submitted to the Royal Statistical Society an estimate of the national wealth at $82,300,000,000, and the national income at $10,140,000,000. At the present time the national wealth of the United Kingdom may be safely computed at $120,000,000,000, and the national income at $18,000,000,000. In other words, if we accept and stabilize the new valuation of money, our post-war national debt will be only equivalent to a sum representing 20 per cent. of the national wealth, and our post-war Budget will not amount to more than 22 per cent. of the national income." Mr. Crammond estimated the pre-war investments abroad at 20,000 million dollars, the war-time sales of these securities at $5,000 millions and the borrowings from abroad at 7,000 millions with loans to Allies and Dominions (excluding Russia) totalling 5,200 millions of what he considered good securities. This would leave a credit on investments abroad over all external liabilities of over $13,000,000,000.

As to gold Great Britain controlled 64 per cent. of the world's output at the beginning of its reconstruction period, together with gold holdings in July, 1919, of $568,558,000 compared with $185,567,000 in August, 1914. It had an immense plant and other resources for increased production and an immense estate awaiting development in the British Empire of pre-war years and in the great new territories such as Mesopotamia of the new period; the empty world markets awaiting British supplies included, also, such home requirements as were indicated by a war-time use of 60,000 tons of steel yearly on British railways instead of the normal 200,000 tons; it had an establishment of new Banking facilities calculated to bring the Foreign or external buyer into financial touch with the British seller with deposits of 9,500 million dollars in 22 banks—an increase of 3,800 millions in two years.

Against these advantages during 1919 was the obvious disadvantage of the $4,500,000,000 Debt to the United States which was largely in short-dated obligations and would naturally be a troublesome element until the United States arranged to fund the indebtedness as a long-term liability; there was, also, $7,500,-000,000 in Treasury Bills and an increase in note circulation with only partial gold backing. British revenues for the year ending Mch. 31, 1919, were $4,445,000,000 and total expenditures—including $11,000,000,000 for final war contingencies—were $12,-900,000,000. The Government's Victory Loan of June-July relieved this situation a little and brought $3,500,000,000 of money to

*Note.—Address before Institute of Bankers, London, Mch. 25, 1919.

the Treasury. New taxation under the Budget gave $545,000,000. and varied economies helped matters for the coming year with an estimated deficit in 1919-20 of only $300,000,000. In 1921 an almost equal condition was expected. The aggregate income subject to taxation in Great Britain during 1919 was $9,850,000,000; the amount actually taxed was $6,635,000,000 and the returns were $1,690,000,000.

The British Commercial Situation in 1919. Obviously, the satisfactory meeting of financial conditions turned upon production and trade. The total Imports of the United Kingdom in the five years of 1914-18 from Foreign countries was £3,332,985,743 or $16,664,928,715; from British countries they were £1,544,364,-793 or $7,721,823,965; from all countries they were £4,877,350,-536 or $24,386,752,680. The total Exports to Foreign countries in the same period were £1,493,123,264 or $7,465,616,320; to British countries they were £857,244,991 or $4,286,224,955; to all countries they were £2,350,368,255 or $11,751,841,275. Imports from Foreign countries in that period increased from $2,544,-000,000 in 1914 to $4,495,000,000 in 1918 and from British countries they grew from $939,000,000 to $2,115,000,000. Exports to Foreign countries grew from $1,295,000,000 to $1,615,000,000 and to British countries from $858,000,000 to $891,000,000. In 1919 there was a tremendous change. In January the Imports were $670,000,000 and in November $715,000,000, or about the same. The Exports grew from $255,000,000 in January to $535,-000,000 in November; an adverse balance of $410,000,000 in January was reduced to $180,000,000 in November.

Meanwhile a systematic campaign to re-capture British supremacy in trade was under way. British commercial missions, un-heralded, were working quietly in all the markets of the world. A mission of six was sent to South Russia to promote trade relations with General Denekine's brief Government. Another mission went to Siberia, while trade experts had, by December, traversed the Balkans, Italy, Germany, South America and other places where British-made goods might expect to find a market. Importers were injuriously affected by the exchange situation of the year and Imports from the United States greatly checked but this proved a substantial advantage to Great Britain along financial lines. The total British Imports in 1919 (Dec. 31) were £1,631,901,864 or $8,159,000,000; the total Exports were £789,-372,971 or $3,991,000,000. ·

There was little pessimism during this year in the nation as a whole—despite abundance of strikers and much industrial strife. F. A. McKenzie, a capable correspondent, put it in "American" language on Dec. 13 (Toronto *Star*) as follows: "The nation is bursting its buttons with its pent-up energy. England has revived its youth. The pessimists and groaners, the Jeremiahs and the Jobs of to-day had better fade away. Every day proofs pile up that they are wrong. Britain is launching out on fresh flights. Men knew this in Germany, and in the schools of Berlin they are teaching English to-day." Lord Northcliffe, in a November interview* with W. P. Hamilton of the *Wall Street Journal,* New York, was clear as to the optimistic outlook of his country and he spoke as controlling owner of scores of daily, weekly or monthly journals. He declared that the country was getting on its feet with wonderful rapidity: "I believe that, almost alone among the peoples of the world, we have passed through the worst of the great strike period, and we have done so not by repressing labour, but by wise co-operation with its organizations." As to the shipping situation, he pointed out that: "We expect very heavy competition at sea, but it is not disturbing our able and far-seeing shipping men. We rely for our supremacy in shipping upon our superior knowledge of a business which we have understood for centuries. Our people like shipping. Our people like being at sea."

In the industrial sphere he was equally hopeful: "A people like ours, backed up by practically every single raw material the world contains, except, I understand, potash, have every reason for the silent confidence they feel in the future. We have, in addition to our supply of raw material, the best-skilled labour in the world. I say without hesitation that, mechanic for mechanic, ours are the best, for we have practically no aliens." In business he also was optimistic: "As bankers, and especially bankers who have to deal with far countries, we are just as good as ever we were. You will find that our 'Big Five' (Banks) are very much alive. . . . I would ask friends in the United States to apply a large amount of salt to any dish served up by young and inexperienced cable correspondents who blow into London, and because they find an absence of the noise and rush to which they are accustomed at home, fail to realize that Mr. John Bull is back at his old stand and is about to give you a thoroughly busy time in many markets." Lloyd's Bank in its December statement announced that reports on business conditions from all leading trade centres such as Birmingham, Manchester, Nottingham, Kidderminster, Newcastle-on-Tyne, Dundee, showed that, in all lines, manufacturers had more orders than they could handle, and that the business being offered from all parts of the world was far beyond present productive capacity.

British Political Matters of Empire Import.   The strength or otherwise of the Lloyd George Government was of importance to the whole Empire. The Premier, himself, had come through the War ranking with Chatham in the annals of military statecraft; in 1919 he came through the first trying year of peace as the dominant figure in European statecraft; in politics he had won the greatest triumph in British electoral history and could afford during this year to lose a few seats or to lose a little popularity in facing the tremendous labour difficulties of the time. The depths of democracy had been plumbed in a vast new elec-

*Note.—Re-published in the *Financial Times,* Montreal, Dec. 13, 1919.

A Western Canada Oatfield—Pilot Mound, Manitoba

torate of men and women and the result was temporary extinction
for the Pacifists, Bolshevists and revolutionary leaders of the day.
Out of 703 members of the House, 338 were new to Parliament
and over 250 had served in the War. On Jan. 11, 1919 the Premier re-organized his Government with the existing War Cabinet
—Lloyd George, Lord Curzon, Austen Chamberlain, Bonar Law,
G. N. Barnes and General Smuts—retained without change. The
chief appointments were as follows:

Prime Minister and First Lord of the Treasury	Rt. Hon. D. Lloyd George, M.P.
Lord Privy Seal and Leader of the House of Commons	Rt. Hon. A. Bonar Law, M.P.
Lord President of the Council and Leader of the House of Lords	The Earl Curzon of Kedleston
Minister without Portfolio	Rt. Hon. G. N. Barnes, M.P.
" " "	Rt. Hon. Sir Eric Geddes, G.C.B., G.B.E.
Lord Chancellor	Rt. Hon. Sir F. E. Smith, Bart., K.C, (Lord Birkenhead)
Secretary of State for Home Department	Rt. Hon. Edward Shortt, K.C., M.P.
Secretary of State for Foreign Affairs	Rt. Hon. A. J. Balfour, O.M., F.R.S.
Secretary of State for Colonies	Viscount Milner, G.C.B., G.C.M.G.
Secretary of State for War and Air	Rt. Hon. Winston S. Churchill, M.P.
Secretary of State for India	Rt. Hon. E. S. Montagu, M.P.
First Lord of the Admiralty	Rt. Hon. Walter Hume Long, M.P.
President of the Board of Trade	Rt. Hon. Sir Albert Stanley, M.P.
President of the Local Government Board	Rt. Hon. Christopher Addison, M.D.
President of the Board of Agriculture	Rt. Hon. R. E. Prothero (Lord Ernle)
President of the Board of Education	Rt. Hon. H. A. L. Fisher, M.P.
Minister of Supply	Lord Inverforth
Food Controller	Rt. Hon. G. H. Roberts, M.P.
Minister of Shipping	Rt. Hon. Sir Joseph Maclay, Bart.
Minister of Labour	Sir Robert S. Horne, M.P.
Minister of Pensions	Sir L. Worthington-Evans, Bart., M.P.
Minister of National Service and Reconstruction	Rt. Hon. Sir Auckland Geddes, K.C.B.
Chancellor of the Duchy of Lancaster	The Earl of Crawford and Balcarres
First Commissioner of Works	Rt. Hon. Sir Alfred Mond, M.P.
Attorney-General	Sir Ernest Pollock, K.C.
Postmaster-General	Rt. Hon. A. H. Illingworth, M.P.
Chancellor of the Exchequer	Rt. Hon. Austen Chamberlain, M.P.
Lord Lieutenant of Ireland	F.M. Viscount French, K.P., O.M.
Chief Secretary for Ireland	Sir James Ian MacPherson, M.P.

At the opening of Parliament on Feb. 11 H.M. the King embodied the spirit and policy of his Government in these words:
"The aspirations for a better social order which have been quick-
ened in the hearts of my people by the experience of the War
must be encouraged by prompt and co-operative action. If we are
to repair the losses and to rebuild a better Britain we must continue to manifest the same spirit. We must stop at no sacrifice of
interest or prejudice to stamp out unmerited poverty, to diminish unemployment and mitigate its sufferings, to provide decent
homes, to improve the nation's health, and to raise the standard
of well-being throughout the community. A large number of
measures affecting the social and economic well-being of the
nation await your consideration, and it is of the utmost importance
that their provisions should be examined, and, if possible, agreed

8

upon and carried into effect with all expedition.'' A period of vigourous reconstruction effort followed with 87 Government Commissions and Committees at work—many of them appointed during the War to prepare for after-development. They were divided into the following main divisions:

Trade Development, under which grouping were 5 Committees dealing with general aspects and 9 dealing with specific phases of the situation.

Finance, with 2 Committees; Raw Materials, with 6 Committees.

Coal and Power, with 2 Committees and 4 sub-Committees; Intelligence, with 2 Committees.

Scientific and Industrial Research, with 2 Research Boards, 5 standing Committees, 7 Research Committees, 4 Enquiry Committees, and 3 Provisional Organization Committees.

Demobilization and Disposal of Stores, with 8 Committees.

Labour and Employment, with 2 Committees; Agriculture and Forestry, with 4 Committees.

Public Administration, with 6 Committees; Housing, with 4 Committees.

Education, with 8 Committees and Commissions; Aliens, with 2 Committees; Legal, with 3 Committees; Miscellaneous, with 3 Committees.

As illustrating the rapidity of demobilization Sir R. S. Horne stated on Apr. 30 that 4,000,000 persons had been demobilized from the Army and Navy; of these 1,000,000 were still unemployed but 80 per cent. of the soldiers, 55 per cent. of civilian male workers in war industries, and 45 per cent. of civilian women workers of the war period, had been absorbed in peace industries. Despite the large unemployed donations, or Government allowances, and the succeeding period of strikes, unemployment at the close of the year was almost normal. In September the Government's general policy was promulgated in a special official publication called *The Future* with the following as the chief items: (1) A National maximum 48-hour week and a living wage for all workers; (2) Whitley Council development and construction of healthy houses; (3) State purchase of mineral rights in coal-mines, a levy on purchase price for social amelioration, and Labour representation on Controlling Boards; (4) Agricultural development and fixed prices for crops for another year; (5) development and control of Electric and Water-power supply; (6) development of Technical Instruction and Research for all classes.

The Trade policy was specific: Free imports (with certain exceptions) from September 1, 1919; no Government support of foreign exchanges except to prevent complete collapse; no dumping of foreign goods for sale at sweated prices; the right to prevent any flood of imports competing unfairly with British goods through a collapse of exchange in the country of origin. There was to be Protection for unstable "Key" industries or products essential for war or for industries which had been so neglected before the War that there was an inadequate supply available; for industries which it was found necessary to foster and promote during the War; for industries that could not maintain the level of production essential to the nation without Government support. Arrangements were to be made for export credits to facilitate resumption of trade with disorganized European countries—representing in pre-war days a total of at least $500,000,000. An illustration of Mr. Lloyd George's character was seen in his response to a popular demand for retrenchment which showed itself at mid-summer. Besides the cutting down of various expenditures he wrote on Aug. 20th to each of his Ministers a letter containing the following clause: "The time has come when each Minister ought to make it clear to those under his control that if they cannot reduce expenditure they must make room for somebody who can. That is the public temper, and it is right." On Oct. 27 it was announced in Parliament that the War Cabinet had ceased to exist and a Cabinet of 20 had been formed by Mr. Lloyd George out of the Government organized in January as follows:

Prime Minister	Mr. Lloyd George
Lord Privy Seal	Mr. Bonar Law
Lord President of the Council	Mr. Balfour
Chancellor of the Exchequer	Mr. Chamberlain
Minister without Portfolio	Mr. Barnes
Lord Lieutenant of Ireland or the Chief Secretary for Ireland	Lord French or Sir Ian Macpherson
Lord Chancellor	Lord Birkenhead
Secretary of State for Home Department	Mr. Shortt
Secretary of State for Foreign Affairs	Lord Curzon
Secretary of State for Colonies	Lord Milner
Secretary of State for War and Air	Mr. Churchill
Secretary of State for India	Mr. Montagu
1st Lord of the Admiralty	Mr. Walter Long
Secretary for Scotland	Mr. Munro
President of the Board of Trade	Sir Auckland Geddes
Minister of Health	Dr. Addison
President of Board of Agriculture	Lord Lee of Fareham
President of Board of Education	Mr. Fisher
Minister of Labour	Sir Robert Horne
Minister of Transport	Sir Eric Geddes

Mr. Asquith and British Liberal Policy. A partial revival of Liberalism took place during the year and the leadership of the Rt. Hon. H. H. Asquith in this respect—though he was for the moment out of Parliament—was energetic in character and explicit in policy. He made a number of speeches—notably at a London dinner on Apr. 11 when he described the December elections as having produced "a top-heavy structure resting upon foundations of sand" and denounced the inclusion of Ireland in the 1918 Conscription Act as unwise, useless and a direct encouragement of Sinn Feinism. He reviewed the governing objects of Liberal policy as follows:

1. The maintenance of the free activity of an unfettered and independent Liberal Party.

2. Determined resistance to all legislation which has for its object or effect the preferential treatment of particular classes or interests.

3. The restoration in the fullest sense, and without any avoidable delay, of political, commercial and personal freedom.

4. Insistence upon the prompt fulfilment of pledges to give Ireland self-government.

5. Relentless warfare against public extravagance, together with the safeguarding of the fiscal system of Free Trade.

6. The pursuit in every sphere of social and industrial life of a national minimum of health, comfort, culture and opportunity.

7. The effective establishment, as guardian and trustee of the relations of all countries, small or great, of a League of Nations.

Other notable addresses were Newcastle-on-Tyne on May 16 and May 17, in London on June 3rd and Leeds on June 19th and at Westminster to the London Liberal Federation on Oct. 21. An insistent point in these speeches was the need to guard England against a return to Protection—with the way paved by Preference—and in the last address mentioned he protested "on behalf of all the principles for which we have been fighting in this War, and which profess to be embodied in the Treaty of Peace, against the money, the material resources or the men of this country being employed in the settlement of what is purely a domestic and internal question for the Russians themselves." He urged reduction of expenditure upon armaments and added, as to other matters: "You have got to choose between an indefinite increase of the income-tax or some form of charge on realized or realizable wealth; there were large accumulations of wealth made during, and to a considerable extent, in consequence of the War, which ought, in justice and in equity, to be made contributory to our most pressing burden—that debt created by the War. In regard to what is called Nationalization, I am not prepared without better evidence to submit the daily details of the working of a great industry to a set of Government officials." On Nov. 27-8 the National Liberal Federation met at Birmingham and passed a series of Resolutions—approved by Mr. Asquith in a lengthy address—which may be summarized as follows:

1. Regarding with grave misgiving the continued disorder in national finance, large expenditures in excess of income and the spending "unnecessarily" of vast sums on military and naval armaments; urging a tax on War Profits, an enquiry into the question of a levy on Capital, an increase in death duties and special taxation upon land and other monopoly values.

2. Declaring that the worker is entitled to a fair share in the product of his industry, and that a minimum rate of wages, with maximum of hours, sufficient to support an average family in a state of physical efficiency and leave a reasonable margin for comfort and leisure, should be fixed for all workers, whether employed by the State or otherwise; approving the Whitley Report and a maximum 48 hours' week and urging establishment of a responsible Tribunal of Labour Arbitration.

3. Welcoming the establishment of the League of Nations as the only method of enlightened international co-operation by which the peace of the world could be secured.

4. Condemning the Government's interference in the internal and domestic affairs of the Russian people and demanding cessation of armed intervention or the supply of munitions to combatants.

5. Approving of Home Rule for Ireland upon the basis of the Government of Ireland Act and along the lines of government in the Dominions.

6. Urging the system of devolution in Parliamentary affairs, Woman suffrage and Proportional Representation.

7. Advocating the immediate provision of 500,000 new houses for the people, greater security of tenure to agricultural tenants and promotion of education in agricultural science; urging support to the movement for small holdings, cottage holdings and allotments, with a thorough taxation of land values as a basis.

8. Affirming continued and unqualified adherence to the policy of Free Trade and condemning Imperial Preference as "uneconomic and dangerous."

9. Protesting against subsidies to any branch of trade or industry unless the profits accrued to the State, demanding thorough reform of the Poor Law, complete popular control of the Liquor traffic and abolition of the State Church in the United Kingdom.

British Incidents of the Year included the official statement in February that the British Government had paid to ship-owners in compensation for British ships sunk by the enemy, while under Government requisition and at direct Government risk, between Aug. 4, 1914, and the Armistice, $520,156,355; the considerable movement of land and of large estates into the market and their sale to Co-operative Associations in towns for food production, to the Government for small holdings and ex-Service men, to existing farm tenants and to land speculators; the Report of the National War Savings Committee under Sir Robert Kindersley showing the amount invested in War Savings certificates as £42,183,718 in 1916, £67,010,817 in 1917 and £108,348,782 in 1918 or a total of $1,087,000,000; the initiation of a movement for organizing the 15,000,000 middle-class people of the United Kingdom in order to fight strikes and high prices; the retirement of A. G. Gardiner from the editorship of the London *Daily News* after a long record of unpatriotic advocacy and a war record of Germanized opinion.

Ireland: Dissensions and Disorders of 1919. Canada took an increasing interest in Irish affairs during this year and its Irish born population of 90,000 was more or less divided in its view of the situation as between Home Rule and Sinn Feinism. Ireland, itself, was a medley of confused thought and action. In the Elections at the close of 1918 the Sinn Feiners had apparently swept the country with 73 members elected as against 6 at the Dissolution of Parliament, 6 Nationalists compared with 76, and 26 Unionists as against 18 Unionists and 2 Liberals. The popular vote, however, was not so sweeping; out of 1,937,245 registered voters 971,945 actually voted for Sinn Fein candidates or were in constituencies which elected Sinn Feiners by acclamation; 235,206 voted for Nationalists or constitutional Home Rulers and 308,713 for Unionists and other candidates—a total of 543,919; the total of those not voting was 421,381 and in such an exciting and stormy election the latter must have been utterly apathetic. There was not, therefore, an actual Sinn Fein majority in the possible vote, though there was one in the actual vote. As the year grew and passed away Sinn Fein appeared to increase in its popular membership and strength—partly through the vacillating policy of a British Government which hated coercion, only adopted it when it seemed absolutely necessary and abandoned it at the slightest excuse; partly because of United States encouragement of sedition and partly because of reflex action from the world's general unrest.

The General Condition of Ireland in 1919. Irish prosperity was freely admitted at this time with a trade in 1914 between Great Britain and Ireland of $675,000,000 which had increased to $820,-000,000 in 1918; there had been no conscription during the War and the grand total of Ireland's direct contribution of men was 145,860 with perhaps 40,000 more, composed of men in the British Army and Navy and Reservists, compared with Scotland's total of 620,000 from about the same population; there had been practically no food restrictions as in England and everywhere else, and food had been very plentiful; there was great industrial activity in Belfast, Londonderry and Larne, both during and after the War; prices of farm lands, which had doubled in value during 15 years, were in 1918-19 steadily rising.

Under the Land Purchase Act of 1903 which enabled the farmer to buy his holding from the landlord on easy terms by purchase money advanced from the State and repayable by a terminable annuity containing interest and principal, over 400,000 tenants had become owners and the British Government had advanced a total of $610,000,000; in these purchases the old-time curse of absentee landlordism had become practically eliminated with two-thirds of the country passing under the operation of the Act. Similarly, there had been much improvement in conditions through the operation of the Labourers' Cottages Acts, under which many thousands of cottages with plots attached were provided for rural labourers. In this way, by 1918, 35,409 cottages had been built and 5,057 were under construction—the great bulk of them being in Munster and Leinster. For these really artistic little homes the workman paid one shilling a week rent. As to the slums of Belfast and Dublin it was true that conditions were and had been bad—as bad as in London or New York. But Ireland was so essentially an agricultural community that agitation and legislation alike had been directed more to the land and the peasantry than toward industry; in 1919 vigorous efforts were made to change these conditions but there were landlord profiteers in these cities as well as elsewhere!

It is interesting to note and was not generally known in Canada that the whole cost of Irish primary education at this time fell on Votes of Parliament—the United Kingdom taxpayer—and totalled $16,945,000 in 1919. In England and Scotland about 50 per cent. of the cost of Education rested on the local ratepayers; the Irish ratepayer paid nothing. At the same time the appointment of teachers (about 13,000) was in the hands of the local authorities—usually the priests; incidentally, it may be added, the British taxpayer paid the cost of the Irish Police service—$11,940,000 in 1919. An illustration of pre-war conditions of prosperity which further developed during 1914-18 was the fact that between 1881 and 1914 the Irish deposits in P.O. Savings Banks increased from $8,225,000 to $66,515,000; the Irish Bank deposits and private balances from $141,445,000 to $309,775,000; the number and values of horses, cattle, sheep and pigs from

8,848,765, worth $361,353,280, to 10,576,892 worth $435,712,425. The values in 1919 were easily twice this latter amount.

On the other hand it was claimed that British injustice had always been the curse of Ireland and that the reforms of later days should not be considered or allowed to obliterate the historical resentment of the people. The Friends of Irish Freedom—an American organization of German sympathies in the War—made much of the drop in population from 6,800,000 in 1821 to 4,400,000 in 1911. No doubt this was partly due to the decrease of industrial life in Ireland through British competition; just as the partial destruction of British agricultural prosperity was due to a free-trade which worked for the benefit of national industries. No doubt, also, the migration was due in part to the elimination of the small tenant farmer by the Free trade competition of foreign and Colonial wheat which helped the raising of cattle and the restriction of grain-growing. The Land system of Ireland once justly described as perhaps the worst in the world had, after 1870, gradually become one of the best.

It was claimed by Sinn Feiners, and with truth, that in 1896 a Royal Commission presided over by Rt. Hon. H. C. E. Childers, had reported that under existing taxation Ireland was contributing $37,500,000 yearly to the British Exchequer while the cost of governing Ireland was only $27,500,000; the average difference in preceding years had been $13,500,000. Whatever the truth in this moot point the whole system was changed in the next British Budget and the incidence of taxation materially altered, so that incomes were graded, making the greater of more taxable capacity than the lesser, and this so revolutionized the whole condition of taxation in Great Britain and Ireland that the balance shifted the other way. In the fiscal year 1918-19 the figures of Revenue from England, Ireland and Scotland, the amounts allotted for Local expenditures and the sums available for the Army and Navy and for running the United Kingdom as a whole were as follows:

Country	Total Revenue Collected	Contribution By Percentage	Local Expenditure of Revenue	Percentage to each Country	Available for Imperial Expenditure	Percentage
England ..	$3,455,310,000	83·70	$719,287,500	77·53	$2,736,072,500	85·49
Scotland ..	486,607,500	11·70	97,637,500	10·52	388,970,000	12·15
Ireland ..	186,375,000	4·51	110,807,500	11·95	75,567,500	2·36
Total ...	4,128,292,500		927,682,500		3,200,610,000	

It was not alleged that taxation was discriminative as between Britain and Ireland and, according to an official Report in 1912 the Imperial revenues were raised in England, Ireland and Scotland by means of the same taxes, levied at practically the same rates—except that the Land tax, Inhabited House tax, Railway passenger tax and Patent medicine taxes were not levied in Ireland at all. There was in these later years a large excess in British expenditures in Ireland over revenues with Old Age pensions as a factor and the charge of an Irish liability, in this respect, of $15,000,000 to the British Exchequer. Incidentally,

·it may be said that the population of Ireland was one-tenth that of Great Britain while one-fifth of all the Pensioners lived in Ireland and two-thirds of the old people of that country, over 70 years of age, were on the Fund. As to industry Kilkenny carpets and tapestry were famous in Europe up to the beginning of the 19th century; Donegal carpets have long been known all over the world and at Naas in 1903 and again after the War, a carpet-weaving industry had been started; weaving of all kinds and linen and woollen industries were natural to the soil and only required peace and confidence to produce great results; ship-building was tremendously active and Belfast industries crowded with orders. Aside from political lawlessness there was little crime and less vice in Ireland than, perhaps, in any other country.

With all the actual prosperity of Ireland its development was only partial; it had long needed self-government of its own along lines such as those which made Canada strong and progressive; from the days of Gladstone and Parnell to those of Lloyd George and Redmond this object had been hampered by English and Ulster allegations of rebellion and disloyalty which were fortified by unthinking Irish utterances of speech and pen. As a country it had a soil, in parts, of the richest and seas on every side swarming with fish; 20 first-class harbours and many lesser ones from which countless ships could sail and trade; wool and flax of peculiar excellence and industrial aptitudes of the highest; great unworked coal deposits and a produce in meats and other food which were excellent beyond compare. No wonder the people groped for something new; had the American-Irish Commissioners of this year been industrial magnates seeking room for investment and development they could have made great profits with countless benefits to the Irish people. So, also, if English capitalists had gone to Ireland instead of English politicians!

As to historic antagonisms what can be said! They have been bad in Ireland as they once were in England—in the days of Brian Boru's reign in Erin, as in those of the Wars of the Roses or the Stuarts; the anti-Catholic laws applied to England as well as to Ireland and Catholic Emancipation came to both alike at the same time; the racial differences of Ulster and Leinster have been duplicated in many countries and certainly religious animosities have never been confined to Ireland alone. Fifty years ago social conditions still were in a wretched condition; nearly the whole agricultural population were tenants-at-will of, in many cases, absentee landlords and subject to increasing rents and arbitrary eviction. Local taxation and administration were in the hands of Grand Juries appointed from Dublin Castle; Irish Catholic education had no such University system as the Protestants had enjoyed for 300 years in the University of Dublin; there was an established Protestant Church supported by general taxes and representing only 12 per cent. of the population; technical education was inaccessible to the great mass of the people and Irish history, language or literature had no place in

public education. That Ireland for some time had been dead
as the Ireland of Brian Boru or of Cromwell.

Progress of the Sinn Fein Movement. The establishment of
an Irish Republic had, in 1919, become the avowed policy of this
organization and its agitators, of all the extremists in the country,
of the minority who unfortunately, but undoubtedly, did hate
England. At the beginning of the year 20 of the newly-elected
Sinn Fein members of Parliament were in prison—chiefly for
participation in the 1916 rebellion—with 70 others who had shared
in that struggle or broken clauses in the Defence of the Realm Act
—a measure applicable to England as well as Ireland; it was
said at this time by some who had studied the situation that Sinn
Feinism was divided into a really revolutionary section of about
one-third with the majority of the others more or less idealists
who had lost faith in Nationalism and Home Rule and were grop-
ing in the dark for something better. It was announced that the
Sinn Fein members would not attend Parliament and it was
understood that they would form the basis of membership in an
Irish Parliament which it was proposed to constitute in defiance
of existing laws or constitutions. On Sunday, Jan. 5—the
British Government having lifted the ban on public meetings
in order to permit a free general election—there were 70 meetings held to demand the release of Irish prisoners in British
hands.

On Jan. 21 the so-called Dael Eireann—Gaelic for Irish Parliament—met in the Mansion House of Dublin within sight and
sound of Dublin Castle and the Viceroy. It was composed of 25
of the Sinn Fein members elected to the British Parliament and
the proceedings were carried on in what was practically a dead
language—the ancient Gaelic; it was avowedly treasonable in
purpose, and yet, typical of the paradoxical Irish character and
history, it had the toleration of Lord French and his 50,000
British troops. Charles S. Burgess was elected Chairman and
Count Plunkett, Arthur Griffith and Edward de Valera were
appointed to present the claims of Ireland to the Peace Conference
at Paris; prayers were read by the Rev. Father O'Flanagan of Ros-
common who had recently been dismissed by his Bishop for political
activities. It was decided that the Provincial constitution should
include a President with Secretaries of Finance, Home Affairs,
Foreign Affairs and National Defence as a Government. The
names were not announced but an Executive was appointed composed of Edward de Valera (President), Arthur Griffith, Charles
Burgess (Cathal Brugha in Gaelic) Count Plunkett, Countess
Markievicz, John MacNeill, William Cosgrove and Michael Kelly
(Coileain). A "Declaration of Independence" was read in Irish
with the delegates standing and afterwards in English and French;
a similar "Address to Free Nations" for use at the Peace Conference was also read and approved. The "Declaration of Independence" was as follows:

Whereas for seven hundred years the Irish people has never ceased to repudiate and has repeatedly protested in arms against foreign usurpation; and whereas English rule in this country is, and always has been, based upon force and fraud and maintained by military occupation against the declared will of the people: and whereas the Irish Republic was proclaimed in Dublin on Easter Monday, 1916, by the Irish Republican Army, acting on behalf of the Irish people; and whereas the Irish people is resolved to secure and maintain its complete independence in order to promote the common weal, to re-establish justice, to provide for future defence, to insure peace at home and good will with all nations and to constitute a national policy based upon the people's will with equal right and equal opportunity for every citizen; and whereas at the threshold of a new era in history the Irish electorate has in the general election of December, 1918, seized the first occasion to declare by an overwhelming majority its firm allegiance to the Irish Republic.

Now, therefore, we, the elected representatives of the ancient Irish people, in national parliament assembled, do, in the name of the Irish nation, ratify the establishment of the Irish Republic and pledge ourselves and our people to make this declaration effective by every means at our command. We ordain that the elected representatives of the Irish people alone have power to make laws binding on the people of Ireland, and that the Irish Parliament is the only Parliament to which the people will give its allegiance. We solemnly declare foreign government in Ireland to be an invasion of our national right, which we will never tolerate, and we demand the evacuation of our country by the English garrison; we claim for our national independence the recognition and support of every free nation of the world, and we proclaim that independence to be a condition precedent to international peace hereafter; in the name of the Irish people we humbly commit our destiny to Almighty God, who gave our fathers the courage and determination to persevere through centuries of a ruthless tyranny and, strong in the justice of the cause which they have handed down to us, we ask His divine blessing on this, the last stage of the struggle which we have pledged ourselves to carry through to freedom.

The other document claimed that for over 1,000 years Ireland had exercised or claimed independence; that the English "policy of repression, spiritual and material, has ever been active from the first intrusion of English power until the present day;" that though English policy had aimed at "keeping every new accretion of population from without separate from the rest of the nation, and a cause of distraction and weakness," nevertheless the Irish nation had remained one; that the Irish were a democratic people and tolerant toward minorities; that the only British reason for opposition was that separation was incompatible with British security and this, surely, was a negation of national liberty; that England's government of Ireland had been at all times, and was conspicuously, at the present time, "an outrage on the conscience of mankind;" that the results of English rule had been "atrocious and deplorable."

Special emphasis was laid upon President Wilson's declaration for "justice to all peoples and nationalities." During the meeting two policemen were murdered in Tipperary while guarding explosives; following the "Session" Sinn Fein journalistic comment was bitter but, upon the whole, *Nationality* and *New Ireland*, the chief organs, seemed hopeful of Peace Conference intervention and did not advise immediate violence; the Dublin *Freeman* stood for Home Rule in the old sense and the Belfast *Irish News* (Nat.)

feared that rebellion would follow inaction by the Conference. As to this Mr. de Valera told R. F. Couch of the United Press of America cable agency, at Dublin on Feb. 24, that: "If the Paris Conference fails to take steps to extend self-determination to Ireland, violence will be the only alternative left to Irish patriots. This will mean something like continued revolution until Ireland's rights are recognized." Count Plunkett, M.P., in Dublin on Jan. 17 stated, according to *Freeman's Journal*, that Sinn Feiners were not in a panic because of Germany's failure in the War: "Germany has not failed. Germany has established herself as a Republic, and Sinn Feiners might soon claim to be standing beside her as a fellow Republic."

Harry Boland, M.P., declared at Longford on Jan. 5 that: "Sinn Feiners acted on the principle that England's difficulty was Ireland's opportunity and, seeing England at death-grips with another great Power they thought it their time to strike a blow, and they had struck." Varied outrages followed in these months and filled page after page of such weekly or monthly journals as traced the record of the movement—killing of policemen, shooting of soldiers, murder or attempts on the life of magistrates, assaults in large number, boycotts, threats of a myriad nature, the stoppage of sport and hunting; many Courts Martial were held and arrests made while on Feb. 4, De Valera escaped from Lincoln gaol where he was under sentence for life. On Mch. 6 there was another turn of the British wheel of policy and the announcement made that all Irish prisoners in Great Britain would be released. Meanwhile, on Feb. 24, J. T. O'Kelly had arrived in Paris as "the envoy of the Irish Republic" to the Peace Conference with, presumably, a passport; on Mch. 21 Father O'Flanagan was refused a passport to the United States! On Apr. 9 the Supreme Council or Executive of the Sinn Feiners met in Dublin and De Valera in an address said: "As far as I know, and I should know a great deal more than most people who are talking, Germany neither fooled, nor attempted to fool Ireland. Germany has not betrayed Ireland." It was announced at this time that a $500,000 Loan would be issued—one-half for internal subscription and one-half abroad.

Labour was also brought into the arena so far as was practicable. Socialists and Bolshevists of varied grades joined the movement though Sinn Feiners, as a whole, were not Socialists; the Transport and Working Union which James Connolly led in 1916 was, however, almost solidly Sinn Fein and a general strike occurred in Limerick against proclamation as a Military area; a section of agitators took up Bolshevism and, on May 11, Miss Sylvia Pankhurst at Dublin urged the establishment of Soviets and Government by the workers. As the year went on outrages continued with more police murders—18 in all, by its close—shooting of farmers and workmen here and there, seizure of munition stores and raids for arms, burning of buildings, etc.

The Government dealt with these conditions so far as Tipperary was concerned by suppressing the Sinn Fein organization, the Gaelic League, the Irish Volunteers, and all kindred organizations. Between Apr. 1 and June 30 there took place 120 outrages of an agrarian nature and 76 of a purely Sinn Fein character. J. A. Burke, M.P., told a meeting at Thurles on May 25 that the lives of all police joining the force since the establishment of the "Republic" were forfeit: "If any man shoots or otherwise destroys one of them, he may rest easy in his conscience, for he is only carrying out the sentence already passed on him by the Republican Government. Now, with regard to the Irish Volunteers, I don't believe in talking a lot about fighting and about shooting. I believe if you have anything to say about using a gun, the best way is to let the weapon speak for itself." Lawlessness continued in various parts of the country, especially in County Clare which was taken over by the Military on Aug. 8— police murders, raids on barracks, firing on soldiers, shooting of farmers, boycotting, rioting, etc.

On Sept. 10, after holding various so-called sittings, the Sinn Fein Parliament was officially suppressed by Government raids upon leaders of the movement carried out over a wide area; meetings of the Dail Eireann were prohibited under the Crimes Act and the other Sinn Fein organizations suppressed in Cork, Limerick, Dublin and Clare. A number of M.P.'s were arrested while further police murders, raids and outrages were recorded. Speaking at Wallasey, Ireland, on Oct. 22, F.M. Lord French said: "Our great difficulty is that a new element has arisen in the already complicated vortex of Irish politics—a new party which claims nothing but complete separation. That is the so-called, self-constituted, and illegal Sinn Fein 'Government,' which possesses a great secret army which they call the Irish Volunteers. Attached to this army are bodies of men who are nothing more or less than assassins, whose business it is to commit outrage and murder on police and soldiers, and on any of the community who question their decrees or their orders, or endeavour in any way to oppose them. The result is that a complete system of intimidation exists throughout the whole population."

Two months later (Dec. 19) a bold attempt was made to murder the Lord Lieutenant; 4 bombs were thrown from behind a hedge in Phoenix Park; one of the men concerned was shot by the Police but the rest escaped. Following this outrage all Ireland was brought under the Crimes Act and all Sinn Fein organizations suppressed. The close of the year saw, also, a new Home Rule effort at Westminster with the official Sinn Fein statement that they "took no interest in it." At the same time Arthur Lynch, ex-M.P., who fought with the Boers against the British, told a New York audience on Dec. 30 that, though he favoured an Irish Republic, he did not believe the Sinn Feiners could succeed because (1) there was no carefully thought out plan; (2) there could be no success or settlement that was not fair to Ulster; (3) there was too much of the religious element in the

question and very few Protestants, such as some of the great
Irish leaders of the past, were in the movement; (4) the British
Labour party had not been cultivated.

The Church and the People of Ireland.   The already difficult
position of the Roman Catholic Church in Ireland grew greater
with every month of 1919. As a religious organization it stood,
fundamentally, for law and order and loyalty; as the National
Church of 3,242,670 people out of 4,390,219 it could hardly
keep clear of so widespread a movement as that of Sinn Fein;
it had in 1910 (*Catholic Cyclopaedia*, Vol. VIII.) 1,087 parishes,
3,688 priests and 543 Convents, with many monasteries, in the
country. In 1916-17 the Irish Hierarchy had denounced rebellion but supported Home Rule and in 1918 they denounced Conscription and the Sinn Fein movement;[*] in 1919 without official
recognition of Sinn Feinism they supported the recognition of
Ireland as a nation—not as a Republic.   On Mch. 4 Cardinal
Logue issued a Lenten pastoral in which he denounced Socialism
as a "species of Bolshevism, the blood-stained career of which
has shocked the sensibilities of Christendom, reviving in the twentieth century, in exaggerated form, the worst horrors of the
French Revolution" and deprecated Sinn Fein drilling as dangerous.

On June 24 a general meeting of the Hierarchy was held
at Maynooth with H. E. Cardinal Logue presiding and 25 pre-
lates present. A statement was unanimously issued announcing
support for any scheme that would satisfy the legitimate aspirations of Ireland and bring peace and contentment to her people:
"The existing method of Government cannot last.   It substitutes
government by constraint with all its evils, for government by
consent with all its blessings."   Military rule was denounced
and self-government demanded: "It is the rule of the sword,
utterly unsuited to a civilized nation, and supremely provoca-
tive of disorder and chronic rebellion. The acts of violence, which
we have to deplore, and they are few, spring from this cause, and
from this cause alone."   Over-taxation was charged against the
British Government and failure to promote suitable schemes of
reconstruction and development; exercise of undue power and
domination was declared to be an unmixed evil "though so long
as it lasts, our faithful people should not allow any provocation
to move them to overstep the law of God"—the patience of Belgium under German rule was specified as an inspiration.   The
following statement was made, in conclusion, (with, also, profound
thanks to the people and Congress of the United States for sympathy and support):

Ireland is a distinct and ancient nation, and it is vain to hope that
things will go well for Ireland or for England until Ireland's rights are
duly recognized. She is fully entitled to a government that will be the
free choice of all her people. Her right is to be the mistress of her own

destiny. With the deepest affection for all her inhabitants of every persuasion, and in pursuance of the duties of our high trust in the interests
of peace and religion, we desire to state, with all the earnestness we can
command, that now is the time for doing justice to Ireland as a nation.

It will be noted that there was no direct reference to Sinn
Feinism or a Republic; indeed a Nationalist believer in Dominion
Home Rule could have said as much. Many of the Hierarchy
denounced current crime and lawlessness though they did not
reach to its roots. Dr. Browne, Bishop of Cloyne, for instance,
issued a letter regarding the Fermoy murder of soldiers on Sept.
7th in which he described the act as "a fearful tragedy, a savage
crime, which cries for vengeance from God and ordered society."
Following the attempt on Lord French's life Cardinal Logue
telegraphed to His Excellency congratulations on his escape and
issued a Message declaring that Ireland was subjected to "harsh
trials and drastic repression;" that "We have been treated like
children, our nurses dangling toys and taxing their ingenuity
to keep us quiet;" that there should, however, "above all be no
reprisal because 'that way ruin lies'." It was considered significant
that the Church refused its burial ceremonies to the attempted
murderer who was killed in the bomb-throwing episode. On the
other hand Bishop Fogarty of Killaloe supported Irish independence as did Bishop Cohalan of Cork and others and Archbishop
Walsh of Dublin wrote to Cardinal O'Connell of New York on
Nov. 10 as follows: "I wish to contribute 100 guineas (£105 sterling) to the Irish National Fund inaugurated under the auspices
of the elected body known as Dail Eireann, our Irish Parliament.
I cannot but think that, as far as your people of Irish race are
concerned, their knowledge of the fact that I have subscribed to
the Fund would be of at least as much help as any money subscription of mine could be."

American-Irish Envoys in Ireland. Into the midst of these
troubles was interjected a visit of investigation and propaganda
by three prominent United States advocates of Irish separation.
Michael J. Ryan, Edward F. Dunne, ex-Governor of Illinois and
Frank P. Walsh, were appointed by an Irish Race Convention
at Philadelphia on Feb. 22-23 to go to Paris and do what was
possible to obtain Irish recognition at the Peace Conference; they
decided soon after arrival there to also visit Ireland with the
object, afterwards stated by Mr. Walsh, of "conferring with President de Valera upon the question of securing international recognition of the Irish Republic." For some reason best known to
itself the British Government permitted this and, though a military
prescription of meetings and processions prevailed at the time,
did not interfere with their speeches and the ensuing demonstrations. On May 4 the Commissioners paid a hurried visit
to Belfast and were entertained by the local Sinn Feiners—Mr.
Ryan speaking to the toast of the Irish Republic. At Dublin on the
5th, they were welcomed by the republican leaders and were
driven around in motor cars decorated with flags of the United

States and the "new republic" while Messrs. Ryan and Dunne addressed a great crowd and demanded the right of self-determination and a republican form of government for the Irish people; indirectly they pledged the support of the United States.

For some days they saw, studied, aided and strengthened every element looking to separation and, on May 8, were received in public state by the "Irish Parliament"—without any Government intervention! Mr. de Valera welcomed them and observed that as he looked during the past few days on the flag of the Irish Republic and the flag of the great Republic of America floating side by side, he could not help thinking what an appropriate combination they made. Mr. Ryan, in reply, indicated his point of view very clearly: "It is because of the triumph of the two great principles of religious liberty and protection of American industries that America has wrested from England the control of the markets of the world. This Irish Republic of yours is as yet a thing of the spirit, but it is certain to conquer. As the mighty Caesars fell before the Apostles of old, so will fall before you the might of England." Other parts of the country were visited, great receptions accorded the Americans and, in one night ride from Athlone to Galway, the roads were illuminated by watch-fires on the surrounding hills.

The Delegates claimed, and it was not officially denied, that their passports were given them at the request of President Wilson with the approval of Mr. Lloyd George; the result was a wave of belief in Ireland that Sinn Fein was going to succeed, that it had won the support of the United States and the fear of England, that a republic and not Home Rule must now be the "irreducible" minimum of the Irish people. This visit did more to strengthen the movement than any other event of the year. No doubt pressure from President Wilson had made the visit possible and the pending of greater issues had made the British Premier give way; perhaps it was the compromise for not officially receiving De Valera and the others at the Conference! On June 6 the American Commission on Irish Independence, as they called themselves, sent a Report to President Wilson, Mr. Lansing, U.S. Secretary of State, and Mr. Lloyd George, which stated that they had toured the four Provinces of Ireland and conferred with President de Valera; described various alleged incidents of their tour and increased the "English garrison" to 100,000 while presenting 47 statements of unproven cruelties and outrages by the "tyrannical" British Government.

Sir Ian MacPherson, Chief Secretary, characterized the document on its receipt as "so extravagant and unwarrantable as to be ridiculous" while Mr. Ryan, in an interview with the New York *Tribune* on his return (June 2), described Ireland as follows in words which must have made his Report seem very ridiculous: "There are more crimes, more laws violated and more persons arrested in a large American city in one week than in all Ireland in a year. Ireland is prosperous, even though taxes

are high, and she has plenty of food. All classes of the Irish
people, merchants, farmers, leaders of industry, are eager for a
settlement." English opinion was illustrated by the London
Star (a Radical and strong Home Rule paper for many years)
which declared on June 16: "The *Star* has always fought for
Irish self-government and against coercion of every brand. It
has severely censured the miserable muddle and mess for which
British politicians are responsible, both before and during the
War. But our sympathy with the legitimate aspirations of
Irishmen does not stifle our respect for the truth, and we warn
our American friends that this Report is a tissue of mendacities."
On June 14 Sir Ian Macpherson issued a 12-page Memorandum
in reply which presented many proofs to meet the 47 allegations
in the Report. There is only space here for one illustrative
charge and reply—the 47th:

(47) With a ferocity unparallel-led even in the history of modern warfare, within the past few days men and women have been shot down in the streets of Dublin.	(47.) Unfortunately four police-men and a girl have been so shot in the streets of Dublin within the past few days by a number of Sinn Fein prisoners. who rescued a Sinn Fein prisoner from the police. The police fired no shots.

The Irish Problem and the United States. Driven by politics,
by an Irish population which was greatly exaggerated as to numbers and influenced by a spectacular and vehement group of Irish
agitators the United States in 1919 took steps in respect to Ireland such as no country had ever yet attempted in connection
with the internal problems of a friendly Power. The Census of
1910 showed 1,352,155 men, women and children in the United
States who claimed Ireland as their birthplace, 2,141,577 with
parents who were both born in Ireland and 1,010,628 of whose parents one was born there. It is probable that a fair proportion of
the adults in this group were more American than Irish; in any
case they exercised a political influence quite disproportionate to
their numbers but also quite obvious. They, of course, had the
support of German-Americans and their organizations; they also,
naturally, drew to themselves that considerable portion of the
American people which still distrusted or disliked England and
her Empire. Whatever the elements of strength they were strong
enough as a political force to make the presentation of Irish problems to the Peace Conference a serious issue and to largely
aid in the defeat of the Treaty and the League of Nations at
Washington.

There was little limit to the language of Irish enthusiasts in
the United States during the year. Dr. Patrick McCartan, the
"Envoy of the Provisional Government of Ireland," stated at New
York on Jan. 5 that: "We in Ireland are not afraid of shedding
blood in our righteous cause and if England attempts to interfere with the establishment of our republic, it will be a declaration
of war on her part, and the blood that will be spilled will be on

her hands." He declared that the American-Irish had already raised a Fund of $8,000,000 to help the republicans at home. At a Convention of the Irish Race held in Philadelphia (Feb, 22-24) with 5,000 present, the Very Rev. P. E. Magennis of New York, President of the Friends of Irish Freedom, declared that: "We have wept enough for Ireland, we have gloried sufficiently in Ireland; now our duty is to work for Ireland, and to work in such a way that the world shall understand that our work is the work of men who can die for Ireland." Archbishop Dougherty of Philadelphia prayed for a free Ireland and speeches of the strongest kind followed from ex-Mayor J. P. Grace of Charleston and Judge D. F. Cohalan of New York.

The leaders of Roman Catholicism in the United States were, indeed, conspicuous in this connection and at the above Convention Cardinal Gibbons moved and carried a Resolution calling upon the President and Congress of the United States "to urge the Peace Conference now in session at Paris to apply to Ireland the great doctrine of national self-determination." His speech was an eloquent appeal to Americans to support the cause of Irish "freedom." It was endorsed by Archbishop Messener of Milwaukee. The Delegates then pledged themselves to raise a fund to promote "the freedom of Ireland" and $1,250,000 was at once subscribed; an elaborate Declaration of Principles was approved which stated that "a state of war, therefore, exists between England and Ireland, which in the interests of the peace of the world the Peace Conference cannot ignore."

At New York on Mch. 17 a parade of 35,000 Irishmen carrying thousands of Irish republican flags and a multitude of Sinn Fein mottoes were reviewed in front of St. Patrick's Cathedral by Governor Smith, Archbishop P. J. Hayes, the new head of 1,325,000 Catholics, Mayor Hylan, W. R. Hearst and Judge Cohalan. In a letter to the Rev. F. P. Duffy, Archbishop Hayes, on June 29, declared that the United States "is not forgetful or ungrateful and its influence will be potent in helping to bring peace and freedom in that Island to whose heroic sons it owes so much in peace and war." Cardinal O'Connell at Boston and other places stated that America had won the War for world liberty and the freedom of Ireland had become her affair. Following this came an appeal for $2,000,000 from New York by the Friends of Irish Freedom and the lavish publication of advertisements saying, amongst other things, that a free Ireland would trade with the United States instead of England and give to Americans a new and great market! On June 17 the American Federation of Labour Convention in Atlantic City urged the United States Government to recognize "the existing Irish Republic."

In June Edmund de Valera, "President of the Irish Republic," arrived in the United States; how he escaped from prison in England, openly attended a Sinn Fein Parliament meeting in Dublin to welcome the American-Irish envoys, and was then allowed to cross the Atlantic, was one of the mysteries of British policy. Born in New York and therefore an American citizen —as he had never sworn allegiance to any but an unrecognized and phantom republic; his father a Spanish native of a South American country and his mother an Irish-American; he, himself, was brought up in Ireland and had first come into prominence in the 1916 rebellion. After some weeks spent quietly at Washington and other centres, with a visit to Cardinal Gibbons on June 20, De Valera arrived at New York on June 22, took a suite of rooms at the Waldorf-Astoria as "President of Ireland," and proceeded to make things lively with the assistance of Irish organizations and of Diarmuid Lynch, M.P., and Liam Mellowes—two Irishmen of 1916 fame who had been in the country for some time.

De Válera announced on the 23rd that he hoped to float in America a $5,000,000 bond issue "to bear interest six months after the British forces have evacuated Ireland" and to obtain American recognition of the "Irish Republic;" a little later he stated that the "Republic" would assume the $500,000 bonds of the Fenian Brotherhood of 1866—which had attempted the invasion of Canada. Arrangements were at once made for a tour of the United States and speeches in succeeding months were delivered to large audiences in all the chief centres of the Republic. There were some interesting things said in these speeches. Addressing the Massachusetts Legislature on June 30 he declared that in some parts of Ulster "small majorities were opposed to an Irish Republic." To 12,000 people at New York on July 10 he stated that Irishmen "wanted their country" and bitterly attacked the British Government. Resolutions were passed denouncing the League of Nations as "a device to stifle the conscience of Christendom by prohibiting any nation from taking action to end atrocities perpetrated on peoples held in subjection against their will by an alien Government;" protesting against the League as a "scheme to fasten upon the United States the abhorrent task of maintaining the integrity of far-flung possessions of the great empires of the world," and demanding formal recognition of the "Irish Republic" by the United States.

At Chicago on July 13 an open-air meeting of 50,000 people cheered the "President" for 30 minutes according to the American custom, hissed the names of Wilson and Lloyd George, acclaimed Mr. de Valera's demand for United States recognition of the "de jure" government of Ireland. Congress was urged to "recognize the Irish republic as now established," to establish trade relations with Ireland for the benefit of American commerce and labour, and to oppose the League of Nations as an organization which would "guarantee the world supremacy of the two remaining autocratic Empires of the world—Great Britain and Japan." At a Convention of the Ancient Order of Hibernians of the United States and Canada at San Francisco, on July 18, the League of Nations was opposed by Resolution and, in an address, De Valera showed a willingness to plunge the world in war again: "In order that

Poland might be freed, three mighty empires had to fall. With the triumph of Poland before us, no one can feel that Ireland is going to fail. It may be necessary to have another period of conflict and world's strife to change the old order." In New York on Aug. 4, after a month's speech-making, the "President" stated on several occasions that the next war would be between England and Japan on the one side and America on the other.

Varied meetings and receptions and demonstrations of the year ended on Dec. 7 with an Irish Race Convention attended by 1,200 delegates and addressed by Mr. de Valera after Judge D. F. Cohalan had declared that: "So long as men are governed by ambitions and interests there will be war. We have started on the commercial war that always precedes the war of arms." Spain, Holland, France, Germany and Austria had all been· rivals of England and been overthrown: "The markets of the world are not great enough to overcome the surplus of both England and America." The "Irish President" was officially received and welcomed by the Governor of Massachusetts and other States and by the Mayors and Councillors of many cities while Resolutions of support were passed by the New York Board of Aldermen and other public bodies.

Meantime, also, the United States had been taking official action. Congress first of all, however, refused the plea of Porto Rica and the Philippines for independence; in the latter case a joint Session of special House and Senate Committees told the Philippine Commission—backed by many meetings and the Resolutions of representative bodies in the Islands—that they were "not sufficiently impressed" by the arguments used. On Feb. 6 the Foreign Affairs Committee of the House of Representatives passed, almost unanimously the following Resolution for concurrence by the House and Senate: "That it is the earnest hope of the Congress of the United States that the Peace Conference now sitting in Paris, in passing upon the rights of the various peoples, will favourably consider the claims of Ireland to the right of self-determination." This was carried in the House (Mch. 4) on motion of H. D. Flood of Virginia by 216 votes to 41 and in the Senate (June 6) upon motion of W. E. Borah by 60 to 1— Senator John Sharp Williams. In form the latter motion was slightly different and it will be noticed that in none of the Resolutions was the word "Republic" actually used—it was camouflaged as self-determination, etc. The Resolution was as follows:

That the Senate of the United States earnestly requests the American Peace Commission at Versailles to endeavour to secure for Edward de Valera, Arthur Griffiths and Count George Noble Plunkett a hearing before said Peace Conference in order that they may present the cause of Ireland. Resolved, further, that the Senate of the United States express its sympathy with the aspirations of the Irish people for a government of its own choice.

Meantime, a curious admission was made by President Wilson in the report of an interview at Paris on June 11th with F. P. Walsh and E. F. Dunne, the Irish-American Commisioners. It was presented to the Senate Foreign Relations Committee on Sept. 6 and not denied. There was (1) the following remark by the President to Mr. Walsh: "We were well on the way of getting Mr. de Valera and his associates over here when you made it so difficult by your speeches in Ireland that we would not do it; it was you gentlemen who kicked over the apple cart," and (2) the following comparison by Mr. Wilson: "Suppose that during our war of the rebellion an Englishman had declared that the South had a right to secede, or sided with the South and had gone into the South while the rebellion was on, or immediately before the rebellion, would not our Government have said that he was fomenting the rebellion?" In a prepared statement at San Francisco on Sept 17 President Wilson intimated a new and very dangerous power for the League of Nations—one enabling it to interfere in the internal affairs of any nation in the world:

1. It was not possible for the Peace Conference to act with regard to the self-determination of any territories except those which had belonged to the defeated Empires, but in the Covenant of the League of Nations it has set up for the first time, in Article 11 a forum to which all claims of self-determination which are likely to disturb the peace of the world, or the good understanding between nations upon which the peace of the world depends, can be brought.

2. My position on the subject of self-determination for Ireland is expressed in Article 11 of the Covenant, in which I may say I was particularly interested, because it seemed to me necessary for the peace and freedom of the world that a forum should be created to which all peoples could bring any matter which was likely to affect the peace and freedom of the world.

Following up this statement Senator T. J. Walsh, Montana, endeavoured to get the Senate to declare that the United States should bring the question of Irish freedom before the League of Nations as soon as it became a member. At intervals, also, during the year, Representative W. E. Mason of Illinois tried to get through a Bill to formally recognize the Irish Republic by voting funds for appointment of a United States Minister and Consuls to Ireland. To the latter proposal George L. Fox of New Haven, Conn., in Committee on Dec. 12, compared the situation of Ireland with that of the Southern Confederacy during the Civil War when Great Britain withheld recognition from the Confederacy even after it had held the Union armies at bay for four years; "Recognition is asked for Ireland, although it has never had an effective army." British opinion of this American campaign was soberly and infrequently expressed; two or three references may be quoted. The Manchester *Guardian*, an extreme Pacifist organ, said on June 25th; "Americans cannot help but appreciate the feelings of the English people as they read of the honours heaped on him who inspired rebellion in the midst of war and who did all in his power to help the enemy. While Oxford honours Pershing, New York welcomes De Valera." The London *Graphic* (May 5) dealt with the general issue as follows: "If any of the States of America were again to demand the right to secede from the Union, it is certain the American people would be bitterly indignant if such a demand received any kind of official encouragement from Great Britain. We apply the same standard of judgment to American interference in our affairs."

Ireland and the Viewpoint of Ulster.   Meanwhile, the question of the Irish Protestant majority of Ulster, or minority of Ireland as a whole, was being discussed but not as the crux of the situation; it had got beyond this. The question of the Belfast Covenanters having the right to fight for their union with Britain; the general problem of religious fears and animosities involved; even the bitterness aroused by questions of partition and of the districts and areas to be excluded were forgotten in the wide outburst of republican advocacy. Still, the constant quotation of Sir E. Carson's fiery 1913 speeches against Home Rule continued; references to his visit to the Kaiser at Hamburg—a matter not unusual with British leaders in the days before the War but a dangerous habit as Lord Haldane had occasion afterwards to realize—were numerous; the statement of the *Irish Churchman* (Nov. 14, 1913) that "We have the offer of aid from a powerful Continental monarch who, if Home Rule is forced on the Protestants of Ireland, is prepared to send an army sufficient to release England from any further trouble in Ireland," was frequently quoted. Sir Edward, himself, was not as continuously aggressive as in previous years; perhaps he felt that Home Rule had become an impossibility. On July 12, however, he dealt in old-time vigour with the American situation:

There is a campaign going on in America, fostered by the Catholic Church, which will soon be joined by the Germans and their funds in order to create a great anti-British feeling. Heaven knows I want good feeling between America and this country. I believe the whole future of the world probably depends upon the relations between the United States and ourselves, but I am not going to submit to this kind of a campaign, whether for friendship or any other purpose. I seriously say to America to-day: 'You attend to your own affairs; we will attend to ours. You look after your own questions at home; we will look after ours.' We will brook no interference in our own affairs by any country, however powerful. It is not for that we waged the great war of independence which has been concluded.

As to the local situation he was explicit: "I tell the British people from this platform here in your presence to-day—and I say it now with all solemnity—I tell them that if there is any attempt made to take away one jot or tittle of your rights as British citizens and the advantages which have been won in this war of freedom, I tell them, at all consequences, once more I will call out the Ulster Volunteers." This speech was debated in the Commons on July 16 upon motion of J. R. Clynes (Lab.). Sir Gordon Hewart, Attorney-General, described the threat as hypothetical and contingent upon an impossibility; no law had been broken. The *Daily News* (Pacifist and pro-German in the War) vigorously denounced Carson (July 17), declared he should be in gaol, and added: "A corrupt Government cannot proceed against a rebel with whom its own members have been in collusion." The London *Times*, which contended that a settlement must be imposed on Ireland, as an agreement was impossible, declared that Ulster had the right to ask for the safeguarding of her liberties but with that done, Great Britain had the right to insist that Ulster should, if necessary, remain a part of Ireland.

As to the basis for these passionate demands of Ulster—just as vigourous as those of the old-time Nationalists or the new-born Sinn Fein—W. R. Moody, an American journalistic visitor to Ireland, put the issue as follows in the Springfield *Republican* and St. John *Standard* of Jan. 24: "The North does not ask for capital or for favours; it asks to be let alone. The North is not a country rich, agriculturally; its natural resources are few but, thanks to the industry and resourcefulness of the population, it has been made into the very heart of Ireland. Through generations they have been loyal, and have assumed that their union with the United Kingdom would be undisturbed. Surely in justice to them the principle of self-determination should be applied." There was "no surrender" in the succeeding Carson attitude and on Sept. 2nd at Belfast he told his Council that: "We dissolved our organizations when the War commenced. Set to now in all our districts and revive them again."

Unionist Ulster was usually taken to include the Counties of Down, Antrim, Armagh, Londonderry, Tyrone and Fermanagh with Cavan, Monaghan and Donegal as doubtful and divisible. How the trade of the whole country could be directed and developed from Dublin without reference to the great port of Belfast, its industries and its control of the avenues of trade with Scotland, was a problem; how the varied interests of two such divergent communities, with two distinct governments, were to be run without friction under Home Rule was a riddle. If the republican dream could be realized Ulster would have to be abandoned by Great Britain and conquered by the new republic; if that wild contingency arrived the golden egg of industry and the 75 per cent. of Ireland's taxable wealth would be destroyed. At the same time Belfast was dependent for much of its trade upon southern Ireland and the removal or practically expressed hostility of that section would greatly injure its prosperity.

Such were some of the seemingly insoluble problems presented by Ulster, to the framers of the new Home Rule Bill of 1919 and the Sinn Feiners, equally. The Irish Unionist Alliance of which Lord Farnham was Chairman, issued a statement at the close of the year (Dec. 12) declaring that as Unionists they had refrained from all political activity during the War; that Home Rule was now a dead cause which the Irish would not themselves accept and that it had always been a ficticious demand and a *camouflage* for separation; that a reign of terror had been set up in Ireland by organized intimidation, by armed raids on lonely farms and houses, by callous murders of isolated police constables; that there were, approximately, 1¼ million Unionists in Ireland including 400,000 in the Southern Provinces; that the Celtic character knew no compromise and that England's ultimate choice must be made between the maintenance of the legislative union, or the surrender of Ireland and Irish loyalists to those who stood for themselves alone, to whom the Imperial idea was anathema, and who were declared to be the avowed enemies of the Empire.

To New York in December, 1919, and later on to Canada, came a Delegation of 7 members of the Ulster Unionist Council— William Coote, M.P., Rev. Alex Wylie Blue and Rev. William Corkey (Presbyterians), Rev. F. E. Harte, M.A., Rev. Edward Hazelton and Rev. C. Wesley Maguire (Methodists) and Rev. William Crooks (Episcopalian). They arrived at New York on Dec. 5 and issued a statement of which the chief paragraph follows: "Our mission is to say to America that the Sinn Fein movement in Ireland, which is spreading its propaganda in America, is not a solution of the Irish question; that it is radical and destructive in its methods; that it is conducting in Ireland a campaign of coercion, threat and assassination; and that it is not supported nor respected, now, by the better type of people whether Catholic or Protestant; that it was the party of rebellion during the War; that it supported and furthered the cause of the foe; that it was a traitor to the Allied cause. It is a movement akin to the Bolshevik republic in Russia. The methods are alike." In an interview given at New York to the Toronto *Telegram* Mr. Coote gave the following reasons why Great Britain could not permit a separated Ireland:

> Apart from economic conditions, the advantages of which are, for the greater part, on the side of Ireland, political and strategic reasons demand that Britain can never permit Ireland, or any part of the Island, to secede from the United Kingdom. As the people of America know, Ireland is placed alongside Great Britain. In some parts only about 20 miles of water lie between each coast line. You can look from Ireland and see the fields and houses on the Scottish coast and the lessons of the War teach us that we cannot have another Heligoland in the Atlantic Ocean. What would have happened during that strenuous time if Ireland had been dominated and ruled by the spirit of Sinn Fein? She would have been in active alliance with Germany; her coasts would have been the natural harbours for German submarines, replenishing their stores of petrol from the Irish people. There is no question that if such had been the case Great Britain would have been paralyzed, if not destroyed, by a German invasion; in all probability no American troops would have been allowed to land in France, and the history of civilization and of the world would be a different record.

British Policy and Proposals for Ireland. Meanwhile the Lloyd George Government and the British authorities had to deal with this new burden added to their tremendous and vital task of national reconstruction and helping to set the world in order; of holding in leash the passions and prejudices of Central Europe and Russia, which the War had so greatly inflamed, and weaving together the divergent interests of 40 nations in a world lately at war; of guiding in safe and reasonable channels the Nationalist, or separatist, or merely restless and futile impulses of alien races in India and Egypt, the Near East and South Africa. If mistakes were made they were inevitable at such a time; if delays occurred in settling so complex a problem as Ireland they might well be condoned. The Government had to face conditions illustrated, and since then intensified, by such publications on the one hand, as the famous *Green Book* of 1886 containing extracts from hundreds of disloyal Irish speeches which largely caused the defeat of Gladstone's policy of that time or, on the other hand, *The Complete Grammar of Anarchy* and *A Hand Book for Rebels*, published in 1918, which gave hundreds of extracts from Unionist and Carsonite speeches inciting to violence and civil strife of another kind.

There were as many proposed settlements as there were differences of opinion. Lord Northcliffe, early in the year, stated his opinions to an American newspaper syndicate as including (1) no coercion of any portion of Ireland; (2) the right of Ireland to fiscal autonomy; (3) Ireland to be enabled to develop political institutions as free as Canada; (4) English manufacturers to establish great factories in Ireland; (5) a tunnel from Ireland to the Scotch coast; (6) English capital to do in the scientific development of Ireland what it had done in other British countries. Lord Wimborne in *The Times* (Mch. 28) urged the carrying out of the Irish Convention of 1917-18 Majority opinions: "The Convention, after 8 months of session, had come within measurable distance of argumentative agreement. Opposition to its findings became either tacit or tactical. Considerable majorities supported its main theses. Outside there was general enthusiasm for the great compromise among all men of moderate opinion. Labour, north and south, was warmly favourable. Sinn Fein abated its pretensions. Even Ulster had made up its mind that a new order was impending, and the more modern exponents of its doctrines were in part reconciled to the inevitable."

On Jan. 23 a new organization for Home Rule within the Empire, called the Irish Centre Party, was formed at Dublin with Stephen Gwynne, ex-M.P., as Chairman; about the same time Lord Midleton, a Unionist leader in Southern Ireland, seceded from the Irish Unionist Alliance and formed the Unionist Anti-Partition League; Lord Haldane was in Dublin at the close of January as the Viceroy's guest and showed considerable political activity while General Sir Hubert Gough was announced as a convert to Home Rule and a member of Mr. Gwynne's Society. On Feb. 17 Sir Ian MacPherson, Chief Secretary, outlined in Dublin certain Government policies and views as follows:

The fate of Ireland is in the hands of the Irish people. Political and economic disturbances will retard the realization of its legitimate industrial ambitions.

An interim grant of £250,000 has been made for the immediate needs of demobilized men and others in need of work.

Any scheme of reconstruction advanced for Great Britain will advance *pari passu* in Ireland.

Ireland has secured housing legislation to suit her own requirements, and she would be wise in continuing that policy.

A system of fixing 'reasonable rents' to be carried out by the Local Government Board, with the co-operation, if necessary, of local authorities with subsidy where necessary to cover the difference between the economic rent and the reasonable rent.

Ireland to participate in the benefits of a Ministry of Health. A bill will be introduced for the medical inspection of schools and school children.

General development schemes, land, transit, light railways, afforestation, etc., will be equally applied in Ireland and to England.

To secure accurate representation of public opinion the principle of Proportional Representation to be applied to Irish local elections.

The United Irish League of Great Britain, though a shadow of its former strength, held a Convention at Leeds on June 7 with T. P. O'Connor as Chairman and Joseph Devlin present; the Sinn Feiners in England called themselves the Irish Self-Determination League. Meanwhile, the definite idea of an Irish Dominion patterned, in the main, upon the institutions of Canada and Australia, had been developed out of many tentative preceding discussions. On Apr. 15 Sir Horace Plunkett, Chairman of the futile Irish Conference, wrote *The Times* declaring that there was no longer any use in offering a restricted form of self-government and that the ripe moment of April, 1918, at the close of the Conference, was gone forever: "Ireland must be given the status of a self-governing Dominion. Upon the strategical questions raised by the propinquity of the two islands the Peace Conference in being, and the League of Nations to come, will make it easy to avoid conflict between British and Irish opinion. The Convention was clear and unanimous upon the necessities of Imperial defence as long as there is any Empire. As to fear of a hostile fiscal policy in Ireland, my own belief is that a contented, self-governing, Ireland would at once enter into commercial arrangements with Great Britain which would be tantamount, in practice, to the present system of Free Trade. Partition, in the only thinkable form of County option, I believe to be neither desirable, nor anywhere in Ireland desired. I admit fully the claim of part of Ulster to special consideration based on the difference of its economic life from that of the rest of Ireland. Within the scope of a Dominion there is ample room for provincial rights; but, if one thing has been made clear by all that has happened in the recent attempts to deal with the Irish problem, it is that, while there may be many solutions, there is but one Ireland." He proceeded to form the Irish Dominion League and was joined by Lord Ashbourne, Sir Algernon Coote, Sir T. Grattan Esmonde, Lord Fingall, Capt. Stephen Gwynne, Brig.-Gen. T. D. Hammond, C.B., Lord Monteagle, the O'Conor Don; these and 50 other prominent gentlemen signed a Manifesto, published on June 28, which contained a careful statement of policy:

In the status of a self-governing Dominion we find all essential conditions supplied. It recognizes our distinctive nationality; it offers us an equal place in a great Commonwealth of free nations; and, our demand once conceded, it will enable us to cultivate friendly relations with them all. We wish Ireland to take her part in guiding the foreign policy of the Commonwealth and preserving the world's peace. Hence we claim for her the same place within the League of Nations as the Dominions overseas.

Let us, then, be clear as to what we mean by the political status we claim for Ireland. As a self-governing Dominion, Ireland would cease to be represented at Westminster; but she would be represented along with the other self-governing Dominions in the League of Nations, and in whatever Imperial Conference, Council or Parliament may at any time be established. All Irish legislation would be enacted in Ireland. The Irish Parliament, through an Irish Executive responsible to it, would have complete control of all internal government, and would fix, levy, and collect all taxes, including duties of Customs and Excise. It is more than probable that the Irish Parliament would find it to its interest to conclude a Free Trade agreement with the country from which Ireland derives most of the raw materials for her industry, and in whose markets she sells most of her produce and manufactures.

Lord Northcliffe supported the general idea of a Dominion of Ireland as did Joseph Devlin, W. Butler Yeats and T. P. O'Connor; the Sinn Fein organs and, especially, *New Ireland* denounced the proposal and said that only an Irish Republic would suffice; the latter journal stated that an Irish Parliament's first act would be to proclaim a republic; the *London Times* of July 24 prophesied and urged the creation of Provincial Parliaments for Ulster and the rest of Ireland with, in each case, a State Executive, an all-Ireland Parliament of one Chamber based on equal representation of the two States and meeting alternately in Dublin and Belfast, with also, continued representation at Westminster. Following the formation of his League and the publication of its weekly organ *The Irish Statesman*, Sir Horace Plunkett put up a vigourous personal campaign for the Dominion idea in the teeth of both Carson and Sinn Fein opposition; Mr. Lloyd George alleged in the Commons on July 21 that Ireland was not a nation because of the existence of Ulster. On Oct. 14 the first meeting was held of a Cabinet Committee on the Irish question with Walter Long, Lord Birkenhead, Edward Shortt, H. W. L. Fisher, Sir L. Worthington-Evans, Sir Auckland Geddes, G. H. Roberts, F. Kellaway, M.P., F.M. Lord French and Sir Ian Mac-Pherson as members. In succeeding months every effort was made to find a reasonable basis for a new Home Rule Act.

In the Commons on Dec. 22 Mr. Lloyd George outlined his new Home Rule proposals preceded by the statement that there were three basic facts in the situation: ''Three-fourths of the population of Ireland are not merely governed without consent but manifest bitter hostility to the Government. The grievance is not on material grounds—Ireland was never so prosperous; it is based on the claim of Irishmen to the right to control their own domestic concerns without interference from Englishmen, Scotsmen, or Welshmen. That is one 'basic fact.' The other is that a considerable section of the people of Ireland are just as opposed to Irish rule as the majority of Irishmen are to British rule.'' The third and, also, a fundamental condition was that ''any arrangement by which Ireland is severed from the United Kingdom, either nominally or in substance and fact, is fatal to the interests of both.'' The War had taught this lesson: ''If we had had there a land over whose harbours and inlets we had no control, you might have had a situation full of peril, a situation that might very well have jeopardized the life of this country. The area of submarine activity might have been extended beyond the limits of control, and Britain and her Allies might have been cut off from the Dominions and from the United States. We cannot enter upon that course, whatever the cost. I think it is right to say here, in face of the demands which have been put forward from Ireland with apparent authority, that any attempt at secession will be fought with the same determination, with the same resource, with the same resolve as the Northern States of America put into the fight against the Southern States. It is important that that should be known, not merely throughout the world, but in Ireland, itself."

Subject to these basic facts the scheme proposed for introduction at the 1920 Session of Parliament included two Legislatures and Governments—one for the Northern or Ulster area based on the 6 Counties and eliminating, wherever practicable, Catholic communities and bringing Protestant communities from couterminous counties—and the other covering, broadly, Catholic Ireland; the right of the two Parliaments to meet and create a single Irish Legislature and, meanwhile, the creation of a Council of Ireland made up of 20 members from each Legislature and a Chairman appointed by the Crown; the right of restricted representation (42 members) at Westminster to be retained; the two Irish Governments to have control of all duties and taxes in excess of a current contribution of $90,000,000 a year for Imperial services; a British grant of $5,000,000 to each Parliament to cover initial expenditure and a permanent free grant of existing Land Purchase annuities totalling $15,000,000 per annum; taxing powers equivalent to those of State Legislatures in the United States and a Joint Exchequer Board to settle future rates of contribution and taxable capacity; the big taxes—income, excess profits, supertax, etc.,—to be levied by the Imperial Parliament which also would control Customs and Excise. The division of powers was to be as follows:

Irish Parliaments.	Imperial Parliament
Education and Local Government	The Crown and Issues of Peace and War
Land and Agriculture	
Roads and Bridges and Transportation	Foreign Affairs and imposition of Customs and Excise
Old Age Pensions and Municipal Affairs	Army and Navy and Defence
Local Judiciary	Treason; Trade outside Ireland
Hospitals and Licensing	Navigation and Merchant Shipping
Law and Order Machinery including the Constabulary	Wireless and Cables
Housing and Labour Legislation	*Post Office and Coinage, Trade Marks
Insurance	and Light-houses, Higher Judiciary

Thus was the 5th Home Rule policy launched; the others included that of Gladstone-Parnell in 1886, Gladstone-Parnell in 1893,

*Note.—Reserved until agreement was reached between the two Irish Legislatures.

Asquith-Redmond in 1912, the Conference-Plunkett Report of 1918. The Premier, in his comments, declared that: "If the people of Ulster and the rest of Ireland unite, they must do so of their own accord. To force union is to promote disunion. Lord Durham's attempted plan to force Quebec and Ontario to join in the same Parliament had to be abandoned. Separate Parliaments had to be given them, and it was only after that was done that Confederation became possible." London newspapers were, on the whole, favourable in their comments though few were optimistic as to the success of the plan; Irish comment was largely hostile with little said as yet by the Unionists and Arthur Griffith, "Acting President of the Irish Republic" declaring there was "nothing for Irishmen to discuss:" impartial opinion hoped for it a fair chance and felt that it was a remarkable step in advance to come from a Government containing many life-long opponents of Home Rule.

The plan, itself, was based, in some of its new points, upon Peace Conference experiences with small Nationalities in Europe. Lord Northcliffe, though an opponent of the Government, declared on Dec. 30 that "the scheme as outlined is based on sound principles." In Parliament on Nov. 24 the Irish Secretary presented a Bill for Irish Educational reform and national schools —probably the most dangerous action which could have been taken at a juncture when Irish unity was sought; seemingly quite futile if Education was to come under the new Irish Parliaments, as announced, a little later. Inevitably the Irish Hierarchy was thus given a new object for suspicion—a part of the natural and world-wide Catholic dislike for secular State education.

Canadian-Irish Opinions and Action. Two extremes of thought developed in Canada as they progressed in Ireland—Ulster being represented by the Orange Order and Sinn Feinism supported at various Irish meetings. In Montreal a mass-meeting was called for Jan. 9 with the issue of a circular declaring that the condition of Ireland was a scandal and disgrace and Mr. Lloyd George "a demagogue and charlatan;" that ("Self-Determination for the smaller nations gives Ireland an equal right with others to enjoy the long-delayed satisfaction of her national aspirations;" that "Freedom without stint and without measure, is the only policy for England to employ." The meeting was held at the Monument National with several thousand enthusiastic Irishmen present. Dr. J. K. Foran, K.C., of Ottawa presided and the speakers included the Chairman, E. B. Devlin, M.P., Dr. J. J. E. Guerin, F. P. Curran, K.C., and C. J. Foy, K.C., of Perth. The latter's speech may be illustrated by his statement that, after the Easter uprising of 1916 which was "a blot on the escutcheon of England" there sprang into existence the Sinn Fein movement—"the best and most logical movement that Ireland has ever had." He declared that "Sinn Fein taught the doctrine of self-respect and self-confidence." A Resolution was unanimously passed declaring:

That this mass meeting of citizens of Montreal, irrespective of creed or race, deems it expedient that on the occasion of the general re-adjustment of European affairs by the Peace Conference the cause of Ireland and her future status be taken into practical consideration, with a view to the immediate securing for her of the same rights, guarantees and liberties as are proposed to be accorded to the smaller nations of Europe; That such rights, guarantees and liberties take the form of self-government according to their respective requirements and ideals, the assurance of which to the smaller nations the statesmen of Great Britain declared to be one of the principal motives actuating the Allies in taking up arms in the recent War.

An important ensuing comment upon the conditions dealt with was that of the Toronto *Globe* (Jan. 22): "Ireland must remain an integral, if self-governing, portion of the United Kingdom and the British Empire, and when the wave of Sinn Fein hysteria has passed, as it will, her sober second sense will accept this rôle, which is the only one possible in her own interests. Historical, geographical, and commercial reasons make her separation from Great Britain unthinkable." Another was at a banquet in Perth on Jan. 14 when strenuous protests were expressed against the views expressed by Mr. Foy. At Ottawa, on Feb. 27, the "case for Ireland" was presented, under the auspices of the Ancient Order of Hibernians, by Mr. Foy as Provincial President of the Order, Hon. J. Hall Kelly, M.L.C., of Quebec and Rev. Father Kavanagh of Almonte. Mr. Hall Kelly said, during his speech, that: "The Irish people voted for the Sinn Fein party and the Irish people want it. If I had the privilege of being over there fighting for Ireland; if I had a voice in Irish affairs, I would be in favour of the Sinn Fein movement, for it is the only movement that will solve the Irish question." Mr. Foy again defended Sinn Feinism. The Resolution passed did not, however, touch the republican issue: "We hold that the claim of Ireland to the freedom and common justice obtainable in the modern state should be the immediate concern of every loyal subject of the British Empire;" Sir R. Borden was asked to use his influence at the Peace Conference to obtain for the Irish people a voice in their government and destiny. The meeting closed with "God Save Ireland."

At Montreal on Mch. 17th there was the usual Irish demonstrations—with some additions; the parade was led by a large green banner flanked by the flags of the "new republic." In Toronto on Apr. 10 a mass-meeting was held with the republican banner of green, white and orange carried across the platform amidst cheers; with speeches by C. J. Foy, Rev. Father L. Minehan, Lindsay Crawford and the Chairman, W. J. Balfe. The following Resolution was approved with unanimity: "That this meeting protests against martial law in Ireland and the denial of freedom to that country, as being subversive of the democratic principles for which this war was fought, and demands that Ireland's case be heard by the Peace Conference so that the justice of her claims may be judged by that tribunal of the nations." Mr. de Valera announced in New York on June 25 that a portion of the "Irish Loan" would be floated in Canada but the results were not announced; at a small meeting in Montreal on July 27 it was decided to send an invitation to De Valera to visit Canada. At the 15th Annual Convention of the Ancient Order of Hibernians in St. Thomas on Aug. 19-21, President C. J. Foy urged freedom for Ireland: "If Ireland were free she would forget and forgive and become the right hand of England."

Colonel Arthur Lynch, ex-M.P., and ex-Boer soldier, told a Toronto audience on Nov. 8 that he wanted a chain of republics instead of an Empire, that Ireland could win nothing by force against the might of England, that a successful attempt to boycott English trade would end in Irish starvation. Rev. Father Minehan in a Toronto address on Dec. 2 declared the British Government of Ireland to be the worst in the world except that of Turkey; he made the interesting remark that the Sinn Feiners "did not desire separation but affiliation with Britain on terms of equality.* The Irish Catholic press of Canada was naturally Home Rule in policy; some of it during 1919 was rather extreme in its opinions. The *Catholic Register* of Toronto blamed Britain for everything; on Jan. 9 it declared that "rebellions were fomented" and then mercilessly extinguished in blood; on Sept. 25 it quoted George Washington in 1788 as follows: "Patriots of Ireland! Champions of liberty in all lands!—be strong in hope! Your cause is identical with mine."

Heated language from the Orangemen of Canada was heard during the year with H. C. Hocken, M.P., Grand Master, conspicuous in his opposition to any form of Home Rule. As he put it at Ottawa on July 30 to the Grand Lodge of B.N.A., so in varied phraseology did the leaders of the Order throughout the country: "Whatever the future may hold for Ireland, the people of Ulster may depend upon the Orangemen of Canada giving them all the support within their power. Sinn Fein rebels shall not rule Ulster. To place a million loyal citizens under the heel of Sinn Fein would be the blackest crime ever committed by any Parliament. Home Rule is a dead issue, made so by the treason and rebellion of its advocates."

India in 1919; Constitutional Reform and Nationalism. Canada was interested in India during the year because of the tremendous experiment in self-government which was being launched; because of the curious forms assumed by Nationalist agitation amongst a few educated leaders in a mass of uneducated, intensely ignorant and yet, in their own way, intelligent people of Oriental ideas and temperament; because of the extraordinary nature of the British effort to establish Western ideals and practices of government amongst 300,000,000 of people steeped in 3,000 years of Eastern autocracy; because, incidentally, Canadian trade with India had increased from $6,603,666, in 1914 to $9,854,038 in 1918 and was still growing in 1919; because a representative Famine Relief Committee with

*Note.—Toronto *Star* report, Dec. 8, 1919.

headquarters in Toronto and Rev. Dr. W. H. Griffith Thomas, Chairman and D. A. Cameron Hon.-Treasurer, had worked hard to raise funds for the famine of this year in the Central and North-West Provinces; because, also, the splendid record of the Indian Empire in the War had awakened a measure of admiration and of interest as to the development and character of its varied races.

The official facts regarding India's contribution to the British Empire's war action were published in a despatch from General Sir Charles C. Monro, Commander-in-Chief, dated Delhi, Mch.19, 1919. It showed that troops from India, British and Indian, were engaged in every theatre of war, from Belgium to Siberia, besides supplying garrisons at several colonial stations; while in India itself the effort of the Munitions Board and other agencies was no less remarkable. As an example it may be said that during the War 1,855 miles of railway track, 229 locomotives, and 5,989 vehicles were sent out of the country, while the clothing factories, in one month, produced 2,000,000 garments. General Monro made the following statement: "On the outbreak of war, the combatant strength of the Indian Army, including reservists, was 194,000 Indian ranks; enlistments during the War for all branches of service amounted to 791,000, making a total combatant contribution of 985,000. Of this number 552,000 were sent overseas. As regards non-combatants, the pre-war strength was 45,000; an additional 427,000 were enrolled during the War; and 391,000 were sent overseas. The total contribution of Indian *personnel* has thus been 1,457,000, of whom 943,000 have served overseas. Casualties amounted to 106,594 which include 36,696 deaths from all causes." Lord Chelmsford, the Viceroy, stated to the Legislative Council on Feb. 19 that India's contribution included £21,000,000 worth of hides, 200,000 tons of railway sleepers, and 42,000,000 articles of military clothing. To quote the beautiful words addressed to England by Nizamat Jung, a native Judge of the High Court of Hyderbad:

O England! in thine hour of need,
When Faith's reward and valour's
 meed is death or glory,
When Faith indites, with biting
 brand,
Clasped in each warrior's stiffening
 hand, a nation's story;

Though weak our hands, which fain
 would clasp
The warrior's sword with warrior's
 grasp
On victory's field;
Yet turn, O mighty Mother! turn
Unto the million hearts that burn
 To be thy shield.

Thine equal justice, mercy, grace,
Have made a distant alien race
 A part of thee.
'Twas thine to bid their souls rejoice
When first they heard the living voice
 Of Liberty.

They, whom thy love hath guarded
 long;
They, whom thy care hath rendered
 strong
In love and faith,
Their heartstrings round thy heart
 entwine,
They are, they ever will be, thine
 In life—in death.

How far such poetic generalizations were true need not be minutely investigated; the proofs were in the war record of a million men and in the other millions which might readily have been obtained; the doubts are in the ever-present element of easily-led and irresponsible millions of illiterate people. Canada, during this period, kept up a Hospital at Nasik in Bombay and heard a series of able lectures at Toronto University from Dr. J. N. Farquhar, a British student of Indian life.

Disorder, Agitations, and Conflicts of 1919. Despite the *Pax Britannica* which kept peace between rival races and creeds and controlled the animosities of Caste, the unrest caused by the War, the echoes of Germany's varied propaganda of rebellion, were bound to find a place in India during the year; these were added to by famine conditions and the Influenza which swept away 5,000,000 of people in a few weeks; they were helped by the restlessness at first evoked by the Montago-Chelmsford reform plans of 1918 and legislation of 1919; they were accentuated by the absolutely necessary Rowlatt Act for the suppression of brutal political crime and a poisonous German propaganda and sedition which, in such soil as India afforded, would soon have produced anarchy. As to this last factor the Government of India issued a statement on Apr. 19 which summarized the situation.

The Governor-General-in-Council thinks it necessary to reiterate here the following salient facts concerning this Act. It is specifically directed against revolutionary and anarchical crime, and can only be brought into force in any locality when it has been proved to the satisfaction of the Governor-General that such crime, or movements tending to such crime, exist. . . . Its first part merely provides for the speedy trial of certain grave offences. In the second and third parts provision is made for preventative action, similar to, but much more restricted in scope than, that now provided by the rules under the Defence of India Act against persons suspected of revolutionary or anarchical crime. Action cannot, however, be taken against any individual without the previous order of the local Government. . . . Not only do the terms of the Act definitely exclude its use in any case not falling within the definition of anarchical or revolutionary conspiracy, but the Government has given the most categorical pledge, which the Governor-General takes this opportunity to reiterate, that the tenor and intention of the Act will be scrupulously safeguarded should occasion arise to put it into operation.

The Governor-General thinks it unnecessary to detail here the deplorable occurrences resulting from the agitation against this Act. The offences which have occurred in Delhi, Calcutta, Bombay, and Lahore have one common feature—they are the unprovoked attempt of violent and unruly mobs to hamper or obstruct those charged with the duty of maintaining order in public places. It remains for the Governor-General to assert in the clearest manner the intention of the Government to prevent by all means, however drastic, any recurrence of these excesses.

Meantime, the Indian National Congress had met at Delhi at the end of 1918 with some thousands of delegates in attendance; it was a Congress notable for the abstention of the "Moderates" in Hindu thought and politics and for the presence of hundreds of peasants who spoke various languages and understood nothing of the proceedings. The Hon. Mothan Malaviya presided and offered loyal and dutiful greetings to His Majesty upon the successful termination of the War: "Indians are particularly glad to think that, while despotic monarchs are disappearing the King-Emperor sits ever more firmly in the affections of his people."

He thought India's representation at the Peace Conference should be more numerous and, referring to India's contributions to the War, he asked how far India would share in the fruits of victory; he hoped that the principles of autonomy and self-determination would be extended to India. The places of men such as Hume, Mehta and Gokhale were taken by extremists such as Besant, Pal and C. R. Das; one Resolution demanded immediate and' full responsible government for the Provinces, another urged the repeal, of the Rowlatt Act and all laws regarding seditious utterances, while still another wanted the release of all prisoners under War and defence measures; B. G. Tilak, M. K. Gandhi and S. H. Imam, leaders in the wilder movements of the day, were suggested by motion as additional members of the Peace Conference from India and that Conference was asked to apply to India "the principle of self-determination."

A very different meeting was that of the Conference of Ruling Princes and Chiefs at Delhi on Jan. 27, 1919, which urged the creation of a Chamber of Princes, approved of direct political relations between important States and the Government of India and expressed appreciation of the elevation of S. P. Sinha to the Peerage and the appointment of Indian representatives at the Versailles Conference. Following these meetings came the violent incidents already referred to—the disturbances at Amritsar in the Penjaub where three Bank managers were burned to death and at Ahmadabad in the Bombay Presidency. Elsewhere, also, on this date of Apr. 6—"the day of humiliation and prayer" in protest against the Rowlatt legislation—attempts were made to stir up trouble and M. K. Gandhi, in particular, led a considerable but not lasting movement of "passive resistance" against the laws regarding sedition. Some disturbances occurred at Calcutta, Lahore and Viramgam but they were not serious. On Apr. 11 the City of Bombay stood for a day on the brink of a bloody riot but it was averted by a mingled display of force and practice of restraint; there followed the invasion of the Indian borderland by Afghan tribesmen and a brief war with the new Amir of Afghanistan. The causes of the whole trouble—quite compatible in such a myriad and varied population as India possessed with the preceding loyalty of the war period—were well explained by Sir William Meyer, Finance Minister, in a Montreal interview on May 9:

Had we been only anxious for the exploitation of the natives we should not have set up our educational standards, but rather cultivated native ignorance; but, as you know, the policy of England, wherever she has had to govern native races, is to set them on their feet; to encourage wholesome manhood, and to introduce such measures of self-rule as would be compatible with native genius. For the present unrest there are many causes. There is the general hysteria universally expressed as one of the results of the War; the restiveness of the Mahommedan population, which numbers some 80 millions, in respect to the possible drastic treatment by the Allies of the Turks; the scarcity, not of food, but of money to buy it; and the new law—the Rowlatt law, which enables the authorities to hold court "in camera," and examine cases of sedition without being compelled

9

to abide by the silence or testimony of hostile witnesses, who have a habit of telling the story of crime to the officials at the first blush, and then denying in court that they know anything about it. Then, there was the disintegrating influence of Mrs. Besant, who stirred up the people in behalf of Home Rule. Add to all this the effect of agitation by the intelligencia class, upon the unthinking multitudes who are unthinkably credulous, and you have an explanation of the situation.

Back of all was the German war-time propaganda which had been succeeded in 1919 by Bolsheviki propaganda and Turkish efforts to undermine Mahommedan loyalty; frequently there were found evidences of seditious work financed by Hindu revolutionists and their Irish and German allies in the United States; Sir George Lloyd, Governor of Bombay, distinctly hinted at a sinister revolutionary organization worked from without and within India as being behind the troubles of April. The chief incident of these disturbances was the drastic action of Brig.-Gen. R. E. H. Dyer at Amritsar on Apr. 11. He was in command of the 45th Brigade at Jullmider and issued a proclamation that in view of the heated state of public opinion there should be no public meetings; he went to Amritsar with 120 British troops and two armoured cars and there found an insolent, unruly mob which he dispersed with difficulty; then faced another mob of 5,000 with a force of 25 British riflemen and 65 Indian troops and the armoured cars; at this point he ordered fire to be opened without further notice and fired all his ammunition into the mob with a result of nearly 500 killed and 1,500 wounded.

His defence was as follows: "In my view, the situation at Amritsar was a serious one indeed, and communications I received from the neighbourhood were indicative of a serious rising. It was, in fact, a widespread movement, and a military situation not confined to Amritsar. . . . I looked upon the crowd as rebels, and I considered it was my duty to fire, and fire well." Lord Sydenham, a one-time Governor of Bombay, told *The Times* that in the opinion of Englishmen in India this action had checked an uprising and saved thousands of lives while the British press of India was inclined to defend the General's action; nothing, however, could convince British home opinion, when it finally became known, that the action was necessary or aught but a wholesale massacre.

Mr. Montagu's Constitutional Act. The reforms and new measure of self-government proposed by Lord Chelmsford and the Rt. Hon. E. S. Montagu, Secretary for India, in their 1918 Report* were widely and continuously discussed—by everyone in India capable of thought and by many incapable of it—before Parliament finally disposed of the legislation of 1919 which was based upon it. The Moderates were largely in favour of the proposed reforms, with support from men like Sir Dinshaw Wacha, Sir Bepin Bose, S. N. Banerjea, T. B. Sapru and Sir N. Chandavarkar and journals such as *The Servant of India* and *the Indian Social Reformer;* the extremists opposed them but in doing so

---

*Note.—See section on India in 1918 Volume of *The Canadian Annual Review.*

split some of their own organizations while the masses hardly understood what it all was about.

A British Government Committee under the Presidency of Lord Southborough investigated the franchise proposals of the Report and recommended that women be excluded from voting for the present; approved an electorate for Provincial purposes of over 5,000,000; recommended separate communal electorates for Mahommedans, and also Sikhs in the Punjab, for Indian Christians in Madras and for Europeans and Anglo-Indians with certain exceptions; proposed special representation of special .interests, including commerce and industry. The Government of India severely criticized many of Lord Southborough's proposals. Another Committee under the chairmanship of Lord Crewe and with Agha Khan as a member, reported on relations between the Home Administration and the Government of India while still another with Lord Esher at its head dealt with administration and the organization of the Army in India. In the House of Commons on June 5 Mr. Montagu supplemented his famous pledge of Aug. 20, 1917, as to "substantial steps" toward Indian self-government by an historic speech upon the 2nd reading of his Government of India Bill. His intention was proclaimed in the clearest words:

I take it that Parliament, or at any rate this House, will agree that the policy of the pronouncement of Aug. 20 must be the basis of our discussion—the progressive realization of responsible government, progressive realization, realization by degrees, by stages, by steps—and those steps must at the outset be substantial. . . . We have promised to India and given to India a representation like that of the Dominions on our Imperial Conference. India is to be an original member of the League of Nations. Therefore I say, whatever difficulties there may be in your path, your Imperial task is to overcome those difficulties and to help India on the path of nationality. . . . In order to realize responsible government, and in order to get devolution, upon which there is general agreement, you must gradually get rid of government by the agents of Parliament and replace it by government by the agents of the representatives of the peoples of India. In other words, you have to choose your unit of government and you have got in that unit to create an electorate which will control the Government . . . The policy of complete local self-government was adopted by Lord Ripon in 1883, and we are now proceeding to carry it out, after a delay of something like 35 years.

The general development was to be along the lines of the Morley-Minto Councils, of Provincial government in the first place, of a gradual training of the electorate, of varied administrative changes and reforms. The first electorate would consist of about 5,000,000 persons. The measure passed its 2nd reading by unanimous vote and was then referred to a joint Committee of the Lords and Commons which went thoroughly into the Bill and made certain suggestions which were duly incorporated in the measure. It also heard Indian representations asking for Indian Ministers in the Government at Calcutta as well as in the Provinces and non-Brahmin communal representation; the European Association of India protested that the Bill meant the very reverse of self-government for 90 per cent. of the Indian people;

leaders of the past and present in the government or life of India were heard including Sir James Meston, B. G. Tillak, Mrs. Besant, Sir Michael O'Dwyer, and others; many Englishmen in India contended that it meant the creation in all the Provinces of small oligarchic governments. The Viceroy intimated on Nov. 3rd that a Chamber of Princes would be established as an advisory body.

The Bill in broad, general terms created Provincial Governments with a Governor, Ministers and Legislature of two Houses in each case; an All-India Legislature including an Assembly and a second Chamber; the establishment of a Public Service Commission to control the Civil Service of India and definition of powers and authority by an immense number of rules and various checks; the modification of control by the India Office at Whitehall over Indian affairs; the provision for a Commission of Enquiry into the operation of the system at the end of 10 years. On Dec. 23 H.M. the King-Emperor issued a Royal proclamation signifying his assent to the Act and declaring that: ''The Act, which has now become law, entrusts elected representatives of the people with a definite share in the Government and points the way to a fully responsible Government hereafter. . . . If, as I confidently hope, the policy which this Act inaugurates should achieve its purpose, the results will be momentous in the story of human progress.'' His Majesty stated that the Prince of Wales would, personally, inaugurate the new constitution of British India. Thus was initiated the boldest and most dangerous policy ever propounded by a Government; certainly the greatest experiment in constitutional rule ever attempted. The objections to it were well stated by Sir Michael O'Dwyer before the Parliamentary Committee as follows:

An Indian province needs a united government; this gives it a divided government.

An Indian province needs a strong government; this gives it a weak one.

An Indian province needs a government capable of prompt action; this leads to delay and friction.

An Indian province needs a simple system of government; this involves extreme complexity.

An Indian province needs a cheap system of government; this involves a very costly one, with elaborate methods of taxation and finance which will certainly not make for economy.

An Indian province needs a government which commands the confidence and ready support of the Services; this tends to divide and disintegrate the Services by making them serve two masters.

An Indian province needs a government which secures good administration to all; this gives power to a small section and endangers the interests of the masses.

South Africa in 1919; The Separationist Campaign   During 1919 the Union of South Africa was face to face with one of the many results of the World War—a stirring up of racial animosities, a revival of old-time Boer prejudices and anti-British feelings, a direct and open agitation for the establishment of a republic. At the same time, through General Botha, the Prime Minister, it was proving itself to be, in government, a sane, loyal, member of the British Empire; through General Smuts, in London and at Paris, it was asserting and receiving a power which no independent community of South Africa could ever have hoped for or could obtain uuder a condition of separation. At the Peace Conference General Smuts, who was also a member of the British War Cabinet and Minister for Defence in the Union Cabinet, held a conspicuous place and was one of the fathers of the League of Nations—in a practical, constructive sense—more so than President Wilson himself and ranking in this respect with Lord Robert Cecil.   .

General Smuts and the League of Nations. In a pamphlet issued early in January he reviewed the proposed policy and described its essentials—based upon the fact that the War had swept away all combinations of peoples which were founded on exploitation of weaker nationalities, and had left the British Empire as "the only embryo League of Nations because it is based on the true principles of national freedom and political decentralization." Like President Wilson, he regarded this project as "the primary and basic task" of the Conference. His comparison of the Empire and the League, as proposed, was most comprehensive:

> It would be interesting to compare the functions here ascribed to the League to the working arrangements of the British Empire. In the first place, in both cases the ultimate authority of common action is a Conference of the principal constituent States. In the British Empire the common policy is laid down at conferences of the Imperial Cabinet, representing the United Kingdom, the Dominions, and India, while executive action is taken by the individual Governments of the Emipre. In the second place, the minor constituents of the Empire, consisting of Crown colonies, protectorates, and territories, are not represented directly at the Imperial Cabinet, but are administered or looked after by the individual principal constituent States referred to, just as it is here proposed that the Powers should, under the League, look after the autonomous undeveloped territories. In the third place, the economic policy of the open door and the non-military policy here advocated for these autonomous or undeveloped territories are in vogue in the analogous British Crown colonies, protectorates, and territories. It is therefore clear that the broad features of the two systems would closely resemble each other. And it is suggested that where the British Empire has been so eminently successful as a political system, the League, working on somewhat similar lines, could not fail to achieve a reasonable measure of success.

Late in March General Smuts was sent by the Conference leaders to Hungary on a special mission; in London on July 17, before leaving for South Africa, he issued a Message which contained some interesting views. He declared "the appeasement of Germany" the first essential for peace and new prosperity and urged that encouragement be given to the Ebert Government; he thought a sobered, purified Soviet rule in Russia better than anarchy and civil war; he declared that the Irish issue was "beginning to poison our most vital foreign relations" and urged a British policy in Ireland similar to that accorded Bohemia by the Conference. From Johannesburg, on Nov. 20, General Smuts —who had become Prime Minister—issued an appeal to the American Senate not to reject the Treaty and the League: "No nation put more faith, more effort into the construction of the League than America. It now only remains to ratify and pass the Covenant. Other nations have approved it. Even distant Asia is represented; Japan has given her approval, while America alone hesitates and falters. Will the great leaders now lag behind the ranks? I cannot believe it. I cannot believe that America will, after all, block the way—that the purely American viewpoint will be allowed to over-ride the wider interests and necessities of our own civilization in the greatest crisis in history."

The Nationalist Movement in South Africa. Meantime, the Nationalists had continued their propaganda or racial assertion and anti-British statements; in January their policy took the form of vehement effort to state the case for South African independence before the Peace Conference; the Colonial Secretary (Mr. Walter Long) in a despatch published at this time stated that under the South African constitution, the South African Government and Parliament alone could be regarded by the British Government as authorized to speak on behalf of the people of South Africa; in February it was announced that the Nationalists would send a Deputation to England and Paris, anyway, and seek to get a Republic declared or recognized. A vigorous debate followed in the House of Assembly at Cape Town on Feb. 14 and lasted several days. Sir Thomas Smartt, Leader of the Opposition, moved that the House condemn the agitation which was being carried on for the dissolution of the Union and the severance of the existing connection between South Africa and Great Britain. He expressed the opinion that such agitation, if persisted in, would lead to civil war and bloodshed and asked where the liberties of South Africa would be at this time but for the British Navy: "These people who are trying to break up the Union are a section of one section of the people of South Africa." He appealed to the other Dominions and asked if Australia, New Zealand and India were not interested in the tremendous strategic importance of South Africa in the southern seas.

The Acting-Premier, Hon. F. S. Malan, Minister of Education, Mines and Industries, moved in amendment that: "The House, while welcoming all constitutional development which would make the Union in the fullest sense a self-governing Dominion, emphatically condemns the present agitation for the disruption of the Union and the severance of the connection between South Africa and Great Britain and also repudiates all attempts to invoke interference from any outside Power." Lieut.-Col. F. H. P. Creswell moved a long amendment to this motion declaring (1) that the status of the Union, as a self-governing Dominion within the British Commonwealth, secured to its peoples the fullest power to deal with all questions affecting their national development and also safety against external danger; (2) that the status established by the South African Act was accepted by the leading representatives of the two races, as a settlement of racial quarrels which had affected their progress and peace for over a century; (3) that the permanent welfare of the people demanded unremitting attention by Parliament and people to grave domestic, social, economic and land problems.   It concluded as follows: "The House, accordingly, records its conviction that the present movement for the abrogation of the South Africa Act, and the disturbance of the existing status of the Union, having particular regard to the circumstances in which the movement originated, will inevitably endanger the country's peace and result in continued neglect of pressing domestic concerns with disastrous consequences."

General J. B. M. Hertzog, the Nationalist leader, opposed these motions as did his followers; urged the right and necessity for establishment of a South African Republic and the separate right of the Transvaal and, especially the Orange Free State, to secede from the Union and the Empire; declared that the Union did not possess freedom, because Great Britain dictated who should be Governor-General and the British flag flew in South Africa.   The Rt. Hon. J. X. Merriman who, in earlier days, was considered a Radical and freely accused of disloyalty, claimed that the Union Parliament had greater freedom than the Transvaal republican Volksraed of independence days and asked what tangible advantage could emerge from a republic.   The only effect would be to break the country in two sections.   Moreover, the Nationalists left the natives and coloured people out of account.   Sir Thomas Watt, Minister of the Interior, declared that it would be impossible for any League of Nations to treat South Africa with such consideration or so sympathetically as Great Britain had done; while Colonel the Hon. H. Mentz, Minister of Lands, speaking as a former Transvaal republican, declared that as long as Great Britain kept faith he would keep his word given at Vereeniging.   Eventually, the Smartt Resolution was withdrawn and that of Mr. Malan carried by 78 to 24.   The Senate passed a similar Resolution by a very large majority.

A series of Loyalist meetings followed throughout the country; at the first one in Cape Town on Feb. 20, Sir N. F. de Waal declared that a large section of the Dutch were in accord with the British element and determined to maintain the Union.   The Nationalist delegation to Europe was led by General Hertzog and included N. C. Havenga, Senator A. D. W. Wolmarans, Dr. F. W. Reitz and Dr. D. F. Malan, F. W. Beyers and E. C. Jansen; it booked passage by the *Durham Castle* but the seamen refused to carry "rebels" and Admiral Fitzherbert, with characteristic British courtesy, offered to convey the delegates to England on the cruiser *Minerva;* with characteristic qualities of a different kind the offer was declined on the ground that the cruiser did not have baths and other conveniences!   On Mch. 2nd the Delegation sailed on a Dutch steamer for New York; in the Assembly on the 3rd, Tilemann Roos, the Transvaal Nationalist, declared that if the Nationalist mission to Europe failed they would continue to agitate with a view to obtaining a majority in Parliament and gaining the independence of South Africa constitutionally.

England was reached in due course after a brief period in New York where the Delegates were officially ignored; in London on June 5th they were received by the Prime Minister. General Hertzog based his plea for Independence upon the feelings of the Dutch population and, when asked as to the racial allignment of the Union Cabinet had to admit that it stood 8 Dutch to 3 Englishmen. He declared that: "The old population has decided to continue pressing its claim to Independence, and the old population, while continuing to do it, will still keep along constitutional lines, and the old population, sir, I feel and I think you feel too, eventually will win, We are here to-day to ask you that the wrong which was done in 1902 may be undone as to the two Republics." Mr. Lloyd George, in his reply, said that General Botha, the South African Premier, had specially requested that the Delegation be heard and he proposed to give them the viewpoint of the British Government.

He pointed out that they confessedly represented the wishes of a party whose adherents were almost entirely drawn from the older Dutch-speaking population of South Africa and who were in a political minority of the Union Parliament; that, on Mr. Hertzog's own admission, the native population of South Africa was definitely against Independence, and wished to remain within the British Empire; that British South Africans, whose intolerant attitude was complained of, had accepted the settlements of 1906 and 1910 with wonderful loyalty and "it was surely a great testimony to their good-will that for the last 10 years a predominantly Dutch Government had been in power in South Africa, which largely derived its power from the votes of British South Africans;" that he could not see how it was possible for the British Government to reopen a great settlement because of political issues which had developed between different sections of the South African people themselves. As to the rest: "The view of the British Government is that the Union of South Africa rests on a fundamental understanding and agreement between the British and Dutch elements of the people of South Africa, in which both made sacrifices and surrenders for the attainment of a great common ideal, and that it cannot be dissolved by the one-sided action of either element without the consent of the other. We could not agrée to any action which means the disruption of the Union."

In conclusion the Premier said: "I would point to the status which South Africa now occupies in the world. It is surely no mean one. As one of the Dominions of the British Commonwealth, the South African people control their own national destiny in the fullest sense. In regard to the common Imperial concerns, they participate in the deliberations which determine Imperial policy on a basis of complete equality. In the greatest Conference

in history South Africa is represented by two statesmen of in-
dubitably Dutch origin, who have won for South Africa an extraordinary influence in the affairs of the world.   It is futile
to believe that South Africa can ever return to that isolation
which was possible a century ago.   The world has become too
knit together; the action of one part impinges too directly and
too rapidly on the fortunes of every other part for any nation
to keep outside the great common current of human affairs.   The
formation of the League of Nations is the recognition of this
inexorable fact; and in the future League of Nations South Africa
will have the same membership and status, and far more influence,
than any of the other States which are outside the ranks of the
five Great Powers.''   The Peace Conference refused to hear the
Delegation and, early in September, they were back in South
Africa; a banquet at Pietermaritzburg (Sept. 5) to welcome them
was seriously disturbed by hostile crowds of workmen.   As a party
they vehemently opposed the German Peace Treaty—both in
Parliament and the country.   It was one of the most cruel documents of history, they alleged, and some Nationalist members
declared that it would be degrading to vote for it.   The Treaty
was approved by 84 to 19 in the Assembly and by 30 to 5 in the
Senate—the minority in each case being Nationalists.

Government Changes and Political Issues.   Meantime, General
Botha had left England early in July, after his work at the
Imperial War Cabinet and the Peace Conference, with a farewell
Message in which he eulogized Britain's part in the War and
the Peace, and concluded as follows: ''I go back to South Africa
more firmly convinced than ever that the mission of the British
Empire now and in the time to come lies along the path of freedom and high ideals.   Britain is the corner-stone upon which
our civilization must rest.''   At Pretoria on Aug. 28 there came,
with tragic suddenness, an attack of Influenza and death to this
great statesman of the Empire—great as an enemy, great as a
friend, great in his statesmanlike grip upon local and world conditions, great as a general in the service of his own people and of
the Empire.   His funeral on the 31st was the occasion of the
most imposing demonstration in South African history with
mourning people for miles along the route.   General Smut's eulogy
was a most eloquent one: ''Only recently Botha saw the whole of
Europe torn by wild passions, and he returned to South Africa
more than ever convinced that salvation and healing would only
be found in a new spirit of humanity and in forgiving and forgetting old differences and wrongs.''   H.M. the King sent a message to Lord Buxton, Governor-General: ''Not South Africa alone,
but the Empire at large, will mourn the loss of a loyal citizen,
chivalrous soldier, and high-minded statesman.''

At the age of 49 Jan Christian Smuts became Prime Minister
of the Union after he had won an international reputation as
a general and statesman; in his first speech in Parliament, in
that capacity, he moved the ratification (Sept. 8) of the Peace

Treaty and declared that South Africa must remain a part of the Empire, and that it could not secede; the Union must not be torn apart by Nationalism. He was explicit as to the right of secession and, in reply to a direct question, replied, "Absolutely and decisively No," and then added: "Our Constitution is laid down in writing, and our Constitution in Clause 19 says that the legislative power of the Union consists of a Parliament of the Union, composed of the King, the Assembly, and the Senate. It is impossible and unconstitutional for either of these parts to secede from the other. The Assembly cannot secede from the King. Of course, by means of revolution you can do that sort of thing, but you cannot do so by constitutional means." Coming to a second question, whether the right of veto still existed and whether the King could veto a law for the secession of the Union from the Empire, there was, he said, no doubt as to the answer: "On an ordinary law there is no such thing, in reality, as veto, but on a question like this it is not only the King's right but, according to the Constitution, it is his duty to keep himself in place and connected with the Union." On Sept. 17 he clearly defined his own policy and indicated a coming general election:

I would ask for the recognition of three fundamental positions. In the first place, I ask that we agree to abide by the British connection, and that we agree not to question it any longer. The British League of Nations, to which we already belong, and the new world system, to which we shall soon belong, give us ample scope as a free nation. In the second place, I would ask that we should also accept as fundamental the principle of frank, honest, whole-hearted co-operation between the white races. I for one could never again be a party to any policy which divides South Africa or tends to divide it on racial lines. The co-operation of the past ten years since Union I desire to strengthen and develop. And lastly, I would ask us to recognize that the great task before us is no longer racial, but has become industrial. The great World War has resulted in conditions which give us a unique opportunity to develop this country and to push ahead with a forward industry and development policy. Let us honour and preserve our sacred national traditions, but let us go beyond that, and join in the great work of the world.

Sir Thomas Smartt and Colonel Creswell, Labour leader, endorsed the Premier's views. General Smuts started shortly afterwards on a speaking tour and at Cape Town on Sept. 26 laid emphasis upon South Africa's immense potentialities, which, he claimed, made it the richest mining country in the world: "There is one continuous coal field here and in Rhodesia, which will not be exhausted in a thousand years, and, in the long run, will prove more valuable than gold or diamonds." At Camaroon he described his view of the British Empire as being an alliance of which the King was the bond: "Under this alliance we keep together, protect and help each other financially, with advice and otherwise, each according to his own light. You do not need to have a republic to be free. You are free in the British Empire." A Nationalist Congress on Oct. 10 took a directly opposite view of the situation and upon this issue was fought the ensuing Election:

1. All laws of the Imperial Parliament affecting South Africa should be declared null and void, as the Union Legislature alone has the right to legislate for South Africa.
2. The Union Jack to be supplanted by a separate flag.
3. The Union to send its own Ambassadors to foreign countries, where desirable.
4. The Governor-General to be nominated by the Union Government.
5. South Africa no longer to use English coinage or the coinage system.
6. The King's veto to be exercised only in the same manner as in the United Kingdom.
7. The stationing of British troops within the Union to be prohibited.
8. No Union Minister to participate in the proceedings of the Imperial Cabinet.
9. The Union to have exclusive control of its foreign policy.

At a Bloemfontein Nationalist Conference (Oct. 16) General Hertzog postponed rebellion for the moment: "The time is not yet ripe for active steps to achieve the country's independence, but we have the right to work until we can say—The time has now arrived." He further declared that he regarded the Union's constitution as nothing but "a scrap of paper," stating, for the time being, how the people in South Africa wished to be governed; but "as soon as the nation's will changes, then it is for the Government, Parliament, and King to alter the scrap of paper accordingly." A Unionist or Opposition Conference at the same place on Oct. 21 followed and passed a Resolution in favour of the vigourous development of the agricultural resources of the country by means of closer settlement and the systematic and continued introduction of British settlers; it also favoured the taxation of land values and approved the recent speech of General Smuts. Sir Thomas Smartt was appointed Chairman and declared that Britishers in South Africa and the Dominions were not going to allow a band of disappointed politicians to disintegrate the Empire: "There may arise a position in which it will be necessary to fight and fight we will." At a Congress of his own South African Party—Pretoria, Oct. 30—the Premier asked for the co-operation of other parties and appealed to the whole population to support the policy of the Government and to devote themselves to the great tasks of peace, agriculture, and mineral development.

Incidents of the year included the assumption by the Prime Minister of the new Portfolio of Foreign Affairs in addition to that of Defence and the passage of a Woman Suffrage proposal in the Assembly by 44 to 42; an increase in Canadian trade with British South Africa from $383,261 Imports in 1914 to $545,723 in 1918 and from $3,834,592 Exports in 1914 to $5,101,614 in 1918; the statement by Lloyd Harris of Canada in a letter dated Jan. 30 that South African representatives in London thought Canada's trade with South Africa could be very largely extended as the Union would have to purchase enormous quantities of goods from the United States and that they would prefer to have these purchases made from Canada; the statement as to the famous Witwatersrand gold mines that white employees in 1918 numbered

22,632 with wages of $43,200,000 and 179,276 coloured persons with wages of $27,070,000 and a total output of £34,823,017, or $174,-000,000, which produced a total working profit of $37,000,000; the increase in trade for the first six months of 1919 over those of 1914 was $95,000,000 or from £50,086,413 to £69,063,018.

Australian Conditions and Elections of 1919.

Events in Australia interesting to and associated with questions of Canadian development were many in this year and included reconstruction, Labour troubles, Tariff issues, Trade expansion and general elections. Like Canada the Commonwealth had come out of the War with many general officers, though the Australian Imperial Force, or A.I.F. was commanded at first by one of the most popular of British generals, Sir William Birdwood. He was replaced by two Corps Commanders of Australian origin—Lieut.-Generals Sir John Monash, K.C.B., K.C.M.G., and Sir J. J. Talbot Hobbs, K.C.B., K.C.M.G. Other well-known Australian officers of the period were Major-Generals Sir J. Gellibrand, K.C.B., D.S.O.; Sir Thomas W. Glasgow, K.C.B., C.M.G., D.S.O.; E. G. Sinclair-Maclagan, C.B., D.S.O.; Sir N. R. Howse, V.C., K.C.B., G.C.M.G.; Hon. Sir J. W. McCay, K.C.M.G., K.B.E., C.B.; Lieut.-General Sir H. G. Chauvel, G.C.M.G., K.C.B.; Surgeon-General Sir C. S. Ryan, K.B.E., C.B.; Colonel Sir H. C. Maudsley, G.C.M.G., C.B.E.; and Brig.-Generals W. R. McNicoll, C.M.G., D.S.O.; J. H. Cannan. C.B., C.M.G.; William Alexander, C.B., C.M.G., D.S.O.; A. J. Bessell-Browne, C.B., C.M.G., D.S.O.; W. L. H. Burgess, C.M.G., D.S.O.

At the close of the fiscal year June 30, 1918, there were 106,239 war-pensioners on the Australian List who had drawn $10,000,000 up to that date and included 39,809 incapacitated soldiers with 30,664 of their dependents and 39,766 dependents of deceased soldiers. The religious affiliations of 323,106 Australian officers and soldiers included 163,081 belonging to the Church of England, 60,603 Roman Catholics, 47,850 Presbyterians with 44,230 Methodists, Congregationalists and Baptists. During this year arrangements were made for providing houses for soldiers and their dependents at an estimated capital outlay of $125,000,-000; $50,000,000 were appropriated for purposes of demobilization and re-education; grants were made to settle soldiers on the land totalling $100,000,000; by the end of June 190,000 had been demobilized and despatched to Australia and the remaining 80,000 rapidly followed. The Federal repatriation policy included the following details:

1. The establishment of curative workshops attached to the hospitals for re-education, for the study of natural aptitudes and for familiarizing the wounded soldier with the use of artificial limbs or exercising injured limbs.

2. Arrangement with private employers to enable men to get the more advanced training—the employers paying a wage appropriate to the value of the actual work and the Government paying the difference between that and the current recognized wage.

3. The provision of facilities for young men who went to war in the middle of their apprenticeships to complete their tuition, the Government supplementing their wages to enable them to do so.

4. The establishment of hostels or homes for voluntary occupation by those permanently incapacitated, with a special allowance payable by the Repatriation authority to friends or relatives taking care of such men.

5. The establishment of a factory for the manufacture of limbs with branch factories in the different States, not only to make but also to repair and renew artificial limbs.

6. The encouragement of small rural industries for soldiers such as hog-raising, the Government guaranteeing a market and organizing and handling the sale of the produce with, also, the promotion of co-operative organization among such settlers.

7. Loans upon liberal and attractive terms for the purchase of homes in urban areas.

During the year an Advisory Committee appointed by the Department of Defence—consisting of Lieut.-Gen. Sir C. B. B. White, Military Advisor to the Government, Maj.-Gen. J. G. Legge, c.b., c.m.g., Maj.-Gen. Sir J. W. McCay and Hon. G. Swinbourne—reported as to a new Militia system along the following lines: (1) Establishing a concentrated course of training and shortening the period previously adopted by several years; (2) organizing the forces of the Commonwealth on Divisional lines with the formation of machine-gun and other new units sufficient to complete six divisions of infantry and two of Light Horse; (3) establishing the Australian Air Service on lines already approved by the Commonwealth Ministry; (4) organizing Divisional headquarters and the creation of skeleton staffs, comprising highly-skilled permanent and militia officers; (5) erecting in central positions, suitable ordnance stores and other buildings necessary for the storage of war materials and equipment; (6) developing the activities of the Arsenal Department along lines which would ensure a reserve stock of shells and other ammunition and enable Australia to undertake the manufacture of all essential munitions of war.

The Government and Policy of W. M. Hughes. During the early part of the year Mr. Hughes was, with Sir R. Borden and General Smuts, a most conspicuous figure in the Peace Conference; the Hon. W. A. Watt was Acting-Premier in Australia and Rt. Hon. Andrew Fisher High Commissioner in London. Mr. Hughes represented the practically unanimous opinion of the Commonwealth in demanding that control of the former Pacific possessions of Germany should be in British or Australian hands and he fought for this contention with vigour and success. Though opposed to any Mandatory scheme, he accepted the final compromise which gave Australia full practical power and the League of Nations certain nominal rights. The Australian Premier and General Botha agreed in contending that mixed international control or influence in the government of a country was sure to create friction and had always done so in Turkey, Egypt and other regions. President Wilson wanted the League to share in this control and, with the United States a powerful member of that body, the Mandatory plan did promise to give American representatives a finger in the government of many and distant regions of the earth; fortunately the varying rules of application to these territories made the control under British mandate almost absolute.

Japan got the Caroline and Marshall Islands because of the war-time treaty with Great Britain which had given the aid of the Japanese Navy in the Pacific to the Allies. Mr. Hughes, however, opposed successfully the proposed Japanese clause in the Covenant which would have established international racial equality and affected the right of the Dominions to exclude Japanese settlers. To the press on Mch. 27 he said: "We cannot agree to the insertion of any words in the Covenant or in the Treaty of Peace that would impair or even question our sovereign rights in regard to any and every aspect of this question. I cannot but regard the proposed amendment as an effort to establish a principle under which, ultimately, some nations would find their internal policy as to immigration and nationalization challenged by the League at the instigation of one of its members." By the close of 1919 the Japanese had established in the Marshall Islands of the North Pacific a great commercial and shipping centre and, by virtue of the enormous union wages, demanded by Australian sailors and ship-workers, were competing in various directions with the Commonwealth itself.

Mr. Hughes believed the League of Nations to be an injurious factor so far as the British Empire was concerned and an influence, in particular, for the weakening and hampering of its Naval power. At a farewell banquet given to him in London on July 1st he based his faith for the future not on the League of Nations, but on the "Triple Alliance" of Great Britain, France and the United States. Meantime, at the opening of the Australian Parliament on June 26 Mr. Watt had outlined Government policy with a review of demobilization and repatriation work and the statement that the Government's ship-building plans would be continued. The policy of the Government was to continue the Commonwealth line of steamers, and to build larger and faster vessels for overseas trade, and so assure satisfactory shipping at reasonable rates to exporters of primary products. The Australian Wheat Board had 2,000,000 tons of wheat on hand, and 8,700,000 tons were being held for the Imperial Government. The Wheat Board overdraft was £18,800,000. Amongst the business foreshadowed were tariff changes which would preserve manufactures started during the War, encourage basic industries upon which the national safety depended, and develop Australian production; improvement of the Industrial Arbitration Act; legislation respecting Naturalization to better safeguard national interests; the closer inspection and control of immigrants.

Mr. Hughes and Sir Joseph Cook, his associate at the Peace Conference, had, meanwhile, left for home on July 8 after the former had been entertained at luncheon by the King and Queen and been made a British K.C. in formal and stately fashion. The Premier was welcomed in Australia with much cordiality and some hostility and found a very mixed political situation which included questions of high cost of living, profiteering, heavy taxation, industrial strife, soldiers' grievances, tariff revision, Bolshevism, naval expansion, inter-State disputes and reconstruction problems. Enthusiastic scenes of personal popularity marked his reception at Freemantle, Melbourne, Bendigo, Sydney and other points, with clear evidence that the returned soldiers or "Diggers" were strongly behind him. In Parliament on Oct. 7 the Premier moved a constitutional amendment giving the Commonwealth power to deal with all industrial matters, whether affecting one or more States, to control combines, trusts and monopolies, and also to make arrangements regarding the production, manufacture and supply of goods; it was to be voted on in a Referendum and went to the country at the close of the year.

On Oct. 13 the Budget of Hon. Alex. Poynton showed total revenues for 1918-19 of $220,300,000 and expenditures of $225,000,000—$100,000,000 being due to the war. The total war expenditure was stated at $1,557,000,000 of which $230,000,000 had been paid out of revenue; the estimated deficit for 1919-20 was $16,000,000 and the Public Debt of the country on June 30, 1918, was £262,542,646 and of the States £380,539,441 or a total of $3,245,000,000—$645 per head. The Government's shipping programme provided for a fleet of 50 cargo carriers at a cost of about $50,000,000. The original fleet, bought by Mr. Hughes, cost $10,000,000; 14 wooden ships ordered in the United States, $5,000,000; six steel ships being built in Australia $4,500,000; 14 other steel vessels to be constructed in Australia $10,850,000; two wooden ships (Australia), $675,000; four steel ships of 12,800 tons (Australia), $8,000,000; and five of 12,000 tons (Great Britain), $10,000,000.

Meantime an Inter-State Commission on Profiteering had described 25 woollen mills as making an annual profit of $769,000 in 1914 and an average yearly profit in 1915-16-17 of $2,000,000 —an increase of net profit to capital from 13·44 per cent. to 31·33 per cent.; 14 hosiery and knitting factories as increasing their profits on capital in the same period from 12·07 per cent. to 25·73 per cent.; the manufacturers of clothing for soldiers as realizing net profits of 13 per cent. in 1914, 29 per cent. in 1915, 39 per cent. in 1916 and 25 per cent. in 1917. The Tariff policy of the Government was based upon (1) the necessity for the preservation of industries which had been brought into existence in Australia during the War; (2) the encouragement of new industries which were contemplated; (3) the extension and diversification of existing industries. On Apr. 29 a Deputation of British manufacturers in Australia waited upon the Hon. W. M. Greene, Minister for Trade and Customs, to ask for substantial and effective preference for British manufacturers of at least 20 per cent. over foreign goods. The Deputation urged that Great Britain's sacrifices in the War entitled her to protection against the competition of other countries which had not been so seriously affected. The Deputation further asked for, practically, the prohibition of traffic in German goods. Mr. Greene replied that the Commonwealth Government was endeavouring to give Great Britain the fullest preference, but that Great Britain should reciprocate.

According to a London *Times* correspondent from Sydney on Apr. 19, Australia years before this time was largely Free-trade: "To-day there are only a very few free-traders left in the Commonwealth. The overwhelming majority of the people favour the building of a tariff which will enable local industries to struggle into existence." In August the Australian Industries Protection League was formed at Melbourne and endorsed by the Acting-Premier (Mr. Watt) who had hitherto been a Free-trader; in 1917-18 $25,000,000 of Japanese manufactures had reached Australia and this fact helped the new proposals as did an increasing domination of the market by American manufacturers; in 1918-19 the import of Textiles increased from $75,000,000 to $130,000,000, that of apparel, including boots and shoes, with oils and leather and paper, doubled, that of metals and machinery rose from 48 to 84 millions. The policy of the Government became clear though not yet put into exact fiscal form. It did, however, create a Bureau of Commerce and Industry to encourage production and expansion of trade and improve industrial methods and sent Mark Sheldon as Trade Commissioner to the United States with orders to push operations there.

The General Elections of 1919. Mr. Hughes was, again, the central figure in this contest; he had the Liberal party support under Sir Joseph Cook and an old-guard of moderate Labour behind him. The Opposition was made up of organized Labour so far as the great bulk of its officials and agitators was concerned, of an Irish Home Rule and largely Sinn Fein element which was very strong in Australia under the leadership of Archbishop Mannix, of Socialists and Bolshevists and O.B.U. in many varieties; the nominal leader was Hon. F. G. Tudor, the practical fighting chief was Hon. T. J. Ryan, Premier of Queensland. The latter had tried many local experiments in State Socialism, a few had been successful but the most of them were subjects of bitter controversy. The Government platform was one of aid to the returned soldier and suppression of the profiteer—by Royal Commissions and a Referendum; the claim that in 1919-20 the ordinary Government expenditure would be only $2,500,000 more than in 1913-14; opposition to extreme Socialistic schemes and to an alleged alliance between organized Labour and the Sinn Fein; industrial and shipping development with moderate Protection; organization of Industrial Councils and an Industrial Court for the Commonwealth; Bond gratuities to returned soldiers of $125,000,000; the declaration that Labour's Socialist schemes involved an enormous expenditure and a yearly deficit of $150,000,000; the setting up of machinery under which wages might be automatically increased as the cost of living rose.

Messrs. Tudor and Ryan issued a Manifesto accusing the Government of sacrificing "White Australia" to the Japanese and of gross extravagance; promising high Protection, effective anti-profiteering legislation, nationalization of shipping, complete self-government and unlimited legislative powers in Australian affairs; advocating abolition of the Senate and State Governorships. The binding tie of the Opposition was a slogan of "Defeat Hughes at any cost"; organized Labour had expelled him from its ranks three years before and it was bound to "get him" at this juncture if at all possible.   Mr. Hughes' description of the Labour policy was "prodigality, disloyalty and utter lack of constructive statesmanship"; an Irish Convention, in Melbourne on Nov. 3rd, passed Sinn Fein Resolutions and publicly supported De Valera with Mr. Ryan as Chairman and the warm support of Archbishop Mannix; of this combination Mr. Hughes made the most.   A factor which no one thought much of, was the Farmers or Country Party which, in a Manifesto, drew special attention to Australia's towering debts and expenditure, the decrease in producers and production, and the increase in city populations at the expense of the rural communities.   It urged increased production and an economical Government, and declared that the primary producers would not stay on the land if excessive taxation and exactions continued.   The consolidation of Federal and States Debts, a vigorous policy of Immigration from Great Britain and extension of Federal shipping construction were urged.   The returned soldiers as a whole supported Mr. Hughes with five Generals and a number of soldiers running in his interest.   The Elections were held on Dec. 13 and resulted in the return of Mr. Hughes with 40 Nationalists, or Liberals, or Hughes-Labourites; 9 of the Farmers' party, who were in the main Hughes' supporters but who intended to act separately; 26 organized Labour and anti-Hughes Opposition. Messrs. Glynn and Webster of the Government were defeated; Messrs. Tudor and Ryan of the Opposition were elected; Generals Cox, Ryrie and Elliott were elected.   The Senate stood 35 Nationalist and one Liberal.

Australian Conditions and Statistics.   During the year official statistics showed that the area of Australia was 2,974,581 and its population 5,030,479; that six cities contained 41·90 per cent. of the population with Sydney placed at 792,700 and Melbourne 723,- 500; that 3,667,672 of the people were born in Australia, 452,295 in England and Scotland and 139,434 in Ireland; that the value of agricultural production in 1917-18 was $289,000,000, of Mineral products $127,000,000, of Pastoral production (wool) $468,500,000, of dairy, poultry and bees $156,000,000, of manufacturing $349,- 000,000; that over half the Import trade and more than two-thirds of the Export trade were with the British Empire; that the Government Railway mileage in 1917-19 was 22,181 and the gross earnings $121,500,000, working expenses $88,000,000, net earnings $33,000,000; that in 1918 the total Deposits in cheque-paying

Banks were $1,123,500,000 and in Savings Banks $581,000,000; that the total Pensions in 1918 were 125,299 and the amount involved $19,737,000; that there were in the Royal Australian Navy in April, 1915, 1 battle cruiser of 19,200 tons, 5 light cruisers and a number of torpedo boats, gun-boats, destroyers, etc.; that there were in the Commonwealth 1,186,540 employees of whom 581,755 were members of Trade Unions with 20,459 unemployed in the first quarter of 1919; that in 1914-18 there were 1,945 strikes in Australia with 8,533,061 working days lost and an estimated loss in wages of $24,000,000; that in 1917-18 there were $44,000,000 worth of spirits, $52,000,000 of beer and $33,000,000 of tobacco consumed in Australia; that in the season 1918-19 the total production of raw wool was 3,431,018 bales of which the United Kingdom took 2,721,166 and the United States 348,387 bales.

Australian Incidents of the Year included the re-appointment for a year of Sir R. C. Munro-Ferguson, G.C.M.G., P.C., as Governor-General of Australia; the successful completion of an aerial passage to Australia from England by Capt. Ross Smith, M.C., D.F.C., A.F.C., and his brother Lieut. Keith Smith in a Vickers-Vimy machine and the knighting of the two aviators (K.B.E.) by the King; the return to Canada in August of D. H. Ross, for many years Canadian Trade Commissioner in Australia, with a view to interviewing manufacturers and exporters interested in Australian trade and with trade statistics showing an increase from $5,600,000 in 1913 to $12,250,000 in 1917-18; the announcement in September that the New South Wales Government had decided a living wage in that State to be $18.50 per week in place of $14.40 with an estimated addition of $30,000,000 to industrial production; the efforts of the Commonwealth Government Line, running from the United Kingdom and the Continent to Australia, to obtain shipping business and the specific detailed advantages offered in circulars by H. B. G. Larkin, General Manager; the appointment of Adrian Knox, K.C., of Sydney, as Chief Justice of the Commonwealth in succession to the Rt. Hon. Sir Samuel Griffith, who had resigned; the deaths during the year of Hon. Alfred Deakin, ex-Prime Minister, on Oct. 7, Sir Phillip O. Fish, ex-Premier of Tasmania, Hon. Robert Harper and Sir Simon Fraser, Hon. William Kidston, ex-Premier of Queensland, James F. Archibald, founder of the famous *Bulletin*, Sir E. M. Nelson, K.C.M.G., manufacturer, and Sir Samuel M'Caughey who left an estate of $28,000,000.

Relations with or Conditions in, Other Empire Countries. The Island Colony of Newfoundland—which ranked in 1919 as a Dominion of the Empire—despite its small population of 250,000—had a prosperous year, marked, however, by much political strife and varied changes of government. It was very proud of its War achievements and of the record won by the Royal Newfoundland Regiment in Gallipoli and on the Western front. Though the Island had no pre-war military force except some naval reservists and boys' brigades, it contributed to the fighting forces of the Empire, in 1914-18, 11,922 of all ranks, including 9,326 men for the Army, 2,053 men for the Royal Naval Reserve, 500 men for the Newfoundland Forestry Corps, and 43 nurses. The Newfoundland Regiment furnished a battalion for the Gallipoli campaign and sent 4,253 men to France and Belgium, suffering casualties of 1,195 killed, dead and missing with 2,314 wounded and 152 prisoners; it won a V.C., 28 M.C's and 6 Bars, with 151 other Imperial decorations, 21 Allied decorations and 22 Mentions in Despatches.

Canadian and other forces were said to have 3,000 Newfoundlanders in their ranks and monetary contributions from a not very rich population totalled $490,000 with a large quantity of Red Cross material and comforts for the troops. At a dinner given in London on May 17 with Lieut.-Col. W. H. Franklin, D.S.O., C.B.E., Commander of the Royal Newfoundlanders in the chair and Lord Morris, ex-Prime Minister of the Island, present, the strong hope was expressed that the Regiment would in some form be preserved; Sir Edgar Bowring, High Commissioner, declared that its complete disbandment was unthinkable; by the close of the year it was deemed impossible to maintain it. It may be added that Pte. Thomas Ricketts, the V.C. winner, was said to be the youngest holder of that honour in the British armies— 15 when he enlisted as a stoutly-built private; at 17 he held the highest of war honours, with the D.C.M. and the golden star of the French Croix de Guerre and had won the personal congratulations of the King.

Politics and Changes of Government in Newfoundland.   Sir William Lloyd, Premier of Newfoundland, attended by special invitation the Peace Conference of 1919; on the 1st of January he had been sworn a member of the Imperial Privy Council; at home Sir Michael P. Cashin, Minister of Finance, was Acting-Premier. The latter was in Montreal in February and told the press on the 5th that the fishermen of Newfoundland were very prosperous and that they embraced the greater part of the population—apart from those engaged in the business affairs of the Colony. The increasing prices paid for fish had been an impetus to prosperity and the majority of the fishermen were saving money while many now owned their own sailing vessels on the fishing banks. Incidentally, he stated that Canadian banks had been very successful in Newfoundland and had won the full confidence of the people. The trade of the Island was described as the best in its history and there was a surplus of revenue over expenditures. The Budget of May 14 showed an actual surplus of $1,170,000 for the fiscal year of June 30, 1918 and one of $1,900,000, estimated, for the coming year with savings of the people during 1918 stated at $5,000,000.   A Government Loan of $5,000,000 in 5½%, 20-year bonds at $102.44 and interest, was announced and duly sold; the Public Debt was $45,000,000.

Meantime, friction had been developing between Messrs. Lloyd and Cashin and, on May 20, a most unique scene occurred in the Legislature. According to the St. John's *Daily News*, Sir Michael Cashin, who had just resigned from the Coalition Government in which his followers were a majority and who, also, was the oldest member of the Assembly, arose and moved that "the Government as now constituted does not possess the confidence of the Members of this House." He said that he had supported the National or Coalition Government since 1917 and claimed that it had faithfully performed the work which it was called upon to undertake; but that there was no confidence existing between the two factions composing it, and that it would be better for the country and for all concerned if they at once separated.

The Premier, Sir William Lloyd, began to explain the circumstances under which Sir M. P. Cashin had resigned from the Government, but the Speaker reminded him that there was no seconder to the motion. The House sat in silence for a few minutes and then the Premier rose and seconded the motion himself. John Currie, Leader of the Opposition, said that his party was prepared to vote for the Resolution, and could do so consistently because it had not had any confidence in the Government during the past two years. The motion was thereupon carried without a division. Sir Michael was then called upon by the Governor, Sir C. A. Harris, K.C.M.G., C.B. C.V.O., and the following new Ministry announced: Premier and Minister of Finance, Sir M. P. Cashin; Minister of Justice, Hon. A. B. Morine; Colonial Secretary, Hon. J. R. Bennett; Minister of Public Works, Hon. William Woodford; Minister of Shipping, Hon. J. C. Crosbie; Minister of Fisheries, Hon. J. C. Stone; Minister of Militia, Hon. A. E. Hickman; Minister of Agriculture, Hon. W. Walsh; Ministers without Portfolio, Hon. W. J. Ellis, Hon. John Currie and Hon. A. W. Piccott.

General elections followed on Nov. 2nd and a keen though not unusual sectarian issue preceded the contest. Lord Morris who, as Sir Edmund Morris, had for many years been Prime Minister, was a Roman Catholic as was Sir Michael Cashin who, after the brief Lloyd *regime* had now succeeded him; in the population of the Island only about one-third held to that faith. The Hon. R. A. Squires, who had left the Lloyd Government in 1918, was now Leader of the Opposition and a prominent Orangeman; he also had the support of Hon. W. F. Coaker, leader of the Fishermen's Protective Union. Both sides had full tickets in the 18 constituencies and both sides were optimistic; a point which did not appear in outside comments was the charge that the Lloyd Government had been unduly influenced from capitalistic sources. In the final result the Government was defeated by 24 out of 36 seats—with 18 of the former total going to the Fishermen's Union. Mr. Squires was called upon to form a new Cabinet and, like his following in the House, it was largely representative of Protestantism and Labour. It was sworn in on Nov. 17 as follows:

Premier and Colonial Secretary ....Hon. Richard A. Squires, LL.B., K.C.
Minister of Marine and Fisheries ....Hon. W. F. Coaker
Minister of Justice ....Hon. William R. Warren, K.C.
Minister of Finance ....Hon. H. Y. J. Brownligg
Minister without Portfolio ....Hon. Walter W. Halfyard
    "   "   ....Hon. Arthur Barnes, LL.D.
    "   "   ....Hon. George Shea
    "   "   ....Hon. Alex. Campbell, M.D.
    "   "   ....Hon. Samuel J. Foote, K.C.

    Outside the Cabinet
Minister of Public Works ....William B. Jennings
Minister of Shipping ....William H. Cave
Minister of Agriculture and Mines ....James MacDonnell

Resources and Progress of Newfoundland. The Island not only progressed in its trade and revenues and fishing interests in 1919 but in other respects also. Sir Edgar Bowring, who had been appointed High Commissioner late in 1918, told the London press on Jan. 30 that: "Our fishermen, who nearly all own their own houses and land enough to supply their own needs in the way of vegetables, lend a hand at lumbering in the winter when the forests supply abundance of employment. The iron mines, again, are an important industry. We supply the great steel works in Cape Breton with their raw material, and during the War our people did a great deal to increase the supply of steel by enlarging the output of the mines. There is ample employment in the Island at good wages. No one earns less than 8s. a day. The cost of living is rather cheaper than it is here (England). Rents and taxes are much lower, and food and clothing cost about the same. The great paper-mills that have been established at Grand Falls not only employ numbers of hands, but also provide a market for the smaller spruce which can only be used in the mills. Here, too, I may point out that water-power is abundant and electricity very cheap. I have been all over the world, and I think Newfoundland compares favourably with other Dominions in the advantages it offers to settlers, especially to those with a little capital. Land is granted to settlers at a nominal figure."

Among the chief commodities for export were cod-oil for tanning purposes, cod-liver oil, hair-seal leather for fancy goods and canned lobsters. In London on Mch. 13 he pointed out that a thousand miles of railway had in recent years been built and operated and that transportation was good; that the development of Newfoundland's water-power was worthy of notice with one-third of the Island under water and numerous falls from which power could be had; that not only St. John's but the smaller towns were lit by electric light; that in the fisheries the old-time methods were disappearing, the oars and the sails were being done away with and the motor-engine taking their place with the result that fishing was becoming more certain and the men were returning to it; as to the great paper and pulp industry, the product of their mills could not be beaten anywhere and, while there were two large companies operating at present there was room in the Island for two thousand. Owing to its greater nearness to England Newfoundland would be the landing and jumping-off place for the Aviation development of the future. In *The Times* (June 21) Sir Edgar touched another point:

There is unquestionably in Newfoundland a large section of highly mineralized country which only needs thorough examination to show that there is great value in the deposits of iron, copper, silver, lead, chrome-iron, and coal. We have them all, we believe, in large and workable quantities. The development which so far has resulted in the export of minerals has been confined to the copper ore exported from Tilt Cove (which has been worked since 1864), Little Bay, and Bett's Cove; iron pyrites from Pilley's Island; and iron ore from the well-known deposits of Bell Island, in Conception Bay, from which the annual exports of ore in recent years have amounted to more than a million tons. As regards coal, in many parts of the Island there are indications of coal deposits that may prove to be of inestimable value, and at the present time some of these deposits are in the course of being examined.

The great attractions of Newfoundland as a sporting country, as a centre for salmon and trout fishing and shooting—as a land of fishing rivers and caribou hunting—became better known at this time and were widely advertised by the Government. As to trade the exact figures of expansion showed Imports for June 30, 1914, of $15,793,726 and in 1919 of $33,297,184; in Exports the respective figures were $15,134,543 and $36,784,616; the total increase in six years being from 30 to 70 millions. A war condition was shown in a decrease of Imports from Great Britain totalling $2,000,000 with an increase from Canada of $7,500,000 and from the United States of $11,000,000; in Exports the important changes were to countries other than these and the total increase was $17,500,000.

Newfoundland Incidents of the Year included the resignation of Sir P. T. McGrath, K.B.E. as President of the Legislative Council,—a post which he had held since 1912 with, also, the Chairmanship of the Pension Fund—upon the defeat of the Cashin Government; an address by Hon. W. F. Coaker (Nov. 27) stating that the export duty on Iron-ore from the Wabana Mines—which supported the Nova Scotia Iron and Steel concerns—would be increased; the fact of influenza and small-pox in the winter of 1918-19 having wiped out almost the entire population of northern Labrador amid conditions of terrible hardship; the suit instituted by Harriet D. Reid, daughter of the late Sir R. G. Reid, chief owner of shares in the Reid-Newfoundland Railway which were valued, before distribution, at $15,000,000, for an accounting as to the control and action of the Executors—Sir W. D. Reid, R. G. Reid, H. D. Reid and Lord Shaughnessy—in respect to an estate composed of $7,302,500 worth of these shares; the claim of Dr. W. T. Grenfell, C.M.G., Labrador Missionary, that stories of the bleak and barren nature of this Atlantic strip of North America—still belonging to Newfoundland—were exaggerated and that the fisheries and water-powers of the region were of enormous value; the final decision of Newfoundland and Canada to refer disputes as to boundary lines in this territory to the Privy Council in order to ascertain what the location and definition of the boundary as between Canada and Newfoundland in the Labrador Peninsula actually was under existing statutes, Orders-in-Council and Proclamations.

In June it was intimated that the French Government had not responded favourably to informal proposals as to the annexation of the Islands of St. Pierre and Miquelon to Newfoundland. The Prince of Wales' visit to the Colony on Aug. 12-13 was a great success with tremendous enthusiasm shown by the people, decorations in every part of St. John's and the usual official programme with regattas and races and a visit to the fishing regions. An important movement during the year was that of Co-operation which affected five concerns in the Island covering fishing, publishing, electric light and ship-building. The chief of these interests was the Union Trading Co., Ltd., with $100,000 capital, organized by Mr. Coaker in the interests of the fishermen and starting in 1911 with $8,000 cash and bringing the men, in 1919, an additional profit on their fish of 20 per cent. The old-time question of Confederation with Canada was not an issue in this year and prosperity was too much in evidence to make any change popular; at the same time, the growth in trade and travel and educational influences between the two countries provided an increasing basis for closer relations.

New Zealand Leaders at Versailles and in Canada.   The Rt. Hon. W. F. Massey, Premier of New Zealand, had a notable part in the Imperial War Cabinet of the closing months of 1918 and at the Peace Conference of 1919. He and his associate, Sir J. G. Ward, had a place at Versailles far out of proportion to the population and power of their great little Dominion of 1,000,000 people and it was obtained for them by the pressure and *prestige* of the Imperial Premier. Technically, only Mr. Massey was a representative, practically Sir Joseph Ward became one whenever necessary through appointment as one of the British delegates. Mr. Massey was one of the British delegates on the important Committee as to Responsibility for the War with attendance at 25 Sessions where he fought energetically to bring Wilhelm II. to trial for his international offences; both leaders took high stand for Australasian or British acquisition of the German Colonies. On June 13, prior to their return to New Zealand, the two Ministers were entertained in London by Sir Thomas Mackenzie, High Commissioner, and Mr. Massey declared himself a firm believer in the League of Nations; if, however, it was to be successful it must have armed force behind it; and it must be remembered, too, that the League would not make war impossible, nor would it come into existence fully matured; he hoped it would be very successful but "we must not allow ourselves to be lulled into a false sense of security." As to the arrangements made regarding Samoa the people of New Zealand and the people of the islands of the Pacific were going to be navigators in the future; he believed New Zealand would become the head of a most important British Island Federation in the Pacific. On Oct. 19, it may be added, the New Zealand House passed a Bill accepting the Mandate for Samoa.

Mr. Massey returned *via* Canada and Sir Joseph Ward *via* the United States. The former was at Halifax on July 4 and told of New Zealand's part in the War: "Three-quarters of the 120,000 enlistments were voluntary. Three thousand, whom the New Zealand Government were unable immediately to equip and incorporate in her own force, joined the British forces. The New Zealand of the future would carry an annual Pension Bill of over two millions sterling; its compulsory military training system had enabled the Dominion to occupy Samoa with 2,000 citizen soldiers immediately on the outbreak of hostilities." On July 9 the Premier was the guest of Toronto and was entertained to luncheon at the Royal Canadian Yacht Club by the City. At Vancouver on July 15 he told the Canadian Club that this was not the last war and it was not Armageddon: "The Germans were Huns 2,000 years ago and they are Huns to-day; they will be Huns a thousand years from now, and until the Day of Judgment and after. I have seen the industrial establishments of Northern France ruined and broken by German guns and other German methods for no other purpose than that France should not compete with German industries for years after the War. I have no faith in the regeneration of the Germans." He believed they were already at work on new engines of destruction. Writing a little later from Wellington (Sept. 4) to a correspondent at Edmonton, Mr. Massey stated that: "While it is impossible to prevent prices from rising in war, we have succeeded in keeping the increase in this country below that of any other part of the Empire; there is provision in the statute book for a fine of £200 in the case of an individual, and £1,000 in the case of a Company, where it can be proved that profiteering has taken place."

Political Changes and Elections in New Zealand. On Apr. 10, 1919, Prohibition was defeated in a general Plebiscite by a few thousand votes—the Civilian population giving a majority of 11,967 for it and the soldier vote a majority of 15,260 for continuance of the License system; there was no finality in the vote as a Plebiscite was to be taken every three years. Prohibition in this case involved compensation, not to exceed $22,500,000, with 1,200 licenses in existence of which the fees went to the Municipalities; Mr. Massey stated in Paris on Feb. 19 that if it failed to carry, a vote would be taken on state control or ownership. As the year grew a measure of discontent with the Massey-Ward Government developed; it found expression in serious Railway strikes, in unrest as to the increased cost of living, in the organization of a National Alliance of Labour with a section which repudiated Arbitration, conciliation or mediation in Labour disputes, in a feeling that neither trade nor industry was expanding as it should do under Peace conditions.

In August Sir Joseph Ward, Minister of Finance and formerly Liberal leader, retired from the Ministry with other Liberal members, on the ground that its coalition work ceased with the War and that an election was inevitable because already two years over-due under War conditions and agreements. The retiring Minister announced his policy as including the establishment of a State Bank, the Nationalization of coal mines and flour mills, the continuance and expansion of Imperial Preference, with additional duties on imports from countries not members of the League of Nations, Proportional representation for city and suburban electorates—with extensions as the growth of population justified, also vigourous land settlement plans, increased railway construction, and restrictions on profiteering. The country should not undertake a local Navy, but should support a suitable scheme for Empire protection in the Pacific. Under his reconstruction Mr. Massey gave Sir James Allen, the able defence Minister of the War period, the Department of Finance. The Elections took place on Dec. 18 and the Premier swept the country with his Reform party. He carried 48 seats, the Liberals obtained 19, the Labour Party 11 and there were 2 Independents. Sir Joseph Ward, Sir James Carroll and G. W. Russell were, themselves, defeated.

New Zealand Incidents of the Year included the publication on Feb. 14 of an official Report issued by the Defence Department which showed the splendid war record of the Dominion. Prior to the War 10 per cent. of the population had been considered a maximum mobilization of forces; yet New Zealand mobilized for service 11·4 per cent. of her total population while over 50 per cent. of the males of military age were actually sent into camp, and the number shipped overseas totalled 100,444. The total casualties at Gallipoli, the Somme, Messines, Passchendaele, and the German and British offensives of 1918, were 42,800 with 16,302 deaths. Trade statistics showed an increase during the war period from $150,000,-000 to $175,000,000—the whole exportable meat and dairy production being bought by Great Britain; at Bisley on July 19 Sergeant Loveday of New Zealand won the King's Prize; during 1916-17 the wool clip of the Islands, also purchased by the United Kingdom, totalled 185,000,000 pounds sold at an average price of 14·74 pence and in 1918-19 the total was 205,000,000 pounds at an average price of 15·25 pence—in that period the British Government had paid $192,000,000 for this wool. In August the New Zealand Board of Trade reported results of an investigation into the Dominion coal production of about 2,000,000 tons a year as showing that: "Though the supplies of coal have not been so regular and uninterrupted as should have been the case with less industrial friction, neither the owners of the mines, nor those actively engaged in the management and direction of the industry, nor the workers in the mines, nor those engaged in distribution, have received remuneration that should be regarded as unduly high in existing conditions"; this Board recommended some form of Nationalization as urgently needed and upon this the Ward party based a clause in their platform.

Importance of the West Indies to Canada. This was not realized by Canadians very fully or generally. To a Northern country the advantages of close association with a Southern climate, area and production were really very great; in the case of the United States they had long been proved to its people and the world. H. J. Crowe, the Canadian champion of Confederation as between Canada, Newfoundland and the West Indies, put this point very well in a Toronto interview on Dec. 5: "The importance of these tropical Islands is not properly appreciated in Canada. We Canadians at present import $108,000,000 worth of tropical products yearly, the greater part from, or rather through, the United States, thus piling up exchange against us. Our imports from the West Indies directly total but $22,000,000 annually. A large part of the 300,000 tons of shipping of the new Canadian Government Merchantile Marine cannot be better employed than in direct trade with the British West Indies, and would have the coincident advantage of supplying a new line of trade between the West Indies and Britain *via* Canada. Even without political union, the tariff preference can be made a potent force for commercial union between Canada and the Indies, although, of course, we will not get maximum benefits until political union is consummated. There must be political union to make commercial ties binding and permanent. Experience has proven the fact. But as England can consume all the tropical products Canada does not absorb, the tariff preference would provide return cargoes for the steamers carrying fruits, etc., from the Islands, thus producing true Empire interchange."

Canada was, in 1919, active in seeking trade in Europe against keen competition; yet its people had, at their very doors, a market of 2,000,000 British consumers who were buying products freely from the United States which Canadian producers could supply. The American Fruit Trust was, according to Mr. Crowe, in control of the Canadian market and was using the West Indies as an adjunct in supplying Canada. *The Canada-West India Magazine* published by the Canada-West Indian League of which T. B. Macaulay, Montreal, was President, urged the commercial side of this policy during 1919 with much vigour. In February Capt. J. M. Reid of British Guiana gave, in this journal, the following condensed figures as to the West Indies:

Colonies	Aggregate Trade Sterling	Population	Area in Sq. Miles	Revenue in Sterling
Bahamas	£ 807,746	55,944	4,493	£ 90,472
Leeward Islands	1,797,058	127,189	704	190,060
Windward	1,851,766	175,278	524	227,170
Trinidad	9,557,902	371,876	1,868	1,064,596
Barbados	4,058,311	184,259	166	311,303
British Guiana	6,230,010	313,859	82,480	669,385
Total	£24,302,793	1,228,405	90,235	£2,552,986

He wanted a Federation of the Islands with British Guiana and closer trade relations with Canada. John R. Reid, a late President of the Ottawa Board of Trade, after close-range study of the situation, expressed opposition to political union (January issue of the *Magazine*) but thought: (1) That a feeling in favour of a commercial federation of the Islands, by means of which co-operation and co-ordination of aim and effort might be obtained, was fast gaining ground; (2) that what the Island leaders in affairs, political and commercial, desired most was, firstly, adequate transportation facilities, and, secondly, the fullest and most satisfactory trade arrangements as to exports and imports; (3) that they favoured Canada and, those with whom he had conversed, were strongly desirous of an increased interchange of products. On Feb. 13 the Town Council of Montegobay, the second town of Jamaica, unanimously passed a Resolution pointing out that because of the increase in the cost of Jamaican products passing through American clearing-houses to Canada, and that as Canada was not connected with any tropical countries from which she could draw her raw materials, the Government should be approached to bring about a Confederation with Canada.

At Montreal on Mch. 18 the West India League tendered a luncheon to Mr. Macaulay who was leaving for the Islands on a mission of enquiry; in his speech the President pointed out that Canada and the West Indies belonged to the same great Empire family, and each was nearer to the other than to any other part of the British Empire while none of their products were competing products. He declared that if free trade could be established between the two, on a reciprocal basis, Canada would get an exclusive market of an additional 2,000,000 people, while the West Indies would get an exclusive market of about 8 millions. At the present time, the West Indies had before them examples such as Porto Rico, which through its free market in the United States, was prospering exceedingly. A free market for West Indian products in the United States was not so advantageous as a free market in Canada, for a large proportion of the United States, such as Southern California and the Southern States generally produced commodities identical with those of the West Indies, and were thus in competition. He was opposed, personally, to political union as being "difficult and ridiculous," because of "the great distance of these Islands from Canada, because of the lack of knowledge of each other's needs, and because it would be unwise for either to attempt to control the Government of the other."

In British Guiana, Bahamas, British Honduras, Trinidad, Jamaica and Barbadoes, Resolutions were being freely and sometimes officially passed at this time in favour of the commercial policy; it was stated that the Islands were only scratched so far as their natural resources were concerned and that, for instance, they only produced 300,000 tons of sugar, while if fully developed, British Guiana alone, could produce 4,000,000 tons. On the other hand the West India Islands as a whole did a large business with the United States and many feared serious injury in this respect from closer Canadian relations. As a matter of fact, there was already a Reciprocity Treaty in force since Apr. 9, 1912—originally negotiated between Canada and Trinidad, British Guiana, Barbados, St. Lucia, St. Vincent, Antigua, St. Kitts, Dominica and Montserrat. The arrangement provided for a mutual Preference by way of a reduction of 20 per cent. from the general tariff schedules on a limited list of commodities. Grenada afterwards granted concessions to Canada while the Dominion gratuitously extended preference to the Bahamas, Bermuda, British Honduras, Grenada, Jamaica and Newfoundland for a period of three years.

Jamaica and the others mentioned, however, remained fearful of United States retaliation and did not return Canada's generosity. Under this partial Reciprocity, trade developed steadily from a total of $6,900,940 of Canadian exports to the British West Indies in 1911-12 to $11,921,116 in 1917-18 and of $8,490,878 Canadian imports from the Islands in 1911-12 to $18,252,381 in 1917-18. Increased values of course, accounted for much of this growth. The United States undoubtedly considered the Islands at this time as geographically tributary and economically dependent upon them and, during the war period, their trade increased with the Islands at the expense of Great Britain in particular. Lower costs of production in the United States, closer proximity in a shipping connection, and comparative indifference in Canada, were probably the chief factors in promoting American influence.

Meanwhile, Mr. Macaulay had been touring the Islands and on his return told the Montreal journal of his League (May) that he went to the West Indies a pronounced advocate of Commercial Union, and had found no real reason why such an arrangement should not be brought into effect. But, he also reported that, after discussing the matter with many of the leading men of the West Indies and British Guiana, he believed the first step in this direction should be an increase of the Preference from the present 20 per cent. to 50 per cent. In Commercial Union discussions the question of taxation to replace duties was a serious one in the Islands; at Ottawa it would involve 1½ millions of revenue on sugar alone: "On the other hand, all recognize the benefits which would accrue by a far greater development of trade between Canada and the West Indies than at present obtains. The United States is forging ahead by leaps and bounds in securing the trade of the West Indies, whether British or not, and the prospects are that unless some greater preference is granted on both sides, the West Indies may ultimately be British in name, but owned by the United States."

Following this came the British preferential policy and its vital influence upon West Indian sugar. A meeting of the British Guiana Chamber of Commerce and other bodies on May 9 expressed "deep appreciation of the granting of preference on Colonial products by His Majesty's Government," and its belief that "such preference will stimulate the production of commodities necessary to make the Empire self-supporting." Mr. Macaulay's addresses throughout the Islands were followed by speeches from Mr. Crowe in favour of closer political relations. At Kingston, Jamaica, on Apr. 23 he summarized the advantages —to the Islands—as follows:

1. Canada would give you a free market—the greatest growing market in the world for tropical products.

2. She would provide new transportation facilities and assist you in development with her capital and energy.

3. She would use her influence and great power in the Mother Country to assist you in securing the maximum preference for your tropical products, particularly sugar.

4. She would meet the deficit in your revenue caused by the free entry of Canadian manufactured and agricultural goods, which, in turn, would greatly reduce your cost of living, and increase your productive power.

5. She would give the British manufacturer in your market a preference of 33 1/3 per cent. over foreigners which he does not enjoy to-day.

6. She would give you a Provincial Government so that you could direct and control your local affairs, and also representation in Parliament at Ottawa, where you would have a voice in directing the affairs of all British America.

Mr. Crowe added: "Sir Robert Borden, our Prime Minister, has authorized me to say, that if the people of the British West Indies, after carefully considering the matter, decide to unite with Canada, he will not only receive, but welcome official Delegates and, with his Cabinet, discuss the terms of confederation in a broad, Imperial way, because he believes such a union would be in the interests, not only of the British West Indies and Canada, but of the Empire as a whole." The chief political difficulty in the way was the question of representation at Ottawa and especially that of the coloured race; Mr. Crowe proposed to overcome this by the Provincial Governments appointing from their members of Legislatures an Ottawa representation in the Senate. The Montreal *Journal of Commerce* (June 17) deprecated this policy but declared that the Commercial Union advocated by Mr. Macaulay ought to be within the reach of statesmanship at no distant day; the movement, however, was one in which the initiative must be taken by the smaller colonies. As a matter of fact and figures, Canada imported $108,000,000 of products from other countries such as the West Indies produced and in small part sent to Canada in these years.

Sir Edward Davson, of London, President of the Associated Chambers of Commerce of the British West Indies, was in Montreal on June 17 and dealt with a new and important factor which had developed: "This is the Preference just granted by the Mother Country on Colonial products. As, in the case of sugar, this is considerably greater than that given by Canada, it must mean that the West Indian crop will go to England and not to Canada as heretofore. I hope, therefore—and this is one of the objects of my visit here—that it may be possible for Canada to meet the new conditions by giving an equal preference on sugar to that of the Home country. The loss of the sugar crop would mean the absence of return freight by the Canadian-West Indian Steamship Line, which is subsidized by the Canadian Government. This, in turn, would endanger the continued supply of Canadian products to the West Indian markets. There is another point connected with this matter of the British Preference. The West Indies propose, in return, to grant a substantial Preference to the Mother Country; and I think it would be regretful if such a Preference were not also extended to Canada.'' So far as these various proposals involved free trade between Colonies and the Sovereign Power there were plenty of precedents—the Tunisian, Algerian and Corsican products into France, the African Colonies of Spain and the Mother Country, the United States and Porto Rico, Hawaii and the Philippines.

Lord Rothermere's proposal, in a press interview of Sept. 15, that the Bermudas, Bahamas and some other West India Islands— but not Jamaica—be given the United States in liquidation of the British war debt to the Republic, excited comment far out of proportion to its importance. Though not taken seriously in England, it was so taken in both Canada and the United States. The latter country discussed it as worthy of consideration and there was reason for this—absolute control of the Caribbean Sea would be commercially and strategically of enormous value to the United States; Professor W. R. Shepherd, of Columbia University, had urged it strongly in 1917 as an absolute necessity to the Republic. Jamaica, at this time, was greatly under the influence of United States business connections; the U.S. Fruit Company controlled and shipped the fruits of the Island and was called a great Trust by Canadian visitors and commentators upon the situation. The Island, itself, was the Gibraltar of the Caribbean seas in more ways than one; its control by Britain or Canada was of importance to the continental and sea distribution of power.

H. J. Crowe in discussing the Rothermere suggestion at Montreal on Oct. 13 said that West India's choice lay between absorption by the United States, or confederation with Canada: "United States interests are making tremendous efforts to subjugate the West Indies in an economic way. Already the chief export of Jamaica has been completely captured by an American Trust. Attempts to create competition in the banana business are ruthlessly crushed by this monopoly which has reduced the producer to economic slavery, and has made this valuable article of food, which should be on every poor man's table, a luxury to the consumer. If the West Indies were federated with Canada, the free interchange of commerce that would follow would lower the cost of living in both countries, and with Canada's bargaining power with other nations to back up the West Indies in the markets of the world, the present stagnation of these strategically situated, rich, tropical, British possessions, would be changed to a state of abundant prosperity."

Protests as to the Rothermere idea followed from various sources and especially (Oct. 24) the West Indian Chamber of Commerce at Kingston, Jamaica. On Oct. 31 a cable came to the latter body

from the Colonial Secretary: "With reference to your telegram of
the 24th October pray assure Jamaica Imperial Association that
His Majesty's Government have no intention of ceding Jamaica or
any other West India colony to any other Power.   Gladly welcome
this expression of the deep attachment of Jamaica to the Empire
of which it has been so long a valued member, and they trust that
the tie which binds Islands to the Mother Country will never be
severed."   Meantime, Jamaican imports from the United States
had been 54·6 per cent. in 1915, 57·4 per cent. in 1916 and 70·1 per
cent. in 1917.   Writing on Oct. 22 to the members of the Government and others in Jamaica, Mr. Crowe defended at length his proposals for union with Canada and added:

As a result of a recent conference I had with the Ministers at Ottawa,
and the President of the Canadian National Railway and Steamship Service,
I am in a position to state that our Dominion Government are desirous of
offering all the transportation facilities required for handling the trade of
Jamaica, at rates that would be in the interests of your producers and consumers, and of cultivating the closest friendly relations between the two countries.   In addition to furnishing steamers for conveying bananas and other
tropical products to Canadian ports, they are prepared to put on all the
refrigerated cars necessary for the delivery of fruit to the West, as far as
Winnipeg.   In order that you may appreciate the magnitude of the Canadian
Government's transportation system, I beg to state that they now have 20,000
miles of railway and 300,000 tons of shipping, and the latter will be steadily
enlarged.   I doubt if there is an organization in the world that owns and has
such complete control over as vast a transportation system.

The possible exports from the British West Indies at this time
included hides and skins from Bermuda; sponge, hemp, shell, fine
woods for furniture, fish, salt and cocoanuts from Bahamas; cocoa,
coffee, fruit, ginger, cattle, hides, logwood, rum, tobacco, sugar, salt,
cocoanut, etc., from Jamaica and dependencies; cattle, cocoa, sugar,
cotton, limes from Leeward Islands; Cocoa, cotton, spices, fine
woods, etc., from Windward Islands; cotton and sugar from Barbadoes; sugar, cocoa, cocoanuts, fine woods, asphalt, crude oil from
Trinidad and Tobago; Sugar, rubber, cocoa, mahogany from
British Honduras; Sugar, fine woods, rice and minerals from
British Guiana.   Yet the total imports by Canada in 1918 were
$2,954,528!

THE PRINCE OF WALES IN CANADA

The Prince's Tour of Canada; His Welcome, Personality and Speeches. The Royal Tour of this year was not the first in Canadian annals but it was, for many reasons, the most memorable. The charming and youthful personality of the Prince combined with great personal tact and a rare capacity for public affairs were apparent from the first moment of his landing on Canadian soil; the difficulties surrounding his visit at a time of general unrest, when men's minds were attuned to conditions of war and strife rather than of loyal tribute and kindly hospitality, were equally obvious; the importance of bringing home to the popular consciousness a living expression of the vital link of Monarchy, in that chain of Empire which girdled the globe, was clear to thinking men. In character and conduct, in manner and bearing, in a mingling of dignity and democracy, in speeches of obvious statecraft and simple eloquence, in unassuming and perfectly natural joy at meeting the people—young and old, rich and poor, millionaire and workman—the Prince of Wales proved himself worthy of his high position, worthy of his national traditions, worthy of the Empire's greatness.

King Edward VII., when Prince of Wales, had visited Canada in 1860 and been accorded a welcome which fitted his gracious and pleasing personality; King George V in his sailor experience had touched the shores of the Dominion upon at least six occasions, though his only official visit was during the Empire tour on the *Ophir*, in 1901, when T.R.H. the Duke and Duchess of Cornwall and York* visited the Eastern Provinces of Canada and were given a loyal and hearty welcome. Other Royal personalities from the days of the Duke of Kent, father of Queen Victoria, down to H.R.H. the Duke of Connaught, in recent years, have made Canada their home for a time; but it remained for the 1919 incumbent of a position and title which have held great places in British history since the exploits of Edward, the Black Prince, to visit every centre of the Dominion—the West as well as the East—and to stamp his personality, his opinions, and his position, upon the greater Canada of a newer day. He came with a reputation for shyness in public life, for gallantry in the field of battle, for unostentatious simplicity in life and manner, for sympathetic bearing and popular characteristics. At the front as he, himself, put it, he had "found his manhood"; he proved it, also, there and amid the large responsibilities of the Empire tour which began in 1919.

During his war experiences he had served in turn on the Staffs of Sir John French and Sir Douglas Haig; he was for some time with the Canadians and Sir Arthur Currie and with the Australians and New Zealanders; he served as any other officer, was constantly under fire and ran exactly the same risks, with countless stories

*Note.—See *The Canadian Annual Review* for 1901.

[272]

H.R.H. THE PRINCE OF WALES
At Lethbridge, Alberta, 1919

H.R.H. THE PRINCE OF WALES
Reviewing Kilties, Victoria, B.C., Sept. 24, 1919

told of perils actually met; he won the M.C. and the French Croix de Guerre and came out of the War a Major in the Army and a Lieutenant in the Navy.   As a sportsman the Prince was at this time efficient at cricket, cycling, diving, driving, riding, football, golf, hunting, polo, motoring, running (long distance), shooting, skating, swimming, tennis and yachting; in Aviation he took great interest and Lieut.-Col. W. G. Barker, V.C., D.S.O., D.F.C., upon many occasions took the Prince up with him and at times across the German lines; in 1918 he had begun to take part in public functions as representing the King and in the making of speeches on a variety of subjects.   The other titles of the Prince at this time were Duke of Cornwall and of Rothesay, Earl of Chester and of Carrick, Baron of Renfrew and Lord of the Isles, Great Steward of Scotland; he was Grand Master of the Order of St. Michael and St. George and of the Order of the British Empire and a Knight of the Garter; as Duke of Cornwall his income approximated $500,000 a year derived from rents and royalties in the coal mines while he also owned considerable areas of land in the County of Cornwall, in Devonshire, in Somerset and in London.   Of him Maj.-Gen. Sir David Watson, commanding the 4th Canadian Division, wrote to the Montreal *Star* on Aug. 2nd:

During the months that he had been closely identified with the Canadians, he clearly demonstrated a keen knowledge of military matters, a sense of humour that was most gratifying, and a charming personality that won for him the genuine esteem of all elements in the Corps.   His example of devotion to duty and gallantry in the line, was particularly appreciated, and very frequently his persistent exposure to danger was a constant source of anxiety to all concerned.   But he went about the lines most unaffectedly, not in any way with a view to heroics, or for the purpose of making capital or securing popularity, but, by his modesty and charm inspiring a confidence and instilling renewed energies and vigour, that were generally appreciated.   The Canadian Corps will always feel that he has been in every way a Man's Man, honourable in all his conduct, gallant to a degree, unassuming and modest as a soldier, and a true comrade and gentleman in every sense of the word.

Preliminaries of the Royal Visit.   The Prince was with the Canadians at Mons and at Bonn in Germany; on May 7 at Witley Camp in England His Royal Highness presented Colours to the 25th, 27th, 28th, and 29th Canadian Infantry Battalions and told them that: "Whether in attack or defence, in trench warfare or raids, you won renown and future generations will recall your noble deeds in the battles of the Somme, on Vimy Ridge, around Lens, Passchendaele, Amiens, and Arras, and will jealously treasure the memorable traditions you hand down to them."   Brig.-Gen. Alex. Ross, who was in command, referred to the personal interest shown by H.M. the King, the Prince and the Royal family in Canadian troops and added: "The recollection of the Royal Family and the Empire which we will carry with us to our various homes—from Nova Scotia on the east to British Columbia on the west—will do much to cement those bonds of Empire which this great War has shown to be so real and binding."

10

On May 20th the Prince addressed a Canada Club dinner in honour of General Currie and gave the first definite announcement of his coming visit in a few words at the close of his speech: "I was almost going to say good-bye, but that would have been a most inappropriate term for me to have used, because I am very glad to be able to take this opportunity of announcing to-night that I am coming over to Canada very soon. I hope to sail in less than three months' time. Naturally the prospect of a visit to the great Dominion would have delighted me under any circumstances, but I shall enjoy it all the more now, and I am looking forward very much to seeing so many old friends again, and I hope to make many new friends as well. It is true that I shall be setting foot on soil that is new to me, but Canadian soil will not seem strange, because even in the company of several of you here to-night, I have wandered over the battlefields of Flanders, which have seen the exploits of the Canadian battalions, and by the memory of their gallant dead who rest there would seem to have a just claim to be regarded as the very soil of the Dominion, itself." In the Commons at Ottawa on the same evening it was announced that the King, in a despatch to the Governor-General, had intimated that the Prince would leave in August and would open the new Parliament Buildings.

On June 6 the Prince was the guest of the Canadian Officers' Club at London and was presented by Sir Arthur Currie with a Loving-Cup in remembrance of the period passed with the Canadian Corps at the Front. In his speech the General quoted a South African who said to him a few days before while listening to the Prince at the Guildhall: "It is a funny thing, Currie, but what binds you to me is that young man." Sir Arthur went on to say that it, indeed, was marvellous when one considered the extent of the British Empire and the number of different peoples within its borders "how much of the bond which held it together was the sentiment centering around the Royal Family?" The Prince spoke of his coming visit with obvious interest. At a later and most gorgeous function (May 29) His Royal Highness was admitted to the Freedom of the City of London and during a rather notable speech referred, in afterwards much-quoted words, to what had been said of his services at the Front: "The part I played was, I fear, a very insignificant one, but from one point of view I shall never regret my periods of service overseas. In those four years I mixed with men. In those four years I found my manhood." On July 27 he was appointed Colonel-in-Chief of the Prince of Wales Leinster Regiment—the Royal Canadian Regiment originally organized in Canada during the Indian Mutiny.

The departure of the Prince took place from Portsmouth on Aug. 5th and he sailed on H.M.S. *Renown*—a great battleship of 794 feet in length, 90 feet in breadth, a displacement of 25,500 tons and a speed of 32 knots an hour with, in this case, arrangements made for the comfort of the Royal guest along lines of simplicity and naval custom. He was accompanied, as an escort, by two other cruisers, H.M.S. *Dauntless* and H.M.S. *Dragon*. The King and

Queen with other members of the Royal family saw the Prince off and *The Times*, in its ensuing editorial, referred to this first stage in his projected tour of the Dominions: "He stands pre-eminently for the promise and the hope of the Empire. No former Heir to the Throne has shared, as he has shared on the threshold of manhood, in the trials, the sorrows, and the triumphs of our race. At the Front, the Prince—chafing, as every one knows, under the necessary restraints of his position—succeeded in sharing to the full the life of all arms. . . . Since the Armistice the Prince has devoted himself, with all his young energy and modest zeal, to public duties. His record of work done, already, is astonishing in its variety, and his manner of doing it has been invaluable—the manner of a man unspoilt by a great position, who has learnt in the hardest of schools the priceless lesson that the man's the man. . . . The Prince stands, as we have said, for the future of the whole Empire, on which, we believe, greatly depends the future of civilization and the true welfare of mankind. He represents the faith of the race in disciplined liberty, in devotion to duty, in an abiding sense of responsibility, and consideration for others—the great virtues in whose spirit the British Army fought and conquered."

The arrangements made for the Canadian Tour covered a period of 4 months and included the details of a trans-continental trip and an incidental visit to the United States. The Chief of Staff to His Royal Highness was Rear-Admiral Sir Lionel Halsey, K.C.M.G., C.B.; the Private Secretary, Sir Godfrey J. V. Thomas, Bart.; the Equerries were Capt. Lord Claud Hamilton, D.S.O., M.V.O., and Capt. the Hon. P. W. Legh; the Naval A.D.C., Commander Dudley North, C.M.G., and the Military Secretary Lieut.-Col. E. W. M. Gregg, C.M.G., D.S.O., M.C. The Canadian Government appointed Maj.-Gen. Sir H. E. Burstall, K.C.B., K.C.M.G., A.D.C. to accompany the Royal visitor during his tour and in a considerable part of it the Hon. Martin Burrell, Member of the Government, was with the Royal party. Officially Lieut.-Col. the Hon. H. G. Henderson represented the Governor-General and Sir Joseph Pope, K.C.M.G., C.V.O., I.S.O., the Government of Canada in the trip from Halifax to Ottawa; the Dominion Archives were represented by A. G. Doughty, C.M.G., LL.D., and the Canadian Physician attached to the Staff was Maj.-Gen. J. T. Fotheringham, C.M.G., M.D. At the desire, it was understood, of the Prince, no Lords-in-Waiting were appointed and the suite was smaller than had been the case in preceding Royal visits. Elaborate arrangements were made by the Press of the world to have the fullest possible reports of the Tour and the following were the chief British, Canadian and American correspondents:

Correspondent	Journal	Correspondent	Journal
Gerald Campbell	London *Times*	Everard Cotes	Reuter's Agency
Warner Allen	London *Morning Post*	F. Hillier	London *Daily Mail*
W. T. Massey	*Daily Telegraph*	John Bassett	Canadian Press Ltd.
Percival Phillips	*Daily Express*	Joseph Barnard	French Canadian Press
Douglas Newton	*Daily Chronicle*	Fred Griffin	American United Press
Ernest Brooks	Press Photographer	George N. Holmes	American Internatn'l

Arrival of the Prince; Welcome to Canadian Shores. St. John's, Newfoundland, the Atlantic outpost of Canada and the oldest British territory on the continent—though not, technically, a part of the Dominion—had the first opportunity of receiving the Royal visitor. The official arrival was fixed for August 12 and, on that day, St. John's was lavishly decorated with fir branches, flags, and arches; the latter spanned the streets, were perched across the roads which climbed the steep slopes and took the form of green castles of fir, turrets and battlements and gates of spruce, while one was made of cod-fish casks; there were various other decorations of splendid furs and feathers. An informal landing was first made at Topsail, a fishing village in Conception Bay, where some hours were spent in walking and seeing something of the very fine scenery at that point. St. John's was reached on the following day with the *Dragon* conveying the Prince as the greater battleship was too large for the Harbour; a beautiful and impressive scene was rendered more so by decorations and cheering crowds at every vantage point. After landing, Addresses were presented by the Commercial community and by the Provincial Secretary representing the Government. A series of formal and informal events followed which included a Luncheon by the Governor, Sir Charles A. Harris, the laying of a Methodist Episcopal College corner-stone, presentation of life-saving medals to 35 heroes who had aided in rescuing survivors from the wrecked liner *Florizel* in the preceding year, inspection of the Houses of Parliament and an afternoon garden-party, a round of golf at the Country Club and an informal Dinner and dance at night. The Prince slept in the same room as his Grandfather sixty years before. There was, also, a parade with brilliant illuminations at night.

St. John, New Brunswick, was the point of landing on the Canadian part of the continent and preparation for the event had been elaborate. The Prince was borne into the Harbour by the *Dragon* and at 11 o'clock on Aug. 15 he was greeted on landing by H.E. the Duke of Devonshire, the Hon. William Pugsley, Lieut.-Governor of the Province, Rt. Hon. Sir Robert Borden, Premier of Canada, the Hon. W. E. Foster and members of his Government, Mayor R. T. Hayes and the City Council, Brig.-Gen. A. H. Macdonell, c.b., c.m.g., d.s.o., and his Staff, Governor Milliken of the State of Maine representing the United States Government. Everywhere within sight crowds of people were massed from all parts of the City and Province. A thousand children sang songs of loyal welcome, a guard of honour from the gallant 26th Battalion was reviewed, the crowds cheered with unusual force and enthusiasm, young ladies dressed to represent the various Provinces of Canada were presented, and the Royal car, with Canadian dignitaries following, paraded through dense crowds to the Armoury where Addresses were received from the Province and the City. The former was presented by Mr. Premier Foster and in his reply—a first speech upon Canadian soil—the Prince, after reference to his father, the King, and His Majesty's appreciation of Canadian progress and war services, added this personal touch: "I greatly appreciate your reference, too kind although it be, to my own services as a junior officer in the War. My first real knowledge of the splendid nations of the British Empire was formed, gentlemen, in the trenches, camps and billets of the western front. Comradeship in the field is the surest of all roads to understanding between men of different climes and ways of life, and I have come thereby to know my brother Canadians in all the conditions incidental to service in the field, and in and out of the line."

A tribute to New Brunswick's war record followed with, also, some words of Imperial thought: "I agree with you, Mr. Premier, that common service and common sacrifice have drawn the nations of the Empire even more closely together than before. We have seen our British principles and ideals sharply outlined in the burning light of a supreme emergency, and we have learned more clearly thereby what the unity of the British Empire means, both to ourselves and to the world at large." The Civic address read by Mayor Hayes was replied to in a similar strain of thought with appreciation of the reception given by "this City of the Loyalists." The first important function was the presentation of colours to the famous 26th Battalion under command of Lieut.-Col. W. R. Brown, D.S.O., with a speech from the Prince in which he described in detail the war record of the Regiment and declared that New Brunswick had a right to be proud of it; decorations were then presented to a number of veterans and Mrs. E. Atherton Smith, Regent, Mrs. J. H. Frink, and Mrs. Pope Barnes, officers of the I.O.D.E. Chapter which had supplied the Colours for the Battalion, were presented to His Royal Highness. Riverview Memorial Park and the Soldiers Civil Re-establishment Hospital were then visited and a bronze tablet presented by the Women's Canadian Club, as a Memorial to New Brunswick's fallen soldiers, was unveiled at the Post Office building.

A Luncheon given by the Provincial Government followed, with the leaders of Provincial life and thought present, together with the Governor-General and the Dominion Premier and the Lieut.-Governor, Hon. W. Pugsley, in the chair. Mr. Premier Foster proposed the toast to the Prince and with loyal words of welcome expressed this thought: "We are convinced that a thorough and intimate knowledge of the thought and spirit of the Overseas democracies is an essential requirement for one who may assume the duty and responsibilities of the British sovereignty." His Royal Highness in reply referred to his coming tour, to his relations with Canadian soldiers, to the gallant record of New Brunswick's troops, to his local welcome and added, in words which were afterwards repeated and echoed throughout the Dominion: "I want Canada to look on me as a Canadian, if not actually by birth, yet certainly in mind and spirit—for this, as the eldest son of the ruler of the great British Empire, I can assure you that I am. I value my

Canadian friendships deeply; I hope to make more; and it will always be my earnest endeavour to prove myself true to those friendships and worthy of your trust.''

In the afternoon the Prince drove through crowded streets, under varied arches of welcome and through several suburban villages to Rothesay where, at Government House, a large and brilliant garden-party was held; the Lieut.-Governor and Mrs. Pugsley with the Duke of Devonshire receiving beside His Royal Highness. After this function he returned to the *Dragon* and early next morning sailed for Halifax. The popularity of the Prince in this first point of his tour was instantaneous and universal with all classes and kinds of people. Press correspondence began in a strain which grew familiar, after a time, from inevitable repetition, in the pen sketches of similar conditions. One of the best personal descriptions of what was called "the Sunshine Prince" was sent to Canadian papers from St. John by a Staff reporter on Aug. 16 and it gave first impressions in rather vivid and unaffected words:

It is strange and hard to explain the way this sunny boy grips you. It isn't his smile alone by any manner of means. It isn't that he is fair and good to look upon—fair as the morning sun rising over distant hills—fair-haired, fresh-faced, clean-looking, healthy and wholesome. It isn't that he is unaffected and boyish and that a sort of pity grips your heart when you think of the weight of responsibility his slender young shoulders must bear, and of the ceremonial oppression that attends his great tour through his great Dominion. It isn't because you know, some way, that he is a real man, capable of playing, and having played, a man's part. Some way or other it's his sincerity and his naturalness. It's written all over him. It speaks out in every gesture and proclaims itself in the tones of his voice. A fine boy, a real man, the Prince is a strange mixture of sheer boy and polished man of the world.

The capital of Nova Scotia and greatest of Canadian sea-ports gave an elaborate welcome to the Prince. In its waters he transferred to the *Renown*, which had come on from Newfoundland, and steamed up the splendid Harbour, followed by the other cruisers and received with salutes from French and Italian battleships which happened to be in port. As it was Sunday, the Prince only landed for a walk at the North-West Arm and paid an informal visit to Point Pleasant Park, the Citadel and the dockyard. In the evening McCallum Grant, Lieut.-Governor, Hon. G. H. Murray, Provincial Premier, Brig.-Gen. H. C. Thacker with several visiting officers, were entertained at dinner on the battleship. Sir Robert Borden was unable to be present owing to a strained ankle from an accident on the steps of the Halifax Club. The ships in the Harbour were vividly illuminated in the evening and at 10 o'clock the next morning His Royal Highness landed officially as guns boomed out and the sun, itself, came from behind the clouds and joined in a formal welcome expressed by abundance of flags and bunting and elaborate decorations. The official leaders were there, a guard of honour from the Garrison was inspected and the sergeants picked out, asked as to their services and shaken hands with; then the Prince departed for the Parliament Buildings where addresses were presented by Mr. Premier Murray on behalf of the Province and by Mayor J. S. Parker for the City.

To the former the Prince replied with references to the beauty and charm of Halifax, the historic interest of Nova Scotia, the splendid troops of the Province and Dominion, the visit of the King in 1901 to Canada; to the latter he spoke of Halifax as "a bulwark of the British Empire in the West," as having long and proud association with the Royal Navy, as the chief port of Nova Scotia and the Eastern gateway of the great Dominion. After this came a visit to the North-End Military Hospital, a drive around the devastated areas of the great Explosion, an inspection of Veterans, Boy Scouts and Cadets and a visit to Camp Hill Hospital. A Luncheon given by the Provincial Government at the Wægwoltic Club followed and, in his attractive and simple speech, the Prince referred to several local matters, to the war services of Nova Scotians, and added: "Besides those who served in His Majesty's forces overseas, I should like to pay a tribute to those who remained at home and did such splendid work in keeping your industries going and supplying the army with the munitions of war. I congratulate you all most heartily on your splendid efforts for the British cause." In conclusion he reiterated the thought which became dominant in so many after speeches: "I come to Canada as a Canadian and I want you all to look on me as such. It is true that I was not born on this side of the water, but I have the mind and spirit of a true Canadian and I shall always try to live up to this."

Following this was a brief visit to the Studley Quoit Club where an unstudied welcome won an informal speech and, shortly after, he laid the foundation stone of the Woman's Residence at Dalhousie University. On this occasion the Prince warmly endorsed the principle of higher education for women and expressed great admiration for the noble part which the women of Canada had played in the Great War: "I have been fortunate enough to meet many of them on the Western front, doing splendid work in nursing the wounded, serving our soldiers in canteens, and generally helping to win the War." Then came the laying of the foundation stone of a Navy League Home for Sailors with the local President of the League, F. T. Warren, as the Prince's cicerone and a public reception at Government House where everyone was welcomed, in a style of most approved democratic informality, and a hearty handshake given by the Prince to a steady stream of people in all sorts of costumes and in every walk of life. The flow seemed endless until, finally, the doors had to be closed, with great crowds still clamouring outside to see and meet the Royal visitor; he came out, however, and spoke a few words of greeting and thanks. Though slow in its enthusiasms and not eager in its welcomes, Halifax had by this time taken the Prince to its heart. A State dinner and dance followed with Miss Grant, the Lieut.-Governor's daughter, as the first unmarried girl with whom His Royal Highness danced in

Canada. Later the Prince returned to his battleship and steamed for Prince Edward Island.

At Charlottetown on Aug. 19 he received a welcome which perhaps was more spontaneous, from the first, than that of St. John or Halifax—showing the cumulative effect of personality under such conditions. With the reception to the Prince was combined the celebration of Peace and the cheering of a little Island which sent 5,000 men to the Front. The Royal visitor landed at noon with rich shields and banners and fluttering flags, thousands of eager faces and voices, and the roar of bands and pipers to welcome him; the official greetings were tendered by Chief Justice J. A. Mathieson, Administrator, Hon. A. E. Arsenault, Premier and Mayor Wright. After a drive through crowded streets and cheering people to the Parliament Buildings, Addresses were presented from the Province and the City and a brief, appropriate speech made in reply to each; many citizens were presented and the Prince was then driven through ever-crowded streets to Victoria Park where he decorated a number of battle-scarred veterans and inspected their ranks with, also, bodies of Boy Scouts and Cadets; at the Prince of Wales' College a Luncheon was tendered by the Government with the Administrator in the chair, and a short, sympathetic speech from the Royal guest, including the declaration that "I come to you, not as a stranger, but as a Canadian." Visits were then paid to the Woodman Fox-farm, to the Government Experimental Farm and to the Driving Park where trotting races were in progress and a Royal box had been prepared. The races were obviously enjoyed; the last function of the day was a garden-party given by the Administrator and Mrs. Mathieson with nearly 1,000 guests present; at 6 o'clock the Prince rejoined his ship and started on the journey up the St. Lawrence to Quebec.

The Royal Reception at Quebec. The Ancient Capital of an historic Canada was ready to give the Prince a warm welcome and, by Aug. 21, when he came, old streets and new were alike aflame with flags and bunting, stately buildings were profusely decorated, the famous and beautiful Dufferin Terrace was bedecked with bright colours, the King's wharf, where the landing took place, was gay with pennants and emblems of the Allies, the chief streets were marked by several splendid arches of evergreens, the City was thronged with visitors. The formal reception began at the Wharf as the Prince left behind the stately pageant of sea and sky and ships which the superb scenery of the St. Lawrence at Quebec always affords to Royalty and stepped upon a red carpet, encircled by tropical plants, to be met by H.E. the Duke of Devonshire, H.E. Cardinal Bégin, the Lieut.-Governor, Sir Charles Fitzpatrick, the Premier, Sir Lomer Gouin, the Anglican Bishop, Dr. Williams, Brig.-General J. P. Landry and the Mayor of Quebec, H. E. Lavigueur, M.P. With the Prince was Sir Robert Borden who had not yet recovered from his Halifax accident. At the Pavilion various presentations were made, the guard of honour inspected and then, through narrow streets, amid cheers given to a fleeting figure in a fast motor-car, the Prince was driven to the Citadel where a State Dinner was given by the Governor-General and Duchess of Devonshire; brilliant displays of fireworks and electrical illumination followed and were repeated from the battleships in the River while the always beautiful panorama of Quebec became even more splendid.

In the morning of the 22nd the Prince of Wales received an official welcome at the Parliament Buildings where Sir Lomer Gouin presented the formal tribute of the Province with passing references to the Duke of Kent, an ancestor of His Royal Highness, who had lived so long in its vicinity, to King Edward the Peacemaker who had honoured the City in his youth and to the present King who had been there on several occasions; with, also, a warm personal welcome by "this Province which prides itself upon its unswerving loyalty to the British Crown." In French the Prince replied with a reference to the historic loyalty of Quebec, to the intrepid conduct at the front of the gallant 22nd Regiment, to the Frenchmen who first brought to this continent the blessings of Christianity and civilization, to the sagacity of the system which, long years after, united the two Canadian races: "We owe the success of this wise policy to your own statesmen, Lafontaine, Cartier and Laurier, no less than we owe it to the statesmen of the other Provinces. I am firmly convinced that an era of long and glorious prosperity is about to open for the great nation born of this union and forever united to the other great nations of the British Empire."

Mayor Lavigueur, in the Civic address, declared that "all Canadians are proud of the support which they have given and of the blood they have shed for the defence of the Empire." A brief reply was accorded and then distinguished citizens were presented. On the way from this function the Prince placed a wreath upon the Champlain monument in front of the Chateau Frontenac; at Laval University he spent an informal hour of great interest inspecting the Royal charters, and historic documents and pictures, and conversing in French with the Cardinal and Rector and other ecclesiastics who were present; a Luncheon followed which was given by the Prince on board the *Renown* to the Governor-General and other official and ecclesiastical leaders of the Province.

In the afternoon, amid ever-present throngs and an ever-increasing volume of cheers, the Prince laid a beautiful wreath upon the tomb of Montcalm and a similar tribute on the monument to Wolfe; he unfurled a silken Union Jack to fly over the battlefields of Quebec at a function initiated by the National Battlefields Commission and presided over by Sir George Garneau; he reviewed the Great War Veterans and decorated a number of heroes from the Western front; he unveiled three tablets at Quebec Bridge in honour of the engineers who had designed and built the structure and formally inaugurated this great Bridge in which he "saluted the indomitable genius and the bright destiny of the Canadian nation—the imperishable jewel of the British crown.'' Great crowds were everywhere, the day was a public holiday, the welcome was enthusiastic to a degree; there was an afternoon informal diversion for tennis and in the evening a dinner at the Garrison Club with Major A. E. Doucet presiding; following this was a Reception at the Citadel by the Duke and Duchess of Devonshire for which 600 invitations had been issued.

On the following day (23rd) His Royal Highness visited the Ursuline Convent and Hôtel Dieu of historic memories and, accompanied by Sir Charles and Lady Fitzpatrick, Sir Lomer Gouin, and attended by his suite, went by special train to Ste. Anne de Beaupré, where he was welcomed to the famous shrine by the Redemptionist Fathers, with peeling bells and strains of the National anthem; a fairly decorated village with people *en masse* in the streets added their tribute. From here he motored to Montmorency Falls and visited St. Mary's (English) Church where he was met by the Lord Bishop of Quebec and wrote his name in a Bible under that of another Edward, Prince of Wales; a game of golf at the Quebec Golf Club and a State dinner at Spencer-Wood, the Lieut.-Governor's residence, followed. On Sunday the 24th, the Prince attended service in the Church of England Cathedral; after luncheon at the Citadel and a good-bye visit to the *Renown,* which was to cruise to the West Indies and meet the Prince some time hence in New York harbour, he left to take his train for Toronto. As at St. John and Halifax and Charlottetown, there followed a Message of thanks and appreciation to the people of the Province. In this case it was more elaborate than usual and paid special tribute to the soldiers of Quebec in general and the 22nd Battalion in particular; to the people of France and that section of the Canadian nation whose ancestors came from France. Once more he called himself a Canadian "equally in touch with both of the great races" which had built up Canada.

The Prince of Wales in Toronto. From Quebec the Prince entered upon his period of land travel—the 8,800 miles which it was estimated he would traverse—and started westward to visit Toronto as the first of over 50 Canadian cities and towns which he was to see in the next three months. According to figures published in the New York *Tribune* of Aug. 18, the Royal train was composed of nine steel cars drawn by Engine 2,300, the most powerful locomotive yet turned out by the Angus Shops in Montreal; the equipment was luxurious and the Prince occupied a special car, *Killarney,* lent by Lord Shaughnessy for the purpose; the train was said to be valued at $780,000! It awaited the Prince at Three Rivers and he was in Toronto on the morning of Aug. 25, after a rapid journey during which the correspondent of the London *Daily Chronicle* stated that "there were many moments when he heard the ghosts of cheers seeping in through the windows" and that at these wayside stations in the darkness of the night, all along the route, people had gathered to give the Prince a passing cheer as he rushed along at 60 miles an hour.

The Queen City was in gala attire with the business part of its streets a mass of bunting and flags and decorations; with the residential streets showing flags profusely and many great buildings specially decorated for the electric displays which were a marked feature of the visit. Here for the first time His Royal Highness was in khaki—the uniform of a Captain in the Army; at the seaport towns he had been in Naval uniform. Throughout the balance of the tour khaki was the favourite garb with, occasionally, civilian clothes. At the station he was received by the Lieut.-Governor, Sir John Hendrie, the Premier, Sir W. H. Hearst, the Mayor, T. L. Church, Brig.-Gen. John A. Gunn, commanding the Military District, and others. The guard of honour was commanded by Major Hugh W. Niven, D.S.O., M.C. With the roar of a Royal salute and the cheers of the crowd echoing behind him, the Prince drove to Government House and thence, after a brief interval, to the Parliament Buildings where he received the Provincial, Civic and other addresses—about 27 altogether. In his replies to the first two —presented respectively by Sir William Hearst and Mayor Church —the Prince complimented Toronto upon its soldiers and its progress, the Province upon its record in the War and in history, in natural development and in the upbuilding of Canada: "In this Dominion you have an opportunity given to few peoples in the history of the world. You have already proved yourselves a nation in the terrible ordeal of war, for you have played your part as such, not only in the struggle' itself, but in the long negotiations which have ended in the Peace of Versailles. A splendid future awaits you as a great self-governing nation, with British institutions, British ideals and undiminished loyalty to the British Commonwealth and Crown."

St. David's Society and the Welshmen from Wales received the honour of an impromptu speech; the large children's choir which sang patriotic songs for the Prince, received similar personal thanks. The women were conspicuous in the presentation of Addresses with Mrs. H. D. Warren representing the Toronto Women's Patriotic League; Lady Pellatt the Girl Guides; Mrs. John Bruce the I.O.D.E.; Lady Gibson the National Council of Women; Mrs. J. W. Garvin the Women's Canadian Club. Other organizations represented were the Methodist Church, the Anglican Synod, the Salvation Army, the University of Toronto, the Jewish Community, the Canadian and Empire Clubs, the United Empire Loyalists and Grand Orange Lodge, St. George's Society and Sons of England, St. Andrew's and Gaelic Societies, the Grand Army of Canada. The Address of the Methodist Church of Canada, presented by the Rev. Dr. S. D. Chown, was very expressive and the following clause may be quoted: "We recognize in Your Royal Highness an exalted symbol of the unity of the great Empire to which our people are all proud to belong, and it is our sincere desire and prayer that through the potency of your personality, under the high calling of the Almighty, the world-wide dominions of the Empire may become closely knit together, and that more than ever it may attain the glory of moral leadership of the world."

From an official welcome the Prince left for his first great popular greeting in Toronto at the National Exhibition Buildings; for the first time in its long history the institution was opened by an Heir to the Throne with 100,000 people cheering the slight figure of the Prince as he spoke briefly at the formal function, or attended the Luncheon, or traversed the grounds and buildings. At the Luncheon, as elsewhere, President T. A. Russell presided and the speeches were very informal, the Prince saying that: "I want you to look at me as a Canadian, as one of yourselves, as one deeply interested in the welfare of Canada. If you will do that I can promise you that it will always be my endeavour to be worthy of Canada's friendship and Canada's trust. Besides being Canadians we are all Britishers which, for lack of a better expression, means loyalty to the British flag and to British institutions—in other words, citizens of the British Empire. I am a Britisher through and through, and I know of no place where I could feel prouder to say so than in Toronto." So it was at the opening ceremonies which were brief and to the point with a climax of cheers and an ever-growing enthusiasm in the crowds.

The next event was the laying of the corner-stone of the new club-house of the Royal Canadian Yacht Club which was performed at 4 o'clock in the presence of a fashionable throng of people; then came the popular public Reception at the City Hall. There, for over an hour, the Prince shook hands with a steady stream of people said to number 2,187 and including men and women, young men and girls, children and aged veterans—including especially George Richardson, a V.C. of Mutiny days. But this was not the end of it for many thousands more wanted to shake hands and in one of his sudden, and soon to be numerous changes in routine ceremonial, the Prince decided to say a few words to them from the City Hall steps which he did: "I wanted to shake hands with all of you who could come in, but I am afraid time will not allow of it. I am sorry to disappoint you and sorry to disappoint myself. I thank you for your wonderful welcome which I shall never forget." As he drove away through the great throng, he stood in the car and gripped the hands of those held up to him— men, women and children—receiving, meanwhile, such an ovation as Toronto had perhaps never before given. A State dinner and small dance at Government House followed in the evening.

The second day in Toronto included a visit to St. Andrew's Military Hospital, the Dominion Orthopædic Hospital outside which 5,000 school children waited to cheer him, the Toronto General Hospital and the Hospital for Sick Children to which he had already sent a lot of toys and dolls; with, everywhere, sympathetic words and actions for the patients and wounded men and little children and with crowds, great or small, on every street, while the cheers seemed to grow in volume as the days passed; the Prince in his later drives standing up in the motor-car and waving his hand in a sort of informal salute as he swept through the throngs. In the afternoon a brilliant Convocation was held at the University and President Sir R. A. Falconer, on behalf of the University, conferred upon him the Hon. degree of LL.D., preceded by a speech in which the President referred to the 6,000 men given by the institution to the War and the 600 of these who would never return. In his reply the Prince paid tribute to the soldiers of the institution, to the "famous University," itself, to its splendid anti-toxin Laboratory—established by Col. A. E. Gooderham, to its Salonika Hospital in the War. A Military dinner presided over by Brig.-Gen. J. A. Gunn, C.M.G., D.S.O., and a dance at the R.C.Y.C. closed the functions of the day with a needed touch of lightness and informal pleasure.

The Prince rested the next morning and played a round of golf at the Lambton Club; at one o'clock he was created a Barrister-at-Law of the Province and made a Bencher of the Law Society of Upper Canada; John Hoskin, K.C., LL.D., officiated and a luncheon at Osgoode Hall followed with a brief and admirable speech from the Prince. Then came another visit to the Exhibition with a renewed and wildly enthusiastic greeting from massed crowds of humanity. Decorations and medals were given to returned soldiers; Addresses were presented to the Prince by the Army and Navy Veterans and Fenian Raid Veterans; horses and cattle in the ring were viewed, Boy Scouts and Girl Guides inspected and the work of the Vocational Training Department examined. It was in riding on horseback through the throngs at this time that the Prince received the greatest of personal ovations and found it almost impossible to retain his seat with the eager crowds pressing and cheering around him—intensely anxious for a glimpse of his face or a shake of the hand which he gave to every one within reach. A final drive around the City with eager greetings by new and cheering crowds followed; for over two hours he motored slowly through many streets lined with from 200,000 to 300,000 people and shook hands with thousands while waving one hand in a gay and informal salute to the others; in the evening the Prince found himself too exhausted to keep further engagements which had been made; late that night he left for Ottawa. A farewell Message to the Mayor stated that: "I desire to express through you to the people of Toronto my warmest thanks for the very wonderful welcome which has been accorded me during my visit to your great city. No words of mine can properly express all I feel, but I leave Toronto very happy. I wish I could greet the people of Toronto as they have greeted me. I look forward eagerly to my next visit."

National Reception at Ottawa; Welcome at Montreal. The Capital City had been preparing for days to receive its Royal guest when he arrived at 11 o'clock on the morning of Aug. 28; it

was in gala attire with 20,000 people on Parliament Hill and
thousands lining the streets from the Station; it had become known
that the Prince had expressed personal wishes for a public reception where he could meet and shake hands, as far as possible, with
everyone; the usually cold and formal Ottawa crowds were excited
and enthusiastic from the first moment of his arrival.   While the
Royal train waited at Manotick, near Ottawa, for the time to
formally enter the city, the Prince took a walk in the country
accompanied by one of his Aides and received many a courteous
welcome from the farming people in the vicinity—one . little girl
shyly presenting him with a basket of ruddy apples which were
smilingly accepted.   At the Ottawa station he was formally
received by Sir Robert Borden, Prime Minister, General Sir Arthur
Currie, Members of the Government, Harold Fisher, Mayor of the
City, and other officials and military dignitaries.   Inspection of
the guard of honour followed and then a drive to Parliament Hill
with tumultuous cheering and acclaim all along the route; the
Prince standing most of the way and saluting the crowds with an
informal wave of the hand.

On a dais in front of the new Parliament Buildings, His Royal
Highness was tendered an Address by the Prime Minister which
proffered the official welcome of the Dominion in fitting terms and
received a reply couched in characteristic language and delivered
with the ready, pleasant and natural manner which was becoming
so familiar to the Canadian people.   The Government's Address
was signed by Sir Robert Borden and Hon. Martin Burrell and its
vital clause was the following: "The notable development in the
status of the great Dominion has tended to strengthen the influence
of the Crown in binding together all the nations of the Empire
through the tie of a common allegiance in which the united purpose and endeavour of all the British peoples find effective expression."   Upon this point the Prince, in his reply, said: "I am
conscious that this lays upon me, as His Majesty's heir, a very grave
and also a very inspiring responsibility. . I therefore greatly prize
the opportunity which you have given me of seeing all parts of the
great Dominion for myself, making a real acquaintance with its
people, and acquiring a first-hand knowledge of its splendid prospects and resources."   On the platform were the Duchess of Devonshire, Mr. Speaker Rhodes, Hon. W. L. Mackenzie King, Bishop
Roper of Ottawa, Col. J. G. Foster, U.S. Consul-General, Members
of the Government, the Mayor and Mrs. Fisher, and many others;
H. E. Lavigueur, M.P., Mayor of Quebec, was amongst the notables
as he had also been at the functions of Quebec and Toronto.

Everything was officially and carefully arranged, but after the
Addresses were disposed of conditions changed.   The Toronto
Globe, in its Ottawa correspondence, described what happened as
follows: "Neither police nor guards nor fixed bayonets availed to
keep the great crowd from sweeping round the Pavilion once the
people had caught a glimpse of that warm, ingenuous and infec-
tious smile.   They simply swept the guards away, and rolled round

the platform like surf against a rock in the sea.   Ottawa went wild,
and that is saying something, for Ottawa is not usually a demonstra-
tive city."   There was, in fact, difficulty in completing the inspection of Boy Scouts and Girl Guides which followed.   This condition prevailed, more or less, throughout the Royal visit; the progress of the ensuing passage away from Parliament Hill was a case
of wildly excited, surging, cheering crowds of people, pressing close
to and following the carriage in which the slight figure of the Prince
stood saluting or waving his hands.   In the afternoon there was a
large and fashionable Reception at Government House with the
Duke and Duchess of Devonshire and the Prince of Wales receiving
the hundreds of representative people who had been invited; in the
evening a dinner was attended at the Country Club with a delight-
ful dance in which the Prince took his full share and obviously
enjoyed himself.   On the following day, after a quiet morning, a
Government Luncheon was attended at which the guests were
leaders in the official life of Ottawa.   Sir Robert Borden welcomed
His Royal Highness in a speech of some length and, after speaking
of the Prince's personal qualities and career, he made certain elaborate references to constitutional conditions as seen by him:

> The Prince comes to us as a Canadian in another and even higher sense.
> With the growth and development of self-government in the great Dominions
> it has come to pass that the tie of a common allegiance is the chief bond
> which unites the nations of the Britannic Commonwealth.   For each of these
> nations there is but one Crown, acting in each Dominion and in every Province
> or state upon the advice of Ministers responsible to the people and invested
> with their mandate.   Thus throughout the Empire there is created a direct
> and perfect relation between the Crown and the people.   The King, acting
> through his Ministers is the executive head of Government in each Domin-
> ion.   Fulfilling the will of the people in the selection of his advisers, he
> stands above party or faction, the acknowledged head of the State.
> During the progress of the War more perfect co-operation became neces-
> sary and was attained.   The guiding principle was laid down that within
> our Commonwealth of nations equality of nationhood must be recognized,
> preserving unimpaired to each Dominion the full autonomous powers which
> it now holds and safeguarding to each by necessary consultation and by
> adequate voice and influence, its highest interests in the issues of war or
> peace.   For each nation complete control of its own affairs; for the whole
> Empire necessary co-operation, according to the will of the people, in all
> matters of common concern.

In his reply the Prince recognized the new status of the Dominions as self-governing nations and added: "At the same time, the
War has shown that the nations of the Empire can combine to act
as a single State in defence of their common institutions and ideals.
This was the feature least expected by our enemies and most effective in saving the liberties of the world.   It must now be our aim
to maintain our unity in the more complex conditions of peace,
for on our unity depends, not only the security of British institutions, but the peace of the world."   Mr. Mackenzie King followed
in an eloquent tribute to the young Prince: "The Sir Galahad of
the Royal Household, the young knight, our future King, whose
joy is in the service of others.   And, as Sir Galahad, through his

pure life and noble deeds, was rewarded by the vision of the Holy
Grail, so, too, we pray and believe that in the time appointed it will
be yours to win the radiance of a people's love and devotion which
makes a lasting glory around the throne.''

In the afternoon the Prince left the higher altitudes of Empire
politics and, at the Civic reception, came into touch during an
hour's hand-shaking with the masses of the people—2,536 by actual
count.   The Ottawa *Journal* described the scene as follows: ''In
spite of the rush and the necessity that each make way for the one
behind, His Royal Highness was able to clasp each hand, speak a
kind and courteous word to the aged, and went out of his way to
shake the tiny hands of the citizens of the future, as, cooing and
staring, round-eyed, they were carried past in their mothers' arms.
At least 100 infants under a year old were thus honoured.''   One
aged lady, Mrs. Wooley, stated, as she passed, that she had shaken
hands with three generations of Royalty and urged His Royal
Highness to ''hurry up and get married'' and continue his line, as
she had hopes of greeting a fifth Royalty.   Coming from this
function he was given another of those ovations which were becoming characteristic of the once staid capital and, in front of the City
Hall, the Prince spoke briefly to the great crowds: ''I should like
to have shaken hands with all of you.   There has, however, been
very little time, and I have only two hands and can only use one at
a time.   I can only say how very happy I am to be in Ottawa, what
a wonderful time I am having, and how much I appreciate your
wonderful reception.''   Saturday, the 30th, was a day of rest with
a round of golf in the afternoon at the Royal Ottawa Golf Club;
on Sunday the Prince attended St. Bartholomew's Church and
called on Lady Laurier and Lady Borden.

On Sept. 1st the stately ceremony of laying the corner-stone of
the Victory Tower in the new Parliament Buildings was performed.
It was a beautiful day and the scene was unusually splendid
even for a city whose natural beauties have few rivals and where
great functions were not infrequent.   Under an imposing panoply
of blue and gold, lined with white velvet and garlands of evergreen,
surmounted by a blaze of Union Jacks and Allied flags, with the
Royal Standard floating above all, stood the Prince of Wales at
11.30 in the morning and around him were the leaders of Canadian
public life, its thought and its progress, with 35,000 of the men,
women and children of Ottawa massed in front.   Before the actual
ceremony Sir Robert Borden spoke of the history associated with
the Buildings which had been burned and reconstructed during the
years of war, described the work of the Fathers of Confederation
and thanked His Royal Highness for doing what his Father had
done in 1860: ''We thank him for his presence in which we find a
happy augury of our future relation to the Empire.   Through this
stately portal will pass those who in the wonderful years to come
shall debate and mould the policies of the greater nation that is to
be.   Here will be shaped the destiny of a country which in the
lifetime of some child within the sound of my voice may perhaps

surpass in wealth and population the Motherland from which our fathers came.''

Amid a hurricane of cheers the Prince responded and then declared the stone ''well and truly laid.'' In his brief speech he referred to Sir R. Borden as ''the only Prime Minister in the Empire who was Prime Minister before the War, throughout the War and at the signature of Peace'' and declared that ''Canada has grown so rapidly in the last half-century, and accomplished so much, that no one can set limits to her future power and development.'' After this the Prince unfurled a flag—a Union Jack on a white ensign with his own coat-of-arms on the fly—intended to inaugurate the National Victory Loan campaign and to be the first of a series of Prince of Wales Flags to be awarded to cities and districts exceeding their quotas; later he inspected the Ottawa veterans of the War and gave decorations to many who had won honours in the struggle; passing from the Hill he drove out of the still-cheering crowds along the bright blue waters of the Ottawa to Government House for lunch. Thence, in the afternoon, he was back amongst an enthusiastic and eager throng engaged in the sports of Labour Day at Lansdowne Park and received another ovation; from there he drove to Hull, the manufacturing suburb of the Capital, on the Quebec side of the border, and, amid happy, cheering, French-Canadians he had another heart-felt greeting.'' On the scarlet steps of a dais outside the City Hall Mayor Archambault presented an Address in French to which the Prince replied in the same language; a galaxy of pretty girls, dressed to represent the Allies, shared in the ceremony, and four tiny girls contributed garlands of flowers linked together by crimson streamers; here, also, the Prince held an open reception and shook hands with throngs of people; he reviewed the War veterans, visited their Club, shared a loving-cup with them and made a little speech; he passed out of sight, presently, standing in the car and waving to the delighted people.

On the following day His Royal Highness was in Montreal—a hasty visit, not on the official Itinerary, before leaving for the West. He arrived at 10.30 in the morning and found the C.P.R. Station beautifully decorated, the bells in all the churches ringing, the factory whistles shrilling their welcome and sirens on the river-craft echoing back the sounds, while a great crowd awaited him whose demonstrations the police found it hard to control. Up Windsor Street as far as the eye could reach, were dense throngs of people, flags waving and fluttering in the warm sunlight, bunting and banners that blurred the blue of the sky-line. In the station enclosure were Mayor Martin and some of the Aldermen, Archbishop Bruchési, Lord Atholstan, Bishop Farthing, Sir Vincent Meredith, Sir F. Williams-Taylor, E. W. Beatty, President of the C.P.R., and many others. Dressed in plain tweeds the Prince's ensuing drive through the City was supposed to be informal; it was, also, and essentially, a people's reception of the Royal guest; cheer after cheer, ever growing in volume, greeted him as the procession passed along its 30 miles of route with Windsor, St. Catherine and Bleury streets gaily decorated; the roads along the mountain-side were crowded and the scene beautiful, the East-end joined in the acclaim and in Lafontaine Park hundreds of children had a riotous time; dignified Dorchester Street and the suburban shades of Westmount gave a continuous welcome.

At the Cartier Monument a brief stop was made and Miss Hortense Cartier, a daughter of the Statesman, was presented to the Prince. A Civic luncheon followed on the summit of Mount Royal with a number of representative guests present and a brief Address read by Mayor Mèdéric Martin, which gave the Prince "loyal, hearty and loving welcome" to Montreal; the Hon. Charles Marcil, M.P., proposed his health in words appreciative of this inter-lude in an official programme and with the declaration that "to-day, you have captured the heart of the city, as you have indeed that of the whole Dominion"; there followed a statement that Canadians all, "regardless of the lands from which our fore-fathers come, are proud of being British subjects." After days crowded into a few hours the Prince left in the afternoon for the West. An interesting incident of this visit was connected with the Luncheon. Before the speeches had begun His Royal Highness took his silver pencil and jotted down on the back of his *mēnu* card a few notes of what he wanted to say. When he had finished he crumpled up the card and was about to throw it under the table, when Archbishop Bruchési, who was sitting next to the Prince, asked for it as a souvenir of the occasion. The Prince promptly smoothed it out and gave it to the Archbishop, who was delighted to find that the Royal visitor not only spoke French perfectly, but that he also thought in French, for the "points" he had jotted down were all in the French language.

Northern Ontario and the Gateway of the West. The Northern country, commencing at North Bay and running around the shores of Lake Superior in regions of growing industrial development, obvious mineral resources, and untold riches in fish and game for the sportsman, was next seen by the Prince, with Winnipeg as the immediate objective. At North Bay, on Sept. 3rd, 10,000 people greeted the Royal visitor; Mayor John Ferguson read an Address, upon a decorated platform of the C.P.R., and received a brief reply. At Sudbury decorations were bestowed upon a number of soldiers and a drive taken through the town. Another Address and reply and a reception by 5,000 people, were crowded into less than an hour; there, and at Verner, Coniston and other stations, decorations, surging school children and cheering crowds or groups of people, marked the passing of the Prince. Sault Ste. Marie was a blaze of colour on the 4th, arches spanned the streets, an Address of welcome was presented by Sir William Hearst, the War veterans were inspected together with local patriotic organizations and a body of Indians from the Garden River Reservation, the great locks and canals were visited, the plant of the Algoma Steel Corporation was inspected.

At the three larger places, where stops were made, there was the same element of personal welcome, the same handshaking and mixing with delighted crowds, which had marked the eastern visits. From here the Prince left for three days' fishing at Lake Nipigon—a famous Northern resort for sportsmen. It was a private excursion with Indian guides and the waving of formal life and public stress for a brief period; he returned fit and hard and happy and passed in a moment, on Sept. 8th, from vast solitudes of rock and forest and water to the modern industrial life of Port Arthur and Fort William, the head cities of the Great Lakes. At the former place Mayor Edward Blaquier presented the usual Address as did Mayor Murphy at Fort William; in both cities the Prince mingled with the crowds, shook hands with large numbers of people, heard thousands of children sing, drove through decorated streets and cheering people; at Port Arthur he presented war medals to soldiers and at Fort William visited the Grain Elevator of the Ogilvie Company and saw their methods of handling Western grain.

He was welcomed at Winnipeg with the declaration by the *Free Press* (Sept. 6) that "the reception given to the Prince of Wales on his visit to Canada is a triumph greater than he, himself, or anyone in the country anticipated; that he has won the hearts of the Canadian people is demonstrated in the most convincing manner wherever he goes and his tour through the Dominion is one continuous round of affectionate acclaim." He reached the Gateway of the West at 10 o'clock on the morning of Sept. 9 and was formally welcomed by the Lieut.-Governor, Sir James Aikins, Chief Justice the Hon. W. E. Perdue, Mayor C. F. Gray, Maj.-Gen. H. D. B. Ketchen, D.S.O., and others. He reviewed the guard of honour, which included two winners of the V.C., and then drove through crowded streets and roars of cheers to the Parliament Buildings; the local press stated that in the area around the junction of Main Street and Bannatyne Avenue 60,000 were massed; at this point 2,500 school children sang patriotic greetings.

The Addresses which were presented included one from the Province signed by Hon. T. C. Norris and Hon. J. W. Armstrong which declared that "the heart of Canada beats true to the Motherland and to the Royal family"; that from the Mayor and Council described the citizens as determined "to uphold constituted authority" and "maintain inviolate British institutions"; that from the Synod of Rupert's Land, signed by Archbishop S. P. Matheson, expressed special appreciation of the timeliness of the Royal visit—a gracious event with a profound significance to the people; the Provincial Chapter of the I.O.D.E., through Mrs. C. H. Campbell, dealt with its work for "one flag, one throne, one Empire"; the Imperial Veterans, the Army and Navy Veterans, the Salvation Army and the Jewish Citizens joined in addresses of welcome and loyalty. The procession through the city was led by 100 scarlet-coated Mounted Police and excitement was so great at times as to be almost dangerous. A Montreal *Star* correspondent described the departure from the City Hall as follows: "As the Prince descended the steps there was no restraining them. Like a huge sea breaking the dykes they swept the police aside and cut off the Prince's carriage. He was swallowed up in an inextricable medley of waving, shouting, wildly excited people. Progress was impossible. Hands were stretched out to him on every side. The Mounted Police had literally to ride the people down to pull him clear." Elsewhere, there were similar scenes; the local papers declared that the City had never witnessed anything like it.

Following the Addresses came a visit to the University of Manitoba with an inspection of veterans and presentation of war decorations, and a Luncheon given by the City authorities where the Prince stated that: "I feel that the splendid spirit that has made possible the growth and development I see all around me here, constitutes a summary of the powers of mind and intellect which have made this great Dominion what it is to-day"; a visit followed to the Manitoba Military Hospital at Tuxedo with, also, the formal opening of a Red Cross Lodge or Club for convalescent soldiers; then came the opening of an Exhibition of Naval Pictures at the Board of Trade building. In the evening there was a State dinner with H.E. the Governor-General also present, the members of the Provincial Government, Mayor Gray, General Ketchen and President J. A. MacLean of the University with many others; following was a Reception and dance attended by 500 of Winnipeg's social circle and in the dancing His Royal Highness joined with zest.

Meantime the City was looking like fairyland with buildings aglow with electric light and whole highways of brilliant illumination turning night into day. At the Tuxedo Hospital the Prince had his hand and arm put under X-Ray treatment to see if the injury from continuous hand-shaking was serious; during the balance of the Tour he had to more or less use his left hand. During the Red Cross ceremony of the day and following an Address signed by Noel Marshall, Chairman of the Canadian Executive and Mrs. A. M. Plumptre, Secretary, His Royal Highness accepted a Life membership and jewelled badge. On Sept. 10 the Prince began the day with a game of golf at the Country Club and then visited the Grain Exchange, stepped into the bedlam of the grain pit and bought 500 bushels of oats for October delivery. A little later he delivered his first formal address to a Canadian audience and the first given in Canada, under this popular form, at a Luncheon of the Winnipeg Canadian Club in the Royal Alexandra auditorium. R. W. Craig, K.C., was in the chair and the guests numbered 700; the decorations included a crimson crown diademed with incandescent globes while flowers were everywhere, together with flags and one great Imperial banner. The address was informal, natural, sincere and the following quotation illustrates its style:

"The West of Canada has a special interest for me. It is the place which, above all others, offers opportunities to the young man. It is going to count tremendously in the future of the British Em-

pire—in fact, it is the western frontier of the Empire. As a young
man, as a Britisher, and as a Canadian, it appeals to me enormously. I know I am going to have a very good time in the West."
References followed to the War, the grain productiveness of this
great region, the need for steadiness in these days of reconstruction, the place of the ocean and the Navy in Canadian life: "As
your great Railways link the various portions of the Dominion,
making possible the progress, development and growth of Canada,
so the oceans link together the parts of the Empire. But the ocean
is no good to us if we do not rule it; and we cannot rule it if we
have not got a Navy. Well, we have got a Navy—a Navy which
has always been considered the finest in the world; and never has
it shown this more than during the great War." Following this
incident was another of the public Receptions which the Prince insisted upon and the people enjoyed; here 10,000 attended and
packed the grounds of Government House while the Royal guest
stood upon a raised platform and saluted slightly for an hour and
a half to a rapid stream of people; afterwards a brief speech was
made to the crowds and a special reception given to 60 Americans
who had come from Minnesota and North Dakota to see the Prince.
He left the City at 6.40 with boisterous farewells from other great
crowds *en route* and at the station—cheers following the Royal
train as it steamed out from this first and greatest City of the
Prairies.

The Prince on the Prairies: A Western Welcome. Saskatoon
was the next of the Prairie cities to formally welcome the Prince and
it gave him an unprecedented reception—even for that home of
hospitality, the West. From the rich country around farmers
poured in to help pay honour to their future King and, according
to the press, fully 30,000 were in the town when His Royal Highness arrived on Sept. 11. The usual Address was presented by
Mayor F. R. McMillan and replied to; a number of returned soldiers
were decorated and a visit paid to the University of Saskatchewan
where the Chancellor, Sir Fred. Haultain, delivered an address of
welcome. Passing again and again through surging, cheering,
crowds the Prince then was driven out to the Exhibition grounds
where, for the first time in his life, he witnessed a Stampede in
which cowboys and buckaroos from all over the continent performed weird feats of horsemanship; "stunts" of skill and courage
typical of the dying rancher days of the wild West; the riding of
bucking bronchos, steer-throwing, riding of untamed horses, las-
sooing contests with wild horses. Presently the Prince asked for
a broncho and, in his civilian clothes, amidst the wildest cheers from
20,000 spectators, he rode the length of the course and back again
—and straight into the hearts of the people. As his car drove
away from the grounds the cowboys formed a dashing escort around
it; and the cheers of the crowd followed with vigourous Western
spirit. One of the incidents of the visit was the passage of his car
between living walls of school children, a quarter of a mile long

and all waving flags. As the Royal train had rushed through villages and tiny settlements on the way to Saskatoon, it was greeted at many places by cheers and the singing of the National anthem; as it passed out again into the night from that city, the faint sound of cheers everywhere greeted the sleeping Prince and his rushing train; near Viscount, Sask., there stood on the roof of his little homestead a solitary figure in khaki outlined against the sky, completely equipped, even to his "tip" helmet, and as the Prince's train passed he brought his rifle to the salute.

On the way to Edmonton, in the Royal dining car, the Prince, was given a Moving Picture exhibition of his own Tour up to date; he arrived at the Alberta capital about 9 o'clock on the 12th preceded by the gymnastics of a whirling aeroplane; the formal reception included His Honour R. G. Brett, the Premier, Hon. Charles Stewart, Mayor J. A. Clarke, Brig.-Gen. H. F. McDonald, Chief Justice Horace Harvey. The guard of honour was first inspected and then 1,500 veterans of the G.W.V.A.; 5,000 school children, massed at the station entrance, burst into wild cheering as they saw the Prince who stopped his car, stood up and waved his hand to them. At the Parliament Buildings Mr. Premier Stewart presented an Address which expressed confidence that "the bonds of Empire unity will be strengthened by your coming into actual contact, on their own territory, with the several Provinces of the great Dominion." To the Premier and the Province the Prince spoke briefly: "I am conscious of the closest kinship with the spirit of freedom and enterprise which breathes so strongly throughout the West, and I see all around me in Edmonton the evidence of the spirit in its most vigourous form. Your great war services have proved that this activity, wonderful as it is, is not self-centered and that the Province is truly conscious of its obligation to Canada as a whole and to the world-wide commonwealth of which Canada is part." A Civic address was also presented.

There were gathered outside 10,000 persons who gave the Prince a wildly enthusiastic greeting; shortly afterwards he was laying the corner-stone of a Memorial Hall for the Veterans of the War and he also officiated at the depositing of the 49th Regiment flags in the Parliament Buildings; at 1 o'clock he was entertained at Luncheon by the Provincial Government. In his speech he repeated the claim to be a real Canadian: "I have the Canadian spirit so strongly within me that I must repeat myself. Now, I am doing my best to become a Westerner. I do not think this should be difficult, because I am a young man and the West is above all things a land of youth." After a reference to the new national position of Canada the Prince added: "You have the history of British institutions on the northern part of this great continent to make or mar, and I know from what you have achieved in the past and from your magnificent records in the War that British institutions, British unity and the British flag are safe in your keeping." Inside the Buildings he tried to shake hands with all those presented but had to give up after a time. A few hours at golf followed in the

afternoon with the presentation of a party of Indian chiefs from the
Stoney Plain Reserve; a dinner at Government House and a Ball
at the Parliament Buildings, where the Prince danced till one
o'clock, closed the day's events.

On the following morning an Hon. degree of LL.D. was conferred upon the Prince by the University of Alberta. The President, Dr. H. M. Tory and the Chancellor, Hon. C. A. Stuart, delivered brief addresses descriptive of the University and its progress,
its war achievements and its history.   Judge Stuart referred to
the Royal guest as "the heir to the greatest of earthly thrones—
the only throne, perhaps, which the War has left more deeply rooted
in the affections of the people" and his visit as an addition to the
great traditions of the University.   A Civic luncheon followed at
which the Prince described Edmonton as "the City of Youth"; as
he left this function to open a ball-game at Diamond Park between
Calgary and Edmonton, huge crowds greeted him everywhere;
after "pitching" in a way to delight the fans and the people, he
stayed for a while to watch the game; the rest of the afternoon was
spent at golf at the Country Club with attendance in the evening at
a banquet of 300 members of the 40th Battalion, a brief speech and
great difficulty in getting away from his loyal comrades of the
Front.   The Prince left the City at 11 p.m. with crowds around the
train, bouquets thrown into the car and even, as it moved away
amidst a roar of cheers, hands thrust up for one good-bye shake
from the smiling visitor.   The enthusiasm was specially notable
amongst the young people and, as one writer said, the people were
quite ready to give the City to the Prince and if there was anything
else he wanted he was welcome to it.   The Edmonton *Bulletin* put
it as follows: "Never before among the older people has so much
enthusiasm been roused over one individual, as has gone out to
this Royal lad, while the younger people are absolutely devoted to
him.   The visit just concluded will be talked of for generations to
come, for the Prince has won a place in the affections of the people
from which he will never be ousted."   It may be added that the
decorations were many and effective, the flags and bunting and
arches gay and bright, the illuminations at night sparkling and
glowing in their welcome.

It was Sunday morning when His Royal Highness, "smiling,
debonair and democratic" as one newspaper put it, stepped from
the train at Calgary and was received by the Lieut.-Governor,
Mayor R. C. Marshall and other representative citizens.   It was a
beautiful day and a beautiful scene; a cordon of returned soldiers
and a great crowd greeted the Prince, though the cheers were not,
at first, very ready in coming; later, and very soon, this changed as
the personality of the Royal visitor made itself felt and, from
block to block, the volume of sound grew greater until the Prince
stood up and bowed and waved his hat to a roar of enthusiastic
welcome.   Divine service at the Protestant Cathedral conducted
by Bishop Pinkham, followed and afterwards a Memorial screen
was dedicated in honour of soldiers fallen in the War.   In the

afternoon the Prince—who had a suite at the Palliser Hotel—paid a visit to the Country Club and on his way there was met by a troop of Boy Scouts who obtained permission to drag his motor-car over a bridge and into the Club grounds. The Colonel Belcher Military Hospital was also visited with the usual informal chats between Prince and patients. A quiet garden-party and dinner followed at the Ranchers' Club.

On Monday 35,000 people welcomed the Royal guest at the Calgary. Exhibition grounds, joined a large gathering of school children in singing, "O Canada," while the Prince stood at attention, and then gave him an ovation. Military veterans and organizations were inspected, including Cadets and Boy Scouts and a group of Nursing sisters and, with many of the latter, the Prince shook hands. The Civic address contained an eulogy of the four Western Provinces as containing the World's greatest grain-producing plains and stock ranges, as well as unlimited wealth in coal deposits, minerals, immense lumber areas and all the riches of the seas. In his reply he declared that: "A grave responsibility rests upon you which will demand the co-operation of all classes and parties and a common determination on the part of the whole community to keep the wider interests of Canada and of the British commonwealth in the forefront of their aims." Many War decorations were then conferred and as the Prince left in his car there was a terrific outburst of cheering. At the Civic luncheon, a little later, a very definite reference to Western problems was made by him for the first time in this Tour:

The farther I travel through Canada the more I am struck by the great diversities which it presents. Its many and varied communities are not only separated by great distances, but also by divergent interests. You have much splendid alien human material to assimilate, and so much already has been done toward cementing all parts of the Dominion that I am sure you will ultimately succeed in accomplishing this great task; but it will need the co-operation of all parties, of all classes, and of all races, working together for the common cause—Canadian nationhood under the British flag. Serious difficulties and controversies must often arise, but I know nothing can set Canada back except the failure of different classes and communities to look to the wider interests of the Dominion, as well as to their own immediate needs. I realize that scattered communities, necessarily pre-occupied with the absorbing task of 'making good,' often find the wider view difficult to keep. Yet I feel sure that it will be kept steadily before the eyes of the people of this great Western country, whose very success in making the country what it is proves their staying power and capacity.

Another incident of the day was turning the first sod for a G.W.V.A. Club-house; a visit was also paid to the Army and Navy Veterans and to the local re-training centre of the Soldiers' Re-establishment Department—Sir James Lougheed, the Minister, being with the Prince on this latter occasion. In the afternoon His Royal Highness, with a few of his Staff were motored to George Lane's well-known ranch, the "Bar-U," near High River, and there he spent a day in rest and another in seeing a round-up of 3,500 cattle and sharing in the cow-boy sports which included a long ride from the corrals in a heavy rain-storm; he also had a short trip to shoot wild ducks and a 5-mile run before breakfast in real running togs. At High River, *en route,* a warm welcome was given by 5,000 people and a tree planted by the Prince in the school grounds with 1,000 cheering children around him. On Tuesday the 16th, he was back at Calgary in the evening for a brilliant Ball at the Armouries with 1,500 guests and here the Prince danced till 2.30 in the morning when he left, amidst ringing cheers of farewell, to take his train. At Banff, on the 17th, a picturesque escort of Stoney Indians met and surrounded the Prince as he proceeded to the Park and, after the Commissioner had presented an Address, His Royal Highness was made, with pomp and ceremony, a Chief of the tribe under the name of "Morning Star," and, during a brief period of thanks, wore the great feathered headdress of his rank. In the next 24 hours he played golf, danced informally in the evening and enjoyed a brief rest. The Royal train left for Lake Louise on the 18th and at Hector the Prince left the train and rode through the superb scenery of the Kicking Horse Pass, to Field, on horseback. At this latter point a walk of 10 miles was taken to Emerald Lake with exercise and splendid scenery combined; on the 20th Golden was reached with a resumption of formal receptions and popular welcomes and an informal review, *en route,* of the Middlesex Regiment which was returning home from Siberia by way of Canada; at Revelstoke, a few hours later, and at Kamloops on the 21st, the Prince was enthusiastically received; at other and smaller points people cheered the passing train as it rushed on its way to the Pacific.

The Prince on the Pacific Coast. On Sept. 22nd, the Prince of Wales reached Vancouver, the end of his long Western trail, as one writer put it, and was able to stand upon the shores of the Pacific and, as he, himself, said at a Civic luncheon, look across its broad waters and see two other British democracies building up a pure British civilization under the Southern Cross. It was an almost English climate which welcomed him; there was a warm-hearted greeting of cheers and a booming of guns to meet him as he left the train and was formally received by Mayor R. H. Gale and his Council, Brig.-Gen. R. G. E. Leckie, D.O.C., and other officials. together with Admiral Hugh Rodman of the U.S. Navy, whose flagship was in port. The guard of honour was inspected and the Royal procession was then formed, preceded by Mounted Policemen in their scarlet coats with others around the Prince's motor-car, with aeroplanes circling aloft and streets gaily decorated in flags and coloured bunting and spanned by arches of welcome. The route taken was thick with cheering people, school children waving flags lined the streets for miles, spectators were perched upon every available place or building or point of vantage; in the beautiful Stanley Park, with its massive trees of fir and spruce, the scene was very striking.

Here a platform decorated with maple leaves and exotic plants stood in the misty sunlight with a pathway, hedged in by the glistening bayonets of red-coated Highlanders, up which the Prince walked to receive the Civic address.   The usual ceremony was added to by a splendid choir of children singing patriotic songs with a background of sentinel trees and a great massed crowd who cheered and sang "Rule Britannia" with alternating enthusiasm.   A visit to the Military wing of the General Hospital followed with a hurried trip to Point Grey where the Prince laid the corner-stone of a new School; an inspection of veterans was the next incident with the conferring of many War decorations; a little later he was at the Hotel Vancouver where a whole floor had been reserved for the Royal guest and his suite.   A brilliant Civic luncheon followed with 400 present who represented the municipal, business and professional interests of Vancouver and, for the first time during the Tour, the women of the City; Mayor Gale presided with His Royal Highness on one side and Admiral Rodman of the U.S. Pacific Fleet on the other.

In his speech the Prince paid high tribute to the Railways which had done so much in building up the West—to the brains, enterprise and endurance of "the great men who have linked up the Atlantic and the Pacific by penetrating the dense, rough wooded country of the east, traversing the great prairies and finally piercing one of the three most massive mountain ranges of the world." He mentioned his own up-bringing in the Royal Navy as adding interest to his visit and to the opportunity of aiding in the local welcome to Admiral Rodman; paid tribute to the Canadian, Australian and New Zealand troops in the War and to the memory of General Botha who had just passed away; reiterated his intention of making another visit to Canada soon, described Western Canada as "the trustee of British allegiance and British institutions" upon the continent and urged all to work together for "Canadian nationhood under the British flag."   Admiral Rodman, in responding for "The Allies," declared that "had the Grand Fleet not done its full duty the War would have ended in a few months with a German victory."   Decorations were then given to 111 officers and men with Brig.-Gen. Victor W. Odlum receiving his C.M.G. and D.S.O.

Following these functions the Prince visited and inaugurated the new quarters of the Navy League and in the evening, after a game at the Shaughnessy Golf Club and dinner at the Vancouver Club, he attended a Military Ball in the Arena with 10,000 persons present in the galleries, or on the floor, and with dancing kept up till an early hour in the morning.   Meantime, American visitors had been swarming into the City in numbers estimated to run from 8,000 to 15,000 and the Pioneers of British Columbia had forwarded an Address of loyalty to the King and pride in their Province.   On the 23rd the Prince was off early in the morning for a game of Badminton and a walk with some of his Staff; later he visited the famous Hastings Mill and then received a great number of people at the Arena and inspected Imperial Veterans and War

Nurses at the Pier on his way to the *Princess Alice* which took him across the Straits, to Victoria, in the afternoon.

The Capital City was reached about 5 p.m. and the Prince welcomed by a myriad of small craft in the harbour, with Royal salutes from the guns of the Garrison Artillery, whistles from boats and factories, cheers and waving handkerchiefs from people on the boats, on the wharves and at every vantage point in sight.   He was formally greeted by Sir F. S. Barnard, Lieut.-Governor, Hon. John Oliver, Premier of the Province, Mayor R. J. Porter, Brig.-Gen. R. P. Clark and many others of note; after the National Anthem had been played the Prince inspected the guard of honour, the Boys' Naval Brigade and the Artillery unit; the Royal procession then formed and passed through cheering crowds to Government House where the Prince stayed during his visit.   At 10.30 the next morning (Sept. 24) he was at the Parliament Buildings where the Provincial and Civic addresses were presented and replied to and in front of which the War Veterans, Cadet Corps, Boy Scouts, Girl Guides and other detachments were inspected.   The Provincial Address was signed by the Premier and Hon. J. D. MacLean, Provincial Secretary, and was significant in its reference to the War: "We rejoice that the victory which has been vouchsafed to us will prepare the way for a closer union of the component parts of the Empire, born of the comradeship and co-operation of the past five years."   To it the Prince replied with an eulogy of the pioneers of the coast and a recognition of the Province as always a firm and vigourous upholder of British allegiance and British ideas: "It was staunch and trusty in the old Colonial days and it has been as staunch and trusty ever since."

At 11 o'clock the Prince laid the corner-stone of the statue of Queen Victoria in the Parliament grounds and at noon held a public Reception in the Parliament Buildings attended by the usual thousands of citizens; following this was a Military luncheon at the Barracks given by Brig.-Gen. R. G. E. Leckie and his Staff. Most of the afternoon was spent at golf and in the evening he attended a State dinner at Government House; at 10.30 he was at the greatest Ball ever given in the City with the Empress Hotel as the centre of a scenic splendour which only the mingling of natural beauty, water scenery, electric lights and manifold decorations could effect.   The Prince danced until 2 o'clock.   Other incidents were a visit (Sept. 25) to the Military Hospital at Esquimalt with the usual sympathetic, friendly talk with the patients and a call at the Red Cross Hut with presentation of the Nurses; an informal speech to Navy League members at the Sailors' Club in the same suburb of the capital with a visit to the students at the Royal Naval College; an official inspection of the Dockyard and decoration of local War heroes and a visit to the Yarrow's ship-building plant. At Victoria early in the day the Hostel for Wounded Soldiers was visited.   On the following day 300 miles of Vancouver Island were traversed with the Royal train stopping at Duncan, Ladysmith,

Nanaimo, Parkville, Qualicum and Courtenay; at all these points
His Royal Highness was welcomed by cheering crowds and delivered a short speech of appreciation; he visited a Hospital at Comox
and stayed over at Qualicum long enough to have a half-hour
dance, which had been arranged at another Hospital in his honour,
with the Nurses as partners.

Saturday and Sunday were intended to be days of rest but on
the former (27th) the Prince managed to see the Home Products
Fair and to be interested in the various organizations which had
stalls of exhibits. The rest of the day was largely devoted to golf;
on Sunday he paid informal visits—in one case, unexpectedly, to
St. Joseph's Hospital and the Aged Women's Home and also
received a deputation of Indian chiefs who presented a loyal
Address. Other incidents of the Victoria visit included a picturesque ceremonial in connection with the Reception at the Parliament Buildings where a group of I.O.D.E. Chapters of the City
raised their standards in honour of the Prince, and the Regents,
at his request, were afterwards presented to him. Another was
a lavish and spectacular display of fireworks in his honour by
Japanese residents. On the 29th the Prince was back again in
Vancouver with an official visit to South Vancouver and Burnaby;
in each municipality there were many and gay decorations, formal
addresses and cheering crowds with surging school children to a
total of 6,000; a feature of the South Vancouver reception was a
loyal Address from the Hindus.

Later in the day New Westminster contributed a reception of
tremendous enthusiasm as the Prince motored in from Vancouver
12 miles away; the streets were lined with crowds and the Fair
ground, where Addresses were presented and the Exhibition
formally opened, was a mass of cheering people. From this point
a journey was taken to the beautiful and fertile fruit valleys of
British Columbia. Vernon was reached on the 30th and gave an
enthusiastic and hospitable welcome, Kelowna and Penticton, Sum-
merland, Peachland and Okanagan Landing all had their glimpse
of the Prince who during one day traversed Okanagan Lake in a
local steamer and drove 60 miles through rich orchards and groups
of cheering people; at Lavington, 12 miles from Penticton, he unveiled a Soldiers' monument and, everywhere, was greeted with
special interest by the soldiers themselves. At Nelson on Oct. 1st,
as at many other places, the Royal visit was made a children's day
with holiday surroundings and cheer; Balfour Sanitarium, an
institute at Kootenay Lake under the Ottawa Government, was
visited near here and in the afternoon some hours were spent at
golf.

From the Rocky Mountains to Winnipeg. From Nelson the
Prince started through the Mountains, on his return journey to the
East, with Macleod, Alberta, as the first important stop; here on
Oct. 2nd the usual Address was received with cheers from the wait-
ing crowds of people; near Lethbridge, later in the day, he was

specially welcomed by the Bloods, a tribe of the Blackfeet Indians, who, at their Reserve, made the Prince a Chief with the title of Mecasto or Red Crow; a formal Address was also presented to him upon the lofty roof of the Board of Trade Building at Lethbridge. Medicine Hat was reached on October 3rd and a tower of flame sent up from its great gas resources as a new form of welcome, a parade followed through the town, a Civic address was presented and veterans decorated. The Prince also inspected local industries where natural gas was utilized for power. Here, as at other points for some time previously, he used his left hand exclusively; there was a great crowd in the town from the country around and the children were much in evidence. From Lethbridge the Prince sent a lengthy message to the Government and people of British Columbia: "I can now say most sincerely that the rich experiences of the past ten days will never be effaced from my memory. I have been enabled to grasp something of the nature of your resources and of the splendid energy with which you are developing your great timber, fishing, mining and agricultural industries. I have been deeply impressed with the splendid scenery of the country which, go where one may, makes so constant and irresistible an appeal to the eye and mind. But my strongest and longest memory will be those evidences of generous hospitality, of fine loyalty to British institutions, and of inspiring optimism, which I met everywhere."

Saskatchewan welcomed the Prince on Oct. 3rd with enthusiastic greetings as he came from Alberta and passed through Swift Current, Tompkins, Maple Creek and Gull Lake where short stops were made; nearly 100 per cent. of the population attended and some brief ceremonial was given to supplement the cheers of the crowds and their elaborate preparations. Moose Jaw presented a splendid welcome on the morning of the 4th including the exhibition of a Table of Plenty, emblematic of Western agriculture and production, an ovation from massed crowds as he drove through the streets; with thousands of farmers present from the country around and streets decorated with sheaves of grain which covered the electric standards from base to top. Many preparations had been made at Regina and the capital of the Province saw the greatest and most enthusiastic throngs in its history when the Prince of Wales arrived on the afternoon of Oct. 4th. The weather was beautiful and His Royal Highness was received at the station by the Lieut.-Governor, Sir R. S. Lake, the Premier, Hon. W. M. Martin, the Mayor, Henry Black and Commissioner A. B. Perry of the R.N.W.M.P. As he drove through the great crowds to the Parliament Buildings the cheering was remarkable; when he reached the platform or dais erected outside the Buildings, 10,000 people shouted themselves hoarse while 3,000 school children waved little flags and a large number of Boy Scouts added a touch of the picturesque to the brilliant uniforms of the Mounted Police, to the background of the great stone building with its beautiful tower and the scenic effect of Wascana Park, to the huge arch of oats and wheat erected by the Government, to the flags and bunting which were waving everywhere.

After reviewing the guard of honour the Prince ascended the dais while the children sang "God bless the Prince of Wales" and received the Provincial address in the course of which Mr. Premier Martin said: "We fully realize that the British Empire and indeed the whole civilized world, is now face to face with economic and social problems of great complexity due to the long duration and vast extent of the armed conflict now closed, and beg to assure Your Royal Highness that the citizens of this Province are prepared to do their part in the solution of all such problems with the same spirit of earnest endeavour, sacrifice and loyalty as was manifested by them during the War. . . . We feel that one of the results of the War has been a greater binding together of the widely scattered units of the British Empire, and that this visit of Your Royal Highness to Canada is additional influence towards closer unity still." In replying, His Royal Highness touched the latter point: "I know that you in this Province are working whole-heartedly for British institutions and Canadian nationhood and that amidst the many and important domestic questions with which you have to deal, the broader interests of the British Empire will always be kept in mind."

The Civic address breathed sentiments of loyalty and was briefly responded to; the Prince then inspected the men of the Royal Air Service, members of the Great War Veterans' Association—in which latter he accepted Life membership—and the Army and Navy Veterans and shook hands with the whole 500; about 40 V.A.D's were inspected and the 26th Battery reviewed while the Collegiate Cadets and Boy Scouts received expressions of approval; decorations followed for about 50 War heroes and the Prince then visited the school children's stand and announced a full holiday for them amidst great rejoicing. During his visit in Regina the Prince had stayed at Government House and on Sunday he rested as far as possible. Incidents of his stay included a view of the British Naval pictures at the Barracks and tea with the Patricia Club, the opening of the new Club-rooms of the Veterans, attendance at St. Paul's Church on Sunday morning and a visit to the Earl Grey Hospital in the afternoon with the usual gracious kindliness to patients and nurses. He, also, inspected the R.N.W.M.P. Barracks and Headquarters for the West and the splendid Mounted Police who were there—the red-coated riders of the Plains whose history includes a record of skill, courage and achievement unique in character. On Monday the Prince left for three days of duck shooting from a camp at Leader's Point in the Qu'Appelle valley and had much success, with a record which proved him a crack shot; several functions intervened such as a reception in the Edenwold district and a ride of 14 miles to Fort Qu'Appelle to visit the Soldiers' Sanitarium and be greeted by singing and cheering school-children *en masse*. Late on the 9th he was back in Regina and left on the C.P.R. for Brandon, Man.; there on the 10th and at Portage la Prairie a little later loyal receptions were accorded. At Portage 1,500 children sang "O Canada," Mayor J. H. Metcalfe presented an Address to which the Prince briefly replied and then invested a number of soldiers with War decorations and planted a maple tree in the Collegiate Institute grounds.

Winnipeg was reached later in the day for an informal and private visit with only two functions accepted—the one a Military banquet and ball in the evening and a Luncheon on Saturday as the guest of about 500 prominent citizens of Winnipeg and the Province. On the former occasion 450 guests were present with Brig.-Gen. H. D. B. Ketchen, D.O.C., presiding—the only civilians invited being Sir James Aikins, Hon. T. C. Norris and Mr. Mayor Gray. The Ball was attended by 600 officers of war experience and as many ladies; the Prince danced till early in the morning. At the Luncheon the address of His Royal Highness was the most elaborate so far given during the Tour; it touched various national and Imperial issues and breathed the Western spirit to a degree. To quote his own words: "The atmosphere of Western Canada appeals to me intensely; the free, vigourous, hopeful spirit of Westerners not only inspires me, but makes me feel happy and at home. I think the Western spirit is very catching; anyhow, I know I have caught it. I shall return to the Old Country realizing that the Western Provinces are going to play a very important part in the future history of the British Empire, and that they carry correspondingly great responsibilities."

This point was clinched by a statement which created wide interest and comment: "I want to feel I have a home in the West and to give the little help I can to the development of the whole country. With this end in view, I have made arrangements to purchase a small ranch in Alberta, and I hope that I shall also, incidentally, be able to help a few ex-service men by employing them on the ranch." As to the rest: "This vast Western country is the youngest part of the great Canadian nation, just as the Dominion is one of the youngest and most important pillars of the Empire. We are all joined together in one great British commonwealth and the freedom we enjoy in every part of it is a noble inheritance of the past, strengthened and enriched by our united and victorious efforts in the Great War." A visit followed, over Sunday, to the shooting lodge of George F. Galt at Lake Francis; on the 13th the Prince returned to the city and left for the East. Meantime it became known that the new Royal ranch was the somewhat famous Bedingfield run near George Lane's "Bar U" at High River; that it was the intention of the Prince to breed only pure-bred stock and that some of the best would be imported at once; that the ranch would be run along business lines and would make it additionally desirable and necessary for personal visits to the West.

Ontario Tour of the Prince. Back from the West, His Royal Highness first stopped at Cobalt, the historic centre of the mineralized areas of Northern Ontario (Oct. 16) and one of the banners of welcome read: "The town is ours, paint it red or any old colour." The miners gave him ringing cheers and plentiful gifts of silver or golden nuggets; he descended into the bowels of the earth and saw the processes of mining 600 feet deep in the O'Brien mine—dressed in oilskins and carrying an acetylene torch; the Coniagas mine was inspected and others visited while underground cheers echoed in the depths as he ascended the shafts to daylight; a drive for miles followed over rock-bed roads to get a general view of the whole district; there was, of course, an official welcome and a review of veterans. At Porcupine a similar experience in the gold mines was had and brief stops were made at Timmins, New Liskeard and lesser towns. From this district the Prince passed on in the night toward Hamilton—with a stop-off at Gravenhurst—and this important industrial centre of Ontario was reached at 1.30 p.m. with an informal reception at the station; the afternoon was spent at the Country Golf Club and the evening in attendance at a Ball given by the Wentworth Women's Historical Society. The invitations to this function had been limited to 400 and a beautiful little souvenir book was presented to the Prince by Mrs. John Crerar who had danced with King Edward during his famous Tour of 1860. The Royal guest chose his own partners and danced every dance until three in the morning.

The next day (18th) was the formal welcome to a city gaily decorated and crowded with ever-cheering people. At 10.30 the Civic address was presented at the City Hall by Mayor Booker with others by the Canadian Club, the Women's Canadian Club, the Irish Protestant Benevolent Society, St. George's Society, the I.O.D.E., the Jews of Hamilton, and St. Andrew's Society. Only the Civic document was read and to it the Prince replied briefly. Through cheering thousands and streets decorated with streamers, bunting and flags, he then passed to the new Memorial School which was formally declared open amid a vociferous welcome from a massed chorus of children singing patriotic songs; the splendid Hamilton Memorial Hospital was then formally opened and the Mountain Sanitarium for Soldiers visited; Lunch was taken at the Tamahaac Club, the Veterans were reviewed afterwards and 133 decorated and tea was taken at "The Homestead" with Mrs. William Hendrie. A Civic dinner followed at the Royal Connaught Hotel with a brief speech by the Prince, who left a little later for Niagara Falls. The correspondent of the Toronto *World* said of the Ambitious City's celebration that: "Never in the history of Hamilton was there such a reception tendered to any one man, or, as a matter of fact, to any group, or upon any particular occasion. Hamilton took the Prince to her heart royally and loyally. From the time he stepped off the Royal train until he left after the Civic banquet, the citizens shook hands with him, cheered him, admired him and learned to love him."

At 11.30 Saturday night (18th) the Prince arrived at Niagara Falls by the G.T.R., was met by Sir Adam Beck and members of

H.R.H. The Prince of Wales at Guelph College

the Ontario Park Commission; he pressed a button which for the first time flashed brilliant electric lights upon the Falls and then watched the beautiful scene in entranced interest for an hour. On Sunday he followed the route of the great River by street car for some distance, descended by the Incline Railway and gazed upon the Whirlpool Rapids, crossed the Aerial tramway high over the scene of gloomy grandeur, visited the Ontario Power Company's plant, drove to Queenston Heights and viewed Brock's Monument. Everywhere there were crowds, pressing and cheering around him; the evening was spent quietly at the Clifton House. On Monday morning there was a children's- holiday and demonstration; the ensuing bestowal of decorations on War veterans was performed amidst enormous crowds from the American as well as Canadian side of the River—Mayor H. P. Stephens in his Civic address referring to this feature of the reception. At noon the train was taken for Brantford with brief and enthusiastic receptions at Vineland and Grimsby; half-an-hour was spent at St. Catharines where 4,000 people acclaimed the Prince at the station while he reviewed Cadets, Boy Scouts, War veterans and shook hands with as many people as possible; brief stops were made at Paris and Kitchener where crowds turned out to see and cheer.

The industrial life of Brantford was hardly seen by the Prince in the afternoon of Oct. 20 but he received the usual official welcome, conferred military decorations at the Armouries, held an informal reception and received a hearty welcome from crowds of the people in sunlit streets. He visited the little chapel built in the days of George III. for the Mohawk Indians and registered his name, after that of his Royal Grandfather, and inspected the Communion plate and Bible presented by Queen Anne to the Mohawks of her day; visited the grave of Brant, the loyal Indian Chief of Revolutionary days and, in the main square of the City, accepted, with due ceremonial, a Chieftanship in the famous Six Nations with the title of Dayrohasereh or ''Dawn of the Morning''; drove to the Bell Memorial and inspected the Army and Navy veterans. At Guelph, on the 21st, thousands stood in pouring rain to welcome the Prince as he left his train to go to the City Hall and cheered him as he stood on the platform outside and received a formal Address. After the presentation of medals to War veterans, a visit was made to the Speedwell Hospital—along streets lined with cheering children—where a bust of King Edward VII. was unveiled.

The Ontario Agricultural College, for which Guelph was famous, and which the Prince had already stated he was looking forward to seeing, was next visited. An informal luncheon and a brief speech in Macdonald Hall followed with President G. C. Creelman in the chair, and the Prince stated that he was no longer an academic observer, but a farmer himself: ''I have just bought a ranch in southern Alberta, which I do not mean to leave entirely to others to work. I hope to come and learn for myself, and in that capacity I shall look for help and advice at Guelph. I hope

11

that I shall be able to show in a few years that I have made good and that I have money in the Bank!'' A patriotic reference was made to Trafalgar Day, the memory of Nelson and the record of the Navy. This visit to the residence building of the girl students, his cordial speech and manner, ensured the Prince a most enthusiastic reception from thousands of young Canadians there and throughout the College. For a time he was surrounded by girls who were photographed with him and sang ''For he's a jolly good fellow'' when he was leaving.

At 2. p.m. the Royal visitor left for Stratford and all along the line in Ontario during the day or through the night, crowds of people gathered at the stations, from miles around, to see the Prince if possible or, in any event, to send a cheer after him and his rushing train. Stratford, London, Woodstock, Ingersoll and Chatham all had him for a brief space during the afternoon and evening of the 22nd. At Woodstock the Collegiate Institute gave a vociferous welcome and amongst the decorations were Union Jacks nailed to the trees; in Chatham an Address was received and veterans and Boy Scouts inspected during a brief hour; in London the streets were black with people and the Prince's motor so crowded it could hardly make progress. The Western University students contributed a loyal and noisy welcome; a dinner was given at the Tecumseh House and a reception held at the Armouries; the formal Civic address was presented by Mayor C. R. Somerville at Victoria Park where a great crowd had gathered and thousands of school children sang songs; Boy Scouts, Girl Guides and the Naval Brigade were reviewed and a maple tree planted. At the Civic dinner the Prince referred to the industries whose centres he had recently been visiting: ''A young nation like this, with its enormous promise, cannot afford to be one-sided, and Canada's natural resources assure her a great industrial as well as a great agricultural development. With your coal, your minerals and your great resources of water, oil, natural gas and other forms of power, you are sure of a splendid industrial future.''

The decorations here included a white arch covered with laurel wreaths and some of the buildings were simply swathed in bunting. In the morning of the 23rd the Prince played golf at the Country Club, attended a military luncheon with Brig.-Gen. L. W. Shannon in the chair, inspected the War veterans on Carling's Heights and conferred 61 decorations; in the evening Windsor was reached and through massed and cheering crowds the Prince passed to the lavishly decorated Armouries where, on a special dais, he received the formal welcome of the border cities of Ford, Walkerville and Sandwich as well as Windsor. A public Reception followed which lasted for an hour and a dinner at the Essex Country Club ended the day. On the 24th decorations were conferred at the Park and the colours of the 99th Battalion deposited in All Saint's Church; a motor-drive was taken through the border cities, some schools and a hospital visited. In the afternoon the Royal visitor spent an hour at Galt where an immense throng welcomed him, with people

from neighbouring centres and thousands of school children, sharing in the reception. A visit was paid to the G.W.V.A. Memorial
Home; at the Armouries a Civic greeting and more cheers from a
great crowd welcomed him.

The week-end was spent at Kingston where on the 25th, the
Prince was met at the station by Mayor H. W. Newman, Maj.-Gen.
V. A. S. Williams and others, by the usual cheering crowd and
school-children; the Civic address followed an inspection of the
guard of honour and a visit then was paid to the Ball grounds
where His Royal Highness kicked off a ball for the contestants; the
Royal Military College was the next point of inspection and under
the guidance of its Commandant, Maj.-Gen. Sir A. C. Macdonell,
the Prince toured the buildings, reviewed the Cadets and presented
Colours. At 6.30 p.m. Queen's University conferred upon
him the Hon. degree of LL.D. with the new Chancellor, E. W.
Beatty, presiding and Dr. Bruce Taylor officiating as Principal;
later a Civic dinner was attended and in the evening an informal
dance at General Williams' residence. On Sunday the Prince
attended service at St. George's Cathedral and afterwards drove to
Cataraqui Cemetery where he placed a wreath of roses on the grave
of Sir John A. Macdonald. He dined with officers of the Horse
Artillery and visited the Military Hospitals. On the 26th an hour
was spent at Brockville en route to Montreal, the usual ceremonies
were gone through, the veterans of the City and County, under
Major T. W. McDowell, v.c., d.s.o., inspected and many decorated.

The Royal Visit to Montreal. From Brockville to the Quebec
metropolis, at all kinds of places in Ontario or Quebec, big and
little, English and French, some kind of welcome was given to the
Prince; the desire to shake his hand seemed universal, the habit of
cheering him had always been spontaneous, it was now becoming
fixed. At Montreal from Oct. 26 to Nov. 2, the welcome was wild
in its enthusiasm and continuous in its manifestation. On the day
of his arrival he was met by a salute of guns from the mountain, by
steam whistles, automobile hooters, church bells, a roar of cheers
and an aeroplane over the Windsor station; the building, itself, was
a riot of flags and bunting and the reception in the station was a
formal and Military one; outside, the guard of honour was inspected while cheer after cheer rent the air, hats were tossed on
high, women waved handkerchiefs and flags, children screamed at
the top of their shrill young voices. In a motor-car bearing the
Royal Standard, way was slowly made through the packed streets
to the accompaniment of a welcome which could not have been
exceeded and which Montreal had, perhaps, never equalled.

As the Royal car passed through the streets, the air was filled
with coloured streamers and confetti until the whole scene was a.
tangled web of colour. Up town or down town, in the business or
other streets, in English or French districts, the enthusiasm was
the same and there was no cessation till the City Hall was reached.
Here there was a red and gold canopy above the steps of the en-

trance with illuminated decorations; in the Hall, itself, the Address and reply were given in the presence of a distinguished gathering led by the joint Chairmen of the Reception Committee—Sir H. Laporte and Lord Shaughnessy. Mayor M. Martin presented the Address clad in his fur-trimmed robes of dark blue with golden chain of office and in its terms declared that the War had given the British soldiers "innumerable opportunities for showing their valour, and that their acts of heroism could not be counted." Canadians also, had distinguished themselves and now, "as soon as Peace is signed, Your Royal Highness comes to further tighten, if possible, the bonds that unite us to the Mother Country, and to cement the union between the two great races forming the majority of the Canadian people." A loyal Address was also accepted (in Arabic) from the Syrian Orthodox Church of North America. The St. George's Society address, after reference to the soldiers and the War, concluded with a demand that British peoples keep the faith: "O God, save all England, centre now and symbol of an Empire far beyond our dreams and bless her with Thy Holy Hand." From here the Prince passed to the Ritz-Carlton Hotel where a suite of rooms had been prepared for him, and in the evening held a Reception at the City Hall where 8,000 people were presented and filed past him with an almost continuous salute by right or left hand; by this time it must have been physically impossible for the Prince to shake hands with very many. The Victory Loan campaign for Montreal was, also, inaugurated by the Prince earlier at a meeting in the Windsor Hotel presided over by Lord Shaughnessy—with reports that Beauce County had won the first of the Prince of Wales' honour flags in Quebec.

On the following day he attended a Civic luncheon at the Place Viger Hotel with 500 representative men present and the Royal table a bower of American beauty roses. The Hon. Médéric Martin, M.L.C., and Mayor, presided and the health of the Royal visitor was proposed by Hon. Charles Marcel, M.P., who concluded by saying: "The memory of your visits will remain graven in the annals of this city as are those of your grandfather and father. We have honoured in you the personification of all that is noble and inspiring. We pray Divine Providence to vouchsafe to you a long and happy life to enable you to carry out to its full fruition the great mission entrusted to you." The Prince commenced his reply in English and finished in French. He dealt largely with the unity of races—England and Scotland, South Africa and Canada as examples: "The union between England and Scotland has lasted through centuries. The union between British and French races in Canada has only lasted half a century, but who can doubt that the union in Canada will produce as great, as powerful and as united a nation as the British nation itself. . . . What is the secret of the success of British policy in this respect. I can say that the secret in Canada is the same as it is in Great Britain. It lies in freedom of speech, freedom of language and mutual respect for each other." This evoked enthusiastic cheers, the audience standing and waving napkins or handkerchiefs. An expressed hope of an early return to Montreal was added and greatly cheered.

Following this function was another passage through great cheering crowds to Lafontaine Park where several thousand troops were inspected; back, then, went the Prince through continued ovations and along Sherbrooke Street to the Art Gallery where he received an Address from a large number of women's organizations, represented as the Women War Workers of Montreal, and conferred War decorations upon 150 officers and men; the Prince of Wales Hospital on Drummond Street was then opened and in the evening a Military Ball attended at the Windsor Hotel. Here, from 9.30 until about three in the morning, the Prince danced; the decorations, arrangements, costumes, uniforms, were all alike, brilliant. On the 28th he formally opened the Canadian War Memorials Exhibition and conducted other functions; on the 29th he was in the Eastern Townships, of English and Loyalist settlement, and stopped at St. Johns, Farnham, Magog, Sherbrooke, Lennoxville, Richmond and St. Hyacinthe; formal Addresses of loyalty, cheering crowds and informal exhibitions of loyal enthusiasm were everywhere tendered.

At Sherbrooke, the largest of these centres, the whole town was on the streets. Children threw kisses to the Prince, and adults shouted and cheered as the car bearing the Royal Standard passed along; the horses of the special policemen were a smother of flags. Opposite the stately church of St. Jean an aged priest waved his barret and shouted "Vive le Prince" as long as the procession was in sight; at the Armouries, where the Prince was presented with an Address and War decorations conferred, Bishop Larocque, Mgr. Tanguay and many other ecclesiastics were on the platform. St. Hyacinthe gave an evening reception and was ablaze with electricity and light; Farnham contributed a large and notable crowd of pretty girls and it was said that some of them went back into the line and were presented half-a-dozen times—one girl gave the Prince a rose and dozens of others immediately begged him for a petal; at Richmond there also was a night display of electric lights and here another public reception was held and the Prince seemed to rejoice in meeting all who could be crowded into the time available. He was back in Montreal in time to attend a gala performance at the Princess Theatre with a drive from the Bonaventure station which gave a repetition of preceding crowds and enthusiasm; from the theatre he attended a private dance at the residence of Sir Mortimer Davis.

On the following day (30th) His Royal Highness came into close touch with other sides of the life of Montreal—the sporting fraternity, the Laval students, the English business section, and the working people. At lunch with the National Athletic Association he met the sporting enthusiasts and watched 30 picked athletes at work; at Laval University he was received by Rev. Canon Chartier and was given an ear-splitting welcome by the students while confetti and coloured ribbons poured on him from all quarters—in Convocation Bishop Gauthier presented an Address to which the Prince replied in French; a visit to the English suburb of Westmount followed and here the school-children shared in the ovation to the Royal visitor and the latter took tea at the Convent Ville Maria where there was a guard of honour of St. Louis Cadets. At Notre Dame de Grace Park the Prince unveiled a Memorial to soldiers who had fallen and was formally received by H. J. Gagne and Capt. the Rev. Frederick Hingston, Principal of Loyala College; Verdun, the French-Canadian working-men's suburb of Montreal then gave a vigourous, enthusiastic, massed reception and added an automobile full of roses to a collection of flowers which, in these four days, would have filled a Dreadnought; the crowds were so dense that the Prince could hardly get through and he stood in his car—after the Address had been accepted—and waved his hand until he was out of the district. A newspaper man's comment may be quoted here from the Toronto *Star* of Oct. 31:

It is a very wonderful thing, this Montreal enthusiasm. Sometimes the fervour and emotion of it catches one in the throat and if it were not that one has a certain distraction in watching for 'Copy' it might overwhelm. It is a very remarkable experience driving day after day, through densely-packed, cheering, excited streets. The effect on the Prince must be very great. Outside the physical exertion, the nervous strain of the surcharged, emotional atmosphere must be very trying. How such a slightly-built boy can stand up to it the way he is doing will be a mystery always. His fine physical condition alone makes it possible.

A dinner at the Mount Royal Club was attended later and in the evening a Citizens' Ball at the Windsor and a dance given by the Grand Army of Canada were graced for a time by the Prince's presence. In the morning of the 31st he was the guest of the Harbour Commission (W. G. Ross, Chairman), inspected various great public works and laid the corner-stone of the Sailors' Memorial (a monument to the bravery of merchant seamen) at Victoria Pier; after inspecting a guard of honour from the Boys' Naval Brigade a visit to the Khaki Club followed and here he shook hands (using the left one) with hundreds of War veterans and unveiled a Memorial tablet; the McGill University was then visited and the Hon. degree of LL.D. accepted at the hands of Dr. F. D. Adams, Acting Principal, together with an eloquent Address of loyal and Imperial thought from what was described as, "in a sense, the National University of Canada"; 1,000 Boy Scouts were also reviewed on the University Campus. The Baron de Hirsch Institute was then visited and a dinner attended at the St. James' Club. On Saturday there were no formal engagements but an informal call was made on Lord Shaughnessy and President E. W. Beatty at the C.P.R. Offices to express thanks for their many courtesies during the Tour of Canada; similarly, H. R. Charlton, of the Grand Trunk Railway, had been called to the Royal car and presented with a pair of crested gold cuff-links. Luncheon was taken with Major A. R. Chipman and 14 others at the Military Club and in the evening a dinner given by Hon. W. J. Shaughnessy at the Mount Royal Club was followed by an informal dance at Lord and Lady Shaughnessy's.

After attending service at St. George's Cathedral on Sunday morning—conducted by Rev. Dr. Symonds—the Prince called upon Archbishop Bruchési who had been ill for some time, at the Hotel Dieu, and had written expressing his great regret at not being able to share in the public welcome to His Royal Highness. In the course of the interview His Grace said: "I was anxious to tell you all my admiration and all my gratitude for the fine speech you delivered at the Place Viger Hotel. What you have said about harmony between the two great nationalities who form the bulk of the population of this Dominion is the full expression of our sentiments and our wishes. Let me tell you that your speech will be frequently quoted, even when you are King of England, as a gospel of peace." About 3 o'clock in the afternoon the Royal train steamed out of Windsor Station with a still-continued ovation from thousands of people; every point of view from the Ritz-Carlton to the Station had been crowded and at the latter point the people still were jammed in cheering masses; inside, a score of little crippled children from the Memorial Hospital, by the Prince's special request, had awaited him and proudly presented souvenirs prepared by their own hands; a guard of honour from the famous 22nd Battalion was in attendance and as the train rolled out flowers were thrown on to the platform of the car and eager hands reached up which the Prince gripped as the train moved out. A passing visit was paid to the Macdonald Agricultural College at St. Anne's, not far from Montreal, where this famous institution accorded the Prince a rollicking reception in which the girls and young men joined with equal vigour. Dr. F. H. Harrison, the Principal, presented an Address and afterwards the returned soldier students hoisted the Prince on their shoulders and carried him out to his car; he also visited St. Anne's Military College before proceeding on his way to Toronto.

Farewell Visit and Speech in Toronto. The Prince of Wales arrived in Toronto early on the 3rd of November and spent most of the day resting at Government House. In the afternoon he played racquets at the University Club and a private dinner-dance was given in the evening by Lady Hendrie. On the 4th a great meeting of the combined Empire and Canadian Clubs was held in Massey Hall and His Royal Highness delivered a speech which will live in Canadian history and long in the memories of those who heard it. Major E. Percy Brown, President of the Canadian Club, occupied the chair, and with him was R. A. Stapells, President of the Empire Club, and a large gathering of Toronto's representative citizens—including E. C. Drury, Premier-elect, and Sir William Hearst, the retiring Premier of the Province. Major Brown spoke briefly and effectively and first paid tribute to some of the founders of the Clubs who were on the platform—F. B. Fetherstonhaugh, J. Castell Hopkins, Lieut.-Col. J. Cooper Mason, D.S.O., J. P. Murray, and Lieut.-Col. C. R. McCullough. In his speech the Prince spoke of this "wonderful Canadian welcome," and then stated that so cordial had been his reception in August that ever since he had had to use his left hand! He referred to his Tour of the country and the impressions it had made upon his mind: "It has enabled me to realize that the notion that the East is purely the industrial part of Canada as opposed to the West, which is the agricultural part, is wrong, and I know now that the agricultural product of Ontario is the largest in the whole Dominion, and that your agricultural activity is as important as your industrial activity." He had become a farmer in a small way himself but, he assured them, he would be a very simple sort of farmer and not interfere in politics! After a tribute to the farmers in general, he went on: "I know they will always remember to think of the wider interests of the nation as well as of their own. It takes all kinds of interests to make a great nation, and Canada cannot afford to be one-sided. I hope, therefore, that Ontario will set the lead by showing that all classes may pursue their own legitimate interests without forgetting the welfare of the Dominion and of the Empire as a whole." A statesmanlike reference to Imperial conditions and the Monarchy, as an institution, was then made:

The old idea of an Empire handed down from the traditions of Greece and Rome was that of a Mother country surrounded by Daughter states, which owed allegiance to that Mother country. But the British Empire has long left that obsolete idea behind, and appears before us in a very different and far grander form. It appears before us as a single State, composed of many nations of different origins and different languages, which give their allegiance, not to a mother country, but to a great common system of life and government.

The British Dominions are, therefore, no longer colonies; they are sister nations of the great British nation. They played a part in the War fully proportionate to their size, and their international importance will steadily increase. Yet they all desire to remain within the Empire, whose unity is shown by common allegiance to the King. That is the reason why, if I may be personal for a moment, I do not regard myself as belonging primarily to Great Britain, and only in a lesser way to Canada and the other Dominions. On the contrary, I regard myself as belonging to Great Britain and to Canada in exactly the same way. This also means that when I go down to the United States next week I shall regard myself as going there not only as an Englishman and as a Britisher, but also as a Canadian.

This new situation, he pointed out, involved responsibilities as well as power: "Unity and co-operation are just as necessary now in peace times as during the War. We must not lose touch with each other or we shall lose all that we have won during the last five years by our common action and effort against the enemy." A further and personal reference concluded a speech in which every sentence was marked by cheers and which showed, in every word, careful thought and considered phrase: "I am not conceited enough to accept this welcome as in any way personal to myself, and I realize that it has been given me as the King's representative coming to Canada as the heir to the Throne. My first visit to the great Dominion has made me realize more fully than ever what a great privilege and what a great responsibility all that confers upon me, and I value these welcomes all the more highly because they have come from the Canadian nation as a whole, from all sections of the community, whatever their race, whatever their party, whatever their education.   I ask myself, what does that mean? It means that the Throne stands for an heritage of common aims and ideals, shared equally by all sections, all parties, and all nations within the British Commonwealth.   No Government represents or stands for all parties or all nations within the Empire.   But there is a common sentiment which is shared not only by all nations within the Empire, but also by all political parties within each nation, and I realize that this same sentiment has been expressed in the wonderful welcomes given me in Canada as heir to the Throne.''   Later in the afternoon an elaborate ceremony of decoration was carried out by the Prince at the Parliament Buildings where, in the Legislative Chamber, 270 persons received Orders and medals conferred by H. M. the King for War services.   Early the next morning the Royal train left for Ottawa and the sleeping Prince passed quietly away from the City which had given him so many and such cordial greetings.

Farewell Speech at Ottawa.   In the afternoon His Royal Highness arrived at the capital and passed through cheering crowds to his automobile and thence to Government House.   Before his arrival at Ottawa the Prince had called in the *personnel* of the Royal train, numbering over 100, who had travelled so many thousand miles with him, thanked them individually, shook hands with each one, presented a souvenir or gift to the chief of each department and to A. B. Calder, who was in charge of all, a handsome piece of jewelry.   A dinner-dance at the Country Club was the event of the first evening in Ottawa.   On Thursday evening (Nov. 6) the Prince attended a May Court Ball at the Chateau Laurier; on Friday a Royal investiture was held at Government House and Maj.-Gen. E. W. B. Morrison was knighted by the Prince with the insignia of K.C.M.G.—the first knighthood he had ever conferred —and the same Order was accorded Maj.-Gen. Sir Henry Burstall, K.C.B., while various lesser Honours were conferred; in the evening a dinner-dance was given by the Duke and Duchess of Devonshire; on Saturday a notable speech was made at the Canadian Club luncheon and in the evening Lady Violet Henderson entertained in honour of the Prince at the Country Club; on Sunday morning (Nov. 9) His Royal Highness attended service at St. Bartholomew's Church where he unveiled a window erected by H.R.H. the Duke of Connaught in memory of members of his Staff in Canada who had fallen in the War, and MacKay Presbyterian Church where he unveiled two other War Tablets; in the afternoon he visited the G.W.V.A. Club-house, accepted Life membership, made a brief speech and shook hands with the 400 members present.

The Canadian Club Luncheon was informal but crowded and enthusiastic with 2,000 of Ottawa's most representative people pre-

sent and President J. E. Macpherson in the chair.   The Prince, in
kindly language and informal terms, thanked the Canadian Government for the admirable arrangements of his Tour; thanked the
Railways for the care and consideration shown to him in a journey
which had grown from the expected 8,800 miles to one of 12,000
miles; thanked, above all, the people, for their wonderful welcomes,
their hospitality, their letters: "I know that they come from the
whole nation without distinction of race, party or education, and
that they have been given to me as the King's son, coming to
Canada as heir to his Throne.   I value it all particularly highly
because I know it expresses the same common sentiment which made
Britishers stand together in the Great War, and which will keep
them solid and united for all time."   He repeated his Toronto
statement: "I regard myself as belonging to Canada and the other
British Dominions in exactly the same way as to Great Britain, and
when I go to the United States on Monday I shall go there not only
as an Englishman and a Britisher, but as a Canadian and a representative of the whole Empire."   On Monday morning the Prince
left for Washington in the Private car of the United States President, which had been sent forward for the purpose, and cheer after
cheer rang out from massed thousands at the station as the Royal
visitor left and made one last effort, from the rear platform of the
moving train, to shake hands with some of the eager people.

   The Prince of Wales in the United States.   The visit of the
Prince to the Republic was brief but important; it was only an
incident in the main Tour but it helped to promote good-feeling
between the Republic and the Empire.   He was officially received
at Rouse's Point, N.Y., on Nov. 10th by Mr. Secretary Lansing of
the U.S. Government, accompanied by Maj.-Gen. Biddle and Rear-
Admiral Niblack; 12 pretty girls held aloft a Canopy formed of
two great British and American flags sewn together.   With the
Royal suite were R. J. Chamberlain, Special Canadian Commissioner of Police, and several Police Inspectors.   From the border
the route was straight to Washington which was reached on the
11th.   In the absence of President Wilson, through illness, all
functions were somewhat curtailed but the Royal visitor was met
at the station by Vice-President T. R. Marshall, General Pershing
and other officials, together with Viscount Grey, the British Ambassador, and driven to the home of Mrs. Belmont, which had been
reserved for his use; despite the rain, large crowds were in the
streets.

   Formal calls followed on President Wilson and Mr. Secretary
Lansing; on the 11th His Royal Highness visited and informally
addressed the National Press Club and attended a banquet given
by the Vice-President of the United States.   In his address at
this latter function Mr. Marshall said: "I cannot forget that, while
we hesitated, while we doubted, while we wondered, England put
her back to the wall and stood upon the far-flung battle-line of
Europe, making freedom and Christian civilization possible even

for the American republic. I shall not say that it was altogether altruistic. There may have been some segment of self-defence in it. But may God give us all, when the time of self-defence comes, the same high altruistic ideals as those of the British Empire.'' In his reply the Prince referred to the President's illness and the recent death of Mr. Roosevelt and added:

As you know, I have recently been travelling in Canada, and I am the richer since that three months' journey by a wonderful experience. I come here, therefore, not only as an Englishman and as a representative of the British Empire but as, also, a Canadian who is as intimately and personally concerned as you yourselves in the life of this North American continent. The British Empire is held together by the common aims and the united sentiment of five sister nations, all of which are devoted to the same cause of democratic self-government. But Canada shares with the United States the splendid territories of this rich continent.

She is divided from you by no physical barrier, no military line, no frontier other than a boundary guaranteed by international law and good will. North of that frontier we cherish our British institutions, our British form of freedom, our British allegiance to the King. South of it you cherish equally the institutions into which the American citizen is born. The forms are different, but the human aim of both systems of government is the same.

To the Press Club he issued, at their request, a brief Message for the newspapers to deliver to the people. After referring to personal meetings with American troops in France and Germany and the services of American naval forces on the sea the Prince went on: ''Now that I am really here in the United States I feel that my anticipations will be completely fulfilled. Your institutions, your ways of life, your aims, are as democratic as ours, and the atmosphere in which I find myself is the same invigorating and familiar atmosphere which I have always noticed in my American friends.'' During the three following days of his visit in Washington the Prince visited 2,000 wounded soldiers in the Walter Reed Hospital, inspected the National Red Cross Headquarters and work, visited the new Lincoln Memorial, attended an official reception at the Congressional Library where members of the Cabinet, Congress and Diplomatic Corps were presented, conferred British decorations on nearly 100 American officers and men, took tea with President and Mrs. Wilson (13th Nov.) and had a chat with the invalid ruler, motored to Mount Vernon and laid a wreath on Washington's Tomb, attended informal dances at the homes of Mr. and Mrs. Joseph Leiter and Mrs. Marshall Field, held a reception at the British Embassy and attended a dinner-dance there and paid a visit to the Annapolis Naval Academy before leaving on the night of the 14th for a few days' rest at Hot Sulphur Springs, Va.—calling on his way upon Cardinal Gibbons at Philadelphia.

During his visit at the Capital the Prince was supposed to have shaken hands with 10,000 people, his popularity grew each day though there was a tendency on the part of his hosts to keep him away from the crowds through non-public announcement of engagements; outside the Belmont mansion the crowds were continuous during almost the whole visit. In fair Virginia the Prince had a very pleasant time; it was a strictly "incognito" visit though, needless to say it was not observed so far as the exhibition of public interest in the Royal visitor was concerned; he danced and golfed, had special swimming lessons and walked and rested from the tremendous nerve calls of the last few months. One of the many small functions he attended was a tea dance given by Mrs. H. H. Rogers, Jr., of Washington and New York.

Then came five strenuous days in New York—from Nov. 18 to the 23rd; with the *Renown*, which had reached New York harbour, as his home during the visit. He arrived at Jersey City from Washington at 11 in the morning and was received by Rodman Wanamaker and a special Reception Committee; from the Battery up Broadway to the City Hall there were great crowds, fairly elaborate decorations and considerable cheering—the Prince standing in his car and saluting. At the City Hall Mayor J. F. Hylan presented an Address dealing chiefly with the United States' share in the War, recognized His Royal Highness as "the distinguished representative of a people who, allied with other powers, fought in deadly struggle to vindicate the liberties of mankind" and referred to the "mighty powers" put forth by the United States; he then conferred the freedom of the City upon the Prince. In his reply the latter expressed pleasure at following the gallant King of the Belgians in receipt of this honour and added these tactful words: "I already have the privilege of being a freeman of the City of London, and so it is a special privilege and pleasure for me to-day to become a freeman of the City of New York, because London and New York, both great business centres, both of them great seaports, are so closely connected in the financial business of the world. Upon the stability and upon the prosperity of those two great cities depends, to an extraordinary degree, the welfare of all continents."

A passage through crowded streets followed to Grant's Tomb where the Prince deposited a wreath; later he returned to the *Renown* for luncheon and entertained the Mayor of New York, Mr. Wanamaker, Archbishop Hayes, and other notables of the City; afterwards he received a delegation of the Inter-Racial Council, reviewed a troop of Boy Scouts and was, also, presented with a Bible by Bishop Charles S. Burch on behalf of the New York Bible Society—with a long introductory speech; he accepted a commemorative medal from the New York Numismatic Society; in the evening he dined with Mr. and Mrs. Henry P. Davidson and officials of the American Red Cross at the Waldorf-Astoria Hotel with, afterwards, attendance at a Gala Concert in the Metropolitan Opera House. During the day the Prince issued a Message to the New York newspapers expressing appreciation of the cordial reception given him by his new "fellow citizens." The following day saw a review of the British War Veterans of America, visits to Trinity Church, the historic edifice of Washington's day, the Woolworth Bulding, from which he saw a wonderful view of the city and harbour, the Produce and Stock Exchanges where the roar of speculation was seen and appreciated, and the Sub-Treasury of the United States.

A Luncheon of the N.Y. Chamber of Commerce followed with A. E. Marling, President, in the chair, and an address from him of most friendly international character concluding with the hope that "our two countries may be united in a bond which naught shall ever sunder." Again, in his reply, the Prince touched a vital point: "The Great War has revealed many things to us, but it has revealed nothing more clearly than the closeness with which the welfare of our two great nations is interlocked. Your prosperity is essential to ours, and ours to yours." Lord Grey of Falloden, who was with His Royal Highness, as British Ambassador, spoke briefly. In the afternoon the Fox Academy of Music entertained the Royal guest as it had another Prince 60 years before; afterwards he attended the Horse Show at Madison Gardens, visited the New York Public Library and the Metropolitan Museum of Art; in the evening he was the guest of a New York Societies' dinner followed by a Ball at the home of Mrs. Whitelaw Reid whose husband had been a popular United States Ambassador in London.

The Dinner embodied the tribute of 8 British or semi-British organizations and was held at the Waldorf with speeches by William Howard Taft, President J. Grier Hibben of Princeton, Alton B. Parker and President J. H. Finley of New York University. Mr. Taft declared that the time would come when the people of the British Empire and of the United States would be found marching side by side in the cause and triumph of world peace. The Prince's speech was a pleasant one and avoided serious topics; he did, however, express the hope that he would be in the United States again before long. He visited West Point Military Academy on the following day and was given a great reception by the Cadets and was back in time to give a dinner on his battleship which included Brig.-Gen. and Mrs. Cornelius Vanderbilt, Mr. and Mrs. Otto H. Kahn, Mrs. H. H. Rogers, Jr., Mr. and Mrs. Joseph Leiter, Mr. and Mrs. Felix Doubleday, Mr. and Mrs. W. K. Vanderbilt, Jr., and half a dozen daughters of these well-known people including Miss Millicent Rogers whom he had met at Washington and in Virginia. Afterwards he had a box at the Ziegfeld Follies where some of his guests joined him.

On the following morning (21st Nov.) the Prince visited Oyster Bay and deposited a wreath upon the grave of Theodore Roosevelt and afterwards lunched at Piping Rock Country Club where 700 members gave him warm greetings; in the afternoon he gave a Luncheon on the *Renown* to 1,000 New York School children—the selection being made by picking honour-graduating pupils from each of the 24 high schools. It was a charming function with little speeches of intense feeling from a representative of the girls and one for the boys; the Prince spoke informally and happily and said in conclusion that "the *Renown* is a large ship, but she is not half large enough to hold all the thousands more of you that I should have liked to have asked on board." In the evening he dined with the Pilgrim's Society of international fame at the Plaza and visited the Hippodrome and then attended a Reception at the 7th Regiment Armoury given by Rodman Wanamaker. The Pilgrim's dinner was a great function with a thousand guests and Chauncey M. Depew in the chair who said, in his address, that none of their recent distinguished visitors had appealed to Americans as had the Prince of Wales: "He has grasped and tactfully interpreted our American ways and habits of looking at things. He has won our hearts. He carries home our appreciation, our affection, and a lasting memory."

In his reply the Prince referred to the peaceful relations of Canada and the United States and added: "I have asked myself how that ideal has been attained here, so much in advance of international conditions in other parts of the world, and I think the answer is quite clear. It has been attained because you on your side of the international boundary and we Britishers on ours have, under somewhat different forms, the same political faith, the same human aims, and the same practical ideals." On Saturday, the 22nd, an Investiture was held with much ceremony on the *Renown* and a number of American generals, officers and men, were given decorations in the name of the King—from the insignia of a Knight in the Order of St. Michael and St. George, given to Maj.-Gen. G. W. Goethals, to the D.C.M. pinned on the breasts of gallant soldiers in the ranks, or the Royal Red Cross given to devoted nurses. A final incident was the review of 5,000 Boy Scouts and Girl Guides.

Then, at 4.45 in the afternoon, came the city's farewell with salutes from passing river craft, cheers from the crowds who lined the Battery piers, and a continuous bedlam of automobile horns as strings of cars moved along Riverside abreast of the *Renown,* and the booming of guns from the Wadsworth and Hamilton forts. There was issued to the press a Message of farewell in which the Prince said with natural simplicity: "I refuse entirely to say good-bye, whether you like it or not, I am going to pay the United States another visit as soon as I can, because I like it so much and because I wish to see more of the country and its people, including the great West." The press comments upon the visit were all kindly and some enthusiastic; popular comment said that he was welcomed as warmly as was General Pershing on his return from the War; the New York *Times* of the 23rd emphasized in him "the great gift of personality." It declared that: "For women he has the grace, the dignity, and the charm of the Princes of legend and romance; for men he has the qualities of good sportsmanship and good fellowship."

Arrival at Halifax; Farewell to Canada.   On Nov. 24 the Prince in his great battleship was once more off the Citadel and City of Halifax; after luncheon he landed informally, played a game of his favourite "Squash" at Artillery Park, and late in the afternoon attended a *dansant* given by Mrs. Charles Archibald. A farewell dinner was given by the Dominion Government in the evening at the Halifax Club with the Prime Minister, Sir Robert Borden, in the chair and H.E. the Duke of Devonshire and a notable gathering present. The Premier proposed the Royal toast with emphasis upon the .value of constant personal inter-course between the Sovereign and his people in Canada; the Prince in a farewell which he described as *au revoir* used words of which the chief thought was as follows:

This, my first visit to Canada, has done two things for me which will influence the whole of my life. In the first place, Canada has given me such wonderful welcomes throughout my travels all the way across the Dominion from Halifax to Vancouver and back, she has shown me such kindness and hospitality, she has, in fact so thoroughly spoilt me that I have been feeling more and more at home all the time. The result is that I am not only intensely Canadian now, but that I shall feel a Canadian all the rest of my life, and I shall never be happy if too many months elapse without a visit to my home on this side of the Atlantic.

The other thing which this first visit has done for me is to give me a thorough understanding of all that Canada stands for on the North American Continent. I realized that pretty fully before I left Ottawa a fortnight ago, but I realize it even more fully now since my visit to the United States. You are the guardians of British institutions upon this continent, and your development as a Nation of increasing power and influence will be one of the most important factors in determining relations between the British Empire and the United States.

A brilliant Ball followed at Government House with 500 guests present and in the morning the ever-active, never-wearied Prince landed at 10.30, inspected his Military and Naval guards of honour, laid the corner-stone of a Tower and Town Clock at the Citadel with due ceremony; visited, officially, the Convent of the Sacred Heart and the School for the Blind, received an enthusiastic wel-come from the students of Dalhousie College and visited the Chil-dren's Hospital where he shook all the little patients by the hand; inspected the Halifax Ladies' College and watched a drill by the girls; gave a luncheon on board the *Renown* to 30 representative guests and, at 3 o'clock on Nov. 25th, on board his great grey cruiser, he was steaming for the Atlantic amidst volleys of cheers from the shores, the roar of cannon, and the whistles of shipping in the Harbour. Messages of farewell and thanks were issued to the Governor-General and to the Lieutenant-Governor of Nova Scotia; to his "comrades-in-arms," the men and women of Canada who served in the Great War; to the Boy Scouts and Girl Guides of Canada.

To H.M. the King Sir Robert Borden sent a cable conveying his warm congratulations upon the remarkable success of the Royal Tour and the wonderful impression made by the Prince upon the people: "The visit has had a distinctly steadying effect, and must serve to strengthen the ties which unite Canada to the rest of the Empire." To it His Majesty replied that the Queen and himself were greatly pleased at these generous words about the Prince: "We are proud that it is to his personality that you so largely attribute the success that has crowned his efforts. I

earnestly believe that this renewed association between my Family
and the people of Canada will strengthen that unity of Empire
upon which, please God, a great and glorious future may be assured. George R. I." His Royal Highness arrived at Portsmouth
on Dec. 1st and was welcomed home with brief ceremony; shortly
afterwards he was received at the London station by the King
and Queen, and leaders of British life and thought, after what
the press described as a 15,000-mile tour. At a great Mansion
House luncheon on Dec. 18 the Prince delivered an important
speech reviewing his experiences and repeating the ideals of Empire
expressed in his Toronto and Ottawa speeches— with additions
necessary for the information of the Mother-land—and urging
a domestic policy throughout Empire countries of ensuring happier
conditions of life to men and women and children:

Our Empire implies a partnership of free nations, nations living under
the same system of law, pursuing the same democratic aims, and actuated
by the same human ideals. The British Empire is thus something far grander
than an Empire in the old sense of the term, and its younger nations—
Canada, Australia, New Zealand, South Africa, and India—are now universally recognized as nations by the fact that they are signatories to the
Peace Treaties which they fought so magnificently to secure.

The people in the Old Country must realize that the patriotism of the
Dominions is national patriotism and not mere loyalty to Great Britain.
It is loyalty to their British institutions, it is loyalty to the world-wide
British system of life and government; and it is, above all, loyalty to the
British Empire, of which Great Britain, like the Dominions, is only one part.
I have also learned that the loyalty of the Dominions is, in a very special
sense, loyalty to the Crown—and the Crown represents the unity of the
Empire. The King, as constitutional Sovereign of the Empire, occupies
exactly the same place in Canada and in the whole British Empire as he
does in Great Britain, and his House, although originally founded in Great
Britain, belongs equally to all the other nations of the Commonwealth.

AGRICULTURE: THE ORGANIZED FARMERS

Agricultural Conditions: Wheat and Dairying, Prices and The Farmer. The estimated capital invested in Canadian agriculture was, in 1918, as follows: $2,792,229,000 in Improved lands, $927,548,000 in Buildings, $387,079,000 in Implements and $1,102,261,000 in Live-Stock or a total of $5,209,117,000; the average increase in the value of farm lands, including farm buildings, was 36·8 per cent. in the five years of 1914-19 or from $38.00 per acre in 1914 to $40.00 in 1915, $41.00 in 1916, $44.00 in 1917, $46.00 in 1918, to $52.00 in 1919. The values of Canadian Field crops were $638,580,300 in the year the War commenced, 1914, and after that they steadily increased in totals as follows: $825,370,600 in 1915, $886,494,900 in 1916, $1,144,636,450 in 1917, $1,367,909,970 in 1918 and $1,452,787,900 in 1919. The average values received by farmers per bushel—according to the Dominion Bureau of Statistics—for their five chief products in 1913 and 1919, respectively, were as follows: Wheat 67 cents and $1.90, Oats 32 cents and 78 cents, Barley 42 cents and $1.15, Potatoes 49 cents and 95 cents, Hay and clover $11.48 per ton and $20.68. The lesser grains, etc., increased in greater proportion: Peas $1.11 to $2.00, Flax 97 cents to $3.75, Buckwheat 64 cents to $1.50. The values of the chief crops in 1914-19 were, in detail, as follows:

Crop	1914	1915	1916	1917	1918	1919
Wheat:	$196,418,000	$312,569,400	$344,096,400	$453,038,600	$381,677,700	$373,086,000
Oats:	151,811,000	176,894,700	210,957,500	277,065,300	331,357,400	320,686,000
Barley:	31,557,000	26,704,700	35,024,000	59,654,400	77,878,670	67,086,000
Rye:	1,679,300	1,899,900	3,196,000	6,267,200	12,728,600	14,804,000
Peas:	4,895,000	5,730,700	4,919,000	10,724,100	7,873,100	7,466,000
Beans:	1,844,300	2,206,800	2,228,000	9,493,400	19,283,900	7,242,000
Buckwheat:	6,213,000	5,913,000	6,375,000	10,443,400	18,018,100	16,967,000
Mixed Grains:	10,759,400	10,034,700	9,300,900	18,801,750	18,951,000	39,779,000
Flax:	7,368,000	15,965,000	16,889,900	15,737,000	40,726,500	25,376,000
Corn for husking:	9,808,000	10,243,000	6,747,000	14,307,200	24,902,800	15,864,000
Potatoes:	41,598,000	35,964,000	50,982,300	80,804,400	102,235,300	124,707,200
Turnips, Mangolds, etc.:	18,934,000	16,560,000	14,329,000	29,258,000	52,252,000	52,365,900
Hay and Clover:	145,999,000	155,807,000	168,547,900	141,376,700	241,277,300	341,869,200
Fodder corn:	15,949,700	16,999,100	9,396,000	13,884,900	29,489,100	32,140,500
Sugar Beets:	651,000	775,500	440,000	793,800	1,845,000	2,191,700
Alfalfa:	3,095,600	3,402,000	3,066,000	3,041,300	7,968,500	11,677,400

The question of prices received by the farmer for his crops was much discussed during these years but the public had little actual

information to go upon; what the Farmers' organizations knew
they did not make public in any greater detail than did the
Manufacturers. The average for wheat, according to Dominion
Government statistics, year by year was as follows: 1914, $1.22 per
bushel; 1915, 83 cents per bushel; 1916, $1.31 per bushel; 1917,
$1.94 per bushel; 1918, $2.02 per bushel; 1919, $1.90 per bushel.
Yet in 1917 the price guaranteed by Government for the highest
grade was $2.21 a bushel, in 1918 $2.24, in 1919, $2.15, which
eventually became $2.30.   As to the export price, according to
the table of yearly totals quoted below, from the Government
trade returns, the figures varied from about $1.00 in 1915 to
$1.10 in 1916, $1.29 in 1917, $2.40 in 1918 and $2.30 in 1919.
The average export price in the United States in 1918 was $2.00
and in 1919 $2.40. Flour exports also increased in price from an
average of $6.00 in 1915 and 1916 to $6.75 in 1917 and $10.00
in 1918 and 1919.   The actual Export totals from Canada were
as follows:

Year Mch. 31	Wheat Bushels	Wheat Value	Flour Barrels	Flour Value
1915	73,918,885	$74,298,548	4,952,837	$24,610,946
1916	157,745,469	172,896,445	6,400,214	35,767,094
1917	189,643,846	244,394,586	7,425,728	47,478,474
1918	150,392,087	366,341,565	9,981,148	95,896,492
1919	41,808,897	96,985,056	9,196,489	99,981,659

This export trade for the five years ending Mch. 31, 1919,
totalled 613,503,634 bushels of wheat and realized a price of $955,-
411,200; the average rate, therefore, was only $1.55 per bushel;
the average rate for the flour exported was $8.00 per barrel. For
years of heavy warfare, great transport difficulties, insistent demand, this was far from being an excessive figure—though it is
equally clear that the large profits came in the last two or three
years.

Meanwhile, during this period, the values of Live-stock had
also steadily increased from a total of $725,530,191 for Horses,
Cattle, Sheep and Swine in 1914 to $1,296,602,000 in 1919; to
this increase Horses contributed $63,000,000, Cattle $411,600,000,
Sheep $35,000,000 and Swine $59,700,000. The apparent increase,
therefore, in values of Field Crops in 1919 over 1914 was 814 millions or 127 per cent., and of Live-stock 571 millions or 79 per
cent.; that of Farm-lands under cultivation, taken at the average
increase per acre of 36 per cent. estimated by the Government,
would be over $1,000,000,000; a total increase in values of $2,385,-
000,000, in five years, for about 1,000,000 farmers or an average
distribution of $3,575 amongst the 667,000 farms of Canada.   It
will be seen that the Field Crops of Canada averaged $2,100 in
1919 to each farm in the country with an average value in Live-
stock of nearly $2,000.

Other incidents of Agricultural condition included a production of Creamery butter in 1918—the latest official figures—of
93,266,876 pounds valued at $41,845,164 compared with 69,730,899
pounds valued at $20,332,399 in 1915; a production in 1918 of

174,881,957 pounds of Factory cheese valued at $39,457,358 compared with 139,897,519 pounds in 1915 valued at $20,649,354; a production in 1918 of $5,740,898 worth of Condensed milk, of $4,048,055 worth of Evaporated milk, of $1,388,248 worth of milk powder, of $395,529 worth of whey butter and casein; a total for all Dairy products in 1918 of $92,875,252. There was a wheat product of 1919 remaining in farmers' hands (Mch. 31, 1920) of 34,837,000 bushels or 18 per cent. of the entire crop with 35,989,-000 bushels in Elevators and flour mills and 6,498,000 bushels in transit—a total of 77,324,000 bushels compared with 118,543,000 bushels in 1919; Exports of food products in the year of Mch. 31, 1919, totalled $358,746,756 compared with $196,909,312 in 1914—though the actual export of wheat and flour, in quantities, decreased from 289,794,162 bushels in 1915-16 to 155,235,260 bushels in 1917-18 and an estimated 90,000,000 bushels in 1918-19; the claim was made by H. Higginbotham, Secretary of the United Farmers of Alberta, that 125,576 farmers enlisted in the Overseas forces during the War— 70,155 volunteers and 55,421 draftees.

The Canadian Farmer as a Class.   The official figures given above would seem to indicate great agricultural prosperity in Canada but, as against the statistics, there were substantial drawbacks.   The lure of the City continued to draw young men from the farms as it did from the towns and villages—though the situation never became as bad as in Australia where out of less than 5,000,000 people 1½ million were to be found in two of its cities; the bright lights and perhaps brighter lives and certainly higher wages appeared to attract the rural youth like a magnet; farm labourers grew more and more difficult to obtain as industrial and war wages grew greater; those who were available demanded the highest wages while the farmer shared in the payment of high prices for clothing, boots and shoes, harness, waggons, implements; as his income grew the farmer wanted the same privileges and luxuries, or whatever they might be called, as the city man with better furniture, and pianos, organs, gramaphones, and the telephone; while motor-cars and motor trucks became part of the life of thousands of farm homes.

As to farm help the official figures of average wages showed that in 1914 male workers received, in the summer season and including board, $36.00 per month and in 1919 $78.00 per month while females obtained $19.00 and $43.00 respectively; the rate per annum (including board) grew from $323.00 for males and $189.00 for females in 1914 to $764.00 and $465.00 respectively in 1919; at the same time the average value of the board per month grew from $14.00 for males and $11.00 for females to $24.00 and $19.00 respectively. As a matter of fact, in the harvest season when labour was vital—especially in the West—wages went up to $4.00 and sometimes as high as $6.00 a day; all official figures in these pages may be taken as a minimum. It was claimed that farm values did not constitute realizable profits and that few Ontario farmers, for instance, made more than $1,000 a year over their expenses while many others were losing money; that there was as great variability amongst farms and farmers and their incomes as amongst city business men and that, as an illustration, a survey of Dundas County dairy farms showed the following averages of net income—from which clothing, fuel, groceries and lighting would have to be deducted: On farms of 21 to 45 acres, $399; on farms of 46 to 60 acres, $555; on farms of 61 to 75 acres, $853; on farms of 76 to 90 acres, $983; on farms of 91 to 110 acres, $1,080; on farms of 111 to 135 acres, $1,061; on farms of 136 to 160 acres, $1,460; and on farms of over 160 acres, $1,738.

As in all occupations, everywhere, much of course depended on individual efficiency and the average cost of producing milk —as an example—on these farms ran from $1.27 to $3.72 per 100 pounds with the difference turning on the quantity of milk given by the cows. There were at this time innumerable estimates and guesses as to the profits of farmers and manufacturers respectively; two such reputable journals as the Montreal *Gazette* and the Montreal *Witness* fought it out on the basis of 80 per cent. increase in the prices of farm products and 170 per cent. in those of industrial products. By the former it was claimed* that from April, 1914, to March, 1919, the price of 15 farm commodities, consisting of grains and fodders, increased 87 per cent.; 17 animal agricultural commodities increased 77 per cent.; and 9 dairy commodities increased 78 per cent.; on the other hand it was alleged that 221 other commodities, which the farmer had to buy, increased 170 per cent. In this connection the *Grain Growers Guide* of May 14 gave the following summary of prices payable by the farmer in the West for agricultural implements in 1914 and 1919:

	Prices 1914	Prices 1919
Binder	$ 165.00	$ 260.00
Mower	60.00	82.65
Rake	36.00	54.45
Gang Plow	93.25	130.00
Sulky	50.00	80.00
Walking Plow	18.50	27.50
Set Lever Harrows	34.40	50.60
Set Wooden Drag Harrows	24.75	30.00
Cart	28.50	40.00
Seed Drill	137.00	206.85
Float (home-made)	6.00	10.00
Waggon	95.00	150.00
Set Sleighs	41.00	47.00
Jumper	29.50	30.60
Buggy	110.00	138.00
Tools	5.00	10.00
Fanning Mill (32-inch)	35.50	45.50
Cultivator	72.00	100.00
Hay Rack	9.00	16.50
Total	$1,050.40	$1,508.55

*Note.—Estimates of the Labour Department, Ottawa.

It was contended, also, that if the farmers were making such great profits as were stated there would be a rush from the city to the country instead of the other way; this statement, however, probably overlooked the attractions of city life—exaggerated as they were to the far-away view. An extreme agricultural viewpoint may be quoted in the following illustration taken from the prosaic life of the hog and editorially described in the *Farmers' Sun* of Toronto (Oct. 1, 1919): "Those hogs that for several months were fed expensive feed and cared for by expensive labour and shipped by expensive freight, sold at expensive commission by the farmer for about 18 cents a pound. When next the hogs were seen they were labelled bacon (first-class) 70 cents; bacon (Wiltshire) 55 cents; hams, 55 cents; loins of pork, 44 cents; legs of pork, 45 cents; now, who is most to blame: the farmer who bred, nursed, fed, doctored, shipped, risked and sold the hog, or those who added from 26 cents to 52 cents a pound to the price?" There was no doubt in 1919 as to the increased cost of feed for animals, of labour for the farm, of fertilizers for the crops, of material and equipment for buildings, of machinery for cultivation purposes just as there was no doubt of the increased price of farm products. There, was, also, no doubt of the enormous markets and demand awaiting Canadian agricultural products—in 1918, for instance, Canada's export of beef was only 2¼ per cent. of British requirements; pork products only 8½, butter 1½, condensed milk 6¼, eggs, 1¼. Wheat was exported to the extent of 42¼ per cent. of what was needed by Great Britain, barley, 14%, oats 38%, and rye 4 per cent. The export of cheese, amounted to 67 per cent. of Great Britain's needs.

Meanwhile, agricultural conditions in other directions were varied during 1919. The War as well as the attractions of city life had drawn on farm labour; extended individual farming on a large scale was developing and George Lane of Alberta or Seager Wheeler of Saskatchewan or R. W. E. Burnaby of Ontario were no longer isolated agriculturalists on a big scale; farmers were spending more, and very largely, on power machinery and other aids to production with a proportion on living betterments; the idea of class or farm organization had grown with great strides while agricultural co-operation for selling products and buying supplies developed in every part of Canada; farmers had been quick in their appreciation and use of the automobile and at the beginning of 1919 Saskatchewan, which was essentially an agricultural Province, had one for every 14 persons, or the largest proportion in Canada; soldier settlement on farms was growing greatly with total Government loans of $53,000,000 called for; Specialties in crop were being successfully developed as in flax, tobacco and sugar-beets.

The farmers, of course, like every other class in the community, came under criticism during the year and, as they acquired influence in politics and government, were bound to face still more of it. In the Commons on June 24 H. H. Stevens of Vancouver attacked the management of the Elevator Companies at the head of Lake Superior on the subject of overages as to which he charged that, in 8 years, more than $10,000,000 worth of grain had been "illegally appropriated by the public Elevators" and in this he included the Grain Growers' Grain Company for an amount estimated at over $500,000 which, he said, brought their estimated earnings in 1916-17 up to 187 per cent. for the year. In reply Hon. T. A. Crerar pointed out that these overages and all the operations of the Elevators were under control of, and strict supervision by, the Board of Grain Commissioners; moreover, the Elevator warehouseman or Company had to make good every bushel of shortage in his Elevator and he should have the right to participate in any surplus which might develop; Mr. Crerar, on the 26th, gave a detailed statement of the Grain Growers' Elevator profits, including overages, as follows: 1912-13, 15·01 per cent.; 1913-14, 14·50 per cent.; 1914-15, 11·46 per cent.; 1915-16, 30·01 per cent.; and 1916-17. 23·25 per cent.; Mr. Stevens re-affirmed his figures in detail and claimed that the difference between them arose because Mr. Crerar based his profits upon the usual $100,000 allowance for investment in an Elevator and that this particular one was leased. The Acting Minister (Hon. A. K. Maclean) in his speech did not condemn overages; he described them as a growth and custom under which a part of charges were paid in kind and which would change in time to a cash system.

Others attacked the farmers for an alleged failure to pay their share of the Income Tax and Sir Herbert Ames in the Commons on June 19 stated that the farmers and their families were 54 per cent. of the population and that out of the 31,130 Income Tax payers of 1918 there were only 3,623 farmers or 14 per cent. of the number and that they paid 3½ per cent. of the total. F. R. Lalor replied to this charge as follows: "Although not a farmer, I represent a farming community. The farmers are prosperous—we will admit that they have done well during the War; prices are good. But I have thought it over carefully, and I do not know five farmers in the County of Haliburton who have an income of $5,000. It is all right to look over the list of Income Tax payers and say that not enough farmers are paying the Tax, but it must be acknowledged that farmers with incomes of $5,000 to $10,000 are scarce in Canada. A farmer thinks he is doing well in the Province of Ontario if he is making $1,000 a year over and above his living expenses." Much was said about the farmer and his motor-car and not very much about the practical necessity of an automobile to an up-to-date business farmer. But, in any case, the proportion of owners outside of Saskatchewan, where wide spaces made it an essential, was not as large as represented. The Ottawa *Farm Journal* made enquiries in the rich Ottawa Valley and found that out of 1,000 farmers 63 per cent. answered and that of these only 24 per cent. had automobiles—it is, also, interesting to note that only 41 per cent. had organs or pianos.

The Government and the Canadian Farmer.   The Report of the Minister of Agriculture for Mch. 31, 1919, with Hon. T. A. Crerar still in charge of the Department, dealt largely with war work and the policy of the Dairy Produce Commission of 1918; with dairy conditions, Experimental Fruit stations, cold storage requirements; with the Seed Commissioners' branch and its work of Seed production, markets intelligence, Seed testing, inspection and purchase, the holding of 400 Field-crop competitions and 153 local Seed Fairs, during the year; with the Live-stock branch which dealt in Horse-breeding, pure-bred cattle and sheep, the co-operative marketing of wool, the Poultry Division and promotion of stock and egg raising and marketing; with the Dominion Experimental Farms, the issue of 18 Bulletins or special pamphlets and the carrying on of important work, experiments and discoveries in the Chemical Division—as to fertilizers, economical production, analysis of samples, meat inspection, etc.; with the work of the Field and Animal Husbandry, Horticultural, Cereal, Botany, Forage plants, Bee, Tobacco, Entomological and other Divisions; with the Health of Animals branch dealing with hog cholera, mange, sheep scab, anthrax, tuberculosis, meat and canned goods, and other subjects vital to the farmer.   The allotment of the year under the Agricultural Inspection Act was $1,100,000 and this was allocated to the different Provinces as follows: Agricultural Colleges and schools $291,702, Instruction and Demonstration $597,712, Women's Work $31,510, Elementary Agricultural Instruction $154,076 and Veterinary Colleges $25,000.

The Board of Grain Supervisors continued during 1919 to exercise important functions with authority granted by Order-in-Council of June 11, 1917, which gave it full powers of enquiry and investigation as to grain supplies and conditions; the right from time to time to fix the price at which grain stored in any Elevator could be purchased and the conditions as to price, destination or otherwise under which grain might be removed from such Elevator; authority to prescribe what grain should be sold to millers or milling firms in Canada or elsewhere and what should be sent to the United Kingdom and the Allied Powers.   Its members included Robert Magill, Winnipeg, (Chairman); H. W. Wood, Carstairs, Alberta; S. K. Rathwell, Moose Jaw, Sask.; J. C. Gage, W. A. Matheson, W. R. Bawlf and James Stewart of Winnipeg; Lionel H. Clarke, Toronto; W. L. Best, Ottawa; Joseph Ainey, Montreal; F. W. Riddell, Regina; J. P. Jones, Fort William.   This body did an important work in regulating and adjusting and helping the sale of Agricultural products—especially wheat.   Its work was supplemented in Europe by the appointment of Dr. J. W. Robertson, C.M.G., to represent Canada on the Food Section of the Supreme Economic Council at Paris and by the appointment (late in 1918) of H. W. Wood, Alberta, to represent the Grain Producers of Canada, and W. A. Dryden, Brooklin, Ont., the Live-stock interests; Dr. Robert Magill, the grain distributing interests; James Fisher, Winnipeg and N. P. Lambert of the

Council of Agriculture; on the Canadian Trade Mission to London. Later on the Board was partly superceded by the Canadian Wheat Board.

In a Report submitted during August, Dr. Robertson—who was, also, Canadian Director of Food Supplies in Europe—described negotiations as to promoting trade in bacon and frozen beef with the United Kingdom and, in the latter product, with Italy and Belgium; arrangements for the sale of stockers to help in restoring the dairy herds of France and Belgium and representations as to the British removal of restrictions on the importation of Canadian Live-stock—the latter effort failing because of an indirect policy of protection for the British farmer as to which Canadians could hardly complain; plans for an agricultural export policy to aid the restoration of Roumania, Greece and Poland. The Imperial Government had some good reasons for its Cattle embargo apart from the natural wishes of its farmers. There were, undoubtedly, varied dangers from contagion in the United States operative through Canada's 3,000 miles of unprotected frontier; it had, also, an established policy as against the live-cattle of all countries and Canada could show no particular reason why it should be an exception. The almost priceless British herds of pedigree live-stock which served not only to preserve and enrich British stock but acted as the fountain head of pure-bred stock throughout the Empire had suffered once, in 1865-66, from a cattle plague when the total deaths exceeded 118,000; in other years losses from imported foot and mouth disease were estimated, in 1873, to total $55,000,000. The result had been the exclusion legislation of 1873 which no British Government afterwards cared to touch—aside from the obvious fact that the British farmer benefitted in pocket from the exclusion of competitive live cattle. A statement was current in 1919 that, in the 1917 War Conference or Cabinet, Sir Robert Borden had been given a pledge that the Embargo would be removed; as a matter of fact, neither the Canadian Premier nor any of his colleagues made this assertion and no proof was ever offered as to the contention; the statement did not appear in the published reports of either Conference or Cabinet.

Early in 1919 the question of marketing the 1919 wheat crop commanded the close attention of the Government and the farming community in particular; it was not yet known whether the Allied Powers would purchase their wheat supplies under controlled conditions, as in the later war years, or whether normal trade conditions would develop. Then followed a curious complication—Dr. Magill declared that the Canadian market had been declared open; Lloyd Harris, Chairman of the War Trade Commission in London, claimed that Canadian wheat should be sold to England and neutral countries only; the Government authorized the Commission to sell 50 or 75 million bushels along this line. Involved in this was the vital question of price as well as the respective selling methods by Government, Commission, or private competitive action. The United States Government had fixed the minimum price for the American crop at $2.15 per bushel and then increased it to $2.26 and arranged for its marketing under Government direction; the Canadian Government, for various reasons, could not see its way to do this and a wide discussion took place during these months in agricultural circles; further complications followed upon the closing of the United States ports and railways to the transport of Canadian grain because of the limited tonnage at command of American shippers—a policy which, of course, caused much agricultural inconvenience while working to the ultimate good of Canadian ports and steamship and railway interests.

The retirement of Hon. T. A. Crerar on June 4 for reasons of a fiscal and general nature, made the appointment of a new Minister of Agriculture necessary; for a couple of months Hon. J. A. Calder was Acting Minister and on Aug. 2 Dr. Simon Fraser Tolmie, of Victoria, was appointed to the post.   Dr. Tolmie operated a farm on Vancouver Island with special attention to live-stock and was a veterinary surgeon by profession and a member of the Commons since 1917.   He was described by the Victoria *Colonist* as "safe, sane and practical to a high degree;" he was sworn in on the 12th and returned to Victoria for his bye-election; the vote cast on Oct. 27 was 7,105 for the new Minister and 5,026 for T. A. Barnard— a Labour and Soldier candidate. The latter was in favour of the Recall system and his resignation (if elected) was held by the Federated Labour Party—a product of British Columbia O.B.U. propaganda—and he, himself, was a confirmed Pacifist, though he had Major R. J. Burde, M.C., as one of his active aides as well as the Vancouver Socialist, Dr. W. J. Currie.   Dr. Tolmie promised immediate construction of the Esquimalt Dry-dock and his Agricultural views were afterwards presented in the *Agricultural Gazette* for November:

Not only must we bring about a better Inter-Provincial relationship in commerce and continue our dealings with the neighbouring Republic, but we must also develop the overseas markets and especially establish trade with the Mother Country.   I believe that the time has arrived when the agricultural interests of Canada should have the very best man available located in London to look after our business and to see that our goods are placed on the market in the best possible shape.   It is the aim of the Government to locate for the farmer the best markets, keep him appraised of their state, and informed on all points pertinent to his business.   I favour the enlarging of our cold storage facilities for overseas shipping and believe that this will be a step in assisting us to compete with foreign countries. We cannot control export prices, but we seek to place our goods economically on foreign markets and thus increase our ultimate returns.

In July Sir George E. Foster, Minister of Trade and Commerce, called a Conference at Ottawa to discuss grain prices, finance and selling conditions and questions of transportation. For the past two war-years prices had been fixed in Canada as in the United States; the War was over, however, and under ordinary conditions the un-economic fixation should cease and normal laws of supply and demand be allowed to operate.   But the war disturbance of markets and prices and conditions continued and it was felt in many quarters that an open market would introduce fluctuations and speculations which would be dangerous; it was suggested as an alternative that the Canadian Government should establish a minimum price for the new season's wheat in order that the grower might be assured of a fair return, and a basis of selling be established. Any reasonable minimum might be exceeded in practice because the Canadian surplus would fall far short of European requirements and the American Government was bound to realize as nearly as possible the price paid its own farmers and its crop would chiefly determine foreign prices.

Financing the crop also had to be considered as a vital matter of Government concern. The amount required would be great—perhaps $300,000,000—and there was already a large national deficit. Hon. T. A. Crerar, President of the United Grain Growers, James Stewart of the Grain Commission, and H. T. Robson of the British Export Mission in New York, E.W. Beatty, President of the C.P.R., James Carruthers, Montreal, J. A. Maharg, M.P., of the Saskatchewan Grain Growers, C. B. Watt, of the Dominion Millers' Association, W. A. Black of the Ogilvie Milling Co., and Dr. J. W. Robertson, were amongst those at the Conference on July 28. After careful discussion and due deliberation by the Government, it was announced in the press of the 30th that a policy had been decided upon as follows:

(1) A Board to buy and market the crop of 1919 with a "probable" guaranteed minimum price of $1.75 per bushel—afterwards fixed at $2.15 with pooling additions.

(2) A cash payment on account to be made to the farmer at the time he sold his wheat.

(3) The wheat crop of Canada to be sold by the Board at the prevailing world prices, and the surplus proceeds, after expenses were deducted, to be distributed to the original sellers of the wheat in proportion to grade and quantity.

(4) No speculating on Exchanges, or profiteering by handlers, to be allowed in disposing of the wheat crop of 1919 to the disadvantage of either producer or consumer.

(5) A direct and immediate cash sale by the farmer, and a speedy movement of the crop along the usual channels of transport.

Action was at once taken to forbid trading in wheat futures on the Grain Exchanges; it was stated that the establishment of the new Board would not interfere with the work of the Board of Grain Supervisors in respect to that portion of the crop of 1918 delivered by August 15. The new Board, however, would have sole authority to deal with the crop of 1919, and with such portion of the 1918 crop as might be undelivered by Aug. 15. The Order-in-Council approving this decision was passed on July 31st and the Canadian Wheat Board constituted, with its *personnel* announced a week later, as follows: James Stewart, of Winnipeg (Chairman); W. A. Matheson, Winnipeg; H. W. Wood, Carstairs, Alta.; W. A. Black, Montreal; N. L. Patterson, Fort William; W. L. Best, Ottawa; F. O. Fowler, Winnipeg; C. B. Watts, Toronto; W. H. McWilliams, Winnipeg; Joseph Quintal, Montreal;

Col. J. Z. Fraser, Burford, and F. W. Riddell, Regina. The Board had the following powers:

1. To take delivery of wheat in Canada at any point and to pay, by way of advance, to the producers or other persons delivering wheat to the Board, such price per bushel as shall be approved by the Board and the Governor-in-Council and to provide for the issue of Participation certificates to persons entitled thereto.

2. To sell wheat so delivered to millers in Canada for milling purposes at such prices and subject to such conditions as the Board sees fit, the price of sale to millers being governed as nearly as may be by the price obtainable at the same time in the world's markets for wheat of equal value, regard being had to the cost of transport, handling and storage.

3. To store and transport such wheat with a view to the marketing of same.

4. To sell wheat so delivered in excess of domestic requirements to purchasers Overseas or in other countries, for such prices as may be obtainable.

5. To fix maximum prices or margins of profit at which flour and other products made from wheat delivered to millers may be sold, and to fix standards of quality of such flour.

6. To purchase flour from millers at prices to be fixed by the Board and to sell same in Canada or in other countries.

7. To take possession of and to sell and deliver to millers, or to purchasers in other countries, wheat stored in any elevator, warehouse, or on railway cars or Canadian boats.

8. To control by license or otherwise, the export and sale of flour out of Canada.

9. For the purpose of performing its duties under this Order to allocate Canadian lake tonnage and to distribute cars for rail shipments.

The Participation certificates enabled the farmer to share in the final distribution of the pooled receipts for the whole crop. Other Government action of the year included the appropriation, while Mr. Crerar was Minister, of nearly $1,000,000 for the construction of a Government Cold Storage plant at Montreal; a meeting of the Minister and officials of the Department on Feb. 18-20 with representatives of Provincial Poultry Associations to consider means for increasing the supply of eggs in the country, and for improving the quality of Canadian eggs placed on the market; the decision to leave gasoline farm tractors costing less than $1,400 on the free list for another year, together with meat cattle; new regulations issued by the Department in May which covered construction and equipment, operation and maintenance, of stockyards with improved conditions in the handling of stock; the establishment, through the Dominion Bureau of Statistics, of improved methods in the collection and publication of Agricultural figures—a difficult matter with so individualistic an industry; regulations for the establishment and maintenance of herds of cattle accredited free of tuberculosis in order to facilitate the sale and export of cattle to the United States; the extension of time for the importation of Oleomargarine into Canada until Aug. 31, 1920, and for its sale until Mch. 1, 1921.

The discussion of Daylight Saving legislation in 1919 was active with the farmers—organized and otherwise—apparently opposed to it; the young people in the cities who gained an extra hour in the evenings were favourable to it; the mothers and women generally, who in many cases had another hour added to their day's work and clipped from their children's sleep, were very doubtful about it; many employers were in favour of it because the morning was the best time, physically, for a man's labour. The Government at first took no action and on Mch. 27 Major R. C. Cooper moved a Resolution in the Commons that the Act of 1918 should be re-enacted; he contended that the cities and the miners were especially favourable, that the United States was continuing its law and that if Canada did not do so the result would be confusion. The Hon. R. Lemieux was favourable to the proposal as was S. W. Jacobs who quoted a British Parliamentary Committee Report on its advantages; E. W. Nesbitt, H. C. Hocken, P. R. Du Tremblay, H. H. Stevens, Hon. W. S. Fielding, S. J. Crowe, A. E. Tripp, C. G. Power and F. N. McCrea supported it in brief speeches while 30 Members spoke against it including Sir Thomas White and Hon. F. B. Carvell. R. C. Henders specified 300 Western Resolutions against it and the bulk of the opposition was avowedly based on the attitude of the farmers who, it was said, objected because Daylight Saving added an hour of darkness instead of daylight to the farmers' day; because farmers shipping milk or other perishable food supplies must meet trains an hour earlier; because farm children frequently went long distances to school, and their mothers would have to get them ready by lamplight; because during the haying and harvest it took hours for the dew to evaporate so that hay or grain could be baled or stacked, or binders operated; because the hottest part of the day was from 12 to 1 o'clock "old time" and under "new time" a farmer must send his hands and his horses to the field during the most intense heat; because farmers who had large areas of hoe-crops thereby lost an extra hour in the morning on account of the dew, etc.; because it interfered seriously with harvesting operations for the same reason and because farm labour near the towns was also greatly interfered with. The arguments in favour were, in the main, that it had proved a success in 12 European countries and that uniformity with them and the United States was desirable; that it would save the people money in gas-bills and coal and electricity and promote home gardening; that it would add to the time for healthful sports and out-door recreation and substitute for workers an hour in the cool morning for one in the hot afternoon. The motion was lost by 105 to 50. The Railways and most of the Cities continued the new time; the Government took no action.

Meanwhile, an important matter of Government policy developed in regard to the export and import of wheat and wheat flour. Under the Order-in-Council of Dec. 4, 1917, and following upon similar United States action, these products had become free of duty between the two countries; shortly afterwards, according to a statement by Hon. J. D. Reid in Parliament on Oct. 9, 1919, the United States Government annulled the existing law by a regulation prohibiting such importations without license, and by refusing to grant such licenses; on Sept. 4, 1919, the Canadian Government had also placed an embargo on the export of wheat to or import from the United States. It was announced at Ottawa on Nov. 24 following that the United States would take off its embargo on Dec. 15. As to the reasons for the original imposition and the current action, Sir John Willison made the following statement on Dec. 15:

The embargo was imposed by the United States Government, not for the benefit of Canada, but as a deliberate, calculated policy in the interests of the United States itself. It may be remembered that at the time the embargo was put into effect hundreds of thousands of barrels of Canadian flour had been sold to the United States buyers. The embargo prohibited the sending of this flour across the international boundary and the United States Food Administration refused to issue permits for such importation except at the Administration's own price, which was substantially below the price at which such contracts were made. The embargo on the importation of wheat and flour into the United States will be withdrawn on Dec. 15, solely because United States millers find that their soft winter wheat does not make a satisfactory product and the stronger Canadian wheat is needed to improve its quality and increase the bread yield.

The Farmer and Government Price Policy. The year began with Dr. R. J. McFall acting as Dominion Cost of Living Commissioner in succession to W. F. O'Connor, K.C., who, in 1918, had created much disturbance, in many quarters, by investigations and comments regarding high prices. Dr. McFall intimated (May 16) that there were two strong reasons for the situation: "There is an absolute scarcity of food materials in the world to-day. With regard to wheat, Canada of course has a surplus, but that does not count, because we are all in the world market. There is an absolute shortage of meat. The second reason is the inflation in currency due to the rush to get war contracts. Men are bidding against each other and paying any price. There are many more dollars run through the printing press than there were a few years ago." On May 30th, 1919, a Select Committee of the Commons was appointed with G. B. Nicholson, Chairman, for the purpose of "enquiring into the prices charged throughout Canada for foodstuffs, clothing, fuel and other necessaries of life, and as to the rates of profit made thereon by dealers and others concerned in their production, distribution and sale; also as to rentals of dwelling houses in industrial centres of Canada and rates of return of capital invested, therein, with a view to effecting a reduction in such prices and rentals." The Committee had its 1st meeting on June 4 and held a number of others with examination of various witnesses; out of it grew the Court of Commerce. It was composed as follows:

G. B. Nicholson	H. C. Hocken	A. B. McCoig
H. H. Stevens	D. Sutherland	E. B. Devlin
J. F. Reid	Hon. W. S. Fielding	T. A. Vien
J. M. Douglas	A. Davidson	W. D. Euler
F. L. Langdon	E. W. Nesbitt	J. E. Sinclair

The Report of the Committee was presented to Parliament on July 5th. Its conclusions, in the briefest form, were that (1) having in mind the service which the consuming public demand, the margin between the actual cost of production and what the consumer pays for such commodities was reasonably narrow; that (2) after careful investigation, and hearings of representatives of Government departments and offices, Farmers' organizations of all kinds, dairymen, millers, packers, cold-storage men, grain dealers, consumers and commission merchants, it found the production cost or price paid to the farmer for beef, hogs, cattle, lambs, dairy products, eggs, etc., was from 100 per cent. to 115 per cent. greater than it was five years before and that the prices of hogs had increased by 125 per cent. on an average, beef cattle, 110 to 125 per cent., dairy products, on the butter-fat basis, and eggs from 100 to 110 per cent. above normal; that (3) it would be unwise or disastrous to fix a price for any of these foodstuffs or to place an embargo on exports and that there could be no material reduction in price except by increased and cheaper production or reduction in the cost of distribution; that (4) in the abattoir and packing-house business, in the milling industries, dairy products and eggs, while there may have been isolated cases of undue profits and other cases where poor business methods had resulted in high prices, "on the whole the business has been carried on a margin of profit reasonably close to actual cost"; that a Board of Commerce should be created which would continue and extend the work done not only by this Committee but by the various control systems the Government had put into operation during the War. It was stated that the publicity given to the investigations of such a Board should have a steadying effect: "Its powers of regulation applied to trade practices and agreements will speed reform, and large questions of policy where trade tends to combinations and restrictions may be submitted to the Board for advisory action."

Following this the Government introduced and carried a Bill for the creation of a Board of Commerce which was called a Combines and Fair Prices Act and which defined combines as (1) mergers, trusts and monopolies, or (2) a relation resulting from the purchase, lease or other acquisition by any person of any control over or interest in the whole or part of the business of any other person, or (3) any actual or tacit contract, agreement, arrangement or combination which had, or was, designed to have, the effect of limiting facilities for transporting, producing, manufacturing, supplying, storing or dealing; preventing, limiting or lessening manufacture or production; fixing a common price or a resale price or a common rental or a common cost of storage or transportation, or enhancing the price, rental or cost of article, cost of storage or transportation; preventing or lessening competition in, or substantially controlling, within any particular district, or generally, production, manufacture, purchase, barter, sale, transportation, insurance or supply; or otherwise restraining or injuring commerce. The expression "Combine" was not to include the combination of workmen or employees for their own reasonable protection. The Board of Commerce was given the administration of this Act with powers of investigation and prosecution; the right to check undue accumulation or with-holding from sale of any necessary of life; power to restrain and prohibit unfair profits on necessaries of life or other practices which might unduly enhance prices; authority to order any cold-storage plant, packing-house, cannery, factory, mine, and warehouse or other premises, to make detailed returns. In case of infraction of the Fair prices section of the Act the Board could hand its papers over to the Provincial Attorney-General for prosecution, or order discontinuance of the practice, with a penalty not exceeding $1,000 a day for disobedience (after 4 days' notice) or imprisonment for not over two years. The Board, as constituted on Aug. 13th, was made up of Hon. H. A. Robson (Chairman), Winnipeg; W. F. O'Connor, K.C., Ottawa; F. A. Acland, Deputy-Minister of Labour —shortly afterwards succeeded by James Murdock, Toronto; and Capt. William White, Secretary. The 1st meeting was at Ottawa on the 14th and co-operation was at once arranged with a similar Board in the United States for a continent-wide campaign against high prices; sugar, milk, clothing, meat-packing and drugs were the chief subjects of enquiry or action during 1919.

In December official statements were issued by the Board which (1) defined its position as a fully organized independent Commission, with supervision and control over the profits of dealers in necessaries of life, and over combines, including trusts and mergers affecting articles of commerce; (2) described its jurisdiction in profits as covering food, fuel and clothing; (3) declared that the adjudication of the Board to the effect that, in a particular case there was profiteering, would form the basis of a criminal prosecution with the further declaration that this would be conclusive proof of the offence when the offender came to be tried in the criminal Courts; (4) stated that its jurisdiction extended to the matter of unreasonable accumulation of necessaries and covered the hoarding of food for an advance in price, or the cornering of food in order to raise prices. It was noted on Dec. 9th that despite the high prices undoubtedly prevailing, profiteering, so-called, or the taking of unjust profits, was not, in the Board's opinion, as common or nearly as common, as many had charged or claimed.

On Dec. 27 it was announced that enquiry would be made as to the Tariff—whether any were abusing it or perverting it to a non-intended end, or exacting under its cover greater profits than they were entitled to. Meanwhile the Board had met at Toronto, Hamilton, Montreal, Halifax, Regina, Edmonton and Ottawa; it issued an Order in Toronto on Nov. 21 fixing the maximum cost of ready-made suits and overcoats by limiting the gross profits on each suit or overcoat sold,—applicable to the city of Toronto only; on the 26th another Order fixed the margin of gross profit allowed to retailers of boots, shoes, rubbers, overshoes, gaiters and other articles, usually sold within retail establishments in Canada, at 33 1/3 per cent.; under an Order of Nov. 24 the margin or gross profit to the retailer on the pork products known as bacon and boned ham, either cooked or smoked, was not to exceed ·20 per cent. of the sale price; at Toronto the Milk Producers or farmers were refused, in December, the right to raise the prices of milk and the current figure of $3.10 per 8-gallon can was approved.

Hostility to the Board was freely expressed by the Farmers' organizations, by the *Grain Growers' Guide* and *Farmers' Sun.* E. C. Drury, of the United Farmers of Ontario, stated at Barrie on Sept. 20 that the agitation by W. F. O'Connor against the price of foodstuffs was simply a red herring drawn across the trail of the real high cost of living at the behest of the manufacturers— not the slightest move having been made against the cotton com- bine, with its 310 per cent. profits; the woollen manufacturers, with their 74 per cent. profits, and the milling trade, with its enormous profits. At Victoria on Nov. 13 the Western Canada Live-stock Union heard vigourous denunciations of the Board from W. H. English, of Harding, Man., and J. D. McGregor, of Brandon—the latter declaring that "the Board has been undoing the constructive work which the Department of Agriculture has been building up for many years and has disorganized the work of the whole country." The creation of this body was not, in fact, popular with either Agricultural or industrial organizations; its efforts to restrict profits and investigate prices were naturally unpleasant to those concerned. It was a Government attempt at regulation and it appeared to prove once more that consumers as between producers, manufacturers and distributors were helpless, unorganized, unappreciative. There was immense discussion and much newspaper publicity for the Board; various enquiries by it of which the people could rarely see any definite conclusion or obtain the actual facts; occasional summary actions by the Board which did good for the moment—from the consumers' standpoint —but seemed to have little result in the end; warnings and notices issued which often seemed to precede fresh rises in price. The Board did good work, its aims were excellent and its policy one of honest effort, but conditions were too much for it* It must be admitted that the farmers' viewpoint as to wheat prices changed constantly and naturally during this war period. A Saskatchewan Commission in 1914 had produced figures showing that it cost at that time 62 cents to produce and haul a bushel of wheat to the initial shipping point; to that figure was added in succeeding years an ever-increasing cost for labour, for feed of animals, for harvesting and threshing and hauling, while additional freight rates were piled upon these figures with extra elevator charges. Early in 1917 the Council of Agriculture suggested to the Govern- ment a flat rate of $1.70 a bushel or a guarantee of price ranging from a minimum of $1.50 to a maximum of $1.90 but Sir George

*Note.—In 1920 Mr. Robson resigned and its enquiries and operations gradually decreased.

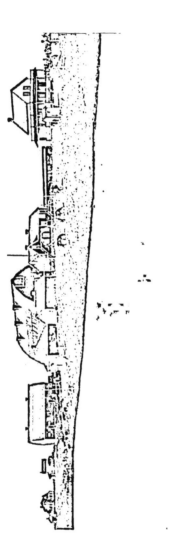

Irrigation Scene in Southern Alberta—A part of the great C.P.R.
undertaking in that Province

Foster would not then go beyond $1.30 a bushel. Eventually Winnipeg Exchange prices went up to phenomenal figures and the first Government fixed rate was $2.21 per bushel; in 1918 it was $2.24½, in 1919, $2.15 with pooling additions and a price charged to millers ranging from $2.30 to $2.80.

The Farmer and the Rise in Prices. This subject was one of vital discussion in 1919 and the increase in all manner of food prices synchronized with the Government's handling of the wheat trade, the demand by many farmers in Canada for a free world market in which they could take advantage of the call for food products and, on the other hand, a demand equally insistent for Government control or price guarantee in order to deal with the uncertain and financially precarious conditions in Europe. From the prices received by the farmer, on his export trade, which averaged in 1915-18 only $1.42 per bushel and from his domestic sales which averaged in the same period $1.28 per bushel, it would not appear that he received the big end of the profits or added unreasonably and improperly to the cost of living. But these official figures did not indicate the prices really received by the farmer though the averages are taken from official figures—the Government's Statistical department and Trade returns. They showed a total wheat crop in 1915-18 of 1,272,402,000 bushels realizing $1,800,486,000 or an average of $1.42 per bushel; the wheat Exports of the same period totalled 612,480,000 bushels valued at $954,908,000; deducting the exports and their values from the total product and values would, apparently, leave the domestic consumption at 659,922,000 realizing $845,578,-000 or $1.28 per bushel.

Where the difference went to between this figure and the Government's guaranteed or fixed prices of $2.21 and $2.24, respectively, for 1917 and 1918, is a problem. Of course Export figures are not always reliable; the supervision is not as strict as with imports where duties have to be collected; quantities and prices may be given carelessly and often overlooked. However that may be, the official figures seem to require explanation in the light of Government rates during these years and the actual prices known to have been realized. If, in the above figures, 1919 exports were included the average of the five years was $1.55 but even this was away below the rates quoted or guaranteed at home. There was no doubt about the world's requirements in 1919 exceeding the supply; hence the economic inevitability of some further increase in the range of prices. Crops also turned out to be less than expected in Canada and the United States while shipment from Australia and India remained difficult, Russia was still a dormant factor and only the Argentine proved a progressive element in supply.

The entire importation of wheat into European countries was under Government control; the United States created a highly organized and well-financed corporation under the Government to dispose of its exportable surplus and the American farmer, if he did not care to sell his wheat to the Government at $2.26 downward, according to grade, could sell it at prices which ran as high as $3.00 a bushel on the Minneapolis market while the Canadian farmer was compelled to sell through the Government at a maximum price of $2.15 and down, according to grade, with pooling receipts at the close of the year which ultimately equalled the United States Government total.   Nearly all the world's Governments during 1919 guaranteed a price for wheat, varying with local conditions, and according to the London *Times** of Sept. 13, they ran as follows:

Algiers $2.86	Denmark $1.97	Portugal $3.85
Argentine 1.56	Egypt 2.67	Spain 3.96
Australia 1.44	France 3.94	Sweden 2.95
Austria 2.21	Germany 2.10	Switzerland 3.25
Brasil 2.65	Holland 3.23	Tunis 3.25
Belgium 2.15	Italy 4.33	United Kingdom 2.23
Canada 2.15	Morocco 1.58	United States 2.26

The farmers of Canada could not fix the price of wheat; they had neither sufficient product nor a great enough organization to do so and even those of the United States had to depend upon their Government to start a great Grain Corporation with Julius H. Barnes at its head; this soon had selling agencies in every European country and power to sell the crop at any figure obtainable and for cash with, also, power under the Wheat Guaranty Bill, if the price demanded were not paid by any particular nation, to prohibit export to that country.   In Canada the Manitoba and Alberta Grain Growers' Associations, the Council of Agriculture, and the Farmers' Association of Quebec opposed a fixed guaranteed price for wheat; the United Grain Growers Ltd., and the Agricultural Societies of Manitoba favoured a different variety of this policy.   The Canadian Council of Agriculture asked for the creation of a Canadian body similar to the U.S. Grain Corporation, and a Government organized selling policy; eventually the Government took the action elsewhere described.
It was said that the price of wheat was not fixed but only a minimum payment to farmers promised until the full result of pooled returns could be received; however that might be, the Government certainly did control the price by its action; it took the matter out of the hands of the farmers as individuals or as organized bodies.   The Government, or the Wheat Board would naturally get all it could for the grain; the more it got and the larger the pooled price the better pleased would be the farmers; inevitably the consumer under such conditions of business might suffer in the end.   Meantime, however, the price was kept from going up, by the closure on any Exchange speculation or sale in the United States, to the extreme American levels or to the heights which the later world shortage might have caused; the consumer, in some degree therefore, benefitted.

---

*Note.—There is a large element of estimate in this, as in many cases initial prices were increased by later pooling results and other conditions.

At the same time the farmer asked for the largest possible initial payment. The Saskatchewan Grain Growers wanted it as near the export value as that value could be ascertained; the United Farmers of Ontario asked the Canadian Wheat Board to make it equal to the United States figure of $2.26; the Alberta bodies poured in Resolutions asking for the United States minimum and the Canadian Council of Agriculture supported this latter contention. The following Resolution on Aug. 1st was passed by the latter body: "In view of the official statement from the Government that a minimum price will be set for the Canadian wheat crop of 1919, and in view of the subsequent reports in the press that such a minimum price would be $1.75 per bushel; the Executive of the Canadian Council of Agriculture desire to state that any such price would be entirely unsatisfactory to the organized farmers of the West and, further, would strongly urge upon the Government that because of the very material shrinkage in the prospective wheat crop of the North American continent in the past few weeks there can be no justification for establishing a minimum price below that now existing in the United States."

On Aug. 18 Sir George Foster announced that the minimum initial payment would be $2.15 while J. B. Musselman, Secretary of the Saskatchewan Grain Growers, declared on Aug. 20, that "comparing it with other food commodities, such as meat, bacon, fruit, breakfast foods, etc., wheat has a much higher value still. If wheat were produced under the Protection given to cottons, boots, etc., and under capitalistic control and by union labour, it would bring to-day not $2.15 at Fort William, but nearer $10 per bushel." At the same time the Royal Wheat Commission in London was stated to have fixed the current price for wheat at a maximum of $1.80 per bushel from Canada and the United States; who was to pay the difference did not appear though W. Sanford Evans, an authority on this subject, declared on Aug. 21st that "Great Britain absorbs the difference between the purchase price and the price necessary to allow for the turning out of the 4-pound loaf for nine pence." He added that in 1918 it cost Great Britain $235,000,000 to make up the deficit between the price it paid for wheat and the price at which the wheat had to be sold to allow for the nine penny loaf. For the farmers it was contended that if large quantities of wheat or flour were exported at a high price the country as a whole would benefit even if the home consumer suffered through an increased cost for the domestic supplies which he required.

Meanwhile, the farmers before and on the Wheat Board were urging the best possible price and, on Aug. 26, H. W. Wood, President of the United Farmers of Alberta, stated that Canadian millers would be asked $2.30 a bushel with prices rising to them as the export prices rose and this was duly carried out. On Sept. 2 a London cable to Winnipeg stated that: "After several weeks of negotiations the Canadian mission in London, acting for the Canadian Wheat Board, has accepted the offer of the British Royal Commission on Wheat Supplies for 500,000 tons of wheat, or approximately 19,000,000 bushels. It was hoped that the Commission would be able to take all of Canada's exportable surplus, but the price asked by Canada proved an insurmountable obstacle, especially when the British were able to purchase in Argentine at a rate of $1.25 a bushel." Following this the United Farmers of Ontario (Sept. 10) asked the Wheat Board to revoke its minimum-payment arrangements. If this were not possible they asked that price-fixing be not applicable to wheat consumed at home and protested against a proposal to prevent the millers from dealing directly with the producers. The Wheat Board was, meantime, allowing the farmer along the American border to sell his grain by waggon-loads in the United States, under permit, and despite the American embargo upon carload sales or export.

By Oct. 30 it was stated that 800,000 tons of Canadian wheat had been contracted for in Europe and paid for in cash but nothing was publicly known as to the prices and the Wheat Board refused to divulge them. With the lifting of the United States embargo at the close of the year the farmers stood to make considerably more on their wheat, the millers to pay more for their supplies and the consumer to pay more for his bread with estimates made that $20,000,000 additional would go to the Western farmer upon his reserve stock of exportable wheat if free trading with the States was permitted. The Wheat Board, it was said, might sell in the United States at the prices to be obtained there and the extra price could go into the surplus above $2.15 to be distributed later amongst Canadian farmers. The United Grain Growers at once (Nov. 30) urged the Board to advance its price to Canadian millers and to permit free trading.

At the close of the year the Department of Trade and Commerce issued a statement that the Wheat Board had handled two-thirds of the exportable wheat crop of 1919 with a total of $48,379,-315 bushels sold of which 33,895,300 went to Great Britain at a realized price of $110,186,265 or $2.30 per bushel; obviously about $7,000,000 was available for distribution to the farmers over and above the $2.15 already paid, with a total price higher, in consequence, than the United States' fixed price. As to the future, it was stated that "sales in the United States will be pooled with past and future European sales to secure equality in price for the Western farmers, whether he marketed before or after the removal of the United States wheat embargo." This would make the final average price still greater. On Dec. 27 the Wheat Board ordered that the price of wheat to the Canadian miller be raised from $2.30 to $2.80 per bushel to partly meet increased prices in the United States and the removal of its embargo on wheat.

Relation of the Farmer and the Consumer. The farmer in Canada is both a producer and consumer but it was in the former capacity that, in these war years and after, he loomed up as perhaps the greatest factor in National conditions. Everybody in the country had to buy or have food and the farmer therefore touched,

in his relations, every household and every individual in the
Dominion.   His prices were vital, with or without economy, they
were fundamental to every interest and industry, to wages and contracts, to construction work and operation, to industries and finance, to Government and war policy.   There was a continuous
rise in his prices, as already stated, but so there was in all other
prices and in all countries.   For much of this he was not responsible because of international demand, Government control and
increasing costs of production; from other increased prices to the
consumer which developed as a result he also suffered and shared
in paying the additional wages to have his implements made, his
clothing and boots manufactured, his goods transported by rail,
or steamer, or motor-truck, or waggon, his farm work done.   The
consumer felt the high cost of bread and milk and other food products; he did not realize that the farmer could not fix his prices
in the same way as factories or merchants regulated theirs; as a
matter of fact, in 1917-18-19 the Government, as representing both
farmer and consumer, more or less regulated or indirectly. controlled the prices of farm products; the Government did not control the prices of manufactured products as a whole.   The Canada
Food Board gave, in its final Report, the following figures bearing
upon these points and obviously taken from the same official source
as are elsewhere compiled in this volume:

Year	Average price of Wheat per bushel	Average price of flour per barrel	Average price of bread per pound	Percentage received by farmer	Percentage received by miller	Percentage received by baker
1913	$0.90	$5.00	5 cents	29	7	64
1914	.95	5.75	5 1-2	30	8	62
1915	1.50	8.50	7	33	10	57
1916	1.65	9.50	7 2-3	36	13	51
1917	1.85	12.50	8 1-3	43	15	42
1918	2.20	11.30	7 1-3	48	7	45

These figures indicate that the farmer in 1919 hardly received
more than one-half the value of his product and that the balance
was divided between the millers and the bakers.   The latter, however, prospered and it seems reasonable to suppose that the farmer
did so also; the capital investment in mills was large compared
with either the farm or the shop and it is clear that if the miller
made big profits, as he did, on his small percentage, the farmer and
baker must have made much more.   On the other hand the
farmer's share of the price received for bread rose in these years
from 29 to 48 per cent., or a little over 50 per cent. of an increase,
the cost of the average family budget for food supplies rose, according to the Department of Labour, between 1913 and 1918, by
almost exactly the same figure of 50 per cent. so that it would
seem the farmer did not get an unfair portion of the general
economic increase.   One of the fundamental causes of high prices
in these years and one which applied to Industries as well as to
Agriculture was the large demand abroad and the consequent
increase in exportation—butter, for instance, between 1914 and
1918 rose by 1,300,000 pounds; cheese by 15,000,000 pounds and
eggs by 4,600,000 dozen from almost nothing; oats by 36,700,000

bushels and wheat by 57,000,000 bushels; flour by 5,500,000 barrels or more than double; bacon from 39 to 199 million pounds and beef from 5,200,000 to 86,565,000 pounds; vegetables from $1,200,000 in value to $19,034,000.

According to a statement of the Department of Labour at Ottawa* prices throughout Canada had risen regularly and steeply from the autumn of 1916 until the end of 1918, when the Armistice led to a decrease in certain lines, and from November until March, 1919, the general level of prices was downward: "In some lines, however, which had not risen greatly during the War, the cessation of hostilities and the assurance of peace caused a more pronounced upward movement to set in, and after March this was greatly strengthened; while in those commodities which had fallen somewhat an upward movement later set in, also, notably in cotton. Foods rose rapidly during the spring and summer months.   The retail prices of foods had fallen slightly in February and March, but rose rapidly during May and each month thereafter during the year, except for a drop in October when many of the new crops were marketed."   Wholesale prices, (which do not really reflect or indicate the retail prices, because of the intervening middleman) showed the following figures, or Index numbers, for all important lines of supply during 1919:

Product	January, 1914	January, 1919	December, 1919	Increase or Decrease between Jan.-Dec., 1919	
Grains and Fodder	140	272	344	I.	72
Animals and Meats	194	343	326	D.	17
Dairy Products	179	294	355	I.	61
Fish	153	268	242	D.	26
Fruits and Vegetables	125	246	286	I.	40
Sundry Foods	112	257	267	"	10
Textiles	135	383	399	"	16
Hides, Leather and Boots..	168	280	377	"	97
Metals	114	242	215	D.	27
Implements	106	241	245	I.	4
Fuel and Lighting	113	246	247	"	1
Lumber	183	279	406	"	127
Paints, Oils and Glass	140	339	425	"	86
Home Furnishings	128	298	352	"	54
Drugs and Chemicals	111	272	214	D.	42
Raw Furs	226	742	1608	I.	866
Liquors and Tobacco	138	258	316	"	58
All Commodities	136	286	322	I.	36

It will be noticed that the greater increases were not agricultural but in the industries associated with building and construction—lumber and paints, oils and glass—and in the leather industries.   The increase in grains and fodder and dairy produce was, however, sufficiently large and it, of course, was fundamental to all industries and interests because of the wages involved.   As to retail prices the figures for 29 foods in 60 cities or towns showed a steady advance long before the War—from $5.48 in 1900 to $7.73 in

*Note.—The Labour Gazette, January, 1920.

1914; the advance from the latter figure to $13.02 in 1918 and $14.70 in December, 1919, was double. In the United Kingdom similar statistics showed the respective increases for 21 foods in 600 centres as from an Index figure of 88 in 1900 to 103 in 1914, 214 in 1918 and 234 in 1919; in the United States dating from 1910, for 17 foods in 45 centres, the increases were from 93 in 1900 to 102 in 1914 and 168 in 1918. Taking the latter country in the 12 months of 1919 the index figure rose to 184.

Meantime, the increase in bread prices was not large though steady; the average cost of making one pound of bread in 1919 ran from 6·946 cents in January to 6·854 cents in April, 7 cents in September and 7:252 cents in December; the actual price to the consumer varied in all the chief centres of Canada: the profits of some millers seemed out of proportion to the prices of bread and wheat—the Ogilvie Company making 72 per cent. of net profits in 1918 with a dividend and bonus of 27 per cent.; the Government action in restricting profits to 25 cents a barrel of flour seemed to make no difference in the price of bread. As to wheat the prices were controlled and regulated by the Government and so with brans and shorts—the former of which was fixed at $37.25 in January 1919 and raised to $45.00 in August, and the latter from $42.25 in January to $55.00 in September—but in the other crops there was much variation. Western barley sold at 75 cents per bushel in January, but reached $1.68 in December, Ontario barley stood at 73 cents in January at Toronto, but reached $1.65 in December. Oats were 63 cents in·January, but rose to 93 cents in December. Flax-seed was $2.93 in January, but reached $6.00 in August then fell to $4.80 at the end of the year. Hay stood at $22.00 at Montreal in January, rose to $40.00 in May, and fell to $20.00 in September, but rose to $25.00 by the end of the year.

During these war-years, the export of flour to the British Empire, chiefly Great Britain, had grown from 4,375,979 barrels, worth $21,956,636, in 1915 to 6,255,804 barrels, worth $67,675,825, in 1919; to Foreign countries, chiefly France, the export had developed in the same period from 576,358 barrels selling at $2,654,310 to 2,940,635 barrels realizing $32,354,834. In animals and meats there was a considerable variation with a later tendency downward in average price. Cattle at Toronto rose from $15.00 per hundred pounds in January to $16.00 in April, falling to $13.50 in October. Beef, dressed, hindquarters, rose from 22-25 cents per pound at Toronto in January to 28-30 cents in July, but fell to 16-20 cents in November. Hogs were at $15.00 per hundred pounds in January, reached $23.75 in July and August, but fell to $15.25 at the end of the year.

The Milk and Butter question in its varied branches was also one of great interest to the farmer and the consumer in 1919. In the previous year the total dairy products in this connection realized $96,930,000 and, in detail, were as follows: butter $41,-750,000, cheese $39,500,000, condensed milk $5,750,000, powdered milk $1,330,000, milk $8,600,000. The estimated production of cheese in 1919, according to the Dairy Commissioner, J. A. Ruddick, was 190,000,000 lbs. with an average value of 27 cents per pound; that of creamery butter 100,000,000 lbs. at an average price of 52 cents; that of Dairy butter 150,000,000 lbs. at 42 cents; that of condensed milk and milk powder 75,000,000 lbs. at about 13 cents—the total estimated value being $176,000,000. Since the War, cheese and butter had doubled in price; in the years 1918-19 the returns from dairy products, according to Mr. Ruddick's figures, almost doubled again in value. Meantime the export of cheese in the fiscal year 1914 was 155 million pounds, in 1918 169 millions and for 1919 was estimated at 145 millions; that of butter in 1914 was 979,000 lbs., in 1918, 5 million pounds and for the year ending Aug. 31, 1919, was 17,537,000 lbs.; 44,338 Cattle were exported in 1914 and 191,359 in 1918. The variations in butter during 1919 were considerable and these prices affected everyone in the country. Official figures, which were, at this time, inclined to be very much below the average of individual experience, put the price at 52 cents in January, 66 in April, 50 in June and 69 in December; but many thousands of people paid up to 75 cents during much of the year.

The Montreal *Star* declared in its Ottawa correspondence of Apr. 28 that: "From enquiries made it is clear that a considerable part of the butter now being sold around 70 and 75 cents was obtained last fall and winter at prices ranging from 45 to 50 cents a pound. The supplies that are now coming in from current production do not, in many instances, admit of such a margin of profit. In the former case, so far as can be learned here, the profiteers are the storage men and others with butter on hand. In regard to the butter now being made, and the prices charged, the retailers are not overlooking their profit and are making out of it fully as much as any other interest." Normally and usually, butter declined in price at springtime but in 1919 the prices increased; it would seem that Canadian dealers, though not shipping butter abroad, expected and obtained the same price they would have got from the imperative demand of Europe had they exported the product. How much of this and other increases was due to cold storage facilities, to farmers holding their supplies individually, or to dealers getting all the product would bring, could only be decided by long and minute investigation. The variation in Cold Storage conditions during 1919, so far as reported to the Cost of Living Commissioner, is clearly shown in the following official figures—in pounds or dozens:

	Feb. 1, 1919	Apr. 1, 1919	June 1, 1919	Oct. 1, 1919	Dec. 1, 1919
Creamery Butter	8,400,060	1,773,290	2,096,671	25,252,983	16,639,818
Dairy Butter ..	698,703	116,963	146,980	1,469,670	900,127
Oleomargarine ..	597,607	339,347	351,118	445,570	482,205
Eggs	414,637	105,030	7,549,451	12,727,072	5,111,864
" Other Storage	1,630,643	697,041	1,121,322	1,040,824	913,445
Cheese	3,485,316	1,499,952	2,983,438	29,697,070	27,018,412
Pork	44,170,344	38,233,491	35,084,771	41,936,810	29,406,080
Beef	52,378,123	44,464,311	26,113,350	24,811,882	41,432,176
Mutton and Lamb	8,303,249	4,456,280	2,030,048	1,899,145	8,048,289
Poultry	5,178,816	3,880,408	1,950,632	691,515	3,110,703
Fish	20,978,767	22,623,815	18,039,200	25,413,417	27,957,178

The stocks of pork and beef held in storage appear to have been very large and more so at the end of winter than at the beginning; the stocks òf butter and cheese toward the close of the year also were heavy and prices were very high. On Feb. 15 R. J. McFall, the Commissioner, reported in this connection that: "These stocks are being held largely in the hope of the revival of the export market. It seems certain that eventually Europe will need all our surplus; at what price no one knows. The hungry consumers fail to gain much comfort from the export market, yet it is to the advantage of all of us to have the export market kept up that we may pay our debts. It is not to our advantage, however, to have domestic prices maintained above the necessities of the export market. The American millers assembled in convention state that wheat and flour prices are considerably above the world's market prices, having been guaranteed by the various Governments. Hog prices are being artificially maintained in the United States, while they are dropping rapidly in Canada; yet the retail price of bacon is being held firm in Canada." He recommended that the order limiting profits should be immediately restored by Order-in-Council and should be rigidly enforced.

The Cold Storage question, as with all "middlemen" issues, was of interest to both farmer and consumer. To a certain extent it was obviously desirable that certain products should be conserved for changing seasons of demand and to preserve them from the heats of summer; but where this necessity ended and when, if at all, the process of enforcing profits rather than preserving food began, did not appear. Dr. C. J. O. Hastings, M.H.O., of Toronto, dealt with this subject on Oct. 10. He described Cold Storage plants as absolutely necessary for the preservation of food which could not be consumed when in season, but strongly objected to such plants being utilized for hoarding the necessities of life in order to allow a privileged few to make large profits: "Under proper regulation, Cold-storage plants could be made an important factor in reducing the present high food prices. Much of the food crops raised on the farms of the country are wasted, and this, added to the amount lost by retaining surplus food products in cold storage, materially contributes to the high cost of living." In the Commons on May 30th Mr. Crerar, then Minister of Agriculture, expressed himself in favour of Municipal Cold-storage plants all over the country as had already been attempted in parts of Western Canada; the Government, he said, had decided to offer to municipalities 30 per cent. of the cost of erection of such plants and had abandoned its policy of extending similar aid to private Cold-storage concerns; it was also stated that former arrangements for supervision of these plants had not been satisfactory, and that the Government was considering the licensing of their warehouses and closer control. The large plant to be erected at Montreal would be under control of the Board of Harbour Commissioners and he hoped to see one at every Canadian port.

Between the farmer and consumer was another middleman of vital importance—the Packer. There were few good words said for him and the burden of many attacks was the charge of monopoly in certain processes of production—after leaving the farmers' hands—and in distribution, with an arbitrary control over prices. The controversy had for a year raged over the William Davies concern and the head of Sir Joseph Flavelle; in 1919 it turned upon certain enquiries made by the National Board of Commerce and the Cost of Living Committee of the Commons. Before the latter body on June 28 it was stated, as to the Davies Company, that it had 65 stores, altogether, with a 1918 turnover of $18,990,271; gross profits of $3,867,597, charges of $2,400,098, and net profits of $467,499. The net profit was 2·46 per cent. on the turnover. Hog products were said to be put into the stores from the Plant of the William Davies Company at possibly half-a-cent a pound lower than they could be put into a retail store not connected with the Company. On Sept. 29 the Board of Commerce issued an order that on and after Oct. 15 the price of pork and pork products was to be set at the figure obtaining on Mch. 10, and that any firm or packing-house charging more than that figure would be considered to be making an unfair and unjust profit.

The official defence of the Packers was issued at once as follows: "Meats now being sold are the product of hogs bought in the past two months during which live hog prices advanced throughout the world to the highest level in history. At present prices these meats are showing heavy loss. The actual facts are that in its most prosperous year the profits of the Packing industry in Canada were less than one-half cent per pound of product sold. If left to take a normal course, prices of product will decline in keeping with the lower tendency of live hogs, and without demoralization of the trade and of the live hog industry, to the detriment of the entire country." Before the Board on Oct. 1st J. S. McLean of the Harris Abattoir Co., declared that the Packing-house performed two main services in Canadian industry: "(a) Domestic—It takes the live-stock produced by the farmer and converts it into meat, thus making it available to the consumer; (b) Exports—It cures and clears to foreign countries the surplus live-stock, not required for domestic consumption." In each of these functions it clearly performed a highly important national service. In six years the exports of Meats to Europe increased 20-fold; in 1918 their value exceeded $100,000,000.

In 1914 Canada had only a small export trade in meat products. However, the scarcity of meat in Europe caused by the War, presented the Canadian farmer with an opportunity. The farmer rose to the occasion. stimulated on the one hand by his desire to assist in the common cause, and on the other hand by what he immediately recognized as a business opportunity. In the packing-house he found at hand an instrument which undertook to get in touch with the buyer of meat abroad, to study his taste in the matter of cure, to secure transport and solve all the other problems incident to developing and carrying through a great enterprise under war conditions. Few people realize how great and vital a service was performed by the packing-house industry during the War.

The broad principles involved were described by E. C. Fox, General-Manager of the Davies Company, as follows: "The packing industry covers the products of live-stock, fats, prepared meats, commodities, produce and inedible materials. The profitable operation of the business depends upon the profits and losses made by each component part—the profits of one branch cannot be read separately from the losses of another. The export packing industry is recognized as one of the staple industries of the country. We do not believe it is possible to segregate and isolate the domestic trade in pork products from export conditions. In both countries we sell to market conditions—each Packer taking the best market he can secure for his products in the Old Country and each Packer determining, according to his own judgment, the prices at which he can sell in the Canadian market." The comparative importance of the export and domestic markets to the Packers was obvious and Lieut.-Col. W. H. Price, M.L.A., had endeavoured to prove before the Board of Commerce on Sept. 27 by the following table that they did not lower prices to the consumers in proportion to the drop in prices by the farmers:

Period, 1919	Live Hogs Per cwt.	Fresh Ham per pound	Fresh Bacon	Cured Ham	Cured Bacon
March 17	$17.45	33½	37½	39	49
March 31	19.00–19.74	34½	38	39½	49½
April 14-28	21.96	39½	38½	43½	51½
May 19	21.60	41½	40½	44½	52
June 16	21.41	42½	41½	45½	52½
June 16-28	21.93	44	43½	46½	54½
June 28-July 10	22.31	44½	43½	48½	55½
July 10-Aug. 9	23.78	46½	45½	50½	57
August 9-25	24.10	46½	47½	51½	59
August 25-Sept. 6	22.65	45½	44½	51	58½
Sept. 6-22	20.67	44½	43½	50½	58½
Sept. 22-Oct. 6 (fixed in advance)	16.75–18.30	41½	41½	49½	53½

As to Milk, the Board of Commerce regulated its price as well as that of bread at certain points during the year; for instance, at Halifax where on Oct. 11, prices were slightly reduced and that of bread fixed at 12 cents per loaf and milk at 14 cents per quart; in Montreal authority was given to raise the price to consumers in October from 13 to 15 cents a quart and to 16 cents in November though statements were submitted by J. A. McBride of that city, to the Board, that out of 495 infants under 2 years of age 40 per cent. were receiving tea and coffee, etc., instead of the vital nourishment of milk, and by Dr. W. A. L. Styles that 65 per cent. of the milk delivered in Montreal was unfit for human consumption; in Toronto, as at other places, strong differences arose between milk dealers and farmers and consumers as to the proper cost of this important food. During October it was proposed by the producers at, or around, Toronto that the wholesale price of milk should be increased to $3.35 for an 8-gallon can or 1¾ cents above the previous winter's price per quart and 100 per cent. increase over that of 1914; it was contended by the Milk and Cream Producers' Association that even then the business would not be profitable.

They alleged that essential supplies had increased to the farmer as follows: Oil-cake from $58 to $94 a ton, hay $20 to $30 a ton, gluten $45 to $60 ton, bran from $38 to $45, and shorts $43 to $55 and $60. The producers or farmers back of the above organization had met on Sept. 14 when a Resolution was moved by R. W. E. Burnaby of Jefferson, and carried, in favour of an investigation into the cost of milk production so that a more amicable understanding might be reached between producer and consumer, and suggesting a Committee to wait upon the Cost of Living Commissioner and to press the proposal upon him. But the milk distributing agencies refused to consider the matter and the Board of Commerce declined to approve an increase during this winter season. The Milk dealers in Toronto claimed, on their part that distributors' profits were greatly diminished owing (1) to the cost per quart having grown from 4·33 cents in 1914 to 7·93 cents in 1919 and the operating cost from 2·33 to 3·71 cents while the selling price had only grown from 7·27 to 11·86 cents with a net reduction in profit from ·61 to ·31 parts of a cent. Meanwhile, milch cows had increased in value from an average of $57 in 1914 to $92 in 1919, and the average increases in the price of milk during 1919 were from 35 to 40 cents per gallon at Montreal; from $2.30 to $3.10 per 8-gallon can at Toronto, and from 50 to 55 cents per gallon at Victoria.

The controversy as between producer and consumer in this respect was pronounced all through the year. In St. John there was a keen discussion of the subject, as at Hamilton, Quebec, Toronto, Winnipeg and Montreal; at Vancouver the Fraser River Valley Milk Producers' Association was charged with fixing prices which the people must pay or go without milk; at Calgary, on Nov. 10, a District Producers' Association was organized and an increase from $3.50 to $4.30 per 100 pounds decided upon; at Truro, N.S., a large meeting of producers in Colchester and Hants Counties organized on Nov. 18 and were told that the Board of Commerce had declined to add a cent to their local price but had cut down the profits of distributors in Halifax; in Ottawa on Nov. 29 the local Producers' Association decided to advance prices to 14 cents a quart or 42 cents per gallon in order "to avert a serious shortage."

The farmers' side of the discussion was given by Hon. Manning Doherty, Ontario Minister of Agriculture, before the Board of Commerce on Dec. 11. He had prophesied this situation two years before when farmers were supplying milk at an actual loss; to-day, he contended, it still was the cheapest food in Toronto. "I, myself, at that time sold all my mature cows and stopped selling milk. Other farmers did the same, with the inevitable result that the supply became less and the prices rose. The prices of all farm products are regulated by the laws of supply and demand. If the public had made dairy farming worth while in the days when prices were low, more men would have continued in the business and dairy products would not be so high to-day. The export of these products do not rob home markets of supplies because there is a very large surplus. Canadians use only a small percentage of what the country's dairies produce and the remainder must go to foreign countries."

Another farm product, as to which there was contention, but no organized action was Eggs which stood at 80 cents in Montreal during January and $1.10 in December with varying prices elsewhere and in between—the lowest on the Toronto market on Nov. 15 being 95 cents and the highest $1.25 per dozen. Up to 1914 the export of eggs from Canada was negligible; in the years from that date to 1918, inclusive, the total was 21,679,359 dozen with the smaller total in 1919 of 733,445 dozen. No doubt this had its effect on prices. Fruit-growing was not so much discussed and the increases in such products as bananas, while hitting the poorer consumers very hard, had nothing to do with the farmers. Apples were high and scarce in the better qualities—partly because of the demand abroad, partly because of the scarcity of labour and growing indifference of the farmer to his orchards, partly because of the extra expense in wrapping and packing. The cost of production, apart from soil and climate, depended upon the variety grown, the availability of labour, the cultural methods used and especially fertilizers—which were very expensive—and the marketing facilities.

The Niagara district of Ontario, the Annapolis region of Nova Scotia and the valleys of British Columbia continued to produce but not to the extent which was possible and desirable; in fact the export decreased from 1,017,336 barrels in 1915 to 405,058 barrels in 1919 while the home demand and price also increased. High prices were influenced by lack of production and increased demand, together with competitive buying from Europe, Australia and New Zealand. Potatoes in February, 1919, stood at $1.25 per bag in Toronto and reached $2.60 in December with a short crop in Ontario and the Western Provinces; the exports in the year ending Mch. 31 were 2,822,550 bushels at $2,832,350 or an average of $1.00 per bushel. There was a movement in the West at the close of the year urging an embargo in the export of potatoes from British Columbia to the United States on account of the existing shortage.

General Interests of the Canadian Farmer in 1919. Meanwhile, the individual farmer had been developing operations along various lines; with more or less aid from Agricultural Colleges and Educational grants by Government, with advice or co-operation from Provincial Governments and his own organizations. In Wool the production for all Canada had increased from 12,000,000 lbs. in 1915, worth $3,360,000, to 20,000,000 lbs. in 1919 valued at $12,000,000—an increase from 28 to 60 cents a pound which did not appear excessive in view of the tremendous demand for woollen goods. The Canadian Co-operative Wool Growers' Co. handled a good deal of this crop and did substantial service to the farmers in price and marketing facilities; in 1918 its sales were 4,400,000 lbs. and in 1919 were estimated at 5,000,000 lbs. while a higher average price was claimed for the wool-growers under this system. Several Provincial organizations—the Sheep Breeders of Alberta, the Provincial Live-stock Associations and the Pincher Creek Wool Growers also handled much co-operative business.

In Flax there was a great demand owing to the elimination of Russia which had provided Britain with 80 per cent. of its supply before the War. Ireland had increased its product but Northern France and Belgium had also been eliminated; hence the effort in 1918-19 to develop the product in Canada and a triumph for the foresight of F. S. Glass, M.P. for East Middlesex, who had for years been urging the cultivation and encouragement of this industry. Mr. Crerar, Minister of Agriculture, stated in the Commons on Apr. 16 that it was largely through the representations of Mr. Glass that an Experimental plant had been established at Ottawa; the work of this plant had been exceedingly successful in developing more advanced processes of handling flax in its various stages; an inventor, assisted by the Government, had completed a machine for pulling flax which would do the work of twenty men; experiments would also be made in the utilization of Western flax fibre for the manufacture of twine. The actual raw material had become a crop of some importance and had increased from 463,359 acres in 1915 producing 6,114,000 bushels and realizing $9,210,400 to 1,093,115 acres in 1919 producing 5,472,800 bushels and realizing $22,609,500. The whole future of the crop depended, however, upon efficient and cheap mechanical aid in harvesting with labour proving increasingly difficult to obtain and handle.

Co-operative marketing was applied very largely in the West to Live-stock as well as to wool. Throughout the country from Winnipeg to the Rockies local live-stock shipping associations were in operation. Many of these were associated with the Grain Growers' movement, but in Saskatchewan stock marketing associations, incorporated under Dominion Act, were doing business on an extensive scale. In Ontario from 200 to 250 organizations were shipping. Many of these latter organizations had their origin in Farmers' Clubs, while others began under the auspices of the United Farmers' Association. In Quebec the Cheesemakers' Agricultural Co-operative Association marketed all classes of commercial live-stock, while the Live-stock Associations handled breeding stock. In the Provinces farther East co-operative marketing was applied more especially to sheep and lambs.

Another agricultural movement of practical character was the Rural credit system of Manitoba. George W. Prout, M.L.A., the father of the policy in that Province, told the Toronto *Globe* on Apr. 5 that the Rural Credits Act, passed at the 1917 Session of the Manitoba Legislature, provided for the organization by

Manitoba farmers of Rural Credit Societies through which the individual shareholders of such Societies could secure short term loans for carrying on or extending their farming operations. The money was borrowed from the Bank at 6 per cent., and the borrower charged 7 per cent.—the difference paying expenses of the Society and augmenting the Guarantee Fund. He explained the scheme as follows:

Each member of the Society takes stock to the amount of $100, and his liability is limited to the amount of his subscribed stock. The Provincial Government takes stock to an amount equal to half that subscribed by the individual members of the Society, and the municipality within the boundaries of which the members of the Society live and carry on their farming operations takes stock to the same amount as the Government. This subscribed stock forms a guarantee fund as the basis for credit, and the Society is enabled to secure credits for its individual members to a total of many times the amount of the subscribed stock. For example, if a Society is organized with a membership of fifty farmers, taking $100 of stock each, it would start with a capital of $10,000, as follows:

Fifty farmers at $100 each	$5,000
The Municipality, half of above	2,500
Government of Manitoba, half of above	2,500
Total	$10,000

It is provided that the municipal subscription needs not be in actual cash, but may be in bonds of the municipality. With such a capital, and the Society becoming responsible for each loan made to its members, after duly passing upon same, it is anticipated that loans to a total of $100,000 could be secured from the bank or banks with which the Society arranges to do business. The Act provides that when 15 farmers in any district have decided to organize a Rural Credit Society they shall make application by petition to the Provincial Secretary, and if the application is in order the Government issues letters patent incorporating the Society.

The total credits of 10 Societies in 1918 were $215,000 and in 1919 of 38 Societies over $1,000,000. Co-operative elevators and sale of farm products had proved successful in various Grain Growing organizations; the elements of co-operative borrowing had been tried in the above policy and in the Manitoba and Saskatchewan Farm Loans Act; the co-operation of Governments and farmers had thus reduced, or standardized, mortgage rates and turned borrowers into shareholders. Another factor which helped the individual farmer at this time was the growth of the Agricultural College movement. At the Ontario Agricultural College, Guelph, there were in the 1919 season a total attendance in regular Courses of 561, and in Domestic Science of 138; at the Manitoba Agricultural College, Winnipeg, there were 226 in the regular Courses, 126 in Home economics and 112 in engineering and general agriculture; at the College of Agriculture, associated with the University of Saskatchewan, there were 212 in attendance and at that of the University of Alberta 125, with 169 other students at the Olds and Claresholm Agricultural schools; at the same College in the University of British Columbia there were 49 students and at Macdonald Agricultural College, St. Anne's, Quebec, there were 157 students in the School of Agriculture, 146 in the Teachers' section and 80 in that of Household Science.

These 2,000 students turned out a proportion from year to year of trained and skilful farmers who could not but be helpful to the industry as a whole in practical work and operation, scientific production and popular leadership. Apart from the Grain Growers and United Farmers' organizations which attracted so much attention and had developed so great an influence by 1919, there were many Associations which had long done good service for the farmers and for Agriculture in general. Those associated with National or Dominion objects, as distinct from Provincial organizations, were as follows, with the elected Presidents for 1919:

Organization	President	Address
Canadian Swine Breeders' Association	H. M. Vanderlip	Brantford, Ont.
Canadian Horticultural Society	E. B. Hamilton	London, Ont.
Canadian Aberdeen-Angus Association	J. D. McGregor	Brandon, Man.
Canadian National Live Stock Record Association	William Smith, M.P.	Columbus, Ont.
Federation of Women's Institutes of Canada	Mrs. Arthur Murphy	Edmonton, Alta.
Canadian Brown Swiss Association	Arthur Galey	Massawippi, Que.
The National Poultry Council	Dr. R. Barnes	Ottawa, Ont.
Western Canada's Dairymen's Association	F. M. Logan	Regina, Sask.
Canadian Society for the Protection of Birds	F. F. Payne	Toronto, Ont.
Canadian Jersey Cattle Club	E. H. Barton	Chilliwack, B.C.
Canadian Hereford Breeders' Association	L. O. Clifford	Oshawa, Ont.
Holstein-Friesian Association of Canada	Dr. S. F. Tolmie, M.P.	Victoria, B.C.
Canadian Ayrshire Breeders' Association	A. S. Turner	Ryckman, Ont.
Canadian Thoroughbred Horse Society	J. J. Dixon	Toronto, Ont.
Clydesdale Horse Association of Canada	William Graham	Claremont, Ont.
Canadian Shire Horse Association	J. Boviand	Brampton, Ont.
Canadian Pony Society	J. M. Gardhouse	Weston, Ont.
Canadian Standardbred Horse Association	Sam McBride	Toronto, Ont.
Dominion Sheep Breeders' Association	W. A. Dryden	Brooklin, Ont.
Eastern Canada Live Stock Union	William Smith, M.P.	Columbus, Ont.
Western Canada Live Stock Union	Dr. S. F. Tolmie, M.P.	Victoria, B.C.

Meantime, there had been organized discussion of Dairying and Live-stock conditions in Canada. The Canadian National Live-stock Association held its 14th annual meeting at Toronto on Apr. 4; the Chairman, William Smith, M.P., referred to the prosperous year through which the members had just passed, and remarked that the ensuing year would be still more prosperous. A Committee was appointed to try and obtain better freight rates for cattle and a Resolution passed asking for an increase in the Government grant to the larger Live-stock shows of $1,500. The Dominion Live Stock Commissioner, H. S. Arkell, called a Conference of representatives of Provincial Governments and Live Stock Associations to meet at Ottawa on May 12-13 to consider action and organization for the sale of Canadian horses and cattle in Europe. Amongst those present were leading officials, farmers and cattle-breeders from all the Provinces with specially large delegations from the West; Dr. J. G. Rutherford presided and Mr. Arkell, in his speech, dealt with the elimination of Russia as a competitor, the British demand for eggs and bacon and horses, and the great desirability for Canada of a lifting of the embargo upon live cattle.

As to countries, he pointed out that: "The United States is

exploiting the market in Europe. Any move on our part to get a part of the European Continental market for our hogs would be unwise as the States produce a fatter hog, and the American hog suits Europeans better. Therefore, we can best concentrate our efforts on the British market, as the United Kingdom is short in supplies of high class products now. I am satisfied that Canada can take Denmark's place in the British market for bacon." Continental Europe wanted horses and Great Britain wanted a certain class which Canada should and could breed and which ran from 160 to 170 guineas in price. He submitted a Memorandum of what ,the Department of Agriculture would do in marketing products and promoting exports for the farmer.

Amongst the other speakers were Hon. Duncan Marshall, Minister of Agriculture at Edmonton, George Hoadley, M.L.A., of Alberta, W. I. Smale, of Brandon; the Hon. T. A. Crerar, Minister of Agriculture, described credit, ocean shipping and salesmanship as the three essentials for obtaining or increasing European trade. Resolutions were passed urging the removal of the British cattle embargo with a guarantee that only Canadian cattle would be shipped from Canada under its conditions; proposing a survey of the Provinces to ascertain what horses, cattle and sheep were available for an export trade; suggesting that representatives of the horse and cattle industries be appointed to accompany Mr. Arkell to Europe in his mission for promoting Canadian Livestock interests abroad. A unanimous suggestion that the Dominion Government should finance sales abroad, on a large scale, was turned down by the Minister as undesirable at this juncture.

Meanwhile, the Executives of the Western and Eastern Canada Live-stock Unions had met at Ottawa a few days before this and organized the Canadian National Live-stock Council with Dr. S. F. Tolmie, M.P. of Victoria, as President and E. L. Richardson of Calgary as Secretary. The National Dairy Council in October decided to work for a National Dairy Show and standardization of Milk in Canada; organized effort along Legislative lines and farm surveys to show cost of milk production; improvement in the work of Dairy divisions of Departments of Agriculture; the checking of dishonest buyers of milk and cream, and the purchase of cream for butter on a quality basis. A Conference was held in Winnipeg on July 18, between representatives of the Dominion and Provincial Governments and the Canadian Railways, to discuss ways and means of relieving the feed shortage existing in a large part of Alberta and Saskatchewan; a basis of agreement and action was obtained. At the annual meeting of the Western Canada Live-stock Union in Victoria on Nov. 12 H. S. Arkell urged development of the export trade in horses and live cattle and the fostering of the chilled meat industry. A National Poultry Conference had been held at Ottawa in February and a National Poultry Council formed with Dr. R. Barnes as President and the following platform or policy:

1. Increased production and economic production—through stock improvement.
2. Quality payment and co-operative marketing.
3. Markets intelligence and standardized product—Government inspected and guaranteed.
4. Service in transportation and perfection in storage.
5. Increased consumption with advertising and salesmanship in the disposal of the product at home and abroad.

The Organized Farmer: Origin and History of the Western Movement. To take men so individualistic in character and habit of mind, so often isolated in home or settlement, so far away from the gregarious instincts and customs of city life as Canadian farmers have always been, and to mould them into great and successful organizations of a business and political nature with, sometimes, a touch of Socialistic thought, was a remarkable achievement. The men of the West who did this were not the first to think of it but W. R. Motherwell, E. A. Partridge, J. W. Scallion, R. McKenzie, and some others, were the first to transmute the idea into practical success. The Dominion Grange in Ontario was the first real Farmers' organization in Canada but it never grew to great public influence; the Patrons of Industry rose and fell in the same Province through building upon the shifting sands of politics before they had time to grow the roots of power. It was the West which first grasped the essence of successful agricultural organization—co-operation for the advancement of the individual welfare of the farmer.

Organization in Saskatchewan, Manitoba, Alberta. Hopkins Moorhouse in his *Deep Furrows*, a really striking book, penned in picturesque language, and with vivid etchings of the life of the farmer, describes the idea as arising in the mind of W. R. Motherwell, then a pioneer farmer of the Qu'Appelle region of Saskatchewan, as he drove over the prairies in the year 1901 and brooded upon the then burning question of the farmers in their struggle for better Elevator facilities and enforcement of existing regulations against the all-powerful Railway of that day. The result was the calling of a meeting in the little prairie village of Indian Head·on Dec. 18 attended by Peter Dayman of Abernethy— where Mr. Motherwell also lived—John Millar, Walter Govan and M. M. Warden of Indian Head, John Gillespie and Elmer Shaw of Abernethy, and Matthew Snow of Wolseley. Organization was effected at once with the men above named as a Provisional Committee for the proposed Territorial Grain Growers' Association; an incident of the meeting was an address from the aged and much respected Senator W. D. Perley who prophesied success to the new movement; C. W. Peterson, then Deputy Commissioner of Agriculture for the Territories, was also present and was suggested for Secretary but the idea of a Government official was at once opposed, and John Millar was appointed, with Mr. Motherwell as Provisional President.

On Feb. 1st, 1902, the first Convention was held at Indian Head with 38 Locals of the new organization represénted and the preliminary choice of officers was confirmed with a first Board of Directors constituted of those mentioned above. The Resolutions passed asked (1) that the Grain Act be amended to empower the Warehouse Commissioner to compel all Railway om anies to erect every approved loading platform, within 30C days after approval was expressed, and legal penalties for infraction; (2) that Railway Companies be compelled to provide farmers with cars to be loaded direct from vehicles at all stations, irrespective of there being an elevator, warehouse or loading platform; (3) that the Grain Act be amended making it the duty of the Railway Agent, when there was a shortage of cars, to apportion the available cars in the order in which they were applied for, and that, in case such cars were misappropriated by applicants not entitled to them, the penalties of the Act should be enforced against such parties. Mr. Motherwell remained President of the organization until it became the Saskatchewan Grain Growers' Association and he, in 1905, was elected to the Saskatchewan Legislature and became Minister of Agriculture in the new Province; E. N. Hopkins of Moose Jaw was his successor with F. M. Gates of Fillmore elected in 1909, J. A. Maharg, afterwards M.P. for Maple Creek, elected in 1912-19. The progress of this, the first great Grain Growers' organization, during the years of its life from 1904 onwards may be seen by a glance at the following table:

	Membership	Life Membership	Fees	Receipts	Expenditure
1904	942	....	$ 471.00	$ 785.76	$ 572.10
1905	1,432	....	717.00	1,017.66	890.17
1906	1,967	....	980.25	1,674.89	898.80
1907	1,961	....	980.75	1,718.25	1,786.43
1908	3,186	....	1,335.40	2,101.90	1,885.67
1909	3,886	339	1,918.00	3,208.29	3,807.52
1910	9,640	692	4,820.80	9,185.69	6,951.15
1911	9,792	778	4,896.00	9,517.06	7,858.12
1912	16,075	....	4,893.71	9,621.26	6,766.15
1913	19,850	....	5,428.25	9,925.19	7,381.02
1914	20,267	947	10,082.80	17,848.54	15,670.16
1915	25,860	....	12,980.00	....	....
1916	25,743	1604	12,852.00	19,204.00	19,248.19
1917	25,404	1822	12,702.00	21,785.47	24,562.28
1918	32,268	2336	16,134.00	27,754.75	32,811.75
1919	33,445	2560	36,820.00	34,468.01	28,581.22

The work of the Association in these years was remarkable and out of its activities or example grew the Manitoba and Alberta bodies; in agricultural trading organizations it was largely responsible for the Grain Growers' Grain Co., the Saskatchewan Co-operative Elevator Co., the Municipal Hail Insurance Association, Regina, and, of course, the Co-operative Wholesale Department of its own Association; in locals or branches it had grown from the original 38 of Indian Head days to over 1,500; the Society and its associated organizations taught Western farmers to realize that they could be a factor of real importance in the affairs of the nation and helped them to know and to trust each other, to act in common where their common interests were concerned; farmers were made to believe that co-operation was the surest road to individual as well as collective success and that legislation was best secured by and through organization.

Following the Indian Head meetings of 1901 and 1902 the next place to organize was Virden, Manitoba, and the pioneer of the movement there was J. W. Scallion who succeeded in forming a strong local Association on Jan. 9, 1903—after a visit from Mr. Motherwell—with himself as President and H. W. Dayton as Secretary. A period of intense organizing activity followed and on Mch. 3-4 Mr. Scallion succeeded in getting together a Convention at Brandon with 100 delegates present representing 26 Locals; the officers elected included Mr. Scallion as President, R. C. Henders of Culross, Vice-President, R. McKenzie, Brandon, as Secretary-Treasurer—all well-known names in the after and greater movement, with D. W. McCuaig of Portage la Prairie as one of the Directors. The stated objects of the Association were "to defend the legitimate interests of the people on the land and to promote the self-development of rural community life." These, the Constitution amplified somewhat, as follows:

To forward in every honourable and legitimate way the interests of the rural population, not in antagonism to other elements of our population, but in cordial co-operation with all.

To promote independent personal thinking upon the questions of the time, to create public spirit and to quicken the public conscience in regard to evils that persist in our present life in order that so far as possible they may be abolished.

To watch legislation relating to the Farmers' interests particularly affecting the marketing, grading and transportation of their grain, livestock and other products. To suggest to Parliament from time to time through duly appointed delegates, as it may be found necessary, revision of existent laws or the passing of new legislation to meet changing conditions and requirements.

To foster and encourage the co-operative methods of distribution of farm products and supplying staple commodities.

Succeeding Presidents were D. W. McCuaig and R. C. Henders, afterwards M.P. for Macdonald. The membership in 1919 was 12,000. The first and almost immediate result of this development was that when Farmers' deputations went to Ottawa or to their Provincial Governments they were received with more respect and their requests in such matters as distribution of cars, freedom of shipment, grading of wheat, inspection of machinery, elevator facilities and other problems relating to agricultural work were either carefully considered, or put on the way to a solution, or a least regarded as subjects worth attention. Politics were carefully avoided and strength of organization cultivated. Those were days of great isolation for the Western farmers, long hauls over the prairies for their grain, great difficulties with and complications over Elevators then largely under railway control, constant friction with the Railways as to cars, grade-weight and price of wheat; they were days of 40-cent or 50-cent wheat and of naturally large powers in the hands of railways, and grain and elevator interests which were, perhaps, even more vital and necessary to the farmer than the latter's very limited product was to them. The Manitoba organization achieved one of the first practical successes of the movement when, in 1910, it compelled the Manitoba Government, in response to a persistent demand and agitation, to accept a policy of Government-owned interior elevators.   An Elevator Commission was appointed by the Government, consisting of D. W. McCuaig, President of the Association, as Chairman, F. B. McLennan and W. C. Graham. Afterwards, however, the Government took the control of affairs out of the hands of the Commission and purchased a large number of elevators at what was said to be an unduly high price; they operated them (176 in number) for two years at a loss and then leased them (1912) to the Grain Growers' Grain Co.

Meantime, in 1906, the Alberta Farmers' Association was organized as the third Provincial unit in the Grain Growers' chain; there was also in existence at that time the Canadian Society of Equity which had been imported from Nebraska by some farmers migrating from that State.   D. W. Warner, Edmonton, was the first President of the Alberta Farmers with Rice Sheppard as Secretary; W. F. Stevens was President in 1907-08 but resigned to become Live-Stock Commissioner for the Province. After continuous effort, the Society of Equity amalgamated in 1908 with the Farmers' Association and the combination became, on Jan. 14, 1909, the United Farmers of Alberta with James Bower of Red Deer as President and E. J. Fream Secretary, with 122 Locals and about 2,000 members; from 1911 to 1914 W. J. Tregillis of Calgary was President, James Speakman of Penhold succeeded him, and in 1916 H. W. Wood of Carstairs became President and so remained in 1919.   The membership of the United Farmers of Alberta in 1918 was 17,000 with 650 Locals; the work done in these years for the farmer was energetic and popular; its characteristics were more political than in the other Provinces, based, perhaps, upon the influence of such American bodies as the original Society of Equity and the later Non-Partisan League which, also, was transplanted from the Western States.   Some of the matters in which it led, or helped, in common with the Saskatchewan and Manitoba organizations, may be summarized as follows:

1. Proving that farmers could co-operate continuously and effectively.
2. Creating a community or class consciousness and a new formula for democracy.
3. Educating farmers along certain defined economic and social lines.
4. Stimulating Co-operative dealing and thus saving locally to the farmer sums of money which in the aggregate of the whole West ran into large figures.
5. Securing special freight rates on seed grain, railway loading platforms and the right to have cars alloted in time as ordered.
6. Obtaining political ends such as Direct Legislation, Prohibition and Women's Suffrage and forwarding such economic projects as Co-operation and Rural credits.
7. Training farmers for public service, for intelligent discussion of public affairs and for independence of Party thought and organizations.

Founding of The Grain Growers' Guide. Following the organization of the last of the three Provincial Associations came the

creation of an organ of newspaper thought.   It had early been
felt by the promoters and pioneers of the movement that a journal
was necessary to deal with Governments and politicians, or Railway and Elevator and grain distributing interests, with whom
they might from time to time differ.   E. A. Partridge was one of
the first to effect practical results and under his direction as
Editor the *Grain Growers' Guide* was started as a monthly
periodical on June 1, 1908, with these expressed objects: "The
purpose of *The Guide's* publication is to aid in the discussion of
the economic and social problems which confront us, to assist in
unifying opinion among our farmers and other workers as to what
it is necessary to do in order that they and we may come to enjoy
to the full the fruits of our labours, and, having thus unified us
in opinions, to serve as a trumpet in marshalling our forces for the
accomplishing of whatever has been decided is best to be done."

For various reasons Mr. Partridge was unable to carry on his
work and the July issue did not appear; a call was made for help
and Roderick McKenzie, Secretary of the Manitoba organization
and at that time on his Brandon farm, was put into editorial
harness; Mr. McKenzie kept the journal going regularly and to
the satisfaction of the Grain Growers interested for three years
when the work of his Provincial Association became too heavy and
his place was taken by G. F. Chipman.

At first the paper was published as the official organ of the
Manitoba Grain Growers' Association, then it was adopted by the
Saskatchewan and Alberta organizations.   Its initial struggle was
against what was termed the Elevator combine and the fight was
a bitter one; the next struggle was against the Tariff as it appeared in 1910 to the farmers of the West and the *Guide* was a
chief factor in organizing the "Siege of Ottawa" when 800 Grain
Growers told the Commons what they wanted in fiscal matters;
then came the Reciprocity struggle of 1911 and strong support
was given the Laurier Government on that issue.   In general
terms the organ set itself to keeping the large, varied and
growing programme of the organized farmers before the public
along economic, political and social lines and it undoubtedly
wielded a considerable influence; its editorial conduct was able
from the point of view aimed at and its weekly circulation in
1918 was stated at 45,000 with ownership of a printing plant
costing $250,000; it exercised a strong influence in the succeeding
discussions, and organization, of the Political movement.

Organization of The Grain Growers' Grain Co., Ltd.   Meanwhile E. A. Partridge of Sintaluta, Sask., had developed his idea of
co-operative trading in grain; at first regarded with doubt as an
impossible though pleasing proposal, Mr. Partridge finally persuaded the 1905 Convention of the Manitoba Grain Growers'
Association to consider the question.   It appointed a Committee
composed of himself as Chairman, with J. A. Taylor of Cartwright
and A. S. Barton of Boissevain as members, to investigate and
report; similar action was taken by the Territorial body at Regina

but with the same expressed doubt and lack of faith. The idea had, meanwhile, been put into operation in a Farmers' Union which had been formed in Texas, U.S., during 1902 by a group of cotton growers; they were joined by men in seven other States and in December, 1905, were able to organize the Farmers' Educational and Co-operative Union of America with, at first, application of their principles chiefly to cotton-growing. Following Mr. Partridge's success at Brandon he organized the farmers around Sintaluta along the same lines; in his Report to the Manitoba Association and to his own Territorial body, bitter hostility was expressed to the methods and policy of the Winnipeg Grain and Produce Exchanges and the farmers were urged to organize along co-operative trading lines.

At Winnipeg on July 26, 1906, this, finally, was done and the Grain Growers' Grain Co. formed with E. A. Partridge as President; John Kennedy, Swan River, Vice-President; W. A. Robinson, Elva, Francis Graham, Melita, T. W. Knowles, Emerson and Robert Cruise, Dauphin, as Directors; with John Spencer as Secretary-Treasurer. The sum of $2,500 was subscribed to buy a seat on the Winnipeg Grain Exchange and to this five Sintaluta farmers contributed $1,500. It was a difficult proposition in those days as the Western Provinces and the Western States, from which so many of their farmers had come, and Ontario to a lesser extent, were strewn with the wrecks of Farmers' organizations; stock, however, was steadily sold, though with little real hope amongst the original subscribers, and business was commenced in September, 1906; by the close of the first year 2,340,000 bushels of grain had been handled with a profit of $790 on an original paid-up capital of $5,000.

Then came a period of struggle with the Grain Exchange, suspension from its privileges and enforced re-instatement by Government action; a period, also, in which the Directors had to give the Bank their own personal security for advances. At the first annual meeting Mr. Partridge retired and was replaced by T. A. Crerar as President and General-Manager and he proved from the beginning, a strong, successful business manager of the enterprise; in 1907 the Company handled 5,000,000 bushels and in 1912 acquired the lease of a Terminal elevator at Fort William; its grain handled there was 16,254,971 bushels in that year, 16,728,996 bushels in 1913, 11,113,922 bushels in 1914, 28,391,277 bushels in 1915, 16,448,023 bushels in 1916 and 12,648,040 bushels in 1917. The total was 101 million bushels in the 6 years.

During these years the Company had obviously prospered and it was really beyond all records in agrarian Co-operative trading. The concern had started with great ambitions but little capital; as it went on acquiring experience of all kinds the grain production and business of the West grew apace; eventually under the able management of T. A. Crerar—who latterly received a salary of $15,000 a year—his assistant J. R. Murray, and a Board of well-known farmers with business capacity, it became an important

institution.   Following its assumption of control over Manitoba
elevators it branched out into Saskatchewan and purchased 30
in that Province with, in 1918, a total of 199 under operation;
in 1912, and in order to meet changing conditions in the grain
trade, the Company leased a 2,500,000-bushel terminal elevator
at Fort William and operated it with yearly growing success as
above stated; in the same year it secured a 300,000,000 feet timber
limit in Northern British Columbia, on the line of the G.T.P. east
of Fort George, and, in 1917, commenced erection of a $250,000
mill and plant at Hutton, B.C., with a capacity of 75,000 feet per
10-hour day, which came into operation in 1918.

In 1912, also, the Company had opened a Co-operative supply
department which by 1917 had a turnover of $3,000,000 yearly
in farm machinery, binder-twine, coal, lumber, flour, fence-mater-
ial, etc.   Export business was taken up in 1913 and, after some
heavy losses incurred in learning a complicated system of operation, the Grain Growers' Export Co. Ltd., was established as
a re-organized method and Harry Stemper appointed Manager.
As the greater part of the continent's grain exports were handled in New York, Mr. Stemper made that city his headquarters
and, in 1915, controlled an export trade of 43 million bushels
which by 1916 had become 90 millions; at this stage in the War
and the entrance of the United States into it, the export business of the Company was taken over by the Wheat Export Co.—
a British Government war business concern.   In 1913 the Company
had also arranged for the carrying on of business as flour, feed
and grain merchants at New Westminster and other Pacific Coast
points.   By 1917 and in 11 years of operation, to quote G. F.
Chipman, Editor of *The Grain Growers' Guide*: "The Company
had built up an enormous business and performed a very wide
service to the grain growers of the prairies and had over 20,000
shareholders.   The Company faced active competition of the
keenest kind in every branch of this work.   It charged competitive prices for all services rendered and made nearly $2,000,000
in profits in 12 years.   These profits were distributed in 10 per
cent. dividends to the shareholders each year and also in very
generous grants to the Provincial Associations in Manitoba, Saskatchewan and Alberta, and for educational work generally."

Co-operative Organization in Saskatchewan and Alberta.
While this was going on other Provincial organizations were
branching out along lines of Co-operative trading activity with
the steadily increasing success of the Grain Growers' Grain Co.
as a natural incentive.   In 1911 the Saskatchewan Co-operative
Elevator Co. was organized as an outcome of the Report issued
by an Elevator Commission which the Provincial Government
appointed in 1910 composed of Dr. Robert Magill, Dalhousie
University, Halifax, Hon. George Langley and F. W. Green, who,
after long and careful study, recommended the creation of a Company controlled by the Grain Growers' Association and aided by
the Government, in the construction or purchase of elevators, with

an advance of 85 per cent. of the cost. The project was approved by the Association after an historic debate in which F. W. Green and George Langley led the forces in favour and E. A. Partridge against—the latter wanting Government ownership of country elevators. Legislation was duly passed and incorporation given on Mch. 14, 1911 with the first elected officials (July 6, 1911) as fol-· lows: J. A. Maharg, Moose Jaw, President; George Langley, Maymont, Vice-President; Charles A. Dunning, Beaverdale, Secretary-Treasurer; James Robinson, Walpole, W. C. Sutherland, Saskatoon, A. G. Hawkes, Percival, J. E. Paynter, Tantallon, N. E. Baumunk, Dundurn, and Dr. E. J. Barrick as Directors. The first elevator was erected at Indi, Sask. in September, 1911 and there were 45 others opened for business in the first year; in 1917 there were nearly 300 under operation while a handsome building had been erected (1915) at Regina as headquarters. The exact figures of progress were as follows:

Season	Shareholders	Elevators	Bushels	Profits
1911-12	2,505	46	3,262,426	$52,461.60
1912-13	8,722	137	25,104,226	167,926.86
1913-14	12,575	192	39,125,788	285,181.61
1914-15	14,742	210	27,407,653	133,745.91
1915-16	18,077	230	48,198,000	557,795.71
1916-17	19,317	258	34,558,687	250,752.88
1917-18	20,683	298	27,066,261	124,811.28

The next organization of this character to be formed was the Alberta Farmers' Co-operative Elevator Co., which was constituted in August, 1913, with W. J. Tregillis, Calgary, as President; Joseph Quinsey, Noble, Vice-President;E. J. Fream, Calgary, Secretary-Treasurer; E. Carswell, Red Deer, Rice Sheppard, Edmonton, P. S. Austin, Ranfurly, J. G. McKay, Provost, R. A. Parker, Winnifred, and C. Rice-Jones, Veteran, as Directors. The mode of operation was much the same as in Saskatchewan; under the local Act the Provincial Government made a cash advance of 85 per cent. of the cost of each elevator built, or bought, by the Company but had no control over location, purchase, price, equipment or capacity; as security the Government took a first mortgage on the Elevator and other property of the Company at a given point, with loans repayable in 20 equal yearly installments. The Act called for 20 Locals to begin with and the Company started operations with 46 and the prompt construction of 42 elevators and purchase of 10 others. The paid-up capital of the concern in the first year was $100,000 and in 1917 over $560,000; the first season saw the handling of 3,775,000 bushels and the second 5,040,000 bushels; a financial difficulty which early developed was met by the support of the Grain Growers' Grain Co. in Winnipeg. Then occurred the death of Mr. Tregillis and, after an interval, the appointment in 1915 of C. Rice-Jones as President and General-Manager, and the handling in that "big crop" year of 19,320,000 bushels with profits for the 4 years' operation of $570,000. In addition to its Elevator business this Company carried on trading in Live-stock and in its first year marketed 141 cars which, in 1917, had risen to 1,242;

it also dealt in the co-operative supply of flour, feed, coal, hay, fruit, lumber, etc., and this branch grew from the use of 100 cars in 1914 to over 1,400 car-loads in 1917 besides a large business in farm machinery. In this latter year the amalgamation of the Alberta Company with the Grain Company of Winnipeg took place.

In Saskatchewan the Grain Growers' Association took a different and more varied line of action than in other Provinces. Up to 1914 it was devoted to educational work and propaganda and had built up a large membership with about 1,000 local Associations and Elevator facilities handled separately. Meanwhile, however, the more or less isolated Locals had been developing collective buying by car-lots in order to reduce prices on such commodities as binder twine, fencing, flour, coal, lumber, etc., and in 1914 the Provincial Association decided to establish a Central wholesale trading department for the service of the local bodies and business was begun at once. The chief products handled were binder twine, coal, fencing material, lumber, trading supplies, apples, flour, feed, potatoes and groceries. When the business began the staff consisted of J. B. Musselman, Secretary and Managing Director, and one stenographer; in 1919 the head office in the Saskatchewan Co-operative Elevator building at Regina comprised over 45 members, while the Winnipeg office of the Association, opened in 1918, had a staff of eight members. At the end of 1914 the sales were $302,000 and the profits approximately $9,000. In the year 1915 the sales increased to approximately $850,000, with a profit of $15,000. In 1916 the sales passed the million dollar mark, with a profit of over $15,000. In 1917 the sales were $1,600,000 and the profits nearly $36,000.

The United Grain Growers Ltd. At this stage, in 1917, the Grain Growers' Grain Co. and the Alberta Farmers' Co-operative Elevator Co. came together in an amalgamation which created much interest. Their relations had always been close and friendly and an effort also was made to get the Saskatchewan Association to bring its business into a common pool but without success for the time being. An Act of Parliament was obtained in June to permit of the amalgamation as the United Grain Growers Ltd., with an authorized capital of $5,000,000.

Arrangements were consummated on Sept. 1, 1917, and the election of Directors resulted as follows: President, T. A. Crerar; 1st Vice-President, C. Rice-Jones and 2nd Vice-President, John Kennedy; C. F. Brown, Calgary, R. A. Parker, Winnifred, Alta., J. J. McLellan, Purple Springs, Alta., P. S. Austin, Ranfurly, Alta., H. C. Wingate, Cayley, Alta., Roderick McKenzie, Brandon, Man., F. J. Collyer, Welwyn, Sask., John Morrison, Yellow Grass, Sask., J. F. Reid, Orcadia, Sask. Mr. Rice-Jones was Acting General-Manager during Mr. Crerar's absence in Ottawa as Minister of Agriculture. After the amalgamation the united concern owned 206 elevators in the three Provinces and leased 137 in Manitoba; owned 223 flour warehouses in the three Provinces and leased 8 and owned, similarly, 181 coal sheds. It had branches of the Live-stock Department in Winnipeg, Calgary and Edmonton with seats upon the Stock Exchanges of Winnipeg, Calgary, Vancouver and Fort William.

This combination of business interests on Aug. 31, 1918, showed Assets of $8,359,176, a paid-up capital stock of $2,159,764, a Reserve of $1,500,000, Profits for the first year of amalgamation totalling $441,760. During the year and under the new conditions the Grain Department had handled 29,879,672 bushels of which 18,000,000 were wheat; the Co-operative Department $5,925,791 worth of flour and feed, coal, twine, wire, fruit and vegetables, lumber, and builders' supplies, machinery, etc.; the Live-stock Department 4,402 cars of animals. The Shareholders' capital and surplus was $4,058,245 or an increase of $573,589 in the year—of this $1,898,482 was composed of surplus earnings and savings over and above dividends; the gross earnings were $3,047,395 and the working expenses $2,256,274 with a dividend of 10 per cent.

A Committee—of its Directors—H. W. Wood, Peter Wright and C. Rice-Jones visited the chief United States Agricultural organizations of 12 States, in 1918, and reported their impressions as to the relative success of Farmers' organizations in the United States and the Canadian West. They found that: "We had been a great deal more successful than they had in the United States, not only in co-operative commercial enterprises, but also in the educational, legislative and economic work of the Associations. We were naturally interested to get them to specify just in what way, and the various opinions expressed practically resolve themselves into the fact that they claim our Associations have been far more successful in securing new legislation and amendments to existing legislation of a nature favourable to the farmers than have their organizations in the United States, and secondly, that the commercial activities of the farmers in Canada have also been more successful than their operations in the United States." They found no State where the farmers obtained such Government assistance in regard to Elevators as was given in Alberta and Saskatchewan and the Americans blamed the entrance of the Farmers' organizations into politics very largely for the result.

The Company by this time controlled 6 subsidiary concerns—the Grain Growers' Export Co., Inc., New York; the Grain Growers' Export Company, Ltd., Winnipeg; Public Press, Limited; United Grain Growers, (B.C.) Ltd.; U. G. G. Sawmills, Ltd.; United Grain Growers' Securities Co. Ltd. and owned a number of shares in the Home Bank of Canada. It may be added that U.G.G. Securities, Ltd., was organized in 1917 for the sale of farm lands on commission and that about the same time the business of Hail Insurance, through general agencies, was added to the other interests of the Company. There were in 1918, 35,000 farmer members behind the Co-operative business of this concern and the total of grain handled in 1912-17 (before amalgamation) was over 100,000,000 bushels.

The Canadian Council of Agriculture. This body was formed at Toronto in December, 1909, with a view to co-ordinating the work of the Grain Growers' Association, increasing and organizing its public influence, and extending its functions beyond the bounds of the West by promoting organization in Ontario and the East. The organization took place at the annual meeting of the Dominion Grange with E. C. Drury, Master, in the chair.   E. A. Partridge, D. W. McCuaig and R. McKenzie were present as Delegates from the West and it was decided on motion of H. J. Pettypiece to form a National organization of farmers to be known as the Canadian Council of Agriculture.   The following objects were stated and afterwards published in the *Proceedings* of the Dominion Grange for that year: (1) To organize the farm population of the Dominion for the study of social and economic problems having a bearing on the happiness and material prosperity of the people; (2) to collect such material from scientific and literary sources, the annals of class movements, and the records of legislative enactments in our own and other countries, as are necessary for the proper information of our people, and to disseminate the same; (3) to formulate our demands for legislation and present them through the officers of the Association to the notice of Parliament and our different Legislative bodies; (4) to encourage the entry of our farmers into active membership in one or other of the political associations, according to individual predisposition, as a means to make the political parties, without distinction, responsive to and representative of the demands of the people who form the bulk of the population; (5) to urge the adoption of co-operative methods by our members (but outside our Association) in the purchase and sale of commodities that equity may be established in the business of exchange.   The Grange in the end, did not affiliate.

It was announced that any association of farmers entirely independent of Government control in the Dominion of Canada and organized to give effect to any or all of the purposes above set forth should be eligible for membership in this Association.   The Saskatchewan, Manitoba and Alberta organizations became charter bodies; in 1916 a re-organization took place so as to admit the commercial associations to membership and the Council then represented the three Western Grain Growers' Associations, the Alberta and Saskatchewan Co-operative Elevator Companies, the Grain Growers' Grain Co., the *Grain Growers' Guide*, the United Farmers of Ontario and its Co-operative concern, the United Farmers of New Brunswick with a total of 90,000 farmers altogether.

Other changes followed such as the amalgamation which constituted the United Grain Growers, Ltd., a restriction of the unit of representation to 4 and the establishment of definite headquarters at Winnipeg in place of the movable head office prior to 1916.   The first President was D. W. McCuaig, then President of the Manitoba Grain Growers; he was succeeded by J. A. Maharg, President of the Saskatchewan body and he, in turn, by H. W. Wood, President of the Alberta United Farmers.   The first Secretary was E. C. Drury of Barrie, afterwards Prime Minister of Ontario, and he was succeeded in turn by E. J. Fream, Roderick McKenzie and Norman Lambert. The work of the Council was largely constructive in policy and propagandist in practice. Its earliest public action of importance was the arrangement of the great Delegation of 800 farmers to Ottawa in 1910 and there followed a vigourous preachment in favour of free trade in Agricultural implements and natural products and for an increase in the British Preference. In 1916 there began a drafting of the Farmer's Platform which it was proposed to make national in scope and character and application and to cover the whole economic, social, and political condition of Canada. It was finally completed in a tentative form and published in December; with very few changes it was endorsed by the Manitoba Grain Growers on Jan. 11, 1917, by the United Farmers of Alberta on Jan. 25, by the Saskatchewan Grain Growers on Feb. 13 and by the United Farmers of Ontario on Mch. 1st.

Then came the closing of the War and the evolution of new problems and plans of reconstruction; meantime, also, several planks in the 1916 Platform such as woman suffrage, prohibition, measures of direct taxation on incomes and business profits, and legislation directed against political patronage, had been carried into effect. It was, therefore, thought desirable in the Autumn of 1918 to revise the Farmers' Platform and bring it up-to-date. This was accordingly done and clauses were added bearing upon Canadian relations with the Empire, the returned soldier, Labour, and such questions as the War-Time Elections Act, Order-in-Council government, Titles, freedom of speech and freedom of the press, and Proportional Representation. The result was approved at a meeting of the Council of Agriculture at Winnipeg on Nov. 29, 1918, and promulgated to the Provincial bodies for final approval, which was unanimously given, during the Winter of 1919. Officially, it was claimed in a pamphlet issued at this time by the Council, that this Farmers' policy would place the country on an economic, political and social basis that would be in the interest not only of farmers, but of the citizens of Canada generally; that the wage-earners, artisans, professional men and trades-people were affected equally with the agricultural classes by the fiscal system prevailing in Canada, and were just as much involved as the farmer in economic and social reforms; that because the organized farmers had initiated and promoted a Federal programme of reform did not prove a desire to create class conflict or gain selfish ends. This National Farmers' Platform was as follows:

1. A League of Nations as an International organization to give permanence to the world's peace by removing old causes of conflict.

2. We believe that the further development of the British Empire should be sought along the lines of partnership between nations, free and equal, under the present governmental system of British constitutional authority. We are strongly opposed to any attempt to centralize Imperial control. Any attempt to set up an independent authority with power to bind the Domin-

ions, whether this authority be termed Parliament, Council or Cabinet, would hamper the growth of responsible and informed democracy in the Dominions.

3. Whereas Canada is now confronted with a huge national war debt and other greatly increased financial obligations, which can be most readily and effectively reduced by the development of our natural resources, chief of which is agricultural lands;

And whereas it is desirable that an agricultural career should be made attractive to our returned soldiers and the large anticipated immigration, and owing to the fact that this can best be accomplished by the development of a national policy which will reduce to a minimum the cost of living and the cost of production;

And whereas the War has revealed the amazing financial strength of Great Britain which has enabled her to finance, not only her own part in the struggle, but also to assist in financing her Allies to the extent of hundreds of millions of pounds, this enviable position being due to the free trade policy which has enabled her to draw her supplies freely from every quarter of the globe and consequently to undersell her competitors on the world's market, and because this policy has not only been profitable to Great Britain, but has greatly strengthened the bonds of Empire by facilitating trade between the Motherland and her overseas Dominions—we believe that the best interests of the Empire and of Canada would be served by reciprocal action on the part of Canada through gradual reductions of the tariff on British imports, having for its objects closer union and a better understanding between Canada and the Motherland and at the same time bring about a great reduction in the cost of living to our Canadian people;

And whereas the Protective Tariff has fostered combines, trusts and "gentlemen's agreements" in almost every line of Canadian industrial enterprise, by means of which the people of Canada—both urban and rural— have been shamefully exploited through the elimination of competition, the ruination of many of our smaller industries and the advancement of prices on practically all manufactured goods to the full extent permitted by the tariff;

And whereas Agriculture—the basic industry upon which the success of all other industries primarily depends—is unduly handicapped throughout Canada as shown by the declining rural population in both Eastern and Western Canada, due largely to the greatly increased cost of agricultural implements and machinery, clothing, boots and shoes, building material and practically everything the farmer has to buy, caused by the Protective Tariff, so that it is becoming impossible for farmers generally, under normal conditions, to carry on farming operations profitably;

And whereas the Protective Tariff is the most wasteful and costly method ever designed for raising national revenue, because for every dollar obtained thereby for the public treasury at least three dollars pass into the pockets of the protected interests, thereby building up a privileged class at the expense of the masses, thus making the rich richer and the poor poorer;

And whereas the Protective Tariff has been and is a chief corrupting influence in our national life because the protected interests, in order to maintain their unjust privileges, have contributed lavishly to political and campaign funds, thus encouraging both political parties to look to them for support, thereby lowering the standard of public morality;

Therefore be it resolved that the Canadian Council of Agriculture, representing the organized farmers of Canada, urges that, as a means of remedying these evils and bringing about much needed social and economic reforms, our tariff laws should be amended as follows:—

(a) By an immediate and substantial all-round reduction of the customs tariff.

(b) By reducing the customs duty on goods imported from Great Britain to one-half the rates charged under the general tariff, and that further gradual, uniform reductions be made in the remaining tariff on British imports that will ensure complete Free Trade between Great Britain and Canada in five years.

(c) That the Reciprocity Agreement of 1911 which still remains on the United State statute books, be accepted by the Parliament of Canada.

(d) That all food stuff not included in the Reciprocity Agreement be placed on the free list.

(e) That agricultural implements, farm machinery, vehicles, fertilizers, coal, lumber, cement, illuminating fuel and lubricating oils be placed on the free list, and that all raw materials and machinery used in their manufacture also be placed on the free list.

(f) That all tariff concessions granted to other countries be immediately extended to Great Britain.

(g) That all corporations engaged in the manufacture of products protected by the customs tariff be obliged to publish annually comprehensive and accurate statements of their earnings.

(h) That every claim for tariff protection by any industry should be heard publicly before a special Committee of Parliament.

4. As these tariff reductions may very considerably reduce the national revenue from that source, the Canadian Council of Agriculture would recommend that, in order to provide the necessary additional revenue for carrying on the government of the country and for the bearing of the cost of the War direct taxation be imposed in the following manner:—

(a) By a direct tax on unimproved land values including all natural resources.

(b) By a graduated personal income tax.

(c) By a graduated inheritance tax on large estates.

(d) By a graduated income tax on the profits of corporations.

(e) That in levying and collecting the Business Profits Tax the Dominion Government should insist that it be absolutely upon the basis of the actual cash invested in the business and that no considerations be allowed for what is popularly known as watered stock.

(f) That no more natural resources be alienated from the Crown, but brought into use only under short-term leases, in which the interests of the public shall be properly safeguarded, such leases to be granted only by public auction.

5. With regard to the returned soldier we urge:—

(a) That it is the recognized duty of Canada to exercise all due diligence for the future well-being of the returned soldier and his dependents.

(b) That demobilization should take place only after return to Canada.

(c) That first selection for return and demobilization should be made in the order of length of service of those who have definite occupation awaiting them or have other assured means of support, preference being given first to married men and then to the relative need of industries, with care to insure so far as possible the discharge of farmers in time for the opening of spring work upon the land.

(d) That general demobilization should be gradual, aiming at the discharge of men only as it is found possible to secure steady employment.

(e) It is highly desirable that, if physically fit, discharged men should endeavour to return to their former occupation, and employers should be urged to reinstate such men in their former positions wherever possible.

(f) That vocational training should be confined to those who while in the service have become unfitted for their former occupation.

(g) That provision should be made for insurance at the public expense of unpensioned men who have become undesirable insurance risks while in the service.

(h) That facilities should be provided at the public expense that will enable returned soldiers to settle upon farming land when, by training or experience, they are qualified to do so.

6. We recognize the very serious problem confronting labour in urban industry resulting from the cessation of war, and we urge that every means, economically feasible and practicable, should be used by federal, provincial and municipal authorities in relieving unemployment in the cities and towns: and, further, recommend the adoption of the principle of co-operation as

the guiding spirit in the future relations between employer and employees—between capital and labour.

7. A land settlement scheme based on a regulating influence in the selling price of land. Owners of idle areas should be obliged to file a selling price on their lands, that price also to be regarded· as an assessable value for purposes of taxation.

8. Extension of co-operative agencies in agriculture to cover the whole field of marketing, including arrangements with consumers' societies for the supplying of foodstuffs at the lowest rates and with the minimum of middleman handling.

9. Public ownership and control of railway, water and aerial transportation, telephone, telegraph and express systems, all projects in the development of natural power, and of the coal-mining industry.

10. To bring about a greater measure of democracy in government, we recommend:—

(a) The immediate repeal of the War-Time Elections Act.

(b) The discontinuance of the practice of conferring titles upon citizens of Canada.

(c) The reform of the Federal Senate.

(d) An immediate check upon the growth of government by Order-in-Council, and increased responsibility of individual members of Parliament in all legislation.

(e) The complete abolition of the patronage system.

(f) The publication of contributions and expenditures both before and after election campaigns.

(g) The removal of press censorship upon the restoration of Peace and the immediate restoration of the rights of free speech.

(h) The setting forth by daily newspapers and periodical publications, of the facts of their ownership and control.

(i) Proportional representation.

(j) The establishment of measures of Direct Legislation through the initiative, referendum and recall.

(k) The opening of seats in Parliament to women on the same terms as men.

The members of the Council in 1918 when these important decisions as to future policy and action were reached included G. F. Chipman, Winnipeg; F. W. Riddell, Regina; J. J. Morrison, Toronto; F. J. Collyer, Selwyn, Sask.; W. J. Healy, *Grain Growers' Guide*, Winnipeg; R. M. Johnson, East View, Sask.; Thomas Sales, Langham, Sask.; W. R. Wood, Winnipeg; C. Rice-Jones, Calgary; J. J. McLellan, Purple Springs, Alta.; J. L. Brown, Pilot Mound, Man.; Rice Sheppard, Edmonton; J. L. Rooke, Togo, Sask.; P. Wright, Myrtle, Man.; J. F. Reid, M.P., Orcadia, Sask.; J. Robinson, Regina; J. W. Leedy, Whitecourt, Alta.; Hon. T. A. Crerar, Minister of Agriculture, Ottawa; N. P. Lambert, (Secretary) Winnipeg; H. W. Wood, Carstairs, Alta.; Roderick McKenzie, Winnipeg; Hon. George Langley, Regina; R. W. E. Burnaby, Jefferson, Ont.; Manning W. Doherty, Malton, Ont.; J. L. Paynter, Tantallon, Sask.; J. R. Murray, Winnipeg; John Kennedy, Winnipeg; P. Baker, Ponoka, Alta.; A. G. Hawkes, Percival, Sask.; J. B. Musselman, Regina. Some slight amendments were afterwards made including one from Ontario which added to the Reciprocity Agreement of 1911 clause the words: "And that any further reduction of the Tariff of the United States towards Canada be met by a similar reduction of the Canadian tariff towards the United States." Another from Alberta was

H. W. Wood

President United Farmers of Alberta and of the
Canadian Council of Agriculture

R. W. E. Burnaby

President of the United Farmers Co-Operative Society
of Ontario; Elected in 1919 President
of the United Farmers of Ontario.

Two Leaders of the Farmers' Party.

approved which substituted for "a graduated personal income tax" the following words: "A sharply graduated personal income tax whereby all would pay a fair tax to the State of as much as 2 per cent. on an income of $2,000, to 10 per cent. on an income of $10,000, increasing in proportion until an income in excess of $100,000 would pay 50 per cent. to the State." To the minor clauses were added a declaration in favour of the Public ownership of the Meat-packing industry and Prohibition of the manufacture, importation and sale of intoxicating liquors as beverages in Canada.

Accompanying the development of this policy was the formation of a Joint Committee of Commerce and Agriculture which included representatives of the Council and the organized Farmers and of the Business interests of the West. The object, as expressed at the initial meeting on Mch. 7-9, 1916, was to bring the Western farming and business interests together from time to time to discuss problems affecting their mutual welfare, in order that in matters where an agreement of opinion was reached, joint action might be taken. The number of representatives was increased to 50, or 25 from each side, and an immediate result was a better understanding as to mortgage conditions with better relations between the Banks and the farmers. Periodical meetings followed and did good service. The Council did not oppose Conscription but it took strong exception to the Government's 1918 policy of removing exemptions and at a meeting in Winnipeg on July 8 passed the following Resolution:

1. That because of the large number of voluntary enlistments from the farms of Canada, the action of the Government in cancelling exemptions has very seriously interfered with production.

2. That the indiscriminate calling of young men bears with exceptional hardship upon the agricultural industry inasmuch as the young people of our farms are qualified to undertake responsible tasks at a much earlier age than others and because the older sons having left the home farms, the responsibility for conducting operations in many cases rests entirely on these young men.

3. That the Government's desire that leave of absence be granted in cases of hardships has very frequently been observed.

4. That before calling up the 19-year or other classes, the Government should hear the Farmers' point of view.

5. That exempted young farmers getting married before cancellation of such exemptions, should be placed in the married class.

6. That training be carried on locally in order that young men could have leave to help in the harvest.

During the War the Council of Agriculture held an important position in dealing with such questions as the fixing of wheat prices and the disposition of flour and grain supplies for the Allies; its influence in such adjustments was considerable and its views or statements concerning Railway rates and problems carried weight with the Railway War Board. The Council in 1918-19 carried on a vigourous campaign against the Tariff and issued pamphlets which described the West as paying a large proportion of the fiscal duties of the whole country—two-thirds of

13

those collected at Port Arthur and Fort William, three-fourths of the sugar duties at British Columbia ports and a proportion of those collected in the East equal to one-half the total collected in the West; claimed that lower Customs duties would mean reduced prices for food and clothing and that profiteering was a chief result of the Tariff and protected capitalism; urged that England be helped in its Free Trade policy and described Direct taxation as the basis of the Farmers' Platform; advocated a new National Policy of freer trade with the following revenue proposals: "Take the revenue from those who enriched themselves during the War. Investigate the holdings of war-stocks as they propose to do in England. Tax the returns from capital, and tax incomes in a way that will bring fair pressure on large and small incomes alike."

The Women's Farm Organizations. It took time for the Women to grasp the importance and value of organization. Individualistic as the farmer by nature was, his wife was even more so; women did not at first like or approve of the meetings which took their men from home and kept them away for many hours in each week. Gradually, however, as farm conditions slowly improved and conditions grew out of the pioneer stages, as tiny settlements became villages or towns and life on the prairie less isolated, as population increased and opportunities and prosperity grew with it, the women came to approve of organization and agitation and co-operation and to believe that all improvements were due to these elements in agricultural growth. Labour-saving devices, conservation of health, better rural schools and higher education, came to be, in their minds, directly connected with better markets, co-operative buying and selling, and better agricultural credit. Back of it all, however, was the desire for social intercourse, the gregarious instinct inherent in women, no matter how isolated or how devoted to home and children.

In 1912 a journalist on The *Grain Growers' Guide,* Miss Frances Marion Beynon, vigourously urged farm women, in a series of able articles, to organize; in 1913 before the annual Saskatchewan Convention, F. W. Green, Secretary of the Provincial Grain Growers, proposed and brought about an accompanying Convention of Farm women at Saskatoon. Instead of being present at the men's Convention as visitors or wives of the Delegates, the women on Feb. 12-14 organized their own meeting and heard addresses from Mrs. A. V. Thomas, Winnipeg *Free Press,* Miss Beynon, Mrs. Nellie L. McClung, Miss Cora Hind, G. F. Chipman, Winnipeg, and F. W. Green. The speeches covered every variety of subject and an unanimous decision was reached to organize a Women's Section of the Grain Growers' Association; a Committee was appointed to make arrangements for organization with Mrs. A. V. Thomas, Mrs. A. G. Hawkes, Mrs. S. V. Haight and Mrs. John McNaughton amongst the members. Mrs. McNaughton of Harris was the first President and for three succeeding years.

After her came Mrs. S. V. Haight of Keeler in 1918 and Mrs. C. E. Flatt of Tantallon in 1919 and the Women's membership in this latter year was 5,000 with 200 Locals.

Meanwhile, in 1913, the constitution of the United Farmers of Alberta was amended to admit women into that organization with the same privileges as men. In 1914 the farm women assembled with the men in annual Convention. In 1915 a still larger number of women were present and this time the majority of the women met in separate Convention and organized the United Farm Women of Alberta with Miss Jean Reid of Alix as President; she was succeeded by Mrs. Walter Parlby of Alix and in 1918 by Mrs. J. F. Ross, Duhamel. The Association numbered 1,500 in 1919 with 120 Locals. The Manitoba women were the last to organize. In 1912 they were admitted to membership on the same terms as men; in 1916 they met separately at the annual Convention and in 1917 elected a Board of Directors to carry on their special work and, in the following year, became the Women's Section of the Grain Growers' organization—in which, however, they retained their individual membership. Mrs. Arthur Tooth of Eli was the first President and her successor was Mrs. J. S. Wood of Oakville. The principles of the Section were defined in its Constitution as follows:

(1) To extend the influence and increase the power of the Association and by special effort to enlist the support and sympathetic co-operation of the women and girls of our rural communities.

(2) Assisting the Association in providing training for leadership for the young people of the rural communities.

(3) The enrichment of rural life, socially and intellectually, by study, discussion, social intercourse, and wholesome, well-balanced recreation.

(4) Education of women and girls for the responsibilities of community life and of democratic citizenship generally.

(5) Making more adequate the educational facilities of the rural boys and girls, and the securing of more intimate relationship between the school and the other units which make up the community.

(6) The safeguarding of the fundamental rights of women and children by more adequate and just legislation, both Dominion and Provincial.

(7) Better provision for the safeguarding of public health, especially of children, and the securing of more adequate medical and hospital facilities for rural districts.

(8) The maintenance and defence of the home as an institution.

(9) Co-operation, where possible, with all organized forces, spiritual or material, which are working for the greatest good of the country and its people.

(10) Larger emphasis upon the finer things of life—"the things that are more excellent."

The United Farm Women of Ontario was organized in Toronto on June 17, 1918 at a meeting of 16 women and 3 men and a Provisional Executive appointed composed of Mrs. G. A. Brodie, Newmarket, President, Mrs. J. N. Foote, Collingwood, Vice-President, and Miss Emma Griesbach, Collingwood, Secretary; Mrs. McNaughtan of the Saskatchewan Association was present and helped in the work of organization—which was greatly facilitated by the right of full membership in the U.F.O. granted to women a few months later; a succeeding Convention (Dec. 17, 1918) included 30 women representing 6 Locals and the Pro-

visional officers were confirmed. The platform adopted specified
these objects: (1) To create a right public opinion amongst women by the study of important local and national questions; (2)
to induce a fuller sense of individual responsibility for community
enterprises and interests, such as better schools, public libraries,
public health and better moral conditions; (3) to help train members to train themselves to think intelligently and to express their
thoughts clearly. Membership increased rapidly and steps were
taken at the 1918 meetings of the organization and of the Women
Grain Growers to form a National organization.

Preliminary action was taken in the constitution of an Inter-
Provincial Council of Farm Women at Brandon on Jan. 8-9, 1919
—following along the lines of the Council of Agriculture. Those
present were Mrs. G. A. Brodie, President in Ontario; Mrs. J.
S. Wood, President in Manitoba; Mrs. John McNaughtan, Hon.
President in Saskatchewan; Mrs. J. F. Ross, Vice-President in
Alberta, and Mary F. McCallum, Associate Editor, *Grain Growers'
Guide.* Mrs. McNaughtan was Chairman and Miss McCallum
Secretary and the meeting organized, temporarily, as the Inter-
Provincial Council of Farm Women with the following objects:
(1) To further the objects of the Canadian Council of Agricul-
ture; (2) to popularize the study of social and economic problems;
(3) to deal with Federal and inter-Provincial matters specially
concerning women and children. Mrs. McNaughtan was elected
President, Mrs. Walter Parlby of Alberta Vice-President and
Miss Mabel Finch of Winnipeg, Secretary, with Miss McCallum
as a member of the Executive. The following Resolution was then
passed:

> Whereas the interest and work of the organized Farm Women are now
> nation-wide and steadily growing in National importance, and whereas we
> believe that this work can now best be furthered by organizing along
> national lines, and whereas we believe, further, that the closest possible
> affiliation with the Farmers' National organization, the Canadian Council
> of Agriculture, is in the best interest of the whole Farmers' movement and
> the nation of which we form a part, we recommend—
> (1) That a Women's Section of the Canadian Council of Agriculture
> be formed; (2) that the Women's Section of the Council of Agriculture be
> composed of one representative from the Executives' of each of the following
> organizations: United Farm Women of Ontario, Women's Section of the
> Manitoba Grain Growers' Association, Women's Section of the Saskatchewan
> Grain Growers' Association, the United Farm Women of Alberta, and one
> representative from The Grain Growers' Guide; (3) that the Women's
> Section of the Canadian Council of Agriculture may meet in joint session
> with the Council for the conduct of such business as may be considered
> to be of common interest, and that the members of the Women's Section shall
> at such joint sessions be accorded all the rights and privileges of members of
> the Canadian Council of Agriculture.

Another Resolution declared that "tolerance should govern all
inter-Provincial relationships." On Apr. 1st the organization met
at Winnipeg in joint session with the Council of Agriculture
and dealt with the final passing of the National Platform; afterwards it met in private session and took up the question of encouraging immigration of domestic help—in which the members
were deeply interested so far as the farms were concerned; they

wrote Mr. Calder, Minister of Immigration, protesting against indiscriminate immigration along this line and asking for the appointment of farm women to go to Britain and select young women suitable for farm work. Mrs. McNaughtan was appointed Convenor of a Committee on Immigration and its associated subjects; Mrs. Wood on Social Service and Mrs. Parlby on Medical Aid; Miss Finch on Young People's work and Miss McCallum on Property laws; Mrs. Brodie on marketing and such subjects as Co-operative business, market fluctuations, grading, oleomargarine, transportation facilities, etc.

The succeeding work of these various organizations—particularly in the West—was remarkable. Their success in a public form was chiefly along the lines of Franchise work, Temperance and Prohibition, and in Public Health campaigns; they co-operated with the W.C.T.U. and other women's organizations and helped largely in obtaining women's franchise in the Provincial arena of Saskatchewan and Alberta; in the same Provinces they influenced the Grain Growers' Conventions to support Prohibition and accompanied various Delegations to the Provincial Governments; in Manitoba special attention was given to Public health and child welfare movements and in Alberta and Saskatchewan the essential need of rural hospitals was the key-note of much work with successful legislation obtained along municipal lines. Improved rural education was everywhere their policy and a matter of earnest effort and included such subjects as Consolidated Schools, improved buildings, hot lunches for children, play-ground equipment; betterment of Social conditions was another object realized in travelling libraries, rest-rooms for women in towns, beautifying cemeteries, establishment of community halls, public meetings and debates and lectures, amateur plays and literary evenings and a general development of social life. Everywhere the organization, like the independent yet similar Women's Institutes of Ontario, did good work and improved the capacity and bettered the life of the women of the prairies.

The Pioneer Farmers' Organization—The Grange. On Nov. 15, 1867, there was formed at Washington, U.S., an Association called the Patrons of Husbandry with its branches to be called Granges; on Dec. 4th following, the National Grange was established—an agricultural, non-political, secret, and non-sectarian body which, by 1872, had 1,704 subordinate Granges including some in Ontario. On June 2nd, 1874, representatives of these latter bodies met at London and organized the Dominion Grange with S. W. Hill, Ridgeville, as Master and Thomas Dyas, London as Secretary. A Declaration of Principles was adopted which defined mutual protection and instruction as the ultimate objects; expressed the desire to bring producers and consumers, farmers and manufacturers, into the most direct and friendly relations, to dispense with middlemen, to oppose the tyranny of monopolies and to fight high rates of interest or exorbitant profits in trade; advocated the teaching of practical agriculture and domestic science in the schools and urged a proper appreciation of the abilities and sphere of women as members of the Order; deprecated interference with politics as an Order but declared the principles of the Grange to be fundamental to honest government.

The motto chosen was: "In essentials Unity; in non-essentials Liberty; in all things Charity." The objects were specified in detail as follows: "To develop a better and higher manhood and womanhood among ourselves; to enhance the comforts and attractions of our homes and strengthen our attachment to our pursuits; to foster mutual understanding and co-operation and to reduce our expenses both individual and corporate; to buy less and produce more, in order to make our farms self-sustaining; to diversify our crops, and crop no more than we can properly cultivate; to condense the weight of our exports, selling less in the bushel, and more on hoof and in fleece; to systematize our work, and calculate intelligently on probabilities; to discountenance the credit system, the mortgage system, the fashion system and every other system tending to prodigality and bankruptcy. We propose meeting together, talking together, working together, buying together, selling together, and, in general, acting together for our mutual protection and advancement, as occasion may require; we shall avoid litigation as much as possible by arbitration in the Grange; we shall earnestly endeavour to suppress personal, local, sectional and national prejudices, all unhealthy rivalry, all selfish ambition; we shall constantly strive to secure entire harmony, good will, vital brotherhood among ourselves, and to make our Order perpetual."

Within five years the Order had 31,000 members scattered over the length and breadth of the Dominion and in 1877 it had been incorporated as "The Grange' in Canada;" about 1,000 branches were organized at one time or another and in 1898 there were about 70 in good working order in Ontario. Any large growth, however, had ceased by this time in Canada though in the United States the Order continued to prosper fairly well and had at one time 1,000,000 members and in 1919 still had a large number. Some commercial undertakings were attempted in Ontario—the Grange Wholesale Supply Co. of Toronto, the Grange Mutual Insurance Co. of Owen Sound, the Grange Trust Co. of the same place and the People's Salt Co. of Kincardine. Only the last one was able to survive the fate which has come to so many similar institutions in the States and in Canada. During these 40 years of life in Canada the Grange had the following Masters—as the Presidents were termed:

1874-78	S. W. Hill	Ridgeville	1894-95	Dawson Kennedy	Peterborough
1879-80	H. Hilborn	Uxbridge	1896	George E. Fisher	Freeman
1881	W. M. Blair	Truro, N.S.	1897-98	W. F. W. Fisher	Burlington
1882	Alfred Gifford	Meaford	1899-03	Jabel Robinson	Middlemarch
1883-84	Jabel Robinson	Middlemarch	1904-05	Henry Grose	Lefroy
1885	Robert Wilkie	Blenheim	1906-08	J. G. Lethbridge	Strathburn
1886	Robert Currie	Wingham	1909-10	E. C. Drury	Crown Hill
1887-88	Chas. Moffatt	Edge Hill	1911	N. E. Burton	Port Stanley
1889	George Copeland	Hespeler	1912	Henry Glendinning	Manilla
1890-91	Henry Glendinning	Manilla	1913-14	W. C. Good	Brantford
1892-93	Peter Hepinstall	Fordwich	1915	W. E. Wardell	St. Thomas
		1916-19	J. C. Dixon	Moorefield	

At the 33rd annual Session of the Grange, Toronto, Dec. 4-5, 1917, the Declaration of Principles had a "Political Section" added with the preliminary re-assertion, as a part of its organic law, that the Association could have no politics: "Yet the principles we teach underlie all true politics, all true statesmanship, and, if properly carried out, will tend to purify the whole political atmosphere of our country. For we seek the greatest good to the greatest number. But we must always bear in mind that no one, by becoming a Patron, gives up that inalienable right and duty, which belongs to every citizen, to take a proper interest in the politics of his country. It is the duty of every member to do all in his power, legitimately, to influence for good the action of any political party to which he belongs. It is his duty to do all he can to put down bribery, corruption and trickery; and see that none but competent, faithful and honest men, who will unflinchingly stand by the public interests, are nominated for all positions of trust; and to have carried out the principle which should always characterize every Patron, that 'The office should seek the man, and not the man the office'."

While the Grange took no part in Elections it did, in later years, advocate certain political principles and frequently sent Deputations to the Governments concerned. It was strongly opposed to everything savouring of militarism and in 1909 denounced the proposal to build or maintain a Canadian Navy; it favoured Provincial ownership of long-distance Telephone lines and the principle of Direct Legislation through the Initiative and Referendum; it opposed Bounties or bonuses to special industries and supported Free trade and Reciprocity with the United States. For many years the *Farmers' Advocate* was the official organ of the Grange; later the *Farmers' Sun* of Toronto became its organ and this journal expressed the strongest possible views upon public questions and party politics.

The Patrons of Industry in Ontario. The strict avoidance of party politics by the Grange in the greater part of its career left room for effort along that line—especially as farmers in the States began to develop political ambitions. In 1889 branches of the Patrons of Industry were introduced into Ontario by organizers from Michigan and in a few months 200 of them were in existence; the aim of the Order was to advance agricultural interests by independent political action. Late in February, 1890, delegates met at Sarnia and formed a Grand Association for Ontario with Fergus Kennedy as Grand President, C. A. Mallory, Grand Vice-President, and L. A. Welch, Secretary-Treasurer; all connection was severed with the United States organization and on, Sept. 22, 1891, a constitution and platform were approved after submission to subordinate bodies. Efforts were at once commenced to have salt, binder-twine and iron ore placed on the free list and a 25,000-petition was sent to Ottawa; a Grand Association for Manitoba was formed at the close of 1891 with Charles Braithwaite as President; at the annual meeting of 1892 in Toronto

Mr. Mallory became Grand President and 600 lodges were stated
to be organized in Ontario. The platform was made public as
follows:

1. Maintenance of British Connection.
2. The reservation of the Public Lands for the actual settler.
3. Purity of administration and the absolute Independence of Parliament.
4. Rigid economy in every department of the public service.
5. Simplification of the laws and a general reduction in the machinery
of Government.
6. The abolition of the Canadian Senate.
7. A system of Civil Service Reform that will give each County power
to appoint or elect all County officials paid by them except County Judges.
8. Tariff for revenue only, and so adjusted as to fall as far as possible
upon the luxuries and not upon the necessaries of life.
9. Reciprocal trade on fair and equitable terms between Canada and
the world.
10. Effectual legislation that will protect labour, and the results of
labour, from those combinations and monopolies which unduly enhance the
price of the articles produced by such combinations or monopolies.
11. Prohibition of the bonusing of Railways by Government grants
as contrary to the public interest.
12. Preparation of the Dominion and Provincial Voters' Lists by the
municipal officers.
13. Conformity of electoral districts to County boundaries, as constituted
for Municipal purposes, so far as the principle of representation by population
will allow.

Following this the Farmers' Binder-Twine and Agricultural
Implement Manufacturing Co., Ltd., with $100,000 capital, was
formed at Brantford; Petitions, were circulated and signed by
40,000 persons for the removal of duties upon implements, coal-
oil, wire fencing and coal; in 1893 the Manitoba body added
Female suffrage and Prohibition to their planks and in 1894 the
Ontario Patrons decided to place candidates in the field for Parliament and Legislature. The membership reported at this time
was 150,000. For the Ontario elections of 1894 the Patrons
placed 30 candidates in the field and the Grand President issued
a Manifesto declaring the political principles of their organization to be as follows: 1st, the election by popular vote of all
County officers, except judges—such officers to be elected for a
period consistent with proficiency and good behaviour, and subject to clearly defined governmental inspection; 2nd, the abolition of Government House, Toronto; 3rd, the abolition of the
system of the people's representatives receiving special favours
from Railway corporations in the form of free passes, or other
favours; 4th, the taxing of mortgages, stocks, and bonds at their
actual value; and 5th, the repeal of all Provincial statutes giving
special class privileges.

The returns showed 16 Patrons elected and J. L. Haycock
of Frontenac County was elected leader when the Legislature
met. On Dec. 11th, following, a Quebec Provincial Association
was formed with J. M. Varville, St. Philippe, as President; Duncan Marshall was sent to the Maritime Provinces to organize
those districts, if possible, and succeeded in starting a number of

lodges with a Grand Association in P. E. Island of which he was elected President.   Meanwhile a Central Dominion Executive was organized at Toronto with Mr. Mallory as President and L. A. Welch Secretary; in the 1896 Dominion elections the Patrons were not very successful and returned only 4 members from Ontario and 2 from Manitoba; a Grand Association was formed, however, for the North-West Territories while W. L. Smith, Toronto, succeeded L. A. Welch as Secretary. This was the peak of the movement and thereafter it gradually declined in public influence and merged into the regular Parties, until, in the 1902 Ontario elections there was not a Patron elected; eventually the Order disappeared altogether as a Canadian organization.

The Non-Partisan League in Canada and the States.   As the Grange and the Patrons of Industry came from the States to Eastern Canada, so did the Non-Partisan League to the West. It obtained some footing in Alberta and Saskatchewan and came into close association with the United Farmers of the former Province who had, also, absorbed in their time another American organization—the Society of Equity. It was in the main a political Society in its methods and essentially Socialistic in its opinions; it originated in North Dakota in 1915 and had, in a short time, gained 65,000 members there, elected the Governor, secured control of the Legislature and, by 1919, had over 200,000 members scattered throughout the North-Western States; in 1916 S. E. Haight, one of its promoters, came over to Canada, made his headquarters at Swift Current, Sask. and preached unceasingly the Dakota platform—which by that time had extended into other Western States and also Alberta. The membership scheme was original with a yearly Fee of $15.00 out of which the organizer was entitled to a commission of $4 while the balance went into the central fund.   In Saskatchewan one of the demands upon this Fund was made by a small four-page weekly newspaper called *The Non-Partisan Leader*, published in Swift Current as the official organ of the League; later on a similar journal was published in Calgary.   Every farmer could be a member and also an organizer, and thus earn his $4.00 for each new member obtained.   In 1917, there were 3,000 members in Saskatchewan and about 2,000 in Alberta; the organization contested 7 seats in the Saskatchewan elections of that year and elected D. J. Sykes by acclamation. S. E. Haight was President.   In Alberta during the Provincial elections of 1917 Mrs. L. C. McKinney and James Weir were elected to the Provincial Legislature. The platform in the States and Canada was practically the same and these were the main points—the last clause being purely Canadian.

1. Nationalization of banking and credit systems, railroads, telegraphs, telephones, and steamship lines and all other means of public transportation and communication.

2. Nationalization of all industries organized on a national scale, and in which competition has virtually ceased to exist.

3. The extension of the Public domain to include all coal mines, water-powers and forests.

4. A Federal Direct Legislation Act, including the Recall and equal and unrestrained Suffrage for both men and women.

5. A graduated Inheritance tax law; a graduated Income tax law; the enactment of a national compulsory Insurance law covering accident, illness, old age, and death.

6. The "free" administration of justice; the abolition of the Canadian Senate and no Court to be legally competent to declare as unconstitutional any Act of the Parliament of Canada.

The chief success of the League was in North Dakota with extreme Socialism as the platform. Here it succeeded in establishing co-operative stores, obtaining control of newspapers, collecting large funds and getting control of small banks. A. C. Townley was President of the National Non-Partisan League and, during 1918-19, cut a considerable figure in politics; he and his League had a large following throughout the North-Western States though keen exception was taken to their anti-war attitude; in March, 1918, Mr. Townley was for a time under arrest because of alleged association with I.W.W's, Pacifists and pro-German Socialists and the circulation of seditious literature; on May 1st 1918 he admitted before the Military Committee of the U.S. Senate that the income of his organization from membership fees was $1,600,000 a year and that its total investment in Liberty Bonds was $5,000; on July 12, 1919 he was found guilty of teaching disloyalty by a jury of farmers at St. Paul. Under its complete control of the North Dakota Legislature a number of League proposals were put into operation and the Governor of the State, L. J. Frazier, on Feb. 26th, signed laws to establish and operate a Bank of North Dakota; build and operate terminal grain-elevators and flour-mills; establish and operate the North Dakota Home Builders' Association for the purpose of enabling citizens of the State to build and own their own homes; and set up an Industrial Commission to manage these and other industries which the State might decide to operate through unlimited powers granted by 14 amendments to the State constitution.

Under the Banking scheme it was proposed to raise $2,000,000 by floating a bond issue, and that amount was to be the capital of the Bank. The State Industrial Commission was to have direction and charge of the Institution and all State, county, township, municipal, school and other public funds, as well as the funds of penal, industrial and educational institutions, were to be withdrawn from the National, State, and Private Banks and placed with the Commonwealth Bank—a total withdrawal of about $50,000,000. The success of the whole movement turned upon the ability of Mr. Townley who was said by opposing journals to have used $2,000,000 in capturing North Dakota and attacking Minnesota; it was believed that with a clever leader, a large campaign fund, an able propaganda organization and political skill behind the movement,.North Dakota would constitute an object lesson in success and power; hence the interest of the League's extension into the Canadian West and the probability that it might have gone far had the Grain Growers not first captured the field and held

it by skillful management. In Minnesota and Chicago the League
tied up with organized Labour to a considerable extent and its
official points of advocacy were utilized to this end as follows:

1. Employment for all and reduction in cost of living; maintenance of
the earnings of labour and of primary producers; destruction of 'monopoly' extortion.

2. Employment for the unemployed, in co-operation with organized
labour, through Government works in such enterprises as road-building,
forestry and timber and fuel production, flood production and land re-
clamation; the immediate reduction of freight and passenger rates, especially
on fuel and food.

3. Liquidation of the National Debt; to that end there should be an
income tax and inheritance tax; all incomes above $100,000 per annum and
all inheritances above that amount to be appropriated until the Debt is paid;
all incomes not accounted for and all income-producing properties, securities and inheritances not listed for this purpose to be forfeited to the
Government.

Under a Referendum in June, 1919, North Dakota stood by
the Socialist programme; control of the Public Schools, with the
idea of teaching Socialism therein, being the most keenly fought
part of the League's policy. In October investigation into the
affairs of the bankrupt Scandinavian-American Bank of Fargo
showed loans to the League and its subsidiaries of $432,000 and
a system under which $3,500,000 had been obtained from the
farmers in post-dated cheques for purposes of political activity
with 47 weekly and 2 daily newspapers under the financial control
of Townley's National Service Bureau.

Such success as the League had in Alberta and Saskatchewan
was largely due to its support of political methods and was accentuated by the success of its parent organization in North
Dakota and Minnesota. The Grain Growers and U.F.A. up to
1919 absolutely refused to consider this policy or to join the
League in joint action; early in this latter year, however, the
bigger organizations assumed a different attitude and, in Alberta,
the Non-Partisan League practically threw in its lot with the
U.F.A., withdrew its organizers and held up both hands for united
Political action. On Mch. 25 the Medicine Hat Political Conven-
tion of the U.F.A. passed this Resolution: "Whereas the Non-
Partisan League has been very successful in maturing the farmers'
demand for independent political action; therefore we invite our
Non-partisan members to throw in all their resources and influence with this body, and so preserve unity of action." On
May 14 a joint meeting of representatives of the League and the
United Farmers of Alberta approved the proposal that the latter
body should go into politics and declared that "the chief aim of
this movement shall be to change our form of government from the
party system to a business administration, based on the fundamental principles of democracy, by which, ultimately, all schools
of political thought will have due representation in the conduct
of the Government of the country."

H. W. Wood, President of the U.F.A., and James Weir of the
Non-Partisans, had frequently disagreed up to this time—the
latter's views being rather advanced for Mr. Wood; in the new

discussion as to combined action Mr. Weir wanted Non-Partisan League members who were not farmers to be included but this Mr. Wood and his organization did not approve of; in July the League had practically suspended its Alberta activities and its political action was made to harmonize with that of the United Farmers. In Saskatchewan the Grain Growers and the Non-Partisans did not agree at all and, in September 1919, J. B. Musselman, Secretary of the former body, issued a circular-letter repudiating the League's policy.

Formation of the United Farmers of Ontario.   After the subsidence of the Grange as an influential factor and the disappearance of the Patrons, the farmers of Ontario drifted back to their old political moorings and were content to accept the labours of the Departments of Agriculture at Ottawa and Toronto and the work of the Ontario Agricultural College as an expression of their desires for improvement in condition and outlook; discontented spirits found an outlet in the *Farmers' Sun*, which, originally, was started by Dr. Goldwin Smith in 1891 as an expression of his views upon Canadian relations with the United States and Britain. Quietly, however, the idea of a powerful organization was working in the minds of such men as E. C. Drury, J. J. Morrison, W. C. Good, W. L. Smith, and others whose experience dated back to Grange or Patron days; they had learned much from such mistakes as these organizations had made and from the successes of the Western bodies.

Following the failure of the Grange to implement its alliance of 1909 with the other organizations a number of its members at their annual meeting on Dec. 17, 1913, considered the question of consolidating existing societies in Ontario and appointed a Committee composed of H. Glendinning, Manilla, Elmer Lick, Oshawa, H. B. Cowan, Peterborough, E. C. Drury, Barrie and J. J. Morrison, Arthur, to take action.   W. C. Good, Brantford, and Lieut.-Col. J. Z. Fraser of Burford were afterwards added and on Feb. 28, 1914, they issued an invitation to the officers of Farmers' Associations and Clubs, Subordinate Granges and Fruit Growers' Associations of Ontario to a meeting which took place in Toronto, on Mch. 19, with 200 delegates present.   Mr. Drury presided and described Ontario as the weak link in the chain of Canadian Farmers' organizations; this Province, in particular, he declared, should not be importing butter, meats and eggs; he urged co-operation as a general policy and the creation of a Society to be called the United Farmers of Ontario with a United Farmers' Co-Operative Company.   This was finally decided upon and a Board of Directors elected as follows:

President	E. C. Drury	Barrie
Vice-President	G. A. Brethen	Norwood
Vice-President	R. H. Halbert	Melancthon
Director	J. F. Breen	Melancthon
"	John Servius	Warkworth
"	R. H. Johnston	Omemee
"	A. E. Vance	Forest
Director	T. H. Adams	Essex

J. J. Morrison of Arthur was afterwards appointed Secretary-Treasurer. The first Resolutions passed opposed the renewal or granting of a Federal bonus on iron-ore and the imposition of a duty on fence wire and urged that Railway property should contribute to municipal taxes on the same basis as farm property. On Feb. 25, 1915, the first Report of the U.F.O. showed 44 organizations and 2,000 members. Resolutions were passed deprecating the current embargo on export of horses and the proposed imposition of a minimum 25 per cent. wage on the Toronto-Hamilton highway construction as inimical to farm interests. R. H. Halbert was elected President and A. J. Reynolds, Selina, and B. C. Tucker, Harold, Vice-Presidents. In the succeeding year 82 new branches were added and a membership of 5,000 attained though only 100 out of 500 agricultural organizations in the Province had as yet affiliated; Mr. Halbert was re-elected President (Feb. 2, 1916) and 'W. C. Good a Vice-President with Mr. Reynolds re-elected.

Resolutions were passed (1) in favour of reduction of duties on all British goods as a step toward helping Great Britain through her war burdens and strengthening Imperial union; (2) appointing a Committee to study methods of agricultural co-operation; (3) urging a Federal law to abolish the sale, importation and manufacture of spirituous liquors during the War with an after-war popular vote as to its re-establishment; (4) deprecating, as injurious to agricultural interests, "any large enlistment from the farms for Overseas service." In the Spring of 1916 the U.F.O. affiliated with the Council of Agriculture and its 3rd Convention was held on Feb. 18, 1917 with Mr. Halbert re-elected President and E. C. Drury and W. C. Good elected Vice-Presidents. At the next Convention (Dec. 19-20, 1917) the President was again re-elected while Mr. Drury became sole Vice-President. On this occasion Resolutions were passed (1) asking the Departments of Agriculture to assist in solving the Rural problem by conducting investigations similar to those conducted in the United States to ascertain the revenues and expenditures of a large number of typical farms; (2) declaring that "since human life is more valuable than gold, this Convention most solemnly protests against any proposal looking to the conscription of men for battle while leaving wealth exempt from the same measure of enforced service"; dealing with the public impression that some change in Canada's relation to the Empire was necessary and declaring that "the whole question should be fully laid before the Canadian people before Canada was in any way committed in this matter; asking for amendment of the Railway Act so that the Bell Telephone Company would handle the business of the Local and Municipal Systems on the same basis as it did business brought to it by the public, namely, at its usual long-distance rates; requesting a continuance of existing restrictions against the admission and manufacture of Oleomargarine; protesting against the conferring of titles upon Canadians as undemocratic.

There followed on May 14, 1918 the great gathering of farmers at Ottawa to protest against the cancellation of exemptions to farmers and their sons; the U.F.O. and the Western grain growers were behind it and thousands were in attendance with an elaborate Memorandum presented to the Government. The 5th Annual Convention was held in Toronto—as were all the others—on Dec. 18-19, 1918, and the Constitution was amended to increase membership fees from 50 cents to $1.00, to admit women on the same basis as men and to increase the number of Directors from 9 to one for each Provincial Riding. The membership at the close of this year was reported at 30,000.

The Grain Growers Enter Politics. Since 1910 the Western Grain Growers had been verging upon politics; their strength was so obvious and their unity along certain lines of political thought so clear that it was difficult to keep out of the arena; their opposition to the Tariff and advocacy of free-trade and reciprocity did for a time allign them, in practice, with the Liberal party and against the Government, but the War, and then the Union Government arrangement, broke up political affiliations and objects for some years. It was claimed as a powerful argument, in 1919, for new allignments and independent political action, that the farmers and their wives, if organized, would constitute a total of 1,559,000 in Canada compared with mechanics and labourers numbering 1,231,000 and the professional and commercial classes totalling 557,000—the reason for including farmers' wives in this category being that they were to all intents and purposes farm workers —supplying meals for the help, feeding poultry and assisting in various farming duties. Adding 625,000 women, not on the farms and 179,000 widows, these totals would make up a rough estimate of Canadian voting power. In this connection there was published at this time a compilation by C. W. Peterson in his interesting *Wake up! Canada*, showing that in 1918 there were in the Senate and Commons of Canada and in all the Provincial Legislatures a total of 222 Lawyers, 163 of other professions, 329 from the industries and the merchant class, 5 Labourers and 161 Farmers or 18 per cent. of the total representation. The strongest argument against Political action for the farmer was its almost uniform past failure in the United States and in Canada and the Report published in 1918 by a United Grain Growers' Company delegation to the United States said as to this point:

Taking an active part in politics they (Officers of American Farmers' organizations) state has been responsible for the wrecking of more Farmers' organizations in the United States than anything else. Upon our asking why the entry of their organizations into politics resulted in their breaking down, the various opinions of different men, stated briefly, can be summed up in the following:—that immediately an organization entered into politics, all the broken-down and would-be politicians in the country were attracted to it with the object in view of using it for their own ends and very often under the pay or backing of interests entirely opposed to the farmers. The regulations for membership in most of the Associations being practically wide-open, they have found it very difficult to prevent this. Secondly, that the old political parties immediately planned the raising of issues upon which the farmers themselves could not agree, the result being a split in the organizations. Thirdly, because of the impossibility of finding candidates for political office whom the farmers could unanimously support, many farmers either on account of old affiliations with political parties, or personal reasons of disagreement on points of issue, refusing to support the candidate nominated by the Farmers' organizations, this resulting in a further split amongst the members.

The political influence in Saskatchewan over a long period of W. R. Motherwell and George Langley, leaders of the Grain Growers and members of the Provincial Government; the appointment of another leader, T. A. Crerar, to the Government of Canada and his later retirement because of Tariff conditions and policy; the birth of political activity amongst the Farmers of Ontario and the growing power of the Grain Growers in Western provincial politics; the influence of the Council of Agriculture in later Government action and policy at Ottawa, were bound to have an effect along lines of direct political action. It was natural that Alberta should move first; it was the keenest in radical thought and policy and was influenced from birth by the political ideals of the Society of Equity and later on, by the principles of the Non-Partisan League—some of the milder phases of their policy finding place in a fruitful soil; the movement was led in this respect by Mrs. L. C. McKinney, M.L.A., James Weir, M.L.A., and H. W. Wood, who had developed by this time into one of the strongest men in the whole Farmers' organization; it was presented in a definite form by the unanimous Resolution of the Alberta United Farmers, in Convention at Edmonton, on Jan. 21-23. Political action had been warmly endorsed by President Wood, who left the chair to speak for the Resolution, of which the terms were as follows:

Whereas our organization has reached a state of development in freedom from partisanism, in mobilization of thought and numerical strength that political action not only becomes possible, but is now necessary to our continued progress; and whereas the nature of this organization, and the very ground-work of its development, demands that it should continue to be independent of any class or party, and free from any sectional influence to the end that purely democratic and independent political action shall be promoted.

Now therefore be it resolved: (1) We urge the Locals in the various Federal districts to take immediate steps looking to the organization of District units for the purpose of holding at least one Convention each year in each of such Districts; (2) the Central U.F.A. office shall, upon request of 10 per cent. of the Locals in any District, render whatever assistance it can in calling and arranging for such Convention; (3) the primary purpose of such Convention shall be to discuss ways and means of taking independent political action and selecting an independent candidate; (4) each Convention shall be responsible for its actions in putting a candidate in the field, in financing and electing such candidate, but nothing in this Resolution shall prevent any officer of the Provincial organization giving what assistance he can when called upon.

A public meeting followed in Edmonton on Jan. 22 which was addressed by Mrs. McKinney and Messrs. Wood and Weir in favour of this policy and supported by John Kennedy and Roderick McKenzie, two leaders from Manitoba. In an interview (Cal-

gary *Herald*, Jan. 15) Mr. Wood stated that: "The financial institutions of the country are really autocratic and all political
parties are autocratically organized. Our efforts are to discover
some method of eliminating this autocratic party rule and discovering some purely democratic method of taking political action." He declared that the Grain Growers had always aimed
at ultimate political action but had to wait till they were strong
enough. In Ontario, on Feb. 18, J. W. Widdiefield, a United
Farmer candidate, carried North Ontario for the Legislature
over a Government candidate, in a Conservative constituency, by
a majority of over 200 and upon a platform with this declaration: "That hitherto the Agricultural interest has not been fairly
or sufficiently represented in legislation; and by reason thereof
grave errors in legislation have been made, to the great detriment
of not only the farming community, but also, through the farming
community, of the whole nation; that, in order that the farmers
may be properly represented, it is necessary for them to enter the
political field; that their representatives in Parliament should
be non-partisan, and should deal with every question which may
arise upon its merits and from the standpoint of the farmer, showing how it will affect the country as a whole."

At Medicine Hat, Alta., on Mch. 25-26, the first of the District
Conventions was held and H. W. Wood declared that the U. F.A.
had to take a step further, which was a political step: "This was
the first time in their lives that they had been called upon to
build their own political machinery, and the machine was going to
be the people themselves who would be absolutely responsible for
everything they did." The policy was warmly endorsed and an
important Resolution passed supporting the Referendum and
Recall and declaring that a candidate immediately after receiving
a nomination, must sign his resignation,—"said resignation to be
placed in the hands of a Committee of 21 qualified electors, with
the understanding that a failure on his part to advocate and defend, by voice and vote, the principles laid down in the Platform
of the Canadian Council of Agriculture, shall be good and sufficient reason to justify the Committee in calling a Convention to
annul the nomination, or in the case of an elected member, forward said resignation to the Prime Minister of Canada." This
action was very generally adopted throughout the West.

Following this the Council of Agriculture decided at Winnipeg
on Apr. 1st that Provincial organizations could take such political
action as they chose and immediately afterwards the Manitoba
Grain Growers' Executive (Apr. 4) declared by Resolution that
if the representatives of the Province in Parliament should refuse
to support, actively, the Farmers' policies the District Associations should immediately take steps to call Conventions of all the
electors in their constituencies who supported the principles of
the Farmers' Platform, and make arrangements to nominate, finance
and elect a candidate in support of this platform. In Alberta
during the next two months political discussion was continuous

and, during June, Grain Growers' Conventions were held in every Federal constituency of the Province and the machinery created and organization started for the nomination and election of a farmers' candidate at the next general election. The nominations were not actually made but the other important preliminaries were carried out with enthusiasm.

On July 25 a Convention was held at Calgary composed of the Executive officers of the 12 constituency organizations and the U. F. A. Political Association was organized with O. L. McPherson, Vulcan, appointed Chairman and H. Higginbotham, Secretary of the U.F.A., as Secretary; Mr. McPherson was, later on, elected President for the year with an Executive composed of Archibald Muir, Provost; W. D. Spence, Calgary, Mrs. G. F. Root, Westaskiwin and Donald Cameron, Elnora. The Farmers' Platform was unanimously adopted, addresses were given by H. W. Wood of the U.F.A., Thomas Sales of the Saskatchewan Grain Growers and G. F. Chipman of the *Grain Growers' Guide* and the payment of Directors, when engaged in the political work of the Association, was fixed at $6.00 per day. The following formal objects were specified:

1. To constitute in itself a medium through which the various Federal and Provincial constituencies' political organizations may act collectively where their common political interests are concerned.

2. To establish a Bureau for the collecting and disseminating of statistics and other information bearing on the political welfare of the people.

3. To assist the various Federal and Provincial constituency organizations to co-operate with other groups having similar aims and to inspire and supervise political organization in the Province.

4. To promote the formation of a National Farmers' Political organization.

Meantime, similar action was taking place in the 16 Federal constituencies of Saskatchewan with Thomas Sales of Langham and J. B. Musselman, Secretary of the G.G.A. active in organization work. The Grain Growers in all the Federal constituencies, except Humboldt, met and created the necessary Executives and their Chairmen came together at Regina on July 31st, with other representative members of the G.G.A., and A. G. Hawkes of Percival acting as Chairman. A Resolution was passed stating that at all these constituency Conventions, held under the auspices of the Saskatchewan Grain Growers' Association, the delegates had expressed in no uncertain terms their lack of faith in the existing political parties and their conviction that it would not be possible to secure through any of them legislation which would give effect to the new National Policy laid down in the platform of the Canadian Council of Agriculture, and deciding, therefore, to perfect a Provincial organization for the purpose of nominating and electing representatives to Parliament "free from allegiance to any existing political parties and who stand for the enacting of legislation that will give effect to the new National Policy."

The creation of a National organization was also urged and J. M. Pratt of the *Grain Growers' Guide* stated that the Alberta farmers were raising a fund of $280,000 to forward these objects. Thomas Sales of Langham was elected Provisional President of the new organization; W. J. Orchard, Tregarva, Vice-President; Thomas Teare, Marquis, R. M. Johnson, East View, and J. B. Musselman, Regina, as Directors. Plans of organization were at once developed including a canvass of the Province by 2,000 persons for funds to carry on the future campaign; on Sept. 17th 67 accredited delegates of the new Party and 6 members of the Saskatchewan Grain Growers met at Regina; Thomas Sales and W. J. Orchard spoke at length as did O. L. McPherson of the Alberta body, W. R. Wood, Secretary of the Manitoba Grain Growers, Norman Lambert of the Council of Agriculture and J. B. Musselman. A constitution was enacted which declared that (1) the sole purpose of the movement was to secure the election to Parliament of suitable persons pledged to use their vote in Parliament and their influence in support of the principles enunciated in the Platform and (2) that "all members of all classes, regardless both of vocation and of former political affiliations, shall be eligible for any office or for Parliamentary candidature provided they desire the enactment of legislation giving effect to these demands." After five busy Sessions the following Executive was elected: President, W. J. Orchard, Tregarva; Vice-President, Thomas Teare, Marquis; A. Baynton, Carlton; Mrs. John McNaughtan, Harris; R. M. Johnson, Eastview; J. B. Musselman, Regina; Geo. F. Edwards, Markinch.

Meanwhile, Manitoba had taken somewhat similar action. The leaders of its Grain Growers were in favour of the movement and, no doubt, the matter had something to do with Mr. Crerar's retirement from the Government; most of the 15 Dominion constituencies organized, as in the other Provinces, and Mr. McKenzie stated on Oct. 9 that they all would have Farmer candidates at the next election; as in Saskatchewan and Alberta the cost of conducting the campaign was to be arranged for previous to the nomination by a canvass of the electors in each constituency for contributions to the election expenses. A meeting of Delegates from the whole Province was held on Oct. 17, under a call from W. R. Wood, Secretary of the G.G.A., which vigorously attacked the Tariff; organization was effected and arrangements made for a series of 40 meetings to educate the electorate.

Into the rather heated political atmosphere of Saskatchewan and Alberta was then projected a Dominion bye-election in the former case and a Provincial one in the latter. The Martin Government in Saskatchewan had during the year alligned itself again with the Liberal party; Hon. W. R. Motherwell, the founder of the Grain Growers' movement had, in 1918, resigned as Minister of Agriculture; Assiniboia, an old-time Liberal seat, had been vacated by J. G. Turriff upon his elevation to the Senate. It was made a test election as to the power of the new organization; O. R. Gould of Manor, President of the Political Executive in the Riding, was nominated on Sept. 25 as the candidate and a campaign fund of $6,000 was announced; on the 26th W. R. Motherwell was nominated by the Liberals to oppose him. In the ensuing fight Mr. Gould held many meetings and had many active supporters; Mr. Motherwell wielded the power of an experienced speaker and of a Liberalism so enthusiastic in conviction that he had given up his position as Minister because of the support given by the Government, at that time, to the Union Government; he also had the backing of three Provincial Liberal members whose ridings were included in Assiniboia; the riding itself had always gone Liberal by 800 or 900 votes though, on the other hand, it was almost entirely agricultural in character.

Incidents of the campaign included elaborate addresses at Estevan and other places by Mrs. W. R. Motherwell; the declaration in an advertisement published by the Assiniboia Liberal Association that the Grain Growers essay into politics was "the most dare-devil act of political bucaneering ever attempted in Canada;" the statement by Mr. Gould that his opponent during the War had "placed partisanship before patriotism" and the claim by him that the United States got 80 per cent. of its revenue from direct taxation, Great Britain 81 per cent. of its vast revenue by the same method, while Canada got 78 per cent. of its revenue through the Tariff or indirect taxation; the fact that the returned soldiers largely supported Gould and the common assertion that the Austro-Germans in the Riding supported Motherwell; the evolution of hostility in the Great War Veteran weeklies of Winnipeg, Regina, Saskatoon, Calgary and Edmonton and, in some of the Labour journals, against the Farmers' organization; the strong opposition expressed by Hon. Walter Scott, ex-Premier of Saskatchewan, in his support of Mr. Motherwell, to the Nationalization of railways and his prediction at Carlyle on Oct. 25 that the present Farmers' movement would suffer the fate of the Patrons of Industry. The speakers were very numerous, as the contest developed, and Hon. Frank Oliver, Hon. W. Scott, A. R. McMaster, M.P., I. E. Pedlow, M.P., supported Mr. Motherwell while J. A. Maharg, M.P., E. A. Partridge, H. W. Wood of Alberta, Thomas Teare, John Kennedy, Norman Lambert, J. B. Musselman, supported Mr. Gould. On Oct. 27 the latter was elected by the overwhelming majority of 5,224 votes—7,712 to 2,488 and Mr. Motherwell lost even his deposit.

In Ontario, on the same day, the United Farmers carried Glengarry-Stormont where Wilfrid Kennedy was elected by a large majority, as was T. W. Caldwell, President of the New Brunswick Farmers, in Carlton-Victoria. Following this initial triumph of the Farmers' movement came the victory won in Ontario over the Hearst Government and a minor but important success in Alberta. Here the U. F. A. had decided to contest the Cochrane seat in the Provincial Legislature with Alex. W.

Moore as its candidate; E. V. Thompson was the Liberal candidate
and a vigourous fight was put up by the Stewart Government;
Mr. Moore was elected on Nov. 3rd by a majority of 145. The
Provincial Government, in a speech by Hon. Duncan Marshall,
at Cochrane on Oct. 15, pointed to its action in turning over one
entire Provincial Agricultural school for the training of soldiers
and their wives. He went into detail as to the aid afforded farmers
through the Farm Machinery Act and the Hail Insurance Act; the
abolition of the bonus system in creameries, and the establishment, instead, of an excellent system of grading and marketing
of dairy products; the rapidly-increasing number of agricultural
schools throughout the Province under the Government system of
"bringing the schools to the boys and girls" of Alberta. H. W.
Wood led the Farmers' forces and at Crossfield on Oct. 21st made
these references in a much-debated speech:

> We, as a group of farmers, are affected alike by wrong economic condi-
> tions. That gives us a common viewpoint. Labour is affected in a different
> way. That gives them another viewpoint. We can scarcely organize with
> a common viewpoint. Now, when we get all of our classes properly organized,
> and we learn and develop leadership amongst our class that is capable of
> representing us intelligently, and we select the best representatives of each
> class, and we get Proportional representation, then each class will send re-
> presentatives commensurate with its strength. These representatives will
> go down there (to Parliament or Legislature) not as hired lobbyists, but
> belong as a body to their class, ready to defend the interests of their class
> with their lives. We go down there as farmers, we ask something we are not
> entitled to! The other classes are just as thoroughly organized as we, and
> they will resist any unjust demands, and that resistance of each other will
> eventually bring them to a common level, on which these great class differences
> .will be settled, and they will never be settled any other way.

On Nov. 11 the Canadian Council of Agriculture met at
Winnipeg with Hon. T. A. Crerar and R. McKenzie present from
Manitoba, J. A. Maharg, and J. B. Musselman from Saskatchewan,
H. W. Wood and others from Alberta, J. J. Morrison, R. H. Halbert and R. W. E. Burnaby from Ontario, Mrs. John Mac-
Naughtan, Mrs. J. S. Wood, Mrs. G. A. Brodie from the Women's
organizations. R. M. Johnson of Saskatchewan stated that $50,000
had been collected there for Provincial political purposes, and
Mr. Crerar stated that in Ontario more than 55 per cent. of the
Farmers' support came from the Conservative element. A Resolution was passed as follows: "Whereas the new National Policy
advocated in the platform of the Canadian Council of Agriculture
is based upon the broad, national, economic interests of Canada
without respect to any particular class or occupation; and whereas
political organization has been promoted within the Provincial
bounds of Alberta, Saskatchewan, Manitoba and Ontario; and
whereas conditions now demand the better co-ordination of the
political effort organized thus far for the purpose of electing
supporters of the National Policy to the Dominion Parliament:
Be it resolved that the Executive of the Canadian National
Council of Agriculture be instructed to invite representation

from the Provinces named herein, to a Conference for the consideration of these matters." A succession of speeches by Hon. T. A. Crerar followed—Brandon, Nov. 18; Regina, Nov. 26; Kentville, N.S., Dec. 12 and Truro, Dec. 15; Toronto, Dec. 19. The North Ontario bye-election for the Commons also developed into a keen fight with R. H. Halbert, President of the United Farmers of Ontario, as the Farmers' candidate, and his election by over 100 majority in a strongly Conservative seat, was the last in a chain of 1919 successes.

THE 1919 RECORD OF FARMERS' ORGANIZATIONS

The Canadian Council of Agriculture. At a Winnipeg meeting of this Executive body on Apr. 1st Women's organizations were for the first time represented and Resolutions were passed urging the Dominion Government to compel the Railway Board to rescind its order establishing Daylight Saving on the Railways; declaring that it should take over control of oil properties and production in Alberta; favouring the proposal for Political action and the nomination of Federal candidates; urging the Dominion Government to provide for the removal of the 7½ per cent. war tax with a substantial reduction in the Protective tariff; opposing the appointment of a Tariff Commission and proposing certain amendments to the Canada Grain Act. At a meeting on July 8-10 it was decided to engage a French-Canadian to carry on Publicity work through French-Canadian newspapers, under the direction of the Council and the United Farmers of Ontario, and to have literature published in the French language for use amongst the French-Canadian settlers in the Western Provinces.

A message was sent the Dominion Government urging investigation as to Cattle-feeding conditions and the drought in Alberta and parts of Saskatchewan with co-operative action between the Governments suggested. An invitation to attend the Liberal Convention at Ottawa was declined and a Resolution passed urging the taxation of all Dominion War bonds. On Aug. 1st the Council sent a Resolution to the Government declaring that because of the very material shrinkage in the prospective wheat crop of the North American continent in preceding weeks there could be "no justification for establishing a minimum price below that existing in the United States." On Aug. 14 N. P. Lambert, Secretary, addressed a long communication to the Wheat Board elaborating this point and urging various arguments in its favour. An elaborate Memorandum on policy was sent to the Liberal Convention at Ottawa which reviewed the economic conditions and requirements of the country; declared that Agriculture was the fundamental industry of Canada and that upon it depended national prosperity; stated that it was being "taxed exorbitantly" by the Tariff and regretted the abnormal growth of cities and urban centres—in the three Western Provinces 92 per cent. in 10 years as against 52 per cent. for rural districts; urged a "low customs tariff and direct methods of taxation," a Federal tax on unimproved land values, Government ownership of all transportation systems on land, air and water and Proportional Representation. Another Session in November was the largest one in its history with H. W. Wood, President of the Council and of the U.F.A., in the chair and representatives present from all the organized Provinces.

Political action was the chief subject of discussion and R. M. Johnson reported for Saskatchewan with $50,000 of funds collected; J. J. Morrison for Ontario stated that 45 members had been elected to the Legislature and 166,000 votes polled for the U.F.O.; a Resolution was passed in favour of a Conference on Political action. Other motions declared the Council out of sympathy with any restriction on the free exportation or sale of standard stock food and refuse or other screenings; declared that the actions of the Board of Commerce had "done much to unsettle and demoralize production of foodstuffs—especially in the Livestock industry;" stated that Lake shipping and coast-wise traffic in Canada should be under control of the Railway Commissioners. An important discussion took place at this time based on H. W. Wood's Crossfield speech as to classes. At Winnipeg on Nov. 17 he repeated his statement and declared that "Government by representatives of economic groups is inevitable" and that the Grain Growers was "an economic class organization." Mr. Crerar at Regina on the 19th speaking of the Grain Growers' platform, denied that it was of a class character: "We do not want class movements in Canada. We do not want them in the making of our laws or administration of the governmental business of the country."

The Saskatchewan Grain Growers' Association in 1919.

This pioneer body opened its 18th annual Convention at Regina on Feb. 18, 1919, with 2,000 delegates in attendance and J. A. Maharg, M.P., in the chair. Its Executive report dealt with the high cost of labour and the greatly increased cost of living; the increase in passenger and freight rates and the uncertainties arising out of unstable markets and insufficiency of supplies; the shortage of labour upon the farms; the serious crop failure over large portions of the Province and the disruption of all kinds of collective activities because of the terrible epidemic of Influenza which had swept across the Province. Heavy losses in binder-twine order cancellations and the need of larger capital for the Co-operative trading Department were specified and criticisms by the Retail Merchants' and Hail Insurance Associations for alleged hostility were reviewed. The Auditors' Report showed that the Association had $400,107 worth of merchandise on hand with Assets of $588,160 and Liabilities of $510,887 and a net loss of $7,434 in the Trading Department. The Rev. Dr. S. G. Bland delivered one of his radical speeches and urged strenuous political action for the regeneration of Canada; the Hon. W. M. Martin, Provincial Premier, dealt with policies of reconstruction, and immigration, and increased production, and pointed to the farmers as 72 per cent. of the population of the Province.

There was no Presidential address in view of Mr. Maharg's recent return from Europe. E. G. Hingsley, Manager of the Saskatchewan Municipal Hail Insurance Association, reported a deficit of $200,000 but stated that during the six years ending 1918 the private Companies had received premiums of $8,900,000 and had paid out in losses a total of $4,500,000; the difference, out of which the cost of administration had to be allowed, was $4,400,000. During the same period the Municipal Association had received $5,400,000 in taxes and had paid back in losses slightly over $5,000,000—the remaining $400,000 representing the cost of administration. Mayor Henry Black and D. M. Balfour, President of the Board of Trade, Seager Wheeler of Rosthern, and Hon. George Langley, Minister of Municipal Affairs, spoke while 40 Resolutions were considered; Mr. Musselman announced a division of his duties and the appointment of S. G. Lowthian as Treasurer of the Association. The chief subject before the Convention was the re-organization of the Trading Department with a capital of $500,000 in order to promote greater strength and efficiency; there was to be an issue of Debenture stock, limited to Members of the Association, and carrying a guaranteed interest of 6 per cent. with provision for an additional 2 per cent. before profits were distributed; a warehouse was to be erected in Regina for the purpose of supplying commodities at wholesale rates to Co-operative stores and Locals; a total of $60,000 was at once subscribed.

The revised Platform of the Council of Agriculture was read and discussed and unanimously approved. An amendment demanding Unrestricted Reciprocity with the United States was voted down after Mr. Maharg had pointed out that this would automatically mean Free trade with Great Britain in the light of other clauses in the Platform. Addresses were delivered on the second and third days by Hon. S. J. Latta, Minister of Highways, G. F. Chipman of Winnipeg, G. W. Prout, M.L.A., in Manitoba, on Rural Credits and James Somerville of Moose Jaw on the Saskatchewan Labour Party. The latter told a restless audience that Labour was becoming impatient and unless it could secure assistance from the producers it would use methods which might not be advantageous to all concerned. Constitutional means had failed to secure reforms: ''Labour men had more strings on them than farmers and this accounted for their failure very often; the press distorted Labour's view and labour was thus discredited. Bolshevism, although denounced in this country, was not understood. The Farmers' Platform did not go far enough to receive the support of labour. The people of the Old Country under low tariff were no better off than the people here under high protection. Labour wanted the nationalization of natural resources, while the farmers were only willing for some of them to be nationalized.''

Resolutions were passed urging completion of the Hudson Bay Railway; asking amendments to the Provincial Telephone Act following a Convention of Company delegates; re-affirming the stand of 1918 on the Language question in the schools; approving of Provincial-owned stockyards and Co-operative abattoirs and cold storages; protesting against increase in price of implements; calling for a Dominion Act to standardize all food production machinery; approving continuation of baking and milling tests of wheat by Government; conferring free Life memberships on returned soldier-farmers; asking extension of the Parcel post as an antidote to increased Express rates; asking a Dominion investigation into the leather trade with the object of restoring the price of green hides and leather to normal proportions; declaring that Canadian citizenship should only be conferred on men of foreign birth who would obligate themselves to bear arms; asking repeal of an amendment to the Stray Animals Act, which would make the Herd law obligatory in Northern Saskatchewan; favouring the continuance of total Prohibition; censuring certain printed forms of Implement dealers which called for 9 per cent. interest. It was also resolved to ask the Government to take steps, without further delay, to fix the price of the 1919 wheat crop on the same basis as that of 1918 and another motion approved the Government's establishment of a Cold-storage warehouse at Montreal and urged the need of similar facilities at other ocean ports.

It was decided, as an Association, not to enter the political field but to provide facilities which would enable the farmers of any Federal constituency in the Province to get together and organize themselves for the purpose of electing to the House of Commons a representative prepared to support the Farmers' National political platform. It was also decided to use only the English and French languages in Association publications. J. A. Maharg, M.P., was re-elected President for the eighth time and A. G. Hawkes, Vice-President; J. B. Musselman remained Secretary. Though the Association as a body did not technically enter the political arena, the organization formed at Regina on Sept. 17-18 .was practically an adjunct with official representatives at the meeting and on the new Executive. The Liberty Drive of Oct. 15, under direction of R. M. Johnson, Pasqua, and J. M. Pratt of *The Guide*, was very successful with indications that, eventually, the $300,000 aimed at for a political fund would be obtained.

The Women's Section of the Grain Growers met separately, at the same time, with Mrs. C. E. Flatt. in the chair. Addresses on the foreign settler problem were given by Dr. J. T. M. Anderson, Provincial Director of Foreign Education, and Mme. Breychinsky, an Ukrainian of Canora, and the following Resolution was passed: ''Whereas under the School Act, as it now exists in this Province, children are compelled to attend school only until they are 14 years of age, and whereas under the law many children leave school lacking the facts of elementary education; Be it resolved, that the Department of Education be petitioned to amend the Act so that each child be compelled to remain in school until the age of 14 years, and as much longer as is necessary to reach the standard of the fifth grade.'' Many Reports as to work amongst the schools were submitted and Mrs. Flatt of Tantallon was re-elected President. Resolutions also were passed asking the Dominion Government to send farm women to Britain to secure domestic help for farm women; declaring that the father and mother were joint partners in the care of their children and should have equal rights and responsibilities in their custody and maintenance, until ordered otherwise by a Court to which both had equal access; urging that youths under 18 should come under jurisdiction of Juvenile Courts; describing it as a first duty of Dominion and Provincial Governments to provide for the care of all mentally defective persons by means of industrial colonies; urging a health certificate as to fitness for marriage to accompany all marriage licenses.

The 9th annual meeting of the Saskatchewan Co-operative Elevator Co. Ltd., was held at Regina on Nov. 26, 1919, with 277 delegates present and the statement that within nine years, the Company had expanded from 46 elevators with 2,580 shareholders, to 316 elevators with 63,813 shareholders. In the year of July 31, 1919, the large total of 21,841,556 bushels of grain was handled with an elevator at Estlin holding the record, for the season, with 238,750 bushels. Over 50 per cent. of the grain handled by the Company's Interior elevators and over the loading platforms passed through the Farmers' own Terminals. Preparations were announced as well under way to double this latter capacity which would give a total of 5,200,000 bushels. The establishment of a Flour mill of large capacity was discussed but decision postponed. The Hon. C. A. Dunning, Provincial Treasurer and 1st General Manager of the Company, spoke and the Board of Directors was re-elected as follows: J. A. Maharg, M.P., James Robinson, A. G. Hawkes, Hon. George Langley, W. C. Mills, H. C. Fleming, John Evans, J. B. Musselman and Thomas Sales.

The annual Report for July 31 showed Assets of $5,370,412 including Country Elevators $421,850 and Terminal Elevators $2,085,620 (both less depreciation); the Liabilities included loans and accrued interest from Provincial Government $2,176,960, a subscribed capital of $3,190,650 and paid-up capital of $1,122,312; the Reserves were $1,069,591, the net profits for the year were $193,599 and the cash dividend 8 per cent. F. W. Riddell remained as General Manager, James Robinson as Managing Director and W. C. Mills Secretary. Resolutions were passed (1) declaring that "we favour the national marketing of our grain through a body similar to the Canadian Wheat Board, on which the farmers shall have adequate representation" and (2) stating that in view of the United States having removed the embargo on the importation of wheat in Canada, "it would not be fair for the Canadian Wheat Board to allow individual marketing of wheat across the boundary in car-load lots, but that the usual 'across the boundary traffic' be permitted to continue."

The United Farmers of Alberta in 1919.

H. W. Wood as President of this organization, as President, also, of the Council of Agriculture, was conspicuous in all the inter-Provincial and Western farm discussions of the year. At a meeting of the Alberta Federation of Labour in Medicine Hat (Jan. 8) he spoke as to a proposed amalgamation of these bodies, deprecated undue haste in the matter and described the mutual desire to eliminate poverty as the only reason for union; he urged free discussion combined with tolerance. The U.F.A. met in its 11th annual Convention at Edmonton on Jan. 21-23 with Mr. Wood in the chair and a formal welcome from Lieut.-Governor R. G. Brett, Mr. Premier Stewart and Mayor J. A. Clarke; the Premier's advice was "to till all you can and employ all you can;" Roderick McKenzie spoke for the Council of Agriculture and J. W. Leedy for the Directors.

Mr. Wood, in his Presidential address, reiterated his well-known views: "We have no well-grounded hope that the idea of rule by right of money is yet even seriously wounded. But the democratic forces of Canada are more determined than ever before to go on till Canada is made a democracy in reality, a democracy in which the people will rule, and money and the 'Great National Interests' over which has been cunningly built so much camouflage, will serve the people. The land of democracy which the people are demanding involves a complete readjustment of present class and national relationships, especially those involving economic affairs." He urged the returned soldier to go on the land and the various Governments to aid him; he declared agriculture to be "the paramount national institution of Canada''; he deprecated the farmers asking for a fixed price on wheat because ''the sooner the prices adjust themselves on the basis of supply and demand, without discrimination for or against any industry, the better it will be for all legitimate industries.'' H. Higginbotham, in his 1st report as Secretary, described the receipts of the Association as increasing in 1918 to $17,935 or double those of 1917; the membership was 17,850 and the new Locals totalled 84; appreciation was expressed of the services of C. Rice-Jones and E. J. Fream in respect to the Military Service Act. Other Committees reported and addresses were given by W. R. Ball, Mrs. L. C. McKinney, M.L.A. and John Kennedy, Winnipeg; J. W. Leedy, late of Kansas, criticized the Canadian banking system as a monopoly and Vere Brown of the Canadian Bank of Commerce, defended it; Hon. G. P. Smith, Minister of Education, and Jean Masson, from Quebec Farmers' Co-operative interests, also spoke.

The Farmers' Platform was adopted by the Convention and a Resolution supporting Political action by the farmers approved. Mr. Wood defined the latter position as follows: ''We must have absolutely independent action. No action must be taken which does not afford the fullest expression of our democratic principles. The machinery of our movement must be started at the very bottom among the people. This object can be reached by the formation of political districts to carry out the wishes and desires of the people in the line of political action.'' A broad basis of democratic co-operation with other bodies should be sought. Some criticism and dissatisfaction were expressed as to the *Grain Growers' Guide,* 'in its treatment of Alberta subjects and farmers, and a motion was passed asking the Executive to report at the next meeting. After a long discussion on Government price-fixing for wheat the motions to that end were shelved but the following approved: ''That legislation be passed confining the dealing in all grain in Exchanges or elsewhere, to cash and sales for actual future delivery of grain and grain products; and that steps be taken to provide the necessary credit to finance all farmers who have grain for sale until such time as they desire to sell it.'' H. W. Wood, of Calgary, was re-elected President and P. Baker, Pomona, Vice-President. The Executive included, also, W. D. Trego, Gleichen; H. Greenfield, Westlock; Rice Sheppard, South Edmonton; Mrs. W. H. Parlby, Alix. The Directors included A. Rafn, Bon Accord and

H. E. Spencer . . . . . Edgerton	Geo. F. Root . . . . . Wetaskiwin
W. F. Bredin . . . . . Bredin P.O.	Geo. G. Huser . . . . . Crossfield
F. W. Smith . . . . . . Sedgewick	G. D. Sloane . . . . . . Cayley
Chas. H. Harris . . . Oyen	L. Peterson . . . . . . Barnwell
Jos. Stauffer . . . . . Olds	Mrs. J. F Ross . . . Duhamel
G. A. Forster . . . . . Nateby	Mrs. Paul Carr . . . . Birdsholm

Resolutions were passed favouring a higher grading for seed oats; protesting against farmers with loans on their farms having to finance seed-grain advances through the Mortgage Companies; opposing the continued importation of Oleomargarine and urging an amended Railway Act to compel better cattle-guards; demanding that women be allowed the right to sit in Parliament on equal terms with men and vigourously opposing Daylight Saving; protesting against the operation of the Alberta Land Tax as discriminating against rural land; asking that qualified chiropractors be allowed to practice in the Province; urging the Dominion Government to assist the chilled meat trade with Great Britain; asking the Government to at once proceed to complete all railroad lines (branch, connecting, and feeders) that had already been commenced together with water-power operations either for domestic or irrigation purposes; demanding that the Goverment grant ''some tangible consideration'' to parents of boys killed in the War; favouring the putting into operation of the Provincial Farm Loans Act and approving Mothers' Pensions; asking for the Provincial licensing of machinery Companies with compulsion as to carrying stocks for repairs. These were the chief Resolutions passed out of 139 presented; many of the latter not being even considered from lack of time. A report from the Committee on Credits—J. W. Leedy, Rice Sheppard and W. R. Ball—was approved as follows:

> Whereas, the present system of Chartered Banks is not able to meet satisfactorily the credit requirements of the Agricultural industry; threfore, be it resolved, that the Convention recommends in the interests of agricultural development that the present banking system be supplemented by a System Bank, created by the Provincial Government which Government shall have plenary power to create, regulate and control, with minimum requirements of $10,000,000 paid-up capital and with power to take deposits; and further, we recommend that the Bank Act of Canada be amended to give the Provincial Legislatures full power to issue charters for such banks as are here described.

Later on in the year H. W. Wood, President of the U.F.A., suggested the promotion of ''group organization'' in the churches. In a paper read to the Presbyterian Synod at Calgary on Oct. 27, he said: ''The Church has been laying the foundation of individual regeneration for 19 centuries. Has not the time come when she can safely begin to build a super-structure of social regeneration? The group organization now developing everywhere is entirely different in character from the individualistic idea of the past. It represents the people merging their individualism into the organized group to make the group the unit of strength rather than trying to act as a mob of individuals.'' The future of the world would, he declared, be decided by the group system—a conflict between God and Mammon, Humanity and Animalism, Democracy and Autocracy. J. H. Woods of Calgary replied from the standpoint of Christ coming to save individual souls, not communities! Speaking at Calgary on Nov. 4, Mr. Wood again defined his views on class matters as follows: ''I believe that in class organization lies our only hope of reaching democracy, but our organization is founded on opposition to class domination or class legislation.''

About this time the U.F.A. was promoting a chain of organization amongst milk producers and shippers, with active co-operative societies at work in or around Calgary, Lethbridge, Medicine Hat, Didsbury and Edmonton. The co-operative Creamery butter movement had failed in Alberta but it was hoped to make this scheme successful and H. Higginbotham of the U.F.A. stated on Nov. 26 that the Fraser Valley (B.C.) Producers' Association was doing great work: ''Controlling the supply and itself receiving the profits from the highest markets, it is able in turn to help the ordinary cream shipper whose product goes entirely into the manufacture of butter. Officials of the Fraser Valley organization estimate that the farmers in Alberta lose $1,000,000 annually on the side of their dairy products through not being organized.'' A great increase in membership took place during the year and the total was stated at its close as 26,000.

The United Farm Women of Alberta met with the U.F.A. on Jan. 21-23. Mrs. Walter Parlby presided and reviewed the work of the year. The need for drastic action to secure more adequate medical aid in the rural districts was taken up at length; ''We have reached the stage in this Province where we have at last established the principle that the care of the public health is the duty of the state. Let us go a step farther and demand a state system of medical and nursing aid, which will give the state a mobilized force of the most highly trained men and women, filled with enthusiasm for service, and guaranteed adequate remuneration for their service; let us demand a Federal Department of Public Health with a Bureau of Child Welfare to correlate the health-work of the different Provinces.'' Closer study by women of the Farmers' Platform was urged; Mrs. G. F. Root of Wetaskiwin, spoke of the need for women's organized work in the Province and Mrs. Nellie McClung upon general matters.

The policy of the organization was further dealt with in an address by Mrs. Parlby before the men's Association. As she put it to them: ''Tired out wives do not make the best companions, the best mothers, or the happiest homes, and the more interests a farm woman can bring into the farm home from the outside, whether from meetings or any other form of recreation, the greater measure of contentment is likely to be found in that home, and the less hurry there will be on the part of the boys and girls to get away from it. Therefore, I would once again ask each of you men to encourage your wife to become a member of our organization.'' The Report of Miss Mary W. Spiller, Provincial Secretary, showed 55 new Locals and 489 new members with a total of 1,303. The officers elected for 1919 included Mrs. Walter H. Parlby, Alix, as President and Mrs. J. F. Ross, Duhamel and Mrs. Paul Carr, Birdsholm, as Vice-Presidents.

Resolutions were passed opposing Daylight Saving legislation and asking the Provincial Government for compulsory supervision of school play-grounds by a teacher; urging homesteading privileges for women on an equal foot-ing with men and demanding National Prohibition of intoxicating liquors; requesting that registered nurses be permitted to qualify as midwives and be licensed to practice as such, and that the Provincial Government under-take to supply both medical practitioners and service nurses, prepared to act as midwives, in all those districts not supplied by independent workers; urging that ''in view of the literary, historic and ethical value of the Bible and the fact that a large percentage of the children of Alberta are growing up in ignorance of its teachings,'' the Department of Education be asked to select a series of Scripture readings for use in the schools; ad-vocating the standardization or nationalization of Education with uniform text-books and, as far as possible, a uniform system of training for rural school teaching in Canada together with the creation of a Canadian Bureau of Education.

The Manitoba Grain Growers' Association in 1919.

The 16th an-nual Convention was held at Brandon on Jan. 8-10 with R. C. Henders, M.P., in the chair. His Presidential address contained strong appeals for a new democracy and denunciation of ''class privileges and oppression'' and of ''a parasitic class who claim as a right the privilege of taking a dishonest toll out of the labour and sweat of their fellow-men.'' His conclusion was as follows: ''I believe that the Grain Growers have within them the potency and power that will make possible a democratic state, a state which in my opin-ion can be established without an intervening period of revolution. I believe further that the people of rural life, through our organization, are the proper persons to whom we must look for the carrying out of this important programme.'':

Addresses were given by W. J. Black, Chairman of the Soldiers' Land Settlement Board, Principal J. B. Reynolds of the Agricultural College and by Mr. Premier Norris who denounced the ''unjust fiscal system'' of the country and the great injustice of the too-high freight rates. A. G. Hawkes of the Saskatchewan organization, Jean Masson of Montreal, on the Quebec Farmers' co-operative interests, Hon. Dr. Thornton on Education in Mani-toba and Miss Mary P. McCallum on Woman's work in the Farmers' movement also spoke. The Farmers' Platform was approved with a few amendments of which most were afterwards included in the revised document; G. W. Prout, M.L.A., spoke on his Rural Credit system in Manitoba and Hon. Ed-ward Brown, Provincial Treasurer, in explanation of the 30-year Farm loan system; William Ivens, the Socialist-Soviet leader, also spoke and a Resolu-tion was passed in favour of ''closer co-operation with Labour Unions and returned soldiers.'' Other Resolutions were passed as follows:

1. Protesting against the recent increase in Freight rates.
2. Urging the Dominion Government to extend and elaborate the systems of milling and baking tests of wheat.
3. Asking the C.N.R. to provide enough rolling stock to supply as many cars as the C.P.R. under similar conditions.
4. Urging that a department specifically devoted to the study of social, educational and economic problems of rural life be estab-lished at the Manitoba Agricultural College.

5. Demanding that the Government should so revise the laws pertaining to the sale of grain and produce that the rights of the seller may be properly protected to prevent the recurrence of such losses as had been sustained by farmers in the default of the Canadian Farmers' Hay and Produce Exchange.

6. Petitioning the Legislature to enact at its next Session that the present School Library policy be supplemented by the inclusion of a special grant of dollar for dollar to assist any school district which raises a local fund for the enlargement and maintenance of a real Community Library.

7. Opposing Daylight Saving and urging the Government not to re-enact it.

8. Asking for immediate completion of the Hudson Bay Railway.

9. Urging permanent enactment of Liquor restriction measures with ultimate complete Prohibition.

10. Re-affirming the Association's policy as being opposed to any form of Protection and, therefore, as not asking for a fixed price for wheat in 1919.

A Political action Resolution similar to those of the Saskatchewan and Alberta bodies was passed, after discussion, with an amendment to the clause requiring a pledge from M.P.'s to support enactment of the Farmers' Platform at the next Session of Parliament by adding the words "unless some great National issue which supersedes all domestic issues should arise." This was done at the suggestion of President Henders who was also a Member of Parliament. W. R. Wood, Secretary, reported 7,600 members and urged a greater proportion out of the 51,000 farmers of Manitoba. J. W. Scallion, Virden, was re-elected as Hon. President, R. C. Henders, Winnipeg, as President, J. L. Brown, Pilot Mound, as Vice-President and W. R. Wood, M.L.A., of Winnipeg, as Secretary. The following District Directors were appointed: Provencher, C. L. Stoney; Lisgar, Peter Wright; Souris, O. A. Jones; Brandon, D. G. McKenzie; Portage la Prairie, P. D. McArthur; Neepawa, A. J. M. Poole; Marquette, Bert Griffiths; Dauphin, B. J. Avison; Nelson, W. I. Ford; Selkirk, W. H. French; Springfield, Bruce Eadie; Macdonald, Andrew Graham.

A Conference of Manitoba Secretaries was held at Winnipeg on June 4-5 and was notable for the bringing of the Churches into the economic issue by W. R. Wood. He first denounced the "essential immorality" of Protection and then added: "Our people need to be enlightened and convinced that the protected interests oppose everything in the way of economic progress. These interests are found relating themselves to the religious life of the country, their leaders appearing prominently in special religious efforts, but constantly using their influence to secure that the Church shall not deal with the economic wrongs of the people." Political action was approved and immediate organization urged at this meeting. Following this incident a controversy arose over the action of President Henders in voting on June 18 against the McMaster amendment to the Budget in the Commons, which urged immediate reduction of duties and, on the 19th, against Mr. Maharg's motion that the duty on plough's should be brought down to the same figure, namely 15 per cent., as the duty on harvesters, drills, horse rakes and cultivators.

The Board of Directors met on July 23 and received a note from Mr. Henders stating that his position had been misunderstood and his motives misjudged and that he felt he should retire. A Resolution was passed regretting the circumstances but declaring that: "While we fully appreciate the long years of faithful service as rendered our organization, yet, after careful consideration, we cannot in any degree accept his attitude on the Tariff in the recent Budget debate and vote. We therefore repudiate his stand, accept his resignation, and reaffirm our adherence to the principles of the Farmers' Platform." Oct. 15 was "Liberty Day" in Manitoba; it was organized by the Grain Growers for a "drive" along the lines of enlarged membership in both men's and women's Sections; it was utilized to educate

the people in the new Political developments. Results were slow in coming
in but were encouraging, with meetings held all over the Province.

The Women's Section met also at Brandon (Jan. 8-10) with Mrs. Brodie,
President in Ontario, Mrs. Flatt in Saskatchewan, and Mrs. Ross, Vice-
President in Alberta, amongst the speakers. Mrs. J. S. Wood was in the chair
and a number of business-like reports were submitted; Miss Mabed E. Finch,
Secretary, reported a membership of 477 with 35 new sections formed in
the year. Mrs. Wood, in her address, urged cottage hospitals as fitting memorials of the war-dead and wanted a membership equal to that of the men
and a voice in framing policies and organization. Resolutions were passed
urging the establishment of a Federal Bureau of Health and asking for a
Provincial training school for nurses to meet such experiences as that of
Influenza; urging the Provincial Legislature to make and enforce laws by
which all mental defectives would be segregated and made wards of the
State; proposing that health certificates for both sexes be produced when
applying for marriage licenses; urging a Child Welfare campaign for Manitoba. Mrs. Wood was re-elected President, Mrs. Arthur Tooth of Eli, Vice-
President, and Miss Finch Secretary.

United Grain Growers' Company in 1919. The 2nd annual meeting of this corporation was held at Winnipeg on Nov. 27-28 with C. Rice-
Jones, General Manager, in the chair because of the absence of President
T. A. Crerar through illness. E. J. Fream read Mr. Crerar's address which
showed profits of $148,549 and a dividend of 6 per cent. for the year ending
Aug. 31. The volume of grain handled was 22,203,207 bushels in 16,115
cars, compared with 29,000,000 bushels in the first year of united operation—
the Grain Growers' Grain Co. and the Alberta Co-operative Elevator Co.
In the Co-operative Supply Department the volume of sales was over
$6,000,000; in the Live-stock section the Company handled 5,257 cars of
cattle, sheep and hogs at the Stock-yards of Winnipeg, Calgary and Edmonton
as against 4,402 cars in 1918; the Grain Growers' Export Co. at New York
was reported as prosperous and the Public Press and *Grain Growers' Guide*
as having made exceptional expansion. The gross earnings of the year were
$2,851,577, the expenses and fixed charges $2,711,161; the current assets—
funds, bonds, stocks, supplies—were $4,712,964; the capital assets—elevators,
machinery and warehouses—were $3,207,303; current liabilities were $2,549,-
261 with "contingent liabilities" of $724,947 and capital liabilities—includ-
ing Debentures, Mortgages, capital stock and surplus—were $5,371,006.
The Reserve was $1,500,000 and was explained as being made up of profits re-
tained in the business and invested along with the capital of the Company.
The By-laws were amended to permit of borrowing up to $12,000,000 and a
Resolution approved allowing employees to purchase stock in the Company.
Another motion declared that the domestic price of wheat to millers should
reflect its export value and that an advance of several cents a bushel meant
a negligible increase in the price of bread and that, therefore, the Canadian
Wheat Board be "urged to advance the domestic price of wheat whenever the
exportable price justifies such an advance."

United Farmers in Other Provinces. The United Farmers of New
Brunswick were organized in May, 1918, and modelled after the Grain
Growers and Ontario organizations; at the close of 1919 it had a paid-up
membership of 5,000 farmers, in 65 Locals, scattered over the Province;
a system of Co-operative chain stores was established in January, 1919, with
a capital of $9,000 and beginning at Woodstock as the United Farmers'
Co-operative Co., N.B., Ltd. The Manager was S. H. Hagerman and the
President of the Company C. L. Smith of Woodstock. The 2nd Annual
Convention was held at that place on Mch, 20 with John Kennedy, Winnipeg, and Jean Masson, of Montreal, present; there were 300 delegates in
attendance representing 25 branches and a Platform was drawn up and
approved; President T. W. Caldwell, Florenceville, devoted his address largely to denunciation of the Tariff and the advocacy of Prohibition and was
afterwards re-elected President. The Platform was as follows:

1. Authorizing County Conventions to nominate candidates for Federal and Provincial Houses and authorizing each County to raise the necessary funds.

2. Opposing all bribery and corruption in Elections.

3. Urging that wilderness and unimproved land be taxed in proportion to the tax on improved land and certain changes be made in the registry of mortgages.

4. Proposing an Act of the Legislature compelling any trunk telephone to give proper connection with Local or Farmers' lines for a reasonable toll, and demanding an investigation before Telephone rates be raised.

5. Suggesting that any man 18 years old be allowed to homestead 100 acres of land and a returned soldier 200 acres with the privilege of buying 100 acres additional in the Province.

6. Favouring an Abattoir, establishment of a cold storage plant and a Stock-yard in the Maritime Provinces.

7. Declaring that Provincial and Federal representatives should pledge themselves to resign on being presented with a petition signed by 60 per cent. of the members of the U.F. of N.B.

8. Supporting total Prohibition and a Provincial plebiscite; favouring Provincial roads improvement and the use of auto taxes for such purpose with a uniform system of breaking winter roads.

9. Appointment of a Farmer as Provincial Minister of Agriculture and a Secretary of Agriculture who should be a Farmer and, also, the son of a farmer and a graduate of the College of Agriculture.

10. Urging a rural daily delivery of Mail Service.

11. Adopting the Platform of the Council of Agriculture, with the exception of the National ownership clause.

On Nov. 26 a protest was forwarded to the Dominion Government against the proposal to constitute a permanent Tariff Commission in Canada. Meanwhile, Mr. Caldwell had been elected M.P. for Carleton-Victoria and on Dec. 10 Hon. T. A. Crerar and G. F. Chipman, Winnipeg, addressed a farmers' gathering at Woodstock and the audience was told that the combined membership in the Farmers' bodies of the West and Ontario totalled 130,000 with 58,000 shareholders in the Co-operative Companies of the West. The United Farmers of British Columbia had been organized in 1917 and held a Conference at Smithers on June 24, 1919 to consider local conditions, to arrange for amalgamation with other Provincial agricultural bodies—including the B.C. Dairymen's Association, the Farmers' Institutes and the B.C. Fruit Growers' Association. During the balance of the year the Committee appointed and composed of J. W. Berry, C. E. W. Griffiths, James Bailey, William Harrison and C. E. Barnes, had the matter in hand and hoped for an organization, eventually, of 10,000 members.

On July 2, 1919, the United Farmers of Quebec were organized at Montreal with 400 present and Joseph Forget of St. Janvier in the chair. Mr. Forget was elected Hon. President, Napoleon Lachapelle Hon. Vice-President, Anthine Ares, President with a Board of Directors representing 14 agricultural centres in the Province. A Resolution was passed advising the Dominion Government that in the national interest farmers should be enabled to conduct their business without the control or fixing of prices on the products of the farm; that production should be based upon the needs of the Export market and that supply and demand should not be artificially regulated in such a way as to discourage production.

The United Farmers of Ontario in 1919. The central event of this organization's history during 1919 was its success in the Provincial elections and this will be dealt with under Ontario affairs. But aside from this it made much progress and had a notable record. On Mch. 6 it was announced that a subsidiary concern of the U.F.O.—the Farmers' Publishing Co., Ltd.,—had purchased the *Farmers' Sun* which, since 1891, had been an

unofficial organ of certain agricultural interests, of the Free trade and Reciprocity ideas of the Patrons of Industry, and from 1896, when he became its
largest shareholder and until his death, of Dr. Goldwin Smith's opinions: The
President at this stage was W. D. Gregory, of Oakville, the Vice-President and
Managing Director was Gordon Waldron of Toronto, W. L. Smith was a
frequent editorial contributor. Early in September the 1st annual meeting
of the new Company was held and showed the postage of 24,000 copies a
week; the new Directorate included Lieut.-Col. J. Z. Fraser, Burford, as
President, Manning W. Doherty, Brampton, Vice-President, J. J. Morrison,
Toronto, Secretary-Treasurer with A. A. Powers, Orono, and W. C. Good,
Paris. Toward the close of the year the journal became the official organ
of the U.F.O., and in December J. C. Ross, a well-known newspaper man of
Montreal, was appointed Managing Editor.

On Apr. 8th a delegation, said to represent the U.F.O. and 10,000
farmers and led by R. H. Halbert, E. C. Drury, J. J. Morrison and others,
waited on the Provincial Government and opposed the construction of a
Provincial Highway under existing conditions. On May 2nd a delegation led
by Manning W. Doherty for the United Farmers, asked the Dominion Government to erect and operate an Interior Terminal Elevator for the service of
Ontario, particularly Central and Western Ontario, to include it as one of
the chain of elevators operated by the Board of Grain Commissioners and
to follow the lines of those in operation at Calgary, Saskatoon and Moose
Jaw in the Western Provinces. A little later, before the Industrial Relations Commission, W. C. Good stated he represented 1,000 U. F. O. Clubs in
the Province and 30,000 members and that the plight of farmers was
serious: "Good labour is not available, and poor labour is getting higher
rewards in the city. The high cost of farm production is due to the Protective tariff and the city worker is bent on a policy inimical to his own
interests by looking at money wages, rather than real wages. Co-operative
methods in industry, a marked reduction of the Tariff on all necessities of
life, and the prevention of speculation in land would be effective methods
of reducing the cost of living." J. J. Morrison pointed out that rural
Ontario had lost 37,563 of population in the years 1916 to 1918 while the
urban population had increased by 35,288. Following the election of over
40 members to the Ontario Legislature, President Halbert carried North
Ontario (Dec. 9) for the Dominion Parliament and E. C. Drury was selected
as Leader of the U.F.O. and became Premier of the Province. Meanwhile,
on Aug. 1st, the following platform was adopted at a meeting of the Executive of the U.F.O. and the Executive of the Political Committee of the
Farmers and duly promulgated—upon it the U.F.O. fought the Provincial
elections of 1919:

> Whereas the rural population of Ontario has been declining
> for many years, being now 139,000 less than it was in 1881 and
> this in spite of natural increases in population, immigration, and the
> extension of settlement; and whereas rural life has been rendered
> difficult and trying, and farm production has been checked; and
> whereas the recent condition in the rural districts is justly attribut-
> able to the unequal rewards of farm and town industry, owing to
> the dominance, in Parliament and Legislature, of privileged urban
> interests; and whereas the Provincial public debt has increased at
> an alarming rate (now exceeding 100 million dollars) and the annual
> expenditure of the Province has increased almost five-fold in the
> last 15 years; and whereas both of the old parties are responsible for
> this state of affairs; We, therefore, the United Farmers of Ontario,
> deem it our duty, to ourselves and the Province, to seek indepen-
> dent representation in the Legislature, with the following objects:
> 1. To cut out all expenditures that are not absolutely essential.
> 2. To abolish the system of party patronage.
> 3. To limit Governmental activity respecting commercial co-
> operation to legislation facilitating co-operative effort, to the keeping
> of accurate records, and to general education along co-operative lines.

4. To provide equal educational opportunities for all the children of all the people, by greatly extending and improving educational facilities in the rural districts.

5. To substitute for the policy of expensive Provincial highways a policy of organized continuous road maintenance, and of making good roads for all rather than high grade roads for a few, the cost of road construction and maintenance being equitably distributed between city and country.

6. To promote a system of Forestry which will maintain and increase the public revenues from this source, protect and perpetuate our forest resources, re-forest the waste places of Old Ontario, and encourage municipalities to engage in forestation enterprises.

7. To encourage and cheapen Hydro-Electric development and maintain effective public control over it.

8. To enact and enforce such prohibitory legislation against the liquor traffic as the people may sanction in the approaching referendum and as lies within the power of the Province. Prohibition is an integral part of the Farmers' Platform, and the U.F.O. will use its influence in that direction.

9. To extend the policy and practice of Direct Legislation through the Initiative and Referendum.

10. To apply the principle of Proportional Representation to our Electoral methods.

The 6th annual Convention of the U.F.O. was held in Toronto on Dec. 17-19 with 2,000 Delegates present and R. H. Halbert, M.P., in the chair. In his address Mr. Halbert did not mince words or phrases: ''I appeal to every farmer and every worker to join at once and get ready for the great battle which is before us. As Lincoln is reported to have said: 'No country can exist half slave and half free.' Neither can we exist in Canada to-day and enjoy any freedom unless the ever-increasing power of the moneyed aristocracy is overthrown. The man who would be free, himself must strike the blow. Stop lamenting about our ills, do not look for a Moses from those who are now on our backs, to bring us out of Egyptian slavery. We must do it ourselves. Let all who can take his or her part in the battle. We are only at the beginning of things in Canada to-day.'' He warned the members against commercializing the organization too much or becoming intoxicated with success.

J. J. Morrison, Secretary, submitted a Report showing 1,130 Clubs associated with the U.F.O. compared with 620 in 1918 and an increase in membership from 25,000 to 48,000: ''This year we have had no Province-wide Conventions, but we have had a series of meetings embracing 64 nominating conventions, followed by hundreds of other meetings where public questions of the day were discussed upon their merits by farmers, who have rapidly developed from shrinking rural workers to self-respecting citizens, determined that Canadian public affairs shall be conducted upon a higher plane and that special privileges shall be banished from our midst.'' The receipts of the year were $32,164 and the disbursements $17,074. As to other associated organizations, Mr. Morrison spoke of: ''The United Farm Women of Ontario, our great helpmate and co-worker, which though only a little more than a year old is becoming firmly entrenched among the rural women of the Province; the United Farmers' Co-operative Co., Ltd., with 5,000 shareholders, which shows a gross turnover of business this year amounting to $8,500,000, including 1,000 tons of binder-twine, representing $500,000; and the business of its Live Stock Department, where in the period from Feb. 20 to Nov. 30, 3,682 cars of live-stock were handled amounting in value to $7,500,000, while eight stores are being operated with great success at outside points; the Farmers' Publishing Co., Ltd., with over 1,700 shareholders, now owns and operates *The Farmers' Sun*, with a circulation of over 30,000 at present, and which is likely to be increased to 50,000 in the near future.''

An interesting incident of the Convention was the reception accorded Hon. E. C. Drury, Premier, and the members of his Government. In the speeches which followed, points of policy were enunciated as follows: "Government grant for 20 per cent. of cost of township roads, with loans for backward townships, repayable in five years; a cheaper form of Provincial highways, with much greater mileage in every County; an eventual increase of auto licenses from $12 to $15 to provide funds for township roads and no Quebec-to-Windsor 'slab of concrete;' simpler laws and Court procedure; refusal of licenses to race-meets, where betting is allowed, and development of the Housing Commission." The Hon. T. A. Crerar, M.P., also addressed the Convention and was hailed as "the future Premier of Canada." Some of his statements were as follows: "It is not so much the amount of taxes you raise as the manner in which you raise them; when you raise your revenues by direct taxation you make better citizens of your people. . . . I am not one of those who believe that any one class, whether farmers or labourers or manufacturers, should have the whole say in any Government; I do say our farmers have not had a fair share in the Government of Canada; Protection is a weapon created by legislation to keep goods out of the country in order to benefit the manufacturing class."

During the Convention meetings various changes in the U.F.O. constitution were discussed; proposals to reduce the number of Delegates and for an increase in Fees were defeated and it was decided to have Directors from each Federal constituency instead of from counties; $748 was voted to the Toronto Sick Children's Hospital and Mr. Morrison drew attention to the fact that 20,000 members did not subscribe to *The Farmers' Sun;* an application for Provincial incorporation with a Charter similar to that of the Dominion Grange was approved. Mr. Halbert retired in the election for President and R. W. E. Burnaby of Jefferson was elected over W. A. Amos of Palmerston; the latter was chosen Vice-President and J. J. Morrison re-elected Secretary with expressions of appreciation for his immense work in organization and in the Elections. The Executive was as follows: Harold Currie, Strathroy, Herbert Hoover, Harold, Mrs. G. A. Brodie, Newmarket and Mrs. H. L. Laws, Cayuga. Resolutions were passed as follows:

1. Favouring the abolition of the Senate and urging this policy for inclusion in the Farmers' Platform.

2. Declaring that a system of long term loans for farmers at reasonable rates of interest, is essential to the proper development of the agricultural industry of this Province, and asking the Provincial Government for a bill providing for some system of long term rural credits.

3. Asking the Railway Commission for a grinding in transit rate for Ontario wheat similar to that granted Western wheat.

4. Requesting that the pre-war freedom of the press be re-established and approving a Dominion Conference to co-ordinate Political action plans.

5. Protesting against the expense of the Wheat Board being charged to the Farmers and asking a special Provincial grant to transport scholars to consolidated schools in New Ontario.

6. Urging the Provincial Government to provide better roads in Northern Ontario so as to encourage the settlers and requesting action to prevent the wanton destruction of shade and ornamental trees upon our public highways by electric, telephone and telegraph Companies.

7. Approving the principle of a uniform rate for power supplied by the Hydro-Electric Power Commission, and asking that the Province assume control of, and as soon as possible proceed to develop, all the water power available in order to supply the demands of the various municipalities in the Province.

8. Viewing with alarm the proposed policy of Hydro Radials involving the expenditure of millions and intending, in many instances, the duplication of present railways and asking that the Legislature move slowly in this matter.

14

9. Proposing that provision be made for the election as Directors of a number of employees and superintendents of the Canadian National Railways from among their number, by themselves, and that in the appointment of the remainder of the Directors care should be taken to see that the chief sections of the country served by the Railway are represented on the Directorate.

10. Suggesting a postponement of the proposed sale of the T. and N.O. (Provincial) Railway to the Dominion Government.

11. Approving "Local option in Taxation."

12. Reciting the long struggle for local telephones and urging the Dominion Government for legislation ensuring to all Local systems the long-distance connection at regular long-distance rates.

13. Approving the selection of Mr. Drury as Leader in the Legislature and impressing upon the new Government a sense of its responsibilities.

The United Farm Women of Ontario (1919) met in their 1st annual Convention at the same time as the U.F.O. with Mrs. G. A. Brodie in the chair and 46 delegates registered while the President's opening address stated there were 50 Societies affiliated compared with 3 a year before. It was proposed to concentrate their work on improvement of rural schools and homes, the removal of disqualifications of women as rural school trustees, especial attention to the Educational system, learning the views of the Legislature on questions affecting women, the appointment of County police matrons and the placing of labour-saving devices on the free list. Most of the women speakers laid stress upon the need of improved electrical and other conveniences for household work on the farms. Mrs. Brodie also addressed the men's Convention in Massey Hall and described her ideal Consolidated School as follows: "A big building in ten acres of land, with room for games; a resident master, well paid; a surrounding community with a community church and a community pastor educated for rural leadership; a people taking a sympathetic interest in rural life."

Miss Emma Griesbach, as Secretary, reported on the work of the year and announced her resignation; the new officers elected were Mrs. G. A. Brodie, Newmarket, President; Mrs. J. N. Foote, Collingwood, Vice-President, and Mrs. H. L. Laws, Toronto, Secretary-Treasurer. There were various interesting speeches made by women and one very radical one by Mrs. David Annis of Woodville, who declared that: "I would advocate, as the ultimate height of farm women's aspirations, the abolition of the Senate, the abolition of the Lieutenant-Governor's post, the abolition of the million dollar Government House, the abolition of the Navy, and the doing away of the post of Governor-General." The following Resolutions were passed: Requesting that such change be made in the law as will permit anyone domiciled in Canada to become a naturalized citizen on personal request for the same; (2) urging that the right of municipal franchise be extended to farmers' wives under the same conditions as to farmers' daughters; (3) endorsing the extension of the Co-operative movement to include such branches of household work, as may be found practical, for the relief of the domestic labour situation and for the help of the farm housewife in particular; (4) asking that graded readers in History and Geography be prepared for elementary schools, in which the pioneer history of the Province shall be given prominence; (5) proposing a standing Committee to make a reality of Co-operation between producers and consumers by bringing the National Council of Women and the U.F.W.O. together; (6) urging the Ontario Government to give J. J. Kelso the financial assistance and encouragement necessary to do effective work, and that County Councils be urged to equip and maintain Children's Shelters in their respective Counties.

The United Farmers' Co-operative Co., Ltd. (1919) held its 6th annual meeting in Toronto on Dec. 16 with R. W. E. Burnaby in the chair and the statement that in 6 years their business had grown from $33,000 to over $8,500,000. He declared that: "One of the chief reasons for rural depopula-

tion is that agriculture has not proven as profitable as have other industries in
the towns and cities. The product of our labours and our position generally
has been one of exploitation by unnecessary middlemen. By wasteful methods
of distribution, both in our buying and selling, we have suffered untold loss.
The cost of our produce has likewise been unduly increased to the consumer.
The object of the United Farmers' Co-operative Co. Ltd., is to overcome
as far as possible these wasteful and expensive methods of distribution and
thus bring the producer and consumer closer together to the mutual advantage
of both.''

The Company, he added, was owned and controlled by farmers and
all its shareholders were farmers; it was divided into three Departments—
Live-stock, Co-operative Trading and Commission; over 100 cars of live-stock
had been handled in a day. He added the assertion that ''the object of
the Company is not to make money, but to save money for our patrons,
whether they be shareholders or not''—the latter having no privileges except
a 7 per cent. dividend upon shares which could not exceed 10 in number while
a new By-law would provide for the distribution of the Company's profits
to its customers who were shareholders, members of the U.F.O. or holders of
special profit sharing certificates. Mr. Burnaby pointed out that ''until a
few months ago the policy of the Company was to sell goods to our Clubs at
as near cost as possible, charging only sufficient profit to cover overhead
expenses.'' But this had been found unpopular with local and wholesale
merchants as well as manufacturers: ''After very careful consideration
your Directors have decided to adopt the selling method practised by nearly
all the big Co-operative organizations in England and Europe. Goods are
sold at about their established retail selling value and at the end of each
year the net profits are distributed to each patron entitled to share therein
in proportion to the amount of his or her purchases. The same method is
adopted for all Clubs and all stores and all the business of each Department.''
W. C. Good, in his address, urged that the affiliated Clubs and Societies should
be turned into local commercial Societies toward which the U.F. Co-operative
Co. might act in the capacity of a wholesale society.

Eight branch stores were reported—Seaforth, Fenelon Falls, Smith's Falls,
Cobourg, Kingston, Aultsville and Toronto; a 7 per cent. dividend was declared
and the total sales reported as $33,000 in 1914, $226,000 in 1915, $410,385 in
1916, $918,197 in 1917, 1,765,378 in 1918 and $8,500,000 in 1919. As to
detail, the annual Report showed that in the Live-stock Department, which
had only opened up 8½ months before at West Toronto, 3000 cars of live-
stock had been handled and sold for $6,467,957, with a handsome profit to
the Company. The Commission Department, which took the place of the
commission merchant, was said to give promise of becoming a big factor in
the development of the Company, an instance mentioned being the sale on
Dec. 12 of 50 cars of flour and feed. In the Co-operation Department, which
handled groceries, implements, etc., either through branch stores or Clubs,
it was stated that at first the business ran behind but was now in a healthy
condition.

The net profits of the whole business for the year were $16,021 and
its assets $283,893; during the year T. P. Loblaw had been appointed Gen-
eral Manager of the Company; the Directors elected at this meeting were
R. W. E. Burnaby, A. Van Allen, R. J. MacMillan, John Z. Fraser, H. V.
Hoover, Arthur Cruise and W. C. Good; A. A. Powers was elected President
and Elmer Lick, of Oshawa, Vice-President. In connection with the organization of retail grocery stores under the auspices of the Company, Mr. Loblaw
told the *Financial Post* on Mch. 22 that: ''There is no intention of adopting
any policy of unfair competition, that is the members of the organization
will not be supplied with goods at figures lower than ordinary retail prices.
The Farmers' Clubs that are the nucleus of the organization may buy through
the Company in any quantity that they may require, but, irrespective of
quantity, the goods will be delivered at the regular retail price.''

INDUSTRY: THE ORGANIZED MANUFACTURERS

The Industrial Situation: Manufacturers and the Country. Twelve years of industrial development in Canada, 1905-17, as given in Census statistics, showed wonderful progress; it was not all due to the War or to tariffs, and even the keenest opponent or critic would hardly say it was mainly due to profiteering or improper methods; it was obviously the result, as a whole, of keen personal perception of opportunities, of the wise use of increasing capital, of a Protection which granted some new or infant industries time and place for development, of the natural growth of a new country; misuse of the Tariff, selfish or profiteering War action, had their places of influence but business capacity and enterprise were the more powerful factors.

The capital invested grew from $846,585,023 in 1905, to $1,994,-103,272 in 1915, and to $2,772,517,680 in 1917; the employees on salaries or wages increased from 392,530 to 514,883 and then to 693,071, respectively; the wages and salaries paid grew from $165,-100,011 to $289,764,503 and then to $553,228,620; the value of the products increased from $718,352,603 to $1,407,137,140 and then to $3,015,506,869. By 1919 these statistics must have grown very much greater but official returns are not available. The gross value of goods made in Canada, in 1917, amounted to $3,015,506,-869, and the cost of materials was $1,602,820,631, leaving the total net value added by the process of manufacture as $1,412,686,238 or $5,449,098 more than the gross value of all production in 1915.

The invested capital of Canadian industrial plants in 1917 was $2,772,517,680 of which (a) land, buildings and fixtures amounted to $998,351,070; (b) machinery and tools to $567,262,538; (c) materials on hand, stocks in process, finished products, fuel and miscellaneous supplies, to $745,546,310, and (d) cash, accounts and bills receivable to $461,357,762. The amount of capital invested in the leading industries was (1) Electric light and power, $356,004,-168; (2) Pulp and paper, $186,787,405; (3) Hog products, $149,-266,019; (4) Cars and car works, $98,274,585; (5) Steel furnaces and rolling mills, $91,894,777; (6) Flour and grist mill products, $72,573,982; (7) Agricultural implements, $70,493,801; (8) Foundry and machine shop products, $69,915,032; (9) Car repair shops, $68,763,298; (10) Slaughtering and meat-packing, $68,145,347. The 15 leading industries, with their gross value of production during the Census years of 1905, 1915, and 1917, were as follows:

	1905	1915	1917	% Increase 1915-17
Food products	$173,359,481	$388,815,362	$754,637,940	94·09
Textiles	85,982,979	144,686,605	265,448,585	83·46
Iron and steel products	53,012,689	120,422,420	400,385,086	232·48
Timber and lumber and their manufacture	112,545,298	123,396,686	225,522,189	82·76

	1905	1915	1917	% Increase 1915-17
Leather and its finished products....	42,132,007	71,086,644	104,804,689	47·53
Paper and Printing	33,749,020	74,098,398	148,896.426	100·48
Liquors and Beverages	14,894,819	84,859,927	29,935,226	14·18
Chemicals and allied products	15,728,306	45,410,486	133,618,658	194·35
Clay, Glass and Stone products	13,968,400	27,244,813	32,374,060	18·88
Metals and Metal products other than steel	50,923,144	90,943,378	171,650,905	88·75
Tobacco and its manufactures	15,274,928	28,987,250	46,786,233	61·40
Vehicles for land transportation	37,396,802	73,875,212	197,488,770	167·32
Vessels for water transportation.....	1,943,195	8,419,648	37,244,678	342·32
Miscellaneous industries	66,249,895	134,268,231	386,420,242	180·78
Hand trades	1,689,195	40,729,180	80,864,273	98·54

There are some interesting deductions from these statistics and perhaps the chief is the fact that the capital invested more than doubled between 1905 and 1915—before the War had produced any great effect upon industry—and it increased again by one-third in the years 1915-17 when the War had begun to impress itself clearly and strongly upon all phases of industrial life; wages and salaries, similarly, doubled in the first 10 years and doubled again in the two years of active war; the value of the products also doubled in each of these periods. When the crash of world-war came to Canada in 1914 and finance, industry, nations, trembled in the balance, it required courage, skill and care to keep the wheels of commerce turning; it required still more of these qualities to turn industry into new lines and to make a profit and an ever-increasing production to meet the calls of war. Plants had to be changed for all kinds of delicate and complex operations, new and varied machinery bought and applied, experts in methods and conditions employed, new processes studied and applied, financial conditions of new and complicated nature mastered, and rapidity of work combined with precision of judgment in production. When the Armistice came a somewhat similar process had to be gone through except that the technique of change was better understood, the processes perhaps easier and the world conditions less difficult—except in the adjustment of wages.

The manufacturers, also, had more funds and greater holdings of cash or liquid securities with, it was estimated by the Royal Securities Corporation of Montreal, $100,000,000 more cash and liquid assets than 4 years previously, in 1914. Larger capital and greater resources, therefore, made conditions of change easier in 1919 than in early war days while the light supplies of general merchandise in store and the open markets at home and abroad for nearly all products—aided by continued Government credits—all contributed to set going the flood of industrial prosperity which came to Canada in the year after the War and enabled the manufacturers to obtain high prices and pay high wages and assimilate the labour of the returned soldiers.

The greatest difficulties were in the Iron and Steel industry which, naturally, had devoted most attention to war production and had the greatest adjustments to make; contrary to the experience in practically all other directions, its plants during 1919 were only working to about 50 per cent. capacity; at its close, however, a great change was visible and prosperous developments on the way. As general production increased in these years and prices grew with the demand, and wages with the cost of supplies, exports also grew and, as with the farmers, very greatly; in 1919 they kept up much better than did those of Agriculture—Manufactures.decreasing in the fiscal year (Mch. 31) by $91,000,000 and Agricultural products, including animals, by $257,000,000. The totals of Industrial export in 1914 were $67,602,238 and in 1915 $95,068,525; then the War began to have its effect and in 1916 they were $250,052,223, in 1917 $487,312,766, in 1918 $660,840,430, in 1919 $571,498,678. Accompanying this process was a large increase in the importation of raw materials and this, as well as extravagance in importing luxuries and Britain's temporary shortage of cash, were large factors in the exchange situation with the United States. The condition of the chief Canadian industries in 1918, when the Peace revolution came, may be seen in the following table of preliminary 1918 returns to the Dominion Bureau of Statistics:

	Capital Invested	Em-ployees	Salaries and Wages	Materials Used	Value of Products
Cotton Textiles	$53,796,894	17,000	$ 9,327,343	$34,289,862	$66,899,328
Agricultural Implements ...	74,410,603	10,095	10,282,589	17,819,840	34,853,673
Hosiery and Knit Goods....	31,092,866	11,327	7,280,902	26,527,287	45,755,129
Bakery and Confectionery.	40,272,206	19,106	14,201,767	51,153,127	85,555,848
Meat Industry	86,969,756	11,917	12,178,385	171,028,104	229,231,666
Woollen Textiles	19,268,202	5,557	3,793,925	15,801,474	25,063,515
Foundry and Machinery ..	84,122,446	26,482	28,986,306	27,788,059	82,493,897
Fruit and Vegetable	16,252,986	5,795	2,834,287	15,019,746	23,685,467
Wood Distillation	3,512,573	675	781,485	3,819,731	7,684,123

The greater industries started into the changes of 1919 with prosperous records—the following being notable increases of dividends during 1918; Laurentide Pulp, which increased the annual rate from 10 per cent. to 11 per cent.; Ogilvie Milling, 10 to 12 per cent.; Lake of the Woods, 8 to 12 per cent.; Dominion Textile, 7 to 8 per cent.; Canadian Converters, 4 to 5 per cent.; Canadian Cottons, 4 to 6 per cent.; Kaministiquia Power, 6 to 8 per cent.; Penmans, Ltd., 4 to 6 per cent.; Price Bros., 6 to 8 per cent.; Riordon Paper, 6 to 10 per cent.; Shredded Wheat, 6 to 8 per cent.; Lyall Construction, 4 to 8 per cent.; B.C. Fisheries, 4 to 5 per cent.; and Asbestos Corporation, preferred, 4 to 6 per cent. Of those Companies which began paying regular dividends in that year, the most notable were the Asbestos Corporation, common, 5 per cent.; Brompton Paper, 5 per cent.; Canadian Machinery, 2 per cent.; Dominion Glass, 4 per cent.; Provincial Paper, 4 per cent.; St. Lawrence Flour, 6 per cent.; Wabasso Cotton, 6 per cent.; and Woods Mfg., 7 per cent. The Government helped in the readjustment during 1919 and by arrangements for national credits promoted trade with Great Britain, Belgium, Roumania and Greece; reconstruction provided many more men who were readily absorbed while higher prices met the demands for more and better wages; large ship-building developments were a feature of the year with both Government and private construction proceeding actively and gradually helping in the initial transportation difficulty; British manufacturers visited Canada and urged exportation of Canadian products to meet demands which they themselves could not for a time satisfy while F. W. Field and other British Trade Commissioners pressed home a knowledge of British requirements and conditions; United States industries and American capital came into Canada steadily to take advantage of (1) the better Labour conditions in Quebec and (2) the British Preference tariff of the present and expected future.

During the previous dozen years about $600,000,000 of United States capital had been put into Industrial branches and interests in Canada. The *Monetary Times* of Toronto, in a carefully compiled list on May 9, 1919, specified 388 manufacturing plants in Canada associated with similar concerns in the United States and having an investment of $264,939,592; some of these industries had become wholly Canadian in character with little of the original investment in control—the majority, however, were acknowledged branches of American concerns controlled, and owned in the main, by United States interests. In 1919 the Canadian border towns, of which Windsor was the centre, benefitted greatly through the investment of this capital; their population in some cases more than doubled in five years, with Windsor and the neighbouring municipalities of Ford, Walkerville, Sandwich, and Ojibway boasting 180 operating industries; so in Welland and other places—notably Hamilton which received $50,000,000 of such investments and a dozen important American Companies in 1919; the Foreign department of the Merchants Bank of Canada estimated that on Aug. 31 of this year there were 426 important American industries operating in Canada—chiefly in Ontario and Quebec—with new ones coming in every month.

Some of the later plants to come were the Carr Fastener Co. of Boston, with a branch at Hamilton, and the Sherar-Gillett Co. of Chicago, at Guelph; the Canadian Products, Ltd., subsidiary of the General Motors Corporation, at Walkerville; the Sunbeam Chemical Co. of Chicago, at Toronto, and the Firestone Tire and Rubber Co., of Akron, Ohio, at Hamilton; the Norton Co. of Worcester, Mass., at Hamilton, and the Columbia Gramaphone Co., at Toronto; the Jenckes Co., of Rhode Island, at Hamilton, and the Burroughs Adding Machine Co., of Detroit, at Windsor; the Nyando Pulp and Paper Co., of Rochester, N.Y., at Fort William, and the Kenworthy Bros. of Stoughton, Mass., at St. Johns, Que.; the Mead-Morrison Co. of Boston at Welland; the Robbins and Myers Co., of Springfield, Ohio, at Brantford; the Western Clock Co., of La Salle, Ill., and the Nashua Gummed and Coated Paper Co., of Nashua, N.H., at Peterborough; the Hoover Suction Sweeper Co., of Canton, Ohio, at Hamilton; the Lindsay Wire Weaving Co., of Cleveland, at Niagara Falls; the International Paper Co., at Three Rivers, P.Q. During the year Sir J. W. Flavelle sold large holdings in the Wm. Davies Co., Ltd., to Toronto and American interests while Chicago firms also acquired control of the Union Stock Yards, Toronto. As a result of prosperous conditions in general, industrial stocks rose steadily and the comparison of some of the larger ones during six months of the year was as follows:

	End of 1918	July 12 1919		End of 1918	July 12 1919
Dominion Steel	62½	71¾	Canadian Cottons	68	86
Steel Co. of Canada ..	64	78½xd	Montreal Cottons	58½	69
Canada Cement	65	70xd	Dominion Textile	100½	118½
Can. Locomotive Co...	63¾	83	Wabasso Cotton	61	88
Canadian Car	80½	41	Penmans	79½	94
" Pref.	84¾	98	Laurentide Power	61½	74
Can. General Electric..	104	112	Montreal Power	87½	92¾
Laurentide	196¾	222xd	Shawinigan	117¾	123
Riordon	117½	141	Ames-Holden, Pref. ...	65¾	99
Spanish River	18	44½	Canada Steamships ...	45¼	51¾
" " Pref. ..	64½	108xd	" " Pref.	78½	83¼
Lake of the Woods ...	166	180	Dominion Canners ...	84½	57
Maple Leaf	136½	175¼xd	" " Pref.	70	76
Ogilvie	220	255	A. MacDonald	20½	35
St. Lawrence Flour ...	96	112½	Consolidated Smelters..	23½	81¼

Questions of profit and capitalization and prices were frequently raised during the year in connection with manufactures as well as with retailers and farmers. There was no doubt as to individual industrial prosperity throughout the country; there was no doubt as to the larger concerns and their increases in net working capital. Price Bros. and Co., for instance, between their fiscal years of 1913-14 and 1918-19 increased their net working capital[*] by $2,279,-913, the Steel Company of Canada by $7,589,585, the Nova Scotia Steel and Coal Co. by $7,507,391, the Dominion Iron and Steel by $11,103,044, the Dominion Textile by $6,048,740, Canadian Cottons, Ltd., by $1,540,703, Canada Cement Co. by $4,515,470, Canadian Car and Foundry by $4,964,719, Ogilvie Milling Co. by $5,319,005, Penmans, Ltd., by $2,054,745. This indicated a process of growth in the main healthy, and one which produced by 1919 much industrial independence of borrowed capital; dependence upon the Banks was a condition of real danger in 1914 when the war crisis struck the Manufacturers. Many smaller industries attained a proportionately strong position and the chief reason that the new conditions of Peace were so easily met, without vital strain upon labour, Government, or Banks, was the prosperous condition of Industry. How far this increasing capitalization was desirable was a subject, like that of Bank amalgamation, of considerable discussion in 1919. The capitalistic side was well put by the Ottawa *Journal* of June 26, following a discussion in Parliament:

No progress in industry is possible without increased capitalization. This axiom must hold good whether capital is supplied by a Vanderbilt or applied by a Co-operative society. A plumber who sets out to stop a leak has to have solder and a soldering iron. These represent capital. Real capital in industry means always tools and material of some sort, whether it be a soldering iron or a blast-furnace, a handful of solder or a million tons of coal, a dollar to buy a hammer or a bank credit of a million dollars to buy everything that a big industry may need.

Suppose that any Company, making high profits, should instead of capitaliz-

---

*Note.—Royal Securities Corporation, published in *Financial Times*, Montreal, Aug. 2, 1919.

ing them in its own business, buy Bank stocks or Government bonds with them. Would not the Company be entitled to the dividends on the stocks or bonds? If, instead, a Company prefers to re-invest its surplus profits in its own business, and thus promotes industry and increases employment, is it not as much entitled to dividends as if it had used the profits to buy somebody else's stock or bonds?

Profit and profiteering are not synonymous terms though often used at this time to signify the same thing. In shipbuilding plants in the United States during certain stages in the War many mechanics were paid at the rate of $7,000 to $9,000 a year; in other cases coloured workmen made as high as $175 a week. Such "profiteering" was no doubt due to special opportunity, or physical fitness, or mental adaptability; the manufacturers who succeeded in Canada or Great Britain or the United States in this period owed their profits to similar conditions. Whether those profits or the wages indicated took an undue amount from Governments and people involved in the War, or from people at home who purchased some of the products thus made, is another and more difficult question. Evidence before the Cost of Living Committee at Ottawa showed some excessive industrial profits; it was claimed that the maximum profit taken by the Canadian manufacturer was 15 per cent. The large volume of profits was often due, as in the Wm. Davies case, to a small margin on a huge turnover—the profits of this latter Company in 1918 being only 2·23 per cent. of the turnover and that of the Lake of the Woods Milling concern 2·43 per cent. Some important Industrial appointments of 1919 were as follows:

Company	Position	Name	Hdqrs.
Consolidated Mining & Smelting Co.	President	James J. Warren	Toronto
Imperial Oil Co.	President	C. O. Stillman	Toronto
"	Vice-President	A. M. McQueen	Toronto
Armstrong-Whitworth of Canada	Director	H. H. Vaughan	Montreal
" "	Director	Lawrence Russell	Montreal
Ames-Holden, McCready, Ltd.	President	T. H. Rieder	Montreal
" "	Director	W. A. Black	Montreal
Maxwell Motor Co. of Canada	President and Gen'l Manager	George W. Parks	Windsor
Chalmers Motor Co. of Canada	President and Gen'l Manager	George W. Parks	Windsor
Canadian General Electric Co.	Vice-President and Chairman	A. E. Dyment	Toronto
" " "	Director	W. L. Matthews	Toronto
" " "	Director	Stephen Haas	Toronto
Dominion Coal Co., Ltd.	Director	George Caverhill	Montreal
Canadian Locomotive Co.	Director	James Carruthers	Montreal
" "	Director	M. J. Haney	Toronto
Can. Consolidated Rubber Co.	Director	Lieut.-Col. Herbert Molson	Montreal
Whalen Pulp & Paper Mills, Ltd.	President	Sir George Bury	Vancouver
" "	Director	I. W. Killam	Montreal
Imperial Oil Co., Ltd.	Director	Victor Ross	Toronto
International Petroleum Co.	Director	Victor Ross	Toronto
Dominion Glass Co., Ltd.	Director	John Baillie	Montreal
Ogilvie Flour Mills Co.	Director	R. R. Dobell	Winnipeg
Can. Steel Tire and Wheel Co.	Vice-President and Manager	F. J. Buller	Montreal
Abitibi Power and Paper Co.	Director	Alex. Smith	Chicago
Abitibi Power and Paper Co.	Director	W. A. Black	Montreal
Riordan Pulp and Paper Co.	Director	J. W. Parkinson	Boston
Riordan Pulp and Paper Co.	Director	Brig.-Gen. J. B. White	Montreal
Lake of the Woods Milling Co.	Director	R. Wilson Reford	Montreal
Lake of the Woods Milling Co.	Director	W. E. Allen	Winnipeg

Progress of the Greater Manufacturing Industries   Electricity and water-power were at the base of much Industrial success in 1919 and immediately preceding years.   More than two-thirds of the total power used in Canada was from this source, and the Dominion Water Power Branch presented several reports pointing out new sources of power.   The immense undertakings at Niagara, on the St. Lawrence, at Shawinigan, at Grand Falls, and in British Columbia were well known and Canada was, probably, the foremost country in the world in this form of development.   Ontario at this time was producing 985,060 h.p., Quebec 842,761 h.p., British Columbia 312,423 h.p., the total, according to latest returns being 2,305,310 h.p., which the Water Power Branch estimated as only 12 per cent. of the total available power in the Dominion.

On Jan. 1, 1919, official figures stated the total capital invested in Central Electric stations as $401,942,402, of which $356,547,217 represented the investment in power development, and transmission, and distribution systems and $45,395,185 the miscellaneous supplies and working capital.   The commercial or privately-owned stations included 71·7 per cent. of this total capital investment and the municipal or publicly-owned stations 28·3 per cent.   The total number of persons reported as employed in the industry was 9,696 with salaries and wages amounting to $10,354,242.   There were in 1918, $43,285,405 invested in the Electrical Apparatus industry with $8,456,705 paid out in wages and a total product valued at $30,045,399.   According to 1917 Census returns the horse-power used in industrial plants in that year was 3,667,269.

Fuel was one of the great industrial problems of 1919.   The production of the country was almost stationary—in 1914 13,637,520 tons and in 1919 13,676,300 tons; the Imports of coal in 1910 were 10,170,122 tons valued at $27,526,678 and in 1919 21,411,813 tons valued at $70,603,005; yet, though double in quantity, the supply did not keep up with the demands and there was trouble during much of the year.   Canadian industries wanted more and more fuel, more and more electric energy, as their production expanded; while the United States output of coal decreased owing to strikes while similar troubles in Alberta reduced the Canadian output in one month (August, 1919) by 441,013 tons alone; transportation difficulties added to the difficulty in the United States and, toward the close of the year, it required all the energies of C. A. Magrath—appointed Fuel Controller on June 11, 1917—and the continued interchange of views between the Governments concerned, to relieve the situation which developed.   Soft coal used by industries, railways, etc., was most affected and the situation in November and December was serious, with three weeks in which practically none of this fuel came into Canada.

On Nov. 15 H. A. Harrington, Ontario Fuel Administrator, took over the coal in storage or on transit in that Province and the Dominion Government put an embargo on export while the Railways cut off many passenger trains. Up to this time the receipt of coal from the United States was only 70 per cent. of that in 1918. Even negotiations for a time failed and all industries were more or less held up. Early in December some emergency coal began to move across the border and, in a couple of weeks, it was doing so freely but the whole situation showed how unpleasantly close was Canada's dependence upon American coal despite her possession of the greatest reserves of coal in the world. Consumption had increased over 10,000,000 tons between 1914 and 1919 yet production remained almost stationary. Incidentally, the value of Electrical power development in this connection was fully illustrated and James White, Vice-Chairman of the Conservation Commission, made the following suggestions on Dec. 27:

1. The public development, under comprehensive plans, of the total regulated flow of our water-powers so far as such development is economically feasible, also that water be conserved by the creation of storage reservoirs.

2. The establishment of central coking plants, in which all bituminous coal shall be coaked before being used as fuel. By constructing these plants near our larger cities the gas will be available for heating and domestic use, thus reducing the demand for coal for this purpose. The other by-products, coal tar and ammonium sulphate, would also be recovered. At present, owing to the consumption of the new coal by our industries, railways, etc., these by-products are largely wasted.

3. The development of super-power stations at mine entries in the West, where water-power is not economically available. From these stations steam-generated electric power could be distributed by transmission lines to municipalities within a radius equal to that of the Ontario Hydro-Electric Commission's line from Niagara Falls to Windsor, Ont. Large amounts of slack or waste coal accumulate at the mines. Where possible this waste should be used for power generation.

Chemical products had a great development in these years and this was illustrated in the exports of Drugs, dyes and chemicals which increased from a value of $1,730,203 in 1913-14 to $17,053,-074 in 1918-19. S. J. Cook, Chemist in charge of a Laboratory at the Department of Trade and Commerce, Ottawa, stated in a London *Times* survey of the situation (Sept. 6, 1919) that one of the most conspicuous developments in Canada at this time was the erection of the world's largest glacial acetic acid plant, built for war purposes, at Shawinigan, Quebec, where an entirely new process, beginning with acetylene, was carried out. Acetone and several smaller products were also produced, while magnesium was made, electrolytically, from its fused salts. At Niagara Falls there was an adaptation to the manufacture of fixed atmospheric nitrogen as cyanamide, the lime-nitrogen fertilizer, and its conversion into ammonium salts. Among electric-furnace products native to Niagara and Shawinigan were aluminous abrasives, ferro-silicon, etc. In the manufacture of munitions of war there arose a demand for acetic acid and acetone which stimulated the wood distillation industries of the country. Salicylic acid and the well-known acetyl derivative, popularly known as aspirin, were also made in Canada, while coumarin, benzoic acid, benzoate of soda and benzaldehyde were further names in the list of new Canadian chemicals.

The Agricultural Implement industry made progress with, in 1918, a capital investment of $74,410,603, salaries and wages of $10,282,539 and products valued at $34,853,673; the exports (Mch. 31) of 1919 were $8,043,296 compared with $2,802,096 in 1915. The Imports were $4,944,278. Leather was the basis of many important industries—notably boots and shoes—and was much discussed during 1918-19 as a result of the steady rise in prices and alleged shortage in material. Leather and its finished products had a production in 1910 of $62,850,412 and in 1915 of $71,036,644; Boots and shoes constituted $33,987,248 and $34,064,696 respectively of this latter total. In 1918 the total for boots and shoes was $43,332,932. The exports were comparatively small—$1,130,334 in boots and shoes, $3,680,794 in manufactured leather and $8,756,918 in unmanufactured leather, with $7,700,029 in hides and skins. These figures indicate expansion but nothing to equal the demand and the rise in prices; there was also an import of boots and shoes in 1919 of $2,694,106, of manufactured leather, $3,612,178 and of unmanufactured $7,856,609, with hides and skins totalling $5,426,008.

Rubber supplies during 1919, as in preceding years, were said to be very short but the Ames-McCready firm of Montreal added a section of rubber manufacturing to their boot and shoes department without reference to this subject at the annual meeting; their total surplus in 1917 was $197,303, in 1918 $304,094, in 1919 $323,322—a total of $830,730 in the three years; with an increase of 27 per cent. in the volume of business, however, the profits remained about the same. The Canadian Rubber Consolidated Co., at their meeting on Apr. 22, showed sales in 1918 of $18,785,640 with net profits of $1,604,851, compared with $1,208,018 in 1917, and liquid assets of $11,297,468. According to the *Financial Times* (Apr. 26) the net profits after the usual deductions, and after providing for the preferred dividend, were equal to 46 per cent. on the Company's common stock, compared with 35·6 per cent. in 1917, 22·1 per cent. in 1916, and 12·2 per cent. in 1915. The Goodyear Tire and Rubber Co., of Toronto, showed sales (Sept. 30, 1919) of $12,839,123 with net earnings of $1,324,328 compared with $760,997 in 1918.

It may be noted here that wholesale leather and shoe firms of the West organized, on Dec. 17, as the Western Canadian Leather and Shoe Finders' Association with S. McCracken of Calgary as President. W. J. Heaven of the Tanners' section of the Toronto Board of Trade made the statement in Toronto on the same day that: "We started off at the beginning of the year with hide prices slightly lower, with packer and other hide prices remaining fairly stationary until the month of March, when they commenced to move upward, and during the month of April they surpassed any prices reached during the war period. They continued to advance during May, June and July, until they reached in July the unprecedented price of 55 cents per pound for cattle hides and $1.00

per pound for calf skins, which at the first of January were quoted at 29 cents and 34 cents respectively.'' They were, therefore, 50 per cent. higher than at the beginning of the year and, he added: ''There are immense quantities of leather yet to come out of the yards which will be made from hides bought at the top of the market, and under these circumstances tanners will not be anxious to make much reduction in prices.''

An industrial and general factor of much interest was that of Automobiles and the increase in purchase and use of these vehicles was enormous—50,489 in 1913, 67,414 in 1914, 87,673 in 1915, 120,498 in 1916, 198,739 in 1917, 269,727 in 1918 and an estimated total in 1919 of 352,700. The imports of freight motors in 1919 totalled $2,274,748 in value, of passenger cars $5,326,510 and parts thereof $6,660,770—the latter of course for putting together as Canadian machines. The exports in freight and passenger cars totalled $7,303,678. The capital invested in the Canadian industry was $36,977,979 in 1918 and the production was $72,286,040. The business was a healthy one and, as in so many other lines, the demand from abroad kept the home market from being thoroughly stocked. It was estimated that $370,000,000 worth of passenger and other motors were owned in Canada at this time and the collateral business of rubber tires and gasoline was large. The Ford Motor Car Co. of Canada, in its latest annual statement, manufactured 39,412 cars of which 17,880 were exported; most of the Companies enlarged their plants as with the Olds Company, or built new factories and, amongst them, the Gray-Dort at Chatham, Willys-Overland at West Toronto, the Briscoe and the Reo. It is interesting to note that General Motors, Inc., of Boston, the great American concern, had, in 6 months of 1919, net profits of $48,000,-000 or $13,000,000 more than in the whole year of 1918.

The Flour-milling industry made great progress in 1919; official figures of investment for 1918 showed $78,144,461 and a production of $261,915,071 with cost of materials, mainly wheat, totalling $218,237,250. The Ogilvie Flour Mills Co., Ltd., reported for Aug. 31, 1919, assets of $16,411,240, net profits of $817,-516 with a Rest account of $2,500,000, a Contingent account of $2,500,000, a working capital of $7,379,006; for the same fiscal year the Lake of the Woods had total profits of $756,616, a year's surplus of $203,616 and a total surplus of $982,414 with a working capital of $2,152,188; the Western Canada Flour Mills Co. showed a surplus profit of $104,431 with a working capital of over $1,000,-000; the Maple Leaf Milling Co. absorbed the Campbell Flour Mills, Ltd., with a combined capital of $6,000,000 and a milling capacity of 18,000 bushels a day. The Ogilvies paid a dividend in 1919 of 12 per cent. with a bonus of 1 per cent. but it was intimated that the profits came from investments rather than the flour business. The Exports of wheat flour in 1919 (Mch. 31) totalled $99,931,659 in value. The subsidiary industry of Bakery and Confectionery had an investment in 1918 of $40,272,208 and a production of $85,555,848.

The Steel industry was and is a vital one to Canada; in this year it was prosperous but with continued difficulty as to supplies of raw material, wages and transportation. The trade in iron and steel products and the manufactures thereof totalled $220,335,562 in 1919 (Mch. 31) and of this record figure $161,619,050 were imports. Of exports the United Kingdom took $9,550,774, the United States $22,078,394 and other countries $27,087,335. The Government during the year discontinued work on the $5,000,000 ships' plate mill at Sydney, N.S., and this left the Ship-building industry dependent on the United States for these supplies. According to David Carnegie of the Imperial Munitions Board, (Jan. 27, 1919) Canada had increased her steel production per annum from one million tons before the War to 2¼ million tons; the United States steel production had increased from 32 million tons to 45 million tons, and Britain's from 7½ million to 12 million tons per annum.

As to the future Mr. Carnegie added: "Britain has a capacity for steel production exceeding her pre-war capacity by 62 per cent., while Canada's capacity has increased 125 per cent. If Canadian manufacturers will follow Britain's example by determining to supply its domestic trade more fully than in the past, Canada will go a considerable distance in using its surplus steel capacity. Canada should have at least one structural mill for rolling heavy structures. The home demands, alone, of the Electrical industry for higher quality steel sheets is not by any means insignificant. The growing demands for alloy steels for motor cars, tractors, and all kinds of engines and high-class machinery, where excessive wear calls for a better and more enduring steel, should arouse the most earnest attention of the makers of electric and crucible steel. The importation into Canada of tool steel, file steel and files, spring steel and springs should be reviewed by the makers of high-class steel." Canada was and is dependent upon the United States for most of its raw material in this Industry; more than 1,000,000 tons of steel per annum was made from imported ore and nearly two-thirds of the fuel used was imported also; only an insignificant amount of nickel was refined in Canada until serious operations began in 1919. Despite these drawbacks, however, the export total of iron and steel products was $58,716,503 in 1918-19 compared with $11,374,981 in 1913-14 with the main details in 1918 and 1919 as follows:

	1917-18	1918-19
Agricultural implements	$4,797,757	$8,023,833
Bars and rods	7,716,318	7,844,044
Billets, ingots, blooms	2,299,378	2,270,721
Ferro-silicon, etc.	2,436,752	2,502,571
Firearms	1,326,796	1,860,279
Hardware, n.o.p.	1,071,974	2,631,893
Machinery, all kinds	3,448,407	7,048,797
Scrap, iron or steel	1,756,657	1,282,825
Tools, hand or machine	1,101,960	2,132,671
Wire and wire nails	8,949,304	7,789,188
Other iron or steel	6,811,043	12,335,933

In the larger Steel Companies there was much talk during the year as to a great coming merger—the Dominion Steel, Nova Scotia Steel, Steel Company of Canada, and Canada Steamships—with total assets of 215 millions and funded or capital issues of 153 millions; toward its close it was known that an English group of capitalists headed by Grant Morden and represented in Canada by Roy Wolvin had acquired large interests in the Dominion Steel Corporation. This Company had net earnings in 1918 (Mch. 31) of $11,050,112 and in 1919 of $8,768,054 with net profits of $7,601,-660 and $5,470,468, respectively, or of 23 per cent. and 17 per cent. on its common stock. The working capital in 1919 was $14,039,-837 compared with $951,729 in 1913. During the year of 1919 $9,000,000 were spent on betterments. The N.S. Coal and Steel Co. had profits of $3,535,525 in 1918 compared with $236,261 in 1914, and net profits of $1,716,492; its 1918 surplus was $886,492 and the total $2, 616,584. The net working capital was $9,101,185 and the total assets $36,288,917.

A dispute broke out in 1919 between the Dominion Coal Co. (subsidiary of the Dominion Steel Corporation) and the N.S. Steel and Coal Co. over the latter's application to the Nova Scotia Government on Feb. 17, 1919, for a re-adjustment of the respective Company holdings of coal areas in the Sydney coal field. The application was framed upon the hypothesis that the coal-field of the Nova Scotia Co., so far as it was possible to mine coal economically, was exhausted and that it would be to the advantage of that Company and not a detriment to the Dominion Company that a re-adjustment should be compulsorily made by Legislative enactment. An exchange of certain areas was proposed and vigourous opposition offered on the ground that the Dominion Company's inshore areas, containing millions of tons of excellent easily-won coal, could not fairly be exchanged for submarine areas that had not been proved and could not be proved to contain coal. It was also claimed by the Dominion Coal Co. that its coal areas in North Sydney were vital to the maintenance of its industries. D. H. McDougall, President of the Nova Scotia, declared on the other hand that the re-adjustment would mean that each Company would have its areas so adjusted as to enable it to get its coal at the lowest possible figure, and would thus do away with the payment of tribute to other's in order to get to some distant coal areas. This issue, no doubt, had something to do with the succeeding merger discussions.

Of other Companies the Steel of Canada had a most prosperous year in 1918 and the net profits for that calendar year were $5,367,-120 compared with $539,811 in 1914 or an increase of 900 per cent. As the *Financial Times* of Apr. 19, 1919, put it: "Taking into consideration the large excess expenditure in connection with the building of coke ovens as well as the large amount set aside for depreciation, together with the substantial cash payments made on new properties, and for liquid investments, the earnings of 15·7 per cent. on the $11,500,000 of common stock, constitute a very

satisfactory performance.   Reserves at the end of 1918 totalled
$7,696,257, compared with the total of $622,453 in 1914, while the
profit and loss surplus at $7,322,872 compared with $1,258,430 in
1914.''   The working capital was $12,222,202 as against $4,976,-
871 in 1914.   Steel and Radiation, Toronto had in 1918 the best
year in its history with net profits of $481,464; Canadian Locomo-
tive had profits of $892,976 in 1919 compared with $134,613 in 1915
and a balance at profit and loss of $1,366,794 as against $142,321
while earning 27·8 per cent. on common stock and increasing its
working capital, in the year, by $1,865,926 or over 170 per cent.

Canada Iron Foundries, Ltd., had in 1919 (Sept. 30) a working capital of $2,237,134 compared with $1,899,815 in 1918 and earnings, without depreciation charges, of $489,943 while its preference
and common shares of an original par value of $10 were worth
$100.   The Canadian Car and Foundry Co., Ltd., for 1919 (Sept.
30) showed profits of $2,993,470 with a total surplus carried for-
ward of $7,061,556 and reserves of $5,123,455, with 7 plants running
and orders in hand for $8,000,000.   Incidents in the Iron and
Steel industry included British requirements for 35,000 trucks; the
branch organization and partial construction of work in Toronto
of Baldwin's Ltd., a great British concern with $25,000,000
capital and 14,000 workmen and a proposed construction in Canada
of a $10,000,000 Steel-rolling mill; a first run of pig-iron made
from British Columbia resources and smelted at Vancouver; the
location at Goderich of the Lake Huron Steel Corporation—a $15,-
000,000 concern with American capital behind it and B. H.
McCreath of Toronto as the chief promoter.   A supplementary
industry was that of Foundry and Machine shops with an investment of $84,122,446 in 1918 and products of $82,493,897.

The Textile industry had a very great success during the later
war years and in 1919 with, however, difficulties in getting adequate cotton machinery, in a limitation of working hours to eight
and the consequent cutting-down of production, an increase in
overhead expenses and advances in the price of raw cotton.   Prices
of products were higher than ever owing to these conditions and the
huge demand from abroad, and the mills had more orders than they
could fill.   The output of Canadian cotton mills according to a
statement by Sir Charles Gordon in the Montreal *Gazette*, after the
close of the year, increased from $27,000,000 in 1914 to $65,000,-
000 in 1919 and the estimated number of spindles increased by
90,000 and the operators by 1,500.

As to profits Sir Charles had this to say: ''They have been on a
conservative basis when compared with the enormous profits which
have been made in other countries by every cotton manufacturing
concern, and the prices of cotton goods in Canada, during the period
in review, have in many cases been lower than the same goods could
have been bought at in either Great Britain or the United States,
notwithstanding the fact that it costs some 20 per cent. more to
produce cotton goods in Canada.   The policy of the Canadian cot-

ton mills has been to re-invest a very considerable portion of their earnings in betterments to the properties.'' In the chief Textile concerns the sales and profits increased between 1914 and 1919 as follows*: Canadian Cotton—sales $3,500,476 to $10,828,326 and profits $411,104 to $1,563,108; Dominion Textile—sales $8,899,719 to $23,666,216 and profits $1,196,990 to $3,434,752; Montreal Cotton—sales $3,017,704 to $5,917,519 and profits $383,177 to $720,649; Penmans—sales $4,071,634 to $8,648,382 and profits $444,054 to $1,953,643. The Assets of these 4 Companies and of the Canadian Converters and Wabasso Company totalled $60,000,000 in 1919 and their total surplus exceeded $11,000,000.

For the year of Mch. 31, 1919, the exports of woollen goods was $3,518,850 and of cotton goods $2,859,241—much less than in 1918 when war requirements induced a large special export; the imports of raw cotton in 1919 were 113,723,536 lbs., valued at $34,008,824. The importation of Textiles (wool and cotton) Mch. 31, 1919, $168,878,366; 1915, $76,992,361. Canada was thus pressing toward development of two great industries; the capital investment of 1918 in Cottons was $53,796,394, the total of salaries and wages was $9,227,343, the total product was $66,399,228 and the cost of materials $34,289,862. In Woollen goods there was similar progress though on a smaller scale. The total investment in 1918 was $19,268,202, the salaries and wages paid $3,793,925, the product $25,063,515, and the cost of materials $15,301,474 and there were in Canada 140 woollen and weaving mills with 2,000 looms and 100,000 spindles; in subsidiary industries there was a considerable product. Women's wear, in the clothing section, had a capital of $25,351,755, salaries and wages of $3,255,855, a cost for materials of $25,692,926 and a product of $46,890,971; Men's wear showed an investment of $33,376,469 with products of $48,779,393, salaries and wages of $4,078,785 and a cost for materials of $25,422,103; Woollen yarn had a capital of $3,767,390, cost of materials $4,311,902, salaries and wages of $521,968 and products valued at $6,499,445; Men's furnishings showed a capital of $12,647,413, wages and salaries of $3,261,922, materials used of $10,527,796 and products totalling $17,876,956; Gloves and mitts had an investment of $6,291,269, Hats, caps and furs of $14,431,530 and Hosiery and Knit goods $31,092,866. The cost of labour for these three latter industries was $13,641,139 and of materials $40,602,242, the total product was $73,945,785.

The trouble as to prices and production in cotton goods was explained by Sir Charles Macara, the great English manufacturer, to a correspondent on Jan. 31 as follows: ''The number of spindles in the world is approximately 144,000,000. Let us take 5 per cent. for depreciation or renewals. This would mean that an equivalent 7½ million spindles would have to be installed each year to maintain the industry. During the War there have been practically no renewals, so that on that account the world may be said to be 30,-

*Note.—Compiled by H. H. Black, Montreal Editor *Financial Post*, Toronto.

000,000 spindles in arrear. We have to consider, too, the losses that
have to be made good in France, in Belgium, and in Russia."
This, he thought, meant scarcity and high prices for some years.
Early in the year arrangements were made through the Minister
of Trade and Commerce as to an order for $3,180,000 worth of
Canadian woollen products for Roumania with, later on, a supplementary order for $700,000 and a Belgian order for $500,000;
price lists of the Textile mills fell 10 per cent. to 20 per cent. in
April but, later on, they rose again and, as to woollens, the later
restriction in supplies of high grade worsted cloths from British
and French mills effected a change in that industry.

The Wood and pulp and paper industry of Canada in 1919
expanded by leaps and bounds. The capital investment (1917)
was $149,266,019, the wages and salaries paid $39,193,711, the cost
of materials was $58,403,316 and the value of products $115,884,-
905.   In 1918 the investment had risen to $180,017,173 and the
production to $144,908,864 with wages, etc., $49,011,735 and cost of
materials $68,498,820.   The rise in prices, which continued in 1918
and 1919, was illustrated by the above increase in the value of products compared with $68,815,472 in the 1915 Census returns. There
were, in 1917, 2,879 operating plants and in 1918, 3,086. As to
Pulp-wood, the United States was, in 1917, supplying one-fifth to
one-third of its requirements, and over 11 per cent. of its wood-
pulp needs, through importations from Canada and this process
greatly increased in the next two years. As Clyde Leavitt, Chief
Forester of the Conservation Commission, put it on Sept. 27, 1919:
"If these growing requirements are to be met continuously, in addition to meeting the increasing demands for pulp and paper from
Great Britain and other European countries, steps must be taken
to retain our forest lands in a continuously productive condition.
Canada is a pulp and paper country *par excellence,* and the amount
of business she can do in the future will be limited only by the
supply of raw material."

Studies made by this Commission showed that the current
methods of cutting were not satisfactory in this respect and that
insufficient measures for re-afforestation were being developed.
Yet, in the United States, it was authoritatively stated that the bulk
of the original supplies of yellow pine in the South would be exhausted in 10 years, and within five to seven years, more than 3,000
manufacturing plants would have to go out of existence there.
Already American paper manufacturers were embarrassed for supplies.   For the year of Mch. 31, 1919, the Canadian exports of
pulp, paper and pulp-wood were $99,259,166, compared with $71,-
755,325 in 1918, $52,924,888 in 1917, $36,141,665 in 1916, $31,561,-
810 in 1915 and $26,428,630 in 1914.   Of the 1919 total Paper
stood for $49,165,795, wood-pulp for $45,706,771 and unmanufactured pulp-wood $15,386,600; of the Printing paper exported in
1918-19 the United States got $36,031,358 out of a total of $40,-
718,021.   As to the latter product, the Canadian Pulp and Paper

Association urged consumers in Canada to buy the home product but the import continued to increase—$6,848,422 in 1917 $7,516,398 in 1918 and $9,044,390 in 1919.

The Paper industry by 1918 stood upon a high level with an invested capital, in combined pulp and paper mills, of $241,344,704, wages and salaries payment of $26,974,226, materials used totalling $37,549,336 in paper mills, and $29,825,142 in wood-pulp manufacture, and a production of $76,700,913 in paper and $42,608,521 in wood-pulp of all kinds. The paper mills numbered 31, pulp-mills 37 and combined mills 26, or 94 altogether. As to sub-divisions in the Paper industry Newsprint in 1918 took 689,847 tons valued at $38,868,084, or $56.35 per ton; Book and writing paper 48,141 tons at $9,310,138 or $193.40 per ton; wrapping paper and boards 104,440 tons at $9,189,914 or a combined value of $177.62 per ton. In November 1919, the Canadian production of Newsprint was running at 2,775 tons a day with the following as the largest producers: Abitibi, 240 tons; Belgo-Canadian, 200 tons; J. R. Booth, 150 tons; Donnacona, 100 tons; Fort Frances, 150 tons; Laurentide, 225 tons; Ontario Paper, 225 tons; Pacific Mills, 200 tons; Powell River Co., 225 tons; Price Bros., 250 tons; Spanish River, 500 tons.

After a prolonged, triangular controversy running through 1918 and 1919 between Manufacturers, Newspapers or publishers, and the Government, as to whether the price of Newsprint in rolls to Canadian publishers should remain at the $69 per ton fixed by Commissioner R. A. Pringle, or should be increased to $80, as the Manufacturers suggested, or be reduced to $50, as the Publishers urged, it was decided in December, 1919, by the Paper Control Tribunal which had been appointed by the Government late in 1918 to investigate the matter. Under Government control the rate per ton, at first imposed in 1917, was $57 and then rose to $69, was reduced on appeal to $66, stood during 1919 at $69, and was now increased to $80. Market conditions at this time were about $90 a ton so that the announced lifting of control in 1920 would involve still higher prices. The situation at the close of 1919 was one of many complications. It was claimed that the cost of newspaper production had increased 100 per cent. during the year in the United States with conditions not quite so bad in Canada; on the other hand, it was said that much of the material in Sunday issues and huge supplements might be eliminated and the cost saved without injury to the public with the shortage of print paper, as a matter of fact, bringing this about to some extent; the consumption of pulp-wood from Canada and in Canada was steadily increasing— a total of 1,000,000 cords in 1917 over 1914 and much more in the next two years; authorities asserted insistently that there was a coming famine of pulp supplies for this continent unless Canada's resources were conserved and developed. On the other hand, all kinds of new uses were being found for pulp and Sir George Bury, head of the Whalen concern at Vancouver, declared on Sept. 16 that:

The pulp industry is in its infancy. It is in the same position as steel was 25 years ago. Paper made from pulp has been employed to make wheels on Pullman cars. In a few years everything we wear will be made of pulp. Five years from now the housekeeper will have all her kitchen utensils made of pulp. The laundry will largely disappear because our under-clothing, shirts, collars, table-cloths, napkins, etc., will be made from pulp. British Columbia will produce the pulp for the world because nowhere else in the world is there grown better wood than the Sitka spruce found on the British Columbia coast. I believe that pulp will finally solve the high cost of living.

As to Companies in this great industry, the Spanish River Pulp and Paper Mills, Ltd., had a capital stock of $13,700,000, a net revenue in 1918-19 of $2,757,964, or $1,000,000 more than in the previous year, with a net surplus for the year of $1,456,921 and $2,368,222 carried forward—compared with a surplus of $268,330 in 1915. The daily capacity of its three mills at Sault Ste. Marie and two other points was 1,120 tons of Newsprint, pulp-wood and sulphite and it employed 6,570 men. The Brompton Pulp and Paper Co., Ltd., East Angus, held 311,768 acres in Quebec containing 2,700,000 cords of pulpwood and 350,000,000 feet, B.M., of saw-logs with earnings which increased from $200,794 in 1913 to $1,051,-274 in 1918 and assets of $12,338,773. The Abitibi Power and Paper Co., Ltd., of Montreal, controlled 1,000,000 acres of pulpwood limits under Ontario Government lease, in the Abitibi region of Northern Ontario, with control of 5,000,000 cords of paper-making woods and 15,000,000 more available in the vicinity of Iroquois Falls where its mills had a capacity of 130,000 tons; its capitalization was $7,000,000; its Funded Debt $6,350,700, the net earnings for 1918 were $1,174,621 and the stock rose during 1919 from 50 to about 187. At the close of the year the Company announced reorganization as the Abitibi, Ltd., with $31,000,000 capital of which $1,000,000 was preferred.

Price Bros. and Co., Ltd., of Quebec, were at this time 100 years old and their timber holdings were estimated at 7,000 square miles of freehold and Crown lands, containing a large quantity of merchantable timber and 20,000,000 cords pulpwood; the supply of raw material was considered practically inexhaustible, as a careful system of conservation and renewal was carried out. The earnings of the Company increased from 4·67 per cent. in 1914 to 18·55 per cent. in 1918; the capital stock was $5,000,000 and the bond issue $5,172,000; the profits for the year of Feb. 28, 1919, were $1,493,961 and the total surplus $2,874,224. The Laurentide Power Co., Ltd., of Grand Mère, Quebec, held timber limits of 2,500 square miles with large available water power; in 1919 it earned 19 per cent. on its common stock and the average earnings for 1912-18 were 11·85 per cent.; the capital stock was $9,600,000 with bonds of $565,778 outstanding. For the year of June 30, 1919, the profits were $2,955,978 and the total surplus carried forward $2,857,204, or 28 per cent. of the combined capital and funded obligations; 1,000,000 young trees had been planted during the year and the working capital was $7,238,086.

The Wayagamack Pulp and Paper Co., Three Rivers, held 1,121 square miles of spruce and pine limits along the St. Lawrence said to contain over 4,000 million ft., B.M. of various woods; its capital stock and bond issues totalled $8,395,000 and the earnings of 1918 were $1,057,742, while the net working capital was $1,230,650. The Riordan Pulp and Paper Co., Ltd., held rights in 1,184 square miles of Quebec timber limits; its net earnings in 1918 were $1,651,250 compared with $375,862 in 1914, and the capital stock was $5,500,000 with bonds of $6,090,000; the total surplus carried forward was $2,218,379. The Chicoutimi Pulp Co., with headquarters at Chicoutimi, had net profits of $819,596 in 1918, great holdings of timber limits and of water and electric power; it was subsidiary, with 4 other Companies, of the North American Pulp and Paper Companies' Trust at Montreal; during 1919 the Saguenay Pulp and Paper Co. was organized as one of the combined subsidiaries with an issue of $5,000,000, 6 per cent. serial gold bonds and the possession of large pulp resources and mills and water powers. According to a statement of the *Financial Post*, Toronto, (Sept. 27, 1919) the 10 leading Pulp and Paper concerns of Canada had a combined capitalization in 1918, or 1919, of $95,000,000, combined profits of $13,230,950, a working capital of $19,100,000, a surplus on hand of $14,927,006, assets of $130,739,800 with an average dividend of 5·3 per cent.

Industrial incidents of the year included the opening of an office in London, England, by the Shawinigan Water and Power Co., for the purpose of developing the sale of carbide of calcium, acetic acid, etc.; a steady growth of Canadian Phonograph production and sales which helped to meet the large import from the United States; the absorption by the Dominion Canners, Ltd., in British Columbia of the Vantoria Canning Co., the Kelowna Packers, Ltd., and the Food Products, Ltd.; the Report of the Canada Cement Co., for 1918 of net earnings of $2,215,708, a surplus carried forward of $2,677,643 and a net working capital of $5,007,914; the increasing sale of lands by the Hudson's Bay Co., and the transfer of its old-time empire in the West to incoming settlers, with a continued development in its great chain of stores, and profits for 1919 of $801,910 with a sale of 285,561 acres at $5,015,355; the placing of orders by all the leading Pulp and Paper interests for new machinery and equipment; an effort by the Alberta Foundry and Machine Co. to make farm tractors for the West; the continued construction of great plants, open-hearth furnaces, ore and coal-docks, immense blast furnaces, etc., at Ojibway by the Canadian Steel Corporation—a subsidiary of the United States Steel Corporation; the transfer of the Dominion Bridge Company's attention to machinery for paper mills in place of munitions' machinery, and of the Canadian Locomotive Co. from heavy shells to car-building, the Willys-Overland from aeroplane motors and munitions to its own specialty of automobiles. It may be added that the Meat industry of Canada was a most important one and its official statistics, as given out for 1918, vital to the country. The total number of packing plants was 67 and abattoirs 11, the capital invested was $86,969,756, the wages and salaries paid were $12,173,385 in the year, the animals slaughtered numbered 3,449,-107 and the total cost of these animals in dressed weight was $171,-023,104, the total product was $229,231,666.

Manufac-turers and the 1919 Problems of Prices and Values.   Did the Manufacturer unduly enhance prices during the later years of the War and in 1919, or make improper profits, or take advantage of a Protective tariff to oppress the consumer? The organized farmer, the Free-trader, and the Liberal politicians claimed that he did; the public, as a whole, listened to this contention and to other attacks upon Farmers and Middlemen and was inclined to criticize all classes; as, however, the manufacturer had concrete plants and products and organization with known profits and frequently obvious wealth, he had to bear the brunt of the blame for what was, in the main, though not in many details, a world condition. That there were profiteers, was clear to all who observed the suddenly-acquired wealth of the war-period; that they often were manufacturers did not necessarily involve condemnation of a whole class, because much of the new capital was not industrial in origin and some of the men who plunged into war industries were not manufacturers by occupation. As to prices, it seems obvious that in the War and after the war manufacturers varied in their raising of rates with a natural though regrettable tendency to apply export prices to domestic supplies. There was not a definite, fixed rule, however, which would have made things clear; in 1919 everything fluctuated. Elbert H. Gary, President of the United States Steel Corporation, presented an important point of view—applicable to Canadian conditions as to the United States—in an address as President of the American Bar Association:[*]

Prices of commodities are too large in many cases; and the average designated general level is too high. They are not regular and are not relative. Some have advanced 50 per cent., others 200 per cent. Many small articles, bringing immense sums in the aggregate, have been advanced beyond all reason because the facts escape exposure and public criticism on account of the smallness of the items. The middleman is charged perhaps 50 per cent. advance, adds this increase to his previous selling price, and then insists upon and secures 100 per cent. advance on the whole.

There has been no level, but rather a changing, irregular range of prices. The producer of an article of food increases the selling price to a purchaser who is a manufacturer of an article of clothing; the latter increases his price to the producer who has fuel for sale; this one increases his selling price to the builder of a dwelling house; then an increase by the owner is passed on to the tenant, who is a labouring man working for the seller of food, the point where the illustration commenced; the workman then increases his rates for compensation accordingly. One and on all have been going, some at a faster pace than others, and, of course, there results confusion, inequalities, unreasonable prices and economic disturbances.

---

*Note.—Published in full by *Financial Post*, Toronto, Sept. 6, 1919.

This was in part a manufacturer's side of the case; the middleman had another story to tell but there was undoubtedly much of general truth in the statement. In what seemed a profiteering branch of the question in 1919 trouble lay in the attempt to dispose of goods made from the high-priced raw material of the later war years at war-time prices—when new raw material was on a lower range; considerable stocks were thus held in certain cases and the Reports of the Cost of Living Commissioner indicated a strong belief that prices also were being held up on some articles of food and shelter as well as of manufacture. That manufacturers were not uniform in any advance of prices was evident from the Department of Labour's Index figures of commodity prices in August, 1918, and August, 1919, which indicated that in this 12-month period, average prices in Textiles declined from 372 to 362 and metals and implements from 266 to 214, while leather, boots and shoes, etc., rose from 285 to 425 and furniture from 276 to 381. At the same time, grains and fodder and animals and meats rose while dairy products and miscellaneous foods declined.

In the United States the Federal Trade Commission reported to Congress on Aug. 6 that the rise in the price of boots and shoes was due to "unwarranted increase" in the price of hides, "exceptional profits" to the tanners, an "unusual margin" to the manufacturers, and prices charged by retailers which were "not justifiable." Conditions were not dissimilar in some Canadian industries —perhaps there was an all-round tendency in this very direction; to assess the individual blame would be difficult. A tentative effort was made by the Board of Commerce and, in the production of boots, alone, it was found that 11 different persons or agencies were involved and that each had to get a profit as follows: the farmer or cattle man; the buyer of hides; the wholesale dealer in hides and his assistants; the tanner; the tanner's workman; the leather merchant (wholesale); the boot manufacturer; his workmen; the wholesale boot and shoe dealer; the railways, which at different times had transported the hides, the leather, or the boots; the retailer, who in a particular case, at Calgary, made $5.00 gross profit on a $15.00 pair of shoes.

Food and boots went up in price during 1919; so did gas and street car tickets over the continent as a whole; coal increased steadily but it was from well-known causes—strikes and lessened production, higher wages and, according to W. G. McAdoo, ex-United States Secretary of the Treasury "shocking and indefensible" profits by the owners in 1917; lumber and wheat went up—everything from pins to locomotives advanced in price; even silver at Cobalt rose from 54 cents an ounce in 1914 to 96 cents in 1918, $1.13 in August, 1919. Meantime, there was profiteering in rentals and even higher costs in transportation and distribution of everything. Manufacturers shared in the process and, obviously, some prices would continue high until the shortage in world supplies was caught up with; high prices for export very largely controlled domestic rates and the Government, in the interest of the country as a whole, encouraged sales abroad of specific products at high prices; if lower rates had been fixed on a lower level at home, it is clear that there would have been a rush of products to the seaboard and scarcity in the country.

The Cost of Living Commissioner and the Manufacturer. This official, Dr. R. J. McFall, who succeeded W. F. O'Connor, k.c., in the position early in 1919 and who was replaced in many duties by the Board of Commerce, made various statements during the early part of the year and some charges—as to Cold Storage and the Canners and Refiners being in combines, notably. On June 7 he submitted a Report to the Minister of Labour as to Textiles and clothing and stated that the situation regarding woollens and worsteds was that Canada was more heavily supplied with. the raw material than ever before in her history with prices very much lower than last autumn; the finished cloth was coming on the market more freely than when the looms were engaged in weaving khaki cloth, and it was sold in the spring of 1919 by the manufacturer, to the wholesaler so as to reach the wearer in the autumn, at lower prices than the finished material in the season of 1918. In many instances Canadian cloth for suitings and over-coatings was going forward for sale by the wholesaler at an eight to ten per cent. decrease.

Apparently, however, the wholesalers were loaded with old stocks of the higher priced materials, which they desired to sell to the public at the old prices. In the case of cottons the manufacturers' prices had also declined since autumn, and the stocks coming ahead for retail sale had cost the middleman decidedly less than earlier stocks. The retail price of such commodities should, Dr. McFall declared, have been reduced. Yet the evidence given showed that, in many. cases the retail price was more than double the manufacturers' price and that the margins taken by the middlemen were greater than the whole amount that went to farmer, manufacturer and labourer. This statement appeared to throw a rather striking light upon the question of relative profits. Following this there were many criticisms of the above conclusions and Dr. McFall on Aug. 5th issued a brief statement to the press: "In the evidence brought out before the Cost of Living Committee my assertion was fully substantiated that Canadian manufactured cloth for suits to be sold during this Fall was sold by our manufacturers, this spring, at prices from 8 to 10 per cent. below their previous lists. It was brought out in testimony, before the Committee, that the 3½ yards of the finest domestic material necessary to make a suit of cloth amounted only to $17.50 at the cloth manufacturers' prices."

On July 25 Dr. McFall stated in an interview that he had required the leading manufacturers and wholesalers of all important products to submit sworn statements as to financial conditions and profits during the past seven years and his conclusion, as stated, was this: "Leading members of some lines of industry and commerce have, as we very well know, reaped harvests since the War began, yet to conclude that all classes in business life have done so is utterly unfair.   It is safe to say that not only are there members of every line of business who have played absolutely fair, but there are also great groups whose yearly balance sheets show very little change in profit during these last seven years."   In the case of Sugar, wherein shortage was great at times, and the price at the end of 1919 was striking toward very high points, there was the usual conflict of statement between refiners and wholesale and retail grocers; it was complicated by questions of production and export prices from Cuba, intermediary costs in the States, shipping and transport difficulties and costs, duty at the border and Government arrangements and negotiations with the United States. The half-dozen sugar Refineries in Canada bore the brunt of the blame and Dr. McFall issued a statement on Aug. 11 declaring that:

Sugar supplies in Canada are being artificially restricted and sugar prices are being unwarrantably advanced by combines and conspiracies which are absolutely pernicious and unlawful.   The attempt has been made to blame the shortage of refined sugar on excessive exports, but the latest available Customs records show that the excess of our imports over our exports is very much greater than usual; the sugar coming into Canada to stay is sufficient to supply decidedly more, not less, than our customary requirements.   In spite of labour difficulties and well-timed closing of plants, sugar has been refined lately in Canada at a rate in excess of our requirements.   Yet we have a shortage!

Increase in consumption through the demand for candy and sugar, in varied forms, to take the place of liquor-drinking as well as for preserving and canning, and strikes for excessive wages which compelled the closing-down of plants, world shortage in general, were some of the reasons advanced by the refineries.   On Sept. 3rd the Board of Commerce restricted the legal profits of refiners to two-fifths of one cent per pound, by wholesalers to not more than 5 per cent. commission, and by retailers to one cent per pound as the only permitted profit.   It may be added that the London *Economist* in its review of 1919 conditions, gave the sugar (cane and beet) crop of the world as 18,400,243 tons in 1917-18, 17,853,730 tons in 1918-19 and an estimated total for 1919-20 of 17,178,763 tons. As the average yearly increase in consumption before the War was 500,000 tons or a total in the 5 years of 2,500,000 tons and, as the actual loss in production was over 3,000,000 tons during that period the fact of a real shortage may be understood and the cause of higher prices largely explained—especially as the demand increased in 1919 away above the normal pre-war limit.   These facts would seem to lessen the force of Dr. McFall's conclusions.   Canada's investment of capital in Sugar refineries (1918) was $37,256,851, the yearly payment of wages, etc., was $2,626,889 and the cost of materials used $45,403,037 while the production of the refined article was $58,812,219.

The Parliamentary Enquiry and the Manufacturers. The High Cost of Living Committee of the House of Commons is referred to at length in the Agricultural Section, but its relation to industrial matters needs brief consideration here. Two or three cases of what looked like high profits came before it in June under investigation by R. A. Pringle, K.C., Government Counsel. F. G. Daniels, General Manager of the Dominion Textile Co., testified on June 18 that the earnings for the year of Mch. 31, 1919, were $3,-434,752 and the net profits, after all deductions, $1,559,888 on a paid-up capital of $2,440,000 and subscribed capital of $7,500,000 with $1,559,888 added to a surplus of $2,189,194; W. E. Paton, Manager of the Paton Manufacturing Co., Sherbrooke, Quebec, testified that the paid-up common stock of his Company was $600,-000 with net earnings in 1915 of 26·15% ; in 1916, 35·38% ; in 1917, 48% ; in 1918, 17·07%, and in 1919, 72·9 per cent. ; in both of these cases the reason lay largely in the purchase of raw material at a low price and the holding of it at advancing and very high prices. It may be added that there were reserve funds of $644,594 used in the Paton business which would reduce average profits by half and that these funds were the accumulations of 50 years. Mr. Paton when asked why the difference should not go to the consumer, made a remark which was widely misquoted: "Our mill was not built for the glory of God, but to make money for the shareholders; we have been very successful in making it, but for as much as eight years at a time the shareholders had to take their dividends out in prayers."

The other fact which caused wide discussion was in the evidence as to the Ogilvie Milling Co. (June 23) which showed a rest reserve of $2,500,000 and a contingent reserve of $1,596,407 on Aug. 31, 1918, on a capital of $2,500,000 common, $2,000,000 preferred and $2,350,000 bonds; profits of $1,955,414 and net profits of 72 per cent. on the common stock, with 27 per cent. paid in dividends. W. A. Black, General Manager, claimed that this did not affect the public as the profit was only 2·06 per cent. on the turnover of $56,750,000 and should be calculated in that way. E. W. Nesbitt, a member of the Committee, added that retailers were showing a turnover profit of 12 per cent. without popular criticism. Similarly, it appeared that the Harris Abattoir Co. of Toronto made 61 per cent. on its capital of $880,000 in the year ending March 31, 1918, and yet its profit per pound on meat was only one-fourth of a cent. Manufacturers were not alone in making profits, however, the Alberta Pacific Grain Co. of Calgary clearing a 15 per cent. dividend in 1914-15, 18 per cent. in 1915-16, 26 per cent. in 1916-17 and 34 per cent. in 1917-18. Two Reports of this Committee were submitted by G. B. Nicholson, Chairman, to Parliament on June 26 and July 5, respectively, after holding 36 sessions and hearing 66 witnesses under oath. It recommended the creation of the Board of Commerce, elsewhere dealt with, declared that the fixing of prices on farm products, or the placing of an embargo on farm exports, would be disastrous and stated that, while there had been cases of undue inflation in prices and some profiteering, ''the margin between the actual cost of production and what the consumer pays for such commodities is reasonably narrow.'' Certain statements and conclusions were especially important along industrial lines:

1. In the abattoir and packing house business we find that without question the large Companies are making a lot of money in the aggregate; they are doing this because of the efficiency of their methods and their large turnover.

2. In the milling industries the same conditions prevail. The gross margin covering cost of milling and the profits made is about four-fifths of ' one cent a pound of flour, while the net profit averages about one-tenth of one per cent.

3. In the case of butter your Committee find that the creameries are taking cream from the farmers and manufacturing it into butter at a gross cost of 3¾ to 6 cents a pound, varying according to locality and distance the cream has to be hauled.

4. In the case of boots and shoes the goods go largely, directly from the factory to the retail stores, where an average spread of from 30 to 50 per cent. is made for staple lines and a much higher one in special lines.

5. In staple goods such as woollens, cottons, etc., the spread from the factory to the retailer is about 75 per cent., namely, 15 to 25 per cent. to the wholesaler and an average of 50 per cent. to the retailer. In the main the evidence shows that notwithstanding these high gross margins the net profit is small when computed either on capital or turnover.

The retailers were said, with exceptions, to be keeping reasonably close to actual cost and there was said to be no real hoarding in the country. Obviously from the facts brought before this Committee and the Board of Commerce, the difficulty as to adjusting the cause of the increasing prices at this time as between the manufacturer, the farmer, the distributor, the retailer and other intermediaries, was increased rather than diminished; every one evidently had a share but the question of proportion was unanswered.

Manufacturers, Retailers and the Board of Commerce. This Commission, whose creation and operations are referred to in another Section,* had much to do with the Manufacturer as well as the Farmer in 1919. Composed of H. A. Robson, K.C., (Chairman), W. F. O'Connor, K.C., and James Murdoch, it was appointed on Aug. 13 and held sessions at most of the centres of Canada, appointed a number of local Commissioners, investigated all kinds of interests and industries, and stirred up an infinite variety of questions in the public mind with an occasional answer in the form of regulated profits. It did all that it could do and regulated some profits in public while indirectly controlling many others. The Board was attacked by farmers and retailers and manufacturers, alike, and W. F. O'Connor, K.C., the Vice-Chairman, came in for some personal criticism. The Chief Commissioner received $10,-000 a year and the others $8,000.

Mr. O'Connor did not mince words upon occasion and, in Toronto on Sept. 11, stated that: ''The primary object of my visit

*Note.—See pages 334-7 of this volume.

to Toronto and Hamilton is to spy out the land and see if it is possible to do with a number of commodities what the Board has done in regard to sugar, to establish a fair profit, and if there is any exceeding of that profit, criminal prosecution and gaol. To do this the Board admits is impossible unless it has the co-operation of those engaged in trade. The (retail) trade seems enthusiastic in favour of this co-operation. The Board intends to drive rivets in the prices, and see they don't go higher, and to help drive them down." The sugar action referred to was a restriction imposed on Sept. 3rd upon legal profits of refiner, wholesaler, and retailer.

Major J. L. Duncan, K.C., acted as Commissioner for the Board in Toronto; Lieut.-Col. H. D. Hulme in Vancouver; James Auld in Winnipeg, and Major Duncan Stuart at Calgary; J. F. Frame, K.C., acted as Counsel to help its operations on behalf of the Governments of Saskatchewan and Alberta, H. W. Whitla, K.C., for the Manitoba Government and J. S. Lundy was appointed by the Ontario Government for a similar purpose while Lieut.-Col. W. H. Price, M.L.A., represented the Department of Justice. Many manufacturers and retailers were examined but an enquiry into wholesale operations, as between manufacturers and grocers, was refused on the ground, as stated by Mr. O'Connor on Oct. 24, that "the existing system of distribution is not against the interest of the public" and that "constant supervision, on the part of the State, of the costs and profits of manufacturers, wholesalers, jobbers, retailers and others will enable the affording of adequate relief in cases where it may be required." Profits on footwear were fixed at 33½ per cent. retail (Nov. 26) and the profits on men's ready-made clothing in Toronto were fixed at not more than 26 per cent. on the sale price up to $25 and above that at not more than 33½ per cent.

Meantime, the public enquiries of the Board seemed to reflect more upon the retailers than the manufacturers. In Toronto on Oct. 10 the boot and shoe firm of D. D. Hawthorne and Co. reported, as jobbers, a net profit in the past year of $190,000, and a net profit between 1912 and 1919 of $800,000. A. E. Grainger, of the T. Eaton Co., Ltd., on the same day stated, as to their boot and shoe department, that the turnover was, in 1918, double that of 1913 while the scale of profits remained the same—with samples submitted which showed a high-grade man's shoe bought at $11 and selling at $16; another bought at $8 and selling at $11.50; boys' boots bought at $4.50, $5.75 and $6.75 and selling at $6.50, $7 and $8.50; children's shoes bought at $4.80, $3.20 and $2.50, and selling at $6.85, $4.35 and $3.35. J. A. Walker of the Walker-Park Co., testified that a pair of shoes which cost $9.94 to manufacturers sold to the wearer at from $14 to $15; C. B. Lowndes of Lowndes Co., Ltd., (wholesalers) stated on Oct. 8 that in men's clothing their gross percentage of profit on sales was 25 per cent. on some lines, 29 per cent. on medium lines and 32 per cent. on higher lines with 49 per cent. on the manufacturing cost; T. Engel, a boot and shoe dealer in Regina, stated on Oct. 16 that on working shoes he figured

about 40 per cent. profit, on children's the same, on rubbers from
35 to 40 per cent. and on fine shoes 50 per cent.; T. Campbell, a
retail dealer in Edmonton, stated, there, on Oct. 17, that hats
which once sold for $4.50 were now being sold at $8.50, and that
the retailer was "only getting about 45 per cent. profit on the
cost."

J. J. Hayes, Manager of the Hudson's Bay Co. store at Calgary,
testified on Oct. 23 that his department carried $58,000 worth of
men's clothing and $15,000 worth of boys' with an average profit of
32 per cent. in the former and of 29 per cent. in the latter and with
gross profits for the department ranging from 10 to 65 per cent. He
added that: "A workingman's suit is marked up in the neighbourhood of 40 per cent. and the better lines of suits from 60 to 65 per
cent. Mackinaws costing $9.40 are sold for $15.00." On one line
of mackinaws he admitted 94 per cent. profit; Ripway suits bought
at $31.95 they sold for $60. Another firm in Calgary, MacLeod
Bros., men's furnishings, showed that from sales amounting to
$500,000 they had cleared a net profit of $20,538. The cost of the
goods sold was $246,761, and the gross profits thereon were 33 per
cent. Major Stuart, who was conducting the enquiry, intimated
that in comparison with some profits these were very low. In
Toronto, during November, 5 manufacturers, 12 retailers and 4
jobbers were examined and the latter showed an average profit
of 20 per cent.—15 per cent. from the manufacturer and 5 per
cent. from the customer.

Major Stuart reported at length upon his Western investigation
for the Board. He found in respect to 9 boot and shoe men of
Calgary that they had made a profit of $224,521 on boots and shoes
costing $446,949 or a profit, on cost, of 50 per cent. and, on sales, of
33½ per cent.; that profits in clothing to the retailers ran from
30 to 94 per cent. and that nearly all dealers stated that their aim
was to get 50 per cent. gross profit on cost; that it frequently ran
higher (much higher, in fact) on some lines. The Commissioner's
general view was this: "Prices seem high. The rates of profit
seem high; 92 per cent. profit on a pair of boots, and 84 per cent.
on an ordinary man's suit, even if a little smart, and 90 per cent.
on a young man's mackinaw, seem too high." On Dec. 12 the
Board issued a report of its first 4 months of work and, in conclusion, made this statement: "The Board is pleased to be able to
observe, as a result of its preliminary survey of business conditions, that despite high prices undoubtedly prevailing, profiteering, so-called, that is the taking of unjust profits, is not, in the
Board's opinion, as common, nor nearly as common, as many have
charged or claimed."

The retailers did not like the conclusions or statements given
above; they complained that sufficient allowance was not made for
overhead expenses; a Toronto clothier stated in the press of June
10 that woollens and trimmings had increased in cost fully 200 to
300 per cent. since 1916, and labour at least 50 to 75 per cent.;

J. A. Banfield, President of the Dominion Board of the Retail Merchants' Association, at Brandon, told the 5th annual Convention of· that body that: "The retailer must dance to the music of the manufacturer; the manufacturer to the raw producer; and that brings us back to labour"; the real issue was said to lie in raw material as, for instance, cotton rising since the War from 10 to 32 cents a pound, wool 18 to 50 cents, flax for linen and woods for furniture in tremendous increases; the demand for fancy boots and clothing and the best of everything was blamed for much of the trouble. Mr. O'Connor (Oct. 25) made a public plea for the wholesale grocer as a necessity and benefit to the public: "He carries many hundreds of lines. He imports from many foreign countries. When he imports he does so in large quantities. Importing and carrying in large quantities he obtains for the benefit of the community which he serves the lowest possible rates. He carries, on credit for a time, the retailers whom he serves. Being relatively fewer than the retailers he saves for the manufacturer the trouble and expense of book-keeping forces, credit men, and that sort of thing."

E. M. Trowern, Secretary of the Retail Merchants' Association pointed out (*Monetary Times*, July 25) that: "It is not generally known that there are many more millions of dollars invested in distribution than there are in either manufacture or production. It could not but be otherwise; merchandise must always be manufactured ahead of the immediate demand. Goods produced or manufactured in Vancouver are of no value to people residing in Halifax unless they are transported to the latter point. To do this, it requires negotiation, purchase, transportation, warehouse facilities, retail facilities, etc., and final delivery to the ultimate purchaser in single items. A host of transactions take place before the goods are finally delivered. All these separate transactions cost money and take time and intelligence in addition to capital, which cannot be regarded in any other light than 'accumulated industry.'" He argued, convincingly, that retailers were necessary and deserved reasonable profits; but neither he nor Mr. O'Connor indicated any reason why they should receive extreme profits. As to the Retail Merchants' Association, Dr. McFall, Cost of Living Commissioner, made a much-discussed statement at Ottawa on Aug. 12 to the effect that the Board of Commerce would deal with the activities of a body which, he alleged, was "openly and secretly fighting the Co-operative Societies of Canada"—the latter he described as a most effective weapon against the high cost of living.

Scientific Research: Its Influence upon Canadian Industry. The Canadian Council for Scientific and Industrial Research of which Dr. A. B. Macallum, F.R.S., was Administrative Chairman and which worked under the authority of the Department of Trade and Commerce, made much progress during the year. It was an honourary and advisory body created in December, 1916, for the primary purpose of working along lines of War industry; its final development made it an efficient aid to the industrial work of the Reconstruction period. The earliest essential effort was to make clear to the public the necessity for improved technical knowledge in every industry; the advantage of science to the manufacturer in the development of new or improved materials —as with current improvements in glassware, tool steels, light steels for motor cars, magnetic materials of high quality, aluminium and other alloys, ferrous and various organic products; and the finding of new means and processes for cheapening production. There were elements of importance in its work, also, to the financier and, of course, to the educationalist.

Dr. F. D. Adams, F.R.S., pointed out during this year that amongst the results of far-reaching importance achieved by Research in fields apart from technology, but of the greatest general importance, were the prevention of malaria, the construction of the Panama Canal, and the developments of aviation dependent upon the petrol motor. So with Tuberculosis and its cure, the effect of fatigue upon efficiency in labour and many other studies. Great Britain in 1918 appropriated $5,000,000 for its Research Council and membership in this organization became of a co-operative character, divisible into industries, with each firm subscribing to the general fund accorded the privilege to (1) put technical questions and to have them answered as fully as possible; (2) to recommend specific subjects for research and, if the Committee or Board considered the recommendation of sufficient general interest and importance, the research to be carried out without further cost to the firm; (3) to use patents or secret processes resulting from all researches undertaken either without payment for licenses, or with only nominal payment; (4) to ask for a specific piece of research to be undertaken for its sole benefit at cost price. In the United States at this time there were 2,000 Research laboratories in connection with large industrial concerns and, according to a statement by Dr. Macallum, more than 50 individual firms who each expended $25,000 to $500,000, annually, on this work. Australia, New Zealand, South Africa and Japan were all, in 1919, active in their efforts. Germany had long been a standing example of success in certain defined lines. Dr. Macallum reviewed the position of Canada as follows on Jan. 2, 1919:

In resources of capital and materials, in all the natural advantages for industrial supremacy we are in an enviable position as compared with our trade competitors. But in regard to the vital question of scientific organization of our industrial processes, of finding new uses and, hence, new markets for the raw materials and the by-products of manufacture, and of keeping pace with the advances made in other countries through Research, we have as yet hardly touched the fringe of opportunity. Confronted with this situation and with a slowly awakening public and individual realization of its portent, the main task of the Council this past year has been, while carrying on the immediate needs of Research work with the means at hand, to pave the way for meeting adequately the urgent needs of the future. The goal has been a supply of trained men for Research work and the enlistment of industrial organizations in co-operative effort to solve common problems, the solution of which lies in the application of science to industry. The great forward step taken has been to promote the establishment of a Central Research Institute at Ottawa, combining the functions of the Bureau of Standards at Washington and of the Mellon Institute at Pittsburg.

At this date the Council issued a Report as to Chemical industries in Canada which showed the influence of science and research upon their development, in the past few years, with 634 chemical product plants in operation; Canada was urged to preserve the wartime development of this important and vital industry and to direct it along essential lines of peaceful work; if manufacturers, representing the financial and natural resources of the country, and chemists, with their scientific training, would use their imagination and initiative and pool their abilities for the common good "there will be built up in Canada in the years to come a Chemical industry of which not only the chemists and manufacturers, but the people, will have reason to be proud." The Report of the Council for the year of Mch. 31, 1919, referred to the work of Dr. F. D. Adams and Dr. J. C. McLennan, overseas, and described a great variety of subjects and projects which the organization or its members were dealing with.

Prof. Stansfield of McGill was stated to have advanced far in the investigation of reducing low-grade iron ores to an industrial basis; experiments in wheat breeding were well under way with a view to obtaining a variety which would ripen early, be wholly rust-resistant, and have good milling and baking qualities; valuable results had been obtained from an enquiry into the discolouration of canned lobster and as to methods for systematically improving that industry; elaborate investigations into the curing of fish and methods in other countries had been carried on; the utilization of lignite ores in the West had been elaborately studied and money appropriated by several Governments for a carbonizing-briquetting plant in Saskatchewan capable of turning out 30,000 tons of briquettes which were equivalent in thermal value, pound for pound, to anthracites; the subject of industrial alcohol, its uses and improvements, was effectively studied and recommendations made as to its manufacture; utilization of fish waste had been thoroughly investigated and the value in Canada stated to be very great, with demonstrational work carried out and practical data, as to this important new industry, obtained and other practical operations well under way.

·The establishment of a National Research Institution was urged along the lines of the Bureau of Standards at Washington with an appropriation of $500,000 asked for, and the control of the Institute to be vested in the Council. Forestry work had been largely carried on and provision was made for 20 studentships and 5 fellowships in Canadian Universities along lines of trained research with initiative and independent scientific thought as the first qualifications. To assist in this the Council instituted Bursaries, ten in number, to be awarded for 1919 to ten graduates whose attainments in science and expressed aims were such as to justify their

J. MURRAY CLARK, M.A., K.C., LL.D.
President of The Royal Canadian Institute, 1919
A Leader in the Scientific Research Movement
and in that for a United Empire

PROFESSOR J. C. McLENNAN, O.B.E., LL.D., Ph.D., D.SC., F.R.S.
University of Toronto
A Distinguished Canadian Scientist

being selected. In December, 1919, it was announced that the Research Council was co-operating with the Dominion Government in studying the problems of aerial navigation in Canada; that it had made provision for 40 bursaries, studentships and fellowships, to be awarded to qualified Science graduates of Canadian Universities in 1920 who would train for service in scientific research; that grants had been made to aid in the investigation of a number of industrial problems and among them one for the investigation of a suitable slag for smelting Canadian ores.

It was stated that other grants had been made: (1) to Prof. Stansfield, of McGill, for his investigations in the reduction of iron ores by gases and the electric furnace; (2) to Capt. F. M. Dawson for investigation of the character of cement in relation to its hydration and its physical properties; (3) to investigate the nutritional diseases of the fox, which were so serious a handicap to the fox-breeding industry. During this third year of its work the Council had carried further the researches described above as under way in 1918; had installed successfully its briquetting plant at Estevan, Sask.; had appointed a Fuel Research Board for Western Canada to standardize the coals and lignite of Alberta; had given attention to the conservation of the supply of Helium in Canada, and urged that measures be taken to preserve public control of this rare and valuable gas of which, as yet, the Dominion was the only source in the British Empire; had made a grant for an investigation of the properties of Helium, under direction of Prof. J. C. McLennan at the University of Toronto.

Meanwhile, the Royal Canadian Institute of Toronto, under the Presidency or leadership of J. Murray Clark, K.C., M.A., had been doing an excellent work in encouraging Research and scientific activity along various lines. Science, scientific studies and addresses, industrial research in many original forms had long been the special work of this body; its annual *Proceedings* had become a store-house of useful fact and scientific analysis or exposition; men such as Sir William Logan, General Sir Henry Lefroy and Sir Sandford Fleming had been distinguished members along lines of accomplished and notable effort. Mr. Murray Clark though not a practical scientist was an enthusiastic believer in its value and as far back as 1894 had begun to urge Scientific Research and continued to do so until in his Presidential address of 1918 he had especially urged the study, use and development of electric water-power. Associated with him in the Institute's later work along the purely practical lines of scientific effort was Prof. J. C. McLennan of Toronto University whose war services in Britain and France were important and very widely known; it was generally supposed that he would have been knighted for these services had the Ottawa Parliamentary action not been taken.

Under date of Nov. 22, 1919, and in view of his return to Canada during the year to resume his duties at the University, the Lords of the Admiralty wrote Prof. McLennan to express their "great

15

obligation": to the University for making it possible for the Admiralty to have the benefit of his services during a period of two years. It was stated that for the first part of this period Professor McLennan had been associated with the Board of Invention and Research, and was responsible for work of the highest value in connection with the development of important war material. In addition, he had entered upon valuable researches into Helium gas, the importance of which was, to some extent, made public in Canada and Great Britain: "Since January last Professor McLennan has acted as Scientific Adviser to the Admiralty, and his scientific ability and practical experience have been of great value in the elaboration of permanent arrangements for applying scientific research to Naval problems." No other details were mentioned but it was understood that Prof. McLennan had worked out a scientific scheme for closing the straits of Dover to submarines and that, after August 1918, no enemy craft as a consequence had entered those waters. Meantime he had in July been awarded the Silver Medal of the Royal Society of Arts for a paper on Science and Industry in Canada.

Speaking to a Special Committee of Parliament at Ottawa on May 28 Dr. McLennan sought to impress upon the members the desirability of establishing a Central Research Laboratory where Canadian scientists could work to increase Canada's industrial products; such an institution he believed would be the basis of a new industrial and economic system. As to Helium gas, and as illustrating the importance of research, he stated that: "In the spring of 1916, it was found that the largest supply of natural gas in Canada, namely, that located at Bow Island, Alberta, contained a little over 0.36 per cent. of Helium. This is a comparatively small and apparently insignificant amount, and yet I may tell you that this wonderful gas was so rare and so costly that, at pre-war prices, the value of the supply of it which escaped into the air from the furnaces and stoves of Calgary, and other houses on the pipe line, was $50,000,000 per day. By the developments which have taken place, during the past two years, the cost of producing the gas in a pure state has been reduced, roughly, 100,000 times." It had, therefore, become possible to use it in place of hydrogen for certain Aircraft.

High tribute was paid to Prof. McLennan at London on Sept. 26 by Hume Cronyn, M.P., who stated that when the War had been going on for a few years the Professor had outlined some ideas on sea fighting to the Canadian authorities without much attention being paid to them; he then went to England where, after repeated efforts, he got his ideas before the Naval experts. A number of them were found to be good and he was put on the regular staff of the Admiralty. He requisitioned vast quantities of explosives and, after repeated tests, made a discovery that almost solved the Submarine question for Britain. Prof. J. C. Fields, F.R.S., of the Toronto University who followed J. Murray Clark as President of the Institute, told that body on Nov. 10 that the highest function of a University was to give opportunity for Research work and to train men for that work.   He pointed to the scientific greatness of France and the engineering and constructional greatness of England; declared that Germany, even during the War, conserved her brain power by keeping her scientifically-trained men out of danger; that she was now in a position to re-assume some, at least, of her scientific supremacy.   Meantime an important address had been delivered by Dr. G. E. Hale, Hon. Chairman of the U.S. National Research Council, before the Ontario Legislature on Apr. 13th.   It dealt with the influence of Scientific investigation and the essential value of co-operation in the international study of astronomy, physics, variation of latitude, the study of sediments, chemical subjects, marine-temperatures, engineering, etc.

In March a Special Committee of the Commons was appointed with Major Hume Cronyn as Chairman and, at its first meeting on Mch. 17, heard Dr. A. B. Macallum describe the current situation in Canada.   He stated that there was a great dearth of trained research workers in Canada—enough at present to supply only about two per cent. of the industrial needs and that in all Canada there were only 37 industrial firms doing anything in the way of original research work, with about 50 men available for the adequate treatment of research problems.   Other incidents of the year included an address (Jan. 30) on the strengthening of the Science departments of Canadian Universities by Dr. Bruce Taylor, Principal of Queen's, Kingston, before the Toronto branch of the Manufacturers' Association with the statement that research would play a great place in industrial supremacy and economy of production; the evolution at a Walkerville plant of a number of new chemical products and the formation at Montreal, on May 16, of the Canadian Institute of Chemistry with Dr. J. Watson Bain of Toronto as Chairman.

The Canadian Manufacturers' Association in 1919.   This powerful body had an importance far beyond its membership—though the 3,530 who belonged to it in 1919 showed an increase of 1,100 per cent. since its incorporation in 1902.   It did not compare in this respect with the 100,000 who filled the ranks of the Grain Growers and United Farmers, or the 50,000 who belonged to the I.O.D.E. or the Navy League.   But it had become a great business organization run by business men on business lines; it stood for policies which represented the personal interests of all members as well as what they claimed to be the general interests of the country; its members were, as a rule, men of wealth and employers of labour and of more or less influence in their different communities.   The industrial business of Canada which they represented, or led, had grown between 1900 and 1917, according to W. J. Bulman, President, in his 1919 address, in the following proportions.

	Per cent.		Per cent.
Establishments	185	Number of Employees on Wages...	100
Capital	520	Wages paid	410
Employees on Salary	140	Value of Products	526
Salaries paid		305 %	

Its policy in 1918-1919 included special encouragement of growth and organization in the Western Provinces and establishment of Industrial interests there side by side with Agriculture; support to proposals for a Bankruptcy law, uniformity in Commercial law, an Act for promoting Technical education; the maintenance of a Canadian trade mission in London and encouragement to Shipbuilding; approval of the Government policy in restricting Immigration and the promotion of Scientific research; Tariff protection for all Canadian interests.   Its position in this latter respect will be separately considered.   In January the Toronto Branch got into co-operation with the G.W.V.A. to promote the employment of returned soldiers and, in Winnipeg, on ·Feb. 1st a joint Committee was appointed for a similar purpose; in the general matter of Reconstruction J. S. McKinnon, Vice-President, elaborated the Association's policy in the March number of *Industrial Canada* as being steady work for, and co-operation with, the returned soldier.

He defended the Manufacturers from the charge of war profiteering: "During the War the manufacturers had to master the great problem of making munitions.   This was entirely new work. They had to find out how to make shells.   They had to get the machinery and learn how to use it.   They had to build plants to house their operations.   They had to secure help when the Army was making most insistent demands for recruiting.   They had to find money to finance their contracts."   At the close of the struggle they were employing 700,000 people and had produced $1,200,-000,000 of war supplies.   In the making of Munitions, he claimed, there were three classes: (1) a few who made good profits, largely as a result of their own enterprise and ability though the Excess Profits Tax took away all profits above 11 per cent., and had secured from business men $65,000,000; (2) the class of manufacturers who fell below the 11 per cent. and made an average profit; (3) the class of manufacturers, of whom there were not very many, who did not succeed in making any profits and, instead, suffered losses.

Much interest was taken by manufacturers in the establishment by legislation early in this year of a Government Department of Industries in British Columbia with a Minister in charge and a Deputy who was to be known as the Industrial Commissioner—the Department to have power (1) to provide for Industrial research and co-ordinate industrial effort; (2) to acquire and utilize in manufacture the knowledge and experience of other countries; (3) to carry out an economic survey of the natural resources of the Province; (4) to furnish advice as to the best way of meeting industrial problems, promote improvement and facilitate establishment of industries; (5) to co-ordinate various industries and to bring together producer, manufacturer and purchaser; (6) to publish technical, scientific, and statistical information and encourage industrial study and research; (7) to aid by Provincial loan or guarantee approved industrial enterprises.   Government plans for water-power development in Nova Scotia and New Brunswick were approved by the organization; in Ontario the Toronto Branch co-operated with citizens' organizations and the G.W.V.A. in promoting soldiers' vocational training; it also supported, by Executive resolution on Apr. 22, the continuance of Daylight Saving.

The annual Convention of the general organization was held in Toronto on June 10-12 and its members spoke of themselves as representing the 700,000 workers in Canada factories who supported at least 1,300,000 dependents.   As a business organization the C.M.A. was divided into the Transportation, Legal, Tariff, Insurance and Commercial Intelligence Departments with 35 Trade Sections united in one Trade Department; the General Manager was J. E. Walsh, the General Secretary J. T. Stirrett and each Department had a Manager; the organ of the Association was *Industrial Canada* which, like the *Grain Growers' Guide*, of Winnipeg, was devoted to the interests and objects of its own organization. There was an Ottawa office, and during the year 1918-19, new Branches had been established at Sherbrooke, Que., Brantford, Ont., Niagara Falls, Ont., and Victoria, B.C.   The 3,500 members represented the majority of Canadian manufacturers but there still were 1,500 eligible for membership; Toronto contributed 833, Montreal 604, the Prairie Provinces 498, Hamilton 215 and British Columbia 58 to the total of members; the yearly revenue from fees was $84,594, and a new annual fee was approved at this meeting bringing up the total to $137,414; five new Divisions were constituted—the Maritime Provinces, Quebec, Ontario, Prairie and the Pacific.

The Presidential address by W. J. Bulman of Winnipeg dealt with War and Peace conditions and Reconstruction and with the extreme Labour element which he denounced strongly: "Briefly, they consider that only certain manual labourers have any rights either to control property or to have any share in the government. They believe that all other classes should either be 'abolished,' or brought under the control of their Committees.   They do not believe in private property, or bank interest, or capital.   All these things should be 'abolished.'   They ask that 'the instruments of production' shall become common property.   They specifically state that all farms should be confiscated, and given to the poorer agricultural labourers."

He dealt with conditions in Russia under Bolshevism, and as to the Canadian manufacturers and their employees in general, he was explicit: "Nearly all the heads of Canadian industries were once workmen themselves.   They have risen to their present positions by ability, perseverance and thrift. The most difficult thing to get to-day is managing ability. The directors of Canadian industries are not trying to keep men down, they are trying to fit them to assume the responsibilities of management. They are eager to find ability, to reward it, and to place it in responsible positions where it will share in the control of industry. The purchase of stock is open to employees in many industrial Companies, and employees have the same opportunities as other men who have succeeded, to save and invest their money. Thrifty workers aspire to be property-owners, or, in other words, capitalists." The Tariff was treated at length. Reports of Committees followed—Insurance by W. H. Shapley, (Chairman) Legislation by Sam Harris, Transportation by W. R. Breyfogle, Membership by W. G. Laidlaw, Tariff by E. J. Davis. An address was given by Lloyd Harris, Chairman of the Canadian Mission in London, in which he dealt with the war-stripped nature of the British market and its demand for Canadian manufactures as well as natural products; woollens, clothing, cottons, paint and varnish, boots and shoes, had all benefitted in the sale of Canadian-made products in the Motherland. Resolutions were passed by the Association as follows:

1. Pledging co-operation and support to the Dominion in its efforts to secure a more complete knowledge of industrial conditions and better relations between employers and employees.

2. Endorsing the British idea of gradual changes, only, in the constitution of society or form of government and recording its opinion that all those persons who attempt to undermine the existing form of government in Canada with the substitution of any other form of government should be summarily punished, and that if they are aliens they should be immediately deported.

3. Declaring that constant and adequate police, fire, water and other protection are indispensable wherever people live in close proximity and that, as grave dangers to life and property, and injury to the public welfare immediately result from any interference with the continuity and adequacy of this protection, therefore, the Dominion Government should enact legislation necessary to prevent strikes among Civic employees.

4. Urging the appointment of a Permanent Tariff Board and approving substantial inter-Empire Customs preferences.

5. Deprecating the removal of the tariff on United States tractors and opposing "any further acquisition or operation of Railways by the Dominion Government."

6. Urging the Government, in view of the exchange situation, particularly, to continue encouragement of Export trade.

7. Approving the Dominion Technical Education Act and urging the Provinces to avail themselves of its facilities.

8. Pledging support to the coming National Conference on moral education in the schools.

9. Urging continuation of the Conservation Commission and praising its work.

10. Deprecating the continued fire-losses of Canada and asking for Government investigation.

11. Endorsing the United States National Association of Manufacturers in its opposition to any substitution of the Metric system for the existing British standard of weights and measures.

During the annual banquet of June 12, Mr. Lloyd Harris spoke again on his Trade mission; G. B. Nicholson, M.P., on the causes of

Labour unrest which he considered to be (1) nervous war-strain, (2) Economic pressure and (3) the irresponsible agitator; W. C. Good, a leader of the United Farmers, on the Tariff with the description of agriculture as the greatest of primary industries and manufacturing as the greatest of the secondary industries; Mayor M. A. Brown, of Medicine Hat, who dealt with Western industrial development, and Dr. R. G. Brett, Lieut.-Governor of Alberta, who spoke for that Province.   The officers elected for 1919-20 included an Executive Council, comprised of 9 appointed members—J. H. Sherrard, and Sir C. B. Gordon, Montreal, P. W. Ellis, W. K. George and R. S. Gourlay, Toronto, C. A. Burge and R. Hobson, Hamilton, H. Cockshutt, Brantford, and E. G. Henderson, Windsor; 5 elected members from the Maritime Provinces, 12 from Montreal, 6 from the rest of Quebec, 17 from Toronto, 5 from Hamilton, 18 from the rest of Ontario, 10 from the Prairie Provinces, 3 from British Columbia; Thomas Cantley, S. R. Parsons and W. J. Bulman *ex officio* as Past Presidents.   The Chairmen of the Committees were chosen as follows: Tariff, E. J. Davis, Newmarket; Transportation, Burton S. Harris, Toronto; Legislation, Sam Harris, Toronto; Insurance, H. W. Fleury, Aurora; Membership, H. A. Telfer, Toronto; Publishing J. F. MacKay, Toronto; Commercial Intelligence, E. Holt Gurney, Toronto; Industrial Returns, C. H. Carlisle, Toronto.

Incidents of the year in this connection included the establishment at Montreal and Toronto of branches of the Canadian Association of British Manufacturers with the following objects: To further the interests of British trade throughout the Dominion of Canada, and to affiliate with and work in concert with kindred associations in other centres of the Dominion having similar objects. It included as members (a) British manufacturers and wholesale exporters from the United Kingdom and (b) representatives and agents of such British manufacturers and wholesalers.   An agreement was also reached between the Federation of British Industries and the Canadian Manufacturers' Association through a scheme for interchange of information and other means of mutual assistance. The C.M.A. was to keep the Federation fully informed (as far as they had information available) as to: (a) Supplies of raw materials in Canada useful for manufacturing processes in the United Kingdom; (b) requirements of the Canadian markets which could not be supplied by Canadian manufacturers themselves, including such goods as were at present obtained from the United States; (c) details of the organization of the C.M.A., and (d) standing of Canadian firms.   The F.B.I., on the other hand, undertook to obtain for the C.M.A. when required: (a) The names of British firms desirous of purchasing raw materials from Canada; (b) firms willing to supply the needs of the Canadian market; (c) details of the organization of the F.B.I.   The organizations were to work together in a friendly and personal, as well as organized, way.

The Tariff: Attitude of the Organized Manufacturers.

The Canadian Manufacturers' Association, like the United Farmers in their more recent political campaign, held strong fiscal opinions; it had been expressing them in varied forms of influence and by Resolution for many years though, as an organization, it had never gone into politics, as such, or publicly supported any one political party; it had long opposed, and continued to do so in 1919, any steps toward Free Trade or Reciprocity with the United States.   Early in this year a Memorandum was submitted by the Association to the Government declaring that the establishment of Preferential Tariffs throughout the British Empire was "necessary to the permanent progress of Canada"; that under such a system there would be immediate and extraordinary increases in industrial production; that great numbers of United States industries would establish large works or branch factories in the Dominion to get advantage of the Preference.   Why, it was asked, should merchandise from foreign countries enter British dominions in general at the same rates of duty as applied on inter-Empire shipments of goods produced within the Empire?: "That policy does not develop or consolidate our Empire, but does unnecessarily strengthen other great trading nations which systematically pursue this special policy of tariff preferences for their own merchandise when interchanged between their own outlying dominions."   The large preferences given United States trade in the Philippines, Alaska, Hawaii, Porto Rico, etc., were specified in this connection.

To the promulgated Farmers' Platform, which is given elsewhere in full, strong exception was taken in a statement signed by the General Manager of the C.M.A. and issued late in January—especially to the demand for immediate removal of certain duties, Free trade with Britain as an ultimate policy, and Reciprocity with the United States.   The first and immediate objection was that this was a time of reconstruction when courage and initiative and united effort were needed and when fundamental tariff changes would, it was claimed, curtail investment and employment, enterprise and trade, and produce or promote unemployment and consequent unrest.   As to finances and duties, the argument used was as follows: "During the last fiscal year the total Dominion Government revenue was $260,778,952, of which $116,577,066 was collected by the Customs tariff and $45,018,562 by the special War tariff.   The total Federal revenue, from all forms of taxation, was only $214,182,156, and of this amount the Tariff collected over 75 per cent.   In view of the fact that, last year, the Tariff provided over 61 per cent. of the total revenue of Canada, and over 75 per cent. of the total secured by all forms of Federal taxation, it seems reasonable to suggest that we should not throw away this means of securing revenue until we have found something which can be guaranteed to take its place, especially in view of the Dominion

Government's announcement that a revenue of $450,000,000 will be required." It was alleged that the Farmers' proposals of a tax on unimproved land, an inheritance tax with extensions of the Income and Corporation Profits taxation, could not be depended upon to meet the situation; Canadian progress under Protection was reviewed and the work of manufacturers in the War eulogized. It was claimed by S. R. Parsons and other C.M.A. speakers that no Income tax, either in Canadian or American experience, really reached the farmers and that removal of all duties would simply leave them as a large untaxed section of the community. *Industrial Canada*, in its April issue, stated that the following interests required Protection just as much as the Manufacturers:

1. Seven hundred thousand men and women working in Canadian factories.

2. The wholesalers and retailers and their employees, who distribute the products of the Canadian factories.

3. The farmers who sell 80 per cent. of everything they produce in Canada.

4. The railway and steamship Companies and their employees who carry Canadian goods.

5. The bankers, brokers, and commission agents, and their employees, who finance Canadian industry.

6. The innumerable investors who own stock in Canadian manufacturing concerns, but who are in no sense manufacturers.

7. All others—doctors, lawyers, insurance men, publishers, etc.—who make their living, directly or indirectly, from industrial concerns and the industrial population.

On May 15 the Toronto Branch of the C.M.A. passed a Resolution which was almost identical with one previously approved by the B.C. Fruit Growers' Association and the United Farmers of British Columbia and which protested against "any interference with the Tariff of Canada until a Commission is appointed to thoroughly investigate and to devise a tariff which will be equitable and just to all classes and that will best serve the welfare of the country as a whole." In his Presidential address, W. J. Bulman had spoken to the C.M.A. of the revived freer-trade and reciprocity agitation and told the organized farmer that his movement would suffer the fate of similar agrarian agitations in the United States and that as industries grew in the West so would a desire and need for protection of local markets; he declared that "we want to retain in Canada our own citizens, to provide them with employment at fair wages, to build up a diversified nation, to develop our raw materials and our natural resources through the efforts of Canadians, and to secure the rewards of industrial enterprise for Canadians"; he urged creation of a Tariff Commission with the object of finding what tariff and what fiscal policy would do most to make Canada a great and prosperous nation within the British Empire; he urged a greater Preference and closer inter-Empire trade relations.

In the annual Report of the Tariff Committee L. L. McMurray, Chairman, submitted an argument against freer trade with the United States, based upon the exchange situation and the fact that

Canadian exports to the Republic in 1914-19 totalled $2,111,924,191 and its imports therefrom $3,465,340,469—a balance against the Dominion of 1,300 millions; he urged Imperial Preferential duties and especially with the West Indies.   In the pages of *Industrial Canada* for October J. R. K. Bristol, Manager of the Tariff department, presented in elaborate form the official arguments for Protection which may be summarized as follows: (1) The need of Protective tariffs to promote and permit of negotiations with other countries for mutually beneficial trade arrangements; (2) the fact of nearly all countries having intricate and complex tariff schedules which they would not lower even at the wish of so powerful a free-import country as Great Britain; (3) the statement that tearing down the Canadian tariff fences would be like turning on to a flat country all the power dams of the world and the obvious impossibility of Canadians meeting such competition when even England had found she no longer could do so; (4) the allegation that all nations devoted only to cultivation of natural resources were in a stagnant, backward, unprosperous condition—with Russia and Ireland as illustrations; (5) the fact that investments of 3,000 millions and 2,000,000 people depended upon Canadian industries.   Finally, Mr. Bristol said:

In this connection I ask you to remember the fact that this Dominion at present represents a comparatively narrow ribbon of populated country stretching from the Pacific to the Atlantic Coast for 3,000 miles along the northern border of the United States.   In the United States, near this border, throughout its entire length, there are powerful industrial groups, with an immense domestic market, built up and nourished by high protection.   These industries everywhere can strike the Canadian ribbon by means of a short northerly freight haul.   But the domestic market for Canadian producers entails the longer and more expensive east or west freight haul.   Moreover, Canadian production is enhanced in cost by Customs revenue duties on machinery, plant, materials and fuel for manufacturing of a class and kind not obtainable in Canada.

The organ of the C.M.A. in its November issue editorially urged that the Canadian Government should appoint a permanent Tariff Board to act in an advisory capacity to the Government: "This Board should make a scientific study of the Canadian customs tariff and also the tariffs of other countries with which Canada trades.   It should familiarize itself with cost of production and other factors affecting manufacturing.   It should frame such a Tariff as would safeguard the best interests of the country."   The Resolution of a Senate Committee in May urging this policy, was endorsed.   On Nov. 25 a C.M.A. delegation, led by President T. P. Howard, waited upon the Government and asked that: (1) The proposed Ministerial enquiry into the Tariff, promised Parliament by Sir Thomas White, be abandoned; (2) that the whole question of Tariff revision be left in abeyance for the present; (3) that a permanent Tariff Commission be appointed with investigatory and advisory powers to deal with the Tariff upon a purely economic and scientific basis.   The Government promised consideration, except as to the Enquiry, which was a settled matter of policy.

The Canadian Reconstruction Association. This industrial and fiscal organization continued during 1919, under the Presidency of Sir John Willison, to do an important work. It claimed to have helped in promoting the formation of a Department of Industry in Alberta and the appointment of a Provincial Industrial Commissioner in Manitoba; at a meeting of its District Committees in Montreal on Feb. 1st satisfactory reports of progress were presented; a national advertising campaign was inaugurated by the Council of the Association and advertisements presenting the policies and arguments of that body appeared in the daily press and Farmers' weeklies; in the Head Office at Toronto an Information service for members was established together with a special Industrial service for particular trade groups; 30,000 copies of an article on Bolshevism, reprinted from the *Canadian Magazine*, were distributed with a publication on the organization of Women's work; a vigourous protest was made by letter and otherwise against the proposed double taxation of branches of American industrial firms in Canada—by the United States as well as Canadian Government.

During the year C. F. Roland, Secretary of the Western Committee of the Association, visited Brandon, Regina, Moose Jaw, Medicine Hat, Calgary, Vancouver, and Victoria, seeing prominent men in the various centres and obtaining pledges of support. As a result of conferences in Vancouver it was decided not to create a separate British Columbia Committee, but to recommend extension of the Western Office to include that Province, while appointing an assistant Secretary to deal with British Columbia questions. It was further recommended that this Provincial branch should appoint three members to the Western Committee, one of them to represent it on the Executive Board of the Association. Mr. Roland reported later that 32 Western Boards of Trade and municipalities had passed Resolutions endorsing the aims and objects of the Canadian Reconstruction Association. Meanwhile a series of circulars and bulletins, dealing with Western problems and general reconstruction activities, had been published fortnightly, and over 28,000 publications of this nature distributed in a few months.

The Secretary and the Western Committee during the year dealt with development in special industries—potato flour, hemp, Kaolin, clay, pottery, flax straw utilization, etc.; it urged enhanced production in field and factory and was active in support of housing plans and legislation; it consistently pressed for a scientific utilization of natural resources, the establishment of better relations between capital and labour, development of the home market and purchase of Made-in-Canada products. It campaigned energetically against Bolshevism and distributed 250,000 leaflets summarizing the Overman Report to the United States Senate; it facilitated the use of natural resources scenes in Moving Pictures and instituted enquiries into comparative retail selling prices of manufactured articles in Canada and the United States and the problem of providing Canadian credit for foreign purchases in the Dominion. An interim Report as to the first point stated that:

1. Canadian retail selling prices of manufactured commodities in most cases are substantially lower than retail selling prices in the United States, *plus* the Canadian import duty.

2. Many commodities manufactured in Canada and protected by a tariff on imports are sold to the Canadian consumer at prices as low, and not infrequently lower, than retail selling prices in the United States of comparable commodities, even without considering the duty.

Dominion incorporation was granted to the Association in May for the purposes of further scientific and industrial research; any work of a patriotic or philanthropic nature tending to promote the industrial and agricultural interests of Canada; an educational campaign to maintain industrial stability, and to insure the continued prudent treatment of problems of reconstruction after the War. The Provisional Directors were Sir J. S. Willison, Toronto, S. J. B. Rolland, H. R. Drummond, Hon. C. P. Beaubien and Hon. N. Curry of Montreal. Besides Sir John Willison, the officers of the Association were Lord Shaughnessy, Hon. President, Sir Augustus Nanton and W. J. Bulman,

Winnipeg, H. R. Drummond, Montreal, J. F. Ellis and W. K. George, Toronto,
Vice-Presidents, and A. N. Worthington, Secretary.

In other directions the Association worked along specific lines. It emphasized the necessity for development of export trade, domestic industrial
expansion, and improvement of relations between employers and employees.
Early in the year, it prepared and circulated about 6,000,000 small pictorial
cards to manufacturers, employees, and purchasers, urging public support of
the home market and purchase of Made in Canada products. It made a
further direct appeal of the same nature to the general public through full-
sized bill posters in cities and towns throughout the Dominion and utilized
motion pictures in order to stimulate public interest in the national value of
industrial development; they covered a variety of subjects including iron and
steel, grain and milling, woollens, agricultural implements and electric lamps,
pulp and paper, sugar, cocoa and chocolate industries. These pictures were
shown throughout the year, in 75 per cent. of the cities, towns, and villages
of the Dominion which had motion picture theatres and were seen by over
three-quarters of a million people weekly. By its advertising campaign conducted in March and April the Association emphasized the alleged danger to
labour, to production, and to industry of any radical revision of the Tariff
downward, and in this connection made a statement as to agricultural implements and prices intended to show that the Canadian price was not the United
States price *plus* the duty. Including the publications already mentioned the
Association issued nearly 7,000,000 copies of pamphlets, bulletins, and other
material during 1919.

**Proceedings
of the
Alberta
Industrial
Congress.** An Industrial incident of the year was the Congress held in a series of Sessions in Alberta which
lasted from Aug. 11 to Aug. 16 and included Medicine
Hat, Lethbridge, Calgary—where the business and
speaking sessions were held—and Edmonton. It was
preceded by a Conference held at Edmonton on Feb.
3rd which was largely organized by Mayor M. A. Brown of Medicine Hat, who described its objects as follows: "We want to build
up industry in this Province. We want to do everything possible
to assist in that great work. We want the Legislature to give us a
Department of Industry—a live, progressive Department organized
on such lines that it can assist and promote industrial growth."
Industrial Research was, also, a subject of close discussion. Lieut.-
Governor Brett, Charles Murphy of the C.P.R., W. A. R. Kerr, Acting-President of Alberta University, gave addresses and there was
an important attendance of Mayors and representatives from many
Municipalities with, also, H. W. Wood of the United Farmers.

Following this and the organization of Western Industrial effort
through the Canadian Reconstruction Association, an Industrial
Development Association, of which M. A. Brown of Medicine Hat
was Chairman, and other bodies, preparations were made for the
greater meeting. It was called by special circular issued in June
from Edmonton with a card of welcome and invitation from Mr.
Premier Stewart; addresses were promised by a number of prominent manufacturers in Canada and the United States and by bankers, railwaymen and other leaders; 20,000 invitations were issued
and the organization work was conducted by J. M. McGreevy, under
the auspices of the Industrial Development Association of which
the principles included development of the industrial resources of
Western Canada, stimulation of interest in and knowledge of manu-

facturing, and effort to counteract the existing tariff cleavage between East and West.

At the Calgary meeting on Aug. 13th M. A. Brown presided, addresses of welcome were delivered by the Lieut.-Governor and Mr. Premier Stewart and by Mayor Brown who said: "The subject uppermost in everyone's mind at the present time is how the country may pay its great war obligations; this can only be done by intensive development and it is clear that development is not intensive in this country; everybody knows that the greater portion of the resources of Canada are still undeveloped; the time has arrived when we should be more than producers of raw materials and we should produce the finished article for the world's markets.   To convince the world of these facts we have called this Industrial Congress."   There was a great array of speakers.   Dr. A. B. Macallum, f.r.s., of Ottawa declared that Alberta's coal supply would last only 5,000 years with the present population and 2,000 years with a population of 20 millions; Eugene Coste, the Provincial Engineer, said that Alberta had the biggest oil fields in the world, 1,600 miles by 3,000 miles wide; A. E. Warren of the National Railways, defended Nationalization and T. M. M. Tweedie, m.p., welcomed the American delegates.

G. E. Whitehouse, a British visitor to Canada, on the invitation of the Dominion Government, said: "In my journey through this great country I have found that Canada produces many things which Great Britain can buy; Great Britain produces many things which Canada wants.   Let us do much more business together. Business is the most easily understood and most straight-forward method of intercourse which civilization has discovered."   J. E. Walsh of the Canadian Manufacturers' Association submitted figures of the Industrial development of the West—the three Prairie Provinces—which showed 429 establishments and a capital investment of $9,229,561 in 1900, 902 establishments and $84,479,837 in 1910, 4,082 establishments and $197,475,107 investment in 1917. He stated that 160 eastern manufacturers had offices or distribution depôts in the West.   R. C. Haskins, Vice-President of the International Harvester Co., Chicago, spoke and a message was read from J. Ogden Armour of the Chicago Packing interests; D. B. Dowling dealt with Alberta coal areas which he compared to those of Wales; James White, of the Conservation Commission, dealt with Alberta's Power in water, coal and natural gas and stated that in the world as a whole there were 75,000,000 horse-power which had been developed, and of this 29,000,000 was used in the United States, 13,000,000 in the United Kingdom and 6,000,000 in the British Dominions and dependencies.

J. A. Cunningham, a British Columbia manufacturer, stated that there were a number of articles which should be manufactured on the coast or in Alberta—for instance, $78,000,000 worth of paints and oils which passed through Vancouver and Seattle each year to be manufactured in the East and were then shipped back to the West again—so in the case of rubber and silk.   Senator G.

D. Robertson, Minister of Labour, stated that the Government was supporting International unionism and spoke highly of its strength and good management and of its sane programme. The United Mine Workers of America, he said, had a membership of 500,000 in Canada and the United States and as they had promised to rebuild the coal industry in Alberta, they should have the support of the Province if they kept their promise. Captain Robert Dollar spoke on Opportunities in the Far East and declared that Canada must have ships: "More than ever in the future is commercial prosperity going to depend on the merchantile marine, and if Canadian trade is to grow, you must be in a position to do your own carrying."

Dr. R. D. MacLaurin of the University of Saskatchewan dealt with Scientific Research and stated that though Canada was richly endowed in coal, oil and iron, yet its people "imported 98 per cent. of their petroleum products at an annual cost of 30 millions of dollars; 95 per cent. of their iron ore and iron products, at a cost of 177 millions, and over 50 per cent. of their coal, at a cost of 71 millions, making a total of 278 millions." As a matter of fact, he believed the imperative need in Canada was a national economic policy based on the scientific development and utilization of its natural resources. H. A. Lovett, K.C., of Montreal, Dr. John A. Allen of Alberta University and Finley P. Mount, an American manufacturer, spoke and the latter addressed the agricultural interests: "Your farmer must learn, as ours has long since learned, that industrial development is his best friend, and his best paying investment. As the market at his door increases, so will the value of his products and his farm increase. As new industries are built up in your communities, new opportunities for profit and enjoyment of life are created. Your foreign market for your agricultural products is now good, and it is reasonable to suppose it will be a good market for some time to come, but eventually your reliance must be on your home market."

Prof. R. C. Wallace, Commissioner for Northern Manitoba, described the resources and coming development of that region; R. H. Campbell, Director of Dominion Forestry, discussed the high prices paid in Alberta for lumber, as compared with Ontario, and thought that this could be remedied by direct importation from the States and the Coast of the raw lumber. James Ramsay, M.L.A., Edmonton, D. C. Coleman of the C.P.R., William Toole, President of the Calgary Board of Trade, Lieut.-Col. Nelson Spencer, M.L.A., Lieut.-Col. J. S. Dennis of the C.P.R., R. T. Riley of Winnipeg, H. A. Craig, Deputy-Minister of Agriculture for Alberta, were amongst the other speakers at this remarkable gathering. There were 1,500 present at the various meetings and arrangements were made for a permanent Secretariat to perpetuate the Congress and its work; it was said to have been the most successful gathering of the kind in Alberta's annals with 25 millionaires present; a fund of about $50,000 was guaranteed for the next meeting which was to be a combined one of Alberta and British Columbia.

LABOUR: THE ORGANIZED WORKMEN

Socialism and Labour: The I.W.W., Bolshevism and the O.B.U. Labour in Canada and in all countries during the War, and in the social disturbances following the War, was divided into two classes: (1) The moderate, thoughtful, industrious, working-man anxious to improve his position by all fair means and taking full advantage of the strike weapon to obtain better working conditions and wages but with no revolutionary principles or policies and with his fair share of national patriotism, love of home and regard for the rights of others—a large majority in English-speaking countries; (2) the idle or shiftless workman, the scheming or unscrupulous and often very clever leader, the honest but misguided labourer who accepted theories plausible in appearance but impossible of application, the believers in exaggerated class consciousness—a combination which helped to create Communists, Anarchists, Bolshevists, I.W.W's, O.B.U's, and all the variety of Red Socialists who, in 1919, were helping to keep the world in miserable unrest.

The Socialism which, at this time, appealed almost altogether to the workingman and found so prominent a place, under so many names, in so many countries, was based upon the theories and doctrines of Karl Marx as embodied in his 1848 Communist Manifesto and it included: (1) Abolition of property in land and application of all rents of land to public purposes; (2) a heavy progressive or graduated income tax; (3) abolition of all right of inheritance; (4) confiscation of the property of all emigrants and rebels; (5) centralization of credit in the hands of the State, by means of a national bank with State capital and an exclusive monopoly; (6) centralization of the means of communication and transport in the hands of the State; (7) extension of factories and instruments of production owned by the State, the bringing into cultivation of waste lands, and the improvement of the soil generally in accordance with a common plan; (8) equal liability of all to labour and the establishment of industrial armies—especially for agriculture. The International organization which, since 1872, had striven to bring together the Labour socialists of all nations upon this platform, and under the Red flag of anti-nationalism and prohibited patriotism, was superceded by War conditions and the fact of the German Socialists standing by their Government in its onslaught upon world liberties; it was revived by the success of Marxian doctrine in Russia and the world-wide propaganda of unrest and revolution which followed.

Socialism in the United States and Canada. Outside of Germany, Socialism during the War was Pacifist, pro-German and opposed in all countries to necessary war-action and policies, such as Conscription, which developed from time to time. In the United States it stood, with certain powerful exceptions such as Spargo and Walling, for extremist thought in every direction and supported the German organizations there, the Irish Sinn Feiners, and the I.W.W. As to the latter, the Socialist Party of America on Dec. 15, 1918, issued a declaration through its National Executive that "the Socialist party repeat the declaration of support of all the economic organizations of the working-class and declares that listings, deportations and persecutions of the I.W.W. constitute an attack upon every American working-man." This organization stood by Mooney, convicted of throwing bombs in a San Francisco procession, and endeavoured to precipitate a general strike to obtain his release; it endorsed Victor L. Berger, the German-American who was expelled from Congress for disloyalty; it boasted amongst its leaders Debs and Emma Goldman, John Reid, the unrecognized Consul-General of the Russian Soviet to the United States. Out of it grew in 1919 a still more extreme section which stood for the organization of Workmen's Councils as in Russia; for recognition of and propaganda about the mass organization of the working men as instruments in a class struggle for seizure of all power in the State; for the creation of an industrial republic. A kindred organization called the Socialist-Labour Party of the United States had issued a platform on Apr. 30, 1916, with the following clause: "We hold that the true theory of economics is that the means of production must be owned, operated and controlled by the people in common. Man cannot exercise his right to life, liberty and the pursuit of happiness without the ownership of the land and tools with which to work." In 1919, there were 250 newspapers in the United States advocating all the varieties of Socialism and in almost every language. The New York *Forward,* in Yiddish, had a daily circulation of 200,000 and the New York *Call,* also, a very large patronage. In Australia and Canada, as well as the United States, Socialism started the One Big Union upon the non-constructive foundation of the I.W.W. The Socialist Party of Canada issued a platform* in the following terms:

We, the Socialist Party of Canada, affirm our allegiance to, and support of, the principles and programme of the revolutionary working class.

Labour, applied to natural resources, produces all wealth. The present economic system is based upon capitalist ownership of the means of production, consequently, all the products of labour belong to the capitalist class. The capitalist is therefore master; the worker a slave.

So long as the capitalist class remains in possession of the reins of government all the powers of the State will be used to protect and defend its property right in the means of wealth production and its control of the product of labour.

The capitalist system gives to the capitalist an ever-swelling stream of profits, and to the worker, an ever-increasing measure of misery and degradation.

*Note.—Pamphlet circulated in 1919 by Edmonton Local No. 1 of the Alberta Executive Committee of the Socialist Party.

The interest of the working class lies in setting itself free from capitalist exploitation by the abolition of the wage system under which this exploitation, at the point of production, is cloaked.   To accomplish this necessitates the transformation of capitalist property in the means of wealth production into socially-controlled economic forces.

The irrepressible conflict of interest between the capitalist and the worker necessarily expresses itself as a struggle for political supremacy.   This is the Class Struggle.

Therefore, we call upon all workers to organize under the banner of the Socialist Party of Canada, with the object of conquering the political powers, for the purpose of setting up and enforcing the economic programme of the working class, as follows:

1. The transformation, as rapidly as possible, of capitalist property in the means of wealth production (natural resources, factories, mills, railroads, etc.) into collective means of production.

2. The organization and management of industry by the working class.

3. The establishment, as speedily as possible, of production for use instead of production for profit.

All the varied and different forms of aggressive Socialism in 1919 had one common aim under many names—the control of the country, of all classes, of all nations, by the workingman.   J. S. Woodsworth, a Vancouver Socialist and a leader in the Federated Labour Party of British Columbia, quoted its platform in the B.C. *Federationist* of Feb. 7th as follows: ''The Federated Labour Party is organized for the purpose of securing industrial legislation and the collective ownership and democratic operation of the means of wealth production.''   He then defined their principles in the following terms: ''The ultimate object of the Party is the collective ownership and democratic operation of the means of wealth production.   This involves a complete revolution in our whole economic and social structure.''

The I.W.W. in the United States.   This organization of ''shock troops'' in the cause of Socialism was formed in Chicago at a meeting on Nov. 29, 1904,. called ''to discuss ways and means of uniting the working people of America, on correct revolutionary principles, regardless of any general Labour organization of past or present and only restricted by such basic principles as will insure its integrity as the real protector of the interests of the workers.''   A Convention followed on June 27, 1905, and the Industrial Workers of the World was duly launched with a platform of the purest Marxian Socialism* and the following preamble: ''The working class and the employing class have nothing in common.   Between these two classes a struggle must go on until all the toilers come together, take possession of the earth and the machinery of production and abolish the wage system.''

The organization grew in strength and, under the leadership of W. D. Haywood, in violence with, later on, the issue of an official pamphlet in 1918 which declared that: ''As a revolutionary organization the Industrial Workers of the World aims to use any and all tactics that will get the results sought with the least expenditure of

---

*Note.—See *The Canadian Annual Review* for 1918, Labour Section.

time and energy. The tactics used are determined solely by the power of the organization to make good in their use. The question of 'right' and 'wrong' does not concern us. No terms made with an employer are final. All peace, so long as the wage system lasts, is but an armed truce." In 1919 the official journals of the I.W.W. were *The Rebel Worker,* published in New York with the sub-title of "Organ of Revolutionary Unionism" and *The One Big Union Monthly,* issued at Chicago by the Executive Board of the I.W.W.; hundreds of thousands of workmen in and out of the United States received these journals regularly. *The National Labour Digest* of San Francisco on July 1, 1919, published these extracts from recent issues:

(1) Men work too hard. They work too long. They produce too much. They are too damned faithful.

(2) The working class of the world no longer stops in its demands at mere hours, pay and conditions, but demands the control of industry, and through that, the further power of directing every social institution.

(3) Read the I.W.W. programme. Study the O.B.U. *Monthly* and find out how to be free men. Why be cringing beggars longer? Take, don't ask!

(4) We are facing a Revolution. It is up to you to subdue the mad dogs of capitalism and open the gates of freedom.

During the year this organization was in the van of Socialistic effort. It inspired the anarchistic Omaha riots; the Seattle attempt at establishing a Soviet and a real revolution which Mayor Ole Hanson so vigourously dealt with; the O.B.U. and its efforts to capture the government of Winnipeg and other Canadian centres; the many strikes which were precipitated first, with reasons stated afterwards; the desperate effort to obtain control of the American Federation of Labour and the attempt to dominate the Police force in cities such as Boston. Everywhere it took advantage of current unrest and Bolshevistic propaganda; everywhere it was beaten in the end. The Rev. Dr. R. S. McArthur, of New York, stated in Ottawa on Nov. 10 that: "The Labour trouble in the United States is not due to the desire to secure shorter hours or larger wages—that is a pretence. It is not the real cause, which is much deeper. It is an effort on the part of the I.W.W., who are the Bolshevists of the United States, to overcome the United States Government."

On Mch. 10, A. S. Burleson, U.S. Postmaster-General, submitted a Memorandum to the Senate Overman Committee in which he stated that the I.W.W., Anarchists, Socialists, etc., had found a common aim and were perfecting an amalgamation with one object, and one object only in view, namely, the overthrow of the Government of the United States by means of a bloody revolution and the establishment of a Bolshevist republic: "The organization of Industrial Workers of the World is perhaps most actively engaged in spreading this propaganda, and has at its command a large field force known as recruiting agents, subscription agents, lecturers, etc., who work unceasingly in the furtherance of 'the cause.' This organization also publishes at least five newspapers in the English language and nine in foreign languages.'' W. B. Wilson, U.S. Secretary of Labour, defined the situation as follows at Boston on Apr. 23: ''The I.W.W. undertake to destroy the profits—to reduce the production of the individual and to increase the cost. With properties practically destroyed the I.W.W. believe that they could take them over and run them for their own profit.''

The Lusk Committee in the New York Legislature and the Overman Committee in the Senate at Washington conducted elaborate enquiries which brought out many facts as to the revolutionary character of the I.W.W. and its seditious work. In the summer of 1919 they devoted their energies to stirring up and organizing the negro. Early in August it was announced that the I.W.W. was flooding the negro sections of Philadelphia and New York with circulars worded in violent language and sometimes illustrated with cartoons of the most vicious conception. In every instance, the negro was urged to join the I.W.W. and in some cases to ally himself with other bodies of Bolshevist sympathies. Then came the great steel strike organized and conducted by William Z. Foster in the most approved I.W.W. manner. He was a well-known Syndicalist or believer in the control of industries by workers organized in unions for each separate industry—the mines for the miners, the railways for the railwaymen, etc. It was a variation only from the slogan of all industries owned by the workers as a class.

His book upon Syndicalism was of a distinctly revolutionary nature and, writing in *Solidarity*, an I.W.W. organ, at Chicago on Nov. 4, 1914, he had shown where his sympathies were and what his policy was: ''I am satisfied from my observations that the only way for the I.W.W. to have the workers adopt and produce the principles of revolutionary unionism—which I take is its mission —is to give up the attempt to create a new labour movement, turn itself into a propaganda league, get into the organized labour movement, and by building up better fighting machines within the old unions, than those possessed by our reactionary enemies, revolutionize these unions, even as our French syndicalist fellow-workers have so successfully done with theirs. Yours for revolution.'' He accordingly organized the Steel men and though the strike failed it was not his fault. Such, in brief, was the record of the I.W.W. in 1919; it was important to Canada because of its parentage to the O.B.U. and the critical developments in the West during the year.

Bolshevism in its 1919 Developments. The Soviet rule of Russia, the clever ruse of autocratic rulers and Socialistic adventurers acting as leaders of the workmen, the idea of class warfare preached by Marx and practised by Lenine and Trotzky in its cruelest forms, the collapse and ruin of the great country which had been Russia, at the hands of a very limited section of the proletariat or workers, affected every other country in the world and influenced, directly or indirectly, the thought and policy of all Labour organizations, Governments and political parties in 1919. It increased the un-

rest of the war period and made Peace appear like another war
while it greatly strengthened the violent elements in all Labour
movements.   Large bodies of workmen in Britain, the United
States and Canada refused to believe the reports of those who had
escaped from blood-soaked Russia; they accepted the alleged
theories of the Socialist leaders there and declared the press and
the people who described the terrors to be tools of the capitalists.
Yet a collection of authentic reports presented to the British House
of Commons on Apr. 29, 1919, accepted as correct by Government
and members alike, and officially published, indicated conditions
hard even to describe in veiled language.   R. H. B. Lockhart got
a letter through to Mr. Balfour from Moscow dated Nov. 10, 1918,
which may be summarized as follows:

1. The Bolsheviks have established a rule of force and oppression unequalled in the history of any autocracy. Themselves the fiercest upholders
of the right of free speech, they have suppressed, since coming into power,
every newspaper which does not approve their policy.

2. The right of holding public meetings has been abolished. The vote
has been taken away from everyone except the workmen in the factories and
the poorer servants.

3. The worst crimes of the Bolsheviks have been against their Socialist
opponents. Of the countless executions which the Bolsheviks have carried out
a large percentage has fallen on the heads of Socialists who had waged a
lifelong struggle against the old *regime*.

4. The Bolsheviks have abolished even the most primitive forms of
justice. Thousands of men and women have been shot without even the
mockery of a trial, and thousands more are left to rot in the prisons under
conditions to find a parallel to which one must turn to the darkest annals of
Indian or Chinese history.

5. The Bolsheviks have restored the barbarous methods of torture and
have established the odious practice of taking hostages. Still worse, they have
struck at their political opponents through their women folk.

6. The avowed ambition of Lenine is to create civil warfare throughout
Europe. Every speech of Lenine's is a denunciation of constitutional methods,
and a glorification of the doctrine of physical force.

7. In order to maintain their popularity with the working men and
with their hired mercenaries, the Bolsheviks are paying their supporters enormous wages by means of an unchecked paper issue, until to-day money in
Russia has lost all value.

In the raids carried out by the United States Government during 1919 many documents were seized showing the teachings of
Bolshevists and one was a Manifesto of the Federation of Unions
of Russian Workers in the United States and Canada which urged,
amongst other things, the capture of all products and means of
production; liberation of all political prisoners and blowing up of
all barracks; the murder of law-enforcing officials and the burning
of public records; destruction of fences and all property lines and
of all instruments of indebtedness.   F. A. Blossom, Editor of *The
Labour Defender,* an I.W.W. organ, stated on Jan. 5 of this year
that Bolshevik elements were forming Soviets, secretly, in cities
all through the United States, that there were 68,000 members in
Canada, and that in Mexico and South America Bolshevism was
particularly active.   In the Report of the U.S. Senate Committee

with Hon. L. S. Overman as Chairman and signed also by Senators W. H. King, J. O. Wolcott, Knute Nelson and Thomas Sterling, the whole record and character of the Bolsheviki were dealt with and two elaborate volumes of evidence printed.   The conclusions of the Committee stated that a few of the fundamental facts relating to Bolshevism and the Russian Socialist Soviet Republic showed that: ''It is the dictatorship of a class and is not a democratic form of government.   In its actual application it has become an autocracy of a few individuals who exercise their authority and suppress all opposition by fear, terrorism, and force.   It has developed into as much of an autocracy, though more cruel in its methods, as the monarchical government of the Czar's *regime*.''

The Report explained how this small minority of a great people had held power: ''The Bolsheviki have inaugurated a reign of terror unparalleled in the history of modern civilization, in many of its aspects rivaling even the inhuman savagery of the Turk and the terrors of the French Revolution.   Under the evidence, your Committee has been compelled to impose the responsibility for this terrorism upon the Government, itself, rather than attribute it merely to the excesses of individuals and groups.   In Bolshevik Russia every instrument available for the exercise of force and power is in the possession of that Government, and those opposed to the Government or who fail to render it whole-hearted support are completely suppressed and absolutely powerless.   The Government is more highly centralized and less restricted in the exercise of that centralized power than was the Government of the Czar.''   The result of the system was that the dictatorship, utilizing Lettish troops and Chinese labourers as well as German and Austrian prisoners, and criminals discharged from the gaols, as a Red Guard for the enforcement of its decrees, promptly secured possession and control of: ''All arms and ammunition, and practically all foodstuffs and commodities essential to the maintenance of life; all clothing and household goods necessary for warmth and health; all gold, silver, and specie, including jewelry, ornaments, gold and silver plate.   Disfranchisement of all but a class of the workers and Soviet soldiers, confiscation on a wholesale basis, seizure of the land and the Banks, and the issue of unlimited and worthless paper money accompany the process.''   The following points were described as the programme of Bolshevism:

(1)   The repudiation of democracy and the establishment of a dictatorship.

(2)   The confiscation of all land and the improvements thereon and of all forests and natural resources.

(3)   The confiscation of all live-stock and all agricultural implements, and of all Banks and banking institutions and the establishment of a state monopoly of the banking business.

(4)   The confiscation of all factories, mills, mines, and industrial institutions and the delivery of the control and operation thereof to the employees therein.

(5)   The confiscation of all churches and all church property, real and personal, and of all newspapers and periodicals and all mechanical facilities and machinery used in the publication thereof.

(6) The seizure and confiscation of all public meeting places and assembly halls, and of all transportation and communication systems.

(7) The confiscation of the entire estate of all decedents, and a monopoly by the State of all advertisements of every nature, whether in newspapers, periodicals, handbills, or programmes.

(8) The repudiation of all debts against the Government and all obligations due the non-Bolshevik elements of the population.

(9) The establishment of universal compulsory military service regardless of religious scruples and conscientious objections, and of universal compulsory labour.

(10) The abolition of the Sunday school and all other schools and institutions that teach religion, and absolute separation of churches and schools.

(11) The establishment, through marriage and divorce laws, of a method for the legalization of prostitution, when the same was engaged in by consent of both parties.

(12) The refusal to recognize the existence of God in its governmental and judicial proceedings, and the arming of all so-called, ''toilers'' and the disarming of all persons that had succeeded in acquiring property.

(13) The discrimination in favour of residents of cities and against residents of the rural districts through giving the former five times as much voting power as was accorded to residents of rural districts in such elections as were permitted.

(14) The disfranchisement of all persons employing any other person; of all persons receiving rent, interest, or dividends; of all merchants, traders, and commercial agents; of all priests, clergymen, or employees of churches and religious bodies.

(15) The denial of the existence of any inalienable rights in the individual citizen, and the establishment of a judicial system exercising autocratic power, convicting persons and imposing penalties in their absence, and without opportunity to be heard.

Soviets were by this time established in most of the cities of the United States and Canada and in many English centres; on the Clyde Bolshevists caused many Labour troubles to shipping during the War and, with other English extremists, were in alliance with the Spartacans at Berlin. Speaking in the Commons, on May 29, Winston Churchill, Secretary for War, described the situation as follows: ''Bolshevism is not a policy, it is a disease. It is not a creed, it is a pestilence. It presents all the characteristics of a pestilence. It breaks out with great suddenness; it is violently contagious; it throws people into a frenzy of excitement; it spreads with extraordinary rapidity; the mortality is terrible; so that after a while, like other pestilences, the disease tends to wear itself out. In its first stages, Bolshevism offers a considerable attraction to the worst elements in an uneducated people like the Russian masses, especially a people who have been long and cruelly down-trodden. They are able to stop working; they are able to take possession of whatever they can find; they can enter the houses of the wealthy and of the middle-classes and of the classes who can read and write, and take the food and the liquor and the clothing and the furniture; they can trample down every vestige of authority; and they can go off and enjoy their plunder. But this only carries them on for a certain number of weeks. The plunder is soon eaten up or wasted, and the accumulated wealth of years can be consumed or rendered unavailable in a very short time. The truth is revealed that the property of the rich only meets, for a very few weeks, the needs of the poor. . . . But by the time this is discovered the whole machinery of production has been destroyed. All relations between man and man have been poisoned. The whole organization of society, and all its scientific apparatus, has been destroyed.''

During 1919 Bolshevists and the I.W.W's, German Socialists and extremists of all kinds—English radicals, Russian reds, Swedish and other devotees of Marx—combined to cause trouble wherever possible in the United States and Canada. It was hard to differentiate between them. Seattle, in the United States, found its counterpart in Winnipeg, Canada; the writings of William Z. Foster of the United States Iron and Steel Workers, who precipitated and guided the steel strike, found many echoes in Vancouver and the West. Foster, in his book on *Syndicalism* described his policy as follows: ''To organize the working people into great syndicalist organizations—revolutionary labour unions. The political state as at present constituted must be blown up, wrecked and cast aside. The way to accomplish this is by direct action—the general strike. Labour must not stop to choose its weapons in its struggle against the great industrial organization of to-day and the state as a whole. All considerations of ethics and morality must be discarded as so much dead wood, as so many fetters blocking labour's liberty of action.''

At Vancouver ''Jack'' Harrington, a local leader of the Socialist movement, stated on Feb. 23 (*B.C. Federationist*, Feb. 28) that ''the bourgeoisie was getting worried about Bolshevism,'' and that the idea was spreading everywhere. He then denounced Lloyd George and President Wilson and added this interesting touch: ''The latter is the son of a Presbyterian preacher and if there is anything lower than that I'd like to know it.'' Dr. W. J. Curry on the same day (Sunday) in a Vancouver theatre remarked that he was losing faith in political or moderate action: ''Seeing who are the enemies of the Bolsheviki it's time for us to admit we are their friends. The Bolsheviki are not angels; they may often seem to be demons, just like in certain conditions we would be.'' In closing, he added: ''It may be a rough road, and stained with blood, we don't know. But we hope the people here may have the intelligence to unite and make resistance impossible.'' This was the sort of thing behind some of the Winnipeg strike leaders.

As A. S. Burleson, United States Postmaster-General, put it in a statement on Dec. 22, so it might have been said as to these Canadian elements: ''The doctrines of the Bolsheviki, Communists, anarchists and kindred organizations are being spread broadcast throughout the United States by agents of revolutionary socialism, co-operating for the purpose of precipitating a revolution through violence and by unlawful and unconstitutional means.'' He pointed out that ''the ultimate object of this movement is to create an international revolutionary party to overturn the governments of the entire world and establish an international communist government for the world, and that the publications forming this propaganda in many cases subtly guard their utterances, but that they are, nevertheless, united in publishing the same character of matter."

In Great Britain the extremists called the Labour branch of the movement "Direct Action" or the use of the strike as a political weapon with which to obtain such ends as the cessation of military operations in Russia.   The extremist leaders were Bolshevists in varying degrees.   J. Ramsay Macdonald stated in the Glasgow *Forward* of June 7 that Russian Bolshevism was "a dictatorship of the Intelligenzia"; Robert Williams, Secretary of the National Transport Workers' Federation, declared at Manchester on June 21 that "Bolshevism is only Socialism with the courage of its convictions"; R. C. Walhead of the Independent Labour Party, on the same occasion described Lenine as "the greatest man the War has produced"; Robert Smillie, the Miners' chief, and Philip Snowden favoured a policy of direct action; Tom Mann in the *Daily Herald* (Labour organ) declared on Oct. 31 that "the purpose of Trade Unionism is the achieving of workers' control in workshops and the industries as a whole."   He added that: "There is nothing in the I.W.W. doctrine to which I do not subscribe."   But these men could not carry British labour as a whole with them and on Sept. 9th the Trade Union Congress by clever manipulation of its voting power evaded a decision on the question of "direct action" in the nationalization of mines' issue and Robert Smillie thereafter declined greatly in influence.   He had tried to force the issue, and failed, with all the chief leaders of Labour against him—Clynes, Thomas, Thorne, Sexton, Blachford, Roberts, Henderson.

The One Big Union in Canada.   This body during the year was organized in British Columbia where Labour leaders such as W. A. Pritchard, J. S. Woodsworth, A. S. Wells, E. T. Kingsley and R. P. Pettipiece with their organ, the *B.C. Federationist*, were all extreme Socialists; it guided the policy of the B.C. Federation of Labour and the above newspaper, it captured a majority of the Winnipeg Labour party and it had elements of support in many other Canadian centres.   The attitude of these leaders has been indicated by extracts already given in these pages and E. T. Kingsley, a clever Socialist writer and President of the B.C. Federated Labour Party, on June 1st gave another point of view in addressing a large Vancouver meeting where he stated that: "No living thing works unless it is enslaved.   But just as soon as men were enslaved by Capitalism, it became necessary to invent some word to express their misery and their agony—and that damned word was W-O-R-K."

The *B.C. Federationist* on Jan. 10 observed that everything was going well with "the slave class" and then added: "It is impossible to demand too much, because nothing short of the whole shooting match is of any use.   It is now realized that compromise is impossible, between the working class and the master class.   It is a fight to a finish, a fight to the death." Meanwhile, in Australia, the One Big Union had got together all the extremists of the Labour movement there and had organized them on Nov. 16, 1918, into a Congress of the O.B.U. which, incidentally, cabled congratulations to the Bolsheviki of Petrograd, sang the Red Flag and expressed, by Resolution, hopes for the success of "revolutionary propaganda amongst all the peoples of Europe." Final organization was effected in a Conference at Melbourne on Jan. 11, 1919, which made direct action, workers' control of industries, with sympathetic or general strikes, and antagonism to regular Labour Unions, a part of its policy.* The chief clauses in its platform were as follows:

(1) Capitalism can only be abolished by the workers uniting in one class (conscious economic organization) to take and hold the means of production by revolutionary, industrial and political action.

(2) The rapid accumulation of wealth and concentration of the ownership of industries into fewer hands make the trade unions unable to cope with the ever-growing power of the employing class.

(3) These conditions can be changed, and the interests of the working class advanced, only by an organization so constituted that all its members in any one industry, or in all industries, shall take concerted action when deemed necessary, thereby making an injury to one the concern of all.

(4) We hold that as the working class creates and operates the socially-operated machinery of production, it should direct production and determine working conditions.

Technically, this body was called the Workers' Industrial Union; popularly it was termed the One Big Union. It was so termed, also, by the *Federationist*, the *Western Labour News* and other extremist organs in Canada. The movement, however, as in Canada, proved hostile to and did not receive the support of organized Trade Unionism. Following these developments and aided by such publications as *The One Big Union* issued from I.W.W. headquarters at Chicago, it was decided by a considerable membership in the British Columbia labour circles to break away from the Trades Council of Canada and to join hands with the stormy elements in the Alberta Federation of Labour and with R. B. Russell, Rev. William Ivens and other Winnipeg leaders of the extremist type. Arrangements were made for the B.C. Federation of Labour to hold its 9th annual Convention at Calgary where a Committee had already arranged for a Western Conference on One Big Union matters and as a protest against the moderation of the Quebec, 1918, meeting of the Trades and Labour Congress.

Proceedings at the Federation Convention on Mch. 10-11 opened with J. Taylor, Vice-President, in the chair and 87 Delegates present. The first and chief Resolution was discussed at length but carried unanimously as follows: "That this Convention lays down as the future policy the building of the organizations of workers on industrial lines for the purpose of enforcing, by virtue of their industrial strength, such demands as such organizations may at any time consider necessary for their continued maintenance, and well-being, and shall not, as heretofore, attempt to persuade Legislative

*Note.—For the full platform see *The Canadian Annual Review* for 1918, page 306.

assemblies to amend, add to, or take from existing statutes, allegedly
called Labour laws." Many Resolutions were offered as to a six-
hour day and the following was approved on the understanding
that it was only a temporary measure of relief: "That this Convention go on record as demanding a six-hour day of five days a
week, to come into effect June 1st, and that intensive educational
propaganda be instituted to that end." Another Resolution sent
greetings to the Soviet leaders of Russia and demanded the refusal
of Labour to handle munitions intended for that country; others
called for united action on the part of the workers to secure the
release of political prisoners, for the lifting of the censorship, and
for the raising of a fund to defend members of the working-class
arrested for having banned literature in their possession.

A motion calling for separation from the regular American and
Canadian Trade organizations was approved but referred to a vote
of the membership for ratification; May 1st was urged for selection as the official Labour Day and another motion declared that
the Capitalist was the only alien in the community and should be so
dealt with by law; greater co-operation between soldiers and workers was urged. John Kavanagh of Vancouver was elected President and A. S. Wells Secretary-Treasurer. The tone of the Convention was one of vigourous hostility to employers and capitalists
and all classes except that of the workers. A. S. Wells made this
comment: "We have got to have an organization whereby, when
the time comes, when we have reached that point where we are
going to take over and operate the wheels of industry—which time
we have talked about so long. At that time we will have to have
an industrial organization similar to that which has proven of
such a benefit in Russia." W. A. Pritchard did not believe in
asking for a six-hour day: "As far as I am concerned, we are not
interested in the business of telling anybody he can buy off our
revolution. We must bring it on in the first place, and when it
comes, the historic conditions being ripe, talk about buying it off,
they could not stop it." There was a good deal of ability shown
in these debates—of which many pages of a *verbatim* report appeared in the Vancouver *Federationist* and the *Western Labour
News*—but with the exception of speeches by J. H. McVety they
were along the line illustrated by the above quotations and the
O.B.U. principles generally.

On Mch. 13th most of the Delegates from this meeting attended
the opening of the Inter-Provincial Western Conference in the same
city. David Rees, Vice-President of the Trades and Labour Congress of Canada and Chairman of the Committee which had called
the gathering together, (V. R. Midgley, Vancouver, F. Wheatley,
Bankhead, Alta., H. Perry, Regina, and E. Robinson, Winnipeg)
acted as temporary Chairman: 237 Delegates were seated including 85 from British Columbia, 89 from Alberta, 17
from Saskatchewan and 46 from Manitoba; R. J. Tallon of
the Calgary Trades and Labour Council, was elected Chairman,

V. R. Midgley of Vancouver, Secretary, and J. Kavanagh Chairman of the Resolutions Committee. The first Resolution was unanimously carried with little debate, as follows: "That the aims of labour as represented by this Convention are the abolition of the present system of production for profit, and the substitution therefor of production for use." The second one declared: "That this Convention recommend to its affiliated memberships the severance of affiliation with their International organization and that steps be taken to form an industrial organization of all workers, and that a referendum on the question be taken at the same time and that the question be submitted to the entire Canadian membership." Another Resolution demanded immediate lifting of the Government's censorship of the press, that all political prisoners be released and that a referendum asking for a general strike in this connection be taken on June 1 if the demands were not granted and a six-hour day accepted. Amid loud cheering and without discussion the following motions were adopted:

1. Whereas, holding the belief in the ultimate supremacy of the working class in matters economic and political, and that the light of modern developments have proved that the legitimate aspirations of the Labour movement are repeatedly obstructed by the existing political forms, clearly showing the capitalistic nature of the Parliamentary machinery, this Convention expresses its open conviction that the system of industrial Soviet control by selection of representatives from industries is more efficient and of greater political value than the present form of government.

2. That this Convention declares its full acceptance of the principle of 'proletarian dictatorship' as being absolute and efficient for the transformation of capitalistic private property to communal wealth, and that fraternal greetings be sent to the Russian Soviet Government, the Spartacans in Germany, and all definite working class movements in Europe and the world, recognizing they have won first place in the history of the class struggle.

3. That the interests of all members of the working class being identical, that this body of workers recognizes no alien but the capitalist; also that we are opposed to any wholesale immigration of workers.

4. That this Conference places itself on record as being in full accord and sympathy with the aims and purposes of the Russian Bolshevik and German Spartacan revolutions.

A six-hour day in all industries to come into effect on June 1st was also approved. A Central Executive Committee of five was then elected, composed of W. A. Pritchard and V. R. Midgley, Vancouver, R. J. Johns, Winnipeg, J. R. Knight, Edmonton, and Joseph Naylor, Cumberland, B.C., to carry on the One Big Union movement and to obtain a favourable response to the proposed Referendum as to which arrangements were placed in their hands. In the *B.C. Federationist* of Mch. 28 appeared a leaflet issued by this Committee which appealed to "the workers of North America" to support the scheme of organization planned by this Calgary Conference for One Big Industrial Organization and to oppose the craft system of unionism and the American Federation of Labour organization. It declared the latter to be against mass action (revolution) or general and sympathetic strikes and to be a "moss-covered and age-old institution"; "In Britain the shop stewards;

in Australia the Workers' Industrial Organization; here, One Big Union." Two days later E. T. Kingsley of the Federated Labour Party told a Vancouver audience: "I stand for One Big Union—for the specific purpose of conquering the reins of power, by peaceable means if possible; and if not, by some other means." The platform of the Party which the above speaker led had the following clauses:

The ultimate object of the Federated Labour Party is the complete overthrow of the present system of property and wealth production, which is based upon the exploitation of labour under the hand of a ruling class. In this we realize and emphatically assert our solidarity with the revolutionary working class of the entire world. As such revolution cannot be accomplished except by the working class becoming master of the State, the supreme instrument whereby the ruling class subjects the workers to slavery and exploitation, we pledge ourselves to the work of education and organization to the end that control of the State may be obtained, if possible, by the exercise of constitutional means. With that control in the hands of a revolutionary working class all obstacles in the pathway of human freedom and progress may be swept aside.

In succeeding months correspondence made public at the Winnipeg trials for sedition showed R. J. Johns, William Ivens, Gordon Carscaden and Carl E. Berg—two professed Bolsheviki and the latter a delegate at the Calgary Convention—V. R. Midgley, J. Kavanagh, as all talking Bolshevism and varied kinds of revolutionary doctrine. On June 4-5 a Conference was held at Calgary to complete the work of the Convention, to report the results of the Referendum, which were not made public, and to promulgate a platform which, though not given much publicity in the press of the country, was given in full by the *B.C. Federationist* on June 13. This Constitution of the One Big Union started with the following Preamble: "Modern industrial society is divided into two classes, those who possess and do not produce, and those who produce and do not possess. Alongside this main division all other classifications fade into insignificance. Between these two classes a continual struggle takes place. As with buyers and sellers of any commodity there exists a struggle on the one hand of the buyer to buy as cheaply as possible, and on the other, of the seller to sell for as much as possible, so with the buyers and sellers of labour power." It went on to declare that: "The One Big Union, therefore, seeks to organize the wage worker, not according to craft, but according to industry; according to class and class needs, and prepare ourselves for the day when production for profit shall be replaced by production for use." Membership was made open to all wage-earners and elaborate details as to management and organization followed. Such was the situation which preceded and accompanied the famous Winnipeg strike of 1919.

The Winnipeg Strike: The O.B.U. Defeated. This struggle was not an ordinary Labour fight for better wages or improved conditions; it was a deliberate effort by an extremist element in the Labour ranks to acquire control of Labour organizations and capture the government of Winnipeg by means of a general strike, or series of sympathetic strikes, which would compel, by absolute force, the surrender of the city into their hands and set loose elements which, it was hoped, would do the same thing elsewhere and, eventually, overthrow the existing system of National government and replace it by one of workmen only. It was not successful—apart from the final powers of law and order which were not strongly utilized from Ottawa—because the great middle class in the community took things into its own hands, won over the reasonable working-men and returned soldiers and defeated the movement; with also, substantial aid from the Mounted Police, from the determined attitude of Mayor C. F. Gray and from the position taken by the Norris Provincial Government. It was a class which the Marxian and Syndicalist, Socialist, I.W.W. and O.B.U. entirely overlooked in their literature and speeches; it was made up of neither workmen nor capitalists but just the ordinary and, somewhat numerous, citizens between those two classes.

The Strike movement was led by Rev. William Ivens, M.A., B.D.—still a recognized Minister of the Methodist Church—and R. B. Russell, and it developed at first along quite ordinary lines. Under the surface, however, there was very active work going on amongst an extreme radical or red element similar to that represented at the Calgary Convention and in Vancouver propaganda. William Ivens as protagonist of the movement was assisted by certain "intellectuals" of the type of Rev. Dr. S. G. Bland, who afterwards moved to Toronto, and he led the press and pulpit and platform work while others of foreign extraction such as Sam Blumenberg, laboured amongst the foreigners and lower-class workmen; the Winnipeg Trades and Labour Council, on Jan. 21, threatened by Resolution a general strike unless the Government removed its ban upon seditious literature; all kinds of trades joined the Labour organizations at this juncture—many of which had hitherto resisted all efforts to that end; the Socialists and Bolsheviki and German elements talked loudly and circulated Bolshevistic literature and precipitated a riot on Jan. 26—in which a band of veterans swept the city and cleared out or destroyed a lot of foreign, pro-German and Socialistic quarters.

At a meeting in the Labour Temple addressed by Rev. Dr. Bland and Mr. Ivens on Feb. 16, the latter declared that under the proposed new system: "All you have to do is to walk into any industry, tell the owner you are going to take it over, and it is done." The work going on at this time was illustrated by correspondence made public in the later trials of Winnipeg seditionists. One was a letter from R. B. Russell dated Jan. 30, 1919, in which he said: "At the last Trades and Labour Council meeting we had a great victory and killed the Labour party for sure. If you send us down 500 copies of the 'Soviets at Work' we will get them out amongst the soldiers and see if it helps." Another dated Mch. 31 acknowledged one describing the success of the Calgary Convention and the O.B.U. which stated that "I have just got in a shipment' of Bolsheviki funds." Russell asked the writer for 20,000 copies of speeches to distribute and added: "I note the substantial financial aid you are receiving and no doubt it will all be needed to carry on our propaganda." On Apr. 23 the Civic Employees' Union in Brandon initiated a strike and by means of sympathetic strikes all but paralyzed the business of that city; at Regina on Apr. 29 a big meeting of the local Trades and Labour Council supported by unanimous motion the O.B.U. policies.

On May 1st, by simultaneous action, the Metal Workers and Building trades of Winnipeg, 6,000 workers in the Metal trades of Toronto and 3,000 men in the building trades of Ottawa went on strike. The Winnipeg strike was to be preliminary to the general strike proposed by the Calgary Convention for June 1st, but afterwards postponed to July 1st; any others which could be arranged would be so much the more helpful. The dominant figure in the Metal trades and Council at this time was R. B. Russell whom the Winnipeg *Free Press* described (June 13) as "an open, avowed and blatant revolutionist," and who, on Dec. 22, 1918, in the Walker Theatre, had declared that a revolution was about to take place in Canada in which the workers would triumph and the capitalists would be in the same position as those in Russia. "The blood that is spilled in Canada," he continued, "will depend on the working class. We must establish the same form of government as they have in Russia so that we may have a Russian democracy here."

The dominating principle presented by the Metal workers was a right of Collective bargaining under which agreements were not entered into between employer and employees only, but were to be subject to the ratification of a Central Metal Trades Council of workers. The three ironmasters of Winnipeg,—the Vulcan Iron, the Manitoba Bridge Co., and Dominion Bridge Co.—while willing to negotiate with their own men, refused to do so through the medium of the Metal Trades Council. They maintained that this body comprised men whose work was not related directly to the crafts in their shops and that, also, the greater number of the men on the Metal Trades Council were employed in railway iron shops where the element of competition in the price of product did not enter to such a degree as in their firms. Back of it all was a struggle between Craft Unionism, or Unions formed of employees in a single firm, as accepted by the American Federation of Labour and the Canadian Trades Congress, and the radical spirits of the I.W.W. and O.B.U. who wanted the Unionism of entire industries which could easily combine to control the employers in each industry and then, by general strikes, in all industries. The Winnipeg *Strike Bulletin* No. 8, of May 26, defined this issue as follows: "Collective bargaining has only one meaning, namely, the right of Labour to form any kind of organization it desires and to make such affiliations as it is deemed necessary."

The Metal Trades Council embraced 19 Unions; its demands included an 8-hour day with a 44-hour week and wage increases up to a rough total of 85 cents an hour; these the employers were willing to consider but Collective bargaining, as interpreted by the Council, they were determined not to accept—they would deal only with Committees from their own shops.   On May 1st when the 2,000 metal workers went out (the Railway metal employees did not do so) the building trades also struck to enforce a wage schedule but without any reference to the Collective bargaining issue.   The Winnipeg Trades and Labour Council, controlled by its President, James Winning, Alderman Ernest Robinson, its Secretary, and R. B. Russell, had, meanwhile, endorsed the Metal workers; according to the Winnipeg *Free Press*, the Winnipeg *Citizen* in its first issue of May 21 and the *Grain Growers' Guide* of the same date, William Ivens in more than one speech declared that Winnipeg was then under Soviet rule.   As illustrating the views of a man who for a time was a sort of Dictator in Winnipeg, a quotation may be given from the *Industrial Banner*, Toronto, of May 2nd.   This journal—edited by James Simpson—described the speech as "a scathing indictment of capitalism" and as delivered a short time before in the Labour Church, Winnipeg.   Its conclusion was as follows: "Such is the damnable system that to-day has its avaricious claws upon every phase of life.   It robs the worker at the cradle, the sick bed, the meal table, the street car, and on the clothes he wears.   When he works he must pay tribute.   Upon his coal, and his gas, and his meat, and his tobacco, the levy is also made.   Then, when weary at last he lies down for his last long rest, the grimy fingers are put upon his coffin and his pall."

Much unrest developed, with great rapidity, in Winnipeg and on May 7 the Trades and Labour Council called for a ballot on the question of a general sympathetic strike to aid the demands of the metal and building trades.   The vote of 52 affiliated unions was 11,112 in favour, to 524 against, with 17 Unions not reported.   The Winnipeg Firemen voted 149 to 6 in favour of the strike; the retail clerks, 450 to 10; Carmen's local, No. 371, 706 to 68; Winnipeg police, 149 to 11; bakers and confectioners, 272 to 2; cooks and waiters (partial vote), 278 to 0; carpenters, 371 to 4; teamsters, 611 to 3.   The T. & L. Council order of May 13th followed and stated that: "A general strike has been called of all organizations affiliated with the Council.   The strike will take effect at 11 o'clock on May 15th.   Every organization but one has voted overwhelmingly in favour of strike, and the biggest strike in the history of Winnipeg will take place as above stated.   No exceptions are anticipated in this strike.   All public utilities will be tied up in order to enforce the principle of Collective bargaining."   Mr. Premier Norris and Mayor Gray did their utmost to avert this final issue and, from May 12, daily conferences were held with the Labour leaders; a meeting was finally arranged between the disputants but the Metals Council would not arbitrate the Collective bargaining issue and the Building trades would not arbitrate their wages schedule.

The general strike was, therefore, commenced on May 15 with the veterans of the city—estimated at 16,000—describing themselves as neutral and the local G.W.V.A. afterwards passing a Resolution in favour of Collective bargaining.   Mayor Gray at once issued an address to the citizens calling for maintenance of order and co-operation to this end with the statement that: "Should any acts be committed that savour of lawlessness I will act swiftly and surely and will use to the full the powers vested in me by the voice of the people."   There were many expressions of fear as to conditions in North Winnipeg where lived thousands of alien enemies and the *Free Press* of the 15th declared that: "Within our borders there are men willing to commit crimes of any degree of atrocity that will bring them profit or satisfaction and they are subject to no restraint except lack of opportunity and fear of punishment." The management of the Strike was placed in the hands of a Committee of 5 men—James Winning, President of the local Trades and Labour Council and H. G. Veitch, past President, Ernest Robinson, Secretary, R. B. Russell of the Metal Workers, and Andrew Scoble of the Street Railwaymen's Union; subsequently 9 others were added and William Ivens as Editor of the *Western Labour News*, supplied a publicity propaganda and a most influential end of the Strike.   A total of 30,000 men were out by the close of May 15, who included employees of all manner and kind of private business institutions, factories, warehouses, stores and shops, and of the following public and quasi-public utilities and essential industries:

> Firemen and High-pressure Water Works' Employees.
> Electric Light and Power Operators.
> Street Cleaners, Scavengers, etc.
> Electric Railway Employees and Postal Workers.
> Building Engineers, Caretakers, and Elevator Operators.
> Freight Handlers and Express Company Employees.
> Truck Drivers, Carters and Delivery Staffs.
> Telegraph and Telephone Operators.
> All Creamery and Milk Handling Employees.
> Storage Plant Employees and Millers and Bakers.
> All Butchers and Packing House Employees.

The Police and Waterworks' employees went technically on strike, but remained at their posts for the time being—"By permission of the Strike Committee"—with water pressure reduced to less than normal.   On the third day of the general strike, by calling out the pressmen, the Committee also suppressed the daily newspapers, and all other regular publications—excepting only the Labour journal.   The immediate result of the strike was that, on the afternoon of the 15th, the citizens found themselves unable to get a meal in a restaurant, to ride on a street car, to go to a picture show, to live the life they had been accustomed to.   There was a great effort to lay in supplies of bread, flour and other necessaries and a situation akin to panic prevailed for a time and was succeeded by a condition of much suffering and privation—especially

Factories of Gutta Percha & Rubber, Limited, Toronto, Canada.

where money or credit was not readily available, and milk an essential—as with children. The Central Strike Committee took charge of the Labour Temple and, whether actually called a Soviet or not, it certainly acted as one, and asserted distinct authority as the ruling factor in the situation.

What followed was described in a special issue of the *Free Press* on June 27: "This Committee first decided that it would be well to have the picture houses and the other theatres open in order that the people might be kept to some extent off the streets. The theatres were, therefore, opened again with display signs and the wording—'Open by special permission of the Strike Committee.' There were no deliveries of milk or bread on Friday morning (16th) with the exception of those maintained by smaller dairies and bakeries. The result was that there was acute suffering among families with small children and at some hospitals and institutions. In this connection all classes suffered and the Strike Committee was quick to see that it would smash its own case if the necessities of life were to be cut off. The result was that the Committee ordered the bakers and bread and milk drivers to return to work, and by Saturday, the 17th, deliveries were again being made. Cream was held to be a luxury and was not allowed. The bread and milk delivery waggons carried signs: 'Permitted by authority of the Strike Committee.'"

The extent to which the strike leaders were at first willing to go was illustrated in this, the calling out of the milk workers, and the current attempt to establish depôts in which preference would be given the families of the strikers—as in Petrograd and Moscow—and thus help in the process of coercion. Let the *Strike Bulletin* of May 17 afford an additional review of the result: "After making a thorough investigation of the depôt scheme, we found it would be impossible to distinguish between the sick children, owing to the fact that it would take days to establish a card system and reports were fast coming in of children on the verge of death for the want of milk. We then decided to open up the supply of milk through the regular method of supply." Meanwhile Winnipeg was without a daily paper and so remained from May 16 to May 22—the printers staying at work under their agreements but unable to really help because the pressmen and stereotypers had ignored theirs and joined the strikers. The Police force remained on duty but, as members of a Union affiliated with the Trades and Labour Council, did so on sufferance and this phase of the situation was not a pleasant one to citizens generally.

Incidents of the first few days included the handing to each worker as he left the C.P.R. shops, of a number of pamphlets issued by the Socialist party and copies of the Socialist *Bulletin*, printed under Winnipeg date line, and containing articles signed by Nicholai Lenine and L. A. K. Martens, representative in the United States of the Russian Soviet; the declaration of attitude by a mass-meeting of Great War Veterans (May 15) through a Resolution de-

16

claring full sympathy with the purposes of the strike as meeting
the general needs of the people, but pledging every legitimate help
to preserve law and order; the Strike order (May 17) that several
cafés should be opened, but that waiters must not serve anyone not
wearing a Union badge and, if any remarks derogatory to the
strike should be made by the owner, the café was to be closed; the
statement by Hon. N. W. Rowell in Parliament on May 16, as to
the Postal employees that the Government considered their action
entirely without justification, and were standing absolutely behind
all the employees who remained to perform their duty in the service of the Dominion at Winnipeg; the remark on May 16 by R.
B. Russell to the City Council, as to closing down the newspapers,
that "we know the effect a newspaper has in moulding public opinion and that, in the past, such opinion has been moulded against
our class."

   With all organized labour in the City on strike, except the
Police and Moving Picture employees, "by permission," it appeared
necessary to make compromise arrangements and the Mayor, on
the 17th, in conjunction with the Strike Committee, planned for the
baking of bread and arranged for milk supplies, but with the provision that at each depôt all applicants for milk must sign a card
that it was for the use of infants under three, for invalids, or for
the hospitals.   The going out of the Telegraphers following that of
the Postal employees, isolated the City as if in a siege and the only
news getting in or out was by hand delivery or by personal journey
to or from another town.   Meanwhile, 3,000 troops were at the
Barracks under command of Brig.-Gen. H. D. B. Ketchen, and the
Mounted Police force was greatly strengthened while citizens were
unpleasantly reminded that in the similar and recent struggle at
Seattle 20,000 troops had been employed.   News also came from
other Western centres that the O.B.U. proposals had carried generally and that sympathetic strikes were possible all through the
country.

   In the Senate (May 21) Sir James Lougheed stated that the
Government had taken all necessary steps to maintain law and
order: "It has within the City a number of troops, sufficient, I
venture to say, to suppress any rioting or disturbances.   The
90th Regiment, the 79th, the 100th, the 106th, the Fort Garry
Horse and the 13th Battery—all these units, up to strength, are in
the City and, in addition, there are ample reserves made up of
civilian units.   In addition there are a number of Northwest
Mounted Police."   William Ivens, as head of the Strikers' Press
Committee, acted as Censor and Main Johnson, of the Toronto *Star*,
stated in a despatch on May 19 that he had either to submit it for
censorship or send the news from a point in Minnesota, which latter
he did.   According to a despatch in the Montreal *Star* of the same
date from Brandon, Mr. Ivens had addressed 3,000 strikers on the
18th and stated that a new Soviet government was being established, that it would shortly regulate all the cities of Canada and

would be instituted without violence. He added that two representatives from the City Council would be invited to the Trades Hall to sit on the Labour Directory with the members selected by the Strike Executive.

There was little concealment at first as to this intention and a *Free Press* fly-sheet of the 20th stated that at the above meeting Ernest Robinson made the following remarks: "I say that, geographically speaking, this strike will continue until it extends from Halifax to Victoria. We have received word from all intermediate points between here and the coast that Winnipeg is the leader, and that they will follow Winnipeg's example and do as we do. We have withdrawn labour from all industry, and it will stay withdrawn until the bosses realize that they cannot stand against the masses of labour. If we can control industrial production now, at this time, we can control it for all time to come, and we can control the Government of this country, too." Every effort was made during these days to persuade the Railway trainmen to join the strike and they could have tied up transportation and still further isolated the city; eventually, however, they refrained. On the 18th Mayor Gray issued a statement that water, milk, general food supply, fire and police protection would be supplied the citizens of Winnipeg. At the same time, he admitted that some anxiety might be felt that "we are securing these rights at the present time by the sufferance of some other authority than the constituted authority of the City government."

On the 19th *The Citizen* appeared as the organ of the Citizens' Committee of 1,000 which, meanwhile, had been organized to protect public rights as between the two main contestants—employers and employees. This Committee, with A. L. Crossin as Chairman, had headquarters in the Board of Trade building and it soon became a powerful body with 10,000 members. It undertook to provide volunteers for the fire brigade, to patrol the streets at night, to put a stop to an epidemic of false fire alarms that was one of the incidents of the early days of the strike, to help man the public utilities and to provide cars for the transport of special constables to any part of the city where trouble might arise. A first result of its operations was the withdrawal of the offensive "permit cards" by the Strike Committee; aided by an intimation from the Provincial Government to the theatres that as they were carrying on business under licenses issued by the Government, they had the choice of taking down the permit cards or of having their licenses cancelled. The second week of the strike saw a resumption of retail business activities of a minor sort but with continued restriction of wholesale trades. The chief point at issue had now developed into a question of the use or otherwise of the Sympathetic strike as a weapon to enforce the principle of Collective bargaining —or indeed any other principle. The Provincial and City authorities took the line that no settlement was possible until the sympathetic strike, as a menace to the citizens of the present and future, was declared off and put aside as a Labour weapon. The following partial statements, with two columns of similar announcements, from the Strike Committee, which appeared in the *Western Labour News* at this juncture showed who was governing the City:

Permission to handle troop trains by the Railways was granted.

A request was received from the United Press that messages be allowed over the wires to Canada and the U.S.A. subject to same being subjected to the Press Committee.   It was agreed that a Committee of four take charge of this matter, and that permission be granted, and that the same despatches be sent to the *New York Call.*

It was decided that no milk Companies should deliver cream during the strike.

Permission was granted to run the Deaf and Dumb School, providing nothing is done in matter of operating Normal School.

A further illustration was to be found in a letter from the Strike Committee, addressed on May 10 to the Oil Companies, Ltd., and announcing the following decision: "First, that all farmers be supplied with the necessary coal oil to meet their requirements; second, that the military, police, doctors, health officers and hospital cars must be supplied with the necessary gasoline for professional services; third, that chauffeurs, in industries which have permission to operate, must have a special permit from the Central Strike Committee." Commenting upon this, Mr. Premier Norris declared that the right and power of the City Council to govern the City was directly challenged in one of its most vital functions, and that further negotiations were, for the time, useless.   On the 22nd Mayor Gray issued a statement declaring that: "The constituted authorities are determined to stamp out the Bolsheviki or Red element in Winnipeg.   The town is open; all business may go ahead as in the past.   No one section of the public has any right to dictate food terms to any other section of the public.   This principle will be strictly adhered to by the constituted authorities." At the same time, Eaton's store began deliveries again and the delivery of ice was attempted.

Senator Robertson, Minister of Labour, and Mr. Meighen, Minister of the Interior, also arrived from Ottawa and, coincident with this R. B. Russell told a strike meeting that "a Dominion-wide settlement on the principle of Collective bargaining must be reached before the general strike here is called off," and that 26 Canadian cities were ready to join in the demand.   The *Citizen* responded with the declaration that: "This is not a strike; it is just plain, ugly revolution.   Two-thirds of the Unions now on strike have struck in defiance of their International, knowing that they sacrifice strike pay and that they lose all the benefits they have been paying for thirty or forty years."   The visiting Ministers soon got into conference with Provincial and Civic and Military authorities, Strikers' and Citizens' Committees; their first action was to issue a statement as to the Postal Service denied the citizens since May 15, without reference by employees to any grievance of their own and on a purely sympathetic issue. For this they had dislocated and paralyzed the public service, and were now told that those returning before 12 o'clock noon of the 26th inst. would be re-instated but all failing to resume their duties by that hour would be definitely refused a place in the Federal service. The Manitoba Government served a similar notice on its Telephone operators.

As a result, some of the Postal and Telephone employees who had struck returned to work, and a number of new employees were taken on to fill the places still left vacant, and these, with the volunteer workers, gave a certain measure of postal service—chiefly the business mail that had arrived in Winnipeg. A little later the railway mail clerks of the District went out but returned (May 31) on an intimation from Senator Robertson that they would forfeit their positions. The *Western Labour News* followed (May 23) with a declaration that capitalists must be made to stop profiteering, to reduce prices and to pay the War Debt: "Labour will have to compel action on their part. To do this it must organize its forces and then it must act in unison. That is the reason for the general strike. The fight is on. It overthrew the government in Russia, Austria, Germany, etc. It has compelled drastic innovations in Britain. Now it has Winnipeg in its grip." Meanwhile the *Free Press,* in its first new and partial issue since the 15th, had struck out, in a "Dream of the Winnipeg Soviet," and in terms of denunciation referred to the "Red" leaders and the extremists amongst the rank and file: "These gentry really dreamed of taking over the wholesale houses and similar institutions, doling out food and the necessities of life to their adherents, and compelling the rest of the community to go on their knees for the right to live"— along the lines of Lenine and Trotzky.

On May 26th the City Council by a vote of 9 to 5, passed a Resolution to prohibit the principle of the Sympathetic strike among Civic employees, with particular reference to the members of the Fire brigade and also declared that all employees who had gone on strike should be notified forthwith of their dismissal from the service of the city. At the same time, Mr. Robertson, Minister of Labour, sent a telegram of vital importance, to the Mayor of Calgary, in which the following statement was made: "Events have proved conclusively that the motive behind the general strike, was the purpose of assuming control and direction of industrial affairs; also municipal, Provincial and Federal activities so far as they were being carried on in this city, and with the avowed intention of extending that control in a wider field. I have no hesitation in stating that the One Big Union movement is the underlying cause of the whole trouble, and that the Winnipeg general strike deserves no sympathy or support from Labour organizations outside." In *The Citizen* of the 26th Hon. Arthur Meighen was reported as saying that: "It is up to the citizens of Winnipeg to stand firm and resist the efforts made here to overturn the proper authorities." Senator Robertson also declared in the same issue that: "I will make no effort to settle this strike until all public utilities which the Strike Committee has tied up are operating normally." He also issued a statement on this date as to Collective bargaining:

The employers, parties to the original disputes, the President of the Canadian Manufacturers' Association and the Citizens' Committee, as constituted since the strike occurred, all agree to the principle of Collective bargaining, namely, the right of any individual to belong to a Labour Union if he so desires and the right of employees to bargain with their employers concerning matters affecting any individual plant or industry. The Central Strike Committee, however, interpret the right of Collective bargaining to mean that the Central body have the power to approve or reject any agreement that may be satisfactory to the employer or classes of employers and their employees, which, if granted, would have the result of enabling any Central Committee, entirely outside the industry or craft affected, to dictate the acceptance or rejection of any agreement. It therefore means, instead of giving to the workmen in any individual plant or industry the right of collective bargaining with their employers, depriving them of the right and places them entirely in the hands of a Central body, which principle the Citizens' Committee of Winnipeg, the Provincial and Federal Governments agree cannot be accepted.

Events now moved rapidly and seriously. On the 28th the City Council urged the Manitoba Government to institute legislation making sympathetic strikes illegal in the Province and Mr. Meighen returned to Ottawa; at Ottawa (27th May) Sir Robert Borden announced in Parliament that "we are absolutely determined that law and order shall be maintained and, consequently, we are of the opinion that members of the Civil Service cannot be permitted to dislocate the public service under the conditions which have arisen." Meanwhile the Railway running trades offered to act as Mediators and negotiations were renewed after an interval of deadlock; on the 30th a procession of about 1,000 returned soldiers, sympathizing with the strikers, waited upon Hon. T. C. Norris and urged a Provincial law legalizing Collective bargaining as understood by the strikers and another Deputation of about 2,500 on the 31st were told that nothing could be done till the sympathetic strike was called off; the action of these men was repudiated by the G.W.V.A. and other Veteran Associations and on June 1st Senator Robertson returned to Ottawa.

Before doing so he stated that the end was in sight and added: "The promoters of the general strike in Winnipeg now sit in the ashes of their folly. In responding to the call to strike a majority violated and repudiated their obligations to their own trades unions and to their employers. Individually and collectively they wilfully discarded their agreements. In a general sympathetic strike the force is directed against the whole community, who are innocent of any responsibility for the offence. Public indignation is immediately aroused because of the inconvenience, loss and suffering imposed upon innocent people. Therefore, Sympathetic strikes must always fail. Socialism has long recognized that Trades unionism is an impossible bar to its revolutionary progress and now seeks through the One Big Union movement to undermine and destroy the Labour organization whose policies are to regard its obligations as sacred and inviolate.   Employers must not mistake the defeat of the general sympathetic strike as a defeat of organized labour.   On the contrary, Labour will emerge from the conflict strengthened from the wisdom gained from its experience.''

On June 2nd, 3,000 soldiers and strikers again paraded and waited upon the Premier with a polite request that he should resign as being incompetent to handle the strike situation; the Police Commission at this time ordered the members of the Force to sign a new contract precluding the Sympathetic strike and with dismissal as the result of a refusal—so with Firemen and other employees of the City Council.   On June 3rd, 700 out of 10,000 members of the G.W.V.A. passed a Resolution of strike sympathy and on the 4th the Executive of this body met, repudiated the above Resolution and declared that ''this Association can no longer remain neutral and is unqualifiedly ready to suppress alien and other agitators, Bolshevism, and any attempt to introduce Soviet principles in Canada''; on the 6th the Mayor issued a proclamation, in view of the tension of feeling existing, which forbade all parades; several hundred soldier-strikers decided to disobey and marched through the City led by R. E. Bray, one of the Strikers' Executive; they were met near the City Hall, however, by a solid line of constables stretching across Rupert street and, after a futile protest, retired.

To the Toronto *Star* of June 7 W. R. Plewman sent a despatch describing conditions at that time: ''Lawlessness and disorder are rampant throughout the city all day and every day.   Men and women are wantonly assaulted upon the streets.   Men, women and children are attacked and threatened while going about their lawful avocations.   Postmen, carrying mail to strikers' houses, are daily beaten.   Yesterday a mob went to the house of one postman, damaged fences, trampled the garden and terrorized the man's wife.   The Crescent and other creamery concerns have been forced to throw thousands of gallons of milk into the sewers because they were not allowed either to distribute it or to make it up into by-products.''   Following this the Mayor was assaulted by two strikers but not seriously injured.   At this time, also, an unpleasant situation developed by the Strike Committee again calling out the bread and milk workers; a situation partially met by volunteer labour and the distribution of milk from the schools.   Meanwhile Mounted Police Patrols were appearing in the streets; on the 9th the whole Winnipeg Police force was dismissed by the Commissioners because of their refusal to sign the pledge as to Sympathetic strikes and the striking Postal employees still out were also definitely dismissed.

The strike was nearing its end, however, and a staff correspondent of the New York *Tribune* on June 8th observed that ''the battle with the Soviet'' had been won and that 75 per cent. of the returned soldiers were now opposing it; that ''the fight against the Soviet idea which lay behind the attempt to tie up the whole city, though probably not half of the strikers knew this, has been long and bitter, and skillfully handled"; that Winnipeg had shown that it could live without "Labour" though it had lost millions of dollars, suffered great discomfort and had been badly scared.   On the 8th, also, Telephone operators were informed that only a portion could be re-instated.   The first street fight of the period took place on the 10th with Sergt. F. G. Coppins, v.c., acting as a special policeman, seriously injured in a riot which lasted three hours and was only ended by the Mounted Police with difficulty clearing the streets. The Mayor issued a warning that sterner measures would be used, if necessary, and on the 11th Chief Macpherson of the Police force was dismissed and replaced by C. H. Newton who proceeded to reorganize the whole body.   Meanwhile, on June 7th, the National Local of the Brotherhood of Railway Carmen had passed a Resolution declaring that "this organization goes on record as repudiating all those resolutions relating to Bolshevism and Spartacanism passed at the Calgary Convention; and that no alien enemy be admitted to this Union unless he can show credentials from the Alien Investigation Board."

At the same time, the Mediation Committee from the Railway Brotherhoods announced that they had so far been unsuccessful in settling the Metal trades dispute which had preceded the general strike.   The Metal trades managers, while accepting the principle of Collective bargaining, had declined to deal with the striking employees except through the various international organizations with which they were connected.   The Committee, however, kept at it. Meanwhile, sympathetic strikes had developed in Toronto where, by the middle of June, 12,000 men were out; in Brandon where many trades went out again and at Edmonton where a walk-out of local Unions took place on May 26 as the result of a strike vote; at Calgary on the same date, and after a vote of the Unions, a number struck, but, as in Edmonton, only partially.   The Regina Trades and Labour Council refused to issue a strike order and that of Saskatoon ordered their men out.   Nominally, these strikes were for the general 6-hour day proposed by the Calgary Convention; practically, they were in sympathy with Winnipeg.

This latter was the view taken by Vancouver where a Central Strike Committee, after the favourable vote of a majority of the Unions, ordered the men out in a "general strike" on June 3rd with this statement: "Will the workers of this country be willing to have their last vestige of freedom stripped from them? Winnipeg first, the rest of the cities in their turn, if the Winnipeg workers are defeated.   The issue is the right of the workers to Collective bargaining through whatever organization they deem best suited to their needs."   The Metal Trades Council in this city, in calling out their men, denounced Senator Robertson's definition of Collective bargaining and gave theirs as follows: "That the workers of any trade, craft, industry, profession or calling, having proved that they have organized the workers in that particular trade, craft, industry, profession or calling as they deem fit, to the extent of a majority of those so employed, shall be considered as an organized body of workers, and shall then be in a position to negotiate with the employers of that particular trade, craft, industry, profession or calling as to wages, hours of employment and general conditions of employment." Thirty organizations went out in part and a certain number were "exempted."

Meantime, another clash between strikers and constables occurred in Winnipeg on June 11th; a rumoured strike of the Railway men caused much worry and a small minority did go out on the 13th with considerable dislocation of train services as a result; on the 16th a substantial move toward settlement was made when the metal trades employers—the Vulcan Iron Works, Manitoba Bridge Co., and Dominion Bridge Co.—gave out for publication a statement defining the extent and character of the Collective bargaining they were prepared to see applied in the shops under their control and with approval by the Minister of Labour, the heads of the Railway Brotherhood organizations and the Western Managers of the Canadian railway Companies. The terms of this understanding included first a recapitulation of the Dominion Order-in-Council of July, 1918 which declared that: "All employees have the right to organize in trade unions and this right shall not be denied or interfered with in any manner whatsoever, and through their chosen representatives should be permitted and encouraged to negotiate with employers concerning working conditions, rates of pay, or other grievances." This, it was stated by E. C. Barrett, H. B. Lyall and N. W. Warren, representing the three Iron and Steel Companies of the original strike, would be generally accepted and they outlined their own views in elaboration of this point with the following clauses as the most important:

1. Employees shall not be discriminated against by employers, or other employees, on account of membership or non-membership in any craft or organization.

2. The members of the various trade organizations employed in the undersigned metal trades shops shall have the right to present and negotiate schedules covering wages, hours and working conditions, with individual employers or collectively with the employers of the metal trades.

3. The employees who are members of the various metal trade organizations in the contract shops (not including railway shops) shall have the right to elect representatives from among the employees of the firm or firms involved.

After agreements were reached in the way indicated, differences, adjustments and negotiations could proceed between the Company or Companies and (1) the Crafts' Committees concerned or (2) the representatives of all the Unions employed by the firm or firms involved, or (3) the Metal trades organizations in general; no strike or lockout to take place in the interim. The Railway Brotherhoods signed an approval of this understanding through their local chiefs and recommended its acceptance. Meantime, men were drifting back to work in various trades and on June 17 a large force of Mounted Police and constables arrested the leaders of the strike and rushed them out in motor-cars to Stony Mountain Penetentiary. The men concerned were Rev. William Ivens, Editor of the *Western Labour News* and Pastor of the Labour Church; R. B. Russell, Secretary of the Metal Trades Council; Alderman John Queen, Advertising Manager of the Labour journal; Alderman A. A. Heaps, R. E. Bray, and George Armstrong. Four Russians—alleged Bolshevists—were also arrested, including Moses Charitonoff, Editor of *The Working People,* a Ruthenian paper. The homes were searched and many documents and much seditious literature seized; the Labour Temple was, also, raided with similar results.

Indignation was expressed by all striking organizations throughout the country and by some not on strike; varied threats were heard of a general strike and the Ottawa Government received many telegrams; the Toronto *Star* (June 18) looked forward to "a great Strike Trial" and described the arrests as a very serious step which was bound to antagonize organized labour. Senator Robertson, in an interview, pointed out that the original dispute, apart from the Postmen, did not come under jurisdiction of the Government but that latterly the trainmen who went out had made the strike a national affair; the Sympathetic strike had also altered conditions and the Government had been gathering information as to whether or not the strike arose out of an ordinary industrial dispute, or whether other and sinister motives were involved. The result of this procedure in general and, no doubt, of the arrests in particular:

Amply warrant the conclusion that a seditious conspiracy was contemplated by a portion of the members of the Central Strike Committee who were believed to be revolutionary and dangerous in their tendencies. It being apparent that a reasonable settlement of the metal trades dispute would not result in settling the strike and because of the persistent and insidious propaganda and misrepresentation that were being spread abroad, especially among the railway employees with a view to extending the strike and utterly dislocating transportation, the Federal Department of Justice, through its authorized representatives, properly decided to take into custody those held to be responsible for seditious conspiracy.

The Minister added that in the correspondence seized was a letter addressed to Russell and acknowledging receipt of Bolshevik money. Tom Moore, President of the Trades and Labour Congress of Canada, stated at the same time that: "The Winnipeg labour leaders have not seen fit to communicate with the Dominion Congress during the strike, and they have departed from constitutional authority. When the strike was called without reference to constituted labour, we gave the labour men in Winnipeg a clear field—the matter was not in our hands." Following the arrest and disclosures of alleged sedition, Rev. William Ivens was, on June 19, expelled from the Methodist Ministry by the Manitoba Conference with a refusal to "locate" him. The *Labour News* at once declared that there would be no strike settlement until the prisoners were set free; they had merely "voiced the demands of the workers and endeavoured to organize the growing sentiment of revolt." In the Commons Sir R. Borden on June 20 stated that the men were arrested under the criminal law of the country, upon the charge that they had engaged in a seditious conspiracy, and they were placed under detention upon that charge. In Calgary on the same day W. A. Pritchard of Vancouver was arrested on the same charge as the others. In Winnipeg on the 23rd another O.B.U. leader, J. S. Woodsworth of Vancouver, a one-time Methodist minister who had taken Ivens' place on the *Western Labour News,* was also arrested and the journal, itself, suspended under orders from the Department of Justice. The *Western Star* was at once issued in its place.

A serious riot occurred in Winnipeg on the 21st with one rioter —a foreigner—killed and 33 other casualties of which 16 were in the Mounted Police. Great crowds had gathered to witness a proposed and illegal parade; after more or less serious mob actions and violence, the Riot Act was read by the Mayor while Mounted Police and Special Constables and a force of Militia were requisitioned to maintain the law and his proclamation; the Police then rode through or fired upon the angry, fighting mobs and gradually dispersed them, making about 100 arrests; after the worst was over, large military forces with machine guns appeared on the scene. A further Proclamation was issued, forbidding all public, open-air meetings until further notice. As to the fighting itself, there was no doubt of the reality and of its leadership by aliens. The Toronto *Telegram's* staff correspondent dealt with it as follows: "Big Austrians were everywhere, throwing and shooting, seemingly indifferent to danger, and resolved only upon dragging down some officer to death. . . . The red-coats had just swept into Main Street and galloped forward with pistols drawn. They were literally surrounded by yelling, shooting, throwing aliens. Half a dozen red coats were on the ground at once and their companions were themselves fighting for their lives with baseball bats."

In the Commons on June 23rd Hon. N. W. Rowell stated that: "The first shots were fired by the mob and the Mounted Police only fired in self-defence. The information we have is that the Police acted with great coolness, courage and patience." The Minister of Labour was in the City and the action of the authorities was approved by him and the Provincial Attorney-General, as well as the Mayor. The end practically came on June 25 when Ernest Robinson, Secretary of the Strike Committee, addressed the Provincial Premier as follows: "I am instructed by the Central Strike Committee to notify you that a Resolution has been passed officially declaring the Sympathetic strike off on Thursday, June 26, at 11 a.m. We now make formal application to your Government to appoint a Royal Commission having the widest powers of enquiry." How keen the feeling had become by this time was indicated by a summary of "three facts" in the *Free Press* of June 26:

The first fact which is not to be blinked, however unpleasant it may be to some people, is that the strike was wrong. It was a wanton, unnecessary assault upon the community by unwise labour leaders who were drunk with a sense of power and really imagined that they could force this community to yield to their dictatorship by the application of force. The second fact is that the strike was a progressive and increasing failure and that it has ended in the complete defeat of those responsible for it. It was defeated by the refusal of the authorities to abdicate their functions and by the public-spirited action of tens of thousands of citizens in backing up the authorities. The third fact is that the strike was not ended by an arrangement of any kind; it was not called off on conditions. The strike was called off because it was an open and notorious failure and no other course was open to those who were directing it.

The Hon. T. C. Norris at once agreed to the appointment of a Royal Commission and named Hon. H. A. Robson, K.C., for the position. He added that: ''The Government throughout has taken the position that the calling off of the Sympathetic strike was a condition precedent to any action on its part. To my mind, it has been abundantly proved that the general sympathetic strike is wrong and futile, that the lesson has been learned and that such a strike is not likely to recur in the future.'' His Government promised an immediate programme of road-building, telephone and hydro-electric construction which would eliminate the danger of unemployment. Many of the workers returned at once to work though many Civic and Government and other positions had been filled permanently; on July 2 more seditious documents were seized in a raid on the Labour Temple and the homes of 30 Winnipeg Socialists and Ukrainian Social-Democrats; on the same day the Metal workers returned to work and so did the building trades; on the 3rd R. J. Johns gave himself up, and F. J. Dixon, M.L.A., who had kept out of prominent association with the strike, but whose views and efforts were well known, with the notorious Sam Blumenthal, were also under arrest and bail.

These men completed the list of those whom the authorities believed guilty of sedition and who were to come up for trial—Queen, Heaps and Bray had been out on bail for some time and were in Ontario telling the people their view of the strike. In Toronto on July 8 a tour of Ontario was announced; William Ivens, also on bail, was again acting as Editor of the Labour News; at Moose Jaw on July 11 J. S. Woodsworth was reported as saying (Globe despatch) that F. J. Dixon should be at Ottawa ''because the Federal authorities control the military and the courts, and Labour is not going to get what it wants until it in some way gets control of the military and the courts''; an interesting sidelight was given by A. A. Heaps at Montreal on July 12 when he declared that ''we were having beautiful weather and we were having a beautiful strike, when the citizens butted into the game and began to attempt to assert their authority.''

Meanwhile, in an elaborate letter written on June 24 by President Moore of the Trades and Labour Congress to E. Robinson, Secretary of the Winnipeg T. and L. Council, he had presented very clearly the attitude of organized labour toward the Strike and its leaders. Mr. Moore first dealt with the general insubordination of the Winnipeg Council; its refusal to call a meeting of trade unionists for him to address on any of three days—May 10, 11 or 12; the refusal of the Council and of Russell and Armstrong to give him any information, when in Winnipeg on those dates; the open repudiation of the autonomy of each craft union to decide for itself whether its members would take part in a Sympathetic strike; the repudiation of the control of International executives as to granting or withholding sanction for a strike by their Winnipeg local unions and a repudiation of the Trades Congress and its Executive.

The Congress, therefore, could do nothing in the Strike but, as to its further evolution of policy, he was explicit: "The principle involved in a Sympathetic strike is one contrary to our policy, involving as it does the putting on one side agreements entered into between respective trade unions, and thus destroying the principle of Collective bargaining." Future action depended upon "(1) passing of Resolutions by your Council that they renew their allegiance to the Trades and Labour Congress and its principles; (2) that they advise all local unions to place themselves in the hands of their International executive, agreeing to abide by the decision of such Executive and the constitution of their respective craft unions; (3) that they repudiate any connection with the O.B.U. and its policies of massed action; (4) that the Trades Council and all local unions affected by the strike pass Resolutions pledging themselves to observe the inviolability of agreements entered into between workers and their employers; (5) that the full autonomy to decide their own action according to the laws laid down in their respective constitutions shall be restored by the Trades and Labour Council of Winnipeg to each local union affiliated therewith." Mr. Moore added the statement that "repudiation of self-constituted authority turns organized effort into mob rule."

Echoes of the Strike: The Sedition Trial. On July 3rd the 13 men—R. B. Russell, Wm. Ivens, R. J. Johns, W. A. Pritchard, John Queen, A. A. Heaps, G. Armstrong, R. E. Bray, Blumenberg and Charitonoff and three other Russians—who had been held on a charge of conspiring to execute seditious intentions, were remanded in Police Court and bail for those out on $2,000 was raised to $4,000 each. By July 22nd, when the preliminary hearings began before Police Magistrate R. M. Noble, the number had sifted down to the first 8 named above with F. J. Dixon and J. S. Woodsworth up for separate trial. The evidence turned chiefly upon revolutionary talk and advocacy with the differences between a sedition which invoked, or paved the way to, violence and a theoretical advocacy which led nowhere in particular. It involved the alleged Bolshevism shown in speeches by all the men on trial at different times, before and during the strike, and their relations to the One Big Union which, it was claimed, involved the introduction of the

Soviet system and the rule of the nation by and for the labouring class alone. Much proof was offered, also, as to the power wielded or attempted by the Strike Committee and as to its practical usurpation of Civic authority. In the proceedings which followed E. J. McMurray, K.C., was Counsel for the prisoners and A. J. Andrews, K.C., and J. B. Coyne, K.C., for the Crown.

The testimony was both interesting and important but only a few outstanding statements can be given here. Mayor C. F. Gray swore on July 28 that the city was practically under the control of the Strike Committee from June 10 to June 20; that R. B. Russell had admitted early in the strike that the iron-masters were willing to bargain on a collective basis; that Ald. John Queen had declared against constituted authority at a Committee meeting in the City Hall; that R. B. Russell had stated, at a meeting of the City Council, that the Police were left on the street by permission of the Strike Committee. On July 31 documents seized at Calgary, Edmonton and Vancouver were put in evidence including a letter of Jan. 3rd, 1919, from R. B. Russell to J. R. Knight, an Alberta leader of the O.B.U., which said: "I see arising out of the unemployment, now beginning to make itself manifest, the most glorious opportunity to show the plug worker that the only solution to the question is by continually pointing to him the situation in Russia." Another of Nov. 29, 1919, referred to a coming Alberta Labour Conference and added: "You can readily realize we could pack it with reds and no doubt start something. Yours in revolt, R. B. Russell." Writing to V. R. Midgley, the Vancouver leader of the O.B.U., Knight said on Apr. 24, 1919: "The meeting was unanimous for the O.B.U., and the vote will be at least 75 per cent. in favour. Russell, Johns, et al. are on the job day and night, and are sending a steady stream of propaganda literature throughout the east."

W. E. Davis, of Minneapolis, testified to hearing Rev. Wm. Ivens on May 16, the day after the strike was called, refer to the Committee's control of everything and add: "The storm is about to break and this time the lightning is about to strike upward instead of downward. I think the Parliament Buildings on Kennedy street would make a good Labour Temple, and the way things are going we will soon move in." Various letters seized in the Winnipeg raids were read with such statements as: "Report satisfactory from Red point of view; We want to use some Russian methods; Capture reins of Government," and others signed "Yours for Revolution," "Yours in revolt," "Yours for Socialism." The names of Russell, Johns and Pritchard were the most frequently mentioned of the defendants in these propaganda letters. A policeman and detective, W. H. McLaughlin, testified on Aug. 5th as to a scheme to seize the Barracks with the help of 4,000 men which was described to him by R. E. Bray and known to Ald. Heaps; notes for a speech, in Ivens' hand-writing, were put in evidence on Aug. 12—seized at his home—which read: "Still the workers cling to constitutional reform. This in spite of the fact that the capitalists control the military and use it against the worker. The only alternative—revolution by any means necessary, bloody or bloodless.''

The hearings concluded on this date and the 8 leaders were committed for trial at the October Assizes; on Aug. 14th bail was refused by Mr. Justice J. D. Cameron upon the ground that the men had broken their promises, when released on bail the first time, to abstain from taking an active part in the labour unrest and had, by public speeches and other activities, carried on a campaign of an indiscreet nature; at the same time it was announced that Sam. Blumenberg and Moses Charitonoff would be deported to Russia—for reasons not very obvious or clear this was not done. A meeting with indignant speeches followed (Aug. 17) addressed by Rev. Dr. S. G. Bland and J. S. Woodsworth who dealt at length with the evil work of those who were trying to ''crush the Russian experiment in democracy''—Dr. Bland denouncing the refusal of bail and urging a better treatment of foreigners. In Toronto on the same day, Mrs. George Armstrong, wife of one of the Winnipeg strike leaders, echoed this thought in different form: ''They say one of our strike leaders was a German. I don't care what a man is if he's white under the skin and a worker. The only alien enemy we have in Canada is the capitalist and the strike-breaker.''

Strenuous efforts followed to obtain the release of these men and at a mass-meeting in Winnipeg on Aug. 31st F. J. Dixon, M.L.A., declared that a 24-hour strike would be called throughout Canada on Sept. 17th; many telegrams of protest were sent to the Government and the United Mine Workers at Sydney, N.S., threatened to tie up the local mines. Eventually, the men were released on bail and at once held meetings of denunciation and O.B.U. advocacy; in Winnipeg on Sept. 14 a meeting was addressed by six of the released prisoners and Resolutions passed condemning Judge Cameron and urging the withdrawal of the Robson Commission; Mr. Ivens, the Strike Censor, denounced the Dominion war censorship and described the Canadian press as capitalistic sheets which could not tell the truth while R. B. Russell declared that the O.B.U. would soon be organized amongst Canadian railwaymen.

Following this the Trades and Labour Congress went on record at Hamilton on Sept. 27 as demanding a fair and impartial trial for the Winnipeg general strike leaders; Wm. Ivens was, on Oct. 6, nominated by a Winnipeg Convention as the Labour candidate for Mayor but retired in favour of S. J. Farmer; he was in Toronto, Montreal and Ottawa a little later collecting defence funds for the coming trial and addressed crowded meetings. J. S. Woodsworth spoke at Calgary, on Oct. 29, and declared that: ''Although the British flag flies over this country, most of it is owned by Wall street financiers. I am not worrying as to whether they keep me in the Penitentiary or not—we'll win anyway. I don't think that the workers of this country will let us stay in anyway''; at Winnipeg on his return Mr. Ivens was welcomed by a large meeting addressed also by W. W. Lefeaux, Assistant Editor of *One Big Union Bulletin*, and F. J. Dixon, M.L.A.; in the current Mayoralty elections Mayor Gray, standing for re-election, declared (Nov. 5) that every man on the Labour ticket was an O.B.U. member.

On Nov. 26 the indictment against the 8 strike leaders came before Mr. Justice T. L. Metcalfe and it was decided to try R. B. Russell first. The testimony was of the same nature as in the preliminary hearings, with 1,700 documents submitted which had been seized in various raids and with Robert Cassidy, K.C., and E. J. McMurray, K.C., acting for the Defence, and A. J. Andrews, K.C., and J. B. Coyne, K.C., for the Crown. Various letters between Russell and J. R. Knight which had been seized at Edmonton on June 1st, were put in as evidence on Nov. 29. One written by Russell early in the year was typical: "I expect we will now be confronted with the horrors of peace and it is to be hoped that the Reds will wake up now and get in all the propaganda that can be expounded 24 hours per day. I suppose you will have seen the trouble we are having with the Charitonoff case and as we have something like a bill of $1,000 to date I hope you will be able to get around and dig up something from the slaves who come within your grasp."

In another dated Jan. 3rd, 1919, and addressed to C. E. Stevenson, Dominion Secretary of the Socialist Party at Vancouver, Russell said: "I have also good news from Toronto. The Machinists' Union held a Convention about three weeks ago and decided to issue a paper. The Comrade who edited the *Marxian Socialist* up until the time it was banned has been appointed Editor and the intentions are to get the same line of stuff off so you can figure the rest yourself." All through the correspondence extreme Socialism, the O.B.U., Bolshevism and the Reds were interchangeable terms. To get control of the Trades and Labour Council for the Reds was one aim clearly specified; that they had such control in Calgary, Edmonton and Vancouver was indicated; that Russell and R. J. Johns finally obtained it in Winnipeg, late in 1918, and held it during the strike was proved by various witnesses. Mr. Andrews stated for the Crown (Dec. 4) that his object was to prove that the intentions of Russell and those connected with him were: (1) To stir up strikes; (2) to set class against class with the object of starting a revolution; (3) to bring about in Canada a Soviet form of Government by means of a general strike.

J. Edward Bird, one of the Defence counsel, stated that they would endeavour to prove that the arrest of the eight strike leaders was ordered for the purpose of breaking up the strike and not as a result of any criminal offence; Mr. Bird and others, also, sought to show that it was really the Socialist Party which was being tried. Various letters showed the close association of Russell with J. F. Maguire, an official of the Socialist Party at Edmonton and Tom Beattie of the United Mine Workers at Calgary. Maguire wrote to Russell on Jan. 12, 1919, that: "We have just returned from the Alberta Federation of Labour Convention. . . . We gave the Bolsheviki the finest boost that has been accomplished for some time. Wherever possible, get Reds to be the delegates (at Calgary). We must plan to have a bumper meeting when we all are in Calgary, and then, surely, this is one place that we can paint Red.'' Beattie wrote Stevenson that: ''The remedy, we all know, is to capture the reins of government, etc., but how? Certainly not by the ballot. The only way we will ever get anywhere is by the use of force. The time is coming when there will be riots and petty little revolutions here and there all over the country.''

On Dec. 5th Sergt. F. W. Zaneth testified in Court that, while posing as a Socialist at Calgary: ''Joe Knight of Edmonton told me that the Ordnance Department of District 18 had received a carload of rifles, and added: 'We should keep our eyes on them, as we may need them some day.' '' A speech by J. R. Knight at the Calgary Convention was also put in as showing the connection of these different leaders with O.B.U. and Bolshevism: ''The Socialists are distinguished from the other working class parties by this only: (1) in the national struggle of the proletarians of the different countries, they point out and bring to the front the common interests of the entire proletariat, independently of all nationality; (2) in the various stages of development which the struggle of the working class against the *bourgeoise*, have to pass through, they always and everywhere represent the interests of the movement as a whole.'' Bolshevism he defined as a world-wide movement and as the beginning of practical Socialism: ''It is a mighty achievement, and by working hard among our fellow-men you will begin to realize that you must take similar steps yourselves. It is only when you are going to command and control the means of wealth production, socialize the resources of this world, that you will have command of democracy.''

Much evidence was adduced as to privations under the conditions imposed by the Strike Committee. L. H. Parker testified on July 23 that he was refused milk for his dying wife by the Crescent Creamery until he got a permit from the Strike Committee. James Carruthers of this Company stated on Dec. 8 that he wrote letters to the Trades and Labour Council and the Strike Committee asking consideration for the innocent babes, the sick in the hospitals and the wounded soldiers, who would suffer greatly if the milk supply were cut off; that to these letters no attention had been paid. Dr. M. H. Gardiner, a Dentist, on the same day, testified that he had asked consideration for patients of doctors and dentists in connection with the cutting off of the water supply but was told by the Strike Committee that it could not make exceptions—''that it was inevitable when great issues were involved that some should endure hardship and even death.'' Extracts, on the 12th, were read by Mr. Andrews from the Winnipeg *Strike Bulletin* of which the following is one: ''The great underlying problem of the Labour movement is to transfer control of wealth production from the parasite masters to the actual producers—the working class. That is what the One Big Union proposes to do. That this One Big Union proposition is revolutionary, going to the very root of the

matter, is apparent from the attitude of the capitalists themselves."
Many witnesses testified as to many speeches by the other men under
arrest, as well as Russell, with a distinctly seditious tone indicated.

The Defence opened on Dec. 16 with a claim that one of the
Crown's witnesses named Dashaluk had been bribed with a promise
of $500 for his evidence and with a protest by J. E. Bird against
the use of catchwords such as Bolshevism—a subject of reproach,
as he put it, often becoming later a badge of honour.   The Citizens'
Committee was placed on the same level as the Strike Committee;
if one was a Soviet so was the other.   R. B. Russell testified (Dec.
17) that he was a Socialist and a supporter of the O.B.U.; that the
principle underlying the latter was the amalgamation of various
trades in one industry, otherwise known as industrial unionism;
that a sympathetic strike was only held on grievances involving big
issues and its origin in some dispute arising between the employer and employees over a principle which, when it is seen by the
unions generally as about to be defeated, is made to include all
unions; that he had tried to arrange a meeting to commemorate
Luxemberg and Liebnecht, the German Spartacists, but that the
Police interfered; that Armstrong and Johns were members of the
Socialist Party but not Heaps, Queen or Ivens; that force was advocated by the I.W.W. but not by Socialists and that, under certain circumstances, he approved of the Russian Soviet system.   Mr.
Russell admitted and defended as historically accurate the follow-
ing from the Preface to the 4th edition of the Manifesto of the
Socialist Party of Canada:

> One more illusion, indeed, we may put from our minds, if we ever had it
> —that of a peaceful revolution.   The master class, capa le of sending millions
> to slaughter in the field for the extension of its profitsb is capable of making
> examples of an industrial city for the retention of its property in the means
> of production.   To expect them to give up their ownership with any good
> grace is to credit them with grace beyond reason.

He also stated that "a general strike, if successful, must
paralyze all industries."   Another item of testimony was that
"people had little enough at present in the way of property as the
C.P.R. owns most of the property in this country."   This statement
he reiterated!   On Dec. 19 F. J. Dixon, M.L.A., stated that
the reports and assertions of witnesses as to Ivens' speech regarding Parliament Buildings and the Labour Temple were false; he
admitted that during the strike he had written numerous articles
for the *Western Labour News*.   The strike, he said, in common with
all strikes, was intended to paralyze industry.   The more inconvenience caused the more effective was the strike.   James Winning
followed (Dec. 21) and admitted that the O.B.U. had tried to get
control of the Trades and Labour council, that a vote was taken on
the matter and that the O.B.U. won.   Other witnesses were heard
and the case went to the jury on Dec. 24th.

In a 4-hours' summing up Judge Metcalfe spoke of sitting on
the case day and night for 23 days, enlarged upon points of law
involved in the indictment and declared that it was illegal for

men to conspire to commit acts that would injure the general citizen; stated that intimidation during a strike and picketing were illegal under the Canadian law.   He added: "An intention to incite people to take power in their own hands or an intention to cause a tumultuous riot, is a seditious intention. If the words used are calculated to cause a disturbance, the speaker of them must be held responsible for whatever follows as a result of his speech."   He reviewed the evidence as to all the 8 leaders and clearly indicated the opinion that most of them were guilty of sedition.   A. J. Andrews in his speech had already urged the fact of wide conspiracy, as proven by the correspondence, words and acts of the Winnipeg men and others.   He named Knight and Berg of Edmonton, Stevenson and Kavanagh of Vancouver, Cassidy, of North Bay, and the other seven accused.   He said there was a common understanding between them all which, from the evidence the jury could not fail to see.   Extracts from Socialist organs and leaflets and pamphlets, the *Red Flag*, the *Socialist Bulletin*, and the *Strike Bulletin*, of several cities were read to prove a Dominion-wide propaganda.

Mr. Cassidy spoke 3½ hours for the Defence and strove to prove that the Strike was for legitimate labour reasons only; the Jury, after a short period, brought in a unanimous verdict of guilty, under the terms of the indictment: (1) For seditious conspiracy in general form and (2) in specific form with overt acts at Walker Theatre meeting, Jan. 22, 1918, at Majestic Theatre, Jan. 19, 1919, in helping to form the O.B.U., in participation at the Calgary Convention, publication and distribution of seditious literature and the Winnipeg general strike; (3) conspiracy to carry into effect a seditious intention by bringing about an unlawful Sympathetic strike; (4) seditious conspiracy to organize an unlawful combination or association of workmen and employees; (5) for an effort to bring about a formation of an unlawful combination or association for the purpose of controlling all industries, and of obtaining property belonging to others and of compelling compliance with the demands of such association (O.B.U.); (6) conspiracy to bring about, unlawfully, changes in the constitution and to enforce the Soviet form of government in Canada by unlawful means similar to those employed in Russia; (7) for trying to commit a "common nuisance" by bringing about a general strike.

The sentence was 2 years in the Penitentiary.   Protests were strenuous and immediate.   At the Labour Church, Winnipeg, (Dec. 28) Wm. Ivens declared that: "In the sight of a judge and jury Bob Russell is a condemned, guilty man, but in the sight of Almighty God he is innocent," while a man in the audience rose and said that "Jesus Christ was a martyr and so is Bob Russell!"   Alex. Ross, M.L.A., Calgary, an opponent of the O.B.U. and the Socialists, declared that: "The sentence passed on Russell can only be regarded by Labour as a challenge.   It is the first time an active member of a labour union has been sentenced because of his advocacy of a sympathetic strike.   The strike is our only weapon of defence, whether sympathetic or otherwise." In Montreal on the same date J. S. Woodsworth denounced the verdict and sentence and described the O.B.U. as merely an industrial organization; stated that "the one compensation for being in gaol was that one acquired the trust of the labouring people"; declared that no free speech existed to-day, and that the great industries, monopolized by a few in-dividuals, constituted but a new form of slavery. The case went on appeal to another Court and Tom Moore, President of the Trades and Labour Congress, refused to comment on it but declared that: "Sympathetic strikes accomplish nothing. The process of direct action by organized labour antagonizes even those who are friendly to Labour. Direct action is negative action and invariably brings the workers into conflict with their own friends." The summar-ized opinion of the Toronto *Globe* was that there ought obviously to be a limit to the right of strike by persons discharging absolutely essential public functions, provided they were guaranteed redress of their own grievances—by fair and impartial adjudication.

Echoes of the Strike: In Winnipeg. The Royal Commission appointed by the Provincial Government and composed of H. A. Robson, K.C., met on July 24 and adjourned to permit of Labour's case being fully prepared, with T. J. Murray, K.C., as Counsel and C. P. Wilson, K.C., appointed by the Government to also act for Labour. As the Commissioner put it: "It is certainly impossible to believe that the whole vast number of strikers were seditious and those who disclaim that charge should take advantage of the opportunity and do so publicly." On the 30th Labour was ready with its case and H. R. Maybank, a C.P.R. yardman, showed how nearly the transportation interests of the West were to being tied up when 86 per cent. of the running trades had voted to join the strike but the International Grand Lodge at Cleveland had refused its consent. James Winning declared that Labour was very much dissatisfied with existing conditions, largely owing to unemploy-ment, high cost of living, profiteering and refusal by some employ-ers to recognize Collective bargaining, as well as inaction on the part of the Government. Reports of large profits being made by industrial concerns had increased this discontent, and it was felt that the greater portion of such profits should go into wages. He stated that the Union men were disappointed because the Govern-ment did not take over railways, packing plants and other indus-tries of that kind. The Enquiry proceeded for some time but no Report was presented during the year.

On July 29 the long struggle in the Winnipeg Trades and Labour Council between moderates and extremists came to a head in the decision of a stormy meeting of 120 members to join the One Big Union. The total membership was about 350, James Win-ning was in the chair, the standing vote showed an unstated major-ity. An O.B.U. constitution was then read and accepted and the Winnipeg Central Labour Council constituted; W. A. Pritchard, O.B.U. organizer, was present as was R. B. Russell and the propèrty of the old Council was turned over by Resolution to the O.B.U. R. A. Rigg, as Deputy in Winnipeg of the Dominion Trades and Labour Congress, intimated that the Trades Council would still carry on and the new organization be repudiated; on Aug. 1st he re-organized the Trades and Labour Council at a meeting, with 92 delegates present, representing 8,000 workers who adhered to the International Union; James Winning was re-elected President and Ernest Robinson Secretary. Mr. Winning resigned a few weeks later and was succeeded by A. G. Cowley. The two organizations then settled down to a persistent fight for membership and Labour approval with the Trades Council established in its old quarters in the Labour Temple and the *Western Labour News* again directly under its control. The O.B.U. were in the same building, however. Wm. Ivens was at once dismissed from his charge of the journal and Ald. W. B. Simpson appointed its Manager. On Aug. 19 both bodies protested against the refusal of bail for the strike leaders.

On Aug. 20th 5,000 men and women met and turned the Citizens' Committee of strike days into the Canadian Citizens' League. A. K. Godfrey presided and A. L. Crossin presented a platform for the new body which he described as "the vital business of every man and every woman who believes to-day in the preservation of our social life as organized, but now threatened by the doctrine of force insidiously spread over this country." The temporary officers chosen included Isaac Pitblado, K.C., as President and Mr. Godfrey 1st Vice-President; the officers formally chosen on Sept. 22nd were as follows: President, Dr. J. Halpenny; Vice-Presidents, A. K. Godfrey, Dr. W. F. Taylor and Major N. K. McIvor; Hon. Secretary, Fletcher Sparling; Hon. Treasurer, J. C. Waugh. The Platform was as follows:

(a) The inculcation of the best Canadian ideals; the cultivation of respect for Canadian law; the proper maintenance of constitutional government and the combatting of all forms of propaganda tending to subvert our established Canadian institutions.

(b) To create a deeper interest in public affairs, particularly in those Civic departments essential to the protection of life and property, and to create among the citizens a greater interest in the selection of Civic representatives and officials.

(c) To study economic principles as they relate to general employment and industrial questions; to disseminate reliable information on this subject and to cultivate a better understanding and closer relationship between employer and employee.

(d) To advocate and assist the formation of a National Organization throughout Canada.

The Mayoralty election which followed was fought solely on the Strike issue with S. J. Farmer—on retirement of Wm. Ivens—as the Labour candidate and C. F. Gray seeking re-election. Mr. Farmer's Committee was headed by F. J. Dixon, M.L.A., and Mayor Gray told a workers' gathering of 3,000 men, who would not listen to him, on Oct. 20 that: "I want to tell you of my intention to run again so that you can organize your strongest against me. I'll fight you like hell.'' To the press he added: ''I will go to places where I have been invited and be glad to attack the Reds on their own battleground.'' He said that much criticism had been levelled against him because of his attitude during the general strike and he desired that the whole people of the city should have the opportunity of either vindicating or disapproving his action. This courageous course made the issue clear—Sympathetic strikes and the O.B.U. against International Labour Unions, ordinary Labour policy and the ordinary citizen. Behind the Mayor was the new Citizens' League which stated the issue on Nov. 19:

> The Radical-labour candidates stand for class rule in the administration of the affairs of the city. The Citizens' candidates say the people shall rule, regardless of class. Between these two theories of Civic government there is no possibility of compromise. These candidates of the Radical-labour element and their supporters proclaim that 'this contest is the second chapter of the strike,' that their supporters must 'vote as you struck.' The same forces are behind them that stood behind the O.B.U. with their Red followers in the strike last summer. They glory in the turmoil their efforts provoked in June. That is the issue they have again raised. They want no other and the citizens accept the challenge.

Mr. Farmer, himself, resented being called a ''Red'' and had not usually been classed with the extremists; he was chiefly known as a Single-tax advocate and anti-Conscriptionist. All but two of his Aldermanic slate were, however, supporters of the O.B.U. and all that it meant; they fought the issue under the name of the Independent Labour Party which the *Free Press* and the League and the Mayor declared to be *camouflage* for the One Big Union. It was the hottest election in Winnipeg's history and the issue was carried into the School Board contest as well as that of the City Council with the claim of the Citizens' League that the success of Mr. Farmer and his friends would mean ''the instant affiliation of those public servants, charged with the protection of our lives and property, with a class organization pledged to desert its post in defiance of all obligations, at any and all times, on the beck and call of the autocrats of the O.B.U.'' The result on Nov. 29 was not absolutely conclusive but it settled the issue for the moment. Mr. Gray was re-elected by 15,630 votes to 12,514 but the Council was equally divided between Citizens' League and Labour with a casting vote to the Mayor. The former body elected F. O. Fowler, ex-Mayor F. H. Davidson and 2 others, with 3 sitting on a two-year term; Labour elected John Queen and 2 others with 4 sitting on a two-year term; on the School Board the Labourites only carried one seat. A curious feature of such a campaign was the fact that out of 60,000 registered voters not 30,000 fulfilled their duties of citizenship.

Echoes of the Winnipeg Strike: Trouble Elsewhere. So far as the Winnipeg strike was due to general unrest it had duplicated conditions all over Canada; so far as it was due to deliberate propaganda the same statement applies. Reference has been made to the strikes which were a more or less direct result of the Winnipeg struggle—Toronto, Calgary, Ottawa, Brandon, Saskatoon, Vancouver. The most important of these were the Toronto and Vancouver incidents. In the former city the Metal Trades Council ordered the strike of May 1st in sympathy with their fellow-craftsmen of Winnipeg. R. C. Brown, President, and others concerned were very frank in their statements and, according to *The Globe*, a mass-meeting on the 1st heard outspoken language from James Simpson, the Socialist leader, in Toronto: "He demanded the complete destruction of the Capitalistic system 'in its entirety' and declared that the voice of the working masses was becoming more insistent every day, and that soon, very soon, if the working people organized, the Utopia of absolute freedom for all, plenty of the good things of life for the humblest workers, and the crushing of present-day 'democracy' would have arrived." Russia was specified as an illustration of the advance of Socialism and the foreigners and aliens in Toronto as a product of real brotherhood.

John McDonald, Vice-President of the Metal Trades Council, declared that his one desire was to see the One Big Union behind the Council, for if an organization of its character was bad for the employing class it must be good for the workers! He added that Socialists held the chief posts in local unions because the workers realized their knowledge of economic problems. The editorial comment of *The Globe* (May 3rd) upon the inception of this strike was succinct: "Organized labour in Toronto, though the great majority of its members have no Bolshevist sympathies and believe in adhering to the methods of the past, is being imposed upon by glib mischief-makers who hate trade unionism, which they regard as an outworn device retarding the 'proletarian' dictatorship that they would set up by violence if they dared." Included in the metal workers were machinists, moulders, engineers, boilermakers, shipbuilders, blacksmiths, and others to a total on May 5th of 5,000; 11,022 other trades were awaiting settlements between their Unions and the employers with 4,150 still under standing agreements.

R. C. Brown, for the Metal Workers, stated the issue as follows on May 16: "The Metal Trades Council of Toronto, representing several of the basic industries of the city, urge Government adoption of the 8-hour day immediately. We speak for the workers engaged in these industries, and we believe we speak for practically the entire rest of the working citizenship of Canada, comprising 6,000,000 people, more or less." In the next few weeks every trade was restless, strikes were in the air, O.B.U. talk was heard widely and, on May 17, at a Queen's Park demonstration, Mr. Brown went so far as to say that: "The capitalists will get such a dose of Winnipegitis before this is over that they will never forget it." A message came from Ernest Robinson, the Winnipeg strike leader, on the 23rd, declaring the situation there to be "a fight to the finish," stating that "an ultimatum has been laid down to the Civic and Provincial authorities," and urging Toronto to take a general strike vote and put it into effect.

On May 28 a deputation of 23 men representing the City Council, the Employers' Association, the Metal Trades, and other interests, waited by appointment on the Premier at Ottawa and discussed the issue of an 8-hour day and 44-hour week. By this time also, another one had developed, as in Winnipeg, and recognition of the Metal Workers' Council, which had been organized by six crafts in the Metal trades within the past year, was demanded; Collective bargaining had been recently introduced as a vital question. The delegation to Ottawa failed to reach any agreement; in Toronto, meantime, a General Committee had been formed of 15 men representing as many trades; on May 29 they issued a statement that "the general Sympathetic strike called for May 30th" would exclude certain classes of workers, with the curious combination of bakers, policemen, fire-fighters, sewage plant operators, theatrical stage employees, public school teachers, College professors, clergy of all denominations, doctors and all hospital help, in order that "no harm shall befall the general public." It was added that "the above mentioned workers have received notice from the General Strike Committee that they are to remain at their posts."

Of this Strike Committee Harry Gray, machinist, was Chairman and 14 of the members were British born—chiefly English. On the 29th, also, the Committee turned down an offer from the Employers' Association to arbitrate the 44-hour week claim; on the 30th about 8,000 men altogether were out with 10,000 more reported as undecided and a total of 25,000 in the city; the strikers included 4,500 metal workers, 2,500 garment workers, 1,000 Massey-Harris men with about 230 factories closed down and 50 shops but it was nothing like a general strike and, from the Winnipeg standpoint, was a failure from the first. Mayor T. L. Church at once issued a request for law and order: "The Government should force all parties to settle these industrial troubles in the usual way by conciliation and arbitration. Law and order must be preserved at all costs and the public will be protected." A new journal, the *Ontario Labour News*, declared that what the workers got would have to be fought for: "The strike which is taking place to-day represents a new phase in working-class organization—a desire not only to increase wages, but a protest against a system that allows men to live in luxury whilst others groan." The strike was, however, a failure as a general one though the Street Railway Union of 2,200 men went out on June 22 by a vote of 1,370 to 75 and stayed out until July 4, when they returned to work with a new wage schedule; this left about 8,000 men from the Metal trades and Garment makers still on strike but the latter went back after a while and, though the Metal workers did not, as a Union, return to work during the year, many of the men did so.

Meanwhile the sympathetic or general strikes in the West had not been very successful. On July 27 the charter of District 18 of the United Mine Workers of America was revoked on account of its connection with O.B.U. organization and views; the strike, however, which had been standing since May 24 continued until the middle of August. The rule under which expulsion took place was as follows: "Any member accepting membership in the Industrial Workers of the World, the Working Class Union, or any other dual organization not affiliated with the American Federation of Labour, shall be expelled from membership in the United Mine Workers of America." A settlement of this issue was reached on Dec. 20 and under it the miners received an increase of 14 per cent. in wages but only members of the U.M.W. were to be allowed to work in the mines of District 18. Senator Robertson took an active part in this matter in order to meet the imperative demand for coal. He explained at this time that it was obviously impossible to recognize two organizations as having jurisdiction to negotiate wage agreements for the same workmen; that the U.M.W. of A. had a well-established reputation for respecting and fulfilling agreements; that the O.B.U. had, by its acts and the utterances of its leaders, indicated no tendency to respect or fulfill any contractural obligations, and was wholly unreliable and untrustworthy.

In Calgary, itself, the City employees twice voted against supporting a sympathetic strike and, by June 12, the C.N.R. and Dominion Express strikers there had returned to work with negotiations going on as to a few others, who were still out, while conditions in the City were normal. In Edmonton, out of 37 Unions, only seven were from the beginning in sympathy with Winnipeg; about 1,600 men were involved and many Unions, which did go out partially, returned to work within a few hours or days—dairy workers, firemen, cooks and waiters, city employees, etc.; by June 18 only six trades were still out and they gradually returned to work. The Vancouver strike threatened for a time to be more serious as many of the workmen were O.B.U. in sentiment and unflinching in their sympathy with Winnipeg extremists. The Winnipeg appeal for a general strike here and elsewhere was contained in Strike Edition No. 17 of the *Western Labour News*: "The workers must act in unity throughout the whole Dominion and make the partial paralysis of industry complete from coast to coast. Not one wheel must turn anywhere for anything." Calgary and Edmonton and Toronto had responded in part and, on May 28, a special secret meeting of the Trades and Labour Council of Vancouver was held. Afterwards it was announced that a ballot would be taken on the question of striking. No specific issue was outlined in connection with the balloting, but on the following night the Council, at a public meeting, adopted the following as their objectives:

1. The immediate re-instatement of the Postal workers on strike in Winnipeg and settlement of the Postal workers' grievances.
2. The right of Collective bargaining through any organization the workers deem most suited to their needs.
3. Pensions for soldiers and their dependents on the basis laid down by the Soldiers' organizations and the minimum recognition for overseas to be a grant of $2,000 gratuity.
4. The nationalization of all cold storage plants, abattoirs and elevators, with a view to obtaining control of food storage.

5. The enactment of legislation for a six-hour day in all industries where unemployment is prevalent.

It was decided that the strike should begin on June 3rd, if a majority of the Unions and a majority of the individual workers voted affirmatively and, at a mass-meeting on the night of June 2, the Strike Committee announced that the necessary majorities had been obtained, but refused to divulge the figures. When published in July they showed that, out of approximately 16,000 union men in Vancouver, 5,804 cast ballots and of these 3,305 voted to strike and 2,499 against striking. Between 10,000 and 11,000 men were actually called out. No serious disorders took place during the strike which was purely a sympathetic one, with no pending disputes, and the Collective bargaining demanded in Winnipeg recognized locally some time before this. Postal employees refused to go out though most of the Civic employees did; the Street railway men struck but their services were largely replaced by jitneys; the waterfront and shipping were badly tied up for a time.

A Citizens' Protective League was formed with Mayor Gale as Chairman and, when the Strike Committee threatened a Telephone strike if the jitneys were not called off, the City Council accepted the challenge and were given enough helpers to carry on the service. The Strike Committee had early undertaken to censor the press and on the 4th the *Sun* had to close down because the printers declined to set a certain editorial denouncing the strike as a revolutionary move. A few days later the *Province* also suspended over a somewhat similar issue, but the *World* made some form of compromise which enabled it to continue. Owing to these difficulties the Citizens' League began on June 16 to publish a daily *Bulletin* reviewing the strike situation and exposing the motives of those who inspired it. Then followed the Winnipeg collapse and the calling off of the general strike; for a time the Vancouver men continued and the Loggers were called in from the camps with picketing of an aggressive nature carried out along the waterfront. After several assaults had occurred there the Mayor forbade picketing and, finally, when the street car men and civic employees decided to return to work, the Strike Committee threw up its hands, on July 3rd, and all strikers were ordered back.

The Employers' Association had, meantime, decided on June 25, that "all Union men who broke their agreements by going out on strike must admit the same on being taken back and that when employers were recognizing Union obligations the following points should be kept in mind: (1) It is desirable to support those men who have retained their affiliations with Unions in good standing with the Internationals; (2) that under no circumstances do we recognize affiliations with the so-called O.B.U." On June 23rd a belated sympathetic strike developed at Victoria of 5,000 members affiliated with the Metal Trades Council but its collapse followed the close of the Winnipeg struggle. There were other strikes going on during these months—Saskatoon, Welland, Montreal, Port

Arthur, etc.—but conditions were not special or of national importance.

After the Winnipeg Strike: The O.B.U. This strike was to have been the proof of power for the One Big Union; the stepping stone to great strength and a propaganda which, it was hoped, would sweep through the Labour Unions of Canada; the beginning of the end for Capitalism and for the International unionism which refused to recognize the I.W.W. and the O.B.U. Its progress was watched with keenest interest, and its expansion east and west into a general strike assisted in every way possible; its development and temporary successes used to assist O.B.U. membership and propaganda. Different methods of organization were adopted in different places. In Winnipeg, on June 29, an Ex-Soldiers' and Sailors' Labour Party was organized with certain special items of advocacy in its platform and then a part of the formulæ of the O.B.U.: "Public ownership of all abattoirs, elevators and cold storage plants and of all lands, mines, forests, railroads, telegraph, telephone, and essential public utilities, including power franchises; direct legislation through the initiative, referendum and recall and proportional representation with grouped constituencies, and the abolition of all Protective tariffs within the Dominion."

An effort was made to form in Toronto a Council of Workers and Soldiers as in Russia but, while many talked O.B.U. doctrines, the majority was against them and no public organization was effected. O.B.U. *Bulletins* appeared weekly in many centres and other Socialist sheets sprang up over night all through the West. The Edmonton *Soviet* was a sample which, in its Apr. 24 issue, urged all workers to obtain and distribute, in shops and factories, the *Revolutionary Age*—a United States journal printed "in the interests of Socialism and explaining Bolshevism"—and other Bolshevik pamphlets. The *B.C. Federationist* put up a strenuous and able fight for O.B.U. organization in British Columbia and succeeded in arousing a strong sentiment in its favour with numerous public meetings in Vancouver and other places such as Prince Rupert. Its point of view was frankly Bolshevistic with the Soviet Republic (May 2, 1919), "like a ray of light in a wilderness of darkness and chaos," to become "a sure beginning to the end of capitalism." So, as a writer in the *Western Labour News* echoed on May 16: "One Big Union is greater than one big army and more effective than one big Government. One Big Union has but to name a day, an hour, a minute, and behold, as the smallest unit of time is reached, a whole nation is paralyzed."

As a result of the work of Pritchard, Kingsley, Woodsworth, Kavanagh, Wells, Pettipiece, Richardson, Curry, Harrington, and others, the vote of the Labour Unions of British Columbia showed a majority for the O.B.U.; while a number of centres between Port Arthur and the Coast (excluding Winnipeg) also voted for the organization after the Calgary Convention; 188 Unions were stated to have given a favourable majority and 70 an unfavourable one—

24,239 to 5,975 out of 41,365 voting strength. A second Conference was called by V. R. Midgley, Secretary, to meet at Calgary on June 4th and at this meeting the Constitution elsewhere referred to was drawn up. At this period the *One Big Union Bulletin* of Chicago was claiming daily triumphs in the Canadian West; "Apr. 4, 10,000 mine workers in Alberta; Apr. 18, endorsement at Port Arthur, Winnipeg, Vancouver and Victoria; May 2, Edmonton claimed." The Regina Trades and Labour Council had on Apr. 28 unanimously endorsed the O.B.U.; a little later the Vancouver Council joined the circle of approval.

From Chicago there came also to the West a large chart printed on the back of a Manifesto issued by W. D. Haywood, General Secretary of the I.W.W., and recently sentenced to 20 years in gaol for sedition. This chart took the form of a large circle, above which was printed "One Big Union" and "Industrial Workers of the World." The circle was divided into six sections and developed a scheme by which the organizers hoped to govern the Dominion, the United States and other countries, under their proposal. These six Departments and their various sub-sections all radiated from the centre in which was to sit the ruling spirits of the I.W.W. and O.B.U. with all subordinate officials and ruling bodies to be composed of workmen. One of these documents was found amongst R. B. Russell's papers in Winnipeg.

O.B.U. organizers were, meanwhile, going through the West and coming as far east as Montreal and Toronto. At Calgary on June 21st E. T. Kingsley of Vancouver[*] told an audience that "if the great Allies would only take their dirty noses out of Russia the peasants would clean up that country in a short time"; he urged the burning up of all paper money and added that "we all ought to be in One Big Union; its purpose should be the mastery of the earth and everything that is on it"; the settlement of a strike, he added, was "only an armistice or truce." Incidentally, the 12th annual Convention of the Workers' International Industrial Union at New York on June 29 was told by the General Secretary, H. Richter, that it was "the original I.W.W." and was so called until 1915; its object now was the creation of "One Big Union" and "a Dictatorship of the Proletariat." He congratulated Winnipeg upon its "virile class spirit." At Butte, Mon., on July 7 a State Convention adopted much of the Canadian O.B.U. constitution and speakers urged the members to prepare for the coming Revolution. Early in July a conference of Delegates elected by British Columbia metaliferous miners was held in Nelson for the purpose of forming a mining department of the O.B.U.; the constitution as laid down by the General Executive was adopted and the organization entitled District No. 1 of the Metaliferous Miners of the O.B.U. A. G. Harvey was elected Chairman; the Fernie Miners, however, refused to join and the stern action of the U.M.W., later on, decided the issue.

---

[*]Note.—Calgary *Herald*, June 24, 1919.

In other directions the movement made a certain amount of progress. Three Unions at Fort William joined the O.B.U. early in October and a Central Labour Council was formed similar to that of Winnipeg; Edmonton organized a similar body shortly afterwards while R. J. Johns, acting as O.B.U. organizer, persuaded the Machinists of Saskatoon to take a charter from his Association; the Vancouver T. and L. Council remained O.B.U. up to the end of the year and the British Columbia Secretary, V. R. Midgley, stated on Nov. 14 that the Order had 30,000 members in Canada with most of the B.C. Lumber Workers' Union still on their books and branches in Toronto, Montreal and Hamilton; District No. 1, O.B.U. Mining Department, was re-organized at Calgary on Dec. 3rd with Henry Beard of Michel as President and the Victoria (B.C.) unit was active; the *B.C. Federationist* published on Oct. 17 a series of points for Sunday School instruction which portrayed in simple language the doctrines of class hatred, right and wrong as merely matters of opinion, the father of the child a slave if a workman, etc.

Other incidents of the year included the withdrawal of the B.C. Federation of Labour from the A.F. of L. (Oct. 10); the large vote polled in the Victoria bye-election by T. A. Barnard who ran against Hon. S. F. Tolmie as candidate of the Federated Labour Party and its platform of securing industrial legislation and "the collective ownership and democratic operation of the means of wealth production"; the passage of a Resolution by the District Labour Council of Toronto on Mch. 25 declaring in favour of collective ownership of national industries; the declaration by James Simpson in the Labour Temple, Toronto, on Apr. 13 that their object was revolution by education and organization and that Socialism, in other words the acquisition of the means of production by the producers, the workers, was as inevitable as light after the night; the victory for the "Red" element in the election of John Munroe as President of the Toronto District Labour Council over A. E. O'Leary, on July 17, and of A. W. Mance as Secretary; the charge made during this contest by James Simpson that O'Leary and Hevey (Secretary) were disloyal to the Council and treacherously serving the purposes of the Employers' Association— and an ensuing law-suit.*

Meanwhile, the failure of the Winnipeg and other strikes had produced a reaction which was helped by the vigourous fighting of the Trades and Labour Congress, the attitude of its President, Tom Moore, and the opposition of the American Federation of Labour. The powerful Railway Brotherhoods refused to consider the O.B.U., the Typographical Union declined its invitations, the Montreal Trades and Labour Council opposed it by substantial majorities, several Calgary and Vancouver Unions of importance refused to come in and Bolshevist-O.B.U. literature, left on street cars, was destroyed by the conductors, the G.W.V.A. Executive repudiated

---

*Note.—Mr. Simpson was found guilty of libel in 1920 and mulcted in large damages.

its Bolshevistic principles and the Alberta Miners returned to the U.M.W.A. The Winnipeg Council, however, openly came into the O.B.U. circle and the fight there and in Vancouver between rival bodies of Union thought lasted throughout the year. The Victoria Council hesitated for a time while the Toronto Council refused to consider it though James Simpson had declared through his *Industrial Banner* as late as June 20 that: "The Winnipeg strike has suddenly become, to labour and all true democrats, a national issue. Liberty is at stake, and the bludgeon methods that have been resorted to are already having an effect that could hardly have been foreseen."

Late in July the Street Railway Union of Regina withdrew from the local Council because of its O.B.U. action; from Australia came a Manifesto of the Australia Workers' Union explaining the sabotage dissension and general madness of I.W.W. and O.B.U. action in that country and warning Canadian workers against its agitators. An illustration of this was given by R. P. Pettipiece at a Vancouver meeting on July 27 when he dealt with redcoats and their "dirty work" and declared that the power of the State must be captured: "If they refuse to let go, they have provided us with a whole lot of precedents as to what we can do with them." The Ottawa Trades and Labour Council elected a majority against the O.B.U.; the Vancouver Council was outlawed by the American Federation of Labour and the Dominion Trades Congress; J. R. Knight of the Edmonton O.B.U. came to Toronto in August to organize, and had a decidedly cool reception; the return to work of the Drumheller (Alta.) miners on Aug. 11 marked a decided victory over the O.B.U. which had kept the strike alive for months— P. M. Christophers, their local leader, severing his connection with the Order; in Vancouver at this time the important and radical Longshoremen's Union decided to stay with the International as did the Civic Employees' Union while the Electrical workers and Steam engineers reversed their previous O.B.U. votes.

International officers of the A.F. of L. and the U.M.W. swarmed into the West and precipitated further defeats for the movement while the statement was spread abroad that the O.B.U. was illegal; on Aug. 20 the Toronto T. and L. Council refused to hear speakers from this body; in Vancouver evidence was made public on Aug. 23 showing that a Russian group in the O.B.U., who had been arrested on July 19, had arranged to establish terrorism on a large scale, if the recent strike had been successful, with dynamiting of Banks and general looting as parts of the project. Following these incidents the O.B.U. forces steadily disintegrated with the International organizations increasing daily in strength. The Edmonton T. and L. Council threw off its O.B.U. affiliations, most of the Vancouver Unions gradually returned to their A.F. of L. allegiance as did those of Victoria in the main; the Regina Council re-affirmed its allegiance to the International by a vote of 25 to 1 on Aug. 25; the Ottawa Street Railwaymen's Union refused by vote on Sept. 5 to have anything to do with the O.B.U. or to allow

its propaganda to be read at any meeting of the Union and ordered
the burning of any that had been received; at this time, also, the
pressmen and shipwrights of Vancouver decided to sever their connection with the O.B.U.; at the 3rd annual meeting of the National
Labour body, Montreal, on Nov. 15, relations with the Order were
voted down by 76 to 54; on Dec. 19 W. H. Armstrong, Director of
Coal Operations in the West, met a re-organization of the O.B.U. at
Drumheller Mines with a "check-off" system which required Operators to deduct U.M.W. dues and assessments from wages in all
Western mines and forward these to Union headquarters—thus
excluding members of all other organizations from the mines.

Organiza-
tions in
Canada: The
Trades and
Labour
Congress. The 8th annual Report of the Labour Department, Ottawa, showed that, at the beginning of 1919,
there were 248,887 members of organized labour Societies in Canada as against 204,630 a year before and
143,343 in 1915; that there were 2,274 local trade
unions with 1,328 located in 31 cities and 32,422
members reported from Montreal, 18,834 from Toronto, 12,050 from
Winnipeg and 15,459 from Vancouver; that the majority of the
International labour organizations operating in Canada provided
for the payment of benefits to members on a varying scale with, in
1918, a total disbursement in the United States and Canada combined of $12,679,934 in death benefits; that the Canadian member-
ship in American Unions, chiefly the A.F. of L. and the U.M.W.,
was 201,432 with 31 independent bodies in Quebec which had a
religious element in their platforms.   Statistics given the House
of Commons on Apr. 28, 1919, showed that there had been in
Canada 1,938 labour disputes between 1901 and 1918 with 10,910
employers and 511,609 employees involved and 12,818,850 working
days lost.   Averaging the wages lost in this period would give a
total of at least $50,000,000.   F. A. Acland, Deputy Minister of
Labour, in reviewing the general situation, estimated the average
workman's family budget of expenses—food, fuel, rent, clothing
and sundries—at $35.17 per week in August, 1918, compared with
$22.15 in August, 1914.

Policy of the Trades and Labour Congress.   Through its President, Tom Moore, its recognized policy of close relations with the
American Federation of Labour and its annual meetings and
clearly defined action, this body held a wide and increasing influence in Canada during 1919.   The fact became conspicuous in its
fight with the O.B.U. and other serious propaganda of the period.
Mr. Moore proved, during this year, a sane and respected leader
of his organization; his chief critics were the extremists who had
been defeated at the 1918 Congress and who branched out into
O.B.U. activities as a result.   He stood for various controversial
doctrines and, for instance, favoured Government ownership of
Banks but he was opposed to general or sympathetic strikes and
against all appeals to force or revolution.   He stood for unioniza-

tion of the Teaching profession and the Police and at the Police enquiry in Toronto (Feb. 14) stated this definition: "From the Trades Union standpoint, workers are those dependent upon the price of their labour for a livelihood, the line of demarcation being usually drawn when the worker reaches the control of others as foreman, superintendent or manager."

He believed in persistent reform and not in delayed action: "I tell you," he said to the Canadian Club, Toronto, on Mch. 17, "if you are content to wait indefinitely you will have the upheaval in Canada as they had it in Russia and everywhere else." But he was optimistic as to this, approved the Whitley industrial policy for adjustment of Labour troubles, and believed in the nationalization of mines and water-powers, forests and raw materials. In this connection he declared that: "Industry should be the servant and not the tyrant of the masses. We want to see greater opportunity for women and children with greater freedom for the workman and security against unemployment; we want to see the day of joint co-operation when the profits of invention and improvement which the workers can devise, shall be reaped by the workers themselves." He, and P. M. Draper, Secretary of the Congress, with J. T. Gunn of the Toronto Labour Party, and others, were free in denunciation of Bolshevism and all its works; he opposed Mackenzie King's idea of four elements in the industrial controversy and saw only two—the employer and employee; in a Labour Day speech at Toronto on Sept. 2nd he declared that there could be "no progress except by orderly development" and "no short cuts to a higher civilization."

The 35th annual Convention of the Trades and Labour Congress of Canada was called to meet at Hamilton on Sept. 22-27 in a communication which described this as a period of transition and confusion, declared the question of International Trades Unionism as the vital point for discussion at the meeting and urged the need of increased labour organization to meet capitalistic combinations of wealth, talent and legal acumen. The Convention met, with Tom Moore in the chair and formal greetings from Mayor C. G. Booker, Hamilton, Sir W. H. Hearst, Provincial Premier, and Hon. G. D. Robertson, Minister of Labour; Fraternal delegates from the National Women's Trade Union League, the British Trades Union, and the A.F. of L. also spoke and there were 901 delegates present. The Report of the Executive Council reviewed the year's events and policy and made the following reference to current misuse of the strike weapon: "A number of leaders of labour and those who follow them have been repeatedly warned of the economic danger of too frequent or too wide a use of the strike weapon. They have been told that it is inimical to production and to the best interests of the nation, and so will ultimately rebound upon themselves. They have not, however, been sufficiently warned of the danger they run of spoiling their final and best weapon of defence by its too great use and in attempts to force by its means decisions that such a weapon ought never to be used to obtain. The strikes that are proposed to-day by some of the wilder spirits are very different things from the legitimate trade union strike—the cutting-off of the supply of labour until the price goes up.   They are intended for political purposes; to force the country by the cutting-off of supplies to agree to political policies which the country does not want and will only accept under compulsion.''

The O.B.U. was referred to in explicit terms of regret that 10,000 organized workers should have been swept off their feet by its promises: ''The futility of the One Big Union methods should have been apparent from the beginning, founded as it was on force and intolerance of the chosen leaders of the Labour movement, repudiating the organizations from which they drew their financial and numerical strength, preaching class hatred throughout the country and gambling their whole future on the success of sympathetic and national strikes.   Prompt measures were taken to check the inroads of this disruptive movement, though not before many labour unions had suffered financial and other losses.''   P. M. Draper as Secretary-Treasurer, reported receipts of $41,786 and an investment of $5,000 in Victory bonds with $14,599 on hand and $10,000 in the reserve fund.   He stated that the affiliations of the Congress included a Canadian membership of 60 national and international organizations with 4 Provincial Federations of Labour, 50 Trades and Labour Councils and 69 Federal labour unions under charter from the Congress.   The total membership was 160,605 or an increase in the year of 43,107 and the salary of the President was increased to $3,600.

An Immigration Committee expressed opposition to any bonusing schemes for the introduction of industrial workers into the country and urged abolition of bonuses to booking agents; a Housing Committee recommended that the Federal Government should establish a system of loans to those desiring to build homes, through the chartered banks, at a low rate of interest and under conditions that the workers could avail themselves of and that where it was desirable to create a Commission to control construction there should be an equal representation of workers; a Special Committee emphatically protested against any Legislative restriction on the right of the Police to organize and affiliate with the Congress and pledged its ''full support to the Police forces of the Dominion in the maintenance of their rights''; R. A. Rigg of Winnipeg, Deputy to the President in the West, dealt with the alleged failure of the O.B.U. scheme there, but added that ''discontent of a very deep-seated character is widespread and the demands for a more aggressive effort to promote the interests of the toilers, as against the rapacious greed of privilege, call for the closest attention.''   A Resolution in favour of Home Rule for Ireland, along the lines of Dominion constitutions, was adopted after an amendment replacing Home Rule by the word ''Independence'' had been defeated.   Other Resolutions were, in part, as follows:

17

1. Declaring that the Executive Council, so long as the Industrial Disputes Investigation Act is in force, should obtain amendments which would bring within its provisions Civic employees—including policemen, firemen, and the letter carriers of the Dominion.

2. Stating that the Congress should support the Winnipeg strike leaders so far as obtaining a fair and impartial trial was concerned.

3. Declaring that the logical development of united action in the use of economic power was within the International trade union movement where ample scope was provided for the united action of various trades with common interests and with the strength of International unions behind them.

4. Stating that free speech, free assembly and a free press were absolutely necessary in Canada to the best interests of the workers.

5. Favouring for returned soldiers the graded scale of gratuities proposed by the G.W.V.A. at Calgary—$1,000 for service in Canada, $1,500 for service in England, $2,000 for service in France.

6. Asking amendment to the Immigration Act so that before deportation of an alien a fair trial should take place.

7. Urging the Federal Government and Provincial Legislatures to adopt legislation for a maximum 44-hour week for all workers and a wage that would allow of a reasonable standard of living.

8. Asking that legislative facilities be provided for the incorporation of Co-operative societies, organized for public service, equal to those which had long existed for the incorporation of joint stock companies, organized to make private profit for shareholders out of the general public.

9. Putting the Congress on record as being in favour of the right of Collective bargaining; the interpretation of same being on the lines of Metal Trades and Building Trades Councils, with strictly organized labour representation.

10. Requesting cancellation of the Order-in-Council putting a ban on seditious literature and requesting release of persons imprisoned for this offence.

11. Declaring the Congress to be against military intervention in countries which, after the termination of the world conflict, changed the form of their social structure, and in favour of the self-determination of nations.

Thirty minor Resolutions were approved and 20 others sent to the Executive Council or Provincial Executives. Tom Moore was re-elected President, Arthur Martel, Montreal, H. J. Halford, Hamilton and A. J. McAndrew, Moose Jaw as Vice-Presidents, with P. M. Draper as Secretary-Treasurer. James Simpson and David Rees (Vice-President) were amongst the defeated candidates. During the speeches the O.B.U. came in for much denunciation—especially at the hands of the American fraternal delegates who also deprecated political Labour parties; Ben Tillett, M.P., from England, strongly supported labour in politics as did many Ontario delegates; David Rees of Vancouver, the O.B.U. supporter who had tried but failed to get through the Executive a motion in favour of Workers' and Soldiers' Councils of the Russian pattern, was described by the President as "revolutionary"; the Congress Executive was given power to suspend or revoke the charter of any Council or Union advocating secession from International unions or forming independent or dual organizations; George Armstrong of Winnipeg failed to get serious consideration for a Soviet Resolution.

It may be added here that the American Federation of Labour, which largely influenced and backed up the policy of this Congress and with which its affiliations were so close, met in its 39th annual

Convention at Atlantic City on June 9-23 with 557 delegates present representing 3,260,068 members, and with Samuel Gompers presiding. Matters affecting Canada included the decision to discontinue a contribution of $500 hitherto made to the T. and L. Congress for legislative purposes and arranging instead that the Federation should pay a regular *per capita* sum to the Congress on the Canadian membership; the passage of a Resolution describing the O.B.U. as preaching an "untried and unsound doctrine," of another refusing to endorse the Soviet principle of rule in Russia, and of one disapproving the O.B.U. Industrial control scheme; the adoption of other Resolutions endorsing the League of Nations by a large majority; prohibiting Trades Council from taking Strike votes, disapproving Prohibition by 26,476 to 3,997 votes, affirming the right of self-determination for Ireland and disapproving the Sympathetic strike.

Various Federations of Labour—Provincial branches of the Congress—held Conventions during the year. One at Fredericton on Mch. 19-21 passed Resolutions declaring that motormen and conductors should have 14 days' compulsory training before going on duty on any Electric railway; that the Government should take over and control all Cold storage plants; that the Proportional representation system of election be adopted for Federal and Provincial elections; that Labour should be represented on all public boards appointed by the Provincial Government. Varied Provincial matters were dealt with and C. A. Melanson was elected President. Reference has been made elsewhere to the B.C. Federation meeting at Calgary; in Halifax on Feb. 27 to Mch. 4 a Nova Scotia Federation was organized with C. C. Dane as President.

Resolutions were passed by this body in favour of a 36-hour week; the payment to women of equal wages with men for equal work; the appointment of mining inspectors from the ranks of the men and by their vote; Government ownership of public utilities and the abolition of the Provincial Legislative Council; the placing of a union label on all manufactured goods, where feasible, and the abolition of all child-labour under 16 years of age; free and compulsory education and the abolition of property qualifications in candidates for public office; the adoption of Proportional representation in those constituencies which could be suitably grouped together; total exclusion of Asiatic labour, and prohibition of prison labour in competition with the free labour market; adoption of the Initiative, referendum and recall principles in application to all public offices. The Alberta Federation met at Medicine Hat on Jan. 6 with 125 delegates present and a stated increase of 4,000 in its membership; the Resolutions passed were chiefly Provincial in scope and Frank Wheatley was elected President over J. R. Knight. A long Resolution of sympathy with the Russian and German Bolshevists was, however, carried; this question evoked bitter contention between the extremists or "Red" faction and the moderates led by Alex. Ross, M.L.A., and A. Farmilo.

The United Mine Workers of America. This organization had a stormy career in Alberta and British Columbia during the year 1919. Its 16th annual Convention was held at Calgary on Feb. 17-26 with 60 delegates present. The annual Report approved of agreements being made with W. H. Armstrong, Director of Coal Mine Operations, rather than with the employers and stated that in the past year's disputes 163 decisions were in favour of the men, 96 in favour of the operators and 62 compromised. Resolutions were passed in favour of the nationalization of drug stores and hospitals; the recognition of chiropractors; the election of mine inspectors by miners and their payment by the Government; the abolition of permits to fire bosses, mine managers and store engineers; the adoption of a general strike, when necessary; and against the introduction of Orientals into mines or their entry into the country.

A Resolution was introduced in favour of the abolition of the contract system of mining and, after a long discussion, the Convention declared itself as being opposed to this system; pledged itself to use every means to hasten the day of its abandonment and to have copies of the Resolution sent to all the Labour bodies of North America. Another Resolution was passed relating to Mothers' pensions which demanded that all married women be paid a monthly salary by the Dominion of Canada and that for each child a monthly allowance be paid to the mother for its keep until the child was 16 years of age if a boy, and 17 years of age if a girl. P. M. Christophers was elected President and Edward Brown, Calgary, Secretary-Treasurer and membership was reported as having increased 4,000 in the year. During the greater part of 1919 the miners were on strike, and a majority of them were in sympathy with the O.B.U.; their charter was at one time taken away from them but eventually they returned to work and to their allegiance and the O.B.U. was, with slight exceptions, abandoned.

The parent body in the United States met in its 27th Convention at Cleveland on Sept. 9-23 with 2,000 delegates present representing 500,000 members in the United States and Canada. The following reference was made by J. L. Lewis, Acting President, to the O.B.U. struggle in District 18, Alberta: "Later it became apparent that the President and members of the Executive Board of District No. 18 were in harmony with this false propaganda. As a result the membership, led astray by their false leaders, voted to affiliate with this so-called organization and a District-wide strike was entered into against the coal operators and the Dominion Government. The agreement under which the District was working was arbitrarily repudiated and all men ordered to stop work. Engineers, firemen, pumpmen and other men necessary to protect the mines were withdrawn and inestimable damage was done the properties. The strike became effective on June 23, 1919. The International Board on July 12 authorized the sending of a Commission, to District No. 18 to take charge of its affairs. They found that the President and other officers were members of the One Big Union and had, under the provisions of the constitution forfeited their claim to affiliation with the United Mine Workers. The Commission accordingly recommended the revocation of the District charter, which action was taken on July 28, 1919." A little after this meeting the matter was satisfactorily adjusted and the O.B.U. routed. As to District 26, Nova Scotia, the following references were made:

Our membership will recall with interest the struggle made to organize the miners of the Maritime Provinces of Eastern Canada. In 1910 our International Union expended vast sums of money to accomplish this purpose, and without avail. Of recent years the miners of this District, recognizing the necessity for a union, organized the Amalgamated Mine Workers of Nova Scotia, after which they began to appreciate the need for affiliation with the United Mine Workers of America. A year or more ago recommendations were made to the International Union to issue a charter of affiliation to this organization.

Meanwhile the N.S. United Mine Workers had held their Convention at Sydney on Aug. 25, 1919, with 97 delegates representing 12,417 members present. The constitution was amended in order to make it conform to the international constitution of the U.M.W. of America. The Executive were instructed to notify all coal companies that after Jan. 1, 1920, the members of the Union would refuse to push boxes any longer. It was resolved to put forth efforts to have the ton of coal, as produced by the miners, reduced from 2,240 to 2,000 pounds—the miners being usually paid by the ton. Political action to secure working class representation in the Dominion and Provincial Legislatures was recommended and the programme of the Canadian Labour Party was approved.

The Canadian Federation of Labour and Other Organizations.
The 11th annual Convention of the Federation met in Toronto on Sept. 2-5 with 53 delegates present representing 2,887 members. Resolutions were passed asking (1) the Federal Government to repeal the law under which labour leaders could be deported without a jury trial and to release "brother workers" in Winnipeg; (2) urging the establishment of a 44-hour week and a minimum wage in accordance with the cost of living as proven by the statistics of the Labour Department; (3) declaring that all profits exceeding 10 per cent. should revert to the Government and thus help reduce the taxes. President Jabez Shaw declared that: "Canada's labour men are now able to conduct their own unions, manage their own affairs, control their own funds, decide when to strike, and make their own agreements without the assistance of the American Federation of Labour or any outside body." Successful organization work was reported from Toronto, Hamilton and Guelph and an address was heard from J. R. Knight, O.B.U. organizer. M. F. Tumpane of Toronto was elected President.

The Workers' Educational Association, formed in Toronto, had originated in England in 1907 and branched off to Australia. It was established to provide opportunity for workers to obtain the benefits of University education, and to assist them to acquire the knowledge essential to intelligent and effective citizenship. To that end, Political and Economic Science, History, English Literature and other subjects were taught under special arrangement. Sir Robert Falconer and Toronto University gave the movement their support in 1919. The Ontario Labour Educational Association held its 17th annual Convention at Stratford on May 24 with 500 delegates present and J. F. Marsh, Niagara Falls, in the chair. The Executive Report dealt with the movement for independent political action and stated that 19 new branches of the Independent Labour Party had been organized. Preliminary steps had been taken toward the organization of women workers. A motion introduced by the Toronto Women's Labour League was carried urging that no married woman be permitted to have employment in industrial and commercial plants if her husband was making an adequate wage for the upkeep of the home.

The 8-hour day was approved by Resolution for immediate adoption; other Resolutions declared in favour of investigation into the exploitation of workmen by the Medical profession, of Mothers' Pensions and for stronger beer under the Prohibition Act. Vigourous action was taken by this body against the imprisonment of those convicted of possessing or distributing seditious literature. The 10th Convention of the Canadian Brotherhood of Railroad Engineers was held at Ottawa on Sept. 29th to Oct. 3rd with 145 delegates present. A. R. Mosher, President, denounced the O.B.U. movement and a surplus revenue of $10,000 was reported with 95 divisions in good standing and a 2,800 increase in membership. A Resolution was passed permitting Sympathetic strikes only upon a two-thirds' majority vote and another approving affiliation with the International Brotherhood of Railway and Steamship Clerks, Freight Handlers and Express and Station Employees. The National Catholic Union of Quebec Province (French Canadian) met at Quebec on Sept. 4 and passed Resolutions of which the most important was one denouncing proposals for Free schools, Compulsory education, or "Neutral" schools where no really religious instruction was imparted. This Union was stated to have about 18,000 members in Quebec with 30 affiliated organizations; according to a statement by Abbé Fortin, its Chaplain, there had not been a strike within its ranks during 5 years while the wages of the Union members were advanced 30 per cent. in that period.

Labour organizations all through this year showed a strong tendency toward political party action. The Independent Labour Party of Ontario won a number of seats in the Ontario elections and its Toronto branch presented an elaborate municipal-labour programme to the electors in December; it decided also to co-operate for electoral purposes with the Canadian Labour Party and at its 3rd annual Convention on Nov. 16 elected J. H. Ballantyne President; the latter joined with James Simpson, H. J. Halford, J. J. Morrison and others in organizing an Ontario Section of the Canadian Labour Party which issued a preliminary platform in very general terms proposing to secure "for producers by hand or by brain the full fruits of their industry and the most equitable distribution thereof"; an Alberta Branch was organized along the same lines; and the New Brunswick Federation of Labour declared in favour of local political organization as did a Labour Conference at Halifax.   Associated with a vital Labour issue was the Convention of Dominion Police Chiefs at Calgary on Sept. 15-16 when a Resolution was passed asking for legislation forbidding the unionism of Police forces in affiliation with any other Union body; it was stated at this time that 37 cities in the United States had Police Unions affiliated with the A.F. of L.

The Government and Labour: The Royal Commission and Industrial Conference.   The Government had especially difficult Labour problems to deal with in this year; they were aggravated by an unusual unwillingness to accept the compromises so vital to the conduct of self-governing and constitutional liberties.   The Hon. G. D. Robertson, Minister of Labour, grew in popular estimation through his handling of the issues involved while strenuous activities in the Winnipeg strike period and in other problems proved him a capable Minister.   He was in favour of the Whitley Industrial Councils—as he put it on Feb. 21 in an interview: "We feel that organization by industries rather than by individual business is the correct method.   Such co-operation secures better standardization of labour conditions, an advantage to all the parties in industry."   Senator Robertson was Chairman of a Government Labour Committee created in May, 1918, and composed of the Minister and a *personnel* which was considerably changed by an Order-in-Council of Feb. 16, 1919.   Its membership then included the following:

Hon. G. D. Robertson	Ottawa	Hon. J. A. Calder	Ottawa
G. Frank Beer	Toronto	Calvin Lawrence	Montreal
Prof. R. M. MacIver	Toronto	Tom Moore	Ottawa
J. A. Stevenson	Winnipeg	Wills MacLachlan	Toronto
John Lowe	Valleyfield	Mrs. Rose Henderson	Montreal
W. D. Tate	Halifax	David Carnegie	Ottawa

This body had much to do with succeeding plans and Conferences.   Various discussions of the Labour condition and unrest took place in the Commons—notably on May 27th when the Prime Minister made a statement as to Government-Labour policy at the Peace Conference and as to current conditions at home.   In reference to the action of Postal employees in Winnipeg and their restlessness elsewhere, Sir Robert Borden explained that: "The Government of this country is in an entirely different situation from a private employer.   The Government employs persons who are servants of all the people of the country.   It differs from a private employer in many respects, but especially so in two important respects.   In the first place, the duties for which public servants are employed have a direct relation to the maintenance of law and order and, as well, a direct relation to the operation of public services which are necessary for the convenience of the people. But, in addition to that, it does not employ these people for any purpose of private gain or private interest; it is acting merely as the representative of the people as a whole, under the mandate, and only so long as it has the mandate, of the majority of the people's representatives in Parliament." A general strike was described as involving some of the methods of modern war and as constituting a mockery of all Peace efforts.

On the *Aquitania* (May 26) just before reaching Halifax, the Hon. A. L. Sifton referred to the strike situation with this comment: "If the laws are wrong there is a constitutional way of changing them; if a Government is bad it can easily be disposed of; but there is no possibility of Canada succeeding and developing its great natural resources as it should except under settled principles and proper administration of law and order." Upon another point Hon. A. K. Maclean, K.C., Acting-Minister of Labour, stated on May 28th that the B.N.A. Act did not give the Dominion Parliament power to enact an 8-hour day; the power lay with the Provinces. On June 2nd M. R. Blake precipitated a long debate upon the Winnipeg strike and general situation. He reviewed the condition of Labour affairs in various countries and freely denounced sedition and sympathetic strikes; Ernest Lapointe, one of the leaders of the Liberal party, was inclined to support the ordinary Labour view and denied that the Labour leaders at Winnipeg or Toronto were Bolshevists. He criticized Senator Robertson for his despatch to Mr. Gompers on May 29 requesting his influence as head of the International Unions to defeat the general strike plans; as to the 8-hour day, he admitted grave doubt regarding the Government's power but declared that it should and could be enacted for all Public Works.

There was a long ensuing debate with Lieut.-Col. G. W. Andrews, D.S.O., member for Winnipeg, declaring that the Sympathetic strike and the O.B.U. were a natural and logical sequence of Labour organization and of the instinct of co-operation and brotherhood and of standing together in an emergency. He preferred, however, the establishment of a Court of Arbitration with compulsory powers. The Government took a firm stand upon the Postal matter and eventually the strikes and troubles passed over in that connection. On June 14 Sir Robert Borden issued an Appeal to the public for steadiness in outlook and action and, above all, for work and production. The credit of the nation, the comfort of the people, the well-being of all classes were at stake:

Many employers of labour have undertaken work at little or no profit in order that their lines of industry might afford every possible opportunity for employment. Efforts to provide employment will obviously be of little avail if the energy of the country is exhausted in lockouts or strikes occasioned by differences which ought to be composed by peaceful methods and without constant interruption of the nation's task. The industries of the country have a very direct and intimate relation to each other, and serious disturbance or stoppage of work makes its effects felt in every allied or related industry. . . . Lockouts and strikes are almost as destructive as war itself, in the waste and loss which they occasion, and in their disturbing influence upon the industrial life of the country. Never was there greater need for steadfast self-control, wise forbearance and a just spirit of conciliation.

Meantime, the Liberal Opposition had taken a rather interesting position on the Labour question. It had elected a Leader whose attitude was cleverly and clearly stated in his elaborate volume upon Labour problems published in 1918 and, more succinctly, in a study of the subject presented to the Empire Club, Toronto, on Mch. 13, 1919. In both cases Mr. Mackenzie King claimed that there were four factors or parties to the question: (1) Labour which supplied the muscular and mental energy necessary to effect the transformation of products; (2) Capital which provided the raw materials, tools, appliances and equipment, essential to industrial processes and the advances for food, clothing and shelter required by Labour pending distribution of the finished product; (3) Management or personal service of a high order essential for guidance of the business, conduct of co-operation between Labour and Capital in the process of production, and maintenance of right relations with (4) the Community. The latter was the primary entity of organized society under whose sanction all industry was carried on and continuous co-operation in production, distribution and exchange became possible. The Labour Resolutions of the Liberal Convention of 1919 declared that Labour was more than a commodity or article of commerce and urged (1) the adoption of an 8-hour day or 48-hour week and of a weekly rest of 24 hours—Sunday whenever practicable—and (2) the introduction into industrial government of principles of Labour and Community representation and part control. There were many lesser planks of policy but these were the important ones.

At Ottawa on June 6th a Special Committee of the Commons recommended amendments to the Criminal Code which should declare Associations proposing to bring about any Governmental, industrial or economic change within Canada, by use of force, to be unlawful. A Government Bill followed giving the Government power to deport anarchists and alien revolutionaries and, on June 7th, it was given three readings and received the Royal assent all on the same day. The above Committee Report was adopted by the House, on motion of Hon. H. Guthrie (June 10), who declared that "in Canada to-day there exist many Associations and Societies developed and organized for the purpose of carrying on a dangerous propaganda, and which, if permitted to pursue their purpose unhindered or unchecked, may ultimately prove a serious menace to our free institutions and to the authority of government in this country."

To help in the administration of the Employment Offices organized, under a 1918 Act, the Minister of Labour on May 12-14 held a first Conference at Ottawa of the Employment Service Council of Canada with 26 representatives present from Employers' Associations and Labour organizations, from the Great War Veterans and the Labour Departments of Provincial Governments. Resolutions were passed in favour of abolishing all private Employment agencies; urging Government aid in adjusting public works and the purchase of supplies to the total volume of employment in the country; asking for a Section in the Council for professional and business placements and Divisions for juvenile and handicapped workers; appointing a Committee to consider University courses on Employment management.

Meantime, it may be added, many industrial or business concerns were voluntarily adopting special policies for improvement of labour conditions. The Massey-Harris Co., Toronto, established a Pension Fund, admitted employees as shareholders and created a Works Council; the B.C. Electric Co. assisted its employees to obtain building sites and erect homes; the Robert Simpson Co., Toronto, the Alaska Bedding Co., Montreal, the Ideal Bedding Co., Toronto, and Ryrie Bros., Toronto, adopted a Profit-sharing system; the Ontario Hydro-Electric Commission established a Pension system and the Taylor-Forbes Co., Guelph, the L. K. Liggett Co., Ltd., operating 19 stores in 7 cities, the Murray-Kay Co., Toronto, and the Goodyear Rubber Co., organized Insurance schemes for their employees; the Imperial Oil Co., continued to work out its effective Industrial relationship plan. As to the much discussed 8-hour day the Minister of Labour was able to report in September that about 47 per cent. of 615,000 workers, employed by 6,250 firms in Canada, already had this policy in operation.

The Royal Commission on Industrial Relations. Early in the year the Government felt the necessity of a careful and authoritative enquiry into Labour conditions throughout the country and, on Mch. 22nd, Senator Robertson submitted a Report recommending the calling of a Royal Commission to (1) consider and make suggestions for securing a permanent improvement in the relations between employers and employees; (2) to advise methods for ensuring that industrial conditions affecting relations between employers and employees should be reviewed from time to time by those concerned, with a view to improving conditions in the future. It was suggested that the Commission should make a survey and classification of existing Canadian industries; obtain information as to the character and extent of organization already existing among bodies of employers and employees respectively; and investigate available data as to the progress made by established joint Industrial Councils in Canada, Great Britain and the United States. This was approved by Order-in-Council of Apr. 4th and the Commission constituted as follows:

Hon. T. G. Mathers ..Winnipeg Hon. Smeaton White .. Montreal Charles Harrison, M.P.. North Bay	} Representing the Public
Carl Riordon ....Montreal Frank Pauzé.........Montreal	} Representing the Employers
Tom Moore ....Ottawa J. W. Bruce ....Toronto	} Representing the Employees

Chief Justice Mathers was appointed Chairman, and Thomas Bengough, Toronto, Secretary. The enquiry opened at Victoria, B.C., on Apr. 26, following, and was completed at Ottawa on June 13th; 70 sessions were held in 28 industrial centres from Victoria, B.C., to Sydney, N.S., and 486 witnesses examined. In his opening address at Victoria the Chairman described the lines of investigation as follows: Organization and classification; unsatisfactory conditions and Labour troubles; remedies applied or suggested; Profit-sharing, Bonuses, and Co-partnership; Joint Councils; general comment or suggestions and Mental attitude. Statements were freely invited without oath, or formality, or interruption. The first result was that a vast mass of digested and undigested, relevant and irrelevant, valuable and worthless material was evoked which the press distributed in varied forms; the next result was a natural though temporary enhancement of unrest in public thought while the final end was the production of a really valuable and helpful statement and Report.

In this document, which was presented to Parliament on July 1st, the Commissioners declared that serious unrest undoubtedly existed, and that it was more pronounced in the West than elsewhere; that it was largely due to upheavals in Europe and the consequent state of the public mind; that the workers of Canada were devoting much thought to the study of economies and to a greater extent than the employers; that the majority of the workers did not believe in extreme ideas or measures but would welcome co-operation and industrial peace until, by a gradual process of evolution, "a system may be ushered in by which the workers will receive a more adequate share of what their labour produces." The chief local causes of Labour unrest were described as follows: "Unemployment and the fear of unemployment; high cost of living in relation to wages and the desire of the worker for a larger share of the product of his labour; desire for shorter hours of labour and denial of the right to organize, or refusal to recognize Unions; denial of Collective bargaining; lack of confidence in constituted government and insufficient and poor housing; restrictions upon the freedom of speech and press, and ostentatious display of wealth; lack of equal educational opportunities."

In amplifying these points it was stated that in practically every Province there was a great scarcity of labour on the farms; that an increasing number of the farmers would gladly employ men by the year and that in some cases provision had been made for a married man with a separate dwelling; that existing unemployment was, in a measure, due to the curtailment of production in some industries because of the lack of ocean tonnage; that owing to the unsettled conditions, there was a great reluctance on the part of those possessing unemployed capital to risk it in new enterprises or in the expansion of those already established; that everywhere high cost of living and a deep-rooted belief in profiteering in the necessities of life were assigned as chief causes of current unrest; that there was a settled conviction in the mind of the worker that he did not get a fair share of the value which his labour produced.

It was stated that employers could be divided into three classes: (1) Those who denied the right of their employees to organize and who took active steps to prevent such organization; (2) those who, while not denying this right to their employees, refused to recognize organization among them and persisted in dealing with them as individuals, or as Committees of employees, without regard to their organized affiliations; (3) those who not only admitted the right of the employees to organize, but recognized and bargained with their organizations on behalf of their employees. There were not many in Canada of the first class, there were a large number of the second and to the third class there belonged the great Railway, telegraph and mining companies and many building trades.

Collective bargaining was described as a policy in use by both employers and employees and as applied in varied forms; it was defined as "the negotiation of agreements between employers or groups of employers, and employees or groups of employees, through the representatives chosen by the respective parties themselves." In its conclusions the Commission strongly recommended the Whitley principle of Industrial Councils with specific plans and operations adjusted to meet special conditions local to Canada; a Labour or Industrial Conference at Ottawa was suggested and legislation, Government action, or enquiry with a view to legislation, along the following lines was recommended:

Fixing of a Minimum wage, especially for women, girls and unskilled labour.

Maximum work-day of 8 hours and weekly rest of not less than 24 hours.

State Insurance against unemployment, sickness, invalidity and old age.

Proportional representation.

Regulation of public works to relieve unemployment and help for the building of workers' Homes.

Establishment of a Bureau for promoting Industrial Councils. Restoration of fullest liberty of freedom of speech and press.

Recognition of the right to organize and of Unions.

Payment of a living wage, Collective bargaining and extension of equal opportunities in Education.

Steps toward establishment of Joint Plant and Industrial Councils.

The above Report was signed by the Chairman and Messrs. Riordan, Harrison, Moore and Bruce. Senator White and Mr. Pauzé submitted a special document laying stress (1) upon the claim that Labour only wanted an 8-hour day as a step toward one of 6 hours; emphasizing the value of piece-work in production and in practice as shown in Quebec; doubting the practicability in Canada of the Whitley plan and expressing approval of the Colorado plan under experiment by the Imperial Oil Co.; declaring that many of the conditions complained of were Provincial, local, or Civic in character; opposing State schemes of Insurance against unemployment and old age as unnecessary. Mr. Riordan submitted a few personal observations in which he declared that the basic trouble was that the worker did not feel satisfied with the living he got from his work and that the evidence, throughout, showed that merely raising wages would not give the worker a better living and that this could only be obtained by dealing with wages and the cost of living together: "The share of the worker can be increased only (1) by increasing the wealth to be shared by decreasing waste; (2) by decreasing the share of the other parties to the production of wealth, and (3) by reducing to a minimum the share of those who are not parties to the production of wealth."

The National Industrial Conference.   Following the Royal Commission Report and as an outcome of its recommendations, a Conference was arranged and called for Sept. 15-20 to meet at Ottawa. It was referred to in the closing Speech from the Throne on July 7 as follows: "Having regard to the necessity of avoiding industrial disturbance and with a view to ensuring more stable relations and a better understanding between employers and employed, my Advisers intend to summon in the early future a representative Conference for friendly and intimate discussion of such questions, and for the consideration of the Report of the Industrial Relations Commission and of the proposals therein set forth."

Under the terms of a succeeding Order-in-Council of July 17 employers and organized labour were each entitled to select 60 representatives to appear for them at the Conference, the selection to be made through their different Associations, and in such a way as to make the gathering representative of the various branches of trade and industry.   An invitation was also extended to the members of the Royal Commission on Industrial Relations and to the members of the Labour Sub-Committee of the Cabinet, on whose recommendation the Royal Commission was established; provision was made for the representation of engineering and technical organizations.   Final arrangements for the Conference were placed in the hands of a joint Committee of employers and employees with C. A. Magrath as Chairman and the following members: C. H. Carlisle, Toronto, E. G. Henderson, Windsor, F. P. Jones, Montreal, R. A. Rigg, Winnipeg, Gus Francq, Montreal, and W. R. Rollo, Hamilton.

The Agenda for consideration included the Labour features of the Peace Treaty, the condition and codification of Canadian labour laws, the Report of the Royal Commission, the question of Minimum wages, the right to organize with recognition of Labour unions and Collective bargaining, the general relations of employers and employees.   The Conference at its opening meeting was presided over by Senator G. D. Robertson, Minister of Labour, with Gerald H. Brown as Secretary; the Delegates present at this or subsequent meetings were numerous and prominent with 72 representing the Employers, 79 standing for Labour and 30 for the Public; a message was read from the Prime Minister, who was to have presided, expressing regret for his absence, through illness, and reviewing the situation as a whole.   Sir Robert Borden was clear and explicit in terms.   He declared that employers must realize that out of the horror and welter of this War new ideals had been evolved and new conditions established:

Industrial development and supremacy have sometimes been purchased at a price greater than any people can afford to pay. Labour is something more than a commodity. The physical well-being and the moral welfare of the people should go hand in hand. Standards of living which are regarded as satisfactory in some industrial communities of the world cannot be tolerated in this country. The employer, if he is wise, will concern himself with all the recommendations and suggestions laid down in the Peace Conference. . . . On the other hand, there are considerations which the labour organizations of the country will do well to bear in remembrance. Full right of organization on the part of both employees and employers has become so well recognized a principle that those who do not accept it are in a small and short-sighted minority. The rights of both employees and employers are thus moulded and governed by agreements reached through negotiations between such organizations in the different trades. But there can be no hope of the co-operation and confidence which are not only desirable but vital unless obligations thus entered into are maintained inviolate and unbroken on both sides.

The Premier's final conclusion was that the waste of 5 years' war must be made up through increased production and this could not be achieved in shorter working hours unless increased efficiency gave an additional output. Addresses followed from the Hon. A. L. Sifton, Hon. N. W. Rowell and Hon. W. L. Mackenzie King. The Liberal leader was elaborate in his presentation of opinion; he urged uniformity of standards in industrial regulation; argued at length as to the presence of four factors in the problem—capital, labour, management and the community; preferred an appeal to Reason in all controversies to the Prussian appeal to Force and described industrial war as having the same origin as international war; declared that industry in its final analysis existed for the sake of humanity and not the reverse. David Carnegie spoke of the Whitley Councils and W. Jett Lauck and Warren D. Stone upon United States labour conditions. The Delegates were divided into three Groups—(1) The Employers; (2) The Employees; (3) The Public.

The first Group included all the leading industries and interests of Canada with such representative manufacturers and business men as T. P. Howard, G. M. Bosworth, F. G. Daniels, F. L. Wanklyn and F. P. Jones, Montreal; S. R. Parsons, Hugh Blain, A. Monro Grier, K.C., Toronto; T. R. Deacon, W. J. Bulman, J. H. Ashdown, J. A. Banfield, Winnipeg; J. J. Coughlan, Vancouver; W. S. Fisher, Sackville; F. H. Whitton, Hamilton; J. Fraser Gregory, St. John; E. G. Henderson, Windsor; G. M. McGregor, Ford; Henry Bertram, Dundas; D. H. McDougall, New Glasgow. The second Group was represented, amongst others, by Tom Moore, P. M. Draper, A. R. Mosher, W. L. Best, Ottawa; Arthur Martel, J. T. Foster, James Murdock, Montreal; James Winning, R. A. Rigg, Winnipeg; J. H. Kennedy, A. E. O'Leary, James Simpson, D. A. Carey, Toronto; R. J. Fallon, Calgary; James Somerville, Moose Jaw; J. E. Tighe, St. John; W. R. Trotter, Helena Guteridge, Vancouver; W. R. Rollo, J. A. Flett, Hamilton; Joseph Gorman,

Cobalt; J. A. Gillis, Sydney; E. S. Woodward, Victoria. Of the third Group H. J. Daly, G. Frank Beer, Sir John Willison, Toronto; C. A. Magrath, Ottawa, Mayor T. D. Bouchard, St. Hyacinthe; Arthur Roberts, K.C., Bridgewater, N.S.; R. W. Wolvin, Halifax, and Thomas Cantley, New Glasgow, might be mentioned with, also, members of the late Royal Commission.

The speeches covered every variety of labour or industrial topic and, as a rule, were conciliatory in tone; the Labour men stood out clearly along specific lines of economic argument and were, in some respects, the best speakers; the industrial leaders and business men presented elaborate statements and were shrewd and keen in their knowledge of special interests but did not always cope with the workers in their clever and enthusiastic presentation of the one side; in the meeting place it was significant that, naturally and without arrangement, the Delegates divided and employers took one side of the Chairman while labour delegates took the other. As to details of discussion the right to organize was largely but not wholly recognized and the employers contended especially for the right of men not to organize; there was sharp division on the 8-hour day proposal and approximation on the Minimum wage subject; there was agreement on Proportional representation and the principle of Industrial Councils.

As to speakers E. G. Henderson for the Manufacturers and Tom Moore for Labour spoke upon several occasions; J. W. Bruce, a good speaker, dealt with Law codification from the Labour standpoint and J. R. Shaw of Woodstock, a Manufacturer, was somewhat aggressive in his answering arguments; Mr. Shaw was the recognized leader of the Employers and Mr. Moore of the Labour group.   J. A. McClelland presented the case for an 8-hour day to which Mr. Shaw and M. P. White replied; R. A. Rigg spoke on the same subject and Miss Guteridge of Vancouver handled it with eloquence; Colonel Carnegie spoke sympathetically, from experience at Hadfields' in Sheffield, and J. H. Ashdown favoured the policy, while Hon. C. A. Dunning of Regina feared its effect on Agriculture; E. G. Henderson and James Winning of Winnipeg disagreed rather strenuously.   The Minimum wage project evoked favourable speeches from Miss Guteridge and E. Parnell of Winnipeg with E. M. Trowern opposing.   W. L. Best and R. A. Rigg presented the case for rights of organization and Collective bargaining with C. H. Carlisle, S. R. Parsons, J. R. Shaw and F. P. Jones in opposition and Dr. D. Strachan of the Imperial Oil Co. as partly favourable.   Mr. Mackenzie King and Mr. Moore debated the Rockefeller plan which the former strongly supported.   At the close of the Conference (Sept. 20) speeches were made by Sir William Hearst, Premier of Ontario, and Hon. T. C. Norris, Premier of Manitoba, amongst others.   Finally, it was found impossible to obtain unanimous reports on Hours of labour; Employees' right to organize; Recognition of labour unions; and Collective bargaining.   In other directions substantial success was achieved.   Reports were submitted by Committees and adopted or amended or rejected—the conclusions reached having the force of Resolutions. Those adopted unanimously were as follows:

1. Suggesting the appointment of a Dominion Board, with Provincial representation, to deal with the advantages of uniformity in the laws relating to the welfare of those engaged in industrial work.

2. Welcoming the declaration of the Prime Minister that a Speakers' Conference would be called to investigate the merits of Proportional Representation and declaring that there were defects in the existing Canadian system of electoral representation.

3. Declaring that there was urgent necessity for greater co-operation between employer and employee and that this co-operation could be furthered by the establishment of Joint Industrial Councils; recommending that a Bureau be established by the Department of Labour to gather data and furnish information, whenever requested by employers and employees, or organizations of employers or employees, with a view to helping, when desired, in the formation of such Councils.

4. Approving the appointment of a Board or Boards to enquire into State Insurance against Unemployment, Sickness, Invalidity and Old Age, and recommending that such Board or Boards be representative of the interests participating in this Conference, viz., the Government, the public, the employer and the employee, as well as of the women of Canada; suggesting that the subject of Widows' pensions be added for consideration.

5. Declaring it expedient that Minimum rates of wage should be fixed throughout Canada for women and children, whether employed at a time rate or according to any other method of remuneration; pointing out that such laws had been enacted in five Provinces; recommending to the Governments of all Provinces, which had not adopted Minimum Wage laws for women and children, a speedy investigation of the necessity for such laws, and, if so found, the enactment of legislation; advising that, if at all possible, these laws should be uniform in terms and method of application.

6. Asking the Dominion Government to appoint a Royal Commission, composed equally of representatives of Labour, Employers, and the Public, to investigate wages to unskilled workers and issue a report; urging Provincial Governments to investigate and deal with the alleged low remuneration paid to female School teachers.

7. Declaring that this Conference, ''recognizing that much industrial unrest, economic loss and social suffering has resulted from land speculation, poor and insufficient housing, and high rents, heartily commends the action of the Dominion and Provincial Governments in their united efforts to improve housing conditions and to provide facilities for the proper and satisfactory housing of our people and recommends increased co-operation of, and investigation by, the Dominion and Provincial Governments to find a satisfactory solution of the problem.''

8. Asking the Government of each Province in Canada to establish Compulsory education for full time, at least up to and including the 14th year, and for part time in cities and towns for the two ensuing years; and that, in all Provinces, Education, in all grades, be made free, so that the child of the poorest paid worker be given the opportunity of reaching the highest educational institution.

9. Urging the removal of war-time restrictions upon freedom of speech and liberty of the press, but recognizing, also, that no person had a right to do anything that was liable to incite the people to commit unlawful acts and that a line must be drawn between liberty and license.

10. Suggesting that all Governments, through public works and otherwise, aid in preventing serious unemployment and approving the general employment policy—through a single agency—of the Provincial Governments.

In the case of the 8-hour day matter, the Employers' Committee reported in favour of a Government Commission composed of an equal representation of employers, and employees of the various industrial, producing and distributing industries, to undertake investigations as to the adaptability of the hours of labour principles of the Peace Treaty to the different industries of Canada. The Employees' Committee agreed with the recommendations and finding of the Royal Commission on Industrial Relations, urged the adoption of an 8-hour day by law throughout the Dominion, with due regard and recognition of the Saturday half-holiday, and stated that in industries subject to seasonal and climatic conditions, such as farming, fishing, and logging, if it could be established by investigation that the operation of such law was impracticable, then exemption should be granted such industries. In this case the 3rd Group suggested Government legislation as to all industries where the 8-hour day was established by agreement and, after investigation by a Commission, the extension of such law to other suitable industries.

As to the three other and basic matters under consideration an Employers' Committee reported that employers admitted the right of employees to join any lawful organization; that employers should not be required to recognize unions or to establish "Closed Shops"; that employers insisted on the right, when so desired, to maintain their plants as "Open Shops," by which they meant that no employer should discriminate against any employee because of the latter's membership or non-membership in any organization, and no employee should interfere with any other employee, because of the latter's membership or non-membership in any organization; that employers should not be required to negotiate except directly with their own employees or groups of their own employees. An Employees' Committee reported on this subject that the Conference should declare in favour of (1) the right of employees to organize or form themselves into Associations for lawful purposes; (2) the recognition of labour unions or the right of employees to recognition by their employer or employers, for the purpose of mutually arranging rules and regulations governing wages and working conditions; (3) the right of employees to Collective bargaining or the negotiation of agreements between employers or groups of employers, and employees or groups of employees, through the representative or representatives chosen by the respective parties themselves—entering into agreements and bargaining collectively with an Association or Union or Employees not to mean recognition of the "Closed Shop," unless the agreement so provided; (4) urging Governments to enact legislation applicable to industries within their respective jurisdiction and making it unlawful for any employer to discharge or refuse to employ or in any manner discriminate against employees merely by reason of membership in labour unions or because of legitimate labour union activities outside of working hours. The Employees' Committee and the 3rd Group agreed that the findings of the recent Royal Commission should be put into effect at once on all Government works or bodies where the principles of democratic government could be applied.

Canada and International Labour Conferences of 1919.   The Peace Conference and the Labour clauses of the League of Nations brought Canada into the limelight of International labour developments; the general wording of those clauses is recorded elsewhere in this volume;* the Hon. N. W. Rowell, K.C., declared at Montreal on Dec. 19, 1919, that "the object of the International Labour Organization, which is associated with the League of Nations, is to promote industrial peace, based on social justice, by improving through international agreement the conditions under which men live and labour." On July 28 to Aug. 2 an International Federation of Trade Unions met in Congress at Amsterdam, Holland, and terminated the old pro-German International Secretariat. Great Britain, the United States, France, Austria, Germany and some other countries were represented and Mr. Gompers, for the Allied nations, failed to get through a Resolution admitting German agression in the War—except so far as Belgium was concerned. Karl Legien, President of the Conference and President of the German Federation of Trade Unions was thanked by various unions represented at the Congress for financial assistance given in the days of German pre-war propaganda. A Resolution was approved as to attending the Washington Conference—provided the Germans, Austrians and Russians were admitted; W. A. Appleton, a British delegate, was elected President. Canada was not represented but was so at the preceding Trades Union and Socialistic Conference at Berne in February when Gustave Francq was the representative of its Labour interests.

The **United States Industrial Conference.** Canada was not directly represented or concerned in this gathering but, indirectly, all American labour movements affected Canadian conditions at this time, and the Conference in question was undoubtedly influenced by the Ottawa meeting which, in fact, was told by Mr. Jett Lauck of the U.S. War Labour Board that "intense interest was being felt in the United States as to its proceedings and outcome." In calling the Conference President Wilson set forth its objects as follows: "For the purpose of reaching, if possible, some common ground of agreement and action with regard to the future conduct of industry, I desire to obtain the combined judgment of representative employers, representative employees, and representatives of the general public conversant with those matters." Its constitution was very similar to that of Ottawa and at the 1st meeting on Oct. 6th, at Washington, Franklin K. Lane, Secretary of the Interior, was appointed Chairman, B. M. Baruch Chairman of the Public group, H. A. Wheeler of the Employers' group and Sam Gompers of the Labour group.

Speeches were moderate in tone and the subjects were almost identical with those at Ottawa—right of wage-earners to organize, right of Collective bargaining and right to be represented by per-

*Note.—See League of Nations Section, Pages 87-98.

sons of their own choosing in negotiations with employers; freedom of speech, of the press, and of assemblage; right of employers to organize and bargain collectively; a Minimum eight-hour day. In addition to these Mr. Gompers, on behalf of Labour, asked for payment of a living wage, equality of wages for men and women in similar work, prohibition of labour for those under 16 years of age, prohibition of immigration for 2 years and a National Conference Board to provide for the systematic review of industrial relations and conditions. Resolutions endorsing the right of Collective bargaining and arbitration in the current Steel strike were voted down with the Public and Employers' groups standing together.

An appeal from the President for general action and unity came at this juncture and then Mr. Gompers moved that: "The right of wage-earners to organize without discrimination, to bargain collectively, to be represented by representatives of their own choosing in negotiations and adjustments with employers in respect to wages, hours of labour and relations and conditions of employment, is recognized." This was supported by the Labour and Public groups but defeated by one vote and the Labour group then withdrew from the Conference; adjournment followed on Oct. 23 after the Employers' group had approved a plan presented by the Secretary of Labour (W. B. Wilson) for the creation of a Board composed of an equal number of employers and employees in each of the principal industries and a Board for miscellaneous industries, the members to be selected in such manner as the employers and employees might respectively determine, to deal with the adjustment of Labour disputes.

International Labour Conference at Washington. This gathering was an outcome of the Versailles Peace Conference and a part of the recognized machinery of the League of Nations which included a yearly Conference, with the first to be held at Washington in 1919, and an International Labour office at Geneva, Switzerland. The details of the meeting were arranged by a Committee on which Sir Malcolm Delevigne was the British member and Dr. J. T. Shotwell the United States representative, with one member each from France, Italy, Japan, Belgium and Switzerland. Arthur Fontaine of France was Chairman and it was decided that the Conference should be held at Washington on Oct. 29 and be composed of four representatives of each of the members of the League of Nations, of whom two should be Government delegates and the two other delegates representing, respectively, the employers and the workpeople of each of the nations concerned. Each delegate could be accompanied by advisers, who were not to exceed two in number for each item on the agenda of the meeting. The questions to be discussed included (1) application of the principle of an 8-hour's day or of a 48-hour's week; (2) the question of preventing or providing against unemployment; (3) women's employment, under various conditions relating to health and fitness; (4) employment of children and the question of prohibiting night-work for women and the use of white phosphorus on matches.

The Chairman selected by the Conference at its initial meeting on Oct. 29 was Hon. W. B. Wilson, U.S. Secretary of Agriculture and the Vice-Chairmen Rt. Hon. G. N. Barnes, Great Britain, Jules Carlier, Belgium, and Léon Jouhaux, France.   H. B. Butler, c.b., of England was appointed Secretary-General.   Thirty-eight countries were represented at the Conference and 122 Delegates with 150 Advisers were present.   The Committee in charge of arrangements acted under Article 393 of the Peace Treaty which provided that of the 12 persons representing Governments on the Governing body of the International Labour Office, 8 should be nominated by the member-nations of chief industrial importance and 4 by member-nations chosen at the forthcoming Conference.   The original eight nations were Great Britain, United States, France, Italy, Belgium, Japan, Switzerland, Germany, if admitted, or if not, Spain. Canada addressed a protest to Lord Milner, Secretary for the Colonies, and presented its claims as an industrial nation superior to several mentioned above and to others who might be selected by the Conference.   Protests also came from India, Poland and Sweden; Australia and South Africa did not send Delegates. Eventually, Canada was given a place amongst the four chosen by the Conference; this governing body was really a sort of Executive Committee and the appointment gave the Dominion a conspicuous place.

The Canadian delegation was one of the most complete and best-informed representations in the gathering and included the Hon. G. D. Robertson, Minister of Labour, and Hon. N. W. Rowell, President of the Privy Council as Government delegates, with F. A. Acland, Deputy-Minister of Labour; L. G. Christie, Legal Adviser, Department of External Affairs; D. A. Cameron, m.l.a., Sydney, and Hon. C. W. Robinson, Moncton; Hon. W. L. Mackenzie King, Ottawa, and Louis Guyon, Deputy-Minister of Labour, Quebec; Hon. T. H. Johnson, Winnipeg, and T. M. Molloy, Secretary, Bureau of Labour, Regina; Hon. C. R. Mitchell, Edmonton, J. D. McNiven, Deputy-Minister of Labour, Victoria; and Gerald H. Brown, Ottawa, as Advisers.   The Employers' delegate was S. R. Parsons, Toronto, and the Advisers were Sam Harris, J. G. Merrick and J. T. Stirrett, Toronto; E. Blake Robertson, Ottawa and J. B. Hugg, Winnipeg.   The Workers' delegate was P. M. Draper, Ottawa, and the Advisers: Tom Moore, Ottawa, Arthur Martel, Montreal, Robert Baxter, Sydney, David Rees, Vancouver, and Mrs. Kathleen Derry, Toronto.   Major L. L. Anthes and T. A. Stevenson of Toronto were also present on behalf of the Dominion Government.   On the Commission of Selection, or Organization, Canada was represented by Senator Robertson and Great Britain by Sir Malcolm Delevigne, D. S. Majoribanks and G. H. Stuart-Bunning.

The chief subject of discussion was the 8-hour day.   Rt. Hon. G. N. Barnes of Great Britain moved on Nov. 4 that ''the draft Convention of the 48-hour week prepared by the International Organizing Committee be adopted by the Conference as the basis for discussion, but that its application to the tropical and other countries referred to, in Article 405 of the Peace Treaty, be referred, in the first instance, for consideration to a Special Committee, which shall report to the Conference." Mr. Barnes argued for this policy in preference to an 8-hour day and declared that while increased production was necessary it could only be secured through a better organization of industry and by humanizing conditions of labour. Long hours of work would not contribute to that end and the adoption of a basic 8-hour day would not give workers the leisure which they desired and needed: "It is true that an 8-hour day, if spread evenly over a week, makes a 48-hour week. But there is no reason why it should be spread evenly over every day in the week if industries can be better served otherwise." P. M. Draper from Canada led in the succeeding issue by a query as to how far acceptance of the motion would bind the delegates exclusively to the 48-hour week. Could amendments for a 44-hour week be subsequently submitted?

Mr. Barnes stated that the Peace Treaty laid down the principle of an 8-hour day or a 48-hour week: "The Organizing Committee put this forward as the basis of discussion in a 48-hour week. I take it that the Convention would be open to amendment only in so far as amendments are compatible with the principle of a 48-hour week." Mr. Draper objected to this: "I believe if we are nailed down to the proposition that we can only have a 48-hour week or an 8-hour day, that it opens the door for allowing certain industries to work nine, ten, eleven or twelve hours a day—it makes no difference so long as the 48 hours per week have been worked!" The Canadian Labour group wanted an 8-hour day and a 44-hour week. Finally, after prolonged discussion extending over a week, and upon motion of Hon. N. W. Rowell, a Committee of 15 members was appointed to deal with the question; three Canadians were included—Senator Robertson, P. M. Draper and S. R. Parsons; Thomas Shaw, M.P., of Great Britain, was Chairman and its Report was submitted on Nov. 24.

It proposed an 8-hour day and 48-hour week in all industrial undertakings, public or private, and to all branches thereof of whatsoever kind, other than undertakings in which only members of a family were employed. A number of stated and rather important exceptions were made, commerce and agriculture were excluded, and July 1st, 1921, was set as the date of operation. Overtime was authorized in certain exceptional cases and regulations were to fix the maximum hours of overtime in each case and the rate of overtime pay was not to be less than time and a quarter. The matter of countries with special climatic and industrial conditions such as Japan, India, South Africa, etc., was dealt with by a Sub-Committee and certain modifications in each case suggested. The Report and Convention, as defined, were adopted by 82 to 8 votes and the Sub-Committee's report was, also, approved.

There was no very close co-operation between the Canadian delegates and those of Great Britain and India; in fact, the former voted against the opinions of British Government representatives from London and India in favour of making the minimum age of employment for children in India 12 instead of 9 years. It was pointed out by one Hindu delegate that raising the age limit to 12 would be more disastrous to the children than otherwise; children, it was said, would be thrown on the streets in a country where, by reason of its peculiar customs, mothers did not have the necessary control.   On the question of unemployment and immigration from country to country the Conference decided (1) in favour of the prohibition of employment agencies which charged fees, and where they did exist to require them to operate under State license: (2) in favour of the prohibition of the recruiting of bodies of foreign workers in any of the States ratifying the unemployment conventions, except after consultation with the employees and workers in each country; (3) in favour of the establishment of an effective system of unemployment insurance, managed either by the State itself or by state-aided associations; (4) advising that the members of the International Labour body should take measures with a view to co-ordinating the execution of work undertaken by, or on behalf of, the state and by public authorities, with a view to reserving as far as practicable such work for periods of unemployment and for districts most affected by such unemployment.

It was also proposed that the question of migration and the protection of foreign workmen should be considered by an International Commission which, while giving due regard to the sovereign rights of each State, should report on measures for the protection of these workers; that European membership in the Commission should be limited to one-half and that nations receiving immigration should control the right of admission and degree of citizenship to be accorded.   Resolutions were passed restricting work in connection with the health of women wage-workers and recommending either maternity benefits or a system of State insurance.   The employment of children in industry was fixed at a minimum age of 14 years with the proviso, also, that children under 12 should not be employed (1) in factories working with power, and employing more than 10 persons; (2) in mines and quarries, on railroads, or on docks.   Night work for young persons employed in industry was prohibited for minors under 18 years of age, with certain exceptions as in industries where, by the nature of the process, or to avoid a waste of fuel or material, work had to be carried on continuously day and night.   Recommendations were approved for the special protection of women and children workers against lead poisoning and the danger of anthrax infection; the use of white phosphorus on matches was forbidden.

Final measures were taken to create the Governing Body for the International Labour Office composed of 12 members representing the various Governments, together with 6 others representing employers and 6 representing workers with Sir Allan Smith and G.

H. Stuart-Bunning representing Great Britain; Albert Thomas was elected Provisional Director-General and Arthur Fontaine Chairman—both of France; Canada was included amongst the 4 countries whose representatives were chosen by the Conference— after a prolonged struggle and a vote in which the Dominion came third in the list with Spain, Poland and Argentina as the other three. It may be added that during the Conference it was decided, almost unanimously to admit German and Austrian delegates but that they were unable to arrive in time. The United States Government was not represented because of its attitude on the League of Nations and the American delegates did not take an active part nor were they represented in appointments to the Governing Body.

Speaking on his return to Toronto at a Manufacturers' meeting on Dec. 18, S. R. Parsons gave the following reasons for opposing an 8-hour day at the Ottawa and Washington Conferences: Shortened hours would necessarily curtail production and the world was in terrible need; nations were not suffering from long hours of labour but for food and clothing; Canada and the United States could supply much of that need and ought to do so and, even if agriculture were not included, the Dominion as a young, undeveloped country would be hard hit by any restriction of industrial hours. Limiting work would be the death of small nations and industries and would not settle industrial unrest; "Un-economic regulations will never bring about social welfare for any class."

EDUCATIONAL INTERESTS AND INSTITUTIONS

Educational Problems and Conditions: In Canadian Provinces. Education is one of the subjects which, in Canada, are allotted by its constitution (the B.N.A. Act) to the control of the Provinces—subject to the maintenance of the rights and privileges of denominational and separate schools as existing at the time of Confederation or admission of the Provinces. Its problems are those connected with the varied languages and customs of settlers in the West; the divergent ideal of the Catholic Church as to religious instruction in schools and the Protestant principle of national non-sectarian instruction; the question of French language instruction in communities outside of Quebec where French-Canadians reside, and the miscellaneous difficulties arising from a large but sparsely populated country. The Provincial control of Education, while it ensures local and specific care and attention involves, also, an inevitable lack of uniformity in system and a great divergence in method with many varieties of instruction in general subjects.

The General Educational Situation. The latest Census figures (Calendar year 1910) showed that in a total school population of 1,154,307, 79·83 per cent. attended school for some period in the year; that in this percentage of attendance, between 7 and 14 years, the record by Provinces was as follows: P.E. Island 84·60 per cent.; Ontario 84·27; Nova Scotia 82·86; Quebec 80·96; New Brunswick 80·05; British Columbia 75·33; Manitoba 74·64; Saskatchewan 66·71 and Alberta 62·83 per cent. Viewing the figures in another way they showed that, of the total number of children between 7 and 14, Ontario had 157 per 1,000 who were not attending school, Quebec 190, New Brunswick 200, Nova Scotia 171 and P.E. Island 154 children; British Columbia had 247, Alberta 372, Saskatchewan 333, and Manitoba 254 children per 1,000 of this age, who did not attend school in the year 1910. These figures have to be judged in the light of varying conditions. Children might go to school one year and not the next, teachers might be scarce or absent, local conditions changed from year to year. Nevertheless the figures were not satisfactory. Taking Canada as a whole, the percentage between 7 and 14 years not attending school was 20·17; the percentage from 15 to 17 years of age attending for some part of the year was 27·14 per cent. and not attending at all 72·86 per cent. In 1911 statistics as to illiteracy were collected and they showed that out of a population of 5 years of age, and over, 5,622,932 could read and write out of a total of 6,323,135 and that 667,340 or 10·55 per cent. could neither read nor write. The reading and writing dealt with in these figures was, of course, slight and crude in degree.

[520]

By the year 1919 all the Provinces, with the exception of Quebec, had laws for Compulsory school attendance, uniformity in the training of teachers, in text-books, in the grading of children. Upon application, the Provincial Governments afforded financial assistance for the erection of new schools, where settlement warranted it, or where increased attendance demanded a larger edifice. Large numbers' of new schools were built from year to year throughout the country, and especially in the ever-growing Western Provinces. Nature study, manual instruction, school gardens, domestic science and technical education were taken up energetically, whilst agriculture formed a more and more important item in the curriculum of all the schools. In the cities and towns of the Dominion no expense was spared in the erection of handsome, spacious school buildings, where health conditions were a prime consideration and even artistic taste a factor. The general welfare of the pupils was studied in the plans of construction, while medical officers and health nurses supervised their personal well-being in most of the Provinces. The majority of the rural schools were ungraded—with several small classes taught by one teacher and fully trained teachers available, though in decreasing proportion, from the Provincial Normal Schools.

The child from the farm received a fairly good education where he took advantage of it and could then, if his parents desired it, enter upon the more advanced courses of the High School, or take up, intelligently and scientifically, in an Agricultural College the study of that first of all industries. Every Province possessed finely equipped Agricultural Colleges, with up-to-date Faculties and scientific farming experts, where the most progressive and modern methods of agriculture were taught with, frequently, the degree of Bachelor of Scientific Agriculture conferred at graduation. Winter sessions were held in most Provinces, where short courses were given, imparting training to boys and girls, over the public school age, in intelligent farming and scientific methods, domestic science and other phases of farm work. These courses proved of immense interest and value, and were, upon the whole, appreciated by agricultural communities. Educational statistics of the Dominion in 1916—the latest available in this complete form—showed the following facts:

Province	Teachers	Pupils	Expenditure
Nova Scotia	3,019	109,189	$ 1,575,562
New Brunswick	2,161	66,548	1,146,883
Quebec	7,982	251,492	11,463,623
Ontario	12,080	508,522	13,351,905
Manitoba	2,991	103,796	6,658,230
Saskatchewan	4,949	119,279	8,163,897
Alberta	4,607	99,201	6,121,614
British Columbia	1,902	59,800	3,216,350
Total	39,691	1,317,827	$51,698,064

Educational Problems of the Day. The leading Educationalists of Canada have, as a rule, had high ideals but their realization has been hampered by unavoidable difficulties.   The vital importance of Education has been an obvious basis of their work but the people could not, and cannot, always be got to see it when the question of municipal expenditure came up and a multitude of isolated, sparsely settled, rural school districts had to deal with a financial problem.   The question of training teachers and paying them so as to make and keep the profession attractive was and is another serious question.   The training difficulty was met by steadily increasing appropriations and the establishment of Normal Schools in all the Provinces; the matter of payment is still a serious problem, with the Provinces slowly increasing the salaries and municipalities still more slowly responding to the same appeal, but with remuneration in almost all other occupations increasing at a greater ratio. In 1915, for instance, the highest salary for male teachers (1st class certificates) in Ontario Public Schools was $1,433 and for females $668; in Quebec Catholic Schools it was $676, in P.E. Island $775, in Nova Scotia $871; in Manitoba the average salary was $768 with a few running from $1,000 to $3,500; in Saskatchewan the highest was $1,298 and in Alberta $1,120.   In all of these Provinces there were considerable advances by 1919.

Another problem was the small percentage of young people attending High Schools—about 10 per cent. in all Canada—with hardly one out of a hundred passing into the Universities.   As illustrating the value of this higher education it was stated in 1919 by the U.S. Bureau of Education that at the ages of 21 to 25 the earnings per week of those with only a primary education ran from $9.50, at the former age, to $12.75 at the latter, while the returns for those having a High School training ran from $16.00 to $31.00 respectively.   In Canada the High Schools were at this time fairly well equipped and, according to Sir Robert Falconer, President of Toronto University,* their laboratories were up-to-date for instruction in Science, and the average of standards and quality of the education given was fully equal to that of the United States, and, in the best schools, would bear comparison with the instruction given in English schools.   The teaching of languages was not, however, as good as it should have been.

Canada in this connection fell more or less into the continental sweep of an educational thought which Dr. P. P. Claxton, U.S. Commissioner of Education, defined in Toronto on Apr. 23, 1919: "Education is not education until it becomes vocational.   It has everything to do with the production of wealth and, therefore, in order to overcome the huge financial losses occasioned by the War there must be a more concentrated educational programme."   The old educational ideal was to teach the child how to live; the new and powerful tendency in Canada, as well as the United States, was to teach him how to make a living.   The over-loading of the curriculum in Canadian schools was and is a condition of inevitable criticism; everyone who did not like, or care for, or appreciate a

*Note.—*The Veteran*, Ottawa, January, 1920.

particular subject wanted it excluded while the principle applied to likes as well as dislikes and to inclusion as well as exclusion. Instruction in all manner of public issues and personal interests—Civics and Prohibition, patriotism and economics, music and singing and physical culture, elementary science and horticulture, botany and picture study, commercial subjects and business courses, nature studies and gardening and drill—was a growing and distinct feature of Canadian education and it is hard to criticize the subjects in detail.   Yet the great essentials of reading, writing, arithmetic, geography, history, grammar, languages, manners, could not but be crowded, somewhat, in their treatment or the child be overladen with work.

Certainly, the average Canadian pupil of this period had no such list of readings and studies in literature as the average child in English schools.   It must be said, also, that not enough attention was paid in Canadian schools to the manners of the children, respect for age and experience was not inculcated, the desire to train boys in freedom of thought and speech often resulted in laxity, if not license, of language and manner.   The combination of politeness with perfect independence was too often disregarded as an ideal condition and the hardly probable extreme of servility was avoided by the too frequent appearance of the other extreme of rudeness.   After all has been said, however, Canadian education by 1919 had achieved a great record and a place of much value in the training of Canadian youth; it was improving in many details and growing gradually better with every turn of time; the expenditure of $50,000,000 a year was a considerable one for seven or eight millions of people and the pride of the ordinary teacher in his or her profession was remarkable.   The all-round level of education amongst the people was good and growing better.

Separate Schools in Canada.   This question of denominational schools was not an active one in 1919, comparatively; as a matter of fact, it was a permanent issue associated with all the tangible and intangible differences of race and creed which time might soften but not, apparently, eradicate.   Manitoba, Quebec, Nova Scotia, Ontario, Alberta and Saskatchewan had all faced this issue from time to time; Ontario in 1919 was the chief centre of controversy. As Bishop M. F. Fallon of London put it to an audience in Massey Hall, Toronto, on Feb. 13, so the Catholics of Canada felt, upon the whole, regarding this subject: "Education and salvation cannot be separated.   Education is the unfolding and strengthening of the whole being.   The highest in the world have been made so through an education which did not mean merely storing the memory and sharpening the wit.   It means that no child shall have a perverted will or a crooked mind.   The heart and the soul are to be developed as well as the body.   The child should be taught love, admiration, sacrifice and courage.   He must be taught that the highest thing is not to be found here, but that there is something higher.   The only atmosphere for the education of a Catholic child is a Catholic atmosphere and this was one of the earliest declarations of the Church.''

Such was the basis of his Church's view that schools must be religious as well as secular; while this was considered essential in primary schools Bishop Fallon, in a Pastoral letter of Aug. 8, intimated that at a later stage another course could be taken: "It may happen that for one reason or another parents will not feel able or inclined to send their children to a College or Convent. In such instances the High Schools and Collegiate Institutes should be made use of. Catholic money has helped to erect these schools and Catholic money contributes to their upkeep.'' In such cases the Parish priest should, he added, visit regularly these schools, either personally or by his delegate, organize the Catholic children for religious instruction and take his place as a matter of right in the life of the institutions. So, in regard to Technical Schools. In Quebec the language issue was super-added to that of the Church.

The extreme Protestant view was strongly put during the year by the Orange Order which, in Saskatchewan, demanded the abolition of Separate Schools and French language instruction; in Nova Scotia urged better enforcement of the non-sectarian School Act and everywhere advocated one language and one school for the whole Dominion. In the Commons on May 14 J. W. Edwards evoked a debate by suggesting the establishment of a non-sectarian School system throughout the Dominion such as existed in the United States and Australia. He mentioned the fact that when Upper and Lower Canada were united in 1841 there was a Roman Catholic majority of 100,000 and that the Separate School Act of 1863 for the Province of Ontario was carried by the Quebec majority in the united Legislature; he declared the greatest human agency for eliminating the differences which divided the Canadian people was a non-sectarian national school system; he favoured the creation of a Dominion Bureau of Education, not to take away existing Educational rights, but to supervise and co-ordinate their application; he suggested a Conference in Ottawa of leading educationalists.

J. A. Robb responded with a very full statement as to the liberality of French Catholic policy and action toward Protestant education in that Province. The Hon. R. Lemieux followed in an historical review of the compromises in this respect which had permitted Canadian Confederation to become a fact and the conclusion that: "The Separate School system is the only one suitable to our conditions, historically it is the best, and if we value our national existence we should see to it that in every school, whether Catholic or Protestant, there is religious tuition. Religion is needed in the world, Mr. Speaker. Human agencies alone will not be able to stop the fury of the revolutionary wave that is sweeping Europe to-day. I repeat, religion is needed.'' R. K. Anderson of Halton replied and voiced the full demand for non-sectarian national schools which, he said, was growing all over the country: "Our public school is a national issue, and should be made a national institution, purely Canadian, and undenominational in its character. Any influence that favours segregation, that divides our population into classes on any claim of expediency, of self-interest, of community interest, or of denominational interest, is dangerous and obnoxious.'' He claimed that while the illiterates in the United States were 7·7 per cent. of the public, in Quebec they were 12·66 per cent. and in three of the Western Provinces over 13 per cent.

H. C. Hocken, Grand Master of the Loyal Orange Order, reviewed conditions as he saw them in Quebec, quoted translations of alleged anti-British material from French Canadian school text-books, indicated the racial difficulties in the West, and urged the need for national schools. In the Senate on Apl. 30, Hon. R. H. Pope brought up the same subject in a Resolution demanding the establishment of a national compulsory school system for Canada. His speech was largely an argument regarding conditions in Quebec. On May 21 Hon. P. A. Choquette declared that no attempt to set aside the provision of the Constitution giving Provinces control of Education could succeed but he favoured the creation of a Central Educational Committee at Ottawa with power to apportion educational grants, and would go so far as to agree that this Committee should have the power to bring teaching, apart from religious instruction in the various Provinces, into uniformity, so that pupils might be moved from one Province to another and fit into the same grades they had left. It would, he thought, be a good thing if pupils of other Provinces could be sent to Quebec and acquire the French language and a knowledge of the French people. The debate was continued on June 24 when Hon. L. O. David pointed out that this Compulsory proposal was now under enquiry and consideration in Quebec; attendance at the schools there, however, was so good that he doubted its necessity. The Resolution was withdrawn.

The difficulty in Manitoba where Roman Catholics had to support their own Separate Schools and, at the same time, contribute to that of the Public Schools, was not a factor in Ontario where taxes were allotted in accordance with the religion of the ratepayer. But there was trouble as to the allocation of taxes from Companies whose shareholders were of mixed faith and it was claimed by the *Catholic Register* of Jan. 23 that out of 10 properties assessed for school purposes to a total of $40,000,000 and including the Toronto Railway, Consumers' Gas, Toronto Electric Light and Bell Telephone, every cent went to the Public Schools though millions worth of the stocks were held by Catholics.

Meantime, the Ottawa Separate School controversy between its internal elements of Irish and French Canadian feeling as to language in education, and the local French Canadian struggle with the Ontario Government over Regulation 17, had been going through a new phase. Financial failure, due to the removal of Government support because of refusal by Separate School Trustees and schools to obey the Provincial Government regulations, as to French language instruction, brought the English-speaking teachers and their supporters to the point of asking the Government, by a Delegation on Jan. 24, to appoint a Commission to take over this branch of the Separate schools.   The Injunction restraining the School Board from borrowing money was making the situation an impossible one; Rev. Father Whelan supported the idea of a Government Commission to administer the schools.   On July 29 the Judicial Committee of the Privy Council in London commenced hearing an appeal, in the case of the Catholic School Trustees of Ottawa against the Quebec Bank and others—in which the Trustees had failed in 1918 to obtain from Ontario Courts the right to get back certain moneys used by the *ultra vires* Provincial Government Commission of 1915 to run the schools with.

Sir John Simon and Senator N. A. Belcourt, K.C., appeared for the appellants and W. N. Tilley, K.C., and McGregor Young for the Ontario Attorney-General.   Decision was given on Oct. 23 with Lord Haldane, Lord Buckmaster, Lord Dunedin and Rt. Hon. L. P. Duff (Canada) present, and the appeal dismissed.   About the same time Mr. Justice Rose in the Ontario High Court (Sept. 26) disallowed the Ottawa School Board's request for the right to borrow $75,000, to keep its schools going, on the ground that he was unable to find that the Board was conducting the schools according to law.   At the close of the year (Dec. 21) Rev. Father J. J. O'Gorman, in his church at Ottawa, urged the settlement of the troubles by the establishment of two mutually independent Separate School Boards in Ottawa, one English and one Bi-lingual, entirely distinct in management, finance and property: "For many years the Catholics of this city, English-speaking and French-speaking, have each had their own parishes, and no friction has arisen as a result; for the same number of years the Catholics of this city have had their schools joined under a mixed French and English Board, and the sad result is known throughout Canada."*

The National Conference on Education. During 1918 this Conference had been under way with a temporary organization centred in Winnipeg and composed of Sir James Aikins, Lieut.-Governor, as Chairman, W. J. Bulman Treasurer and Prof. W. F. Osborne, Secretary—the latter making a tour of Canada and obtaining the necessary support for the project.   It was financially backed by a Dominion-wide effort of the Rotary Clubs which, under the leadership of Rev. Dr. E. Leslie Pidgeon, obtained enough to cover all expenses and leave about $25,000 for continuation of its work.   The idea at the root of the Conference was the relation of Education to citizenship and it was officially called for Oct. 20-22 in order (1) to direct public attention to the fundamental problems in the educational systems of Canada; (2) to consider education in its relation to Canadian citizenship; (3) to undertake the establishment of a permanent Bureau to guide and assist the educational thought

*Note.—See *The Canadian Annual Review* for 1914, 1915, 1916, 1917, 1918 Ontario or Quebec Sections.

of the country. The Chairmen at different periods of the Conference were Sir James Aikins, who delivered the opening address on Oct. 20; the Hon. Dr. R. S. Thornton, Manitoba Minister of Education; Prof. Carrie M. Derick of McGill University; Hon. W. M. Martin, Premier and Minister of Education, Regina; Mrs. George H. Smith, Educational Secretary of the I.O.D.E.; St. Catharines; W. J. Bulman and Archbishop Matheson of Winnipeg. The chief subjects announced and authoritatively dealt with were as follows:

Subject	Speaker	Address
Moral and Spiritual Lessons of the War	The Rev. Dr. C. W. Gordon	Winnipeg
The School and the Development of Moral Purpose	Dr. Theodore Soares	Chicago
The School and the Development of a National Character	Sir Robert Falconer	Toronto
Essential Factors in Education	Dr. Helen MacMurchy	Toronto
Auxiliaries to the School in Moral Training, Y.M.C.A.	Taylor Statten	Toronto
The Function of the Public School in Character Formation	J. F. White, LL.D.	Ottawa
Education and Reconstruction	Peter Wright	Newport, Wales
The School and Industrial Relationships	Dr. Henry Suzzallo	Seattle, Wash.
The Basis of Moral Training	Michael O'Brien	Toronto
The Right of the State to concern itself with Character Education	Dr. Milton Fairchild	Washington
The School and the Newer Citizens of Canada	Dr. J. T. M. Anderson	Regina
The School and Democracy	President John H. Finley	Albany, N.Y.
The Ethics of Christ in the Life of a Nation	Very Rev. Dean Tucker	London

There were 1,200 delegates in attendance from every part of Canada with many from the United States and a few from Great Britain. The keynote of the gathering—which was officially termed a National Conference on Character Education in Relation to Canadian Citizenship—was struck by Sir James Aikins in his opening address: "No democratic nation can make headway or attain greatness which permits its people to grow apart from each other by being divided into classes distinct and mutually exclusive. No such nation can succeed and allow itself to be dominated by a class of wealth, a group of labour, a union of farmers, an assembly of athletes, a society of intellectuals or a body of religionists." All sorts of statements were made in the ensuing discussions and most varied views expressed. Denominational religion was excluded from the discussion but the principle of religion could not be eliminated and Rev. Dr. J. J. Tompkins of St. Francis Xavier University, Antigonishe, sent a paper in which he urged that "God should not be ruled out of the child's life and that His inclusion was the beginning of all morality" while the Very Rev. Dean Llwyd of Halifax pleaded for "the existence of a spiritual part in man as distinct from the material aspect of his being, for the existence of the moral sense in human personality, for the predominating right of that moral sense to be regarded in the battle of life."

The Rev. Dr. H. P. Whidden, M.P., of Brandon, suggested that there should be introduced into all the homes of the country, from Halifax to Vancouver, good books written by Canadian authors. The Rev. Dr. C. W. Gordon urged (1) the re-affirmation of conscience as supreme in human conduct; (2) the supreme worth of humanity and of comradeship; (3) the supreme place of religion in character-making and nation-building. President Suzzallo of Washington University defined co-operation as the great essential; Peter Wright of England urged an international system of school readers; Mr. Premier Martin of Saskatchewan wanted practical aid to meet practical difficulties and pointed out that the average shortage of teachers in his Province, over a 10-year period, was 750.   Rev. Dr. John McKay of Manitoba College declared the teaching of morality from text-books had been a failure in Japan and France; he believed the essential point was the development in the child mind of a sense of the reality of the Unseen and of the personal existence in society of the living God.

Dr. Finley declared democracy could not succeed without education; W. M. Davidson, M.L.A., Calgary, stated that the weakness of the Canadian system lay in poor payment of teachers; Mrs. L. C. McKinney, M.L.A., Claresholm, Alta., described the home, the church and the school as the inseparable trinity of democracy.   Dr. Milton Fairchild denounced Socialism and argued that without wealth and the lead of those who had organizing ability and financial genius, a nation could not get a living for everyone.   Permanent wealth was essential to the development of the higher elements of national civilization, art, science, history, literature, religion, education and research and to the accumulation or preservation of these things from generation to generation.   Dr. Soares declared that "democracy must learn to accept the guidance of expert authority"; Dr. J. T. M. Anderson stated that illiteracy in Canada represented a yearly loss of $75,000,000 in production and that 85 separate languages and dialects were spoken in the three Western Provinces.

It was decided to make the Conference permanent and the Report of the Organization Committee was adopted declaring that a National Council in Character Education should be created with duties involving the realization of the Resolutions of the Conference, and preparation for a similar Congress to be held three years hence; that the National Council should consist of 50 members, 36 of whom were to be nominated, four from each Province, and that these 36 should nominate the remaining 14; that this Council should meet at least once a year with an Executive Committee of the Council to consist of nine persons.   The Council was duly appointed and a Resolution passed as follows: "That this Conference puts itself on record as recognizing the necessity for the deepening and the strengthening of the moral and spiritual factors in our national education alike in the school, the church and the home, and instructs the newly appointed National Council to make a consideration of the problems herein involved a first charge upon its deliberations." Other Resolutions may be summarized briefly:

1. Recommending to the Federal Government the adoption of a distinctive Canadian flag.

2. Declaring it in the best interests of the whole country that a high type of rural schools be developed and that, as a means to this end, Continuation work in rural schools be encouraged.

THE VERY REV. WM. R. HARRIS, D.D., LL.D., D.LITT.   THE REV. JAMES B. DOLLARD, D.LITT.

TWO DISTINGUISHED CANADIAN AUTHORS OF 1919

3. Suggesting that, with a view to strengthening Canadian citizenship there should be held under Dominion Government auspices an appropriate function in each community, preferably on Dominion Day, for the public reception into citizenship of those who had met all the conditions of naturalization.

4. Recommending that in the schools the spirit and practice of co-operation in games and in class-work be encouraged rather than those of competition.

5. Favouring the study of both English and French in all Canadian secondary schools and universities.

6. Declaring that it is the duty of the Federal Government to assume without avoidable delay its fair share in the financial burden, incidental to the Canadianizing of an immigrant population, by providing suitable special Dominion grants to be expended and administered by the Provincial Governments concerned.

7. Urging all Educational bodies to deal frankly and publicly with reductions in rank or dismissals of teachers.

8. Expressing hearty approval of all auxiliary agencies such as the Boys' Brigade, the Boy Scouts, the Cadet Corps, the Canadian Standard Efficiency Training, the Girl Guides, the Little Mothers' League, and the Canadian Girls in Training, which aid in developing among children of school-age physical fitness and the spirit of service and citizenship in the community.

9. Recommending that a complete system of medical and dental nurses be organized in every Province, for both rural and urban schools and also that provision be made for the adequate and specific training of all teachers in the principles and practice of hygiene.

10. Urging a strict censorship of moving-picture posters and advertisements; emphasizing the great educative influence of these moving pictures for good or evil and urging improvement in the standards; asking for the securing of more pictures depicting Canadian and British life and sentiments.

11. Urging enlarged opportunity for the education and training of teachers and raising of the standard of education for admission to the teaching profession.

12. Declaring that provision for state aid should be made for parents who would otherwise be forced through economic necessity to take their children away from school during the compulsory period.

The composition of the Conference and its thousand registered delegates was very representative. Six of the nine Provinces sent their Ministers of Education. Many Provincial Education Departments were represented by administrative officials and there were inspectors, superintendents, principals, teachers and trustees of public and separate schools in large numbers; the Universities and Colleges were ably represented by Presidents and Professors and the Churches were conspicuously present. Leaders of religious education were there and ministers of every denomination, including Roman Catholic. Besides these the following organizations in different sections of Canada sent Delegates: Rotary Clubs, Canadian Clubs, Women's Canadian Clubs, Kiwanis Clubs, Trades and Labour Councils, United Farmers, United Grain Growers, Local Councils of Women, W.C.T.U., Y.M.C.A., Y.W.C.A., Social Service Councils, Boy Scouts, Child Welfare Agencies and Women's Institutes. The influence of the gathering was considerable, the comments upon its success and value by those in attendance enthusiastic.

18

Technical Education in Canada. This subject was largely a matter of Provincial policy and enactment until 1919; nearly every Province expended some money yearly upon Technical training in its lower or higher forms. Manitoba had an Industrial Training School at Portage la Prairie with 64 boys under instruction in 1919; Nova Scotia a Provincial Technical College, 9 local technical schools with 1,509 students and 29 Mining Schools with 289 pupils in 1919, a School of Art and Design and Provincial Directors of Manual Training; Quebec had a Polytechnic School at Montreal with 115 students in 1918-19 and 17 Technical and Art Schools with 3,642 pupils; together with an efficient Science Department in McGill University, a Commercial and Technical High School, and a School of Higher Commercial Studies affiliated to Laval. Ontario went into this subject upon a large scale as became its industrial importance; it had in 1919 eleven industrial, technical and art schools with 155 teachers and 4,739 pupils; A. H. Leake, Inspector, reported 100 Manual Training centres in operation with a Farm Mechanics course recently introduced in High and Continuation Schools; a Summer School for Technical teachers was held in Toronto during July with 40 teachers attending the five weeks' course; there were 95 Household Science centres in the Province. F. W. Merchant, Director of Industrial and Technical Education, reported for 1919 that 13 evening Technical schools were opened during the year and classes in Marine engineering established at 6 Lake ports with others for Masters and Mates while the Department of Education had given liberal grants for technical buildings and equipment.

Action at Ottawa had been urged for some years, with pressure from the Manufacturers' Association and other industrial and labour organizations and various public bodies, but it was held up by the War. In the Commons on May 16, 1919 the Hon. J. A. Calder, Minister of Immigration and Colonization, gave notice of Resolutions and legislation providing for the promotion of Technical Education upon a national scale with the appropriation for that purpose of $10,000,000 to be apportioned as follows: $750,000 for year ending Mch. 31, 1920; $800,000 for 1921, and $900,000 for 1922; $1,000,000 for 1923 and $1,100,000 for 1924 and a like sum for each year up to and ending Mch. 31, 1929. These moneys were to go (1) in a fixed sum of $10,000 to each Province yearly and (2) the balance to be allotted to the Provinces as grants payable quarterly in proportion to population as at the last Federal Census—provided a similar sum was expended by each Province within each year specified. In determining the grant payable annually no account was to be taken of any liability or expenditure incurred by the Province for the acquisition of land, the erection or improvement of buildings, or the supplying of furnishings or equipment for any institution established prior to Apr. 1, 1919. The payments were to be made under the following conditions:

All payments shall be applied and used for Technical Education in the manner agreed upon by the Minister and the Government of each Province; every such agreement shall be approved by the Governor-in-Council.

Not more than 25 per cent. of the grant shall be applied for acquiring land, erecting, extending or improving buildings or supplying furnishings and equipment.

There shall be forwarded to the Minister annually, by each Province taking advantage of the Act, a report setting forth the work done in such Province in promoting Technical Education.

The Minister shall be the sole judge of all questions and differences that may arise under the proposed legislation or under any agreement made in pursuance of the proposed legislation.

The Resolutions were approved and became law as The Technical Education Act of 1919. Agreements were made during the year with some of the Provinces—notably, Ontario, whose first appropriation was $224,382. The general object of these grants was to fit young persons for useful employment in vocational, technical or industrial pursuits; the age limit for entrance was 13 years with 3rd class passage from an elementary school; the expenditures were limited to buildings and equipment, payment and training of teachers. The Administration of the Act was placed under the Minister of Labour and Prof. L. W. Gill of Queen's University, Kingston, was appointed Director of Technical Education. This legislation enlarged the area of discussion and was generally approved; it helped, also, in the vocational work for returned soldiers.

The general subject, with special reference to Textiles, was discussed by the Ontario Educational Association on Apr. 24 at Toronto; in connection with the Canadian Textile Institute a meeting was held in Toronto on Sept. 6 addressed by Prof. A. F. Barker of Leeds, the Hon. H. J. Cody, Minister of Education, and Sir Robert Falconer. The speakers all looked forward to Ontario becoming an industrial centre in this respect and Dr. Cody urged that the study of the scientific character of raw materials, study of technical processes, training in administrative and executive matters, study of the dyeing industry and various forms of applied chemistry and engineering, should have a place in the equipment of the proposed Textile School.

Educational Issues and Conditions in Ontario. The problems of this Province were associated in 1919 largely with rural conditions, the influx of people from the farms to the cities, the question of education as a help away from the farm or from manual labour, the problem put by J. H. Putnam, Inspector of Schools, Ottawa, in *The Globe* of Dec. 29 as follows: "Too often the country school has been so divorced from the life interests of the country people that its pupils have insensibly come to feel dissatisfied and ashamed of their homely but wholesome life and surroundings. They have embraced the first opportunity to escape to the cities. Had they been properly educated or had their parents been properly educated, they would have become partners with their fathers in dairying, poultry-keeping or the production of honey or fruit." How to combine instruction in the love of rural life with knowledge of other things which might easily be made to appear more attractive to the youthful mind was the question! How, in the cities, to combine rudimental learning in the things of life with training along technical and industrial lines was another problem!

The Hon. Dr. H. J. Cody, in his annual Report of Mch. 19, 1919, as Minister of Education for Ontario, touched many sides of the situation as then developed: "We construe Education to mean more than the impartation of knowledge and the training of the mind. Its broad scope covers bodily health and fitness, mental culture, devotion of spirit and social efficiency. The German educationalists think of civilization in terms of intellect; the British in terms of character. Which ideal is the safe and worthier, history has already pronounced. Efficiency in itself is no more moral than lightning. From what motive does it spring? To what aim is it directed? The proper place of efficiency is as the servant of a moral ideal." In 1918 there were in the Province 14,422 teachers and 591,283 pupils as compared with 5,049 teachers and 407,339 pupils in 1867. The schools in 1918 numbered 6,950. The teaching of Agriculture at this time was steadily extending with 1,020 Public and Separate Schools, qualifying for grants, compared with 33 in 1911; 588 had school gardens and 432 home gardens while 28 High Schools taught Agriculture compared with 11 in 1915.

The Minister recognized the rural school problem but found much hope in the Consolidated school principle: "All consolidations will be voluntary and must be duly approved by this Department. Better roads, increased means of rapid transportation, wider distribution of electric power will make life in the country more attractive than ever. There will be more of community spirit. Such a Consolidated School, with its assembly hall, should become the local community centre; and with its graded classes, better teachers, larger numbers, higher average of attendance, and advanced courses, it would bring the advantages of a High School education almost to the doors of the boys and girls on the farm." Encouragement of Industrial and Technical schools was a part of Dr. Cody's policy, and improved attendance regulations was another, with higher salaries to teachers as an essential:

The teacher, after all, holds the key to the educational citadel. On his or her personality largely depends the training of the child. Everything that tends to raise the status of the teaching profession makes directly for the improvement of education. On the teachers is being thrown to-day a burden which should be borne also by the other educational factors of the community—the home, the church, and the press. Salaries commensurate with their services, and their public recognition by the community as a most honourable profession, will increase their teaching power.

Efficient Inspectors, the addition of women to School Boards, the development of Public Libraries, were other points in Dr. Cody's platform. A Deputation from the Ontario Educational Association waited upon the Minister on Jan. 25 and made a number of suggestions including one as to amending the Truancy Act so that any child attending school could be compelled to attend regularly, though under 8 years of age and protesting, also, against the placing of History on the list of examination papers for junior High School entrance. On Apr. 8 Dr. Cody spoke at length in the Legislature and outlined his views and prospective policy. He declared that drastic legislation was not necessary; many of the features, for instance, of the Fisher Bill in Great Britain were already embodied in Ontario laws. What was needed was development in the existing machinery of the Department with some minor legislation dealing with Consolidated Schools, a measure regarding the attendance of youths between 14 and 18 and promotion of rural libraries; he believed most of the educational problems of Ontario could be solved by the expenditure of money. In 1912 there had been $1,900,000 spent on primary and secondary education, and this year there would be over $3,000,000 spent for the same purposes.

Some improvement in regulations and text-books might be desirable and would be undertaken, but he added: "I do not want Inspectors or teachers to feel that they are the slaves of the letter, and thus kill the spirit. I want them to feel that the text-books and regulations are instruments and not masters." The Department of Teacher Training was to be made independent of the Technical department; special training would be given Inspectors and revisions in the courses of study arranged. It was proposed to make a combination of grammar and composition in the elementary school courses. There had been too much physical and scientific geography in these classes and this would be corrected. Plans also were under way for specialized Secondary and Agricultural schools and specialized Commercial and Technical schools.

The legislation carried by the Minister during the year was important and included (1) amendments under which arrangements were facilitated for medical and dental inspection in the Public and Separate Schools; (2) an Act respecting Compulsory school attendance which provided that every child in the Province of Ontario between 8 and 14 years of age should attend school for the full term during which the school of the section or municipality in which he resided was open each year, unless excused for sufficient reasons; (3) a measure as to Consolidated schools which provided that agreements could be entered into for the consolidation of school sections composed of portions of townships and incorporated villages, or for the consolidation of any of these with any of the others and an appropriation of $100,000 for the purpose; (4) an Act respecting Compulsory school attendance of adolescents beyond the age of 14 either for full or part time. This latter measure was regarded by Dr. Cody as most important with its main provisions as follows:

That every boy and girl in the Province up to the age of 18 years must either be employed or go to school; that when employed there must be part-time attendance at school classes—400 hours a year between the ages of 14 and 16 and 320 hours a year between 16 and 18; that this attendance must be during the day-time, and not at night after the boy or girl has done a full day's work; employers to make provision for the part-time employment of adolescents so that they may attend class; that all municipalities of a population of over 5,000 must provide such classes for part-time study; such study to be divided into (1) Continuation of elementary education; (2) commercial and trade preparatory classes; (3) commercial and extension classes.

Another measure facilitated the formation of rural libraries and an additional grant of $250,000 was given to assist rural schools in increasing teachers' salaries.   On July 19 Dr. Cody announced certain changes in Lower School courses of study: (1) Limitation in study of the World War to its suitable perspective in connection with British, Canadian and Modern history; (2) certain changes in the course in Arithmetic and provision of a more practical course in business forms; (3) simplification in Physics and Chemistry courses; (4) request to teachers to relieve, wherever possible, the burden of home work in the lower forms.   In September the teachers of Continuation Schools, High Schools and Collegiate Institutes were instructed to ease up in the home work which they had been accustomed to give students.   In his Circular the Minister said: "The home work assigned to junior pupils is often too great in amount and too difficult in character.   The pupils in the lower forms are at a critical period in their lives when nature's energies are largely needed for physical development.   There must be time for rest and recreation.   The Principal, therefore, should consider it an important part of his duty to keep in close and careful touch with the home work required by the members of his staff."

In October the Consolidated Schools were re-organized and new regulations issued.   They covered the selection of a school site, to consist of five acres of ground including playgrounds, garden plots, area for experimental agriculture and a small forestry lot: the location, size and equipment of the building and related matters; an equipment, unless the Minister should otherwise decide, for the teaching of manual training, household science and agriculture with the inclusion of a piano or other musical instrument, a projection lantern or moving picture machine; there was to be provision for the collection of the children by vans which would traverse the main roads carrying all those who were living more than a mile from the school.   The financial provisions gave a fixed grant of $2,000 to each Consolidated School in actual operation before Dec. 22, 1921 with a specific building grant to be paid under certain conditions.   At this point came the defeat and retirement of the Hearst Government; there was much talk for a time of Dr. Cody remaining as a non-political chief under the new Administration but it was decided otherwise; in any event, the new Minister had the benefit of the trained mind and services of A.H.U. Colquhoun, LL.D., Deputy-Minister, who had held that office since 1906.

On Dec. 14 a Deputation of Provincial teachers waited on Hon. H. R. Grant, the new Minister of Education, and asked for a minimum salary of $1,000 for those holding a permanent certificate and $800 minimum for those having interim certificates (1st year) and $900 for those in the 2nd year.   The 1st annual Report of the new Minister covering the affairs of 1919 dealt, in the main, with conditions under his predecessor.* In it, however, he expressed the new views of a new Government with the condition of rural schools as the pivot of his policy. Mr. Grant first dealt with the School statistics of 1918—the latest year available—and pointed out that the rural schools numbered 5,757 with at least 5,000 of these as one-teacher schools; that the sum spent upon them totalled $5,700,000 of which the School sections contributed over $3,000,000, the Townships $1,807,000 and the Legislature $698,000; that, of this, $3,744,635 went in salaries to teachers and that the value of rural school property was $12,600,343. On the subjects of Rural salaries and Consolidated Schools the Minister was explicit:

RURAL TEACHERS' SALARIES. The salary scale for teachers has improved year by year, but the unprecedented economic conditions of the present time render it inadequate. The rural schools are taught chiefly by women teachers. But 6·27 per cent. of the teachers in them are males. The average salary of the woman teacher has increased from $382 in 1908 to $609 in 1918, and, as everyone is aware, a remarkable improvement has since taken place. As long, however, as urban salaries are so much better— the average salary for the woman teacher in urban schools in 1918 being $882—the rural school will continue to suffer from frequent changes and from the difficulty of securing and holding the most experienced teachers. The salary is not the sole factor in this condition, but it is the most potent. My own experience of rural conditions leads me to the conclusion that the comfort of the teacher must also be closely looked after.

CONSOLIDATED SCHOOLS. The problem of consolidation of schools is complex, varied according to the locality, and aims not at cheapness but betterment. It is not the fashion of Ontario to adopt drastic changes heedlessly. The people have been accustomed for generations to local control of their section schools. The campaign for consolidation must be one of exposition and persuasion. In Ontario, consolidation of schools, as a practical reality, is new, although, of course, the policy is not new in other communities. In 1919 there were 13,000 of these schools in the Republic and 43 States have adopted it as their policy. In the Canadian Provinces, Manitoba has about 100 consolidated schools and Alberta about 60. Ontario has been less easy to convince, because the conditions are widely different from those in the younger Provinces and because each school section has a tradition to which its people are attached.

In seven places consolidation was under way and he hoped the movement would spread as being conducive to greater efficiency in teaching; the larger number of pupils created increased interest and emulation; reductions in absence from school registered 50 per cent.; closer expert supervision and improved buildings and equipment became possible; reduction in expense was obvious. Mr. Grant considered that the Continuation Schools required special attention: "The Inspectors report a scarcity of teachers and a low salary scale. Probably one-half the attendance in these schools consists of pupils whose parents are engaged in agricultural pursuits, and the upbuilding of these schools is, therefore, part of the whole rural school problem. The complaint is general that the Continuation Schools receive inadequate financial support for the

*Note.—The Report was dated April, 1920.

work they have to do, and it is the duty of the Legislature to remedy these conditions.'' He corrected an impression that only a small portion of the Public school pupils went on to the High Schools; as a matter of fact, the average showed 87,200 entering the Elementary schools every year and 14,656 the Secondary schools. Higher salaries in all schools were declared essential; the encouragement of Technical and Industrial training was urged; promotion of the Public Library service advised and a revision of the Act indicated. The military service of Ontario teachers in the War was stated as 573 with 85 killed and 148 wounded; 36 decorations were granted. The Statistics of the schools for 1918 were given as follows:

PUBLIC SCHOOLS

Number of Public Schools	6,136
Enrolled Pupils	457,615
Average Daily Attendance	261,164
Number of Teachers	11,419
Number of Teachers who attended Normal School	8,862
Average Annual Salary—Male Teachers	$1,226
Average Annual Salary—Female Teachers	$707
Amount expended for Teachers Salaries	$8,323,816
Amount expended for all purposes	$13,707,165
Cost per Pupil (enrolled attendance)	$29.95
Number of R.C. Separate Schools	559
Number of Enrolled Pupils	71,302
Average Daily Attendance	40,535
Number of Teachers	1,526
Amount expended for Teachers' Salaries	$703,335
Amount expended for all Purposes	$1,469,558
Cost per Pupil	$20.61
Number of Protestant Separate Schools	6
Number of enrolled Pupils	437
Number Night Elementary Schools	13
Number of Enrolled Pupils	671

SECONDARY SCHOOLS

High Schools and Collegiate Institutes	164
Number of Pupils enrolled	30,732
Average Daily Attendance	24,500
Number of Teachers	1,088
Average Annual Salary	$1,565
Amount Expended for Teachers' Salaries	$1,637,476
Total Expenditures	$2,586,114
Cost per Enrolled Pupil	$84.15
Number of Continuation Schools	136
Pupils in Attendance	5,006
Average Daily Attendance	3,773
Number of Teachers	234
Amount Expended on Teachers' Salaries	$234,976
Total Expenditures	$332,853
Cost per Pupil	$66.49
Number of Night High Schools	25
Pupils Enrolled	4,485
Number of Teachers	153
Industrial, Technical and Art Schools	47
Pupils Enrolled	21,472
Number of Teachers	766
Total Expenditures	$493,200

The total enrollment of Pupils in all schools was 591,283 or 22 per cent. of the total population; the Expenditure was $18,588,890 or $6.90 per head of the population; the Attendance in rural schools (1918) was 217,129 or 41·05 per cent. of the total attendance compared with 57·88 per cent. in 1903; the Attendance in urban schools was 311,788 or 58·94 per cent. compared with 42·12 per cent. in 1903. Of the Teachers 1,068 were males and 11,877 females while 1,099 held 1st class certificates, 9,018 2nd class and 1,247 3rd class. As to special institutions the Ontario School for the Deaf had 277 pupils in 1918 with an average annual cost per pupil of $392.95; the Ontario School for the Blind had a total attendance of 128 in 1919 and an expenditure of $66,874. There were in 1919, 43 Collegiate Institutes, 36 High Schools, 59 Public Schools and 14 R. C. Separate Schools with Cadet Corps—a total of 150.

The Ontario Library statistics of 1918 showed 242 Public Libraries in the Province with 445,090 volumes and a circulation of 535,367 books, the total expenditure was $40,561 and the amount spent on books $12,721, the Legislative grant for 1919 was $8,291. The Free Public Libraries numbered 183 with volumes totalling 1,407,666 and circulation 4,759,049, the total expenditure was $578,865 and $57,182 was spent on books; the 1919 Legislative grant was $24,510. W. O. Carson, Inspector of Public Libraries, dealt in his annual Report with the amendments to the Act which permitted an increased Library rate in municipalities, the success of the *Ontario Library Review*, the work of the Travelling Libraries, the value of the Training School for Librarians. He described the Public Library as follows:

It is an educational institution and a necessary part of an educational system. It supplements the work of schools and serves students who do not attend school. It is an active promoter of popular education. Five kinds of service are usually given by the modern library: (1) reference service, from the answering of simple but not unimportant questions to furnishing extensive information; (2) lending books for home study; (3) lending books for recreative reading, from which there is a greater educational value as a by-product than is generally supposed; (4) special service to children, including the story-hour; (5) providing reading rooms with periodicals and newspapers.

The 19th annual meeting of the Ontario Library Association was held in Toronto on Apr. 21 with an address by Hon. Dr. Cody, Minister of Education. Other addresses of the Session were "The Public Library and the Foreigner," by Miss Norah Thomson, B.A.; "Book Reviewing," by Peter Donovan of *Saturday Night*; "The Public Library of To-morrow," by Miss B. Mabel Dunham, B.A.; "The Days of Reconstruction," by Sir John Willison. Dr. Cody stated that the expenditures on Library work during the years of the War had increased 44 per cent., while the use of books had increased 53 per cent.; about 10,500 books were made available for military camps during the period. Travelling Libraries during the past year had increased about 14 per cent. F. P. Gavin, B.A., Windsor, was President for 1919. On Sept. 10 there was opened in

Toronto the School for Professional Training of Librarians when Dr. Cody described the Public Library as a great popular University extension movement.

The Ontario Educational Association met in its 58th annual Convention at Toronto on Apr. 22 with Rev. James Buchanan of Toronto in the chair and addresses of welcome from Hon. Dr. Cody, Minister of Education, and Principal Hutton of Toronto University.   Dr. Cody referred to the Superannuation Act of Hon. Dr. Pyne and to certain necessary amendments which had been passed; he also dealt with the re-construction of the Ontario College of Art which had trained in its time over 1,300 pupils and described it as growing apace under the management of G. A. Reid, R.C.A.   Dr. P. P. Claxton, U.S. Commissioner of Education, Prof. Paul Balband from France, Dr. O. C. J. Withrow on Social Hygiene, Taylor Statten on Training for Boys, addressed the Convention.   Many speakers, on varied subjects, addressed the different Sections; almost everyone of the 40-odd speeches or papers would deserve reference or quotation if space permitted.

Resolutions were passed by the Public School Section (1) asking that History, as a subject, be reinstated in Part I of the Entrance examination and that the course be simplified; (2) requesting the Minister to make the essential qualification for a Public School Inspector's certificate "successful public school experience rather than mere academic standing"; (3) urging that a course in Health, including the teaching of the facts of reproduction, the natural laws controlling them and the results of breaking these laws, be established in all the Normal Training Schools; protesting against melodramatic and comic picture shows, the manufacture and sale of cigarettes, the comic supplements appearing in some Canadian papers; declaring that before people are allowed to marry they should present a certificate from a qualified medical practitioner that they are mentally and physically qualified for the rights of parenthood.   W. F. Moore, Dundas, was elected President for 1919-20, Henry Ward, Toronto, Treasurer, and R. W. Doan, Toronto, who was attending his 41st meeting of the Association, was re-elected Secretary.   A Resolution was passed approving and pledging support to the League of Empire's proposal to establish in London a Club-House for Overseas Teachers visiting the capital —as a memorial to Overseas teachers fallen in the War.   The following heads were elected in the different Departments and Sections:

Elementary Department	N. C. Mansell	Sault Ste. Marie
Public School Section	A. E. Bryson	Cobalt
1. Principals	John Munro, B.A.	Hamilton
2. Rural School Teachers	J. A. Short	Swansea
3. Primary Teachers	Mary A. Rowe	Brockville
Kindergarten Section	Grace Loucks	Ottawa
Household Science Section	Miss Pritchard	Owen Sound
Technical and Manual Arts Section	Alfred Howell	Toronto
Reformed Spelling Section	Prof. D. R. Keys, M.A.	Toronto
Hygiene and Public Health Section	Wallace Seccombe, D.D.S.	Toronto
League of Empire Section	Principal Hutton, LL.D.	Toronto
Home and School Council Section	Mrs. A. C. Courtice	Toronto
Collegiate and Secondary School Department	A. P. Gundry, B.A.	Galt

Modern Language Section	Prof. M. A. Buchanan, Ph.D	Toronto
Natural Science Section	Arthur Smith	Toronto
Classical Section	Prof. G. Oswald Smith	Toronto
Mathematical and Physical Section	W. L. Sprung, M.A.	Stratford
English and History Section	George Malcolm	Toronto
Commercial Section	W. M. Shurtleff, B.A.	Kingston
Continuation School Section	H. E. Thompson	Toronto
High School Principals Section	A. M. Overholt, M.A.	Brantford
Supervising and Training Department	N. McDougall	Petrolea
Inspector's Section	C. W. Mulloy, B.A.	Aurora
Training Section	Dr. W. J. Karr	Ottawa
Music Section	A. T. Cringan	Toronto
Trustees' Department	Rev. W. M. Morris	Orangeville

Quebec and Compulsory Education. The chief educational question of the year in this Province was that of Compulsory education. Those who urged this policy were earnest in their belief that it was needed and would be beneficial. Those who opposed it believed that it was unnecessary and that the school system of the vast majority being a religious one it was to the interest of the Church and its Curés, in all the parishes, to keep the attendance up to the mark; that as a matter of fact and according to the 1917-18 figures the averages of attendance at the Catholic schools was 346,125 out of a total of 435,903 or 79·40 per cent., while in Protestant schools it was 43,645 out of 57,130 or 76·40 per cent.; that the primary authority over the child was the parent and not the State and that, as the Rev. Father H. Lalande, S.J., claimed, in a Montreal address on Jan. 23, "if the State assumed any direct authority there would at once be a clash with the parental authority, and if the State insisted there would have to be a sacrifice of the parents' natural right which would lead to dangerous doctrines of communism and socialism"; that, as he also stated, the object of education was to make honest and useful citizens for which literacy was not an essential accompaniment and that for children intended for manual labour or the farm, 4 or 5 years at school was sufficient.

It was also alleged that, in Quebec, families were very large and it would be an exceptional hardship if all the children had to go to school; that the present situation compared favourably with other Provinces where Compulsory education was in force and that the non-attendance amounted to 22 per cent. among children from 5 to 7 years, of 5 per cent. among children from 7 to 14 years, and 52 per cent. among children from 14 to 16 years; that at the age of 14, as *La Patrie* put it at this time, the large majority of children were capable of doing useful work and the pressing necessities of life in many cases, and the desire for money in others, caused scores of parents to take their children out of school, the boys being placed in wage-earning positions, the girls kept at home to help with the housework. On the other hand, there were strong expressions of opinion in favour of the proposal which, hitherto, had chiefly been urged by enthusiasts like Godefroi Langlois in *Le Pays* or Dr. J. T. Finnie in the Legislature. In this body on Jan. 29 T. D. Bouchard, who had latterly taken up the subject with great zeal, attacked C. J. Magnan, Inspector-General of Catholic Schools and charged him with designedly moulding the school statistics to serve his purpose in opposing this policy; the discrepancies quoted did not, however, seriously affect the totals and, later in his speech, Mr. Bouchard stated that the child population of the Province was actually 73,321 more (Federal Census) than the Provincial statistics gave. He attacked, also, the "indifference, negligence and egotism" of parents and charged that the French people did not occupy on this continent the place they should in the economic, commercial, industrial and political field owing to lack of Education.

Meanwhile, a largely-signed and influential petition had been prepared in Montreal and was presented to Archbishop Bruchési on Jan. 18 by a Delegation of prominent Catholics—Senators F. L. Béique, C. P. Beaubien and R. Dandurand; L. E. Geoffrion, ex-President Chambre de Commerce, J. V. Desaulniers, President of one Section of the Catholic School Commission, and A. W. Patenaude of another. The Petition asked the Archbishop to urge upon the attention of the Catholic Committee of the Council of Public Instruction, the desirabilitiy of obtaining a Compulsory school attendance law and declared that, in taking such action, the Province would be following the course of all progressive countries. Amongst the signatories were the members of the Deputation and Lord Shaughnessy, Sir Alex. Lacoste, Hon. E. L. Patenaude, Hon. J. M. Wilson; Judges Eugene Lafontaine, Thomas Fortin, L. P. Demers, Charles Archer, L. T. Marechal. L. L. Loranger; Lieut.-Col. Clarence F. Smith, Edouard Montpetit, F. J. Bisaillon, Dr. A. Hingston, J. A. Vaillancourt, O. S. Perrault and C. H. Catelli.

The Archbishop promised to submit the request after Mr. Patenaude had presented school statistics showing the large numbers of children that left school after a year or two years' attendance. Senator Beaubien also urged the necessity of Technical education and pointed out that a solid primary education was a pre-requisite. The Protestant Council of Public Instruction had already supported this policy; on Jan. 31 a large delegation of Labour men, claiming to represent 1,000 local unions, (International) and 125,000 Labour men—in other Provinces as well as Quebec—urged the Provincial Government to enact laws establishing compulsory and free education with uniformity of text-books throughout the Province; demanded that all persons under 21, employed in any kind of work, be forced to at least attend night schools; asked for the appointment of a Minister of Public Instruction. Incidentally, they requested 2½ per cent. alcohol in beer. Sir Lomer Gouin stated that this latter point was under Federal jurisdiction and Hon. L. A. Taschereau announced that a Deputy-Minister of Labour would be appointed shortly. Later in the day a Deputation from the National and Catholic Labour Unions urged the Government not to grant Compulsory education and they argued that the time was not ripe for such a law and that, in fact, it was not needed. Catholic Commercial travellers, a little later, also petitioned the Government against this policy.

On Feb. 5 the Catholic Committee of the Council of Public Instruction discussed the matter for hours and approved a Resolution of Hon. T. Chapais and Hon. J. M. Tellier that the Superintendent of Public Instruction should enquire, by every means in his power, and with the aid of the Prime Minister and his colleagues, as to the reliability of the School statistics furnished by the Inspectors. When this was done the Council could deal with the subject more satisfactorily. There were present Archbishops Bruchési and Roy, 9 Bishops and 11 prominent Judges or other laymen with Hon. C. F. Délage, Superintendent of Public Instruction, in the chair. At Farnham on Feb. 12 Hon. S. A. Fisher (Protestant) urged Compulsory education: "The Legislature has been increasing the educational grant continuously for many years, but the School Boards have not been increasing theirs in proportion. The Commissioners should raise more money. Nothing good can be done without spending money." In the Senate on Apl. 30th, Hon. R. H. Pope dealt with this subject and declared that lack of provision for Compulsory attendance of children at school had resulted in the withdrawal of Quebec children in large numbers after the first few years of schooling; altogether too many had left after the third and fourth years and he compared this attendance with somewhat similar conditions in Ontario as follows:

Quebec	Protestant	Roman Catholic	Ontario	Attendance
First year	14,756	155,376	Primary	131,844
Second year	8,843	97,947	First reader	72,898
Third year	8,377	75,247	Second reader	102,972
Fourth year	8,142	44,045	Third reader	100,023
Fifth year	6,464	17,468	Fourth reader	90,050

Senator Pope claimed, also, that the Quebec *Year Book* gave the School population of the Province in 1916-17 as 543,873; the School attendance in that year was 464,447 and the number not attending school at all was therefore 79,426; there should be added to these 58,000 who only attended school one year. Hon. C. P. Beaubien claimed (May 15) that Quebec was first amongst the Provinces in its school attendance with the proportions in 1916-17 as follows: Nova Scotia 63 per cent.; New Brunswick 65 per cent.; Manitoba 54·05 per cent.; Saskatchewan (1911) 58 per cent.; Alberta 60 per cent.; British Columbia 78 per cent.; Canada, as a whole 58 per cent.—the Province of Quebec 77 per cent. On May 15th the Catholic Committee of Public Instruction decided to press the proposed enquiry and make it a thorough analysis of conditions and a Sub-Committee was appointed for the purpose composed of Mgr. Emard, Bishop of Valleyfield; Mgr. Bruchesi, Archibishop of Montreal; Mgr. Ross, of Rimouski; Rev. Father H. Desrosiers, Principal of the Jacques-Cartier Normal School, Montreal, and Hyacinthe Fortier, M.P. Other incidents of the discussion were the defeat of T. D. Bouchard in St. Hyacinthe during the general elections and the election of Judge Lafontaine as Chairman of the Montreal Board of Catholic School Commissioners; in Montreal during September a large increase in the pupils of almost every school in the city was reported.

Meantime, the question of Teachers' salaries had been raised and considerably discussed in the Provincial Legislature, the press and on public occasions. The average situation, of course, could not be compared with other Provinces as there were 1667 male teachers in Orders and 4,338 Nuns teaching in the schools of Quebec who drew very little pay and in some cases none. The average salaries had, in any case, increased for male teachers in Catholic schools from $703 in 1912-13 to $890 in 1917-18 and for female teachers from $163 to $213; the average in Protestant schools had grown for male teachers from $1,400 to $1,643 and for females from $469 to $606. Bound up with the question of salaries was the shortage of teachers and a Deputation to the Government on Jan. 17th declared that many Protestant schools, especially in the rural districts, were closing for lack of teachers; a minimum of $500 for elementary teachers and $700 for those holding model school diplomas was urged.

Mr. Délage, Superintendent of Public Instruction, drew attention to this subject in his annual Report for 1918-19: "Notwithstanding the good work of the Catholic and Protestant Boards of Examiners, and of the Normal Schools, real nurseries for the training of teachers, notwithstanding the sacrifice the Directors make to put them on a good footing and the Government's offer of awards, the number of teachers tends to diminish. The scarcity is already felt in many places." He urged $300 as a future minimum salary. In Montreal, a little later, a new Protestant scale was granted with a minimum for women of $850 and a maximum of $1,250; there followed a strong Catholic agitation for increases with a Delegation to Hon. L. A. David, Provincial Secretary, on Oct. 18 which claimed that the annual minimum salary for Catholic teachers in Montreal was $700 for males and $500 for females, and the maximum from $1,400 to $1,700 with an average to all teachers in Montreal of $1,100. They asked for an increase of $400; Judge Lafontaine, meanwhile, had suggested in the School Board, as a help toward solution, the dismissal of 238 male teachers and the appointment of female teachers in their stead. In November an all-round increase of $100 was decided upon, to be granted if power were given to increase taxes and it was pointed out that two small increases had already been given during the year; at the same time strong ground was taken against any organization or unionization of teachers. The official Quebec statistics of the year 1917-18 compared with 1916-17 were as follows:

CATHOLIC AND PROTESTANT ELEMENTARY SCHOOLS

	1917-18	1916-17
Total of schools under Control	5,332	5,287
Number of Independent Schools	76	80
Pupils of schools under Control	202,649	206,133
Pupils of Independent Schools	6,308	5,433
Catholic Pupils	208,606	211,242
Protestant Pupils	351	324
Average attendance of Pupils	158,799	162,084

Total of male and female lay Teachers	5,803	5,782
Number of male Teachers in Orders	107	117
Number of Nuns teaching	825	815
Total of Protestant Elementary Schools	695	714
Protestant Pupils in Elementary Schools	37,273	39,606
Catholic Pupils in Elementary Schools	1,301	1,565
Total of Pupils	38,574	41,171
Average Attendance of Pupils	29,520	31,030
Total of Male and Female Lay Teachers	1,454	1,466

CATHOLIC MODEL SCHOOLS AND ACADEMIES

Number of Model Schools under control	573	566
Number of Independent Model Schools	112	113
Pupils of Model Schools under control	94,831	93,111
Pupils of Independent Model Schools	9,287	9,517
Catholic Pupils	103,846	102,326
Protestant Pupils	272	302
Total of Pupils in Model Schools	104,118	102,628
Average attendance of Pupils	83,533	83,322
Total Number of Teachers	1,022	1,019
Number of Catholic Academies under control	179	156
Number of Independent Academies	179	171
Pupils in Independent Academies	26,845	25,892
Catholic Pupils	99,556	90,376
Protestant Pupils	330	344
Total of Pupils in Academies	99,886	90,720
Average attendance of Pupils	85,003	77,748
Pupils in Catholic Model Schools and Academies..	204,004	193,348
Grand Total of male and female lay teachers	1,396	1,356
Number of male Teachers in Orders	1,667	1,521
Number of Nuns teaching	4,338	3,963

PROTESTANT MODEL SCHOOLS AND ACADEMIES

Number of Model Schools under control	42	40
Protestant Pupils in Protestant Model Schools	5,157	4,960
Catholic Pupils in Protestant Model Schools	228	243
Average attendance of Pupils in Model Schools	3,920	3,976
Total Number of Teachers	290	178
Number of Protestant Academies under control ...	30	31
Number of Independent Academies	....	....
Total of Protestant Academies	40	41
Protestant pupils of Protestant Academies	10,212	11,747
Catholic pupils of Protestant Academies	376	355
Total of Pupils in Protestant Academies	10,588	12,102
Average attendance of pupils	8,282	9,308
Grand total of Pupils	15,973	17,305
Total of male and female lay Teachers	604	618

CATHOLIC CLASSICAL COLLEGES

Number of Classical Colleges	21	21
Pupils in Commercial course	2,192	2,599
Pupils in Classical course	5,430	5,729
Total of Pupils	7,622	8,128
Average attendance of Pupils	6,956	7,454
Total of Professors	747	747

The total of teachers in all schools and colleges was 18,403, of whom 8,079 were religious in their Orders or vocations; the school contributions of the Province included $6,832,844 from municipal taxation, $376,097 from monthly fees, $5,196,359 from independent subsidized schools and $2,145,976 from all Government sources —a total of $14,551, 277. Upon the general question of inter-Provincial education Léon-Mercier Gouin, a rising young lawyer of Montreal, addressing the Empire Club, Toronto, on Nov. 27, said: "Let our French-speaking students come to Toronto and to Kingston; let them learn here the English language, and also our Canadian ideal; let them become acquainted with you, and also with your aspirations; and in the same way, let your College men come to Montreal and to Quebec—they will be welcome if they wish to come. . . . If scholarships were founded in Quebec allowing let us say, ten French-Canadians to come and study in Ontario either letters or sciences, we would enjoy immediately immense advantages; and in the same way if your own people would come to our Colleges in Quebec to become acquainted with French literature—and also with our French-Canadian literature, which indeed exists—then we would easily find the means of a real, effective and powerful *bonne entente*, and as we could have an exchange of students, so also we ought to have an exchange of professors."

Schools in the Maritime Provinces. Dr. A. H. MacKay, Superintendent of Public Schools in Nova Scotia, since 1898, in his Report for the year of July 31, 1919, had to deal with a reduced enrollment for the Province of 875 girls and 240 boys due to abnormal weather, the Influenza and an average shortening of the school term. The statistics of the year showed 1,797 school sections and 124 without schools as against 85 in 1918; 2,812 schools in operation or a reduction of 47 with 3,012 teachers as against 3,037 in 1918; 1,640 Normal-trained teachers, 163 male teachers and 2,849 female, 565 new teachers; as to service there were 942 of 1 year or under, 668 of 1 to 3 years, 548 of 3 to 5 years, 474 of 5 to 10 years, 289 of 10 to 20 years, 219 of 20 to 30 years, and 63 of 30 years or over; the registered Pupils in the 1st quarter of 1919 were 91,123, 2nd quarter 97,843, 3rd quarter 102,125 and 4th quarter 67,088 with decreases in each case running from 5,255 down to 900: the total of Pupils in common school grades was 97,844, in High School grades 9,138 and in Technical Schools 2,608 or 109,590 altogether.

There were 81 school gardens, 729 members of Cadet corps, 1,579 teachers in ungraded schools and 1,433 in graded; the total value of school property was $4,137,743 and of all property in Sections $139,271,595; the Expenditures by the Province were $432,496, by municipalities $204,519, and by Sectional assessment $1,460,577; the distribution of School-books by the N.S. School Book Bureau was 215,041, including Common and High School text-books and Teachers' text-books, at a cost of $38,968. Special institutions of the Province were the School for the Deaf in Halifax with 78 in attendance, the School for the Blind with 153 under instruction, the Victoria School of Art and Design with 79 students enrolled. The Normal College reported for 1918-19 an enrollment of 255 and the

Principal, Dr. David Soloan, urged better surroundings for his students:

Admittedly the occupation they propose for themselves cannot be classed as gainful in any large sense. It is beyond 'contradiction, therefore, that state authorities owe it to the young people training for the public educational service to ensure not only the physical comfort necessary to successful study but an environment calculated to refine and to improve socially. The public has not yet intelligently and squarely faced the matter of a supply of teachers. Present conditions point to the vital necessity of their doing so. And one of the factors that will have to be considered early is the proper housing and social training of the student-teachers at the Normal College.

Early in the year the Halifax *Herald*—opposed to the Government of the day—initiated a vigourous campaign against the Provincial School system (Feb. 8; Feb. 15; Feb. 26) with the claim that seven-eighths of the School sections were providing for less than one-third of all the pupils; that out of 109,032 pupils enrolled during 1917 there were 5,941 who attended school less than 20 days, 11,577 who attended only from 20 to 49 days, 16,323 who attended only from 50 to 99 days; that there were 33,841 pupils, or more than one-third of all the enrollment, who attended school less than 99 days during the year; that the County Academies and other secondary-schools of the Province were taught largely by those who had merely completed the secondary-school courses, and that none but a College graduate should be permitted to teach a County Academy or secondary-school, or any school authorized to educate those who intended to teach others; that the training of the teachers was superficial, inadequate, and entirely unspecialized, and that only a little over 8 per cent. of the total school population ever reached the secondary schools. The most serious allegation and condition however, was poor pay and the fact that teaching had lost its attractiveness as a permanent profession—a condition, of course, not confined to Nova Scotia.

The other side of the question was presented in the Legislature by Hon. R. M. MacGregor, for the Government, on May 5th. During the year $1,372,000 had been spent upon Education or $3.76 *per capita*. This was lower than in the United States, but the people of the Province were not so wealthy. An important feature of the year had been an increased attendance in the Schools of Mechanical and Domestic Science. Teachers' salaries had also been advanced by $120,000, before the new scale advocated by the Council had come into effect, and the Municipal School Fund had been raised from thirty-five cents to fifty cents *per capita*. He laid particular emphasis upon the Technical College which, because of war conditions, had been obliged to depart from its original purpose of providing an Engineering course. It had been a centre of patriotic activities and its whole equipment and staff was now devoted to the service of the Invalided Soldiers' Commission for the re-education and retraining of disabled men who were unable to resume their former occupations. He also touched upon the Bilingual schools, of which there were 140 in Nova Scotia, and said that the problem had been solved by the use of French readers in the first four grades and English text-books in the higher grades. Teachers' salaries still were too small but, the Minister added, there would be a substantial increase beginning with the opening of the next school year in August.   J. C. Tory followed and wanted French and Spanish substituted for the dead languages and a Minister of Education appointed.

In New Brunswick Dr. W. S. Carter, Chief Superintendent of Education, reported for the year of June 30, 1919, that there were 1,959 Schools in the 1st term and 1,950 in the 2nd; 2,078 and 2,107 Teachers, respectively, and 62,324 and 64,920 Pupils respectively; there was an all-round decrease.   The chief subjects taught in common school grades, so far as numbers of pupils, were concerned were physical exercises, morals, reading and spelling, grammar, history, drawing, writing, singing, arithmetic, geography, health and nature lessons, with sewing, knitting, Latin and French as optional and only the latter subject taken to any extent.   The average salaries of teachers ran from $1,523 in grammar schools and $901 in Superior schools to $1,200 for 1st class (male), $506 2nd class, $389 3rd class, with $705 for 1st class (female), $427 2nd class and $332 3rd class.   The increase in these different classes over the salaries of 1909 were respectively as follows: $439, $212, $559, $154, $127, $310, $138, and $113.   The Provincial grants showed $1,153,163 voted at annual school meetings, $99,097 from County School Funds and $277,995 paid out by the Education Office of the Government.   The Provincial Normal School report of Principal H. V. B. Bridges showed in 1919 an enrollment of 275 students, or an increase of 22, with an increase, also, in French or Acadian students.

During this year the New Brunswick Teachers' Association made a strong effort to obtain increases in salaries.   This body was formed in 1918 with Berton C. Foster, M.A., LL.D., of Moncton, as President and its platform included the following items: (1) To strive, in harmony with all educational authorities, for the advancement of sound education in the Province; (2) to awaken and promote a healthy professional spirit and to encourage a higher standard of efficiency; (3) to use all legitimate means to increase the salaries of teachers and other members of the Association, in order that the best talent may be attracted to the teaching profession and retained in it; (4) to unite in a combined effort for an enlarged and adequate Pension scheme.   One of their strong arguments was that the 18 leading Educationalists of the Province, from the Chief Superintendent down, averaged salaries of $1,800!

In Prince Edward Island the annual Report of the (Acting) Chief Superintendent of Education, H. H. Shaw, showed for the year of Dec. 31, 1918, a total of 468 schools and 596 departments, 597 teachers and 17,861 pupils enrolled; the average daily attendance was 11,334, the Government expenditure on schools was $173,-579 and that of the Districts $94,967; the average salaries paid to teachers ran from $705 down to $195; the most largely patronized subjects of instruction in different grades were writing, arithmetic, grammar, history, geography, spelling, composition, drawing and physical training. There were 23 vacant schools which, Mr. Shaw urged, should be amalgamated with other districts; a number of Boys' and Girls' Clubs had been formed to promote studies in elementary Agriculture at home—growing roots and vegetables, caring for live-stock, poultry, etc.; physical training was stated to be compulsory and reference was made to "startling facts" as to so many young men having proved ineligible for military service. In this Province during 1918 a Teachers' Union had been formed with the object of raising the status and salaries of the profession. Mr. Shaw said of this: "Improvement in any direction is at present retarded, if not blocked, by the comparatively low salaries paid the teachers. Hence, to meet this condition, a schedule of salaries has been drawn up and agreed upon by the members of the Union, as the minimum rates of salary on which they can decently live. Their demands cannot be considered unreasonable."

Education in Manitoba During 1919. Robert Fletcher, Deputy-Minister of Education, in reporting to the Minister for the year of June 30, 1919, dealt first with the inevitable Teacher problem: "Our teacher supply has not been adequate, and it was necessary in order to meet the situation to issue during the year over 400 permits to untrained people. Manitoba trains in her Normal Schools a sufficient number to meet all requirements, yet the exodus to other occupations, the inevitable claims of matrimony and the steady drain to the Western Provinces where more money is paid are causing the situation to become more acute. Those who leave are not always the novices fresh from training, but include many of our most experienced and competent people. This difficulty is not felt in the larger centres, which offer better salaries, permanent tenure of office and, in the city of Winnipeg, provision for retirement. The permits issued are all for rural districts, where the untrained represent more than 25 per cent. of our total teaching force. We have in Manitoba 1,526 one-room schools with an enrollment of 39,835 pupils and an average attendance of 19,685. It is these children who are suffering under present conditions." Better salaries was the remedy urged; the Permit teacher was described as an unmitigated evil.

As to other matters, Mr. Fletcher pointed out that Medical inspection was fast becoming a reality with 43,950 children examined once during the year and 6,964 twice and 49 nurses giving all their time to the work; Dental inspection had been started in Winnipeg with 3,292 examined. The total expenditure on Education for the year of Nov. 30, 1918, was $1,391,678 of which $912,492 went to the Schools and the balance to the Industrial Training School, the School for the Deaf, the School Attendance Branch, and Neglected Children, with $148,913 to the University of Manitoba and $200,859 to the Manitoba Agricultural College. Consolidation continued to gain ground with more than 100 schools so organized while the Municipal School Board idea gained slowly in rural favour.   Dr. Daniel McIntyre, Superintendent of Winnipeg Schools, reported 41 schools with 705 teachers, salaries totalling $944,750, an enrollment of 15,676 boys and 15,829 girls with a daily average of 22,252.   The total distribution of free text-books in the Province was 55,036, the attendance at the Industrial Training School, Portage la Prairie, was 89 and at the Manitoba School for the Blind the number was 151; the total attendance at Intermediate High Schools, Collegiate Institutes and Technical High Schools was 5,687 with 114 such schools and 270 teachers.

The School statistics of the Province for 1919 were as follows: School population 138,352 and total registration of pupils 114,662; average attendance 72,072, number of Districts 2,017, school departments in operation 3,256, school-houses 1,784; the teachers employed were 3,097 of whom 524 were males and 2,573 females with 81 having Collegiate standing, 351 1st class certificates, 1,603 2nd class, 849 3rd class, 53 specialist and 160 interim; the value of school-houses was $12,980,053 and total assets $15,960,670.   An important legal decision of the year was given in two Mennonite cases (Hildebrand and Doerksen) wherein these Russian settlers claimed that they could not be compelled to send their children to school and test cases were submitted to the Court of Appeal.   The decision unanimously rendered by Chief Justice W. E. Perdue and Justices J. D. Cameron, A. Haggart and C. P. Fullerton was that (1) the Government of Manitoba had the right to pass in 1916 the School Attendance Act under dispute; (2) that this Act was binding on the Mennonites in the Province, who came to it in 1874, despite their claim of alleged special privileges granted under the Order-in-Council of Aug. 13, 1873; (3) that the Government of Manitoba had full power to legislate as to school attendance and education in respect to these settlers.

The case had been decided on Aug. 12th and under the judgment a right to appeal direct to the Imperial Privy Council was refused; it was carried on, however, to the Supreme Court of Canada.   In the Legislature on Jan. 30 Hon. Dr. R. S. Thornton, Minister of Education, delivered an elaborate address on Educational conditions and reviewed the Government statement of 1914 that (1) it was the first duty of the Government to bring suitable educational facilities within the reach of all the children in the Province, and (2) that the teaching of English should be made obligatory in all public schools.   He observed that under then existing regulations, out of 1,685 one-room schools, there were on June 30, 1915, 421 Bilingual schools—French, German, Polish, Ruthenian; there was a whole system of Bi-lingual operation from Normal Schools down. He then proceeded as follows:

Our first step after the repeal of the Bi-lingual clause in the law was to remove the machinery that had been shaping and making for Bi-lingualism. The Bi-lingual text-books were disposed of; the schools were all brought under the care of the General Inspectors; the Mennonite and French Normal schools were dispensed with; all students were required to take all their examinations in English; no permanent teaching certificates were granted except to British subjects, and all teachers were asked to take the oath of allegiance before entering on their duties; the Polish and Ruthenian Training schools were closed. In the work of reconstruction we had to consider the training of new teachers, and the providing of adequate living conditions for teachers so that we would be able to secure and retain their services; in three years we have added 120 school-rooms, providing accommodation for 6,000 additional children and, during the year, there have been built in connection with the schools 22 teachers' residences making a total of 67 to date.

The question of Municipal School Boards referred to in the Deputy Minister's Report involved the bringing together of various school districts of a municipality under a single local control. As the Department pointed out in urging the policy: "With it will come better teachers, well-equipped for their work and with longer tenure of office. . . . The collection and handling of taxes will be simplified. Accounting will be greatly improved. Greater care will be exercised in the location of new schools which will be made to serve larger groups, with transportation supplied as required. It will also be possible to provide a municipal high school at a convenient point." On Sept. 2nd it was announced that 200 schools could not re-open for want of teachers and 5,000 children were thus left without instruction; according to Mr. Fletcher school boards lacking vision, and paying inadequate salaries, were largely responsible for this shortage of teachers.

In this connection the Winnipeg School Board on Oct. 14 recommended an all-round increase in salaries of $100 and at Brandon on Oct. 17 the new Provincial Commission appointed to investigate the question commenced its labours; it was composed of A. E. Hill (Chairman), S. H. Forrest, Souris, Thomas A. Neelin, Mineota, J. A. Glen, Russell, Mary M. Dawson, Crystal City, and P. H. Harris, Secretary. At the annual meeting in Winnipeg, on Dec. 30, of the Manitoba Teachers' Association Resolutions were passed approving of the movement to organize an Association of Teachers' Federations embracing the four Western Provinces and declaring that $1,200 should be the minimum wage for holders of permanent 2nd class professional certificates. Other motions passed included a recommendation for the exchange of literature between the Western organizations with a view to securing unity of aim; in favour of the establishing of a Chair of Pedagogy in the University of Manitoba; approving of the creation of a Teachers' Bureau when the financial condition of the Federation would permit; calling for a certificate showing that teachers coming in from outside points had given two years' services, satisfactory to an Inspector, before they were granted a permanent certificate. H. W. Huntley of West Kildonan was re-elected President.

Educational Conditions in Saskatchewan. The racial and language problems of this Province made its educational system difficult to adjust at times; the importance of these issues was recognized by the Prime Minister (Hon. W. M. Martin), holding, as did his predecessor, the Portfolio of Education. There were in the Province 40,000 people who did not speak English; many others spoke it slightly but were more or less illiterate with, in the 1911 Census, 13·7 per cent. so recorded. Mr. Premier Martin spoke on Apr. 22 at Regina and reviewed, especially, the Dr. Foght Report of 1918 which recommended the Municipality as the unit of school organization—a plan strongly favoured by Manitoba educationalists. Mr. Martin did not altogether approve of it: "Personally, I think the time for the passing of the little rural School Boards has not arrived. If these are done away with, the result will be that a great deal of the local interest now taken in the local school would also be done away with. A great many districts have paid off all their indebtedness but others have great debts still. In such a change the difficulty of adjusting financial matters would be great."

As to the Consolidated School, Mr. Martin stated that the Department favoured the system, but the policy of forcing or actively encouraging consolidation had not been adopted because of the difficulty of financing these schools in the great distances of Saskatchewan. He stated that in 1917 there were 70 per cent. of the pupils of the Public Schools in the first four grades, five per cent. in grade eight and only five per cent. in the High School grades. In rural districts it was established that but one pupil out of every 129 was doing High School work. The Department, in order to encourage attendance at the High Schools had decided to give a grant to every town and village school which had 15 pupils taking such work and including Grade 8 pupils. Mr. Martin dealt at some length with the problem of permanency in the teaching profession: "The number of teachers who leave the profession each year, is reaching appalling figures with one-third of the Saskatchewan teachers changing annually." As a result the Department was forced to issue permits and about 1,000 had been given in 1918, while the average for the last ten years was 750. Statistics were quoted which showed that in the years 1916-17-18, 1,440 teachers entered the Province and only 153 were lost to the other Provinces. In this same period 4,605 teachers had taken licenses in Saskatchewan; about 3,000 had been trained in its Provincial Normal Schools during the same length of time; 55 had been transferred to Manitoba while Saskatchewan received 433 back from that Province.

In the succeeding Session of the Legislature the Premier put through several important Educational amendments. The Secondary Education Act was amended so that every High School which wished to take up fourth year work, must employ three members, at least, on its regular teaching staff while a Collegiate Institute must have 75 pupils who had passed Grade VIII instead of 50. The School Act was changed to provide (1) that a declaration of naturalization, as well as the oath of allegiance, was necessary for all Trustees, under a penalty for non-compliance of a $100 fine;

(2) that power be given to Boards of Trustees to co-operate with one another in the erection of a teacher's residence, and to furnish and maintain the same on such terms as were mutually agreed upon; (3) that power be granted to a Board of Trustees, or a group of them, to provide for medical or dental inspection, or to employ a school nurse or a special instructor in household science, manual training or agriculture. An important Language amendment, or rather new section, was passed:

Except as hereinafter provided, English shall be the sole language of instruction in all schools, and no language other than English shall be taught during school hours; (2) in the case of French-speaking pupils, French may be used as the language of instruction, but such use of French shall not be continued beyond Grade I and, in case of any child, shall not be continued beyond the first year of such child's attendance at school; (3) when the Board for any district passes a Resolution to that effect, the French language may be taught as a subject for a period not exceeding one hour in each day as a part of the school curriculum, and such teaching shall consist of French reading, French grammar and French composition; (4) where the French language is being taught under the provisions of sub-section (2) or (3) hereof, any pupils in the Schools who do not desire such instruction shall be profitably employed in other school work while such instruction is being given.

As to this, it made a vital change in the status of French-speaking pupils of primary schools. Since 1905 it had been permissible for the taxpayers of any School District to make provision for a course in French in the primary grades which their children attended. The new law reduced the time in which such instruction in French could be given in the primary grades to one hour. This particular legislation was strongly criticized in French-Canadian circles, and in Quebec. Stewart Adrian, Provincial Grand Master of the Orange Order (Mch. 5) praised the Martin Government for having stopped the teaching of foreign languages in the elementary schools of Saskatchewan but disliked ''the special privilege extended to the French language'' and urged further agitation so that the English language only could be used as a medium of instruction in all schools. The School Grants Act was amended so as to permit grants for noon-day lunch in Continuation and Night schools and the Attendance Act was changed to permit of enforcing a fine of $10 for neglect in sending a child to school, regularly, by means of distress levy or sale of goods and chattels when necessary.

As to Teachers' salaries the discussion was continuous. In 1917 the male teachers, with 1st class certificate, received an average of $1,353 in urban centres and $950 in rural, and female teachers $930 and $871 respectively; 2nd class teachers (male) received $1,100 and $894 respectively and female teachers $844 and $849; 3rd class teachers (male) received $887 and $864 and female teachers $784 and $818 respectively; Provisional teachers (male) received $940 and $881 respectively and female teachers $785 and $884. On Sept. 5, 1919, W. J. N. McNeely of the Teachers' Exchange Department of Education stated that Saskatchewan salaries in the rural districts ranged from $900 to $1,000 for teachers holding a 3rd class certificate; from $1,000 to $1,200 for 2nd class teachers and from $1,100 up for 1st class teachers. In a number of cases, in foreign settlements, teachers this year were being paid $1,300 a year in addition to securing a house rent free and free fuel. This Exchange was a new organization of the Department to secure and locate qualified teachers, to help teachers as a body in obtaining higher remuneration, to assist the School Trustees in giving it and to promote co-operation between them. Formed early in 1918, it had within a year placed more than 1,000 teachers in positions.

Speaking at Swift Current on Oct. 3 Mr. Premier Martin stated that the Department of Education was prepared to give abundant assistance to the proposed teachers' Pension scheme as soon as the teachers of the Province were ready to endorse a definite plan. Since the direct enforcement of the Compulsory Attendance law, he said that a very gratifying increase had been noted in all Sections. As to the Mennonites, the Department would insist that there be but one School law for all and they would have to conform to regulations in sending their children to the schools erected for them on the Mennonite settlements: "These people are here and they are going to remain. It is folly to talk of having them deported in large bodies. They have been here a long time and while they are deluded in thinking they have special privileges in Saskatchewan over other citizens, at the same time we have got to use reasonable toleration in our treatment of them." They held the same delusion as to guarantee that was so summarily dealt with in the Manitoba Courts and gave the Premier and his Department much trouble for a time—especially in the colony south of Swift Current. Mr. Martin's own reception in the district was hostile and inspection of the schools was found difficult; Bishop Wiebe personally refused to co-operate in sending the children to the new schools which were being built and operated by the Department. On Sept. 25 forcible measures were taken to have the Attendance Act respected.

An encouraging statement as to foreign settlers in general was issued by the Education Department on Oct. 30th: "Of 177 schools in Ruthenian settlements, only 28 have engaged teachers holding provisional certificates or permits, while out of 178 schools in German settlements, only 12 of the teachers are not fully Normal-trained. When it is remembered that 418 provisional certificates have been issued throughout the Province up to Oct. 25 it is clear that the Trustees in the non-English schools are not only eager to obtain fully qualified teachers, but are willing to pay good salaries." Meanwhile, Dr. J. T. M. Anderson had been appointed Director of Education amongst "the new Canadians" of the Province with a policy which he had outlined in February as follows:

To ensure the obtaining by every child in our schools of an adequate knowledge of the English language and the training necessary for good Canadian citizenship. In order to accomplish this, every school in non-English districts will be supplied with strong Canadian teachers and these will be provided with comfortable, home-like cottages and paid salaries of at least $1,500. These schools will become community centres where instruction in Canadian civics and customs, housekeeping, poultry-raising, etc., will be encouraged; field day sports and picnics will be held to introduce the people to the social side of Canadian life and night schools to overcome the alarming illiteracy of the adults; text-books will be prepared for the use of these adults which will breathe the true spirit of national life and where local School Boards are dominated by foreign-born trustees, who will not comply with the School Act and regulations, they will be relieved of their duties and an Official Trustee appointed.

On Nov. 16 A. H. Ball, Deputy-Minister of Education, stated that there were in the Province 4,297 school districts including 3,900 rural schools and 397 urban schools. All schools had the same curriculum and, with one or two exceptions, the pupils in all the schools used the same text-books. The School Attendance Act was enforced through centralized control and Saskatchewan was the first Province in the Dominion to appoint a Director of School Hygiene and he had done excellent work. It was also stated that 154 new Public Schools had been opened during the year and that there were 31 Consolidated Schools in the Province. There were, also, 20 Separate Schools—16 Roman Catholic and 4 Protestant. Toward the close of the year the Department, through D. P. McColl, Superintendent of Education, was dealing with extensions in the High School course to include certain phases of industrial work and those approved by the Minister included (1) studies in Agriculture and Home Economics; (2) two-year courses in commercial and manual training to be extended to 3 years; (3) pupils completing any of these industrial courses, with such additional subjects of a general nature as were prescribed for general culture, to be admitted to the 2nd class session of the Normal School and, on passing, be given 2nd class certificates and certificates in the special work taken.

The various Educational bodies dealing with the interests of the 138,000 pupils (1917) and 5,700 teachers of the Province included the Saskatchewan School Trustees' Association which met in Regina on Jan. 22-23. It showed a notable sweep of sentiment for one language in the Schools compared with its previous year's Convention of the opposite type of thought. The chief Resolution, swiftly adopted with one dissentient, declared that "whereas it is commonly admitted that the French-Canadian holds no legal right to language privileges in Saskatchewan, and whereas 13 or 14 other nationalities form a part of our body politic, therefore, be it resolved that the language privilege granted to the French in our midst is prejudicial to the best interests of our commonwealth." Another motion urged that no private elementary school, academy or college be permitted in the Province of Saskatchewan, except under license. Finally, it was declared that no person should be eligible for School Trustee who could not read and write English. J. F. Bryant presided and there were 1,000 registered delegates with addresses delivered by Sir Richard Lake, Lieut.-Governor, Dr.

H. W. Foght of Washington, D.C., the Provincial Premier and W.
D. Cowan, M.P.

The French-Canadian School Trustees' Association met at Regina on Feb. 19 with 200 delegates present and passed Resolutions
declaring that French-Canadians were determined that their
children should learn English and that the natural law under
which education was a sacred right of parents should be respected
by the authorities; protesting against Resolutions passed by the
above Convention as likely to prolong racial divisions; asking that
teaching of French be facilitated in French-Canadian districts and
recommending a minimum salary for teachers and the establishment of a Pension system; urging that the Educational system of
the Province be placed under the control of a Council of Public
Instruction composed of two sections, one Catholic and one Protestant—as in Quebec. It may be added that in Mr. Martin's
absence during the year Hon. S. J. Latta was Acting Minister and
that on Mch. 18 H. H. Smith, B.A., Saskatoon; T. H. McGuire, K.C.,
LL.D., Prince Albert; William Grayson, K.C., Moose Jaw; Rev. D.
Gillies, B.A., Regina; George H. Ling, M.A., PH.D., Saskatoon, were
appointed members of the Provincial Educational Council.

Educational Conditions in Alberta. In this Province, as elsewhere in the West, the Government fully recognized the great value
and necessity of Education and the Minister in charge at this
time, Hon. George P. Smith, was enthusiastic in his effort to keep
the Provincial system along lines of progress with, in 1919, an increase of the Educational appropriations for the year of one-third
or nearly $500,000; this was applied chiefly to the promotion of
general efficiency and partly, also, to meet the needs of 150 newly-
established schools. As to this, the Minister stated in a press interview on Jan. 9th that the Government aid for Education in the
various Provinces of Canada per pupil was as follows: Saskatchewan, $8.78 per pupil; Alberta, $6.05; Manitoba, $4.82; New Bruns-
wick, $3.16; Nova Scotia, $2.47; Quebec, $2.25; Ontario, $1.47. On
the 13th Mr. Smith laid before a Convention of Provincial School
Trustees in Edmonton a plan for promoting Technical training.
He proposed that three small towns, in close vicinity, should combine to get a teacher who would travel amongst them, giving a couple
of days' instruction at each place; the schools would get a certain
grant toward the teacher's salary, and also towards equipment;
there should be an official appointed by the Government for purposes of inspection and co-operation. In isolated country places
the people should be encouraged to get teachers who would qualify
for this work and such teachers would be given a bonus of $100 to
$150, and the school a small grant for equipment. To a Farmers'
Convention on the same day the Minister reviewed the situation as
follows:

The greatest problem to be faced was that of the rural schools in the
Province. Two-thirds of the children of Alberta got their education in
the rural schools. Less than five per cent. of these children enjoyed the

privileges of secondary education. Consolidated Schools were the only medium to extend secondary advantages to rural districts. The great drawbacks to such schools were the heavy costs and the difficulty of imperfect roads. Another big problem was the difficulty of enforcing school attendance in rural districts. While the Province did as much as possible, so many lived so far from schools that it was impossible to enforce attendance, either on moral or statutory grounds. Canadianizing the great mass of foreign and alien people constituted still another problem. Any man or woman attaining citizenship without becoming familiar with the English language was working under a handicap. Yet it was from such classes that there came the most trouble in enforcing school attendance. Out in the more isolated districts where conditions were least desirable was where, generally, the least qualified teachers were found. The need for more men in the teaching profession and the value of returned men in this work were recognized by the Department of Education. The salaries were scandalously low and in this respect the school situation was alarming. There was no good reason why so many schools of the Province should be closed. Hundreds were in this condition. The Department had done all that was possible in the matter; yet 300 teachers would leave the Camrose Normal School in a few days and not one had a position guaranteed. Farmers and school Trustees must help to solve the difficulty.

The difficulties in Alberta were due, largely, to isolation, great distances and sparse population, insufficient inspectors and inadequate salaries. The Minister in various speeches laid stress upon the value of returned soldiers in this respect. At Edmonton on Feb. 21 he said that provision was being made for their co-operation and it was possible for them to enter the Normal Schools without fees and further financial assistance would be given by Government loans to be paid back on easy terms. Another plan for meeting this problem was taken up by the Department—the provision of houses, for teachers, of varying size and costing from $1,000 to $1,800; under new legislation carried by the Minister of Education the Province was to pay one-third of the cost of the building and essential furnishings, with the District providing the balance. At the 1919 Session, also, the appropriations for Education were approved and amounted to a 40 per cent. increase, with a total of $1,700,000; the extra sum being derived from the Supplementary Revenue tax.

Of this additional half million dollars, four-fifths went to providing better schools and education among the farmers; while the city schools received 60 cents per day or $120 a year for 200 teaching days, the country schools received $1 a day or $200 a year. The Consolidated School Act was also amended to facilitate Co-operation and avoid troubles which had hitherto arisen between town and country districts; the Department also initiated a policy of two-roomed schools to meet the crowded pressure in some districts—under this policy the Province bore part of the increased cost by providing a double grant for the second teacher and an extra grant of $250 to furnish the second room so that it might be used also as a community hall. In October about 40 such schools were under way. Through an increased vote of $50,000 for school inspection the number of Inspectors was increased from 24 to 35.

Mr. Smith was in Toronto on Aug. 12 and told the press that he was studying the question of Technical education with a view to the establishment of a Provincial Institute of Technology and Art in the city of Calgary. As to the general situation in Alberta he stated that the Government inspection of private schools had resulted in the elimination of all unnecessary or undesirable ones; there were now only 18 private schools in the Province and half of the teachers in these were University graduates. Of the so-called Hutterite invasion of Alberta, the Minister said that they were giving no trouble to the educational authorities. The law provided for the appointment of a Trustee over each district, and schools had been erected with returned soldiers in charge; the prejudices of these people were being disregarded and they were conforming to the regulations of the Department. The Institute project was proceeded with and on Nov. 21 a Conference was held at Calgary regarding details and prospects.

The Minister's Report for the calendar year 1918 included a statement by J. T. Ross, Deputy-Minister, in which the salary situation was once more analyzed: "The meagre salary paid the teacher, and the lack of permanency of his position, except in city schools, has been responsible for driving many teachers out of the profession, and thus depriving the children in many districts of that continuity in their studies which leads to thoroughness and rapid progress. The opinion prevails in many school districts that any person can teach school, and this leads trustees to engage untrained and inexperienced teachers at minimum salaries." He stated that the Department of Education secured a supply of teachers from the other Provinces and at least 300 of these, who had standing entitling them to teach in Alberta, were placed in the rural schools of the Province; 467 were trained in the Normal Schools in 1918, and of these 60 were males and 407 females. The War seriously affected the attendance of men at Normal Schools, and only 14·74 per cent. of the total attendance was males, while in 1912 they had formed 28·05 per cent. of the total attendance.

There still was a shortage of 800 trained teachers and for these vacancies certificates were issued to students. The minimum yearly salary at this time in an ungraded school was $840; the age limit for compulsory education was 14 years; during 1918, 16 Consolidated schools were established, making a total of 54. Statistics of the year showed 48,880 enrollments in rural schools and 62,229 in urban schools; the daily average attendance was, respectively, 28,961 and 39,527 and the total number attending was 111,109; the number of teachers was 5,652, the total expenditure on salaries $2,860,351; the number of School Districts was 2,971 and the new ones in the year 192; the value of School buildings and grounds was $14,863,976 and of School libraries $191,387; the number of schools in operation was 2,766 and the departments 3,933—an increase in the former case of 295 and in the latter of 436.

Of Educational organizations the Alberta Teachers' Alliance met at Calgary early in the year representing a membership of

1,000; T. E. Stanley, Calgary, was elected President. Amongst the Resolutions passed were the following: (1) asking all School Boards to admit teachers or an advisory committee of teachers at the School Board meetings; (2) opposing Daylight Saving; (3) making it an obligation of members of the Alliance to refrain from speaking disparagingly of teaching as a profession and declaring that members of the Alliance would not receive into full fellowship, on the staff of a school, teachers who were non-Union. This Union organization made great progress during the year and in September urged upon all School Boards the adoption of a new self-renewing contract, which would provide security of tenure for the teacher by making it impossible to dismiss him except for proved inefficiency or misconduct, or to transfer him without his consent.

This contract also embodied a Provincial wage schedule of which the main feature was a minimum wage, for all Public School teachers, of $1,200 per annum with liberal increments for experience and efficiency. This minimum was $350 in advance of the statutory minimum. The employment of a permanent Provincial organizer was decided upon and District Secretaries were appointed to ensure a more intensive organization in every section of the Province. The Alberta Teachers' Association met at Calgary on Oct. 31 and passed Resolutions declaring that oral French should be commenced in Grade VII, where school organization would permit the employment of a special teacher, or where the regular teacher was qualified; that no class-room should contain seating accommodation for more than 35 pupils; that the time had come for a Canadian Educational magazine. The latter was a Primary Section motion. Frank Speakman was elected President.

The Northern Alberta Teachers' Association met in Edmonton on Nov. 6 and the Minister of Education told them that at present the number of teachers admitted to training schools was less than half the number required, and they were entering in constantly decreasing numbers. Recently the Government of Alberta had established a plan whereby students aspiring to the teaching profession, but with insufficient means, could borrow enough money from the Government to put themselves through the Normal School. As a result Mr. Smith said that, within a week, at two Normal Schools opening with 180 students, 115 more were added to the rolls. He also announced that it was the intention of the Department of Education to supply a Flag to every school in the Province and that the Department would insist on each school having a flag-pole: "We will select suitable dates, say about 20, throughout the school-year, on which the flag will be raised. These dates will be occasions on which British peoples made unselfish contributions to human liberty." An incident of the year was the enforced retirement in June of Dr. Norman F. Black, Principal of the Regina Collegiate Institute, after 10 years' service, and as a result, apparently, of differences between himself and Peter McAra, Chairman of the Board.

Education in British Columbia During 1919. The British Columbia system was established in 1872 and amended in many important respects by the Provincial Acts of 1891 and 1896. The chief executive officer was the Minister of Education, assisted by a Chief Superintendent; the enrollment of pupils in 1917 in all schools was 65,118, the teachers numbered 2,124, the Government expenditures were $1,609,124 and those of the municipalities and rural districts $1,637,539. The B.C. School Teachers' Association met at Victoria on Sept. 17, with Mrs. Irene Moody in the chair, and discussed at length, but without definite conclusion, the question of Bible reading in the schools, the financing and maintenance of High Schools by the Government, the necessity of Technical education. The B.C. School Trustees' Association, which met at Vancouver on the 19th, was inclined to be critical of the Minister of Education (Hon. J. D. McLean) and Dr. Alex Robertson, Superintendent of Education; a motion was voted down which declared that funds for Educational purposes should be a common charge upon all persons earning a separate livelihood and be levied as a poll-tax. Consolidated Schools were approved. An organization which made great headway in this Province during the year was the Parent-Teacher Federation with Mrs. J. Muirhead as President. Its central idea was that children could not properly be taught in the mass. Each child's temperament and disposition should be taken into account. Close relations between teacher and parent were, therefore, said to be essential, with the following results:

1. There would be a better understanding between teacher and parents and instead of fault-finding and unfair criticism on the part of many parents, there would be sympathy and co-operation.

2. Inadequate equipment in the school would be recognized by parents, the agitation for better things come from them direct, and the whole electorate become educated in school needs.

3. Parents, who occasionally attended school, would see that no child could be at its best unless sufficient sleep had been secured and would also see the necessity of children attending with regularity and punctuality.

In the School year 1918-19 the total enrollment was 72,006, the average daily attendance was 56,692, the total number of teachers 2,332 of whom 197 were in High Schools, 957 in City Graded Schools, 549 in Rural Municipality Schools and 629 in rural and assorted Schools.

The Universities and Colleges of Canada in 1919. The Higher Educational system of Canada is an interesting study of growth in new communities with the background and inspiration of a great new country. It has had a century's record of slow development and, in the end, a result of substantial achievement. Primarily the system is based upon British ideas and traditions. Latterly it had, super-imposed upon these, a fabric of up-to-date, modern, technical, commercial, industrial, agricultural and business instruction; in effect it has combined something of the best in both British and American institutions. It is, in all the Provinces, the apex of a theoretical structure in which the Public School and High School lead gradually to the University; practically, things have not quite worked out as expected. There were in 1919, 20 Universities in Canada with endowments totalling $22,000,000 and buildings valued at more than $28,000,-000; Government yearly grants of $1,400,000 and a total income of 3½ millions; a total teaching staff of 1,800 and students numbering (1916) 16,000. The Colleges of Canada, including Denominational, Agricultural, Technical, Military, Naval, Dental, Medical, Veterinary and Pharmacist, numbered 43; their teaching staffs totalled 600 and students (1916) 7,500; the value of their endowments and lands and buildings was $21,000,000 and total Income $1,700,000.

These institutions of Canada were, in 1919, keeping up many of the traditions and much of the culture of the Old World; they were trying, also, in an age of development and industry, commerce and invention, to keep up with the practical realities around them; they were being guided by public opinion to give in some measure a final touch of knowledge to a great process of development in agriculture, in the building of railways, in the sinking of mines and scientific work of Mining, in the transforming of water-power into plants of electric energy, in the organization and technique of finance and industry, in the transformation of the raw material into marketable, usable, products. As was pointed out in the Winnipeg *Free Press* of July 28, the University ought to be closely related to all these great movements: "It should provide trained minds, minds that can see and judge, minds that can lead and invent, that are resourceful, liberal, determined, trustworthy, progressive. It should be able to point out the most effective methods by which great undertakings can proceed, and the most favourable conditions in which they can be developed into their greatest usefulness."

This was not exactly the mission of Oxford or Cambridge; it was claimed to be, in part, the mission of Toronto and McGill and Queen's. During later years in Canada the Universities and Colleges had another duty thrust upon them by events—aiding the reconstruction of the returned soldier; they had lost many splendid young men in the War and sent probably 16,000 to the front in the four years of struggle; they did much to help their students when returning from service. A Conference of University representatives was held at Ottawa on Jan. 16 with such well-known heads of institutions present as Sir R. Falconer, Toronto, L. S. Klinck, Vancouver, W. C. Murray, Saskatoon, W. A. R. Kerr, Edmonton, R. Bruce Taylor, Kingston, C. C. Jones, St. John. It was finally decided by Resolution that: "It is in the best interests both of the nation and of the returned soldiers that educational facilities be provided for all returned men who will desire them, and are deemed capable of taking advantage of such as are provided, and that these facilities should be adequate as preparation for the life or vocation which they intend to follow when returning to civil life.''

The same principle, it was said, should apply to all persons whose University courses, including under-graduate or post-graduate work, had been interrupted by enlistment, and it was suggested that men be selected by the Department of Civil Re-establishment, on the recommendation of the University or College concerned; that the Government of Canada should become responsible for the expense incurred by such University in providing adequate preparatory instruction; that such training should not be necessarily limited to the duration of one academic year; that the Department of Labour should organize a special Branch to deal with unemployment in the professional classes and to collect information regarding all men who desired teaching positions and University appointments.   On May 23 another Conference—the 6th annual one of Canadian Universities—was held at Quebec with President Stanley Mackenzie of Dalhousie in the chair and Toronto, McGill, Ottawa, Trinity, McMaster, Laval (Montreal), Laval (Quebec), Bishop's, St. Joseph's, Victoria, Manitoba, British Columbia and Alberta represented by Presidents or Professors.   The general opinion was expressed that the Dominion Government should extend financial assistance, of at least a million dollars, to help the Universities in completing the education of ex-soldiers and enabling all boys of 18 up to 19 years, who had enlisted, to have the opportunity of a higher education.   A Committee was appointed to wait on Sir Robert Borden and present this view, and on July 31st a letter to the Premier was made public under the signatures of President Falconer and the representatives of Alberta, McGill, St. Francis Xavier and Laval with the following proposal:

The Government should grant to every returned soldier who can prove his need and his capability, maintenance and fees for at least one year.   The sum of at least $350 would be required for subsistence, and at the highest the fees should not average more than $150.   In view of the fact that there are probably at least 1,000 returned soldiers now in the higher educational institutions of Canada and about the same number undergoing instruction either in the Khaki University or in British Universities, it is probable that not less than 2,500 or 3,000 may be expected to seek an education next Winter in our Canadian institutions.   The amount therefore required for carrying out this scheme should be placed at $1,500,000.

In this connection the Imperial Government plan for providing assistance for the higher education of returned officers and men was broadened to include facilities for study in Universities and other educational institutions of the British Empire overseas and Lord Milner enquired from Canada what concessions would be made in return.   A reply was sent by the Governor-General to the effect that the Canadian Universities would welcome all such students and give to those recommended by the British Committee full credit for work already done in British Universities.   Ex-officers and men of British nationality domiciled in the United Kingdom, who had served in the British Forces, were therefore eligible

THE HON. SIR HENRY LUMLEY DRAYTON, K.C.M.G., M.P.
Appointed Dominion Minister of Finance, 1919

THE HON. WM. LYCN MACKENZIE KING, C.M.G. M.A. M.P.
Elected Leader of the Liberal Party of Canada in 1919

for money grants to enable them to pursue their studies in Canada. The chief net result of voluntary action along Reconstruction lines in Canadian Universities was as follows:

University of Alberta—special short courses in agriculture covering five months for all returned men referred by Department of Soldiers' Civil Re-establishment. Special classes from May 16 to September covering preparatory or matriculation work for returned soldiers, to enable them to enter University in fall. No fees charged.

University of Manitoba—Courses leading to matriculation for High School graduates. Special tutorial courses for students in first and second year Arts and Science whose terms have been interrupted, to enable them to complete their year before fall session. Entrance at any time and withdrawal as soon as studies satisfactorily completed. No fees charged.

University of Saskatchewan—Courses leading to matriculation in any one of the Faculties in which the requirements are reduced. Special summer school course from July 2 to Aug. 9, in which student may choose the particular subject he desires to study. No fees charged.

Queen's University—Courses leading to matriculation for anyone who lost time on war service admitted to certain preparatory work which qualifies for entry as undergraduates. Every student who was overseas granted a bonus on each examination in arts and science. Summer session in Applied Science opened on Apr. 28, counting as a full University year.

University of Toronto—Courses in preliminary work starting in April and September for entrance upon the regular work in the various Faculties in October. Men must be high school graduates. Fees, $15.00 for each term of approximately three months. No general regulations—each case considered on its own merits.

McGill University—Classes leading to matriculation. Entrance requirements modified for returned soldiers. Special coaching classes for those who failed in subjects during year and any others wishing to take advantage of same to enable them to save their year. This to be carried on for next session and perhaps the following. No fees charged for above classes.

Meanwhile, the question of payment for Professors and Staffs was under discussion. Conditions were better than in the United States where 256 representative Colleges, employing 8,030 teachers, expended $13,388,000 in salaries during 1917 or an average of $1,667 a year. None-the-less, however, Canadian University men found it increasingly difficult to get along while increasing salaries were a further drain upon University finances. Hence the value to Canada of the share of its Universities in the Carnegie Foundation Pension Fund under which the Staffs received a retiring allowance of 60 per cent. of their salaries. Early in 1919 a new plan was inaugurated by the Foundation under which Life insurance and Annuity policies at cost were provided to Professors and members of the teaching staffs of about 70 Universities in Canada, the United States and Newfoundland. Hence, also, the welcome accorded the announcement (Dec. 24) that J. D. Rockefeller had given $100,-000,000 to the Rockefeller Foundation to raise the salaries of College Professors in the United States with this additional clause: "The Canadian people are our near neighbours. They are closely bound to us by ties of race, language and international friendship, and they have, without stint, sacrificed themselves and their youth and their resources to the end that democracy might be saved and extended. For these reasons, if your Board should see fit to use

19

any part of this new gift in promoting Medical education in Canada, such action would meet with my cordial approval." Dr. George E. Vincent, President of the Foundation, stated that $5,000,000 would be set apart for the work of Canadian Medical Schools.

Another subject which came up in 1919 was the need of University co-ordination throughout the Dominion. As with elementary education some institutions had been Provincialized by policy and the Confederation pact; the schedule of studies and practices of instruction were different in some Provinces. Dr. George B. Cutten, President of Acadia University, suggested (Montreal *Star*, Feb. 11) that a Central Department or Bureau should be established at Ottawa for purposes of co-ordination in higher education and for inspiration, consultative and advisory operation. In June Lord Beaverbrook, who was visiting his former home in New Brunswick, made arrangements to offer five scholarships for University courses annually and for competition among the High School graduates of New Brunswick; the scholarships were to be held at any Canadian University and be of the value of ' $325 a year for the period of a whole course in Arts, Theology, Law or Medicine, Civil Engineering, etc.

University incidents of the year included the conferring of an Hon. D.D. by the University of Glasgow upon Rev. C. W. Gordon, B.A., D.D., LL.D., F.R.S.C., of Winnipeg; the awarding of an Hon. LL.D. by the University of Edinburgh to Brig.-Gen. A. E. Ross, C.B., C.M.G., and of an Hon. D.D. to Sir R. A. Falconer, Toronto; the grant of an Hon. D.D. by Oxford to Rt. Rev. E. J. Bidwell, Bishop of Ontario. An interesting yearly episode in University life was resumed in 1919 by the election of Rhodes Scholars which had been postponed during the last year of the War. Only one Canadian scholar—H. C. Warburton of P.E. Island—was killed in action during the great struggle but A. N. Carter, J. B. Clearihue, P. E. Corbett, W. F. Dyde, W. S. Kent-Hughes, C. W. B. Littlejohn, H. G. Nolan, H. S. Smith, G. S. Stairs won the M.C. on active service, W. B. Hurd the O.B.E. and J. M. Macdonell the M.C. and Croix de Guerre. The Rhodes Scholars selected for Canada (1918 and 1919 appointment) were as follows:

Institution	Name
University of Manitoba	G. P. R. Tallin
" "	C. Rhodes Smith
University of Saskatchewan	C. Boville Clark
University of British Columbia	J. Hamilton Mennie
" " "	Capt. Sherwood Lett, M.C.
University of Alberta	Capt. H. A. Dyde, M.C.
" "	Allan Harvey
McGill University	T. W. L. MacDermott

The Khaki University of Canada, which did such good work in England during the War was, in the summer of 1918, taken into the Canadian Military Forces as part of the regular establishment and it carried out an important work during the period of demobilization with Dr. H. M. Tory, President of Alberta University, as Director. The instruction was given by educational officers in the individual battalions, but in the camps and hospitals of the Forces, Special Colleges with teaching staffs, libraries and buildings were established. Men whose college courses in the Canadian Universities had been interrupted by enlistment were concentrated in the Khaki College at Ripon. Here there were 800 University students following regular University courses of study and covering the work of the 1st and 2nd years in Arts and Applied Science, one year in Law and in Medicine, three years in Theology, and two years in Agriculture. The instruction was provided by a staff of about 70 University-trained men. For the more advanced students courses were arranged in various British Universities and were attended by 355 students and accepted as the equivalent of one year's study at Canadian Universities. Including all branches of training—lower and higher education alike—the aggregate attendance in these institutions—which were closed in July, 1919,—was 641,137 at lectures and the total in regular courses 50,189; the cost of operation was $500,000. Similar educational services were established in the contingents from New Zealand, Australia and South Africa and, later in the Imperial forces where they became a permanent part of the training of British soldiers.

The University of Toronto in 1919. The report of the Chancellor of the University, Sir Edmund Walker, C.V.O., for the year of June 30th, showed a gross revenue of $993,715 and total expenditures of $1,191,602—the deficit of $206,869 being charged against a special Legislative grant of $200,000 and a balance of $51,044 from the previous year's grant. Sir R. A. Falconer, President, reported a Staff of 459 including 63 Professors, 42 Associate and 31 Assistant-Professors, and the total inclusive of 57 on active service. Reference was made to the deaths of Prof. A. H. F. Lefroy, M.A., K.C., and R. A. Reeve, M.D., LL.D., one-time Dean of the Medical Faculty and to the retirements of Dr. Alfred Baker, Dean of the Faculty of Arts, Dr. W. H. Ellis, Dean of Applied Science, Dr. B. E. Fernow, Dean of the Faculty of Forestry and Dr. Alexander McPhedran, Professor of Medicine for 19 years. The following appointments to the Chairs named were noted: A. Carruthers, M.A., Greek Literature; C. A. Chant, M.A., Ph.D., Astrophysics; J. H. Faull, B.A., Ph.D., Botany; D. R. Keys, M.A., Anglo-Saxon; J. J. R. McLeod, M.B., Ch.B., Physiology; Alex. Primrose, C.B., M.B., Surgery; Dr. Duncan A. Graham, Medicine.

The total registration of students, including the Summer Session, was 3,356 with 1,449 in Arts, 97 in Graduate courses, 828 in Medicine, 323 in Applied Science, 418 in Faculty of Education, 12 in Forestry, and 254 in Department of Social Service. The total enlistments of graduates and undergraduates in the War was stated at 5,681 with 608 killed on service and 884 wounded. In his comments Sir Robert Falconer described the complexities caused by the return of men from the Front and the generous arrangements made for their educational advancement; paid tribute to the services of the Connaught Antitoxin Laboratories in the preparation and distribution of Influenza vaccine and to the continued Research support of Lieut.-Col. A. E. Gooderham in placing at the disposal of the University a finely-equipped laboratory for conducting investigations in the process of fermentation; stated that in the Faculty of Medicine the outstanding event was the gift by Sir John and Lady Eaton, of $500,000 for the establishment of a full-time Professorship of Medicine—a gift which established the Faculty amongst the leading Medical Schools of the continent. It was in the form of a $25,000 annual payment for 20 years beginning on Jan. 1, 1919, and one of the conditions was that the Governors of the University should continue to spend annually upon the Department of Medicine not less than was spent at the time that the gift was made. Special attention was to be given to the Department of Pediatrics and to the teaching of Clinical medicine as well as the laboratory side of the subject. Dr. Falconer also mentioned the special research work and valuable series of lectures arranged by Prof. J. C. Fields, F.R.S., and the Royal Canadian Institute, as well as the legacy of $50,000 left to found two Fellowships by the late Dr. W. J. Mickle of London. The financial statement of the University showed Endowment and other Funds totalling $7,376,887; the Librarian, H. H. Langton, reported 156,540 bound volumes and 51,356 pamphlets.

There was published early in 1919 the 4th Edition of the *Varsity War Supplement*, a handsome pictorial and literary presentment of what the University had done in the War—edited by Sidney Childs and with articles by the President, Sir Edmund Walker, Archbishop Bruchési, and others. Succeeding incidents included an address to the students by Principal Bruce Taylor of Queen's in which he described a University as not a great medical school, nor was it a great law school, it was an atmosphere: ''It is a place where men see things and dream dreams—it exists to make you cultured men and women.'' A decision was announced suspending military and physical training for the season and the statement made in February that Brig.-Gen. C. H. Mitchell, C.B., C.M.G., D.S.O., would, upon his return from the Front, take up the post of Dean of the Faculty of Applied Science; the series of lectures on Philosophy in the Middle Ages given by Prof. Maurice de Wulf of the University of Louvain and now of St. Michael's College, Toronto, was an incident of interest; the Report of the University Hospital Supply Association issued by Lady Falconer, President, showed total receipts of $121,107; the initiation in April of a campaign by the University Alumni Association to raise $500,000 for a Memorial to the graduates and under-graduates of the University, who had given their lives in the War, promised to be successful; the appointments of John McNaughton, M.A., LL.D., of McGill as Professor of Latin and of Dr. George R. Pitrie as Professor of Pediatrics were announced. On June 5 a special Convocation was held when the following Honourary degrees were conferred:

LL.D.	President John Grier Hibben	Princeton University
LL.D.	John Davison Lawson	University of Missouri
LL.D.	Alex. Fraser, Litt.D., F.S.A.	Ontario Archivist
LL.D.	Thomas A. Kirkconnell, B.A.	Lindsay Collegiate Institute
LL.D.	Rev. Donald McGillivray, M.A., D.D.	Missionary to Shanghai
LL.D.	Alex. McPhedran, M.D.	Toronto
D.Sc.	Robert R. Benseley, B.A., M.B.	University of Chicago
D.Sc.	Frank R. Lillie, B.A., Ph.D.	University of Chicago
D.V.S.	John G. Rutherford, C.M.G.	Ottawa

The final enrollment of students in October for the 1919-20 Session showed 3,492 compared with 3,051 in 1913-4 with hundreds of war veterans included. It was stated on Oct. 7 by the Toronto *World* that 1,200 returned men were then at the University, that $20,000 had already spent on their training, with classes running at a loss in order to help those who were unable to pay their way, and that the Ontario Government had declined Sir Robert Falconer's proposal of a $500 per head grant. On Oct. 11 it was announced that Prof. A. P. Coleman, M.A., Ph.D., F.R.S., had been appointed Dean of the Faculty of Arts. A special Convocation was held on Oct. 14 to hear Cardinal Mercier and to confer upon him an Hon. LL.D.; a similar function had been attended by H.R.H. the Prince of Wales on Aug. 26. On Nov. 11th Hart House, the munificent gift of the Massey Foundation to the University of Toronto, was formally opened when Chester D. Massey, Chairman of the Foundation, handed over the building to the Chairman of the Board of Governors of the University, and His Excellency the Duke of Devonshire declared the building formally open. Following this incident came a special Convocation (Nov. 11) when the Hon. degree of LL.D. was conferred upon General

Sir Arthur Currie, G.C.M.G., K.C.B., Brig.-Gen. C. H. Mitchell, Maj.-Gen. J. T.
Fotheringham, C.M.G., M.D., Prof. J. C. McLennan, F.R.S., Maj.-Gen. W. G.
Gwatkin, C.B., C.M.G., and that of M.A. was given Major T. W. McDowell, V.C.,
D.S.O., while Miss Edith C. Rayside, R.R.C. was made an Hon. Master of Household Science. Sir William R. Meredith presided and H.E. the Duke of Devonshire was present. The latter also laid the foundation stone of the War
Memorial Tower to be erected at the corner of Hart House and to link that
building with the main structure—the outcome of the efforts to raise $500,000
mentioned above.
     Of institutions affiliated to the University of Toronto, Victoria
College was a prosperous Methodist institution with a record of 608 on
active service, 66 on its Honour roll of dead and 73 winning decorations; the students in 1919 numbered 369 and the Staff 27, with Rev. Dr. R.
P. Bowles as President; Acta Victoriana was a most successful College
journal and the income of the institution for the year of July 31 1919, was
$143,268 with assets of $1,934,749; on Feb. 26 H.E. the Duke of Devonshire
was entertained at Luncheon and the annual Convocation was held on Apr.
25 with the Hon. degree of D.D. conferred on Rev. James L. Stewart, B.A.,
of the West China Mission, Rev. George N. Hazen, B.A., Sarnia, and Rev.
Trevor H. Davies, Toronto; during the year Rev. J. W. Macmillan, B.A., D.D.,
of Winnipeg was appointed Professor of Sociology and Rev. F. W. Langford,
B.A., M.B.E., Associate Professor of Religious Pedagogy.   St. Michael's
College, Toronto, had 170 students in 1919 and early in the year had a
series of important lectures from Prof. Maurice de Wulf of Louvain; late
in the year Sir Bertram C. A. Windle, M.A., M.D., D.SC., F.R.S., F.S.A., of Queen's
College, Cork, was appointed Professor of Anthropology. Trinity College,
a Theological institution of the Church of England and one of the Arts
Colleges of the University, had, in 1919, 150 students and a project under way
for a splendid series of buildings in Queen's Park. Knox College, a Presbyterian institution federated with the University, had in this year, 90 men
preparing for the Ministry of the Church; the College had Rev. Dr. Alfred
Gandier as Principal and lost by death during the year Professors Robert
Law and J. D. Robertson with appointments which included Rev. William
Manson, M.A. of Glasgow, as Professor of New Testament Literature; at
the Convocation of Oct. 7th the Hon. degree of D.D. was conferred upon
Rev. George J. Ross, Union Theological Seminary, New York.

McGill University, Montreal, in 1919.

The annual Report of this
institution for the year of Aug. 31, 1919—the 90th in the educational history
of the University and the 98th since its foundation—was submitted by Dr.
Frank D. Adams, Acting Vice-Chancellor and Principal. The first and outstanding matter dealt with was the illness which came suddenly to Sir William
Peterson, K.C.M.G., LL.D., on Jan. 12 and resulted in his retirement on May 1st
following. His eminent services of 24 years as Principal were fittingly referred to in a Minute by the Governors of the University in which they eulogized
his work, his patriotism, his character, his scholarship. The Rt. Hon. Sir Auckland ,C. Geddes, K.C.B., M.D., British Minister of National Service who, at the
outbreak of the War was Professor of Anatomy in the University, was offered
and accepted the position of Principal and Vice-Chancellor but was compelled
by the emergencies of the situation in Great Britain to respect the Prime Minister's urgent request for him to remain longer at his post in London; it was
decided to grant a year's leave of absence and Dr. F. D. Adams, F.R.S., Dean
of the Faculty of Applied Science, was appointed Acting-Principal.
     During 1919 the Board of Governors lost by death George E. Drummond
and by resignation Sir Herbert B. Ames;· Dr. P. B. Mignault, K.C., resigned
as Professor of Civil Law on appointment to the Supreme Court of Canada
but took over the Chair of Legal Ethics; Dr. J. G. Adami, F.R.S., resigned
after long service as Professor of Pathology to accept appointment as Vice-
Chancellor of the University of Liverpool, Prof. John MacNaughton in order
to go to Toronto University, and Prof. Howard Barnes on account of ill-
health; the death of Charles H. Gould on July 30 removed an official who had

done great service to the institution and the country—increasing the McGill
Library from a small collection to nearly 200,000 volumes.   Important appointments included S. E. Whitnall, M.A., M.D., B.Sc., to the chair of Anatomy in
place of Sir Auckland Geddes; John Tait, M.D., D.Sc., to that of Physiology
and Horst Oertel, M.D., to that of Pathology; Lieut.-Col. A. S. Eve, C.B.E., M.A.,
D.Sc., F.R.S., was appointed Director of the Department of Physics, and H. A.
Smith, M.A., Professor of Common Law; Gerhard R. Lomer, M.A., Ph.D., was
appointed Librarian.

The McGill Siege Battery (No. 7) returned on May 11 and was duly
welcomed home; the total enlistments of the University in the War were stated
as 2,529 graduates, under-graduates and past students (including 90 members
of the Staff) with 341 killed or died of wounds and 522 wounded, with, also,
382 Honours won.   It was stated in the Report that Physical training was
compulsory and would remain so while Military training would be amongst the
recognized options; the Service Department under J. H. T. Falk, as Director,
was reported as very successful with 14 students taking the full course and
110 one or more of the Special courses of lectures; the degree of Bachelor of
Commerce was established in connection with the affiliated School of Commercial Studies and its courses were extended to cover Banking, Insurance and
Accounting.   The enrollment of students for 1918-19 included 369 in Arts,
20 in School of Commerce, 240 in Applied Science, 460 in Medicine, 59 in
Dentistry, 18 in Pharmacy, 52 in Law, 104 in Music, 122 in Agriculture, 142 in
School for Teachers and 112 in Household Science—a total, with some miscellaneous subjects, of 1,708; the degrees conferred during the year were 194 of
which 56 were in Arts and 77 in Medicine and Surgery.   Other appointments
not already mentioned were D. S. Laird, M.A., as Professor of Education, and
Robert Summerby as Professor of Cereal Husbandry; Representative Fellows
elected were Gregor Barclay, B.A., B.C.L., Lieut.-Col. J. J. Creelman, B.A., B.C.L.,
K.C., D.S.O., and A. T. Bazin, M.D., D.S.O.   The Endowment Funds of the University, or as it was, technically, the old-time Royal Institution for the Advancement of Learning, totalled in 1919 $20,999,746, the Receipts were $995,342 and
disbursements $994,724.

Like Toronto, McGill made special arrangements and gave varied privileges
to returned soldiers; in February a course of free public lectures was given on
"Government" by the Faculty of Law and covering Empire, Dominion, Province, City and Judicial systems; in London on Apr. 4 a Dinner was given to
Sir Auckland Geddes in honour of his McGill appointment with a speech from
him in which he declared that there was no factor more important for the
peace of the world in the future than the development of cordial relations
between the two English-speaking peoples, and that "on our side Canada is
the key to that position with the Universities of Canada holding the key;" at
the University Convocation of May 22nd a farewell message was read from
Sir William Peterson and it was announced that the Carnegie Foundation had
granted him $4,000 a year retiring allowance; on July 22nd, following, Sir
William was presented with an illuminated Address and a mink-lined motor
rug by the Faculties of the University.   In the Address it was stated that:
"The well-known and widespread reputation of McGill University throughout
the Empire is in appreciable measure due to your rich scholarship, your administrative ability, and, above all, to your patriotic and Imperialist attitude.
And, what your colleagues have always deeply appreciated in you, their Principal, is your assertion and championship of the freedom of academic thought."

On Oct. 31 a Royal Convocation was held and the Prince of Wales admitted to the Hon. degree of LL.D.; in the Address presented the Prince was told
that McGill, alone, amongst the greater Universities of Canada depended
almost entirely on private benefaction.   The attendance of students during
1919 broke all records and the Registration in the Session of 1919-20 was 2,656
compared with 1,426 in 1917-18 and 2,058 in 1913-14 before the War.   In the
1919-20 enrollment there were 516 in Arts, 90 in the School of Commerce, 643
in Applied Science, 642 in Medicine, 93 in Dentistry, 33 in Pharmacy, 136 in
Law, 111 in Music, 157 in Agriculture, 80 in Household Science and 146 in
School for Teachers.   It may be added that Prof. A. S. Eve was admitted as a

F.R.S. during the year and Dr. G. E. Armstrong elected President of the American Surgical Association.

Of the affiliated Theological Colleges the Congregational institution had a new Principal during the year in Rev. Dr. David L. Ritchie and its attendance numbered seven; the Presbyterian College had a registration of 51 and the Wesleyan College, of 59.

Queen's University, Kingston, in 1919. Principal R. Bruce Taylor, M.A., D.D., in his first annual Report, dealt with a registration of 1,425 students in 1918-19 as compared with 1,227 in the previous year; with the retirement of Dr. James Cappon as Professor of English Literature after 31 years' service, of Dr. A. P. Knight, Professor of Physiology for 27 years, and of Dr. W. L. Goodwin, Professor of Chemistry, after 36 years service; with the appointment of N. L. Bowen, M.A., B.Sc., to the Chair of Mineralogy and C. W. Drury, B.Sc., Ph.D., to that of Metallurgical Research; with details of the 1918-19 Registration which showed 513 in Arts, 100 in Science, 237 in Medicine, 138 in Education and 155 in Banking; with the success of the University in meeting the conditional gift of $500,000 from the late Dr. Douglas based upon a similar sum being contributed in Canada—a result achieved partly through the generosity of the Carnegie Foundation in promising $250,000; with the position of the Faculty of Education which would cease to exist at Queen's as well as in Toronto if the current proposals for a Central Teachers' Training Institute under Government control at Toronto were carried out.

The objections to this latter policy were stated as follows: ''It has been a great thing for teachers of the High Schools that they had to have some University training, for life in the University implies a conflict of opinion and a widening of friendship that makes for catholicity and a generosity of view. If, however, this double rampart is to be erected, and the training of teachers is to be confined to an Institute directly under the control of the Department of Education, teachers, who already tend by their profession to be isolated from their fellows and to become narrow-minded, will be exposed in a still larger degree to those influences which tend to hinder them from being citizens of the world. In its more limited aspects, too, this policy, if it be carried through, will be injurious to Queen's, which has so worthy a record in the educational policy of Canada. More and more, the University will lose touch with those High Schools in which it has found its best recruiting ground for students.'' The Principal also drew attention to the new salary arrangements under which the salary of a full professor should reach $3,500, of an associate or a professor not in charge of a department, $2,900, of an assistant professor $2,400, and of a lecturer $1,900.

The Carnegie Foundation Pension, already accepted by Toronto, was described as under consideration: ''Should this scheme be adopted, a professor under the age of 40, would pay 5 per cent. of his income and the University another 5 per cent. to the subsidiary Company to be created by the Carnegie Corporation. The unofficial suggestion has been made from New York, that the Trustees might set aside for this purpose $50,000 of the new Endowment, and that to this the Carnegie Foundation might add another $20,000 or $25,000.'' There would also be the grant of $125,000 a year from the Provincial Government for the past and present years and the $50,000 endowment of a Research Chair by G. Y. Chown. The revenue of the University for the year of Mch. 31, 1919, was stated at $278,717 and the expenditures $281,137, the Assets were $1,773,317. It may be added here that the Registration for the Session of 1919-20 was 2,468—984 in Arts, 378 in Science, 228 in Medicine, 112 in Teaching, 455 in Banking and the Summer Session with 219 in Arts and 96 in Science.

Speaking at the Empire Club, Toronto, on Jan. 30, Dr. Bruce Taylor advocated the establishment in Britain, and in all the Dominions of the Empire, of a British Empire University Chair for one of the Universities in each of these countries, and which would give instruction regarding the character and development of British institutions within the Empire, and the international relationships of its Dominions. A little later the Principal expressed regret (Ottawa, Feb. 20) that the Dominion Government had not given Queen's a fair place in its Scientific Research Council arrangements and stated that Queen's University was putting on a special summer course- in Engineering to enable returned men to save a year in their course.   The Government had been asked to pay the salaries of the Professors required for the summer work, but had refused to do so.   Dr. A. B. Macallum denied any favouritism in respect to the Council work but the reply was that Queen's was originally omitted from the Council, while two other Universities, Dalhousie and Saskatchewan, which had done little research work, were given representatives.

Meantime, Edward W. Beatty, K.C., President of the C.P.R., had been elected Chancellor of Queen's in succession to the late Dr. James Douglas and R. A. Stapells, a prominent business man of Toronto, to the Board of Governors.   A banquet was tendered to Mr. Beatty in Montreal, on Apr. 8, by the local Queen's Alumni Association; in his address Mr. Beatty stated that the Universities, while still the seats of learning in this country, were rapidly taking the functions of public service institutions, in that they helped to supply to the young men and women the ideals and standards which made for the best Canadianism.   At the Spring Convocation of Queen's on Apr. 30 the Hon. degree of D.D. was conferred upon Rev. George Duncan, M.A., B.D., Montreal, and Rev. Robert Laird, M.A., Toronto; that of LL.D. upon Prof. William J. Alexander, PH.D., Toronto; J. Murray Clark, M.A., K.C., lately President of the Royal Canadian Institute, Toronto, and Prof. William Nicol of Queen's. In his speech Dr. Murray Clark drew attention to an interesting historical point which he had already dealt with in addresses and papers: ''When a Court of Judicature was established in what is now Canada, it was directed that the 'Lawes of Virginia' should be .the rule or pattern.   At that date, 1721, Virginia was still British.   The Virginia Charter provided that settlers should have all the privileges of Englishmen in such ample measure as 'if they were born and personally resident in England' and, mark the words, 'should be governed by such Statutes as they should choose to establish for themselves,'—thus anticipating the self-government which now prevails.''

It was announced that the million dollar Fund was practically complete and that $40,000 had been secured for building a Women's Residence; D. M. McIntyre, K.C., and Alex Longwell, Toronto, were added to the Board of Trustees.   Succeeding incidents included the appointment in August of Capt. J. D. Craig as Professor of Classics and Prof. John B. Black of Glasgow as Professor of Modern History; the organization of a Department of Commerce and provision of Courses in Banking and Finance, Accounting and Auditing, Commercial and General Business, Foreign Trade and Public Service.   On Oct. 16 an impressive Convocation was held to formally inaugurate E. W. Beatty, K.C., as Chancellor and Robert Bruce Taylor, M.A., D.D., LL.D., as Principal.   Many Hon. degrees were bestowed to mark the event and addresses given by Mr. Beatty and the Principal, by Hon. H. J. Cody, and Hon. Mackenzie King. The LL.D. degrees were as follows:

Hon. Frank Carrel	*The Telegraph*, Quebec
Philip D. Ross	*The Journal*, Ottawa
H. M. Nimmo	*Saturday Night*, Detroit
Frank D. Adams, F.R.S.	McGill University, Montreal
Sir R. A. Falconer	University of Toronto
Edward W. Beatty, K.C.	Montreal
President P. Godfrey	Drexel Institute, Philadelphia
Prof. T. F. Holgate	Northwestern University
President A. C. McGiffert	Union Theological Seminary, N.Y.
Provost E. F. Smith	University of Pennsylvania
Prof. R. M. Menley	University of Michigan
Prof. J. E. Woodbridge	Columbia University, N.Y.
G. Herrick Duggan	Lachine, Quebec
Maj.-Gen. J. T. Fotheringham, C.M.G.	Ottawa
Dr. L. Harwood	University of Montreal

Prof. Stephen B. Leacock ....McGill University
Miss A. E. Marty ....Inspector of Public Schools, Toronto
Hon. W. L. Mackenzie King ....Leader of the Opposition, Ottawa
Hon. G. D. Robertson ....Minister of Labour for Canada
Dr. F. J. Shepherd ....Montreal
Brig.-Gen. the Hon. A. E. Ross, M.L.A...Kingston
Hon. William James Roche ....Chancellor of Western University

Lieut.-Col. the Rev. Alex. M. Gordon, M.C., D.S.O., Ottawa, was made an Hon. D.D. Incidents of the year included the decision of the Carnegie Foundation of New York to aid the proposed Pension fund of the University with a grant of $25,000; the announcement that the late Dr. James Douglas, Chancellor of the University, had left $150,000—besides his other benefactions —to Queen's for a Library building; the continued consideration of the project to establish in Ottawa the Medical branch of Queen's University in conjunction with the new Civic hospital at the Capital and the determined opposition of Dr. J. C. Connell, Dean of the Faculty; the request for additional Government aid—an increase from $125,000 to $165,000 a year—presented to Mr. Drury and his Cabinet on Dec. 12 by a Deputation headed by Brig.-Gen. A. E. Ross, M.L.A., who stated that of the 812 High School and Collegiate Institute teachers in Ontario who were University graduates, 247 came from Queen's, while out of 93 graduates of Universities acting as School Inspectors, 53 were graduates of Queen's.

Laval University—The University of Montreal.

Laval University, Quebec, founded in 1852, and Laval in Montreal, founded in 1878 as a branch of the former institution, have had a history wrapped up with the whole modern life and thought of the Province of Quebec. Of Laval in Quebec André Siegfried, the French scholar and statesman, said in his 1906 study of Canadian life and affairs: ''To understand, indeed, all the charm which breathes from this ancient institution one must visit the historic structures of the Grand Seminary, which stand haughty and venerable upon the rock of Quebec. One must traverse the interminable and sombre corridors like those of a convent or a fortress, lighted here and there by narrow windows through which one suddenly perceives, as in a dream, the marvellous panorama of the river. One must see pass in these ante-chambers, in these old-fashioned and sombre class-rooms, the processions of students, half lay, half ecclesiastic, with their curious uniform belonging to another age. One must, especially, have conversed with the ecclesiastics who are the instructors, so French in language, so Canadian, so Catholic and withal so remote and different from our modern European France.''

Both institutions had Faculties of Theology, Law, Medicine and Arts; the Quebec University granted as many as 18 degrees and the latter 12—conferred until 1919 through the Quebec institution; the teaching staff at Quebec numbered in 1916, 140 and at Montreal 304; the number of students at Quebec in 1918 was 1,288 with Mgr. Francois Pelletier, M.A., as Rector and in Montreal they totalled 4,205 with Rev. Emile Chartier, M.A., LL.D., Ph.D., as Secretary-General. During 1919 the Holy See granted Laval of Montreal complete autonomy and it became an independent French-Canadian Catholic University. The announcement was made on May 10th by Bishop Gauthier, Vice-Rector, with the additional statement that it would, in future, be called the University of Montreal. On Nov. 22 the main building of the University at Montreal, containing the Medical departments, was destroyed by fire. The damage was estimated at $400,000 and was covered by insurance. Many valuable paintings, photographs and other irreplacable articles were very largely saved but the Laboratory, with much and priceless material, was wholly destroyed while archives and records and books which could never be replaced also were lost.

On Nov. 28 at a meeting in the Archbishop's Palace it was decided that the University should be at once re-buildt and that a minimum of $2,000,000 would be needed with a maximum placed by Sir H. Laporte at $4,000,000. A

General Committee was appointed composed of Mgr. Gauthier, Auxiliary Bishop. Hon. F. L. Béique, Z. Hébert, Lieut.-Col. C. F. Smith, Dr. J. J. E. Guerin, Senator J. M. Wilson, J. L. Perron, K.C., Beaudry Leman, Sir H. Laporte, A. P. Frigon and others. A plan of campaign to raise the money was arranged and Mgr. Gauthier chosen as President of the Committee; of the Executive Committee General A. E. Labelle was Chairman, A. P. Frigon, General Director, and Léon Trepannier and Edouard Montpetit, General Secretaries; the Hon. Treasurers were Beaudry Leman and Tancrède Bienvenu while Léon-Mercier Gouin was President of a Committé. des Conférences. The first step was to obtain a free site and this the City Council was willing to grant; the next was to obtain help from the Provincial Government and Legislature. As the Montreal *Star* of Dec. 12 pointed out: "There is a French-speaking population of a million or more in and around Montreal, that is, in the immediate vicinity of such a University, and probably twice as many to whom the University of Montreal would be an intellectual centre and permanent inspiration. Unfortunately, the French-Canadian population does not possess the wealth which, gathered in a few hands, can produce the gifts of millions required for the very costly enterprise represented by great buildings and the requisite equipment of a thoroughly modern university—and nothing else will serve."

Sir Lomer Gouin accepted the Hon. Presidency of the Committee and made a general statement (Dec. 12) which indicated the necessary support. It was in reply to a Delegation headed by Bishop Gauthier which waited upon the Government and was supported by the general sympathy of the members of the Legislature in the request for aid. The Bishop pointed out that the fire had only precipitated the question of finding a new home for the University, because the old building was far too small for the big increase in students that had already taken place, and those who desired to attend the different Faculties. In Law alone they had 94 new pupils this year and in Medicine there were 75 new students. He spoke of the needs of the University itself, of the desire to establish new Faculties, such as Comparative Legislation, Political and Social Economy, Foreign languages and Scientific Research, and also emphasized the need for an Hostel for the students, where the priests in charge could exercise control and encourage discipline. He showed that the students came from all parts of the Province and the majority from outside Montreal. Senator Béique declared that the City would have 2,000,000 population in ten years and that the need of a great French-Canadian University was steadily growing; the hope of the speakers was to get $2,000,000 by public subscriptions and $1,000,000 from the Government.

The Premier in his reply said that to his mind three millions would not be enough, and he thought their ambition should be to fix their objective at $5,000,000, and even then they would not have too much. The Government would give substantial help. The campaign was proceeding at the end of the year with $100,000 pledged at the initial meeting by six persons.* Meanwhile, the Legislature was asked for incorporation of the University of Montreal to include Laval University at Montreal, the Law Faculty of Laval University at Montreal, the Medical Faculty of the institution, and the Dental, Veterinary and Pharmacy schools. Archbishop Bruchési and the Bishops of his ecclesiastical district also issued a signed statement as to the appeal of the institution for help: "The University ought to maintain and to kindle among us a Catholic sentiment which is found in public life as well as in the private life of the citizen. It ought, while retaining fidelity to the Church, to arouse the true patriotism which preserves all the traditions of the foundations of our faith, of a charity that is alive, of continuous labour, of unblemished honour and of perfect loyalty. It is for the advantage of your families that you will labour for the new University. As a matter of fact in every country it is the University, its attitude of mind and its teaching, which give us an opportunity of gauging the moral and intellectual development of the people. It is also the hearth from which the light shines that guides and kindles the patriotism of our citizens. It is the fortress which jealously preserves the treasures of our beliefs and of our traditions."

*Note.—Early in 1920 a total of $4,000,000 was subcribed.

It may be added that Laval, Quebec, gave its Hon. LL.D. in this year, to W. H. Moore, Toronto, author of *The Clash.* According to a statement by Archbishop Bruchési in the Toronto 1919 *Varsity Supplement,* nearly all the students in the Montreal and Quebec institutions who were preparing for the secular professions—about 700 in each University—had enlisted for active service; the Canadian Military Hospitals at St. Cloud and Joinville spoke to all Canada for the Medical element.

Four Western Universities. The University of Manitoba, Winnipeg, was founded in 1877 and in 1919 had Faculties in Arts, Science, Law, Agriculture, Engineering, Medicine, Architecture and Pharmacy; its teaching Staff totalled 42 and the students numbered (1918) 800; the value of its endowments was $890,000 and its Income $175,000. It had now, after many years of struggle and even disputes as to jurisdiction and control, attained a recognized position of Government support. Incidents of the year included the appointment of Prof. J. N. Finlayson of Dalhousie to the Chair of Civil Engineering; the change of Manitoba Medical College from a status of affiliation to that of a Faculty of Medicine in the University with Dr. S. W. Prowse as Dean; the retirement of Sir Augustus Nanton from the Board of Governors and appointment of T. J. Murray; the Registration of students in September was the largest on record with much congestion in space resulting and the need of new buildings emphasized. At a meeting of the Board of Governors on Oct. 9 the Minister of Education (Dr. Thornton) assured them of the support of the Government in the immediate erection of a temporary structure on the University campus to meet the need for additional laboratory and lecture-room space. The permanent buildings on the Tuxedo site would be constructed as soon as conditions permitted. The President, Dr. James A. MacLean, reported late in December that there were 1,450 students in attendance.

Of the affiliated institutions it may be said that Wesley College (Methodist) received in June a Report from the Saskatchewan Conference Commission, appointed in 1918, to enquire into the enforced and much-discussed retirement of Rev. Dr. S. G. Bland from the College. The dismissal was found to have been for retrenchment purposes although Dr. Bland's public utterances were admitted to have been the subject of much criticism and the cause of withdrawal of considerable support from the College. At Wesley on Apr. 27 Rev. Hamilton Wigle, President of Mount Allison College, was made an Hon. D.D.; Rev. A. E. Hetherington of Vancouver was appointed Professor of Religious Education; Principal J. H. Riddell stated that the $30,000 deficit of 1918 had been reduced to $3,000 and that the College had contributed 384 men to the War of whom 51 would never return. Manitoba College (Presbyterian) welcomed a new Principal on Oct. 15, in the Rev. Dr. John MacKay of Vancouver, who, in his inaugural address denounced German Socialism and declared that the Church should strive for "the universal recognition of the value and rights of the individual." The Manitoba Agricultural College was described by Principal J. B. Reynolds on Sept. 28 as based upon the model of the Guelph institution while those of Saskatoon and Edmonton were more of the American type. Its functions he analyzed as follows: "(1) To develop technical efficiency or manual skill in the arts of farming and housekeeping; (2) to teach the sciences that relate to farming and housekeeping, so that the labour on the farm and in the house is intelligent and well-directed; (3) to teach economics of the home, of the farm, of the market, so that the resources of the farm and the home may be skilfully managed; (4) to teach sociology and citizenship, so that rural citizens may learn the art of living together and not apart and that schools and churches and clubs may instruct their minds and enrich their lives."

The University of Saskatchewan, Saskatoon, faced a stormy incident during 1919 in the dismissal of four of its Professorial Staff owing to differences with the President, Walter C. Murray, M.A., LL.D.—a widely respected and cultured educationalist. Those concerned were Ira A. MacKay, LL.B., PH.D., Professor of Law, R. D. MacLaurin, B.A., PH.D., Professor of Chemistry, J. L. Hogg,

Ph.D., Professor of Physics and S. E. Greenway, Director of Extension Work. The announcement was made by the Board of Governors on Aug. 13 with a published statement which included correspondence showing dissatisfaction with existing conditions in the minds of the four officials. It appeared that there was a dispute between Mr. Greenway and the President—the former having advised Hon. C. A. Dunning, Acting Minister of Agriculture, that loyalty was lacking in the institution and that only a few of the Faculty had confidence in the President. On Apr. 9 the University Council met and passed the following Resolution: "This University Council wishes to go on record as affirming its confidence and loyalty to the President and resents any imputation of disloyalty or lack of confidence in the President or his conduct of the University and congratulates him on the splendid results achieved during his ten years' service." It was supported by 27 votes with four members not voting. Each of the four stated to Prof. Arthur Moxon that their attitude was caused entirely by disagreement with Dr. Murray's policy in matters not very clearly explained and that they had no personal charges to make. Later, Mr. Greenway did make allegations as to his Extension figures being changed when reported to the Government.

On Apr. 22 D. P. McColl, for the Board of Governors, asked each Professor to state reasons, if any, for dissatisfaction with the management; all but four expressed satisfaction and the replies of the latter were divergent and not very explicit—Prof. MacKay declaring that while excellent work was being done in seven specified departments he did not approve of conditions in five others. The Board met again on July 10 and passed a Resolution stating that, after a careful investigation of the statements made and criticisms offered they were of the unanimous opinion that the 4 Professors should be granted leave of absence, with full pay for specified periods, on condition that they accepted the offer of the Board on or before Aug. 1, 1919, and intimated to the Secretary their intention to retire from the service of the University at the end of the said leave of absence. This proposal not being accepted, the Board on Aug. 11th removed these officials from the service of the University—the dismissal to take effect on Dec. 1st, 1919. The comment of the Regina Leader (Aug. 15) upon the issue was that: "The statement issued by the Board of Governors will satisfy any unprejudiced mind that no other course remained open to them, if they were to faithfully discharge their duty of protecting and promoting the best interests of our Provincial higher institution of learning. The evidence is quite convincing that these men were not only not loyal to the President of the University and their fellow-colleagues of the Faculty, but that they had assumed a position of disregard and almost contempt for the Board of Governors, were conniving at the downfall of the President, and had made charges against him and the general administration of the University which had no foundation in fact."

This trouble created wide controversy and the Graduates' Association issued on Nov. 12 a circular expressing doubt as to the justice of the Board's action in dismissing these gentlemen and urging all members to attend the meeting of Convocation called for Nov. 19. On this occasion Sir Frederick Haultain, Chancellor of the University, presided and each of the 4 men presented long statements. Dr. MacKay charged the President with exercising autocratic powers in government and in determination of policy. He declared that though there were five constituted bodies in the University, practically the entire task of direction, management, and policy descended upon the shoulders of the President and he proposed as a remedy that the office of President be bifurcated by the appointment of a Controller, whose functions would be similar to those of the City Commissioner and would leave the President free to direct the more important educational policies of the institution. After a 12-hour debate a Resolution was passed deprecating the manner in which the four Professors were dismissed from the Faculty of the institution. At the close of the year the resignation of Professor MacKay was announced with a published statement from the Staff of the University (Dec. 18) that there was "complete co-operation and harmony amongst the members of the several Faculties."

Incidents of the year included a special Matriculation course for returned soldiers and a Registration in March of 263 students in Arts, 142 in Agriculture, 37 in Law, or a net total (less duplications) of 430; a registration also of disabled soldiers, taking vocational courses, of over 300 and of 400 in courses for Gas Engineering, with a total attendance in excess of the 1,000 reported for 1918; an appeal by Dr. T. A. Patrick of Yorkton, in seeking re-election to the Senate of the University, for making French obligatory for matriculation and for all degrees where it now was optional—even, if necessary, at the cost of making Latin optional where it now was obligatory; the establishment of a short course for teachers and others to be held at the University, July 2 to August 9, with two groups of courses offered, one for teachers, the other for candidates for a University degree; the later organization of three short courses of instruction on internal combustion engines, including automobiles; the letting of contracts in July for construction of new Physics and Engineering buildings at the University, the structures to cost $400,000 and to be of the same materials and in the same style of architecture as the original University buildings. It may be added that at the annual Convocation Hon. E. L. Wetmore was given the Hon. degree of D.C.L. and that during the year J. T. Hebert, B.A., LL.B., was appointed to the Department of Law and A. C. McGougan, B.A., Ph.D., Head of the Department of Physics. The University lost 66 students killed in action during the War and its soldier representatives won 34 decorations. Emmanual College, Saskatoon, was a Church of England institution affiliated with the University; its students in 1919 numbered 20 and the graduates at Convocation on May 5 were 11; Rev. George F. Trench, M.A., was Principal and a new appointment of the year was Rev. L. H. C. Hopkins, M.A., as Professor of New Testament Exegesis.

The University of Alberta, Edmonton, had a Staff which numbered 43 and students, registered in 1919, totalling 618 while Law lectures were given in Calgary and Edmonton by 17 honourary lecturers selected from the local legal profession. Donations were received during the year of two aeroplanes from the British Air Ministry and a gift of $12,000 from the Alberta Pharmaceutical Association to aid the work in Pharmacy and, with financial assistance from both the National and Provincial Governments, the University undertook to give a special short course in practical agriculture for returned soldiers. In order to further assist men whose academic work had been interrupted by enlistment, the Department of Education organized a special summer course of instruction in High School branches to the end of Grade XII, or the first year in the University; a course of Lectures on ''Merchandizing'' was also established upon request of the Retail Merchants' Association. An interesting incident was the Conference of June 23-29, called at the request of the United Farm Women, for the purpose of offering some light and leading to young people on the farms who had been compelled to leave school early and had lacked opportunities for self-improvement. A surprising degree of interest was shown and 105 students were enrolled. The Summer School of Teachers held at the University was also very successful with 345 in attendance and 4 of the University Departments contributing Instructors.

This year, for the first time, arrangements were made under which the University put on courses in French, Latin, Mathematics and Physics to count towards the degree of B.A.—each course to count as a half year's credit. Twenty-two students were registered in these courses. New buildings for Mining, Engineering and Agriculture were completed in 1919 and the erection of another for the Faculty of Medicine was under way. Final figures of contribution to the War showed an Honour roll of 436 with 58 dead on active service and 38 decorations won. In August President H. M. Tory, M.A., D.Sc., LL.D., F.R.S.C., returned from Overseas where he had acted as Director of Educational Services for the Canadian Army and President of the Khaki University of Canada. During his absence W. A. R. Kerr, M.A., Ph.D., Dean of the Faculty of Arts and Sciences, was Acting-President. The Department of Extension Work, in connection with Travelling Libraries, popular Reading courses, Visual Instruction, material for Debating and public discussion, was continued on an extended scale.

On May 15 the 9th annual Convocation of the University was held and Dr. Kerr, the Acting President, Hon. G. P. Smith, Minister of Education, Hon. C. A. Stuart, Chancellor of the University, delivered addresses, while degrees, prizes, scholarships and medals were duly awarded the winners of the year—including 24 in the B.A. course. Dr. Kerr reported an anxious year, a depleted staff and student circle owing to war calls and, then, a sudden increase until at the close of the current Session there were 595 registrations or 77 per cent. more than the previous year. In July, and in accordance with changes made by Legislative enactment, a new Board of Governors was constituted as follows: Chief Justice Horace Harvey (Chairman), the President and Chancellor of the University, L. M. Johnstone, K.C., Lethbridge, and Dr. J. D. Harrison, Edmonton (6 years); Mrs. Walter Parlby, Alix, and Miss Isobel Noble, Daysland (4 years); W. E. Hay, B.A., Medicine Hat, and James Ramsay, M.L.A., Edmonton (2 years). In September the appointment was announced of Duncan A. McGibbon, M.A., Ph.D., to the Chair of Economics, John J. Ower, B.A., M.D., as Professor of Pathology, Dr. Frank Wyatt to the Department of Soils in the Faculty of Agriculture, and R. S. L. Wilson as Professor of Civil Engineering, while a number of members of the Staff returned from war service abroad. The College of Agriculture opened on Nov. 8 with 34 registrations.

Of the affiliated institutions Alberta College (Methodist) had new buildings which cost $200,000 and occupied a conspicuous place on the University grounds; it was given a new Principal in 1919, Rev. A. S. Tuttle, M.A., and had a registration of 300 students. Alberta College, North, under its Principal, Rev. F. S. McColl, B.A., had a registration of 1,550 students compared with 550 in 1914 and with accommodation greatly over-taxed; Robertson College (Presbyterian) had Rev. Dr. J. M. Millar as Acting Principal who, in October, was confirmed in his appointment while the College continued in 1919 to co-operate with Alberta College in Theology; Mount Royal College, Calgary, under Principal the Rev. Dr. G. W. Kerby, made marked progress during the year.

The University of British Columbia was an integral part of the public educational system of that Province and, as such, had aimed, since its inauguration in 1915, to complete the work begun in the Public and High Schools and to render service through further channels of teaching, research and extension. The students in attendance for the 1919-20 course totalled 890. One of the problems which this institution had to face was the tendency of students at Victoria to go to Eastern or United States Universities instead of the Provincial institution and it was stated at a meeting of the Public School Board there (Apr. 23) to be due to the fact that students could only take one year of local college work instead of two, as in the days when the High School was affiliated with McGill. It was also alleged that the course of Applied Science was a year longer at Vancouver than at either Toronto or McGill. The basic reason, however, was the lack of adequate buildings and of courses which had to await greater local development. So far all that was possible had been done with the limited resources of a sparsely-peopled Province.

A much-regretted incident of the year was the death of Dr. F. F. Wesbrook, the first President of the institution; he was succeeded in June by Leonard Sylvanus Klinck, B.S.A., Dean of the Faculty of Agriculture. In his place Prof. F. M. Clement, B.S.A., of the Department of Horticulture, was appointed. During the Summer the new President spent two months in the East and on his return stated that Governments, business, and the freedom of financial operation, were depleting University Staffs everywhere: "The scarcity of men of professional capacity and a corresponding strong demand for their services by the Universities is the outstanding feature of Canadian and American university life to-day." At the 5th annual Convocation on Sept. 23 Dr. R. E. McKechnie, Chancellor, presided and the University Honour roll in the War was reported as 504 with 62 Decorations won. The Registration for 1919-20 was 681 in Arts and Sciences, 164 in Applied Science, 45 in Agriculture or a total of 890 with 640 in Short Courses; the record of Registration since the beginning showed the remarkable progress of the University despite the difficulties mentioned above—379 in 1915-16; 434 in 1916-17; 674 in 1917-18; 1,152 in 1918-19; 1,530 in 1919-20. During this period a Forest Products Laboratory had been established and a Science building erected and the total of Government grants in 1916-19 was $1,505,684; the members of the teaching Staff at the close of 1919 was 70.

Dalhousie and the Maritime Universities. The 1919 annual Convocation of Dalhousie University took place on May 13 and the President, Dr. Stanley MacKenzie, stated that 65 young men of this University had given their lives on active service with 45 others winning decorations on the battlefield and that the old University building on Carleton Street would in future be known as the Forrest Building, in honour of the veteran President of other days, John Forrest, D.D., D.C.L., LL.D., whose *régime* had begun and ended there. The Hon. degree of LL.D. was conferred upon Rev. Clarence MacKinnon, D.D., Principal of Halifax Presbyterian College, and Melville Cumming, B.S.A., Principal of the N.S. Agricultural College, Truro. On June 10 the Faculty of the University and the members of the Dalhousie Hospital (No. 7) Unit met in a Dinner to Lieut.-Col. John Stewart, the first Commander of Canadian Stationary Hospital No. 7. New members of the Board of Governors were appointed at this time—Hon. R. G. Beazley, M.L.C., and T. Sherman Rogers, K.C.; J. A. Dawson, PH.D., was appointed to the Chair of Biology and Major R. A. Spencer, M.C., and Bar, to that of Civil Engineering; the enrollment at the close of the year was 611, or 50 per cent. greater than the record pre-war attendance, with 134 in Medicine, 53 in Dentistry, 234 in Chemistry, and the balance in Arts, Engineering, Law and Pharmacy—all sections overflowing with students and every class-room taxed to the uttermost; upwards of 200 returned soldiers were on the list.

The great Dalhousian event of the year was its Centenary celebration. Founded in 1818 by George, 9th Earl of Dalhousie, Governor-General of British North America, "for the education of youth in the higher branches of science and literature," based upon the plan and principle of the University of Edinburgh, and (Letter to Lord Bathurst, Colonial Secretary, Dec. 14, 1817), "open to all occupations and sects of religion, restricted to such branches only as are applicable to our present state, and having the power to expand with the growth and improvement of our society," the institution had through a hundred years of struggle and success nobly lived up to its objects and ideals. On May 22, 1820, the corner-stone of the University building was laid by Lord Dalhousie and on Jan. 13, 1821, the Governors of the University were duly incorporated; in 1863 it was re-organized and began the modern period of progress which was most marked after the appointment of Dr. Forrest as President in 1885. The celebrations included a great Convocation on Sept. 11 when Dr. Stanley MacKenzie occupied the chair and spoke briefly of the spirit and purpose and life of Dalhousie; Prof. Archibald MacMechan followed in an eloquent word picture of the Founder of the institution; Prof. Howard Murray dealt with the history of the University in a discriminating, authoritative and interesting statement; many recipients of the Honourary degree of LL.D. also spoke. The list of those in receipt of this honour were as follows:

Rt. Hon. Sir R. L. Borden	..Ottawa	Murdoch Chisholm, M.D.	....Halifax
Richard B. Bennett, K.C.	....Calgary	Chief Justice R. E. Harris	.Halifax
Hon. William J. Bowser, K.C.	Vancouver	Isaac Pitblado, K.C.	.......Winnipeg
Archbishop Neil McNeil	....Toronto	Rev. John Pringle, D.D.	....Sydney
President H. S. Pritchett	..New York	Prof. W. T. Raymond	....Fredericton
President J. G. Schurman	..Cornell	Principal S. N. Robertson	..Charlottet'n
President Harry P. Judson	..Chicago	Prof. James Seth	.........Edinburgh
Dr. David Allison	.........Sackville	Prof. Simeon Spidle	.......Wolfville
Charles H. Cahan, K.C.	....Montreal	Col. John Stewart, M.D.	....Halifax
George S. Campbell	......Halifax	Rev. Dr. J. J. Tompkins	....Antigonishe
Lieut.-Col. Thomas Cantley	..N. Glasgow	Frank Woodbury, D.D.S.	....Halifax

The first seven were conferred *in absentia*. A banquet followed with Dr. G. S. Campbell, Chairman of the Board of Governors, presiding and a toast list which included 7 representatives of United States Universities, one of British and 15 of Canadian institutions. On the 12th there was a procession of 500 students of the day, and of yesterdays, passing with the ancient tablets of the Old building for dedication to the use of the new one which was to be erected at Studley; an impressive scene was the brief and emotional address of Dr.

John Forrest, President *emeritus* and modern Father of the University; speeches, music and dancing made up a final fête. It may be added that 54 degrees were conferred in 1919 and 2,277 since foundation.

The University of New Brunswick, in its academic year of 1918-19, had a registration of 70 which was still affected by war conditions but, in November, the Chancellor was able to report an enrollment of 170 for 1919-20 or the largest on record. The annual Encænia was held on May 15 with 11 graduates and a special Convocation on Dec. 3rd conferred the Hon. LL.D. degree upon H.E. the Duke of Devonshire. During the year Earl O. Turner became Professor of Civil Engineering, A. V. S. Pulling was appointed to the Chair of Forestry, J. A. Spaulding, PH.D., to that of French and German and E. L. Harvey to that of English. All but the last were Americans—owing, no doubt, to the attractiveness offered by other fields to available Canadians. At the close of the year a Fund of $75,000 was initiated to establish a Memorial to the 34 students or graduates killed in the War and $30,000 was speedily contributed. A handsome and elaborate *Memorial Magazine* was issued in this connection which gave details as to the men who had sacrificed their lives and mentioned 33 War decorations as won by Alumni of the University. On Apr. 12 the St. John *Standard* urged the Government to give a larger grant than the current $20,000 a year to the University and thus enable it to become the leading institution in the Maritime Provinces.

King's College, Windsor, N.S., the oldest educational institution of British America, founded in 1789, received in 1919 a bequest of £15,000 from Lady Haliburton, widow of Lord Haliburton who had been a grandson of "Sam Slick" and was, himself, a graduate of King's; on May 8 the annual Encænia was held with Rev. Dr. T. Stannage Boyle presiding and 18 degrees bestowed with the Hon. D.C.L. given to Rev. W. R. Hibbard, M.A., Rothesay, and Rev. A. W. Smithers, M.A., Fredericton, and that of Hon. D.D. granted Rt. Rev. Dr. J. F. Sweeny, Toronto,—the total to date was 1,163. Mount Allison University, Sackville, opened on Sept. 23 with a registration of 242 students compared with an attendance of 166 in the 1918-19 Session; during the year Edgar Allen, M.A., Ph.B., was appointed to the Chair of Biology and Rev. James King, M.A., PH.D., as Professor of Religious Education.

Acadia University, Wolfville, had an attendance of 335 students and its subsidiary institutions, the Ladies' Seminary and the Academy, had 409 and 296, respectively, or a total of 1,040 with about 100 deductions for duplication; about 100 returned soldiers were in this total and were reported by the President, Rev. Dr. G. B. Cutten, as doing splendid work with one year's free tuition accorded; the war record was nearly 700 enlistments, 63 dead in action and honours or decorations won by 80 with a memorial Gymnasium under construction. During the year Acadia made a precedent by appointing Dr. John D. Logan Special Lecturer on Canadian Literature; Dr. W. J. Wright was appointed Professor of Geology. At the 81st Convocation, on May 28, the Hon. degree of M.A. was conferred on J. W. Dewis, M.D., Boston; D.D. on Rev. Bowley Green, Moncton; D.C.L. on H. T. Ross, Montreal; LL.D. on Lieut.-Governor MacCallum Grant and D.Sc. on Principal F. H. Sexton. The President announced benefactions of $35,000 from Senator N. Curry, $33,000 from J. D. Rockefeller, $10,000 from W. H. Chase, Wolfville, and also $5,000 from Senator W. Dennis—the latter to found a Scholarship in memory of the late Edward Manning Saunders—and $10,000 from "a Friend," Halifax, towards the purchase of a Library of Canadiana. Degrees conferred in 1919 were 34 and the total since 1838 to date was 1,615.

Other Canadian Universities and Colleges.

The University of Bishop's College, Lennoxville, received a Royal charter in 1853 and in 1919 it had a teaching staff of 10 with 72 students in attendance at the 1919-20 session; at its Convocation of June 19, 12 degrees were conferred and the Hon. D.C.L. bestowed upon Rt. Rev. W. C. White, Bishop of Newfoundland, Hon. W. G. Mitchell, K.C., Provincial Treasurer of Quebec, and Maj.-Gen. Sir H. E. Burstall, K.C.B.; at this time the Rev. Dr. R. A. Parrock, Principal since 1907, resigned and became Vice-Chancellor with Rev. Canon H. H. Bedford-

Jones, M.A., D.D., Toronto, appointed in his place; the Honour roll of this English Church institution in the War was 117 with 23 killed in action. McMaster University, a Baptist institution of Toronto, founded in 1857, had a depleted attendance during the War but in 1919 returned to pre-war figures in its attendance with 235 students—so also with its affiliated College at Woodstock; there were 40 graduates in 1919 and on May 7 the Hon. degree of D.D. was conferred on Rev. M. B. Parent, M.A., of Roxton, Que., and Rev. J. F. Vichert, M.A., Colgate University, with that of LL.D. upon Rt. Hon. D. Lloyd George, Prime Minister of Great Britain; during the year the Alumnæ Association succeeded in collecting funds for a Women's Residence.

Western University, London, of which Sir Adam Beck was Chancellor and Mayor C. R. Somerville President of the Board of Governors, had under way in 1919 a new Medical building to which London had given $100,000 and to which the Hearst Government was, on Mch. 12, asked by a Delegation headed by Bishop Williams (Anglican) and Bishop Fallon (Catholic) to grant $150,-000; in September Dr. L. P. Shanks of the University of Wisconsin was appointed head of the Department of Romance Languages; the students for 1919-20 numbered 250. In August Mr. Somerville, who had lost his son in the war, retired and was succeeded by Arthur T. Little. It was announced in October that Bishop Fallon of this city had a large educational policy under way involving the construction of Fallon Hall, as a School for Boys, the bringing of L'Assumption College, Sandwich, and the Ursuline Academy, Chatham to London with new buildings, and the enlargement of St. Peter's Seminary—for all of which the Bishop was said to have a Fund of $500,000. Huron College, the Anglican institution of London, had a largely depleted record of attendance during the War with every available man under enlistment; the students of 1919, however, totalled 23 and there were evidences under Principal the Rev. Dr. C. C. Waller of distinct progress; the institution was affiliated with Western University and its Theological course was an effective one.

The University of Ottawa, Ottawa, (Catholic) had in its 1919-20 Session 700 students and a Staff of 65. Brandon College, Brandon, Man., (Baptist), of which Rev. H. P. Whidden, D.D., M.P., was Principal, had an enrollment in 1918-19 of 323 and in 1919-20 of 400; a Slavic department was organized during the year and of the 150 students of the College in residence 80 per cent. were enrolled in Bible and Mission classes; 40 returned men were in attendance and 35 were upon the Honour roll of killed in action; a Forward Movement was started for $300,000 as an endowment and building Fund. The 8th annual Report of Regina College, Regina, (Methodist) showed prosperous conditions with $15,000 paid on its Debt, and a total enrollment of 600 students. Loyola College, Montreal, made a stirring campaign for funds in April 1919 and came out of it with $328,721 and the declaration at a banquet on May 7 by Rev. Father Fillon, Provincial of the Order of Jesus, that the day of Bilingual Colleges and Universities had passed and that Loyola would become "a great English Catholic University"; Archbishop Bruchési was Hon. President of the Executive Committee of the Fund and J. T. Davis General Chairman, with Rev. Father Hingston, S.J., Head of the College and recently back from the War, as a chief worker; the College was opened in 1906, had sent a large contingent to the War, and now maintained a Convalescent Home for soldiers. In the Maritime Provinces there were other successful institutions which should be mentioned. The University of St. Francis Xavier, Antigonishe, of which Rev. Dr. H. P. MacPherson was President, had 131 students in 1919 and conferred 16 degrees; the Presbyterian College of Halifax had 14 students, the College of Ste. Anne at Church Point 60 students, the Holy Heart Seminary, Halifax, 68 students and St. Mary's College 17; St. Dunstan's University, Charlottetown, had in its 1919-20 season, 271 students.

DOMINION GOVERNMENT AND POLITICS

Sir Robert Borden as Prime Minister in 1919. The Canadian Prime Minister who had lived and worked through all the strenuous years of war and into the reconstruction period of 1919 had characteristics which were clearly stamped upon the history of the times and of his country. They may not have included the magnetism or the picturesqueness which marked Sir John Macdonald and Sir Wilfrid Laurier but they certainly commanded the loyalty of his party and the respect of the people. The Peace Conference at Versailles took up the Premier's time during the first part of this year and during its early months Sir Thomas White was Acting-Premier; later on, Sir George Foster held the reins for a time. Sir Robert's career at the Peace table has been dealt with elsewhere; it was one of dignified action and ultra Canadian policy, it commanded the respect of Empire and Allied delegates alike.

His practical refusal of the important post of British Ambassador at Washington showed an unusual disregard for one of the prizes of political power; its proffer proved the high opinion of his ability held in the higher British circles. Determination, persistence, courage, were the qualities which his friends and admirers credited him with; indolence, indecision, lack of strength, were the allegations of his political enemies. The only answer necessary to the latter charges may be found in Canada's patriotic plunge into the War and its Government's early record of difficulties surmounted; in the history of the organization and maintenance of the Union Government; in the call of Parliament and Cabinet and the majority of public opinion in 1918 and in 1919 for his retention in office.

Sir Robert Borden was welcomed home to Ottawa on May 26 after declining a public demonstration at Halifax and his chief comment in response to a Civic address was that he remained an optimist as to Canada and her possibilities: "I am confident that the men who performed so splendidly in the armies of Canada and on the battlefield of the world will be a controlling, steadying and dominating influence for law and order and will co-operate, without regard to race and creed, to enable Canada to accomplish the high destiny which is hers." Succeeding statements and speeches were marked by the careful thought which stamped his whole character. The Winnipeg and Toronto strike situation was met with determination but without aggressive action; his advice in the critical times of May and June were summed up on June 2nd as "keep your heads" and a statement of the belief that Canada, despite prevailing unrest, was better off than any other country; the Reconstruction and Land settlement policies were developed with skill and suc-

[578]

cess; the handling of Parliamentary opinion and policy was marked by diplomacy and illustrated in his treatment of the difficult Titles question, which he directed from London, with a result which may or may not have been desirable but which certainly tided over a Parliamentary crisis.   His appeal to the country, in a press message of July 14, as to the Labour and industrial situation commanded public respect and his policy of organizing a Board of Commerce to control profits and the calling of a Labour-Industrial Conference to discuss abnormal conditions of unrest and economic disturbance, were points of high policy.   In his statesmanlike Message to this Conference, Sir Robert pointed out the vital import of increased production:

The relation of the output to the fixed or overhead charges directly and materially affects the cost.   Moreover, the industries of Canada are not yet organized or developed upon the vast scale reached in some countries with which we are called upon to compete in the world's markets.   In such countries an enormous output materially reduces the cost of the finished article.   If we cannot sell to advantage the industries concerned must develop a lower cost of production or they must discontinue.   This increased relative efficiency is as important to Labour as to Capital, and it is as essential in the office of the management as on the floor of the factory.

It was inevitable that rumours of his retirement should be numerous during this year; he had more than once in Caucus and Parliament intimated his willingness to resign, his more than readiness to make way for others.   But the pressure was and remained too strong for him to have his way; despite war-weariness of responsibility, the ill-health which troubled him after returning from London and Paris, the accident at Halifax on Aug. 17, the illness which came to him on Sept. 5 and affected his health through the balance of the year, he continued to hold his post and lead his Party.   There was much talk during these months of Sir Thomas White as a possible Prime Minister, of Sir George Foster, of Hon. Arthur Meighen, of Hon. J. A. Calder, of Hon. N. W. Rowell and others, but there was no united call for anyone but himself.   On June 26 a Unionist caucus was held for the purpose, generally understood, of deciding upon the formation of a permanent Unionist Party as a development out of the war purposes and tenure of the Unionist Government.   It was the first caucus of the Session attended by Sir Robert and in his speech he re-expressed his desire to retire from the Premiership after the strenuous life of the past few years.   At the same time he did not wish to be construed as evading any responsibility or retiring, so to speak, in the face of the enemy.   The caucus would not hear of the suggestion for a moment and Sir Robert did not press the point.   A Resolution was carried, amid enthusiasm, urging continuance of the Party as a permanent entity in politics and the taking of steps necessary to that end.   A reconstruction of the Cabinet and an autumn Session were announced.

Meantime, the Premier and his Government were fighting external difficulties and Parliamentary differences within the party over the Grand Trunk legislation and Prohibition; in a letter dated Nov. 1st and read in the Senate on the 5th, Sir R. Borden pointed out that he was not only in favour of the Railway arrangements but had, in fact, initiated negotiations in London two years before. This Railway policy was, in itself, a big thing and, in years before the War, the Government acquisition of the C.N.R., of the G.T.R., and the Grand Trunk Pacific would have been deemed a sufficient achievement for the life of a Government and for years of Parliamentary struggle. Speaking to a Railway Brotherhood gathering at Ottawa, on Dec. 8, the Premier made this reference to the responsibilities thus assumed:

The efficiency of transportation in Canada is an essential factor in the national life. Railways, waterways and highways all have their part. From conditions which have gradually developed during many years has arisen the result that about one half the total railway mileage of Canada is, or shortly will be, in the ownership of the State. You must realize, and I hope you will agree, that this condition emphasizes the importance of devising some means by which this great, essential, and national, activity shall not be interrupted or prejudiced by disputes between employers and employed. If, between jealous and sometimes antagonistic nations, the principle of settling international disputes by peaceful methods has been acknowledged and adopted, surely disputes between employers and employed can be investigated and adjusted by means other than those which may bring upon the whole people distress and suffering comparable to that entailed by war. So far as railways in the ownership of the State are concerned, their duty is, on the one hand, to the public whom they serve, and on the other hand to the employees who also serve the same public. So that, in this instance, employers and employed alike serve the people as a whole.

During these months Sir Robert had been suffering from continued ill-health; practically, it was a breakdown from the high strains and tremendous work of the war years; renewed assertions of his retirement appeared in the press only to be met by appeals to continue in harness. During October and November he had been in the South and returned improved in health but not sufficiently so to endure the work and worry which awaited him on Nov. 26 when he arrived in Ottawa; on Dec. 15 it was announced that a relapse in health had occurred and that he must retire at once or withdraw for a prolonged period from active leadership. The statement made public on Dec. 18 was that, after examination, his physicians had emphatically advised that "the condition of his health absolutely forbade him to continue at present the discharge of his official duties, and that continuance therein would inevitably result in a serious and permanent impairment of health and eventually in complete incapacity for further work."

The regret expressed in the newspapers was general and the importance of the Premier's work fully recognized; pressure by letter and telegrams urged some compromise in the matter of retirement while, on the other hand, the recent bye-elections had indicated a decidedly doubtful attitude in the public mind as to the Government, itself. On the 18th it was stated that Sir Robert would, at the earnest wish of his Cabinet, remain as the titular head of the Government and leave Ottawa for a space in order to see if rest and recuperation would restore his health. The official announcement was that: "Sir Robert Borden is naturally reluctant either to continue duties for which the condition of his health unfits him, or to retain his position as head of the Government while absenting himself for a considerable period from his post. On the other hand, the views of his colleagues have been urged with such force and unanimity that he finds himself unable to disregard them. He has, therefore, concluded, at their request, to take such rest from active work as may prove necessary, during which period effective arrangements will be made for the discharge of the duties which otherwise would be incumbent upon him. The period of his absence from duty will necessarily depend upon his progress toward recovery, and, in the end, the condition of his health will determine his resumption of official duties or his retirement therefrom."

Changes in the Government; Incidents of Administration. Meanwhile, there was noticeable a tendency toward retirement amongst members of the Government. The Hon. T. A. Crerar, Minister of Agriculture, resigned in a letter of June 4th in which he assigned the Budget and its fiscal policy as his reasons; amplified later by speeches along the lines of the Farmers' Platform and its Free trade and Reciprocity policy. He paid high tribute, however, to the Premier's "courageous facing" of war responsibilities and the "fine manner" in which he had represented Canada abroad. Mr. Calder took over the Department for a time. On July 7 Sir Thomas White wrote to the Prime Minister reminding him of a promise made months before to relieve him of his duties and pointing out that his health had been impaired by the long strain and heavy responsibility which had rested upon him continuously during the period of the War; stating, also, that personal affairs which, for the past eight years of public life had been almost wholly neglected, demanded immediate return to private business.

There was no doubt as to the facts in this connection; the miserably inadequate salaries granted Cabinet Ministers at this time made it impossible for them to properly maintain their positions in the strenuous life of the capital without private means; the heavy work of the Departments and Government in general made it equally impossible to attend to outside or personal business. There was widespread regret expressed at the retirement of this Minister; it was regarded as a distinct national loss and his war services in finance constituted a record of which Canada did not fail in current appreciation. He had been hailed in many quarters as the coming Prime Minister; even his retirement did not prevent this possibility being discussed. On Aug. 2nd the resignation became operative—though Sir Thomas retained his seat in the House; Mr. Meighen, meanwhile, had acted as Minister. Sir Henry Lumley Drayton, K.C., who, since 1912, had been the effective and efficient Chairman of the Board of Railway Commissioners, was appointed to the position and sworn in on Aug. 2nd; Hon. F. B. Carvell retired at the same date as Minister of Public Works and was appointed to succeed Sir Henry Drayton; at the same time Dr. Simon Fraser Tolmie of Victoria was appointed Minister of Agriculture and sworn in on Aug. 12th; on Sept. 2nd Hon. A. L. Sifton, Minister of Customs and Inland Revenue, replaced Mr. Carvell as Minister of Public Works and Hon. J. D. Reid, Minister of Railways, took charge of the Customs Department. Later on Sir H. Drayton was elected by acclamation for Kingston and Dr. Tolmie re-elected in Victoria.

The Government's financial policy in this year had, meanwhile, been guided by Sir Thomas White with distinct success. He moved in Parliament on Apr. 10 for a War vote of $350,000,000, and it was later approved by legal enactment, to meet expenditure connected with the War and the demobilization of the forces or expenses growing out of the War. The Minister, on Apr. 10, declared that the financial situation was serious: "Our future depends upon our increased production and our ability to find markets for it; and these markets cannot be found under present conditions, unless credits are extended by us. If the Dominion Government to-day said: 'No more credits for the purchase of our wheat, flour, and cheese, and the products of our manufacturers,' you would have a panic in this country." In his Budget speech on June 5th Sir Thomas stated the National Debt before the War as $335,000,000 and, after Demobilization, as probably $1,950,000,000; of Canadian securities $150,000,000 were outstanding in Great Britain, $362,000,000 in the United States and $1,510,000,000 in Canada; the annual interest payable before the War was $12,893,804 and in 1919 $115,000,000, with existing Pensions of 30 millions and a probable future total of 40 millions; the cost of demobilization and gratuities was estimated at $300,000,000 and the total Expenditure for 1919-20 at $620,000,000 with an estimated Revenue of $280,000,000.

As to the Tariff the Minister said: "We propose to wholly repeal the British preferential rate of 5 per cent. Further we propose to partially repeal the intermediate and general tariff rate of 7½ per cent."—at present in effect upon a specific List of foodstuffs and manufactures. The Resolution presented also provided for a reduction of five cents per pound in the British preferential, intermediate and general tariff rates on roasted or ground coffee, and three cents per pound under the British preferential tariff on British-grown teas. The free importation into Canada of wheat, wheat flour and potatoes from countries which did not impose a custom duty on such articles grown or produced in Canada was also enacted. There was, also, an alteration in the rates on soda ash and specific, instead of *ad valorum,* duties were levied on pig lead, zinc, spelter and copper ingots; arrangements had been made with the Railways for reduction of rates on Agricultural implements between East and West and lower Tariff rates on Implements, therefore, became possible with a total reduction in the rate of from 32½% to 50%, with a similar reduction on farm waggons.

In the case of Cement, the war customs duty was repealed and the general tariff rate reduced to 8 cents per 100 pounds or by 8 cents from the existing general tariff rate. The total estimated loss in revenue from these Tariff reductions was placed at $17,000,000. Sir Thomas stated the revenues received in 1915-19 from the Special War Tariff at a total of $150,000,000; he hoped for a general revision of the Tariff in 1920. There was an increased Income Tax, on all corporations, of 10 per cent. on net income instead of 6 per cent.; in the case of individuals the normal rate of 4 per cent. was to be levied upon all incomes over $1,000 but not exceeding $6,000; in the case of unmarried persons and widows or widowers without dependent children, and upon all incomes exceeding $2,000 but not exceeding $6,000, in the case of all other persons; there was to be a normal tax of 8 per cent. on all incomes exceeding $6,000 and the Surtax was to commence at $5,000 instead of $6,000 with increase by graduated and large increases, in particular, over $100,000—running from 56 to 65 per cent. upon all amounts in excess of $150,000 per annum.

The Business Profits War Tax was renewed for the calendar year 1919; the cost of the War to Canada was given, up to Mch. 31, 1919, as $1,327,273,848 and the ordinary expenditure during the same period—beginning Apr. 1, 1914—was $832,757,589 with $180,277,873 additional expenditure which would ordinarily be charged to capital account; the Bank savings of Canada since the first year of war had increased by $588,000,000 and the total Dominion notes outstanding on Mch. 31, 1919, were $298,058,607 while the gold held against them was 38·92 per cent. It would, Sir Thomas stated, be necessary to float one more War Loan in Canada. After considerable debate, the Resolutions were agreed to on June 19 with an amendment by A. R. McMaster, in the following terms, voted down by 120 to 70—after 14 Unionists had supported the amendment and 2 Opposition members (W. D. Euler and F. McCrea) had opposed it:

That the proposals of the Finance Minister are unsatisfactory. They offer no curb against extravagance. They utterly fail to take any adequate steps to relieve the present high cost of living. They give no definite promise of Tariff revision downwards; that, to relieve the present situation, the Tariff should be so framed as to free the food of the people and the machinery used in the development of the natural resources of Canada, together with the raw material entering into the manufacture thereof: To take off or substantially reduce, as speedily as may be expedient and just to all interested, the duties upon all other necessaries of life; that also, the reciprocal offer of trade with the United States should be accepted, and a general downward revision of the Tariff undertaken forthwith in conformity with the principle herein enunciated.

Following the Budget came the 3rd Victory Loan. Though originated and planned under Sir Thomas White's administration, it fell to Sir Henry Drayton to develop and encourage the effort to meet the heavy obligations then outstanding. On Aug. 1st a meeting of the 1918 Committee was held at Ottawa and, by request of the Government, the Dominion Executive of that most successful campaign, with its $695,000,000 subscribed, was re-constituted. E. R. Wood, Toronto, once more became Chairman, J. H. Gundy, Toronto, Sir Augustus Nanton, Winnipeg and J. M. Mackie, Montreal, were appointed Vice-Chairmen; A. E. Ames, Toronto, was Chairman of the Dominion Administrative and Finance Committee, J. H. Gundy, Toronto, of the Special Subscriptions Committee, W. N. McIlwraith, Toronto, of the Dominion Publicity Committee and W. S. Hodgens, Toronto, of the Dominion Business Committee. Publications were at once issued showing that of the $610,000,000 accepted from the 1918 Loan subscriptions $312,000,000 had been paid for War and Demobilization expenses in Canada, $59,000,000 for the Service Gratuities, $207,750,000 advanced to Great Britain and the Allies, $9,000,000 granted the Halifax Relief Fund and $21,350,000 advanced for purchase of the B.C. Salmon Pack, for Imperial shipbuilding, and for purchases of various raw materials of war manufacturing.

Back of Canada, as security for such a Loan, were the values of yearly production (field crops, mines, fisheries and forests) which, in 1916, were 1,292 millions and, it might have been added, with the inclusion of industries and live-stock, over 4,800 millions. The National wealth of Canada was stated at 19,000 millions. The Loan asked for was in the form of $300,000,000 5½ per cent. gold bonds—part in 5-year bonds due Nov. 1, 1924, and part in 15-year bonds due Nov. 1, 1934; the issue price was 100 and accrued interest and it was intended to meet, firstly and primarily, $210,000,000 of incurred obligations. In Toronto, on Oct. 16th, Sir H. Drayton and, on Oct. 22nd, Sir T. White, addressed special audiences in favour of the Loan and the former was at Montreal on the 23rd with his official maiden speech in that city; the Minister of Finance then went West and, beginning at Winnipeg on Oct. 27th, spoke at Brandon, Regina, Edmonton, Saskatoon and other points upon the same subject: Hon. W. L. Mackenzie King and Hon. T. A. Crerar wrote letters in support of the Loan; Hon. E. C. Drury, the new Ontario Premier, told an audience at Barrie on Nov. 3rd that the country was on the edge of a time of depression, that "the time will come, not very far off, when wages will have dropped and the value of a bushel of wheat gone to one-half the value it is now and then the Victory bonds will be a most valuable security to hold." The subscriptions, which had opened on Oct. 27th, were closed on Nov. 15th and the finally announced results—compared with 1918—were as follows:

Province	No. of Applications		Amount Subscribed	
	1918	1919	1918	1919
British Columbia	80,315	55,373	$ 36,683,900	$ 36,411,915
Alberta	56,813	30,543	18,979,250	17,178,900
Saskatchewan	77,328	34,122	26,072,450	21,712,650
Manitoba	86,972	52,782	44,030,700	41,642,200
Ontario	542,648	455,489	336,055,350	355,739,050
Quebec	161,822	139,938	180,868,450	162,032,150
New Brunswick	31,957	21,778	17,002,550	15,635,050
Nova Scotia	61,040	36,398	33,221,550	28,521,900
Prince Edward	5,406	4,229	3,011,050	3,158,400
Total	1,104,296	830,602	$695,870,250	$682,032,215

At this time, and following the continued increase in Imports from the United States over and above the Exports, Canadian rates of exchange fell steadily till, in December, the Canadian dollar was worth only 90 cents in New York and was being refused altogether on some railways and in many cities. On Dec. 12th the Finance Minister stated that $20,000,000 in gold was being shipped to try and rectify the situation but it proved to be insufficient and the excess of imports from the Republic over exports by Canada stood at 1,750 millions for the years 1913-19. Government incidents of a financial nature, during the year, included agreements with France and Roumania under which credits were to be extended to a total of $25,000,000 each for the purchase from Canada of raw materials, foodstuffs and manufactured goods in fixed proportions; the statement by Sir James Lougheed on Sept. 25, in the Senate, that similar credits had been arranged with Greece and Belgium to a total for all four countries of $100,000,000 with $6,000,000 allotted to Italy and that the amount actually paid by Canada under the contracts was $1,008,021 to Belgium and $5,053,656 to Roumania; the statement that the gross Debt of Canada on Aug. 1st, 1919, was $2,907,-667,041 and the net Debt $1,670,263,691 with the latter figures reaching $1,838,131,058 on Dec. 31st, 1919. It may be added that the Canadian Failures in the calendar year 1919 were $12,952,123, or almost exactly the amount of the year 1909 and comparing with $30,741,292 in 1914 and that the Canadian Bank Clearings of the year totalled $16,709,598,898 or $2,945 millions more than 1918.

Of other and individual members of the Government, or their Departments, only a little can be said here; the work of the Ministers of Agriculture and Labour, Railways and Reconstruction, are dealt with separately. The position of Hon. N. W. Rowell, as a former Liberal leader in Ontario, at a time when Messrs. Carvell, White and Crerar had retired, and the creation of a permanent Unionist Party was mooted, had elements of difficulty in it: the Toronto *Globe* of July 15th charged Mr. Rowell with having abandoned his principles and "crossed the floor" of the House to the Conservatives. Speaking at Okanagan, B.C., on July 25th the Minister replied by asking if the Liberal organ had changed its views as to the need of Union Government; if it thought he should withdraw his support from the Government on the Prohibition issue, on the development of a great Government-owned and operated system of National railways, on its Labour platform, or the Peace policy, or the League of Nations scheme, or its Nation-Empire proposals.

At the National Liberal Convention on Aug. 6th many attacks were made upon Mr. Rowell—notably by H. H. Dewart, M.L.A., E. M. Macdonald, M.P., and Ernest Lapointe, M.P. Mr. Rowell, however, went on his way without apparently worrying over the matter and kept a position high in the councils of Unionism and in the confidence of the Premier with frequent references in the press—pro and con—to his possible accession to power as Unionist leader. He distinguished himself at the Washington Labour Conference, made a number of effective speeches during the year and led the hosts of Prohibition at Ottawa; on Oct. 6th he officially welcomed the King and Queen of the Belgians at Niagara Falls, Ont., for a brief and passing hour on Canadian soil; he addressed the 40th international Convention of the Y.M.C.A. at Detroit on Nov. 20th and declared that militarism was again threatening the world with war but that "by putting our weight and our influence against armaments, against the revival of militarism, against these curses that would align young men of our nations one against the other, this continent has it in its power to make a great contribution to the solution of the world's problems."

The Hon. Arthur Meighen, Minister of the Interior, was a favourite in the Conservative element of Unionism for the post of Prime Minister; his logical and effective speeches, his industry and high administrative qualities created and retained confidence. His annual Report, showed for 1918-19, a Dominion Lands revenue of $3,539,927 and gross receipts from all Departmental sources of $10,-339,210; a surveyed land area in the three Prairie Provinces of 191,005,786 acres and unsurveyed 263,783,892 acres; large sales of land during the year including 285,561 acres by the Hudson's Bay Co. at $4,978,950 and, by the C.P.R., 602,555 acres at $10,580,669 with total sales to date valued at $35,037,422 for the Hudson's Bay, $113,708,234 for the C.P.R., and $46,000,000 for the C.N.R. and other companies. This Minister also had charge of the National Parks and the Yukon. Mr. Meighen was in the West during January and spoke at several points before returning; he was in Winnipeg during the strike period and on Aug. 25th spoke at Medicine Hat and on the 27th, with Mr. Calder, at Lethbridge; he asked an audience at Woodstock, N.B., on Oct. 25th where class politics would end—if the farmers combined, might not the rest of the country combine against the farmers!

Mr. Carvell, Minister of Public Works, made a few speeches during the year and always said something practical or interesting. He stated at Ottawa on May 12th that the new Parliament buildings had cost $8,000,000 and might cost $10,000,000 owing to the sensational advance in building material and wages. At an Ottawa meeting on Feb. 13th he declared that "there is a great deal too much talk in some of the newspapers and amongst the public about the troubles of the returned soldier," and added his belief that money could not be better expended, for both value and for unemployment, than in the making of good roads; at Kingston on Feb. 15th he stated that wages could not come down unless the cost of living took a drop, and the cost of living would not decrease materially until wheat became cheaper. He disapproved the fixation of prices. The Report of this Department, after Mr. Sifton had taken it over, but for the year ending Mch. 31st, showed expenditures of $21,395,500 on Public Works of which $3,181,348 was on Harbour and river works, $7,466,679 on Public buildings and $8,492,503 chargeable to War appropriations.

During the latter part of 1919 Sir George Foster was for some time Acting-Premier with Hon. A. K. Maclean as Acting-Minister of Trade and Commerce; he only spoke a few times during the year with, however, one eloquent address to the Canadian Club, New York, on Nov. 22nd; he issued a Message to the people for Peace Day, July 19th, in which he eulogized Canada and Canadian soldiers but urged Canadians not to forget "the preponderant part taken by the countries of the Empire in the world struggle by land and water, in air and under sea, nor the tremendous expenditure by them in blood and treasure so freely offered and so bravely borne." Mr. Calder as Minister of Immigration, controlled a policy which was one of restriction rather than the unlimited encouragement of the days of Sifton and Rogers; his great organizing ability and Western popularity made his continuance in the Cabinet after Mr. Crerar's retirement a most important matter for the Government; he was supposed to be one of three or four possibilities for the Premiership. In August he made a tour of the drought areas of Saskatchewan and Alberta and promised measures of relief which were afterwards carried out.

The situation as to Immigration was complicated. There was great need for workmen in the cities and the factories, for labourers on the farms, for domestics in the homes; yet there were 300,000 returned soldiers being demobilized and strenuous opposition by Labour Unions to any encouragement of immigrant workmen; transportation difficulties also were great. The official statistics for the years of war showed 144,789 in the year ending Mch. 31st, 1915, 48,537 in 1916, 75,374 in 1917, 79,074 in 1918 and 57,702 in 1919. For the calendar year 1919 the total was 117,633. Of the latter 57,251 were from the British Isles and chiefly soldiers' dependents with 52,054 from the United States—largely farmers and their families who were stated to have brought cash and effects into the country totalling $18,419,406. In the 10 years ending Mch. 31st, 1919, 162,523 intending immigrants had been rejected at the United States border and 8,756 at ocean ports, with the restrictions and tests becoming more stringent and more effective every year.

At the same time, there was a continuous emigration from Canada not recorded in any official Canadian figures but appearing in United States returns as immigrants to that country. The total so given was 82,215 in 1914-15, 101,551 in 1915-16, 105,399 in 1916-17, 32,452 in 1917-18, and 22,446 in the calendar year 1919. If these figures were accurate they indicated a distinct war condition in migration as, in 1918, restrictions were imposed upon the emigration of able-bodied men from Canada. In 1918-19 Canada lost many foreigners by emigration as did the United States; large numbers of Austrians, Italians, Greeks, etc., left for their home countries. The population of the Dominion at the close of 1919 was estimated at 8,835,102. Mr. Calder's policy in this year was to encourage farmers and farm help and domestic servants and to discourage skilled or unskilled labour of the artisan class until all

returned soldiers were settled and the demobilization of both soldiers and workers disposed of.   W. W. Cory, C.M.G., Deputy-Minister of Immigration and Colonization, in his Report for the year
of Mch. 31st, 1919, stated that 9,466 women and children, dependents of returned soldiers, had been brought back with, probably,
35,000 still in the United Kingdom.

During the year the Minister retired about 100 employees who
had outlived their usefulness and divided the country into three
Districts—the Eastern, Western and Pacific, with an Immigration
Commissioner in charge of each.   W. R. Little was appointed for
the Eastern at Ottawa, Thomas Gelley for the Western at Winnipeg, A. L. Joliffe at Vancouver for the Pacific.   Mr. Calder, also,
carried through Parliament amendments to the Immigration Act
which gave him, or the Government, absolute authority and control
over this subject.   The new Act gave power to prohibit or limit in
number for a stated period, or permanently, immigrants of ''any
nationality, race or religious sect, or of any specified class or occupation''; it gave specific powers to deport foreigners working for
social disorder or revolution; it imposed a literacy test applicable
to persons over 15 as to knowledge of reading with special powers to
the Minister, in application of the clause—though, it may be added,
the United States had recently repealed a Literacy clause as keeping
out desirable people; it enlarged the list of causes, such as insanity,
alcoholism, or disease, under which immigration rights could be
refused; it gave the Government power by Order-in-Council to
prohibit persons from entering Canada for either a stated period
or permanently, and for any reason which might be deemed advisable; it had a naturalization clause which declared that ''when any
citizen of Canada who is a British subject by naturalization, or
any British subject not born in Canada having Canadian domicile,
shall have resided for one year outside of Canada, he shall be pre-
sumed to have lost Canadian domicile and shall cease to be a Canadian citizen for the purposes of this Act.''   Following this enactment new regulations were imposed in London and amongst them
the following as advertised in the British press:

At all times and in addition to the literal rendition of the terms and
prohibitions of the Canadian Immigration Act, the Canadian Department of
Emigration and Colonization will continue to exercise its sovereign discretion
and jurisdiction as to who shall or shall not be allowed to land in Canada.

The Department knows that industrial workers are being sought here by
Canadian industrial concerns, but all such must seek the consent of the Department at Ottawa before they can be landed in the Dominion.   This Department, acting in conjunction with the Canadian Department of Labour, will
control the movement which might otherwise result in persons going to Canada
under inadvisable and disappointing conditions.

Canada wants farm workers at any time of the year they can be placed.
Canada wants household workers of the right type at all times and Government Conductresses are appointed on specified steamers to afford protection
en route for all unaccompanied women and girls, whether they be going out to
marry, going to work, going to live with friends or relations.   The British
Overseas Settlement office is giving free transportation to Imperial ex-service
men and women, which means third-class on the British railway and third-

class on the ocean to a port in Canada. For certain specified women ex-Service war workers, and in accepted cases, that Office issues a coupon ticket book from which the Booking Agent will take the British Government Order for the third-class ocean passage.

In addition to the prohibitions of the Canadian Immigration Law set out in the circular of the North Atlantic Passenger Conference No. 13/19, every immigrant 18 years or over is required to possess in his or her own right $25.00; every child between 5 and 18, $12.50. Double these amounts when landing between 1st November and last day of February, inclusive.

In specific details the Minister and his Department arranged to aid the immigration of British ex-Service men and gave them the same privileges under the Land Settlement Act as to Canadian veterans except that they were required to pay 20 per cent. instead of 10 per cent. on the purchase price; Mr. Obed Smith, Commissioner of Emigration in London, announced on Oct. 4th that the Ministry of Immigration would maintain the same attitude and policy as before the War in that only workers on the land and household workers were needed in Canada or should be encouraged to emigrate; neither ex-Service men nor women, he added, would obtain free transportation until approved by the Canadian representative in London. Meantime, co-operation had been arranged by Mr. Calder and J. Bruce Walker, the Publicity Commissioner at Winnipeg, between the Western Railway and Land Companies and the Government, for promotion of agricultural immigration from the United States—the difficulty in this connection as to Great Britain being that only a limited number of about 1,000,000 persons were engaged in Agriculture.

Meantime, British women Commissioners had been sent out to report as to Canadian conditions, in this respect, to the Overseas Settlement Committee while the Salvation Army also undertook active operations as to emigration from Great Britain; in August, Lieut.-Col. J. Obed Smith returned from London and visited Canadian centres east and west in order to investigate local requirements; for three days (Sept. 9-12) 16 women, representing the greater Women's organizations of Canada, were in conference at Ottawa with the Minister of Immigration as to the situation. A permanent body was formed, entitled the Canadian Council of Immigration of Women for Household Service and composed of a representative from each of the National bodies and from each Province in which a Hostel for the care of women immigrants was established. Lady Falconer of Toronto was elected President, the Western Vice-President was Mrs. McNaughton and the Eastern, Mrs. Vincent Massey; the supervision of Hostels and the disbursement of Government subsidies, with the making of recommendations to the Minister, were the duties of the organization. It may be added that, with the specified approval of Mr. Calder, an Order-in-Council was passed on Mch. 26th allowing British Hindus residing in Canada "to bring in their wives and minor children"—with limitation to one legal wife. On May 1st, after much trouble and controversy over a considerable immigration, into the West, of Hutterites, a sect in North Dakota similar to the Mennonites, an Order-in-Council was passed forbidding the immigration of Doukhobors, Hutterites and Mennonites.

As to other Government incidents it may be said that Hon. P. E. Blondin, Postmaster-General, reported through his Deputy, R. M. Coulter, for the fiscal year 1919, that 12,290 Post Offices were in operation and 181,505 rural mail delivery boxes; that the net Revenue was $21,602,712 and Expenditures $19,273,553; that there had been an issue of 9,100,707 Money Orders totalling $142,375,808 in value with a balance on Mch. 31 of $41,654,960 in the P.O. Savings Bank. The 1st Annual Report of the Dominion Statistician (R. H. Coats, F.S.S.) was issued under the Trades and Commerce Department, and dealt with the origin, purpose and organization of the Dominion Bureau of Statistics; there was tabled in the Commons an official statement on Mch. 12th as to 4,147 employees in the permanent Inside Civil Service and 18,593 in the permanent Outside Service with, on Apr. 1st, 1918, 6,324 temporary employees of the Inside Service, 12,555 of the Outside and 13,000 rural Postmasters or a total of 54,619 persons; the closing was announced on Dec. 31st, of the war-time Department of Public Information—the duties still needed being carried on within the Department of External Affairs; an arrangement was made under which the Civil Service bonus of $10,000,000 granted by Parliament was to be distributed by the Civil Service Commission; an important historical speech was delivered by Sir Edward Kemp, Minister of Overseas Military Forces, in the Commons on May 27th in which he reviewed with elaboration and care the war policy and administration of his Department in England.

An interesting discussion developed in many quarters during the year as to the use of Commissions and Orders-in-Council by the Government in time of War and still, to a considerable extent, utilized in days of Reconstruction. From a statement afterwards presented to Parliament* it appears that in 1914-19 there were 84 Commissions appointed either by Parliament or the Governor-in-Council and including 19 under the Labour Department, 19 under the Marine Department, 8 in the Post Office and 7 under the Justice Department; on July 3rd Mr. Rowell, President of the Privy Council, presented a statement as to Orders-in-Council for the years 1914-19 showing a total for the five years of 35,142 with 1,253 under the War Measures Act. With the close of 1919 many of these were discontinued and of those under the War Measures Act only 9 remained in operation. The yearly average of these Orders, outside of the War Measures Act, was not much larger than usual; in 1910 under the Laurier Government there had been 4,769 and in 1911, 5,732. Sir George Perley, High Commissioner in London, returned to Canada in July for a visit—the second one since war began in 1914. The Commissions appointed during the year included the Mathers' Labour Commission, the Royal Labour Com-

*Note.—Mch. 18th, 1920.

591 CHANGES IN THE GOVERNMENT: INCIDENTS OF ADMINISTRATION 591

mission, the Board of Commerce, and the Canada Wheat Board which have been dealt with elsewhere.

The Hon. W. E. Middleton, Toronto, and Hon. J. A. Chisholm, Halifax, were appointed on Aug. 14th to enquire into and report upon the allegations of impropriety or mis-conduct made in respect to the administration of The Military Service Act at the Guelph Novitiate in 1918. There was a prolonged enquiry in the course of which Sir Sam Hughes and the Counsel making the charges agreed that Hon. C. J. Doherty, Minister of Justice, had no personal object in respect to the much-discussed raid and that, as General Hughes put it: "If he had forty sons, he would have offered them all in connection with the War that has just closed." The Report was made public on Nov. 4th and exonerated Mr. Doherty of all blame and described his action and that of General Mewburn as proper and right under the circumstances; Capt. Macaulay, the officer who conducted the raid, was criticized for tactlessness and harshness and the Jesuit Society was recognized as "an Order of an exclusively religious character." An Inter-Department Committee was appointed by the Government composed of Sir Joseph Pope, Maj.-Gen. W. G. Gwatkin, Thomas Mulvey and Dr. A. G. Doughty, to devise and procure satisfactory Armourial bearings for the Dominion of Canada.

Of other Commissions Hon. D. Murphy, H. H. Watson and F. W. Welsh of Vancouver were appointed to investigate into and report concerning the relations between the firm of J. Coughlan & Sons, of Vancouver and their employees; Dr. J. G. Rutherford, C.M.G., Ottawa, J. S. McLean, Toronto, J. B. Harkin, Ottawa, and Vilhjalmur Stefansson were made Commissioners to report upon the potentialities of the Arctic and Sub-Arctic regions of Canada in the development of Musk Ox and Reindeer herds for commercial and national purposes; the Hon. W. B. Chandler, Fredericton, was appointed to report as to complaints concerning the treatment of women passengers, (soldiers' dependents) on the *S.S. Scandinavian* and Dr. J. G. Rutherford to enquire into Racing and betting conditions in Canada; Hon. F. E. Hodgins, Toronto, was appointed to enquire into alleged ill-treatment of the men of the C.E.F. while on board the transport *Northland* from Liverpool to Halifax, and Hon. D. M. Eberts, of Victoria, to report upon the administration of Fisheries in the Barkley Sound district of British Columbia; Judge J. A. Barron was appointed to enquire into the cessation of the Toronto Street Railway Service on Sept. 3rd, 1919. The chief Government appointments of the year were as follows:

Member of King's Privy Council for Canada	Hugh Guthrie, K.C., M.P.	Guelph
Senator of Canada	Col. Gerald V. White	Pembrooke
Senator of Canada	William Proudfoot, K.C.	Goderich
Member Board of Pension Commissioners	Major Stanley B. Coristine	Ottawa
Commissioner of Customs and Deputy-Minister of Inland Revenue	Robinson R. Farrow	Ottawa
Assistant Chief Commissioner Railway Board of Canada	Simon J. McLean	Ottawa
Member of Canadian Trade Commission	Rhys D. Fairbairn	Toronto

Commissioner of North-West Territories.William W. Cory, c.m.g .... Ottawa
Director of Dominion Experimental
  Farms ....E. S. Archibald, B.A., B.S.A......... Ottawa
Deputy-Minister of Agriculture ......Dr. J. H. Grisdale .... Ottawa
Canadian Director of Food Supplies...Dr. J. W. Robertson, c.m.g .... Ottawa
Superintendent of Dominion Peniten-
  tiaries ....Maj.-Gen. W. St. Pierre Hughes.... Ottawa
Deputy-Master of the Royal Mint (Im-
  perial Government) ....A. H. W. Cleave.................. Ottawa
Dominion King's Counsel ....Hon. T. H. Johnston .... Winnipeg
Special Counsel, Soldier Settlement
  Board ....William F. O'Connor, k.c.......... Ottawa
Member National War Savings Commit-
  tee ....William K. George .... Toronto
Hon. Physician to H.E. the Governor-
  General ....Maj.-Gen. J. T. Fotheringham, c.m.g. Ottawa
Hon. Aide-de-Camp to H.E. the Gover-
  nor-General ....Lieut.-Col. M. C. Edwards, D.S.O.... Ottawa
Hon. Aide-de-Camp to H.E. the Gover-
  nor-General ....Col. J. L. R. Parsons, D.S.O., C.M.G.. Ottawa
Hon. Aide-de-Camp to H.E: the Gover-
  nor-General ....Col. F. M. Gaudet, c.m.g.......... Montreal
Hon. Aide-de-Camp to H.E. the Gover-
  nor-General ....Lieut.-Col. L. R. la Flèche, D.S.O.... Montreal
Hon. Aide-de-Camp to H.E. the Gover-
  nor-General ....Col. G. Godson-Godson, D.S.O...... Ottawa
Senator of Canada ....Hon. Thomas Chapais, M.L.C., LL.D.. Quebec
Canadian Trade Commissioner to FranceLieut.-Col. Hercule Barré, M.C..... Montreal
County Court Judge of Renfrew....Evan H. McLean .... Renfrew
County Court Judge of York ....Emerson Coatsworth, k.c........... Toronto
County Court Judge of District No. 6,
  N.S. ....Allan Macdonald .... Antigonish
District Judge of Acadia, Alberta...Lieut.-Col. J. D. R. Stewart........ Calgary
District Judge of Calgary, Alberta....William Roland Winter .... Calgary
Puisne Judge of the King's Bench,
  Quebec ....Hon. R. A. E. Greenshields........ Montreal
Puisne Judge of the Superior Court,
  Quebec ....Eratus E. Howard, k.c............ Montreal
Junior Judge, County Court of York..James H. Denton .... Toronto
Deputy-Judge, County of Hastings....Samuel S. Lazier .... Belleville
County Court Judge of Kent ......John J. Coughlin .... Kent
County Court Judge of Carleton ....Ranald D. Gunn .... Carleton
County Court Judge of Waterloo ....Edward J. Hearn .... Toronto
3rd Junior Judge of County of York..Charles H. Widdifield .... Toronto

The Militia Department and General Mewburn's Policy.   The demobilization of the Army and the re-organ- ization of the Militia were associated problems of the year and both were in the hands of General Mewburn; as to the former, complete plans had been made be- fore the war ended with machinery well organized for the purpose.   Canada was divided into 22 dispersal areas with stations and each soldier was enabled, so far as was possible, to select the area he wished to go to, and arrangements were made, accordingly, subject to the preference given organ- ized units originating at specific points.   By Sept. 20, 1919 the total troops embarked from Overseas since Nov. 11, 1918 was 264,045 and the total number demobilized was 338,833.   The Minister was able to state in the Commons during October that, in the handling of this large number of men, not a single life had been lost through accident at sea; three casualties occurred by derailment of a train. At the above date there were 6,598 men in Canadian Military Hospitals.   In his annual Report for Mch. 31, 1919, General Mew- burn stated the Militia expenditure of the year at $3,444,954 and the War expenditure at $377,120,138—the former comparing with $10,998,162 in 1913-4.   The first matter of the year, apart from demobilization, was the re-organization of the Permanent Militia or regular Canadian Force; it had done splendid service at the Front and of its 300 officers fully five-sixths went Overseas with all the men who could be spared; all its larger Units, including the Royal Canadian Dragoons, Strathcona Horse, the R.C.H.A. and the Royal Canadian Regiment, greatly distinguished themselves. In March its re-organization was effected on a basis of 5,000 men as follows:

Cavalry.—The R.C.D. with headquarters and two squadrons (Toronto); the Strathcona Horse, headquarters and two squadrons (Calgary).

Artillery.—R.C.H.A., brigade headquarters and three batteries (Kingston); R.C. Garrison Artillery, regimental headquarters and five companies, with four coast defence companies and one heavy battery (Halifax, Quebec and Victoria).

Royal Canadian Engineers.—Two companies (Halifax and Victoria).

Infantry.—R.C.R., regimental headquarters and five companies (Halifax); Princess Patricia's, regimental headquarters and four companies (Toronto).

Only officers and men who had served Overseas were admitted to the new Force which was 2,000 larger, as an establishment, than in 1914; the terms of enlistment were for two years, and renewable, with regimental pay similar to that of the C.E.F. The following detachments, other than those mentioned above, were authorized: Army Service Corps, permanent Medical Corps, Veterinary Corps, Ordnance Corps and a military staff corps of clerks. A vigourous recruiting campaign was also initiated. On June 24, the House of Commons discussed General Mewburn's proposal to double the strength of the Permanent Corps of Canada and make the total force 10,000. It was opposed by A. R. McMaster, W. F. Nickle, and J. A. Robb. The Minister pointed out that the force proposed was a relatively small number compared with the area of the Dominion: "I regret to say that I am confirmed in that belief by events happening all over the world, the troubles arising to the south of us and the troubles arising in different parts of Canada." General Mewburn estimated that 7,000 men would be needed and, by the close of the year, 6,277 were distributed throughout the 11 Military districts of the country while a Machine Gun squadron, or brigade, was under arrangement for each of 14 Canadian centres. The subject had been debated again in the House on June 24th and the Minister's policy approved, on a vote of 56 to 34, with Hon. T. A. Crerar, Dr. Michael Clark and W. F. Nickle joining with the Opposition.

The re-organization of the Militia was a more complicated matter. Early in the year the Government approved a Commission composed of Maj.-Gen. Sir W. D. Otter, K.C.B., C.V.O., (Chairman) Maj.-Gen. W. G. Gwatkin, C.B., C.M.G., Commander of the General Staff, Maj.-Gen. Sir E. W. B. Morrison, K.C.M.G., C.B., D.S.O. and Brig.-Gen. A. G. L. McNaughton, D.S.O., to enquire into conditions in this respect and to give, as General Mewburn announced on Feb. 14th, "special consideration to the problem of re-organization of the Active Militia upon a plan which would at once preserve the history of Militia regiments and perpetuate the identity of Overseas Battalions." The great difficulty in the way was to preserve the home and local and historic identities of existing Regiments

20

with those of the newer Battalions and products of the World-War. There was, also, the standing of officers having long militia experience or experience in South Africa with the vital need for recognition of the services of men who had been leaders at the Front and had gained honours in the great struggle; equally important was the allotting of colours and battle honours to the Militia or War regiments—many of the former having records to be proud of in the earlier military history of the Dominion.

Meanwhile, on Feb. 7, a sum of $142,850 had been set aside by Order-in-Council for allowances to Militia regiments as a help in the pending re-organization; in succeeding months the Otter Commission visited the headquarters of Canadian Military Divisions, called together the Militia officers and those of the C.E.F. and discussed the best method and system of co-operation; in Artillery and Machine Gun units there was no serious difficulty as pre-War affiliations and conditions did not enter into the matter. In Montreal, at a Conference on Sept. 9th, the proposal most favourably regarded was that the City Regiments should be continued as at present with their names, records and other traditions intact; the suggestion was made that Overseas battalions should become absorbed into the strength of the mother regiments, still preserving their Overseas identity as battalions forming part of the original regiments from which they had been organized, in part, at least. On Nov. 15th the re-organization of the Militia Council was announced as follows:

President ....Maj.-Gen. the Hon. S. C. Mewburn, C.M.G., M.P.
Vice-President ....Maj.-Gen. Sir Eugene Fiset, C.M.G., D.S.O.
Inspector-General ....General Sir A. W. Currie, G.C.M.G., K.C.B.
Adjutant-General ....Maj.-Gen. E. C. Ashton, C.M.G.
Quartermaster-General .....Maj.-Gen. Sir H. E. Burstall, K.C.M.G., C.B., D.S.O.
Finance Member ....Brig.-Gen. J. G. Langton.

The Minister was, meantime, having much difficulty in obtaining the necessary funds. On a pre-war basis it had cost ten million dollars annually to maintain the Permanent forces and Militia; since that time the rise in the cost of materials, food, transportation and accommodation for horses, men, and material was estimated by the Department at 110 per cent. Taking the future, on the basis preceding the War, the cost would be $25,000,000 and it was at this figure that the Militia estimates for 1920 were placed—with a section of opinion in Parliament, as before the war, inclined to criticize the Militia on general principles. Incidents of the year included the purchase by the Department of war-time buildings and improvements at Long Branch and Camp Borden, Ont.; the announcement in January that Officers whose service in the C.E.F. had ceased would be permitted to retire retaining their rank, if recommended and qualified under specified regulations as to service, age, etc.; the statement in a Parliamentary return of June 13th that a much-discussed, alleged, Report by Lieut.-Col. J. S. Jenkins of enquiry into Overseas Military conditions was never completed or made because the work of the Committee was unfinished when the Armistice came and demobilization began; the active advocacy by Brig.-General W. A. Griesbach, C.B., C.M.G., D.S.O., M.P., of a Military Service scheme based upon the assumption that all male citizens of Canada should be liable to give military service to the State in time of war and to be trained in time of peace to give such service when called upon, with the declaration that these principles should be incorporated in the law and policy of Canada; the announced changes in King's Regulations to provide that the establishment of Majors-General should be 25, of temporary Brigadiers-General not more than 50 and of Colonels 100; the official statement from the Department that up to Aug. 31st, $75,179,396 had been paid in Gratuities to returned soldiers with $45,000,000 yet to be expended and that the amount of Separation Allowances paid (almost complete) was $104,291,440; the announcement by the Department on Sept. 29th that the King's certificate or discharge would be issued through the Militia Department to all soldiers who, after service, were discharged as medically unfit or to those who, while not serving in a theatre of war, were discharged as a result of disabilities caused by air raids, naval bombardments, etc.   The following were appointed General Officers Commanding Military Districts in 1919:

District	Headquarters	Commander
No. 1	London,	Brig.-General H. A. Panet, C.B., C.M.G., D.S.O.
No. 2	Toronto,	Maj.-General J. H. Elmsley, C.B., C.M.G., D.S.O.
No. 3	Kingston,	Brig.-General Victor A. S. Williams, C.M.G.
No. 4	Montreal,	Brig.-General C. J. Armstrong, C.B., C.M.G.
No. 5	Quebec,	Brig.-General J. P. Landry, C.M.G.
No. 6	Halifax,	Brig.-General R. C. Thacker, C.B., C.M.G., D.S.O.
No. 7	St. John,	Brig.-General A. H. Macdonell, C.M.G., D.S.O.
No. 8	Winnipeg,	Maj.-General H. D. B. Ketchen, C.B., C.M.G.
No. 9	Victoria,	Maj.-General R. G. E. Leckie, C.M.G.
No. 10	Regina,	Brig.-General Alex. Ross, C.M.G., D.S.O.
No. 11	Calgary,	Brig.-General A. H. Bell, C.M.G., D.S.O.

Reconstruction Plans; Pensions and Land Settlements. In 1919 the Departments and work of six Ministers were more or less concerned in the returned soldier and Reconstruction and, before the creation of the Repatriation Committee of the Cabinet, some of these functions and duties overlapped; in the public mind there was always a good deal of confusion.   The Ministry of Soldiers' Civil Re-establishment, formed early in 1918, with Sir James Lougheed as Minister, included Hugh Clark, M.P. as Parliamentary Secretary, F. Gerald Robinson as Deputy Minister and E. H. Scammell as Assistant Deputy; its duties covered Hospitals, Convalescent Homes and Sanatoria for invalided troops, vocational, educational and other training for returned and discharged men, provision of employment and assistance in rehabilitation for civil life; it controlled the work of the Invalided Soldiers' Commission and of the Board of Pension Commissioners. The Minister of the Interior, Hon. Arthur Meighen, had charge of the Land Settlement Board; the Hon. N. W. Rowell, President of the Privy Council, was also in charge of the Department of Public Information; the Hon. T. A. Crerar as Minister of Agriculture and the Hon. G. D. Robertson as Minister of Labour were concerned, respectively, in Land Settlement and in Unemployment problems; the Hon. J. A. Calder, Minister of Immigration, was Chairman of the Repatriation Committee of the Cabinet.

This body, by the time Reconstruction had reached its critical stages, when an average of 2,000 troops a day were arriving in Canada for months at a time, had done much to co-ordinate the policies of the different Departments and other agencies handling the repatriation problem; to co-ordinate the machinery created for carrying out these policies; to inform the public as to what was being done so as to secure the co-operation of different classes in the country. Speaking in Toronto on Jan. 10 Mr. Calder gave a full and valuable statement of national conditions and Government plans which greatly helped to clear the air. This was repeated at Quebec on Feb. 6th. The Department of Soldiers' Civil Re-establishment was divided into three sections: Medical Service, the retraining of disabled men, and the problem of bringing undisabled men into touch with opportunities for employment. By June, 1919 there were 9,132 patients in charge and under necessary treatment by the Medical Service; in the Training branch 10,858 men were under instruction with 3,720 graduated; in the Information and employment section 150,297 soldiers had been interviewed, 85,622 requests for information answered, 80 free Government employment bureaux established from coast to coast, 37,681 applications for placement received (May 24, 1919) and 22,958 or 75% arranged.

On Mch. 1st, 1919, new regulations were enforced under which (1) additional medical treatment benefits were made available for all returned soldiers; (2) further facilities were placed at the disposal of soldiers so disabled by war service that they were unable to follow their pre-war occupation and consequently required retraining; (3) increased pay and allowances were granted discharged members of the Canadian forces who had been so disabled by war service that they were unable to carry on their pre-war occupations, whilst undergoing re-training. These allowances were increased by 20% in the case of single men and from 18 to 40% in the case of married men and, in the latter cases, were calculated upon the number of children. In September Hon. Mr. Rowell presented legislation to the Commons and Sir James Lougheed to the Senate confirming reciprocal arrangements with the Imperial Government as to British reservists in Canada and Canadian soldiers in Great Britain. Mr. Rowell stated that in the week of Sept. 6th, 12,230 patients were under treatment in the Hospitals and he added this pledge: "The Government has undertaken to provide that every man who has served in the Canadian forces and who suffers at any period of his life from disease or disability, contracted or aggravated by service in the field, shall have free medical treatment and that during the period of his illness, no matter when it occurs, he shall receive the same pay and allowances to provide for himself and family as he would have received had he continued in the Army.''

The number of men receiving training on Aug. 31st was stated as 11,134 and those who had completed their courses 5,955; for the six months ending Aug. 31st, 9,793 had submitted themselves for employment while the Civil Service Commission had appointed 5,320 to positions and the Department of Re-establishment 3,000. It may be added that up to Nov. 20th following 6,676 returned soldiers had been placed by the Department or Government agencies on Farms, 977 in logging work, 2,275 in mining, 191 in Fishing and 24,049 in Manufacturing establishments. The question of increased gratuities to returned soldiers was a vital topic of the year and deputations, earnest appeals and organized effort by a section of the Veterans urged $2,000 as the sum desired for each soldier who had seen service in France, $1,500 for those who had got no further than England and $1,000 for those who served in Canada—a national liability of $1,000,000,000. Hon. Mr. Calder pointed this out on Nov. 5th and, in submitting the Report of a Parliamentary Committee of enquiry into the matter—of which he was Chairman —stated that the annual interest alone would be $55,000,000. In the case of a special plan proposed by the G.W.V.A. and including schemes for lands, loans, housing, investment and removal of debts, the country would need about $400,000,000 to carry it out; the plan submitted by Colonel J. W. Margeson, President of the Ottawa branch, G.W.V.A. and a member of the Pensions Board, would mean an outlay of $200,000,000.

The Minister explained what had already been expended and estimated total expenditures to the end of the current fiscal year (Mch. 31, 1920) as follows: Pensions $53,536,498 with an annual estimated outlay of $30,000,000; gratuities $153,686,557, and return fares of dependents $1,916,578; Department of Soldiers Civil Re-establishment $57,045,664, and Soldier Settlement Board $48,-228,103 with cost of Labour Bureaux $383,331. Estimated expenditures in the future included an additional $101,771,896 for Soldiers Settlement and $25,000,000 for settlement with Imperials; $50,000,000 for Department of Soldier's Civil Re-establishment and $40,000,000 for unemployment. The summary of all expenditure was $491,540,623, with $263,000,000 of this needed for actually planned work. The Gratuity proposals were, therefore, thoroughly impracticable and the Government was doing all that the country would desire it to do in view of financial conditions and national responsibilities: ''If it is the view of this Parliament that there should be a further general distribution of grants or gratuities to all of the ex-members of the Forces, then there is but one thing for Parliament to do, and that is to say so very clearly and plainly. And if Parliament comes to that conclusion then there is only one course and that is that some other Administration must carry on.''

Mr. Mackenzie King moved the referring back of the Report for further consideration but, after debate, this was rejected by 100 to 35 and the Report accepted.

Parliament appropriated $40,000,000 under its Committee's recommendation for the re-establishment of returned men and the expenditure of this money was put in the hands of the Canadian Patriotic Fund organization; it was to be applied in relief of emergencies, for actual unemployment and for cases where insufficient money was earned to support families, etc. At the close of the year an Order-in-Council put the Canadian members of the Imperial forces and their dependents on the same level as to gratuities, pensions, etc., as those of the C.E.F. Incidents of the year in this general connection included a policy of industrial training for boys under 18 who had enlisted in the C.E.F.; the statement before the Calder Parliamentary Committee on Sept. 29th by Major L. L. Anthes, of the Re-construction Department, that there were over 30,000 returned soldiers then without employment—Ontario having 12,090, Manitoba 4,151, Nova Scotia 4,025, British Columbia 3,850 and Quebec 3,244 with other small totals; the fact that up to July 1919 the United States had provided the sum of $18,000,000 for vocational training of returned soldiers and Canada, $32,000,000; the statement of T. A. Stevenson, on his return from an official enquiry in Great Britain (Aug. 29th), that "there are as many men in training in Canada to-day under our rehabilitation organization as there are in the United Kingdom although enlistments there were 14 times as great as Canada's and casualties nearly 20 times as many."

On Feb. 12th the resignation of H. J. Daly as Director of the Repatriation Committee and appointment of Lieut.-Col. Vincent Massey as his successor were announced; the retirement of Lieut.-Col. F. McKelvey Bell, M.D. as Director of Medical Services, and replacement by Col. E. G. Davis, C.M.G., M.D., followed; the resignation of Major J. L. Todd from the Pension Board, the appointment of Major S. B. Coristine and the later retirement of J. K. L. Ross, Chairman of the Board, took place with the appointment on Aug. 2nd of Lieut.-Col. J. T. C. Thompson, D.S.O., as Chairman of the Board, and Lieut.-Col. J. W. Margeson as a member. Finally, on Dec. 21st, an Order-in-Council approved a War Service Gratuity, payable to the naval and land forces of Canada in place of Post Discharge pay; the amount to be paid was graduated up to six months pay and allowances, exclusive of subsistence allowance, or allowances in lieu of rations and quarters, and according to the length and nature of service.

In the matter of Pensions Canada's estimate during 1919 was for $30,000,000 a year with an expected increase to $40,000,000 in the near future. An important organization had been built up in this respect, with the Board of Pension Commissioners at its head, composed of three men who were each appointed for ten years. The head office was at Ottawa and there were 17 branch offices in the principal centres throughout Canada. These local branches received applications from soldiers' dependents for pensions, sent visitors to call on pensioners in their homes, held medical re-examinations and dealt with complaints.   The Board kept representatives travelling from coast to coast interviewing pensioners and addressing organizations interested in their welfare.   On Jan. 6 a British official statement showed weekly pensions and allowances as follows: Canada, 47s. 11d.; United Kingdom, 40s.; New Zealand, 40s.; South Africa, 40s.; Australia, 30s.; United States, 28s. 10d.   On Mch. 31st, 1919, the exact official figures at Ottawa showed the total number of disability pensioners as 44,726 (not including widows and children), with a yearly liability of $7,476,167 and the total of dependent pensioners as 16,888 with a yearly liability of $9,636,-939.

In Parliament during June a special Committee was appointed to deal with Pensions of which Hon. N. W. Rowell was Chairman and it reported on June 24th provisions for increased payments in the form of a year's bonus in specified cases and of other general increases with the addition of 2,000 more pensions to Imperial Reservists in Canada; the Bill embodying these proposals was passed with little opposition.   On Sept. 26th an official statement was issued by the Pension Board that "Canada is at present paying war pensions to nearly 90,000 individuals, at an annual cost of over $24,000,000 and, under the Pensions Act which became effective on Sept. 1, the majority of these will receive bonuses and increases which, in the aggregate, will involve an additional annual expenditure of $4,000,000."   At the close of the year the Board was reorganized as a Civil rather than Military body with the Commissioners devoting their whole time to their duties.   At the same time an arrangement was made under which the Canadian Board was empowered to act in Canada for the British Ministry of Pensions.

The Land Settlement Board, of which W. J. Black was Chairman, continued its 1918 work and had, in the current year, a record of marked accomplishment.   It was found necessary, early in 1919, to broaden and vary the original plans in view of the fact that only a limited amount of suitable homestead land was available for Soldier settlement, and that some Crown lands were held by the Provinces while homesteading did not suit all returned soldiers. It was, therefore, proposed in March that the Provincial Governments should co-operate with the Soldier Settlement Board in acquiring suitable lands at present held uncultivated by private owners; the lands so bought to be re-sold to the soldier at cost price with payments extended over 20 years or longer.   Hon. Mr. Meighen, as Minister of the Interior, had this matter under his jurisdiction; with the basis to go upon that out of 273,444 members of the C.E.F. who had been written to 87,771 had expressed a desire to take up Agriculture or stock-raising.   At Winnipeg on Jan. 31st the Minister delivered an address of remarkable force and lucidity urging the claims of the returned soldier upon the public and the Provinces; the responsibility of his Department and the Board lay in agricultural training, where necessary, of returned men and the providing of land, giving assistance in financing and subsequent supervision.

On May 12 Mr. Meighen introduced a measure in Parliament which passed in due course. It extended the scope of the legislation, passed in 1917, by which Dominion lands within 13 miles of a railway were made available for Soldier settlement, and provided for the purchase of privately-owned lands in any Province for resale to eligible soldier settlers. It also enabled the Soldier Settlement Board to compulsorily purchase lands which were held to be retarding agricultural development. All Canadians in all the services were eligible together with widows of such persons and the Board could loan up to $4,500, repayable in 25 annual installments, with interest at the rate of 5 per cent. amortized. For the purchase of live stock, implements, etc., it could loan up to $2,000 repayable in 4 equal annual installments, beginning the third year, with interest at the rate of 5 per cent. but with no interest charged for the first two years. A further sum of $1,000 could be loaned for permanent improvements, repayable in 25 years, at 5 per cent. The Act also provided Agricultural training for eligible soldiers, not ready to go immediately on the land, and for the payment of allowances for the settler and his dependents during the time of training.

Before this legislation passed Mr. Meighen told the House on June 23 that $14,467,974 had been appropriated by the Board and its branches of which $9,000,000 had been spent on land and $5,-000,000 on stock and equipment with 4,269 loans approved and 12,594 settlers granted certificates for settlement out of 17,109 applicants. On Aug. 4th Mr. Meighen was able to state at Port Credit that "the Dominion of Canada has placed more men on the land than all the Colonies of the Empire put together, with Great Britain thrown in and the United States on top, and more than all that total by 50 per cent." Up to Dec. 15th, 1919, the Board had provided loans aggregating $51,572,332 to 17,218 returned soldiers who were settling on the land—the average loan being $2,934. It had granted 5,433 soldier entries approximating 869,000 acres of free lands in the Western Provinces, and about two-thirds of the grantees had exercised their civilian homestead rights, which meant an additional 575,000 acres, or a grand total of 1,444,000 acres. It had dealt with 42,630 returned soldiers who had applied for certificates qualifying them to become beneficiaries under the Act and, of these, 32,363 candidates had received certificates.

Political Conditions in 1919: Position of the Liberal Party. The Government during this year faced a steadily growing division in public sentiment and it lacked the internal cohesion which formerly came from Party loyalty, Party principles and Party patronage. A Conservative wing of Unionism, led by Hon. Robert Rogers, wanted the old Conservative rule back again and the elimination of Liberals from the Government. His policy, as presented to a Toronto audience on Mch. 11th, included maintenance of the National Policy of protection, and continuance of the War-Times Election Act in some form which would exclude aliens from voting. As to the farmer, he would provide him with a better Home market: "The duty of the Government is to see to it that our raw materials, which are our natural resources, are developed and that blast furnaces are put to work in all parts of the country in order that the manufacturer may be supplied with raw material as cheaply as possible, and that he may be able to turn out Canadian-made implements without the handicap of having to pay a heavier price for raw material than the American manufacturer." Cheaper Implements would, he claimed, be one result.

At Winnipeg, on May 9th, Mr. Rogers declared that the Union Government had failed in grappling with preparations for Peace and urged Conservative organization. Canada's first duty was to the returned soldier, its second was to correct "the unbridled manipulation by jobbers, by traders and by profiteers," that had resulted in an unbearably high cost of living. In Toronto the Central Conservative Association on July 24 stood for a straight Conservative party ticket in that City at the next elections and, on Aug. 25th, Mr. Rogers suggested in Winnipeg the formation of a National Committee, representative of the Conservative Party, from the various Provinces of Canada which, when organized, would direct and manage the work of general organization everywhere. At a succeeding Convention of the Manitoba Provincial Conservative party, Sir Robert Borden's name was left off the list as Hon. Patron.

Meanwhile, Mr. Crerar had left the Government and been given the practical leadership of the Farmers' party; he gathered increasing *prestige* from month to month through the increase of his farmers' following in Parliament—by attrition from Government ranks and in bye-elections to about 15,—while the Ontario elections made him at once an important political figure, hailed in agrarian circles, as the coming Premier of Canada. In the Commons F. F. Pardee, and Hon. W. S. Fielding alligned themselves once more with the Liberals and 12 Western Unionist Liberals broke away on the Budget division; while the Manitoba Grain Growers forced R. C. Henders, M.P., to resign his Presidency because he had supported the Government and the Budget. The Liberal Party was not in a strong position at the beginning of the year. Sir Wilfrid Laurier was leader and his personal magnetism and popularity had pulled it through the difficult period of Warfare into the still more vexed political days of Reconstruction; here the Farmers' organizations and success drew, probably, more from the ranks of Liberalism than from the Conservatives.

Speaking to the Eastern Ontario Liberal Association formed in Ottawa on Jan. 14th, Sir Wilfrid threw out an olive branch to Unionist Liberals and supported a platform of (1) generous treatment to returned soldiers and their dependents; (2) restoration of the British preference to its pre-war status, admission of foodstuffs

free of duty from all countries which admitted Canadian foodstuffs
free in return, and progress toward freer trade generally, step by
step; (3) democratization of Labour and repeal of the War-times
Election Act; (4) abolition of government by Order-in-Council
and of censorship of the press; (5) support of the League of
Nations.   Following this a Central Ontario Liberal Association
was formed at Toronto with W. E. N. Sinclair of Oshawa as President—one of the Resolutions passed demanding repeal of the Privy
Council Appeal with, also, a declaration by Hon. George P. Graham
that a re-union of the Liberal party was essential.   East Elgin
Liberals, at St. Thomas on Jan. 22nd, recommended the adoption
of the Farmers' Platform in complete form.

On Feb. 17th Sir Wilfrid Laurier passed away at Ottawa after
a stroke of paralysis which attacked him on the 15th.   No
measure of national respect that could be offered was lacking in
the State funeral which was accorded the dead leader on Feb. 22nd;
in the tributes of personal affection shown by letters and telegrams
which poured in for days and the procession of 45,000 people who
passed the stately catafalque in which his remains lay at the Victoria building where Parliament had been sitting; in the cablegram from H.M. the King declaring that "Canada will mourn for
one who dearly loved his country and will remember with pride
and gratitude his great powers of administration, genius and leadership," and other messages from British statesmen and Empire
leaders; in the procession along the two-mile route from the Victoria Museum to the Basilica, thronged by tens of thousands of
devoted admirers paying their last tribute to the "Old Chief"; in
the solemn Requiem Mass at the Basilica celebrated by Mgr. di
Maria, Papal Delegate, and the splendid panegyrics of Mgr. O. E.
Mathieu, Archbishop of Regina, and the Rev. Father J. E. Burke
of Toronto; in the Parliamentary tributes of Sir Thomas White
and Hon. Rodolphe Lemieux—the latter's words such as only an
eloquent French-Canadian could have used.   The passing of the
brilliant Liberal leader was not easily forgotten and, later in the
year a movement developed to erect a national monument over his
grave in Notre Dame Cemetery; a strong Central Committee was
formed in Ottawa with Hon. S. A. Fisher as Chairman and $30,000
as the objective.

This event worked great political changes and, in the House of
Commons on Feb. 24th, a Liberal caucus selected Daniel D. Mc-
Kenzie, a notable and hard-hitting Liberal member from Cape
Breton since 1904, as Opposition leader in the House, pending the
call of a National Liberal Convention.   At a banquet in Montreal
on Mch. 22nd Mr. McKenzie made it clear that he was simply Leader for the current Session.   On May 17th, following, Liberal
leaders from eight of the Provinces conferred at Ottawa with Mr.
McKenzie, appointed a National Committee to make preparations for the coming Convention and issued a call for Aug. 5-7th.
Apart from the Convention ensuing Liberal incidents included

the Party triumph in P.E. Island and Quebec where a clean sweep was made in each Province; the keen attacks made by Mr. Hartley Dewart, as Provincial leader in Ontario, upon Mr. Rowell and the expressed hostility of *The Grain Growers' Guide* to the Liberal policy; the defeat of W. R. Motherwell, Liberal candidate, in the Saskatchewan bye-election which gave an indication of the Farmers' attitude; the issue of two pamphlets as Party literature giving the substance of speeches by W. T. R. Preston—at Orono on Feb. 14th and at Peterborough on June 21st—attacking the Borden Government for alleged electoral frauds in connection with the 1917 general elections; the rise of Ernest Lapointe into prominence as a Quebec Liberal leader and his triumphant election in Quebec City as successor to Sir W. Laurier; the appointment at the close of the year of Andrew Maydon, M.A., LL.B., Ottawa, as General Secretary of the National Liberal Committee and of John Lewis, a well-known Toronto journalist, as Editor of Liberal Publications.

The Liberal Convention of 1919: Mackenzie King as Party Leader. The question of a successor to Sir Wilfrid Laurier was the dominant one in Liberal thought during several months of 1919. Should he be a French-Canadian or an English-Canadian; should he continue the traditions and sentiment of Laurier leadership or branch out into the new conditions of a troubled time; should he be an elderly and experienced politician, versed in all the codes of political life and steeped in Parliamentary precedents, or a young, active and untramelled spirit; should there be a new policy with a new leader to meet new conditions? Such were the questions in a thousand forms of fluctuating discussion with, perhaps, the pivotal point resting in the hope of combining Western Liberalism with that of Quebec in the future electoral struggle. D. D. McKenzie was chosen as House leader and the big questions shelved for the coming Convention while a Party caucus on Apr. 3rd arranged the preliminary details of representation so as to include all the Liberal members of the Senate and Commons and all Liberal candidates defeated at the 1917 Elections; Liberal Premiers or Opposition leaders in the Provinces and the Presidents of 9 Provincial Liberal Associations; three delegates from each constituency to be elected at a local Convention to be called for that purpose and six from seats entitled to 2 representatives; the Liberal members of each Provincial Assembly, and Liberal candidates defeated at the last Provincial election in each Province, acting jointly, with power to select from among themselves a number of delegates equal to one-fourth of the total number of representatives in each Provincial Assembly. Women were entitled to be elected as Delegates and an invitation was extended to the Canadian Council of Agriculture, the Dominion Trades and Labour Congress, the Great War Veterans' Association, and the Canadian Railroad Brotherhoods to send representatives for the purpose of presenting such views as these National bodies might desire prior to the drafting and adoption of a National Liberal platform. The Liberal press was urged to attend.

Liberal meetings were held all over the country and delegates chosen; at a Conference in Ottawa on May 17th it was stated that Unionist Liberals were generally co-operating and were disposed to bury their Conscription differences; the Western Provincial leaders appeared willing to abandon their support of Union Government and resume their Liberal support. In the press preceding the gathering, which was officially called by Mr. McKenzie on May 9th for Aug. 5-7th, the most discussed possibilities as Leader were Hon. W. S. Fielding, Premier of Nova Scotia for 12 years, and Minister of Finance for 15 years, Father of the Reciprocity policy of 1911; Hon. George P. Graham, member for a time of the Ontario Government, leader for a time of the Ontario Opposition, member of the Dominion Government in 1907-11; Hon. William M. Martin, member of the Commons for 8 years and Premier of Saskatchewan since 1916; Hon. William Lyon Mackenzie King, C.M.G., M.A., LL.B., PH.D., 8 years Deputy-Minister of Labour, M.P. in 1908-11, and Minister of Labour for three years. Mr. McKenzie himself had many friends and followers with Mr. Fielding as, apparently, the press favourite for the position.

Suggestions poured in upon the Committees in charge and the Toronto *Globe*, in its Ottawa despatch of July 31st stated, that "the tendency in nearly every suggestion is to ask for a greater control by Canada, progressively, of looking after her own foreign affairs, a continual restriction in the appeals to the Privy Council, until Canada stands at last, without doubt, as an independent nation, linked only with the other nations of the Empire by ties of sentiment and a common Sovereignty." The Chairman of Committees selected prior to the meeting of the Convention were as follows: Laurier Resolution, Hon. S. A. Fisher; Trade and Commerce, A. R. McMaster, K.C., M.P.; Soldiers' Problems, Hon. Dr. H. S. Béland; Organization, Hon. J. R. Boyle; Railway and Transportation Problems, Hon. G. P. Graham; Labour and Labour Problems, Hon. Mackenzie King. Out of the mass of conflicting thought expressed prior to the meeting came the clearly defined fact that Quebec would not ask for or expect a French-Canadian leader and an obvious difficulty in electing Mr. Fielding because of his occasional support of the Union Government and his attitude in favour of Conscription.

When the Convention opened on Aug. 5th at Ottawa the Premiers of 8 out of 9 Provinces of Canada were present—Gouin of Quebec, Murray of Nova Scotia, Foster of New Brunswick, Bell of P.E.Island, Norris of Manitoba, Martin of Saskatchewan, Stewart of Alberta, Oliver of British Columbia. The Farmers' Party was not represented nor were the Labour Unions officially. There were 1,400 delegates present with Quebec totalling about 460 and Ontario 450 and the Convention was called to order by Hon. Charles Murphy; Mr. McKenzie then proposed Hon. G. H. Murray and Sir

Lomer Gouin as joint Chairmen in a brief speech; in a short opening address Mr. Murray declared that ''we can agree, now that the
War is over, that the usefulness of a Union Government is gone and
that in dealing with domestic affairs the old system of Party government gave a higher sense of responsibility on the part of men
for their country, and will give us a more effective and more economical Administration.'' During succeeding proceedings announcements from the chair were made in English by Mr. Murray
and in French by Sir Lomer Gouin.

The first Resolution, moved by Sir Allen Aylesworth and Hon.
R. Lemieux, dealt with the death of Sir Wilfrid Laurier and reviewed his 32 years of Party leadership, stated that ''his life was
spent in the service of his country and his King,'' and declared
that his greatest work was bringing the two great races of Canada
into harmony. It was adopted by a silent, standing vote. The
Convention was then addressed by Capt. R. L. Calder, M.C., a Delegate, on behalf of the Grand Army of Canada; in the afternoon
brief addresses were given by Hon. J. H. Bell of P.E. Island, Hon.
W. F. A. Turgeon, Saskatchewan, Hon. John Oliver, British Columbia, and Hon. Dr. H. S. Béland, Quebec; at the close of the first day
it was generally believed that Mr. Martin was the favourite for
leader while Mr. Lemieux was stated to have quoted Lady Laurier
as expressing Sir Wilfrid's desire to have Mr. Fielding as his successor. Mr. Martin, however, would not allow his name to go before
the Convention and remained firm in this determination; Sir
Lomer Gouin supported Mr. Fielding.

A Tariff policy was decided upon the 6th after keen discussion
in Committees and in the Convention with Mr. Oliver opposed to
its terms as savouring of class action; he urged that all the necessaries of life, all tools, implements and machinery used by the people, should be free of customs taxation; Kirk Cameron, a Montreal
manufacturer, urged the Convention to not altogether repudiate
Protection. But strong speeches by A. R. McMaster and Ernest
Lapointe carried the day for freer trade and only a few hands went
up for proposed amendments of a moderating type. As finally
carried, the Resolution, presented by Hon. George Langley and Hon.
P. J. Veniot, was as follows:

That the best interests of Canada demand that substantial reductions of
the burdens of customs taxation be made with a view to the accomplishing of
two purposes of the highest importance: (1) Diminishing the very high cost
of living which presses so severely on the masses of the people; (2) reducing
the cost of the instruments of production in the industries based on the
natural resources of the Dominion, the vigourous development of which is essential to the progress and prosperity of our country.

That to these ends wheat, wheat flour and all products of wheat, the
principal articles of food, farm implements and machinery, farm tractors,
mining, flour and sawmill machinery and repair parts thereof, rough and
dressed lumber, gasoline, illuminating, lubricating and fuel oils, etc., nets, net
twines and fishermen equipments, and fertilizers, should be free from customs
duties as well as the raw material entering into the same; that a revision
downward should be made and substantial reductions should be effected in the
duties of wearing apparel and footwear, and on other articles of general con-

sumption (other than luxuries), as well as on the raw material entering into
the manufacture of the same; that the British preference should be increased
50 per cent. of the general tariff.

That the Liberal party hereby pledges itself to implement by legislation
the provision of this Resolution when returned to power.

In the evening Messrs. King, Graham, and McKenzie spoke upon
different Resolutions with Mackenzie King in the lead as to oratory
and with a tribute to the late Leader which evoked tremendous
cheering.   His Labour Resolution was unanimously approved and
its chief clauses were as follows: (1) Approving the general principles of the Labour Convention of the League of Nations Covenant;
(2) urging the introduction into the control of industry of a principle of representation whereby labour and the community, as well
as capital, might be represented; (3) declaring that, so far as practicable, there should be Federal and Provincial co-operation for an
adequate system of Insurance against unemployment, sickness, dependence in old age, and other disability, which would include Old
Age pensions, Widow pensions, and Maternity benefits; (4) favouring representation of Labour on Federal Commissions pertaining
to labour matters and representation of Labour on the Board of
Directors of the Canadian National Railway; (5) urging that the
system of re-training soldiers unfitted for their past work because
of physical injuries be extended to disabled workers in industry;
(6) advocating more effective restriction of Chinese immigration,
Federal incorporation of co-operative associations, the acceptance
of the principle of Proportional Representation; (7) urging immediate and drastic Government action as to the high cost of living
and profiteering; (8) asking for a discontinuance of government by
Order-in-Council and a just franchise and its exercise under free
conditions.

An important Resolution of the second day was presented by
Hon. R. Dandurand and E. M. Macdonald as follows: "That no
organic change in the Canadian constitution in regard to the relation of Canada to the Empire ought to come into effect until after
being passed by Parliament, and ratified by vote of the Canadian
people on a referendum."   To this W. D. Gregory, K.C., of Toronto,
a devoted follower of the late Goldwin Smith and John Boyd, of
Montreal, President of the Canadian National League, proposed to
add the words: "That we are strongly opposed to any attempt to
centralize Imperial control."   Following an eloquent speech by
Mr. Lemieux in which he denounced Imperialism and "Downing
Street" and Centralization, the amendment and motion were enthusiastically approved and combined.   Another Resolution, proposed by Messrs. Graham and Lemieux and carried without discussion, declared that the Liberal policy of construction of the
National Transcontinental Railway had been thwarted in its objects
and results by the Borden Government; that the Government's policy in subsidizing and lending money to the Canadian Northern
had been unbusiness-like and required investigation; that the present system of managing Government Railways of 15,000 miles in

length was "unwieldy, inefficient, and extravagant," with public
ownership and operation not receiving a fair trial; that the Government had neglected its duty in not providing adequate facilities
and ocean tonnage for after-war needs and had thus failed to protect the trade and transportation interests of Canada in a critical
period; that the Convention believed that "a wise and economical
development of our natural resources" and a judicious and vigourous immigration and colonization policy, coupled with stringent
economy and efficient management in every department of Government, would solve the transportation and other difficult problems now confronting the country.

The Resolution on Reciprocity was presented by Mr. Fielding
and duly carried. It expressed regret at the defeat of the 1911
Agreement with the United States as "a sacrifice of the best interests of Canada for distinctly partisan ends"; declared that Canada
regretted the pending repeal of the U.S. Reciprocity Act at Washington but had no cause for criticism as it had been kept for 8 years
on the statute books; that "we, as Liberals, again place on record
our appreciation of the object of the said Agreement and our faith
in the principles of friendly international relations underlying it,
and we express our earnest hope that there will be a renewed manifestation by the two Governments of a desire to make some similar
arrangement." Another motion presented by Hon. S. A. Fisher
urged (1) that in the interest of agricultural production and development it was expedient to encourage Co-operation and induce
greater investment in farming, and it was therefore deemed expedient to utilize the National credit to assist Co-operative agricultural
credit Associations to provide capital for agriculture at the lowest
possible rates; (2) that it was expedient to extend the principle
and system of Canadian Government elevators and to provide
interior and terminal cold storage warehouses equipped for the
assembling, assorting, preparing, storing and grading of food products supplied to the farmer at cost of operation; (3) that it was
expedient for the Government to arrange for the distribution of
fertilizers at the lowest possible cost.

A Committee on Banking was approved following Mr. Fisher's
declaration that the present system was designed to benefit commercial rather than agricultural interests. The Hon. W. E.
Knowles moved a Finance Resolution pointing out (1) that the
present burden of National Debt was $220 on each man, woman and
child in the Dominion with annual interest charges of $15 per head;
(2) that the estimated expenditure for the current fiscal year would
be $800,000,000 or $100 per head of the population with an expected deficit of $300,000,000 or $62.50 per head; (3) that national
disaster would follow if the present policy were not changed and
urging "exercise of the severest economy" and an equitable and
effective imposition and collection of graduated taxes on Business
Profits and on Income—applicable to all incomes above reasonable
exemptions—together with taxes on luxuries. Lieut.-Col. J. L.

Ralston, D.S.O., presented the Soldiers' policy of the Convention which included the following clauses:

1. Approving the adoption of a system of cash grants to the soldiers and dependents of those who had fallen in addition to the present gratuity, and to any pension for disability resulting from service.

2. Placing the whole matter of the education of the returned soldier in the hands of competent educational authorities to provide for the co-ordination, improvement and extension of a system both vocational and general.

3. Providing that any increased cost of Insurance in favour of the dependents of the soldier should be borne by the State where such increase arose from disability incurred during the War.

4. Declaring that such pensions and allowances be granted as shall enable soldiers or their dependents to maintain a liberal standard of living—with special references to the training of disabled or partially disabled soldiers and the degrees of capacity for work, uniformity in medical examinations, better employment agencies and application of this Resolution to sailors, aviators, nurses and Canadians serving with Imperial or Allied forces.

A Resolution was passed in favour of Dominion legislation to supplement and enforce all Provincial measures for bringing about complete prohibition of the Liquor traffic. The Premiers of Alberta and Saskatchewan presented a Resolution declaring that "the Provinces of Manitoba, Saskatchewan and Alberta should be granted "the ownership and control of the natural resources within their respective boundaries on terms that are fair and equitable with reference to all other Provinces of the Dominion." Another Resolution presented by W. T. R. Preston, and duly approved, declared that in the 1917 Elections there had been a conspiracy to carry out an elaborate system of frauds in connection with the military voters' part of the War-Time Elections Act, and demanding a Commission of Enquiry. Another motion presented by John Boyd, Montreal, and Donald Downey, Vancouver, recognized that the crown of Sir Wilfrid Laurier's life-work and the dearest wish of his heart was the establishment of racial concord and national unity throughout the Dominion and, therefore, emphatically condemned "all attempts to create racial discord and national disunion." Other Resolutions included the following:

1. Expressing "devotion to the person and office of His Gracious Majesty King George the Fifth and appreciation of his untiring efforts during the War in promoting harmony throughout his Dominions and also its unalterable attachment to the British Empire and to our own beloved Canada."

2. Expressing gratitude to the "valiant Canadian Army for its splendid share in the great victory."

3. Pledging a "vigourous prosecution of the measures best calculated to conserve the life and improve the physical standard of our Canadian citizenship."

On Aug. 7th balloting took place upon the question of Leadership with Mr. Mackenzie King leading on the first ballot which stood 344 for him, 297 for Mr. Fielding, 153 for Mr. McKenzie and 153 for Mr. Graham with a second ballot standing as follows: King 411, Fielding 344, Graham 124 and McKenzie 60. The 3rd ballot was destroyed, after being partially taken, because of Mr. Graham's withdrawal; the 4th ballot met the same fate through

Mr. McKenzie retiring and, on the 5th ballot, W. L. Mackenzie King was elected Leader by 476 votes to 438 for W. S. Fielding. After the great roar of cheers announcing the result had passed, Mr. Fielding, in a few earnest and felicitous words moved that the choice be made unanimous; it was supported by Messrs. Graham and McKenzie and then, after the singing of the National Anthem and O Canada! the new Leader spoke in terms of tactful reference and forceful thought. Incidents of the Convention were many and interesting and reference should be made to a preliminary gathering of the Quebec delegation on Aug. 5th when L. A. David, M.L.A., for Terrebonne, made what the press called a Nationalistic speech and urged the Quebec members to withdraw while Ernest Lapointe replied in characteristic form with almost unanimous acceptance*; the presentation of an elaborate statement from the Canadian Council of Agriculture explaining their platform and reasons for not being represented; the personal interest taken in Mackenzie King's descent from William Lyon Mackenzie, his grandfather of Upper Canada rebellion fame; the fact of such Liberal leaders as Mowat, Blair, Joly, Cartwright, Mills, Paterson, Tarte and Laurier having passed away since the 1893 Convention with N. W. Rowell and Clifford Sifton absent for Unionist reasons. It may be added that the Secretaries of the Convention were Duncan C. Ross, M.P., and Lucien Pacaud, M.P.

The new Liberal leader took charge of the Party with many things in his favour. He had an university education and a trained mind, an active political record, much experience along lines of Labour administration and problems; he had health, strength and comparative youth with marked literary and speaking ability. His handicaps, politically, were association in 1915-18 with the work of the Rockefeller Foundation in New York as Director of Investigation of Industrial Relations which was a matter easily capable of political misapprehension and his colourless public attitude in respect to the War—excepting a share in the Election of 1917 as a supporter of Sir W. Laurier and opponent of Conscription. As to the first, he did good work of a high character— one result being the publication of *Industry and Humanity,* an able treatise upon the Labour question—and as to the second he afterwards explained the personal and family responsibilities which prevented action. Meantime, he had, early in 1919, addressed a number of meetings, chiefly on Labour issues—Reform Club, Montreal, Jan. 11th; Empire Club, Toronto, Mch. 13th; Newmarket Electors, Mch. 15th; Quebec City public meeting, Mch. 28th; Montreal meeting, Mch. 30th; Toronto Liberals, Apr. 7th. In May and June he was in England studying Reconstruction and Labour questions there.

Following his election as Leader and the generous comments of the press upon his abilities and great opportunity he received various expressions of popular confidence. The Montreal City Council

*Note.—Ottawa *Journal,* Toronto *Globe* despatch, etc.

passed a unanimous Resolution on Sept. 8th declaring its "deep satisfaction" at his selection as Liberal leader, recognizing his "sterling qualities as a statesman" and congratulating him upon the mark of confidence given by the Liberal party.   He delivered an able speech upon the Rockefeller Foundation and Labour issues at the Ottawa Industrial Conference in September and accepted, a little later, the Liberal nomination in Prince County, P.E.I., after declining to run in Stormont-Glengarry against a Farmers' candidate.   He spoke at Summerside on Oct. 2nd and, as elsewhere, was very conciliatory to the Liberal-Unionists: "Are we to believe that these men and women of Liberal convictions numbering themselves by thousands, were not honest, were not conscientious, were not patriotic in the votes they cast, in the light of the knowledge they had at the time, and the circumstances as represented to them?"   But, he declared, the time had now come for them to return.   He was elected by acclamation on Oct. 20th and meanwhile, on Sept. 20th, he had accepted a nomination to run for North York in the next Federal elections.   In the House he made his maiden speech as Leader on Oct. 23rd during the Grand Trunk Pacific debate.

Dominion Parliament and Legislation; Bye-Elections of the Year.   The continued loosening of Party ties—originating in War conditions and Union Government—created various complications in the bye-elections of this year.   Oct. 27th was fixed as the date for 8 contests which, it was obvious, would afford some indication of the trend of public thought.   Two of them went by acclamation and, no doubt, by arrangement between the Party whips—in Kingston on Oct. 20th Sir H. L. Drayton, the new Minister of Finance and in Prince's, P.E.I., Hon. Mackenzie King, the new Liberal leader, were elected without opposition.   In the other six ridings there had been a net Liberal majority of 1,425 in 1917 with Quebec East, Liberal, by acclamation.   The result of the bye-elections was distinctly in favour of the new Farmers' party. J. W. Kennedy was elected in Stormont-Glengarry over Brig.-Gen. C. L. Hervey, D.S.O., (Ind.-Cons.); O. R. Gould in Assiniboia over W. R. Motherwell (Lib.); T. W. Caldwell in Carleton-Victoria over Lieut.-Col. W. W. Melville (Unionist), and in place of Hon. F. B. Carvell.   The only Liberal elected was Ernest Lapointe in Quebec East over F. X. Gallibois (Ind.) and the only Conservative Hon. S. F. Tolmie in Victoria over T. A. Barnard (Lab.).   The election in North Ontario was postponed owing to the sudden death of W. J. Cowan, the Unionist candidate, but R. H. Halbert, President of the U.F.O., defeated the new Unionist candidate, N. D. McKinnon, by a majority of 185.

The first Peace session of Parliament since 1914, the 2nd Session of the 13th Parliament of the Dominion, was opened by H.E. the Duke of Devonshire on Feb. 20th with a Speech from the Throne which referred to the close of the War and the policy of the Peace Conference, the re-adjustment of business and reconstruction generally; promised some important legislation and declared that "the deeply loyal' and earnest co-operation of the Overseas Dominions and Dependencies with the Mother Country must more firmly cement for all time those ties which bind the Empire in indissoluble union. The spirit born of common sacrifice, suffering and heroic endeavour will also, it is confidently hoped, permanently unite the Allies by the bonds of a great memory and tradition, and effectually promote the formation of a League of Nations which will ensure for all time the peace of the world." For the first time in 45 years the Commons met without Sir Wilfrid Laurier and the Chamber was draped in mourning with flowers at the vacant chair; Sir Thomas White acted as Government leader and paid generous tribute to the late Liberal statesman as did others in the. Commons and Sir James Lougheed in the Senate. The Address was moved by Major D. L. Redman of Calgary and Capt. R. J. Manion of Fort William and, after a long debate, was approved without division on Mch. 18th.

Legislation initiated by the Government and passed during the ensuing Session was varied and important. The creation of the Board of Commerce, charged with the administration of the Combines and Fair Prices Act which was concurrently passed for the investigation and restraint of combines, trusts, etc., and the checking of excessive profits; the Soldier Settlement Act of Hon. Mr. Meighen and General Mewburn's Bill for an increase in the Permanent Force; the Budget proposals of Sir Thomas White with appropriations totalling $851,000,000, his renewal of the Business Profits Tax and increases in the Income Tax; Mr. Guthrie's Anti-Sedition Bill, Mr. Calder's Technical Education grant of $10,000,-000 and his Immigration Act, have all been dealt with under specific headings. During the Session Mr. Ballantyne obtained an appropriation of $40,000,000 for his ship-building schemes and $90,000,-000 was voted to Public Works—including a Loan of $35,000,000 to the Canadian National Railways and $35,000,000 for Railway equipment with a part of the balance for works of usefulness and value undertaken, especially, to aid returned soldiers and prevent unemployment; $50,000 was voted for continuance of the Canadian War Mission at Washington under some form of permanent Peace representation; in accordance with an Order-in-Council of Dec. 3rd, 1918, the House approved a vote of $25,000,000 to further the Housing plans of the Government—the building of dwellings for workingmen through advances to the Provinces.

A most important measure was that rendered necessary by the national acquisition of the Canadian Northern Railway and subsidiary systems and their re-organization as part of the National Government Railways. A Bill was passed incorporating the Canadian National Railway Co. and providing for nomination by the Governor-in-Council of a Board of Directors with definition of their duties and functions. Provision was made for regulating capital, stock, the payment of Directors, etc., and the Governor-in-Council was empowered to operate further railway properties or works which might become the property of the Government. An amendment to the Railway Act appropriated $200,000 a year for ten years to aid in actual construction work for the protection, safety and convenience of the public, at highway crossings or railways at rail-level. Hon. Mr. Rowell carried a measure creating a Department of Public Health to be presided over by a Minister of the Crown with a Deputy-Minister and Staff. The duties and powers of the Minister were to include all matters and questions relating to the promotion and preservation of the health of the people of Canada, and particularly the following: Co-operation with Provincial and other Health authorities; conservation of child life and child welfare; inspection and medical care of immigrants and seamen; supervision of public health on railways, boats, ships and all methods of transportation; supervision of Federal public buildings and offices with regard to the health of Government employees; administration of the statutes bearing on Public Health; collection, publication and distribution of information as to good health and improved sanitation. A Dominion Council of Health was also provided for.

Hon. Mr. Guthrie had a Bill amending and consolidating the Naturalization Acts for the purpose of bringing Canadian legislation into conformity with that of the Imperial Parliament on this subject. The Highway Bill, carried by Hon. Dr. Reid, was designed to promote and assist the building and improving of highways throughout the different Provinces of the Dominion and provided for payment to the Provinces of $20,000,000 over a period of five years beginning Apr. 1, 1919, with the condition that any highway for which money was granted should be constructed or improved in accordance with an agreement between the Minister of Railways and the Province in question—the aid to be 40 per cent. of the actual and necessary cost. On Mch. 20th Sir Thomas White introduced and carried a Bill ratifying the Government action in appointing on Mch. 7th a Receiver for the Grand Trunk Pacific Railway and declaring the works of the G.T.P. Saskatchewan Railway to be "for the general advantage of Canada." The Hon. A. K. Maclean provided an Air Board Act for the creation of a Board of Aeronautics composed of 5 or 7 members; the Chairman to be a Minister of the Crown and the Departments of Militia and Naval Service to have representation. The Board was to supervise all matters relating to aeronautics and study its development in Canada and other countries; to construct and maintain all Government aerodromes and air-stations, and control all aircraft and equipment for His Majesty's service; to operate such services as might be approved, and prescribe all aerial routes. It was to have power to regulate and control aerial navigation over Canada and its territorial waters, to license pilots, register aircraft and air-stations and to control aeronautics generally.

Mr. Rowell, in another Bill, re-constituted the Board of Pensions with three Commissioners and a Chairman who were to hold office for 10 years at $5,000 salary each and the Chairman $7,000; Pensions were also varied and increased. An increase in the force of the R.N.W.M.P. was authorized, the pay increased and its duties extended as the Royal Canadian Mounted Police. Mr. Guthrie's Bankruptcy Bill was an important step in advance. One of its objects was to give uniformity throughout the Dominion to all matters pertaining to bankruptcy and to abrogate or place in abeyance existing Provincial laws on bankruptcy and insolvency; in the drafting of it an effort was made to provide a uniform law for the various Provinces with all preferences and priorities between creditors abolished and an expeditious means of administering insolvent estates provided. It applied to all corporations, with the exception of banks, railways, trust and insurance companies, and to all persons, except farmers and wage-earners earning less than $1,500 a year.

A measure of Dr. Reid's provided, as to Electric and Power Companies, that no Company should acquire, construct or maintain any plant, line, or other equipment within the limits of a municipality without the consent of the municipality—subject to appeal to the Railway Commission—but it was defeated in the Senate. Other measures introduced but not carried included the Civil Service Amendment Act of A. K. Maclean; the re-creation and amendment of the War Purchasing Commission and Mr. Meighen's Act to disqualify Military defaulters from voting for 15 years and from holding Government office or employment; W. F. Nickle's Bill creating a Canadian Divorce Court and the Prohibition measure ratifying certain Orders-in-Council passed by the Government, under authority of the War Measures Act, for the purpose of restricting, during the War and for 12 months thereafter, the manufacture, transportation and importation of intoxicating liquors. This latter Bill passed the Commons but was destructively amended by the Senate which refused to withdraw its amendments though the Government would not accept them. The Consolidated Railway Act which the Commons amended so as to subject Companies like the Toronto and Niagara Power to the municipal control over streets was also rejected in the Senate and this clause eliminated in the Commons in order to get other clauses through.

Resolutions were passed including that on Titles, elsewhere dealt with, and that on Daylight Saving in which a proposal to re-enact the Bill was defeated by 105 to 50. A Bill respecting Copyright, introduced in the Senate by Sir James Lougheed, was held over. During the Session D. D. McKenzie acted as Opposition Leader and the Houses were prorogued on July 7th with a Speech from the Governor-General in which reference was made to the great volume of legislation passed, to the rapid completion of the task of demobilization and to Government efforts at vocational training and reconstruction. It was declared that: "From the War Canada emerges with the proud consciousness that in fulfilling her duty to civilization and humanity she has taken a high place among the world's nations.'' Following the close of the Session W. F. Nickle, M.P. for Kingston, resigned his seat. The chief debates or discussions of the Session were as follows:

Subject	Introduced by	Date
Death of Rt. Hon. Sir Wilfrid Laurier	Sir Thomas White	Feb. 25
Speech from the Throne	Daniel Lee Redman	Feb. 25, 26, 27, 28, Mch. 3, 4, 6, 7, 10, 11, 12, 13, 14, 17 18
Grand Trunk Pacific Railway Co.	Sir Thomas White	Mch. 20, Apr. 3
Good Roads	Hon. J. D. Reid	Mch. 21, June 23, July 2
Alien Enemies—Treatment of Soldiers	H. S. Clements	Mch. 24
Garden Villages for Soldiers	H. M. Mowat	Mch. 24
Canada's Claim to War Indemnity	P. R. DuTremblay	Mch. 24
Tariff Reduction and U.S. Reciprocity	Sir Thomas White	Mch. 25
Daylight Saving	Sir Thomas White	Mch. 27
Civil Service Positions	F. B. McCurdy	Mch. 31
Ministers of the Crown	Wm. D. Euler	Mch. 31
Advances for the purchase of Seed Grain	Hon. Arthur Meighen	Apr. 1
Georgian Bay Canal	C. R. Harrison	Apr. 2
Bank Mergers in Canada	Hon. R. Lemieux	Apr. 2
Department of Public Health	Hon. N. W. Rowell	Apr. 4, 10
The Guelph Novitiate	Lieut.-Gen. Sir Sam Hughes	Apr. 7
Military Service Act	Sir Sam Hughes	Apr. 9
War Expenditure	Sir Thomas White	Apr. 10, May 7, 8,
Canadian National Railway Co.	Hon. J. D. Reid	Apr. 11, 23, 24, 25, 28, May 6
Conferring of Titles on Canadians	W. F. Nickle	Apr. 14, May 22
Fibre Flax Production	Samuel Francis Glass	Apr. 16
Efficiency in Civil Service	Michael Steele	Apr. 16
Immigration Act Amendment	Hon. J. A. Calder	Apr. 29, 30, May 1, 9,
Bankruptcy Act	Hon. Hugh Guthrie	May 1, 2, 9, 15
Control of Aeronautics	Hon. A. K. Maclean	May 5
Dominion Forest Reserves and Parks	Hon. Arthur Meighen	May 12
Proprietary or Patent Medicine Act	Hon. A. K. Maclean	May 15
Dominion Water-Powers Act	Hon. Arthur Meighen	May 16
Railway Act Consolidation	D. D. McKenzie	May 20,28, June 4, 27
Prohibition	Sir Thomas White	May 13
		May 21
Canada Shipping Act Amendment	Hon. C. C. Ballantyne	May 26, June 5, 24
Administration of the Overseas Forces	Sir Thomas White	May 27
Civil Service Act	Hon. A. K. Maclean	May 28
Industrial Unrest in Canada	M. R. Blake	June 2
The Budget	Hon. Sir Thomas White	June 5, 9, 10, 11, 12, 18, 16, 17, 18, 19
Technical Education	Hon. J. A. Calder	June 5, 20
Purchasing of Departmental Supplies	Hon. N. W. Rowell	June 6, 21, July 2,
Sedition and Seditious Propaganda	Hon. Hugh Guthrie	June 10
Act Respecting Divorce	William F. Nickle	June 20
Soldiers' Settlement on the Land	Hon. Arthur Meighen	June 23
Canada Grain Act Amendment	Hon. A. K. Mclean	June 24, 26
Militia Act Amendment	Maj.-Gen. S. C. Mewburn	June 24
Income War-Tax Act	Sir Thomas White	June 24
Customs Tariff Act Amendment	Sir Thomas White	June 25
Pension Act Amendment	Hon. N. W. Rowell	June 25, 27, 28, 30
Naturalization Act	Sir Robert Borden	June 18, 21, 26, 30
Judges Act Amendment—Salaries	Hon. Arthur Meighen	June 28, July 1
Port of St. John	Hon. C. C. Ballantyne	June 30
High Cost of Living	G. B. Nicholson	July 1
Post Office Appointments	Hon. N. W. Rowell	July 1
Criminal Code Amendment	Hon. Arthur Meighen	July 1
Board of Commerce Act, 1919	Hon. Arthur Meighen	July 3, 4,
Newsprint Control—Powers of Commissioner	Sir Thomas White	July 4
Electric and Power Companies	Hon. J. D. Reid	July 4
Combines, Monopolies, Trusts and Mergers	Hon. Arthur Meighen	July 4
Dominion Elections Act Amendment	Rt. Hon. Sir Robert Borden	July 5

A special Session of Parliament was opened on Sept. 1st by H.E. the Duke of Devonshire with a Speech from the Throne in which he referred to the visit of H.R.H. the Prince of Wales and indicated the purpose of the Session as being ratification of the Treaty of Versailles. The Address was moved by Rev. Dr. H. P. Whidden of Brandon and J. C. McIntosh of Nanaimo, B.C., and approved without division on Sept. 17th. The Peace Treaty was discussed at length and passed after an important debate which is dealt with in the first part of this volume; on Sept. 12th Hon. N. W. Rowell made an elaborate speech upon the Gratuity question with all kinds of documents quoted and facts adduced as to Pensions and gratuities and allowances and Land Settlement in Canada and other countries. The chief legislation of the Session was that dealing with the acquisition of the Grand Trunk Railway System. The Resolutions authorizing an agreement to this end, between the Government and the G.T.R., were presented by Hon. J. D. Reid, Minister of Railways, on Oct. 15th.

In his speech Dr. Reid explained the $70,000,000 advances to the Grand Trunk and the G.T.P. in 1909-18, the necessity for taking over the latter road in 1918 and the advantages of purchasing the former at this time and thus establishing a great National railway system in Canada. Sir Thomas White and Mr. Meighen spoke on the 16th, with others pro and con, and the Resolutions were passed (Oct. 17th) on division. The Bill confirming the acquisition was then read a first time. On the 2nd reading (21st Oct.) D. D. McKenzie presented an Opposition amendment declaring that "the Bill proposes an uncertain but very large addition to the Debt of the Dominion"; that a measure of such wide-reaching character and large importance required "a study by the House and the people that cannot possibly be given in the closing days of the Session"; that the present Session of Parliament was called for a special purpose which had already been accomplished; that under such circumstances the introduction by the Government of a measure of such great importance as the acquisition of the railway and property of the Grand Trunk Company of Canada was "improvident and inexpedient."

This was negatived by 91 to 61 and Hon. W. S. Fielding on Oct. 31st proposed, on the 3rd reading, that a Commission be appointed to enquire into the affairs of the Grand Trunk Railway prior to its acquisition but it was defeated by 91 to 50; Mr. Mackenzie King then moved an amendment referring the Agreement, when made, back to Parliament for ratification but this was negatived by 90 to 55; J. A. Campbell proposed that the value of the 4 per cent. guaranteed stock of the Railway (£12,500,000) be referred to arbitration and this amendment was defeated by 83 to 57 while another by J. J. Denis declaring that no award by arbitrators should be final until approved by Parliament was negatived by 85 to 53; a motion by G. W. Parent declaring that the ownership by the Canadian Government of the American section of the Grand Trunk Railway would involve this country in international troubles "respecting labour administration and public policy" and asking an assurance that the Government would not take over such lines, was defeated by 87 to 43; a final six months' hoist moved by J. A. Robb was also beaten by 84 to 53. The Bill then passed both Houses.

The measure itself authorized the acquisition of all the capital stock of the G.T.R. system—£49,573,492—excepting a guaranteed 4 per cent. stock amounting to £12,500,000; upon this latter the Government was to guarantee dividends at 4 per cent. as well as the interest upon present Debenture stocks outstanding of £31,926,125; the value of the Preference and Common stocks of the G.T.R., outstanding at a face value of £37,073,000 were to be determined by a Board of three Arbitrators and new guaranteed stock then issued by the Government to the value so designated; a Committee of Management was to be formed consisting of five persons, two to be appointed by the Grand Trunk, two by the Government, and the fifth by the four so appointed, to insure the operation of the Grand Trunk System (in so far as it was possible so to do) in harmony with the Canadian National Railway—the two systems being treated in the public interest, as nearly as possible, as one system. Various other clauses of the proposed Agreement were specified and the Government and Grand Trunk Company authorized to enter into and sign such an agreement. The following were the chief debates of this Session:

Subject	Introduced by	Date
Speech from the Throne	Dr. H. P. Whidden	Sept. 2, 5, 15, 17
The Peace Treaty	Rt. Hon. Sir R. L. Borden	Sept. 2,4,8,9, 10, 11, 12, 23
Great War Veterans' Gratuity	Hon. N. W. Rowell	Sept. 12
Gratuity Question	J. A. Currie	Sept. 16
Board of Commerce	Hon. C. J. Doherty	Sept. 19, 30
Houses for Soldiers	H. M. Mowat	Sept. 22
Criminal Code Amendment—Electrocution	H. M. Mowat	Sept. 22 Oct. 7
Navigable Waters Protection	Hon. A. L. Sifton	Sept. 23
Manipulation of Soldiers Votes, Alleged	D. D. McKenzie	Sept. 24, 25, Oct. 1, 2
Battle Casualities, Canadian	Lieut.-Gen. Sir Sam Hughes	Sept. 29
Treatment of Returned Soldiers	A. E. Fripp	Sept. 29
Canada Wheat Board	Sir George Foster	Sept. 30 Oct. 9
Adulteration Act Amendment—Bran and Shorts	Donald Sutherland	Oct. 1
Civil Service Act, 1918—Amendment	Hon. A. K. Maclean	Oct. 2, 10
R.N.W.M.P. Act Amendment	Hon. N. W. Rowell	Oct. 3
Intercolonial Railway	D. D. McKenzie	Oct. 6
Oleomargarine; Manufacture and Importation of	Hon. Hugh Guthrie	Oct. 7, 9,
Grand Trunk Railway, Acquisition of	Hon. Arthur Meighen	Oct. 10, 15, 16, 17, 20, 21, 22 23, 24, 27, 28, 29, 30, 31, Nov. 3, 4, 8
Meat and Canned Foods Act Amendment	Hon. A. K. Maclean	Oct. 20
Soldiers' Civil Re-Establishment	Hon. James A. Calder	Nov. 5, 6, 7,
Canada Temperance Act Amendment	Hon. C. J. Doherty	Nov. 8

Incidents of the Session included the passage of Hon. A. K. Maclean's Bill providing for a re-classification of the Civil Service; a heated scene in the House when D. D. McKenzie read a telegram purporting to be signed by Hon. Arthur Meighen and sent to Sir Robert Borden on Nov. 30th, 1917, asking him to allot 1,000 soldier votes (cast in the trenches during the current elections) for division amongst specified Manitoba ridings and which Mr. Meighen described, when the original was submitted to him in the House, to be a forgery; the official statement in the House on Nov. 3rd that the Committee in charge of the construction of the new Parliament Buildings included Hon. A. L. Sifton (Chairman) with Messrs. Reid, Ballantyne, Calder, Lougheed and Robertson of the Government, and Senator Watson, as members and J. A. Pearson and J. O. Marchand as Architects; the Government's legislation amending and extending the Canada Temperance Act so as to make it applicable to Provinces instead of Counties and enabling a Province, if the majority of its Dominion electorate should so decide in a Referendum, to prohibit the importation as well as manufacture of intoxicating liquors; the fact that Mr. McKenzie, Opposition Leader, for his two Sessions in this year drew two salaries and indemnities making a total of $19,000 or $4,000 more than the Prime Minister; the valuable Report of a Senate Committee presided over by Hon. J. S. McLennan which dealt with and presented proposals for the betterment of the machinery of Government—the enhancement of Ministerial responsibility to Parliament and the making easier of Parliamentary control over Ministerial action. The House was prorogued on Nov. 10th by H.E. the Governor-General with further reference to the Prince of Wales' visit and an expression of satisfaction at the acquisition of the G.T.R.

Political Affairs and Incidents: The G.W.V.A. and I.O.D.E.   In addition to the Prohibition legislation mentioned above the Government passed an Order-in-Council on Feb. 11th, at the suggestion of the Minister of Militia, imposing stiff penalties upon the sale of liquor to officers or men in uniform and providing that any person, other than a medical officer, physician or surgeon, whether licensed to sell liquor or not, who should sell liquor to soldiers in uniform, was to be tried by military court martial and sentenced, if guilty, to 12 months' imprisonment or a fine of $300, or both.   On Oct. 14th an official statement was given in the Senate showing that between Apr. 1st and that date there were 424 illicit stills in Canada compared with 27 in the years 1916-18 while 316 such stills were seized as against 22 in the preceding period.   Dec. 31st, 1919, was the last day upon which the War-Time Prohibition Act was operative in Canada while the United States distilleries were only given to Jan. 17th, 1920, to dispose of their entire stocks.   Hence it was that the close of the year saw many worried Prohibitionists in Canada and many who were not of that school of thought, ready, for a time, to rejoice.

The question of National health was much discussed during the year and reference has been made to the organization of a Department of Health in the Dominion Government.   Early in July the Hon. N. W. Rowell assumed charge as Minister and Lieut.-Col. John A. Amyot, C.M.G., M.B., of Toronto, was appointed Deputy-Minister.   In this connection social hygiene had been dealt with at a Conference called by the Acting-Premier—Sir Thomas White —at Ottawa on Feb. 3rd, with many Provincial representatives and leading medical officers present and Hon. J. A. Calder and Hon. W. D. McPherson presiding alternately; a basis was laid for some of the later work of the Health Council, and Resolutions were passed in favour of compulsory, standardized, treatment of venereal diseases with prevention of quack treatment and infection and rigid rules as to notification—also as to the desirability of making remedies, such as Salvarsan, cheaper through Government rights of production.   The 8th annual meeting of the Canadian Public Health Association was held in Toronto on May 27th, when a Resolution was passed in favour of the Government manufacture of Salvarsan and Dr. H. E. Young, Victoria, was elected President; in Ottawa on May 30th a National Council for Combating Venereal Diseases was organized with Hon. W. R. Riddell, Toronto, as Chairman, and a representative Executive appointed with Capt. Gordon Bates, Toronto, as General Secretary.

Meanwhile Mr. Rowell had combined his Health programme with enforcement of Prohibition by undertaking in October to reduce by legislation the use of drugs such as cocaine and opium which were being used in considerable quantities and to meet the charge that Prohibition had increased this use of drugs to an alarming degree.   On Oct. 8th there met at Ottawa the Dominion Council of Health which had been formed under Government auspices and which included the Deputy-Minister and the Chief Health Officer of each Province.   Amongst those present were Dr. J. A. Amyot, as Chairman; Dr. J. S. W. McCullough, Ontario; Dr. Elzéar Pelletier, Quebec; Dr. W. H. Hattie, Nova Scotia; Hon. W. F. Roberts, New Brunswick; Dr. H. E. Young, British Columbia; Dr. Gordon Bell, Manitoba; Dr. W. C. Laidlaw, Alberta; Dr. M. M. Seymour, Saskatchewan; Prof. J. C. Fitzgerald, Toronto; Tom Moore, President Trades and Labour Congress; Miss Helen Y. Reid, Canadian Patriotic Fund, Montreal; Mrs. H. E. Todd, President Canadian Women's Institutes.   The chief subject of discussion was venereal disease and $10,000 was appropriated for the Council to commence a nation-wide campaign of information and propaganda; $10,000 was also voted the National Council for combatting this Disease.   Of the main sum, $180,000 was proportionately, assigned to the Provinces, and their representatives assured the Department of general co-operation along the same lines.

The Great War Veterans and Other Military Bodies.   This organization held an important place in public discussion during the year and, according to C. G. MacNeil, Dominion Secretary-Treasurer, it had on July 31st, 1918, 125 branches and 16,000 members and on July 31st, 1919, 525 branches with 250,000 members.*   Early in the year Mr. MacNeil had left Regina to take up his new appointment as National Secretary and received, on Jan. 13th, high tributes to his organization work in Saskatchewan from Mr. Premier Martin, W. D. Cowan, M.P., Harris Turner, M.L.A., and others, at a farewell dinner.   On Feb. 10th the Association presented to the Dominion Government a number of Resolutions forwarded by branches in the West, which urged the deportation of undesirable aliens, an examination into the

*Note.—Letter to Author Sept. 22nd, 1919.

loyalty of those suspected of enemy sympathies and the curtailment of certain civil rights for those who were permitted to remain in the country. On Mch. 11th Mr. MacNeil appeared before a Parliamentary Committee on Soldiers' Pensions and stated on behalf of the G.W.V.A. that the Pension scale should be based upon the cost of living in various parts of the country and, therefore, could not be uniform throughout Canada; a totally disabled man with a family of five, should receive $1,400 or $1,500; as to orphan children, they should be given equal educational advantages with those children whose parents were alive and they should receive a pension up to 21 years of age.

The great question of the year for the Association was that of a War bonus to returned soldiers. What was called the Calgary Resolution had been unanimously passed at a large general meeting of members of the G.W. V.A. in that city on Feb. 23rd; it suggested a cash grant of $1,000 payable to each member of the C.E.F. who had served in Canada, $1,500 to all who served Overseas and $500 additional to those serving in an actual theatre of war—besides any regular gratuity or pension for service disability. It was approved by many branches and was the basis of a prolonged agitation; there was, also, much internal opposition as voiced by *The Veteran*, the chief organ of the Association, in its declaration of May, 1919, that a total of 1,000 millions, which it would cost, was prohibitive to the country, that the Government aid to Land Settlement should be further encouraged and met favourably by the veterans, and that this, with an effective educational and vocational policy, and some scheme of industrial loans, should be sufficient. On May 16th a Deputation of the G.W.V.A. interviewed Sir Thomas White and General Mewburn and discussed demobilization problems, Pensions, and the proposal of a further post-discharge bonus, running from $1,000 to $2,000. As to the latter subject, Sir Thomas pointed out that such a Government obligation of $850,000,000 was at this time out of the question. At an Executive meeting of the Association held at Ottawa on June 9th a tentative statement of general principles was approved and issued to the branches for consideration at the ensuing Vancouver Convention of June 30th.

The 3rd annual Convention was held at Vancouver on June 30th to July 5th with 270 delegates present from every Province of the Dominion. W. P. Purney, President, in a thoughtful address described the chief aims of the Association as consideration for the widow and orphan and the care of disabled veterans; the satisfactory rehabilitation, as speedily as possible, of all comrades who were able to take their places in the industrial and other life of the country. The following was the first Resolution and was carried unanimously: "That this Association is fully in sympathy with that portion of organized labour which is striving to better the conditions of the working men through lawful and constitutional means and which is in no sympathy, whatever, with factions controlled by extremists who strive by all means to overthrow British institutions and incessantly breed discord and advocate riot or revolutions; and that we are unalterably opposed to all capitalistic combines which seek, by economic or financial pressure, to control, to an unwarranted degree, the governing bodies of this fair Dominion to the detriment of the majority of the people of Canada."

Other approved motions declared in favour of "a steeply graduated income tax" and of taxing all war bonds, beyond the total face value of $10,000, held by individuals, firms and corporations; supported the suggestion that all cold-storage plants, owned by private corporations, should be taken over by Provincial or Municipal bodies at the earliest possible moment; urged the immediate deportation of alien enemies and asked that no child labour be permitted under 16 years of age; petitioned the Government to appoint a permanent Commission, composed of representative producers, manufacturers, wage earners, and such experts as might be deemed necessary, to investigate and fix the cost of production, of manufacture, of transportation and of the sale of all essential commodities of life—the Commission to prepare a schedule of all such costs, profits and wages for the sanction of Parliament which should then be embodied in a statute with heavy penalties for its violation. Other Resolutions were as follows:

1. Asking for Women franchise on same basis as for men and endorsing the principle of Proportional Representation for the House of Commons.

2. Suggesting that all Civil servants, entitled to superannuation, be replaced by returned men.

3. Asking for a longer period of training in the Vocational department with properly qualified craftsmen in charge.

4. Urging immediate steps to establish a Canadian Air Force under national ownership, control and operation, with the workers sharing in the management.

5. Demanding the immediate adoption by Government of a system of bonus payments as the most satisfactory and effective means of re-establishing the soldiers; declaring that such bonus should be on an equitable basis limited only by the country's ability to pay, with classification, distribution and administration to be agreed upon and decided by a Joint Parliamentary and G.W.V.A. Commission; stating that such bonus should be in addition to any gratuity or pension resulting from disability received on active service.

6. Favouring the equalization of pensions by raising the rank and file to the basis of the commissioned officer.

7. Declaring that Pensions should be increased to meet the increasing cost of living and apply proportionately to the allowance for dependents; that Pensions for orphan children were inadequate and should be increased and extended to the age of 18; that permanent Medical Boards should be established in each Military District and a pension be given to widows and children even if the marriage were contracted up to seven years after date of discharge; that a pension should be given widow and children in the event of death from any cause within six months of discharge.

8. Urging that Canadians in the Imperial forces be given same pensions and allowances as those in the C.E.F.

9. Recommending the enactment of a Minimum wage and Insurance against old age, illness and unemployment; suitable housing for all, and that all loans for building purposes be made direct by the Federal Government to the ex-soldier applicants; stringent restrictions upon Immigration and naturalization.

10. Urging better Educational conditions, such education to include instructions in governmental problems and citizenship and an extended scope for better agricultural and artisanship education.

11. Asking that the Soldiers' Land Settlement Act be amended and enlarged to permit of loans being made on city, town or village properties to returned soldiers for the purpose of building or buying houses, or for the purpose of paying off present liabilities and making improvements to present homes—the rate of interest, terms of re-payment, etc., to be the same as pertaining to farm lands.

12. Suggesting that all arable lands not utilized by the Indians be acquired, on fair terms, by purchase or otherwise, and that, until such terms were arranged, there be no further alienation of Indian lands and that all leased lands be re-inspected and re-classified immediately.

13. Declaring that all lands, patented, or unpatented, held by undesirable aliens, Doukhobors, Hutterites and Mennonites, should be declared settlement areas; service in the C.E.F. held equivalent to residence duties.

14. Asking for the compulsory registration of all enemy aliens in Canada, and this registration to involve a rigid medical examination with mental tests, and urging the Government not to encourage immigration during the coming year or to grant subsidies for the purpose.

15. Expressing disappointment with the administration of the Department of Soldiers' Civil Re-Establishment and asking for the appointment of a Minister responsible to the Commons.

16. Requesting the Minister of the Interior to put into force a plan by which all unpatented swamp, marsh and muskeg lands, within 20 miles of a railroad, be made quickly and easily available for acquirement by returned soldiers.

17. Asking the Government to provide Life insurance at cost for disabled men on the basis of their medical examination on attestation.

18. Endorsing the general principles of the British Whitley Council plan.

The chief debate of the session was on the Calgary Resolution, backed as it was by all Alberta and by many other branches; the final compromise (Resolution No. 5) was received with gratification. W. P. Turney was re-elected President and R. B. Maxwell and S. Stalford, Vice-Presidents. The Executive included C. E. Doherty, for British Columbia; T. Dace, Alberta; G. W. Andrews, D.S.O., M.P., Manitoba; H. H. Bamford, Saskatchewan; R. D. Ponton, Ontario; A. Mackenzie Forbes, Quebec; W. D. Tait, Nova Scotia; L. Duffy, New Brunswick; D. E. Palmer, P.E. Island. A request to send representatives to the Liberal Convention at Ottawa was declined. Incidents of the year in the G.W.V.A. included the success of its monthly publications—the *B.C. Veterans' Weekly*, the *Western Veteran* of Alberta, the *Manitoba Veteran* of Winnipeg, *Harris Turner's Weekly* of Saskatoon and *The Veteran* of Ottawa; the first annual meeting of a United Kingdom Branch in London on May 3rd with A. A. Gemmell, late of Calgary, elected as President in succession to C. F. Gifford; the affiliation of the Canadian Association with the British Great War Veterans of America on Sept. 2nd—the latter becoming a sort of American Command of the G.W.V.A.; the letters of Sir Robert Borden to C. G. MacNeil (Aug. 27th and Sept. 5th) declaring that the Gratuity of December, 1918, had been considered generous by the G.W.V.A., that the financial condition of the country "precluded any larger or further gratuity," and that the Government saw no necessity for a Committee or Commission to enquire into the subject; the speech of Mr. Rowell in the House on Sept. 12th which satisfied the Veterans that, whatever might be done in the future, the Government in the past had dealt generously by them; this Mr. MacNeil admitted while the appointment of a Committee removed the chief grievance of the moment. To this Special Committee of Parliament on Oct. 6th the G.W.V.A. submitted the following basic table for proposed re-establishment:

Year of Enlistment	For service in Canada	Year of Arrival	For service in England	Year of Arrival	For service in France
A 1914.....	$500	F 1914.....	$1,000	L 1914.....	$1,000
B 1915.....	400	G 1915.....	800	M 1915.....	800
C 1916.....	300	H 1916.....	600	N 1916.....	600
D 1917.....	200	J 1917.....	400	O 1917.....	400
E 1918.....	100	K 1918.....	200	P 1918.....	200

Following the Report of the Committee, leaders of the G.W.V.A. expressed keen dissatisfaction and W. D. Tait, R. B. Maxwell and D. Loughnan resigned as an Advisory Committee of the Government's Repatriation organization. Meanwhile, many who opposed the Bonus idea had expressed themselves strongly and Major D. L. Redman, M.P. of Calgary declared on Nov. 10th that: "I have always fought the Bonus because I regard it as an effort that would result in taking money out of the mouths of widows and orphans in order to parcel it out among men who have absolutely no disability and can best advance their own interests and the interests of their country by getting to work." On Dec. 6th President W. P. Purney issued an appeal to all returned soldiers to join the G.W.V.A.

An outcome of this agitation was a movement led by J. Harry Flynn of Toronto, formerly Sergeant in the C.E.F.; the men behind it were a small minority of the returned soldiers and of the G.W.V.A., but they created a good deal of turmoil for a time. Following the Government's decision not to grant the gratuity a mass meeting of 5,000 men was held in Toronto on Sept. 7th, *The Globe* was attacked for opposing the gratuity and a Returned Soldiers' Gratuity League or, as it was later on termed, the United Veterans'

League, was formed; another gathering on Sept. 11th, presided over by Mayor T. L. Church, passed a Resolution along the Calgary lines and was addressed by Stewart Lyon of *The Globe* in opposition and explanation; similar meetings were held at Halifax and Ottawa and another at Toronto, on the 15th, when Secretary W. E. Turley of the Provincial G.W.V.A. was refused a hearing.   Mr. Flynn was made President of the new organization on Oct. 3rd and his attacks upon the G.W.V.A. and the Government were frequent and vigourous; some of the leaders of the former responded and David Loughnan, Editor of *The Veteran*, described J. H. Flynn as an American and "a demagogue." A journal called *The Veteran Democrat* was started on Oct. 1st to advocate the $2,000 gratuity and had a brief but energetic life.   At this time T. O. Cox, for the Government Department concerned, replied to Mr. Flynn's statement that only $600,000,000 would be required with definite statistics showing that 368,052 men served in France and that at $2,000 each the total would be $736,104,000; that 50,000 served in England and at $1,500 this would be $75,000,000; that 172,520 served in Canada or $172,520,000—a total of $983,624,000.   Mr. Flynn was heard by the Parliamentary Committee on Oct. 1st and threatened political action if the policy were not accepted.

Another organization of returned men was the Grand Army of Canada, founded in 1918, with the general object of aiding soldiers and their dependents and supported by a publication called the *G.A.C. Journal;* it had one curious declaration in its list of principles—"that a serving class is a disgrace to our civilization''; the President in 1919 was S. J. Brown, Toronto, and the Secretary, W. J. Carmichael.   As a body it strongly supported the Calgary proposals and backed up Mr. Flynn's efforts while its Platform, issued in September, advocated all forms of public ownership, increased gratuities, pensions and preferences for soldiers, an 8-hour day and repeal of the Ontario Temperance Act, establishment of the Initiative, Referendum and Recall, with Proportional Representation.   A Convention, on Dec. 10-11th, passed Resolutions in favour of equalizing gratuities to Imperial reservists, nurses, etc.; declaring that no person or group in Canada should be permitted to enjoy civil and political rights or privileges who were not prepared to fulfil, in letter and spirit, the obligations and duties of native-born British subjects; favouring a continuance of the grant of Honours by the King and reconsideration of the recent Parliamentary Resolution.

The Army and Navy Veterans of Canada with W. J. Tupper of Winnipeg as President, increased their membership and influence in 1919.   Toronto organized a branch with Lieut.-Col. A. J. McCausland as President; the Winnipeg Unit on May 13th denounced Bolshevism and the Winnipeg Trades and Labour Council; the 2nd annual Convention for the Dominion was held at Montreal on July 23-25th with President Tupper in the chair.   Resolutions were passed (1) expressing loyalty to the King and his Throne; (2) asking the Government to take up in a practical way the high cost of living and curse of profiteering; (3) condemning in the strongest terms the doctrines of Bolshevism and anarchy, with emphatic opposition to the One Big Union as calculated and intended to cause strife and disturbances; (4) asking that any soldier or sailor who had homesteaded should have his time of service count on the homestead duties whether he made entry before enlistment or afterwards; (5) supporting a special cash bonus of $2,500 to disabled soldiers and men who had served in France; (6) demanding a Referendum in each Province as to light beer and wine licenses.

The Imperial Order Daughters of the Empire.

The I.O.D.E. as it was known all over Canada, exercised considerable public influence in 1919, had a prosperous year and did much good work along the lines indicated in its aims and objects of stimulating loyalty to the Throne, fostering union amongst the daughters and children of the Empire, diffusing education as to Empire history and conditions amongst the people, and taking action of a varied patriotic nature as required by circumstances.   The 19th annual meeting was held at Montreal on May 26-31 with Mrs. A. E. Gooderham in the chair.   The President's address referred to her 18 years' association with the Order, her 8 years in the Presidency, and her desire now to retire from active leadership; paid high tribute to the late E.F.B. Johnston, K.C., for his services to the Order and to the memory of Mrs. P. D. Crerar; described the past year as perhaps the hardest in the history of the Order for those concerned in the management. The French Relief Scheme had been carried through successfully: ''A small portion of France was set aside, and will be known as 'The Daughters of the Empire Sector,' and we experienced the joy of doing something by our own initiative for our splendid ally. All that now remains to be done is to arrange for a permanent record of the names of the Chapters who gave assistance, through our own French Relief scheme, to suffering France.'' During the War the I.O.D.E. had raised over $5,000,-000 for patriotic purposes.

Mrs. Gooderham urged a welcome and kindly treatment to the English brides whom Canadian soldiers were bringing home and pleaded for the loyalty of members to the Order, its leaders, and its work: ''We need a spirit of loyalty that will not be modified or warped by personal animosities or prejudices. In a large organization like ours it is not possible that our opinions regarding policy and methods will always be harmonious. But we can always be fair and just in our judgments, if we endeavour to understand those with whom we disagree. In an organization like the Daughters of the Empire, prejudices and personal dislike should not be permitted to control our course of action. I hope that none of us will ever give our new President and her associates cause to feel that, no matter what they may suggest, the plan will meet with opposition, not helpful criticism. I hope that my successor will never be given reason to feel that her mistakes—and mistakes may be made in all sincerity—will be welcomed and magnified.'' Mrs. Clark Murray, founder of the Order, spoke briefly, a Resolution of deep regret at the death of Mrs. P. D. Crerar of Hamilton was passed and loyal messages despatched to Their Majesties the King and Queen; an address was delivered by Lady Baden-Powell on the Girl Guide movement.

Mrs. Gooderham submitted a careful and detailed statement in reply to certain accusations made in a printed statement issued by Lady Kingsmill of Ottawa; the latter's statement was also read. This difference of feeling and opinion between Lady Kingsmill and Lady Pope of Ottawa on the one side and the President on the other, coloured the proceedings of the 1919 as it had those of the 1918 annual meeting and was greatly magnified in the press. The questions at issue included the charge that two Resolutions were omitted from the official Minutes; that Lady Kingsmill had personal difficulty in obtaining access to these Minutes and was eventually given a *verbatim* copy at a cost of $50; that a certain Report had not been included and that she had difficulty in seeing certain letters at the Head Office; that there was an effort by the President and Executive to change the form of distribution in the French Relief scheme. Mrs. Gooderham declared that there was only one Resolution omitted and that it had been previously rescinded; that the Report in question had been taken away from the President's table with no copy available. except a private one which she had to hold in view of the charges being made; that the Minutes were in constant use and could not be carried away by anyone and that a copy was therefore the only way of meeting Lady Kingsmill's request; that there had been no change in policy in the French matter and that she had always acted for the I.O.D.E. and for it alone.

The Report of the National Treasurer, Mrs. John Bruce, for the year of Apr. 30th, 1919, showed a total of $1,138,205 raised by the Chapters during the year. The chief subject of discussion was the proposed National War Memorial of the I.O.D.E. As presented by the Executive the proposals dealt with the raising of a Fund of $500,000 as a Memorial to Canadian soldiers who had died in the War to be expended as follows: (1) To endow a chair or lectureship in one of the Canadian Universities for the teaching of the History of the Empire and to provide a centre of research into its political and economic problems; (2) to place in the schools reproductions of the Canadian War Memorial Pictures painted for the Dominion Government; (3) to promote courses of illustrated lectures on the history and geography of the Empire; (4) to place in all schools attended by children of foreign-born parents a Daughters' of the Empire Historical Library; (5) to found University scholarships for sons and daughters of soldiers or sailors killed in action, disabled, or dying after the War from wounds.

Lady Borden, on behalf of the Laurentian Chapter, Ottawa, objected to the first clause and declared that the noblest purpose for which this Fund could be used would be the provision of educational advantages for as large a number of the sons and daughters of the men who had served in the Naval and Military Forces as the limits of the Fund would permit. Mrs. R. R. Morgan, on behalf of the Saskatchewan Provincial Chapter objected, also, to this clause because Lectures were not always desirable or successful and because "the Saskatchewan Chapter looks forward with apprehension to a scheme which involves the bringing of influential men from without the Dominion to mould public opinion—especially in matters of government." Finally, the following Resolution was unanimously carried:

That a Fund be raised by the Daughters of the Empire in Canada to promote the educational work of the Order as a Memorial to the Canadian men and women who have died so gloriously in the defence of the Empire during the present War, this Fund to be expended in the following ways:

(a) To found scholarships of sufficient value to provide a University education, or its recognized equivalent, available for and limited to the sons and daughters of: (a) the soldier or sailor or men of the Air Force killed in action or who died from wounds, or by reason of the War, prior to the declaration of peace; (b) the permanently disabled soldier or sailor; (c) the soldier or sailor who, by reason of injuries received in service overseas, dies after the declaration of peace while his children, or any of them, are of school age. In those Provinces where other organizations or institutions have made similar provision, these scholarships will not be given.

(b) Post Graduate Scholarships along the lines set out in the plan proposed by Saskatchewan, but from a national fund, to be distributed among the Provinces.

(c) A Travelling Fellowship, to be competed for by the I.O.D.E. and Provincial scholars.

(d) A Lecture Foundation in Canada for the teaching of Imperial History.

(e) To place in schools selected by the Departments of Education of every Province, some of the reproductions of the series of Canadian War Memorial Pictures, painted for the Dominion Government by leading artists of the Empire, to commemorate Canada's part in the War.

(f) To promote courses of illustrated lectures, free to the children of Canada, on the history and geography of the Empire.

(g) To place, within the next five years, in every school in Canada, where there are children, of foreign-born parents in attendance, a Daughters' of the Empire historical library.

Following this came a visit and address from H.E. the Duchess of Devonshire. The officers elected for 1919-20 included Mrs. John Bruce, Toronto, as President; Mrs. E. F. B. Johnston, Toronto, Lady Pope, Ottawa, Mrs. Graham Thompson and Mrs. Angus MacMurchy, Toronto, and Mrs. R. R. Morgan, Regina, as Vice-Presidents; Mrs. D. McGillivray, National Secretary; Mrs. Arthur Pepler, National Treasurer; Mrs. J. A. Stewart, Organizing Secretary; and Mrs. G. H. Smith, Educational Secretary. The suggestion was made by Lady Pope and approved that a Provincial Chapter for Ontario be organized; the Executive was instructed to appoint a Committee to consider amendments, etc., to the proposed new Constitution; the resignation of Miss Constance Boulton as a protest against criticisms of Mrs. Gooderham was not accepted; re-affiliation with the National Council of Women was approved and a War Memorial Committee appointed with Mrs. G. H. Smith as Convenor, Mrs. Bruce and Mrs. Gooderham and various Provincial officers as members, with others to be elected by Primary Chapters and the sum to be raised settled at $500,000; the Government was asked to aid in establish-

Paper Mill of the Spanish River Pulp and Paper Co. Ltd., at Espanola
in Northern Ontario

ing a Canadian National University at Ottawa and to make the removal of
the embargo on Oleomargarine permanent; a long Resolution was passed in
favour of Child Welfare work—including a Dominion Health Department, a
Child Welfare Bureau, Provincial and Municipal propaganda and a nation-
wide Child Welfare Week. Incidents of the meeting included addresses by
Mrs. Julia W. Henshaw of Vancouver as to war relief service in France, and
Lieut.-Col. J. M. Elder, M.D., C.M.G.; the statement that there were 45,000
members in the I.O.D.E.; the Report from Mrs. G. H. Smith as to Educational
work which showed a remarkable effort at placing handsome pictures of a
patriotic character in the schools and a persistent campaign of education in
Empire subjects amongst the school children of Canada. Toward the close
of the year the Memorial campaign was well under way with $75,000 pledged
by Toronto Chapters; on Dec. 2-5 a Dominion-wide appeal was made for
$500,000 with about half the amount realized.

Canadian Railway Policy and Conditions in 1919. The Dominion in this year assumed serious responsibilities along lines of Railway ownership and con-
trol; the Minister of Railways and Canals (Dr. J. D.
Reid) had the difficult task of re-organizing and, in
large part re-creating, the whole fabric of administration for a great continental system of Government
railways out of a combination of Government and private lines with
hitherto competing interests; in this the Minister had the assistance
of able Railway men in general and of D. B. Hanna, President of
the Canadian National Railways, in particular—at the same time
he inherited, the difficulties of the Canadian Northern and the
Grand Trunk as to insufficient rates and interest burdens. The
Canadian Government Railways in 1919 technically did not yet
include the Canadian Northern, the St. John and Quebec or the
Grand Trunk; they did include the Intercolonial and its Windsor
Branch, the N.B. and P.E.I. Railway, the P.E.I. Railway, the International, Hudson Bay, Vale Railway, St. Martins, Salisbury and
Albert, York and Carleton, Moncton and Buctouche, Elgin and
Havelock, Quebec and Saguenay, National Transcontinental and
Grand Trunk Pacific. For these lines—many of them very small
—the total operating revenues for the year of Mch. 31st, 1919, were
$38,063,664, the operating expenses $43,854,802, and the deficit
$5,791,138; the St. John and Quebec had a revenue of $137,665 and
expenditures of $268,602; the Canadian Northern system for the
year of Dec. 31st, 1918, had operating revenues of $47,310,011 and
expenditures of $45,662,275 with interest as additional.

Of conditions in the ensuing fiscal year of 1919-20 Dr. Reid
made the following statement in the Commons on July 7th: "It
is estimated that the loss on the Grand Trunk Pacific will be
about $9,000,000, and the loss on the Canadian National Railway
System as a whole, say roughly, $19,000,000, or a total of $28,000,-
000. The following is a summary of the moneys to be supplied to
the Board of Directors to meet the expenditures enumerated: Loss,
$28,000,000; construction on the Canadian Government Railways,
$11,121,000; Canadian National Railway construction and better-
ments, $21,421,000, or a total of $80,542,000."

21

As to mileage the Government Railways, as stated above, totalled 4,213 and with sidings, etc., 5,366; the C.N.R. System 9,574 miles; the Grand Trunk 3,578 miles in Canada; the G.T.P. and branch lines 2,830; or a total under Government control at the close of 1919 of 21,348 miles. The total operating mileage of all Canadian lines (June 30th, 1918) was 38,879 or, with 2nd track, sidings, etc., 50,853; the capital totalled $1,999,880,494 of which $877,600,613 was in Stocks, $216,284,882 in consolidated debentures (C.P.R.) and $905,994,999 in Funded debt; the total aid given to Railways in Canada was $218,714,318 by the Dominion, $37,437,895 by Provinces and $17,914,836 by municipalities; the total of Land grants was 44,096,989 acres, the executed Guarantee bonds by the Dominion totalled $183,532,523 and by Provinces $174,955,872. The passengers carried in 1918 were 50,737,294 and the freight traffic carried 127,543,687 tons (2,000 lbs.); the total equipment was 5,756 locomotives, 6,376 passenger cars and 228,133 cars in freight and other service. The question of Government ownership was debated during the year but not widely; public opinion ran strongly in favour of the policy and the Parliamentary discussions on the one side were somewhat perfunctory; E. W. Beatty, of the C.P.R., contributed the ablest of the arguments and speeches against assumption of what he feared were undue national responsibilities; this view was supported by the Montreal and Quebec Boards of Trade and by the Montreal *Star* and Montreal *Gazette* and various financial papers; the financial failure of Government operation during war-time in Great Britain and the United States was a chief argument used.

The Board of Railway Commissioners exercised its usual important functions during the year with Sir H. L. Drayton as Chairman until his entry into the Government and then with Hon. F. B. Carvell—the other Commissioners being A. C. Boyce, A. S. Goodeve, J. S. McLean and J. G. Rutherford. During the year the Board (Apr. 11th) declined to interfere with the action of Canadian Railways in advancing clocks on their systems to conform with Daylight Saving time in the United States; on May 14th it granted the Bell Telephone Co. a 10 per cent. increase in exchange rates and an increase in long distance, or a total addition to income of $1,100,000; in June, owing to the coming lapse of the War Measures Act, the Railway Act of Canada was amended so as to give the Board, under this Act, powers to fix, determine and enforce just and reasonable rates, and to change and alter rates as changing conditions or cost of transportation might from time to time require.

On July 19th the Board issued its judgment on the application of the Express Companies for increases in rates, and of municipalities for increased deliveries. It was stated that the Railways and Express Companies were carrying on business at a large loss and increases were allowed in the general merchandise express scale to an average of 45·94 per cent. in Eastern Canada; 23·75 per cent.

on the Prairies; and 11·48 per cent. in British Columbia.   The higher rate of increase in Eastern Canada resulted from the abolition of discriminatory rates and extension of equal treatment to all districts.   The new Chief Commissioner heard cases for the first time at Ottawa on Sept. 16th.   Speaking at Victoria, B.C., on Nov. 25th Mr. Carvell spoke seriously of the car shortage: "The fact is that between 21,000 and 22,000 more Canadian cars are on United States rails to-day than there are American cars on Canadian rails. At least one-tenth of the cars owned by Canadian railroads are locked up in the United States, and we are afraid to let more go there.   It is one of the most serious problems before us.".   It may be added that the Canadian Railway War Board was re-organized in November and from Dec. 1st became the Railway Association of Canada with H. G. Kelley as Chairman of the Executive.

The 4th annual Report of the Canadian Northern Railway System for the calendar year 1918 was issued on Sept. 15th, 1919, and signed by D. B. Hanna, President.   The gross earnings were $49,-062,712 including $1,752,700 of Interest received; the working expenses were $45,662,275 and the Interest charges $17,898,246 or a net deficit of $14,497,809.   As to this Mr. Hanna stated that it was hoped the 1918 increases in freight rates, to meet those in the United States following the application of the McAdoo increases in wages to Canadian railways, would have proved a set off.   But the result was quite different: "Supplements have been issued from time to time augmenting the allowance to various classes of employees, shortening the hours of service, and generally adopting the 8-hour day, with many other specific improvements in working conditions, all having the immediate effect of largely increasing the compensation of employees.   The result of this was that at the end of the calendar year the pay roll of the Company, which had previously averaged $1,890,000 per month reached the enormous total of $2,815,000 per month, equivalent to an additional $925,000 per month, representing an increase of almost 50 per cent. over the wages paid up to the date the McAdoo Award took effect."

It was pointed out that the use of the Canadian National Railways as a collective, title covering both the C.N.R. and the Government lines, had been authorized by Order-in-Council on Dec. 20th, 1918, and by a 1919 Act of Parliament; the Canadian National Railway Co. had been incorporated to operate all the Railways under Federal control.   The Assets of the C.N.R. were stated at $622,-753,529 with a surplus over Liabilities of $17,932,244; the Funded Debt of the Company was $128,543,062 and of affiliated Companies $125,186,538; early in the year the Toronto Suburban Railway (Electric) running to Guelph was purchased.   Speaking at Vancouver on Apr. 4th D. B. Hanna stated that: "When the Government took possession of the Canadian Northern they came into possession of a property that, mile for mile, is laid in such territory as will produce in time the maximum amount of traffic and, given the same time as has been given the C.P.R., its gross earnings west of

Port Arthur will be largely in excess of the C.P.R.'' By the close of 1919 the Canadian National Railways, in the broad sense of the combination, covered 22,375 miles and represented an investment of $1,300,000,000.

The Canadian Pacific Railway in 1919 had a prosperous year* with net earnings of $32,933,036, a net Surplus of $844,249 and Assets of $1,078,777,358; the net increase in working expenses over 1917, largely due to additional cost of wages, was $38,152,706; its total mileage in Canada on Dec. 31st was 14,006 and in the United States 4,853 miles or about the same as that of the National system when in full working order. During the year the new President, E. W. Beatty, K.C., performed efficient work in the management of the Railway, took an active part in presenting to the public the principles of Railway action and policy in this country, and urged in a number of speeches the necessity of caution in Government assumption of Railway ownership. At a Thorold banquet on Feb. 3rd he stated that during the War the Company had lost 13 ships by enemy action, carried over 1,000,000 troops and passengers by sea and 4,000,000 tons of freight; helped to raise the 1st Canadian Railway Construction Corps and constructed and equipped the first Commissary cars made in Canada for the transporting of troops, the first hydraulic hay press in Canada for use in the transportation of hay to Great Britain, and had first initiated the employment of women labour on a large scale.

At the 3rd annual banquet of the Company to its officials (Mch. 23rd) Lord Shaughnessy and Mr. Beatty delivered notable addresses and the Conference, held at the same time, with 500 officers of the Railway in attendance, was a development of great importance and interest. At Montreal on May 7th before his Shareholders; at Victoria on May 29th before the Canadian Club; at Nelson, before the B.C. Associated Boards of Trade, a little later; at Calgary on June 3rd before the Canadian Club, and at Edmonton, on June 4th, in a press interview; in a Saskatoon interview on June 5th and at Winnipeg on June 7th; at a Quebec Board of Trade banquet on Oct. 1st, and in Montreal on Oct. 23rd, Mr. Beatty emphasized his opinions as to the danger of a too extensive Government ownership and control of railways in a country such as Canada. When action was finally taken and the issue settled for the moment he declared that success for the National Railway system was imperative: ''I can say with perfect candour and honesty that no one desires its success more than I, and this is a hope which I think can fairly be re-echoed by anyone who desires the burdens of this country to be as light as possible, and the freight and passenger rates as low as possible.''

C.P.R. incidents of the year included the publication of a handsome brochure by its London Office giving portraits of 144 men of the European staffs of the C.P.R. and Dominion Express who had served in the War.—23 having been killed in action and the service

*Note.—For full reports and official statements see *Supplement* to this volume.

of all covering 10 battlefronts, the Navy, and the Air Service; a presentation in London on July 5th by the Staff of the C.P.R. to Sir George McLaren Brown—European General Manager for the Company—and Lady Brown; the appointment on Dec. 8th of Sir John Eaton of Toronto as a Director of the Railway; the wide use in England of a magnificent cinometograph record of the Prince of Wales' trip across Canada *via* the C.P.R. In Montreal on Apr. 6th an action was entered against the C.P.R. Company by the Dominion of Canada to have the Minister of Finance appointed custodian for 143,676 C.P.R. shares valued at $22,000,000, the property of enemy shareholders, and held on the New York register of the Company in the names of those who, presumably, were enemy aliens. Action was taken under the Enemy Trading Act of 1914 and involved arrears of dividends as well, or a total of $38,325,100. Judgment was given for the Government on Apr. 23rd and a transfer of stock order issued by Mr. Justice Duclos.

The Grand Trunk Railway in 1919 passed out of private Company control to that of the Government after an historic career of useful service to Canada and of difficulties in expansion which, eventually, were too great to overcome. Since early in 1918 the negotiations for purchase had been proceeding, with offers and counter-offers; the crisis had come through the Grand Trunk Pacific when it was placed by the Government in the hands of a Receiver—the Minister of Railways—for inability to meet interest payments; in September conferences took place at Ottawa between Sir Alfred Smithers and H. G. Kelley representing the G.T.R. and members of the Dominion Government at which an agreement was reached and announced by Hon. Arthur Meighen on Oct. 10th; Parliament passed a Bill authorizing the Government to accept this Agreement and to take over the whole system.* According to official figures, the operated mileage of the G.T.R. in 1918 was 3,529 in Canada and 419 in the United States and, under American control, 99 miles in Canada and 1,246 miles in the United States; the mileage under G.T. Pacific was 2,817 in Canada—the total in Canada, therefore, was 6,508 miles and in the States 1,665. The Funded Debt of the System, including G.T.P. and American lines, was $448,703,356, the common stock $118,209,695, the Guaranteed and Preference notes $133,286,651 and, with Equipment notes, the total Securities held by the public were $707,929,817.

From Mch. 10th, 1919, the Government operated the Grand Trunk Pacific, its branch lines, telegraph, steamship, hotels and other enterprises. The Grand Trunk Directors declared that they were forced into the whole agreement and sale by war conditions and Government pressure. As Sir A. W. Smithers, M.P., Chairman, put it on June 30th: "We are in our present position to-day from circumstances entirely beyond our control—namely, enormously increased expenses arising from high wages and increased cost of material, and not being allowed sufficient increase of rates to meet

*Note.—See Parliamentary record, Pages 615-16.

the increased expenditure.   In one way or another, the Governments of Canada, America, and Great Britain have had to assist the railways under present exceptional conditions, and the only railway left to its own resources is the Grand Trunk Railway, the oldest railway in Canada, which has rendered 65 years of service and received practically no assistance from the Government in all that long period.''   Strong opposition to the Government policy in this respect was expressed by large financial interests and, especially those of Montreal, with both Board of Trade and Chambre de Commerce against it; by the Quebec Division of the Canadian Manufacturers' Association, and by the Liberal party in Parliament as to various clauses and conditions of the Agreement; by the Montreal *Star* and *Gazette*, *La Patrie* and *Le Canada*, the Quebec and Regina Boards of Trade—the chief point being that the Dominion, as primarily responsible for the G.T.P., should take it over and leave the Grand Trunk alone; in the Senate Hon. G. G. Foster and Hon. R. Dandurand of Montreal, Hon. F. Nicholls, Toronto, and Hon. George Gordon, Sudbury, fought the measure; it went through in due course, however, with public opinion as a whole favourable.

Incidents of the year included a record of G.T.R. war activities showing $1,000,000 paid to enlisted employees and contributions of $370,000 to Canadian Patriotic and Red Cross funds; the contribution of 5,357 employees to active service of whom 350 were killed, 800 wounded and 60 decorated; gifts by employees of $550,-000 to the Patriotic and Red Cross Funds and $7,750,000 in subscriptions to Victory Loans; the handling of over 850,000 troops and transportation of immense quantities of ammunition.   In December W. P. Hinton was elected a Director.   The annual Report of the Grand Trunk Company for the calendar year 1919, compared with 1918, was as follows:

1918		1919
£13,655,225	Gross Receipts	£14,125,553
10,979,960	Working Expenses at the rate of 89·58% compared with 86·75% in 1918	12,645,152
£1,675,265	Net Traffic Receipts	£1,480,401
181,887	Income from Rentals and hire of Equipment	179,459
£1,857,152	Total Net Revenue	£1,659,860
	Add—	
44,981	Sundry Interest and other Receipts	44,981
263,085	Debenture Stock	263,085
104,615	Balance of General Interest Account	264,185
£2,269,833	Net Revenue Receipts	£2,232,111
1918		1919
	Charges—	
£70,000	Rents (Leased Lines)	£70,000
1,357,025	Interest on Debenture Stocks and Bonds of the Company..	1,357,024
504,162	Interest on Secured Notes	527,482
336,846	Estimated Loss on Lines in United States taken under Federal control by the United States Railroad Administration	276,461
£2,268,033		£2,230,968
1,800	Leaving a surplus of	1,141
£2,269,833		£2,232,109

THE PROVINCE OF ONTARIO IN 1919

The Hearst Government: The Legislature and Political Affairs. The year commenced with two bye-elections of considerable interest—North Ontario and St. Catharines. In the former a vacancy had occurred by the death of W. H. Hoyle (Cons.) elected in 1914 by a good majority; the candidates were J. W. Widdifield, Liberal and U.F.O. against Major H. S. Cameron, Conservative. In the latter, a strong Conservative riding, also vacated by death, F. R. Parnell (Cons.) was running against W. E. Longden (Lab.). Several Ministers took part in the contests and Mrs. Rose Henderson, a Montreal woman of extreme Labour views, came up to help Mr. Longden in St Catharines. The Government took the line presented by Sir William Hearst, in a Toronto speech of Jan. 14th, and urged the splendid war record of the Administration, the proposed Housing policy, the establishment of employment bureaux, the extension of roads and construction of bridges, proposals for increased technical education, the Land Settlement scheme for soldiers; the Premier also stated, on Jan. 16th, that private licensed vendors of liquor in Ontario would be abolished and instead of the several existing agencies—Toronto, Hamilton, London, Ottawa, Kingston, Windsor—in operation throughout the Province the Government would take over the business itself.

In North Ontario the United Farmers put up a vigourous fight and Hon. T. W. McGarry on Jan. 28th pointed to the Government's successful imposition of taxation on the great sources of wealth, the large estates which were compelled to pay Succession duties, the great corporations which furnished a fair revenue to the Province; the increase in expenditures for agriculture and education, the development of the northern country and the making of good roads. At St. Catharines on Feb. 7th Mr. McGarry promised (in view of the Influenza epidemic) that the Government, in taking over the vendors' stores would provide proper measures to permit the obtaining of liquor for medicinal purposes; he stated that $14,-000,000 would be expended in the coming year on public works which would employ much labour. On Feb. 18th the result showed Mr. Widdifield elected in North Ontario by 3,965 votes to 3,547 and Mr. Parnell in St. Catharines by 5,154 to 4,980.

In the next few months the Premier and his Ministers made a number of speeches on public policy. The Hon. H. J. Cody spoke at Ottawa on Feb. 6th in a notable discussion of Educational problems and a description of the new and progressive policy which he proposed to carry out; he followed this up at other meetings. Sir William Hearst stated at Toronto (Feb. 12th) that the Government

had decided to proceed with the expenditure of approximately
$25,000,000 on buildings and various construction works of which
the T. and N.O. Railway stood for $1,000,000, in buildings, exten-
sions and improvements, and the Hydro-Electric Power Commission for a minimum capital outlay of $9,000,000.   From time to
time other Ministers—Hon. F. G. Macdiarmid, Hon. W. D. Mc-
Pherson, Hon. I. B. Lucas, Hon. G. Howard Ferguson, Hon. G. S.
Henry—spoke at meetings in connection with either the Prohibition
Referendum or the coming Elections.   On Feb. 25th Dr. G. C.
Creelman, for two years Commissioner of Agriculture, resigned to
devote his whole time to the Guelph College of Agriculture of which
he was President, and was succeeded by C. F. Bailey, Assistant
Deputy-Minister; on Sept. 26th Brig.-Gen. A. E. Ross, C.M.G., M.D.,
M.L.A., since 1911, was appointed Minister without Portfolio.

Departmental Reports and Statistical Detail.   Hon. G. S. Henry
submitted his Report, as Minister of Agriculture, for the year Oct.
31st, 1918, sometime in the year 1919—no date given.   It dealt
with a record year in production of field crops, Departmental work
in securing and distributing labour, in operating tractors, in extension of the arrangement for granting loans for seed purposes, in the
organization for backyard gardening and vacant lot cultivation, in
publicity work through farm papers and in a general use of motion
pictures.   The attendance at the Guelph Agricultural College was
stated as 1,722 with, for the first time, a Short Course in agriculture
for women.   During 1919 the Department continued to issue Bulletins and publications helpful to farmers such as the following: Judging Vegetables by A. H. McLennan, B.S.A.; The Apple Maggot, by L.
Caesar, B.S.A., and W. A. Ross, B.S.A.; Farm Crops, by C. A. Zavitz,
B.S.A., D.SC.; Hay and Pasture Crops, by Dr. Zavitz and W. S. Squir-
rel, B.S.A.   Of the agricultural legislation of the year, for which
Mr. Henry was responsible, an Act was passed authorizing the
establishment of Community Halls and Athletic Fields in rural
districts.   It empowered the Minister to make a grant of public
funds to a township establishing a community hall and an athletic
field; the grant was limited to 25 per cent. of the cost of the building exclusive of land, and was not to exceed $2,000; debentures
could be issued by the Township to provide its necessary funds.
The Minister was also authorized to make a similar grant to any
Consolidated School providing these facilities.   Other measures
were as follows: (1) providing for the purchase of all Cream for
sale, shipment or manufacture on the basis of the fat contents; (2)
specifying regulations as to the branding of Live-stock; (3) providing that successful students at the Ontario Veterinary College
should be entitled to a diploma granted by the University of Toronto
conferring the B.V.Sc. degree.   The Ontario official statistics of
Field crop production in 1919 were as follows, with values as
given by Dominion Bureau of Statistics:

Field Crops	Acres	Bush.	Yield per Acre Bush.	Total Value
Fall Wheat	619,494	15,051,708	24	$29,519,000
Spring Wheat	361,150	5,646,544	15	17,182,000
Barley	569,188	13,183,757	23	17,215,000
Oats	2,674,841	78,388,018	29	71,876,000
Rye	140,072	2,219,042	15	3,279,000
Buckwheat	178,569	4,071,959	22	5,584,000
Peas	127,253	1,816,517	14	4,180,000
Beans	22,920	288,480	12	1,039,000
Corn for Husking	221,004	15,152,475	68	18,790,000
Mixed Grains	628,761	19,785,287	31	26,672,000
Flax	13,717	129,461	9	450,500
Alfalfa	146,790 (tons)	314,419 (tons)	2	6,851,000
Hay and Clover	3,508,266 "	5,588,804 "	1	115,161,000
Fodder Corn	399,549 "	4,013,946 "	10	25,304,000
Potatoes	157,286	15,144,921	96	20,820,000
Sugar Beets	24,500	9,586,495	391	2,606,000
Turnips, Mangolds, etc.	123,029	42,756,000	348	14,027,000

The acreage under orchard and small fruits was 282,250, the
number of Horses in the Province on June 30th was 719,569 and of
cattle 2,927,191, of sheep 1,101,740 and swine 1,695,487—the total
value according to Federal figures was $384,266,000, or an increase
of $140,000,000 since 1914; the number of Poultry in the Province
was 11,705,809.   Through G. A. Putnam, Superintendent of
Women's Institutes, these important organizations were given every
encouragement and in this work the Department of Education aided
that of Agriculture.   In 1918, 75 Demonstration lectures were given
and a Summer Series of meetings arranged for 1919 with an attendance of 40,000 and 130 courses in a few months; on Apr. 6-8th a
Conference was held in Toronto and many subjects of vital interest
discussed including public health and child welfare, education, immigration, agriculture and home economics; later in the year a Convention was held at London (Oct. 22-23rd) and another in Toronto
(Oct. 28-29th); the President of the Ontario Section of the Federated Women's Institutes of Canada—of which Mrs. E. F. Murphy,
Edmonton, was President—was Mrs. William Todd, Orillia, and
the Secretary Mrs. B. O. Allen, Fort William; the 1918 membership of the Institutes was 30,069, the total of all meetings held was
12,719 and the attendance 250,579.   The Statistics Branch of this
Department issued a valuable Report for 1918 showing the value
of Farm lands, Buildings, Implements and Live-stock in the Province as $1,633,413,528 or an increase of $153,000,000 since 1914
with chattel mortgages of $2,320,325 against the Farms and $23,-
809,234 against all other occupations in the Province.   The Department also aided the chief Farmers' organizations and the heads
of these during 1919 were as follows:

Ontario Agricultural and Experimental Union...Hon. Nelson Montieth ....Stratford
Ontario Vegetable Growers' Association ....W. S. Evorall ....Beamsville
Ontario Corn Growers' Association ....R. W. Kindser ....Blenheim
Fruit Growers' Association of Ontario ....J. E. Johnston..........Simcoe
Entomological Society of Ontario ....Prof. Lawson Caesar ....Guelph
Dairymen's Association of Eastern Ontario .....R. G. Leggett ....Newboro
Dairymen's Association of Western Ontario .....Frank Boyes ....Dorchester
Ontario Beekeeper's Association ....James Armstrong ......Selkirk
Ontario Swine Breeders' Association ....William Jones ....Mt. Elgin
Ontario Large Yorkshire Breeders' Association...J. O. Stuart ....Osgoode
Ontario Sheep Breeders' Association...........G. L. Telfer ....Paris
Ontario Cattle Breeders' Association..........John Gardhouse ....Weston

Ontario Horse Breeders' Association	William Smith	Columbus
Ontario Horticultural Association	William Hartry	Seaforth
Ontario Fairs Association	L. J. C. Bull	Brampton
Ontario Farm Drainage Association	S. W. Hyatt	Mt. Bridges
Ontario Winter Fair Association	J. D. Flatt	Hamilton
Ontario Creamery Association	William Newman	Lorneville
Ontario Ploughmen's Association	W. C. Barrie	Galt
Ontario Hereford Breeders' Association	J. E. Harris	Kingsville
Ontario Berkshire Breeders' Association	H. A. Dobson	Cheltenham
Ontario Poultry Association	G. G. Henderson	Hamilton
Ontario Veterinary Association	Dr. Campbell	Toronto

The Hon. W. D. McPherson, as Provincial Secretary, reported for the Children's Aid Societies of Ontario under J. J. Kelso's administration with 948 children cared for in 1918; the 2 Hospitals for Feeble-Minded and Epileptics showing 1,192 patients and those for the Insane with 6,172 patients; the 98 public hospitals in Ontario, including 11 Sanatoria for Consumptives, 68 private hospitals, 39 Refuges, 31 orphanages, 2 convalescent homes and 31 County houses of refuge, with 112,431 patients under treatment during 1918 at a total cost of $5,763,924. The administrative work of the Provincial Secretary, with his jurisdiction over the License Department, the Municipal Auditor and the Housing Act, though reported for 1919 by Hon. H. C. Nixon, the new Minister, pertained in the main to Mr. McPherson's period of administration. The 4th annual Report of the Board of License Commissioners (J. D. Flavelle, Chairman) Apr. 30th, 1919, showed 2,547 convictions and 479 dismissals under the Ontario Temperance Act compared with 3,285 and 668 respectively in the previous year; the Provincial revenue from fines was $231,833 and $204,514 respectively and the expenses of enforcement $126,580 against $118,982 in 1917-18; the Municipal revenue from fines was $437,812 and $338,228 respectively. As to the Government Dispensaries, established as a result of 1919 legislation, they were reported as conducted under an exacting system of inspection with business transacted in 7 months, up to Dec. 31st, 1919, of $2,010,404 and gross profits of $713,168. J. A. Ellis, Director of the Bureau of Municipal Affairs, reported for 1919, to Hon. Mr. Nixon, that the Housing Board had been organized in March, 1919, with Loans totalling $3,677,974 up to the close of the year and 1,184 houses constructed, at an average cost of $3,106, with a total of $10,629,000 appropriated by Order-in-Council and $941,640 approved for houses not yet erected.

Mr. Macdiarmid, Minister of Public Works and Highways, received from Dr. W. A. Riddell, Superintendent of Trades and Labour, a report as to 11 Government Employment Bureaux which had handled in the year of Oct. 31st, 1918, 26,407 applications for work from men and 15,617 from women; 41,525 notifications of help wanted (men) and 23,844 for women with a total appointed to positions of 23,217 men and 21,569 women. For 1919 plans were made upon a basis of 35 Offices. The 1918 Report of W. A. McLean, Deputy-Minister of Highways (Apr. 11, 1919) showed an expenditure on Roads by Township Councils of $1,768,785 with 9,500 miles of Provincial county roads also designated for improve-

ment under the terms of an increased Government grant of 60 per
cent. of expenditure; the total spent on these County roads was in
1918 $2,226,899 of which $1,482,610 was for construction and $744,-
289 for maintenance and of this total $815,439 came from Provincial
subsidies; the County work included metalling of 215 miles, grading 321 miles, and bridges constructed 93, with 900 culverts.   The
Provincial Highways project of the Government was described as
follows:

The main line of the Provincial Highway System from Windsor to
the Quebec Boundary, with branches to Niagara and Ottawa, constitutes a
series of important market roads, to which is added the traffic from numerous towns, cities and shipping points linked together along the route. The
future potential traffic of the route is very great. Within 12 miles of the
route is 52 per cent. of the total population of the Province, and over one-
third of the rural population. It passes through 12 out of a total of 23
cities in the Province, containing 84 per cent. of the city population. The
Provincial Highway passes through Counties possessing 54 per cent. of the
total farm property and producing 51 per cent. of the total field crops of the
Province. Section by section it forms a series of most important market roads
for local farm traffic. Residents on and adjacent to these roads are entitled
to its proper maintenance for their market traffic. These roads must be so
built as to carry all the heavy traffic which is flowing over them (or which will
flow over them when improved to a reasonable standard), or else the farming
community along them is unfairly penalized for residing on them.

Mr. McLean also dealt with motor vehicles, showing a passenger
car registration of 101,845 and of motor trucks numbering 7,529—a
total increase in the year of 25,584; the passenger cars owned in
Ontario cities was stated at 36,699 and in towns, villages and townships at 64,900.   The 13th annual Report as to Game and Fisheries
(31st Oct., 1919) was made to the new Minister, Hon. F. C. Biggs,
and showed a revenue of $346,197 and expenditures of $185,247;
Provincial fisheries were stated to give employment to 3,918 men
with $2,694,104 invested in the industry; moose, deer and caribou,
beaver, and musk-rats were reported as plentiful together with
partridge, and pheasants in certain districts; a large Fish hatchery
was under construction at Fort Frances and a qualified Fish Cul-
turist had been appointed to look after the large yearly distribution of fry, etc.; the Fish Sales branch handled 3,155,902 lbs. and
made a profit of $70,207 on a total business of $403,521; the value
of the Fish caught in 1919 was $3,175,110 with a total of $74,322,013
since 1870.   Under Mr. Macdiarmid, and then Mr. Biggs, was the
Timiskaming and Northern Ontario Railway Commission (J. L.
Englehart, G. W. Lee and Hon. R. F. Preston) which reported for
1919 463 miles in operation, a revenue of $3,136,752, expenses of
$3,076,130 and net earnings of $53,153.

Mr. Howard Ferguson, Minister of Lands, Forests and Mines,
received the 1919 Report of T. W. Gibson, Deputy-Minister, giving
statistics for 1918, and including various valuable articles on Mines
and minerals in the Province—Peat, the Abitibi-Night Hawk Gold
Area, Cobalt, the Larder Lake Gold Area, etc.   In this year the
Ontario output was $80,308,972 or 11·3 per cent. increase in value

over that of 1917 which had exceeded 1916 by 10·3 per cent.; the
number of employees was 16,226 and the total of wages paid $20,-
698,119. The increase was in metallic minerals—chiefly Gold,
which rose from $5,529,767 in 1914 to $8,502,480 in 1918, Silver
$12,795,214 to $17,415,882 and Nickel $5,136,804 to $27,840,422.
The total increase in all Minerals between 1914 and 1918 was $34,-
013,013. The advance figures of 1919 production were as follows:

Metallic	1918	1919
Gold	$ 8,502,480	$10,451,688
Silver	17,415,882	12,913,316
Copper in matte	8,262,360	2,740,663
Nickel in matte	26,578,200	7,990,403
Iron, pig	1,364,736	1,200,793
Nickel, Metallic	1,262,116	3,931,055
Sundries	2,792,285	2,272,824
Metallic total	$66,178,059	$41,500,742
Non-Metallic		
Clay Products	$ 2,018,450	$ 3,093,262
Cement, Portland	1,910,839	3,659,720
Lime	872,177	1,235,736
Natural Gas	2,498,769	2,383,394
Petroleum, crude	781,097	632,789
Salt	1,287,039	1,395,368
Stone, building, trap, etc.	869,239	1,068,957
Sundries	3,893,303	2,261,746
Non-metallic total	$14,130,913	$15,730,972
Metallic total	66,178,059	41,500,742
Grand total	$80,308,972	$57,231,714

The producing Gold mines in 1919 numbered 5 in the Porcupine
area and of this Hollinger produced $6,655,781, the Dome $1,279,-
341 and McIntyre $1,955,769; three in Kirkland Lake district and
three in neighbouring areas. In Silver the six Cobalt mines, Coniagas, Kerr Lake, McKinley, Mining Corporation, Nipissing and
Trethewey, distributed $3,524,241 to shareholders in 1919 or a total
to date for this area of $78,334,762 with shipments (1904-19) valued
at $182,039,972. Mr. Ferguson's Report for the year of Oct. 31st,
1919, showed 49,704 acres of agricultural and town-site areas sold
for $48,119; settlers in the North numbering 539 with patents for
55,000 acres and Provincial lands under license totalling 16,231
square miles; a total revenue for the Department of $2,755,736 and
disbursements of $1,536,766.

The Ontario Railway and Municipal Board (D. M. McIntyre,
Chairman) reported for 1918 to Mr. Lucas, Attorney-General, as
to 529 formal applications for decision with 74 of them involving
the validity of debentures valued at a total of $5,273,742; the acci-
dents on Provincial Railways numbered 426 injured with 22 persons killed. On Feb. 3rd, 1919, the 5th annual meeting of the
Ontario Safety League, aided by the Government and supervised
by this Board, was held at Toronto with 130 delegates present and

the report of much good work done in educating the public as to the need of care in travelling, walking, driving, motoring, etc. Mayor Church of Toronto was elected President. The most important act of the Ontario Railway Board in 1919 was the order to the Toronto Railway Co. on June 23rd to forthwith operate an ''adequate service'' during the strike of that period; the succeeding order on the 26th taking over the Street Railway system upon failure to so operate and appointment of R. C. Harris (*protem*) as General Manager; the offer of the Board to the striking workmen of 50 cents an hour for 3 months, 52½ for the next 6 months and 55 cents thereafter—a considerable increase; the acceptance of this decision by the T.S.R. Company and resumption of control on July 8th. This Board also controlled 628 Telephone Companies or Systems in the Province.

Miscellaneous Reports included that of James Clancy, Provincial Auditor, as to certain over-rulings of Treasury Board orders, etc.; that of J. Bruce Macdonald, Inspector of Division Courts, dealing with 338 offices in the Province; that of A. R. Boswell, K.C., Superintendent of Insurance, as to 2 Provincial Life and 2 Joint Stock Fire Insurance Companies and 71 Purely Mutual Fire Companies with 148,617 Policies in force, a net amount at Risk of $341,798,832, a total Income (1918) of $884,229 and expenditures of $846,796; that of the Workmen's Compensation Board (Samuel Price, Chairman, and G. A. Kingstone) with, in 1919, a total of $4,192,859 awarded in benefits for 44,260 accidents of which 429 were fatal, an estimated 500,000 workmen under protection of the Board, and an average rate of assessment upon employers of $1.22 per $100 of pay-roll; that of Dr. J. W. S. McCullough as Deputy-Registrar-General, showing 64,729 birth registrations in 1918, 19,525 marriages and 43,038 deaths with 7,337 of the latter due to Influenza and 4,660 to Pneumonia; that of Hon. C. A. Masten, Commissioner, as to Insurance laws in Ontario apart from Life and Marine, with the statement that $1,837,000,000 of insurance was carried on property in Ontario with about $14,000,000 paid yearly by the people, or $5.60 per capita in premiums, $3.60 per head returned for losses incurred. Various suggestions as to management and control of Companies were offered and a general revision of the Insurance Act suggested. The Bureau of Municipal Affairs reported the 1919 population of the Province as 2,621,785 of which 998,597 were in townships, 528,326 in villages and towns and 1,094,-862 in cities. Other statistics (1918) were as follows:

Particulars	Townships	Villages and Towns	Cities
Assessment	$706,635,799	$265,795,177	$1,096,947,589
Municipal Taxes	11,228,811	6,146,674	26,931,590
School Taxes	5,098,924	2,870,186	8,474,887
Debenture Debt	9,788,505	83,270,559	190,265,910
Sinking Fund	174,588	2,826,214	43,452,828

The 1919 Session of the Legislature. The 5th and last Session of the 14th Legislature of Ontario was opened by Sir J. S. Hendrie on Feb. 25th with General Pau of France attending as a visitor.

In the Speech from the Throne His Honour welcomed the close of hostilities, spoke of the Empire as standing "firmly and unitedly for freedom and justice" and referred to the War patriotism of Canada; mentioned the Labour situation of unemployment and promised a programme of industrial and commercial and constructive activity; stated that the Government had entered into an agreement with the lumbermen of the Province, under which a representative was being sent overseas to secure for Ontario a share of the trade in lumber and forest products required to restore the devastated countries; promised Land settlement and Housing legislation and reported work on the Queenston-Chippewa Hydro-electric undertaking as hastening to completion while development at Lake Nipigon, to supply Port Arthur and Fort William, would "shortly be commenced"; announced the paying of allowances to widowed mothers having dependent children, as under consideration and referred to the 1918 agricultural production as most favourable; indicated Educational developments and changes along lines of technical, industrial and vocational training and promised other important measures. A number of newly-elected members were introduced—Hon. G. S. Henry, Hon. H. J. Cody, R. A. Fowler (Lennox) Conservatives; Beniah Bowman, (Manitoulin) the first U.F.O. member; with W. H. Fraser, Liberal, of North Huron, and J. A. Calder, North Oxford.

The Address was moved by Z. A. Hall, South Waterloo, and Irwin Hilliard, K.C., Dundas, and was passed on Mch. 5th, after some debate and the defeat by 58 to 25 of an amendment moved by H. H. Dewart, K.C., and G. C. Hurdman declaring that provision should be made for a preparation of Voters' Lists which would include the names of all women and men over 21 years of age entitled to vote at Provincial Elections. The first important item of Government legislation was Sir William Hearst's Bill for taking advantage of the Dominion's Housing proposals; the Premier explained the policy on Feb. 26th and reviewed the steps leading up to it. The Housing situation had been brought to the attention of the Government in 1918 and a Housing Committee was appointed with a loan of $2,000,000 at 5 per cent. offered by the Province to municipalities on condition that the latter put up 25 per cent. of the amount loaned to builders; the Report of this Committee was a valuable contribution to public thought. Subsequently, the Dominion Government set aside $25,000,000 for this purpose, and of the total about $8,500,000 became available for Ontario. The Premier explained that his Bill authorized the appointment of a local Commission of five—not members of the Municipal Council—in places of over 100,000 in population. No profit was to be made by the municipalities in loaning the money: "It is the intention to give the municipalities the widest latitude in carrying out the provisions of the Act. While plans will be supplied to them, it is not the intention to bind them down to any particular plans or methods, though building schemes will have to be approved by the Municipal Director." It was estimated that a $3,000 home would cost the purchaser $20 a month if payment were spread over a period of 20 years; about 20 municipalities had intimated their intention of coming under the Act and about 20 more were considering the matter.

Paving the way for the administration of this Act, Sir William introduced another Bill to amend the Bureau of Municipal Affairs Act so as to permit the appointment of J. A. Ellis to the position of Director of Municipal Affairs with charge of the preliminary details in connection with the above Act to Provide for the Erection of Dwelling Houses. On the 2nd reading (Feb. 28th) the Premier stated that there was no doubt as to a very serious shortage of moderate-priced houses throughout Ontario, suitable for returned soldiers and working men and women, in almost every industrial centre. As to Toronto, out of 13,544 houses only 36 per cent. were occupied by single families and of the total 1,338 were classed as unfit for habitation. The measure passed with little amendment or criticism after Major J. C. Tolmie (Lib.), had, on Mch. 17th, moved for a grant of $200 to every returned soldier, or parents of a soldier who should take advantage of the Act, and been ruled out of order.

Other legislation included the Bill presented by Hon. I. B. Lucas authorizing appointment of a Provincial Public Trustee to assume the direction of escheated estates—monies that had passed into the possession of the Province because no heirs had appeared to claim them—the estates of lunatics, etc.; ordering the payment into the Treasury of about $250,000 which was held awaiting claimants and transferring, ultimately, the duties fixed under the Charities Accounting Act; safeguarding behests and gifts made to various charities, and, in certain cases, permitting care of private trusts. The Hon. W. D. McPherson presented a Vital Statistics Act revising the existing law, bringing it into harmony with that of other Provinces and clarifying conditions of registration with more stringent regulations and penalties; Sir William Hearst carried measures extending the right of women to sit in the Legislature, to be appointed or elected to municipal office, and to farmers' wives and daughters to sit on School Boards. Amendments were made to the Workmen's Compensation Act (Mr. Lucas) increasing the allowance to widows from $20 to $30 a month, the children's allowance from $5.00 to $7.50, and the maximum to all dependents from $40 to $60—provided that the 55 per centage of average earnings would permit such payments; authorizing, also, the inclusion of persons engaged in clerical work in the benefits of the Act and arranging that the Government in future should meet the entire cost of medical attention. Mr. McGarry had a Bill authorizing the Government to raise money up to $10,000,000 upon the credit of the Province and to make such a loan free of Provincial taxation and Succession duties, with interest at 7 per cent.—the latter clauses being permissive and, it was hoped, not necessary.

The Premier carried a measure authorizing the inclusion in the Cabinet of a Labour representative as Minister of Labour and Mr. Macdiarmid a grant of $5,000,000 to aid in the improvement of public highways, and for the payment of grants, or expenditures for that purpose, as provided by the various Acts; Mr. Lucas carried a Bill by which defaulters under the M.S.A., and persons convicted of seditious or treasonable offences during the War, were disqualified from voting or holding public office in Ontario for a period of 10 years; Mr. McGarry amended the Legislative Assembly Act so as to provide the payment of a $5,000 salary to the Leader of the Opposition; the Highways Act was amended to increase the Government contribution towards the maintenance of County highways to the same basis as the rate for construction or 60 per cent. of the total outlay; the Motor Vehicles Act was amended to make the speed limit in cities, towns and villages 20 miles an hour and 25 miles in the country—a five mile an hour increase. The very important Educational legislation presented by Hon. Dr. Cody has been referred to in the Educational Section and under the terms of several Acts additional facilities for vocational and industrial training for girls and boys, beyond the stage of elementary instruction, were provided, consolidation of rural schools aided, attendance of all pupils in Elementary schools enforced, and increased grants given to rural and technical education.

Other legislation of the Session included the repeal of the Provincial War-Tax; permitted suspension of the manufacturing clause as to poplar pulp-wood and the exportation of that product; amended the Mining Act so that no male under 16 should be employed in or about a mine, or under 18, below ground in a mine, establishing an 8-hour day for underground workers with certain specified limitations and providing various improved regulations for safe-guarding the miner and his work; authorized the Hydro-Power Commission to establish a Superannuation or retiring allowance Fund for its employees and permitted it, with Government approval, "to enter into an agreement with the corporation of any municipality receiving power from the Commission, for including permanent employees of any Company established under The Public Utilities Act, or under this Act, for the management and control of works, for the distribution of electrical power or energy in the municipality, upon such terms as to the contribution by a municipal corporation and otherwise as may be deemed expedient"; amended the Provincial Highway Act so as to facilitate operations, protect construction, and allow the Government to enter into agreements with the Dominion Government under the pending Federal appropriations for Highway construction.

The Mortgage moraterium was renewed by statute amendment for another year; $500 was authorized to be paid to J. M. Delamere, Assistant Clerk of the Assembly, in acknowledgement of 50 years' service; Trustees were authorized to invest in Securities of the United Kingdom and the Dominion, the Provinces or Municipalities of Canada; the Marriage Act was amended to provide for the consent in writing of a parent or guardian of anyone under 18 years of age who was not a widow or widower.   An Act regulating the practice of Optometry created a Board of Examiners to grant certificates for Opticians, with registration rules and fees, and the provision of penalties for irregular or fraudulent sale of glasses; the Loan and Trust Corporation Act was amended in a variety of details and regulations; the Hydro-Electric Railway Act was amended to declare legal, valid and binding certain specified contracts as to Radial railways submitted to and approved by the respective municipalities, when finally passed by the Councils concerned—Port Credit and St. Catharines line and the Welland, Port Colborne, Bridgeburg By-laws; the Assessment and Municipal Acts were variously amended and that of the Municipal Franchise Act so as to give final control to the Ontario Railway Board over the franchise upon any highway within a radius of 5 miles of any city.

The establishment of Community Halls and Athletic Fields in rural districts was authorized and encouraged by a grant of $2,000 in each case; the Factory Act was amended to safeguard the employment of women and girls living in camp communities during the summer season; the Theatre Act was amended to give the Board of Censors absolute power "to permit or prohibit the exhibition of any film or slide in any theatre of Ontario" and power was taken to enforce the playing of the National Anthem at the conclusion of each performance in a theatre; the Fire Marshal's Act was amended to permit the appointment of a Deputy Fire Marshal with deputies, also, in specified Districts and to further safeguard communities from fire.   The Minister of Lands, Forests and Mines was authorized to create Private Forest Reserves subject to the consent of the owner and approval of the Government and another Act regulated the business of Fox-raising; the Teachers' Superannuation Act was amended in certain details and the affiliation of the Toronto Conservatory of Music with the University of Toronto was authorized while the Act relating to the College of Fine Arts was amended so as to re-organize its operation and government; the Public Institutions Act was amended to apply the word "Hospital" to Insane and other similar public institutions and an Act was approved regulating Industrial Refuges for females.

An Act respecting Natural Gas regulated the industry and its supply following upon the Report of an Advisory Board appointed by the Government to investigate the condition of this problem in Ontario which had reported in April and recommended that all natural gas in the Province be conserved and precautions be taken to prevent waste and misuse—allowing for a variation of treatment as between the gas fields of the east and west; that for the present the available supply of natural gas be allotted, so far as possible, for use in the homes; that diligent search for new gas areas and the tapping of the same should be wisely encouraged; that consideration be given to the adjustment of rates and the establishment of an equitable scale of prices proportionate to the cost of discovering, producing and selling this product.

Prohibition and Mr. McGarry's Budget.   The most-discussed legislation of the Session was that touching Prohibition.   The question itself ran all through the debates on the Address and even the Budget debate.   On Mch. 4th Lieut.-Col. H. A. C. Machin, an active Conservative opponent of the policy, dealt with the subject at length, and urged compensation to meet the confiscation of property involved in abolition of licenses; denounced what he described as improper interference with personal liberty in the enforcement of the Ontario Temperance Act; declared that this policy was making people hypocritical and insincere to a degree never equalled before; referred in picturesque style to Societies and persons whom he called "sin-hounds" and whose chief pleasure lay in "chasing sinners" through Legislative enactment and Government regulations.   On Mch. 7th Mr. McGarry announced in Toronto that: "A wide, open, Referendum on the Prohibition question will be taken in Ontario, possibly in September next, for the people to determine what measure they want. Whatever the verdict of the people may be, it will be upheld by the Government and they will be given every opportunity of expressing in the fullest possible manner their desires on this important question."   Successive caucuses of Government supporters followed and, on Apr. 8th, Sir William Hearst told the House that the questions submitted would be in the following form:

1. Are you in favour of the repeal of the Ontario Temperance Act?
2. Are you in favour of the sale of light beer containing not more than 2·51-100 per cent. alcohol weight measure through Government agencies, and amendments to the Ontario Temperance Act to permit such sale?
3. Are you in favour of the sale of light beer containing not more than 2·51-100 per cent. alcohol weight measure in standard hotels in local municipalities that by majority vote favour such sale, and amendments to the Ontario Temperance Act to permit such sale?
4. Are you in favour of the sale of spirituous and malt liquors through Government agencies, and amendments to the Ontario Temperance Act to permit such sale?

The Premier stated that in order to prevent confusion in determining the result every voter should vote on every question, or his ballot would be spoiled: "If the first question is answered in the affirmative, the Ontario Temperance Act will be repealed and the old license law just as it existed prior to 1916, will be revived. If question two is answered in the negative, nothing is required to be done, but if it is answered in the affirmative, the Government will be called upon to at once make provision for the sale of light beer through Government sales agencies. The same course will follow in regard to question three. If the majority vote is in the negative, no action is necessary. If the majority vote is in the affirmative, the Government will be called upon to at once make provision for sale of light beer in standard hotels. Again, with question four, should the affirmative carry, the Government will be called upon to make all necessary and proper regulations for the sale, through Government agencies, of liquor of all kinds for consumption in homes only."

Two Bills were presented—the first, the Temperance Referendum Act, 1919, as outlined, and the other consisting of amendments to the Temperance Act providing for the sale direct by the Government of all liquors that could lawfully be sold under the Act and involving abolition of the sale of liquor by private vendors; the whole machinery in this case would be in the hands of the Board of License Commissioners from whose Government stores all druggists would have to buy their restricted supplies and physicians their limit of 10 gallons. Liquor advertisements were prohibited and medical prescriptions regulated. Hon. Mr. McPherson piloted the latter Bill through the House, and the Premier was responsible for the Referendum measure. In his speech of Apr. 16th Sir William told the Legislature that he stood by the Temperance Act and believed Prohibition would be supported by the people: "This Act has lost my Government support; it has turned many warm personal and political friends of my own into enemies. It has brought me more abuse and criticism, ten times over, than all other political questions combined since I entered public life." Since Dec. 24th, 1917, the importation of liquor containing more than 2½ per cent. proof spirits had been absolutely prohibited by Dominion legislation, and its manufacture since Dec. 31st, 1918; he hoped this condition would continue. There was little expressed opposition to the measure; below the surface there was much opposition in the House and particularly in the Conservative ranks; the Bill finally passed its readings without division or amendment.

Mr. McGarry presented his Budget on Mch. 6th with the announcement of a surplus of $1,809,719 for the year ending Oct. 31st, 1918, which the Treasurer claimed to be the largest in Provincial history and with a statement that the property War tax of one mill on the dollar would be repealed. This Tax had given proceeds in 1915-18 of $8,000,000 and the total war expenditure of the Province in the same period had been $8,400,000 and to date $9,900,000. The ordinary Revenue for the year was $19,270,123 and Expenditure $17,460,404; the total revenue for the war period and for the Hearst Government, in 1914-18, was $64,356,792 with expenditures of $59,389,321. Since 1914, and apart from the War tax, the revenues had increased by over $6,000,000 and the ordinary expenditures by $4,700,000. Amongst the notable items of receipt in 1918 were $1,214,093 from motor licenses, $803,090 from Public institutions, $3,157,566 from Succession duties, while Lands, Forests and Mines realized $2,964,161, Corporations Tax, etc., $1,523,234, and Interest from the Hydro-Commission, $1,412,604. Increased expenditures included $260,000 additional upon Education, $201,000 upon Public institutions, $156,000 upon Agriculture, $270,000 upon Game and Fisheries. In Capital account the expendi-

tures for 1918 totalled $12,442,203 of which the chief items were
$8,569,951 upon the Hydro-electric system, $642,000 upon improved
Highways, $645,000 upon Northern Ontario development, $228,000
upon T. and N.O. Railway, $682,000 upon Buildings and Drainage.
During the year $15,725,000 had been borrowed at from 5½ to
6½ per cent. and the gross Public Debt stood at $75,645,917 on
Oct. 31st, 1918; against this stood Assets of $22,000,000 represent-
ing the T. and N.O. Railway, $36,018,000 representing the Hydro-
Electric system, and minor items totalling $71,000,000—inclusive
of a cash balance in Banks of $5,195,244. Indirect Assets included
$22,000,000 invested in Public buildings with Natural resources
estimated at $503,000,000; indirect Liabilities included guarantees
totalling $19,120,269.

The estimated Receipts for 1919 were $18,408,428 and Expendi-
tures $14,980,406 exclusive of statutory and capital expenditure.
On Oct. 31st, 1919, when the Government was leaving office the
cash balance in the Banks was $7,603,110. C. M. Bowman,
for the Opposition, on Mch. 11th turned the Surplus into a
deficit: "In order to arrive at a true statement of the actual
results of this year's business, according to the manner in which
the Financial statements were prepared under the Liberal administration and by Colonel Matheson, for some few years after he
became Provincial Treasurer, I add to the Expenditures that on
additions to Public buildings, $475,146, also the amount expended
on Northern Ontario development of $645,446, and that on High-
way improvement of $642,208—making a total, for what I claim is
current expenditure, of $20,814,612 as against $19,270,123, or a
deficit of $1,544,488." As to Northern Ontario Mr. Bowman was
very critical: "The policy that has been pursued there has since
1912 been a wasteful and improvident one and, as time goes on, one
that will prove not in the best interests of the North country.
Out of a total of $5,000,000 expended up to the present time, over
$4,000,000 appears to have been spent upon roads exclusively.
Miles and miles have been built where there are no settlers and
where there will not be any for many years."

Opposition Policy and Government Appointments. During the
Session William Proudfoot, K.C., was Leader of the Liberal Opposition and, to a great degree, abrogated the tacit war-time
understanding between Government and Opposition; H. Hartley Dewart, K.C., his energetic lieutenant, did all he could to make
the fighting lively and issues clear for the coming Elections. Mr.
Dewart attacked the License administration at every opportunity
and was keen in his criticism of Unionist Liberals and Hon. N.
W. Rowell; on Mch. 5th he declared that "the Premier of Ontario
and Mr. Rowell went over the top together, and I venture to pre-
dict that they will go to the bottom together"; he precipitated the
first division of the Session on Mch. 5th on the Ontario Election
Act. On Mch. 20th Mr. Dewart attacked License Inspector, Rev.
J. A. Ayearst, and indirectly charged the Attorney General (Mr.

Lucas) with condoning alleged offences in what was called the Homer case: "If Mr. Ayearst is examined before a Committee of the House he will have to admit that he has profited by the earnings of private detectives and that while they were in the pay and employ of a private detective Agency, doing other work, they were retained and employed by him and in the pay of the Department, while he, Mr. Ayearst, received a portion of the earnings of these men." Chief Justice Sir William Meredith was at once appointed a Royal Commissioner to investigate the charges and Mr. Ayearst was suspended from his duties; a little later the Chief Justice announced his decision exonerating, Mr. Ayearst and the Department and the Inspector at once resumed his position. Mr. Dewart (Mch. 20) had also moved that the accounts of the License Board in the Provincial Secretary's Department, between 1913 and 1918, be investigated by a Special Committee but this was defeated by 54 to 15.

As to Opposition policy, in general, during the Budget debate (Mch. 20th) J. C. Elliott and J. A. Pinard (Liberals) moved that the House disapprove of (1) the Treasurer's statement as not fairly setting forth the real character of the Government's financial transactions; (2) the alleged extravagant and wasteful expenditure of public money by the Government, as illustrated by the annual expenditure on Government House when important public services such as Education, Agriculture and Roads were in great need of further funds; (3) the stated concealment of specific and important items of current receipts in respect of Departments under the heading of "Casual Revenue"; (4) the treatment of receipts from the disposal of Capital assets, such as timber, as current receipts, while at the same time treating the payments as on Capital account; (5) the alleged exorbitant cost of Civil Government.

A motion was presented on Apr. 2nd by Mr. Dewart and G. C. Hurdman which declared that: "In the opinion of the House it will be more in keeping with the dignity of the proceedings in the Assembly and with the democratic spirit of our Institutions if the ceremonies at the opening of the Legislature are made less formal in their character and, having regard to the establishment of women upon a basis of Electoral and Legislative equality with men, that the same Regulations as to dress at the opening of the House shall apply to both sexes." A Government amendment was carried, on division, eliminating these references to dress, etc., and congratulating the women of the Province on their splendid sacrifices and services during the War. On Apr. 3rd William McDonald and S. Carter moved, but afterwards withdrew, a Resolution declaring that the representation of the people in the Legislature was "too large, unwieldy and expensive" and asking a reduction to the figure of Ontario representation at Ottawa (82).

T. R. Atkinson and H. Munro moved on Apr. 9th that Reconstruction meant the bettering of general conditions and urged the Government to pass remedial legislation providing for such matters as "a fair wage, fair prices for the products of the farm, encouraging men to go back to the land, pensions for widows with dependent children, the suppression of feeble-mindedness and social diseases." A Government amendment re-capitulated at great length the policy of the Government in recent years, and its programme of accomplished effort, which was carried "on division." Messrs. Proudfoot and Elliott proposed on Apr. 16th that legislation be passed providing for election to the Legislative and Municipal Councils by "a form of Preferential Voting" but, after discussion, the motion was withdrawn; Messrs. F. W. Hay and Dewart also moved an expression of regret that partisan appointments to the Civil Service were still being made and asking for a revision and increase of salaries to the Government officials but it was defeated on division. The Opposition also opposed an increase in the speed time-limit for automobiles.

A Government motion accepted the Insurance Report of Judge Masten and appointed a Committee to consider his proposed amendments to the Insurance law; an afterwards withdrawn motion by Lieut.-Colonels W. H. Price and A. C. Pratt, Conservatives, proposed on Apr. 17th "to memorialize the Government of Canada to institute and have tabulated the profits made during the War by all public contractors on munitions and war supplies with a view to having paid into the Treasury of the Dominion all profits in excess of a fair percentage on invested capital." Incidents of the Session included a Deputation of United Farmers said to represent 10,000 U.F.O. members, which waited upon the Government on Apr. 8th and stated that the proposed Provincial Highway would not be for the benefit of the people but rather for the motor interests; E. C. Drury explained that the financial situation was serious and economy vital, that their objection was not to good roads but to "pleasure roads" or roads run parallel to existing railway lines; the Resolution presented declared that the Highway would not help production in any manner commensurate with its cost or as well as would lines radiating from market centres.

With the Elections in sight and current dissatisfaction with the Prohibition Referendum privately expressed in rumours and varied forms, a Resolution of the Conservative caucus was made public on Mch. 20th which extended congratulations and expressed loyalty to Sir William Hearst "for the eminently able, conscientious and worthy discharge of the onerous duties devolving upon him since his elevation to the office of Prime Minister and, particularly, for his War policies and War work, which have rebounded to the credit of this great Province." In respect to attacks upon Government House Hon. Mr. Macdiarmid pointed out on Apr. 16th that while it had cost $1,098,000 to construct and complete only $238,000 of that amount was paid out of capital expenditure because $860,000 had been realized from the sale of the old Government House property. It was stated on Apr. 3rd that the much-discussed Toronto -Hamilton Highway had cost to Jan. 31st, 1919, $1,088,717, exclusive of the extra cost of widening roadways, storm sewers, etc., which were to be paid by the Radial railway and local municipalities. The House was prorogued on Apr. 24th, with a review of its important legislation, by the Lieutenant-Governor.

The chief Government appointments of the year outside of the change of Government was that of a new Lieutenant-Governor. Sir John Hendrie had retired after serving his 4-year term beginning in October, 1914. He was the first occupant of the new Government House of the Province and had officially entertained the Duke and Duchess of Connaught, the Duke and Duchess of Devonshire, Prince Arthur of Connaught, Theodore Roosevelt and J. H. Choate, Sir Cecil Spring-Rice and others. On Nov. 27th Lionel Herbert Clarke, Chairman of the Toronto Harbour Commission, ex-President of the Board of Trade, member of the Niagara Falls Park Commission, and a public-spirited and well-known business man of Toronto, was appointed to the post and sworn in on Dec. 1st. At this time the Toronto *Star* was conducting a vigourous campaign for the abolition of Government House as an institution; the new Government claimed that the funds received from the sale of the old Government House property were not ear-marked for the purpose of building, or for the upkeep of a Government House, but that the property on which the new Buildings were erected was covered by a stringent covenant restricting the use of the property during 20 years from the date of the purchase in 1909 from other than residential purposes. Official appointments of the year were as follows:

Police Magistrate	J. T. Bridgewater	Dresden
Police Magistrate	I. F. McKinnon	Waterford
Police Magistrate	D. J. Corrigall, D.S.O., M.C.	Port Colborne
Judge of the Juvenile Court	W. P. Archibald	Ottawa
Surrogate Judge County of Wellington	Louis M. Hays	Guelph
Surrogate Judge County of Prince Edward	E. H. McLean	Picton
Surrogate Judge County of Grey	C. F. Sutherland	Owen Sound
Surrogate Judge County of Waterloo	E. J. Hearn	Kitchener
Surrogate Judge County of York	Emerson Coatsworth	Toronto
Sheriff of Simcoe	D. H. MacLaren	Barrie
Ontario Parole Officer	Maj. The Rev. A. R. Lavelle	Brantford
Registrar of Deeds	D. H. McElroy	Carp
Registrar of Deeds	Charles C. Platt	Gore Bay
Juvenile Court Judge	H. S. Mott	Toronto
Chief Coroner of Hamilton	Dr. George S. Rennie, C.M.G.	Hamilton
Division Court Clerk	C. A. Wilson	Campbellford
Division Court Clerk	H. L. Fawthrop	Cornwall
Division Court Clerk	Charles M. R. Graham	London
Deputy Attorney General	Edward Bayly, K.C.	Toronto
County Crown Attorney, Prescott and Russell	Louis Coté	Ottawa
County Crown Attorney, Lanark	J. M. Balderson, K.C.	Perth
Assistant Director, Industrial and Technical Education	Justus C. Miller, LL.D.	Toronto
Director of Training, Education Department	Dr. Sydney Morgan	Hamilton
Governor of Provincial Gaol	Major George H. Basher	Toronto

General Elections in Ontario: Defeat of the Hearst Government. Throughout the first half of the year the coming Elections were discussed as a certainty and the possible allignment of parties viewed with much interest. It was generally believed that, despite the steady growth of the Farmers' movement and the underground note of dissatisfaction in Conservative ranks with the Prohibition policy, the Government would have a major-

ity; the Liberals were hopeful and more aggressive than for years
past.   During this period Sir William Hearst, as Prime Minister,
received many Delegations and made various announcements of
policy in his replies or in other public speeches.   A large deputation from Northern Ontario, on Feb. 28th, representing the mining
and lumber interests of the North, urged the extension of the T.
and N.O. Railway to James Bay, the construction of branch lines
to Gowganda and Kirkland Lake and the building of trunk roads
through partly developed areas.   Careful and immediate investigation by a special expedition into the region was promised.   A
Labour delegation on Mch. 18th asked co-operation in meeting current conditions of unemployment and were promised a speeding up
of public works; on June 6th the Premier told a similar deputation
that he thought the Provincial Government had no authority to
pass laws providing for a 44-hour week and collective bargaining.

The Government Policy in the Campaign.   Speaking at Eugenia
Falls on June 26th, Sir William declared that two principles had
guided him in his Administration—one was to maintain and uphold
the traditions of the administration of Sir James Whitney, and
the other was to increase the fighting strength of the Province
during the War.   As to Prohibition, Provincial legislation had
closed the bars and the liquor shops in order to increase war-time
efficiency, but it was the Dominion Order-in-Council that had
brought about complete Prohibition so that the Provincial Government was entitled neither to credit nor to blame in that respect.   In
an agricultural connection he stated that the total value of the
field crops of Ontario during the 4 years of War was $398,779,646
more than the value during the previous 4 years.   He urged the
Farmers not to go in for political action but to use their influence
through existing parties; he warned them not to allow their organizations to be turned into "*camouflaged* Liberal clubs."   He eulogized Public ownership of Utilities and the Hydro-electric enterprise: "This policy, under the chairmanship of Sir Adam Beck,
has saved millions of dollars, prevented collapse of our industries
during the War and helped to prevent distress and suffering during the fuel shortage."

At Queenston, on July 30th, the Premier said, as to the Ontario
Temperance Act, that he knew of no other Provincial measure
which had "so increased the efficiency of our people, conserved our
national strength, aided thrift, and generally contributed to our
fighting power" as this; in denying Mr. Dewart's charges of a
"deal" with Mr. Rowell and the Unionists through Mr. Proudfoot,
he declared that he had never had any understanding or agreement
with Mr. Rowell, politically, in any way, shape or form.   He quoted
an extract from a biography of H. H. Dewart in Morgan's *Canadian Men and Women of the Times* (1912) which said: "As a
young man was a strong advocate of Canadian Independence and
is still pronouncedly in favour of it," and proclaimed the Conservative policy to be the antithesis of this view.   The Premier

spoke at Mitchell on July 31st, at Stratford on Aug. 1st, at
Marmora on Aug. 20th, at Brantford on Aug. 24th.   Here he
dealt with current criticism of the O.T.A.: "I stood by it in its
inception, and I will stand by it until its fate is decided.   I believe
it has accomplished much good for the people and for the Province.   It increased our economic strength, increased our efficiency,
and generally added to the fighting strength of the Province in
wartime.   It has proven beneficial in both days of turmoil and
reconstruction."

Sir William was at Brampton on the 29th and on Sept. 9th announced that the Referendum would be taken on Oct. 20th; on
Sept. 20th the Central Conservative Association of Toronto passed
a Resolution of confidence in the Administration of Sir William
Hearst: "Called to office at the most critical period in the history
of Canada and faced with unprecedented problems arising out of
the War, he met every issue with courage and determination.
. . . We pledge ourselves to give our united, enthusiastic and
active support to the Hearst Government."   On the 23rd, dissolution was announced with writs returnable on Oct. 20th and nominations one week earlier.   At the same time Brig.-Gen. A. E. Ross
was taken into the Cabinet and the Prime Minister issued a Manifesto declaring that the Elections were called on the day of the
Referendum in order to elicit the largest possible vote on both
issues; to avoid unnecessary expenditure and disturbance of business; and to enable the people to exercise their constitutional
rights and powers at the earliest possible opportunity.

This document was an earnest appeal to the Electors to support the Government on its War record and war expenditure of
nearly $10,000,000; its non-partisan administration of affairs and
support of Hydro-electric power and the Radial railway policy of
Sir Adam Beck; its encouragement of Agriculture with appropriations increasing to $1,675,235 in 1919 and its good roads and
Provincial highway policy; its Workmen's Compensation Act
which had realized for the workmen $9,500,000 to date and for
pensions and medical services was netting them $12,819 daily; its
Northern Ontario policy of new roads and bridges, money advances
to settlers, supplies of seed and live-stock, establishment of creameries and industries, provision of fire protection and improved mining laws; its Educational policy, with current appropriations of
nearly $4,000,000 or one million in excess of 1914, establishment of
a Pension fund for Teachers, encouragement of rural schools and
of agricultural, technical and vocational education, and maintenance of low school-book prices; the work of its Soldiers' Aid Commission.   As to the future Sir William summarized the Government's policy as follows:

The greatest possible assistance to Agriculture in every shape and form
and the faithful enforcement of the people's verdict on the Liquor question.

Vigourous support of Hydro-Electric development and cheap light and
power for our farmers.

Conversion of certain railway lines into Hydro-Electric lines with good roads reaching every part of Ontario.

A Pension Fund for mothers and direct representation of Labour in the Cabinet.

Establishment of a Minimum wage and unification of the Labour laws of Canada on a just and equitable basis.

Such further labour legislation within Provincial jurisdiction as may arise out of the findings of the National Industrial Conference and the International Labour Conference.

Housing accommodation for industrial workers and special consideration to returned soldiers, with Cabinet representation.

A new era for Education with provision of technical and agricultural instruction throughout the Province.

Improvement of transportation facilities in Northern Ontario and conservation of our timber resources, and encouragement to mining.

Measures to reduce the high cost of living and protection of the public health, generous assistance to hospitals and charities, and special care of mental defectives.

Only a brief reference was made to the Ontario Temperance Act: "We pledged ourselves when our soldiers returned to submit the question of the continuance of this law to the judgment of the whole people. This we are now doing. The Government undertakes to carry out the will of the people as expressed in the ballot box, and to do this faithfully, impartially, and fearlessly." During the ensuing campaign stress was laid upon the Government's war record with certain basic facts stated. Ontario gave in men 232,895; in contributions $54,532,188; to Victory Loans $540,465,-550; it provided 50 per cent. of Canada's war effort. The Ontario Government was said to have spent in war work over $10,000,000; maintained in England the most efficient military hospital in Europe; furnished club houses for the soldiers in London and Paris; made gifts of food and guns to the Mother Country; made large grants to the British Red Cross, Belgium, Serbian relief and other worthy patriotic objects. Temperance legislation and administration, Financial policy and progress, Labour legislation and assistance to Agriculture were the other points upon which stress was laid.

Speaking at Sarnia on Oct. 4th the Premier dealt with the alliance in many ridings between Farmer and Labour candidates: "I do not believe in class legislation—not even for the farmers. At the same time, I am a champion of co-operation, of the joint activity of capital, labour, and agriculture. If the farmers seriously enter politics as an independent party, it will prove fatal to themselves and will be demoralizing to the whole structure of government. It would be just as bad for Labour, for you cannot get away from the fact that the people of Ontario want legislation for the whole and not for any one class." He also spoke at Watford on the 4th, at Cobourg and Bowmanville on the 7th, at Brockville on the 8th, at Belleville on the 11th, at Ottawa on the 13th. The nominations on this date showed 105 Conservative candidates, 69 Liberals, 70 United Farmers and 22 Labourites in the field with Hon. Dr. H. J. Cody in North-East Toronto, Brig.-Gen. the Hon. A. E. Ross in

Kingston, W. D. Black in Addington and J. R. Cooke in North Hastings elected by acclamation on the Government side. Sir William afterwards spoke at Chatham on Oct. 14th, at Strathroy and Guelph on the 15th and at his home town of Sault Ste. Marie on the 17th.

Incidents of the campaign were the confidence in the result felt by Sir William Hearst, personally, and his belief that gains from the Temperance forces would more than balance any defections in his own party; the comparative lack of organized campaigning by individual Ministers and their devotion to work in their own ridings with the dropping out of many old-time Conservative members of the House—about two dozen—in favour of farmer candidates, or by defection in party support, or from doubt as to the result; the publication of a letter by E. C. Whitney, brother of the late Premier, urging the return of the Government and describing Prohibition as a wise policy; the vigourous support of the Government by the *Orange Sentinel* on Oct. 16th; the limited part taken either in Province or his own constituency by Sir Adam Beck and the energetic work done in London by the opposing and popular Liberal-Labour candidate, Dr. H. A. Stevenson. On Oct. 16th Sir Adam spoke in London and stated that he was running as an Independent: "I do not object to the Government having a control of the Hydro enterprise, but I object to its becoming a Government department; only as an Independent can I look after the interests of Hydro-Electric Power for the people of the Province in the most efficient manner." Lieut.-Col. A. C. Pratt, M.L.A. (Cons.), vigourously attacked the Government with unproven allegations as to lack of economy at Orpington Hospital in England and with the demand, expressed on Aug. 11th, for an Ontario Conservative Convention to select a new leader; Lieut.-Col. H. A. C. Machin, M.L.A. (Cons.), endorsed this policy and took a strong anti-Prohibition position while Colonel Pratt claimed that 27 members in the Legislature privately opposed the present Leader's Prohibition policy. The Convention idea was also supported by John Allan, M.L.A. for West Hamilton, with the statement of Hon. T. W. McGarry at Marmora on Aug. 20th that: "The Government will continue as it is now with its present leader until we decide to go to the people, and further, there never was a time in a Government which was carrying on the affairs of the country with a majority, when it was necessary to call a Convention."

The Liberal Policy in the Campaign. During the 1919 Session of the Legislature there had been much dissatisfaction with the attitude of William Proudfoot, House leader of the Liberals; his support of the Government's War policy during the War may have been all right but many of his followers did not want it continued in any respect; H. H. Dewart, in particular, was aggressive in his attitude and hostile to the support given by Mr. Proudfoot to Unionism at Ottawa. On June 26th a Liberal Convention was held in Toronto to map out the policy for the coming Elections and to elect a permanent Party leader.   C. M. Bowman, M.L.A., presided and D. D. McKenzie, M.P., was present and spoke, as did W. T. R. Preston; the chief candidates for Leader were Mr. Proudfoot and Mr. Dewart; Major the Rev. J. C. Tolmie and J. C. Elliott; Mr. Proudfoot received 23 votes on the first ballot, Major Tolmie 97, Mr. Elliott 37, Thomas McMillan of Seaforth 8, and Mr. Dewart 147—on the second one H. H. Dewart was elected by 158 to 121 for Major Tolmie and 24 for Mr. Elliott and the choice made unanimous.   Mr. Proudfoot had, meanwhile, retired.   The Liberal press was not as cordial as it might have been.   *The Globe* of June 27th deprecated the selection as "a handicap to the cause of Temperance" and the *Christian Guardian,* organ of Methodism, on July 2nd declared that Mr. Dewart was "regarded generally as the chief representative of the liquor interests in the Ontario Legislature." The London *Advertiser* approved the choice with enthusiasm.   The Toronto *Star* was hostile to Mr. Dewart on the Temperance issue. Personally, Mr. Dewart was a man of ability, a strong Liberal and devoted follower of Sir Wilfrid Laurier.   A large number of lengthy Resolutions were passed at the Convention and may be summarized as follows:

1. Declaring in favour of progressive Temperance legislation to the fullest extent of the Provincial jurisdiction, and pledging all necessary steps to vigourously and effectively carry into effect the will of the majority of the people.

2. Favouring amendment of the B.N.A. Act to abolish the Senate.

3. Urging the importance of Labour questions, favouring the creation of a Labour Department and appointment by the Government of a Provincial Industrial Council consisting of an equal number of employees and employers, men and women, together with a Chairman appointed by the Government, to consider and report on the causes of the present unrest and the steps necessary to safeguard and promote the best interests of employees, employers and the State.

4. Protesting against the Patronage system, suggesting the creation of a non-partisan Civil Service Commission and the purchase of all supplies by Competitive open tender.

5. Objecting to the present system of levying taxes on improvements and urging local option for municipalities to assess and tax improvements, including buildings, business and income, on a lower basis than land.

6. Advocating immediate Labour legislation to include a general Minimum wage for both men and women applicable to all industry throughout the Province; the appointment of a permanent Cost of Living Commission to keep minimum wages and prices upon the level of a respectable livelihood; an 8-hour day for all industrial occupations and for both men and women; better inspection of factories and recognition of Collective bargaining; Insurance against sickness and unemployment, based on the principles of English law; abolition of imprisonment for debt; the increase of the exemption of married men's wages from attachment from $25.00 to $40.00; the revision of the list of articles exempt from seizure for debt, so as to leave secure the actual necessities of home life; Mother's pensions to be administered by the Department of Labour, with power to provide medical attendance and necessaries whenever required and amendment of the Dower Act so as to ensure to every married woman a fair and adequate share of her husband's estate.

7. Condemning the Government for not dealing with the High Cost of Living and for failure in the investigation and prosecution of illegal combines.

8. Declaring for Government control and regulation of cold storage plants, abattoirs and stock-yards.

9. Condemning and urging repeal of the Ontario Election Act amendments "whereby partisan enumerators are appointed to prepare Provincial voters' lists at large and unnecessary expense."

10. Denouncing "the wasteful and extravagant manner in which the millions of dollars designed to open up Northern Ontario are being spent, the miles of roads built where there is no settlement and the neglect of sections where actual settlement is going on"; declaring that these moneys should be handed over to the elected officers of the municipality instead of being expended under the patronage of the local member or defeated candidate; stating that this Northern country, under capable administraiton, would have an enormous development.

11. Advocating for the North country an aggressive policy of expansion and a strong propaganda for immigration and settlement; a "development of the water-powers in unorganized areas by the Province without municipal guarantees"; construction of a chain of fish hatcheries on the inland lakes and provision of adequate transportation facilities to operated mines in remote districts and the testing of new areas by diamond drilling; encouragement of prospecting and help in proving discoveries and conservation of Nickel products for the service of the Province and Empire; a graded mining tax consistent with value of the output and profit realized.

12. Promising, if elected, to begin at once the clearing of timber off suitable farming land in New Ontario; the employment for this work and all other incidental work of only those men who had served their country overseas in the recent War; to open roads, build narrow gage railways, settle communities, open schools, etc., all on the basis of the above system of employment; to encourage men when they had completed their service of one, two or three years, under the Government system, to settle in the country so reclaimed and engage either in trade, manufacture or farming.

13. Declaring for a form of preferential voting which would result in Proportional Representation.

14. Favouring for the returned soldier adequate pensions for the wounded and for the dependents of soldiers and sailors who had been killed; equal pension for equal disability; a Minimum pension of $10 per month; insurance for the enfeebled; provision for settlement of soldiers on land in Old Ontario when desired; promotion of vocational training and preference in all official appointments.

15. Approving the work of the Consumers' Leagues.

16. Declaring for the reservation of all water-powers within the jurisdiction of the Government of Ontario for development; the construction of a system of Hydro-Radial Railways throughout the Province "wherever conditions warrant expectation of successful operation"; the elimination of private monopoly of the Telephone service in the chief centres of population and over wide areas of rural Ontario and the creation, ultimately, of a Provincial Telephone service; refusal to confer franchises hereafter upon private corporations for railway power, lighting, heating, telephone or other services requiring for their successful operation the use of the highways, or which came into competition with similar services owned and operated by public authorities.

17. Approving a system of rural credits for farmers with long-term money at low interest; agricultural schools with demonstration farms to continue education of Public school children; urging a spirit of co-operation between producer and consumer.

18. Favouring Pensions to widowed mothers with dependent children; assistance to unfortunate and destitute women with children; payment by the State of a wage to prisoners to be used for support of wife and dependent children; steps to check infant mortality and care for feeble-minded with a law to prevent marriage of persons having hereditary disease.

19. Supporting Proportional Representation and urging a system of reforestation of waste lands and abandoned areas.

20. Urging a radical change in the school system with a "restoration of simplicity and efficiency in the courses of study" and abolition of all non-essentials; reduction in burden of home-work, larger salaries to teachers and a more adequate Pension allotment; adequate teaching of Agriculture and restriction of the powers of the Educational Department to make changes in the system without Legislative authority.

21. Supporting the immediate and vigourous prosecution of the County Roads system with increased grants for construction and maintenance; with Provincial grants, also, for Township roads and a holding up of the Provincial Highway scheme for further Legislative consideration.

Following this Convention Mr. Hartley Dewart showed energy in pressing his Party's claims and campaign; in the Legislature he was insistent in enquiry, criticism and controversy with the Government; in Toronto, on July 10, he denounced the suggestion to take the Referendum and electoral votes on the same day and keenly criticized the method of preparing voters' lists; at Weston on July 11th he denounced the *Christian Guardian* for alleged misrepresentation and Sir William Meredith for his judgment in the recent Ayearst investigation; he freely and frequently criticized Hon. N. W. Rowell and in turn was arraigned by the Minister in a letter published on July 14th as having led, in co-operation with Mr. Murphy, "all the diverse elements of our population in Ontario hostile to Union Government and to Canada's war policy" and as being "a rising hope of the organized Liquor traffic"; he answered this in a biting speech at Walkerton on July 15th and declared that both Liberal and democratic principles had "suffered much at Mr. Rowell's hands." Mr. Dewart had been at Formosa on the 15th and he spoke at Russell on Aug. 4th; on the 5th he was at East-view, Ottawa, and received a rousing reception at the Dominion Liberal Convention a little later.

He spoke at Chatham on Aug. 16th, in Toronto on the 18th, at Ailsa Craig on the 20th and London on the 22nd—where he dealt at length with the old charge of Nickel being permitted to get out of the country to the United States and thence to Germany; he was at Fergus on the 28th and on Sept. 3rd was elected Hon. Vice-President of a new Provincial Liberal organization of which Mr. Mackenzie King was Hon. President and A. C. Hardy, of Brock-ville, President. At Lanark on Sept. 6th he declared all the United Farmer planks to be already in the Liberal platform and placed the Liberal party on record as favouring Prohibition and determined that the will of the people be carried out; he was in Toronto again on the 9th, at Bracebridge on the 10th, Elmsdale on the 11th, Paris on the 15th, Kingsville on the 16th, Durham on the 18th and Newmarket on the 20th. This covered more than 20 ridings and he was at Whitby on the 29th and other places and in Toronto, again, on Oct. 7th, at Pembroke and Almonte on the 9th, Picton on the 11th, Galt on the 12th, Brampton on the 14th; he was at Massey Hall in Toronto on the 15th.

Incidents of the Liberal campaign included the candidacy of William Proudfoot in Centre Huron as an Independent. He issued a statement defending his support of Union Government and

added: "I was also censured because I voted for the extension of
the life of the Legislature. I so voted because I did not think
that it was in the best interests of the country to bring on an Election during the War. Before taking this matter up in the House
I had a gathering of the Liberal Opposition, and was, by their
unanimous vote, directed as to the action to pursue." J. C. Elliott,
after 11 years in the Legislature dropped out in West Middlesex
and 5 other Liberal members followed his course; the Toronto *Globe*,
while not supporting Mr. Dewart, personally, urged in successive
editorials a varied criticism of the Hearst Government; the Toronto *World* (Cons.) while nominally supporting the Government
gave continuous space to, and approval of, the allegations regarding Nickel and the Germans and thus aided Mr. Dewart's insistence
upon this issue; the latter's charge that the License Board had supplied wine to the Jews of Toronto for festival purposes created a
sensation but was met by the statement that this Vishnick, as it
was called, was obtained for sacramental purposes.

The Farmers and the Campaign. The United Farmers of Ontario proved the possession of surprising strength in the Elections;
they worried the old Parties, hampered their nominations, per-
plexed their leaders and confused the issues. In the old Legislature there were 17 farmers belonging to either one or other of the
two old parties; in the field during this contest 68 official members
of the U.F.O. were candidates. Of the leaders, R. H. Halbert, the
President, had run in North Ontario for the Commons, R. W. E.
Burnaby and E. C. Drury were not candidates, J. J. Morrison, the
Secretary, devoted himself to what proved a most efficient organization of the Province, W. C. Good spoke at various points. Mr.
Drury took an active part as Vice-President of the U.F.O. and
dealt largely with economic problems. At a Toronto meeting on
Mch. 6th, when the Elections were still in the offing, he stated that:
"We are determined—and we are going to get it—to have economic
freedom, and we are going to get rid of the Tariff that has allowed
one class of exploiters to plunder the public on watered stock."
Upon another point he was explicit and declared that Farmers
were frankly hostile to concrete Provincial highways because they
regarded them as needless burdens of expense, created, primarily,
to provide speedways for automobiles, through the Province. He
stated that the interests of the farmer in the country and the
workingman in the city, were so nearly similar that there ought to
be ground for co-operation in changing the existent party rule.

Speaking at Fenelon Falls on June 26th Mr. Drury declared
that: "The U.F.O. and the farm organizations of the West are in
politics to the limit. These organizations have been forced into
this position and there will be no turning back. We are not only
in politics but we have the only really constructive political policy
now before the country—free trade with Britain in five years, free
trade with the United States to the extent provided for by the old
Reciprocity treaty and further free trade with the United States

in all lines the Americans are ready for free exchange with us."
There could, he added, be no amalgamation with "the defunct
Liberal party"; the U.F.O. also stood, "unequivocally, for prohibition of the manufacture, importation and sale of intoxicating
liquor." At Barrie 'on Sept. 20th he stated that Labour was making a mistake in trying to get an arbitrary 8-hour day: "Even
present conditions in towns are drawing men from the country.
How could farmers who are compelled sometimes to work 18 hours
a day be expected to help the 8-hour movement?"

Mr. Morrison spoke frequently during the year. He outlined a
specific line of thought at Mount Albert on Feb. 5, preparatory to
the coming contest: "There was a time when the Province of Ontario
did not have any big Debt hanging over it and I want to point out
to you that 75 per cent. of the representatives in the Legislature,
then, were farmers. As time went by, the reins of power slipped
from the farmers and went into the hands of other people, who were
more used to spending money." At Walkerton on July 31st he
was enthusiastic: "This is a day of action. We are setting out to
revolutionize the politics of this country. I don't care if we
don't win an election; we will build up a strong organization,
which will eventually rule this country." Here he outlined an
argument used everywhere by U.F.O. candidates in the campaign
and applied locally to different Counties: "Where are the girls
and boys who should be here? Gone to the city! Under the policy
pursued by the old parties the concession lines and side-roads have
been bled white, and the smaller urban centres have lost ground,
while the larger centres have been made greater. Only 30 per
cent. of the population of the whole Province is made up of food
producers and these have to feed not only themselves but the other
70 per cent. as well. The high cost of living is a direct result of
this upsetting of the balance in population."

At Listowel, and Barrie, and Prescott, and Fergus, and many
other places he spoke and on Sept. 27th issued a statement replying
to the charge of *The Globe,* that many Conservatives were not being opposed by the U.F.O., with proofs that most of the specified
ridings were urban: "The U.F.O. has been absolutely impartial as
between the two old parties. It has placed candidates in the field
in practically every constituency where, in the judgment of the
farmers of that constituency, the proportion of rural to urban
population indicated they should be represented by the farmer.
There are 68 constituencies of this class and it is expected that
there will be at least 66 U.F.O. candidates in the field." The
policy of opposition to both parties was vehemently urged by Mr.
Halbert and upon several occasions he handled the matter without
gloves. At Erin on July 28th he said: "I regret that some members of the U.F.O. have accepted party nominations. There is
nothing in our constitution to prevent acceptance by a member of
the U.F.O., of such nomination, but a man cannot ride two horses
at the same time and I, for one, am prepared to see that he gets off
one, and gets off quick."

THE HON. ERNEST CHARLES DRURY, M.L.A.
Appointed Prime Minister of Ontario in 1919

Manning W. Doherty and R. W. E. Burnaby made some important speeches during the campaign and the *Farmers' Sun*, which, on Apr. 2nd, became the recognized organ and property of the U.F.O., argued for its platform with ability. It took ground against Socialism and declared on Sept. 10th that: "The platform adopted by Mr. Dewart's Convention contains a complete statement of the Socialistic programme, the enactment of which would ruin the country and reduce the farmers to a distress which they have not yet experienced." In its columns appeared pages of statistics showing the rural decline in population to prove the contention (Oct. 8th) that "urban centres and the Big Interests have, by means of legislation, been placed in a position to attract population from the land." To do this Railway builders had been subsidized, Steel and other interests "fattened on bounties," Manufacturers enriched by the Tariff. The increase in Provincial expenditure from $5,267,453 in 1904 to $24,334,000 in 1918 was freely denounced together with corresponding increases in the cost of Civil Government, the increase in Ministerial salaries ($31,000 to $60,000) and the costs of Departments. On Aug. 13th the Provincial Platform of the U.F.O. was published, as elsewhere recorded.*

The Labour Party in the Campaign. The unrest everywhere prevalent in the early part of this year showed itself in the effort of Ontario Labour to organize along political lines. There were, at the beginning of the year, an Independent Labour Party in Ontario and an Ontario Section of the Canadian Labour Party which claimed to have about 10,000 members. There was, also, the Ontario Labour Educational Association and its organ, *The Industrial Banner*, of which, later on, James Simpson, became Editor. Mixed in with these organizations were many Socialists and this school of thought dominated a great many of the principles advocated. The policy of the I.L.P. was published in *The Industrial Banner* of Jan. 31st, 1919, as follows:

Free and compulsory education—Free education in all institutions supported by the Government and free text-books.

The Public Ownership of all public utilities and natural sources of wealth.

Nationalization of Banking and credit systems.

Direct legislation through the Initiative, Referendum and Recall.

Gradual elimination of unearned increment through increasing taxation.

Equal pay for equal work and abolition of property qualifications for all municipal offices.

Abolition of all election deposits and Proportional Representation with grouped constituencies; Abolition of the Canadian Senate.

No Court to be legally competent to declare as Unconstitutional any Act of the Parliament of Canada.

Amending the B.N.A. Act in order that the decisions of the highest Court of Appeal in Canada shall be final in all matters, civil and political.

That adequate, equal pensions be granted to all disabled soldiers, either officers or men, or their widows and dependents.

*Note.—See historical record of the U.F.O. in Agricultural Section on Pages 399-400.

22

Pensions for mothers with dependent children and Old Age pensions.
Creation of national reserves of coal and timber.

An effort was made by the I.L.P. to carry St. Catharines in the
bye-election and the Secretary of the party—J. T. Marks—with
Mrs. W. F. Singer, Toronto, Mayor M. M. MacBride, Brantford,
Controller H. J. Halford, Hamilton, and Mrs. Rose Henderson,
Montreal, helped in the campaign, as did Tom Moore, President of
the T. and L. Council.   Much elation was expressed at the vote
polled by the Labour candidate who reduced a Government majority of 1,529 to 172.   At a Toronto Convention of this organization
on Apr. 18 the relations of Labour and the Tariff were debated at
length and it was decided to affiliate with the Canadian Labour
Party.   Resolutions were passed as follows: Opposing Daylight-
Saving and urging the release of Eugene Debs from United States
prison; protesting against the sending of troops to Russia and demanding the rescinding of Orders-in-Council against seditious
literature; opposing military training in the schools and favouring
a shorter working day; asking for a Fair Wage Court and a National minimum wage; favouring control of Cold-storage houses by
the Government and equal Pensions for officers and men; asking a
grant of $50 and free Hospital treatment for mothers and a Gov-
ernment guarantee to every child of the necessities of life, medical
care and an unlimited education; demanding unemployment insurance and abolition of the existing system of taxation with substitution of a graded tax on all incomes and lands and graduated Succession duties; condemning the Government's Housing policy and
asking the use of State forests to reduce cost of building houses;
describing the present system of vocational training as a farce.

It was announced that the I.L.P. had 78 branches at this time,
and 90 delegates were present at the Convention with W. R. Rollo,
Hamilton, in the chair.   For the coming year Mr. Rollo was elected
President and J. T. Marks Secretary while affiliation with the
C.L.P. was stated as being for the purpose of united effort in the
coming Elections; the Toronto *Globe* declared the Convention to
have been "inexcusably weak in dodging the Tariff question."
The new Canadian Labour Party was at this time composed of a
combination of Socialists with ordinary Trade Unionists, and
others such as the Fabian Society, with James Simpson as its
leading spirit and Secretary, and it was not completely organized.
The Labour Educational Association of Ontario which met in its
17th annual Convention at Stratford on May 24th, with 150 delegates present, was, in a sense, the parent of both the above organizations; its President at this time was J. F. Marsh, and Secretary J.
T. Marks.   Its chief task was announced as that of affiliating all
the 800 Labour bodies in the Province.   Practically, and for Election purposes, the I.L.P. was the fighting Labour organization of
ensuing months; it formed new branches, increased its membership, nominated candidates, collected funds and promoted joint
action with the U.F.O.

On Dec. 27th, 1918, J. J. Morrison, Secretary of the Farmers, had replied to an expression of hope along these lines as follows: "We feel that closer relation is absolutely necessary between urban and rural labour and that to this end our officials should frequently meet in conference that something more tangible than mere favourable expression might bring about a practical unity." This policy was realized in the 1919 campaign to a considerable extent though the *Farmers' Sun* of June 25th did not seem very sure of the situation: "The capitalists and labourers are only temporary enemies. Their class strife ends at the door of the polling booth, where they join hands to uphold Tariff protection and to keep the farmers in servitude. The farmers are their only recourse to satisfy their exactions of dividends, wages and leisure." In North Oxford, North Grey, Welland, West York, Timiskaming and many other ridings Labour either endorsed the Farmers' candidates or ran one of their own; on Oct. 17th the *Industrial Banner* recommended 32 candidates who were either Labour, Labour-Farmer or Labour-Veteran.

Labour incidents of the contest included the conference at Hamilton on Mch. 16th between H. J. Halford, Mayor MacBride, Brantford, James Simpson, J. H. H. Ballantyne, Toronto, and W. C. Good of the U.F.O., as to combined political action; the strong condemnation of Mr. Simpson's Socialistic views (May 5) by Mayor MacBride, head of the Brantford I.L.P., and afterwards elected M.L.A.; the candidacy of Controller W. D. Robbins as Labour-Government candidate in Riverdale (Toronto) with the general understanding that he would be Minister of Labour if the Hearst Government were returned; the advertised declaration of the Ottawa Labour party in the Ottawa *Journal* that if John Cameron and F. Lafortune were elected locally they would obtain legislation "to abolish the evils of poverty and unemployment and help all to live in well-planned and healthy houses with free education for children including a University training"; the running of a Labour candidate against Sir Adam Beck in London.

Prohibition, Soldiers, Women, in the Election. The Conservative leader in this campaign was enthusiastically a Prohibitionist but promised to carry out the will of the people, as shown in the Referendum, whichever way they voted; the Liberal leader was not personally a Prohibitionist but was pledged to support Prohibition if approved by the people in the Referendum; the U.F.O. were pledged to support Prohibition but were in active antagonism to the Government which had put it in force; the Prohibitionists were unpledged as to party and their supporting newspapers were divided in opinion with *The Globe* criticizing the Government, the *Methodist Guardian* denouncing Mr. Dewart, and the Toronto *Star* (Oct. 6-8th) urging support of Sir William Hearst as the Prohibitionist leader of a party previously opposed, in the main, to Prohibition. Out of this situation anything might develop. So far as the political leaders were concerned the Referendum was left largely to take care of itself; even the Premier, who was whole-heartedly for it, did not appeal to the people on its behalf as he certainly did for the ordinary policies of his Government; the questions were there and the people were left to answer them while it was currently reported that Messrs. McGarry, Macdiarmid and Ferguson of the Government were not personally friendly to Prohibition except as a war-time measure. Messrs. Pratt and Machin, Conservative members of the Legislature, did not conceal their antagonism while Lieut.-Col. Kelly Evans ran in North-East Toronto as an avowed advocate of beer and wine license; the Citizens' Liberty League, of which Colonel Machin was President, stood for an affirmative answer to the Referendum questions and, in particular, for a beer of 2·51 per cent. alcohol contents as compared with 2·75 per cent. demanded by Mr. Gompers and Labour interests in the States.   C. H. Mills, Conservative candidate in North Waterloo, was opposed to the O.T.A. and T. Herbert Lennox of North York did not profess any liking for the policy; the *Methodist Guardian* of Oct. 15th urged the return of the Hearst Government.   The Prohibition Referendum campaign was well organized with all the Temperance forces united and controlled by the Rev. Dr. A. S. Grant and Rev. Peter Bryce; neither money nor pains were spared in organization and the getting out of the vote; a Toronto Referendum Committee was organized and did strong work for Prohibition.

The Veterans took no organized part in the campaign though all parties, in platforms and speeches, appealed earnestly for their support.   The Liberals nominated Lieut.-Col. H. R. Arthur, for Sudbury; Lieut.-Col. E. D. O'Flynn, for West Hastings; Major J. C. Tolmie, for Windsor; Lieut.-Col. T. Bart Robson, for East Middlesex; Lieut. K. S. Stover, for Algoma, and Major Malcolm Lang, for Cochrane.   The Grand Army of Canada tried to carry on along independent political lines and the *G.A.C. Journal* opposed Prohibition; the Lieut.-Col. Dougald Carmichael, D.S.O., M.C., ran in Centre Grey as U.F.O. candidate against the Attorney-General, and Capt. G. B. Little in East York against the Minister of Agriculture; Brig.-Gen. A. E. Ross stood for Kingston again as a member of the Government; in Riverdale (Toronto) Sergt.-Major J. McNamara, D.C.M., ran as a returned soldier candidate and in North-West Toronto Lieut.-Col. H. S. Cooper, M.C. with Bar, stood as a Liberal.

As to Women, there were only two candidates—Mrs. J. Wesley Bundy, President of the Toronto Women's Liberal Association, in North-East Toronto and Mrs. J. C. Sears in one of the Ottawas; Mrs. Ralph Smith, M.L.A., of Vancouver, spoke at Whitby and several other places for the Liberal party, and Mrs. H. D. Petrie sought a Liberal nomination in Hamilton.   Mrs. G. A. Brodie, President of the Women's U.F.O., gave several addresses and at Barrie on Aug. 14th vigorously attacked Protection and the tariff and added: "One thing you men cannot do, you cannot win elections without the help of women who now have half the voting strength of the country. You think your wives will vote as you do, don't you? Don't be too sure of that. We have got you where we want you at last.''

Result of the Elections. When the Legislature was dissolved the standing of the Parties was as follows: Conservatives 76, Liberals 29 and United Farmers 3; in the bye-elections since 1914 the Conservatives had won 12 seats, the Liberals 6 and United Farmers three. A notable feature in the previous Election had been the large Conservative majorities yet, by Oct. 13th in this new contest, 17 Conservative members of that Legislature had either retired from the field or been beaten in Conventions while six Liberals were in a similar position. In the 1919 Elections the Conservatives contested 101 seats, the Liberals 72 seats, the U.F.O. 68 and Labour 24 while Independents ran in 17 seats. When the results became known on Oct. 20th it was found that the Hearst Government was overwhelmed by a group of opposing Parties; that Sir William Hearst was beaten in his own riding by 1,370 majority, Hon. I. B. Lucas in Centre Grey by 474, Hon. W. D. McPherson in North-West Toronto by 1,125, Hon. F. G. Macdiarmid in West Elgin by 1,879, and Hon. T. W. McGarry in South Renfrew by 322; that Sir Adam Beck, the political hero of London, had lost his seat by 1,901 majority and William Proudfoot, ex-Liberal leader, had gone down in Centre Huron by 163; that H. Hartley Dewart, the Liberal leader, had defeated G. H. Gooderham (Cons.) in S. W. Toronto by the immense majority of 7,186, and that J. Walter Curry, K.C., another Liberal candidate, had won in S.E. Toronto by 5,313 majority. It was a political upheaval with hardly two dozen members of the late Legislature re-elected; three clergymen were returned—Rev. J. C. Tolmie (Lib.), Rev. C. H. Buckland (Cons.), and Rev. J. C. Watson (U.F.O.); Toronto elected four soldiers— Cooper, Ramsden, McNamara, Thompson and 14 others were returned throughout the Province; all the avowed anti-Prohibitionists were defeated including Pratt, Machin, Evans and Mills, and both the women candidates; Manning Doherty of the U.F.O. was defeated in Peel by 105 and H. C. Nixon, U.F.O., elected in North Brant by 1,024. As to Parties the Conservatives elected 25 members, the Liberals 29, the United Farmers 45, Labour 11 and Independents 1. The following were the returns by constituencies:

Addington—William D. Black, acclamation, Conservative.
Algoma—K. S. Stover, Liberal, 2,270; John M. Robb, Conservative, 2,226; John E. Wright, U.F.O., 1,900. Majority for Stover, 44.
Brant North—Harry C. Nixon, U.F.O., 3,597; Franklin Smoke, Conservative, 2,573; Uzziel O. Kendrick, Liberal, 1,966. Majority for Nixon, 1,024.
Brant South—Morrison M. McBride, Lab., 6,408; Morgan E. Norris, Lib., 4,031; W. S. Brewster, Cons., 3,326. Majority for McBride, 2,377.
Brockville—Donald McAlpine, Liberal, 4,866; Albert E. Donovan, Conservative, 3,751. Majority for McAlpine, 1,115.
Bruce North—W. F. Fenton, U.F.O., 3,689; Wm. McDonald, Liberal, 3,132. Majority for Fenton, 557.

Bruce South—Frank Rennie, Liberal, 2,727; J. J. Zetter, U.F.O., 1,930; W. D.
  Cargill, Conservative, 1,855. Majority for Rennie, 797.
Bruce West—Alex. R. Mewhinney, Liberal, 3,094; Gideon H. Ruttle, U.F.O.,
  2,993; Chas. H. Green, Cons., 1,696. Majority for Mewhinney, 101.
Carlton—Robert H. Grant, U.F.O., 4,877; Adam H. Acres, Conservative, 3,795.
  Majority for Grant, 1,082.
Cochrane—Malcolm Lang, Liberal, 2,951; Robt. S. Potter, Conservative, 1,831;
  John Vanier, Ind. Liberal, 1,211. Majority for Lang, 1,120.
Dufferin—Thos. K. Slack, U.F.O., 4.117; John Reburn, Conservative, 3,579.
  Majority for Slack, 536.
Dundas—Wm. H. Casselman, U.F.O., 4,792; Irwin Hilliard, Conservative,
  3,268. Majority for Casselman, 1,524.
Durham East—Samuel S. Staples, U.F.O., 1,111; Josiah J. Preston, 808.
  Majority for Staples, 303.
Durham West—Wm. J. Bragg, Liberal, 3,346; John H. Devitt, Conservative.
  2,608. Majority for Bragg, 738.
Elgin East—Malcolm MacVicar, U.F.O., 4,937; Thos. M. Moore, Conservative,
  3,365. Majority for MacVicar, 1,572.
Elgin West—Peter G. Cameron, U.F.O., 7,542; Finlay G. Macdiarmid, Con-
  servative, 5,663. Majority for Cameron, 1,879.
Essex North—Alphonse G. Tisdelle, U.F.O., 6,486; Paul Poisson, Conservative,
  2,638. Majority for Tisdelle, 3,848.
Essex South—Milton J. Fox, U.F.O., 3,558; Lambert P. Wigle, Liberal, 3,428;
  Lewis Wigle, Independent, 1,629. Majority for Fox, 130.
Ft. William—Henry Mills, Labour, 3,745; A. McGillivray, Liberal, 2,232; Chas.
  W. Jarvis, Conservative, 1,298. Majority for Mills, 1,513.
Frontenac—Anthony M. Rankin, Conservative, 3,016; Wm. Fawcett, U.F.O.,
  2,507; Wm. Spankie, 850. Majority for Rankin, 509.
Glengarry—Duncan A. Ross, U.F.O., 4,554; A. J. MacDonald, Liberal, 2,779.
  Majority for Ross, 1,775.
Grenville—Hon. G. H. Ferguson, Conservative, 4,125; G. A. Payne, U.F.O.,
  4,044. Majority for Ferguson (on recount), 81.
Grey North—D. J. Taylor, Labour, 5,659; A. S. Macdonald, 4,461. Majority
  for Taylor, 1,198.
Grey Centre—Dougald Carmichael, U.F.O., 4,363; Hon. I. B. Lucas, Con-
  servative, 3,889. Majority for Carmichael, 474.
Grey South—Geo. Mansfield Leeson, U.F.O., 5,252; David Jamieson, Conserva-
  tive, 4,299. Majority for Leeson, 953.
Haldimand—Warren Stringer, U.F.O., 6,056; Wm. Jacques, Conservative,
  4,066. Majority for Stringer, 1,990.
Halton—John F. Ford, U.F.O., 4,456; Alfred W. Nixon, Conservative, 3,402;
  E. H. Cleaver, Liberal, 3,190. Majority for Ford, 1,054.
Hamilton East—G. G. Halcrow, Labour, 16,012; S. L. Sanders, 8,424; W. L.
  Fitzgerald, 2,146. Majority for Halcrow, 7,588.
Hamilton West—Walter R. Rollo, Labour, 8,722; John MacFarlane, Conserva-
  tive, 4,079; James Dixon, Liberal, 1,675. Majority for Rollo, 4,643.
Hastings East—Henry K. Denyes, U.F.O., 3,641; Sandy Grant, Conservative,
  3,467. Majority for Denyes, 174.
Hastings North—John R. Cooke, Conservative, acclamation.
Hastings West—William Henry Ireland, 5,072; Edward Buckett O'Flynn,
  4,647. Majority for Ireland, 425.
Huron Centre—John M. Govenlock, Lib., 3,193; Wm. Proudfoot, 3,030; Robt.
  W. Livingstone, U.F.O., 2,039. Majority for Govenlock, 163.
Huron North—John Joynt, Conservative, 2,897; W. H. Fraser, Liberal, 2,556;
  R. C. Procter, U.F.O., 2,249. Majority for Joynt, 341.
Huron South—Andrew Hicks, U.F.O., 3,298; F. W. Ellerington, Conservative,
  2,524; John T. Morgan, Liberal, 2,047. Majority for Hicks, 774.
Kenora—Peter Heenan, Lab., 1,870; H. A. C. Machin, Liberty League, 895;
  Alfred Pitt, Cons., 610; A. T. Fife, 405. Majority for Heenan, 975.
Kent East—James B. Clark, U.F.O., 5,374; Jas. N. Mowbray, Liberal, 4,348.
  Majority for Clark, 1,026.

Kent West—Robt. S. Brackin, Liberal, 8,098; Eliott W. Hardy, U.F.O., 5,179; Milton W. Shaw, Conservative, 3,583. Majority for Brackin, 2,919.

Kingston—Hon. Arthur Ed. Ross, Conservative, Accl.

Lambton East—Leslie Warner Oke, U.F.O., 4,575; J. B. Martyn, Conservative, 2,161; Duncan J. McEachern, Liberal, 1,882. Majority for Oke, 2,414.

Lambton West—Jonah Moorhouse Webster, U.F.O., 6,081; James S. Crawford, 4,782; Peter Gardiner, Cons., 4,180. Majority for Webster, 1,299.

Lanark North—Hiram McCreary, U.F.O., 2,881; Hon. Richard F. Preston, Cons., 2,798; Christopher Forbes, Lib., 1,373. Majority for McCreary, 83.

Lanark South—Wm. J. Johnston, U.F.O., 3,872; Jas. G. Gould, Cons., 3,069; Richard Grant, 1,096. Majority for Johnston, 803.

Leeds—Andrew W. Gray, Conservative, 4,351; Jno. P. Sinclair, Liberal, 3,620. Majority for Gray, 731.

Lennox—Reginald A. Fowler, Cons., 2,329; Carleton Woods, Lib., 2,015; Claude B. Bretheu, U.F.O., 1,482. Majority for Fowler, 314.

Lincoln—Thos. Marshall, Liberal, 3,242; Wilson Kline, U.F.O., 2,735; Daniel H. Moyer, Conservative, 2,253. Majority for Marshall, 507.

London—Hugh Allan Stevenson, Labour, 13,008; Sir Adam Beck, Independent, 11,107. Majority for Stevenson, 1,901.

Manitoulin—Beniah Bowman, U.F.O., 2,428; Jno. W. Kinney, Conservative, 1,605. Majority for Bowman, 883.

Middlesex East—Jno. W. Freeborn, U.F.O., 5,463; T. Bart. Robson, Liberal, 2,500; J. E. Robson, Conservative, 2,421. Majority for Freeborn, 2,963.

Middlesex North—James C. Brown, U.F.O., 3,857; Geo. A. Elliott, Conservative, 2,161; Jno. Grieve, Liberal, 1,627. Majority for Brown, 1,696.

Middlesex West—Jno. Giles Lethbridge, U.F.O., 4,394; Daniel C. McKenzie, Conservative, 1,419. Majority for Lethbridge, 2,975.

Muskoka—Geo. Walter Ecclestone, Cons., 3,054; Harmon E. Rice, Lib., 2,764; Dalton J. Armstrong, Ind., 789. Majority for Ecclestone, 290.

Niagara Falls—Chas. F. Swayze, Labour, 4,057; Carlton F. Munroe, Lib., 3,689; Geo. J. Musgrove, Cons., 2,826. Majority for Swayze, 368.

Nippissing—Jos. H. Marceau, Lib., 3,122; James T. Wilson, Ind.-Lib., 2,188; Henry Morel, Cons., 2,046. Majority for Marceau, 934.

Norfolk North—Geo. David Sewell, U.F.O., 4,522; W. E. Sutherland, Conservative, 2,645. Majority for Sewell, 1,877.

Norfolk South—Jos. Cridland, U.F.O., 3,280; Arthur C. Pratt, 1,954. Majority for Cridland, 1,326.

Northumberland East—Wesley Montgomery, U.F.O., 4,521; Alex. Hume, Conservative, 4,434. Majority for Montgomery, 87.

Northumberland West—Samuel Clarke, Liberal, 3,401; Fred. D. Boggs, Conservative, 2,747. Majority for Clarke, 654.

Ontario North—Jno. Wesley Widdifield, U.F.O., 4,162; Jno. Wetherall, Conservative, 3,529. Majority for Widdifield, 633.

Ontario South—Wm. E. N. Sinclair, Liberal, 7,843; Chas. Calder, Conservative, 4,418. Majority for Sinclair, 3,425.

Ottawa East—Jos. Albert Pinard, Lib., 7,309; Videle Lafortune, Ind.-Lib., 2,878; Olivier Durocher, Cons., 1,311. Majority for Pinard, 4,431.

Ottawa West—Hammet P. Hill, Cons., 8,953; Jno. Cameron, Ind.-Lib., 7,856; Geo. C. Hurdman, Lib., 6,526; J. Sears, 2,428. Majority for Hill, 1,097.

Oxford North—Jno. Alex. Calder, Lib., 5,369; Robt. E. Butler, Cons., 3,056; Jno. Scott, Farmer and Lib., 2,852. Majority for Calder, 2,313.

Oxford South—Albert Thos. Walker, U.F.O., 4,452; Victor A. Sinclair, Conservative, 3,835; Alex. Rose, Liberal, 2,888. Majority for Walker, 617.

Parkdale—Wm. Herbert Price, Conservative, 11,091; Jno. Hunter, Prohibition, 4,995. Majority for Price, 6,096.

Parry Sound—Richard Reece Hall, Liberal, 4,618; Jos. Edgar, Conservative, 3,857. Majority for Hall, 761.

Peel—Thos. L. Kennedy, Conservative, 4,562; Wm. J. Lowe, Liberal, 4,457; Manning W. Doherty, U.F.O., 2,345. Majority for Kennedy, 105.

Perth North—Francis W. Hay, Liberal, 6,095; Wm. A. Amos, U.F.O., 4,454; Jas. A. Mason, Conservative, 4,092. Majority for Hay, 1,641.

Perth South—Peter Smith, U.F.O., 5,847; Percy Coupland, Conservative, 3,261. Majority for Smith, 2,586.

Peterboro East—Ernest Nicholls McDonald, U.F.O., 3,623; Jas. Thompson, Conservative, 2,604. Majority for McDonald, 1,019.

Peterboro West—Thos. Tooms, Labour, 4,732; Geo. Alex. Gillespie, Liberal, 4,047; Robt. Jas. Soden, Cons., 2,625. Majority for Tooms, 685.

Port Arthur—Donald Macdonald Hogarth, Cons., 2,578; Jno. Park Mooney, Lib., 2,095; Ed. Jno. Blaquier, Ind., 1,564. Majority for Hogarth, 483.

Prescott—Gustave Evanturel, Liberal, 3,929; Jos. A. Caron, U.F.O., 2,631; Edmund A. Mooney, Liberal, 1,724. Majority for Evanturel, 1,298.

Prince Edward—Nelson Parliament, Liberal, 4,557; Robt. A. Norman, Conservative, 3,612. Majority for Parliament, 945.

Rainy River—Jas. Arthur Mathieu, Cons., 1,420; Ed. J. Callaghan, Lib., 1,068; Jno. F. H. Barber, U.F.O., 1,062. Majority for Mathieu, 352.

Renfrew North—Ralph Melville Warren, U.F.O., 3,979; Ed. A. Dunlop, Cons., 3,749; Thos. H. Moffatt, Lib., 1,954. Majority for Warren, 230.

Renfrew South—Jno. Carty, Jr., U.F.O., 5,426; Hon. Thos. W. McGarry, Conservative, 5,104. Majority for Carty, 322.

Riverdale—J. McNamara, S., 7,472; J. T. Dick, I.-L., 5,873; G. Lockhart, 189; Wm. D. Robbins, C., 5,706. Majority for McNamara, 1,599.

Russell—Damase Racine, Liberal, 6,121; Philias Blanchard, U.F.O., 4,947; S. A. Landry, 1,180. Majority for Racine, 1,174.

St. Catharines—F. H. Greenlaw, Lab., 6,313; F. Raymond Parnell, Cons., 4,422; Jos. Ed. Master, Lib., 2,235. Majority for Greenlaw, 1,891.

Sault Ste. Marie—Jas. Cunningham, Labour, 4,444; Sir Wm. H. Hearst, Conservative, 3,074. Majority for Cunningham, 1,370.

Simcoe Centre—Gilbert Hugh Murdock, U.F.O., 5,234; J. T. Simpson, Conservative, 3,808. Majority for Murdock, 1,426.

Simcoe East—J. B. Johnston, U.F.O., 5,063; J. I. Hartt, Cons., 4,580; D. C. Anderson, Ind.-Lib. 2,773. Majority for Johnston, 483.

Simcoe South—Edgar J. Evans, U.F.O., 2,927; Alex. Ferguson, Conservative, 2,526. Majority for Evans, 401.

Simcoe West—Wm. Torrance Allan, Conservative, 4,491; Richard Baker, U.F.O., 3,606. Majority for Allan, 885.

Stormont—Jas. W. McLeod, Lib., 4,284; Jos. McKillican, U.F.O., 2,946; Duncan A. McNaughton, Cons., 2,731. Majority for McLeod, 1,338.

Sturgeon Falls—Zotique Mageau, Liberal, 2,690; A. A. Aulin, Conservative, 892; Alph. Legendre, U.F.O., 755. Majority for Mageau, 1,798.

Sudbury—C. McCrea, Cons., 3,551; R. H. Arthur, Lib., 3,409; A. T. Sweezy, Farmer and Lab., 1,789. Majority for McCrea (on recount), 142.

Timiskaming—T. Magladery, Cons., 3,092; A. Montgomery, I.L.P. and U.F.O., 3,015; R. Taylor, Lib., 2,520. Majority for Magladery, 87.

Toronto Northeast, Seat "A"—Hon. Henry J. Cody, Conservative Accl.

Toronto Northwest, Seat "B"—Henry Cooper, Lib., 18,522; Hon. Wm. D. McPherson, Cons., 17,397. Majority for Cooper, 1,125.

Toronto Northeast, Seat "B"—J. E. Thompson, C., 13,495; Mrs. J. W. Bundy, L., 8,685; Kelly Evans, I.-C., 8,172; J. W. Buckley, I.-L., 2,910. Majority for Thompson, 4,810.

Toronto Northwest, Seat "A"—Thos. Crawford, Conservative, 18,797; Jas. G. Cane, Liberal, 16,056. Majority for Crawford, 2,741.

Toronto Southeast, Seat "A"—Jno. O'Neill, Lib., 10,037; Jas. H. G. Wallace, Cons., 5,452; A. Ruppert, Lab., 1,063. Majority for O'Neill, 4,585.

Toronto Southeast, Seat "B"—Jas. Walter Curry, Lib., 10,508; Henry C. Schofield, Cons., 5,195. Majority for Curry, 5,313.

Toronto Southwest, Seat "A"—H. Hartley Dewart, Lib., 16,555; Geo. Gooderham, Conservative, 9,369. Majority for Dewart, 7,186.

Toronto Southwest, Seat "B"—Jno. Ramsden, Lib., 12,428; Wm. McBrien, Cons., 7,628; J. MacDonald, Ind.-Lib., 6,457. Majority for Ramsden, 4,800.

Victoria North—Edgar Watson, U.F.O., 3,348; Robt. W. Mason, Conservative, 2,430. Majority for Watson, 918.

Victoria South—Fred. Geo. Sandy, U.F.O., 2,452; Jno. W. Wood, Conservative, 1,103. Majority for Sandy, 1,349.

Waterloo North—Nicholas Asmussen, Ind.-Lib., 5,354; Geo. C. Haehnel, 3,213; W. Snider, Lib., 2,974; C. H. Mills, Cons., 1,487; G. Barbour, U.F.O., 2,211; J. M. Reid, 225. Majority for Asmussen, 2,141.

Waterloo South—Karl K. Homuth, Lab.-U.F.O., 8,074; S. E. Charlton, Lib., 3,836; Z. A. Hall, Cons., 2,641. Majority for Homuth, 4,238.

Welland—Robt. Cooper, Liberal, 5,183; Donald Sharp, Conservative, 3,440; Menno E. Barrick, U.F.O., 1,949. Majority for Cooper, 1,743.

Wellington East—A. Hellyer, U.F.O., 3,279; Robt. Thos. Pritchard, Cons., 2,371; U. Richardson, Lib., 1,623. Majority for Hellyer, 908.

Wellington South—Caleb H. Buckland, 4,362; Samuel Carter, 4,242; John A. Cockburn, 3,060; George E. Heathcote, 223. Majority for Buckland, 120.

Wellington West—Robt. Neil McArthur, U.F.O., 3,379; Wm. C. Chambers, Conservative, 2,810. Majority for McArthur, 569.

Wentworth North—Frank Campbell Biggs, U.F.O., 4,634; Sidney Jno. Rasbery, Conservative, 1,783. Majority for Biggs, 2,851.

Wentworth South—W. A. Crockett, U.F.O., 2,642; Jas. T. H. Regan, Cons., 2,331; Ben. Ed. Thompson, 1,995; S. H. Wilkinson, 664. Majority for Crockett, 311.

Windsor—Jas. Craig Tolmie, Liberal, 10,874; Wm. B. Woolatt, Conservative, 6,225. Majority for Tolmie, 4,649.

York East—Hon. G. S. Henry, Cons., 8,962; Geo. B. Little, U.F.O., 7,290; Robt. J. Gibson, Lib., 6,926; Jno. Galbraith, 1,144. Majority for Henry, 1,672.

York North—Thos. Herbert Lennox, Conservative, 4,139; J. M. Walton, Liberal, 3,853; Samuel P. Foote, U.F.O., 2,869. Majority for Lennox, 286.

York West—F. Godfrey, Cons., 10,436; J. Simpson, Lab., 8,323; F. G. J. Whetter, Lib., 4,935; S. Ryding, 4,087. Majority for Godfrey, 2,113.

Figures published at the close of the year showed that the Conservatives had polled 391,278 votes, with 4 acclamations, the Liberals 333,550 votes, the U.F.O. 258,090, Labour 131,394 and Independents 56,256 votes—or a total of 1,170,569 votes. The Ottawa *Journal* (Nov. 20th) commented on the difference between votes and elected members: "The arrangement of electoral districts in Ontario (and throughout Canada) is such that a farmer's vote has practically twice the effect of the vote of any person resident in cities or large towns. Ottawa, for instance, with 110,000 population elects two members to the Ontario Legislature; Carleton County on one side with 20,000 people elects one member; Russell County on the other side has a population of 40,000 and elects one member." So in the other parts of the Province. Another point of view was that the Conservative party polled 34 per cent. of the total votes cast and received only 23 per cent. of the representation; the Liberal party polled 29 per cent. of the votes and received 26 per cent.; the U.F.O. polled 22 per cent. of the votes and secured 40 per cent. of the representation.

The Referendum was carried on Question I by 772,041 to 365,-365; on question II by 733,691 to 408,266; on Question III by 747,-920 to 383,727; on Question IV by 693,829 to 447,146. These figures, taken from tabulated returns compiled in *The Pioneer* of Nov. 21st, were not official, but were approximately correct. The Premier took his defeat with dignity, and at the Sault, where he first received the news, said in a brief address: "I will not make any prophecy as to what will take place. I thought the Government was going to sweep the country, and I was not alone in that, for a great many Liberals who were supporting me thought so, too. The Temperance Act no doubt had a great deal to do with my defeat, but I did what I felt was right, and if I had it to do over again, I would do the same thing."

Formation and Policy of the Drury Government. Following the Elections much interest was felt in a situation where no one Party had a majority; the only certain point was that all parties but the Conservative were opposed to the Government and that it had the smallest measure of support amongst the three chief sections in the coming Legislature. Under these circumstances the Lieut.-Governor could, constitutionally, have called on any leader who showed a reasonable chance of forming a coalition or upon whom he was advised to call by the outgoing Prime Minister. As a matter of fact, the Lieut.-Governor in a decidedly unusual interview was constitutionally correct in the following statement (Oct. 22nd): "I believe that under the circumstances I can call anyone in the House or out and ask him to form a Government. Of course, it goes without saying that such a man would have to have the support of a majority of the Legislative Assembly in order to carry on."

Sir John Hendrie outlined the general situation as follows: "Now, we have two parties with Leaders, neither of which can form a Government that would have a majority support in the House. We have two class parties, representing and elected to represent, certain classes of the community. It is entirely different to former situations where, with two parties, the one in power was defeated and the defeated Prime Minister advised the Lieut.-Governor to ask the Leader of the other party to form a Cabinet. The result is a move away from party representation toward class or factional representation." To this interview the Liberal leader took exception in a statement issued on the same day: "It is rather early for the Lieut.-Governor, in an inspired interview, to suggest where he will look for a leader or how he will deal with the situation. His natural course is to call upon the successful leader of the Liberal party to form a Government. It will be time enough to discuss the calling in of an outsider when it appears that it will be impossible for the groups to get together in the common cause of establishing popular government."

Mr. Dewart went on to say that as Leader of one of the two Parties in the House when it was dissolved he had the right to be called upon to at least attempt the formation of a Coalition Government: "The Hearst Administration has been overwhelmingly beaten and the principles that the Liberal party has fought for have been vindicated by the election of a controlling group of Liberals, Soldiers, Farmers and Labour representatives. The principles of their policies they hold largely in common. There can be no reason why they should not get together." To this possibility *The Star* (Liberal) took strong exception and claimed (Oct. 23rd) that the people had passed Mr. Dewart and his party by and chosen U.F.O., Soldiers or Labour candidates in preference; the *Globe* contended that it was the Governor's duty to call on whomever the Farmers elected as their leader.   Meanwhile, the Farmer members, with outside leaders of the U.F.O. such as R. H. Halbert, R. W. E. Burnaby, Col. J. Z. Fraser, W. A. Amos, M. W. Doherty, W. C. Good, Hon. T. A. Crerar, M.P., representing Dominion organizations, and James Simpson representing the Canadian Labour Party, had met in Conference at Toronto and on the 23rd issued a statement through J. J. Morrison, Secretary, as follows:

> The members-elect of the United Farmers of Ontario, after due consideration of the matter, have decided that it would be unwise for them to enter into alliance with either of the old Parties as parties. They are prepared to assume the fullest share of responsibility and form a Government in co-operation with such members of other parties as are in sympathy with their platform and principles and are free to give support thereto. In the formation of a Cabinet full consideration will be given to the various interests of the Province.

The question of an Attorney-General was rather difficult as there was not a lawyer amongst the elected members of the U.F.O. and rumour was rife as to the possible selection of a Liberal—J. W. Curry, K.C., being mentioned frequently in the press; it was also pointed out that 7 farmers had been elected as Conservatives and 6 as Liberals which gave farmers, as a class, a majority in the Legislature. The question of Leader was not immediately decided by the Conference; E. C. Drury appeared from the first to be the favourite and there also was a good deal of talk as to Sir Adam Beck; J. J. Morrison was much spoken of in view of his valuable Election services and other names prominently mentioned were Peter Smith, North Perth; Andrew Hicks, South Huron; R. H. Grant, Carleton; Beniah Bowman, Manitoulin; R. W. E. Burnaby and Manning W. Doherty, and Joseph Gridland, South Norfolk; W. I. Johnston, South Lanark, and Earl Biggar, Brantford. No vote was taken, however, and on Oct. 29th the press was advised that Ernest Charles Drury of Crown Hill had been unanimously selected.   At a concurrent caucus of the Labour party a Resolution of endorsement and confidence was passed.   Mr. Drury was 41 years of age at this time and without Parliamentary experience; his father was the late Hon. Charles Alfred Drury, Minister of Agriculture in Ontario during 1888-90 and his ancestors had been farmers in Simcoe County back to Richard Drury who came there from England in 1819; he was a graduate of the Ontario Agricultural College, Master of The Dominion Grange for two years, first Secretary of the Canadian Council of Agriculture and one of the chief influences in organization of the U.F.O.; he had run as a Conscriptionist Liberal for North Simcoe in 1917.   In his speech to the Conference the new Leader said:

I do not entertain any fears regarding the situation. It is true we may be lacking in experience, but the situation is not one which calls for the fine arts of the politician. It is true that, in a sense, we represent the farming community, and in all truth, that section of the people has been in great need for many years of a greater voice in the Legislatures of the Province and of the country, a voice which it is our duty adequately to supply. But in a very real sense we represent not alone the 40 per cent. of the people who are on the farms, but also the great bulk of the common people of all classes, the people who are desirous of good government, of stability, efficiency and economy, and of the fair and equal enforcement of law. Our success, therefore, depends, not on political manœuvring, but on the breadth and fairness of our policy, and on our adherence to high ideals of democracy and public service.

He declared that, if called to power, the Party would "stand for no class legislation"; that it would fearlessly and effectively enforce the decision of the Referendum; that his Government would make an honest attempt "to solve a problem which bears heavily on us all, and which, as wages and prices of farm produce decline, may become an intolerable burden—the high cost of living." Speaking at Barrie on the 30th Mr. Drury declared that "the movement which swept us into power was not alone the farming movement; there was a deep feeling in all sections of the community that Party government had outlived its day." Mr. Drury addressed a Victory Loan mass-meeting in Toronto on Nov. 10th and, after urging public support to the Loan, added: "Ours will not in any sense be a class Government and I wish to say further that we are not out to get things for the farmer that the farmer should not have. We would hold ourselves as a failure if we did not govern in the interests of every class, every legitimate interest, in the Province of Ontario."

Meanwhile, the Hearst Government had been clearing up business with a view to retirement; the Premier had announced his intention to leave public life entirely and Hon. G. Howard Ferguson, senior member of the Cabinet, became, tentatively, leader of the Provincial Conservative party; there was much talk of the Hon. Dr. Cody remaining as a non-partisan Minister of Education but he resigned with the other Ministers; it was generally stated that W. F. Nickle, K.C., ex-M.P., of Kingston, had been offered the Attorney-Generalship of the new Government with Gordon Waldron and W. E. Raney, K.C., frequently mentioned for the post. As to Labour, an early gathering of that Party at Hamilton on Oct. 26th had decided that they would co-operate only with the U.F.O. and it appointed a Committee composed of W. R. Rollo, Hamilton, M. M. MacBride, Brantford, and J. B. Cunningham, Sault Ste. Marie, to confer with a Farmers' Committee—R. H. Grant, Rev. W. Watson and Peter Smith. The Tariff and the 8-hour day were the chief points on which differences might have arisen but they were put aside; a personal issue developed into Mayor MacBride's breaking away from the final Conference of Committees on Oct. 29th with a later endorsation by Brantford Labour. On Nov. 12th it was announced that the Labourites had approved of Messrs. Rollo

and Mills as their representatives in the new Cabinet. On the
14th the Drury Government was announced, and sworn in, as follows:

Premier and President of the Council	Hon. Ernest Charles Drury
Attorney-General	Hon. William Edgar Raney, K.C.
Provincial Secretary and Registrar	Hon. Henry Corwin Nixon
Provincial Treasurer	Hon. Peter Smith
Minister of Lands, Forests and Mines	Hon. Beniah Bowman
Minister of Agriculture	Hon. Manning William Doherty
Minister of Public Works and Highways	Hon. Frank Campbell Biggs
Minister of Education	Hon. Robert Henry Grant
Minister of Labour	Hon. Walter Ritchie Rollo
Minister without Portfolio	Hon. Henry Mills
Minister without Portfolio	Lieut.-Col. Dougall Carmichael

Mr. Morrison, it was understood, had declined a Cabinet post—
believing that his work for the present lay with the U.F.O. A
little later (Nov. 29th) Mr. Mills took over administration of the
Bureau of Mines, Mr. Rollo assumed charge of the Provincial
Board of Health and Colonel Carmichael was appointed a member
of the Hydro Electric Commission in place of the late W. K. Mc-
Naught. Messrs. Drury, Raney, Smith and Biggs, had certain Liberal affiliations in the past; Messrs. Grant, Nixon and Doherty had
some Conservative associations; the others had no known political
ties and none of them had any Parliamentary experience. As to
politics, the Premier, in a Toronto speech on Nov. 17th, declared
that: "Behind our movement for direct political action there was
a widespread belief that our politicians had been absolutely insincere. It was not so much that mistakes had been made, but that
the men who ran our affairs lacked sincerity. The people decided
they would rather have sincere men who might make a few mistakes." He also intimated that with the adoption of Proportional
Representation and a due extension of the Referendum—to both of
which he was committed—the "almost total elimination of the
Party system" was in sight. To the Associated Boards of Trade
on Nov. 20th he said: "You need fear no class legislation. The
Government of this Province has been taken over in a spirit of
public service. The old party system outlived its usefulness.
The new People's party will go forward with a sincere desire to
serve, unhampered by the barnacles, the parasites and the hangers-
on of the old parties." Following the appointments it became
necessary to hold bye-elections and on Dec. 15th Messrs. Smith,
Bowman, Grant, Nixon, Rollo and Biggs were re-elected by acclamation—four of them had preceding majorities running into thousands.*

Succeeding incidents included the effort of the Toronto *Star*
to make the abolition of Government House an issue with editorials
which were backed up by the *Farmers' Sun* and various news
articles urging or intimating action by the new Government in that
direction; the intimation by Mr. Premier Drury on Nov. 25th at
Barrie that the spirit and operation of the Criminal laws should be
changed along the lines of charity and justice with special attention

*Note.—Seats were arranged for Messrs. Drury, Doherty and Raney early in 1920.

to gaols and children.; the Premier's statement on Nov. 26th that he and the Government were behind the Hydro-Electric projects as they had been developed up to the present, and as they showed signs of being developed, to the fullest possible extent that the finances of the Province would permit; the personal act of Mr. Drury, which became public on Dec. 1st, and by which he voluntarily reduced his salary from $12,000 to $9,000. To the Canadian Club, Toronto, on Dec. 3rd, the Premier said that caucus government would be a thing of the past and that he would never resort to patronage to retain office. As to Education: "I don't think our educational policy will be along technical or vocational lines. We don't care about making a good farmer or a good carpenter; the main thing is to turn out a good citizen." On the 5th accompanied by Messrs. Mills and Bowman, Mr. Drury started on a tour of New Ontario. Cobalt and Haileybury, South Porcupine and Cochrane, Timmins and Monteith, Matheson and Swastika, North Bay and New Liskeard and Englehart, were visited; hosts of suggestions and proposals were heard and close attention given to facts and conditions.

At a Dominion Grange banquet in Toronto on Dec. 15th Mr. Drury specially urged good-will toward the United States: "It is part of my religion that I should do all in my power to cultivate good relations between Canada and the United States. We want that boundary kept without gun or fort—not now, but forever." At the annual meeting of the U.F.O. on Dec. 18th a Resolution was passed endorsing the selection of a Farmers' leader to form the Government, re-affirming the Provincial platform of the Association and urging upon the Administration the seriousness of its responsibility and the great trust placed in its hands. The members of the Government as a whole attended the Convention and delivered brief addresses. Other incidents of this period included the non-political banquet given by several hundreds of his friends in Toronto to Sir William Hearst on Dec. 17th, with A. E. Ames in the chair; the issue of a statement by H. H. Dewart on Nov. 29th vigorously criticizing the new Government and "a People's Party which would not allow a lawyer or a doctor, a merchant or a miller, a banker or a manufacturer, or an independent farmer, upon its platform during the whole of the campaign"; the protest in East and North Middlesex against the appointment, by promotion, of Miss Walker as Registrar on the ground of her alleged opposition to the U.F.O. and the Premier's refusal to admit of anything even savouring of political patronage in that connection.

The Hydro-Electric Situation and Radial Railway Policy. During this year the Province, the Government, and the people, had to consider the tremendous developments of Sir Adam Beck's Hydro-Electric policy. There was no doubt of its popularity and of the personal power of the man whose enthusiasm had created so great a factor in Provincial progress; there was, also, no doubt of the large responsibilities which were steadily growing for the people and the Province to bear in the future. The Hydro-Electric Power Commission of Ontario, which controlled the combined Government and Municipal Hydro system of the Province with Sir Adam Beck as its Chairman and driving force, had, on Oct. 31st, 1919, Assets totalling $51,081,982* which included the original cost of the Niagara, Thunder Bay, Severn, St. Lawrence, Wasdell, Eugenia, Ottawa, Muskoka and Rideau Systems, at $19,931,061; the Niagara Power Development works' expenditure to date, at $14,713,970, and the Ontario Power Co. shares, etc., at $11,304,100. Liabilities included cash advances from the Provincial Treasurer of $36,592,816, the Bank of Montreal $1,200,-000, with Debentures of $8,320,900 issued for purchase of the Ontario Power Co. and the new Essex and Thorold Systems. Sir Adam Beck in his Report for the year of Oct. 31st, 1919, reviewed the enormous increases of the past two years in cost of materials and labour, the scarcity and decrease in efficiency of labour, the heavy duties and war taxes, and added:

At the beginning of the year, the Commission fixed a schedule of rates covering the estimated cost of service to all municipalities. These rates brought in a total revenue of $3,729,705, while the actual cost of service was $3,860,700, which includes the total expenses for interest, cost of power, operation and maintenance, amounting to $3,243,329, and all the necessary fixed charges and reserves, such as sinking fund, reserves for renewals and contingencies, amounting to $617,371. After meeting all operating expenses and setting aside the reserves as above set out the expenditures exceeded the revenue by $130,995; the cost of service to all municipalities exceeding the estimates by but 3·5 per cent.

The total mileage of lines built and acquired by the Commission was 2,583 miles. It was claimed in the Ontario Elections that, since its inception, the Hydro-Electric scheme had, so far, saved to the consumers of electric power in Ontario over fifty million dollars and displaced, annually, 5,000,000 tons of coal; that it had developed and distributed 350,000 horse-power to over 230 municipalities, 175,000 domestic consumers and 6,000 customers for power; and that the Queenston-Chippewa undertaking would provide an economical development of 400,000 horse-power with a prospective ultimate development in the whole Province of over 1,000,000 horse-power. Sir Adam Beck at Oshawa on Oct. 10th deprecated this statement as too moderate: "The Hydro is saving the people of Ontario at least $25,000,000 per annum, in addition to a saving in coal of approximately $35,000,000 per annum, while establishing, also, the basis of a perpetual supply."

The Chippewa Power scheme involved the running of a Canal 12¾ miles from Chippewa, about two miles above Niagara Falls to the Niagara River at about one mile above Queenston and was a really great engineering feat, a costly project financially, but an important one for the provision of cheap power to the people. Sir Adam described the situation on Sept. 5th at Toronto as follows:

*Note.—Officially published Auditors' Report of Clarkson, Gordon and Dillworth, Toronto.

"Originally, the undertaking was to cost between $16,000,000 and $18,000,000, and between 175,000 and 200,000 h.p. were to be developed. Subsequently it was decided to double the capacity of the Canal and, although the cost was also doubled, its capacity, instead of being 6,600 second feet will be over 15,000 second feet, and the product of that water will be 500,000 h.p. for peak loads. For ordinary purposes it will supply 425,000 h.p. with equipment installed to develop 525,000 h.p."

This development depended for final operation upon a revision of the Waterways Treaty with the United States; if it were successful in construction and operation it promised to cut the soft coal imports of Ontario in two, fill the greater part of the Province with a tremendous flow of electric energy, and operate fast electric radials throughout the central part of the Province. As an engineering project it involved the taking of water from above the Falls, carrying it *via* the Canal 13 miles to the edge of the deep Niagara gorge, near Queenston, and letting it fall 500 feet to the level of Lake Ontario with immense power extracted from the force of the falling waters. This power would be equal, it was claimed, to 10,000,000 tons of coal or, at 1919 prices, anywhere up to $100,-000,000 a year. Besides this project the Commission was pledged to the St. Lawrence power development with an immediate expenditure of $26,000,000 and a possible total of $300,000,000 by the Dominion and other beneficiaries combined and an expected addition of 1,000,000 horse-power to the resources of the Province.

Meantime, the Radial or electric Railway plans were in a process of steady development but with signs of serious opposition—notably the attitude of the Farmers' organization. The 1919 Report of the Commission stated that, despite war-time limitations in construction, the line from Toronto to Bowmanville, 43 miles, was under way with 14 miles of rails laid between Bowmanville and Whitby, some grading done and some rights of way purchased. Estimates were completed on this route and indicated a cost of $8,360,794 for purchase of rights of way and existing construction, completion of the line to Toronto and provision of the rolling stock and equipment necessary to commence service. The annual revenue was estimated at $1,118,003 and the operating expenses and interest at $1,076,175. Hope was expressed that the Dominion Government would turn over the G.T.R. lines in this district when acquired, and so permit their early operation by electric power besides avoiding unnecessary duplication. For the Toronto-Niagara line two Townships and the City of Hamilton failed in 1918 to carry their By-laws approving the municipal share in the cost but, during 1919, Hamilton and one of the Townships came in; all the Councils between Toronto and St. Catharines then voted to go on without the obdurate Township of Saltfleet and an Order-in-Council was secured authorizing the Commission to issue the necessary bonds and proceed with the construction.

Eight municipalities interested in the 28-mile line between Wel-

THE HON. ROBERT HENRY GRANT, M.L.A.
Appointed Minister of Education for Ontario in 1919

THE HON. MANNING WILLIAM DOHERTY, M.L.A.
Appointed Minister of Agriculture for Ontario in 1919

land and Port Colborne and Bridgeburg, all of which had carried their By-laws in January, 1917, were anxious to have their line constructed, but here, as in respect to construction at Hamilton, the question of Grand Trunk duplication was involved. The Toronto-London line was held up by a few of the 31 municipalities concerned voting against it though 90 per cent. of the necessary guarantees were carried; on the Hamilton-Elmira-Guelph project voting was to take place early in 1920 with a capital cost of $6,530,-659 involved for 75 miles of line with, also, the proposed acquisition of the Guelph Street Railway.   These efforts or arrangements were tentative and preliminary to Sir Adam Beck's great ideal of a Province gridironed by publicly-owned electric lines giving a fast and comfortable service with low rates for passengers and light freight; at the end of this year fully 3,000 miles of these roads, involving an expenditure of $200,000,000, had been asked for by municipalities.   The Commission reported against the building of many of the lines because sufficient business was not in sight to make them pay and it did not press for construction in other cases. Less than 300 miles really went through all the stages necessary before asking the Government to guarantee the issue of bonds by the Municipalities.   The lines which, at the end of the year, the Commission desired to go on with were that of Toronto and Bowmanville, 43½ miles, Toronto and Port Credit, 15 miles, Port Credit and St. Catharines, 60 miles, and Hamilton to Elmira, 78 miles.

The estimated cost of these lines was $30,000,000 and by 1921, as stated by Sir Adam during the Hamilton radial campaign, the total investment in the Hydro-Electric system of Ontario, as a whole, would be $100,000,000.   This fight in Hamilton was a very keen one and the majority on Mch. 15th was 2,737 out of a total vote of 9,607.   At London on Mch. 17th he announced, as a result, the immediate construction of not only the Hamilton and Niagara radial, but also of the Kitchener, Guelph, Stratford and London line, on which the people had voted two years before.   The two lines would be joined between Toronto and Port Credit.   He also stated that the Commission was conducting negotiations with the Père Marquette Railway for the acquisition of that Company's lines between St. Thomas and Windsor, and also for branches serving Chatham and Sarnia.   At this time, also, the Commission refused to sanction the proposed purchase by Toronto of the Toronto and York Radial Railway because it was said the arrangement involved a perpetual franchise for the delivery of freight on the street-car lines of Toronto for the whole 24 hours of every day of the week, and imposed upon the city a perpetual obligation to carry this freight and express at less than cost.

Representatives of the Hydro-Electric Railway municipalities at Guelph, on Apr. 24th, urged the taking over of the G.T.R. by the Federal Government and non-interference by Federal authorities in the development of Provincial water-powers.   Sir Adam, in his speech, protested against what he termed the opposition of the Railway authorities at Ottawa, of Dr. Reid, the Minister of Railways and others, to the Hydro projects—especially the St. Lawrence River branch—and stated, incidentally, that in the Chippewa work the Ottawa powers had mulcted the Commission of 42½ per cent. duty on every item of machinery necessary to bring in to construct the plant. At a Toronto meeting on Apr. 30th he stated that the total present capacity of the Hydro undertakings was 400,000 h.p., with an ultimate capacity of 1,950,000 h.p. The cost was $81,000,000 and in 1921 this would be increased to $110,000,-000 which would not include the St. Lawrence scheme: "We've got to realize on that policy. International it may be; inter-Provincial it is not; Dominion it will never be." There now were 234 municipalities, he declared, linked in the Power project with its privileges going to 1,750,000 people. It had 3,000 miles of transmission lines; 12 systems were being operated by the Commission, and were providing 345,000 horse-power.

At Whitby on May 7th, 325 representatives of municipalities east of Toronto, interested in Hydro radials, met and requested the Dominion Government to hand over to the Hydro Commission, at a valuation, the Toronto Eastern Railway as an integral portion of the radial system which was to connect the Niagara and St. Lawrence districts, or the western and eastern sections of Ontario. Sir Adam Beck stated that when the St. Lawrence power was developed, Ontario would command 1,000,000 horse-power in that locality. He estimated the coal displacement of this power at $50,000,-000 annually. Later in the month it was stated that the Dominion Government had acceded to this request. At a Galt Convention of Western Hydro interests on July 31st, Sir Adam described the policy for that part of the Province as involving the electrification of the Galt and Elmira branch of the G.T.R. which passed through Kitchener, and also the Grand Trunk line from Fergus to Galt via Guelph. The idea was then to proceed to Hamilton, on a new right of way, by a 24-mile short line and in to Toronto. At Stratford on Aug. 29th the Hydro leader addressed representatives of 75 Western Ontario municipalities and in Toronto on Sept. 4th met the delegates to the annual meeting of the Hydro-Electric Railway Association who were vehement in their demand for Government action rather than talk, enthusiastically endorsed Sir Adam Beck in this project and unanimously passed a Resolution calling for prompt administrative action. Sir Adam pointed out that Guelph was still holding up the London-Toronto line. J. W. Lyon, Guelph, the persistent supporter and advocate of the whole Hydro policy, was re-elected President. Speaking at Oshawa on Oct. 9th Sir Adam said:

Toronto is going to have the finest radial system of any city on the continent if we have the courage to carry out our plans. We want a system of railways municipally-owned that will make you independent of the steam roads. Our system will not be under Government ownership but public ownership and, unlike some other systems, there will be no politics connected with it. We have our eye on greater projects still; I mean the St. Lawrence River, and if we have our own way we will build a dam which will regulate the level of Lake Ontario. We are going to make the head of the Lakes the head of navigation and will have a showdown with Montreal. When our plans are completed we will be able to supply power to run all the railways in Ontario and to develop two million horse-power. We want to transmit St. Lawrence power over to connect with the Niagara system at 220,000 volts, and I think I will live to see it.

A meeting at Windsor of 9 Border municipalities on Oct. 25th urged that Sir Adam Beck be offered the Premiership; at Toronto on the 29th he received an ovation, following his London political defeat, from 400 municipal delegates and Resolutions were passed urging his retention of the Chairmanship of the Commission; at Whitby on Oct. 29th he announced an arrangement with Hon. Dr. Reid, Minister of Railways, that the C.N.R. track, which parallelled the Grand Trunk from Bowmanville to Napanee and thence to Kingston, would, in the event of G.T.R. nationalization, be turned over to the Hydro Commission. From these latter speeches the total expenditure on Hydro projects, then immediately in sight, may be summarized as follows:

Present investment—municipalities and Government	$96,000,000
Expenditure in next five years, including the $30,000,000 Chippewa project	54,000,000
Buying out of opposition, nearly	48,000,000
St. Lawrence development Plans	30,000,000
	$228,000,000
Cost of proposed Hydro radials (Estimated)	52,000,000
Total	$280,000,000

Sir Adam was at Galt on Nov. 6th and at London on Nov. 18th where 100 delegates to the Ontario Municipal Electrical Association asked the Government to give permanency to his tenure of office by appointing him Chairman of the Hydro-Electric Power Commission for a ten-year term; at Windsor on the 19th he told the Great Waterways Conference that the power capacity of the waters of the Great Lakes and the St. Lawrence would meet the expense of deepening this great waterway to the sea. He went on as follows: "We are spending $100,000,000 in developing power at Chippewa Falls. That is only a starter. When the authorities at Ottawa discontinue their patronage of private interests in favour of voting money for enterprises such as the St. Lawrence project we shall have the cheapest power, light and transportation in the world." The Eastern Ontario Hydro-Electrical Union was organized at Brockville on Dec. 8th, with 150 delegates present and W. B. Reynolds elected President, and the passage of a Resolution calling on the Ontario Government to develop the Long Sault or some other available water-power in that region immediately.

There was persistent opposition during this period. The *Financial Post* of Toronto was continuous in its criticism and pessimistic outlook; James White, Deputy-Chairman of the Conservation Commission, stated at Calgary on Aug. 13th that improved types of turbines, combined with new methods of utilizing the steam-producing qualities of coal, rendered very insecure the future of hydro-electric power; Dr. J. Murray Clark, K.C., of Toronto, argued at length, in several able articles, for great caution and proved that financial disaster had come to Ontario through the Municipal Loan Fund of the early Fifties which, for a time, was very popular with the municipalities. The U.F.O. Convention of Dec. 18th viewed "with alarm" the proposed policy of Hydro-radials with its expenditure of millions of dollars and feared that in many instances there would be duplication of existing steam railways. But the supporters of the movement had no fears and on Dec. 12th 300 municipal delegates waited upon the Drury Government and asked that the Board of the Hydro-Electric Commission be increased from three to five members appointed for terms that would ensure continuity, that Sir Adam Beck be made Chairman for a term of six years, and that one-half the remaining members be elected by municipalities using Hydro-Electric energy.. The Toronto *Globe* represented much of the press of Ontario in re-affirming (Dec. 27th) its support of the Hydro-Radial line running from Toronto to Bowmanville.

ONTARIO INCIDENTS OF 1919.

Apr. 1—During the Public Accounts Committee enquiry into the Dewart-Ayearst charges, J. D. Flavelle, Chairman of the License Board, stated that over 500,000 physicians' prescriptions for liquor had been passed since September, 1916, and over 1,000,000 quarts sold under these orders with 8,500 committments to prisons under the O.T.A. and $1,250,000 imposed in fines.

Apr. 30—Rev. B. H. Spence was sentenced to a fine of $500 or 4 months in gaol on the celebrated *Parasite* charges for publication of banned literature, but the judgment afterwards (July 30th) was quashed by Judge Morson.

Aug. 29—The Ontario Municipal Association passed Resolutions asking the Government to amend the Assessment Act so as to exempt income from personal earnings of non-householders in rural municipalities; requesting an optional system of municipal government for cities and towns of the Province and the securing of a Report on improvement of the present municipal government system; urging that taxes due for business and income be levied the year in which the assessment was made and that the time for collection be different from the time for payment of taxes on real property; declaring that all by-laws, plans and specifications for the construction of permanent improvements and the issue of debentures, therefor, should be approved by the Municipal Bureau.

Oct. 29—The retirement of J. L. Englehart as Chairman of the T. and N.O. Commission was announced after 14 years of devoted service.

Nov. 20—The 6th annual meeting of the Associated Boards of Trade of Ontario was held at Toronto with President William Taylor of Owen Sound in the chair and among the Resolutions passed were the following: Favouring a report on metals and minerals of Ontario by the Provincial and Dominion Governments and Government aid to establish ship-building in Canada; opposing the leasing of all Grand Trunk lines in Ontario to the Hydro-Electric Commission; opposing business taxation; urging the appointment of a Royal Commission to study the Tariff, and of a permanent Tariff Board; urging legislation to provide for the immediate coinage of pure nickel coins of small denomination; calling for every possible encouragement of Aviation, by subsidy or otherwise, for the commercial and postal services of the Dominion.

QUEBEC AND THE MARITIME PROVINCES

General Conditions in Quebec: Politics and Legislation in 1919. The Province of Quebec in 1919 had a most prosperous year with fine crops, great industrial development and very few Labour troubles; its Government in the 15th year of Sir Lomer Gouin's Administration faced a general election of unique certainty as to result and with an exceptional tribute of popular approval. The largest of Canadian Provinces, Quebec in this year had 24,000,000 acres occupied and 8,000,000 under crop out of a total area of 450,000,000 acres; dairying, which had realized $65,-000,000 in 1918, was prosperous and capable of still greater expansion with cattle valued at $139,119,000 as against $59,334,657 in 1914; with increased values in other Live stock very marked—horses $50,105,892 in 1914 to $62,163,000 in 1919, sheep $3,770,494 to $13,000,700 and swine $9,087,028 to $22,450,000.*

It had 43 pulp and paper mills producing 800,000 tons of pulp and 450,000 tons of paper and paper products valued at $65,000,-000; with 130,000,000 acres of forest-land valued at $575,000,000 and a tremendous development in the pulp-wood industry; with enormous electrical energy estimated at over 6,850,000 horse-power of which 875,000 h.-p. was developed and various growing industrial centres the result—the Shawinigan system alone carrying 205,-000 h.-p. and feeding an area of 4,500 square miles; with industries numbering 7,158 establishments in 1915, an output of $387,-900,585 and a capital investment of $548,902,575—growing greatly in product and importance every year; with a mineral production (1918) of $18,182,179, a Forest product of $40,761,730, a Fisheries product of $3,414,378, butter and cheese valued at $30,033,984, Live-stock worth $252,445,000 and Field crops $271,750,900—a total natural product, with the current Industrial output estimated at $400,000,000, of $1,016,588,171. The Agricultural product of the Province in 1919 was as follows (Federal official figures):

	Area in Acres	Total Yield	Average Price per Bushel	Total Value
Spring Wheat	251,089	4,206,000 bush.	$2.88	$10,010,000
Oats	2,141,107	57,275,000 "	1.06	60,712,000
Barley	234,892	5,844,000 "	1.64	8,784,000
Rye	38,481	578,000 "	2.00	1,156,000
Peas	81,642	1,225,000 "	3.62	4,435,000
Beans	48,202	853,000 "	4.52	3,856,000
Buckwheat	170,043	4,081,000 "	1.70	6,938,000
Mixed Grains	157,637	4,256,000 "	1.50	6,384,000
Flax	11,384	111,000 "	3.91	434,000
Corn for husking	48,608	1,788,000 "	1.84	3,290,000
Potatoes	315,590	57,280,000 "	.85	48,688,000
Turnips, Mangolds	87,496	27,780,000 "	.53	14,723,000
Hay and Clover	4,299,360	6,449,000 tons	20.54 ton.	132,462,000
Fodder Corn	74,007	611,000 "	8.41 "	5,189,000
Alfalfa	28,488	67,000 "	14.22 "	953,000

*Note.—For organisation of Quebec United Farmers see Page 898 and for Quebec Educational Conditions see pages 539-44.

According to a statement by G. E. Marquis of the Provincial Bureau of Statistics, the farms of Quebec, with their improvements, houses, barns, etc., were valued at $72 an acre in 1919 as against $57 in 1918. The average wages, per month, for men, was $76, including board valued at $23, as against $65 in 1918; that of women was $37 a month, including board, as against $33 in 1918. There was an increased production of potatoes in 1919 with high prices, a general cultivation of tobacco with higher prices, a maple crop estimated at 12,157,447 lbs. of sugar and 1,470,775 gallons of syrup, high prices for butter ranging from 52 to 65 cents per pound at the factories, an increasing exportation of milk and cream to the States. In other lines of development, there was much ship-building done at Three Rivers and Lauzon and Montreal with 786 ocean vessels of 2,179,280 tonnage arriving at Montreal and 7,499 inland vessels with a tonnage of 4,357,734—in each case a large increase over the 1918 season.

During 1919 the Hon. J. E. Caron, for 10 years the efficient Minister of Agriculture in the Province, was able to report the production of field crops as a record one, which he estimated on Dec. 15th at $300,000,000 in value, or treble the value of the 1914 product, with a total area under crops placed at 7,935,513 or nearly double that of 1914. In these values potatoes had gone up since 1917 from 25 to 57 millions, turnips from 9 to 18 millions, Hay and clover from 48 to 129 millions. Mr. Caron had always encouraged Farmers' Clubs of which there were at the beginning of 1919, 782 in the Province including 120 Agricultural Co-operative Societies; his appropriations in 1918-19 for these organizations and the general encouragement of Agriculture totalled $488,000 and in 1919-20 $300,000 with $43,000 and $35,000 respectively for Agricultural Schools and $21,000 and $15,000, respectively, for House-keeping Schools; in September, 1919, there were 26 French-Canadian and 44 English Housewives' Leagues or Farmerette Clubs in the Province; the total grants for all agricultural purposes in 1918-19 were $798,000 and for 1919-20 the estimates were $556,500.

It may be added from the valuable volume published yearly by the Bureau of Statistics, and edited by G. E. Marquis, that there were in Quebec at this time 337,483 electric plants with 1,346 miles of transmission lines and 194,836 consumers of electricity; that the Automobiles registered in the Province numbered 786 in 1910 and 26,931 in 1918; that there were (1918) 836 Banks or branches in the Province with a total of Bank Clearings at Montreal, Quebec and Sherbrooke of $5,114,224,491; that there were 108 Mutual Benefit Associations with 134,746 Quebec members, Benefits of $70,855,944 in force and claims paid in 1918 of $2,056,041. The Montreal City and District Savings Bank, a Provincial Institution without a Dominion charter, had 100,000 depositors with a total of $33,808,-573 on deposit and a capital and reserve of $2,831,100; the Caisse d'Economic de Notre Dame de Quebec, founded in 1848 with a view to receiving small deposits from the masses, had a total in 1919 of

$10,317,973; small Co-operative People's Banks numbered 102 and 98 of them reported 27,593 members, 20,672 depositors and $2,513,-405 of Savings with $2,623,095 of Loans.   The population on Dec. 31st, 1918, was 2,432,251 and the municipalities numbered 1,316 with Assets of $150,930,866 and Liabilities of $185,640,500.

The annual Report of the Department of Lands and Forests (Hon. H. Mercier) showed a revenue of $2,510,141 for the year of June 30th, 1919, of which $1,357,996 came from stumpage dues. The Report of the new Minister of Colonization, Mines and Fisheries (Hon. J. E. Perrault) for 1919 gave figures of Mineral production showing a total of $20,701,005 or 10 per cent. increase over 1918 and including Asbestos $10,932,189, Copper and sulphur ore $447,-623, Chromite $223,321, Magnesite $283,719, Mica $224,723, Brick $1,179,624, Cement $4,337,572, Granite $329,992, Lime $521,031, Limestone $903,986, Tile, etc., $412,367.   The enthusiastic Minister of Roads, Hon. J. A. Tessier, showed 210 miles of road constructed in 1918 with a total length of Provincial highways, macadamized or gravelled, of 2,564 miles; his expenditures totalled $611,000 for the year 1917-18 with $1,064,300 under the 1912 Good Roads Act; he looked upon highways as subsidiary to railways, co-operative not competitive, essential as part of a great system of highways, waterways, railways; his appropriations and loans for 1918-19 totalled $2,269,304 with an expected increase of $1,000,000 for 1919-20; the total extent of improved roads in the Province at the close of 1919 was 3,000 miles and the money spent in development was chiefly in a system of main communication roads under Government aid and supervision.

The new Minister of Public Works and Labour, Hon. Antoine Galipeault, dealt in his Report for June 30th, 1919, with 5,251 miles of Railways in operation and the cash Provincial payments since 1867 to 1,631 miles of this total, for redemption of 13,324,950 acres of Land grants, as $4,557,728; with the building of 524 road bridges costing $3,664,799 and 51 under construction at a cost of $732,824; with the efforts of the Department to avert fires and the payment of $24,974 as bonuses to Municipalities, etc., in this connection; with the continued and effective inspection of Hotels and examination of stationary engineers receiving 1,136 certificates and 1,074 renewals; with the continuation of Government insurances on buildings, furniture, etc., totalling for the Province $2,670,100 and premiums of $32,875.   The Minister also dealt with certain improvements in Labour conditions and new laws which were coming into force as to (1) minimum wages for women, (2) forbidding the employment of girls or boys in industrial establishments unless they could read and write fluently and (3) providing for the protection of public buildings against fire and the creation of a Board of Examiners for electricians similar to that established some years before for the examination of stationary engineers.

Joseph Ainey, the new Superintendent-General of Provincial Employment Bureaux, reported 12,876 unemployed as registered during the year at the 5 Government Bureaux and 11,135 vacant places advised by employers with 5,688 persons placed in positions out of 8,871 referred to employers; the Soldiers who registered were 8,189 of whom 4,876 were referred to employers and 3,799 placed.   Felix Marois, Registrar of the Councils of Conciliation and Arbitration, reported as to the strikes in which he had intervened and deprecated strikes in general as ruinous or injurious to all concerned and only right in "extreme cases of unjustifiable refusal to redress wrong."   Incidents of the year included the conversion of the Soldiers' Employment Commission in January into the Quebec Returned Soldiers' Commission composed of Hon. G. A. Simard, M.L.C. (Chairman), Hon. R. Smeaton White and Alphonse Verville, M.P., as members with the object of giving assistance to all returning soldiers of the Province in securing positions in civil life, to keep daily records of the soldiers, and to take up complaints with the proper authorities; the effort of Léon-Mercier Gouin, son of the Premier, to promote good feeling between the Provinces of Quebec and Ontario and an address before the Union Catholique of Montreal on Feb. 9th which expressed views very similar to those addressed by him to the Empire Club, Toronto, on Nov. 27th, following and urging "a closer co-operation between Ontario and Quebec in working for the glory and development of our beloved country."

Other incidents were the speech of Hon. L. A. Taschereau in the Legislature on Feb. 12th in which he declared that there was no racial friction in Quebec, and at the same time urged French-Canadians to teach their children English because Bi-lingual training fitted them better for the battle of life; the appointment of Louis Guyon as Deputy-Minister of Labour and Ivan E. Vallée as Chief Engineer and Director of Provincial Railways; the response of the Province, outside of Montreal, to the Victory Loan of 1919 with subscriptions which reached a total of $35,030,950 compared with $34,520,850 in 1918 and $17,649,550 in 1917; the unveiling on Sept. 7th of the Montreal monument to Sir Georges Etienne Cartier through the pressing of an electric button by H.M. the King at Balmoral Castle, Scotland, with ceremonial local addresses by H.E. the Governor General, and Hon. Thomas Chapais, M.L.A.; the enthusiastic welcome at Montreal and Quebec given to Cardinal Mercier by Church, Government and people on Nov. 2-3.

An interesting view of Quebec and French-Canadians was expressed (1) by Lloyd Harris at Montreal on Dec. 3rd when he said that "the Province of Quebec is the balance wheel of Canada," and (2) by Sir Andrew Macphail when he told the Canadian Club, Montreal, on Nov. 10th and the Canadian Club, Quebec, on Dec. 16th that "The Province of Quebec is the last refuge in America for political sense, good order, freedom and civilization."   On Sept. 18th at a meeting in Montreal called by Fred. Wright, Editor of the *Canadian Municipal Journal*, a Union of Quebec Municipalities was organized in preliminary form with Omer Chaput as Secretary of the Committee; its formation was completed on Dec. 14-15 at Montreal with 380 delegates registered and a constitution framed which included a Board of Trustees and a Board of Directors with a Bureau of Information through which the services of experts in municipal law, engineering and accounting could be secured for the special benefit of, and at no extra cost to, each member municipality.   Hon. W. G. Mitchell, Minister of Municipal Affairs, was elected Patron, Mayor the Hon. M. Martin of Montreal as Hon. President and Mayor Henri Lavigeuer of Quebec, Hon. Vice-President; Mayor Jos. Beaubien of Outremont was President and Mayor R. Prieur, Point-aux-Trémbles, Secretary-Treasurer.

The 1st Legislative Session of 1919.   The first Session of this year was the last of the 14th Legislature of Quebec.   It was opened by Lieut.-Governor Sir Charles Fitzpatrick with a Speech from the Throne which referred to the death of Sir P. E. Le Blanc, Lieut.-Governor, to the end of the War and the heroism of the soldiers of liberty and justice; declared that the Province owed a debt of gratitude to the soldiers and that "my Government intends to offer free lots of land to such as may wish to take up farming, and to devote special attention to establishing employment bureaux in the principal centres of the Province, in order that soldiers, artisans and workmen may more easily and rapidly find work and employment"; stated that the work on "good roads" was proceeding satisfactorily and that the total length of roads improved was now nearly 2,600 miles; declared that road-making in colonization centres was being pushed as actively as possible with the Government· unceasingly devoting its efforts to promoting land-clearing whilst colonization in Abitibi was steadily progressing; described Agriculture as enjoying unprecedented prosperity and the result of the Greater Agricultural Production campaign of the Department in 1918 as having met with unhoped-for results; promised legislation of importance including one to "complete the law already passed" as ·to Prohibition.   The Address was moved by E. Thériault of L'Islet and Henry Miles of Montreal and approved after a brief debate.

The chief subject of controversy in the debate was the recent appointment of Mayor Martin of Montreal to the Legislative ·Council and, on Jan. 22nd, a Liberal member—Georges Mayrand of Montreal—criticized Mr. Martin as having frequently attacked and insulted the Premier in his Mayoralty campaigns and denounced the appointment; Arthur Sauvé, Opposition Leader, followed along the same lines and declared that Mr. Martin, instead of being called to the Legislative Council, should have been brought into Court for his attacks on the members of Legislature.   He demanded an enquiry as to the platform charges of corruption made by Mr. Martin against the Premier, the Government and the Legislature.   Sir Lomer Gouin, in his speech, merely said that: "I am just as sensible as anybody else of my dignity.   Public men are always subject

to attack.   All political men have enemies, but I regarded the interests of Montreal, and I thought that in making this nomination I
was working for the good of Montreal.''   That city was bound to
develop greatly, the Government had given it a new system of
administration, and he considered the Mayor's place to be in the
Legislative Council.   In the Council itself the Address was moved
by Hon. F. T. Savoie and Hon. Frank Carrel and approved without division.

Mr. Sauvé on Feb. 6th again demanded an enquiry into the
appointment and the Martin charges.   In the Council on
Feb. 19th Mr. Martin denied the newspaper reports of his
speeches: ''If I had known anything of malversation by any
members of this House I would not have consented to become a member.''   He spoke at length as to the Aztec deal, the
Fournier case and other matters of Civic controversy and sat down
amidst silence.   In the Assembly on Mch. 17th Mr. Sauvé moved
for a Royal Commission of enquiry into this subject but was ruled
out of order; in the Council on the same day Mr. Martin stated as
to his campaign charges that there were millions involved in the
annexation of Maisonneuve to Montreal, that he had merely quoted
rumours floating around at the time and had no intention of im-
plying that the deal had been put through by fraudulent or dishonest pressure.   Political attacks and insinuations continued, however, chiefly in *L'Evenement*, a Quebec Conservative journal, with
the Premier's name brought in, and to that paper on May 13th
Hon. G. E. Amyot wrote stating that in 1910 he had paid Sir
Lomer Gouin, Premier of the Province, and his partner, L. P.
Bérard, $100,000 for a piece of Maisonneuve land to build a new
factory on, that the land had then greatly increased in value from
its original cost of $33,000 and that it continued to do so
and he was able to sell it in 1912 for $158,000.   He asked if there
was anything wrong in a public man transacting business, or selling
his own property, while Prime Minister!

The Budget was presented on Jan. 30th by Hon. W. G. Mitchell,
Provincial Treasurer.   For the year ending June 30th, 1918, he
had a good report to make: ''During the 4½ years of the period of
the War, knowing that the country was facing unknown burdens
and conditions I, on all occasions, advised economy by Government,
municipalities, corporations and individuals.   This Government
has, I submit, practised such economy, and in fact has made this
its watchword at all times, and has administered the Public funds
with care and foresight, under the wise leadership and capable
guidance of our worthy Prime Minister.   The Province has forged
ahead, and I was enabled at the end of of each year to show a substantial surplus; this year the Province has excelled all other
records in its history and for the year ending June 30 last it has
the very large surplus of $2,134,558.''   The Ordinary revenue for
these years exceeded the estimates by $4,246,226, while the estimate
of the Ordinary and Extraordinary expenditure was exceeded by

only $2,174,620. This difference was due to the Succession Duties exceeding the estimate by $3,336,547: "This excess in receipts enabled us to pay large sums for patriotic and charitable purposes out of the Consolidated revenue, and to further increase the grants to the important public services of Good Roads, Agriculture, Education and Colonization."

The actual revenue in 1918 was $13,806,390, the ordinary expenditure $11,423,497 with $248,334 of extraordinary expenditure and the surplus as above; the Liabilities of the Province were $42,-891,544 and the Assets $10,749,026, the Funded Debt was $38,015,-654 and the unfunded Debt $2,962,574; for 1918-19 the Treasurer estimated an Ordinary revenue of $10,449,393 and Ordinary expenditure of $10,399,345; the abrogation of the Amusement Tax was promised and Mr. Mitchell pointed out, as to a subject of some debate, that in the last 5 years, apart from the Dominion subsidy, the total Ordinary revenue of the Province was $42,354,093 of which Montreal contributed $22,482,144 or 53 per cent.; he estimated that automobile tourists, encouraged by good roads, had spent $1,500,000 in Montreal during 1917 and double that sum in 1918. In this latter connection he stated that the Government since 1912, in its Good Roads policy, had paid the municipalities up to June 30th, 1918, $10,719,936 and on Government roads $6,155,683, with net proceeds for Loans on this account of $5,850,805 out of $20,000,000 authorized. In view of the coming Elections the following table was of interest:

Government Expenditures	1897-98	1905-06	1917-18
Education	$484,260.00	$584,460.18	$1,581,454.80
Agriculture	193,226.97	210,600.00	724,244.64
Roads	4,000.00	8,000.00	1,733,770.30
Colonization	110,250.00	140,500.00	337,261.11
Total	$741,726.97	$893,560.18	$4,376,730.85

The Conservative leader criticized the Budget on Feb. 6th. He claimed that the Government had built up its surplus by refusing to grant increases of $500,000 to employees, by refusing many grants that were urgently needed, and by not making preparations for the great economic changes that were bound to arise. It had obtained the revenue by levying taxes on municipalities which ought to pertain to those municipalities and he specified the tax on automobiles used, for the most part, within specific municipal limits. He laid stress on the spending of $1,346,332 by means of special warrants, and declared they would soon have the Government authorizing new taxation by means of Orders-in-Council! The large receipts and surplus were due, he alleged, to about $3,-000,000 received from the Estate of Sir W. C. Macdonald. He claimed that the Government included in its Assets public works that brought in no revenue and had no negotiable value such as the $3,619,147 spent on the Bordeaux gaol.

One of the chief measures of the Session was Hon. L. A. Taschereau's Bill providing for a Minimum wage for women; it was elaborate and wide in scope and character. It established a Commission composed of three members, one of whom should be the Deputy Minister of Labour or some other person nominated by the Minister, as Chairman, and two others nominated by the Lieut.-Governor-in-Council and one of whom could be a woman.   No member was to be paid a salary but a Secretary could be employed and the Commission was to have jurisdiction over all industrial establishments in the Province, and the right to enquire into the working conditions of all women in any establishment and the wages they received.   If the Commission were of opinion that the wages paid in any case were insufficient, it could order a conference of a specified number of persons, half composed of employers and half of employees, with the addition of a few disinterested persons, to investigate working conditions and wages, and by a majority determine the minimum wages that should be paid in that particular industry; the decision of the conference to be submitted to the Commission who could approve, reject or modify it or order a new conference.   The final decision of the Commission was obligatory with special power to the Minister to act in individual cases of hardship or necessity.

Another measure carried by Mr. Taschereau, as Minister of Labour, was one which prohibited employment of any children under 16 years of age in any class of remunerative employment, whatever, unless he or she could read and write—including work in an industrial plant, service as a bell-boy in an hotel or as a newsboy.   In order to work it was necessary to hold a certificate that he or she had attended school for at least 6 years.   Amendments to the Workmen's Compensation Act provided that in the case of a workman receiving a fixed salary, there should not be counted, in the determination of his annual salary, any remuneration which he might receive for additional work outside of his regular hours of labour; it was also provided that in the case of injuries to a son, who was the principal support of the family, the father could receive compensation.

Other legislation included a Bill changing the name of Fraser-ville back to its original one of Rivière du Loup; another setting aside certain areas of farm lands for free grant to British or Allied soldiers who had been honourably discharged after serving on any of the fronts in the Great War and who were previously residents of Canada; a measure establishing the powers of the College of Dental Surgeons upon a dignified basis and with control over licenses and diplomas; a measure authorizing the appointment of a Deputy-Minister of Labour with control of matters connected with labour, under the direction of the Minister, and with the duties of Chief Inspector of Industrial establishments; a Bill of Hon. J. L. Décarie amending the Public Instruction Act in certain details and one by Hon. W. G. Mitchell amending the Municipalities Act which changed the whole system of voting in such municipalities as desired to borrow money and made it easier for them to obtain approval of by-laws authorizing loans; a Bill abolishing the Court of

Review and another granting large tracts of land in various parts of the Province to certain Railways. .

Under this legislation the Quebec Central got 2,000 acres per mile for 20 miles, the Canada and Gulf Terminable Railway Co. 2,000 acres per mile for 190 miles of road, the Rouge River Railway Co. in Argenteuil and Labelle the same grant for 80 miles, the St. Francis Valley Railway Co. for 95 miles and the Shefford, Bagot, and Missisquoi Line for 75 miles; while an unnamed Railway in the North running for 100 miles from Temiscamingue or Kipawa to the Rivière des Quinze was to get 4,000 acres per mile, and a railway in Abitibi, also unnamed, the 2,000 acres per mile grant. Acts were passed incorporating the St. Felicien and Ungava Railway Co. and the Quebec and Ungava Railway Co. with Lord Templetown and others as incorporators; Mr. Taschereau had a measure taking up the Dominion Housing allotment of $6,600,000 to the Province which provided that municipalities could appoint Commissions to direct the local building programme while the Provincial Government would appoint a Director of Housing and lend the money to the municipalities at five per cent. A general scheme was to be prepared by the Provincial Treasurer, who would make such advances to the municipalities as he deemed proper. Dwellings were not to cost more than $4,500 including values of the land which latter was not to exceed one-sixth the cost of the building; the municipality was not to advance more than 80 per cent. of the total value of the building and lot in the case of persons borrowing money to erect houses on their own lots, or not more than 65 per cent. in the case of houses erected by Housing companies.

The Mining laws were amended by Hon. H. Mercier to better enforce the Crown's royalty rights, taking as a basis the value at the mine of the mineral extracted, without deducting costs of extraction, and giving the Minister power to fix the duration and scope of mining licenses in New Quebec as well as terms and conditions. Acts were passed authorizing erection of the Sherbrooke, St. Hyacinthe and Hull Technical Schools at a cost of $150,000 each and a grant to each school of $10,000 a year. Amongst the measures which failed to pass were that of J. N. Francoeur prohibiting the marriage of first cousins; the attempt by Georges Mayrand to abolish the recently-established Commission system of government in Montreal and cancel the new Tramways Company franchise in that city; the Bill of S. Létourneau incorporating and amalgamating the Montreal Association of Accountants and the Provincial Institute on the ground of monopoly allegations. Incidents of the Session included the eloquent tributes paid to Sir Wilfrid Laurier's memory (Feb. 18th) by Sir Lomer Gouin, Hon. W. G. Mitchell, Arthur Sauvé and C. E. Gault in the Assembly and by Hon. Jules Allard and Hon. Thomas Chapais in the Council, and the suggestion (Feb. 7th) by S. Létourneau that the Government should establish Travelling scholarships so as to enable ten scholars from the Technical schools, the Universities or the Polytechnic schools of the Province, to spend two years in some other country so as to complete their education in science, art or any of the professions.   The House was prorogued on Mch. 17th after a Session in which the Assembly did not record one vote and considered 189 Bills.

The Quebec Prohibition Bill of 1919.   At the beginning of this year the Prohibitionists in Quebec felt sure that the Province would join the rest of Canada in support of their policy; by long, hard fighting they had won 1,090 out of 1,200 municipalities in recent years through Local Option though the gains only represented a half of the actual population as Montreal, Sherbrooke and other centres had not come in; Sir Lomer Gouin had declared himself a friend of Temperance while La Ligue Anti-Alcoolique and the Dominion Alliance and the Anti-Liquor League had all been working in harmony with apparent co-operation between many of the priests and the Protestant ministers.   There followed a keen effort to influence the Legislature for a compromise along the lines of a wine and beer license as against "bone dry" Prohibition which it began to appear the French-Canadian workman did not like.   The legislation of February, 1918, had tightened the laws greatly and promised total Prohibition on May 1st, 1919; since then continuous agitation and effort and influence had been brought to bear on the Government and Legislature and it became more and more clear that public opinion was not in favour of an extreme policy.

The Quebec Brewers' Association published in February a signed advertisement declaring beer to be a wholesome and nutritious food and that its sugars were nourishing and heat-producing, its dextrines and albumens muscle-building foods, its hop extracts appetizing and a useful sedative, quieting to the nerves, its phosphates excellent as a brain food and for building up bone tissue. Delegations, pro and con, waited on the Government which was deluged with telegrams asking for a law which would permit wine and beer after May 1st—one Minister, the Hon. N. Séguin, getting an average of 150 a day from Montreal; Mr. Sauvé for the Opposition declared in favour of a wine and beer license and on Mch. 4th the Government announced its policy.

The Bill introduced by Hon. W. G. Mitchell, Provincial Treasurer, proposed to retain all the Prohibitory clauses of the 1918 measure which was to come into force on May 1st except that the electorate would be given the right, by a Referendum, of saying whether they would like beer and light wines to remain as a beverage.   The Referendum was to take this simple form: "Are you in favour of beer and other malted liquors, and wine and cider, being sold for beverage purposes, providing the maximum of alcohol contained in beer and other malted liquors does not exceed 2·51 per cent., weight measure, and provided the maximum of alcohol contained in wine and cider does not exceed 6·94 per cent. weight measure?"   In his speech on the 2nd reading Mr. Mitchell declared that the Bill completed the intention of the Government as indicated in the Act of 1918, and the undertaking, as continued in the Speech from the Throne, to complete the License Bill. The Government, however: "On account of the many representations that have been made, on account of the thousands and thousands of petitions and telegrams that we have received from all over the country, believes that this question is of such paramount importance and the opinion of the public of the Province is so divided, that we do not think we should be called upon to speak for the people."

He explained that the new Act provided for prohibition of the sale of intoxicating liquor of all kinds and descriptions, except that the Government could authorize a number, not to exceed 25, of vendors who would be placed in charge of depôts established in Montreal and throughout the Province for the purpose of supplying liquor for industrial, mechanical and artistic purposes and for sacramental and medicinal purposes. Certificates were to be signed by doctors or priests or a solemn declaration made of the purposes for which it was to be used with varied restrictions and heavy penalties imposed. If the Referendum should be in favour of beer and wine licenses, the Government would issue about the same number of licenses throughout the Province as existed at present but there would be no bars. Where the Canada Temperance Act was in force the new law would not apply should the wine and beer be carried in the Referendum; if these were carried in Montreal but with a sufficient majority against them from outside to over-balance the City, the latter would have to submit to the Provincial majority. The number of persons authorized to import intoxicating liquor into the Province after Apr. 30th for the purpose of selling the same to authorized vendors and to import beer and other malt liquors, cider and wine was to be limited to ten, and licensed on payment of a fee of $25,000 a year. The quantity of beer permissible on one certificate was not to exceed one dozen pint bottles or ½ dozen quarts. The Referendum was, finally, settled for Apr. 10th and the Bill passed its 2nd reading on Mch. 13th and was through both Houses before adjournment on the 17th.

The ensuing battle was short but vigourous. A Provincial Prohibition Convention was held at Montreal on Mch. 12th to protest against the Government's policy; it declared that the Referendum came at a bad season and left them without time for a great campaign of education. A division of opinion came, also, in many quarters from which support was expected. The Anglican Bishop of Montreal (Dr. Farthing) declared on Mch. 30th that he believed in absolute Prohibition but with Compensation; the Anti-Alcoholique Ligue showed clear differences of view and Victor Morin, its Secretary, stated on Apr. 3rd that "the moderate use of beer and wine will be a strong help against the use of alcoholic liquors" and that the League was founded on the principle of tolerance in regard to fermented drink; a Committee of Moderation was formed on Apr. 2nd at Montreal of those "in favour of the use of beer and wine" with men like Lord Shaughnessy, Sir Alexandre Lacoste, Hon. L. O. David and J. T. Foster, President of the Trades and Labour Council, as Honourary Officers and Joseph Quintal, President of the Chambre du Commerce, as President.

The Hon. Napoleon Séguin, Minister without Portfolio, undertook a personal campaign in Montreal for the beer and wine license and a strong point in his argument was that there were over 20,000 unemployed at present in the City, and that the shutting down of breweries would add about 20,000 more to the total. He claimed that to his influence, at the request of organized Labour, was due the policy of the Government in this respect; he also claimed in his speeches that the clergy were, or would be, behind the opposition to complete Prohibition—though no proof of this was given. He declared, also, that Prohibition put the priests in a humiliating situation as to wine for their sacraments. *L'Evenement* of Quebec opposed Prohibition as undesirable and the G.W.V.A. of Montreal passed a Resolution against it; *La Presse,* and *La Patrie* and *Le Devoir* of Montreal all supported the Government policy and preached moderation and toleration while the French-Canadian Temperance Societies very largely held aloof.

Meantime, the English Prohibitionists held many meetings and distributed immense quantities of literature and several ministers were arrested for doing this, personally, in Montreal without a permit; in their pulpits nearly all the Protestant clergy denounced beer and wine licenses; the priests in most cases were inclined to leave their charges free and no Mandement was issued by the Hierarchy. A Montreal parade on Apr. 10th had some interesting banners: "Let's all go home and let Toronto run the show"; "Home Rule in Old Quebec"; "Vive la France, Long Live Its Wine"; "Look at Bone-Dry Russia." The result of the vote was as follows: Yes, 178,112; no, 48,433, majority for the affirmative, 129,-699. It was estimated that 45 per cent. of the electors cast their votes. Montreal gave a majority of 57,147 for beer and wine compared with 6,000 against Prohibition in the Federal Referendum of 1898; Quebec City's majority was over 7,000; Sherbrooke, Three Rivers, St. John's, Hull and Westmount gave smaller majorities. Women did not vote and the decision did not affect Local Option which could still make these centres "dry" by special vote.

Many reasons were assigned for the result and one of them was the absence from the Province of Archbishop Bruchési whose Prohibitionist views were well known. The Ottawa *Journal* pointed out (Apr. 12th) that the general situation was improved: "The general sale of spirituous liquors comes to an end and the open bar is gone even for the sale of beers and wines. The milder beverages may only be sold and drunk at tables which is certain to greatly curtail consumption and assist in restricting abuses." On June 27th Dr. A. H. Deslogues, Superintendent of Quebec Asylums, in addressing a Quebec Medical Convention, denounced the use of alcohol as poison and a cause of insanity but praised the new Pro-

THE HON. HONORÉ MERCIER, K.C., M.L.A.
Appointed Minister of Lands and Forests for the Province
of Quebec in 1919

vincial system: "This law of temperance, as we may call it will bring the whisky drinkers to prefer wine and light beer or cider, to their poison and the general health will be enhanced. I am satisfied with this mitigating law of prohibition." Toward the close of the year Montreal had 250 beer and wine cafés and 350 grocer's licenses; through the Province a tendency became evident in municipalities to vote themselves "wet" under Local Option in order to get beer and wine licenses and Lachine was one example; many vendors in Montreal did not obey the law as to spirituous liquor or as to the alcohol strength of wines sold.

The Gouin Government and the Electoral Victory of 1919. Sir Lomer Gouin, in his 15 years of power, had won many tokens of popular confidence from the people of Quebec but the situation in 1919 brought him an absolutely unique tribute. Cautious in policy but optimistic in thought and expression; opposed to extremes in sentiment or public action and with a policy which was progressive without being too far in advance of the times; he had held Quebec through the difficulties of the War and kept its confidence in those of reconstruction. His New Year Message to the people of the Province breathed assurance as to its rich resources and prosperous future while the same period brought to him the Grand Cross of the Order of the Crown from the King of the Belgians. He believed in home manufactures. At the inaugural banquet of the Council for the Development of Technical Education at Montreal (May 5th) he declared that: "Canada, and particularly Quebec, exports too much raw material to other countries to be manufactured. We have progressed, it is true. A few years ago we were exporting all our pulp-wood. To-day we are exporting paper pulp and finished paper, but we are still exporting an immense amount of pulp-wood. The situation is the same with other industries." He pointed out that individuality was the great essential. Conferences would create co-operation but individuality evoked inventions and discoveries. These remarks were important in view of the current American effort to get the Quebec embargo on the export of pulpwood from Crown Lands lifted.

During the early part of the year Elections were in the air although the Legislature was only three years old and its predecessors had, since 1899, run an average of 4 years; newspaper rumours also were frequent as to Sir Lomer Gouin going to Ottawa as member of the Unionist Government but they do not appear to have had any foundation. On May 22nd the Premier announced the dissolution of the Assembly with nominations for June 16th in 80 electoral divisions; Charlevoix-Saguenay, Gaspé and Magdalen Islands were given special dates with the general voting to take place on June 23rd. On May 24th *La Minerve* announced the Conservative policy under Arthur Sauvé, who acted as Leader of 7 followers in the Legislature. The first clause dealt with Educa-

23

tion: "Better national education in the schools, a programme better
adapted to our needs, a more serious school inspection, and one
more complete; School Inspectors who will not have under their
jurisdiction 8,000 pupils as to-day, but only enough for them to
look after properly; development of a public educational spirit and
practical encouragement to Arts and Science, with encouragement
to the Technical schools and the School of Higher Commercial
Studies." Others may be summarized briefly:

1. Development of Agriculture, so as to favour intensive cultivation and
small farms. Re-organization of Agricultural Clubs and of all our agricultural system and methods.

2. A Minister of Industry and establishment of a system of Agricultural credits; a Minister of Labour.

3. A more effective policy of colonization of lands with colonization
roads for the farmer and special privileges for the sons of colonists. Special
prizes for dairy industry in the colonization regions.

4. Enquiry into the cutting privileges granted to lumber merchants,
and the restitution to the Crown of property and money belonging thereto.
An end of exploitation.

5. Control of certain Mines and Industries by the State.

6. Development of our water powers with a view to furnishing electricity at cheaper prices to the cities and towns.

7. Simplification of the administration of justice. Fewer laws of
exception; fewer costly trials; fewer functionaries; rigourous application of
the laws to the great as well as to the small.

8. Justice for Montreal and its ratepayers, great and small, and complete enquiry into Montreal relations with the Legislature and Government
during the past 15 years.

9. Complete enquiry into the affairs of the small municipalities asking
annexation to Montreal and in regard to the private legislation concerning
such municipalities.

10. Fidelity to the national ideal which states that Canada belongs to
Canadians and is for Canadians. Provincial autonomy and a Government
and Parliament composed of competent men representing all classes.

11. Reform or abolition of the Legislative Council; General Elections
at fixed dates; bye-elections a month after the seats become vacant. Proportional Representation.

On June 10th the Premier inaugurated his campaign at St.
Rochs, in Quebec City, and dealt at length with the record of his
Government. After a tribute to the late Sir Wilfrid Laurier he
referred to the War cataclysm which had shaken the world and
added: "It was our duty to come before the people in these grave
times to ask for a renewal of our mandate, a vote of confidence, so
that we might continue the work we have undertaken." He
claimed that since 1905 all promises had been kept and more than
kept; from 1905 to 1918 the excess of ordinary revenues over
ordinary expenditure was $11,961,697, being a yearly average of
$920,130, while the Provincial Debt had gone down from $15 per
head to $13.51; there had been a transformation in Education with
the establishment of Normal Schools in the Province to equip men
and women as teachers competent to earn fair living wages; the
$100-a-year teacher had disappeared as in 1912-13 there were 578
teachers receiving from $100 to $125 and in 1917 only five; the
Montreal Technical School was a splendid institution and so recog-

nized and the Paris gold medal had been awarded to the School
for Higher Commercial Studies; Agricultural instruction was being
given throughout the Province to fit city men for the farms and,
in referring to Colonization, he stated that in 1911 there was not an
inch of the rich grounds of Abitibi under cultivation and there was
no population, while to-day there was a population of 20,000 with
fifty new parishes established.

As a party leader and for the Liberal party he took credit for
the institution of Boards of Arbitration and Conciliation for settling disputes; compulsory use of apparatus for preventing accidents; labour inspectors for all public buildings; laws regarding
sanitary arrangements in buildings; establishment of Employment
Bureaux; appointment of a Deputy-Minister of Labour.   Quebec,
he declared, to be above all the Provinces in its Good Roads policy,
while the recent annexation of Ungava had made Quebec the
largest Province in Canada.   The people must, he went on, be
attracted to the land and production enhanced: "To obtain this
end the multiplication and improvement of means of communication is imperative.   The development of this communication will
favour social relations and it will allow the producer to bring his
goods to market.   We wish to spend $5,000,000 in aid of coloniza-
tion to make the land attractive, and I am convinced that from this
encouragement new municipalities will spring up from Gaspé to
the Abitibi."   Temiscamingue was to be opened up and more railways were necessary: "We tried for ten years to have the existing
Railway companies build lines to Temiscamingue, but did not succeed.   We want a railroad to go from Kipawa to Lac des Quinzes.
We want railroad communication between Temiscamingue and
Montreal.   Now, if we are elected on the 23rd of June we propose,
if we cannot induce the Railway companies to do it, to build these
railway lines ourselves."   Hon. L. A. Taschereau also spoke with
L. A. David, K.C., M.L.A., and Hon. N. Séguin.

As to Finance and progress in general, a strong case was made
out for the Government in various speeches by Hon. W. G. Mitchell.
There had been surpluses in every year since 1904-05 beginning
with $48,095 and ending with $2,134,558 in 1917-18 with a total
for the 14 years of $9,100,126; in the 1919 Victory Loan Quebec
had purchased $175,433,000 of bonds and the Imports had increased
in those years from 32 to 180 millions with Exports leaping up
from 37 to 279 millions; the Government payments for Agricultural
development had risen from $218,000 in 1905-06 to $624,551 in
1914-15 with grants to Agricultural Clubs and Societies growing
from $35,000 to $116,000; Mineral production had grown from
$3,750,000 in 1905 to $18,000,000 in 1918.   At Sherbrooke on June
11th Mr. Mitchell stated that as soon as the present wave of industrial unrest had subsided New York and other capitalists had advised him that $100,000,000 was ready for investment in Quebec.
Sir Lomer Gouin also spoke, as he did at Granby on the 12th, and
at a few other points.   But it was not necessary, so far as the

Elections were concerned, and Mr. Sauvé found it desirable to spend most of his time in his own riding.

On Nomination Day (June 16) there were 45 acclamations which included all the Ministers except Mr. Séguin and Mr. Décarie—the latter not a candidate owing to his coming retirement. The only Conservative acclamation was Brig.-Gen. C. A. Smart in Westmount. In Drummond, Montreal-St. George, Quebec and Sherbrooke the Opposition candidates withdrew; in all the other 41 ridings only Liberal candidates were in the field. In the 36 electoral divisions where voting took place 131,084 votes were cast with 1,448 ballots rejected as irregular and the total equal to 53·6 per cent. of the names entered in the lists—Liberals polling 90,651 votes, Conservatives 21,990 and others 16,995. If the acclamations were counted as a unanimous vote the Liberals received 316,624 in the entire Province to 37,987 for the Conservatives and 16,995 for independents. Meanwhile, on the day following the acclamations, the Premier spoke at Montreal as to his policy toward that city. He defended, in particular, the annexation of Maissonneuve, a rich industrial suburb, with fine buildings and sidewalks and public works which could not now be built for double the money cost to Montreal in its assumption of Debt, etc.; as to Maissonneuve Park, Montreal needed parks greatly and this one, it was said, had cost $7,000,000 and would be worth $25,000,000 in 10 years; as to the administration of Montreal, the Commission which the Government had appointed was described as temporary and as having done good work—debentures which had been selling below par were now at a premium. The result of the Elections in detail was as follows:

Constituency	Elected Candidate	Defeated Candidate	Majority
Argenteuil	John Hay		Accl.
Arthabaska	Joseph-Edouard Perrault		Accl.
Bagot	Joseph-Emery Phaneuf	Narcisse P. C. McDuff	769
Beauce	Arthur Godbout		Accl.
Beauharnois	Achille Bergevin	John A. Sullivan	876
Bellechasse	Antonin Galipeault		Accl.
Berthier	Siméon Laferrière		"
Bonaventure	Joseph-Fabien Bugeaud		"
Brome	William Robert Oliver	Charles U. R. Tarte	1,410
Chambly	E. Merrill Désaulniers		Accl.
Champlain	Bruno Bordeleau		"
Charlevoix-Saguenay	Phillippe Dufour	Pierre D'Auteuil	118
		Alfred Moffatt	
		Maxime Morin	
Châteauguay	Honoré Mercier		Accl.
Chicoutimi	J.-Arthur Gaudrault	Honoré Petit	183
Compton	Camille-Emile Desjarlais		Accl.
Deux-Montagnes	Arthur Sauvé (Cons.)	Donat Lalande	811
Dorchester	Joseph O. E. Ouellet		Accl.
Drummond	Hector La Ferté		"
Frontenac	Georges-Stanislas Grégoire		"
Gaspé	Gustave Lemieux		"
Hull	Joseph Caron		"
Huntingdon	Andrew Philps		"
Iberville	Joseph V. A. Forget	Joseph-Aldéric Benoît	115
		Zoël Fortier	
Iles-de-la-Madeleine	Joseph-Edouard Caron		Accl.
Jacques-Cartier	Joseph S. A. Ashby	Louis-Joseph Barbeau	751
Joliette	Pierre-Joseph Dufresne (Cons.)	Joseph-Ernest Hébert	126
Kamouraska	Charles-Adolphe Stein		Accl.
Labelle	Joseph-Honoré Achim	Louis Cousineau	803
Lac-Saint-Jean	Emile Moreau	Thomas-Louis Bergeron	2,442
Laprairie	Wilfrid Cédilot	Omer Poissant	250
L'Assomption	Walter Reed	Edouard Laurion	914

Constituency	Elected Candidate	Defeated Candidate	Majority
Laval	Joseph-Olier Renaud (Cons.)	Thibaudeau Rinfret Daniel Sauriol	424
Lévis	Alfred-Valère Roy		Accl.
L'Islet	Elisée Thériault		Accl.
Lotbinière	Joseph-Napoléon Francoeur		"
Maisonneuve	Adélard Laurendeau (Lab.)	Alphonse-Avilla Desroches Joseph-Napoléon Cabana	1,122
Maskinongé	Rodolphe Tourville	L.-A. Lamy	725
Matane	Joseph Dufour	Joseph Roy Georges Ducasse Joseph-Israel Massé	655
Mégantic	Lauréat Lapierre		Accl.
Missisquoi	Alexandre Saurette	Louis Gosselin Oscar-Alphonse Bérial	327
Montcalm	Joseph-Ferdinand Daniel	Louis-Auguste Laporte... Charles-Édouard Prévost	942
Montmagny	Charles Abraham Paquet	Fortunat Bélanger	190
Montmorency	Louis-Alexandre Taschereau		Accl.
Montréal-Dorion	Aurèle Lacombe (Lab.)	David Giroux Georges Mayrand Louis N. C. de Courville E. Hurtubise	561
Montréal-Hochelaga	Joseph-Hercule Bédard	Francis Fauteux Adélard Jolivet	1,043
Montréal-Laurier	Ernest Poulin	Napoléon Turcot Wilfrid Lajeunesse Lucien Gauvreau	420
Montréal-Sainte Anne	Bernard A. Conroy		Accl.
Montréal-Sainte-Marie	Napoléon Seguin	Alfred Mathieu	796
Montréal-Saint Georges	Charles Ernest Gault (Cons.)	Edward Earl	Accl.
Montréal-Saint Jacques	Irénée Vautrin	Lucien Plante Eudore Dubeau	479
Montréal-Saint-Laurent	Henry Miles	Joseph Altar Budyk Robert Louis Calder	101
Montréal-St. Louis	Peter Bercovitch		Accl.
Napierville	Amédée Monet		"
Nicolet	Joseph (Alcide) Savoie		"
Pontiac	Wallace Reginald McDonald	William Hodgins David B. Barry	225
Portneuf	Lomer Gouin		Accl.
Québec	Aurèle Leclerc		"
Québec-Centre	L.-Arthur Cannon		"
Québec-Est (East)	Louis-Alfred Létourneau	François-Xavier Galibois..	376
Québec-Ouest (West)	Martin Madden		Accl.
Richelieu	Maurice Péloquin	René Larivière	836
Richmond	Walter George Mitchell		Accl.
Rimouski	Auguste-Maurice Tessier		"
Rouville	J.-Edmond Robert		"
Saint-Hyacinthe	Armand Boisseau	Télesphore-Damien Bouchard	520
Saint-Jean (St. Johns)	Alexis Bouthillier	Alfred-Noé Deland	964
Saint-Maurice	Georges-Isidore Delisle	J. Hubert Biermans	892
Saint-Sauveur	Arthur Paquet	A.-Emile Lortie	255
Shefford	William Stephen Bullock	Louis-Joseph Jodoin	1,127
Sherbrooke	Joseph-Henri Lemay		Accl.
Soulanges	Avila Farand	Joseph Elie Arcade-Momer Bissonnette	394
Stanstead	Alfred Bissonnet		Accl.
Témiscaming	Télesphore Simard	Pierre Gélinas	455
Témiscouata	Louis-Eugène-A. Parrot		Accl.
Térrebonne	Louis-Athanase David		"
Trois-Rivières	Joseph-Adolphe Tessier		"
Vaudreuil	Hormisdas Pilon		"
Verchères	Adrien Beaudry		"
Westmount	Charles Allan Smart (Cons.)		"
Wolfe	Joseph Eugène Rheault		"
Yamaska	Guillaume-Édouard Ouellette		"

In Montreal two Labour members were elected while the Conservatives only elected five members in the Province; Arthur Sauvé was returned in Two Mountains and the Government had a majority of 74 when all returns were in. Following the Elections came changes in the Ministry—Hon. Louis Jules Allard, Minister of Lands and Forests, retiring after 14 years' service to become Prothonotary of the Superior Court, Montreal, and Hon. J. L. Décarie, Provincial Secretary, to be Chief Judge of the Court of

Special Sessions at Montreal.   On Aug. 25th a number of changes
were announced.· The Prime Minister gave up the Attorney-Generalship and Mr. Taschereau took it over after 12 years' service as
Minister of Public Works.   Three new men came into the Cabinet
and the re-organization was completed as follows:

Prime Minister and President of the Council	Sir Lomer Gouin, K.C.M.G.
Minister of Roads	Hon. J. A. Tessier
Attorney General	Hon. L. A. Taschereau, K.C.
Minister of Agriculture	Hon. J. Edouard Caron
Minister of Lands and Forests	Hon. Honoré Mercier
Provincial Treasurer and Minister of Municipal Affairs....	Hon. W. G. Mitchell
Minister of Public Works and Labour	Hon. Antonin Galipeault
Minister of Colonization, Mines and Fisheries	Hon. J. E. Perrault
Provincial Secretary and Registrar	Hon. L. A. David, K.C.
Minister without Portfolio	Hon. John C. Kaine
Minister without Portfolio	Hon. Narcisse Pérodeau
Minister without Portfolio	Hon. N. Séguin

Mr. Allard was replaced in the Council by Clement Robillard of
Montreal and, a little later, J. N. Francoeur succeeded Mr. Galipeault as Speaker of the Assembly.   Succeeding incidents of importance included the appointment of a Special Commission for the
revision of the general statutes of the Province in accordance with
the law passed at the last Session and composed of Charles Lanctot,
Deputy-Attorney-General, (Chairman); A. Rives Hall, K.C., Montreal, and L. P. Geoffrion, K.C., Clerk of the Legislative Assembly;
the speech of E. W. Beatty, C.P.R. President, at Quebec on Oct. 1st,
when he said that "the Province offers a great variety of Railway
traffic possibilities with a production of manufactures which is 27
per cent. of that of all Canada; with wood-pulp and paper, 58 per
cent. and 49 per cent. respectively; with dairy products 57 per cent.,
and a live-stock varying from 11 per cent. to 35 per cent. of that
of Canada''; the institution on Dec. 1st of a new and stricter system
of checking medical prescriptions issued for the sale of liquor; arrangements by the Department of Agriculture for an extensive use
of tractors on the farms to be sold to farmers at cost price in order
to make up for the scarcity of horses and the high cost of feed and
to assist in the cultivation of a wider acreage; the suggestion of the
Montreal Chambre du Commerce that a Provincial Department of
Trade and Commerce should be created.   At the close of the year
a very general belief was voiced in the press of Quebec that Sir
Lomer Gouin was to retire and be replaced by either Mr. Taschereau
or Mr. Caron but the belief proved to be premature.

The Meeting of the New Legislature.   The 15th Legislature of
the Province was opened at Quebec on Dec. 10th by Sir Charles
Fitzpatrick, Lieut.-Governor, with a Speech from the Throne which
referred to the Prince of Wales and the loyal greeting given "this
warm-hearted Prince" by the people of Quebec; described as a matter of satisfaction the fact that external ideas and opinions as to the
Province were undergoing a change with growing appreciation of
Quebec as "an economic and moral force alike in its steady progress in every sphere and in the sterling qualities of its inhabitants
with their abiding respect for peace, tradition, good order and the

rights of property"; mentioned the continued progress of Agriculture and the industry as becoming modernized and as more and more prosperous; stated that "in order to enlarge the field of agricultural operations it is proposed to spend $5,000,000 in providing facilities for settlement of new lands" and that a Railway in the Temiscamingue region had become a necessity with the Government taking steps to secure its construction; promised an energetic pursuit of the Government's policy of Road construction and the building of a Bridge over the Batiscan River to complete the Montreal-Quebec highway; stated that the building of the Three Rivers Technical School was completed and that of three others about to be started.

J. N. Francoeur was elected Speaker and, on Dec. 26th, Hon. W. G. Mitchell presented his Budget for the year of June 30th, 1919, showing a Revenue of $12,666,352 and an ordinary and extraordinary expenditure of $12,371,130 with a Surplus of $295,221. The Liabilities of the Province were stated at $43,965,512 and the Assets at $10,930,221; the Funded Debt was $37,716,286 or a reduction in the year of $299,367 while the unfunded Debt was $4,167,298 with cash credits, claims and other Assets of $8,848,295 to counter-balance it. The Treasurer estimated the industrial output of the Province at $500,000,000 for 1919 and pleaded for harmony between labour and capital: "Those who are urging legitimate labour to the belief that revolution as practised in Russia is better than constitutional Government are un-Canadian and unpatriotic. One means disaster for the workingman and the other his prosperity and happiness." He declared that current unrest was due to "too much sectionalism, too much provincialism, too much prejudice, too much narrowness and too little Canadianism and national spirit." As to remedies: "We must co-operate, we must compromise. There must be give and take, the big men giving more than the small men, because they are big." C. E. Gault spoke for the Opposition and maintained that had all accounts been paid there would have been a deficit instead of a surplus shown. He also opposed any immediate borrowing. On Dec. 20th the Legislature adjourned until Jan. 8th, 1920.

Progress and Politics in Nova Scotia during 1919 In Nova Scotia there were all the basic elements of progress in 1919 and, as a matter of fact, its population of 511,176 in 21,427 square miles of territory produced during that year values of over $190,-000,000 with sources of wealth resting in coal-beds linked by water with Newfoundland iron; apple orchards of the richest character, lumber and pulpwood; iron and steel plants, shipyards and refineries in Halifax, Sydney, New Glasgow or Amherst; fishing fleets that worked from a long, indented coast, rich soils abounding in the 700 square miles of the Annapolis and Cornwallis valleys and of which one-tenth was planted and much in "dyked" lands or in a network of "intervales.'' Wild clover pasturage yielded the finest Canadian wool and produce was marketed in Canada and the West Indies, on the United States seaboard and overseas.

The Mineral resources included iron, limestone, gold, molybdenum, manganese, antimony, gypsum, salt, pottery-clay, oil shales and there were vast supplies of coking coal with only one-quarter of the hydraulic energy of the Province developed. Transportation was supplied by cheap water carriage, easy of access from any centre and by 1,784 miles of gulf, river, canal and lake connecting Sydney with Port Arthur; by three transcontinental railways and fifteen lines of ocean steamers. According to the yearly estimate of the Halifax *Chronicle* the products of Nova Scotia in 1919 were valued at $192,197,300 and included Coal $25,000,000; Coke and by-products, gold, gypsum, Building materials and other minerals, $8,913,300; Iron and Steel products $19,000,000; Fisheries $14,-350,000 and manufactures, ships and freights $56,260,000; Farm products $51,034,000, products of the Forest $16,965,000 with Game and Furs $675,000. The Halifax *Herald* estimate of values was $197,632,000 and the total for 1918 was $174,965,314. The field crops for 1919 were officially given as follows—the Dominion estimate of values being $63,187,500:

Crop	Acres	Total Yield	Value
Wheat	31,546	605,610	$1,362,623
Oats	150,010	5,633,078	5,914,731
Barley	11,479	312,096	499,353
Rye and Peas	2,258	46,081	118,891
Buckwheat	18,746	413,694	620,541
Beans	7,321	94,095	564,570
Mixed Grains	5,047	178,024	259,536
Potatoes	50,724	8,561,798	8,561,798
Turnips	18,521	9,996,257	2,499,064
Mangels and other Fodder Crops.	10,118	1,087,173	671,183
Hay	685,915	1,279,836	25,596,730
Vegetables	......	......	1,000,000
Apples	......	1,500,000	3,375,000
Total			**$51,044,009**

The Funded Debt of Nova Scotia in 1918 was $14,527,799 and the Assets of the Province—assessed value of taxable property, coal mines capitalized at 4 per cent. and Crown Lands—$166,152,237. Incidents of the year in connection with material development included the graduation of 16 students at the N.S. College of Agriculture and the grant by Dalhousie University of an Hon. LL.D. to its Principal—M. Cumming, B.S.A.; the annual meeting of the United Fuel Companies at Kentville on June 24th with the report of a prosperous year, a turnover of $2,000,000 handled at an overhead cost of 1·31 per cent. and the re-election of F. W. Bishop as President; the fact that a loss of $3,000,000 in the 1918 Potato rot might have been averted by two or three sprayings of the crop; the passing of a Provincial Act in 1919 for Encouragement of Live Stock Improvement which safe-guarded the breeding of stock and the Government grant of $92,250 for general Agricultural purposes including $39,000 for the College and Farm and $15,000 to Agricultural Societies; the product of Nova Scotian Creameries for the

year of Dec. 1st, 1919, showing a value of $1,303,587 or an increase
of 34 per cent. over 1918; the shipments of Coal for 1919 totalling
4,521,000 tons, or less than 1918, owing largely to strikes—with,
also, the opinion expressed (Dec. 31st) by Hon. Robert Drummond,
an authority on the subject, that this decrease was the last of a
period with increases in the future as probable.

The Government and Departmental Reports.   The Lieut.-
Governor, MacCallum Grant, proved a popular official in this year
and, especially, in his leadership of the reception to the Prince of
Wales.   As President of the North British Society he made an
appeal to the public on May 3rd for support to the N.S. Highland
Battalion (85th) in completing its outfit of Highland garb at a
cost of $10,000; he laid the corner-stone of the new Maternity Hos-
pital of the Salvation Army at Halifax on Oct. 26th, presided at
various meetings and took an interested part in the public affairs
and life of the Province; on Nov. 13th he was the guest of the Vic-
torian Club at Boston, reviewed at length the inter-locking of the
history of Massachusetts and Nova Scotia and urged close and
friendly relations between the two countries; he took great interest
in the Provincial Conference of business interests at Halifax on
Dec. 3-4 and personally appealed to all the Mayors of the Province to see that their towns were properly represented.

The Hon. G. H. Murray, in his 23rd year as Premier, was honoured by a foremost place in the National Liberal Convention and
his inaugural speech at once opened the gathering and marked the
return of his Provincial Government into the ranks of Federal
Liberalism.   In his speech of Aug. 5th Mr. Murray indicated the
re-union of the Liberal party, with Conscription as a dead issue,
and added: "The perpetuation of Union Government in this country under the conditions that we face would be a matter of continual compromise, it would produce much uncertainty in administration, it would have a tendency to give the country unstable Government and it would prevent the development of a sound and
healthy public opinion.   Party government may have its weakness but, take it all in all, it has given better administration under
normal conditions than any other form of political organization."
On Sept. 13th Mr. Murray unveiled a statue of Robert Burns at
Halifax and declared that "by his wealth of human understanding he was enabled in his poetry to tap the universal well-springs of
love and sympathy"; he appealed on Oct. 27th to the Province to
do its part in the Victory Loan and to help ensure the prosperity
of the country and discharge a National duty to its soldiers; on
Dec. 1st he asked Nova Scotia to contribute to the $30,000 Fund
for a Memorial to be placed over the grave of Sir Wilfrid Laurier.

The Report of the Provincial Secretary (Hon. G. H. Murray)
for 1918 (Sept. 30th) showed 122 Companies incorporated during
the year, the registration of 2,814 additional motor vehicles with
387 chauffeurs, the establishment of 36 stations of the Fishermen's
Union during the year, a revenue of $268,678 or an increase of

$101,398; the 7th Annual Report of the Department of Public Health (Mr. Murray) showed a prevalence of smallpox, especially amongst wage-earners who neglected to be vaccinated, with 1,250 deaths from Influenza in the last three months of 1918 and contained a declaration by the Provincial Health Officer that activities of several hundred local Boards should be organized and harmonized, and that unnecessary illness and death were accountable, directly and indirectly, for an economic loss to the Province of more than $10,000,000 annually; the Hon. O. T. Daniels, Attorney-General, submitted the Report of the Superintendent of Neglected and Dependent Children who dealt with 2,340 children in various institutions that cost $235,866 a year to maintain and received $17,400 from the Provincial Government. The Minister of Public Works and Mines (Hon. E. H. Armstrong) reported for 1918 a Coal production of 5,265,404 tons and the sale of 4,613,484 tons of which 2,758,959 tons were consumed in the Province, 882,607 in New Brunswick, 219,184 in Newfoundland, 78,063 in P.E. Island, 134,449 in Quebec and 269,080 tons in the United States; he also dealt with a production of 415,808 tons of Pig-iron, 512,377 tons of Steel ingots, 407,048 tons of Limestone, 584,891 tons of coke, 705,000 gallons of Toluene and 13,379,600 bricks.

Mr. Armstrong also reported as to the administration of Humane Institutions covering 6,698 patients treated in the various general hospitals, while in the Nova Scotia Hospital and the several County asylums there were 2,861 persons under care. Ninety-eight civilian patients were treated at the Nova Scotia Sanatorium, and 69 mothers and 62 children at the Salvation Army Maternity Hospital and Children's Home. In all, 11,788 persons were under care. Mr. Daniels, in his Report as to Rural Telephones, dealt with a system which in 1918 embraced every county in the Province and supplied service direct to 2,220 homes or to over 12,242 people, and indirectly supplied communities where the population, according to the last Census, was 81,500. This Minister also presented the Report of the Secretary for Agriculture which showed that in 1918 the Government had purchased 2,000 tons of fertilizer, 1,600 tons of feeding stuffs, as well as supplies of seed, etc., for the farmers, and that, in addition, bonuses were paid on the purchase by farmers of 278 two-furrow plows, 141 seed drills and other implements while 17 tractors were disposed of to farmers at cost price. The Workmen's Compensation Board reported, in 1919, 70 fatal cases (for part of the year) and 203 in 1918 while the accidents were, respectively, 6,260 and 7,665, the Assessments $920,920 and $1,367,869 respectively, and compensation paid for accidents $183,-272 and $249,920; the Board had a total investment of $2,233,026 as general reserves with Disaster reserves of $310,054 set aside in 1919, and $127,358 in 1918.

Incidents of the year included the Convention of the Nova Scotia Farmers' Association at Truro on Mch. 11-12 and an address by Dr. Cumming on the "Agricola" centenary with the election of

D. R. Nicholson, Coxheath, as President; the 45th annual meeting of the Nova Scotia Fruit Growers' Association at Bridgetown on Jan. 21st and favourable reports of the work of the United Fuel Companies, as its buying organization, with the election of Rev. H. S. Shaw, Waterville, as President; the estimated lumber-cut of the Province for 1919, by Hon. O. T. Daniels, as 300,000,000 feet with home consumption of 100,000,000 feet and total values of $19,965,-000; the issue of a Provincial Loan in June for $1,200,000 bonds at 5 per cent., free from Provincial taxation, with 101·63 offered for $700,000 1-year notes and 98·18 for $500,000 10-year bonds—the latter to retire an issue of 20-year bonds maturing in July; a permission granted the Nova Scotia Tramways Co. by the Public Utilities Commission for an issue of $1,000,000 7 per cent. 3-year notes with the offering made at par and accrued interest; the attacks made upon the Murray Government at Sydney on Aug. 27th by members of the United Mine Workers' Convention who charged specific instances of neglect by Deputy Mining Inspectors and unsympathetic consideration of miners' "demands" by Mr. Armstrong, Commissioner of Mines, with a Resolution in favour of election of the Inspector of Mines by a majority referendum vote of the mine workers of the Province—a man named Barrett stating that he would "like to talk to the Government with machine guns"; the celebration on Oct. 22nd by Hon. M. H. Goudge, for 16 years President of the Legislative Council, of the 90th anniversary of his birth with congratulations from all parts of the Province; the official statement on Sept. 22nd. that returned soldiers had purchased 12,000 acres of land in Nova Scotia. The chief appointments of the year, including that of Chief Justice R. E. Harris as Administrator in the absence of the Lieut.-Governor, were as follows:

King's Counsel	James A. Hanway	Amherst
King's Counsel	Edgar N. Clements	Yarmouth
King's Counsel	Daniel C. Chisholm	Antigonishe
King's Counsel	Robert F. Phalen	North Sydney
King's Counsel	Hon. E. Lavin Girroir	Ottawa
King's Counsel	James W. Maddin	Sydney
Provincial Inspector of Health	James A. Doull	New Glasgow
Clerk of the County Court of Victoria	A. N. MacKenzie	Baddeck
Deputy Registrar-General	Alastair J. Campbell	Halifax
Board of Governors Dalhousie College	Eliza Ritchie, Ph.D.	Halifax
King's Counsel	Wm. H. Huggins	Ottawa
Deputy Stipendiary Magistrate	Walter J. O'Hearn, K.C.	Halifax

The Meeting of the Nova Scotia Legislature.   On Feb. 27th Lieut.-Governor MacCallum Grant opened the Legislature with a Speech from the Throne in which His Honour commented on the fact of the current year marking a century in the life of the Parliament Buildings in which they sat, referred to the Armistice and the gallant part taken by the soldiers and sailors of Canada and Nova Scotia in the great War and mentioned the work of the N.S. Returned Soldiers' Commission, the Government's co-operation with the Federal authorities in establishing Labour Bureaux and the continued use by the latter, at Provincial request, of various institutions such as the Provincial Sanatorium, the N.S. Hospital, the

Technical College and the Agricultural Farm and College.   His
Honour then dealt with the desire of the three Prairie Provinces to
obtain control of their natural resources and stated the policy of
Nova Scotia concisely: "Inasmuch as these Provinces received large
annual grants of money from the Dominion Treasury in lieu of
these natural resources, it is obvious that, if these resources should
be transferred to the Prairie Provinces, and the special subsidies
still continued, there would be a very material change in the financial relations between the Dominion and the Provinces generally.
In such a case, a readjustment of these financial relations would,
in justice to all, be necessary."

The necessity of securing for the public more satisfactory service than was being given under existent conditions by Public Utilities, particularly street railways, was described as of increasing
urgency and a Bill was promised designed to give improved services
under Provincial direction, to facilitate the public ownership of
street railways, where desired, to give impetus to the development
of the water-power resources of the Province and to thus assist in
furnishing the public with light and power under favourable economic conditions.   Extension by legislation of the useful powers
and functions of the Public Health Department was promised and
also of Vocational and Technical training for workers; reference
was made to the Government's generous subsidies during the past
year to meet the shortage of seeds, fertilizers and other necessities
for production and to the excellent crops of 1918; the continued
shortage in mining production was ascribed to a scarcity of miners,
and the lack of adequate transportation facilities; a measure as to
Housing was promised and other legislation indicated.

The Speaker at this Session was the Hon. Robert Irwin, the
mover of the Address was J. J. Kinley of Lunenburg and the seconder H. G. Bauld of Halifax; it passed on Feb. 28th after a brief
debate in which Mr. Premier Murray and W. L. Hall, K.C., Conservative leader, made the chief speeches.   The latter declared the
Educational grant to be totally inadequate and the existing school
curriculum as only designed for the few students who went on to
the Universities*; urged Government Housing operations on a large
scale and more attention to the making and improvement of small
or minor roadways; demanded stricter supervision and control of
Public utilities including Telephone and Tram services, and dealt
with the difficulties between the Dominion and Nova Scotia Coal
Companies; asked for a new and better Franchise Act and approved
every good proposal for helping the returned soldier.   Mr. Murray
in his address stood by his policy as enunciated through the Lieut.-
Governor: "The Government has presented rather a comprehensive
programme.   It is progressive—perhaps radical.   When taxation
is necessary to carry it out it may not be popular.   The subject matter of the settlement of the soldier, the extension of our hospital
system, the Department of Public Health, the control of public

*Note.—For Education in Nova Scotia see Pages 544-6, 575.

utilities, a more aggressive highway policy, are all matters of the highest importance.''

Legislation of the Session included Mr. Daniels' Act to provide for fair rents for dwelling houses and to restrict the eviction of tenants; it was to apply only in a city or incorporated town where the Council had passed a Resolution in favour of its operation. Under its terms no judgment or order for the recovery of possession of a dwelling house, or for the ejectment of a tenant therefrom, could be made so long as the tenant continued to pay rent at a fair and reasonable rate, and performed the other conditions of his tenancy. The Bill was restricted, however, to dwelling-houses in which the poorer class of the community lived. Another measure of importance was the Housing Act intended to take advantage of the Dominion Loan of $2,000,000 to this Province. Under its terms money was to be lent by the Provincial Government to ''returned soldiers, working men and women and those of small means'' for a period up to 20 years at 5 per cent. with a maximum cost of $3,000 for house and land. Municipalities and Companies under Provincial Charter were given the right to acquire land and construct houses under these conditions but the former could not make loans to individuals, firms or companies, except companies incorporated by the Province; the loan to be made to a Housing company was not to exceed 85 per cent. of the value of the land and buildings. A Director of Housing was to be appointed by the Provincial Government and, on July 30th, Wensley B. MacCoy, K.C., was appointed to this position.

Hon. Mr. Armstrong carried a Bill to amend the Town Planning Act so as to extend the time for its application in the Municipalities to Apr. 23, 1921, to provide for the appointment of two Municipal Councillors yearly to the local Town Planning Board and to widen the scope of the Act for rural purposes and the scientific investigation of land throughout the Province. This Minister had another Bill amending the Workmen's Compensation Act with a view to removing ambiguities and preventing abuses in its administration; a number of the changes were accepted without criticism but Hector MacInnes, K.C., and others of the Opposition claimed that some of the clauses would place too heavy a burden upon industry and would equip the Board with arbitrary powers. Important amendments to the Public Health Act proposed by Mr. Armstrong provided for the division of the Province into three general Health Divisions, the establishment of a health clinic in each county, the appointment of a Provincial Health Inspector, three Divisional Superintendents, a Superintendent of Nursing Services, and a Public Health Nurse for every county. Emphasis was also laid upon hygiene in the schools.

Two important Bills dealt with the water-powers of Nova Scotia. They were based upon a Report of the N.S. Water Power Commission of 1917-18, presented in four different statements, and which proved that the Province possessed resources in this respect far in excess of present or probable requirements. The estimates of power given were based on actual measurements of the water available at or near the various sites; new discoveries of power were reported in detail and individual sites described with a total continuous capacity stated at 93,000 h.p. for every hour in the day and every day in the year. The first Government measure in this connection made the Ontario Hydro-Electric scheme applicable in principle to Nova Scotia and clothed the Governor-in-Council with authority to create a Commission into whose hands should be placed the administration and decision as to all matters concerning water-power in the Province—with powers of investigation, facilitation of finance and operation, co-ordination of development work. The 2nd Bill proposed, according to the Minister, to practically repeal the water-power legislation of the 1918 Session so that the Commission plan might be worked out with the sole and exclusive right to use, divert and appropriate any and all water at any time in any water-course in Nova Scotia and vest it forever in the Crown or Government of the Province. Mr. MacInnes and others opposed the Bill as confiscatory in its provisions and as giving the Government the right to arbitrarily take over private property belonging to mills or lumbermen; W. L. Hall, Opposition Leader, denounced the measure as "absolutely unsound and dangerous" and reflecting on the integrity of the Crown and the House and W. L. Kinley, a Liberal member, took similar ground; an arbitration clause was asked for but the Bills passed in due course in a House where the Government had 27 seats and the Opposition 10. The Commission was appointed on Aug. 25th as follows: The Hon. E. H. Armstrong, Commissioner of Public Works and Mines (Chairman); Frank C. Whitman of Annapolis Royal, and Robert H. McKay of New Glasgow.

Other legislation included a measure (Hon. H. H. Wickwire) enabling the Government to share in the Dominion Highway grants and to borrow $500,000 for the improvement of Provincial roads; another, which amended the Revenue Act so as to double the taxation on Banks with large increases on all corporations of a Trust, Loan, or Insurance character. Every Bank doing business in Nova Scotia and having an office or agency in Halifax, with a capital of $500,000 or upwards, was to pay a tax of $2,000 and an additional sum of $200, in respect of each office and agency in the Province up to and not exceeding ten in number, and a tax of $100 for each office or agency exceeding ten; steam and other railways were also taxed at $50 per mile for one track and, where the line consisted of two or more tracks, of $30 per mile for each additional track, owned, operated, or used within the Province. Amendments to the Statute law provided for the escheat of unoccupied lands in the absence of heirs and Mr. Wickwire carried Motor legislation under which chauffeurs' licenses were increased from $2.00 to $5.00 with the enforcement of a technical examination for chauffeurs. License fees for motor trucks were arranged as follows: 1 ton truck, $20; 3

ton truck, $75; all others over 3-ton, $100. There were to be two plates on all cars and the rate of speed was increased to a maximum of 25 miles per hour.

The Submarine Coal Areas Bill (Mr. Armstrong) was an attempt to settle the difficulty between the Nova Scotia Coal Company and the Dominion Coal Company regarding submarine areas which had compelled the closing of several collieries belonging to the former Company and the throwing of several thousand miners out of employment. The Bill empowered the Commissioner of Public Works and Mines, after enquiry and report and approval by the Governor-in-Council, to "make such orders and regulations as he may deem expedient for the purpose of ensuring that such submarine coal-mining area shall be worked in the best interests of the Province"—by some other concern! A Bill presented by Hon. R. M. MacGregor provided for a Commission to investigate the hours of employment of women engaged in industrial occupation and other matters pertaining to such employment, and also as to Mothers' Pensions or Allowances. On Dec. 10th following this Commission was duly appointed: John McKeen, Halifax; Jane B. Wisdom, Halifax, and William B. Scott, Glace Bay, with A. T. Mac-Kay of Trenton as Secretary. Other measures consolidated the Acts relating to Vital Statistics and to Game; an important Bill was that amending the Nova Scotia Temperance Act. Under its terms the latter increased the penalties imposed for infraction, appointed one wholesale vendor for the Province who was to import and distribute all liquor for industrial and medicinal purposes, provided against abuse by physicians' prescriptions and declined a clause allowing the sale of liquors with a low percentage of alcohol —2½ per cent. beer for instance—which F. H. Bell, K.C., of Halifax urged before the House in Committee backed up by C. C. Dane, President of the N.S. Federation of Labour, and Mayor Hawkins of Halifax and opposed by Rev. H. R. Grant of the N.S. Temperance League. Under the Great War Memorial Act arrangements were to be made for suitable memorials to commemorate the participation of the Province in the War. Meanwhile, the House on motion of J. C. Tory, after an effective and able speech, passed (May 6th), unanimously, the following Resolution:

That in the opinion of this House the time has come when the Government of Nova Scotia should press for a settlement of its just claims against the Federal Government in respect to the following matters: (1) compensation as an equivalent for lands reserved for the Provinces of Manitoba, Saskatchewan and Alberta; (2) compensation as an equivalent for cash subsidies paid to the Provinces of Manitoba, Saskatchewan and Alberta, purporting to be in lieu of lands; (3) compensation as an equivalent for land granted the Provinces of Ontario and Quebec in which the people of Nova Scotia have a proprietary interest in common with the people of the other Provinces of Canada; (4) compensation for unfair treatment of Nova Scotia in respect to the public expenditures of the Dominion of Canada since Confederation.

On May 5th the Attorney-General (Mr. Daniels) presented the estimates of Revenue and Expenditure for the current year as $3,-229,896 for the former and $3,223,327 for the latter with an expected surplus of $6,569; the revnue in 1918 had been $2,332,632 and expenditures $2,552,597 with a deficit of $219,965. The chief increase in estimated revenue was from direct Taxation of corporations, etc., through which $271,605 was received in 1918 and $503,900 expected in 1919; municipalities were expected to contribute $455,000 for Highway purposes and an increase of $108,000 was estimated in returns from the Provincial Sanatorium; the revenue from Mines had decreased under War and labour conditions from the 1918 estimate of $765,000 to $656,989 and in 1919 a still smaller amount was looked for—$631,000. The total revenue increase provided for additional expenditure on roads of nearly $200,000 and of $400,000 in other items. The Legislature was prorogued on May 17th.

Nova Scotian Incidents of the Year. The most important of these was the dispute between the Nova Scotia Steel and Coal Co. of New Glasgow and the Dominion Coal Co. of Sydney. In Pictou County the Nova Scotia concern found itself without coal of a nature suited to certain of the more important operations which it carried on. After working its mines in Cape Breton for years, it had reached the end of its holdings in the particular submarine area from which almost its entire supply had been drawn. Adjoining this area was another deposit, or portion of the same deposit, controlled but not worked by the Dominion Company. The Nova Scotia Company applied to the Government and Legislature for permission to extend its workings into that area and declared that unless this permission was granted its entire steel plant would be compelled to close. The Dominion Company naturally refused to consider the handing over to a competitive corporation of property lawfully held for a considerable time and which it planned to work at some unspecified date in the future. In return for the proposed concession, however, the Nova Scotia Company offered to abandon areas which it controlled adjoining Dominion properties in another direction. This, the Dominion Company declined to accept and a long and acrimonius controversy ensued; hence the Bill passed by the Legislature at its 1919 Session which provided that the redistribution of certain coal areas should be left in the hands of the Provincial Minister of Mines who would decide upon the indemnities to be paid or received in the case of any transfer of titles being made.

The 14th annual Session of the Union of Nova Scotia Municipalities was held at Yarmouth on Aug. 27th with President Hiram Goudey in the chair. Addresses were given by W. B. MacCoy, K.C., Dr. W. H. Hattie, H. C. Crowell and others, and Resolutions were passed (1) asking the Provincial Government to appoint a Commission to equalize assessments throughout the Province; (2) protesting against any Federal legislation trenching upon Municipal control of the streets and asking for a protective clause in every future grant of public franchises; (3) declaring that any town unable to raise sufficient funds for school purposes should be permitted to increase the poll-tax to ten dollars for school purposes only. A. J. Bannerman, of Pictou County, was elected President; the 1st Vice-President was Mayor A. C. MacCormack, Sydney Mines, and the 2nd Vice-President Parker Archabild, of Halifax; the Secretary-Treasurer, Arthur Roberts, k.c., of Bridgewater, was re-elected. On Nov. 28th the Halifax City Council passed a Resolution, in view of the Halifax Power Co. being unable to proceed with the development of Hydro-electric power at the North East River, St. Margaret's Bay, asking that the water power be acquired by the N.S. Power Commission and its development proceeded with as a Provincial work.

Other incidents included the appointment of four women (June 2), for the first time in Nova Scotia, to administer oaths, and take and record affidavits and affirmations within Nova Scotian Courts; the riot in Halifax on Feb. 18th which followed a raid upon Chinese cafés in the down-town district and was succeeded by another disturbance on the 19th when, for 1½ hours, the city was at the mercy of a mob, with 9 stores wrecked, $20,000 worth of damage done and a dozen civilians and soldiers injured; the increase in the earnings of the N.S. Tramways and Power Co. from $645,241 in 1914 to $1,325,000 in 1919; the tremendous storm which swept the coasts of Nova Scotia on Nov. 5-6 and demoralized power and lighting, damaged buildings, wrought havoc amongst shipping and covered the shores with wreckage. On Dec. 3rd a Conference was held at Halifax of representative business men from every part of the Province for the purpose of promoting an Old Home Summer and World's Fair—the calling back for a season to Nova Scotia of the tens of thousands of its citizens living in other countries or Provinces. Speeches were made by the Lieut.-Governor, by H. C. Crowell, promoter of the idea, Hon. G. H. Murray, C. L. Martin, Amherst, E. C. Whitman, H. R. Silver and many others and the project given a strong start.

Development and Public Affairs in New Brunswick during 1919.   This Province of 17,910,410 acres in area with only 351,889 people (1911 Census) has had a history and progress and influence out of all apparent proportion to its population. With 11 natural harbours and a coast of fertile fisheries; with 7,500,000 acres of Crown timber lands and 4,500,000 acres of private timber areas; with 10,000,000 acres suitable for mixed farming and 4½ million acres occupied; with abundant water-powers of which 26,113 h.p. are developed and 131,460 h.p. as yet unused; with estimated coal resources of 151 million metric tons and plentiful supplies of gypsum, natural gas, tungsten, copper, brick-clay, antimony, manganese, limestone, oil shales and building-stone; with rich reserves in big game, and fine shooting and fishing, the Province possesses many attractions besides an industrial development in which every year sees steady advance.[*]

[*]Note.—For United Farmers see Canadian Agricultural Section, Page 397 and for Education see Special Section, Pages 546, 576.

The year 1919 was a prosperous one for New Brunswick. Business and industry thrived and the farmers secured a larger return for their labour than ever before; work was plentiful and wages high while the unrest which disturbed so greatly the rest of the world did not make itself felt to any noticeable extent; in spite of the high cost of living, the average householder seemed able to pay his customary bills and still have something left for unusual expenditures. In 1918 the registration of automobiles—a modern test of prosperity—was 6,000 for the Province; in 1919 the number was estimated at 8,000 of which at least 1,000 were in the city of St. John. At the close of the year it was expected that New Brunswick's lumber-cut would exceed all records. Reports received from 29 forest rangers showed a cut of logs in their districts of 229,000,000 feet with 13 other rangers whose reports were not in; when all were received it was estimated that the cut would exceed 300,000,000 feet compared with 202,000,000 feet of sawlogs and about 19,000,000 feet of poles, ties, pulp, etc., in 1918.

On June 3rd representative business, railway, municipal and public men met in St. John and organized the All New Brunswick Tourist, Game and Resources League after a Convention presided over by E. A. Schofield who explained the promotion of tourist traffic, knowledge of Provincial resources, enjoyment of New Brunswick sport, and development of its general interests, as the objects in view. The Hon. W. E. Foster, Prime Minister, endorsed the movement and declared that tourist travel should be encouraged, good roads, good hotels and good public utilities aided by not only officials or public men but by the people in general. After Hon. C. H. Labillois, Hon. P. J. Veniot, Mayor R. T. Hayes and others had spoken, organization was effected with F. B. Edgecombe, Fredericton, as President, a number of representative men as Vice-Presidents and C. B. Allan, St. John, as Secretary-Treasurer. A banquet followed with a strong speech from the Lieut.-Governor (Mr. Pugsley) and a general air of success accompanied the proceedings. Immediate operations were to be along lines of publicity-pamphlets and advertisement of the Province in moving pictures and lantern slides.

Another and old-time institution, the Maritime Board of Trade, met on Sept. 17-19 at Moncton and decided, unanimously, by Resolution in favour of Maritime Union; the development of national ports; division of the C.N.R. into operating units with a Maritime unit including all three Maritime Provinces; Maritime geological research; improvement of connections with P.E. Island; expansion of relations with the West Indies and contiguous colonies. H. J. Logan, K.C., Amherst, was elected President and M. E. Agar, St. John, Vice-President. The St. John Board of Trade was an important business organization of the Province with R. B. Emerson as President in 1919, W. F. Burditt, Vice-President, and R. E. Armstrong Secretary-Treasurer. Its policy during the year included (1) improvement in Customs regulations as applied to entrance and clearance of coastwise craft; (2) Civic betterment along lines of permanent street paving; (3) adherence to Daylight Saving and a request to the Legislature for better fire protection and appointment of a Fire Marshal; (4) opposition to the Dominion acquisition of the G.T.R. and the pressing upon Dominion authorities of Harbour needs and extension; (5) drawing attention to the importance of the local Port.   An export trade growing from 21 to 200 millions in the years 1914-18 was specified and the claim made that St. John was the nearest all-the-year-round port in Eastern Canada to the Canadian West; that it was easy and safe of access at all times; that its low water depth of 32 feet enlarged to 58 feet, or 60 feet at high water, enabled it to be used with perfect safety by the largest steamers afloat; that it was free of ice at all times and, further, that its advantageous situation in relation to the West Indies, Cuba, South America, the Panama Canal, etc., rendered it peculiarly adaptable as a terminal port for steamers running to and from any of these countries.

The Foster Government and Provincial Policy.   Mr. Foster was not greatly troubled by politics in this 2nd year of his administration, with 30 Liberals in the House to 17 Conservatives; but there was a good deal of political fighting and many personalities in the press and during the Session.   The Premier, himself, resumed his affiliation with Dominion Liberalism by attendance at the Ottawa Convention of the party on Aug. 5-7th and at preceding meetings there for organization purposes.   Prior to that, however, he had some trouble with his own fellow-Liberals in St. John arising out of the calling of a local Convention to appoint delegates to Ottawa. Following out the Dominion Liberal idea of recognizing and bringing back the Conscriptionist Liberals, Mr. Foster had been asked to call the Conventions for his Province but that of St. John was arranged without his knowledge or approval.   At its session on June 26th J. F. Belyea presided while Dr. A. F. Emery spoke strongly against Unionist Liberals being admitted and declared that Mr. Premier Foster had voted against the Laurier candidates in 1917; a telegram was received from D. D. McKenzie, the Ottawa leader, specifying Mr. Foster's appointment and expressing a sincere hope that "in interest of Party amicable arrangements may be agreed upon"; a proposal, however, to this end, and for a conference with the Premier, was voted down by a large majority and delegates were duly chosen without his approval.   At a second Convention held, July 10th, on the formal call of Mr. Foster the Premier was made Chairman of what proved a stormy meeting; it declined to say anything about party unity and re-elected the Delegates named at the previous Convention.   Other meetings held throughout the Province were more harmonious.

Mr. Foster took part in many functions of the year and, for instance, opened the Woodstock Fair on Sept. 10th, the Fredericton Exhibition on Sept. 13th and that of Chatham on the 22nd; he was

in Ottawa on Oct. 24th to look after the interests of the Port of St.
John in connection with G.T.R. legislation; he addressed a Liberal
Convention at St. Stephen on Nov. 6th.   In reviewing the policy
of his Government on this occasion he stated that its Crown Land
action was responsible for an increase in revenue of $500,000 to
date and that the increase for this year would amount to $200,000;
that, although not in favour of Government ownership in everything, he strongly advocated the ownership by the people of the
waterways and water-power of the Province and that the Commission recently appointed would work to this end; that the farming
industry was the most important in New Brunswick, that the high
cost of living was due to inadequate production, and that the Government would make this industry more attractive by increased
assistance and inducements to those who wished to take up farming.

Early in the year the Report of the Hon. P. J. Veniot, Minister
of Public Works, was issued with much detail as to 1918 expenditures; the total was $1,374,901 of which $364,902 went for Permanent bridges, $221,718 for Ordinary bridges, $436,547 for Permanent roads and $224,634 for other roads.   This Minister had
been an active politician in past years and the Conservative party
never lost an opportunity to attack him; he was versatile in his
efforts and work during the year.   On Jan. 17th he was at Ottawa
urging the taking over by the Government of the Caraquet branch
line and a generous Federal assistance for good roads in New
Brunswick; on the 18th he addressed a dinner of the Montreal
Reform Club in both English and French; on the 10th of March as
leader of the Acadian people in the Province he joined with Hon.
J. B. M. Baxter, the Conservative leader of the Orangemen, in
assuring the Legislature of their united efforts to do away with
the things which made for strife between the two races.   Another
visit to Ottawa in May evoked an interview on the 12th in which
he said that arrangements had been concluded to obtain New Brunswick's share of the Federal Highway grant.   The Provincial classification of permanent roads had been approved and plans and other
data had been submitted at Ottawa.   The Minister had also taken
up with the C.N.R. Board the question of more favourable rates for
gravel to be used in the construction of roads.   Speaking at the
annual banquet of the N.B. Automobile Association on Nov. 26th
Mr. Veniot reviewed his Roads policy and conditions at length:

New Brunswick maintained her roads without any help from the municipalities.   During the last three years the money obtained for roads in the
Province was $2,125,000, of which only $385,000 had been obtained from the
ordinary revenues; $1,425,000 came from the Automobile Fund fees.   Of this
$1,100,000 had been spent on the trunk and semi-trunk roads, $400,000 on the
by-roads and $180,000 for work done on them.   In 1918 Inspectors were placed
on the roads and the automobile fees had increased marvellously every season
since that time.   To improve 17,000 miles of roads in the Province as some
people were agitating to have them improved, would cost $42,500,000 as there
were 3,600 miles of trunks and secondary trunks and 14,000 miles of roads
and country roads to be fixed.   This the Province could not stand financially
until the people of New Brunswick would do as the people of other Provinces
did—pay more taxes for road improvement.

The Hon. E. A. Smith, Minister of Lands and Mines, in his Report for the year of Oct. 31st, 1919, showed net receipts from licenses, leases, stumpage dues, certificates, etc., of $858,166 compared with $791,027 in 1918—the largest revenue in Provincial history from this source.   The Minister made this comment: "I am glad to report that the new conditions of the Forest survey are not only eminently satisfactory, but have met our best expectations, and the Province is receiving, at last, a full and honest return of the lumber cut upon its Crown Lands.   We have now set up a complete Forest force; every member of which owes his position to his ability and industry, employed as a permanent force throughout the year.   All old methods have been discarded.   At the risk of repeating myself, let me say again, we have been drawing too heavily on our Forests during past years; in other words entrenching on our forest capital instead of being content with the annual increment.   The time is at hand when more conservative methods must be adopted, such as closing out certain hard cut areas altogether in order to ensure a continuous forest crop."   Mr. Smith dealt with the Provincial water powers and expressed regret that there was no adequate legislation for promoting hydro-electric development and that the 1919 Bill to that end had to be held over. Forest fires were referred to with 17 square miles burned over as against 30 miles in 1918.   The estimated returns from Territorial revenue for 1920 was $1,000,000; late in December the Minister was in Toronto to meet Dominion Forestry experts who were consulting there with a view to the adoption of New Brunswick methods in Ontario.   The plan of having all forestry and lumbering operations under control of experts and practical foresters was regarded as a model for the rest of Canada by the Canadian Forestry Association and a Memorandum was placed before the Ontario Government pointing out the excellent results obtained.

The Minister of Agriculture, Hon. J. F. Tweeddale, had a satisfactory statement for 1919 with unceasing activities in every branch of his Department—agricultural census, Live-stock increase and improvement of breed, purchase and distribution of 1,400 purebred sheep, co-operative marketing of wool, the Pig Club work of many boys, the organization of a Cheese Board to aid buyers and sellers, a Sussex Dairy Show and Convention, the work of the Central Creamery at Moncton and establishment of others, the operations of the Poultry Division and formation of Poultry Clubs, development of the apple industry and work of the Provincial Horticulturist, a good honey crop and work of the Apiculturist and of the Beekeepers' Association, growth of agricultural lessons in the schools and extension of Women's Institutes, the success of the 87 school gardens in operation, the activities of the Agricultural representatives in Counties.   During the year the usual working agreement with the Provincial Departments of Nova Scotia and P.E. Island in the operation of a Maritime Dairy School at Truro, N.S., was carried out; the organization of the New Brunswick Dairymen, United, was effected on Mch. 7th at Sussex with F. G. Hugh-son, Cornhill, as President, and the object of promoting the production, manufacture and sale of dairy products with protection for the interests of the industry from a Provincial standpoint—through legislation, co-operation, meetings, study and discussion.

The Cheese and Butter Board was constituted on June 12th with T. G. Perry, Lower Ridge, as President, for the purpose of establishing a regular system of sale for output of the creameries and factories; cheese production of 24 factories totalled in 1919 1,256,-388 lbs. worth $347,772 and the Butter production of 17 creameries was 915,816 lbs. at $504,602. The 1st annual Convention and Dairy Show was held at Sussex on Dec. 3-4th with useful speeches, exhibitions of method and work; appreciation was expressed of Dominion work along these lines and A. E. Trite of Salisbury elected President. Mr. Tweeddale in his Report—which was one of the most complete and elaborate published by any Province in this year—dealt with the work of 153 Agricultural Societies of the Province with their 10,281 members and Government grants of $19,000; he also reviewed, through their Supervisor, the operations of the 132 Women's Institutes with their enrollment of 5,000 members and efforts at gaining for the women of rural New Brunswick a clearer understanding of current problems and better recognition of common rights. At their 7th annual Convention in St. John on Oct. 28th, with Miss Hazel McCain in the chair, a number of valuable addresses were given and Resolutions passed: (1) asking on behalf of the children of the Province for appointment of two women upon the Board of Moving Picture Censors; (2) urging establishment of the kindergarten system in all the schools of the Province and creation of a branch for Kindergarten training in the Provincial Normal School; (3) undertaking the collection of lists of mentally defective in all districts of the Province.

Meetings were held of other Agricultural bodies during the year and Presidents elected as follows: N.B. Agricultural Societies, United, W. H. Moore of Scotch Lake; N.B. Beekeepers' Association, George L. Pugh of Nashwaaksis; N.B. Fruit Growers' Association, Lieut.-Col. O. W. Wetmore of Clifton. Speaking at Fredericton on Sept. 13th Mr. Tweeddale described the great problems of the day as settlement of existing unrest and escape, by increased production, from the "false prosperity" evolved by high prices and borrowed money; the Minister described one unusual item of Provincial policy in its encouragement of wheat production, by a Provincial bonus paid to encourage wheat mills, which he had lately increased from $1,000 for a 25-barrel mill to $2,000 for a 50-barrel mill and under which six new mills would be erected by the close of 1919. It may be added that the Dominion Farm Settlement Board of the Province had by November of this year listed 300 farms for sale in the Province and available for soldiers' occupation. The farms ranged in price from $150 for 35-acres in Queen's County to $20,000 for 300 acres in Albert County. One county,

Madawaska, offered only one farm, while King's County offered 80; the majority were practically abandoned farms. Many of these were occupied by soldiers on a basis of investing 10 per cent. of the price with 20 years to complete payment at 5 per cent. for the balance as a Loan from the Reconstruction Department at Ottawa. The Agricultural production of New Brunswick in 1919 (Federal statistics) was as follows:

Crop	Area Acres	Total Yield Bush.	Average Price per Bushel	Total Value
Spring Wheat	35,641	623,000	$2.32	$1,444,000
Oats	305,484	9,261,000	.98	9,086,000
Barley	10,662	285,000	1.35	385,000
Rye	353	7,000	2.00	14,000
Peas	4,697	69,000	3.03	209,000
Beans	6,409	106,000	5.25	556,000
Buckwheat	74,542	1,871,000	1.36	2,547,000
Mixed Grains	5,297	179,000	1.23	220,000
Potatoes	75,578	10,790,200	.97	10,466,000
Turnips, Mangolds, etc.	24,279	8,898,800	.58	5,155,000
	Tons	Tons	Per Ton	
Hay and Clover	786,175	1,111,000	20.26	22,512,000
Fodder Corn	5,906	30,000	8.00	240,000

The Hon. Dr. W. F. Roberts, Minister of Public Health, was an active member of the Government. The first meeting of the new Bureau of Health was held at the Department on Mch. 3rd with Venereal disease and proposed legislation as the topic of consideration; Dr. Roberts promised a Bill to provide for more nurses and their diversion to danger points in times of epidemic; at the 39th Convention of the N.B. Medical Society, St. John, July 15th, the Minister declared that "the profession, as a whole, must lift itself up from consideration of the individual and treat the whole prospect of human sickness and disability," described infant mortality as at the very base of the health problem with medical examinations of school children as a public health and not an educational measure. The discussions of this body were published in the press and were of obvious value; Dr. G. G. Melvin of Fredericton was re-elected President and Dr. Roberts 1st Vice-President. On July 19th the smallpox "scare" of 1919 had extended to New Brunswick and the Washington authorities, without advice or notice, at once imposed a quarantine. Dr. Roberts telegraphed the Surgeon-General at U.S. Headquarters as follows: "Perfectly willing to submit to such action should conditions warrant, but my Department has been particularly assiduous in combating contagious disease, so that at present there exists practically no smallpox." On the 24th the vaccination regulation was suspended. The Report of the Provincial Hospital for 1918 showed 626 patients with $51,001 as the revenue and $127,298 as cost of maintenance; the Jordan Memorial Sanatorium treated 90 patients during the year. The chief Government appointments of 1919 were as follows:

Recorder of the Supreme Court ....W. H. Harrison ....Fredericton
Judge of Probate for Westmoreland ....Frank A. McCully, K.C. ....Moncton
Judge of Probate for Albert ....W. D. Bennett ....
Clerk of the Legislative Assembly ....George Young Dibblee .....Fredericton
Member Farm Settlement Board ....E. P. Bradt ....Fredericton
Superintendent of Immigration ....Fred. E. Sharp ....Fredericton
Registrar of Deeds for King's ....Lieut. G. B. Hallett, M.C. ..Fredericton

The New Brunswick Legislature in 1919. The 3rd Session of the 7th Legislature of the Province was opened on Mch. 6th by Lieut.-Governor, the Hon. William Pugsley, D.C.L., LL.D., with a Speech from the Throne which referred to the close of the War and New Brunswick's part in the largely-increased production of foods, generous subscription to Victory Loans, wonderful response to the Red Cross and other similar funds, indefatigable personal effort on the part of the women of the Province; mentioned the Royal visit, the great Provincial harvest of 1918 and the Government policy toward Soldier settlers; referred to the demand of the Prairie Provinces at the 1918 Inter-Provincial Conference for control of their natural resources and declared that it had naturally suggested "a re-adjustment of subsidies which would in some way compensate the people of the older Provinces who had not received territorial additions so that they would be amply repaid for the alienation of public Western lands in which they had always had a partnership interest"; expressed regret that the growing coal production of Queen's and Sunbury was to be affected by transportation difficulties and mentioned the coming year as likely to witness very marked progress in the sinking of further oil wells, and in the development of oil-shales in the Province by wealthy and experienced English capitalists; stated that the St. John Valley Railway would soon be in operation from Centreville in the County of Carleton to its point of connection with the C.P.R. at Westfield, a distance of 158 miles, and that the Government had presented its claims for the taking over of the Saint John and Quebec Railway as a part of the Government-owned Canadian National Railway system; promised a considerable amount of legislation. Dr. J. E. Hetherington was unanimously elected as Speaker and the Address was moved by A. A. Dysart of Kent and J. G. Robichaud of Gloucester.

The debate commenced on Mch. 10th with a strong attack on the Government by Hon. J. A. Murray, Conservative leader, who had just recovered from a severe illness and with a review by the Premier of his Government's policy—in the course of which he stated that the total voluntary War contributions of the Government and people of New Brunswick was $37,221,888 including the subscription of $27,000,000 to the 1917-18 Victory Loans. As to the Valley Railway frauds, he declared that it had been proved that "A. R. Gould, when President of the St. John and Quebec Railway Co., in order to obtain a contract for the construction of the Valley Railway in 1912, had been compelled to pay and did, secretly and corruptly, pay approximately $100,000 to J. K. Flemming, then Premier of the Province, which money never was repaid to the Province"; he stated that it was the intention of the Government to prosecute all concerned in this and similar matters up to the limit the law would allow. The Hon. Dr. J. B. M. Baxter replied for the Opposition as did L. P. D. Tilley, K.C., while Hon. Dr. Roberts, Hon. P. J. Veniot and others responded for the Government and the Address passed without division on March 18th.

Of the 127 Bills introduced during the ensuing Session 118 were passed. Amongst the more important items of legislation was Hon. Mr. Tweeddale's Soldiers' Settlement Act under which the Government was to purchase 2,000 acres in lands near the cities or towns for partially disabled soldiers who desired to do gardening, poultry-raising, bee-keeping or to raise small fruits; the lands were to be transferred to the Soldiers' Settlement Board, and not more than $25 per acre was to be paid for them by the Government while provision was made to give those who preferred it a grant of 100 acres of Crown lands.   Hon. Mr. Veniot amended the Highway Act of 1918 so as to suspend for a period the election of by-road and trunk road Commissioners in order to meet the Ottawa authorities in their allotment of money for Highway purposes.   This Minister also amended the Provincial Railways' Act in order to obtain power for the Government to compel the Caraquet and Gulf Shore Railway Co. to put their roadbed in proper condition and to give the public adequate service.

Under the Government's Housing Act authority was given to borrow an amount, not exceeding $1,250,000, from the Dominion Government and to enter into an agreement with the latter Government regarding the loan and the security for its return; to prepare a general Housing scheme for the Province, which would set out the minimum standards, prices of houses and other conditions, along lines laid down in a memorandum prepared by the Federal authorities—the Loans to be repayable over a period of 20 years, with a possible extension to 30 years.   The maximum cost of these houses was to be $4,500 and the minimum $3,000, the building of farm houses was included though not, as yet, agreed to by the Dominion Government; action as to municipalities was voluntary and conditions of agreement with the Provincial Government the same as the latter's terms with the Dominion authorities—only 85 per cent. of the amount required for construction could be loaned and Housing companies could be utilized as well as individuals; repayments by individuals were as low as $20 a month and a Town Planning scheme could be made part of the general procedure.

Mr. Premier Foster presented the N.B. Power Company Bill based on the Currier Commission Report.   It was an elaborate measure but was eventually withdrawn in order to refer the question of a rate base, in its depreciation fund enactment, to the Supreme Court for decision as to the correctness of, or a proper substitution for, the $2,800,000 fixed in the Report.   On Mch. 28th a motion protesting against any Federal adoption of Daylight Saving was unanimously approved; Hon. Robert Murray, Provincial Treasurer, carried a measure to ratify and confirm an issue of $300,000 of 6 per cent. debentures authorized by Order-in-Council of July, 1918; Hon. Mr. Roberts amended the Public Health Act so as to change the membership of District Boards of Health to not less than 4 or more than 6; Hon. Mr. Foster obtained authority to issue new bonds to take up $2,282,000 of Provincial debentures maturing in 1919 and to make short-term loans for not more than three years; Hon. E. A. Smith had a Bill allowing the shipment abroad, under certain cases approved by the Advisory Crown Lands Board, of unmanufactured lumber cut on Crown lands; a Government measure was passed giving women the right to vote on precisely the same terms as men and providing for an early preparation of a Women's electoral list with classifications as spinster, married woman or widow; the Jurors and Juries' Act was amended to increase the age limit from 60 to 65 years.

Other measures included a Sale of Goods Act and a consolidation of the Acts for the Protection of Children; Acts authorizing the Government to borrow $1,050,000 for construction of Permanent Highways and $600,000 for the construction of Permanent bridges; a Bill granting an extension of time for the completion of the St. John and Quebec Railway between Gagetown and Westfield and to make a new agreement in that connection; an Act regulating Provincial Railways and another providing for sale of various small railways to the Dominion Government; amendments to the N.B. Railway Act and establishment of a Game Refuge of 400 square miles for game animals, birds and fish; amendments to the Vocational Education Act and the Schools Act and a Bill creating a Commission to enquire into the question of increased Teachers' salaries. A Resolution was unanimously passed on Apr. 17th regarding two New Brunswick soldiers arrested in England in connection with the Rhyl riots which urged the Ottawa Government to obtain delay in their trial so that (1) proper and sufficient counsel could be supplied for their defence; (2) witnesses in their favour have an opportunity of producing evidence either in person before such Court or by Commission; (3) that (a) such witnesses might, upon request, be sent to England at the expense of the Dominion Government or (b) the said Court be transferred to Canada, where the bulk of the said witnesses now were located. The Legislature was prorogued by the Lieut.-Governor on Apr. 17th with special references in his Speech to the Act to assist the Soldiers' Settlement Board, and to the appropriation made for the purchase of land for soldiers with physical disabilities; to, also, the Act making more liberal provision for the education of the Blind and that respecting jurors and juries, intended to secure the just and impartial administration of the law, both civil and criminal.

Prohibition, Finances, Politics, in New Brunswick. The Prohibition wave had reached this Province in 1916; during 1919 every effort was made by its advocates to give it the force of a tidal current. The St. John District Methodists on Mch. 4th urged that no changes be made in the present Prohibitory laws except to strengthen them; on Mch. 14th representatives of the N.B. Temperance Alliance attended a Convention at Ottawa and pressed their views on the Dominion Government; the Council of this Alliance met at St. John on May 20th, expressed confidence in the result of the Provincial Referendum of 1920 and passed a Resolution asking the Provincial Government to deal with the sale of extracts, essences and tinctures.   Incidentally, the Alliance expressed its congratulations to Rev. W. D. Wilson, Chief Inspector under the Temperance Act, because of "the wise and statesmanlike manner in which he has administered his Department."   Following the request of the Temperance organizations of the Province, the Government decided to take over the sale of the liquor considered necessary for industrial, medicinal and sacramental purposes.

A Government Bill was accordingly passed at the 1919 Session of the Legislature, to become effective upon proclamation, which authorized the Lieut.-Governor-in-Council to take over and thereafter conduct the business of the wholesale vendors in the Province —licensed to sell liquor under the Intoxicating Liquor Act—and for this purpose the Government could appoint a Board of three persons to carry out the provisions of the Act.   The Government was given the right to import, buy and sell liquor for the purposes of the Act, as full and as ample as the right of a wholesale vendor under existent conditions.   Power was given the Government to refit premises to carry on the business and to make rules and regulations respecting the duties of the Board, the verification of the stock of liquor on hand from time to time, the quality of the liquor supplied to the public on medical prescriptions, and the prices to be charged therefor, the sale of extracts, essences and tinctures and for such other contingencies as might arise.   In the original Act provision was made for a Referendum 12 months after peace had been signed or after a sufficient time had elapsed to judge of the working of the Act.   An amendment now provided that at such election the Government could "submit such questions pertaining to the Act as may be deemed advisable."

There was some strong opposition to the Bill and F. L. Potts described the irregular and arbitrary searches of private houses for liquor, declared the agitation to be overdone and the restrictions on essences and flavours as ridiculous and tyrannical; Dr. J. Roy Campbell described the Liquor Act as the most un-British measure ever enacted in the Province—under it people were in utter dread of liquor inspectors and those accustomed to the use of stimulants, on the advice and prescription of physicians, could not travel without fear of interference and insult.   The Act was not put into force and on Oct. 2nd Mr. Premier Foster explained that it was because of uncertain conditions prevailing, on account of the Plebiscite which must take place shortly and because of the Dominion Government's Order-in-Council which prevented the importation or shipment of liquor from one Province to another and which must expire with the declaration of peace.   On July 17th, following, the N.B. Medical Society affirmed by Resolution that: "Alcohol is a necessary drug and should be under no more restrictions than any other drug, that the prices now charged for alcohol and alcoholic stimulants are excessive and that the Government be asked to control the price." It was added that "the liquor now-obtainable is in many cases impure, adulterated and not up to the drug standard, and that the Government is responsible for the quality of alcohol and should put these sections of the Act in force."

Strong feeling was expressed against the Act and objectionable methods of enforcement. Dr. J. S. Bentley, the new President of the Society, in the course of a prepared paper in which he spoke highly of the therapeutic value of alcohol, remarked: "Perhaps nothing has more forcibly brought to every one's attention the necessity for good stimulants for medicinal use than the recent epidemic of Influenza." On Nov. 18th the N.B. Temperance Alliance met at Fredericton, asked the Government to obtain a Referendum under Dominion legislation as to the manufacture and importation of liquor and urged stringent Provincial regulations regarding the use of essences, extracts, etc., for beverage purposes. Donald Fraser, Plaster Rock, was re-elected President. On Nov. 12th the Premier stated in reply to varied rumours that: "The Government will not seek to restrict licensed vendors from purchasing liquor from any source where they can legally do so" and that the Government had refused to accept a proposal that retail vendors in New Brunswick should be confined to making their purchases from the wholesalers of St. John.

The finances of New Brunswick for 1918 (Oct. 31st) showed an Ordinary revenue of $2,258,637 and total Receipts from all sources of $3,667,805 with Ordinary expenditures of $2,223,592 and a total for all purposes of $3,636,854; in the Legislature on Mch. 25th the Provincial Secretary-Treasurer, Hon. Robert Murray, presented the 1919 estimates of Ordinary receipts as $2,064,830 and Ordinary expenditures as $2,054,188; the current Liabilities of the Province on Oct. 31st, 1918, were stated as $783,902 and the current Assets $309,302. Mr. Murray delivered his Budget speech on Mch. 25th and for the first time in the history of the Province he presented a detailed account of the actual business transacted by the Province during the past fiscal year, instead of a mere statement of the cash receipts and expenditures. The close of the War, he said, found the people of New Brunswick prosperous as was shown by their liberal subscriptions to the War Loans, and an increase of $13,-000,000 in the Bank clearings. The chief figures were as given above and, in his 1919 estimates, the Treasurer asked for $10,000 for Immigration and $15,000 to help disabled soldiers to settle on the land. The estimate for ordinary interest was $509,600; in 1918 the ordinary interest charge was $473,000. The estimate for interest on Valley Railway bonds was $187,299; the actual charge in 1918 was $179,000. The estimate for Public Works was $441,600 as against $365,000.

The chief items in the 1919 estimates of Receipts were $637,976 from Dominion subsidies, $809,500 from Stumpage and Forest dues, $110,000 from Motor Vehicles and $75,000 from Succession duties; the chief items of estimated Expenditure were $88,831 on

Agriculture, $298,785 on Education, $127,000 on Provincial Hospital and $441,600 on Public Works. The Bond liability of the Province on Oct. 31st, 1918, was $17,163,089 or an increase of $1,-353,233 in that year and included $9,099,646 of Funded Debt, $2,-113,442 of N.B. Government Stock and $5,950,000 of Valley Railway indebtedness.   Hon. J. A. Murray, Opposition leader, and other critics, proceeded to turn the small surplus into a deficit which the St. John *Standard* (Cons.) had already figured at $195,-000.   The same journal put the capital liabilities of the Province at $19,697,897.   As finally stated at the close of 1919 the Revenue for the year of Oct. 31st was $2,168,822 and the Expenditures $2,-496,508 or a deficit of $327,686; there was a new system of keeping the books and accounts with which the Government expressed much satisfaction; the Opposition produced many instances of apparent discrepancy in figures and reports.   It may be added that in May a Provincial issue of $1,000,000 3-year, 5½ per cent. gold bonds was sold in Montreal and New York for 101.

The prolonged problem of the St. John Valley Railway went through several new phases in 1919.   On Mch. 21st a large Delegation waited on the Government and asked that the Railway be extended without delay from Centreville to Andover which would cost about $1,500,000; on Aug. 21st the first train to pass from Fredericton to St. John over this Railway carried the Lieut.-Governor; Hon. F. B. Carvell, members of the Provincial Government and guests to the number of 40 and the end of the first phase of construction was reached after 8 years of stormy history and muddled politics.   Its construction completed the last link in a railway system which gave the shortest existing route between Quebec and St. John and greatly reduced the mileage over which the Canadian National Railway must haul through traffic between Ontario and the West during the months when the St. Lawrence was closed to navigation.   From St. John to Fredericton by the Valley Railway, from Fredericton to McGivney Junction by the Canada Eastern section of the C.N.R., and from McGivney to Quebec by the transcontinental line of the C.N.R. system was the new route.   The new line was described as having a solid roadbed, substantially ballasted, equipped with heavy steel rails, with low grades and easy curves fitted for the transportation of heavy trains at high speed.   It was also a scenic route of wonderful beauty. The cost, however, had been great—to Mch. 1st, 1919, it was $6,-946,021—and the estimated additional cost of the Gagetown-Westfield section was 289,913; the expected Dominion subsidy for the Line was a little over $1,000,000, and the annual interest charge would be over $300,000.   Meantime, running rights over the C.P.R. from Westfield to St. John were under arrangement but with various delays involved and it was not until Oct. 1st that the St. John and Quebec Valley Railway was actually in operation with a passenger and freight service which, however, still remained irregular for a time.

The Conservative party in New Brunswick was stronger than in many other Provinces at this time but it was hampered in many ways and the attacks of the Liberals and Government supporters upon the preceding Flemming and Murray administrations were continuous; Messrs. J. A. Murray, the Opposition leader, B. Frank Smith and J. B. M. Baxter of the late Government were constantly on the defensive and this, of course, weakened their fighting force. The chief charges and controversy turned upon the so-called Patriotic Potato scandal and the Valley River Railway campaign Funds—with the latter of which, however, J. K. Flemming, ex-Premier, was chiefly associated. As to the Potato matter the Government, late in 1918 had appointed James McQueen, K.C., a Commissioner with sweeping powers of investigation, and his Report was made public on Mch. 18th. He summed up the situation in part as follows: "The Province purchased—in the year 1914—68,603 barrels of New Brunswick potatoes in order that a patriotic shipment of 51,379 barrels might be sent to the Army and Navy of the Imperial Government and to the relief of Belgian sufferers. The amount expended for this purpose was $153,515.75. No tenders were called for, but names of certain persons were selected and these given a preference over all others. Within this circle still another preference was extended, this time to the Hon. B. F. Smith, afterwards Minister of Public Works in the late Government, and one of the present members for the county of Carleton; this privilege (as set out above) never should have been granted, was shamefully abused, and is one of the chief causes for the loss sustained. The number of barrels of potatoes which the Province had on hand after the two shipments were completed, according to the quantity purchased, should have been 17,224. Of this quantity 13,142 barrels were sent to Cuba, 521½ barrels sold to W. D. Mansell, and 100 barrels sold to A. B. Crosby and Co. The balance of these potatoes were not accounted for and, outside of the culls, which were traced to some extent, appear to be a total loss to the Province. A large number of these were sold by Mr. Daggett (lately Secretary of Agriculture) to parties in St. John and were never credited to the Province. The returns for the potatoes so sold (amounting to $8,499.46) never passed through the books of any of the Departments of the Province."

There were an infinite number of complications and details in the story, and incidents in the Report, but the Commissioner placed the final loss to the Province as at least $32,861. Mixed up in the matter and in an effort to conceal or make good the loss was W. B. Tennant of Valley Railway notoriety and the alleged campaign contributions of that Company while J. B. M. Baxter, Attorney-General, was declared to have advised as to procedure, etc. Of the other Ministers concerned, Mr. McQueen said: "That the late Minister of Agriculture, Hon. J. A. Murray, was constantly consulted by his Secretary as to the manner and method in which this Potato transaction was being carried on and is largely responsible for the loss incurred in connection therewith, either through neglect of duty or incapacity; that the Hon. B. F. Smith was advanced by the late Government $2,375.70 on the purchase of potatoes which the Province never received, and the Province also paid $71.85 as interest on his drafts in connection with this potato transaction which he should have paid.'' The first and natural answer to the Report was that it was openly and obviously partisan and this declaration was made and pressed by the *Standard* and other Conservative papers, with vehemence. In detail this view was given by the St. John journal on Mch. 21st as follows:

The McQueen Report, which was ordered for no other purpose than to attempt to destroy the personal and political reputations of a number of active Conservative members, found with respect to these members that J. B. M. Baxter loaned money to J. B. Daggett, which money has not been returned. That J. B. M. Baxter and George B. Jones assisted W. B. Tennant in certain financing. That J. A. Murray had personal, business dealings with the firm of A. C. Smith and Co., which dealings were not of a character in which the Province of New Brunswick was interested in the slightest degree. That B. F. Smith received a couple of thousand dollars more than the Commissioner believes he is entitled to. That Mr. Smith denies this contention and the amount in dispute is subject to settlement by the usual legal process. That Mr. Baxter is out of pocket through his desire to help straighten out an unfortunate complication. That G. B. Jones has accounted for every cent received by him in party funds and has proved disbursements to the full amount.

In the Legislature on Mch. 27th Mr. Premier Foster presented a Resolution recapitulating at great length the charges and statements contained in the Report and concluding as follows: ''That in view of the evidence and findings of the said Commissioner it is the opinion of this House that the conduct of the said members, being highly reprehensible and calculated to lower the character of the public life of the Province, as well as being derogatory to the dignity of the Legislature, merits and receives the censure of this House. Further resolved, that in the opinion of this House and in the interests of public life in this Province, the members named above should resign their seats in this Legislature.'' The former Ministers followed Mr. Foster in defence of what was, in essence, the use of party funds, held and controlled by W. B. Tennant, to meet a loss made by one of the Government Departments—at a time when the then Ministry was greatly discredited by the Flemming and Valley Railway charges and did not wish to give their opponents the slightest additional food for criticism. Hon. B. F. Smith dealt with the Report at great length and pointed out as an important preliminary that he was not even a member of the Assembly at the time of these alleged transactions; the Hon. J. A. Murray made an equally elaborate statement in which he quoted facts to prove that this was the ''threatened vengeance of a discredited politician'' dismissed from office by a former Conservative Government.

Mr. Murray freely admitted, however, an error in judgment— in attempting out of party funds to protect the Province against a

legitimate loss on a business transaction.   In the whole matter he
claimed to have depended on subordinates who had not proved as
capable as could have been desired.   Mr. Baxter spoke eloquently
and clearly in defence of his position—with an admittedly high
reputation at the bar and in person—and defined the affair, so far
as he was concerned, as a reflection rather than a charge.   He had
stood by his colleagues and would do it again; he had given Mr.
Tennant $3,000 of his own money which he then believed to be the
total Potato loss and he did not regret it.   A number of Liberal
speeches followed and the Resolution was carried on a Party vote
of 22 to 14 after a Conservative amendment, moved by J. Roy
Campbell and Dr. W. C. Crockett, had been defeated on the same
vote which declared that "the House is convinced that there was
no intentional wrong-doing" on the part of the Ministers but
regrets that "greater care" was not exercised in the purchase of
the potatoes and that an effort was made to suppress the facts and
circumstances.

That this Report and the action of the House was injurious to
the standing of the Opposition was obvious; one Party organ, the
Fredericton *Gleaner,* urged a change of leader at once and the
Moncton *Times* was apologetic though the *Standard* and most of
the others stood to their guns; there was, also, internal discontent
and F. L. Potts was one of those who thought a change in the
leadership desirable and stated this, publicly, at a St. John meeting called to select delegates for a Provincial Conservative Convention.   This gathering was held on Nov. 6th with delegates present
from all parts of the Province and J. E. McAuley in the chair; Mr.
Murray submitted his resignation as Leader and Albert E. Reilly
of Moncton was nominated but at once withdrew his name; Hon.
J. B. M. Baxter received the enthusiastic cheers of the Convention
but declined to accept leadership upon a matter in which he stood
side by side with Mr. Murray; the latter's name was presented for
re-election and the vote showed only a few dissentients.   A Provincial organization was then formed with A. D. Ganong, St.
Stephen, as Chairman and the following Resolutions were passed:

1.   Pledging the appointment of a practical farmer as Minister of
Agriculture.
2.   Declaring against class control of Government but admitting that
agriculture had not in the past been properly represented and urging Conservative nomination of farmers to control rural seats.
3.   Promising when returned to power to secure information, scientifically collected, as to Provincial water-powers with a view to their utilization and the discouragement of speculative control.
4.   Favouring free school books for all public schools.
5.   Recommending Conservative-Labour candidates whenever possible
and pledging appointment of a Minister of Labour without increasing the
number of Ministers.
6.   Recommending that all general and bye-elections be held on Mon-
days to allow commercial travellers and fishermen opportunity to exercise
their franchise without unduly interfering with their business and that upon
a vacancy occurring in the Legislative Assembly, the bye-election to fill such
vacancy shall be held within sixty days thereafter.

7. Pledging preference in all appointments to men who had served overseas in a theatre of war.

8. Promising to establish schools of technical education, and to introduce technical education in all public schools, so far as possible.

9. Pledging a revision of the Mining laws with a view to greater development of Provincial Mineral resources and approving a Road policy by which the bye-roads would be put in condition and maintained in proportion to the trunk road system.

10. Declaring that, in view of certain anti-French speeches in the Province "this Convention affirms that the policy of the Opposition Party lies in freedom of speech, freedom of language, and mutual respect and that it therefore expresses its disapprobation of all speeches or writings which have a tendency to create discord between the two great races of this Province."

A matter closely associated with politics was the consideration by the Provincial Supreme Court of the long-pending action of the Government against J. K. Flemming for the restitution of monies estimated at $100,000 alleged to have been illegally obtained by the former Premier from A. R. Gould when the latter was President of the St. John and Quebec Railway Co. On June 7th some technical objections raised by Mr. Flemming's counsel were overruled. Later on (Nov. 12th) Government Counsel in this case announced that Mr. Flemming's health had become so poor that he was quite incapable of appearing in Court or of giving evidence; medical affidavits were offered and the case was, therefore, held over indefinitely. As to another suit, respecting the same monies and directed against W. B. Tennant, the Government at this time added a clause to its statement of claims which arose out of the Potato case, and was to the effect that the defendant, Tennant, had made an offer to the late Premier G. J. Clarke, who in 1914-17 had charge of the Government and of all matters relating to the St. John and Quebec Railway, that if the Company for which Tennant was acting should receive a contract for the construction of a portion of the Railway, Tennant would pay certain moneys to various persons to be designated by Clarke; that the contract in pursuance of this understanding was given to the Company represented by Tennant, without tender, and that the Railway company agreed to pay $200,000 more for the work than it would have cost under fair and open competition.

An incident of the year was the investigation into the affairs of the N.B. Power Company which supplied St. John with power, light, gas and street cars by a Royal Commission composed of Henry Holgate, Montreal, Prof. A. S. Richey, Worcester, Mass., and Guy W. Currier of Boston (Chairman). The Report was made public on Feb. 28th and found that the cost of the property of the Company, in service, on Jan. 1st, 1919, totalled $2,800,000 and that this should be accepted as the rate-basis or amount on which dividends were to be provided under any arrangement with the City. This did not include the water-powers, or any lands or expenditures in connection with water-power development. The Commission recommended that the bonds and the preferred stock should stand as valid at a total of $3,100,000, but that the com-

24

mon stock of $2,000,000 should be reduced to $500,000 and that no dividend should be paid upon it until a separate reserve of $300,000 had been built up out of earnings; from this a return on the $500,-000 of common stock could be paid in the course of time.   Other and elaborate procedure as a basis of legislation was added and in the main accepted by the Government as a settlement of the dispute between St. John and the Company but proposed legislation was deferred for a Court opinion as to the rate-basis.   Other incidents included the contribution of $15,000 by the people of New Brunswick to an Endowment Fund for the Blind and the Report of the Workmen's Compensation Board which showed that since the Act came into force on Jan. 2nd, 1919, and up to October of that year, the Board had paid out $34,650 for temporary disability and $4,376 in partial disability.   The total number of accidents during the nine months was 1,750.

Conditions and Affairs in P. E. Island; The Provincial Elections.   The Province was prosperous in 1919 but the people were not altogether contented; high prices and unrest invaded the Garden of the Gulf as they did every other part of Canada.   The Island had an area of 2,184 square miles, near—all of which was suitable for cultivation but with only about half of it actually in field crops; the population was less than 100,000.   It was described at this time as a land for farmers and fishermen; the climate was healthy, fogs were rare, and the winters not severe. There were no mining industries and manufactures were limited; the soil was naturally very fertile and whenever top-dressing was necessary mussel mud—found in great quantities in the bays—was used.   Mixed farming and fruit culture were carried on, and in both forms of agriculture there was much room for development while fruit-growing, especially of apples, offered excellent opportunities and the cultivation of small fruits found a ready market in the adjoining Provinces.   Connected with the mainland by Ferry service and having a Railway from end to end, the Island enjoyed in 1919 exceptional transportation facilities; it, also, offered unusual opportunities for the development of summer resorts in its many bathing beaches and its deep bays and inlets.

In Agriculture and Live-stock the Island held an exceptional position at this time; its cattle, sheep and hogs numbering 119 to the square mile compared with 26 in Nova Scotia and 16 in New Brunswick; Community Breeding Clubs were organized to still further improve conditions and the character of the stock.   The Provincial Department of Agriculture (Hon, M. McKinnon) in its Report for 1918 declared that: "The Live-stock industry of the Province is in a very healthy condition.   Stockmen are attending more carefully to the factors which tend towards improvement while a promising feature of the industry is the number of young men who are establishing pure-bred flocks and herds."   The dairy industry was described as doing well and the high prices of mutton and wool were said to have greatly stimulated sheep-raising; swine were being kept in ever-increasing numbers and co-operative selling of eggs through Poultry Associations was showing good results with 900,000 dozen, or one-half the Island's product, sold in this way during 1918 for $350,000; the trade in horses was growing and under-drainage of farm-land being largely practised.

The 59 Farmers' Institutes in the Province did a limited amount of co-operative buying for their members in feed, fertilizers, seeds, spray materials, etc., with one Institute doing a business of $14,000 in lambs, alone, during 1918; the production of Cheese in that year was 38,075,687 lbs. valued at $538,503 and the Butter produced was valued at $266,490. Fox-farming had a steady development in 1918-19 and the Fur Sales Board reported in September, 1919 that there were 4,000 pairs of foxes in Island ranches, capitalized at $16,000,000, with an annual revenue from foxes and furs of $1,000,000 and a production of 6,000 pelts. It was estimated that in the 1919 Season 1,500 fox-pups were exported from the Island to various places, including Norway and Japan and that Island fox-fur was being sold to a value of $2,250,000 a year. The Field crops of 1919 had the following production, according to Federal statistics:

Spring Wheat	35,595	624,600	$3.25	$1,405,000
Oats	174,987	6,088,000	.85	5,182,000
Barley	5,636	164,000	1.40	229,700
Peas	490	8,100	3.25	26,300
Buckwheat	4,094	87,800	1.50	132,000
Mixed Grains	18,900	848,400	1.22	1,089,400
Potatoes	36,234	4,529,000	.85	3,850,000
Turnips, Mangolds, etc.	12,337	6,396,000	.26	1,688,300
		Tons	Per ton	
Hay and Clover	237,883	428,000	20.00	8,564,000
Fodder Corn	522	6,260	8.00	50,000

Government and Legislation in the Island. The Lieut.-Governor, Augustine Colin Macdonald, passed away on July 16th and, after a period during which Chief Justice J. A. Mathieson acted as Administrator, he was succeeded on Sept. 3rd by the Hon. Murdoch McKinnon, M.L.A., for eight years Commissioner of Agriculture and 22 years member of the Legislature. Politically, the Arsenault Government started the year with a Conservative majority of only 18 to 11 and one seat vacant, in a House of 30 members, and with a leader who had replaced Hon. J. A. Mathieson as Premier in June, 1917. He and his Government had supported Union Government at Ottawa but it did not appear that Island Liberals were any the more inclined to support Mr. Arsenault at Charlottetown. The 5th Session of the 38th General Assembly of the Province was convened on Apr. 2nd and prorogued on May 15th. The chief legislation of the Session included amendments to the Election Act under which returned soldiers were given special voting privileges, the old system of electing Councillors and Assemblymen together was retained and a secret ballot provided for; an Educational Tax Act, imposing a tax on all real property—except in Charlottetown and Summerside—of not less than two and not more than three mills on the dollar of the value of such land, for the purpose of increasing the statutory salaries of school teachers; together with a poll-tax for the same purpose upon rate-payers in Charlottetown and Summerside of not less than two or more than four dollars.

There was a renewal of the War and Health Tax for one year and passage of a Vital Statistics Act with stringent regulations as to reporting births, deaths and marriages. A Sale of Goods Act was passed and a Housing Act along lines similar to those of other Provinces except that the maximum cost of house and land was to be $3,500 and that a farmer, on approval of the Director of Housing, could obtain a loan in order to erect a dwelling-house for the occupation of a married employee; there was, also, an Act to provide for the Prevention and Suppression of Fires and the appointment of a Fire Marshal; an Act relating to Fox Companies provided for mergers and amalgamations, for the sale or surrender of shares at a valuation with payment, if arranged, in cash, or part cash, and part in foxes. The City of Charlottetown was authorized to expend $100,000 on permanent pavements and the total of moneys appropriated for public service was $505,923 with a capital sum of $21,500 and contingent grants for Highway improvements and Mussel mud experiments. The Prohibition Act was amended with changes of which the following were the most important:

1. The Prohibition Commission, consisting of six clergymen—three Protestant and three Roman Catholic—in whose hands the administration of the law was placed by the Government in 1917, was now to import the liquor and have it sold through vendors, who were to be on salary. Heretofore it was imported by a wholesale vendor and sold by retail vendors.

2. The quantity of liquor allowed to be given on any one prescription for medicine from a doctor in any one day was to be 24 ounces, regardless of the distance of the patient from a vendor. Heretofore, when the distance was ten miles or over, 48 ounces could be prescribed.

3. The penalty for first offence was put at $200 to $500 or three to six months in gaol instead of $100 or three months. For a second offence the penalty was to be from 6 to 12 months in gaol without the option of a fine.

4. Any doctor, who in the opinion of the Commission violated the Act with regard to giving prescriptions, was to have his right of issuing prescriptions cancelled.

5. The penalty for forging doctors' certificates was to be a fine of from $100 to $300 for first offence, and heavier penalties for subsequent offences. Provision was made for the inspection and analysis of liquors.

A Petition signed by 600 labouring men of Charlottetown was presented to the Government, asking that "stronger beer" be allowed to be sold. The Temperance people met this with a counter-petition signed by 867 male voters and 1,647 young men and women who were non-voters. A Referendum was provided by another Act to be taken in 1920, at a date to be fixed by proclamation, not later than two weeks before the Session of the Legislature, in order "to ascertain the number of voters within the Province who are in favour of or against the Prohibition Act, 1918, and amendments thereto." Incidents of the year included the passage of a Resolution (Jan. 16th) by the Central Farmers' Institute supporting the United Farmers of Ontario in their demand for reduction of the tariff on farm implements, fertilizers, coal, lumber, cement, oils, etc.; the declaration by the Egg and Poultry Co-operative Association (Jan. 16th) favouring imposition by the Provincial Government of a special Education tax; the opening on Sept. 25th by H.E. the Apostolic Delegate, of Dalton Hall, a Residence for students at Charlottetown given by Hon. Charles Dalton; the establishment of a Teachers' Union and its demand in October for a minimum salary wage running, according to classification and sex, from $425 to $625 which culminated in a strike planned for December and a Government decision to grant the desired schedule; the dedication on Sept. 24th of the new St. Dunstan's Cathedral at Charlottetown, described as the largest in the Maritime Provinces, and built in Gothic style at a cost of $200,000; the formation at Charlottetown of an Industrial Promotion Committee with a view to the development of manufacturing on the Island and a proposal to build a Highway across the Province as a War Memorial.

The General Elections of 1919. The Conservatives of the Island had won a great victory in 1911 with 28 seats to two for the Liberals but in 1915 they had obtained only a tiny majority of 4. In 1919 they had against them the general unrest and high prices countered, however, by unquestioned prosperity; the fact of the Premier, Hon. A. E. Arsenault, being an Acadian and Catholic also raised certain Orange prejudices and grievances—including the appointment of a Roman Catholic and alleged Sinn Feiner as Secretary to the Superintendent of Education in place of a dismissed Orangeman; according to an Orange *Sentinel* review of the Elections (July 31) the Lieut.-Governor was a Roman Catholic as well as his Secretary and so were the Premier, the Clerk of the Legislature and many other officials; 45 per cent. of the Province, however, was Roman Catholic in belief and there were 13,000 French Acadians in that total. The farmers, also, revolted to some extent and sought to have farmer candidates in the ridings though they did not organize a distinct party. There was said to be dissatisfaction with the administration of Public Works—especially with an alleged neglect of roads and with some clauses in the recent Highway Act; the returned soldiers were appealed to by both sides but did not take a conspicuous part in the contest though their voting qualifications were of a special kind—men who went overseas having the right to vote for two candidates in each riding and men on active service in Canada only one vote; the Government's attempt to introduce open voting in its Ballot Act amendments during the Session and its inability to carry the proposal probably injured its *prestige.*

J. H. Bell, K.C., the Opposition and Liberal leader, promised the usual economy and efficiency. A second car ferry steamer was to be put on the Borden-Tormentine route, and the whole of the P.E.I. Railway would be standardized; representation was to be secured on the Canadian National Railway Board with a view to procuring

better transit facilities across the Straits, and lower freight rates
to be obtained for fresh fish. No public moneys were to be expended,
and no liabilities created, unless specifically authorized by the Legislature. A short railway would be built to the Mussel Mud deposits
in Richmond Bay and lower freight rates made for this product on
the Island Railway. School teachers would be given a fair living
wage and the health and patriotic spirit of the pupils promoted.
Revenue and expenditure were to be equalized and unnecessary
officials discharged. All liquors imported for medical purposes
were to be inspected and analyzed and sold at actual cost. Co-
operation with Farmers' organizations throughout Canada was
promised "in their efforts to reduce the high cost of living," to
remove the causes of industrial and social unrest, and to abolish
or substantially reduce import duties on agricultural implements
and the necessities of life. On July 24th the Liberals swept the
Province and only Mr. Premier Arsenault, two of his Ministers—
Hon. J. A. McNeill and Hon. Murdock Kennedy—and J. D.
Stewart were elected on the Government side. The returns were
as follows:

District	Queen's County		District	Prince County	
1st	(C) Hon. Cyrus W. Crosby	Lib.	3rd	(C) Alf. E. McLean	Lib.
	(A) Murdock Kennedy	Cons.		(A) Aubin E. Arsenault	Cons.
2nd	(C) Hon. Geo. E. Hughes	Lib.	4th	(C) Hon. Walter M. Lea	Lib.
	(A) Bradford W. LePage	Lib.		(A) Hon. John H. Bell	Lib.
3rd	(C) Hon. David McDonald	Lib.	5th	(C) Creelman McArthur	Lib.
	(A) Peter Brodie	Lib.		(A) James A. McNeill	Cons.
4th	(C) Hon. Fred'k J. Nash	Lib.		King's County	
	(A) James C. Irving	Lib.	1st	(C) Harry D. McLean	Cons.
	Charlottetown			(A) Daniel C. McDonald	Lib.
	(C) C. Gavan Duffy	Lib.	2nd	(C) James P. McIntyre	Lib.
	(A) Ed. T. Higgs	Lib.		(A) Hon. Robert N. Cox	Lib.
	Prince County		3rd	(C) Hon. James J. Johnston	Lib.
1st	(C) Christopher Metherell	Lib.		(A) John A. Dewar	Ind.
	(A) Hon. Benj. Gallant	Lib.	4th	(C) Wm. G. Sutherland	Lib.
2nd	(C) Wm. H. Dennis	Lib.		(A) Wallace B. Butler	Lib.
	(A) Albert C. Saunders	Lib.	5th	(C) James D. Stewart	Cons.
				(A) Stephen S. Hessian	Lib.

The general belief was that the soldiers voted against the Government and Conservatives complained that they had backed up
the troops at the front and given them reinforcements when the
Laurier Liberals fought Conscription; now, in P.E. Island they had
given them special votes, also, and these were used to put the Liberals into power! There was more than this in the result, however, with 18 Protestant Liberals and 8 Roman Catholic Liberals
returned in a Province which was one-half Catholic. It would
seem that the Orange vote, which in all Canadian Provinces is
largely Conservative, must have supported the Liberals. The new
House, it may be added, included 7 lawyers and 10 farmers with
the balance merchants and professional men. The Arsenault
Cabinet resigned on Sept. 5th, after a delay which the Liberals
strongly criticized and J. H. Bell was at once sent for. Mr. Bell
was a Scotchman and barrister, 75 years of age, and formerly at
different times in the Dominion Parliament and the Provincial
Legislature. The new Government was sworn in on Sept. 9th as
follows:

Prime Minister ....Hon. John Howatt Bell, K.C.
Provincial Secretary-Treasurer and Commissioner
    of Agriculture ....Hon. Walter M. Lea
Commissioner of Public Works ....Hon. Cyrus W. Crosby
Attorney General ....Hon. J. J. Johnston, K.C.
Minister without Portfolio ....Hon. G. E. Hughes
Minister without Portfolio ....Hon. Benjamin Gallant
Minister without Portfolio ....Hon. Robert N. Cox
Minister without Portfolio ....Hon. David McDonald
Minister without Portfolio ....Hon. Frederick J. Nash

All but Mr. Nash had previously sat in the House—the latter was Managing Editor of the Charlottetown *Patriot*, Mr. Lea was a wealthy farmer with large Live-stock interests, C. Gavan Duffy was announced as the coming Speaker. The only bye-election was that of Mr. Crosby who, after a brief contest was re-elected over Thomas Wigmore (Cons.) by a majority increased from 88 to 354. It was claimed in this contest that official figures collected by the new Ministers showed an actual deficit during the 9 months of Jan. 1st to Sept. 9th of $254,000—largely incurred in public works.

THE PRAIRIE PROVINCES OF THE WEST.

**Manitoba:
Its Progress,
Government,
Politics and
Legislation,
in 1919.** This comparatively small Province of the West, with its 25,000,000 acres of estimated arable land out of a total land area of 148,000,000 acres, had only 6,000,000 acres under crop in 1919 but with conditions which ensured prosperity. The timber and pulp resources of its northern region were extensive but still unexploited as were its water powers with the Nelson River capable alone of producing 2,500,000 h.p.; its mineral resources in 1919 were becoming more and more known with extensive deposits of gold and copper north of the Saskatchewan river. The Flin-Flon ore body was alleged to contain over 20,000,000 tons of copper; abundant oil shales were found in the Pasquia hills and gypsum and building stone were produced in considerable quantities elsewhere while molybdenite was found near Falcon Lake. Not since 1888 had Manitoba known anything like a crop failure; in addition to her wealth in farming-land each year brought greater indications of the potential wealth in minerals and lumber of the immense added territory to the north and east referred to above.

The Province marketed in 1919 110,519 head of cattle, 133,000 hogs, 35,000 sheep and 4,000 horses through Winnipeg yards, alone, besides additional interior sales; remaining on the farms were 800,000 cattle, 400,000 horses, 167,000 sheep and 250,000 hogs with more than 3,000,000 poultry. The Dairy returns of 1919, according to the annual, authoritative, statement of the Winnipeg *Free Press*, were $65,017,690 or $12,000,000 more than in 1918 and comparing with a total of $11,351,087 in 1915; there was a new Egg trade of $2,020,579 and the Stockyards of Winnipeg handled a total of $38,-441,364 in value; the Wool product was $1,509,740, Potatoes $21,-851,200 and Hay and roots $34,932,313. Following upon its 1918 agricultural victory when Manitoba had won at the International Soil Products Exhibition of Kansas City, U.S., the first prize for the finest collection of vegetables made by any State or Province in North America, the 1919 Exhibition saw Manitoba winning 7 cups, 4 State championships, 2 county competitions, 34 first class awards, 15 seconds, 10 thirds and a special award for wild game. It also captured first prize for the most attractive exhibit by any nation, Province or State; for an exhibit of small grains (wheat, oats, barley and rye) by a nation, Province or State; and for vegetables by a nation, Province or State; second for the most comprehensive exhibit. The Federal statistics of agricultural production in 1919—sometimes differing, it may be added, in totals from Provincial estimates—was as follows:

Spring Wheat	2,880,301	40,975,800	$1.92	$78,706,000
Oats	1,847,267	57,698,000	.72	41,420,000
Barley	893,947	17,149,400	1.17	20,187,000
Rye	298,932	4,089,400	1.28	5,228,000
Peas	5,666	81,400	2.08	170,000
Mixed Grains	80,355	759,000	1.40	1,068,000
Flax	57,379	520,300	4.26	2,215,000
Potatoes	42,000	5,287,500	.81	4,266,000
Turnips, Mangolds, etc.	6,045	1,118,000	.60	663,000
		tons	per ton	
Hay and Clover	260,878	401,400	16.99	6,818,000
Fodder Corn	16,867	114,500	13.28	1,520,000
Alfalfa	5,181	11,400	22.40	256,300

Provincial Administrative and Departmental Affairs. The most important industry of Manitoba is that of Agriculture and the head of this Department in 1919 was Hon. Valentine Winkler. His Report covering the year of Oct. 31st, 1918, included statements of progress from J. H. Evans, Deputy-Minister, and many other officials. They dealt with Co-operative wool marketing and the shipment of 361,585 lbs. from Winnipeg to Toronto with 925 wool-growers participating in the arrangement; with Live-stock and the estimated total value of horses, cattle, sheep and swine in Manitoba as $465,196,675 and the statement of receipts at the Union Stock-yards, St. Boniface, as 729,599 head in 1918; with 42 Creameries in operation and a production of 8,450,132 lbs. selling at an average price, at the Creameries, of 45 cents or a total of $3,802,-559; with a Honey crop of 944,104 lbs. produced by 921 beekeepers keeping 14,736 colonies of bees. The Weeds Commission (S. A. Bedford, George Walton, H. B. Brown) reported much field work being done, deprecated the apathy of many town Councils and mentioned 60 farm meetings as being held during the winter; the Publications Branch reported excellent work in maps, bulletins and circulars and the Immigration branch specified 5,053 settlers during the year, chiefly from the United States, with 34,575 pieces of literature distributed during 1918; the Game Branch and Demonstration Farm Board also reported.

In the Legislature, on Feb. 5th, 1919, Mr. Winkler reviewed the work of his Department and claimed that the upward bound of the Dairy industry in Manitoba was directly due to the policy adopted by the Norris Government. He reminded the House that in 1912 and 1913, 55 car-loads of butter had been imported and contrasted this with the export in 1918 of 175 car-loads, valued at $11,788,173 or nearly double the value of the export of the previous year. The Minister also referred to the advance in the wool industry and the enhanced prices received owing to the institution by his Department of Co-operative marketing—in 1915 the clip of 69,000 pounds was sold at 25 cents per pound; in the following year the clip handled had increased by 100,000 lbs., and the price gone up to 32 cents; in the next two years the sales amounted to 174,000 and 362,-000 respectively and the price per pound received was 58 cents.

Intimately associated with the work of this Department was that of the Rural Credit Societies operating under a 1917 Act of the Legislature fathered by George W. Prout. It provided for the organization by Manitoba farmers of Societies through which the individual shareholders could obtain short-term loans for carrying on or extending farming operations. The money was secured from the Banks at 6 per cent. by the Society and the borrower was charged 7 per cent. The security of the Banks was the guarantee of the Society as a limited liability concern *plus* the assets of the individual borrower for repayment of his own obligation. In these Societies each member took stock to the amount of $100, and his liability was limited to the amount of his subscribed stock; the Provincial Government took stock to an amount equal to half that subscribed by the individual members of the Society; the municipality within the boundaries of which the members of the Society lived took stock to the same amount as the Government. This subscribed stock formed a guarantee fund as the basis for credit, and the Society was thus enabled to secure credits for its individual members to a total of many times the amount of the subscribed stock. There were, in 1919, 38 operating Societies with 14 others chartered and a total authorized capital of $1,040,000; the Board of Directors of each Society passed upon and recommended credits and the Banks, therefore, had not only a doubled security but also careful preliminary judgments to go upon in granting the loans. Up to Oct. 31st, 1919, the 38 Societies had granted Credits, and money had been borrowed accordingly, for the following purposes:

Purchase of Live Stock	$172,532
Purchase of Machinery	94,155
Putting in and taking off Crop	278,748
Breaking New Land	247,691
Farm Improvements	18,865
Retiring Liabilities and Sundry Purposes	239,885

Of similar character was the Manitoba Farm Loans Association which was still more closely related to the Government. It had commenced operations on Apr. 1st, 1917, and its main objects were to check mortgage companies in their interest rates, to facilitate farm building operations and to lend money to the farmer through the Association at 6 per cent.; Lachlan McNeill was the Government Commissioner. At the beginning of 1919 there were 91 loans in 110 municipalities outstanding to 762 farmers with a total of $2,000,950; under the Act the Association could not pay more than 5 per cent. for its money or lend it at a rate higher than 6 per cent.; the co-operative element came in the fact that each borrower had to be a shareholder in the Association for a specific amount of money. At the 1919 Session the Act was amended to more clearly define the disposition of moneys received from borrowers in respect of annual installments upon their loans and the investment of these funds for the future redemption of outstanding debentures. Arrangements, also, were made with the Workmen's Compensation Board for the custody of $200,000 of its moneys at 5 per cent. For the year of Nov. 30th, 1919, 795 applications for loans aggregating $2,532,800 had been received with $668,900 of applications declined; the total paid to date in Loans was $3,220,950 of which $141,014 had been repaid.

The Hon. G. A. Grierson, Minister of Public Works, in his Report for Nov. 30th, 1918, dealt with the final stages of such buildings as the new Parliament House, the Central Power House, the new Law Courts, etc.; with the Bureau of Labour and Minimum Wage law, the Good Roads Board, the Drainage Districts and Public institutions in general. A. McGillivray, Highway Commissioner, reported progress on the Winnipeg-Portage Highway: "The work of grading the 27½ miles of the St. Francois-Xavier section of this Highway was completed during the year and all bridges and culverts requiring immediate renewal were constructed of concrete. It is the intention of the Municipal Council of Portage la Prairie to complete the grading of the Portage section next year. This section is 26½ miles long and immediately joins the St. Francois-Xavier section on the west. The final completion of these two sections will give a continuous highway from the City of Winnipeg to the west for a distance of 67 miles. The road will be surfaced with gravel. The Council of Portage la Prairie Municipality is financing its share of the cost of this work, together with a large market road system, and the construction of permanent bridges, by the issuance of debentures."

The Commissioner hoped that the Highway would be carried eventually 226 miles to the Western limits of the Province; 141 miles of the road were either constructed or in progress of construction, thus leaving 75 miles which had not yet been taken up by the three municipalities through which they would pass; 50 municipalities had so far taken advantage of the Good Roads Act. In 39 of these, the work done had been in connection with roads and bridges in market-road systems, and in the remaining 11, the work done was on bridge construction only. Fourteen municipalities had issued debentures and proceeded with the construction of comprehensive systems of roads, which it was expected would prove adequate for some time to come. In 25 municipalities, systems which were deemed suitable and sufficient for local requirements, had been defined and the portions of these systems under improvement had been brought within the provisions of the Act. In the matter of Provincial Highways the Government assumed 66 2/3 per cent. of the cost of construction; the balance and the cost of maintenance were borne by the municipalities; so with the cost of bridges and culverts. According to the Chief Engineer, the number of miles of drainage constructed in the 20 Districts of the Province was 2,474 and the acres of land benefitted thereby 2,087,240; F. W. Simon, Architect of the Parliament buildings, stated that he had under the present Government certified $2,500,000 of expenditure to Oct. 31st, 1918; under the Manitoba Factories Act there had, during the year, been 1,853 inspections of 588 establishments with 17,500 employees, and the issue of 1,264 orders as to safety, sanitation or child labour and, under other Acts, 44 bakeries and 763 shops, warehouses and offices had been inspected; the accidents of the year reported were 1,123 and the Elevators inspected numbered 940.

The Minimum Wage Commissioners (Rev. Dr. J. W. Macmillan, (Chairman), Lynn M. Flett, Edna M. Nash, Edward Parnell and James Winning) reported for 1918 the holding of 24 conferences with industries employing women and that out of 4,674 women workers in Winnipeg and St. Boniface 3,664 had been dealt with by the Board; 18 industries had been persuaded to accept the principle of notice before dismissal or leaving. Other reforms had been effected: "We have ordered payments of wages to be made weekly, and immediately after having been earned. We have required a weekly half-holiday for saleswomen who work on Saturday evenings; and one whole day each week for those in places which operate on Sunday. In large stores, where the clerks go to lunch in relays and some have thus an excessively long work-period, we have required a ten-minute interval for rest in the midst of this long period. We have ordered toilet accommodation in connection with all stores, for it was lacking in many of them." Laundry workers and wages had been regulated in Winnipeg, Brandon and Dauphin and wages raised from $6.00 and $7.00 to $8.50 and $9.50 a week; in foodstuff industries $10 had been established as the ordinary minimum, in Departmental stores $12.00 and in retail shops $10.00; in soap and paper-box and drug factories $10.00 was the minimum fixed and in glove, bag, bedding, jewellery, millinery, tailoring and knitting establishments $12.00 was the figure set. In 1919 the minimum rates were raised to $11.00 in those industries which had been placed at $10 or less and in many cases the $12 rate was raised to $12.50; in most cases, also, a nine-hour day was established with 48 hours per week and a Saturday half-holiday. During the year Dr. Macmillan, Mr. Parnell and Miss Flett resigned from the Board.

It may be added that the Public Institutions Board of the Public Works Department reported 825 Insane patients at the Brandon Hospital and 671 at Selkirk with 333 in the Home for Incurables, etc., at Portage la Prairie. To the Hon. Edward Brown, Provincial Treasurer, the Superintendent of Insurance reported on May 1st, 1919, the collection of premiums totalling $8,868,871 and payment of losses on Life, fire, sickness, live-stock, automobile, Employers' liability and other forms of insurance totalling $3,779,326 with 42 Provincially-licensed Insurance companies doing business. Besides those already mentioned there were several important Government Commissions in this Province. The Public Welfare Commission had been created in 1917 and composed of Hon. Thos. H. Johnson, D. B. Harkness, M.A., H. J. Symington, K.C., W. J. Fulton, B.A., J. M. Thompson, A. T. Mathers, M.D., Robert Forke, Miss Ethel Johns, Mrs. S. E. Clement, Brandon, and Mrs. J. Halpenny, Winnipeg. It was required by law to investigate and report to the Lieut.-Governor-in-Council on all phases of charitable and welfare work, both public and private, within the Province. Special attention was given to the unification of effort and to the study of finance, supervision and control in this connection and a Report issued in 1919 defined the following principles:

1. Responsibility of Government in seeing that the primary needs of all children are provided for from some source, and that the reasonable needs of the handicapped and less fortunate of its citizens shall be adequately supplied.

2. That provision of the necessary financial support for an effective Public Welfare system shall have intelligent and methodical direction from the Government. whether the funds are secured from public monies or from benevolent contributions, or from both of these sources.

3. That all the benevolent or welfare activities of the Province, whether public or predominantly public or private, should be subject to the inspection of a public body established by Government, and amenable to Government regulations.

4. That the public body charged with the function of Inspection, Research and Recommendation should be kept distinct from and independent of any administering body.

5. That the Welfare activities of Government relating to neglected and dependent children, delinquents, hospitals, asylums and to all charitable institutions, public and private, should be grouped under one Department or Portfolio instead of being distributed among several Portfolios as at present.

The Mothers' Allowance Commission in its Report for Nov. 30th, 1919, explained that municipalities were required to appoint Mothers' Allowance Committees to receive and investigate applications from prospective beneficiaries under the Act for submission, with their recommendation, to the Commission. The Commission and Committees endeavoured to secure the full co-operation of mothers and children of earning age, and to see that the ability to earn was fostered and encouraged on the part of the mother without neglect to her home or children. The monthly schedule of allowances was carefully revised from time to time and ran, according to rental, for the number of rooms occupied, with $8 to $15 for fuel, and allowance for food and clothing based upon number in family; 1,291 children were thus cared for in the homes of 413 mothers under an average annual allowance of $230 per child as compared with the average in a public institution of $278. In the year 1919 243 new applications were received and 214 granted.

An important development of the year was the Greater Winnipeg Water District and the Commission in charge of its large interests was composed of R. D. Waugh (Chairman) and J. H. Ashdown. It had become by this time one of the chief Public Works on the continent and was one of the five longest water systems in the world. Begun prior to the War and carried on without intermission during its five years, the Aqueduct was an 85-mile concrete structure with contracts awarded in October, 1914, for a total figure of $6,142,640 and preliminary estimates of cost, exclusive of land and interest, as $13,045,600; the total length completed to the end of 1917 was 372,688 feet or 83 per cent., and the amount expended $11,275,587 with securities issued of $10,782,112. The source of supply for the water was Shoal Lake and it had to be carried 85 miles to Deacon—about 10 miles east of Winnipeg; this

Lake (drainage 360 square miles) was a part of the Lake of the Woods which had a drainage of 27,700 square miles. The length of the conduit finally completed was 96 miles and the difference in elevation between Shoal Lake and the Winnipeg Reservoir was 294 feet; the undertaking involved the supply of 85,000,000 gallons of water, every 24 hours, to 250,000 people. Concurrent with this work was the construction of a Government railway and Telephone line running from St. Boniface to Shoal Lake, the carrying of 12,000 passengers in its first year of operation, the opening up and cultivation of much new country with market gardens operated and large timber resources under development—with, also, a Provincial Industrial Farm established.

Still another project was under way in 1919, with private capitalists interested, for the electrical development of water-powers near Winnipeg—Winnipeg River, 509,900 horse-power; Pigeon River, 72,255 h.p.; Mossy, Dauphin, Waterhen and Fairford Rivers, 17,500 h.p. In 1906 Winnipeg had sanctioned the construction of a Municipal electric system which on Apr. 30th, 1919, had Assets of $10,243,773 and a surplus of $104,262 between operating revenues and expenses with 37,809 customers and yearly surpluses ever since 1914; it was estimated that current low rates for electric light and power, compared with other cities, had meant a saving of $5,000,000 a year to the public. Projects were under development before the War at the Great Bonnet Falls, on the Winnipeg River, but changing conditions compelled the Winnipeg Electric Railway interests to call in outside support and the Northern Construction Co., who built a large part of the Greater Winnipeg Aqueduct took up the matter and a $9,000,000 enterprise involving 160,000 h.p. was under way in 1919. In connection with the general Power question the Government put an Act through the 1919 Session to provide for the Transmission of Power throughout the Province, the appointment of a Power Commissioner, the creation of a Provincial system for supply of electric current to localities and interests by means of Power plants established in different parts of the Province and not dependent upon any one system such as that of Winnipeg.

Another Commission was that on Assessment and Taxation appointed in 1918 and composed of Hon. Edward Brown, E. M. Wood, L. W. Donley, Peter Wright, J. W. Breakey, M.L.A., D. D. McDonald, Robert Forke, W. R. Wood, M.L.A., Ald. F. Fowler and H. Pulford, Prof. A. B. Clark, W. J. Christie, J. H. Parkhill, E. Robinson, W. H. Gardiner, J. H. Curle, J. F. Fielde, and N. M. Warren. Early in 1919 the question of Taxation became an acute one, especially in Winnipeg where, it was contended, the city was $92,000,000 over-assessed; a Conference between the Government and City was held on Feb. 14th and consideration of a new system was promised. Following this the Commission was in session at all the chief centres of the Province with E. M. Wood as Chairman and asked a series of very complete and searching questions upon the issues involved. At the close of the year the Report was issued in volum-

inous form.   It gave the population of the Province as 507,904,
the number of resident farmers as 58,875, the area of Taxable land
as 17,669,447 acres, the area under cultivation as 7,051,304 acres,
the total Assessment as $487,531,534, the Taxes imposed as $13,216,-
942 and the Municipal Debenture debt as $56,108,633.   The chief
summarized recommendations were as follows:

1. That all real property in the Province be assessed—Land at its value;
buildings and other improvements at two-thirds of their value.

2. That in urban municipalities, comprising cities, towns and villages,
the basis of taxation shall be: (a) the assessment value of real property; (b)
business; (c) income; (d) special franchises; (e) licenses.

3. That in rural municipalities taxation be on the assessed value of
land only, in the case of farm-land; and on the assessed value of both land
and buildings and on net profits of business and on incomes, in unincorpor-
ated village areas in rural communities where lands are not used for purely
agricultural purposes.

4. That for the purpose of widening the base of taxation an Income
tax be introduced in the urban municipalities of the Province, as well as in
those portions of rural municipalities having urban characteristics.   The tax
to be on all incomes of persons over certain fixed amounts.

5. That a Provincial Tax Commission be constituted at the earliest possible date, with sufficiently wide powers to enable said Commission to fully
and effectually perform its functions.

6. That the statute labour provisions be repealed and that there be
substituted therefor the power to rural municipalities to levy for a limited
amount annually against all ratable property within their respective limits
for expenditure on road improvements.

7. That the poll-tax provisions of "The Assessment Act" be absolutely
abolished at the end of the year 1920.

8. (a) That the School Act be amended making the taxation unit for
rural schools correspond in area with that for municipal purposes; (b) that
the establishment of municipal rural school boards be made compulsory instead
of optional; (c) that in the election of trustees to said Boards, a fair method
be provided to govern in all cases; (d) that when school districts provide the
plant equipment for secondary education. the Department grants to such be
equal to 80 per cent. of the entire cost of operation.

9. That the exemption of church property in urban municipalities be
limited to the church building itself and the land upon which it stands.

Meanwhile, the Norris Government as a political entity had
achieved many practical results since taking office in 1914—establishment of Compulsory education, Referendum on abolishing the
Bar, Woman Suffrage, a Direct Legislation law, laws against Electoral corruption, Workmen's Compensation Act, Minimum Wage
legislation, Settlers' Animal Purchase Act, Good Roads legislation,
Farm Loans and Rural Credit Acts, promotion of Hydro-Electric
development, etc.   During 1919 the Hon. T. C. Norris, as Premier,
had to face the Farmers' movement in the Province and on Jan.
8th he told the Brandon Grain Growers' Convention that "recognition of the difference in interests between eastern, western and middle Canada must be followed by a willingness to compromise.   It
might take the form of readiness to accept a customs tariff of say
12½ per cent. rather than the 25 to 40 per cent. now imposed.   Such
a spirit, fairly met, should enable us to cross over the difficult
period ahead in safety."   Mr. Norris was in Ottawa on Apr. 7th

and stood for moderate counsels in this respect; on the eve of a Western Liberal caucus as to Tariff matters he declared that Manitoba's demand was not exorbitant and that twelve commodities made free, and corresponding markets opened, would go far to satisfy the people—for the present, anyway. At the same time he and Mr. Brown, Provincial Treasurer, and J. A. Campbell, M.P., pressed upon the Dominion the need for completion of the Hudson Bay Railway. Mr. Norris, accompanied by Hon. Edward Brown and Hon. Dr. R. S. Thornton, attended the Dominion Liberal Convention at Ottawa in August, and Manitoba stood distinctly for recognition of the co-operation of Unionist and Laurier Liberals.

Government incidents of the year included the announcement on Feb. 7th of a Commission to conduct the registration of aliens of every nationality in the Province, with Judge R. H. Myers of the County Court as Chairman; the creation by Order-in-Council on May 8th of the Industrial Conditions Commission with Rev. Dr. J. W. Macmillan (Chairman), F. H. Weir and W. C. Angus representing Labour, and W. R. Ingram and L. R. Barrett representing Employers, as members, and for the purpose of research into the high cost of living, into wages paid to all workers in the Province, and into practically all phases of local industrial life; the appointment of a new Advisory Board for Manitoba Agricultural College. The members of this body were John Sweet, Thornhill; Mrs. Leslie of Melita; William Nichol, Brandon; R. M. Matheson, Brandon; Duncan F. Stewart, Thompson; R. J. Avison, Gilbert Plains; John Crawford, Chater; A. D. McConnell, McConnell; Robert Milne, B.S.A., Lansdowne, with Hon. Valentine Winkler as a member ex-officio. The Hon. Mr. Grierson stated in the Legislature on Feb. 11th that in actual construction work $4,373,581 had been expended on the new Parliament Buildings and that an additional expenditure of $1,534,769 would be required, so that by the time the structure was completed approximately $6,000,000 would have been expended; the Report of the Workmen's Compensation Board showed awards of $408,817 in 1918 for disability, medical benefits and pensions with premiums paid by employers or chargeable to self-insurers of $499.430.

Under Government auspices the Prison Farm at Birch River put new methods of treating prisoners into operation with the Parole system of labour found to work satisfactorily; a Permanent Government Committee was appointed in September to confer with a Committee of the Civil Servants' Association and to meet from time to time in order to discuss bonuses, organization of service, classification, salaries, etc.; at Ninette, on a picturesque hill-side overlooking Lake Pelican in the Pembina Valley, the buildings of the Manitoba Tuberculosis Sanitorium were completed during this year and arrangements were also made to bring the 20 or 25 medical students in training at this institution into the plans of the Medical Faculty of Manitoba University; an echo of a famous political and legal controversy was heard on Oct. 3rd when Mr. Justice Curran ordered Thomas Kelly, the Contractor, to pay back to the Government of Manitoba $1,207,351.65, as the amount decided by the Board of Appraisal to have been received by Kelly in over-payments on the contract for the Manitoba Parliament Buildings—with interest at five per cent. from July 1st, 1914; on Dec. 10th Hon. T. H. Johnson, Attorney General, following a statement that there were 5,000 persons of feeble-minded character in the Province, promised that substantial provision would be made by the Government to meet the situation.

An important incident of the year was the decision on July 2nd of the Judicial Committee of the Privy Council that the Manitoba Initiative and Referendum Act of 1918 was *ultra vires*. There were present Lord Haldane, Lord Buckmaster, Lord Dunedin, Lord Shaw and Lord Scott-Dickson. Lord Haldane, delivering the judgment, pointed out that in this measure the Legislative Assembly sought to provide that laws for the Province could be made and repealed by the direct vote of the electors, instead of only by the Legislative Assembly whose members they elected; declared that the whole intention of the Act was to restrict the powers of the Lieut.-Governor and Legislature; quoted Section 92 of the B.N.A. Act which enacted that "in such Province the Legislature may exclusively make laws in relation to matters" coming within certain classes of subject. There were many Government appointments during the year. Major D. M. Duncan, M.A., was appointed and afterwards resigned as Chairman of the Minimum Wage Board; Rev. Dr. J. W. Macmillan resigned as Chairman of this Board prior to Major Duncan's appointment, and at the close of the year G. N. Jackson was appointed; the Elevator and Hoist Board was constituted with Edward McGrath (Chairman) and A. Steventon, W. J. Easterbrook, T. A. Harp and G. W. Murray as members; J. Gordon Steele resigned at the close of the year as Comptroller-General and a Board of Trustees for the Provincial Library and Museum was appointed composed of Messrs. T. C. Norris and J. W. Armstrong of the Government, Hon. James Baird, Speaker of the House, Hon. A. B. Hudson, K.C., Prof. Chester Martin, Dr. Charles N. Bell, and Prof. R. C. Wallace. Miscellaneous appointments were as follows:

Member Fair Wage Board	Arthur J. Bonnett	Winnipeg
Member Fair Wage Board	Charles J. Harding	Winnipeg
Member: Advisory Board, Department of Education	Archbishop Matheson	Winnipeg
Member: Advisory Board, Department of Education	Rev. David Christie	Winnipeg
Member: Teaching Commission	J. Allison Glen	Russell
Clerk of Executive Council	Fred. T. Axford	Winnipeg
Governor, University of Manitoba	John A. Machray	Winnipeg
Governor, University of Manitoba	Thomas J. Murray	Winnipeg
Governor, University of Manitoba	William Iverach	Winnipeg
Medical Superintendent, Brandon Hospital	Major C. A. Barager, M.D.	Brandon
Clerk of the Legislative Assembly	Lieut.-Col. Arthur W. Morley	Winnipeg
Arbitrator under Soldiers' Settlement Act	George A. Metcalfe	Winnipeg
Agricultural Adviser of Rural Credit Societies	R. H. Murray	Tilley
Official Trustee of Various School Districts	Ira Stratton	Winnipeg
Official Trustee of Various School Districts	John Franklin Greenway	Winnipeg
Provincial Psychiatrist	Alvin T. Mathers, M.D.	Winnipeg
Chief Engineer under Electric Power Act	J. Rocchetti	Winnipeg
Trustee: Manitoba Sinking Fund	Austin E. Harris	London
Trustee: Manitoba Sinking Fund	Sir K. W. Price, K.B.E.	London

On Nov. 6-7 a Manitoba Conservative Convention was held at Winnipeg with 130 Delegates in attendance and R. G. Willis of Boissevain in the chair. Hon. Robert Rogers was not present but other leading Conservatives such as W. J. Tupper, K.C., W. J. Bulman, J. T. Haig, E. J. Taylor, K.C., and R. A. C. Manning, were in attendance and the first business was the election of a Leader. R. G. Willis of Boissevain, a well-known farmer, Major Fawcett Taylor, of Portage la Prairie, Albert Préfontaine, the current leader in the House, W. J. Tupper, K.C., and Mrs. James Munro, Winnipeg, were nominated; all withdrew, however, except the first two and Mr. Willis was elected on ballot by an unstated majority. The Provincial organization was re-constituted with Mr. Tupper (a son of the late Sir Charles Tupper) as President, Major Taylor and Mrs. Munro as Vice-Presidents, A. E. Johnston, Secretary and C. F. Mount, Treasurer. W. J. Bulman was elected Patron in place of Sir Robert Borden and E. L. Taylor Hon. President. The Union Government was much criticized and the action regarding Sir R. Borden was significant of the fact that Mr. Rogers and his Dominion Conservative party re-organization views were influential; a Resolution was passed declaring that the Conservatives of Manitoba would favour "a coalition with any political force that promises to defeat the Norris Government"; no definite platform was promulgated but a Committee report denounced the Norris Government for "waste, extravagance and incompetency" while advocating the establishment of a Provincial Ministry of Labour and the abolition of the Municipal Commissioners' tax.

The 1919 Session and Legislature. The 4th Session of the 15th Legislature of Manitoba was opened on Jan. 23rd by Sir J. A. M. Aikins, Lieut.-Governor, with a Speech from the Throne which referred to the close of the War, the coming Peace terms, the gallantry of Provincial soldiers at the Front, the debt due by Canadians to them in this era of reconstruction; dealt with the bitter toll of Influenza but eulogized the brave band of volunteer nurses in Manitoba and the vigilance of the Department of Health; mentioned the work of the Public Welfare Commission, its survey and special classification of mental diseases and the near completion of the Psychopathic Institute which, as part of the Winnipeg General Hospital, would introduce into the new system of treatment the most humane and scientific methods anywhere in vogue and prevent mental cases from passing through the gaols as in the past; specified various activities of the Department of Agriculture and the substantial progress of the industry in general and Live-stock and Dairying in particular; reported a renewal of negotiations for transfer of natural resources from the Dominion and promised some important legislation.

The Address was moved by A. J. Lobb, Rockwood, and Robert Jacob, North Winnipeg. During the ensuing debate Mr. Préfontaine, Opposition Leader, found little to criticize in the Government policy and F. J. Dixon (Lab.) only deprecated the delay as to Direct legislation; Lieut. J. W. Wilton proposed that the Government at once call into consultation the Winnipeg Board of Trade, the Manufacturers' Association, organized Labour, returned Soldiers' Associations and organized Farmers, to decide whether or not the Government could do anything to establish new industries in Manitoba—what industries could be established at once, with fair prospects of success and what form or forms governmental assistance could best take; Lieut.-Col. George Clingan, also back from the Front, eulogized Prohibition and declared that some person or Government should stop the continued process of increase in the cost of labour, in the materials used, in the products sold. The Address was passed on Feb. 7th without division.

The Hon. Edward Brown delivered part of his Budget speech on Feb. 12th and part on Feb. 18th. He first reviewed Manitoba's place in the War as including $5,450,000 raised by a levy upon the rateable property of the Province, and by voluntary and individual subscriptions for the Red Cross organizations of $1,976,000, for the Y.M.C.A. $236,000, for the Navy League and Sailors $205,000—a total of $7,867,000; for Victory Loan subscriptions the total was $76,000,000. He described the new taxes on Amusements, unoccupied lands and rateable property as having been most successful with a total product in 1918 of $897,000. The estimated Expenditure for the year of Sept. 30th, 1918, was $7,571,205 and the actual amount $7,308,680; the estimated Revenue was $7,655,347, and the actual total $7,631,548; the surplus was $322,868 as compared with a deficit of $184,175 in 1917 and of $252,982 in 1916 and with a surplus of $229,931 in 1915—a net surplus for his four years' Treasurership of $115,641. The chief items of expenditure were $1,162,873 upon Education, $585,131 upon Agriculture and Immigration, $1,541,236 upon Telephones and $1,263,793 upon Public Works. The chief items of revenue were $1,425,135 from Dominion subsidies, $334,899 from School Lands, $299,578 from various Fees, $866,941 from Interest, $197,503 from Succession Duties, $540,353 from Corporation and Railway taxes, $134,934 from Amusement taxes, $236,314 from Automobile licenses, $625,000 from Municipal levy, $137,500 from Unoccupied Land tax, and $2,003,307 from Telephone rentals.

The total cash on hand on Nov. 30th was $3,382,671 and the Capital expenditure of the year was $2,056,693. Mr. Brown dealt with the Debt as follows: "The entire bonded indebtedness of the Province has now reached the sum of approximately $33,900,000. Of this amount $19,300,000 is revenue-bearing and represents our investment in telephones, elevators, drainage, judicial districts and farm loans. The net Debt is $14,500,000, and is represented by the public buildings of the Province, together with the money spent under the Good Roads Act. From the net Debt there may be very fairly deducted the cash in hand representing unexpended capital balances, totalling $1,103,000, together with $400,000, part of the proceeds of the Tuxedo property and now forming a sinking fund. These two items will reduce the net Debt to approximately $13,000,000. Our population is 613,000, and it would thus appear that our per capita debt is $21 per head of population. This is among the lowest in the Provinces of Canada. When the present Government came into the office the gross debt of the Province was $27,300,000. Since then there has been added $6,560,000. Of this large sum $4,000,000 has been borrowed for the purposes of the New Parliament Buildings and $1,000,000 to pay the debts of the late Administration. I deemed it important to make a careful review of the various sales of bonds issued since the present Administration took office, and I find that, in all, there have been 14 transactions, two of which were issued bearing 4½ per cent. interest, nine bearing interest at 5 per cent., and three at 6 per cent., and that the average rate for the period, including all charges, was 5·88 per cent.—a record which will compare with any of the Governments in Canada, not excluding the Dominion. In addition, by refunding certain sterling securities and issuing dollar securities instead, the Debt of the Province has been written down by $450,000. The Assets of the Province reach a grand total of $74,000,000, an increase of $4,500,000 during the year.''

During its 4 years rule the purposes of the Government were defined as (1) Improved Education with an expenditure therein of $4,120,000 during that period; (2) the betterment of Agriculture with the establishment of a Farm Loans Association, reduction of cost of money on long term loans, the formation of Rural Credit Societies, the loaning of money in larger volume and at reduced rates to the farmers, the loaning of money directly for the purchase of stockers and female animals and the sale of cows on terms of easy payment to settlers in the newer districts; (3) better Moral and social conditions with legislation providing for Prohibition, Women's Franchise, the Mothers' Allowance, the Health Act, the Workmen's Compensation, the Fair Wage Act, the Minimum Wages, etc. Mr. Brown urged greater industrial development: ''We have all the elements here which enter into successful manufacturing, namely, cheap electric power, a satisfactory labour market, much raw material. Our manufacturers have initiative and enterprise and, given a chance, can produce almost anything made in other parts of Canada, and perhaps in many cases just a little better.'' There were in the Province already 834 establishments with 19,260 employees, a pay-roll of $19,000,000 and products of $62,000,000.

Reference was made to the large wholesale trade, jobbing and merchantile interests of the Province; to the excellent Banking system which had proved a tower of strength to the nation in the War and a condition in which ''the entire cash resources of Canada can be mobilized in 48 hours by a conference of not more than half a dozen men with the Minister of Finance.'' The estimated Expenditure for 1919 was $8,377,000 and Revenue $8,450,000; the

· Municipal Levy was to be reduced from 2½ to 2 mills and $2,420,-
000 would be required on capital account. The actual Expenditures for 1919 (as stated in the 1920 Budget) were $8,544,790 and
Revenues $8,986,076. The Opposition criticism was voiced by P.
A. Talbot (Cons.) on Feb. 19th who claimed that instead of a
surplus there was really a deficit; F. J. Dixon (Lab.) went further
and accused the Treasurer of "padding" the balance sheets. Mr.
Premier Norris replied to the latter allegations, as did Mr. Brown,
in terms of keen resentment on Feb. 21st—the Treasurer declaring
that "the views of Mr. Dixon are too well known and appreciated
at the proper worth by members of the House, and those who know
him about the city, to have any heed paid to them. His attitude
towards the Red Cross organization, Conscription and all other
public matters are repudiated by 99 per cent. of the citizens whom
he is supposed to represent." Public opinion, as a whole, and the
financial press generally approved the financial statement as a good
one. A little later the Treasurer issued a statement explaining the
new Accounting system of the Province which he considered to be
the best in Canada and under which, for instance, the following
revenues given as outstanding and unpaid, were not taken into the
1918 totals though they were certain to come in and would have
swelled the surplus greatly:

Succession Duties unpaid	$281,689
Interest on School Lands outstanding	521,122
Interest on Provincial Lands outstanding	365,559
Or a total of	$1,168,370

The legislation of the year included 130 Bills. The Hon. Mr.
Brown passed an Act which relieved returned soldiers and sailors
from taxes up to an amount of $50 per annum and another measure
established an Alien Registration Bureau; returned soldiers were
given protection from foreclosure of mortgages for one year after
the proclamation of peace and were given a preference in the administration of Housing funds; for the purpose of assisting soldiers in land settlement, an Act was passed giving the Government
power to expropriate vacant land for their use while amendments
to Municipal and Assessment Acts exempted from taxation all institutions owned by, and property held by, Veterans' Associations.
Provision was made through the Attorney-General's Department
for the free administration of the estates of soldiers and under the
Department of Education so that returned soldiers, who had the
necessary educational qualifications, could receive free tuition and
text-books for Normal School courses, together with an advance of
$50 per month, without interest, to assist them through these
courses—the money to be refunded by small installments from their
salaries when they had obtained their certificates and secured positions.

In this connection Resolutions were passed by the Legislature
(1) requesting from Ottawa a substantial increase in the Pensions

of totally disabled men, and for the dependents of deceased soldiers;
(2) asking for readjustment of the scale of pay for vocational students and instructors; (3) urging that funds be made available to
be loaned to returned men for the purpose of building houses or
establishing themselves in business and upon the same basis as that
provided for returned men who wished to settle on farms; (4) calling on the Federal Government to reimburse parents, so far as
monetary consideration could do so, for the loss of sons in the War.
The Rural Credits Act was amended so that the Government could
guarantee indorsements given by any Society providing that the
amount did not exceed a stated sum, and could borrow money by
Treasury Bills up to $500,000, to implement such guarantees or to
make such loans—the object being to make the Societies, if necessary, independent of the Banks; a Treasury Act made provision
so that temporary loans might be negotiated, if required through
the failure of the revenue from unforseen causes, by Order-in-
Council—such loans not to exceed the respective amounts of the
deficiency in the Consolidated Revenue Fund; a similar measure
provided the right to borrow also upon the anticipated receipts for
the current year from the different municipalities and school districts of the Province—such loans not to exceed, in any case, the
amount of the Municipal Commissioner's levy for the year then
current.

The Electrical Transmission Act provided for the appointment
of a Commission similar to that in Ontario (J. M. Leamy was afterwards appointed Commissioner) and the creation of a Hydro system based upon Provincial and Municipal co-operation; the Hotel
Act was amended so as to include in licenses the right to operate
two·pool tables, to prohibit the sale, service or delivery of any
fermented or malt beverage to a minor under 16 years of age, to
forbid the employment of any girl or woman not the wife or
daughter of a licensee in any place where such liquors were sold;
a Poultry Breeders' Act was passed which provided for the incorporation of the Manitoba Poultry Breeders' Association, the organization of local bodies or branches throughout the Province, a Government grant to encourage such societies and to give prizes at
Winter Shows. Another Bill vested the control of the Provincial
Library and Museum in a Board of Trustees, made it a separate
department of the Civil Service and provided for a copy of every
publication printed or published in the Province to be furnished to
the Library; the Elevator and Hoists Act constituted a Board with
power to adopt rules and regulations respecting the construction,
operation, maintenance and carrying capacity of elevators, hoists,
dumb-waiters, and all other hoisting appliances installed in buildings in Manitoba, and provided for the inspection and licensing of
all such appliances and the operators thereof.

The Live Stock Purchase and Sale Act was passed for the purpose of increasing and improving the live-stock of the Province; it
gave the Department of Agriculture power and authority to pur-

chase or raise live stock and to sell the same to *bona fide* farmers actually resident upon farms in Manitoba; it provided that any such sale could be either for cash or partly upon credit, credit to be given only under the Act for a term not exceeding three years and to the extent of not more than 75 per cent. of the purchase price of any animal, with the Department retaining a lien on such animal until full payment was made.   Under the Land Settlement Act provision was made for the appointment of a Board of three members by the Lieut.-Governor-in-Council, to undertake the following duties: (1) To make a list of the unoccupied land in the Province of Manitoba suitable for settlement; (2) to ascertain what portion of the unoccupied land in Manitoba was suitable for agriculture or grazing purposes; (3) to obtain information as to what prices were asked by owners of unoccupied land in the Province suitable for settlement; (4) to place a valuation on such unoccupied land where the owner refused or neglected to supply such information.

A Farm Implement Bill was passed, under strong demand from the farmers, which was designed to prevent misrepresentation on the part of salesmen by creating a standard contract to safeguard the rights of the purchaser; G. J. H. Malcolm had a measure which would enable a single municipality, or parts thereof, to co-operate with other municipalities or the Government in the erection or purchase and maintenance of a Union Hospital; a Government Bill brought the Manitoba Agricultural College under the provisions of the Civil Service Act; the Hon. Dr. Thornton carried a measure regarding the treatment of mentally diseased persons and the establishment of the Psychopathic Hospital as an addition to the Winnipeg General Hospital and providing for such persons to be sent direct instead of going before a magistrate for committal; by amendments to the Good Roads Act the municipalities were empowered to borrow on ten per cent. instead of six per cent. of the assessment and the Minister of Public Works was given power to carry out the improvement or construction of a road where the municipality neglected to do the work—one-third of the cost to be charged against the municipality.

The Barbers' Act provided for a Board, for examination and the issue of licenses, and other measures provided for the establishment of an Industrial Research Bureau, sanctioned borrowing for capital expenditures which amounted to $12,678,000, and amended the Amusements Taxation Act so as to abolish the tax on Theatre seats. The Corporations Act was amended to increase the levy on Banks, Trust and Insurance Companies; a Dower Act was passed to more fully secure a wife's right in the homestead and her one-third share in her husband's real and personal property. An Act respecting Industrial Conditions, carried by the Premier, was intended to aid in settling Labour disputes, and correcting unjust and unfair conditions of employment, by the creation of a Permanent Joint Council of Industry to consist of 5 persons—2 representing workers and 2 employers—with jurisdiction to hold enquiries in Labour disputes, to investigate cost of living conditions, to enquire into the condition, wages, etc., of employees and employment in general, to examine into charges of unfair profits or breaches of contract, to recommend legislation. Other Bills regulated and licensed Produce dealers and enabled municipalities to borrow limited amounts of money for seed grain purposes; gave the Provincial Board of Health special powers in establishing Dispensaries and making regulations for dealing with venereal diseases; dealt with and authorized appointment of a Board of Welfare Supervision, amended the Winnipeg Charter and the Workmen's Compensation Act.

A Resolution was voted down by the Government which required the flotation of Manitoba Government bonds to be done by public tender in future but, following this, the Government approved and carried a Resolution declaring that while the House in general approved the policy of calling for public tenders for bond issues, it did not deem it wise for the Administration to be committed in all cases to such a policy. Another Resolution, passed without division, was that of A. W. Myles and T. G. Hamilton (Liberals) denouncing the "unjust and unrighteous tariff" and demanding from the Dominion Parliament (1) an immediate and substantial all-round reduction of the Customs Tariff; (2) the reduction of the duties on goods imported from Great Britain to one-half the rates charged under the general tariff, and further gradual uniform reduction in the remaining tariff on British imports that would ensure complete free trade between Great Britain and Canada in five years; (3) the acceptance by the Parliament of Canada of the Reciprocity agreement of 1911 and the placing upon the free list of all foodstuffs, not included in the Agreement; (4) the placing on the free list of all agricultural implements, farm machinery, vehicles, fertilizers, coal, lumber, cement, illiminating fuel and lubricating oils and all raw materials and machinery used in their manufacture. During the Session General Pau was received and welcomed by the House and on Mch. 7th two Manitoba winners of the V.C.—Alex. Brereton and Fred. Coppins—were similarly honoured. The House was prorogued on Mch. 14th.

Other Affairs and Incidents of the Year. An important meeting was that of the 16th annual Convention of the Union of Manitoba Municipalities at Winnipeg on Nov. 18-19 with 300 delegates present and J. A. Marion of St. Boniface in the chair. Resolutions were passed (1) requesting the Provincial Government to make it compulsory for all landowners to use .gopher poison in some effective form and pointing out the tremendous loss caused to farmers by these animals; (2) criticizing both Dominion and Provincial Governments for imposing regulations on farmers with respect to noxious weeds and enforcing these regulations by means of Noxious Weed Acts, while at the same time Government lands were nothing more than weed patches; (3) endorsing the principle of establishing some central authority to co-operate with municipal assessors in the matter of assessment and taxation; (4) asking amendment of the Good Roads Act so that cities as well as towns and villages might take advantage of it in building their trunk highways; (5) supporting a Provincial levy of a sufficient amount in 1920 to carry on the work of the Patriotic Fund.   Ald. J. A. Marion of St. Boniface was re-elected President and Robert Forke, Pipestone, Secretary-Treasurer.

Incidents of the year included a Deputation representing the Motor League of Manitoba, the Winnipeg Board of Trade, Winnipeg Automobile Club, Canadian Manufacturers' Association, Canadian Rotary Club, Brandon Board of Trade, Manitoba Good Roads Association, and the Union of Manitoba Municipalities, or about 10,000 people, who waited on the Government on Feb. 19th and asked for Provincial construction and maintenance of the main trunk Highways; on Feb. 27th a Municipal Delegation asked the Government to bear two-thirds of the cost of maintaining Provincial highways and a little later the published plans for roads and bridges showed an early expenditure of $5,000,000 over the Province as a whole; by an' Order-in-Council passed Sept. 17th, the acting Premier, Hon. Edward Brown, and the Provincial Cabinet placed 6,000,000 acres of improved farming lands on the market for returned soldiers.   On Jan. 19th sixty women representing more than 11,000 members of women's clubs in Manitoba waited on the Government and asked for legislation to establish legality of inheritance for foster and illegitimate children; to place foster and illegitimate children on terms of equality with legitimate children; to make it imperative that the paternity of illegitimates be a public record and to provide for the child bearing its father's name; to provide for the wife being entitled to one-third of the husband's estate and her right to will her portion as she chose; to establish the mother's right of guardianship in her minor children.

At the meeting of the Children's Aid Society, Winnipeg, on Jan. 9th, Canon Bertal Heeney stated that over 13,750 little children's lives had been benefitted through the intervention of the Society and almost 4,000 little ones rescued, sheltered, cared for, and given a start on life's journey from its shelters.   Legal guardianship had been assumed in 865 cases, good foster homes secured for 1,056 children, and the Society at this time had 582 children under its care for whom it was legally responsible.   A Convention of Manitoba Teachers, on Apr. 23rd, approved, by large majority, the establishment of a Retirement Fund made up of contributions from the teachers and the Provincial Government with teachers paying three per cent. of salary on all salary received—the contributions to be obligatory, no teacher to be eligible for a pension who had not served at least 15 years in the Province, and the minimum pension to be $500 and maximum $1,000.

In Winnipeg on Nov. 21st the Rice Lake Mine Operators' Association was formed with many properties represented and the object of securing from the Dominion and Provincial Governments necessary improvements in the way of transportation by water and land, mail facilities, telegraph facilities, appointment of a resident Government mining engineer for this important northern region. R. C. Wallace, Commissioner of Northern Manitoba, did much during 1919 to bring the now admittedly great resources of the north before the people of Canada. There was much prospecting and preliminary development work with the Flin Flon and Schist Lake district as most conspicuous and the Athapapuskow, Herb Lake, Copper and Brunne Lake regions becoming well known. Mr. Wallace summed up the situation in the Manitoba *Public Service Bulletin* of October as follows:

The work of the past five years may be characterized as very successful prospecting. In order that successful mining may ensue, railway transportation is essential. Until such transportation is provided, mining operations will be difficult on the gold properties and impossible on the copper properties in the western section of the district. The extent of the Flin Flon property in itself amply justifies the building of a railway. While in the search for copper properties no discoveries have yet been made comparable to the Flin Flon and Mandy properties, prospecting has revealed a very widespread occurence of copper sulphides throughout the mineral belt and, more particularly, on the western section. There is, therefore, ample encouragement for still further and more detailed prospecting for copper ore bodies in the mineral belt and, in certain instances, for the expenditure of capital in the underground prospecting of properties already obtained. As far as gold mining is concerned, interest now centres more especially on unusually large gold-bearing quartz lodes and silisified zones on the Copper and Herb Lake districts. . . . Throughout the belt the iron sulphide bands are remarkable both in respect of distribution and width.

Alberta: Progress, Government, Politics and Legislation in 1919. With 80,000,000 acres of land estimated as suitable for agriculture and only 7,000,000 under cultivation, Alberta had in 1919 the bases for an ever-increasing production and prosperity. With these resources of rich, rolling prairies and great grazing districts, there were considerable quantities of white spruce and pulpwood; extensive water-powers but little developed and numerous lakes well stocked with fish; plentiful supplies of game, vast quantities of coal—estimated at 1,072 million tons underlying 25,000 square miles of surface; immense resources in bituminous sands along the Athabasca River and gypsum estimated at 217,000,000 tons along the Peace River; natural gas flowing from wells in various parts of the Province and oil-fields believed to have immense possibilities. Great irrigation works aided production in the South, immigrants were slowly pouring into the far North, the winters, as a rule, were moderated by the Chinook winds and yet the population was little more than half a million with, in 1918, a production of grain, hay and root crops valued at $128,595,000, animals slaughtered and sold worth $50,000,000, Dairy and other products valued at $35,575,000.

The tremendous increase in grain production typified the possibilities of the future with wheat increasing between 1909 and 1918 from 8,467,799 bushels to 23,751,519 (51,000,000 bushels in 1917) and Oats from 24,819,661 bushels to 60,322,717 bushels; the general average of production per acre over 10 years was 20·34 bushels for spring wheat, 22·61 for winter wheat, 37·65 for oats and 26·81 for barley. In 1919 Dairy production was very successful with a total value of $31,625,000 or double that of 1915 and a total in the years of war, 1914-18, of over $100,000,000. The once Government-owned Creameries had become community-owned operated under Government inspection and instruction. The grade standards for cream and butter were set by the Dairymen's Act and there were in 1919, 55 of these co-operative Creameries in Alberta; with them were 13 privately-owned and operated Creameries in which the owner bought his cream outright and these got the same encouragement and assistance that the Community creameries did. Cheese-making was not popular in Alberta at this time the farmers preferring to raise their young stock and sell cream; in 1919 the 10,000,000 pound product of Alberta creamery butter found a market in the Yukon, the Western States, Montreal, Toronto, the Eastern States, Belgium and Great Britain; the number of dairy cows in the Province in 1919 was 365,596 compared with 192,903 in 1914.

Horse-breeding had always been popular on the Alberta plains because of its well-drained soil, due to a rolling surface and clearly defined slope, a fine quality of grasses, excellent water, a good climate, freedom from epidemic troubles, and the light nature of bronchial or pulmonary disorders. George Lane's ranch at High River was stocked at this time with 1,000 Percherons and pure-bred Clydesdales were well established in the Province—the total number of horses in 1919 being 800,380 compared with 609,125 in 1914 and 254,197 in 1910. The Province was also eminently suited for the production of mutton and wool. The country was slightly rolling and the climate highly favourable for sheep, with foot troubles and epidemic skin troubles practically unknown. The grasses were of the kinds relished by sheep and the cultivated crops required for winter feeding such as hay, the feed grains and roots were easily and cheaply grown.

The market for wool and mutton and for purebred stock was good with about 90 per cent. of the wool clipped, sold directly in primal markets through the Canadian Co-operative Wool Growers' Association, Ltd. The collecting of this wool was done by half a dozen local wool growers' Associations in the Province, and the growth of the industry was shown in the fact of 364,498 sheep in 1919 compared with 155,301 in 1910. The Canadian Co-operative concern was a large one from the beginning with over 1,200 shareholders, a subscribed capital of $71,800 within the first year and the handling of 4,500,000 pounds of wool worth, approximately, $2,-821,000. The 1st annual Convention was held at Calgary on Jan. 16th and an address given by James McCaig of the Alberta Department of Agriculture, dealing with consolidation and co-operative marketing. As to swine, conditions were equally good and Edmonton and Calgary had a great local Packing plant in the P. Burns Company which was known throughout the continent while the Swifts of Chicago had established a large branch concern in each centre. The keeping of poultry was popular and out of 62,000 farms in the Province 50,000 in 1919 reported flocks with a total of 3,172,777 in 1916 and 4,426,373 in 1919. It may be added that Federal statistics for June 30, 1919, gave the values of Alberta Horses as $75,230,000; Cattle $104,804,000; Sheep $5,103,000; Swine $11,140,000.

The Report of the efficient Minister of Agriculture (Hon. Duncan Marshall) for 1918 dealt in part with the drought of that year and the increase in value of the net product in spite of this disability; the Greater Production campaign which had been successful and an arrangement made for the supply of small tractors to farmers at factory price *plus* freight; the Schools of Agriculture at Olds, Claresholm and Vermilion which showed continued success despite a remarkably large Honour Roll and the drain of wartime; the new College of Agriculture which reported 32 students in attendance with steadily-growing equipment and courses of up-to-date character; the Live-stock and Dairy Commissioners and the Superintendent of Fairs and Institutes who described varied conditions of progress or work as did the Seed and Weed Branch, the Poultry Superintendent and Marketing Commissioner, the Chief Game Guardian, and the Crop Statistician; the shipment of Horses in 1918 which was reported as 36,898 and of cattle as 335,194. Mr. Marshall never lost an opportunity of speaking for Agriculture during this year.

At Brandon on Jan. 7th he declared that: "The big thing for Provincial Governments, as I see it, is to give to the boys and girls an agricultural training, especially a training in the breeding and care of livestock, without which there can be no good farming. The big thing for the Federal Government is to take every burden off the farmer in the way of taxation on what he has to buy and give him a free market in all the world, and then, when the farmer is making money, as he will do, tax his income to pay the interest on the War debt." In the Legislature on Mch. 11th the Minister stated that during two years, the total amount guaranteed in loans to farmers under the "Cow Bill," or Live Stock Encouragement Act, was just over two million dollars, the number of farmers served under the Bill was 2,480, and the number of cattle purchased by them over 2,000. Three new Agricultural Schools were under way at this time to be located near Calgary, Youngstown and Raymond, respectively. With these in operation from 700 to 1,100 young men and women would, the Minister declared, be receiving instruction within 2 years for less than $1,000,000 of capital expenditure. On May 1st Mr. Marshall announced that these Schools and the Demonstration Farms would be managed together, with

A. E. Meyer, LL.B., as Superintendent, that W. F. Stevens would take charge of the Northern Peace River work and direct it from Grand Prairie and that S. G. Carlyle would replace the latter as Live-stock Commissioner.

There was, during the year 1919, a greatly threatened and actual shortage of feed and seed in parts of Southern Alberta where the intense heat of June and July burned out certain areas of crop; half a million head of cattle were said to be involved and special measures had to be taken by the Governments—Federal and Provincial—to meet the situation.   In places where a two years' experience had to be faced the position was, in isolated cases, desperate, with farmers and families as well as cattle and stock, threatened by starvation.   One plan of the Alberta Government for alleviating the situation was to import fodder from Manitoba, the cost to be borne one-third by the Federal Government, one-third by the Province, and one-third by the railways.   On July 31st Mr. Stewart, the Provincial Premier, stated at Calgary that 100,000 tons of hay would be purchased for feed purposes by the Government if necessary; at the same time he refused to go beyond the small rancher owning 100 head of cattle or less in the matter of relief, though A. E. Cross, an old-time authority on local conditions, estimated at this meeting that there were from 300,000 to 400,000 head of stock in Alberta, south of the main line of the C.P.R., and that this meant that at least 450,000 tons of feed would be required in that section: "Ranchers either have to obtain feed, ship their cattle to where feed is available or else sell them."

Mr. Marshall stated that buying cattle at low prices from farmers in these straits was little less than stealing and that he would make provision to have a Government man stationed in Calgary to whom farmers, forced to sell their cattle, might apply in order to get the best market prices.   The Premier warned people against panic and its dangers, pointed out pending arrangements of Governments and railways and promised to start road work for the aid of farmers in districts badly affected.   As the summer months passed, however, crop conditions improved though the coming winter was destined to see much privation and a considerable loss in the livestock.   On Oct. 24th Mr. Stewart announced that, by agreement with the Dominion Government, personal relief would take the form of coal and flour.   In organized municipalities, the supervision and distribution of this relief would be in the hands of the various Councils, who would borrow the necessary money, direct, with the guarantee of the Province.   In unorganized districts, the Government would take responsibility for the supervision and distribution of relief through the Department of Public Works, administered by the Hon. A. J. McLean.   The Department of Agriculture already had the matter of seed grain distribution and the locating of fodder for districts where feed was short, well in hand. On Nov. 7th the Lethbridge Board of Trade reported that conditions in Southern Alberta were not as good as they were at that

time last year, but were "a great deal better than press indications
would lead the public to believe." After careful investigation "we
find that the cattle in southern Alberta, numerically, are as numerous to date as they were at the same period last year." The final
crops of the year as recorded in Federal statistics, were as follows:

Crop	Area	Total Yield	Average Price	Total Value
All Wheat	4,282,508	34,575,000	$1.83	$63,348,000
Oats	2,767,872	65,725,000	.64	42,640,000
Barley	414,212	10,562,000	1.86	19,645,000
Rye	83,804	1,173,000	1.42	1,666,000
Peas	1,508	29,000	3.00	87,000
Beans	690	6,900	4.00	28,000
Mixed Grains	26,000	948,000	.83	783,000
Flax	80,690	222,000	4.15	921,000
Potatoes	45,848	8,241,200	.83	6,840,200
Turnips, Mangolds, etc.	17,500	2,768,800	1.06	2,934,900
		tons	per ton	
Hay and Clover	433,296	476,600	20.89	9,956,200
Fodder Corn	900	5,000	10.50	52,500
Alfalfa	21,558	43,000	29.16	1,254,000

Agricultural incidents of the year included the initial operations of the Co-operative Credit Act of 1917 under which W. M.
Seller, Supervisor, formed in 1919 a number of Societies with conditions very similar to those of Manitoba—a membership of 30 to
100 with each member putting up $100 or a total $5,000 in a
Society of 50, the municipality $2,500 and the Provincial Govern-
ment $2,500; the increasing success of the Live Stock Encourage-
ment Act or "Cow Bill" with, in August, 608 Associations, or
about 3,000 families, benefitting by the loans, thus arranged for buying live-stock, to a total in amount of $1,345,350; the Convention at
Medicine Hat on Aug. 6-7 of the Western Canada Irrigation Association, passage of a Resolution asking for Dominion and Provincial
co-operation in development of certain specified agricultural lands
and the election of Hon. Duncan Marshall as President; the statement by H. A. Craig, Deputy Minister of Agriculture, on Aug. 15th
that "Germany has a little less arable land than Alberta, and
France slightly more—we have one-half million population and with
a present revenue of $200,000,000 from agricultural products, we
can form some idea of the population which the Province could sus-
tain were our land all under cultivation"; the purchase of an
Albertan ranch near High River by H.R.H. the Prince of Wales and
the shipment of pure-bred cattle and horses from England to stock
it with.

The Coal production of Alberta in 1918 was 6,148,620 tons—of
which the Province consumed 440,620 tons, Saskatchewan 1,372,439
tons, Manitoba 511,168 tons and Seattle and Spokane 133,276 tons
—and which, despite strikes and transportation difficulties, was
the largest of any Province in that year; with appeals for coal coming in 1919 from Montana and British Columbia, from Eastern
Canada and many other Provinces and States only to be met by
renewed and greater Labour troubles and a frequent cessation of
production with an estimated and reduced product of 5,000,000
tons. Toward the close of 1919 monthly production of bituminous
coal had increased to a total of 281,000 tons in October and 285,530

tons in November. If this production had been maintained steadily throughout each month of the year the total production for 1919 would have been about 10,000,000 tons, which would have more than taken care of the whole requirements of the Provinces of Manitoba, Saskatchewan and Alberta. Development was, indeed, only limited by labour conditions and the demand in these critical years of costly anthracite and transportation was practically unlimited. In this connection the Lignite Utilization Board, a joint Dominion and Saskatchewan institution, was busily at work developing a system of briquetting carbonized lignite which was expected to work tremendous advantage to Alberta as well as Saskatchewan: The West paid $13,000,000 in coal to the United States which, it was said, could all be kept within the country if Alberta would increase a production which, in 1919, was less than 50 per cent. of the capacity of its Mines.

In June the Stewart Government appointed a Commission to enquire into the whole Provincial Coal question, composed of John T. Stirling, (Chairman), Walter Smitten, John Loughran, W. F. McNeill and Harvey Shaw. Its Report was made public on Dec. 30th and stated that Sessions had been held at Edmonton, Calgary, Drumheller, Wayne, Edson, Lethbridge and Blairmore and 74 witnesses examined, together with Resolutions, correspondence, exhibits, etc.; that many Alberta Mines only operated one-half the year or less and that if more continuous operation was obtained, the result would be a reduction in the price of coal to the consumer and steadier employment to the workman; that provisions for settling disputes at the Mines were not satisfactory, living, housing and sanitary conditions, in many cases, not good and educational facilities inadequate; that a considerable loss of market had been sustained owing to (a) cessations of work, (b) shortage of railway cars, (c) misrepresentation as to size and quality of coal, and that existing freight rates militated against the marketing of Alberta coal in Manitoba and the United States; that Mines equipment and power, under the present system, were too expensive and that large quantities of coal had been and were being lost through improper mining methods, as well as through cessations of work; that for the best interests of the mining industry in this Province steps should be taken at as early a date as possible to have the natural resources vested in the Crown in the right of the Province.

A series of detailed recommendations was made (1) as to management of the mines, advertising their product, testing and selling the coal; (2) as to the appointment of a permanent Provincial Mining Commission with power given by legislation to make working agreements and provide for the settlement of disputes, to deal with living and housing conditions and co-operate with the Department of Education in providing educational facilities, to investigate the propriety of opening mines and investing capital under specific conditions and to facilitate market operations; (3) as to the obtaining of an expert to investigate freight rates and traffic movement of

coal; (4) as to the establishment of a Central purchasing agency
and a standardizing of equipment with the organization of better
Hospital facilities.   The close of the year saw many Alberta people
very hopeful that the briquetting experiments would do great things
for Alberta coal and its shipments east and west.

The Stewart Government and Policy in 1919.   The Government
of the Hon. Charles Stewart had a delicate situation to meet in this
year.   Essentially Liberal in policy, it was entirely dependent on
the farmers of the Province for power and the farmers of Alberta
were the most independent, the freest-thinking and most radical of
the entire West.   In 1919 they appeared to have made up their
minds to fight the old parties unitedly so far as Dominion politics
was concerned and this, the bye-elections at the close of the year
seemed to indicate might apply also to Provincial Governments.
The formation of the United Farmers of Alberta Political Association "to inspire and supervise political organizations in the Federal
and Provincial constituencies of the Province," obviously threatened the Stewart Government, though there was at the time no
absolute breach between the Government and the U.F.A. as an
organization; the ensuing defeat of the Stewart candidate in'
Cochrane was very significant.*   H. W. Wood, the U.F.A. President, outside of the Legislature, and James Weir and Mrs. L. C.
McKinney, Non-Partisan members within the Legislature, were
united in opposition to all Party machinery or government.   In
connection with the many Resolutions passed by the United Farmers
of Alberta at their 1918 Convention and afterwards presented to the
Government, Mr. Stewart wrote a letter to the Secretary on Jan.
14th, 1919, which stated that the Hail Adjustment Bureau proposal,
the Provincial Schools of Agriculture matter, the Land-tax for
Telephones, were under consideration by the Government and that
three other matters mentioned were entirely under Dominion jurisdiction.   As to the rest:

1. Use of Blackleg vaccine.   The Department of Agriculture has
recently secured a quantity of germ-proof vaccine and this is now available
at the three Schools of Agriculture.
2. County Agent System of Farm Instruction.   Similar work is being
carried on from the agricultural schools and demonstration farms and it is
the intention to greatly extend this work.
3. Return of R.N.W.M.P.   When this organization was removed from
Western Canada. the Alberta Government protested against the removal and
were forced thereby to establish the Provincial Police.

On Jan. 28th the Legislative Committee of the U.F.A. (H. W.
Wood, P. Baker, H. Greenfield, W. D. Trego, Rice Sheppard, Mrs.
Parlby and H. Higginbotham, Secretary) met the Government in
conference and the latter explained its policy in various directions.
The Premier stated that the Canadian Government Railways had
agreed to lay steel on the Medicine Hat to Hanna line at once; that

---

*Note.—For the history of the U.F.A. and the Western Farmers' movement in
1919, see Pages 357, 379, 383-9, 392-5.

THE HON. WILLIAM EDGAR RANEY, K.C., M.L.A.
Appointed Attorney-General of Ontario in 1919

ROBERT HENRY HALBERT
President United Farmers of Ontario and elected M.P.
for North Ontario, 1919

the Government was trying to get the St. Paul de Métis line to St. Paul, 15 miles beyond the end of the present grade; that they were pressing the Dominion for completion of the Canadian Northern from Whitecourt to Grande Prairie; that they hoped for construction of the E. and D. Line through the mountains. The Farm Loans Act was described as very similar to the Manitoba Rural Credits law and the Government proposed this year to put it in active operation—which was done; the question of relief for settlers in dried-up sections where several crops in succession had failed was described as a difficult proposition which the Government did not care to embark upon; Hon. G. P. Smith, Minister of Education, stated that the Consolidated School Act would be amended so that the rural vote would stand on its own basis apart from urban action and that the rural Trustees' organization should be revived and its representatives, together with the U.F.A. and other interested organizations, be called together for a Conference on Rural Education.

On Feb. 15th a further conference was held and Messrs. Boyle and Marshall stated the Government's opposition to furnishing of Seed grain to the farmers except in cases of exceptional emergency; in reply to Mr. Boyle's statement that if certain amendments to the Hail Insurance Act were put through the private Companies might refuse to do business in the Province, Mr. Wood stated that the farmers would just as soon they did withdraw if unwilling to do business in an equitable way; the Government approved of Mothers' Pensions, of help in First Aid instruction, of a midwifery course for nurses, of venereal disease legislation, of control over the casket monopoly, of Dower Act amendments; it disapproved of legislation as to a Health certificate for marriage, as to chiropractors practising, as the use of educational taxes for consolidated schools, the removal of the tax on improvements, and the licensing of machinery companies.

Early in the year a Provincial Convention of the Liberal party was called at Calgary for Jan. 16-17. As stated in the public notices issued by the Liberal Executive of Alberta, there was to be no restriction on the attendance of delegates and no local conventions or primaries to select delegates to the Convention. Every man or woman voter who wanted to vote and work for Liberal principles was invited and would have equal rights with every other delegate attending. Notwithstanding a bad crop, the Influenza and high railway rates, there was a large attendance with 250 delegates present who included the Premier and all his Ministers; Alexander Allan presided and Mr. Stewart, in speaking, urged union and not disintegration of the forces standing for democracy—under the Liberal banner; Hon. Frank Oliver urged support for the Liberal party because it stood for definite principles and the first Resolution was a long eulogy of the work and character of Sir Wilfrid Laurier, and endorsement of his leadership. There were a number of others passed and the Provincial Liberal Association was re-

25

organized with Dr. Egbert of Calgary elected President; with
Lieut. W. R. Howson and Dr. Oliver Boyd of Medicine Hat as
Vice-Presidents, and O. E. Culbert as Secretary-Treasurer.   The
following is a summary of the Resolutions approved:

1. Demanding repeal of the Dominion War Times Election Act.
2. Asking for the immediate transfer of natural resources to the Provinces, and compensation for lands which had been wrongfully alienated.
3. Approving of a Soldier Settlement policy which would include the
purchase of land, special loans, agricultural surveys, etc.
4. Calling for equality of wages as to men and women for similar service, an 8-hour day for all employees known as industrial workers, total abolition of all child labour, and a Minimum Wage for all industrial workers.
5. Requesting a restoration of the right of farmers to sell seed grain
to one another.
6. Demanding for each Province its fair quota of all the Hospital and
Dental equipment and supplies in use in Canadian military hospitals in
Canada and overseas whenever these supplies and equipment were no longer
required for the C.E.F.—in order to build up Provincial institutions for the
welfare of the whole people; urging both the Provincial and Federal Governments to forthwith deal seriously with the whole Health problem, including
and dealing particularly with the questions of baby welfare, tuberculosis,
venereal diseases, and the proper care of all those, whether infants or adults,
who were mentally deficient, also the aged and infirm; asking for an immediate survey of the Province to ascertain the real facts and requirements along
all these lines with a vigorous policy of research work, along preventative
lines.
7. Declaring that the Federal Government should absolutely prohibit
the manufacture, importation, exportation, storage or sale of intoxicating
liquors within the Dominion of Canada.
8. Asking the Government of Canada to insist that in any of the
treaties or agreements made at the Peace Conference by or on behalf of the
British Empire, there should be, whether directly or indirectly, no trespass
upon or derogation from the powers of self-government heretofore enjoyed
and exercised by Canada; that in any apportionment of war indemnity
Canada should receive her fair share, not as payment for sacrifice made, but
as recognition of the part taken by her in the struggle for world liberty;
that no change be made at any Imperial Conference in our constitutional relations with the Government of the United Kingdom which would impair or
limit in any way our freedom of action or decision as a nation.
9. Condemning the Federal Press Censorship as a species of martial
law and an abuse of power.
10. Endorsing the policy of Hon. F. Oliver in the Edmonton *Bulletin*
as representing "the live principles of democracy."
11. Denouncing the Union Government at Ottawa as having transgressed
the fundamental principles of Liberalism which had been incorporated into the
constitution of the country, and thereby usurped an autocratic power which
Sir R. Borden and his colleagues had since used and abused to the great
detriment of the country.

Following this Mr. Premier Stewart took an active part in
public matters. Addressing a University gathering on Apr. 20th
he urged a return to fundamental things: "We cannot tamper with
religious ideals. When a student leaves here with doubts on religion he has a bad influence. You can argue away the Christian
religion, but you can't replace it." He deprecated the circulation
of bad or false literature, the doubtful moving pictures, and the
shallow vaudeville performances of the day. He was in Ottawa
during May negotiating in Railway matters connected with G.T.P.

absorption by the Dominion and attended a Liberal gathering where he urged the need for adopting, in its entirety, the platform of the Calgary Conference; he expressed at Calgary on July 2nd the belief that, in establishing the proposed Government Technical institution there, it should not be merely a trade school for artisans, but a higher institution of science and technical training, holding the same relation to the engineering branches—chemistry, mining and metallurgy, that the University of Alberta at Edmonton did to law, medicine and such professional branches of learning; with all but two of his Ministers—Hon. C. R. Mitchell remaining as Acting Premier—he attended the Dominion Liberal Convention at Ottawa in August and thus marked the final allignment of his Government against the Unionists which the Calgary Conference had shown was coming; he returned with strong expressions of approval for Mackenzie King as Leader and a declaration that the issue in Canada to-day was Tariff reform and not Conscription as it was in 1917. At Calgary on Aug. 26th the Premier met Messrs. Calder and Meighen of the Dominion Government to discuss the Irrigation problems of the South and, on his return, stated that the Dominion Government would assume the responsibility of the water and of sending out survey parties to lay out the plans but would leave it to the Province to guarantee the bonds and finance the project—an enormous undertaking involving from 10 to 15 million dollars. Mr. Stewart was again in Ottawa during October and on his return (Oct. 9th) stated at Calgary that in case both the Federal Government and the C.P.R. failed to take over or buy the Edmonton Dunvegan and B.C. Railway, the Provincial Government would take steps to meet the interest on the guaranteed bonds of both the E.D. and B.C. and the Alberta and Great Waterways; he also intimated that the Provincial valuation of the former Line was $11,000,000 and of the latter $7,400,000.

Then came the Cochrane bye-election and the Premier's expression of amazement, on Oct. 17th, at the decision to run a Farmers' candidate: "Every cent I own is in my farm. I went into the Legislature to further the agricultural interests of the Province and accordingly my own. It has been my fight ever since I became a Minister to see that the farmers of the Province were having a square deal and I think I have done this with some success." He had always worked in sympathy with the U.F.A. On no occasion had that organization in any representation to the Government been rebuffed or turned down. Generally the Government had accepted its recommendations. The bye-election was caused by the death of Hon. C. W. Fisher, Speaker of the Legislature, who had represented the riding since 1909 with a vote in 1917 of 630 to 469. The two candidates were E. V. Thompson, Liberal and Government, and Alex. Moore, United Farmer, and the issue proved to be a distinct trial of strength between the Government and the Farmers. In Cochrane on Oct. 15th Hon. Mr. Stewart opened the campaign in an excellent speech during which he stated that responsible government must be carried on by Parties, no matter what name they were designated by; that, as a party leader, he conceded the right of any man in his party who felt that the leader was going astray to vote against the leader; that he fully conceded the right of any organization to run another candidate in the riding, but that "no class can make a success, as a class, in trying to run the Government." Hon. Mr. Marshall reviewed the Government's agricultural policy with pride.

At Crossfield on Oct. 21st H. W. Wood, President of the U.F.A., and Mrs. Walter Parlby spoke at length but did not attack the Stewart Government directly; Mr. Moore, the candidate, was explicit in his expressions. He intimated that the Liberals had first sought to join hands with the U.F.A. in the selection of a candidate but balked when they found the candidate would have to place his resignation in the hands of the U.F.A. Executive to be acted on when that body saw fit: "The Liberal Government didn't want a man tied down with the recall." He alleged that under Party government the leaders cared nothing for the rank and file after they were elected and that all legislation was dictated by a small clique in the Cabinet; that the U.F.A. farmers were not out to tear down anything but to help build up. The present system of responsible government was "government from the throne," while the system the U.F.A. Political organization proposed was "direct government from the people." The kind of Government the U.F.A. organization wanted would be based on groups of lawyers, doctors, storekeepers, farmers, etc., with representatives in proportion to their numbers and power based upon the allignment of groups. Mr. Wood did not in his speeches directly attack the legislation or policy of the Government and at Cochrane on Oct. 22nd said: "The Hon. Charles Stewart is an honourable, upright citizen, doing the best he can under difficult circumstances, and I reiterate that"; but party system was the nourishment of his Government and they wanted something else.

An important point in the Government reply to Mr. Moore, and his leaders, was that, if elected, he would, under the Recall plan, not be the representative of all the people of Cochrane, but of a handful of individuals comprising the U.F.A. Executive Committee—practically of the Chairman—and that this was a vital departure from the very foundation of British democratic government which rested on the mutual confidence and respect of the electors and their chosen representatives; the other point was denunciation of Farmers' rule as a class government—Mr. Wood expressed preference for the use of the word "group." There was a keen fight, with the Ministers and U.F.A. leaders speaking almost every night and an unexpected incident was the attack upon Mr. Moore's candidacy by James Weir, M.L.A., Non-Partisan, whose help had been expected by the U.F.A. He refused because of an alleged raising of the "class" question by President Wood, or as he put it in a letter, the attempt to create an "agricultural Soviet." In his campaign Mr. Moore stood upon the Farmers' National Platform as to Tariff, Public ownership, Taxation and Co-operative agencies with a special demand for operation of the Farm Loans Act and Co-operative Credit Act in Alberta, for better rural education, a uniform system of roads under Government supervision, varied regulations as to Public Health, improved rural conditions, and "liberty, equality and fraternity for all."

He was elected on Nov. 3rd by a majority of 145, or 729 to 584. Of the result O. L. McPherson, President of the U.F.A. Political Association, said: "We fought the election on the Government's own chosen grounds—namely, that the Government must be on the old party lines—and our success against the greatest odds possible in this Province, proves that the Government is out of touch with the sentiment of the people." Mr. Stewart declared that his was still a Farmers' Government and would remain one. Mr. Wood declared (Nov. 4th) that the political party system was passing away: "The chief problems facing civilization to-day are problems of class relationship and those problems can never be solved except by organized classes co-operating together."

One of the most active Ministers of the Government was Hon. A. G. MacKay who had charge of Municipal Affairs and Public Health. He was insistent in speech and regulation and legislation —so far as he could obtain the latter—for improved conditions. The great need of Hospitals for such a scattered population and the vital interest of women in the subject were constantly referred to by him and his appeals for the support of the Women's organizations were strongly made. Speaking at Edmonton on Jan. 24th to the United Farm Women, he gave a statistical record of the ravages of Tuberculosis and venereal diseases in the United States and Canada; described the need of care for the mentally defective and his intention to rigidly enforce sanitation laws; urged his plan of municipal hospitals and a Provincial nursing organization; declared as to maternity cases, in pioneer or isolated settlements, that it was the plain duty of the Province to provide a housewife to look after the family and to pay all Hospital and travelling expenses for the mother.

In the Legislature on Mch. 18th he presented amendments to the Public Health Act under which local Boards of Health would be held responsible for local health precautions; a more rigid supervision of Chinese restaurants and other eating and lodging houses be required; local health boards be compelled to report to the Provincial Department so that a staff of sanitary and health inspectors could energetically follow up complaints and see that health regulations were observed. Undertakers and embalmers were to be licensed and charges regulated—even as to the price of caskets; vaccination was to be compulsory except in rural cases where distance from medical attendance would produce hardship. On March 27th the legislation was further explained and amplified into the bases of a great Provincial system of State-fostered and protected public health with a separate Government Department which was given jurisdiction over the Acts relating to Public Health, Nurses, Municipal Hospitals, Venereal diseases, the Medical profession, Pharmaceutical and Dental Associations, Marriage and Vital Statistics; its officials were to be the Minister—a position to which Mr. MacKay was at once appointed—Deputy-Minister, all Boards of Health officers, Provincial Sanitary Engineer and Inspectors, etc.

At this time there were 49 Hospitals in the Province under Government supervision and receiving grants of $100,000 a year. In his speech the Minister said as to Municipal Hospitals that 10 such hospitals would probably be built this year, and many new Districts formed; health inspection of public schools would be urged and carried through at least once annually with specially trained nurses to be made available by the Government for this purpose; infant mortality would be reduced as much as possible by the Province providing service housewives in outlying districts while mothers were removed to hospitals for care, and nurses furnished, later on, for home work; also the progress of tuberculosis would be combatted by the building of a Sanatorium at Bowness, which, although for five years mainly available for returned soldiers, would become the property of the Province after that time for general civilian use. Mr. MacKay stated that out of 8,805 maternity cases in Alberta during 1917 there were 5,202 without medical attendance. It was expected that a dozen trained nurses would take a special course at Alberta University in 1919; the cost of meeting the Influenza epidemic was stated as $25,476 in 1918 with an estimated $50,000 in 1919; Venereal diseases were said not to be very prevalent in Alberta and free clinics not altogether desirable but immediate treatment of cases and notification to Provincial Board of Health to be compulsory.

As to Municipal matters Mr. MacKay intimated at this time that the Wild Lands tax and the Educational tax in municipal districts would hereafter be collected by the municipal councils. As to the collection of school taxes it would be left optional whether they were raised directly through the school trustees or through the municipal council. He had Bills dealing with these points and another with arrears of taxes which, in the year 1918, totalled $1,341,870 or nearly one-half of five rural Provincial taxes—with total Government arrears at date of $2,434,322. For all cities, towns and municipalities within the Province the arrears were $16,000,000 of which Edmonton, alone, provided $6,000,000. Under the new legislation instead of costly and cumbersome tax enforcement proceedings there were to be annual compulsory tax sales. Another amendment for Municipal bodies allowed the payment of arrears of taxes to be spread over a period of 8 years provided each year's current taxes were paid as well.

The Minister of Education (Hon. G. P. Smith) was aggressive in speech and policy during the year.* He promised the U.F.A.

---

*Note.—General conditions as to Education are dealt with at Pages 554-7, 572.

Convention on Jan. 23rd that legislation at the next Session would re-organize the Consolidated School system and improve other educational facilities.   On Apr. 4th he stated the total Educational appropriations for the year—including $339,403 to the University of Alberta—would run up to $1,574,093.   On the 13th he explained his proposed legislation as involving eight new departures in policy: (1) provision of High School opportunity to rural children at Provincial expense by abolishing fees and providing additional grants to public schools doing High School work; (2) generous aid to Technical education in the towns, villages and even consolidated schools and including manual training, household science, commercial courses, music and art, with substantial grants towards teachers' salaries and also equipment; (3) encouragement to construction of Teachers' residences by contribution of one-third of the cost based upon specific terms as to total cost, area of land, and conditions making for a real family home; (4) promoting the engagement of two teachers in schools, where an excessive enrollment existed, through the establishment of two-room schools and generous grants for second teacher epuipment and transportation of children; (5) the establishment of a Community Hall in connection with all rural 2-roomed and consolidated schools, with grants of one-half the cost of equipment; (6) doubling the grant to night classes or schools with a view to encouraging work in non-English districts; (7) establishing a special University course for English-speaking teachers who were recommended by an Inspector and who would undertake to serve at least two years in the non-English speaking schools—the course to be free of all expense either as to tuition or living expenses; (8) loans to soldiers taking a Normal School course.

Four Acts were specifically and largely amended to meet these and other changes and to remodel, in particular, the Consolidated School conditions.   Voting by ballot was established in this latter connection and other conditions made which the Minister hoped would do away with clashes between town and country districts. Mr. Smith made an effort during the year to have every School in the Province provided with a flag.   He, therefore, introduced the policy of supplying a Union Jack, 2 feet wide and 4 feet long, to each district on the recommendation of the School Inspector and in lieu of books or of a portion of the ordinary school grant.   A list of dates on which the flag was to fly was also issued.   This Province had a School Libraries Branch in its Education Department and G. Fred. McNally, Provincial Supervisor of Schools, stated in December that over 1,000 books were carried in stock all the time and that in 1918, 2,500 schools had operating Libraries with 500,000 books valued at $200,000 distributed to them by the Department within the past 5 years.

Political or Administrative incidents of the year included a declaration by the Premier on Oct. 18th in favour of Proportional Representation; the development of active advocacy by an Edmonton weekly journal, *L'Union,* of a policy which involved the uniting of all Belgians, French, and French-Canadians in the Province for the defence of certain political, religious and educational principles; the vigourous attacks upon the Government for its defence, or as it was termed by Conservative and U.F.A. speakers, the "whitewashing" of Lucien Boudreau, Government member for St. Albert, whose drug-store in Edmonton had been under fire as a liquor-selling place and which attacks the *Bulletin* declared to be "a campaign of mud-slinging" without any real basis; an Order-in-Council of Oct. 26th providing an addition to the salaries for employees of the Provincial Government in the form of either bonuses or increases. An interesting incident was the refusal of James Weir, M.L.A., to be bound by any rules in his relations with the U.F.A. Early in the year it had looked like a working agreement between the Non-Partisan League and the United Farmers, then almost like absorption of the former body on the political question, then Mr. Weir broke through the traces at the Cochrane election.

On Oct. 23rd the Dominion and Alberta Governments made an agreement as to a joint relief system in connection with the drought and crop failure in parts of the Province—the Provincial Government undertaking distribution and each Government providing one-half the necessary funds, outside of distribution, with the security of liens taken for relief advances to be in favour of the Government of Alberta except in cases where relief was extended to settlers upon unpatented lands, in which event the security or liens on such unpatented lands would be in favour of the Dominion.   The loans were to be at 7 per cent. and the details arranged between the Minister of the Interior and the Provincial Premier.   Other events of importance included the promise of the Government on Apr. 8th to dismiss all aliens of enemy origin whether naturalized or not, then in its employ, as fast as the Great War Veterans' Association would replace them by returned men qualified to fill such positions—with a similar statement as to married women not in actual need of remuneration from positions held; the Report of the Alien Registration Board at Ottawa which showed 50,549 persons in the Province over 16 years of age and of alien birth; the decision in April by the Judicial Committee, London, in the case of the Toronto General Trusts *vs.* The King which upheld the decision by Mr. Justice Hyndman, confirmed by the Court of Appeal and by the Supreme Court of Canada, that Succession duties could be collected by the Province of Alberta from the estates of persons holding mortgages upon Alberta land, although resident outside of Alberta at the time of decease.

The Report as to Neglected and Dependent Children showed that 1,034 of these, and 513 delinquent children, were dealt with by the Department during 1918 with 182 adopted and 267 placed in private homes; the Report of the Superintendent of Insurance to Hon. C. R. Mitchell for the calendar year 1918 showed 29 com-

panies under Provincial license with $2,862,453 of Fire premiums
and $1,280,572 of losses, $991,085 of Life premiums and $189,225
of losses; the appointment was announced on July 11th of a Royal
Commission by the Government to investigate Municipal Financial
conditions, composed of Chief Justice H. Harvey, Hon. N. D. Beck,
Mr. Justice Hyndman and H. M. Evans.   In connection with a
dispute between the Northern Alberta Natural Gas Co. and the
City of Edmonton as to an increase of rates to be charged the city
for gas, they came to an agreement on Oct. 16th and asked the
Board of Utility Commissioners to consent to a stated increase; the
Board (G. H. V. Bulyea and A. A. Carpenter) stated on Nov. 25th
that it had power to deal with the matter against the contention of
the Attorney General who intimated that he would carry it to
the Court of Appeal; the Court decided on Dec. 28th that the
Public Utilities Commission had no power to authorize any increase
in the maximum price of gas to be supplied by the Gas Company to
the City of Edmonton, under a contract entered into between the
Company and the City, which was later validated by the Legislature.

The 1919 Session of the Legislature.   The 2nd Session of the
4th Legislature of Alberta was opened at Edmonton on Feb. 4th
by Lieut.-Governor Robert George Brett with a Speech from the
Throne which referred to the end of the War, the coming return of
the soldiers to their homes and the Government's effort to assist in
the work of re-construction by establishing a Bureau of Labour;
dealt with unfortunate droughts in Southern Alberta and frost in
the North which had decreased grain production in 1918 though
total values had been higher; described the Influenza epidemic as
proving the need of further health and sanitation laws and promised
some important Bills along this and other lines; expressed the hope
of definite Dominion proposals as to transfer of Natural resources
to the Province.   The Address was moved by J. J. Gaetz of Red
Deer and J. B. Atkins of Didsbury and, after a lengthy debate,
was passed without division on Feb. 17th.

Meanwhile, at a Conservative caucus on the 4th, George Hoadley had been re-elected Leader of the Opposition with Brig.-General
J. S. Stewart declining nomination and Major J. R. Lowery was
chosen as Chief whip; J. E. McNaughton was the Government
Chief Whip.   In his speech on the Address Mr. Premier Stewart
stated that the Government had been obliged to take over the
Lacombe and Blindman Valley Railway and that an extension of
this Line must be constructed with as little delay as possible.   He
spoke of his recent visit to France; of the urgency of re-establishing the returned soldiers in civil life and of the forming of Provincial Labour Bureaux; of the failure of the Provincial Premiers to
obtain control of the natural resources of the West; of the need of
more Asylum buildings at Ponoka; of the proposed Tubercular
Sanatorium to be erected in the spring; of the plans to provide

better school and hospital facilities in the Province.   Mr. Hoadley made a radical speech in part of which he proposed dispensing with the speeches on the Speech from the Throne and have them instead turn entirely upon an initial speech to be made by the Premier dealing with the actual legislation which the Government contemplated.   He contended that higher education was being paid for by those who were unable to take advantage of it.

Legislation of the ensuing Session included 60 Public Bills of which 7 were withdrawn and the following clauses or amendments of various Acts affecting women: Providing for a Register of Nurses to be available in times of epidemic and for a University course for nurses with a diploma qualifying for inspection of children in schools; permitting nurses who had taken a course in Obstetrics and obtained the consent of the Minister of Public Health to practise midwifery where physicians were not available; enabling, under the Mothers' Allowance Act, a widow, and in some cases, a wife, who, having in her custody a child or children under 15 years old, if boys, and 16 years, if girls, was unable to take proper care of them, to receive assistance—one half of the cost of which would be borne by the municipality in which she was resident, and the balance by the Province at large; providing for the care of mental defectives in an institution with a charge of $10 per month to be paid by the municipality in which the defective had last had a usual abode for at least a year, with the municipality entitled to collect this amount from the person legally responsible for the defective's support.

The Municipal Districts Seed Grain Act provided for advances to purchase seed in localities affected by drouth or frost and other Bills dealt with details of repayment, securities, mortgages, etc.; the Vital Statistics Act was amended to divide the Province into registration districts with Registrars and general organization and a compulsory registration of marriages by officiating ministers, etc.; the Act respecting Arrears of taxes has been referred to and there were the usual voluminous changes in the Town and Village and Municipal Acts together with one authorizing investigation and amelioration of financial conditions in certain municipalities under specific conditions; the Educational Tax Act was amended to impose a tax of one mill on the dollar of assessed value of assessable land—the procedure for assessment, collection and enforcement of such tax to follow the provisions of The Wild Lands Tax Act; this latter Act was amended to extend by two months the exemption as to enclosed lands pasturing cattle, horses, or sheep; the Municipal District, Improvement District and other Acts were amended to facilitate the collection of Taxes and especially arrears and so with the Act for Recovery of Taxes.

The Municipal Hospitals Act and others associated with public health have been referred to elsewhere and under the Women's Institute Act a clause provided for incorporation of Women's Institute Girls' Clubs by any eight or more girls of not less than 12 years of age, with such social, literary, educational or recreational objects as were approved of by the Provincial Advisory Board. The Act respecting Purchase and Sale of Eggs provided that no person should buy, sell or have in possession for sale unwholesome eggs and first handlers buying from producers must candle the eggs and reject bad ones; eggs placed in cold storage for more than sixty days must be candled and packed in dry cases with new fillers and flats; inspectors appointed by the Minister were to have power to enter any premises where eggs were sold and inspect all eggs on hand. The Dairymen's Act was amended to provide a standard sample for cream with Inspectors given authority to weigh and take samples of milk and cream, to repeal the $5.00 license fee on Creameries, etc., and to leave the amount to be fixed by regulation; the Irrigation Act, Taber Irrigation District Act and Reclamation Act were variously amended and the Alberta Co-operative Credit Act was changed so that the minimum number for organization was reduced from 30 to 15 farmers, and the subscribed stock from $3,000 to $1,500 with no Society commencing business until it had not less than 20 per cent. paid up. The Societies were also authorized to borrow money for purposes of fire and hail insurance.

Another measure provided for appointment of 3 members of the Provincial bar by the Government as a Board of Commissioners for the promotion of uniformity of legislation in Canada—Commissioners to hold office for three years and to meet annually in conference with the Commissioners from other Provinces for the drafting of such uniform laws. The Public Utilities Board, upon petition from the owners of subdivided lands, or upon giving notice to the parties interested, was empowered to withdraw any lands from the limits of a city, town or village, or to direct that such lands should remain within the limits, and to fix rates of taxation in such cases. By amendments to the Land Titles Act the holder of a mortgage or an encumbrance must elect to take a choice of either foreclosure proceedings, or mortgage sale proceedings and no execution could be registered unless it set forth the full name, residence and occupation of a debtor. Executions against lands were to be re-registered within six years.

The Factories Act was amended to give the Government power to appoint, in any city or town of over 5,000, two persons, one to represent employers and the other to represent employees, and these, together with a third to be appointed by the Government were to constitute an Advisory Committee, whose duty it would be to suggest regulations as to hours of labour and minimum wages. By another Bill the management of the Alberta Police Force was placed in the hands of a Commissioner under control of the Attorney-General; the force of Provincial constables was not to exceed 500, and all permanently employed to be British subjects; in addition, to the duties generally assigned to constables they were given special powers in regard to the enforcement of The Liquor Act.

Other Acts were passed to regulate Billiard rooms and Bowling alleys, to amend the Bulk Sales Act and the Workmen's Compensation Act—fixing the minimum assessment on employers at $2.50 per month with power, if so required by the Board, to deduct from the wages of workmen and pay to the Board an amount sufficient to meet the assessment of any person or persons employed by such workmen.   The Electrical Protection Act gave the Workmen's Compensation Board power to make and enforce regulations with regard to the generation, transmission, transformation, distribution and use of electrical energy in any place or class of places from time to time as such might appear necessary to ensure safety and protection for the workers engaged.   Another measure established the Alberta Government Employment Bureau.

Incidents of the Session included a Resolution presented by W. A. Rae, which was carried unanimously, declaring that the Dominion Government should make no concessions of Petroleum or Oil territory in Northern Alberta in view of pending negotiations as to Provincial control of Natural Resources; a brief debate on Feb. 21st as to the dismissal in 1918 of Hon. C. W. Cross, Attorney General, in which both the Premier and Mr. Cross took part with veiled references made to a letter from Mr. Stewart offering his Minister the post of Agent-General in London prior to the retirement of Mr. Cross; the statement that in the Seed Grain legislation of the year the Government would stand security for advances up to $700,000 while Mrs. L. C. McKinney (Mch. 26th) reproached the Government for niggardliness in voting only $50,000 for Mothers' Pensions—or almost as much as it spent on a corrective institution for children who had gone wrong; a debate on Apr. 6th regarding John A. Reid, the well-known Agent-General of the Province in London, who was appointed in 1918 as Efficiency Officer at $6,000 a year with other Government duties such as the preparation of Alberta's case regarding Natural Resources.

The Public Accounts of the Province were presented to the Legislature on Feb. 19th and showed the Revenue (capital and income) for the calendar year 1918 as $11,028,890 and the total Expenditures $10,676,641 with a surplus of $352,248; the capital revenue and loans were $3,368,128 and capital expenditure $2,372,-835—of which latter Public Works took $716,523, advances to the Farmers' Co-operative Co. $212,085, Telephones $426,750 and Repayment of Loans $918,820.   The Income included Dominion subsidy and school lands of $1,999,771, Succession duties $204,500, Corporation taxes $251,331, Motor vehicle fees $535,310, Theatres Act fees $106,122; the total Income actually collected was $7,660,-761 with $1,866,662 due and outstanding.   The Expenditures on Income were $8,303,805 of which $1,165,973 was interest on Public Debt; $571,057 for administration of Justice and $508,328 for Civil Government; $1,058,762 for Public Works and $1,187,924 for Education; $493,669 for Agriculture and $382,758 for Dairy Work;

Hospitals, Charities and Public Health took $211,819 and Telephones $1,171,687. The Public Debt on Dec. 31st, 1918, was $31,-500,200 with sinking funds of $754,050.

In his Budget speech of Mch. 16th Hon. C. R. Mitchell, Provincial Treasurer, reviewed these figures and estimated the Revenue for 1919 at $9,362,470 and Expenditures at $9,343,309; the actual amount received, as stated a year afterwards in the 1920 Budget, was $9,642,739 and expended $9,525,748. Mr. Mitchell declared that he had obtained an increase of $82,972 in the Federal subsidy owing to increased population and through reasonable pressure had obtained over $3,000,000 of Funds created by the Dominion sale of Alberta School lands. The estimated expenditure on Education would be increased to $1,584,093 and as to Public Works $1,372,190 would be charged to Income and $2,114,300 to Capital. He pointed out that one of his great difficulties was collection of Land taxes which depended very materially upon the seasons. The Government must depend on these taxes to be paid at will, as the only method of collection was by way of enforcements and tax sales after a certain lapse of time. Telephones were expected to bring in $1,625,000 and in the Department of Municipal Affairs the Wild Lands' tax was expected to bring in $770,000, the Educational tax $160,000, and the Supplementary Revenue Act a total of $1,100,-000—a total revenue from the Department of $2,058,000 or an increase of $891,000 over 1918.

Including Victory bond purchases and Red Cross and other contributions, Mr. Mitchell estimated that the Alberta people contributed $42,000,000 to the War effort of the country. The Assets of the Province (1918), stated by the Treasurer as standing against its Debt of $31,000,000, were $135,952,458 made up of public buildings, bridges and roads, investments in Telephones, deposits or accounts in hands of Dominion Government, with unsold Crown lands of 6,909,450 acres valued at $12.00 an acre. James Ramsey replied for the Opposition and deprecated holding a cash balance of $1,-000,000 in the Bank when borrowed money was costing 5 per cent.; urged adoption of the Manitoba system of accounts and defied anyone except a chartered Accountant to understand Alberta's system; if greater economy were not practised he declared people would be kept away from the Province by fear of taxation burdens. It may be added that the Government at the end of the year sought to be reimbursed at Ottawa for the money they had paid out in interest on guaranteed railway bonds, through the default of the G.T.P. Company; that the careful work of the Utilities Commission in safeguarding investors had a good effect in financial centres and that, on Jan. 14th, $1,000,000 of Alberta 20-year, 5½ per cent. bonds were purchased in Toronto by A. E. Ames and Co. at 99·14·

Prohibition, Railways, and Other Alberta Questions. The question of making Prohibition prohibit and the use of liquor in connection with Influenza made up a vital issue of the year.   Mr. Hoadley and the Opposition made the most of the illicit sales and a situation which for the year 1919 were officially stated* to show a total sale through Government, physicians and druggists for medicinal purposes, of $2,150,317 and illicit sales estimated at $3,-500,000—the profit to the Government on its own transactions being $300,000.   In the House on Feb. 6th Mr. Premier Stewart, in reply to criticisms, said that the Government was doing its utmost to enforce the Act; but during the Influenza epidemic large quantities, of liquor were sold under doctors' orders and this made detection more difficult.   It was easy enough to charge that liquor was being illegally sold and used, but it was hard to place the hand of the law upon such traffic: "There is a portion of the population which is determined to damn the Prohibition law in order to have it repealed if at all possible."   It was his desire to have the Act enforced, as was every other statute of the Province, but more men and money were needed.   The return of 300 R.N.W.M.P. would help in the patrol of the Provincial borders where much liquor was being imported.

On Feb. 11th Mrs. L. C. McKinney and James Weir vigourously criticized the enforcement of the Act; A. F. Ewing (Cons.) stated on the 13th that disregard for the law had grown apace and conditions were becoming worse and worse.   The Attorney-General (Hon. J. R. Boyle) went further than the critics themselves on the 14th: "I venture to say that 60 per cent. of the male adults of this Province were guilty last year of some infraction of the Liquor Act.   I don't mean that this number were buying from bootleggers but that they were lying to a doctor, telling him they were sick when they wanted a drink."   He said that much more money and many more detectives were needed for enforcement.   At the same time he added: "It is clear that the consumption of spirituous liquor has been tremendously decreased in the Province under the Liquor Act as enforced.   I am quite convinced that, even with the bootleggers included, there is not more than 25 per cent. of the liquor being consumed to-day that there was before the Act.   It has banished the treating system, the system under which so many men fell victims of bar-room conviviality and herein it has been a real blessing."   During the month of January, 1919, the drug stores of Edmonton sold 214,999 ounces of liquor and those of Calgary 119,255.   Later, in the House, Mr. Boyle said that the difficulty of enforcement was partly due to lack of co-operation from the people and partly to Federal refusal to prevent importation across the borders.

On the 27th a keen debate occurred upon the following clause in a letter written by F. G. Forster, formerly Chief Provincial Inspector, to Mr. Boyle on Nov. 8th, 1918: "I would consider it sensible and advisable to modify your orders to give the local drug-

*Note.—Hon. J. R. Boyle, Attorney General, in Legislature on Mch. 1st, 1920.

gists all the liquor they want.   I do not consider that one-fifth of the liquors going out locally are being used within the meaning of the Liquor Act."   The Minister stated that 148 Provincial police were enforcing the regulations as compared with 50 in Ontario; by the new Provincial Police Act that force was put under the Attorney General, instead of a Commission, and were given large powers of search for liquor; these latter had to be restricted somewhat under the severe criticism which developed.   Mr. Boyle carried a number of amendments to the Liquor Act during the Session of which one empowered the Government to fix the form of prescription to be used by physicians in prescribing liquor and another to fix, from time to time, the price at which liquor should be sold by druggists.   A public meeting at Edmonton on Mch. 7th passed a Resolution asking the Government to regulate the price of alcoholic beverages and prevent profiteering in what was called a medical necessity and urging the right of the people to a good beer containing 4 per cent. alcohol together with stouts and ales; on June 11th the Anglican Synod of Alberta, meeting at Calgary, unanimously resolved that "the Legislature should repeal the Liquor legislation now in force and substitute therefor such legislation as will meet with the approval of the people and find an effectual enforcement."

In the House on Apr. 4th J. G. Turgeon drew attention to the great hardships of people in isolated sections during Influenza, or other sickness, who had no doctors and were debarred from keeping alcohol.   Following these and other incidents there developed a violent controversy over the alleged sale in 1918 of certain liquors to Lucien Boudreau, a druggist of Edmonton, on time instead of for cash as the regulations prescribed.   F. G. Forster was brought into the matter as making the charge and, with the Opposition, did his best to make things unpleasant for the Government; the Government vendor, W. J. Webster, swore before the Public Accounts Committee on Mch. 20th that no liquor had been sold Boudreau except for cash.   A Committee appointed to enquire into the matter reported Mr. Forster's charges disproved; the Opposition on Apr. 15-16, led by A. F. Ewing and J. R. Lowery, after a vigourous debate and with long Resolutions, endeavoured to have this Report reversed; the Government was supported, however, by 26 to 20. At the close of the year the Alberta Medical Society decided to discipline any physicians guilty of infraction of the Liquor Act and the Social Service Council asked for a Federal Referendum on the importation of liquor.

The Railway question continued to be a vital one in Alberta during 1919.   The Northern region, the Peace River country, all the great region on the Edmonton and Dunvegan and B.C. Railway between Edmonton and Grande Prairie depended for development upon either railway construction or the efficiency of existing lines.   Immigrants were steadily entering the North and in the

Grande Prairie district alone there were 150,000 acres of crop with estimates of substantial production. J. D. McArthur of the E.D. and B.C. Railway, stated on Apr. 22nd that extensive improvements would be carried out at once and the 160 miles between Edmonton and Sawridge receive reconstruction attention first; between Sawridge and Burnt River there was considerable work to be accomplished, from Burnt River to Spirit River ballasting would be carried forward and this work also continued down the line from Spirit River to Grande Prairie—a fifty-mile stretch of railway that was badly in need of improvement.

Of the Alberta and Great Waterways Railway, which Mr. McArthur had also built, in the main, it was stated at this time (Apr. 14th) by Norman Harvey, Deputy Minister of Railways, that the bonds were guaranteed for a total distance of 350 miles—Edmonton to Fort McMurray with a branch line to Egg Lake, 41 miles long and 20 miles of siding—and that the total interest so far dealt with was $1,326,151. The mileage between Edmonton and Fort McMurray was 289 miles, and the steel was now laid to Last Caché, within ten miles of the terminus, and the grading completed to the terminus. Mr. Harvey said that 11 miles of the Egg Lake branch had been completed with 30 miles of grading. The interest on bonds was charged up as part of the construction cost and cheques were paid out to the Railway for the total amount of each progress estimate, including interest on the bonds—after assurance that the bondholders had been paid their interest. In August the C.N.R. reported steel within 23 miles of St. Paul de Métis and over 100 cars of material on the ground at Sangudo ready for track extension to Whitecourt. The Railway situation in detail was as follows on Dec. 31st, 1918:

Railways	Authorized mileage par value	Mileage	Executed mileage par value guaranteed	Mileage
Can. Nor. and Can. Nor. West. Railways	$36,066,000	2,292·4	$22,344,250	1,427·37
Grand Trunk Pacific Railway	4,182,500	259·5	4,182,500	259·5
McArthur lines	19,100,000	985	18,820,000	921
Lacombe and Blindman Valley Railway	273,700	89·1	273,700	89·1
Additional light Railways	1,126,800	160·9	....	......
Total	$60,748,500	3,686·9	$45,520,450	2,656·97

Speaking in the Legislature on Mch. 28th Mr. Stewart stated as to the G.T.P. guaranteed branch lines that the Provincial Government would require a strict accounting before any liability for interest on bonds would be admitted under Dominion acquisition. He announced, in regard to the McArthur E.D. and B.C. system, that the Province had assumed full responsibility for allowing interest on bonds guaranteed to be paid on construction estimates, these charges to be taken from the Trust Fund of the Company. On Apr. 9th the Premier stated that there would be an immediate extension by the Government of the Lacombe and Blindman Valley Railway to Rimbey, 20 miles northwest of Bentley, the present terminus of the line; he added that while he was head of the Government there would be no more Railway bond guarantees. In the House on Apr. 17th Messrs. Ewing and Lowery moved, for the Opposition, a Resolution expressing grave disapproval at the policy of the Government in "permitting railway promoters to exploit the credit of the Province without safeguarding the interests of the people" and described the McArthur system as about to collapse with $18,820,000 of Government guaranteed bonds involved; the Government amendment stated the vital need for these railways when the bonds were backed, pointed out that the Government held a first mortgage on the roads and ample security, stated that the Dominion Government should "grant further financial assistance" to these lines.   The amendment was carried by 29 to 17. During the debate W. A. Rae of Peace River described J. D. McArthur as the only railway man who had built new lines during the War, with the money he had made in Railways east of Winnipeg put into enterprises north of Edmonton.   Early in April Mr. McArthur and H. A. Robson of Winnipeg were in Ottawa to see if the Government would grant a Dominion subsidy to the Dunvegan line or incorporate it in the C.N.R.

Irrigation was largely discussed during the year as a result of the drouth and at Lethbridge on Mch. 13th, 500 farmers met and organized an Association to bring about the irrigation of 500,000 acres, and to prepare a programme for consideration by the Dominion and Provincial Governments, which were asked to aid in the scheme, at a cost of $18,000,000.   President G. R. Marnoch, of the local Board of Trade, was the chief mover in the project and the Irrigation Development Association was duly formed.   A telegram from the Minister of the Interior (Hon. A. Meighen) said: "Am ready to undertake surveys for irrigation work referred to provided Provincial Government give clear understanding that responsibility from that on is Provincial and not Dominion, we affording appropriate engineering supervision.   If Province in discharge of such responsibility purchase District bonds and desires Dominion loan against same, such will be considered."   Mr. Premier Stewart did not approve this proposition; if the Province did anything of the kind it would do its own surveying and would not borrow money from the Dominion Government.

In August a letter was made public from Pat. Burns, the well-known cattle man of Alberta, to Lieut.-Col. J. S. Dennis and William Pearce of the C.P.R. irrigation project congratulating them on the splendid work done and expressing regret that he had not earlier appreciated its value: "If this had only been undertaken years ago, there would be no talk these days of a possible shortage of feed for our cattle, pigs and sheep, but it would be now, what it will be in the future, one of the richest localities in America."   On Aug. 23rd Mr. Stewart and other Provincial public men conferred at Calgary with Messrs. Meighen and Calder of the Dominion Government and the chief point at issue seemed to be whether the Dominion Government would, in addition to preparing the engineering and water surveys for irrigation projects, be responsible for the actual amount of water delivered.   There was no question as to the importance of proposed developments and Mr. Meighen himself declared, after driving over a wide region, that "Irrigation was to Southern Alberta what the Hydro-Electric was to Western Ontario."   No concrete Provincial action, however, was taken up to the close of the year.

Of other questions it may be said that the Government on Jan. 30th received the Executive of the Alberta Federation of Labour, and its requests for 27 changes in existing laws and legislation—for amendments to the Factories' Act so that it would be more rigidly enforced and more Inspectors appointed; for an Act to establish and protect the wages of workmen employed on public works and a model license law for barbers; for a Mechanics' Lien Act and that bi-monthly wages be paid to all wage-earners in the Province excepting farm help; for a Department of Labour and provision for Sanitary inspectors in towns, villages and camps; for enforcement of the building trades Protection Act through Government-appointed Inspectors; for free School supplies, free medical, surgical and dental attention, and a maximum 8-hour day for all stationary engineers; for legislation that would legalize the profession of the chiropractors and prevent the use of films in bad physical condition.

The Deputation also requested the Government to take steps against the evil of prostitution by providing the victims with sufficient means to live until suitable and useful occupations could be found for them.   They wanted a Housing Act and a Commission to enquire into the possibility of printing school text-books within the Province.   At their annual meeting (Jan. 7th) the Federation protested against any modification of the Liquor Act and against 2½ per cent. beer; they also demanded a $1,200 salary as the minimum wage for Teachers.   The annual Report of the Workmen's Compensation Board, composed of J. T. Stirling (Chairman), W. F. McNeil and J. A. Kenney, for Dec. 31st, 1918, dealt with 5 months' operation, an assessment of 3 per cent. on the average monthly pay-roll of the industries concerned which totalled, for this period, $94,995, and with claims and medical aid of $13,719. The number of employers within the scope of the Act was 264, the employees numbered 10,259 and the amount of pay-rolls, on which assessments were made, was $5,540,512.

The Telephone question was an issue of the year.   The net earnings of the Government system in 1918 were $619,918 according to Superintendent W. R. Pearce, and the gross earnings $1,-393,543; the total capitalization of all lines was $9,758,970 and the exchange plant and rural plant were reported as not self-supporting.   The Opposition severely criticized the management and especially the failure to set aside an adequate fund for depreciation; Major Lowery claimed in the House on Apr. 7th that a correct plant valuation would show a three or four million dollar depreciation on the $10,000,000 system.   The Premier replied that the

Provincial Telephone system represented an investment of some $10,000,000, with accrued surpluses of $750,000—though he admitted that no amount for depreciation and renewal service had been set aside since the inception of the system. He would, personally, have preferred such a Fund but the $750,000 accumulated surplus would have to be charged up to the capital account of the Telephones to meet the need for depreciation. Mr. Stewart announced an increase in rural rates and Major Lowery contended that the $750,000 surplus should really be one of $1,189,519.

Incidents of the year included the Session at Edmonton on Mch. 19-22 of the Grand Orange Lodge of Alberta with an appeal from Sir James Outram, Bart.,—who was re-elected Grand Master—for a Federation of the Grand Lodges of the Prairie Provinces and a summary of Orange policy as follows: (1) To promote legislation for the amendment of the School Law, by making the English language the sole medium of instruction in every grade and of every School, or institution, controlled by Government; (2) to promote legislation for the abolition of Separate Schools in the Province of Alberta; (3) to take steps to have enforced within the Province of Alberta the laws of the Dominion with regard to the Official use of the English language, only, in all Public forms, documents, offices and assemblies. Following the Bolshevistic Resolutions of the Western Labour Convention at Calgary on Mch. 15th the G.W. V.A., Alberta Provincial Command, passed a motion on Mch. 16th declaring that: "We believe that the action of the Labour Conference in preaching revolution and riot, should be severely condemned and that steps should be taken by the Central Government to either arrest or deport the leading apostles of anarchy, sedition and disloyalty."

The Union of Alberta Municipalities met at Edmonton on Nov. 12th with R. J. Chrystal, M.D., of Carstairs, in the chair and addresses of welcome from the Lieut.-Governor, Premier, and Mayor of Edmonton. W. D. L. Hardie, Mayor of Lethbridge, spoke of City Home Rule and Dr. Whitelaw of Edmonton urged a better conception of Hospitals and their uses. Resolutions were passed asking greater extension of powers to Alberta towns; requesting an Educational Commission for the Province; appointing a Committee to co-operate with the Industrial Research organization; asking for an investigation of Hydro-Electric power possibilities; urging the Provincial Government to continue its fullest financial and moral support both to the Industrial Research Bureau and the Alberta Development Association. Mayor R. C. Marshall of Calgary, was elected President. Notable addresses were given by Hon. A. G. MacKay, J. A. Kenney, C. J. Yorath. It may be added that the Alberta G.W.V.A. elected as its 1919 President E. C. McKenzie of Lethbridge, the Alberta Institute of Chartered Accountants chose J. B. Sutherland as President and the Alberta Land Settlement Association was formed on the 7th with O. N. Gilbert of Calgary as President. Of the Alberta Motor League William Cousins of

Medicine Hat was President.   In connection with motors the Hon.
J. L. Coté, Provincial Secretary, stated on Mch. 19th that in 1906,
41 motor licenses were issued, and in 1918 29,250; in the past two
years they were mainly taken out by the farmers of the Province.
Up to date, 15,500 motor licenses had been issued in the Province
for 1919, as against about 10,000 for the same period last year.

Saskatche-
wan: Its
Progress,
Administra-
tion and
Legislation.
With a total area of 94,000,000 acres suitable for
production and only 16,000,000 acres under cultivation in 1919, this Province of 650,000 people has had
a remarkable record of expansion.   It has become
Canada's greatest grain-growing Province and in 1917
produced 56 per cent. of all Canadian wheat as
against 4 per cent. in 1904; in 1915 it exceeded any State in the
American Union in its production of grain and as to wheat retained
this supremacy in 1916 and 1917.   It has an Elevator capacity for
68,000,000 bushels and the number of its chartered Bank branches
increased from 39 in 1905 to 480 in 1918.   The southern parts are
prairie land and the central and northern parts are wooded, with
many lakes and rivers, and forests estimated to contain from 8,000,-
000,000 to 14,000,000,000 feet of lumber.   Over 1,000,000 horse-
power could be developed from its rivers and the lakes are well-
stocked with valuable whitefish, trout, pickerel and sturgeon.
Over 1,000,000 dollars worth of furs are trapped annually in the
Province and big game is plentiful with herds of caribou in the
north.   Discoveries of gold, copper, iron, coal, glass sands and
other minerals have been made north of the Saskatchewan River
but little development had been done up to 1919; extensive deposits
of lignite coal and pottery and fire-clay are found in southern parts
and indications of oil and gas are numerous.

Agricultural Conditions and the Department of Agriculture.
The agricultural production of Saskatchewan in 1919 included
grain, hay, vegetables, etc., totalling, according to Federal official
figures, $296,882,800; Dairy products valued at $16,769,847 and a
wool-clip of $580,000; Furs and game estimated at $2,000,000.
Garden products at $2,000,000 and Poultry and poultry products
of $8,170,000.   The total value of Live-stock in the Province was
estimated at $268,422,101 according to Provincial statistics and
included 1,092,974 horses and mules worth $163,946,100; 1,379,563
cattle (cows, bulls, calves, steers) valued at $92,760,262; 146,911
sheep worth $2,203,665 and 432,367 swine valued at $9,512,074.
The wheat acreage of 1919 showed a substantial increase over 1918
but the production, owing to drouth in certain sections, averaged
only 8·5 bushels to the acre compared with 10 bushels in 1918.
The total values of all Farm products and stock in 1919 was $636,-
415,107 as against $585,733,357 in 1918 and $609,588,065 in 1917.
Despite the drought-stricken areas the total wheat yield was almost
equal to that of the previous year and a close official estimate was
made by Hedley Auld, Deputy-Minister of Agriculture, when he

.told the Toronto *Globe* correspondent on Aug. 22nd that ''the year was an abnormal one but he confidently expected a crop of 80 to 90 million bushels of wheat.'' As will be seen by the statement of agricultural production which follows, the latter figure was almost exactly attained[*]:

Product	Acreage	Yield	Production	Price	Total value
Wheat	10,587,363	8·5	89,993,685	$2.08	$187,186,865
Oats	4,887,747	23·1	112,156,969	·86	96,454,998
Barley	492,586	18·2	8,970,501	1.40	12,558,701
Flax	929,945	4·8	4,489,761	4.70	21,101,877
Rye	190,482	10·5	2,000,861	1.45	2,900,523
Peas	4,853	12·5	61,000	2.00	122,000
Beans	1,820	10·0	18,000	6.45	116,100
Xd grains	22,017	35·0	771,000	1.50	1,156,500
Potatoes	66,176	100·0	6,617,600	1.00	6,617,600
Turnips	18,982	257·75	3,591,000	1.12	4,022,000
Hay, clover	265,417	1·05 tns.	279,000	17.00	4,743,000
Fodder corn	6,690	12·50 "	84,000	12.50	1,050,000
Alfalfa	11,526	1·60 "	18,400	27.50	506,000

During the year many American farmers and some investors bought up Saskatchewan lands; the Regina *Leader* of Aug. 25th stated that Col. R. J. Cross, a well-known farmer and auctioneer of Estlin, south of Regina, had been active in selling farm lands to farmers from Iowa and Illinois and, during the past six weeks, had disposed of $350,000 worth of Regina district farms. A large single transaction was the purchase by Dr. T. Douglas, of Moose Jaw, from H. O. Hutchins of his farm at Keeler, with its 3,000 acres, at a cost of approximately $150,000. Meanwhile, the Government's Farm Loan Board was lending money to the farmers on terms very similar to those of Manitoba and Alberta. Established in 1917 the idea in this connection and in the Greater Production Farm Loan Bonds, issued under supervision of this Board, was to borrow money from the people of Saskatchewan as a whole and lend it on 1st mortgage to the farmers of the Province; altogether up to the end of 1919 $2,500,000 had been thus loaned at 6½ per cent., and which had been obtained on bonds bearing 5 per cent.— leaving enough to pay the cost of operation. During the War there had been difficulty in obtaining all the money required and the criticism of the scheme offered in certain quarters was that the loans were not made to farmers in isolated districts not covered by the operations of Mortgage Companies—which was the original intention—but that the Board competed in the more accessible and settled districts with the regular companies.

The Provincial Treasurer (Hon. C. A. Dunning) in his Budget speech of Jan. 29th stated as to this Farm Loans policy that: ''We did not expect to do all the business but we did and do hope to exert an influence on the cost of mortgage money to the farmer, and we also hope to affect the terms and conditions upon which he secures mortgage loans. There is ample evidence that we are affecting these conditions. Through our Farm Loans Board we have affected the attitude of the mortgage companies generally

---

[*]Note.—These were Provincial statistics and there is usually a discrepancy between Province and Dominion in this respect; the Federal Bureau of Statistics, however, gives the total for Saskatchewan in 1919 as $296,822,800 which compares with the above total of $338,536,159—a very large difference!

towards farm loans. While the cost of nearly everything in this Province has gone up from 100 to 200 per cent. since the War started, the cost of farm loans has inclined downward rather than upward." The loans themselves were made direct from the Government through the Board and the full amount of the loan, less the expense of getting it through, went to the borrower direct; on a loan of $1,000 the annual payment of principal and interest was $76.58. The members of the Saskatchewan Farm Loan Board in 1919 were J. O. Hettle, Saskatoon, J. H. Grayson, Moose Jaw, and Colin Fraser, Regina.

The Government also did much to encourage co-operative efforts. Under a 1917 Act the Saskatchewan Co-operative Creameries, Ltd., was formed for acquisition or erection of cold storage plants assisted by a Government loan of 75 per cent. of the cost of the plants, re-payable in 20 years, and lent at a rate not to exceed 6 per cent. per annum. After 18 months' operation three large cold storage plants had been acquired and useful egg and poultry marketing departments established. The Saskatchewan Co-operative Elevator Co. was a Grain Growers' project under which the Government advanced 85 per cent. of the amount of subscribed capital, the loans repayable in 20 yearly installments and the interest 5 per cent. In 1918 this Company had 20,683 shareholders, 298 elevators and handled 25,994,552 bushels. Co-operative Wool marketing was another Government enterprise under which a branch of the Department of Agriculture acted as a free wool marketing agency for the sheep men of the Province, who prepared their wool in accordance with directions issued by the Branch, and forwarded it to a warehouse provided in Regina. In 1918 there were 916 consignments of 394,000 lbs. and the average price received per pound by the farmers had risen from 17¾ cents to 61½ cents.

Live-stock marketing was also developed with 9 Associations organized in 1914 which increased to 41 in 1918, and handled 689 cars with $1,558,621 worth of animals. By 1919 legislation, Co-operative Stockyards or markets were established—one at Moose Jaw for the South and one at Prince Albert for the North. The capital stock was fixed at $100,000 and half of it was to be held by farmers while dividends were not to exceed 8 per cent. and the Government assisted the Companies by a cash grant equivalent to one-third of the cost of the necessary buildings, yards, and pens. Both Companies commenced operations during the year with yard facilities adjacent to well equipped private abattoirs. W. W. Thomson, was Director of Co-operative Associations for the Province, and he stated on Aug. 13th that the Wool clip was developing rapidly under above conditions: "Last year the total handled was 916 shipments, of 394,000 pounds. This year, already, we have had 1,066 shipments of nearly 600,000 lbs." Another bit of Government policy was the formation of Institutional Farms, of which C. M. Learmonth was Superintendent, with farms at Regina, Prince Albert, Moosomin and Battleford and special attention given to Live-stock work, the promotion of pure-bred stock and popular instruction in the maintenance of flocks and herds. These and many other branches of Agricultural development were the product of a Department of Agriculture which, for many years under Hon. W. R. Motherwell as Minister and latterly under Hon. George Langley and Hon. C. A. Dunning, had greatly helped the farmers. Two important appointments of 1919 were those of Percy E. Reed as Dairy Commissioner and Lieut. J. G. Robertson, B.S.A., as Live-Stock Commissioner.

The Report of the Minister for the year of Apr. 30th, 1919, was submitted by Mr. Dunning with a preliminary review by F. H. Auld, Deputy-Minister, which showed a good year's work and much development in spite of war calls and drouth difficulties. Reference was made to the Domestic Science Scholarships won by six young women, and to the Dominion Agricultural grant of $81,-728 and the Fund for Agricultural Relief of the Allies, (Chairman, J. A. Maharg, M.P.,) which resulted in a remittance of $19,329 to the Dominion Treasurer on May 23rd, 1919. Of other Reports from officials one of the chief was that of T. M. Molloy for the Bureau of Labour; he had charge of a great variety of matters and commenced with figures as to Lumbering in 1917 which showed a total valuation of $2,036,029 for that year; the Coal Mines Branch showing on Dec. 31st, 1918, 51 mines in operation, 360,081 tons produced in the year, and 532 miners or labourers employed; as Fuel Administrator Mr. Molloy described the fuel dealers in cities, towns and villages as numbering 1,613 and the consumption during the past coal year as 1,650,000 tons; Factory inspection reports showed 208 factories and 3,639 employees inspected with industrial accidents in the fiscal year, 1918-19, totalling 784 compared with 689 in 1917-18; new buildings reported from the five cities of the Province were $2,388,358 in 1918 as against $1,492,778 in 1917; harvest labour returns showed 13,736 employed during the 1918 season with average wages per month of $55 to $65 and wages for servant girls from $30 to $40; new Government Employment agencies were established and 9 were in operation on Apr. 30th, 1919, with 4,409 applications received during the year and vacancies reported as 6,634—female figures were, respectively, 717 and 1,578.

The Chief Game Guardian dealt with violations of the law, publications issued, Lantern slide lectures given on Saskatchewan wild life, licenses issued to a total of 10,914 with a revenue of $24,136 and the work of the Natural History Museum at Regina; he reported that each year there came increasing complaints as to wanton slaughter of big game by Indians and he had had conferences with Federal officials as to the best means of dealing with the problem; Mr. Bradshaw's review of the wild animals and bird-life of the Province was of much interest. M. P. Tullis, Weeds and Seeds Commissioner, reported much work done in enforcing the Noxious Weeds Act with 14 field men supervising the work of weed inspectors, conducting short courses, and directing distribution of seed and feed for the 1919 crop. Edward Oliver, Secretary of the Statistics Branch, reported as to the Land situation which showed 78,836,603 surveyed acres of which 27,133,700 were under Homestead, 5,854,200 under pre-emption or purchase, 2,302,000 under Scrip, special grants, etc., 15,177,063 granted to Railway companies and 3,087,000 to Hudson's Bay Co., 3,932,000 under School Land endowment, 3,009,100 under Timber licenses, and 6,195,700 under Forest reserves and parks; dealt at length with the crops of 1918, with an increased value in the production and price of Livestock in 1918 totalling $21,347,025 and a total of Poultry in the Province numbering, 8,000,369, with 12,382 immigrants into Saskatchewan and 1,280 homestead entries.

W. W. Thomson dealt at length with the important work of the Co-operative Branch which showed in the year 1918-19, 15,132 shareholders in 329 Agricultural Co-operative Associations and a capital invested of $230,000, 41 Associations marketing Live-stock and an aggregate turnover of farm produce totalling $5,278,166. The Agricultural Societies of the Province, with S. E. Greenway, Director, showed 20,336 members, receipts of $382,261, assets of $310,586 and an average membership of 160 in the Societies; Seed fairs, Poultry shows, and Exhibitions of all kinds were a part of their work; the Agricultural Societies' Convention of Jan. 14-16th, 1919, was an important meeting with a Resolution which urged the Dominion Government to aid development of Western Canada's oil resources as an economic measure which would provide cheap supplies for the farmer and reduce the cost of farming operations. J. G. Rayner reported the formation of Boys' and Girls' Clubs and J. G. Robertson, Live-stock Commissioner, described a very flourishing industry valued at $273,592,455 and increasing yearly in numbers and value.

He reported that the average prices for Sheep had increased from $5.70 in 1914 to $14.65 in 1918, for Cattle from $7.20 to $11.60, for Swine from $7.82 to $18.85; that the Live Stock Purchase Act was operating well with 477 farmers in 1918 purchasing cattle, sheep or swine; that the trend in Saskatchewan was from specialized ranching and grain-growing to mixed farming and that the health of animals in the Province was good with many precautions taken; that under the Wolf Bounty Act organized municipalities had paid, in 1918-19, $45,496 for the destruction of 35,-249 coyotes and 6 grey wolves. W. F. Windeatt reported 1,577 cattle brands, 1,017 horse brands with 1,190 renewals. The Dairy Commissioner, P. E. Reed, dealt with 20 co-operative Creameries and 18 private ones in operation, with 5,009,014 lbs. of butter produced valued, with ice-cream and other products, at $3,180,622— the average selling price of the butter being 44 cents. During 1919 the Department issued a number of pamphlets dealing with topics useful to the farmer—Potato Growing by Prof. John Bracken and Plows and Plowing by Prof. J. MacGregor; Weeds, Home Beautification, etc.

On Feb. 12-13 the Saskatchewan Dairymen's Association held its 10th annual Convention at Saskatoon and heard a number of important addresses. Resolutions were passed (1) urging the earliest possible completion of the Hudson Bay Railway in the interests of Western agriculture and Canadian commerce; (2) declaring that any further railway increase in rates on Dairy produce would ruin that industry; (3) asking that dairy butter be handled in grade as was creamery butter and that Ottawa representatives be appointed to take charge of Egg-grading work in Saskatchewan; (4) suggesting that the women and young people of the farms get together in a scheme to advance dairying; (5) urging that the admission of Oleomargarine be again declared illegal and the present order rescinded; (6) asking for the free admission of dairy machinery used in pasteurization. The Saskatchewan Farm Lands Association was formed early in the year with J. H. Haslam of Regina elected President and the following stated objects: ''(1) To promote and encourage the settlement and cultivation of all farms and agricultural lands in the Province of Saskatchewan; (2) to establish uniform commissions and promote a spirit of co-operation among members; (3) to establish uniform customs and regulations, as applied to the sale and leasing of farms and farm lands and to co-operate with Governments and organizations having similar objects.'' The chief Agricultural Societies of the Province, with their Presidents in 1919, were as follows:

Saskatchewan Dairy Association	J. C. Moore	Leask
Saskatchewan Veterinary Association	Dr. J. S. Gibson	Govan
Saskatchewan Aberdeen-Angus Association	James Brown	Neudorf
Saskatchewan Stock-Growers' Association	Jack Byers	Valjean
Provincial Horse-Breeders' Association	R. H. Taber	Condie
Saskatchewan Cattle Breeders' Association	W. H. Gibson	Girvin
Saskatchewan Sheep Breeders' Association	A. J. Quigley	Sintaluta
Saskatchewan Live-stock Board	E. W. Caswell	Saskatoon

The Martin Government and Political Conditions. The Hon. W. M. Martin proved himself a skilful leader of difficult local conditions during the year; he assumed national prominence through the desire of a very considerable group of Liberals at the Dominion Convention to make him Leader of the Party; he continued his vigourous administration of Educational affairs and took over the personal control of Railways, also, during 1919. In the Legislature on Feb. 1st the Premier stated that a scheme was under consideration to assist the children of soldiers killed in the War, or who had suffered disability, to continue a higher course of education beyond the Public School; on Mch. 5th in an interview upon his return from Ottawa Mr. Martin expressed the hope that the natural resources would be returned to the Western Provinces and was inclined to believe that such action would be conditional on accepting a smaller annual subsidy from the Dominion. He was insistent at this time and throughout the year upon the necessity of Tariff changes along free-trade lines. At Tisdale on Mch. 26th he dealt with this question and the general situation of the Province at great length. It was a speech intended to give the people information regarding the Government, its work, policy and functions.

As to finances the Public Debt on Apr. 30th, 1916, was $24,292,000 and on Dec. 31st, 1918, it was $29,636,000 expended as follows: Public Buildings $8,910,000, and Public improvements, roads and bridges, $7,990,000; Telephone system, $7,093,000 and Miscellaneous items—drainage, District bonds, Royal Commissions, City of Regina, Sanatorium, Saskatchewan Co-operative Elevator Co., Farm Loans Board, $5,643,000. Of this Debt $13,160,000 was self-sustaining. As to Reconstruction, he said: "The Provincial Government is giving preference to returned men in the Civil Service, provided they are qualified for the work available, and already 150 are in the employment of the Government. Reconstruction in this Province simply means the beginning of our development again at the point where we left off when war began. We want more railways, we want more and better roads, we want immigration, and we want better schools." In respect to Railways he was explicit: "The condition of affairs in many parts of the Province is lamentable; settlers have gone in ahead of railway construction and in many cases were induced to go with the promise of a railroad; they have waited and waited for years, drawing their grain to market 30, 40 and even 50 miles." No stone must be left unturned to help them.

Regarding roads, etc., he declared that: "There is nothing will do more to develop a new country like Saskatchewan than the construction of good roads. Road building here is, however, unfortunately very difficult and expensive. I think the proper course to pursue is to spend what money we can on the development of a system of main roads, leaving to the local authorities the building of branch roads leading to the main thoroughfares." For the construction, maintenance and improvement of roads and the construction of wooden bridges the money was provided out of revenue and for the building of steel bridges, which were of a permanent character, it was provided out of capital: "During the coming fiscal year, for these purposes, we propose spending $846,630 out of revenue, and $573,000 out of capital." Mr. Martin then urged increased Immigration and, as an aid to this end, said: "I do believe that if the economic conditions of the country are made what they should be by a proper revision of the Tariff downwards, and by the opening of free markets for our natural products to the south of us, people will come here in very large numbers."

Education was dealt with in elaborate detail. Under the School Attendance Act of 1917 there had been 1,500 prosecutions and the Act would be rigidly enforced; through the Teachers' Bureau, of 1918, 256 teachers had been placed and under a special branch of the Department 50 plans had been furnished for rural schools and an organized system of improvement in lighting, ventilation and sanitation established; a Director of School Hygiene was doing good work with a number of nurses under his supervision. So with many other changes and hoped-for reforms. As to the Language question he declared: "The policy of the Government is that every child in the Province must learn the English language. If he knows another language, so much the better, but he must at least learn English; and we made up our minds that whatever steps were necessary to bring about this condition of affairs would be taken." In 1918 there were only 118 schools out of a total of 4,157 in the Province using any foreign language in the school, and then only for the last hour in the day. These figures showed a decrease from 139 in 1917. At the last Session of the Legislature, he pointed out, an Act was passed prohibiting the use of any other language than English during school hours, with an exception made in favour of the French people, on account of their historic position in Canada. The speech concluded with a long reference to the Tar-. iff: "Agricultural machinery, lumber, building material, cement, oils, should be placed on the free list, and in connection with many other items which are the necessities of life, such as boots and shoes and clothing, the Tariff should be very substantially reduced, not only to assist the farmer, but to assist all consumers in the country; the British preference should be substantially increased, and the Reciprocity agreement which is still open to us, should be at once accepted."

On June 16th the Premier took charge of the Conventions to choose delegates to the National Liberal Convention—numbering 65 or 70 from Saskatchewan—and issued an elaborate call to action and organization in which he announced his return to the Liberal ranks with war issues a matter of the past: "Before Union Government was formed, I deemed it to be my duty, on account of the all-important issues which were before the civilized world, to assist the Government of the day in everything that pertained to the carrying on of the War and, since the formation of Union Government, I have endeavoured to co-operate in all matters essential to the proper organization of the country." The present vital needs of the country were food and fuel and Tariff reduction. The latter subject was dealt with at length, the Saskatchewan Liberal platform of 1917 re-stated, and an indirect reference made to the Farmers' movement: "I often hear it stated that the day of party is past; under our system of government this can never be. Party Government has existed in England for two centuries; we have always had it in Canada. Third parties have existed sometimes, but never for any great length of time and never with any marked success. The names of parties may change. There may be realignments, but parties there will always be."

At Weyburn on June 17th Mr. Martin expressed his personal position.clearly: "While I believe that a reorganized Liberal party with a progressive platform is the best medium of expression for Western opinion, I do not intend nor do the people of Saskatchewan intend to slavishly follow the Liberal party or any other party. The people of this country want a clear-cut, low tariff policy." Several other of the 16 Provincial Conventions were addressed by the Premier—notably at Saskatoon on July 7th where he again dealt with the Tariff as the all-important subject of the day. To the Conference, itself, in August, Mr. Martin was accompanied by Messrs. Latta, Knowles and Dunning of the Government and by Hon. Walter Scott, his predecessor, who was appointed from Regina and, at Ottawa he found himself one of five prominently mentioned candidates for the Leadership—Fielding, Graham, McKenzie, Mackenzie King and himself. On Aug. 7th the press reported him as saying: "No, I will not allow my name to go before the Convention. I have taken that position from the start. The opportunities for service are great and I feel much attracted, but I made my decision last May and simply cannot accept."

Meanwhile, Mr. Martin had to face the Grain Growers' movement, as it expanded from an attack upon Federal parties, into one of antagonism to Provincial Governments. In Alberta the Farmers had come out clearly at the Cochrane election; in Manitoba they were divided and not yet in open opposition to the Norris Government; in Saskatchewan their Association had always been closely allied to the Provincial Government with Hon. W. R. Motherwell, their founder, as Minister of Agriculture for many years and Hon. George Langley, one of their leaders, as another Minister. In the bye-elections of the year the Martin Government had no open defeat—Weyburn, vacated by the retirement of Hon. R. M. Mitchell, Speaker of the House, returned C. M. Hamilton (Lib.) by acclamation on July 23rd; Kamsack, a riding of motley racial type, returned Mrs. M. C. Ramsland (Lib.), in succession to her late husband on August 29th, over Corp. W. W. Whelan who ran as an Independent; Kindersley, a part of Assiniboia and the scene of Mr. Motherwell's bitter fight with the Grain Growers' organization, of which he had been head and front for years, elected W. H. Harvey, the Grain Growers' candidate, by acclamation—with the endorsement of a Liberal Convention upon his past Liberal record. As to the Assiniboia Federal election correspondence between Mr. Martin and Hon. W. R. Motherwell which was published on Nov. 18th showed that the latter contested the seat against the wishes of his friends and late colleagues in the Government. There was, therefore, no direct clash between the Grain Growers and the Martin Government; Mr. Dunning was a Minister and a Grain Grower; Mr. Langley was still a Minister, Vice-President of the Co-operative Elevator Co. and Member of the Council of Agriculture.

As to Education* the Premier spoke frequently during the year and his policy regarding English in the Schools commended him even to the fiery spirits of the Provincial School Trustees' Association, when he addressed 2,000 of them on Jan. 22nd. At this Convention, now a vigourous one-language body, where two years

*Note.—See Educational Section, Pages 549-54, 571-3, and for Grain Growers' Association, see Pages 854-5, 885-6, 890-2.

before it had been of polyglot opinion in this respect with P. M.
Friesen as President, J. F. Bryant delivered a powerful Presidential
address and was re-elected by acclamation while the Premier spoke
briefly and was given a hearty reception.   Following up his legislation as to English in the schools—with certain privileges for
French—the Premier had appointed Dr. J. T. M. Anderson as
Director of Education amongst new Canadians or, in other words,
non-English settlements and the latter, during 1919, conducted a
vigourous campaign of English instruction.   At the close of the
year it was announced that since 1905 $13,200,000 had been spent
by the Province upon Education.

As to Railways, Mr. Martin submitted his first Report, as Minister, for the year of Apr. 30th, 1919.   It showed the following
total of Railway lines in the Province: C.P.R. 2,776, C.N.R. 2,226,
and G.T.P.R. 1,168.   The only additional mileage in 1918 was a
total of 50 miles for the whole three Railways; D. C. McNab,
Deputy-Minister, gave statistics showing that the Railways had
695 depôts, 858 loading platforms, 2,077 Elevators, 113 warehouses, 372 Freight-sheds and 504 stockyards.   As to the G.T.P.
and its lines guaranteed by the Province, the Premier stated on
Apr. 4th that if the Dominion Government expected to operate the
G.T.P. branch lines they would have to pay every dollar of the
interest on the bonds guaranteed by the Province: "If the Province
is forced to pay the interest we will exercise our right to the
security and it will be a very easy matter indeed to have the
branch lines operated."   On May 1st the Saskatchewan Government made a payment of interest amounting to $275,000 and an-
other payment came due on Nov. 1st.   Meantime, there had been a
re-organization of Mr. Martin's Cabinet with Mr. Dunning replacing Mr. Langley at the Department of Agriculture, Mr. Martin
relieving Mr. Dunning of Railways and Mr. Knowles taking the
Department of Telephones.   The new Cabinet was sworn in on
Feb. 15th as follows:

President of the Council, Minister of Education and
   of Railways ....Hon. William M. Martin, K.C.
Attorney-General ....Hon. W. F. A. Turgeon, K.C.
Minister of Public Works ....Hon. A. P. McNab
Minister of Municipal Affairs ....Hon. George Langley
Minister of Agriculture and Provincial Treasurer ......Hon. Charles A. Dunning
Minister of Highways ....Hon. Samuel J. Latta
Minister of Telephones and Provincial Secretary ....Hon. W. E. Knowles

Government incidents of the year included the Legislative vote
of $100,000 as a preliminary amount for construction of the War
Memorial Museum to be built near the Parliament Buildings and
under the supervision of Mr. McNab as Minister of Public Works;
the Report of Mr. Knowles, Minister of Telephones, which showed
on Apr. 30th, 1919, a construction work during the year of 2,263
long-distance wire miles, 19 new exchanges and 17 new toll offices
with a total of 70,703 stations giving service in the Province, 238
exchanges and 368 toll offices, a poll-mile long distance length of

4,741 and wire-mile long distance length of 22,415 with 400,000 people said to have access to this service and the statement on July 4th that new and increased Telephone rates would go into force on Sept. 1st; the Report of Mr. Langley as Minister of Municipal Affairs showed on Apr. 30th, 1919, 7 cities, 75 towns, 317 villages, 300 rural municipalities and 4,145 school districts and gave details of population, assessment, tax-rates and Debenture debt with a reference to the retirement of J. N. Bayne who had been Deputy Minister for 10 years; the issue in August of new and elaborate regulations as to the management, maintenance, functions, duties and jurisdiction of Boards of Health, Medical Health Officers and Sanitary Inspectors by Mr. Langley, who was the Minister in charge of the Bureau of Public Health, and Dr. M. M. Seymour, Commissioner of Public Health.

Mr. Knowles, as Provincial Secretary, reported 185 new Companies in 1918-19 with $5,918,500 of capital and 50 extra-Provincial companies with $33,580,000 capital, a Departmental revenue of $1,234,522 of which Motor licenses accounted for $743,954 while Premiums of Insurance companies doing business in Saskatchewan totalled for the year $10,389,846 and their general investments $28,319,145 while the general investments of Loan companies reached a total of $57,051,405. As Minister of Highways Mr. Latta on Aug. 1st reported that the Government had entered into more than 500 contracts, valued at $230,000, with the rural municipalities of the Province for the construction of new roads and for the improvement of existing main roads to form a part of the approved Highways system and that he had under way a large programme of timber bridge construction with $80,000 as the total value of work in hand and $107,000 representing the construction of steel bridges already in hand. During the year Sir Richard Lake, as Lieut.-Governor, took part in many functions and carried out his duties with distinction; the former Premier, Hon. Walter Scott, returned to the Province with health largely restored and resumed his place in public affairs as a strong Liberal, an opponent of Union Government and of the Grain Growers as a "class" party and a supporter of Mr. Motherwell in his Assiniboia contest. It may be added here that Mrs. W. M. Martin, on retiring as Provincial President of the I.O.D.E., was presented (Oct. 30th) with a life membership in the National Chapter and a gift of $800 from the Provincial Chapter, which latter she donated to the Regina Hospital. The crop failure in some parts of the Province caused by draught called for Government action during the autumn and the Bureau of Labour prepared to place 2,000 farmers in temporary employment with an advance of travelling expenses; special relief was granted in flour, coal and clothing, and co-operation arranged with the Dominion Government upon a basis of one-half the cost—the Provincial Government undertaking the distribution. The chief Government appointments of the year were as follows:

Law Officer; Department of Attorney-General	Allan L. Geddes	Regina
Assistant in Agriculture Extension Work.	Andrew M. McDermott, B.S.A.	Regina
King's Counsel	Percy M. Anderson	Regina
King's Counsel	Daniel Buckles	Swift Current
Superintendent of Weyburn Mental Hospital	Dr. R. M. Mitchell	Weyburn
Inspector of Schools	Robert Weir, B.A.	Regina
King's Counsel	Daniel Maclean	Saskatoon
Commissioner of Local Government Board.	J. N. Bayne	Regina
Deputy Minister of Municipal Affairs.	John J. Smith	Regina
Wild Lands Tax Commissioner	George Armstrong	Regina
Director of Town Planning	M. B. Weekes	Regina

Meeting and Enactments of the Legislature. The 2nd Session of the 4th Legislature of Saskatchewan was opened at Regina on Dec. 6th, 1918, by Lieut.-Governor Sir Richard S. Lake who expressed pleasure at the close of the War and reviewed the splendid response of Saskatchewan to the calls of duty; urged the responsibilities of the coming reconstruction period, mentioned the Educational Report of Dr. Foght* and the Ottawa Inter-Provincial Conference; promised some important legislation. The Address was moved by Rev. M. L. Leitch of Morse and G. W. Sahlmark of Saltcoats and, after a brief debate, was passed without division on Dec. 9th. The chief measure discussed before adjournment on Dec. 20th to the 1919 Session was that relating to the English language in Schools.† On Jan. 13-14 a Resolution presented by J. G. Gardiner declared that the War Times Elections Act should be repealed by the Dominion Parliament at the earliest possible moment; Hon. W. R. Motherwell moved in amendment that a deputation be sent to Ottawa to press this upon the Government and to also urge the acceptance of the Provincial franchises as the basis of the Federal franchise; the amendment was defeated by 44 to 4 votes. Another motion reviewed, on Jan. 15th the difficult Railway situation, the uncertainty of Federal policy as to future ownership and control and its effect upon Provincial activities and guaranteed securities and urged the Provincial Government to impress upon the Ottawa authorities the necessity of announcing a definite policy; it was approved without division on the 20th.

Bernhard Larsen (Lib.) moved on Jan. 17th a Resolution declaring that changes should be made in the Banking system of Canada which would "permit of the establishment of local agricultural banks in close touch with local conditions and the needs of the farming industry." It was debated at some length and finally approved. On Jan. 24th a Resolution was unanimously carried urging the Government of Canada to "immediately fix and guarantee the price of wheat for the 1919 crop at a reasonable figure to approximate as nearly as possible to the price fixed and guaranteed by the U.S. Government." Another Resolution unanimously passed urged the Dominion Government to grant Provincial control and administration of the Lands set apart by Parliament as an endowment for School purposes. So with a Resolution of Mr. Motherwell's in favour of the establishment of a Faculty of Edu-

*Note.—See *The Canadian Annual Review* for 1918, Pages 688-9.
†Note.—See *The Canadian Annual Review* for 1918, Page 690.

cation at the University of Saskatchewan and a general betterment of Educational conditions.   On Jan. 23rd a long Resolution of protest against the "present unjust and unrighteous Tariff"
was passed with demands very similar to those of the Grain
Growers' organizations.   It was carried unanimously but, on Feb.
5th, the presentation of these and other matters as an Address to
H.E. the Governor-General describing them as measures of relief
demanded by the people of Saskatchewan from the Federal Government was opposed by Donald Maclean, the Opposition leader;
the vote stood 36 in favour and 5 against what the press called a
"Bill of Rights."   On Feb. 4th a Committee of the House reported
in favour of a Government enquiry at the next Session as to the
practicability of publishing a Hansard of the Assembly.

On Jan. 8th Mr. Dunning stated that Provincial guarantees for
unconstructed C.N.R. lines had lapsed owing to the Dominion acquisition of the Railway; on Jan. 30th he delivered his Budget
speech.   He stated that, including subscriptions to the Victory
Loans of 1917-18, the people of the Province had contributed $54,-
695,000 to the national war effort; reviewed the statistical condition of the Province, the Public Debt and the revenue returns;
stated the gross bonded Debt on Dec. 31st, 1918, as $29,635,906,
the net bonded Debt as $16,476,000 or $22.14 per capita, the portion
of the Debt which was self-sustaining as $13,159,000; intimated
that the capital expenditures in the current Estimates for the year
would increase the Debt by $6,728,000; spoke at length of the
School Lands Fund and stated that there was $6,183,000 in the
Trust Fund arising out of these lands with $4,000,000 in arrears
of payment to the Dominion Government; gave his personal estimate
of the value of lands thus held at $141,000,000.

The Minister stated the loans of the Farm Loans Board up to
date as $3,000,000 and the cost of administration as $26,000.   Later
in the year the Public Accounts showed the revenue for the year
ending Apr. 30th, 1919, as $8,333,758 which included Dominion
subsidy, $2,307,147, and Provincial Taxation, $2,479,708; Licenses,
$979,156 and Fees $918,672.   It may be added that Education
received $1,187,544, Agriculture $197,445 and Public Health $297,-
350 while Public Works cost $822,336 and Public Improvements
$500,704.   The total expenditures were $8,086,756 and were subdivided as follows: Administration $397,485; Protection (Courts,
gaols, Land Titles, etc.) $1,268,213; Developmental (Education,
Public Health, Agriculture, Highways, etc.) $3,496,279; Patriotic
purposes $825,468.*

The legislation of the year included the imposition of a Supplementary Revenue Tax of 4 cents per acre against all lands
situated within rural municipalities and which were not contributing towards the maintenance of the Public Schools; authorized the
purchase of Seed grain to supply farmers under specific conditions

---

*Note.—Budget Speech of Jan. 27th, 1920.

MRS. J. S. WOOD
President of the Women's Section
Grain Growers' Association of
Manitoba

MRS. JOHN McNAUGHTAN
Four years President Women's Section
Saskatchewan Grain Growers'
Association

MRS. G. A. BRODIE
President of The United Farm Women
of Ontario in 1919

MRS. WALTER PARLBY
President United Farm Women of
Alberta, 1919

WOMEN LEADERS IN THE FARMERS' MOVEMENT

of mortgage security while another Act permitted the apprehension and detention of dangerous lunatics and appointment of an Administrator for Lunatics' estates; Wild Lands Tax amendments of detail character were made as well as technical changes in the Vital Statistics Act. The Employment Agencies Act gave authority to close up private labour employment bureaux and another authorized the establishment of Provincial Labour Bureaux in co-operation with the Federal authorities; the City Act was amended to make the maximum limit of the municipal income tax 30 mills on the dollar and to provide that cities should not invest sinking fund monies in municipal or school debentures outside the Province of Saskatchewan; the Government Bill respecting Devolution of Estates provided that the estates of persons dying intestate should be divided equally between the mother and child—when there was only one child; the Trustees' Act was changed to add securities of the United Kingdom and the United States to the list of those in which trust funds could be invested by Trustees; a Venereal Diseases Act was approved based, in the main, upon those of Ontario and Alberta.

A Minimum Wage Act was passed which fixed standard minimum wages, hours of employment and conditions of labour for females. Under its provisions a Minimum Wage Board of five persons was created—two of the Commissioners to be women. The Board was to ascertain and declare what wages were adequate to meet the current cost of living and what were reasonable hours and proper sanitary conditions. The Act applied only to Cities. Amendments of the Municipal Act provided that the home of the soldier should be wholly exempt from taxation in villages, and to the extent of $50 per annum in towns and cities and that this exemption should extend until the year following the discharge of the soldier; the Volunteers and Reservists' Relief Act protected, by amendment, the land of a soldier from sale for taxes from the first day of the year in which he enlisted until the expiration of two years from the date of his discharge; another amendment affecting villages and rural municipalities, only, provided for the making of quarterly payments by the village and the rural municipality to any village school district situated wholly or in part within their boundaries; the Hospital Act was amended to provide a scheme under which Hospital districts could be formed without regard to municipal boundaries and enable the Government to define and establish such districts upon receipt of a petition from the Council of each municipality concerned, or from 25 ratepayers in each municipality or area to be included—the Government to approve other details and a vote then to be taken. The Legislature was prorogued by Sir Richard Lake on Feb. 5th after passing 110 Bills of a public or private nature. A third Session was opened on Nov. 27th but its proceedings more properly belong to the year 1920.

26

SASKATCHEWAN INCIDENTS OF 1919

Mch. 4th.—The annual Convention of the Saskatchewan Municipal Hail Insurance Association decided to take advantage of recent legislation and to make provision to levy a seeded acreage assessment, if necessary, to meet the losses and expenses in full for the year 1919, provided such assessment did not exceed 25 cents per acre. A. E. Wilson, of Indian Head, presided, E. G. Hingley, Managing Director of the Association, reported as to the year's business and its unfavourable nature and Mr. Wilson was re-elected President.

Mch. 5-6th.—The 14th annual Convention of the Saskatchewan Association of Rural Municipalities dealt with over 50 Resolutions and was addressed by its President C. M. Hamilton, M.L.A., of McTaggart, the Lieut.-Governor, J. N. Bayne, and others, with a long and elaborate speech from Hon. George Langley, Minister of Municipal Affairs. The Resolutions passed dealt with all kinds of detail in municipal taxation and assessment, wild lands and homesteads, roads and settlements, schools and telephones, Hospitals, etc. The Association placed itself on record as approving a fixed price for the 1919 wheat crop; declared unhesitatingly in favour of English as the only language of instruction and the only language of study in the elementary schools of the Province; approved continuance of Prohibition as a permanent measure though a substantial proportion of the delegates present did not vote on this question.

Apr. 9th.—The Alien Registration Act showed Saskatchewan to have 48,921 aliens over the age of 16.

May 2nd.—The Minimum Wage Board of the Province was appointed as follows: W. F. Dunn, Moose Jaw. (Chairman); Mrs. M. I. Robertson, Saskatoon; Mrs. A. M. Rothwell, Regina; J. F. Cairns, Saskatoon; H. Perry, Regina, with T. M. Molloy, Labour Commissioner, as Secretary.

May 17th.—The Saskatchewan Retailers' Association affirmed its belief that Prohibition had beneficial results and urged the Government to continue existing enactments.

June 11th.—The Registrar of Vital Statistics issued figures as to the Influenza epidemic of 1918-19 showing a total of 4,322 deaths in Saskatchewan or more than the loss of the Province in the War.

June 25-26th.—The Union of Saskatchewan Municipalities met at Saskatoon with W. W. Davidson of Moose Jaw in the chair and an address of welcome from Sir Richard Lake. Dr. Wilson, M.H.O., of Saskatoon attacked Dr. Seymour's administration of Public Health with vigour, L. A. Thornton, Regina, spoke at length on Taxation problems as did Hon. George Langley, C. J. Yorath, H. G. Wilson, K.C., of Indian Head, and others. Many Resolutions of a Municipal nature were passed.

July 8th.—The Judicial Committee of the Privy Council held that the Surtax provisions of the Saskatchewan Rural Municipalities Act were valid, and, therefore, that the Hudson's Bay Company must pay surtaxes for the years 1914, 1915, 1916 and 1917 to the municipalities in which the Company lands were situated, together with penalties which would add practically 50 per cent. to the amount of the original tax bill, of 1914.

July 31st.—It was announced by the Minimum Wage Board that the Schedule of wages and hours for female workers would be as follows:

Classification	Laundries and Factories	Stores or Shops	Mail Order Houses
1st 6 months	$9.50	$9.50	$8.00
2nd 6 months	11.00	11.00	10.00
3rd 6 months	12.50	13.00	12.00
After 18 months	14.00	15.00	14.00
Length of Week	50 hours	48 hours	48 hours

Minimum wage for experienced females employed in shops, stores and other merchantile institutions in Saskatchewan would be $15 a week—for beginners $9.50 per week, with an increase every three months until one year of service had been completed, when the employee was to be deemed experienced and entitled to the $15 scale.

Sept. 19th.—According to a decision of the Saskatchewan Court of King's Bench notices served on municipalities by Separate Schools asking for an apportionment of Corporation taxes between Public and Separate schools where Corporations had failed to comply with the provisions requiring them to state how their School taxes should be divided, were to be considered "continuing notices" and, therefore, entitle the Separate School Boards to their part of the taxes.

Oct. 27th.—The Regina Trades and Labour Council requested the Government to grant the Minimum Wage Board power to adjust all questions pertaining to industrial female labour and asked that wages of girls in mail order houses be placed on the same basis as girls employed in shops.

Nov. 5th.—The Provincial Presbyterian Synod meeting at Regina discussed the Prohibition situation and various speakers declared that conditions were becoming more scandalous every day and that there was almost as much drinking as in the days of the open bar; while there was much criticism of doctors and druggists. A strong Resolution urging better enforcement of the Act was passed.

Nov. 14th.—It was announced that the total estimated expenditure of the Municipal Hail Insurance Association for the year was $2,167,000, including operating expenses, with the municipalities assessed for a total sum of $2,300,000, of which $1,639,000 had been paid in to the Association. A deficit of $500,000 was expected on the year's business.

Dec. 1st.—It was estimated by the Government's Motor License Branch that 8,000 more motor licenses were issued in 1919 than in 1918 with a total of 58,821.

British Columbia: Progress, Government and Legislation. This great region of mountains and valleys, seacoasts and islands, Mines and Fisheries, Timber and industries, had an Agricultural production for the year 1918 of $49,543,008, or 31·55 per cent. more than in 1917; a Mineral product of $41,083,093 or 11% increase; a Lumbering product of $54,162,523 or 12% increase; a Fishing product of $21,518,495 or 40·50% increase; an estimated industrial product of $50,000,000 or an increase of 37 per cent.—a total of $216,307,119 for a population of less than 400,000 of whom 25,000 were Indians. The Assets of the Province in this year were officially stated as $20,000,000 of a realizable nature with Public Works and other properties totalling $20,000,000 more. According to the Forest Branch of the Department of Lands there were 297 saw-mills and 93 shingle mills in the Province, in 1919, with a capacity of about 2,500,000,000 feet annually and a manufacture, in 1918, of 65,229 tons of paper and 14,380 tons of sulphite; the Fisheries were the largest in the Dominion with immense resources in the thousands of miles of indented sea-coast and an increase in yearly value to $18,000,000—though not an increase of product—and a salmon pack of 1,393,256 cases in 1919; the business of the Province in this year made a substantial advance with Bank clearings in Vancouver, alone, totalling $655,-000,000 or an increase of 110 millions over 1918; the lumbering industry was greatly prosperous with a total valuation estimated by Hon. T. D. Pattullo, Minister of Lands, at $70,285,094 or $16,-

000,000 over the previous year and a total log-scale of 1,758,329,995 feet, with a pulp and paper sale of $12,554,257.

Agriculture was very successful in 1919, with increased product and prices and a 25 per cent. increase in fruit and vegetables; the production of Live-stock in 1919 was $12,437,510, and that of meats $3,730,800; the Poultry production was $3,840,795 and in Dairy products the value was $6,804,364; in vegetables the production was $7,411,195 while Fodders showed a product of $15,012,233 and grains of $6,088,913. The total of all agricultural production in 1919 was $65,384,556 and the importation of agricultural products from other Provinces and the United States totalled $22,734,-150. Industry of many kinds was prosperous with ship-building exceeding that of 1918 by 15,000 tons with 66,000 more tons on order and awaiting completion—wooden ship-building was in doubt but the steel industry far better than expected; wholesale and jobbing trades were very active in 1919 with profitable prices and the retail trade was finding the demand greater than its stocks in hand —with, also, excellent credit conditions.

The preliminary estimate of Mineral production for 1919 showed $3,216,865 in gold, $8,631,205 in copper, $3,871,063 in silver, $1,-658,121 in lead, $2,717,803 in zinc, $12,476,276 in coal and coke— a total of $33,421,333 for all minerals and a decrease of $8,361,141 from 1918. This was due to a cessation of war demands and activities, strikes and labour troubles, and was accompanied by the closing of the Grand Forks smelter and the Phœnix Mine and non-operation of the Greenwood smelter; but there were many signs of increasing activities in other directions, larger operations, successful financing and pending development. Fox-breeding had a considerable development in the Province and an incident of the year was the obtaining by the Department of Lands of an order from the Imperial Government for 70,000,000 feet of lumber; the water-powers of the Province were estimated at 3,000,000, 24-hour, horse-power with 250,000 h.p. actually developed.

The Government of the Hon. John Oliver had over 30 supporters in a House of 46 members with no vital issues to meet during this year except the ever-pressing one of taxes and revenue. There were outside elements of discontent, however,—a noisy Socialist element in Vancouver and on the Island which gave all the trouble possible to Government and business interests but it had only one representative in the Legislature; there was, also, a good deal of dissatisfaction amongst the returned soldiers and, on Apr. 22nd, after a meeting of the Provincial G.W.V.A. in Victoria, a delegation of several hundred waited upon the Ministers and presented a Petition which strongly criticized the Government: (1) for having no definite land policy for the soldiers; (2) for failing to assume liability in the Housing policy of the Dominion authorities; (3) for non-appointment of returned soldier-farmers to the Land Settlement Board and for approving a civilian as Public Utilities Commissioner; (4) for failure to investigate certain charges brought up in the Legislature. The document concluded with a request for the immediate dissolution of the House and resignation of the Government.

Mr. Oliver forwarded a written reply expressing grave doubt as to the representative nature of the petitioners and reviewing the Government's policy in this connection—an advantage for a soldier in purchasing land from the Land Settlement Board of $500 over a civilian; the provision of 22,000 acres, with current improvements costing $500,000, for their settlement; the actual Legislative consent to the Dominion Housing plan and the fact of Hon. Dr. McLean being at this very time in Ottawa to conclude an agreement. As to the appointment of Mayor Gale of Vancouver as Utilities Commissioner, it had been a case of the best-fitted man for the post; in the matter of general appointments the returns showed between July, 1918 and April, 1919, 148 returned men appointed by the Civil Service Commission and 30 civilians. Following this controversy Mayor Gale resigned his post of Commissioner and a returned man was appointed.

The Premier showed no hesitation in denouncing irresponsible labour agitators and, on June 10th, in speaking at New Westminster, declared that: "Engineered by a handful of agitators there is under way throughout Canada a deliberate attempt to overthrow constitutional government and substitute therefor a dictatorship. I am convinced that the Bolshevists are behind all this turmoil." He was, at this time, making a tour of the Interior and at Mission on July 16th used characteristic language: "We had to raise your taxes, and we're going to do it again. If you don't like the Government, or don't trust it, you can put another one in and I would not mind being relieved of the burden." Like all the other Provincial Premiers—except that of Ontario—Mr. Oliver attended the Dominion Liberal Convention and swung in behind the new Leader; while in Ottawa, where he supported Mr. Fielding, a strong effort was made to get the Minister of Railways to take over the Pacific Great Eastern Railway; he succeeded in getting D. B. Hanna, the National Railways chief, to promise an investigation. In September Mr. Oliver, as Minister of Railways, spent a week inspecting the P.G.E. and addressed meetings at Quesnel and other points. He was an active member of the Provincial Taxation Commission which held sittings in the chief centres of the Province during the year and of which Hon. John Hart, Minister of Finance, was Chairman; Mr. Oliver, personally, put nearly every witness through a thorough cross-examination and told every interest concerned that the Government needed all the money it could get. Another B.C. Taxation Commission, appointed in 1917, reported during the year as to plans and methods of taxation.

Government incidents of the year included a visit of the Attorney-General (Hon. J. W. de B. Farris) to England in June to present the Provincial side in an appeal to the Judicial Committee as to the under-surface rights of the Esquimalt and Nanaimo Railway in foreshore lands of Chemainus Harbour; the recognition by Hon. E. D. Barrow, Minister of Agriculture, on July 26th at a Vancouver Convention of the Provincial Civil Service Association, of the right of salaried officials of the Government to organize and co-operate to meet the high cost of living; a three weeks' tour of the North in July and August along the line of the G.T.P. by Hon. T. D. Pattullo, Minister of Lands, and in September by Hon. J. H. King, Minister of Public Works; the statement by Mr. Farris on his return from London that F. C. Wade, K.C., was doing very good work as Agent General and his belief that "the Province has a great opportunity to induce large investments of British capital and to secure a large number of settlers with financial resources behind them"; the attendance of the Attorney General and J. D. McNiven, Deputy Minister of Labour, at the Labour-Industrial Conference at Ottawa in September; the removal of Dr. Alex. Robinson, Superintendent of Education, from his position on Nov. 3rd after 20 years' service, with no reason announced, and appointment of S. J. Willis, B.A., to the post; the creation of a new Department of Industries under the Government with D. B. Martyn as Industrial Commissioner; a visit in November of Mr. Pattullo to Ottawa and arrangement of various matters at issue including better wharf accommodation at Prince Rupert, co-operative publicity action and development of Mount Robson Park. The chief Government appointments of the year were those of Chief Justice J. A. Macdonald as Administrator for a time in the absence of the Lieut.-Governor; the retirement of Sir F. S. Barnard in December and appointment (Dec. 9th) of Lieut.-Col. the Hon. Edward Gawler Prior, one-time Premier of the Province, as Lieut.-Governor; the appointment of Major J. L. Retallack of Vancouver as Public Utilities Commissioner and Dr. David Warnock, O.B.E., as Deputy-Minister of Agriculture. The following were created King's Counsel:

F. Higgins	Victoria	O. W. Craig	Vancouver
A. M. Johnson	Victoria	A. B. Macdonald	Vancouver
F. R. M. Russell	Vancouver	M. B. Jackson, M.L.A.	Victoria
W. G. E. McQuarrie	Westminster	Capt. D. A. McDonald	Vancouver
J. N. Ellis	Vancouver	Douglas Armour	Vancouver

As to Government Reports that of the Hon. Mr. Oliver, Minister of Railways, for the year of Dec. 31st, 1919, dealt with continued construction of the Canadian National terminals at Vancouver, Port Mann, New Westminster and Victoria and expenditures in January-November of $340,740 with an estimated total cost (including Steveston and Patricia Bay) of $9,141,503; continued progress of C.N.P. construction on Vancouver Island from Victoria towards Barkley Sound and of 116 miles of the Kamloops-Vernon line in the Interior; a great deal of operating, maintenance and constructive work on the P.G.E. Railway between Vancouver and Prince George and receipts for the year of $6,600,000 with $4,000,-000 also required to complete the line from Squamish to Fort

George and provide rolling stock and of $18,000,000 to connect the
P.G.E. with the Edmonton and Dunvegan line of Alberta.   The
Minister of Lands (Mr. Pattullo) reported a revenue for 1918 of
$369,392 and dealt with the work of the Soldier Settlement Board,
the Survey Branch and the various lands allotted to returned sol-
diers.   The Minister of Agriculture (Mr. Oliver for part of 1918
and Mr. Barrow for part of the year) submitted reports from the
Deputy Minister (W. T. McDonald) as to the Horticultural Fruit
Inspection, Plant Pathology and Live-stock Branches, and the
Prairie Markets and Coast Market Commissioners; dealt with appropriations for 1918-19 of $219,684, the work of the Statistics
Branch, the Dairy instructor, Apiary inspection and Poultry instructors; the progress of 62 Women's Institutes with 2,428 members and of 154 Farmers' Institutes.

The Report of the B.C. Workmen's Compensation Board showed,
in 1919, 18,185 accidents from various causes with 277 of them
fatal.   During the year 20,766 cheques for compensation to disabled workmen or their dependents were issued by the Board with
a total amount paid to workmen of $1,403,077.   The payments in
3 years of operation were $3,233,009.   The Advisory Council to the
new Industrial Commissioner was constituted during the year as
follows: A. C. Flumerfelt, Victoria; Nicol Thomson, Vancouver; J.
E. W. Thompson, M.L.A., Grand Forks; Major R. J. Burde, M.C.,
M.L.A., Alberni; F. G. Dawson, Prince Rupert.   The organization
was honourary and up to the close of the year industrial loans to a
total of $422,200 were advised, and authorized by the Minister in
charge, out of $2,767,404 applied for.   Mr. Farris, Minister of
Labour, issued his first Report for Dec. 31st, 1918, and gave elaborate statistics of Provincial trades and industries with a Directory of British Columbia labour organizations; the work of the
new Free Employment Bureau was described with 3,990 applications from employers during 5 months, 3,113 positions filled and
1,659 applicants for work unplaced; the strikes of the year were
reviewed and the work of the Minimum Wage Board analyzed.

This Board was composed of J. D. McNiven (Chairman), Helen
G. MacGill and Thomas Mathews, and held a number of conferences during 1918-19 with various industries and issued a number
of orders, fixing the minimum rates in specific industries to all
female employees of 18 years or over—usually at figures adjusted
to the number of months employed and experience gained and including, during 1919, the laundry, cleaning and dyeing industries
with a rate running from $8 to $12 per week; the fruit and vegetable industry at $14 for a week of 48 hours; manicuring, hair-
dressing and barbering and ushers in theatres, etc., $10 to $13 a
week and the same in general manufacturing industries; in public
house-keeping occupation, $14 per week of 48 hours was allowed
less $5.25 for board and to girls under 18 years $12 a week less $3
for board; telegraph and telephone operators $15 a week with
special conditions as to hours and ages; stenographers, book-keep-

ers, etc., $15 a week or $65 a month with apprentices running from
$11 to $14 for a week of 48 hours, employees in the merchantile industry, $7.50 to $11.00 per week under 18 years, and $12.75 over
that age.

The Conservative Opposition to the Oliver Government was led
in the Legislature by the Hon. W. J. Bowser, K.C., ex-Premier of
the Province, who received during this year the Hon. LL.D. degree
from his *Alma Mater*, Dalhousie University, Halifax, and, also,
was re-elected Leader of his Party. The latter event occurred at a
Provincial Conservative Convention held in Vancouver on Sept.
29-30 with 500 delegates present from all parts of the Province.
H. L. Edmunds presided and there was no opposition to the nomination of Mr. Bowser—Lorne A. Campbell of Rossland, who was
nominated, immediately withdrawing. In his speech of acceptance
Mr. Bowser specified 30 points of policy which he hoped the party
would adopt and the chief of these were duly recorded in Resolutions which may, be briefly summarized as follows: (1) That there
should be no further absolute alienation of the natural resources of
the Province and that the Government should, by royalty or otherwise, retain a portion of future grants for the use of the people;
(2) that Oriental settlers should not be given the franchise on the
same basis as white men; (3) that the Government should remove
the University to its site at Point Grey and provide proper accommodation for the students, that its policy and operation should be
kept free of party politics and given entirely into the hands of the
Governors and Senate, and that the annual grant be increased;
(4) that the Hospitals should receive more Provincial aid and that
grants for roads should be spent on that object and not all on
salaries for officials; (5) that aid be given to encourage systematic
exploration with a view to the discovery of bodies of iron ore and
the ultimate establishment of steel industries; that encouragement
be given to the revival of mineral prospecting in the mountains,
and that the Conservative policy of building roads and trails to
prospects and mines be further enlarged; (6) that the Soldiers'
Moratorium be extended for one year and some form of State life
insurance for disabled men be established; (7) that greater Government assistance be given to ship-building and that agriculture
and the mining industry should receive more Government encouragement and aid.

Other Resolutions urged more equitable taxation, control of
smelter rates and strict enforcement of the school and other laws
then being violated by the Doukhobors. The Convention also declared itself in favour of a measure providing full and equal rights
for women in all matters touching inheritance, homesteads, divorce,
separation and the custody and care of children, and repeal of the
present "inequitable" laws. Other things approved of were the
establishment of Normal Schools in the Interior; a change in the
rule of the road so as to turn to the right instead of the left; the
principle of Mothers' Pensions and conservation of child-life; a

revision of the whole scheme of Education in order to make it of more practical value to the child and the sending of students abroad for perfecting in Technical knowledge.   S. L. Howe of Vancouver was elected President of the Provincial Conservative Association and Capt. George Black Secretary.

The 3rd Session of the 14th Legislature of British Columbia was opened by Lieut.-Governor Sir F. S. Barnard, on Jan. 30th with a Speech from the Throne which reviewed War and Peace conditions and specified certain co-operative arrangements with the Federal Government; stated that a large tract of land had been purchased under the Soldiers' Settlement Act in the Okanagan District with appropriations for development work to be asked for; added that a considerable area of Crown lands had been surveyed and reserved for the purpose of soldier settlement and that provision was being made to acquire homesites within or adjacent to cities, with moneys advanced by the Federal Government for Housing purposes to be utilized to erect dwellings thereon; asserted that the Government had been active in urging upon the Dominion the necessity of completing the contractual obligations of the C.N.R. Railway Co., in respect of unfinished work in British Columbia, with good results accruing; mentioned the continued construction of the P.G.E. Railway, specified an arrangement with the other Western Provinces for the standardization of educational text-books and promised considerable legislation.

The Address was moved by F. W. Anderson of Kamloops and F. A. Pauline of Saanich and passed, after prolonged debate, on Feb. 21st without division.   On Feb. 10th a long Resolution was carried specifying in elaborate terms a scale of assistance to soldiers and dependents which, it was declared, the Dominion Government should grant; another was urged in favour of deporting all alien enemies from the Province and preventing immigration of others into the country to which a Government amendment stated that control of Immigration was a matter of Dominion control and the motion was lost by 27 to 14; a Select Committee was approved to receive and consider and report upon the varied schemes for soldiers and reconstruction; a Resolution by F. W. H. Giolma in favour of a Government guarantee to all returned men, of positions previously held in the Civil Service, was met by a Government amendment approving of all Orders-in-Council issued upon this subject and it was carried by 30 to 13.   Hon. W. J. Bowser, the Conservative leader, moved on Feb. 25th a long Resolution asking for an enquiry into the administration of the Prohibition Act but it was ruled out of order and the Chair upheld by 27 to 11.   A Resolution, carried without division, declared that the Federal War-time arrangement with the United States as to discontinuance of naturalization requirements from American citizens should be abrogated; another motion was approved declaring that the "rule of the road" should be changed to conform with that of contiguous Provinces and States.

On Mch. 11th Mr. Premier Oliver and Hon. J. H. King moved a Resolution of gratitude to the soldiers of the Province, a pledge of care for dependents and a preference for soldiers in public positions; the Opposition asked for a definite expression of practical policy but were ruled out of order and the motion passed. On Mch. 17th R. H. Pooley and Dr. W. O. Rose moved an elaborate Conservative resolution of censure on the Government for action and inaction, policy or lack of it, alleged breaking of promises, unjustifiable increase of taxes and unwise imposition of taxation, P.G.E. policy, etc.; Dr. J. W. McIntosh and G. S. Hanes (Liberals.), in amendment reviewed the charges against the Bowser Government in the P.G.E. matter, criticized the Oliver Government for not investigating these allegations and declared that the Legislature had "little confidence in the Leader of the Administration and less in the Leader óf the Opposition"; the motion was ruled out of order after a heated debate. During the Session a multitude of questions were asked and many facts given as to the P.G.E. Railway and its assumption by the Government; continued efforts were made in Resolutions, or in requests for certain persons to testify before the House and its Committees, or in speeches and references, to reflect upon the late Government in that connection but the House showed no desire to revive the question and the Premier, himself, voted on Feb. 20th against one of the Resolutions; the Select Committee appointed to deal with Reconstruction for the soldiers submitted a series of valuable reports detailing and describing various proposals and methods of procedure and treating of the problems and conditions facing the returned man.

Legislation of the Session included a re-enactment of the Vancouver Island Settlers' Rights Act of 1917 which had been disallowed by the Federal Government; a Better Housing Bill designed to permit the Province to take advantage of the plan of the Federal Government to advance $25,000,000 for a Housing scheme, with British Columbia's share about $1,200,000—the terms being similar to legislation enacted elsewhere except that its operation would at first be confined to returned soldiers, with widows given first attention, and then the crippled or physically unfit men; the Depasturing of Cattle upon Crown Lands dealt with grazing and established a system of regulations with penalties for infraction; Hon. Dr. King had a Bill for the construction of works to prevent the encroachment of rivers upon their banks and to provide for Government action following application from a municipality or group of individuals; a Civil Service Superannuation Bill provided a Fund from which would be deducted 4 per cent. of the salary of the civil servants to be kept to the credit of the latter, and on this twice a year, interest at the rate of five per cent. would be credited by the Minister of Finance with a final superannuation allowance of double the sum which the amount at credit in the Superannuation Fund would earn.

Mr. Oliver's Act for the "Initiation and Approval of Legislation by the Electors'' provided for a Petition as to any Specific Act signed by not less than 25 per cent. of the qualified electors of the Province, presented to the Legislature not later than two weeks after the commencement of any regular Session, and verified by the Speaker as to sufficiency of the signatures. In this case, and if the proposed law was not enacted at the Session at which it was presented, and the Attorney-General did not hold that it was *ultra vires* of the Legislature, the Lieut.-Governor-in-Council must submit the law to a vote of the electors at the next general Election. The Act was passed against strong Conservative opposition—the 2nd reading being 21 to 8. There was, also, a Referendum section to the Bill enabling 15 per cent. of the electors to demand that any Act of a current Session be submitted to the people. If then approved by the electors under above conditions, it would automatically, upon proclamation, become effective; if defeated, it was inoperative. A new Municipal Act was passed which included safeguards for municipal sinking-funds and the provision of an official test of securities in which they could be invested; an amendment to the Poll Tax Act extended its provisions to Chinese engaged in certain industries, such as fisheries; an Act to provide for the marking of eggs was to make it clear that Oriental eggs or cold storage eggs could not be sold unless plainly labelled as such; the Supply Bill providing for an aggregate expenditure for the year on current and capital account of $13,469,914, was also passed.

Another Government measure provided for the guarantee of principal and interest of a loan not exceeding $500,000 to be floated by the University of British Columbia Board for the purpose of carrying on building construction at Point Grey. General approval was expressed for an Act creating a Department of Industry for the administration of which the Government was to set aside $2,000,000 to be raised by a domestic loan and to be used in the initiation of industries in the Province in which returned soldiers would be given preferential employment; operation was to be under the Minister of Mines but no separate Department would be created at once. A Public Utilities Commission, with one Commissioner, was created by special Act with powers of supervision over public utilities, their organization, conduct of business, fixing of rates, enforcement of improvements; with appeal from decisions to the Court of Appeal and the definition of such utilities a very wide one. A Library Act was intended to provide a library service for every part of the Province, and to co-ordinate the library work by means of co-operation and Government aid.

The Budget Speech was delivered by Hon. John Hart on Mch. 12th who dealt with the year of Mch. 31st, 1918, which showed a Revenue of $8,882,846 and Expenditures of $8,399,649 with a surplus of $483,196. As to the balance of the year up to Dec. 31st, the 9 months revenue was $9,242,295 and expenditures $7,128,937 with $1,094,663 expended on capital account or a total surplus of $1,019,249. There was on Mch. 31st, 1918, a Public Debt of $23,-

071,936. For the soldiers Mr. Hart stated that funds were needed in order to spend $1,500,000 on productive public works; $500,000 in connection with the Soldiers' Settlement Act; $500,000 on irrigation works, and $1,500,000 on a Housing policy. Later figures showed a still more prosperous financial return for Mch. 31st, 1919, with a Revenue of $10,931,279 and Expenditures of $9,887,744 or a surplus of $1,043,000 and capital expenditures of $2,224,541. Special items of expenditure were Agriculture $228,798, Education $1,831,622 and Public Works $1,851,881. The Liabilities of the Province on Mch. 31st, 1919, were $27,826,561 and the capital Assets were stated at $12,462,701 held by Dominion Government, Sinking funds of $4,886,273 making, with lesser sums, a total of $21,222,394; to this latter total the Government added estimated values of Provincial buildings, roads, bridges, and other properties of $20,392,-363 and showed, therefore, $13,788,196 of excess in Assets over Liabilities; there were also indirect Liabilities or Railway guarantees of $63,902,863. On a $3,000,000, 5½ per cent. issue of 20-year bonds, the Province on Mch. 3rd realized 99·32. The Legislature was prorogued on Mch. 29th.

BRITISH COLUMBIA INCIDENTS OF THE YEAR.

Jan. 22nd.—Chief Justice Gordon Hunter declared in judgment rendered that the Royal Commission appointed by the Provincial Government to investigate the illegal traffic in intoxicants was issued without lawful authority.

Jan. 22nd.—Lieut.-Col. James Slater, D.S.O., was appointed Prohibition Commissioner in succession to W. C. Findlay, dismissed for scandalous abuse of his position—including illegal importation and sale of hundreds of cases of liquor.

Feb. 22nd.—At Revelstoke the Boards of Trade of Eastern British Columbia unanimously passed a Resolution asking for the separation of British Columbia into two Provinces with the Cascade Mountains as a dividing line.

Apr. 22nd.—Mayor Gale of Vancouver stated that there were from 750 to 1,000 general factories in the Province, employing about 18,000 hands with a yearly output of $30,000,000, while the Province imported $20,000,000.

May 3rd.—Peter Veregin, the Doukhobor leader, stated at Grand Forks that their community holdings in Canada were worth $2,000,000 and that they held 40,000 acres in British Columbia and Saskatchewan.

June 10th.—W. C. Findlay, formerly Prohibition Commissioner, for the Province, was sentenced by Mr. Justice Gregory to two years' imprisonment in the Penitentiary, as guilty of abuse of trust.

Oct. 7-9th.—The B.C. Union if Municipalities met at North Vancouver, heard a number of important addresses, passed varied Resolutions and elected J. Loutitt, North Vancouver, as President.

Nov. 3rd.—Hon. J. W. deB. Farris, Attorney General, reviewed at length, in a Nelson speech, the history of Prohibition in the Province, went extensively into the Findlay case and subsequent developments, referred to the great volume of liquor being sold through the drug stores and the Government vendor, on prescriptions, and frankly admitted that conditions were bad—in respect to the volume of prescriptions issued, to illicit trade in liquor, and to the effects of this trade.

Dec. 21st.—The Attorney-General, (Mr. Farris) stated that in the eight months from March to October, inclusive, doctors in British Columbia had issued 188,120 prescriptions for liquor—one Doctor writing 4,000 prescriptions in a month.

The North-West Territories. The million and a quarter square miles of the North-West Territories included in 1919 all Canadian lands and islands north of the Western Provinces and east of the Yukon. Agriculture was confined to a small loop of warmer climatic region extending northwards down the Mackenzie. Internal communication was by dog team in winter, by canoe in summer; external, by steamer 1,400 miles from Fort Smith to Fort McPherson, or by Hudson Bay to Chesterfield Inlet, whence inland navigation was possible for 550 miles by the Thelon. A line drawn from Churchill to the Mackenzie Delta divided the ''barren lands'' from a wood-producing area.

The surface evidence of minerals was abundant and evidences of a great oil field numerous; coal had been discovered along the Mackenzie and on Arctic islands and copper was common along the Arctic shores and on the Government Reserves of mineral rights near the Coppermine River; bituminous shales and limestone, tar and salt springs occurred in the Mackenzie Basin. The lakes teemed with whitefish and trout, the rivers with salmon; cod, seal, and walrus were found in Hudson Bay and the Baffin Bay whaling industry continued to be successful. The Mackenzie Basin was the best fur region of North America with herds of caribou and many moose. The musk-ox was specially protected and Reserves set apart for this valuable animal and for future herds of reindeer.

The Territory of the Yukon. This region was known, economically, as the scene of the Klondike gold discoveries and production of $200,000,000; to the traveller it was interesting as containing Mt. Logan, the highest mountain of North America and many magnificent glaciers. Communication with Dawson, the chief city, was maintained either by the Lynn canal and White Horse railway route or by the Yukon river through Alaska. Though the production had dropped steadily from that of 1900 with its record of $22,275,000, minerals other than gold, especially copper, silver and coal, promised well in 1919 while antimony, bismuth, and platinum had been found. Individual placer claims had by this time been absorbed by corporations and the large amounts of capital invested in hydro-electric dredges, hydraulic washing and water-carrying ditches were proof of the great importance of the Territory in professional opinion. The production of gold in 1918 was $2,248,398 and in 1919 $1,684,048. Only 1,000 tons of coal were mined in 1919 as compared with 3,000 tons in 1918. Of copper ore, 1,147 tons were shipped in 1919, all from the district adjoining White Horse, as compared with 3,057 tons in 1918. The Gold Commissioner in this year was G. P. McKenzie and the Comptroller G. A. Jeckell.

CANADIAN OBITUARY FOR 1919*

Name.	Particulars.	Place of Death.	Date.
Allan, Andrew Alexander...	Allan Steamships Co.	Montreal	Feb. 12
Angers, K.C., LL.D., Sir Auguste Réal	ex-Lieut.-Governor of Quebec; one-time Provincial Premier	Montreal	Apr. 16
Aylesworth, Major Alan Featherston	95th Battalion C.E.F.	Barrie	Aug. 24
Beamish, John	Father of Pythianism in the British Empire	St. John	Oct. 6
Belcher, C.M.G., Lieut.-Col. Robert	Prominent Militia Man	Calgary	Feb. 10
Benson, D.D., Rev. Manley.	Veteran Minister of the Methodist Church	Toronto	July 20
Blackburn, Walter J.	President and Gen.-Mgr. London *Free Press*	London	Jan. 1
Blaine, Col. Arbuthnot	Well-known Militia officer .	St. John	Oct. 19
Blais, Rt. Rev. André......	Bishop of Rimouski	Rimouski	Jan. 22
Booth, George	Manufacturer, and a founder of the Can. National Exhibition	Toronto	Feb. 12
Boulton, Frederick Campbell Melfort	Well-known Stock Broker ..	Toronto	Feb. 2
Boyle, Arthur	Former Dominion Member for Monck	Niagara Falls ...	Dec. 10
Brown, Hon. George William	Veteran Politician of North-West Territories; ex-Lieut.-Governor of Saskatchewan	Regina	Feb. 17
Buck, M.D., M.R.C.S., Anson	Well-known Physician	Palermo	Apr. 18
Burke, Edmund	Prominent Toronto Architect	Toronto	Jan. 2
Campbell, M.D., Donald Alexander	Prominent Physician	Halifax	Jan. 6
Campbell, Prof. Glenn H. ..	Professor of Latin, McMaster University	Toronto	Dec. -
Carney, ex-M.P., Michael ...	Prominent Merchant and Politician	Halifax	Feb. 2
Cartwright, K.C., John Robinson	Deputy Attorney-General for Ontario	Toronto	Sept. 10
Chipman, Lieut.-Col. John DeWolf	Prominent Business and Militia man	Toronto	Sept. 19
Cochrane, M.P., Hon. Frank.	One-time Minister of Railways and Canals	Ottawa	Sept. 22
Colcock, N. B.	Agent-General for Ontario in London	London	Apr. 1
Comstock, William Henry ..	Well-known business man ..	Brockville	Mch. 9
Orerar, Mrs. P. D.	Noted philanthropist and war worker	Hamilton	May 20
Cross, Hon. Alexander George	Justice of the Court of King's Bench, Quebec ...	Rideau Lake, Ont.	Aug. 18
Davis, D.D., Very Rev. Evans	Dean of Huron	London	Mch. 17
Detweiler, Daniel B.	Business man and promoter of The Great Water-Ways Association	Kitchener	Apr. 18
De Varennes, M.L.C., Hon. Ernest	Well-known French-Canadian	Quebec	Jan. 8
Dewey, O. E.	Freight Traffic Mgr., G.T.R.	Atlantic City ...	May 15
Douglas, William James	Gen. Mgr. of Toronto *Mail and Empire*	Toronto	Oct. 19
Drummond, George Edward.	Prominent Business man and financier	London, Eng. ..	Feb. 17
Elliot, Dr. Charles S.	Well-known medical practitioner	Toronto	
Ewing, K.C., William A. ...	Well-known barrister	St. John	Aug. 21
Fisher, M.L.A., Hon. Charles Wellington	Speaker of the Alberta Legislature	Edmonton	May 4
Forget, ex-M.P., Sir Rodolphe	Banker, financier, politician.	Montreal	Feb. 19
Foster, Lady Adelaide (Davies)	Wife of Rt. Hon. Sir George Foster	Ottawa	Sept. 17
Fullerton, K.C., James S. ..	ex-Toronto Corporation Counsel	Toronto	Dec. ..
German, B.A., M.A., D.D., Rev. John Ferguson	Leader in the Methodist Church	Toronto	Dec. 18

*Note.—Owing to error in a despatch to Toronto papers, the death was wrongfully recorded in 1918 Obituary of Hon. Jules Allard, Quebec Minister of Lands and Forests.

[798]

Name.	Particulars.	Place of Death.	Date.
Gibbons, George Sutton ...	Well-known Lawyer of London	Toronto	Oct. 26
Gould, Charles Henry	Librarian at McGill University for 30 years	Montreal	July 30
Graham, K.C., Bruce Thompson	Eminent Criminal Lawyer..	Halifax	Sept. 27
Gribble, Rev. Canon John ..	Well-known Anglican Clergyman	Toronto	Sept. 24
Gundy, William Pearson ...	Well-known business man; member War Purchasing Commission	Ottawa	May 20
Gurney, W. Cromwell	Prominent business man ...	Toronto	Sept. 17
Hamilton, D.D., D.C.L., Most Rev. Charles	Former Anglican Archbishop of Ottawa and Metropolitan of Ontario	La Jolla, Cal'f'a.	Mch. 14
Hanna, M.L.A., K.C., Hon. William John	President Imperial Oil Co. and First Food Comptroller for Canada	Augusta, Georgia.	Mch. 20
Hargraft, Alexander R. ...	Prominent member Winnipeg Grain Exchange	Winnipeg	Aug. 29
Harman, S. Bruce	Well-known Insurance Man.	Toronto	Oct. 12
Harper, B.A., Ph.D., John Murdoch	Canadian Educationalist and Author	Quebec	Mch. 1
Harris, C.M.G., Robert	President of the Royal Canadian Academy	Montreal	Feb. 27
Harris, B.Sc., William Dale.	ex-President Montreal Terminals Railway	Ottawa	Sept. 28
Haselwood, D.D., Rev. James H.	Prominent Methodist Minister	Toronto	Apr. 10
Hebden, Edward Feild	General Manager Merchants' Bank of Canada, 1905-16.	Ottawa	Sept. 30
Holmes, Hon. Simon Hugh.	Former Premier of N.S. ...	Halifax	Oct. 14
Humphrey, Robert B.	Well-known business man .	St. John	Sept. 6
Hunter, Rev. John E.	Evangelist of international fame	Toronto	Mch. 17
Innis, Peter	Former Gen.-Mgr. of Windsor Annapolis Railway ...	Kentville	Aug. 27
Irving, Lieut.-Col. Henry Erskine	Lawyer and well-known Militia man	Toronto	July 4
Johnston, K.C., Ebenezer Forsyth Blackie	Well-known criminal lawyer, Vice-President Royal Bank of Canada	Toronto	Jan. 29
Kenny, John A.	One of the founders of the Winnipeg *Free Press* ...	Winnipeg	Oct. 19
Labatt, Col. Robert Hodgetts	Commanded 4th Battalion, C.E.F.	Hamilton	Feb. 7
Lacoste, Lady Marie (Globensky)	Wife of Sir Alexandre Lacoste	Montreal	Dec. 11
Lafferty, Lieut.-Col. Frank D.	Superintendent Dominion Arsenals	Quebec	Dec. 29
Laurier, P.C., G.C.M.G., K.C., LL.D., D.C.L., Rt. Hon. Sir Wilfrid	Prime Minister of Canada 1896-1911	Ottawa	Feb. 17
Le Blanc, M.L.C., Hon. Isadore	Politician and ship-owner..	Arichat, N.S. ...	June 26
Le Blanc, ex-M.L.A., ex-M.P., Hon. O. J.	ex-Member of New Brunswick Government	St. Mary, N.B. ..	Dec. 14
Lefroy, K.C., Augustus Henry Fraser	Editor Canadian *Law Times*, Professor of Roman Law, University of Toronto ...	Ottawa	Mch. 7
Leonard, James W.	ex-Gen. Superintendent C.P. R.	Brampton	Apr. 28
Linscott, Rev. Dr. Thomas S.	Well-known Publisher	Quebec	Mch. 1
Loucks, Rev. Canon	Well-known Anglican clergyman	Kingston	July 20
Lyle, D.D., Rev. Samuel ...	ex-Moderator Presbyterian General Assembly	Hamilton	Jan. 29
MacColl, Maj. Allan Evan..	Well-known physician, M.H. O. 15th Battalion	Belleville	May 5
MacGillivray, Rev. A. H. ..	President Hamilton Ministerial Association	Hamilton	Nov. 15
McDougald, C.M.G., D.S.O., John	Commissioner of Customs, Ottawa	Halifax	June 14
M'Keever, M.C., D.S.O., Maj. Andrew Edward	Noted Canadian Aviator in the Great War	Toronto	Dec. 26
McKenna, LL.D., James Andrew	Journalist and Member of Indian Commission	Victoria	May 5

Name.	Particulars.	Place of Death.	Date.
McLaren, Hon. Peter	Canadian Senator and Lumberman	Perth	May 23
McMann, Thomas	Prominent Orangeman	Maple Creek	Apr. 15
McNaught, C.M.G., William Kirkpatrick	Member Hydro-Electric Power Commission; Hon. Colonel in Militia	Toronto	Feb. 2
Macdonald, Hon. Augustine Colin	Lieut.-Governor of P.E. Island	Charlottetown	July 16
Mackay, B.D., Ven. Archdeacon Alfred William	Secretary of Provincial Synod of Ontario	Ottawa	Nov. 21
Malloch, B.A., M.D., F.R.C.S., Lieut.-Col. William John Ogilvie	Eminent surgeon during the War	Toronto	Feb. 18
Marshall, ex-M.P., Joseph Henry	County Registrar of East Middlesex	London, Ont.	June 6
Matthews, Wilmot Delour	Eminent financier, ex-President Toronto Board of Trade, Vice-President Dominion Bank	Toronto	May 24
Matthews, James Thorold	Vice-President Matthews Steamship Co.	Toronto	May 19
Meredith (U.E.L.) Mrs. Edmund Jarvis	Daughter of late Sheriff William Botsford Jarvis and grand-daughter of Chief Justice William Dummer Powell (89 years of age).	Ottawa	Sept. 28
Mickle, Hon. Charles Julius	County Court Judge and former Provincial Secretary of Manitoba	Minnedosa	Nov. 9
Murray, Rev. Dr. James	Well-known Presbyterian Clergyman	Toronto	Dec. 18
Neville, K.C., Rufus Shorey	Well-known lawyer	Toronto	Nov. 15
Northgraves, Rev. George Richard	One-time Editor Catholic Record	London	Apr. 26
Osler, Bart., M.D., F.R.S., Sir William	Noted Canadian Physician and Regius Professor of Medicine at Oxford	Oxford	Dec. 29
Paterson, D.D., Rev. Charles Gordon	Well-known clergyman and civic worker	Winnipeg	Aug. 1
Peters, K.C., Hon. Frederick	ex-Premier of P.E. Island	Prince Rupert	July 29
Price, D.S.O., M.C., Lieut. Evan Edward	Distinguished soldier	Toronto	Sept. 11
Ramsay, J.P., F.S.A., William	Prominent in Philanthropic business and financial circles	Scotland	June 17
Read, M.P., Capt. Joseph	Well-known P.E.I. politician	Ottawa	Apr. 5
Reeve, B.A., M.D., LL.D., Richard Andrews	Former Dean of the Faculty of Medicine, University of Toronto	Toronto	Jan. 28
Richardson, Richard Thomas	Well-known Agriculturist	Ottawa	Dec. 26
Robertson, D.Sc., Prof. John D.	Presbyterian Educationalist.	Toronto	Sept. 22
Robertson, J. P.	Provincial Librarian of Manitoba	Los Angeles	Apr. 11
Robertson, William	Prominent business man	Halifax	Apr. 30
Robinson, Hiram	Prominent Lumber merchant	Ottawa	Sept. 9
Roy, Monsigneur Emile	Vicar-General of Montreal	Atlantic City	Apr. 7
Eyrie, William	Well-known business man and philanthropist	Toronto	Nov. 10
Scolefield, Ethelbert Olaf Stuart	Provincial Librarian and Archivist	Victoria	Dec. 24
Seagram, ex-M.P., Joseph Emm	Noted Horseman and Politician	Waterloo	Aug. 18
Seath, M.A., LL.D., John	Superintendent of Education for Ontario	Toronto	Mch. 17
Sellar, Robert	Editor Canadian Gleaner	Huntington	Nov. 30
Sherwood, O.S.A., A.R.C.A., William Albert	Well-known artist	Toronto	Dec. 5
Small, K.C., John T.	Well-known lawyer	Pinehurst, N.C.	Jan. 30
Smith, ex-M.L.A., Charles Napier	Journalist and Liberal Politician	Saulte Ste. Marie	Oct. 29
Somerville, Rev. Dr. John	Treasurer of Presbyterian Church in Canada	Toronto	May 31
*Steele, C.B., K.C.M.G., M.V.O., Gen. Sir Samuel Benfeld	Commanding Canadian and British forces at Shornecliffe	London, Eng.	Jan. 30
Stimson, Lieut.-Col. George A.	Prominent bond dealer and one-time officer commanding the Grenadiers	Toronto	Dec. 4

*Note.—Death recorded in error in 1918 Obituary, Page 751.

Name.	Particulars.	Place of Death.	Date.
Stirrett, Archibald Campbell.	B.C. Manager of Credit-Foncier	Vancouver	Nov. 12
Strathy, Henry Seton	A leading banker and financier	Toronto	Apr. 26
Studholme. M.L.A., Allan	Well-known Labour member for East Hamilton since 1916	Hamilton	July 28
Sumner, T. W.	One-time Provincial School Inspector	Paris, Ont.	Aug. 2
Summerby, William J.	Agent-General for New Brunswick in London	St. John	Nov. 20
Talbot, ex-M.L.A., ex-M.P., Hon. Peter	Senator of Canada	Lacombe, Alta.	....
Taylor, ex-M.P., Hon. George	Senator of Canada	Ottawa	Mch. 26
Treble, Dr. Charles Edward.	X-Ray Specialist	Toronto	Oct. 28
Trenholme, Hon. Norman William	Judge of the Court of King's Bench and Dean of the Faculty of Law, McGill University	Montreal	June 25
Van Wart, T. S. G.	Prominent Western Liberal.	Toronto	Nov. 21
Walsh, Rev. Canon	Well-known Anglican Clergyman and Orangeman	Brampton	Sept. 28
Warman, D.S.O., M.C., Capt. Olive W.	Brilliant air fighter	Edmonton	May 12
Waterous, Julius E.	Well-known Manufacturer...	Brantford	Jan. 12
Weddell, Robert	Well-known Contractor and financier	Trenton	Sept. 9
Wilson, Lieut.-Col. Robert	X-Ray Specialist and Head of Department, Electric Therapenty, Granville (London) Hospital	Toronto	Nov. 1
Windeyer, Lieut.-Col. R. C..	Well-known Militia man	Toronto	May 31
Wright, Alexander Whyte...	Vice-Chairman Workmen's Compensation Board	Trenton	June 12

SUPPLEMENT

Canadian Finances, Resources, Business
Annual Reports and Addresses

Windsor Station and Head Office of the Canadian Pacific Railway, Montreal

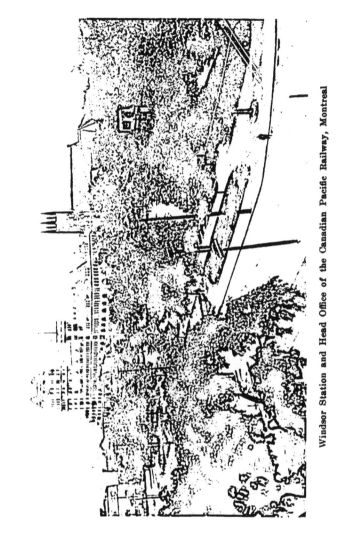

Windsor Station and Head Office of the Canadian Pacific Railway, Montreal

A GREAT CANADIAN INSTITUTION

ANNUAL ADDRESS BY PRESIDENT E. W. BEATTY

AND

REPORTS OF THE COMPANY

THE CANADIAN PACIFIC RAILWAY*

1st Annual Address of E. W. Beatty, K.C., as President of the Company, May 7, 1919. The results of the year's operations were, on the whole, and under the conditions which existed, satisfactory, notwithstanding the shrinkage in the net earnings of $12,043,630, due to the extraordinary increase in wage scales and cost of materials of all descriptions. Over seventy-seven per cent. of the total increase in operating expenses was due to increases in wages alone. The volume, both of freight and passenger traffic, decreased in comparison with 1917, the increase in gross earnings of $5,148,363 being due to increases in rates granted in March and July of last year. The fact that notwithstanding the heavy increases in the cost of operation there was a surplus after payment of all charges and dividends, is another satisfactory evidence of the foresight and wisdom of the Shareholders in having approved substantial expenditures in previous years, which undoubtedly permitted the operations of the Company to be carried on with a cheapness which would not have been possible had such adequate facilities not been provided.

A conspicuous example of the results of such foresight is found in the difference in the cost of rolling stock acquired during the years 1911 to 1914, and the approximate market value of an equivalent amount if required to be purchased in 1918. The rolling stock purchased during the former years, if required to be furnished at the 1918 prices, would have represented an increased cost of approximately $96,000,000. After four years of war, and the existence at times of the most severe climatic conditions, I am happy to say that the physical condition of your property is excellent, and it will not require more than usual maintenance expenditures to ensure its usual efficiency. The results of the operations of the three months subsequent to the conclusion of the fiscal year have been disappointing, but not unexpectedly so in view of the falling off of general traffic during the months of February and March and the inevitable heavy costs of maintenance and operation due to high wages and the high prices of materials. In view of the

*Note.—For a History of the C.P.R. see Supplement to The Canadian Annual Review for 1911; for Lord Shaughnessy's last address as President see 1918 Supplement.

uncertain conditions which succeeded the conclusion of hostilities and the need of providing as much employment as possible, your Directors did not think it wise to make drastic reductions in the number of men employed by the Company, and the shops of the Company have been maintained at full pressure, always on necessary work, but in some cases on work which might have been postponed if the general conditions had warranted it.

Your Directors are of the opinion that a reasonable amount of additional branch line construction should be gone on with as soon as conditions warrant, and the necessary statutory authority is obtained. Resolutions will be submitted for your approval for the construction of the lines which are most urgently required. In this connection, I should point out that in the matter of railway construction the country is faced with a condition quite unprecedented in the recent history of Canada, in that the National Railways and your Company are the only large Companies with resources sufficient to enable them to provide additional railway facilities to any substantial extent. Serious and continuing blunders in railway policy have resulted in the Government being required to assume the ownership at present of 11,400 miles of railway, with the prospect of the acquisition of an additional 6,400 miles. When this acquisition has been accomplished, the principal competing systems in Canada will be your Company and the Canadian National Railways.

I have no apprehension as to the ability of your Company, with its splendid facilities and equipment and loyal and efficient officers and men, to obtain a fair share of the traffic and to handle it expeditiously and well. I have no fear of Government ownership, but Government ownership apparently has some fear of private competition under equal conditions. It has recently been found necessary to give the National Railways privileges in the matter of construction of railways not enjoyed by private Companies and to exempt them from complying in other respects with the existing laws respecting railways. I sincerely trust that this policy of making one law for the National Railways and one for the Canadian Pacific and other private enterprises will neither be continued nor extended, because nothing would, in my opinion, be calculated to destroy confidence in Canadian railway enterprise more than a policy which would confer exclusive and peculiar rights on the National Railways designed to make the competitive conditions unequal.

The subject of Government ownership has received much attention recently, but not nearly as much as the importance of the subject justifies. Notwithstanding our previous experience and that of the United States and Great Britain, Government ownership and operation of railways is to be attempted on a large scale. The situation is full of danger which cannot be avoided or even minimized except by a rigorously independent and non-political administration, which is at least difficult of establishment under our system of Government. This fact must, however, be obvious, that in no other way can the people of Canada obtain a correct appreciation of the results of Government operation of the Systems which are or which may hereafter come into its possession, than by their being administered in strict accordance with the laws of the country under which other Companies have to operate, by their financial and accounting methods being made as precise and as accurate as the law now requires of private Corporations, and by the exact financial results being submitted to Parliament each year.

Different views may conceivably be held as to the wisdom of public ownership and operation of railways. My own views are sufficiently well known not to require repetition, but the fact is public ownership is already here, and experience only will show whether the difficulties I have mentioned in securing efficient and non-political administration can be overcome, and the country receive an adequate service at a minimum of loss. I am satisfied the Government recognize these difficulties and that a sincere and determined effort will be made to meet the situation. It would seem, however, to be obviously wise that the assumption of further obligations should at least be deferred until the practicability of Government administration, or administration under the aegis of the Government (which is quite inseparable from Government ownership) has been demonstrated. In the end, the burden of the enterprises must be borne by the people, and the people are entitled to know whether the method of administration provided and the results of that administration are such as warrant their approval of the continuance or extension of them in the interests of Canada.

The returns from sales of land during the fiscal year just closed have been the largest in the history of your Company, and it is a matter of great gratification to your Directors, as no doubt it is to the Shareholders, that the incessant activities of the Company in the matter of sale and colonization of lands and the promotion of immigration to Canada has had such far-reaching and beneficial results. As a direct consequence of the efforts of the Company, more than 21,000,000 acres of land have been sold to settlers, and more than half a million settlers induced to come to Canada and settle in the Canadian West. The contribution to the exchequer of the country has been thereby increased by many millions. With return to peace conditions I should expect a considerable increase in immigration, and with the vigorous development of the country's natural resources and the necessary extension of the markets of Canada we have every reason for confidence in the future prosperity of the country, even though the present year may be one during which the commercial expansion may be only moderate.

It would not be proper that I should conclude my remarks without a personal reference to your former President, Lord Shaughnessy, who retired from the Presidency during the last fiscal year. It is perhaps not necessary that I should reiterate the inestimable value of his services to the Company from the beginning of his connection with it, but more particularly during the last twenty years, during which time he occupied the position of Chief Executive Officer. It will, however, be gratifying to the Shareholders to know that, great as has been the success of Lord Shaughnessy's administration of the Company's affairs, viewed from a purely commercial standpoint, greater still has been the influence and force of his personal character and ideals and his high sense of duty on the officers and men of the Company, with the result that the Canadian Pacific enjoys an esprit and an ambition for efficiency among all ranks which I venture to think is unequalled, and certainly not excelled, in any corporation in the world. It must be a source of great gratification to Lord Shaughnessy to know, on his retirement from the active work of the Presidency to the more advisory work of Chairman of the Company, that not only was his administration extraordinarily successful, and that he leaves the property in excellent physical condition, but that he created during his tenure of office an organization the ambition of which, and every member of it, is to utilize that property in the closest co-operation and to the full extent of their powers for the benefit of the country and the Shareholders.

Director's 39th Annual Report for the Year ending Dec. 31, 1919.   The working expenses for the year amounted to 81·39 per cent. of the gross earnings, and the net earnings to 18·61 per cent., as compared with 78·10 per cent. and 21·90 per cent. respectively in 1918. The gross earnings of your transportation system during the fiscal year under review exceeded those of any previous year in the history of the Company, and exceeded the gross earnings of 1918 by $19,391,362, but the net earnings were less by $1,569,351. This large addition of $20,960,713 to working expenses is due to the great advance in wages and the increased cost of fuel and other materials. Your Directors cannot hold out any hope of substantial relief for some time to come from these high costs which are reflected so strongly in the operating expenses of the Company, but every effort is being made to offset the effect on your revenues by economy in operation and the extension of the Company's freight and passenger business. It is not to be expected, however, that any normal increase in business can possibly equal the extraordinary increase in wage and other costs which all railway companies have experienced during the past two years.

The sales of agricultural land in the year were 681,763 acres for $13,668,443, being an average of $20.05 per acre. Included in this area were 80,795 acres of irrigated land which brought $52.53 per acre, so that the average price for the balance was $15.68 per acre. There were no sales of Four per cent. Consolidated Debenture Stock, Four per cent. Preference Stock, or other capital securities during the year. The late granting of the necessary statutory authority, combined with difficulty in securing labour and the early setting in of winter in the West, prevented extensive construction during the year of branch line mileage which you authorised at the last annual meeting. Your Directors are of the opinion that reasonable additional construction should be' gone on with as conditions warrant, and your authority will be asked for proceeding with the construction of the following lines and for the issue and sale of a sufficient amount of Four per cent. Consolidated Debenture Stock to meet the expenditure, namely :—

Wymark-Archive Branch, 25 miles.
Rosetown South Branch, 45 miles.
Weyburn-Lethbridge Branch from Altawan to Manyberries, 35 miles.
Moose Jaw Southwesterly Branch from Consul Southeasterly, mileage 35 to 60.
Moose Jaw Southwesterly Branch from Assiniboia Southwesterly, 30 miles.
Leader Southerly Branch, 50 miles.
Duchess or Rosemary North Branch, 34 miles.
Cutknife to Whitford Lake Branch, 40 miles.
An extension of the Swift Current Northwesterly Branch from Empress Northwesterly, a distance of 20 miles.
An extension of the Swift Current Northwesterly Branch from Sedgewick to Vegreville, 54 miles.

Your Directors appreciate that the construction of the above lines can only be proceeded with gradually in view of the probable shortage of labour available for such purposes, but they deem it desirable to obtain your authority in order that the work may be gone on with from time to time as circumstances permit. In order to facilitate the economic handling of traffic in and out of Winnipeg your Directors think it desirable to double-track the line extending from Winnipeg to Molson, and, for the purpose of relieving the main line of pressure of traffic during grain shipping seasons, that capital expenditure should be made on the Bassano Branch, extending from Bassano to Java, with the view of raising it to the standard of the Company's main line, and thus permitting the expeditions and cheap handling of grain and other traffic from points west of Bassano. The estimated total cost of these works will be about $2,000,000, but in the opinion of your Directors the heavy present and prospective traffic in these districts amply warrants the outlay. In anticipation of your confirmation your Directors authorized capital appropriations, in addition to those approved at the last annual meeting for 1919, aggregating $3,359,-000, and subject to your approval have authorized expenditures on capital account during the present year of $9,613,353. Of this amount the principal items are :—

Replacement and enlargement of structures in permanent form	$1,267,144
Additional stations, roundhouses, freight sheds and shops, and extensions to existing buildings	2,009,166
Tie plates, rail anchors, ballasting, ditching and miscellaneous betterments	1,113,599
Replacement of rail in main and branch line tracks with heavier section	979,493
Additional terminal and side-track accommodation	442,363
New coal dock at Fort William Terminals	871,000
Proposed new station and yard changes at Trois Riviéres	500,000
Improvements in connection with Telegraph Service	575,860
British Columbia Coast Service	185,000
Mechanical Department, machinery at various shops	363,236

The balance of the amount is required for miscellaneous works to improve facilities over the whole system and effect operating economies.

Your Directors are making provision for obtaining the following necessary additions to your Company's equipment, namely: 3 dining cars, 43 sleeping cars, 67 air dump cars, 2,500 sixty-ton box cars, 500 refrigerator cars, at a total cost of approximately $13,162,000. During the course of the year the following Steamships were disposed of, namely S.S. Prince George, S.S. Princess Margaret, S.S. Princess May, S.S. Virginian, S.S. Monmouth. The S.S. War Peridot and War Beryl, having a dead-weight tonnage of 10,500 tons each, were purchased.

You will be asked to approve By-law No. 91, repealing By-law of the same number, naming officers authorized to prepare and issue Tariffs of Tolls pursuant to the provisions of the Railway Act of Canada. The lease of the Nakusp and Slocan Railway, extending from Nakusp to Three Forks, with branches to Sandon and White Water, and having an aggregate mileage of 48·47 miles, which was executed in 1895 and under which the railway of that Company was leased to your Company for a period of 25 years from July, 1895, will expire in July of the present year. Your Directors will therefore submit for your approval a new lease of the railway to this Company for a period of ninety-nine years on the usual terms. Appreciating the vital importance to Canada of the success of the Victory Loan of 1919, your Company subscribed to $20,000,000, of which $14,000,000 was taken for the Company's Special Investment Fund.

The Consolidated Mining and Smelting Company, in which your Company has a substantial direct interest through its holdings of Bonds and Stock and upon the success of whose undertaking the prosperity of Southern British Columbia and the consequent traffic for your railway depend to a marked degree, will require during the present year additional sums for needed extensions and additions to its plant. In anticipation of your consent your Directors have decided to advance such amounts as may be required pending the making of capital issues or other permanent financial arrangements by the Consolidated Company. Your Directors regret to report the death on the 24th of May last of Mr. Wilmot D. Matthews, of Toronto, who had been a Director of the Company for thirty-one years, and whose advice and counsel have always been of the utmost value to his associates on the Board. During the year the Hon. James Dunsmuir, of Victoria, resigned as a Director. The Hon. William J. Shaughnessy was elected to succeed the Hon. James Dunsmuir, and Sir John C. Eaton was elected to the Board to fill the vacancy created by the death of Mr. Matthews. The undermentioned Directors will retire from office at the approaching Annual Meeting. They are eligible for re-election: Sir John C. Eaton, Mr. Grant Hall, Sir Vincent Meredith, Bart., Sir Augustus M. Nanton.

For the Directors,

E. W. BEATTY,
President.

MONTREAL, March 15th, 1920.

The accounts of the Company for the year ended December 31st, 1919, show the following results:—

Gross Earnings	$176,929,060.00
Working Expenses	143,996,023.58
Net Earnings	$ 32,933,036.42
Deduct Fixed Charges	10,161,509.77
Surplus	$ 22,771,526.65
Contribution to Pension Fund	500,000.00
	$ 22,271,526.65

From this there has been charged a half-yearly dividend on Preference Stock of 2 per cent., paid October 1st, 1919 .... $ 1,613,638.42

And three quarterly dividends on Ordinary Stock of 1¾ per cent. each, paid June 30th, 1919, October 1st, 1919, and December 31st, 1919 .... 13,650,000.00

15,263,638.42

$ 7,007,888.23

From this there has been declared a second half-yearly dividend on Preference Stock of 2 per cent. payable April 1st, 1920 .... $1,613,638.42

And a fourth quarterly dividend on Ordinary Stock of 1¾ per cent., payable April 1st, 1920. 4,550,000.00

6,163,638.42

Leaving net surplus for the year .... $ 844,249.81
(which amount has been placed in reserve to meet special taxes imposed by the Dominion Government)

In addition to the above dividends on Ordinary Stock, three per cent. was paid from Special Income.

GENERAL BALANCE SHEET, DECEMBER 31st, 1919

ASSETS

PROPERTY INVESTMENT:
Railway, Rolling Stock Equipment and Lake and River Steamers. $546,458,756.20

OCEAN AND COASTAL STEAMSHIPS, Exhibit "A" 29,894,172.43

ACQUIRED SECURITIES (COST):
Exhibit "B" 124,339,836.18

ADVANCES TO CONTROLLED PROPERTIES IND INSURANCE PREMIUMS .. 8,065,575.66

INVESTMENTS AND AVAILABLE RESOURCES:
(Including amount held in trust for 6% Note Certificates, $58,461,538.37)

Deferred Payments on Lands and Townsites	$66,659,982.43
Imperial and Dominion Government Securities..	37,702,580.56
Provincial and Municipal Securities	2,031,721.29
Debenture Stock loaned to Imperial Government	40,000,000.00
Miscellaneous Investments, Exhibit "C," Cost.	31,762,214.85
Assets in Lands and Properties, Exhibit "D" ..	95,211,488.66
Cash	2,969,683.12

276,337,570.91

WORKING ASSETS:

Material and Supplies on Hand	$21,990,868.65
Agents' and Conductors' Balances	3,618,072.48
Net Traffic Balances	809,897.19
Imperial, Dominion and United States Governments, Accounts due for Transportation, etc.	4,176,804.15
Miscellaneous Accounts Receivable	7,576,384.16
Cash in Hand	53,519,420.78

91,691,447.41

$1,078,777,358.79

LIABILITIES

CAPITAL STOCK:

Ordinary Stock	$260,000,000.00
Four Per Cent. Preference Stock	80,681,921.12

$340,681,921.12

FOUR PER CENT. CONSOLIDATED DEBENTURE STOCK 216,284,882.10

MORTGAGE BONDS:
Algoma Branch 1st Mortgage 5 per cent........... 3,650,000.00

NOTE CERTIFICATES 6 PER CENT. 52,000,000.00

CURRENT:
  Audited Vouchers $10,700,097.44
  Pay Rolls 4,637,770.33
  Miscellaneous Accounts Payable 12,006,966.49
                                                   27,344,834.26

ACCRUED:
  Rentals of Leased Lines and Coupons on Mortgage Bonds 570,631.33

EQUIPMENT OBLIGATIONS 7,990,000.00

RESERVES AND APPROPRIATIONS:
  Equipment Replacement .... $ 3,376,703.28
  Steamship Replacement 23,672,436.83
  Reserve Fund for Contingencies and for Contin-
    gent War Taxes 38,219,661.53
                                           65,268,801.64

PREMIUM ON ORDINARY CAPITAL STOCK SOLD 45,000,000.00
NET PROCEEDS LANDS AND TOWNSITES 91,569,596.36
SURPLUS REVENUE FROM OPERATION 127,275,369.53
SPECIAL RESERVE TO MEET TAXES IMPOSED BY DOMINION GOVERN-
  MENT 3,047,871.02
SURPLUS IN OTHER ASSETS 98,093,458.43

                                      $1,078,777,355.79

2nd Annual Address of Mr. E. W. Beatty, President of the Company, May 5, 1920.

The Annual Report of the Company and statements attached, which have been in your possession for some time, reflect very vividly the situation prevailing generally in respect of increased costs of operation. Notwithstanding that the gross earnings of the Company were the largest in its history, and exceeded the gross earnings of 1918 by $19,391,362, the net earnings were less by $1,569,351. The large increase in working expenses of $20,960,713, following as it does an increase of $17,191,993 in the working expenses during the year 1918, or a total increase in 1919 over 1917 of $38,152,706, is a striking example of the effect of the increased cost of wages and material in the operations of a Company—even one conservatively and economically administered as are the affairs of your Company.

While it is a matter of great gratification that, even with these exceptional costs, your Company has been able during the past two years to earn its fixed charges and usual dividends and very moderate surpluses, it is nevertheless important that the relation between earnings and expenses should now receive the most careful consideration. The results of the operations during the past two years show an upward trend in costs, which even extensive increases in gross earnings and effective operating economies, due to heavier loading, larger power and consequent reduced train mileage, have not equalized. For the past sixteen years the freight and passenger rates of all Canadian railways have been subject to review or have been fixed by the Dominion Railway Commission. The rates have been readjusted from time to time, first being lowered and then increased, but the extent of the increase has not equalled the increased costs which have recently been forced upon all Companies, and reductions in which cannot with any confidence be predicted at this time.

During the fiscal year ended June, 1914, the working expenses of your Company, with a mileage somewhat less than the operated mileage of last year, were $87,388,000, while for the year 1919 they had climbed to practically $144,000,000—an increase of 64%. Within that period increases of nominally 40% in freight rates and 15% in passenger rates have been authorized by the Railway Commission. The actual increases owing to the adjustment of rates made by direction of the Board were in fact 30% in freight rates and 10% in passenger rates. The result, therefore, has been that during the past five years the percentage increase in operating expenses was double the percentage increase in tolls accorded to the Companies.

Owing to the parity of conditions existing between the United States and Canada, the Canadian roads were forced, during the War, to put into effect the high wage scales made effective under Government control of the American roads and they were also compelled to continue operating under tariffs of tolls substantially the same as those in force in the United States. These tariffs were entirely inadequate as results in the United States clearly demonstrated. By legislation recently enacted, the American carriers are assured of rates which will return a fixed percentage on the value of the undertakings used in the public service, which will mean a reconsideration of, and increase in, the rates now current in that country. No doubt the necessity of rate adjustments in Canada will be given earnest consideration by the Government and the Dominion Railway Board. While it is not my purpose to anticipate any action which may be taken, it is only proper, I think, to say that a readjustment is amply warranted, both on the ground of the value of the service rendered by the carriers and the cost to them of performing such service.

It is further to be remembered, and I do not anticipate that it will be forgotten, that the value of any enterprise to the people it serves depends greatly upon its ability to progress and develop, and on the maintenance of a high credit, without which such development cannot take place. Waste, extravagance and improvidence must be discouraged, but I can imagine nothing more detrimental to Canada than that its railway systems should be unable to keep pace in their own development with the progress of the country, and that they should be unable to aid that progress by the expansion of facilities, the construction of necessary new lines and by meeting the increasing demands of the public in the way of efficiency and comfort in service.

Based upon accepted principles in other countries governing compensation due to transportation and other public service corporations, the net earnings of your Company have always yielded a moderate return upon the capital actually invested in the enterprise. The railway net earnings of the Company for 1919 represent only a return of 4% on the actual cash invested in the railway itself.

The operations for the year 1919, after the payment of fixed charges and the usual Preference and Common Stock dividends, showed a nominal surplus of $844,249, which has been placed in reserve to meet the special taxation imposed by the Dominion Government, which special taxation ended in 1919. The fixed charges of the Company are low, the interest on the Preference Stock is equally low, and the dividend of 7% payable on Common Stock from railway earnings is moderate. A factor which seems to be lost sight of in these discussions of the relations between expenses and revenues, is the absolute necessity of reasonable surpluses in the case of any corporation conducting an enterprise as extensive as that of your Company. The gross earnings of the Company for the year exceeded $176,000,000 and the surplus, after deduction of the moderate fixed charges and dividends, only amounted to less than half of one per cent. of these earnings.

Considering the importance of reasonable provision for working capital annually from the operations of the Company if its high credit and ability to progress are to be maintained, it will readily be appreciated that the revenues during the past two years have been, to say the least, inadequate.

In the discussion which has taken place as to the desirability, or otherwise, of increased rates and therefore increased revenues to the Canadian railways, two theories are publicly mentioned. The first, that rates should be increased but that any surplus earnings thereby accruing to your Company should be taken back through the medium of special taxes, and the second, that rates should not be increased but that the Government Railways' deficits, if such occur, should be met out of the general revenues of the country. Both theories are, in my opinion, unsound. Rates should be established which represent a fair return for the service rendered, and if by efficiency and economy and the character and extent of its equipment and facilities a Company can render its operations under such rates profitable, there is no warrant for the confiscation of those profits, nor can there be anything but doubtful honesty in the proposal that one Company's revenues accruing to it from service actually rendered by it and well performed should be taken from it to supplement the revenues of a competitor whose operations do not show favourable results. It is scarcely necessary for me to say that the fairness, or otherwise, of any rate basis is not necessarily measured by the strength or resources of a Company, or by the lack of them.

The second theory, that rates should not be increased but that any deficits should be met from the general revenues of the country, is unsound economically and unfair alike to the Government-owned and other railways. It is obvious that any system which permits services to shippers and others to be performed at unreasonably low rates is discriminatory in their favour, and discriminatory against the public whose taxes are increased as a contribution to those who use railway facilities.

In my opinion the rates in this country should be determined having regard to the cost and value of the services rendered by the Companies and to the legitimate needs of the Companies if they are to meet the transportation requirements of the country.

In the Annual Report reference has been made to the Company's irrigation project in Alberta, the construction of which was undertaken some years ago, and in the earlier progress of which some difficulties were met. The project has now become firmly established and the success has been so pronounced during the past few years that further reference to this important undertaking is, I think, warranted. An area of 643,526 acres has been brought under irrigation through the medium of 3,969 miles of irrigation canals and distributing ditches. Of this area 301,382 acres of irrigable land have been sold at an average price of $38.18 per acre. There is still for sale within the block 342,144 acres of irrigable land for which there is at present a very active demand. During the period from the commencement of construction to 31st December, 1919, the Company has expended in connection with the construction and maintenance of these irrigation works the sum of $15,-186,348 and in their operation the sum of $1,761,268.

I look forward to immigration to Canada on a large scale and, while a period of retrenchment and financial conservatism may conceivably be the part of wisdom, your Directors have the same implicit faith in the future growth and prosperity of the country that they have always had, and also the same confidence in the ability of your Company to play an important part in its development and prosperity.

C.P.R. BOARD OF DIRECTORS, 1920.

MR. RICHARD B. ANGUS	Montreal
MR. EDWARD W. BEATTY	"
HON. FREDERICK L. BÉIQUE, K.C., SENATOR	"
SIR JOHN C. EATON	Toronto
MR. GRANT HALL	Montreal
SIR HERBERT S. HOLT	"
MR. CHARLES R. HOSMER	"
BRIG.-GEN. FRANK S. MEIGHEN, C.M.G.	"
SIR VINCENT MEREDITH, BART.	"
SIR AUGUSTUS M. NANTON	Winnipeg
SIR EDMUND B. OSLER	Toronto
COMDR. J. K. L. ROSS	Montreal
RT. HON. LORD SHAUGHNESSY, K.C.V.O.	"
HON. WILLIAM J. SHAUGHNESSY	"
SIR THOMAS SKINNER, BART.	London, Eng.

EXECUTIVE COMMITTEE

MR. RICHARD B. ANGUS	MR. EDWARD W. BEATTY
MR. GRANT HALL	
SIR HERBERT S. HOLT	SIR EDMUND B. OSLER
RT. HON. LORD SHAUGHNESSY, K.C.V.O.	

CANADA'S FINANCIAL POSITION IN 1919

ANNUAL ADDRESSES AND REPORTS

OF

THE CANADIAN BANK OF COMMERCE*

The fifty-third Annual Meeting of the Shareholders of The Canadian Bank of Commerce was held in the banking house at Toronto, on Tuesday, 13th January, 1920, at 12 o'clock. The President, Sir Edmund Walker, having taken the chair, Mr. A. St. L. Trigge was appointed to act as Secretary, and Messrs, A. J. Glazebrook and J. E. L. Pangman were appointed scrutineers. The President called upon the Secretary to read the Annual Report of the Directors for the 12 months ending 29 Nov., 1919 as follows:

The balance at credit of Profit and Loss Account, brought forward from last year, was		$ 1,444,842.68
The net Profits for the year ending 29th November, after providing for all bad and doubtful debts, were		3,074,892.72
		$ 4,519,735.40
This has been appropriated as follows:		
Dividends Nos. 128, 129, 130 and 131, at twelve per cent. per annum.	$ 1,800,000.00	
War tax on bank-note circulation to 29th November	150,000.00	
Written off Bank Premises	350,000.00	
Transferred to Pension Fund	120,000.00	
To adjust British and Foreign investments on existing exchange rates, not otherwise provided	750,000.00	
Subscriptions:		
Salvation Army	$ 5,000.00	
University of Toronto Memorial Fund	2,500.00	
Soldiers' Emergency Fund, Repatriation Campaign	10,000.00	
Navy League of Canada	2,500.00	
Sundry subscriptions	2,000.00	
		22 000.00
Balance carried forward		1,427,735.40
		$ 4,519,735.40

Address by Sir John Aird, General Manager of the Bank. Contrary to the view expressed last year, that it was unlikely that we should again shew such large figures for some years to come, the unexpected has happened, and we have made a new record in both profits and total assets. Undoubtedly the continued high level of prices for commodities of all kinds has left its mark upon the balance sheets of financial institutions, and while this condition continues it will be reflected in the figures of our own annual statement. The net profits have amounted to $3,074,000, after a most careful provision for all the doubtful items among the Bank's assets. These earnings exceed those of last year by $224,000, a satisfactory increase of 7·9 per cent., but which compares with an increase of 8·9 per cent. in assets. The figures show that the forces which have been steadily

*Note.—For the history of this Bank see *The Canadian Annual Review Supplement* for 1910 and succeeding volumes for yearly Addresses and Reports.

reducing the rate of earnings on the services performed by Canadian banks for the public, to which I referred last year, are still actively at work, and it is fervently to be hoped that the keen spirit of competition, so strenuously active in many directions, will not blind Canadian bankers to this tendency of the times. When it is considered that the three million odd dollars that we show as our net profits represent the combined earnings of over 500 offices, and the result of the efforts of a staff of over 4,000 employees, it will be more clearly recognized how meagre is the shewing in comparison with the vast amount of hard labour and heavy responsibility involved. We have paid during the year four quarterly dividends of 3 per cent., or 12 per cent. in all.

Our quick or easily realizable assets have increased by $16,892,-000, and stand at 49·11 per cent of our liabilities to the public. Our holdings of Dominion and Provincial Government securities have increased $10,700,000 during the year, largely represented by our share of advances to the Dominion Government which are being repaid out of the proceeds of the last Victory Loan. Current commercial loans, that is, those current loans not classified as "call and short loans," both in Canada and elsewhere, shew considerable increases, amounting to $20,837,000 in all, which may be considered as another welcome indication of reviving commercial activity. We have disposed of the Eastern Townships Bank building in Montreal during the year, and this accounts for the reduction in Real Estate other than Bank Premises. The increase in Bank Premises Account is due principally to the acquirement of sites for a number of our newer branches, in pursuance of our general policy in this respect. The total of our assets has grown during the year by $39,333,000, or 8·9 per cent., which under the circumstances we consider satisfactory.

Throughout the war the Canadian banks abstained by common consent, from the opening of new branches. Not only was this justified by the uncertainty of the outlook, but the drain upon the manhood of the country for military service was so great that it was only with difficulty that those members of our staff who were left behind were able to cope with the work thrust upon them, even with the assistance of the temporary staff. Accordingly, while the conflict lasted, we could do no more than to keep a record of those places which seemed to offer a promising field, with a view to occupying them when the general situation justified such a step. The programme thus laid down has fully employed our energies during the past year, but is fairly well completed, and now that we have occupied most of the promising new fields in Canada that have been brought to our attention, and have protected our business at those points where such action seemed necessary, we purpose turning our attention to foreign fields. In the meantime the new branches we have opened are, most of them, progressing satisfactorily, and although the initial expenses connected with them are heavy, we look to see them become before long a source of strength and profit.

27

Out of the total of 1,704 officers of this Bank who volunteered for the defence of the Empire, either in the army or navy, we have reinstated during the course of the year 996, and have still to hear from 253 of them. We have been glad to welcome these officers back to our service, and will do all in our power to assist them to become re-established in civil life. It is our hope that in the course of a reasonably short time they will find themselves at no disadvantage as a result of the loss in banking experience which naturally resulted from their absence. The opening of new branches and the expansion of our business have made it possible to take on the staff again all those who apply for reinstatement.

An unlooked for consequence of the war has been the unsettlement of the relations between employer and employed in every walk of life. One of the primary causes of this has been the extraordinary increase in the cost of living, but any one who is forced to grapple with the problems before the employer knows that this can be the cause of only a small part of his difficulties. The deeper and more complex part of them, no doubt, had their origin in that phase of the war, when it took on the aspect of a life and death struggle between the opposing forces. For a time everything had to be subordinated to the turning out of men, munitions and material for use in the war. The Government became, practically, almost the sole employer, the erst-while employer acting as its manager or agent to secure the necessary production. Under these conditions the usual balance-weights and counterpoises of business enterprise were lacking. To secure the necessary production was the only thing that mattered; the cost of doing so was a secondary consideration, and any demands made by employees were granted almost before they were asked. Thus new conditions arose, some shewing marked improvement over those existing before the war, but others such as are foredoomed to failure if put into practice under the usual conditions of peace. It is, perhaps, too much to ask of either employees or employers that they should at once grasp with a clear mental vision all the far-reaching consequences of these changes. Suffice it to say that the adjustments necessary now that business conditions have become more normal are many and difficult, and involve to the utmost a spirit of fairness and a willingness to compromise opposing points of view on both sides. Speaking for our own staff, both permanent and temporary, they have rendered us loyal service in difficult days, and we have sought to give generous and sympathetic consideration to the difficulties which have been particularly their lot, as salaried men and women, during an extraordinary rise in the cost of living.

The condition of the foreign exchanges is one of the problems with which we have had to deal during the past year, and it is one in which the people of Canada are deeply concerned, as it has a very direct effect upon their economic life. Canada is not alone in suffering from the effects of a depreciated exchange, in fact, it is a condition now familiar to almost every country in the world. The artificial expedients which have been resorted to in order to correct the situation, such as the shipping of gold, the sale of securities and an attempt at fixing exchange rates, are inadequate and may even prove dangerous. The rehabilitation of our dollar can only be accomplished by saving, economy and greater production. It has perhaps become fairly generally known among those who take an interest in the matter that our imports from the United States greatly exceed our exports to that country, and that in the case of Great Britain the reverse is true, our exports greatly exceeding our imports. Therefore in the case of our trade with the United States there is a scarcity of bills receivable which we can set off against our bills payable to that country; while in the case of our trade with Great Britain the reverse is true, and the bills receivable exceed the bills payable to such an extent that she has been forced to obtain credit from us for many of her purchases of food-stuffs produced in Canada. There is much more, however, in the situation than this. We have been selling on credit to France, Belgium, Greece, Roumania, and to some extent to Great Britain, manufactured goods, the raw materials of which are largely imported from the United States, and we are called upon to pay for these raw materials in cash. In addition to this, the interest payments on our debt abroad have increased, as well as the heavy shipping charges which have to be paid on water-borne goods. In paying for the raw materials referred to we are forced to use up a large part of those funds ordinarily available to defray the cost of our normal imports from the United States. The scarcity of United States funds has thus been accentuated by the increased demand, while the source from which we have been wont in the past to make up any deficiencies, that is, the balance due to us by merchants and others in Great Britain, is not now available for this purpose for two reasons; first, that Great Britain is not settling in cash as in the past; second, that such part of this indebtedness as might be made available for the purpose is not now acceptable to the United States as payment, because that country has already a surplus of British debts which she is anxious to realize. If to these factors in the problem be added the effect of increased purchases of luxuries imported from the United States in the present era of free and easy spending, an idea will be obtained of at least some of the main reasons for the present situation.

Address by Sir Edmund Walker, C.V.O., LL.D., D.C.L., President of the Bank.

We have passed through a year in which the daily surprises have been as perplexing as during the war, and in which the anxieties have been as great, except that sometimes they affected rather the mere happiness of the world than human life itself. War, however, still continues in many countries, and there and elsewhere many have died from lack of food. The War has been won by the most superb co-operation in the attainment of one ideal—the winning of the war. We may lose all that victory seemed to secure by indulgence in countless theories, many of them aiming at the disintegration of society, instead of again co-operating in one ideal—the restoration of order and the improvement of social conditions, so that the happiness of the greatest number may be secured.   It is not by standing idle while we discuss methods that we can get out of our present troubles. If the call is to "man the life boat" we do not wait for academic discussion before the boat is launched on its life-saving mission, and too much argument between capital and labour just now, is madness in view of what we seek to save. The rising curve of prices cannot be made to turn downward without an increase of production, nor can we face the heavy obligations left by the war except by greatly increasing production.   The man who does not do his best at his particular job is not merely helping to barricade the only pathway that will lead us out of our troubles, but he is helping to raise, or to maintain, the cost of the necessities of life for his own family. I may be called a friend of capital for saying this, but I am on record elsewhere as an advocate of many changes in the present relations of the employee and employer, all of them in favour of the employee.

While we and the rest of the world are failing to produce on a sufficient scale to provide for human comfort and to pay our debts, the price of everything has so increased, that although all clearing-house and trade returns shew higher figures in money, these generally represent transactions based on smaller quantities of merchandise, and because we think in terms of dollars and not of merchandise, we are living in a fool's paradise. The imperious demands of war rapidly raised all prices, and payment was only possible by inflating the currency; unfortunately inflated currency sustains and further increases prices. If with our own currency we bought only goods made in our own country, the minimum of harm would be done, but possessing more currency and fewer commodities than usual, we are acting like the drunken sailor newly come ashore, and buying everything that fancy suggests, whether necessary or not, without regard to whether it is made in Canada or abroad. For every purchase of goods made abroad, whether in Great Britain or China, or anywhere else, we settle through New York, and the rise or fall of the rate of exchange, about which we are so much concerned, is the expression of our failure, or the reverse, to pay cash or its equivalent.   In this connection the speaker has for many years, at these annual meetings, presented the facts of our foreign trade, the peculiarities of our relations with the United States, the sales of our securities abroad to pay for the excess of our imports and the danger of mortgaging the future of our country, and has given frequent warnings as to the character of many of our imports.

The excess of our exports over imports for the year ending 31st March was $343,491,000 as compared with $623,647,000 for the previous year. Although so much smaller than for 1918, the excess was larger than in any previous year. The difference of $280,156,000 is more than accounted for by a falling off of $320,874,000 in our exports to Great Britain, and this again is due to a decrease of $297,893,000 in exports of agricultural products and of $87,318,000 in manufactured articles. For the six months ending in September the exports for the two half years are almost equal, while the imports were $33,571,000 less. It is gratifying to notice that, apart from the decrease in agricultural production, our figures have not been much altered by the cessation of the manufacture of munitions. Food is in greater demand than ever and our factories are behind in the production of almost every line of manufacture, while nearly every form of raw material is difficult to obtain. Our total foreign trade for the fiscal year was $2,176,378,000, as compared with $2,548,-691,000 in 1918.

Let us consider a few items in our imports which at least suggest great possibilities of curtailment, if we are prepared to restrict our pleasures for the common good. Under the head of apparel we bought abroad to the extent of $8,500,000, including headgear alone for over $5,000,000; under fancy goods, $4,000,-000; fruits and nuts, $25,000,000; furs, $4,500,000; gramaphones, over $2,000,000; silk in various forms, $21,000,000; tobacco, nearly $12,000,000; in all, $77,000,000, mostly luxuries. Then we are yearly face to face with enormous imports of material, part of our requirements, of which we already produce, or which it would be natural for us to produce. It is obvious that our national finances would benefit if we could either produce the following items ourselves, or avoid in any way their importation; bricks, clays and tiles, over $4,000,000; coal, coke and charcoal, $79,000,-000; breadstuffs, $26,000,000; all foodstuffs, $121,000,000—much of this is doubtless absolutely necessary, but surely there is room for a large reduction; iron and steel in all forms, $161,000,000, including machinery $45,000,000; textiles in all forms, $168,000,-000; motors, railway cars and other vehicles, $18,000,000.

There is one comforting feature about our trade with the United States. While in 1913 we bought $2.70, last year we bought only about $1.50 of goods for every dollar's worth bought by the United States from Canada. While our purchases have increased in value by 65 per cent, theirs have increased by 180 per cent. Comparing the totals, the imports for 1919 are less by $46,000,000 than in 1918, but as in the item referred to in past years, military stores, there is a decline of $80,000,000 and another decline of $17,000,000 in pork, both due to the cessation of the War, the imports for ordinary purposes are much larger than ever before. The most notable increases are in traction engines, mainly for farming, about $10,000,000, and in raw cotton about $13,000,000.

There are many handsome increases in exports to counterbalance increased imports, but the outstanding feature is the enormous decrease of $295,000,000 in the value of exports of grain, of which $270,000,000 is due to a decrease in export of wheat.   There is a reduction in quantity of 150,000,000 bushels, from 215,000,000 bushels of all grains in 1918, to about 65,000,000 bushels in the year ending March, 1919. In the item, "cartridges—gun, rifle and pistol," which has figured so largely in our exports during the war, there is a decline of $139,098,000.   There is also a decline of $12,000,000 in exports of flax seed. Against the decline in imports of pork there is a corresponding one in exports of bacon, but there is an increase of about $28,000,000 in exports of meats and butter. There is an increase of $14,000,000 in the item of ships sold to other countries. In our imports the totals of increases and decreases are not very far apart, but in exports we have the extraordinary condition of increases amounting to $110,-000,000 and decreases amounting to $443,000,000. Had we been as fortunate in the quantity of merchandise we had to export in the fiscal year ending March, 1919, as we were in the previous year, our financial position would have been very different.

The preliminary estimate of the value of our field crops for the year 1919 is $1,452,787,000, as compared with $1,367,909,000 in 1918, the actual figures for which fell slightly short of the estimate.   There was a decline in the value of grain crops, but a large increase in fodder crops and potatoes. Except in swine there is a slight increase in the numbers of all live stock on our farms. It is difficult as yet to obtain accurate figures as to the production of our mines for the year just closed. We estimated that of 1918 at $220,000,000, and the actual figures were $211,-301,000. For 1919 the best estimate we can obtain is $167,000,000, shewing a falling off of nearly $45,000,000, which is almost entirely in metals. Because of the ending of the war we produced only about half the quantity of nickel produced in 1918; about the same quantity of lead and zinc, at lower prices; less copper, also at lower prices; and less silver, but at higher prices.

The statement of the Public Debt of the Dominion of Canada at the end of November shows a net total of $1,817,839,000, and we are informed that at the end of the fiscal year, March 31st, it will be $1,950,000,000. The estimated net amount due by Great Britain to the Dominion at the end of November is $181,000,000. There is also due by the Governments of four other countries about $20,000,000. These assets are taken into account in stating our net debt. In addition to the debt due by Great Britain to the Government of Canada, there is a debt of $200,000,000 due by Great Britain to the Canadian banks, on which, however, since the close of the year partial payments have been made. The war expenditure of our Government has fallen from a million dollars daily to half a million, but we are still far from normal in this respect. The expenditure for pensions has now reached $3,000,000 monthly. The sales of Canadian securities for 1919 are much larger than in 1918, and there is an important difference in their distribution:

Security	Total Sold	In Canada	In United States	In Great Britain
Government	$781,812,000	$629,562,000	$152,250,000	....
Municipal	27,166,393	18,333,893	8,832,500	....
Railway	35,355,133	5,700,000	24,550,000	$ 5,105,133
Public Service Corporation	20,950,000	11,100,000	9,850,000	....
Miscellaneous	44,100,202	34,595,202	9,505,000	....
Total 1919	$909,383,728 100%	$699,291,095 76:89%	$204,987,500 22:54%	$ 5,105,133 :57%

There is an increase of about $145,000,000 in the total, but the increase in the amount sold in the United States is over $170,000,000. Had it not been for these sales the difficulties in connection with New York exchange would have been much greater.

The difficulties of reconstruction after the great war are even greater than we feared. The whole world is feeling the effect of four years in which ordinary work and economics of life were not merely neglected, but the basis therof was almost swept away. We are short of almost every commodity, the strongest evidence of this being the fact that millions of people in Europe face actual starvation. We cannot re-establish the normal supply of commodities except by working harder than usual, and we cannot lessen the terrible strain of high prices without doing the extra work which will put an end to the lack of commodities. We cannot adjust prices without also bringing about a contraction in the volume of paper money and other instruments of credit, and so far as it is possible to enforce contraction without interfering with the production of what is really necessary, the reduction of prices will be facilitated. In a word, bankers should not aid speculation, or assist ventures which do not directly lead to production. We are still building ships with feverish haste throughout the world, and we ought to be spending large sums on railroads in order that commodities may be freely distributed. The present cost of ocean transportation, quite as much as the cost of goods at the primary markets, stands like a huge barrier across the pathway of return to normal conditions. What is worse, however, is that even present prices, in the natural order of things, will go on rising until the lack in the world's supply of commodities has been filled, and there has been a large contraction in the volume of paper money now in existence.

In the case of many classes of wage earners there has been an adjustment of pay against this increased cost of living, but there are many instances in which there has been either no adjustment or one quite inadequate. There are, however, some classes of earners who are so highly paid, in comparison with the past, that they have unusual spending power, and, along with all the others who have profited unduly by the war, they are spending their money in such a manner as to increase still further the troubles of the less well-off. Apart from this, after the gigantic struggle of the War, the world has slackened its energies and is filled with argument and unrest. All these elements move along an ascending spiral which clearly ends in ruin if we cannot arrest their course.

We know now roughly the cost of the War as represented by our public debt. This debt is held mostly at home but partly abroad. In addition, there were issues of securities made before and during the war by governments, municipalities and private companies, and sold abroad. On the whole of this debt, so held abroad, the annual charge is about $190,000,000 per annum. Of this roughly about $65,000,000 is due to holders of our securities in the United States, and about $125,000,000 to holders in Great Britain and Europe. This debt we can pay only by an excess of exports over imports or by new borrowings. The debt at home is our own domestic affair. Certain citizens have advanced the cost of the war to the nation, and we now have to distribute this cost by taxation over all the citizens of Canada (except those who escape taxation), so as to meet the annual amortization payments. If the annual payments are obtained by reasonably fair taxation, so levied that the taxes do not become a cause of restraining our industries, we shall not fail to win through, but to accomplish this, much study of the subject is necessary. Many forms of taxation not yet in use in Canada will doubtless be employed, in addition to those now in force, but the whole question should be approached without that class feeling which often causes taxes to be so apportioned, that bitterness and a sense of injustice are felt by many who do not object to being heavily taxed so long as those who really can afford to pay their share do not escape. The income tax should be paid by a much larger number of citizens. The tax on surplus profits needs much study: there is all the difference in the world, both in justice and in the interest of the community, between a large aggregate of profit made by a small margin on each transaction and a similar sum made by an unfairly large margin of profit on each transaction. The community may be deeply interested for its own advantage in securing the extension of the first kind of transaction, while no one is interested in the success of the other class except the taxpayer himself. The tax in the end must be borne by our industrial activities, and we are foolish if, in our eagerness to escape our own share, we make such burdens so heavy on others that many of these activities must cease, and commodities that under fair conditions might be produced at home are replaced by imports from abroad.

The usual review of business conditions presented at our annual meetings is of marked interest this year. The unemployment which it was feared a year ago would be widespread, even if only temporary, did not occur except in a few centres of industry. Industrial plants were quickly readjusted to peace time industries and orders for many kinds of commodities poured in beyond the capacity to fill them, not so much, however, beyond the capacity of the plants as beyond that of the men to work them; and, therefore, as we are not satisfying the demand, prices must go on rising. At the same time the demand for housing accomodation and for many other public and private building requirements is greater than the world has ever known before. Surely this all sounds

like the prosperity we so often sigh for, and, indeed, to many it
is a time of large profits or high wages, but the pendulum can
swing only a certain distance in one direction or the other. There
is not much satisfaction in a prosperity which can only be sustained by borrowing more money, nor can our comfort be un-
alloyed if production is insufficient to keep a large part of the
world from starvation.

When the future historian, however, looks back at the events
of the past year, he will not see an irresolute world failing to
take the steps necessary to recover the road to happiness. He
will applaud the efforts of society in Winnipeg, London, Boston
and elsewhere, to defend itself against revolution; he will wonder
at the activity in the shipyards of the world to supply the lack
of transportation; he will see that capital and labour are not
farther apart, but much nearer to reasonable solutions of their
difficulties; he will, indeed, from his lengthened perspective, see
that the chaos following the war is steadily yielding to that great
quality of civilization on which the hope of the world rests, the
love of order. We hear much about the decline in the exchange
value of the pound sterling and more about Great Britain's loss
of ascendency in the world of finance, but if you will read the
report of our London manager you will find no trace of doubt,
no murmur of complaint. Great Britain has accomplished the
most stupendous things in history; the world owes her more in
respect and admiration than it can ever pay; but she asks nothing from others—she is simply clear-sighted and aware of her
enormous obligations, and of what they involve. No one who reads
his statement will find cause for pitying her, she is so strong and
self-reliant; on the contrary, there is abundant cause for pride
that we are part of the great Empire which in the supreme emergency saved the world.

The number of Director's was increased by By-law from 22
to 25 and the new Board elected as follows: Sir Edmund Walker,
C.V.O., LL.D., D.C.L., Z. A. Lash, K.C., LL.D., John Hoskin, K.C., LL.D.,
D.C.L., Sir Joseph Flavelle, Bart., LL.D.., A. Kingman, Hon. W. C.
Edwards, E. R. Wood, Sir John Morison Gibson, K.C.M.G., K.C., LL.D.,
Robert Stuart, George F. Galt, A. C. Flumerfelt, Hon. Geo. G.
Foster, K.C., Chas. Colby, M.A., PH.D., George W. Allan, K.C., M.P.,
H. J. Fuller, F. P. Jones, H. C. Cox, Charles N. Candee, J. S.
Mitchell. Thos. Findley, W. W. Hutchison, H. R. Silver, The Rt.
Hon. Sir Thos. White, K.C.M.G., Jas. A. Richardson, and T. A.
Russell—the last three being new members.

At a meeting of the newly elected Board held later, Sir Edmund
Walker, C.V.O., LL.D., D.C.L., was re-elected President, and Mr. Z.
A. Lash, K.C., Vice-President.

GENERAL STATEMENT
OF
THE CANADIAN BANK OF COMMERCE

29TH NOVEMBER, 1919

LIABILITIES

Notes of the Bank in circulation		$ 30,047,659.66
Deposits not bearing interest	$151,688,481.72	
Deposits bearing interest, including interest accrued to date	241,916,674.29	
		393,605,156.01
Balances due to other Banks in Canada		74,816.06
Balances due to Banks and Banking Correspondents elsewhere than in Canada		8,727,208.45
Bills Payable		441,180.99
Acceptances under Letters of Credit		14,866,446.19
		$447,762,467.35
Dividends Unpaid		4,002.86
Dividend No. 131, payable 1st December		450,000.00
Capital Paid up	$ 15,000,000.00	
Rest Account	15,000,000.00	
Balance of Profits as per Profit and Loss Account	1,427,785.40	
		31,427,785.40
		$479,644,205.64

ASSETS

Gold and Silver Coin Current on hand	$15,425,252.93	
Gold deposited in Central Gold Reserves	6,500,000.00	
Dominion Notes on hand	31,436,349.25	
Dominion Notes deposited in Central Gold Reserves	10,000,000.00	
		$ 63,361,602.18
Notes of other Banks	$ 2,433,211.00	
Cheques on other Banks	14,372,830.21	
Balances due by other Banks in Canada	476.59	
Balances due by Banks and Banking Correspondents elsewhere than in Canada	$10,589,390.95	
		27,395,908.75
Dominion and Provincial Government Securities, not exceeding market value		46,865,379.16
British, Foreign and Colonial Public Securities and Canadian Municipal Securities, not exceeding market value		39,847,537.30
Railway and other Bonds, Debentures and Stocks, not exceeding market value		5,958,791.41
Call and Short Loans (not exceeding 30 days) in Canada on Bonds, Debentures and Stocks		20,750,828.04
Call and Short Loans (not exceeding 30 days) elsewhere than in Canada		24,854,885.75
Deposit with the Minister of Finance for the purposes of the Circulation Fund		881,791.81
		$219,911,724.30
Other Current Loans and Discounts in Canada (less rebate of interest)		$212,188,170.54
Other Current Loans and Discounts elsewhere than in Canada (less rebate of interest)		24,932,369.89
Liabilities of Customers under Letters of Credit, as per contra		14,866,446.19
Overdue Debts (estimated loss provided for)		137,130.65
Real Estate other than Bank Premises		467,650.60
Mortgages on Real Estate sold by the Bank		203,861.18
Bank Premises at cost, less amounts written off		5,858,006.22
Other Assets not included in the foregoing		71,434.27
		$479,644,205.64

B. E. WALKER,
President.

JOHN AIRD,
General Manager.

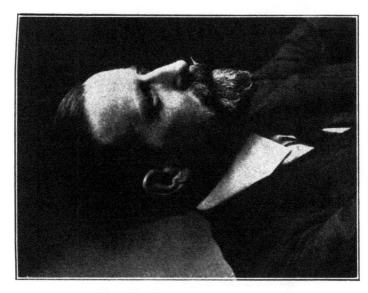

SIR F. WILLIAMS-TAYLOR, D.C.L.
General Manager The Bank of Montreal

SIR H. VINCENT MEREDITH, BART.
President The Bank of Montreal

CANADA'S POSITION AFTER THE WAR

ANNUAL ADDRESSES AND REPORTS
OF
THE BANK OF MONTREAL*

Annual Meeting and Report of the Bank on Dec. 1st, 1919. The 102nd Annual General Meeting of the Shareholders of the Bank of Montreal was held in the Board Room at the Bank's Headquarters. Amongst those present were: D. Forbes Angus, R. B. Angus, S. M. Baylis, E. W. Beatty, K.C., H. W. Beauclerk, D. R. Clarke, Colonel Henry Cockshutt, Huntly Drummond, Edward Fiske, J. Jeffrey Fiske, C. J. Flett, K.C.; Hon. Geo. G. Foster, K.C.; G. B. Fraser, Dr. Wm. Gardner, Sir Charles Gordon, G.B.E.; J. Maxtone Graham, C.A.; Lt.-Col. G. R. Hooper, C. R. Hosmer, L. Julien, Harold Kennedy, T. Marion, Chas. Meredith, Sir Vincent Meredith, Bart.; W. R. Miller, Lt.-Col. Herbert Molson, M.C.; S. Geo. McElwaine, Wm. McMaster, Campbell Nelles, Hugh Paton, John Patterson, Alfred Piddington, Henry E. Rawlings, James Rodger, A. G. Ross, Rt. Hon. Lord Shaughnessy, K.C.V.O.; E. P. Winslow. On motion of Mr. R. B. Angus, Sir Vincent Meredith was requested to take the chair. The Chairman then called upon the General Manager, Sir Frederick Williams-Taylor, to read the Annual Report of the Directors for the year ended 31st October, 1919, as follows:

Balance of Profit and Loss Account, 31st October, 1918		$1,901,613.22
Profits for the year ended 31st October, 1919, after deducting charges of management, and making full provision for all bad and doubtful debts		3,314,227.38
Premiums on New Stock		3,500,000.00
		$8,715,840.60
Quarterly Dividend 3 per cent. paid 1st March, 1919..	$ 572,250.00	
Quarterly Dividend 3 per cent paid 1st June, 1919 ..	600,000.00	
Quarterly Dividend 3 per cent. paid 1st September, 1919	600,000.00	
Quarterly Dividend 3 per cent. payable 1st December, 1919	600,000.00	
	$2,372,250.00	
Amount credited to Rest Account	4,000,000.00	
War Tax on Bank Note Circulation to 31st October, 1919	190,986.17	
Subscriptions to Patriotic Funds	39,750.00	
Reservation for Bank Premises		300,000.00
		6,902,986.17
Balance of Profit and Loss carried forward		$1,812,854.43

*Note.—For History of the Bank see Supplement of *The Canadian Annual Review* for 1910; for preceding Reports and yearly addresses see Volumes 1911-18.

Address by Sir Vincent Meredith, Bart., President of the Bank. General trade in practically all branches has been active and profitable during the year and the Bank has participated in the general prosperity. The balance sheet shows profits in moderate proportion to the resources employed and yet, I trust, not unsatisfactory to the Shareholders. That reaction from the feverish activities and high prices produced by the vast conflict which so many apprehended has not occurred, nor can it be said to be impending. The feeling as to the future is less optimistic than it has been, but the great pressure on our agricultural and manufactured resources caused by home and foreign demand shows no sign of abatement. Though marked by a high degree of prosperity, the year has also been one of world-wide labour unrest, with demands for increased wages and shorter working hours, culminating in strikes and disorder, with resultant decreased efficiency, lessened production and greater cost of output. This unrest may in a measure be attributable to unsatisfactory pre-war conditions, but probably in a greater degree is the result of unsettlement due to the abnormal nervous strain of the great war.

In one important respect, normality has come again—the mercantile sea-going tonnage of the world has been restored to pre-war dimensions and is rapidly being increased, an accomplishment that should soon permit of regularity in the carriage of overseas trade and in a reduction in freight rates and cheapened cost of commodities. The high cost of living, about which so much is being said and for the relief of which so many remedies are suggested, is a world-wide, not a local, condition. It is due in part to the large volume of currency now in circulation, which to a considerable extent must be regarded as credit expansion largely the result of Government borrowings and the disbursement of the proceeds thereof, together with post-war activity.

The deprivations of the past five years have induced an orgy of self-indulgent expenditure by the general public, to which has been added lavish outlay by many people who amassed fortunes during the war. All these are contributing factors, but they affect to only a limited extent the high costs, which are without doubt the direct result of the pressing demands of European countries for commodities of every nature at abnormally high prices. We cannot, therefore, expect any considerable amelioration in living conditions until the world's demands are satisfied and Europe once more returns to an exporting basis. Every effort is being made to this end, but it must of necessity come gradually. Food and prices will without doubt be the soonest overcome, and I think we may look forward confidently to a reduction in the cost of all commodities both at home and abroad after another harvest, to be followed in natural sequence by a reduction to some extent in the scale of wages; but the process promises to be gradual, and marked and rapid decline in the near future do not seem probable.

The foreign trade of the Dominion has been well maintained, and the outlook gives no cause for apprehension of an early recession. The latest available figures, those of the seven months ending October 31st, show imports to have been $543,670,000 and exports $688,890,000. As compared with the corresponding period last year, there was a decline of $16,400,000 in imports and of $31,200,000 in exports, a relatively insignificant decrease, while the favourable balance of trade has this year been $145,200,000. The price index of commodities not having materially varied during the periods under review, the deduction may be made that the volume of our foreign commerce has not greatly changed, although the figures of particular products have fluctuated considerably. Thus, the export of foodstuffs was larger in value by $114,200,000 this year than last, in the seven months, and the export of wood and wood products, including paper, $25,800,000 larger. On the other hand, miscellaneous exports, which include munitions, show a decrease of $141,600,000.

With the exception of the United States, the gold holdings of all the belligerent countries have been depleted during the war to meet adverse trade balances, and their economic condition has been greatly weakened, the value of the pound sterling, in terms of the American dollar, being reduced to $4.00, the mark to 2½c., the franc to 10c., and our own currency by 4% to 5%. The depreciation of currency, however, is not wholly an unmixed evil, as it acts as a corrective to adverse trade balances by checking imports and stimulating exports. In the absence of gold, large issues of paper money have been made necessary in all countries to meet the demand for a circulating medium in consequence of abnormal business activity, coupled with war expenditures. The effect has been the demoralization of all exchanges.

To restore the reserves of metal and provide an effective gold standard correcting the over-issue of paper money will take time, and can only be brought about by economy and increased exports. The stabilizing or pegging of exchange I believe to be inadvisable, owing to its prohibitive cost. In any event, it would be futile to attempt to do so until there is a cessation of Government borrowings. The relation of gold reserve to note circulation is a question on which divergent views are held, one school of economics demanding the restoration and maintenance of an effective gold standard and the other contending that goods and services, combined with gold, form an adequate and more elastic reserve. I am not sure that it is not the part of wisdom to depart from old notions of the rigidity of the gold reserve, and recognize that we are justified in enlarging our note-issuing powers to respond to all legitimate business demands in periods of great trade activity or emergency, provided such expansion is based on self-liquidating securities. If used to cover discrepancies in revenue, it is then a form of inflation wholly unjustifiable, bringing with it, as it does, the well-known evil effects of a depreciated currency at home, besides greatly damaging our credit in the eyes of the financial world.

There are three indispensable factors to the upbuilding of Canada—immigration, production and exports. Immigration during the last five years has been negligible owing to the war. In the first seven months of the current fiscal year, new arrivals numbered 82,893, of whom 42,377 came from Great Britain and 35,949 from the United States. While these figures do not represent a large movement as compared with several pre-war periods, they show a gain of 51,734 immigrants, or about 166 per cent. over the corresponding months last year. After-the-war emigration of foreign-born has taken place in fairly large volume, the exact figures of which are not obtainable. In my judgment, it is of vital importance that our unoccupied areas be settled and made productive with as much rapidity as possible, the future prosperity of the country and ability to meet our debts largely depending on increased production. It is believed that nations will not war again in this generation, and the objection to the incoming of alien people is in consequence mitigated. The combing should not, therefore, be made too fine. The economic gain of a large immigration to develop our basic industries cannot be overestimated, particularly at a time when war has left many nations impoverished in food and denuded of commodities which Canada is capable of supplying.

There is reason to believe that the policy of the energetic Minister of Immigration will be broad-based, and that its fruits will be manifested in an increasing influx of settlers upon the land, of domestic servants, and of artisans and labourers. Indications are already given of a large movement in the spring from the United States into our Western Provinces, attracted by the superior productivity of our soil and its comparative cheapness, and I think we may reasonably hope for a considerable immigration from the countries of our late Allies and from the Scandinavian kingdoms.

The state of the national finances deserves a wider and more profound consideration than the subject appears to receive. The net Debt, which before the war was $331,000,000, had on October 31st last reached the vast sum, having regard to population, of $1,785,000,000, an increase of more than five-fold in as many years. That debt is still mounting, and by the close of the current fiscal year, that is to say on March 31st next, will not be less than two thousand million dollars and probably more. The situation is a serious one, though mitigated by the fact that our Debt is largely internal. We cannot go on borrowing indefinitely, and it is a certainty that we shall have to bear a much heavier burden of taxation than formerly for many years to come. To repeat the formula that has been heard so frequently but to which, unfortunately, sufficient attention has not been paid, relief is to be found in immigration, harder work, greater efficiency, increased production and thrift. To these agencies must be conjoined rigid economy in all private and public expenditure.

There arises in this connection the question of methods of taxation, which may require readjustment to meet post-war conditions. Trade is being hampered by a somewhat penalizing excess business profit tax, and unless this impost is speedily reduced, or abandoned altogether, we cannot meet unencumbered competition on equal terms.   Furthermore, enterprise and expansion are stifled and foreign establishments deterred from entering the Canadian industrial field.   Taxation should be so distributed that it will not have the effect of making this country too dear to live in and thereby divert intending residents to other countries.   Doing away with many exemptions and imposing taxation on all classes of the community who have the ability to pay, and placing a high tariff upon imported luxuries would, I believe, cause little hardship and considerably ease a strained financial situation, besides giving all persons in Canada a more immediate interest in the economical administration of our public affairs.

Canada can and will meet all her obligations, and of her ability to do so no more conclusive evidence need be given than the immense subscription to the recent Victory Loan.   With regard to the subject of foreign trade, it is only a matter of time before increased production will overtake domestic demands, and, unless preparations are made in advance for finding markets overseas for our exportable surplus of raw materials and manufactured goods, our uninterrupted prosperity may be checked.   The needs of foreign countries are great and pressing, and profitable business awaits the Canadian exporter, but it cannot be acquired unless long-term credits are provided.   Our Government has been far-sighted in giving assistance in this direction and, no doubt, is prepared to extend further aid, provided exporters, who reap the benefit, will assume a proportion of the risk.

Self-interest alone would seem to dictate that credit facilities be extended to those countries which can demonstrate their ability to pay if given reasonable time, and we would thus avoid the possibility of abrupt changes in industrial conditions and bring about a gradual return of international trade equilibrium.   I cannot close without voicing what, I am sure, is the feeling of every Canadian—that the recent visit to Canada of His Royal Highness the Prince of Wales not only gave abiding pleasure to every class of our population, but rendered a great and memorable service to the Empire in strengthening the Throne in the affection and confidence of the people, and by drawing still closer the ties which bind the commonwealth of nations over which he is destined to reign.

Address by Sir Frederick Williams-Taylor, D.C.L., General Manager of the Bank.   The economic and financial difficulties that confronted the country during the war have since changed in nature, but have not disappeared by any means. There is an aftermath of problems which Canada must face and in which bankers are vitally concerned. At present there is great trade activity: yet our national debt grows apace, with attendant ills. Therefore, even with a full measure of faith in our country, I find the near future difficult to visualize. We derive a measure of consolation in comparing our lot with that of countries worse off than our own, but contiguity and ambition direct our eyes towards that country to the south which has benefitted so vastly by the war.

It is no reassuring reflection that the United States has already reduced its war debt by some $800,000,000, while we confront an increase of $600,000,000 for the current year. It seems obvious, however, that though fate has treated the two countries differently, any prosperity experienced in the United States must be reflected in Canada. Our true comfort, as well as our pride, is that the Dominion did its duty in the great war as a part of the British Empire. No Canadian would have it otherwise, and therefore we face the cost with stout hearts and the future with watchful serenity. Turning to the special features in our balance sheet and the points of interest arising therefrom, I might say, first, that the absorption of the Bank of British North America has been so smooth and so complete that no ripple appears upon the surface of our affairs. We believe its friends and officers alike feel at home in the Bank of Montreal.

Since presenting the last balance sheet there has been an increase in our capital stock of $4,000,000, with a corresponding increase in Rest Account. Both items now stand at $20,000,000. The increases are primarily in connection with the acquisition of the Bank of British North America. Shareholders of that Bank were accorded the option of taking cash or exchanging their holdings into Bank of Montreal shares on a determined basis. After the allotments had been made under this arrangement, our own shareholders accepted the opportunity of subscribing for the limited remainder of capital shares to bring the whole up to $20,000,000. Our authorized capital is $28,075,000. Many of our banking transactions during the post-bellum year under review were unusual in character and of special interest. They need not be described in a report of this nature. It will suffice to say that they have added to the strength and prestige of the Bank. Our profits for the year have been satisfactory, enabling us to provide the usual return of 12% on capital and make adequate provision for doubtful debts.

It seems to me of sufficient importance to bear repeating that there has been no profiteering whatever by the banks of Canada, for the price of money has not been raised. Alone of all commodities, the cost to the borrower of loanable funds of the banking institutions of this country remains unchanged. Not only is this the case, but, speaking for ourselves, it seems only proper for the shareholders to know that in handling business entrusted to us by the several Governments during the war and since, our policy has been to charge only the narrowest of commissions and minimum interest rates. In many instances, where the services were of a war character, we have acted free of charge. The Bank's earnings have been maintained through fuller employment of our reserves, the ratio of our liquid assets to liabilities being 67% as compared

with 71% a year ago. There has been no restriction of credit to
our commercial borrowers. All legitimate applications of this
nature have been granted. Also we have loaned freely to subscribers against the security of the various war loans, and to Municipal,
Provincial and Federal Governments as required.

It is pertinent to mention that, in the ordinary trade of the
country, money has been made so easily and with so little risk since
1914 as compared with ordinary times that our Banks, in turn,
have operated with unusual freedom from losses. As a measure
of prudence, however, we provide for contingencies, a policy with
which we feel sure you will be in accord. The practical evidence
of Canada's fortunate trade conditions lies in the fact that commercial failures for the twelve months ended 31st October were
766, as compared with 904 for the previous corresponding period
and with 1,669 in our bank year 1912-1913. That outstanding
subject, the high cost of living, has been dealt with by your President, but I might add that the inevitable decline in prices is at
least nearer, and it is to be hoped that the delay is not lulling
dealers into the erroneous belief that the standards of these last
few years will continue indefinitely. Misconception on this point
would constitute a menace alike to borrower and banker. It
seems certain that food prices will drop presently and that all commodities must decline in price; therefore great care and scrutiny
of credits on the part of bankers and other business men are imperative.

Our savings deposits continue to grow satisfactorily both in
volume and in number. The fact that we are custodians of deposits of a special nature inevitably causes our total figures to
fluctuate heavily. Our total deposits are $442,000,000, being $27,-
000,000 less than a year ago. Our deposits ten years ago were
$173,000,000. The total deposits of all Canadian Banks are now
$2,360,000,000, as compared with $2,085,000,000 a year ago and
$832,000,000 ten years ago. Our current loans in Canada also vary
largely in volume. The total is now $164,000,000, as compared
with $146,000,000 at the corresponding date last year. Our pro-
vincial and municipal borrowers continue to exercise caution in
the matter of capital expenditure. Loans in this class aggregate
$15,000,000. The Bank's premises account has been reduced by
$500,000 through the sale of certain banking properties not re-
quired. Among our assets, the item Dominion and Provincial Government securities, including loans to the former, now stands at
$64,000,000. A year ago the total was $46,800,000. The total
holdings of all the banks, as indicated by the Government return
of October 31st, was $361,200,000.

The premium on New York funds, the increase in our National
Debt and in our Canadian currency circulation, are matters of deep
interest and should be studied by all. The purchasing power of
the Canadian dollar in the United States has decreased, as reflected
in the premium on New York funds. A year ago it cost two dollars

to send one hundred dollars to the United States of America; to-day the cost is four dollars and twenty-five cents.   Exchange is now a subject which, as an English authority states, "insists on bringing itself to the attention of all kinds of people who hitherto regarded it as a sort of mysterious cryptogram with which they had no practical connection."   In elementary terms, more money continues to flow out of Canada than comes in, thus creating a net balance against us after taking all transactions into account.   New York being our natural clearing house for transactions with Great Britain and the rest of the world, it is clear that the present extra-ordinary cost of sending money to the United States would not exist but for the fact that we cannot spare the gold with which to pay the net balance in question against this country, while, in com-mon with all countries, our legal tenders are naturally not current abroad.   We should have precisely the same conditions between our own Provinces, were it not that our legal tenders and bank notes are current throughout the Dominion.

It is true the balance of trade was in favour of Canada to the extent of $340,000,000 for the year ended 31st October last, but whereas we paid for all our purchases abroad, we have, in the same period, shipped goods on credit to England and Continental coun-tries to the extent of many millions not easy to estimate, besides sending out of Canada annually about $200,000,000 interest on our recorded indebtedness abroad, mainly to Great Britain and the United States.   These factors alone would not create an adverse exchange to the extent that exists, but, in addition, there are the invisible earnings in the Dominion of foreign business corporations, chiefly American, seeking return to proprietors abroad.   The dis-advantage Canada is under in respect to the premium on New York funds will last until the ebb and flow of such funds are equal. Repayment to Canada of the moneys, aggregating $420,000,000, owed us by Great Britain and the Allies would quickly cause the premium in question to disappear.   We naturally shall be repaid in the fullness of time, but it is well to bear in mind that an alleviation of the penalty can as surely be found by diminution of imported luxuries as it is certain that the penalty, in part, is caused by such importations.   Also, the situation could be relieved by borrowing in the United States, but this course is to be de-precated and would not be a cure, but merely postponement of pay-ments.   As indicated by your President, the true remedy lies in increased production and the economy that would be reflected in resumption of those personal sacrifices of pleasure made during the war.   It is here in place to remark that in the eyes of Europeans the people of North America are extravagant and wasteful.

Since the outbreak of war, Canada has created fresh domestic credit instruments in the form of bonds of $2,100,000,000.   The increase of circulation and of bank deposits followed as a natural sequence.   Our Bank and Government note circulation is now $532,000,000, as compared with $235,000,000 in 1913, an increase of $296,000,000.   In the same period the total gold held in Canada has increased $60,000,000. Canadian provincial government, municipal and industrial public loan flotations, during the twelve months under review, were $117,500,000, of which, in round figures, $90,-000,000 was placed in the United States. The discount on the Canadian dollar attracted material American buying of such securities, especially of those domiciled in New York.

In Great Britain, the dollar exchange situation is the cause of much anxious thought. Meanwhile, the present low value of the pound sterling in America encourages special operations such as the purchase in London of Canadian and American securities. These operations help to correct the abnormal conditions and, granted a reasonable attitude on the part of labour, there is ground to justify confidence regarding future financial and industrial conditions. Considering the time, money continues plentiful in England at moderate rates, and there is no thought on the part of London of surrendering an historic position as the financial centre of the world. As in the previous years of war, our London office has been cut off from the important business of issuing loans for Canadian borrowers, but, on the other hand, it has increased greatly in importance and utility as an administrative centre for our foreign business, and is steadily growing in value to our branches on this side of the water.

The Dominion Government, in July of this year, borrowed $75,-000,000 in New York for refunding purposes. The terms paid by the Government were onerous yet unavoidable. Evidence that the price of issue was in keeping with American market conditions lies in the fact that there has since been no rise in the quoted price. Incidentally it may be mentioned that Canada secured as good terms as in the case of the recent British loan of $250,000,000 in the same market. A sign of the times is the buying power for first-class securities created throughout the Dominion. This is a healthy and desirable condition induced by Government war loans and war savings certificates. It is vital that Canadians should recognize the virtue of saving. As between production and thrift, though they should go hand in hand, the latter is fundamental and leads naturally to the former.

REPORT OF SUPERINTENDENTS ON PROVINCIAL CONDITIONS

Quebec. The cut of lumber during the past season was not as large as usual. Practically all stocks have been sold and shipped out. Prices were high. Labour conditions show improvement and a larger cut is looked for this winter. The demand for pulpwood from the United States was uneven, but stocks have been well disposed of and high prices are expected to be maintained. The paper mills of the Province continue working to capacity, the demand for newsprint and better qualities of print papers exceeding the supply. Manufacturing in nearly all lines has been generally satisfactory, although production is still limited by scarcity of skilled labour and raw materials.

Hay and cereal crops were average. Root crops were large, but potatoes suffered from rot. Pasturage was good, and dairy products will show an increase. With the exception of asbestos, there is little mining done in the Province. Asbestos prices are good and shipments are well maintained. The fur business has been good, and boot and shoe manufacturers find difficulty in supplying the demand. Shipbuilding continues active, a number of large steel vessels having been launched from different yards during the year. The wholesale and retail trade was most satisfactory; collections were good and failures show a decrease. There have been no exceptional expenditures during the year by the Dominion or Provincial Government, and municipalities have limited disbursements to necessary works. Practically no railroad construction was undertaken. There is very little speculation in real estate; values and rentals are both high. General conditions, both in cities and rural districts, are good, with no apparent slackening in trade since the termination of the war. The housing problem is everywhere acute, and those dependent on a fixed income are seriously affected by the abnormal cost of all necessaries.

Ontario. Manufacturing in Ontario has been limited only by shortage of supplies and disturbances in labour. Government credits for goods sold to Europe have stimulated manufacturing, and domestic demands have been insistent. New industries have been started, and a number of successful manufacturing concerns in the United States have been making enquiries with the intention of locating in Ontario. Ontario farmers have been steadily bettering their position in recent years, installing modern equipment and improving their modes of living. The past year has been one of fair crops and high prices. A wet spring was followed by an exceptionally dry summer, and grain crops, with the exception of fall wheat, fell below the average. Root crops were good; corn and tomatoes were a record yield; the season was poor for all fruit except grapes. Cheese production showed a falling off. There is a shortage of hogs; sheep raising is on the increase. The cattle situation is somewhat unsettled, owing to the limited amount of feed available for carrying through the winter.

The production of lumber has been seriously reduced owing to shortage of labour. 1919 has been an excellent marketing year, with heavy sales to Great Britain and the United States, and a steady domestic demand for all classes of lumber. Prices have been unusually high, there is no accumulation of stocks on hand, and notwithstanding the scarcity of labour and increased costs of operating, the year has been a successful one. Pulp and paper have been in large and increasing demand, with soaring prices for the latter. Mining production during the year has been curtailed. The demand for nickel fell off after the Armistice; strikes lessened the silver output. Both these situations are improving and larger production has taken place at the gold mines. Both wholesalers and retailers report it easy to sell goods. Credits are shortened and bad debts negligible. Larger expenditures were generally made by municipalities this year in an effort to overtake works postponed during the war. Population shows a general increase, with a tendency to drift to urban and manufacturing centres. Values in real estate are steadily increasing. So little building took place during the war that there is now a general shortage, particularly in dwelling houses, and in consequence there is much activity in real estate and an improvement in the building trades. There has been a continued extension in hydro-electric power during the past year, and works at Nipigon and Chippewa, as well as at other places less important, will within the next two years add very largely to the available power for manufacturing and other purposes throughout Ontario. Generally speaking, the year has been one of great activity throughout the Province.

Maritime Provinces. The past fishing season has been successful, the catch being almost a record one. Prices are lower, however, and ocean transportation is still restricted. The American, West Indian and Southern Brazil markets will probably take most of the available supply. The output of coal was below last year's figures, owing to a slackened demand, a shorter working day and labour unrest. Steel plants show a decreased output. The construction of the new plate mill at Sydney nears completion, and when in operation will be a factor of great importance commercially to the whole Dominion. The lumber cut was above that of last year and has been largely sold to the British and French Governments at high prices. The demand is good from the United States, but sales have been curtailed owing to transportation difficulties. Labour is more plentiful and, notwithstanding high wages and the excessive cost of provisions, indications point to an average cut this coming winter.

The crop of hay and cereals was above the average. Root crops were again large, but potatoes were slightly damaged by rot. Fruit harvested in good condition was almost a record crop. Manufacturing along conservative lines shows steady progress. Owing to continued excellent prices received for farm products, fish and lumber, and the high wage scale, both wholesale and retail trades have been good, with few and unimportant failures. The Dominion Government expenditures have been largely confined to work on ocean terminals at Halifax and to the dry dock and breakwater at Courtenay Bay, St. John. Provincial and municipal expenditures have been limited to necessary works. A steel shipbuilding plant is being built at Halifax, and four steamers are already in course of construction. Small wooden vessels continue to be built in Nova Scotia and New Brunswick, although the demand is not so good as a year ago. Business in the Maritime Provinces has been little affected by the change from war conditions to those of peace, and trade activity continues.

Prairie Provinces. During part of the past season extensive areas in Saskatchewan and Alberta experienced, in common with the North-Western States, severe drought and loss of crops, but owing to good yields in other areas and to high prices the value of grains raised exceeded that of the year 1915, when the largest crop in the history of the West was produced. Failure of pasture and hay in certain districts caused anxiety to ranchers, and while autumn rains brought relief, the scarcity and high price of feed for winter use forced the sale of some unfinished cattle at prices adversely affected by worse conditions in the United States. The high value of wool has encouraged sheep ranchers to pay prevailing prices for winter feed and carry over flocks. Heavy and profitable yields from irrigated lands are giving a new impetus to irrigation, which already stabilizes the live stock industry in Southern Alberta.

Saw mills were in active operation during the past season and found a ready market at profitable prices. Coal, a most important natural asset of Alberta and Saskatchewan, especially of the former, has not been produced in quantity to equal demand, strikes and labour shortage having reduced the output. There has been renewed activity in the search for oil in Alberta. In Northern Manitoba, gold and copper prospects are receiving increased attention and attracting capital. Results from the summer fishery in the West were satisfactory. The principal source of supply at present is Lake Winnipeg, from which whitefish alone to the limit of three million pounds was taken. Other important fisheries are at Lesser Slave Lake and Lac la Biche. Some progress has been made in carrying out an extensive plan to develop new power at the Winnipeg River, Manitoba. There are many evidences of increase in the population. Immigration desirable in character, although not yet large, shows a substantial increase over last year (1918), while the figures are small compared to pre-war years.

Central city real estate has been firmer in price, and small dwellings are in great demand. Farm lands have sold freely at new high prices. Trade, wholesale and retail, has been good. Manufacturers have operated their plants to capacity or limit of labour, and have found a ready market. The past season witnessed fresh activity in constructing branch railway lines, although all plans could not be carried out owing to shortage of labour. The West on the whole has had a prosperous year, exceptions being the districts in which crops were lost through drought. The two visits of H.R.H. the Prince of Wales were the happiest and most important events in many years.

British Columbia. In the opening months of the year the lumber trade was dull, but in the spring a heavy demand arose in the United States and accumulated stocks were disposed of at rising prices. Great activity prevailed during the summer and autumn. The demand for cedar shingles has been good, and prices have reached unprecedentedly high figures. The outlook for the coming year is exceptionally good, both in domestic and foreign markets. The pulp and paper mills have been busy, and their product is on the increase. Shipments are largely to the Orient and to the Antipodes. The total salmon pack, while not quite so large as last year, brought high prices, and the result proved satisfactory. The halibut fishery is decreasing, due to over-fishing of the banks. All things considered, the fishermen have had a profitable year.

Mining development throughout the Province has been retarded by unsettled labour conditions and the high cost of supplies, and the total output for the year is not expected to be as high as that of 1918. Mining is being carried on in a practical, businesslike manner, and there is no speculation in mining stocks. Grain crops were affected by drought and were below the average. Fruit and vegetables have been good crops with prices ruling high. More attention is being given to agriculture, and farmers and growers generally have had a profitable season. The shipbuilding programme in British Columbia is about finished and new contracts have not yet been made, although negotiations are in progress with that object in view. The industry has been valuable to the coast cities in British Columbia during the past three years. The Government is building a graving dock at Esquimalt and negotiations are being conducted with the Government for construction of a drydock at Vancouver, a necessity for the port.

Wholesale trade has been good and retail trade active. Railway construction has been carried on during the year in extending the Pacific Great Eastern, connecting up the Canadian National Railway between Kamloops and Kelowna, and in extending the local railway on Vancouver Island. Municipal outlays have been restricted to ordinary expenditures. The Dominion Government have in contemplation a considerable expenditure for extension and improvements to Vancouver harbour. The real estate situation has improved during the year; properties have been turning over at fair prices, but without speculative values. Rents have increased, and there is a scarcity of dwelling houses in all parts of the Province. The population has increased, and further immigration is expected during the coming year. Conditions throughout the Province on the whole are better than they have been for some years, and prospects appear good for continued business activity into the new year.

Newfoundland. The estimated catch of cod will be substantially the same as last year, with purchasing prices about 25% less. The comparative export figures to 30th June, 1919, are:

		Quintals	Value
Dried Cod	1919	1,618,770	$24,316,830
	1918	1,821,206	18,829,560
Pickled "	1919	212,253	1,543,232
	1918	195,218	1,023,426

The frozen fish industry is being developed. The output of the Bell Island iron mines was again smaller than the previous year, being 709,300 tons as compared with 751,000 tons in 1918. About the usual amount of lumbering was done. Paper manufacturers are now running their plants at full capacity. Tonnage is available, and stocks have been marketed at high prices. The pulp industry is dull. The take of seals was the smallest on record, probably owing to the limited number of vessels engaged. Manufacturers of clothing, boots, shoes, ironwear, cordage, and so forth, are all making money. Wholesale and retail trades continue good with payments well met. With the high prices obtained for fish and oils, the financial position of the community is generally good. Interest-bearing deposits in banks show an increase of nearly $2,000,000 over last year.

GENERAL STATEMENT

AS ON 31st OCTOBER, 1919

LIABILITIES

Capital Stock		$ 20,000,000.00
Rest	$20,000,000.00	
Balance of Profits carried forward	1,812,854.43	
	$21,812,854.43	
Unclaimed Dividends	8,621.49	
Quarterly Dividend, payable 1st Dec., 1919 —..	600,000.00	
		22,421,475.92
		$42,421,475.92
Notes of the Bank in circulation	$43,922,844.00	
Deposits not bearing interest	129,946,641.02	
Deposits bearing interest, including interest accrued to date of statement	312,655,964.44	
Deposits made by and Balances due to other Banks in Canada	2,110,833.25	
Balances due to Banks and Banking Correspondents elsewhere than in Canada	4,122,490.91	
Bills Payable	4,334,342.79	
		497,093,116.41
Acceptances under Letters of Credit		4,895,505.49
Liabilities not included in the foregoing		894,711.67
		$545,304,809.49

ASSETS

Gold and Silver coin current	$24,742,654.64	
Dominion notes	49,865,151.50	
Deposit in the Central Gold Reserves	25,200,000.00	
Balances due by Banks and Banking Correspondents elsewhere than in Canada	$13,856,808.36	
Call and Short (not exceeding thirty days) Loans in Canada, on Bonds, Debentures and Stocks	2,583,910.00	
Call and Short (not exceeding thirty days) Loans in Great Britain and United States	78,255,625.37	
	94,696,343.73	
Dominion and Provincial Government Securities not exceeding market value	63,984,255.10	
Railway and other Bonds, Debentures and Stocks not exceeding market value	8,517,835.56	
Canadian Municipal Securities, and British, Foreign and Colonial Public Securities other than Canadian	47,041,359.70	
Notes of other Banks	2,744,153.99	
Cheques on other Banks	21,189,104.58	
		$337,960,858.80
Current Loans and Discounts in Canada (less rebate of interest)	164,182,581.03	
Loans to Cities, Towns, Municipalities and School Districts	15,092,718.13	
Current Loans and Discounts elsewhere than in Canada (less rebate of interest)	15,903,424.98	
Overdue debts, estimated loss provided for	549,133.12	
		195,727,857.26

Bank Premises at not more than cost (less amounts written off)	5,500,000.00
Liabilities of Customers under Letters of Credit (as per Contra	4,895,505.49
Deposit with the Minister for the purposes of the Circulation Fund	1,088,166.60
Other Assets not included in the foregoing	162,421.34
	$545,304,809.49

VINCENT MEREDITH,
President.

FREDERICK WILLIAMS-TAYLOR,
General Manager.

BOARD OF DIRECTORS

SIR VINCENT MEREDITH, Bart. - - -	President
SIR CHARLES GORDON, G.B.E. - - -	Vice-President

R. B. ANGUS, ESQ.	HAROLD KENNEDY, ESQ.
H. R. DRUMMOND, ESQ.	COL. HENRY COCKSHUTT
LT.-COL. HERBERT MOLSON, M.C.	E. W. BEATTY, ESQ., K.C.
G. B. FRASER, ESQ.	C. R. HOSMER, ESQ.
LORD SHAUGHNESSY, K.C.V.O.	WM. MCMASTER, ESQ.
D. FORBES ANGUS, ESQ.	H. W. BEAUCLERK, ESQ.

J. H. ASHDOWN, ESQ.

General Manager:
SIR FREDERICK WILLIAMS-TAYLOR

Assistant General Manager and Superintendent Quebec, Maritime, Newfoundland and Mexico Branches:
F. J. COCKBURN

Assistant General Manager and Superintendent Bank of British North America Branches:
H. B. MACKENZIE

Assistant General Manager and Manager London Branches:
G. C. CASSELS

Assistant General Manager and Superintendent Ontario Branches:
D. R. CLARKE

Superintendent Western Branches:
E. P. WINSLOW

Capital Paid Up	$20,000,000.00
Rest and Undivided Profits	21,812,854.43
Total Assets	545,304,809.49

The Bank has 305 Offices in Canada, Newfoundland, United States, Mexico; at London, England, and at Paris, France, with Correspondents in all Countries, offering exceptional facilities in all departments of General and Foreign Banking business.

CANADIAN CONDITIONS AND PROGRESS

ADDRESSES AND REPORTS

OF

THE ROYAL BANK OF CANADA*

Address by C. E. Neill, General Manager of the Bank. The figures of the Balance Sheet submitted to you to-day record the greatest growth of any year since the Bank was incorporated. The total assets are $533,647,084.93, an increase of over $106,000,-000 over the previous year, and it is of interest to know that no portion of this increase is due to the absorption of banks, as has been the case in some previous years. Our deposits are $419,121,399.37, the growth for the year being approximately $87,000,000. During the month of November there were large withdrawals from the Savings Department for investment in the last Dominion Government Loan, but a substantial portion of this amount remained temporarily over the end of our year at the credit of the Government. Our circulation is slightly higher than last year. Current loans have increased $50,109,910.69, but it is satisfactory to note that the percentage to total assets is only 43·75 per cent. The liquid position of the Bank has been well maintained, the percentage of liquid assets to liabilities to the public being 55·03 per cent. Further investments in Dominion and Provincial Government securities to the extent of nearly $9,000,000 have been made during the year.

The capital of the Bank has been increased $3,000,000 since our last Annual Statement, through the sale of 20,000 new shares at $150 per share to our shareholders, and 10,000 shares at $200 per share to the London, County, Westminster and Parr's Bank. The Reserve Fund now stands at $17,000,000, as compared with $15,000,000 last year. Our additional resources have enabled us to show a substantial increase in earnings. Net profits for the year were $3,423,264.34, being 1C·81 per cent. on the average combined capital and reserve, as compared with $2,809,846.24, being 10·19 per cent. on capital and reserve the previous year. The regular dividend of 12 per cent., and an additional bonus of 2 per cent., were paid during the year, and a balance of $1,096,418.74 is carried forward in Profit and Loss Account. I desire to take this opportunity of commending the staff of the Bank. I think I am

---

*Note.—Annual Meeting at Montreal, Jan. 8, 1920. For History of the Bank see *Supplement* to *The Canadian Annual Review* for 1910; for preceding Reports and Addresses see Volumes for 1911-18.

safe in saying that from the highest executive officers to the newest junior, there is the strongest possible feeling of loyalty to the institution, and this is undoubtedly a great factor in our development.

Address by Sir Herbert S. Holt, President of the Bank. The statement today presented is the most satisfactory in our history and fittingly marks our jubilee. In the fifty years since our incorporation we have grown from a local Bank to an international institution with a steadily rising place among the great banks of the world. Our paid-up capital has increased from $300,000 to $17,000,000, our reserves from $20,000 to $18,000,000 and our assets from less than a million to over half a billion dollars. Most of this phenomenal progress has been made in recent years, but tribute is due to the prudence and wide vision of those early administrators who laid so solidly and broadly the foundation upon which we have built. In all periods of grave depression we have never failed to pay a dividend, and only once, and that 34 years ago, have we drawn on our reserve. Throughout our career, advantage has been taken of every favourable opportunity both at home and abroad to extend our operations and to add to our resources. This expansion has proved beneficial not only to the Bank, but to the Dominion. In 1870 our profits were 4 per cent. on our working resources. Now, owing to the volume of business, we are affording increased facilities on a return of less than one per cent. on total assets.

During the year just passed, Canada has again proved her ability to meet every emergency as it arises. Our soldiers have been absorbed into civil life without strain, our industries have been re-adjusted with little unemployment, and the unfailing response of our people to every patriotic call has been shown by the immense over-subscription to the last Victory Loan. Despite an unfavourable harvest in some parts of the West, the country is prosperous and the balance of trade continues largely in our favour. Factors which have contributed to the prevailing high prices are being gradually eliminated. Ocean transportation service will soon far exceed that of the pre-war period and stores which have accumulated in distant lands will, as a result, become readily available. Industrial plants have multiplied and everywhere an army of women workers has been added to the ranks of labour. Moreover, Europe can only ultimately pay its huge debts by a corresponding output of goods. We shall then enter upon an era of greater supplies and keen competition. If prices fall in the future, as seems probable, each dollar made and saved today will then have greater purchasing power. We should therefore strive to produce to the limit of our capacity while markets are high, and exercise the most rigid economy in order that our gains may be conserved.

The Government is still discharging some of the heavy obligations arising out of the war and the net public debt now fast approaches, two billion dollars. There are only two ways of meeting this responsibility; greater industry and less extravagance—prosperity is not unending or national borrowing power unlimited. It is an unvarying economic law, of which we in Canada had a bitter experience following the Civil War, that all conflicts terminate in a period of prosperity and inflation during reconstruction which is succeeded by equal or greater depression. For this inevitable re-action in the future, we should now be prepared, and it is the duty of the Government to set an example to the nation by abstaining from all unnecessary or wasteful expenditure. It cannot be too strongly urged, or too often repeated, that the greatest possible effort must be put forth in every direction if we are to meet the amount required for interest and the redemption of debt. It has been aptly said that Governments have no income outside that of the people, and that the wealth of a country, like that of an individual, can only be built up by spending less than is earned.

In the difficult times ahead, the Dominion holds a commanding position owing to the abundance of its natural resources which need only the touch of energy and capital. The market for pulp and paper continues to expand, the demand for gold and silver adds to the value of our mines, and the soaring prices of coal will hasten the development of water powers. Above all, the expected influx of settlers to the West will further agricultural production, our main source of wealth, and extend our market for home manufactures. Industrially our position is much less favourable. Capital, which is everywhere in demand, is not likely to be attracted to new enterprises, with their attendant risks, so long as it is called upon to bear all the loss in case of failure, and to share its profits with the Government in the event of success. The labour unrest, now almost universal, also acts as a brake upon industrial activity. No employer can profit from dissatisfied labour, and no employee from unreasonable demands.

Europe still affords by far the largest market for our exports, and we have greatly extended our overseas facilities by entering into a close working arrangement with one of England's foremost institutions, the London County Westminster & Parr's Bank, Limited, whereby each will act as agent for the other in those countries where one is established and the other is not. This association has been strengthened by the British bank's purchase through our shareholders, of 10,000 new shares of stock issued at $200 per share on the 16th of April last. The 20,000 shares issued earlier in the year at $150 per share, as announced at our last meeting, were eagerly subscribed by our shareholders. These two new issues increased our paid-up capital by $3,000,000 and enabled us to add $2,000,000 to our reserve. With continued prosperity in Canada and those countries to the south in which we have branches, our business has greatly expanded. A proportionate increase in earnings enabled us not only to declare our usual dividend of 12 per cent., but to announce a Fiftieth Anniversary

Bonus of 2 per cent. on our stock. We realize that our success has been due in no small measure to the efforts of an efficient and loyal staff, keenly interested in our progress and it is with pleasure that we have supplemented the sum granted in midsummer by a Jubilee bonus of 20 per cent. on the salaries of all employees. Between the Executive and the staff there is a feeling of mutual confidence and reliance. There is no position in our service to which the ambitious may not aspire, and the extension of our branches abroad opens still wider the door of opportunity.

Address by Edson L. Pease, Vice-President and Managing-Director. Trade conditions throughout the Dominion continue very prosperous. There have been few failures during the year and general prosperity is indicated by the increase in savings deposits. The decrease in exports caused by the cessation of our former trade in munitions has been in part overcome by greater sales of farm products and pulp and paper. The balance of trade remains largely in our favour, and the general position is shown in the following statistics:

	1918	1919		
Value of Field Crops (Dec. 31)	$1,383,082,000	$1,469,530,000	Increase. $	86,448,000
Bank Clearings (Dec. 31)	13,776,332,000	16,701,173,000	Increase.	2,924,841,000
Note circulation (Nov. 30)	234,983,000	237,547,000	Increase.	2,564,000
Chartered Banks, Deposits (Nov. 30)	2,234,253,000	2,493,570,000	Increase.	259,317,000
Chartered Banks—Current Loans (Nov. 30)	1,239,718,000	1,405,229,000	Increase.	165,511,000
Exports—Merchandise (Nov. 30) 12 months	1,300,761,000	1,251,095,000	Decrease	49,666,000
Imports—Merchandise ·(Nov. 30) 12 months	898,212,000	920,077,000	Increase.	21,865,000
Customs Receipts (Dec. 31) 12 months	154,725,000	169,071,000	Increase.	14,345,000

The Western wheat crop was a disappointment, the yield being 167,000,000 bushels only. The value of the crop, however, between $400,000,000 and $425,000,000, was a record one on account of the high prices prevailing. By order of the Canadian Wheat Board the price of wheat was fixed at the beginning of the season at $2.30 per bushel, and on December 27th last was advanced to $2.80 per bushel, as against $2.25 for the 1918 crop. The large increase in the Bank clearings indicates a material expansion in trade. The growth in deposits is remarkable considering the heavy withdrawals from the banks in connection with the November, 1918, Victory Loan, and the first instalment of the 1919 Victory Loan. Of the latter loan, which amounted to $658,000,000, no less than 63 per cent. has already been paid. The increase in commercial loans indicates no curtailment in this class. In fact there is keen competition for commercial accounts. The percentage of commercial loans to total deposits on November 30, 1919, was 53·85, as compared with 73·53 in November, 1914. Munitions figured in the exports of 1919 to the extent of $44,000,000, while they amounted to $274,000,000 in 1918. The decrease, therefore, in exports of $49,000,000 last year is much smaller than was anticipated. Of the total imports, $920,000,000, no less than $726,000,000 came from the United States, the principal items being iron and steel products, coal, cotton and sugar. We estimate the luxuries and dispensable articles at $88,000,000.

The problem of exchange grows in perplexity. The prevailing rates give additional value to almost all our exports, but our immense imports from the United States are penalized. The return to parity may be a long and difficult process depending in great measure upon European conditions, and the course of American action. The only effective means of checking the advancing rate upon remittances to the United States is to reduce to the lowest possible limit our imports from that country, remembering that the purchase of articles of luxury, or goods that can be manufactured in Canada, by increasing the adverse balance of trade, adds to the premium which we pay on iron, steel, coal, cotton, and other raw materials which are absolutely necessary for the maintenance of some of our industries. There are indications, however, that the present unfavourable position may be somewhat improved in the near future. The British Government has given notice of its intention to make a substantial payment on account of the indebtedness to the banks, and it is expected that within the next four months Canada will export to the United States a large amount of flour.

The President has referred to the prejudicial effect upon industry of the Excess Profits Tax, and I wish to emphasize his remarks. To keep production from falling off and to increase it, thus furnishing full employment for labour, is more essential now than ever. There is no encouragement to enlarge old industries and establish new ones when profits, if made, are to be specially taxed by the Government. The Secretary of the Treasury, in reporting upon the effect of a similar impost in the United States, says that "in many instances it acts as a consumption tax, is added to the cost of production upon which profits are figured in determining prices, and has been and will, so long as it is maintained upon the statute books, continue to be a material factor in the increased cost of living."

The year just concluded has given additional proof of the service to the country and advantage to the Bank of our branches in foreign fields. Prosperity throughout the West Indies and Central and South America is reflected in the growth of our deposits, which continue largely to exceed our commercial loans, the excess on November 29th last being $26,000,000. At a time when the Dominion can sell to the greater part of Europe only on long-term credit, with uncertain prospects of repayment in the case of some countries, the development of markets in these tropical countries which have so greatly increased their purchasing power, is of the utmost importance. We have therefore decided to extend our operations in this direction, and in addition to branches opened during the past year at Rio de Janeiro, Brazil, Buenos Aires in the Argentine, and Montevido, Uruguay, we shall shortly be established at Sao Paulo and Santos in Brazil, and Bogota and Barranquilla, Colombia.

In order to cultivate our rich business possibilities in these foreign lands and to promote reciprocal trade with Canada, we are issuing pamphlets describing their economic resources and import needs, and a Monthly Letter will be circulated reviewing general trade conditions and opportunities. Our new Department of Commercial Intelligence will further provide enquirers with any special information desired, and its scope will be limited only by the demand for its service. Through this bureau, and the financial facilities offered by the Bank, we hope to stimulate the interchange of commodities between these countries of vast potential resources and the Dominion, and enable each to share in the upbuilding and prosperity of the other. We are also co-operating in the movement in favour of closer commercial relations between the Dominion and the British possessions on this continent. These Colonies form one of our natural markets, selling the things we need and buying the staples we have for export. The lowering or removal of customs barriers,and the inauguration of direct steamship communication would result in greatly increased trade and lead to the speedy development of the agricultural, forest and mineral wealth of these Colonies.

The marked feature of British banking during 1919 has been the continuance of amalgamations. At the end of 1918 there were only 34 banking institutions in England, or about one to every 1,300,000 inhabitants, as compared with 19 in Canada, or one to every 450,000. In other words, if we were on a parity with England, we should have only seven parent banks in the Dominion. The British Government realizes that we have entered upon an era of great industrial combinations and that these can only be safely financed by like consolidations of banking interests. The United States Government, which has hitherto opposed all mergers, has awakened to the needs of the times. In addition to the creation of the Federal Reserve system, it is now encouraging its great banks to establish branches abroad and, through its State Department, Consuls, Trade Commissioners, and official publications, is affording them every assistance in its power.

Our Jubilee year marks also the twentieth anniversary of the Bank's entry into Cuba. This event has been commemorated in the island by the opening of our new premises in Havana, a handsome seven-storey structure. The first floor, 100 feet frontage by 150 feet in depth, is occupied by the bank, while the remainder of the building affords spacious office accomodation for the public, all of which is occupied. It gave me great pleasure to attend the inaugural ceremonies which occurred last month. Business in Cuba is very prosperous. Sugar prices are high, and the new crop promises to be one of the largest in its history. The rapid increase of business at our New York Agency, due in large measure to the business generated by our branches, made it desirable to secure to our use for all time the premises occupied by the Bank in William Street. We have, therefore, purchased the building and already four of its floors are required for our

848 THE CANADIAN ANNUAL REVIEW

needs. This being our Jubilee, the Bank has prepared a brief history of the efforts made during the past fifty years to build up a sound and progressive institution, and to promote the commercial interests of the Dominion. A copy will be forwarded to each of the shareholders at an early date. In entering upon our second half century, we are confronted with many problems, which we are confident can be successfully met. We have a notable record behind us, and I believe a still greater one lies before us.

REPORT AS TO PROVINCIAL CONDITIONS

British Columbia. Business conditions in British Columbia steadily improved during the past year. The demand for lumber at the beginning of 1918 was poor, and the outlook somewhat in doubt. Wooden ship-building was drawing to a close, and orders for aeroplane spruce were cancelled. In May, however, a strong demand for lumber developed, principally from the United States. Prices advanced considerably, but shippers were handicapped by the shortage of cars. The 1919 cut will be rather smaller than that of the previous year, which was reported as 1,761,184,000 feet. Pulp and paper mills were busy, with a slightly increased output and advanced prices. The Department of Lands reported the value of lumber produced in the Province in 1918 as $26,219,000 and pulp $10,517,000, the total value of forest products being given as $54,162,000.

The salmon pack was smaller than last year, being 1,393,000 cases compared with 1,600,000 cases in 1918. The Fraser River pack was again a failure, but the increased run of sock-eyes in the Skeena River offset to some extent the shortage in the Fraser. The halibut catch in Prince Rupert district again decreased. Protective measures are evidently necessary to conserve this valuable food product. About one hundred fishing boats are owned in and operated from Prince Rupert. With the exception of silver, the production of all mines was less in 1919 than during the previous year. Labour troubles in the Crow's Nest district was the principal cause of the decline in coal production. Improved methods of treating low grade ores have been introduced and will make profitable the operation of many properties in the Rossland district and in other parts of British Columbia.

Grain crops were about average, with higher prices prevalent. Fruit growers had a profitable season. The large increase expected in fruit production was materially reduced by a heavy frost in October. There was a good demand for live stock at satisfactory prices. A large number of returned soldiers took advantage of the opportunities afforded by the Soldiers' Settlement Board and settled on the land. There is plenty of good land available and conditions are reported excellent for mixed and stock farming. The building of steel ships was continued at Vancouver, Victoria and Prince Rupert. In view of the demand for ships, it is expected that this industry may continue during the coming year. Greater activity in manufacturing was reported,

and a number of new industries were established. The Dominion
Government will shortly commence operations on the new terminals for which $5,000,000 was recently voted by Parliament.
General business was very satisfactory, and the outlook was good
in all lines. Hotels had a record year, and an influx of people
is expected as soon as transportation facilities become normal.
The improvement in real estate continued, but without speculation.
Properties for occupation were purchased for cash. Only a small
amount of building was in progress during the year on account of
the high cost of labour and materials.

Middle West Provinces. Crop results in the Middle Western
Provinces were disappointing. There was partial or complete
failure in Southern Alberta and Central and Southern Saskatchewan, with average to good crops in Manitoba and other districts
of Alberta and Saskatchewan. Seeding conditions in the spring
were favourable, but hot weather followed in May and a dry spell
in June and most of July. Frost also affected much of the wheat
crop in Saskatchewan, while the crops in Manitoba suffered from
rust. Hail losses were also severe in sections of Alberta and
Saskatchewan. The wheat crop was therefore about 167,000,000
bushels only, but high prices more than offset the short crop.
Drought and lack of feed depleted cattle herds of young stock.
Dairying is becoming an increasingly important industry, the
value of products for 1919 being estimated at $57,000,000, or
$7,000,000 in excess of 1918. The Soldier's Settlement Board
approved of 22,151 applications for settlement in the Central
Western Provinces out of a total of 31,807 applications for the
whole dominion. Total loans throughout Canada to returned
soldiers settling on the land amounted to $50,699,000, of which
loans in the Western Provinces were in about the same ratio as
the number of applications. Manufacturing concerns in the larger
centres had a profitable year. There was no shortage of labour.
Lumber operations were relatively unimportant. The cut for the
three Middle Western Provinces was slightly in excess of 1918,
namely :—

Alberta	57,608,725 ft. at $34	$1,958,696
Manitoba	28,006,789 " " "	952,239
Saskatchewan	120,241,573 " " "	4,088,213

Building operations were much below normal for the past
few years and housing accomodation was at a premium. Mining
was confined mainly to coal in Alberta. Labour troubles are
said to have caused the falling off in the production—see the
following table :—

	1918	1919	
Lignite	3,035,061	1,268,239	(9 mos.)
Bituminous	2,982,334	1,477,132	"
Anthracite	131,225	53,109	"
	6,148,620	2,798,480	
Briquettes	100,470	53,109	
Coke	32,858	Nil	

There are believed to be large deposits of copper and gold
in the northern parts of Manitoba but little has been produced

28

to date. Considerable development on certain gold properties is expected during 1919. Alberta has the reputation of having large natural gas deposits, but the permanence of the supply has not yet been established. The same Province produced 13,040 barrels of oil valued at $100,000 during the year ended April 30, 1919, as compared with 8,500 barrels valued at $63,320 during the previous period in 1917-18. Recent statistics relative to fisheries are not available. Considerable herring were caught at the head of the Great Lakes, and the smaller lakes in the northern sections of the three Western Provinces are well stocked and are fished for commercial purposes.

Immigration was more or less stagnant during the war. The Central Western Provinces, however, received 22,267 immigrants from the United States for the ten months ended October, 1919, as compared with 19,649 for the same period in 1918. These immigrants were of a good class, and it is estimated that they brought with them in cash and effects nearly $12,000,000. Trade conditions throughout the year were very satisfactory for both wholesaler and retailer. Failures were light and mortgage companies report that payments compare favourably with previous years, with the exception of southern Saskatchewan, which has experienced a succession of crop failures.

Ontario. General conditions throughout Ontario during the past year were good. There was little unemployment apart from that due to strikes in certain industries, and as a rule high wages were paid. Wholesale and retail trades were satisfactory and few failures occurred during the year. Wholesalers found it possible to do business on shorter credits, as retail dealers sold on a cash basis to a greater extent than formerly. Grain crops, fall wheat excepted, were below the average. This was due to a wet spring and a hot, dry summer. The acreage and yield of fall wheat was double that of 1918. Root crops were good, with the exception of potatoes. Corn was good, and the hay crop above the average in quantity and about the average in quality. The fruit yield was much below the average, with the exception of grapes. Tobacco was satisfactory and sold at high prices. More fall ploughing was done during the year than for several years past. Live stock, especially milch cows and sheep, showed satisfactory increases. Owing to the scarcity of feed, less beef cattle than usual was carried over the winter in some districts. The production of cheese was less than in 1918, but more milk was sold to the condenseries.

Manufacturers had a very successful year. Production was limited only by the shortage of material and disturbed labour conditions. The demand for both domestic and export purposes was excellent, and goods sold at high prices. A number of new factories were, or are about to be, established, many of them as subsidiaries of American companies. Owing to labour troubles and to curtailment of demand for nickel and copper since the termination of the war, the value of the production of minerals decreased nearly $22,000,000 for the first nine months of 1919 as compared with the same period in 1918.

	1918	1919
Gold ....\.	$ 6,875,766	$ 7,574,586
Silver	12,500,980	7,898,220
Nickel (metallic)	214,507	2,732,676
Nickel in matte	20,105,087	5,424,552
Copper in matte	6,820,785	1,908,936
Pig Iron	1,184,120	795,009
Other metals l	1,897,791	1,541,734
	$49,599,036	$27,875,713

The lumber output was considerably less than in 1918 owing to scarcity of labour, high cost of supplies and the difficulty experienced in the fall of 1918 in inducing men to go into the woods during the influenza epidemic. Both domestic and export demand was active at high prices. The lumber cut will probably be larger in 1920. Pulp and paper production was greater than ever and sold at very high prices. The shipyards of the Province were fully employed at remunerative rates. The Ontario Hydro-Electric Commission is engaged on new works at Chippawa which will develop 300,000 additional horse-power at Niagara. The Commission is also building a plant at Nipigon to develop between 60,000 and 75,000 H.P., machinery being installed to produce an immediate increase of 25,000 H.P.

Quebec. Considerable difficulty was experienced last year in harvesting the crops on account of heavy rains. The hay crop was average. The grain crop, although of good quality, gave a light yield when threshed. The heavy crop of potatoes was diminished by rot. Farmers complained of shortage of labour. Exports of grain and dairy products from Montreal were as follows:—

GRAIN AND FLOUR

	1918	1919		
Wheat (bushels)	22,082,000	82,803,000	Inc.	10,721,000
Oats (bushels)	34,748,000	2,448,000	Dec.	32,300,000
Barley (bushels)	2,763,000	10,799,000	Inc.	8,036,000
Rye (bushels)	206,000	776,000	Inc.	570,000
Flour (sacks)	7,419,000	7,721,000	Inc.	302,000

DAIRY PRODUCTS

	1918	1919		
Cheese (boxes)	1,754,000	1,172,000	Dec.	582,000
Butter (packages)	143,400	77,000	Dec.	66,400
Eggs (cases)	77,700	449,000	Inc.	371,300

The large decrease in shipments of oats was due to the absence of British Government orders. The number of ocean-going vessels entering the port of Montreal during 1919 was 786, with a tonnage of 2,179,000, as against 644 vessels in 1918, tonnage 1,910,000. Manufacturers had a record year. Textile companies report that mills were working to capacity, with orders on hand for months to come. The boot and shoe trade was unusually busy throughout 1919, as retailers during the previous year allowed their stocks to get low, hoping for a fall in prices. They were obliged, however, to replenish at the high prices current last year. Both wholesalers and retailers report an extremely active year. A greater proportion of customers availed themselves of trade discounts. Collections were never better than last year and the number of failures was smaller than for the past 25 or 30 years. There was improvement in the lumber business owing to increased space having been available for ocean shipments. There was a firm demand for lumber from the United States. Pulp and paper mills were working to capacity during the past year. The building trades were more active although not yet normal, building not having fully revived. Shipbuilding was not so active, and some cancellations were received for ships for foreign account. There was a little revival in real estate, more sales of city business properties having been recorded.

Maritime Provinces. The fishery industry had a very successful year. The shore catch was small but the deep sea catch was one of the largest on record, the Lunenburg fleet alone bringing in a total 300,000 quintals as against 238,000 in 1918 and 233,000 in 1917. Prices were lower, however, being from $12 to $14 per quintal as compared with $15 in 1918; pickled herring declined $4, and spring mackerel about $10 per barrel. Transportation difficulties are reported to have been almost as great as during the war. The lobster pack is estimated at 130,000 cases as compared with 100,000 in 1918, with prices from 40% to 50% higher.

Farmers had a satisfactory year and obtained high prices for their products. Hay, grain and root crops, with the exception of potatoes, were good. The latter suffered from rot, and the crop was below the average. The apple crop—over 2,000,000 barrels, was a record one. There was a temporary falling off in shipments of apples to the British market. Live stock of all kinds showed a healthy increase and farm labour continued scarce and wages high. The lumber cut exceeded that of 1918, more operators were engaged, and the labour market was easier. Lack of transportation handicapped shippers and to some extent restricted exports, particularly to the United States where a good market offered. Shipbuilding showed a falling off, especially in the case of wooden ships. There was fair demand for smaller trading vessels and fishing craft, and yards handling this class of construction were kept busy. Conditions in the mining industry were similar to those existing in 1918, and the output was about the same. A shortage of labour was again reported. The demand for coal was heavy and prices high. Manufacturers had a good year, the steel and iron industries excepted.

Newfoundland. The total catch of cod was estimated at 185,000 quintals less than in the previous year, having been 1,831,000 quintals only, as compared with 2,016,000 in 1918. The value of the smaller catch, however, was materially greater. Cod oil was in active demand at record prices, namely, between $280 and $290 per ton. The herring fishery is an important one, but the catch, 212,000 barrels, was not as large as in the previous record year. The seal fishery was the poorest experienced, being only 81,293 seals as compared with a normal catch of about 200,000. This is partly accounted for by the small fleet of seven steamers engaged in the fishery as against twenty prior to 1914. The shortage in catch, however, was offset to some extent by the prices obtained for the oil and skins which advanced to figures hitherto unknown. The lobster and salmon fisheries continued to be affected by abnormal conditions in Europe, Germany having been one of the largest importers in pre-war times.

Lumbering was not extensively engaged in during the past year, although the pit prop industry continued to be developed. Shipments were small, owing to a shortage of tonnage. The pulp and paper industries operated successfully during the year. In the vicinity of 700,000 tons of iron ore were shipped from the Bell Island mines during 1919. Coal was discovered in small quantities, for local use only. Manufacturers have been working to capacity. Wholesale and retail trade has been good and obligations have been met satisfactorily.

The following Director's were elected for the ensuing year with, afterwards, Sir Herbert Holt re-elected as President and Edson L. Pease as Vice-President and Managing Director:

JAS. REDMOND, ESQ., Montreal, Que.
G. R. CROWE, ESQ., Winnipeg, Man.
D. K. ELLIOTT, ESQ., Winnipeg, Man.
HON. W. H. THORNE, St. John, N.B.
HUGH PATON, ESQ., Montreal, Que.
A. J. BROWN, ESQ., K.C., Montreal.
W. J. SHEPPARD, ESQ., Waubaushene.
C. S. WILCOX, ESQ., Hamilton, Ont.
A. E. DYMENT, ESQ., Toronto, Ont.
C. E. NEILL, ESQ., Montreal, Que.
SIR MORTIMER B. DAVIS, Montreal.

G. H. DUGGAN, ESQ., Montreal, Que.
C. C. BLACKADAR, ESQ., Halifax, N.S.
JOHN T. ROSS, ESQ., Quebec, Que.
R. MACD. PATERSON, ESQ., Montreal.
W. H. MCWILLIAMS, ESQ., Winnipeg.
CAPT. WM. ROBINSON, Winnipeg, Man.
A. MCTAVISH CAMPBELL, ESQ., Winnipeg, Man.
ROBERT ADAIR, ESQ., Montreal, Que.
T. SHERMAN ROGERS, ESQ., K.C., Halifax, N.S.

STATEMENT OF BUSINESS

For the Year ended

29th NOVEMBER, 1919

Balance of Profit and Loss Account, 30th November, 1918	$ 535,757.19	
Profits for the year, after deducting charges of management and all other expenses, accrued interest on deposits, full provision for all bad and doubtful debts and rebate of interest on unmatured bills	3,423,264.34	
		$ 3,959,021.53

Appropriated as follows:—		
Dividends Nos. 126, 127, 128 and 129 at 12 per cent. per annum	$ 1,866,196.50	
Fiftieth Anniversary Bonus of 2 per cent. to Shareholders	340,000.00	
Transferred to Officers' Pension Fund	100,000.00	
Written off Bank Premises Account	400,000.00	
War Tax on Bank Note Circulation	156,406.29	
Balance of Profit and Loss carried forward	1,096,418.74	
		$ 3,959,021.53

RESERVE FUND

Balance at Credit, 30th November, 1918	$15,000,000.00	
Premium on New Capital Stock	2,000,000.00	
Balance at Credit, 29th November, 1919		$17,000,000.00

GENERAL AND COMPARATIVE STATEMENT

LIABILITIES

	30th Nov., 1918	29th Nov., 1919
To the Public:—		
Deposits not bearing interest	$135,243,278.72	$159,656,229.66
Deposits bearing interest, including interest accrued to date of Statement	197,348,439.20	259,465,169.69
Total Deposits	$332,591,717.92	$419,121,399.37
Notes of the Bank in Circulation	39,880,975.74	39,837,265.74
Balance due to Dominion Government	9,000,000.00	14,000,000.00
Balances due to other Banks in Canada	26,794.90	13,970.86
Balances due to Banks and Banking Correspondents in the United Kingdom and foreign countries	8,068,926.22	7,449,852.43
Bills Payable	316,058.43	806,776.89
Acceptances under Letters of Credit	10,162,629.56	16,467,978.69
	$397,547,102.77	$497,697,243.90
To the Shareholders:—		
Capital Stock Paid up	$ 14,000,000.00	$ 17,000,000.00
Reserve Fund	15,000,000.00	17,000,000.00
Balance of Profits carried forward	535,757.19	1,096,418.74
Dividends Unclaimed	10,122.95	8,203.03
Dividend No. 125 (at 12% per annum), payable Dec. 2nd, 1918	420,000.00	....
Dividend No. 129 (at 12% per annum), payable Dec. 1st, 1919	....	505,319.12
Fiftieth Anniversary Bonus of 2%, payable December 20th, 1919	....	340,000.00
Total	$427,512,982.91	$533,647,064.98

ASSETS

Current Coin	$ 17,488,314.07	$ 17,653,879.92
Dominion Notes	24,686,344.75	26,785,724.00
United States Currency	....	8,746,805.00
Other Foreign Money	....	2,545,138.41
Deposit in the Central Gold Reserves	26,000,000.00	24,500,000.00
Notes of other Banks	10,678,020.86	8,464,200.00
Cheques on other Banks	20,034,899.30	23,757,240.83
Balances due by other Banks in Canada	6,042.80	17,108.80
Balances due by Banks and Banking Correspondents elsewhere than in Canada	10,391,516.44	18,101,378.08
Dominion and Provincial Government Securities, not exceeding market value	36,599,976.37	45,323,598.66
Canadian Municipal Securities and British, Foreign and Colonial Public Securities other than Canadian, not exceeding the market value	29,620,885.90	33,400,542.77
Railway and other Bonds, Debentures and Stocks, not exceeding the market value	15,084,414.64	19,414,891.06
Call Loans in Canada, on Bonds, Debentures and Stocks	10,067,481.94	16,495,614.30
Call and Short (not exceeding thirty days) Loans elsewhere than in Canada	24,374,191.40	33,812,751.53
	$224,982,088.47	$273,908,862.86
Other Current Loans and Discounts in Canada (less rebate of interest)	119,184,715.26	143,259,518.47
Other Current Loans and Discounts elsewhere than in Canada (less rebate of interest)	64,175,163.85	90,210,271.82
Overdue Debts (estimated loss provided for)	388,513.29	365,089.66
Real Estate other than Bank Premises	1,171,181.69	1,495,271.00
Bank Premises, at not more than cost, less amounts written off	6,492,011.85	7,016,444.12
Liabilities of Customers under Letters of Credit, as per contra	10,162,629.56	16,467,978.69
Deposit with the Minister for the purposes of the Circulation Fund	742,818.75	750,000.00
Other Assets not included in the foregoing	213,910.19	178,648.80
	$427,512,982.91	$533,647,084.99

H. S. HOLT,
President

EDSON L. PEASE,
Managing Director

C. E. NEILL,
General Manager

●

STATEMENT TO THE DOMINION GOVERNMENT (CONDENSED)
MARCH 31st, 1920

LIABILITIES

Capital Paid Up	$ 17,000,000.00
Reserve Fund	17,000,000.00
Undivided Profits	1,096,418.74
Notes in Circulation	39,142,342.74
Deposits	448,416,486.87
Due to other Banks	11,865,128.00
Bills Payable (Acceptances by London Branch)	2,070,003.42
Acceptances under Letters of Credit	18,546,725.65
	$550,137,105.42

ASSETS

Cash on Hand and in Banks	$108,365,350.70
Deposit in the Central Gold Reserves	22,000,000.00
Government and Municipal Securities	37,346,341.67
Railway and Other Bonds, Debentures and Stocks	16,358,851.48
Call Loans in Canada	15,308,829.99
Call Loans elsewhere than in Canada	45,365,515.72
	$244,739,889.56
Loans and Discounts	281,817,536.68
Liabilities of Customers under Letters of Credit as per contra	18,546,725.65
Bank Premises	7,701,278.12
Real Estate other than Bank Premises	1,526,798.56
Mortgages on Real Estate sold by the Bank	54,876.90
Deposit with Dominion Government for Security of Note Circulation	750,000.00
Total	$550,137,105.42

AN IMPORTANT BANKING INSTITUTION

ANNUAL ADDRESSES AND REPORTS
OF
THE MERCHANTS BANK OF CANADA*

. The 57th annual meeting of the Shareholders of the Merchants' Bank of Canada was held on June 2nd, 1920, in the Board Room at the Bank's Head Office at Montreal. Among those in attendance were: Sir H. Montagu Allan, Mr. K. W. Blackwell, Mr. Thomas Long, Mr. A. J. Dawes, Mr. F. Howard Wilson, Mr. Farquhar Robertson, Mr. George L. Cains, Mr. Alfred B. Evans, Lt.-Col. Jas. R. Moodie, Hon. Lorne C. Webster, Mr. E. W. Kneeland, Directors, and Messrs. Walter Wilson, John Patterson, Edward Fiske (Joliet), Arthur Browning, A. D. Thornton, Colin Campbell, Thomas Stapleton (Oshawa), R. S. White, S. M. Baylis, W. B. Blackader, David Kinghorn, A. Haig Sims, Andrew A. MacDougall, W. M. Ramsay, T. E. Merrett, A. B. Patterson, P. C. Schaefer, W. J. Finucan, F. J. Shreve, W. A. Meldrum, J. N. Lorrain, J. M. Kilbourn, F. L. MacGachen, J. G. Muir, James Elmsly, H. R. Little, A. McFayden, C. A. Harcourt, R. H. Arkell, W. B. Leitch. On motion of Mr. John Patterson, the President, Sir H. Montagu Allan, was asked to take the chair. Mr. J. M. Kilbourn was appointed Secretary.

Address by Sir H. Montagu Allan, C.V.O., President of the Bank. Despite the fact that operating costs have continued their upward course, the net profits resulting from the year's business were $1,686,156.15, being an increase over last year of $302,586.75. The financial position of the Bank, as reflected in detail in the Balance Sheet before you, will, I hope, meet with your full approbation. In the Directors' Report of a year ago, I mentioned that an issue of $1,400,000 of new stock was being made, and that, owing to the date of allotment, this step would fall for comment more appropriately at the next Annual Meeting. I am now pleased to advise you that the issue was promptly taken up and long since paid for in full by the shareholders. The Paid-up Capital of the Bank, therefore, stands to-day at $8,400,000, while the $700,000 premium received from the new issue and $700,000 transferred from Profit and Loss Account have been added to the Reserve, thus maintaining that Fund upon an equal basis with the Paid-up Capital. You have already been advised that, in line with the growth of the Bank, and with a view of keeping pace fairly and

---

*Note.—For History of the Bank see *The Canadian Annual Review Supplement* for 1910 and for preceding Annual Reports and Addresses see the volumes for 1916, 1917 and 1918.

D. C. MACAROW
General Manager Merchants Bank of Canada

reasonably with the legitimate requirements of our ever-growing clientele, a further issue of $2,100,000 of new stock, upon the same favourable terms to the shareholders, is now under way. This new issue will appropriately be referred to again a year hence. It may be of interest to mention that the Bank's shareholders now number 2,622, as against 2,406 in 1919, and 2,340 in 1918.

At the commencement of the Bank's fiscal year, presently under review, the Directors felt warranted in placing the Dividend on a regular 12% basis, and also, later, in distributing a bonus of 1%, making in all 13% received by the shareholders during the twelve month period. No doubt their action in this respect will have your full approval. During the year we opened 65 Branches, with a number of sub-agencies as feeders, and I may say that results have amply justified our action, as evidenced by the fact that we have only closed 2 Branches during the period. In December last our office in London, England, was opened for business and already gratifying progress has been made in the building up of a London connection, while the facilities afforded our clientele on this side have greatly enhanced the value of the services we are enabled to extend to them. It had been apparent for some time that the growth and increasing importance of the institution called for the completion of our organization by the establishment of an office in the Capital of the Empire. During the year we conceived it to be advisable and expedient, in keeping with modern and approved practice, to liquify to some extent the inactive asset represented by Bank Premises Account, which, as you are aware, must, with the growth of the Bank, be an ever-expanding one. We, accordingly, turned over certain of our premises to a subsidiary company called the Merchants' Realty Corporation, who in turn issued Bonds against the respective properties to the amount of $4,000,000, the proceeds of the sale of which have been appropriately applied. These Bonds are of a serial nature and will be thus automatically amortized as they fall in for payment, control of the property being held by the Bank through the ownership of all the stock of the Company, this being shown upon our books at a nominal figure.

Since the last Meeting, death has removed from our midst Mr. E. F. Hebden, formerly General Manager of the Bank and, for a period, Managing Director. His service in the institution was life-long and in his demise the financial community lost a distinctive and distinguished personality, the Bank an able and experienced administrator. His death is regarded with deep regret by all. The vacancy upon the Board has been filled by the appointment of Mr. E. W. Kneeland, of Winnipeg, a business man of wide experience and influence in the West. In view of the continued growth of the Bank's business, the Directors are of opinion it would be desirable to enlarge the numerical strength of the Board by adding one more to their number, and an amendment to this effect, of the relative by-law, will be submitted for your approval. The name of Mr. Gordon M. McGregor, of Windsor, Vice-President of the Ford

Motor Company of Canada, will accordingly be included in the list, which will be submitted to you in due course. He is a man of high standing in the commercial community, and we are sure of your agreement with the Directors that he will prove an acquisition to the Board. You may be interested to learn that I made a trip last autumn through Ontario and the West—accompanied by some of the Directors and the General Manager. We met all the senior officers, and I have pleasure in saying that I found the trip both inspiring and beneficial to a degree. We have undoubtedly an efficient staff and you will, I am sure, join with the Directors in extending to its members, one and all, a word of cordial appreciation for their capable and loyal services, to which the measure of progress the Bank has enjoyed is in no small extent attributable.

Presentation to Mr. Macarow, General Manager
After my formal address I wish to add just a few words, and I apologize to Mr. Macarow for doing so, because it is somewhat of a personal matter, but I think on this occasion it should be referred to. I wish to say that the day before yesterday I and the members of the Board were notified by a member of the staff of the Bank that a very important affair was to take place in the board room here yesterday afternoon. We attended, and were agreeably surprised to find that the business in hand was a presentation to our General Manager, Mr. D. C. Macarow. I have not secured his permission to mention this matter, but take the opportunity of doing so, because it was a decidedly unique event, of which neither he nor I nor the Directors had any previous knowledge. It turned out to be a spontaneous gift from all the members of the Bank's staff, from Vancouver to Halifax, a magnificent silver tea service, one of the most beautiful things I have ever seen, with other objets d'art.

The presentation was the occasion of several very happy addresses from members of the staff, with an Address which they presented Mr. Macarow, along with their gift, and led to a particularly illuminating reply from the General Manager, which, needless to say, brought down the house. It is with particular pleasure that I inform the shareholders of this event, because it is of interest to you all to know that the General Manager and the staff are in such close accord, and have such friendly personal relations. We of the Board have every confidence in Mr. Macarow, and, from what we saw in the West last year, there was no doubt of the friendly feelings of the staff everywhere towards him. As an evidence of the friendly and confident relations that exist between Mr. Macarow and the staff all over Canada I think yesterday's function was one of the most agreeable and unique I have been privileged to witness for a long time, and I congratulate Mr. Macarow on the regard he has won from the Bank Staff throughout the whole Dominion.

In the first place I must say that the personal onslaught made upon myself by the President is as unexpected as it is kindly. I was deeply touched by the presentation so spontaneously made to myself by the staff throughout the country. I view the presentation with mixed feelings, appreciation of the kindly intent it showed, and doubt as to my own merits. However, I accepted it in the spirit in which it was given, and it will always be one of my most prized possessions. The President's address forms a comprehensive epitome of all the important phases of the·Bank's present position, and has appropriately dealt with or touched upon the several outstanding developments which have taken place during the past fiscal year. I shall, therefore, but add a brief word of amplification as to some features of the statement which it occurs to me may be enlarged upon without unnecessary repetition.

Another Victory Loan last autumn was again heavily subscribed to by the Bank's clientele throughout the country, their total subscriptions reaching the large sum of $41,770,000, practically all of which (conversions being negligible in amount) was a direct charge against our deposits. Yet the resultant heavy withdrawal was not only overtaken, but deposit totals show an increase, in addition, over last year, of $24,900,000. This must be considered a satisfactory achievement, I think. Commercial discounts have, in natural course, advanced also, and the total now stands at $113,198,000, being an increase during the year of $17,324,000. These figures indicate that the Bank is continuing to carry its full share of the load in a period when the support and encouragement of the productive capacity and energies of the country is a matter of paramount importance. If stable conditions are to be reasonably maintained, it is essential that the vital channels of commerce and industry be kept open and, I venture to assert, in functioning as the above figures reflect, the Bank is playing its part to that end.

At last year's Annual Meeting I made reference to our Asset column as representing dollar for dollar of actual value, and I make the same assertion to-day with equal emphasis. The record of growth this year leads me to feel that a few figures showing our progress, taking the last five years as a basis of comparison, may be of some interest to you. The totals and percentages are as follows, based on the year-end figures as at 30th April, 1915, and 30th April this present year:

	1915	1920	Gain
Total Deposits	$64,869,000	$163,080,000	151%
Current Loans and Discounts....	47,401,000	113,198,000	138%
Total Assets	86,190,000	197,387,000	129%

A satisfactory and evenly balanced measure of development, you will, I am sure, agree. If I may be permitted to add a word as to general conditions I will be brief, for the subject has been dealt with from platform, pulpit and press so exhaustively that I cannot say much without wearisome reiteration. I fear it must be admitted,

however, that the progress of this country, and indeed of the world
at large, toward normal peace conditions has not been what we
looked forward to a year ago.   Unsettlement continues, labour and
other difficulties abound, and the dominant need of the time, Production, is palpably inert and backward.   So long as production
lags, so long will high prices and general inflation continue.   Costs
are mounting to ever higher levels and the process of deflation with
the necessary changes in ideas, in habits and in outlook to something
more approaching those of normal conditions can hardly be said yet
to be in real evidence, though sporadic and somewhat spectacular
cutting of prices in certain seasonal lines of manufactured goods
may perhaps be accepted as a psychological sign showing that the
trend, at least, is in the right direction.

The demand for borrowed capital continues to be more or less
importunate and it is in the conservation of credit and the equitable
rationing of it that Banks can play and, indeed, are playing a sound
constructive role.   Legitimate productive enterprises are being
fostered and encouraged fairly, while at the same time a firmly
restraining hand is held upon unproductive, non-essential and
speculative undertakings.   This policy of selective curtailment, so
to put it, operating as it does at the very root of existing evils, and
applied with due judgment, discrimination and consistency, cannot but prove a beneficial corrective and an importantly contributing factor towards restoring, with a minimum of dislocation and
disturbance, healthy and normal conditions in the body politic.

I might here venture to say that it is a matter of gratification
to see our merchantile marine growing apace and to know that the
Government will have, it is understood, some 45 merchant vessels in
commission by the end of July next.   I mentioned last year, and I
reaffirm the opinion then expressed, that there is nothing of greater
national importance than the establishment of our own lines of
ocean transport, and what has been and is being accomplished in
this direction, both by the Government and by private enterprise,
augurs well for the future safety and stability of the country's
trade and commerce.   After what looked like in some respects an
ominous start the crop situation throughout the country now seems
to justify the belief that good yields will be secured this year.
Predictions, however, are futile and we can only nurse the hope that
actual results will fairly measure up to present optimistic estimates.

Certainly, on the theory of averages alone, we are entitled to
look for some redress in the crop situation this year.   Much depends upon it, more especially in view of the disappointing results
of the last two years, and if nature is benevolent in the coming
harvest this country will benefit to an unmeasured extent, and we
shall be reasonably in a position to view the period of deflation,
upon the threshold of which we stand, with feelings of confidence
as to our immediate future—as to our ultimate future there need
be no misgiving, for it must be borne in mind that Canada is a
young and virile country of almost limitless possibilities and im-

mense natural resources awaiting development, that its manhood is strong, enterprising, thoughtful and sane.

While we have our readjustment difficulties to deal with, our progress through the transition period will be orderly and well-conducted if there is a fair measure of mutual appreciation of surrounding difficulties and reasonable co-operation and good will all along the line in surmounting them. In a word, if the wise and reasonable policy so briefly and clearly condensed in the three simple words "give and take" continues to operate with cordial uninterruption we shall move with steady and assured step to the great destiny which lies before us through wide-open avenues of peace, progress and prosperity. Before closing I would like to add my tribute of appreciation to the staff of the Bank for their devotion and efficiency. I cannot do so better than by saying that the President's apt and graceful remarks thereanent have my unqualified and unrestricted endorsement. It is true, indeed, that the progress of the Bank is in no small measure due to the co-operative efforts of a loyal, capable and contented staff. That, I know, we have.

The Directors were re-elected as follows and afterwards Sir H. Montagu Allan was re-elected President and K. W. Blackwell Vice-President:

Sir H. Montagu Allan	Mr. Farquhar Robertson
Mr. K. W. Blackwell	Mr. Geo. L. Cains
Mr. Thomas Long	Mr. Alfred B. Evans
Sir Frederick Orr Lewis, Bart.	Mr. T. Ahearn
Hon. C. C. Ballantyne	Lt.-Col. Jas. R. Moodie
Mr. A. J. Dawes	Hon. Lorne C. Webster
Mr. F. Howard Wilson	Mr. E. W. Kneeland
Mr. Gordon M. McGregor	

STATEMENT OF BUSINESS FOR THE YEAR ENDED 30th APRIL, 1920

THE MERCHANTS BANK OF CANADA

The Net Profits of the year, after payment of charges, rebate on discounts, interest on deposits, and making full provision for bad and doubtful debts, have amounted to	$1,686,156.15
Premium on New Stock	700,000.00
The balance brought forward from 30th April, 1919, was	574,043.32
Making a total of	$2,960,199.47
This has been disposed of as follows:	
Dividend No. 128, at the rate of 12 per cent. per annum.. $238,416.01	
" " 129 " " " 243,726.44	
" " 130 " " " 250,805.76	
Bonus 1 per cent. 83,263.00	
Dividend No. 131, at the rate of 12 per cent. per annum . 252,074.56	
	$1,068,285.77
Government War Tax on Note Circulation	81,138.72
Transferred to Reserve Fund from Premium on New Stock	700,000.00
" to Reserve Fund out of Profits	700,000.00
Written off Bank Premises Account	100,000.00
Contribution to Officers' Pension Fund	50,000.00
Balance carried forward	260,774.98
	$2,960,199.47

Balance, 30th April, 1919 .... $7,000,000.00
Premium on New Stock 700,000.00
Transferred from Profits ....·............ 700,000.00

$8,400,000.00

Average Paid-Up Capital during year $8,230,539.00

STATEMENT OF LIABILITIES AND ASSETS AT 30th APRIL, 1920

LIABILITIES

	1920	1919
1. To the Shareholders:		
Capital Stock paid in	$ 8,400,000.00	$ 7,000,000.00
Rest or Reserve Fund	8,400,000.00	7,000,000.00
Dividends declared and unpaid	338,159.22	194,194.00
Balance of Profits as per Profit and Loss Account submitted herewith	260,774.98	574,043.32
	$ 17,398,934.20	$ 14,768,237.32
2. To the Public:		
Notes of the Bank in Circulation	14,791,027.00	13,316,032.00
Deposits not bearing interest	45,368,876.69	43,552,214.61
Deposits bearing interest (including interest accrued to date of Statement)	114,132,175.79	91,904,993.37
Balances due to other Banks in Canada	2,747,402.86	2,614,696.64
Balances due to Banks and Banking Correspondents in the United Kingdom and foreign countries	831,997.39	105,076.96
Bills payable	....	....
Acceptances under Letters of Credit	2,117,441.21	464,153.05
Liabilities not included in the foregoing	....	....
	$197,387,855.14	$166,725,404.95

ASSETS

	1920	1919
Current Coin	$ 4,193,117.50	$ 4,946,946.33
Deposit in the Central Gold Reserves	7,500,000.00	7,000,000.00
Dominion Notes	8,407,008.25	8,405,602.50
Notes of other Banks	1,170,482.00	985,044.00
Cheques on other Banks	11,098,195.77	6,082,616.99
Balances due by other Banks in Canada	9,400.50	8,215.80
Balances due by Banks and Banking Correspondents in the United Kingdom	445,034.79	123,496.50
Balances due by Banks and Banking Correspondents elsewhere than in Canada and the United Kingdom	1,561,157.87	1,903,040.10
Dominion and Provincial Government Securities, not exceeding market value	7,898,229.90	6,005,573.65
Railway and other Bonds, Debentures and Stocks, not exceeding market value	4,507,688.10	4,119,705.32
Canadian Municipal Securities and British, Foreign and Colonial Public Securities other than Canadian	18,239,204.59	15,238,399.32
Call Loans in Canada on Bonds, Debentures and Stocks	6,471,494.31	5,184,690.71
Call Loans elsewhere than in Canada	6,206,587.78	2,801,857.72
	$ 72,697,546.36	$ 62,750,168.94
Current Loans and Discounts in Canada (less rebate of Interest) $113,198,913.90 Loans to Cities, Towns, Municipalities and School Districts 3,587,491.69	116,786,405.59	95,874,426.04
Current Loans and Discounts elsewhere than in Canada (less Rebate of Interest)	1,117,268.51	832,918.12
Liabilities of Customers under Letters of Credit as per contra	2,117,441.21	464,153.05
Real Estate other than bank premises	604,325.33	782,326.64
Overdue Debts, estimated loss provided for	352,737.25	386,973.56
Bank Premises at not more than cost (less amounts written off)	2,576,630.21	5,253,269.48
Deposit with the Minister for the purposes of the Circulation Fund	377,000.00	366,000.00
Other Assets not included in the foregoing	758,500.68	515,149.12
	$197,387,855.14	$166,725,404.95

H. MONTAGU ALLAN,
      President.

D. C. MACAROW,
      General Manager.

REPORT OF THE AUDITORS TO THE SHAREHOLDERS OF THE MERCHANTS BANK OF CANADA.

In accordance with the provisions of sub-sections 19 and 20 of Section 56 of the Bank Act, we report to the shareholders as follows:—

We have examined the above Balance Sheet with the Books of Account and other records at the Chief Office of the Bank and with the signed returns from the Branches and Agencies and have checked the cash and verified the securities of the Bank at the Chief Office against the entries in regard thereto in the books of the Bank at 30th April, 1920, and at a different time during the year and found them to agree with such entries. We also attended at some of the Branches during the year and checked the cash and verified the securities held at the dates of our attendances and found them to agree with the entries in regard thereto in the books of the Bank.

We have obtained all the information and explanations we have required. In our opinion, the transactions of the Bank which have come under our notice have been within the powers of the Bank, and the above Balance Sheet is properly drawn up so as to exhibit a true and correct view of the state of the Bank's affairs, according to the best of our information and the explanations given to us, and as shown by the books of the Bank.

> GORDON TANSLEY, } Auditors.
> VIVIAN HARCOURT, }

(of the firm of Deloitte, Plender, Griffiths & Co.)

MONTREAL, 25th May, 1920.

EDITORIAL IN MONTREAL *GAZETTE*, JUNE 2nd, 1920

THE MERCHANTS BANK OF CANADA

Canadian banks have enjoyed so long a succession of profitable years that proceedings at annual meetings evoke no discussion, and interest is confined to the observations of high officials upon the general commercial situation. The meeting of Merchants Bank shareholders, yesterday, made no exception to the rule. The institution has had a successful year. The field of its operations steadily widens. In the twelve months to April 30th last, deposits, loans, note circulation, number of branches, and number of shareholders all increased substantially, and these are the items significant of banking prosperity. Profits of $1,686,156 represent a fraction over 10 per cent. on average capital and reserve, and a gain of $302,586 over the preceding year. In common with several other banks, the Merchants has manifested conspicuous enterprise in extending the scope of its business, and in assisting the remarkable expansion of Canadian trade during recent years. In the period under review, 65 new branches were established, and it is a tribute to the good judgment of the management in the past that it was

found desirable to close only two agencies.   To a capital increase
of $1,400,000 last year, there is being added another $2,100,000,
bringing the total up to $10,500,000, supplemented by a reserve of
$9,450,000 out of undivided profits and premiums on stock issues.
In some respects, the popularity of a bank is attested by the number of its proprietors, which, in the case of Merchants, has grown
to 2,622, or nearly 300 more than two years ago, and to these have
been given of late appreciably higher dividends warranted by
larger earnings.   Comparisons are sometimes odious, and distinctions invidious, but noticeable in the addresses yesterday of the
President and of the General Manager was the warm tribute paid
to the staff of the bank; and while doubtless staff loyalty and
efficiency is not exceptional in Canadian banking, it will be gratifying to the proprietors of the Merchants to learn how capably they
are served.

The General Manager, Mr. Macarow, alluded briefly to the annual statement, which tells its own tale, pointing out that the deposits have risen $24,000,000, despite the purchase during the year
of nearly $42,000,000 of Victory Bonds by the bank's clientele, and
taking a survey of progress during the last five years, he was able
to show a gain of 151 per cent. in deposits, of 138 per cent. in loans
and discounts, and of 129 per cent. in total assets, a remarkable
expansion.   Deeper interest attaches to Mr. Macarow's remarks
upon the general trade situation.   His deductions are cautious, as
becomes a banker.   A return to normal conditions is still in the
future: "Unsettlement continues, labour and other difficulties
abound, and the dominant need of the time, production, is palpably inert and backward."   This state of things has existed ever
since the conclusion of the war, and is probably inseparable from
periods of rising prices, expanded circulation, easy credit, and
lavish expenditure.   But the balloon cannot indefinitely go up, and
the bankers' problem is to determine when it has reached a safe
summit, and to prepare the way for a gradual descent.   It happens, perhaps always will happen in circumstances like the present,
that the desirable means of arresting inflation are not being yet generally applied.   Production lingers, and in the words of Mr.
Macarow "so long as production lags, so long will high prices and
general inflation continue."   Higher wages and shorter hours of
work intensify the plight, and Labour has not yet learned the lesson, that the remedy for the high cost of living is not to be found in
increased wages and lessened work.

Mr. Macarow expresses no compunctions as to the future of
Canada commercially.   It has, indeed, become necessary for the
banks to cast an anchor at the windward in order to arrest credit
expansion and to check operations conducive to higher prices, but
there is plenty of banking accomodation for legitimate business.
A policy of "selective curtailment," in the apt phrase of Mr. Macarow, is being adopted towards borrowers, and in his opinion such
policy applied with due judgment, discrimination and consistency,

cannot but prove a beneficial corrective and an important factor
towards restoring, with a minimum of dislocation and disturbance,
healthy and normal conditions.   It would be a happy issue out of
trouble if men would understand that material salvation is to be
found in more, not in less, work, and in longer, not shorter hours
of labor in the production of essential commodities.

Much depends on the character of the crops.   An abundant
harvest will prop the commercial structure and extend the period
of what, after all is said, are good times; but it is yet too early to
prognosticate the yield.   It is much, however, to know that a
promising start has been made.   One subject touched upon by
Mr. Macarow deserves, perhaps, more attention than it has received
outside of political discussion, and that is the importance of the
Canadian merchantile marine.   In a short time there will be 45
steamships in commission, and in another year 60 vessels.   These
ships have exceptional usefulness in the sense that they can be employed to exploit new markets and to bring to Canada needed products not always otherwise obtainable.   The Canadian marine has
already performed good service in bringing sugar from Cuba and
tropical products from the West Indies.   It may be used in regular
routes, in giving continuous communication between Canada and
other countries with which commerce can be exchanged, and the
value of this fleet is not wholly to be esteemed by the profit it may
earn directly from freightage.   Mr. Macarow's last word was a
qualified optimism.   The country will, he believes, surmount whatever difficulties may beset it, if the people exercise mutual co-operation and good will all along the line, and recognize that security
rests in a policy of "give and take."   Crisp and concise in form,
the General Manager's address has struck the salient notes.

GROWTH OF THE MERCHANTS BANK OF CANADA

Year	Paid-Up Capital	Reserve Fund and Undivided Profits	Total Deposits	Total Assets
1890	$5,799,200	$2,340,904	$ 8,754,841	$20,717,737
1895	6,000,000	3,057,277	10,864,304	22,928,248
1900	6,000,000	2,650,686	16,178,408	29,588,531
1905	6,000,000	3,473,197	27,066,248	41,477,589
1910	6,000,000	4,999,297	54,091,275	71,600,058
1915	7,000,000	7,245,140	63,662,368	86,190,464
1916	7,000,000	7,250,984	72,540,828	96,861,363
1917	7,000,000	7,421,292	92,730,935	121,130,558
1918	7,000,000	7,487,978	112,284,675	140,987,544
1919	7,000,000	7,574,043	138,071,904	166,725,404
1920	8,400,000	8,660,774	163,080,452	197,387,855

A RECORD OF GREAT PROGRESS

ANNUAL ADDRESSES AND REPORT

OF

THE DOMINION BANK

The Forty-Ninth Annual General Meeting of The Dominion Bank was held at the Banking House of the Institution, Toronto, on Wednesday, the 28th January, 1920. On motion of Mr. R. S. McLaughlin, seconded by Mr. E. B. LeRoy, Sir Edmund B. Osler occupied the chair, and Mr. C. A. Bogert acted as Secretary. Messrs. Graham Campbell and W. Gibson Cassels were appointed Scrutineers. The Secretary read the Report of the Directors to the Shareholders and submitted the Annual Statement of the affairs of the Bank, for the year ending December 31, 1919:

Balance of Profit and Loss Account, 31st December, 1918			$ 446,503.23
Profits for the year, after deducting charges of management and making full provision for bad and doubtful debts		$1,256,053.83	
Less			
Dominion Government War Tax (on circulation)	$60,000.00		
Taxes paid to Provincial Governments	26,350.00		
		86,350.00	
Making net profits of			1,169,703.83
			$1,616,207.06
Which amount has been disposed of as follows:			
Dividends (quarterly) at Twelve per cent. per annum	$720,000.00		
Bonus, one per cent	60,000.00		
Total distribution to Shareholders of Thirteen per cent. for the year		$ 780,000.00	
Contribution to Officers' Pension Fund		30,000.00	
Contributions to Patriotic and other Funds		10,500.00	
		820,500.00	
Written off Bank Premises		300,000.00	
		1,120,500.00	
Balance of Profit and Loss Account carried forward ...		495,707.05	
			$1,616,207.05

E. B. OSLER,
President.

C. A. BOGERT,
General Manager.

Address by Clarence A. Bogert, General Manager. An analysis of the statement which you will consider to-day shows many features of an encouraging character. At the last Annual Meeting I gave the Shareholders some comparative figures of the Bank's position just prior to the outbreak of the War and as at the close of business on the 31st December, 1918. The changes which took place during that period were of a gratifying

The Dominion Bank, Toronto

nature and the same remark applies to the Bank's activities and the results obtained during 1919.

Much the same conditions prevailed during the period under review as in the previous two or three years. The Bank's funds were well employed, and as no appropriations for doubtful accounts were necessary except for some very nominal amounts, the earnings show a considerable increase. The net profits—after careful revaluation of assets, including allowances for depreciations where necessary—were $1,169,000, an increase of $83,000 over the 1918 profits, being at the rate of 9 per cent. on the Bank's Capital and Reserve, as compared with 8·35 per cent. in 1918. After providing for the 12 per cent. dividend, extra disbursements to the Staff, various forms of taxation and other usual charges, your Directors were able to authorize the payment of a bonus of 1 per cent., and also to appropriate a larger amount to a reduction in Bank Premises account than in any previous year—$300,000, was written off, as against $250,000 in 1918 and $200,000 in 1917.

There have been some important changes in the Bank's Assets and Liabilities—all indicative of expansion and increased strength. The Bank's public liabilities—and I refer especially to the most important one, public deposits—show a notable increase; deposits not bearing interest are $3,200,000 greater and deposits bearing interest have increased $12,000,000. Apart from this, $25,000,000 of deposits, representing payments on the 1919 Victory Loan, were transferred to the credit of the Dominion Government at our Ottawa Branch during the month of December, and nearly half of this amount was disbursed by the Finance Department before the end of the year, otherwise the Bank's total deposits would have shown a greater increase than in any two previous years in its history. Total deposits, for the first time, passed the $100,000,000 mark in 1919.

The Cash Assets of the Bank, i.e., Specie, Dominion Government Notes and the equivalent, amount to $31,900,000, an increase of $3,400,000 over the previous year and equal to nearly 25 per cent. of the Bank's Public Liabilities. Adding to that total the Bank's investment and Call and Short Loans in Canada and Abroad, there are Immediately Available Assets of $70,000,000, which amount represents an increase of $6,500,000, and is equal to 54 per cent. of the Bank's Public Liabilities.

Dominion and Provincial Government securities show a decrease of $1,176,000 from the 1918 figures. The Bank made Short Term advances to the Dominion Government during the last six months of the year of about $12,000,000. On the other hand, the Government retired during the year other obligations amounting to over $13,000,000. Canadian Municipal Securities and British Foreign and Colonial Public Securities are practically unchanged, but it is noteworthy, and a gratifying indication of Great Britain's recuperative power, that of $200,000,000 loaned by the Canadian Banks to the British Government early in the

War, $50,000,000 will be retired during the first five months of
the present year, and it is expected that other further reductions
will soon be made. Railway and other Bonds, Debentures and
Stocks are nearly $400,000 less. The other investments of the
Bank, all of a high-grade character, have not materially changed.
Call and Short Loans in Canada increased nearly $1,000,000 and
Call and Short Loans Abroad increased $3,500,000, occasioned
chiefly by extended activities at our New York and London Offices.

In the Report reference is made to the number of branches
opened by the Bank during 1919, all of which were decided on
only after careful investigation of prospects. Outside of establishing several new offices in Canada at points already mentioned,
an Agency of the Bank was opened in New York City on March
31st last. Desirable premises were obtained in a very central
locality on Broadway near the head of Wall Street and already the
move appears justified by results.

Early in 1919 an important link was made in connection with
the Bank's foreign business, viz., the establishing of reciprocal
relations with the British Overseas Bank, Limited, a new British
corporation inaugurated in May last, chiefly to take advantage of
and assist in the development of Great Britain's foreign trade.
Seven leading institutions are concerned in this Corporation with
assets of over $900,000,000. It is the intention of the British
Overseas Bank, Limited, to gradually establish branches and correspondents in important centres throughout the world and create
a large international business of a lucrative character. Although
this institution is still in its infancy, the Directors and Officials of
The Dominion Bank feel that in the course of time the connection
will provide valuable remunerative facilities and increased benefits
for the Bank.

Although the Canadian banks now provide facilities for the
public unsurpassed, either in the number of offices or banking
machinery, by any other country that we know of, we find that
the remuneration for actual services performed is less by comparison. Rates for commercial loans are practically the same as
prevailed a decade ago, although in the meantime operating expenses have increased enormously, cost of building has nearly doubled
in the last five years and the average remuneration of a bank's staff
is at least thirty to fifty per cent. greater than five years ago.

Under such conditions as these the Banks could not possibly
show the results obtained during the past three or four years,
had it not been for the fact that there has been a continuous demand for all surplus funds from our Governments; on account
of the War all classes of people have made money, borrowers
generally have greatly improved their financial position, and
losses through bad debts have been less than at any time in the
history of Canadian banking.

I think the danger zone in Canadian banking at the present
time is in commercial loans. It takes no special ability to make

judicious selection of a Bank's actual investments, which are, or should be, of high grades, subject to slight fluctuations, and losses or shrinkages—except of a temporary character—seldom occur under this heading, neither does the element of risk enter very greatly into a Bank's transactions of an international character, although depreciation in practically all foreign currencies, with one or two exceptions, has taken place and our financial institutions have been obliged to write down their European securities and balances accordingly. In a Bank's commercial loans, however, the human element always predominates, and at the present time, when practically every line of business has enjoyed three or four years of unequalled prosperity, there is a marked tendency—which is difficult to discourage—to continue purchasing goods and products of all descriptions at high figures, and losses, more or less serious, to individuals and, incidentally, to the Banks, are sure to occur.

Any banker can sit at his desk and decline applications for credits submitted if any element of risk is apparent. This policy will probably keep him from making bad debts, but in carrying it out, he will certainly fail in his duty, not only to the institution which he represents, but to the whole community. There is a risk in every commercial transaction—frequently unforeseen and unavoidable. Doubtful accounts will appear—not preventable either by ability, organization or caution. Manifestly the Canadian Banks, during the re-adjustment period, while perhaps scrutinizing credits with more than usual care, should refrain from leaning the other way. Legitimate development and production are more than ever necessary to prepare for meeting our obligations and to pay interest charges in the meantime. Fortunately the change from abnormal to normal conditions is taking place slowly and, so far, without unfavourable features. We still find extraordinary activity in practically every class of business; a demand for products of every description that cannot be met and a shortage in foodstuffs, raw materials, and manufactured articles. It will certainly take a year or two for supplies to catch up to demands.

Address by Sir Edmund B. Osler, President of the Bank. The Canadian banks have prospered in recent years, but operating expenses continue to steadily increase,—the returns which their shareholders receive, with very few exceptions, fall far short of those of the stockholders of the larger banks in the United States, Great Britain, South Africa, France, Spain and the countries in the Far East.

The Bank has gladly taken back to the service all returned soldiers who wished re-engagement, and has made allowances to them for increases in salary they would have received had they not volunteered. During the war period 436 of the staff volunteered for active service,—over 200 have rejoined the staff, 54 lost their lives, and 12 were permanently disabled and could not return to their duties. The remuneration of Canadian bank staffs generally is steadily increasing, and the Pension Fund makes provision for them in their later years.

The Bank has sustained a severe loss in the death of Mr. W. D. Matthews, its Vice-President. Mr. Matthews had been a Director for over thirty-six years, and Vice-President for eighteen years. He was a man of exceptional judgment, and was cautious in business matters, without being in any way timid. The Bank's activities have, in recent years, become so widespread that it was considered advisable to elect two Vice-Presidents, one of whom should be representative of Western Canada, where our operations are now so very extensive. Sir Augustus M. Nanton, of Winnipeg, has therefore been elected one of the Vice-Presidents, and Mr. A. W. Austin, of Toronto, who is so intimately connected with business affairs in the East, has been elected to the other Vice-Presidency.

While the past year has been a prosperous one for the banks, the future must cause anxiety to all financial institutions. The exchange conditions are serious, and in Canada we must expect a very large amount of money to be withdrawn which has been borrowed from England and from Scotland by the various mortgage companies and loaned on mortgage in Canada. There is no inducement now to send money here from England, and there is every inducement for the English lenders to have their funds returned to England, and take advantage of the very low rate of exchange. I should say between $50,000,000 and $75,000,000 would be a very conservative figure at which to place the amount loaned to the various companies here from Great Britain for investment in mortgages. Some of these companies have already arranged to close up their business on account of these conditions, and this state of affairs, I think, must become more accentuated during the next year or two. No money can be expected from Great Britain for investment in this country until the exchange situation improves.

The larger banks must continue to expand to meet the new trade conditions of the world. Already some have opened foreign offices or made affiliations with foreign banks or financial corporations, and I think this, policy will continue. From all quarters—the pulpit, the managers of financial concerns, railway presidents, the press—comes a warning that there must be economy practised. Extravagance is still the order of the day however and, in my opionion, will continue to be until conditions change and hard times come upon us. Meanwhile all financial institutions should, I think, bear in mind that the existing conditions cannot last, and they must watch closely the trend of events for the next year or two. Canadian banks are at present in a strong position and well able to cope with future problems.

Remarks by A. W. Austin, Vice-President of the Bank. In accepting the position of one of the Vice-Presidents of The Dominion Bank, I felt that it would be a difficult task to perform the attendant duties as well as did the late Mr. W. D. Matthews, who was, I consider, one of the best all-round business men of his day. Mr. Matthews never failed to give of his time and exceptional judgment in the interests of the Bank, and his services were always in demand.

Making special reference to the Province of Ontario, I may say that while crops throughout the Province last year were below the average yield, higher prices have made up for the shortage. Ontario farmers did wonders in food production during the war, but now that the war is over there is a tendency to go easier among them, as well as among non-agriculturists. Large sums have been expended, however, in the common cause in connection with the war, and the loans floated to provide for this expenditure and the interest thereon must be met, and this fact will tend to stimulate agricultural expansion and increase production. The people of Ontario feel a deep pride in their development of agriculture and manufacturing.

One helps the other in establishing our province as easily the greatest economic force within the Dominion; a force capable of generating as much financial power as all the other provinces together. This was clearly demonstrated when in the last drive of the Victory Loan Ontario subscribed for double the amount of all the other provinces. The success of the Sixth War Loan, which was oversubscribed even though not tax exempt, shows the soundness of Canada's economic and financial position. Now we know Canada can finance more of its own undertakings than was dreamed of heretofore. Not only are Canadians absorbing Canadian securities, but Americans are taking them on account of the exceptional profits through the discount in Canadian currency.

The past year will, I am sure, be a memorable one for our General Manager, for under his able guidance the affairs of the Bank have been brought to a splendid state of efficiency, and we have been able to resume the payment of a bonus to the Shareholders. The great success of the Bank throughout the year is also due to the keen interest taken by all connected with it, from the President down to the junior clerks.

Address by Sir Augustus M. Nanton, Vice-President of the Bank. I greatly appreciate the honour of being appointed a Vice-President of The Dominion Bank, but I am not unmindful of what made it possible for me to have that position. As the previous speakers have already told you, Mr. W. D. Matthews was a tower of strength to The Dominion Bank. I was with him when he became ill on the 7th of May last, and in his death I feel that I have lost a most sincere and true friend.

I am one of your Western Directors. I would, therefore, like to say a word or two regarding the West. As to British Columbia, I think it may be said that the business in that province has been prosperous during the last year. The lumbermen were never so busy. They never obtained as high prices in the past as they are obtaining now, and the outlook for that industry is exceedingly good. The fisheries have been satisfactory. The coal mining in British Columbia is, I think, only second in extent, speaking of the coal areas, to that of Alberta. The mines have had their troubles during the past year as they have had in the East, but at the moment they are operating satisfactorily. The fruit industry of British Columbia is one of great importance. For years the results were anything but satisfactory, but last year there was a fruit crop that exceeded, I think, anything in the history of the province. The greater portion of it was safely harvested and sold at exceptionally good prices.

Alberta is a Province of diversified interests. It has coal enough to supply the whole Dominion, but there are two obstacles in the way of shipping it to Eastern Canada—the distance and the difficulty of obtaining satisfactory labour. The crops in that Province, especially in the southern portion, were exceedingly light during the last year, but in the northern part, Edmonton and throughout that district, they were somewhat better. In the Far North—the Peace River District—I saw harvests that were equal to, if not better than, any we have ever had in Manitoba or other Prairie Provinces. The cattle in Alberta have been suffering somewhat this year on account of the poor condition of the grazing ground. The losses, however, are not going to be nearly as great as was at first anticipated. Thousands of cattle have been sold and thousands have been removed to other parts of the country where they have been foddered. As an example of the number that have been removed from that Province during less than the last four months, one Railway Company loaded and moved from points South of Calgary over 135,000 head of cattle.

I would like to remind you of what we hope will be a great asset, not only of Alberta but of the Dominion as well—oil. Systematic boring is now going on throughout the Province of Alberta for oil, where it is believed it will be found, and if it is found, it will mean a source of wealth to the Dominion almost second to none. Irrigation has proved at last to be a great success. It is now being utilized not only by corporations but is under consideration by the Government.

Saskatchewan is largely a grain-growing country. Last year we grew wheat to the value of about four hundred millions of dollars in the whole Dominion. Of this practically half was grown in the Province of Saskatchewan; the value of that produced west of the Great Lakes being some $340,000,000, as against $60,000,000 in Eastern Canada. A few years ago the West was not considered of very great importance in the matter of grain-growing, but things have changed in this respect.

In Manitoba the crops have been fair, but that Province does not now depend upon its wheat. It has gone into mixed farming, and the farmers and business men generally in Manitoba are prosperous. It is only recently that the great mineral wealth of the Northern part of Manitoba has been discovered. Another thing that is of vast importance to that Province is its water power. I think you will find that within a very short period water power in addition to what is now in existence on the Winnipeg River, only some 60 miles from Winnipeg, will be developed to the extent in one instance alone of over 170,000 horse-power, and at a figure considerably less than any other that has taken place, that I can trace, on the continent of North America.

I would like to refer to the live stock business of Western Canada. The stock yards in Winnipeg are about on a par with those of Toronto, while in Calgary and Edmonton they far exceed in volume of business those of Montreal. We have in the West practically half the beef cattle of Canada. Of course you in the East largely exceed us in dairy cattle. _To give you an example of how business has gone ahead, the Bank clearings of Winnipeg to-day are equal to what they were in Montreal in 1911 and far exceed what they were in Toronto in 1915. We are growing somewhat. The immigration to our country is improving, and I am glad to report that the greater number who are now taking up homesteads in Western Canada are of British descent. You wonder why I am speaking of the West and only of the West. My reason is that the business of The Dominion Bank, which comes from Western Canada, now forms a very important portion of that done by the Bank. The President and General Manager will bear me out in stating that the result of the Western business has been satisfactory. You have heard from our worthy President and the General Manager regarding the position of the Bank. They have not given advice directly, but in an indirect way they have given warning, so that I will merely tell you that we in Western Canada are trying to be cautious, but we think the prospects are good.

The following gentlemen were elected Directors for the ensuing year and afterwards Sir Edmund B. Osler was re-elected President and Mr. A. W. Austin, Toronto, and Sir Augustus M. Nanton, Winnipeg, Vice-Presidents: A. W. Austin, James Carruthers, R. J. Christie, Sir John C. Eaton, E. W. Hamber, H. W. Hutchinson, W. L. Matthews, R. S. McLaughlin, Sir Augustus M. Nanton, W. W. Near, Sir Edmund B. Osler, A. T. Reid, and H. H. Williams.

PROGRESS OF THE DOMINION BANK

Date	Paid up Capital	Reserve Fund	No. of Branches	Net Profits	Total Deficits	Total Assets	*Liquid Assets
1875	$ 970,250	$ 225,000	8	$ 138,310	$ 1,747,497	$ 3,653,007	$ 863,721
1880	970,250	355,000	10	103,952	3,246,882	5,501,670	1,855,070
1885	1,500,000	980,000	11	203,496	5,183,675	8,950,580	2,797,536
1890	1,500,000	1,300,000	16	248,584	8,116,875	12,309,378	4,157,143
1895	1,500,000	1,500,000	18	189,561	10,289,165	14,289,165	4,454,751
1900	1,500,000	1,500,000	22	214,342	15,790,401	20,824,147	7,728,675
1905	3,000,000	3,500,000	41	490,495	34,088,108	44,403,739	15,026,076
1910	4,000,000	5,000,000	80	659,300	49,302,784	62,677,830	22,041,300
1911	4,702,799	5,702,799	86	704,045	58,547,865	70,179,552	27,011,053
1912	5,000,000	6,000,000	93	901,539	59,342,436	79,224,680	29,241,840
1913	5,811,344	6,811,344	99	950,402	59,788,590	80,506,462	27,102,876
1914	6,000,000	7,000,000	95	925,364	57,766,996	80,457,109	27,812,110
1915	6,000,000	7,000,000	90	805,123	65,965,597	87,475,126	32,660,400
1916	6,000,000	7,000,000	87	893,502	70,473,614	92,866,692	37,625,896
1917	6,000,000	7,000,000	88	1,005,062	81,948,095	109,436,145	57,660,453
1918	6,000,000	7,000,000	90	1,086,498	96,107,711	133,506,275	63,528,850
1919	6,000,000	†7,000,000	115	1,169,703	111,414,057	143,504,920	70,075,379

*Note.—Liquid Assets include Specie, Dominion Government Demand Notes. Notes of and Cheques on other Banks, Deposit with Central Gold Reserves, Balances due from other Banks in Canada and Foreign Countries, Dominion and Provincial Government, Municipal and other Securities, and Loans on call secured by Stocks and Bonds.

GENERAL STATEMENT

FOR THE YEAR ENDING 31st DECEMBER, 1919

ASSETS

Gold and Silver Coin	$ 1,980,842.69	
Dominion Government Notes	15,843,726.00	
Deposit with Central Gold Reserves	4,100,000.00	
Notes of other Banks	1,170,382.54	
Cheques on other Banks	6,816,287.08	
Balances due by other Banks in Canada	8,857.96	
Balances due by Banks and Banking Correspondents elsewhere than in Canada	1,988,043.83	
	31,903,139.60	
Dominion and Provincial Government Securities, not exceeding market value	8,790,080.39	
Canadian Municipal Securities, and British, Foreign and Colonial Public Securities other than Canadian, not exceeding market value	13,334,525.62	
Railway and other Bonds, Debentures and Stocks, not exceeding market value	1,996,115.14	
Call and Short (not exceeding thirty days) Loans in Canada on Bonds, Debentures and Stocks ..	9,852,534.25	
Call and Short (not exceeding thirty days) Loans elsewhere than in Canada	4,698,984.25	$ 70,075,379.55
Other Current Loans and Discounts in Canada (less rebate of interest)	65,396,248.68	
Other Current Loans and Discounts elsewhere than in Canada (less rebate of interest)	1,050,488.62	
Liabilities of Customers under Letters of Credit, as per contra	1,168,405.41	
Real Estate other than Bank Premises	5,469.57	
Overdue Debts, (estimated loss provided for)	74,566.85	
Bank Premises, at not more than cost, less amounts written off	5,407,180.30	
Deposit with the Minister of Finance for the purposes of the Circulation Fund	304,500.00	
Mortgages on Real Estate sold	22,680.84	
	73,429,540.27	
	$143,504,919.82	

LIABILITIES

Capital Stock paid in		$ 6,000,000.00
Reserve Fund	$ 7,000,000.00	
Balance of Profit and Loss Account carried forward	495,707.05	
Dividend No. 149, payable 2nd January, 1920	180,000.00	
Bonus, one per cent., payable 2nd January, 1920 ..	60,000.00	
Former Dividends unclaimed	4,089.00	
		7,739,796.05
Total Liabilities to the Shareholders		$ 13,739,796.05
Notes in Circulation	9,525,809.00	
Due to Dominion Government	5,000,000.00	
Deposits not bearing interest $37,088,399.96		
Deposits bearing interest, including		
interest accrued to date 74,325,657.59		
	111,414,057.55	
Balances due to other Banks in Canada	878,911.22	
Balances due to Banks and Banking Correspondents		
elsewhere than in Canada	973,956.16	
Bills Payable	197,582.96	
Acceptances under Letters of Credit	1,168,405.41	
Liabilities not included in the foregoing	606,451.47	
Total Public Liabilities		129,765,123.77
		$143,504,919.82

E. B. OSLER,
President.

C. A. BOGERT,
General Manager.

AUDITORS' REPORT TO SHAREHOLDERS

We have compared the above Balance Sheet with the books and accounts at the Chief Office of The Dominion Bank, and the certified returns received from its Branches, and after checking the cash and verifying the securities at the Chief Office and certain of the principal Branches on December 31st, 1919, we certify that, in our opinion, such Balance Sheet exhibits a true and correct view of the state of the Bank's affairs, according to the best of our information, the explanations given to us and as shown by the books of the Bank.

In addition to the examinations mentioned, the cash and securities at the Chief Office and certain of the principal Branches were checked and verified by us at another time during the year and found to be in accord with the books of the Bank.

All information and explanations required have been given to us and all transactions of the Bank which have come under our notice have, in our opinion, been within the powers of the Bank.

Toronto, Janauray 20th, 1920.

G. T. CLARKSON
R. J. DILWORTH } of Clarkson, Gordon & Dilworth, C.A.

A GREAT INSURANCE INSTITUTION

ANNUAL REPORT AND PRESIDENT'S ADDRESS
OF THE
CANADA LIFE ASSURANCE COMPANY

The 73rd Annual Report of the Canada Life— Toronto, Jan. 8, 1920. The Directors have much pleasure in submitting the 73rd Annual Report of the Canada Life Assurance Company, setting forth the financial position of the Company as at the 31st December, 1919. The report of the transactions for the past year shows that the Company has shared fully in the unprecedented expansion that has taken place in the life insurance business. Policies issued during the year, including revivals, amounted to $46,380,774, the greatest volume of new business ever issued by the Company in any year and exceeding the business of the previous year by $20,608,026. The new policies paid for, exclusive of dividend additions, totalled $41,641,877, an increase over 1918 of $17,750,209. The total Assurances in force now amount to $229,794,267.25, showing a most satisfactory increase of $33,813,716.78 over 1918, after meeting death losses, maturing endowments and other terminations of the year.

The total income was $12,012,381.79, representing premium income of $8,046,634.90 (not including payments made to other companies for re-assurances); considerations for annuities $274,517.68; interest income, including profits from sale of securities, $3,618,797.02 and income from other sources $72,432.19. Payments of $6,347,925.75 were made during the year to policyholders and their representatives, and to annuitants. These payments were made in settlement of death claims, matured endowments, dividends, cash values for policies surrendered, and as annuities. The Assets now amount to $69,352,268.23, an increase during the year of $3,404,693.38. In the past year another substantial investment was made by the Company in the Victory Loan of the Dominion of Canada. As in previous years, the Company's securities have been valued on a most conservative basis.

The Policy Reserves, under the same stringent method of valuation as in past years, amounted at the 31st December to $58,066,273, an increase of $3,050,319 over the corresponding reserves of 1918. After allotting $1,587,731.60 to those entitled to share in dividends during 1919, the surplus amounted to $7,187,736.42, out of which $2,515,000 will be paid in dividends to policyholders in 1920. In addition, our contingent reserve of $500,000 has also been maintained. The net surplus earned in 1919 was $1,877,160.47, which is the largest in the history of the Company. Notwithstanding the influenza claims during the early part of the year, the mortality experience of the Company was exceedingly favourable. Your Directors take this opportunity of recording their appreciation of the effective service and co-operation of all who are connected with the Company in Office and Field, including the London Board and Advisory Boards in the United Kingdom. The exceptional progress made during the year, as shown in the satisfactory Report herewith submitted, is due in a large measure to the efforts of the Branch Managers and Field Representatives, and to the efficiency of the Officers and Staffs at Home and Branch offices.

On behalf of the Board,

TORONTO,   HERBERT C. COX,
6th January, 1920.   *President.*

Annual Address by Herbert C. Cox, President of the Company.
The first full year since the signing of the Armistice and the virtual conclusion of peace has brought many problems, some of them as yet unsolved, and many surprises, not all of which have been unpleasant. The best minds are focused upon the former and are bringing to their solution a judgment and experience broadened by the years of warfare and tempered by the new spirit of toleration which these years have created. The readjustments, naturally difficult and tedious, are made more so by the attitude of important sections of the community who should rather facilitate them, but in spite of this some headway is being made. No opportunity should be lost of impressing upon each individual citizen of the Allied countries the vital importance and necessity of the fullest conservation of our resources and the utmost production of which we are capable, if we are not to be outstripped by our recent enemies, who, we are told by the highest authorities, have already addressed themselves to the full limit of their power to regaining what they have lost through and during the war.

The great fever of unrest disturbing the world and upsetting the relation between employer and employee is perhaps a natural outcome of the recent experiences, and it has been suggested that not so much in profit-sharing as in happiness-sharing will be found the solution as between Capital and Labour. Already the creative mind has done much in evolving ways of assuring to the workman a greater share of the wealth which his industry and energy help to create, and many large employers, looking beyond the immediate present, have made through group Life Assurance provision for the families of their employees in the event of the death of the last named. A larger measure of personal contact and understanding between the heads and hands of our great industrial undertakings should do much to smooth out the rough places. The pressing necessity and task with which the Allies are presently faced is, of course, the provision for ultimately meeting the enormous obligations which have been created in carrying on the war. Many authorities favour the funding of all Allied war debts, with a new schedule of taxation in each country and a new tariff to obtain between the allies, the former to be equitable in all regards, and the latter such as to encourage rather than deter trade with each other.   Its supporters believe this method will finally prove to be the solution of the situation.

Our own country has seen a continuance of the expansion already well under way as reflected in the channels of retail trade, in further large increases in bank deposits, in the development of manufacturing industries limited only by the supply of raw materials and labour, and in the growth of live stock and other farm products.   The market for our commodities abroad is wide and urgent, but is hampered by the lack of shipping, and is also unfortunately at the moment more or less dependent upon our ability to provide credit for our would-be customers.   This is, of course, difficult to do in view of the enormous sums required to care for the balance of our own war expenditures and the demands for demobilization and re-establishment of soldiers, but the Government has been able to assist to some extent and will perhaps see its way to help in larger measure when the other obligations have been met.   The Victory Loan, 1919, has afforded appreciable relief, and it is thought it will be the last offering of Government securities in this so-called popular way, any further necessary borrowings of the Government being made in the pre-war method, with the probable difference that much of the funds required will continue to be provided in our own country.   Among the lessons taught Canada by the war are that her resources are much greater than she had realized, that she can furnish her Government with a much larger share of her money needs than had ever been thought possible, that it is good business to be our own bankers, and that the average citizen if he obligates himself to certain fixed payments for saving and investment will meet them regularly and with sureness. The frequency of the Victory Loans has provided him with a channel for thus obligating himself almost to the point of habit, and it would seem that the purchase of Life Assurance may offer the best means of continuing and confirming the habit.

Weather conditions in the Western Provinces were again very unfavourable for the growing crops.   Lack of rain was general, and induced in some districts, which had similarly suffered the previous year, a total crop failure, but the aggregate cereal yield of the Provinces was somewhat better than in the preceding year. This condition has necessarily resulted in delay in the payment of borrowers' interest in some sections.   The loaning companies seek no unfair advantage of their clients, but rather give them ample time and further encouragement through additional advances for the purchase of seed grain where such are desirable and warranted. Ontario, Quebec and the Maritime Provinces had more normal conditions throughout the summer, and their production compares favourably with that of 1918.

Again the fodder difficulty in Alberta is being met as largely as possible by carrying the feed to the stock or by transporting the

stock to the areas where feed is available, although in some instances
the rancher considers it better business to sell his stock than to
endeavour to obtain fodder at present prices.   The United States
produced 10 per cent. more corn than in 1918, while her wheat
yield showed a decrease of the same percentage.   The total value of
her crops is some $700,000,000 in excess of the previous year.   The
European countries involved in the war are fast recovering their
productiveness, and it is said that France and Belgium have good
crops, that traces of the war are being very rapidly removed, and
that there is being brought under cultivation ground which had
been over-run by the forces of the Allies and Central Powers.

In the period from 1898 to 1913 the immigrants coming into
Canada increased from 32,000 to 402,000, dwindling again in the
year ending March 31, 1919, to 37,000.   That the tide has again
turned is indicated by the numbers coming in during the first seven
months of the present fiscal year, namely 82,000, and it is thought
by those in touch with the Department of Immigration that we may
now look for a steady influx, both from Great Britain and the
United States.   It is the policy of the Government, for the present
at all events, to invite and encourage only those who have the
inclination and the qualifications necessary to fit them for work on
the land, as it is realized that in this rural population lies our
greatest aid to higher production, with its effect, in turn, upon
living costs.   Our outstanding need is now, and for many years
will be, "more people" to share in our development and in our
success.   The broadest and most liberal program possible to the
Government in this regard will command a very general support,
and one of our first efforts should be to retain our own young men.

There have been periods in our history when the smallness of
our stature as a nation prevented the realization of the visions of
these boys, and they left us to join the already full-grown Republic to the south, to the great advantage of those United States.
It has been impressed upon us of late, however, that our own country has now attained its manhood and that within its borders lies
not merely potential, but actual wealth.   No longer is it necessary
for our men to seek opportunity elsewhere.   We may well ask the
reason for the prosperity which abounds within the Dominion, and
find the answer in the spirit of progress exhibited by her people
among themselves, the internal trade which we sometimes overlook
in our concentration upon exports and imports.   The thrift of the
people of Canada, as well as their reputed extravagance, requires
some emphasis, and we have in the great volume of Life Insurance
being transacted an evidence not only of immediate savings, but,
what is even more important, a proof of unselfishness and self-
denial which is beyond all praise.   We may with confidence put our
faith in a people who have had the desire to protect their homes to
the extent of new Assurances approximately six hundred millions
of dollars during the past year.   No pessimism as to the quality of
our citizenship can stand against this solid fact.   Men permanently
given to extreme views as to the rights of Capital and Labour, or a

people hard driven and without prosperity, do not set aside their savings for so unselfish a purpose as life insurance.

We are somewhat at a loss to account for the enormous and unprecedented increase in the amount of assurances sold by all the companies in the past twelve months.   True, enlarged selling organizations have worked more intensively, and in ordinary circumstances would have been responsible for a normal advance in production.   The perhaps natural reaction of nervousness following the epidemic of influenza is sometimes thought to have been an important factor, while a much larger demand for business and inheritance tax purposes has been apparent.   None of these, however, offers a quite full explanation of the matter, and it has been suggested that for a parallel we must look to the years during and following the Civil War, when there seemed to be some relation between the production of new Life Assurances and the prices of necessary commodities.   From 1860 to 1880 the amount of life assurance issued annually in the United States followed with peculiar accuracy the rise and fall of commodity prices, and practically the same phenomenon appears both in that country and Canada for the years 1913 to 1919.   If such a relation does exist, and if the corresponding movement in prices and insurance is not merely a coincidence, then we may presumably look for a continued upward trend in the latter, as there does not appear to be imminent any downward movement in the former.

If the demand persists, and we hope it may, the Government and those seeking the protection will look to the properly authorized agencies to supply it.   Can these agencies meet the call without leaning unduly upon their existing members?   It is an open secret that a policy does not become self-sustaining until it has been in force for a period of four or five years, and that in the meantime it must rely upon assistance from the general earnings or surplus, it, in turn, as it becomes older contributing its share of help to the newcomer.   This process can be carried on fairly and without injury to old members up to a point, but beyond that point the care of the new entrant must be to some extent at their cost, since it entails a reduction in the amount returnable to them by way of so-called profits or dividends upon their policies.   What are these profits or dividends?   Simply the refund of portions of the payments made to the companies by the assured which have been found unnecessary in carrying out the contracts.   It is obvious, therefore, that the companies cannot in equity to these old members go on indefinitely undertaking the large volume of business offering by curtailing these profit payments, and it is equally obvious that we must not cease to perform to the fullest extent the function required of us.   In what, then, lies the solution of the difficulty?   The Insurance Act of Canada contains a provision eminently adapted to meet just the situation with which we are confronted, and there appears to be no good reason why all the companies should not avail themselves of it.   It is, indeed, conceivable that its use under a ruling of the Department might be desirable.   Many of the

American States have adopted similar enabling legislation, and it is hoped the remainder will also do so.

In response to a demand from some quarters that the Government should institute a means of furnishing Insurance to our soldiers who are impaired as a consequence of the war, and therefore unable to obtain protection at standard rates, the matter was taken under advisement by the authorities, but the difficulties in the way were numerous and important.   A method by which the companies might be of assistance has been suggested to the Government, and is having consideration.   The market for Group Insurance, under which the employer provides protection for all his employees, has been so insistent and is becoming so wide that the Finance Minister, with the advice of the Superintendent of Insurance, has finally approved a basis upon which Canadian companies and others doing business in Canada may undertake it.   A few of the larger companies, including the Canada Life, have already completed the necessary preliminaries and are now fully prepared to satisfy the requirements of those who seek this form of policy.   This idea of group insurance is one of the newer developments in the relations of industrial, commercial and even financial enterprise, and will, it is thought, have a very marked bearing upon them.   While it is as yet only in its infancy, it is evident that it can be sold with profit to the companies, and its benefit to the purchaser has also been demonstrated.

We must not omit mention of the visit of his Royal Highness the Prince of Wales to Canada and the United States.   His intense personal charm, his alert interest in and appreciation of everything he saw, his unfailing instinctive tact and courtesy to all with whom he came in touch, his facility and aptness in expressing himself under varying and sometimes trying conditions, have made a very lasting impression not only upon the people of both these countries, but upon his countrymen in Great Britain, and cannot fail to have a profound influence upon the future of the nations over which it is his destiny to rule.

In common with other companies, we have shared in the pronounced demand for Insurance apparent throughout the twelve months, and before the end of the year had achieved our objective of Fifty Millions of new business, enabling us to report issued and revived policies of $46,380,000, an amount greatly in excess of any previous year.   Ordinarily this large underwriting would involve an expense which we should have some hesitation in undertaking, but our earnings for the year, to which reference will be made later, have been so extremely satisfactory that we have been able to absorb it without difficulty and without change in the scale of dividends upon existing policies.   Our Insurances in force now total $230,000,000, an increase of $34,000,000, which is a gratifying percentage of the new issues for the year.   While the growth in our Canadian business has been marked, we are happy to report an important improvement in Great Britain, due in varying measure

29

to the maintaining of our dividend scale, to a wider organization and to a greater confidence in things Canadian.

Approaching every applicant with the desire to have him become a policyholder, it is most unfortunate that in some instances the impairments are such that we are unable to accept him. That the number of cases in which this is necessary is only three per cent. of the whole, indicates a consistent endeavour to perform our normal function. The last of our war claims are now being cared for, and we record the total from this source since the commencement of hostilities as $1,800,000. This is a very reasonable amount, being less than one per cent. of our total Assurances, and in meeting it we have had no difficulty or disturbance in regard to other obligations or promises. In the early months of the year we suffered rather severely from deaths resulting from the continuance of the influenza epidemic, but as this cleared away our recovery was so rapid and our normal death losses so much below the amount provided for that we have a saving or profit from this source of $938,000, as against $68,000 for the previous year. In addition to this, the other elements which contribute to surplus have been so favourable that we are able to report the largest surplus earnings in the history of the Company, namely, $1,877,160.

That we have met without hesitation the wholly unlooked for demand upon us in the form of new business, and that we carry forward the above very handsome surplus, which enables us to continue without reduction our usual rate of profit distribution to those policies sharing this year, is altogether gratifying. That the advantage of our strength in this regard has had a perceptible effect upon our success in Great Britain, is already apparent on this continent, and must become of increasing value as the man in the street more fully realizes its significance. The special reserve of $500,000 accumulated during the last five years still remains as a safety valve in the event of any unforeseen demand upon us. This year marks the end of another quinquennium, or five-year period, and we have had the pleasure of allotting to policies, entitled to participate, dividends of which the cash value reaches the highly important total of $2,761,000. A portion of this has already been distributed, the balance to be available during the ensuing year, as determined by the premium due dates of the individual policies to which they apply.

Many years ago this Company adopted fixed quinquennial periods—1899, 1904, 1909, 1914 and 1919—and all policies issued prior to 1900 had their profits maturing in these years, involving at those stated times the division of a very large amount of surplus. In connection with policies issued during and since 1900 the contribution method has been employed, so that this is the last time we shall be called upon to make an unusually large distribution, the sums allotted in future being more evenly divided from year to year. Anticipating the demand likely to arise for group insurance as soon as it should be sanctioned by the Finance Department, we prepared our policy forms and premium rates and had them approved by the Superintendent of Insurance. The rates we have adopted are, we believe, ample to secure us against loss, while being at the same time sufficiently low to enable us to compete on reasonable terms with other institutions.

The requirements of the Government for war purposes have again made a heavy demand upon Canadian life assurance companies, which have responded with subscriptions totalling $51,500,-000. This Company was the largest individual subscriber amongst its fellows, and the second largest in the entire list, applying for $12,500,000, on account of which we have been allotted $7,800,000. While doing our share in this regard we have still been able to take advantage of a favourable market to purchase $1,814,000 of other Government, Provincial and Municipal issues, and to lend $3,525,-000 upon real estate mortgage. The demand for the latter has been much better than in 1918, with the result that we have invested in this way not only our principal repayments, but an additional amount, which gives us a material net increase in our mortgage loans. As we maintain a strong and aggressive loaning organization throughout the Western Provinces, it has been possible for us to take full and prompt advantage of any favourable change in the loan market, and the service thus placed at the disposal of our clients is greatly appreciated and productive of much business.

Crop failures, total or partial, have naturally not been without effect upon interest collections, but these have been considerably better than might have been expected under the circumstances. In any instance where we think the payment of arrears is doubtful the amount has not been included in the asset described as "interest outstanding." May I repeat the statement made last year that our farm loans covering 1,500,000 acres, average about $7 per acre on our own valuation of $20 per acre. Mixed farming is on the increase amongst our borrowers, and must ultimately have a helpful effect upon their interest-paying capacity.

Our mortgage loans, city and farm, now number 8,400 for somewhat over $22,000,000, and add greatly to our earning capacity. That they constitute a very active portion of our assets is indicated by the important repayments which average almost ten per cent. of the principal each year. In other words, experience during the last few years has shown us that we must annually put out three million of new loans to make a net increase of one million. During the war period the high prices obtained for his wheat has enabled the Western farmer to greatly reduce his mortgage indebtedness, and it is perhaps fair to assume that as these prices decline the tendency will be for his borrowings to become more permanent. Another factor contributing to the large repayments is found in our readiness to allow returned soldiers desiring to borrow from the Soldiers' Settlement Board to discharge their loans to this Company without notice or bonus. This action is in line with the general desire to facilitate the early re-establishment of home-coming soldiers.

In transactions involving such a large number of individuals, and covering such an extended area, there must necessarily be some casualties, but we continue to be able within reasonable time to dispose of all foreclosed properties without loss of either principal or interest.

Embarrassment has come to a few Western municipalities following a period of over-inflation, during which large debenture issues were sold in undue anticipation of future development, but presumably under the supervision of their Provincial Governments. Some of these towns and cities have applied to the holders of their debentures for relief and it would seem that this must be afforded in some measure to enable the municipalities to carry on. Every effort has been made, but without avail, to persuade the Provincial Governments to come to the rescue of their respective municipalities, in view of the bearing which these delinquencies will have upon the general credit and borrowing power of the Provinces themselves and their stronger municipalities. The future will doubtless demonstrate to them the shortsightedness of their present policy of aloofness and non-responsibility.

The outstanding feature of the past few years in relation to our investments is the large increase in the holdings of Federal and Provincial Government securities, with an improvement in interest yield upon them from $3\frac{1}{2}$ per cent. to $5\frac{3}{4}$ per cent. Concurrently we have added to our City, County, Township and School debentures, while reducing very materially those of towns and villages and the bonds of Corporations and Public Utilities, following a studied and fixed policy of confining ourselves to what may be regarded as the highest class of Bonds and Debentures.

That our programme in this regard and in relation to mortgage loans has been right is amply proven by the gradual rise in our average net interest rate, which has this year reached the highest point in the Company's history, namely $6 \cdot 06$ per cent. With this rate of earning upon our assets while our reserves are held on a 3 and $3\frac{1}{2}$ per cent. basis you will be readily seized of our unequalled ability to produce surplus. A very instructive chart has been prepared showing the tendency in our interest rate, commencing at $5 \cdot 70$ per cent. in 1889 and diminishing with some fluctuations to $4 \cdot 35$ per cent. in 1900, when it was deemed wise to put our reserves on a 3 and $3\frac{1}{2}$ per cent. basis. The drop in these years was probably due in large measure to high prices obtaining for securities and the very small proportion of mortgage loans on our books. Following a decision to invest more largely in the latter form of security the necessary organization was inaugurated and the curve of our yield rate has been steadily upward until, as I have said, it reaches this year $6 \cdot 06$ per cent. That our ledger assets are cared for at a cost of a trifle less than 1/3 of 1 per cent. is very satisfactory and has an important bearing on this net yield.

Having in mind the insidious effect of the policy loan upon the permanency of the original insurance, there was instituted a systematic effort to stimulate repayments and to discourage new loans, with the desirable result that during the year the one item has offset the other, leaving the total loans of this nature at the same figure as a year ago, and virtually the same as five years ago. At the last annual meeting you were good enough to authorize the creation of a Staff Savings and Pension Fund. You will be glad to know that a large portion of the staff have already become contributors to the fund, and we anticipate that practically all of the male members will do so. As this is the sixth annual statement the present Management has had the honour of presenting to you, perhaps you will permit a very brief review of the progress made in the five full years of its administration:

	1914		1919
New Policies issued increased from	$ 15,000,000	to	$ 45,500,000
Total policies in force increased from	157,000,000	to	230,000,000
Income from all sources increased from	8,500,000	to	12,000,000
Total assets increased from	56,000,000	to	69,000,000
Surplus earned increased from	1,500,000	to	1,900,000
Total payment to policyholders increased from	8,860,000	to	6,847,000

This development has not been accomplished without the material strengthening of our organization, both in the field and in the home office, not without the laying aside of some of the old servants of the Company who had given it faithful and valuable service, not without the adoption of new methods of stimulating our own forces and the interest of their constituents, but it has been brought about, I am happy to say, by the generous and vigourous team-work of the staff at large, by the kindly acquiescence of those who have stepped aside, by the bringing of trained salesmen to an aroused and receptive public, and it has furthermore been brought about at a perceptibly decreased rate of cost which has enabled us to report a largely-increased surplus earning.

STATEMENT FOR THE YEAR ENDING 31st DECEMBER, 1919

RECEIPTS

Balance of Ledger Assets as at 31st December, 1918		$63,251,889.55
First Year's Premiums	$1,719,866.60	
Renewal Premiums	6,440,278.41	
Single Premiums applied to purchase Bonus Additions and Premium Reductions	384,117.98	
Annuity Considerations	274,517.68	
	$8,768,780.67	
Less Re-assurance Premiums	447,628.09	
Total Net Premium Income	$8,321,152.58	
Interest (including Rents)	3,517,392.60	
Profit on Sale of Securities	101,404.42	
Supplementary Contracts	37,660.00	
Amounts left with the Company to accumulate at Interest	19,388.97	
Staff Savings and Benefit Fund Contributions	15,383.22	
Total Income		12,012,381.79
		$75,264,271.34

PAYMENTS

Death and Disability Claims (including $199,288.57 Bonus Additions)		$2,976,492.45
Endowments Matured (including $82,766.59 Bonus Additions)		862,029.59
Surrender Values to Policyholders		983,555.90
Dividends to Policyholders—Cash	$811,427.63	
Cash applied to purchase Bonus Additions, Premium Reductions, etc.	351,073.62	
		1,162,501.25

Annuity Payments	314,243.39
Surrender Values to Annuitants	6,558.64
Supplementary Contracts	37,586.18
Amounts left with the Company and interest	4,958.35
Commissions, Salaries, etc.	1,700,397.21
Taxes, Licenses and Government Fees	164,744.36
(Exclusive of Taxes on Real Estate)	
All other Expenditures	513,206.62
Dividend on Paid-up Capital	150,000.00
Expenditures charged to Shareholders' Account	12,281.85
Amount written off Securities	101,404.42
Amounts adjusted in Suspense	4,037.36
Balance of Ledger Assets	66,271,371.74
	$75,264,271.34

ASSETS

Government Bonds		$12,856,320.49
Municipal and other Bonds, Stocks and Debentures		18,123,529.48
Mortgages on Real Estate		21,065,945.08
Loans on Policies		9,389,316.97
Real Estate (including Company's buildings in Toronto, Montreal, Calgary, etc.)		3,503,801.64
Loans on Stocks, Bonds, etc.	$ 138,943.00	
Loans on Guaranteed Mortgages	1,000,000.00	
		1,138,943.60
Cash in Banks and on hand		273,211.58
Ledger Assets		**$66,271,371.74**

OTHER ASSETS

Premiums in transit, and half-yearly and quarterly premiums payable within nine months, less cost of collection	1,124,965.00
(Reserve on above item included in Liabilities)	
Interest and Rents due and accrued	1,955,931.49
	$69,352,268.23

LIABILITIES

Net Re-assurance Reserve	$58,066,273.08
Instalment Claims Reserve	355,871.00
Contingent Reserve	500,000.00
Staff Savings and Benefit Fund	68,667.62
Claims in course of settlement	520,363.50
Surrender Values claimable on policies subject to revival	271,696.00
Dividends to Policyholders in course of payment	455,693.42
Dividends allotted to Deferred Dividend policies issued on and after 1st January, 1911	314,175.00
Taxes on premiums accrued and payable in 1920	119,952.62
Due on account of General Expenses	23,556.55
Annuity Payments outstanding	36,589.71
Premiums and Interest paid in advance	154,204.56
Shareholders' Account	351,932.26
Items in Suspense	3,602.55
Capital Stock paid up	1,000,000.00
Surplus (including Dividends to policyholders payable during 1920, $2,515,000.00)	7,187,736.42
	$69,352,268.23

C. R. ACRES,   HERBERT C. COX,
       Secretary.   *President and General Manager.*

BOARD OF DIRECTORS

The following Directors were elected for the year 1920:—

HERBERT C. COX   ·   ·   ·   PRESIDENT AND GENERAL MANAGER.
E. R. WOOD   ·   ·   ·   VICE-PRESIDENT.

ROBERT BICKERDIKE, M.P.
ADAM BROWN.
ALEXANDER BRUCE, K.C.
BRIG.-GEN. THE HON. SIR J. M. GIBSON, K.C.M.G.
ROBERT STUART.
DR. JOHN HOSKIN, K.C.

HON. SIR JAMES A. LOUGHEED, K.C M.G., SENATOR.
KENNETH MACKENZIE.
LEIGHTON McCARTHY, K.C.
WM. B. MEIKLE.
J. H. PLUMMER, D.C.L.
H. A. RICHARDSON.

F. LEM. GRASETT, M.B., EDIN. UNIV., F.R.C.S., E.

A REMARKABLE INSURANCE RECORD

ANNUAL REPORT AND STATEMENTS
OF THE
SUN LIFE ASSURANCE COMPANY OF CANADA*

The Directors' Annual Report for the Year 1919.
The outstanding feature of the Company's business for the past year has been a growth and development far in excess of that of any previous year, and surpassing, in some respects, even the highest expectations of your Directors and officers. Conditions were unusually favourable for the writing of new business and the conservation of that already on the books. For the first time in the history of the Company, the applications for new assurances exceeded a hundred million dollars ($100,336,848.37). New policies issued and paid for in cash were 38,774 for $86,548,849.44, an advance of $34,957,457.40 over the figures for the preceding year.

The business in force now stands at 223,622 policies for $416,358,462.05, a gain of $75,548,805.92, or twenty-two per cent. These figures reflect the prosperity prevailing throughout the country, and are evidence also of the high quality of the Company's business. This is further emphasized by the fact that there has been a considerable reduction in the number and amount of policies kept in force under the Company's automatic non-forfeiture provision, and a decrease also in the amount due on such policies.

During the year an arrangement was completed for the re-assurance of the Provincial Life Assurance Company, with outstanding policies amounting to $3,989,423.00. This business was secured on a basis which will benefit the policyholders both of this Company and of the Provincial Company. The income from premiums, interest, rents and other sources amounted to $25,704,201.10, an increase of $4,053,101.41 over the total income for the preceding year. The reduction in the volume of annuity transactions which was so noticeable during the period of the war has now been overcome, and the receipts for last year ($2,103,318.88) show a handsome advance over the previous year.

The total payments to policyholders or beneficiaries for claims by death, maturity of endowments, surrenders, profits, etc., amounted to $12,364,651.15. The claims by death which fell in

---

*Note.—Preceding Annual Reports may be consulted in the 1911-18 Volumes of *The Canadian Annual Review*; a History of the Company will be found in the *Supplement* for 1910.

during the year, though still abnormal, were less in amount than
in the previous year, although the assurances in force were, of
course, for a much larger amount. The influenza epidemic caused
heavy losses during the early months, and a few claims, due to
the war, continued to be notified to us, but the mortality during
the later months was highly favourable. During the year profits
were paid to policyholders amounting to $1,606,503.37, the largest
dividend disbursement made by the Company to its policyholders
in any year. The undivided surplus over all liabilities and capital
stock is $8,037,440.25, the liabilities being calculated by the usual
standards of the Company, which are much more exacting than
those laid down by the Insurance Act. The Company has paid
to its policyholders or their beneficiaries since organization $91,227,-
532.30. The assets now stand at $105,711,468.27, being $8,091,-
089.42 in advance of the previous year. Never in this generation
have such favourable opportunities been presented for securing
high class and remunerative investments. Your Directors have
purchased heavily of high grade bonds, running for long terms,
and preferred stocks of our strongest corporations. The bond
investments of the Company now total $61,686,638.12 of which
$21,215,309.29 are Government securities, chiefly of the Domin-
ion of Canada, $7,687,788.02 Municipal, and $32,783,540.81 bonds
of various corporations. The remaining assets are well distributed
among the various forms of investment permitted under the Insurance Act.

It is a gratification to your Directors to present a report showing such unusual progress and so satisfactory in other respects.

T. B. Macaulay,   S. H. Ewing,   Frederick G. Cope,
        President.   *Vice-President.*   *Secretary.*

**Report of
the Annual
Meeting
of the
Company.**   The Annual Meeting of Policyholders and Shareholders took place in the Company's Head Office
Building on Tuesday, March 2nd, 1920, at 2.30 p.m.
The President, Mr. T. B. Macaulay, occupied the
chair. Mr. Macaulay, in moving the adoption of the
Directors' Report for the year 1919, called attention to the tremendous strides the Company had made during the year and congratulated policyholders and shareholders alike upon the splendid
results achieved. The President also referred to the excellent
services rendered to the Company by the Head Office Staff and
the Agency organization, whose loyal and efficient efforts had made
possible such truly great progress. The motion for the adoption
of the report, which was seconded by Mr. S. H. Ewing, Vice-
President, was carried unanimously. The retiring members of
the Board were unanimously re-elected. At a subsequent meeting of
the Directors, Mr. T. B. Macaulay was unanimously re-elected
President, and Mr. S. H. Ewing, Vice-President for the ensuing
year.

ASSETS

(The market values given are those fixed by the Dominion Government Insurance Department).

Bonds—Government, Municipal, Railway, Gas, Electric and other bonds:

Par Value	$74,666,750.66	
Ledger Value	61,686,688.12	
Market Value	60,766,106.53	
Carried out at Market Value		$ 60,766,106.53

Stocks—Preferred and Guaranteed Stocks:

Par Value	$14,638,798.75	
Ledger Value	12,895,998.31	
Market Value	11,505,667.44	
Carried out at Market Value		11,505,667.44

Other Stocks:

Par Value	$ 3,269,838.33	
Ledger Value	3,739,971.76	
Market Value	4,389,920.00	
Carried out at Market Value		4,389,920.00
Loans on Real Estate, first mortgage		6,850,761.16
Real Estate, including Company's buildings		5,243,319.12
Loans on Company's policies (secured by reserves on same)		12,381,528.95
Premiums reported under Soldiers' and Sailors' Civil Relief Act (U.S.)		806.07
Loans on bonds and stocks		563,186.72
Cash in banks and on hand		481,652.90
Outstanding premiums (net)	$1,699,841.17	
Deferred premiums (net)	620,805.40	
		2,320,646.57
Interest due (largely since paid)		187,876.45
Interest accrued		1,058,933.64
Rents due and accrued		11,612.72
Net Assets		$105,711,468.27

LIABILITIES

Reserves on Life Policies according to the British Offices Om. (5) Table with 3½ per cent. interest on policies issued prior to December 31st, 1902, and 3 per cent. on policies issued since that date (Federal Life policies 3½ per cent.)	$79,517,517.70	
Reserves on Annuities according to the British Offices Select Annuity Tables with 3½ per cent interest	14,112,216.80	
	$93,629,734.50	
Less Reserves on policies re-assured	223,688.60	
		$ 93,406,045.90
Death Claims reported but not proved, or awaiting discharge		1,873,252.23
Extra Reserve for unreported death claims		250,000.00
Present value of Death Claims payable by instalments		685,204.48
Matured Endowments awaiting discharge		283,881.95
Annuity Claims awaiting discharge		80,973.66
Dividends to policyholders awaiting discharge		225,369.63
Profits allotted to Deferred Dividend Policies, issued on or after January 1st, 1911		90,933.28
Accumulated Credits on compound interest policies, etc.		64,799.62
Premiums paid in advance		112,587.62
Sinking Fund deposited for maturing debentures, etc.		146,473.88
Commissions, medical fees, taxes, etc., due or accrued		459,813.85
Shareholders' account, including dividends due 1st January, 1920		44,692.92
Total Liabilities		$ 97,174,028.02
Cash Surplus to policyholders by the Company's standard, as above (Including $382,554.06 payable during first three months of 1920.)		8,537,440.25
Capital subscribed, $1,000,000; paid up	$ 500,000.00	
Net Surplus over all Liabilities and capital stock	8,037,440.25	
Net Surplus over all Liabilities, except capital stock	$8,537,440.25	
		$105,711,468.27

The net surplus over all liabilities and capital stock according to the Dominion Government Standard is $9,026,596.95

INCOME

Life Premiums:

New	$ 3,584,046.35	
Renewals	13,663,710.21	
Single Premiums	686,037.98	
		$17,933,794.54

Thrift Premiums—Renewals	89,479.36
Annuities	2,103,318.88
Accident	21.18
Group Insurance	6,352.00
	$20,082,965.96
Less paid for re-assurances	63,895.96

	$ 20,019,070.00
Dividends left on deposit	2,111.79
Net Income from Interest and Rents	5,489,305.97
Net Profit on Sale of Securities	105,835.74
Receipts towards expenses on premiums advanced under non-forfeiture privilege	87,977.60
	$ 25,704,201.10

DISBURSEMENTS

Death claims, including bonuses	$4,845,060.39
Disability claims	1,070.55
Matured endowments, including bonuses	2,175,218.42
Annuity payments	1,499,502.67
Payments under guaranteed interest policies	34,734.13
Cash profits paid policyholders	1,656,334.29
Bonuses surrendered	80,441.13
Surrender values	1,367,055.05
Surrender values of matured referred dividend policies	705,234.52

	$ 12,364,651.15
Paid for claims on supplementary contracts	45,410.60
Reduction in premiums from application of dividends	91,326.32
Dividend deposits withdrawn	289.50
Dividends on capital, January and July, 1919	78,135.00
Expense account	2,119,486.91
Commissions	2,652,149.00
Medical fees	176,235.35
Taxes (exclusive of those on real estate)	348,827.53
Federal Life shareholders	26,130.25
Written off Securities of Re-Assured Companies	55,169.68
Net Adjustment in Ledger Assets due to change in value of Foreign Currencies	48,107.33

Total Disbursements	$ 17,995,899.36
Excess of Income over Disbursements	7,708,301.74
	$ 25,704,201.10

DIRECTORS AND OFFICERS

T. B. MACAULAY, F.I.A., F.A.S. - President and Managing Director
S. H. EWING - Vice-President.

ROBERT ADAIR	CHARLES R. HOSMER
W. M. BIRKS	ABNER KINGMAN
HON. RAOUL DANDURAND	H. R. MACAULAY, M.D.
J. REDPATH DOUGALL	JOHN McKERGOW
SIR HERBERT S. HOLT	JNO. W. ROSS

Actuary:
ARTHUR B. WOOD, F.I.A., F.A.S.

Secretary:
FREDERICK G. COPE

Treasurer:
E. A. MACNUTT

General Manager of Agencies:
JAMES C. TORY

Comptroller:
H. WARREN K. HALE

Legal Adviser:
J. A. EWING, K.C.

Executive Inspector:
A. B. COLVILLE:

Consulting Medical Referee:
W. F. HAMILTON, M.D.

Chief Medical Officer:
C. C. BIRCHARD. M.B.

A PROSPEROUS CANADIAN INSTITUTION

ANNUAL REPORTS AND ADDRESSES
OF
THE HOME BANK OF CANADA*

The Fifth Annual General Meeting of the Shareholders of The Home Bank of Canada was held at the Head Office of the Bank, 8 King Street West, Toronto, on Tuesday, the twenty-ninth day of June, nineteen hundred and twenty, at twelve o'clock noon. It was moved by Mr. M. J. Haney, seconded by Mr. C. E. P. McWilliams:—That the President, Mr. H. J. Daly, take the chair, and that the General Manager, Mr. J. Cooper Mason, do act as Secretary. Carried. The Secretary then read the report of the Directors, as follows:—The Directors of the Bank beg to submit to the Shareholders the Fifteenth Annual Report for the year ending the 31st of May, 1920, accompanied by a statement of the Bank's affairs and the results of the operations for the year. The net profits for that period, after making provision for bad and doubtful debts, rebate of interest on unmatured bills under discount, cost of management, etc., amount to $268,894.95. This, added to $158,-348.98 brought forward from last year, together with premium received on stock $3,787.92, makes a total sum of $431,031.85, which has been appropriated as follows:—

Four quarterly dividends at the rate of 6% per annum	$117,286.89
Government War Tax on Note Circulation	19,585.36
Reserved for Dominion Government Income War Tax	5,510.61
Reserved for adjustment of exchange rates on British and Foreign balances, and securities	25,000.00
Written off Bank Premises Account	15,000.00
Donations to Patriotic and other Funds	1,875.00
Transferred to Reserve Fund	100,000.00
Balance carried forward	146,873.99
	$431,031.85

During the year the following branches and sub-branches were opened:—

Ontario: Roncesvalles and Neepawa, Toronto; Danforth Ave. and Main St., Toronto; Angus (sub to Alliston); Galetta (sub to Arnprior); Hamilton; London East (sub to London); Sarnia; Shelburne; Windsor.

Manitoba: Bethany; Marquette (sub to Winnipeg); St. James.

Saskatchewan: Amulet (sub to Weyburn); Khedive (sub to Weyburn).

On the 1st of September last the dividend was raised from 5% to 6% per annum, as forecasted by the President at the last Annual

---

*Note.—For particulars of the 14th Annual Report see the 1918 issue of *The Canadian Annual Review*.

Meeting.   There is one change in our Directorate to be recorded.
Early in the year Mr. M. J. Haney resigned from the office of
President and retired from the Directorate, and his place was
filled by the election of Mr. H. J. Daly to the office of President, and
the vacancy on the Board by the election of Mr. J. Cooper Mason.
The regular inspections of the Head Office and Branches have been
made, and Mr. S. H. Jones, the Auditor appointed by the Shareholders, has completed his investigation and has attached his certificate to the statement herewith submitted.

**Address
by Mr.
H. J. Daly,
President of
the Bank.**
This is the first occasion that I have had the honour
of meeting a representative gathering of the Shareholders of The Home Bank of Canada as President of
their institution.   I need scarcely tell you that the
occasion is one in which I take great pride.   It is
about twenty years since I made my first banking
transaction with this institution, and, while I have always followed
its career with a special interest, and been ambitious for a closer
association with it, I had scarcely hoped to so thoroughly realize
those ambitions as to stand before you to-day in my present capacity.   I fully appreciate the honour that has come to me and the
responsibilities my position entails, and I may here give you my
assurance that my duties shall be conscientiously performed with
every respect and regard for your interests and for the welfare of
The Home Bank of Canada.

At our Annual Meeting last June, this chair was filled by Mr.
M. J. Haney, whose resignation was publicly announced early in
January.   At the last meeting of the Board of Directors, attended
by Mr. Haney, he was the recipient of expressions of regard individually from his associates in office, and we also jointly conveyed
to him a small token of our esteem in a formal address.   Many of
you here, who know Mr. Haney personally and recognize the value
of his services to the Bank, will join with me now in again extending to him a word of appreciation.

The report of our affairs before you to-day shows that, during
the twelve months of the fiscal year ending May 31st, The Home
Bank has made uniform and substantial progress.   The period has
been a prosperous one for the banks generally in spite of the economic problems that have arisen as a result of the war and the slow
and uncertain progress made towards the restoration of normal
conditions.   Business interests, and for that matter social and
political interests also, have been passing through a period of
anxiety which is shared by all thinking persons in every walk of
life.   It is a matter of congratulation that our banking system has
proved itself fundamentally sound under an abnormal strain and
has preserved the routine of business and public credit from any
indication of disturbance.

The standing of exchange is, however, a matter which must still
be viewed with some concern, as it is having an effect upon our

Mr. H. J. Daly,
President of The Home Bank of Canada

foreign trade. It presents a problem involving so many factors that no one nation has been able to approach a solution. Measures for relief must be of almost universal application, and the introduction of such measures requires a concerted movement towards adjustment between the nations that, under normal conditions, carried on an active and profitable trade between each other. As this trade was formerly based upon the understanding that the nation owing a debit balance should make settlements with the creditor nation in gold, and as the European nations have not the gold available to tender in payment of such debts, their national currency has so greatly depreciated in the exchange markets of the world as to discourage the foreign buyers and sellers from entering upon trade negotiations. We, in Canada, feel this more particularly in our trade relations with the United States because the discount upon our Canadian money there, through the world-wide relations of that Republic, largely influences the rate of exchange applying also in other European countries against Canada. The subject is becoming better understood on both sides of the line and there is a hopeful sign in the realization by the business interests of the United States that an adverse rate of exchange against Canada operates as a detriment to trade with this country.

Canada is the United States' third best customer, Great Britain being first, France second. Speaking in general terms, Canada buys twice as much in the United States as all the countries of South America combined. The publicity given to these statistics has awakened the American people to the realization of the fact that Canada is a valuable customer, while our own people have similarly become informed that the rate of exchange will advance against Canadian money in the United States proportionately as they buy American goods. We therefore have both the Canadian buyer and the American seller thoroughly informed on the mutual disadvantages of abnormal exchange, and this understanding of the situation should lead to a concerted movement to bring about a more satisfactory adjustment of our international economics.

There probably will be some temporary setback to business through the levy of taxes under the new budget. The difficulties of framing this measure of taxation are generally appreciated, as is evidenced in the willingness of business interests to meet conditions brought about by the application of the new levy. The National Debt is there, to be paid off as expeditiously as may be accomplished without disturbing the accustomed channels of industry and trade. Exports and production cannot be taxed. The presumption is that the tax may be raised from what the people can comfortably spare and what may be added to the overhead charges of the manufacturing and trade without hindering activity in these spheres. The Budget aims in these directions and will in all likelihood be ultimately brought to operate equitably in the minor features of its detail.

A third problem which confronts us is that of Labour. This

has been a vexed question for many years, but those of us who have followed its history can trace the development of a more generous spirit in the contention. It is no longer a war of class against class in this country. Education has gradually removed social antagonism and made the issue one of economics rather than class prejudice. While the prevailing scarcity of farm labour, which is viewed with alarm in the United States, might have had an effect upon agricultural production in Canada, it is a satisfaction to note that according to the Government estimate issued two weeks ago, our acreage under cultivation has not been materially reduced, although seeding was late. The Bureau of Crop Statistics in the United States has reported that while the supply of farm labour is only 72 per cent. of normal, the demand is 53 per cent. above normal. It is estimated by authorities on production in the United States that there is a shortage of 24,000,000 wheat acres in that country, therefore our own estimated shortage of 2,205,000 wheat acres for all Canada is not an unfavourable comparison. When it is remembered that our farmers have to contend with the same awkward conditions that restrict agricultural production in the United States the prospects indicated by the crop estimate show that they have done exceptionally well. Moreover, there appears to be a general increase in acreage for grains other than wheat. The Government estimates have later been supplemented by crop observers in the Provinces of Manitoba, Saskatchewan and Alberta, and their forecasts are even more favourable than the prospects as outlined by the Government schedules.

On the whole we may felicitate ourselves that as a Nation, Canada stands in an exceptionally favourable position. We have a vast extent of territory, much of it practically unexploited while large areas that are thinly populated are readily accessible by rail communication. We have all the facilities for settling desirable immigration and wherever new sections have been opened unexpected natural resources have been uncovered. With our heritage of undeveloped resources and active, healthy-minded people intent upon the solution of economic difficulties, we should assume a position of leadership in the industrial world. We have no serious handicaps to retard our development. When we become united to increase production and the practice of the more simple forms of economy, our progress toward national wealth is assured.

Comments by Lieut.-Colonel J. Cooper Mason, D.S.O., General Manager of the Bank.   From the figures set forth in the Fifteenth Annual Statement of The Home Bank of Canada, placed in your hands to-day, you may judge that the results of our operations for the fiscal year ending May 31st, 1920, have been satisfactory. There are no exceptional statistics presented in the statement. It records a year of normal progress, the most outstanding feature of which is the Bank's favourable position with regard to the proportion of its liquid, or readily available assets, as compared with its liabilities. Approximately 20%, or to be accurate, 19·58%, of our total assets are in the form of cash; while our liquid assets amount to more than half, or 51·73%, of our liabilities to the public, which includes our notes in circulation at the close of the fiscal year, with deposits on that date and the interest thereon; amounts due the Government, and balances due to other Canadian and foreign banks.

This percentage of liquid assets against liabilities has been arrived at by a very conservative estimate of our securities and holdings in this class, so that the proportion of almost 52% is to be read in its true significance as representing a most favourable situation of our affairs. The 1919 Victory Loan was raised during our year's operations and the subscriptions contributed by depositors and customers of the Bank has been reflected in our deposits. The amount of subscriptions actually passing through the Bank to the Victory Loan were $4,843,450, and we have during the period since that loan has been closed recovered the amount that was withdrawn for subscriptions, and actually increased our deposits by $1,099,-830.91. This increase applies to deposits from the public for accounts bearing interest and accounts not bearing interest, and does not include deposits of the Dominion Government. Our net earnings represent 13·72% on Paid-up Capital, or 11·40% on Paid-up Capital and Reserve. Although our operating expenses have been heavily increased, without any proportionate increase being available for advanced rates for loans, our net earnings for the year amount to $268,894.95, showing an increase over last year of $30,141.07.

At our last year's Annual Meeting the announcement was made that a Bond Department had been established at our Toronto Office. After thirteen months of operation the results of the business transacted in this department have completely justified its establishment. It has rendered a needed service to our customers who may contemplate investing in Government War Loan, Victory, or other high-class securities, or who may desire information upon any securities of this form. The service of this department has been made available to all our Branches, and its scope has been greatly broadened during the latter half of the past fiscal year.

Our Department of Foreign Exchange, which was also inaugurated about the time of the last Annual Meeting, has also proved its usefulness and productivity during the past twelve months. In this department we have fully realized our anticipations conveyed to you in our message of the last Annual Meeting. Demobilization was generally completed April, 1919, and since that time our returned men have been pretty well all returned to their former or to other appointments in the service of the Bank. During their absence Overseas they had been retained on the staff register, and have therefore been placed on the same basis of remuneration as though their service with the Home Bank had been continuous.

It has been very satisfactory to note that in spite of the great change in environment our Overseas men have taken up their civilian vocations without any apparent difficulty. Some manifestations of restlessness might have been expected but these have been exceptionally few. In every instance the Overseas men have resumed the practice of banking with increased enthusiasm, and a broadening of their abilities. Special thanks are due to the staff which carried on our banking operations during the period of the war. We were under the necessity of working short-handed, although business was abnormal in its detail. We now have ten branches in Toronto, and with the opening of a new branch on Yonge Street, near Bloor, at an early date, we will have eleven branches in this city.

AUDITOR'S REPORT TO THE SHAREHOLDERS

In accordance with sub-sections 19 and 20 of section 56 of the Bank Act, 1913, I beg to report as follows: The foregoing balance sheet has been examined with the books and vouchers at the Head Office, and with the certified returns from the Branches, and is in accordance therewith. I have obtained all needed information from the officers of the Bank, and in my opinion the transactions coming under my notice have been within the powers of the Bank. I have checked the cash and verified the securities of the Bank, at its chief office, both on the 31st of May, 1920, and also at another time during the year; the cash and securities of one of the Branches have also been checked, and in each case they have agreed with the entries in the books of the Bank with regard thereto. In my opinion, the above balance sheet is properly drawn up so as to show a true and correct view of the state of the Bank's affairs, according to the best of my information and the explanations given to me, and as shown by the books of the Bank.

SYDNEY H. JONES, Auditor.

DIRECTORS ELECTED FOR 1920.

President.	Vice-President
H. J. DALY	R. P. GOUGH

C. A. BARNARD, K.C.   LT.-COL. CLARENCE F. SMITH

HON. A. CLAUDE MACDONELL, K.C.

S. CASEY WOOD   J. AMBROSE O'BRIEN
J. COOPER MASON   FRANK J. B. RUSSELL

OFFICERS.

Inspector:	General Manager:	Chief Accountant:
E. A. KEMP	J. COOPER MASON	O. G. SMITH

Capital Authorised $5,000,000.00
Capital Subscribed, $2,000,000; Paid-up 1,959,073.41
Rest 500,000.00

THE HOME BANK OF CANADA

GENERAL STATEMENT 31ST MAY, 1920.

LIABILITIES.

TO THE PUBLIC—

Notes of the Bank in circulation	$ 1,975,780.00
Deposits not bearing interest	5,002,741.70
Deposits bearing interest, including interest accrued to date of Statement	15,570,158.07
Deposits by and balances due to Dominion Government	3,668,102.56
Balances due to other Banks in Canada	6,448.06
Balances due to Banks and Banking Correspondents in the United Kingdom	80,550.82
Balances due to Banks and Banking Correspondents elsewhere than in Canada and the United Kingdom	544,074.70
	$26,847,855.91

TO THE SHAREHOLDERS—

Capital (subscribed $2,000,000) paid up	$ 1,959,073.41	
Rest Account	500,000.00	
Dividends unclaimed	2,275.53	
Dividend No. 54 (quarterly), being at the rate of 6% per annum, payable June 1st, 1920	29,386.23	
Balance of Profit and Loss Account	146,873.99	
		2,637,609.16
		$29,485,465.07

ASSETS.

Gold and other current coin	$ 183,668.19	
Dominion Government Notes	3,742,564.50	
		$ 3,926,232.69
Deposit with the Minister of Finance as Security for note circulation		105,000.00
Notes of other Banks		392,320.94
Cheques on other Banks		1,338,728.75
Balances due by other Banks in Canada		116,974.88
Due from Banks and Banking Correspondents in the United Kingdom		99,764.20
Balances due by Banks and Banking Correspondents elsewhere than in Canada and the United Kingdom		797,274.99
Dominion and Provincial Government Securities not exceeding market value		1,902,091.14
Canadian Municipal Securities, and British, Foreign and Colonial Public Securities other than Canadian		1,550,903.12
Railway and other Bonds, Debentures and Stocks, not exceeding market value		1,214,524.39
Call and Short (not exceeding 30 days) Loans in Canada on Bonds, Debentures and Stocks		2,445,690.02
		$13,889,505.07
Other Current Loans and Discounts in Canada, less rebate of interest		13,986,605.71
Other Loans and Discounts elsewhere than in Canada		24,786.03
Loans to Cities, Towns, Municipalities and School Districts		260,364.22
Overdue Debts		63,013.70
Real Estate other than Bank Premises		62,939.88
Mortgages on Real Estate sold by the Bank		105,497.14
Bank Premises at not more than cost, less amounts written off		1,030,553.44
Other assets not included under the foregoing		62,197.88
		$29,485,465.07

H. J. DALY,
President.

J. COOPER MASON,
General Manager.

A LEADING CANADIAN INSTITUTION

ADDRESSES AND REPORTS
OF THE
TORONTO GENERAL TRUSTS CORPORATION*

The Thirty-eighth Annual Meeting of the Shareholders of The Toronto General Trusts Corporation was held in the Board Room of the Corporation's Head Office, corner of Bay and Melinda Streets, Toronto, on Wednesday, the 4th day of February 1920. The President, Hon. Featherston Osler, K.C., D.C.L., took the chair, and Mr. W. G. Watson, Assistant General Manager, acted as Secretary of the Meeting. Mr. A. D. Langmuir, General Manager, submitted and commented upon the financial statements showing the operations of the Corporation for the year ended 31st December, 1919.

Remarks by the Hon. Featherston Osler, K.C., D.C.L., President of the Corporation. The Profit and Loss statement and the statement of Assets and Liabilities which have been placed in the hands of the Shareholders inform them more pointedly than any extended explanation of mine could do of the remarkable growth and solidity of the business of the Corporation. The volume of the assets in their charge and under their management now exceeds $101,000,000, an increase of assets over those shown in the preceding year of over $10,000,000. The paid-up capital and reserve are represented by the figures of $3,500,000, and a substantial increase in the earnings of the year has enabled the Directors, after providing for an inevitable increase in the expense of management, to maintain the usual dividend of 10% and to pay, in addition, a half yearly bonus of one per cent., and to carry forward a balance of $265,529. The Directors thought it desirable to carry forward this balance instead of transferring any part of it to the Reserve Fund which already exceeds the Capital Account by $500,000.

Many of us, no doubt, have observed that the Legislature, prompted probably by exposures of mismanagement in the care of some institution, has endeavoured to protect the public by certain requirements designed for the greater security of shareholders and investors. In substance all these requirements had already been observed in the ordinary business of this Corporation and, so far as they were merely formal, have occasioned us no inconvenience beyond the additional labour imposed upon the staff. The continued confidence of the public in the adminis-

*Note.—For particulars of the 37th Annual Report see *Supplement* to the 1918 Volume of *The Canadian Annual Review.*

MR. A. D. LANGMUIR
General Manager of The Toronto General Trusts Corporation.

tration of estates by the Corporation is illustrated by the increase in the number of estates placed in its charge, and this is a subject to which I again invite the attention of the Shareholders, every one of whom, if satisfied by 'the result in his own case with the management of the Corporation, can aid in extending its business and increase its influence.

I cannot, without regret, refer to the loss the Corporation and the Board sustained during the year by the death of the late Mr. W. D. Matthews, whose advice and assistance were much valued by the Board. The illness of another Director, the late Senator McLaren (resulting in his death) and the distance he lived from Toronto, prevented him from giving that assistance which his business experience could otherwise have offered. The places of these two Directors were filled by His Honour the Lieutenant-Governor, Lionel H. Clarke, and Mr. Robert Hobson, of Hamilton.

Address by A. D. Langmuir, General-Manager of the Corporation. It is with a great deal of pleasure and no little amount of pride that your Directors are to-day able to report to you that we have succeeded, during the past year, in registering another milestone in the history of the Corporation, in the fact that our assets have now crossed the One Hundred Million Dollar mark. In this connection it is interesting to note that it took thirty-one years to acquire the first Fifty Million Dollars of assets, and only seven years to accumulate the second Fifty Million. While it has taken thirty-eight years to accomplish this result, in doing so there is another factor to be taken into consideration which is, that in building up this large Trust Estate business, the policy of the management of the Corporation from its inception has been dictated by a high sense of its paramount obligations as a Trustee. It has not used its high power except as incidental to the purpose for which it was created. It has not risked its character and capital or its fiduciary interests by assuming business of a hazardous nature, but has consistently endeavoured in all its aims and undertakings to build up a reputation that would inspire the confidence of the public, and establish the fact that a responsible and well-organized Trust Company—in preference to an individual—is the safest, most economical, and in every other way, the most satisfactory Executor or Trustee to administer estates, and invest and manage Trust funds.

Trust Companies were brought into existence primarily because of the difficulty in obtaining Trustees and Executors having sufficient time at their disposal to accept such responsible positions, and also because even if such people could be found, there was no certainty of permanency. Such reasons hold good just as strongly to-day as ever before; in fact one might say even more so. To-day business men in all walks of life, recognize that a new era has opened up in the world's history. During the year great things have been accomplished as a result of the efforts for a reconstruction of old time methods and understandings, and as a consequence of these new conditions, the time, attention and consideration of individuals towards their own personal affairs will be required more than ever. Primarily the functions of Trust Companies may be described under two categories:—

(a) Those relating to the management and realization of estates, payment of debts, etc., which, speaking generally, are the duties of an Executor.

(b) Those relating to the care, management and investment of Trust funds, which are the duties of a Trustee.

Under the first come such duties as renting houses, making collections, repairs, placing insurance, paying taxes, effecting sales of real estate, realizing assets, conducting businesses, etc., etc., and the distribution of Capital and Income to beneficiaries. And in the second case, the investment and management of Trust funds, collection and disbursement of income, pending the arrival of the period when the distribution of Capital takes place in accordance with the terms of the Will or Trust Deed under which the Trust Company acts. In the selection of an Executor, Trustee, or Agent to fill these duties, too much importance may be given by the person considering the appointment of a Trustee, to the matter of charges for compensation, inasmuch as such fees are not different from those that are allowed by the Courts to individuals. The important point to be determined by the Testator or Settlor is that in the selection of his Trustee he may feel assured that he has fully protected the interests of his family and estate, and that such Trustee can be faithfully relied upon to carry out the conditions and terms of the Will or Trust Settlement Deed. In this connection it should be remembered that a Corporate Executor and Trustee in touch with the market at all times, and being in a position to acquire investments in large amounts, may frequently effect a considerable increase in the revenue of the estate in this way, as well as make advantageous sales of assets that would go a long way in offsetting the Trust Company's remuneration.

While on this subject it will be of interest to the public to learn that the Public Trustee in England, whose fees a few years ago, were fixed at what was considered a cost basis, has found that, in order to take care of the bare expenses of the Department, the charges for the administration of Estates, care and management of Trusts, etc. must be very considerably increased. In his published report for the year ended the 31st of March, 1919, he shows a deficiency of £52,990 or, in other words, that the expenses of his department exceeded his income in one year, on the basis of the fees fixed, by nearly $250,000. It is now found necessary to very greatly increase the original tariff of fees under which it was hoped that the Department might be administered; indeed the suggested new rates, together with the cost to the estates of the work that is farmed out to real estate and other agents, in accordance with their practice, and the charges made for special services such as inspecting property, registration and enquiry fees, etc., will, as we estimate, bring the cost to the estates under the care and management of the Public Trustee up to a figure that will exceed the cost of administering similar estates in Canada under our Trust Company system. The report of the special Committee appointed by the Lord Chancellor to enquire into the organization of the office of the Public Trustee in England, as recently presented to Parliament, provides interesting information on the subject of estate administration, as well as upon the cost connected therewith.

In the administration of a large volume of assets comprised of almost every class of security in which are interested a great number of people, it would not be surprising if differences of opinion sometimes arose between Trustees and beneficiaries in the construction of documents, or in respect to matters of detail connected with the administration of some estates. Such instances, I am glad to say in the experience of the Corporation, have been very few in number.

At the date of our last Annual General Meeting of Shareholders, an Armistice had been arranged between those conflicting antagonists who for over four years had been carrying on a War, the nature of which had never previously been experienced in the world's history. A full year has since elapsed during which interval protracted negotiations have been carried on by the representatives of the nations interested, looking to an arrangement for a settlement of peace terms and conditions that would insure safety and tranquility for future generations. It is a cause for thankfulness to know at this time that such arrangements have been completed, and the Treaty signed, and that the nations of the world may again resume their peaceful pursuits. Concurrently with these negotiations, the world has been undergoing a period of unrest, a result no doubt of the War, and the culmination of those differences which have racked the social and industrial life of the world, and which gave so much dissatisfaction before the War, and indeed are still causing anxiety in our financial, social and industrial life. Nevertheless, great strides have been made during this year of reconstruction towards finding solutions of these difficulties through the good common sense exercised by those saner representatives of the contending interests, who realize that we have entered upon a new era in the world's history; that a new state of society exists having different ideals, and with a very much broader and more generous appreciation of the requirements and necessities of that class of our people who form the greatest bulk of humanity, and upon whose industry and contentment the happiness of the world is dependent. It is to be hoped when our next Annual Meeting takes place that the world will again have become normal, producing the necessaries of life and materials that are so absolutely essential to relieve the burden of debt which has been inherited as a result of four years of destruction.

The Estate Assets now under management of the Corporation aggregate the large sum of $87,763,834.26. Of this amount, investments have been made by the Corporation to the extent of $26,831,455.33. The character of these investments is set forth in the Assets and Liabilities statement, and the balance of the Estate assets is comprised of securities in the original state of investment or condition in which they were taken over, amounting to $59,878,042.27, and are of the following nature:—

Mortgages	$ 6,188,573.29
Stocks and Bonds	35,932,750.83
Real Estate	14,147,787.90
Miscellaneous Securities	3,608,930.25
	$59,878,042.27

In most cases, in connection with these original assets, authority is vested in the Corporation by the terms of the documents under which we act, to retain or realize upon them as the Corporation in its discretion may determine. Of course this is a very great responsibility requiring close and constant attention to all the different classes of securities affected. In some instances, the Corporation's responsibility in exercising this discretion depends on receiving the consent of certain of the beneficiaries interested. It might be interesting to mention that realizations on account of original assets were made during the year just closed of the following classes of securities:—

Real Estate	$1,412,233.94
Mortgages	1,427,731.63
Stocks, Bonds and Debentures	5,861,094.27
Miscellaneous Assets	1,190,513.44
	$9,891,573.28

The investments negotiated by the Corporation now aggregate the large sum of $39,213,884.21, being an increase over the preceding year of $3,418,236.15. While during the past year there has been evidence of an improved demand for mortgage loans, the repayments made continue abnormally large, but with the tide of immigration again commencing to flow towards Canada, and building operations becoming more active, a very substantial improvement should be experienced in the demand for this class of investment. In this connection, however, too great caution cannot be exercised at the present time, in scrutinizing values placed upon farm lands in the Western Provinces. With the high prices prevailing for farm products at the present time, and the inflow of people from the South with greatly enlarged ideas of farm land values, an enormous expansion in values is taking place in these Provinces as a result of such influences; and while at the present prices of farm produce such values might be upheld, judging by past experience, we must in time look for more normal conditions, and very considerably reduced prices for all those commodities, the sale of which, at the present time, is bringing to our farmer friends such substantial profits.

With regard to real estate conditions which have prevailed throughout Ontario during the year 1919, I may say that not for many years has there been such an active demand for residential property, due of course entirely to the lack of building during the War period. Every advantage was taken of these conditions to dispose of estate properties which were held for sale by the Corporation. With regard to business property conditions were not so favourable, particularly in the early part of the year, and some difficulty was experienced in keeping space fully occupied. A distinct improvement developed during the year, however, so that at the close of 1919, there was little or no warehouse or office space available in Toronto for rent. The indications are that this coming year, in view of the difficulty in finding suitable locations, an active market may be looked for in all branches of real estate.

Our plan of Guaranteed Investment has met with much favour during the past year, the amount entrusted to the Corporation for investment in this plan having increased over that of last year by $1,290,675.61. I have no hesitation in recommending this form of investment to all people who have surplus funds for investment. The rate of interest return is equivalent or better than that received from Dominion of Canada War Bonds, and investors are relieved from all care and responsibility of any description in connection with the investment.

It was then moved by Mr. Herbert Langlois, seconded by Mr. Roderick MacLennan, and resolved that the following Shareholders be and the same are hereby appointed Directors for the current year, namely: Hamilton Cassels, K.C., LL.D.; His Hon. Lionel H. Clarke; Hon. W. C. Edwards; Wellington Francis, K.C.; Brig.-Gen. Sir John M. Gibson, K.C., K.C.M.G., LL.D.; Arthur C. Hardy; Robert Hobson; John Hoskin, K.C., LL.D.; Lieut.-Col. R. W. Leonard; Thomas Long; J. Bruce Macdonald; Hon. Sir Daniel H. McMillan, K.C.M.G.; Lieut.-Col. John F. Michie; E. T. Malone, K.C.; Sir Edmund B. Osler; Hon. Featherston Osler, K.C., D.C.L.; J. G. Scott, K.C.; Sir Edmund Walker, C.V.O., LL.D., D.C.L.; E. C. Whitney; H. H. Williams. At a subsequent meeting of the Directors the following officers were elected:—President, the Hon. Featherston Osler, K.C., D.C.L.; Vice-Presidents, Hamilton Cassels, K.C., LL.D., and Brig.-Gen. Sir John M. Gibson, K.C., K.C.M.G., LL.D. The Inspection Committee was re-elected, namely: Hamilton Cassels, K.C. LL.D., Chairman; Brig.-Gen. Sir John M. Gibson, K.C., K.C.M.G., and Wellington Francis, K.C. The following members were elected to the Advisory Boards at Ottawa, Winnipeg and Vancouver:

Ottawa—W. D. Hogg, K.C., Chairman; Sir George Burn, Nelson D. Porter and Alexander Maclaren.

Winnipeg—Hon. Sir Daniel H. McMillan, K.C.M.G., Chairman; H. H. Smith, W. H. Cross, and Frederick T. Griffin.

Vancouver—A. H. Macneill, K.C., Chairman; Eric W. Hamber, F. B. Pemberton, and R. P. Butchart.

STATEMENT FOR YEAR ENDED 31st DECEMEER, 1919

ASSETS

Capital Account:—

Mortgages on Real Estate	$ 1,947,240.85	
Government and Municipal Debentures	401,065.37	
Loans on Debentures, Stocks and Bonds	279,750.31	
Loans or Advances to Trust Estates and Guaranteed Mortgage Accounts under Administration by the Corporation	376,987.50	

Real Estate:—

Office Premises and Safe Deposit
Vaults at Toronto and Ottawa $725,000.00
Accrued Rents re Offices and Vaults
at Toronto and Ottawa 4,975.22

	729,975.22	
Cash on hand and in Banks	147,618.42	
		$ 3,882,637.67

Guaranteed Account:—

Mortgages on Real Estate	$ 7,045,987.67	
Government and Municipal Debentures	2,240,597.18	
Loans on Debentures, Stocks and Bonds	90,800.00	
Cash on hand and in Banks	99,174.73	
		$ 9,476,559.58

Estates, Trusts and Agencies:—

Mortgages on Real Estate	$ 13,521,364.92	
Government and Municipal Debentures	11,053,176.32	
Stocks and Bonds	1,273,711.56	
Loans on Debentures, Stocks and Bonds	983,302.53	
Sundry Assets	4,965.84	
Cash on hand and in Banks	1,049,370.82	
	$ 27,885,791.99	

Original Assets, including Real Estate, Mortgages, Debentures, Stocks and Bonds, etc., at Inventory Value	59,878,042.27	
		$ 87,763,834.26

Total	$101,123,031.51

LIABILITIES

Capital Account:—

Capital Account	$1,500,000.00	
Reserve Fund	2,000,000.00	
		$ 3,500,000.00

Dividend No. 94 due January 2nd, 1920	$ 37,500.00	
Bonus of One per cent. payable January 2nd, 1920	15,000.00	
	52,500.00	
Interest in Reserve	35,000.00	
Appropriation for Federal Income Tax and Sundry Accounts	29,608.65	
Profit and Loss	265,529.02	
		$ 3,882,637.67

Guaranteed Account:—

Guaranteed Funds for Investment	$ 9,476,559.58	
		9,476,559.58

Estates, Trusts and Agencies:—

Trust Funds for Investment or Distribution	$ 27,885,791.99	
Inventory Value of Original Assets of Estates and Agencies under administration by the Corporation	59,878,042.27	
		87,763,834.26

Total	$101,123,031.51

COMPARATIVE STATEMENT

Showing the growth of Assets under the care of the Corporation during the last Nineteen Years

1900	$ 16,047,394.97	1910	$ 41,601,297.63
1901	19,236,224.55	1911	45,086,659.99
1902	19,988,827.45	1912	53,852,564.15
1903	21,054,495.09	1913	63,055,883.97
1904	22,747,029.78	1914	67,421,090.99
1905	29,096,478.11	1915	71,869,470.10
1906	31,408,279.39	1916	77,180,513.63
1907	32,909,902.68	1917	83,286,782.89
1908	35,161,646.79	1918	90,832,629.80
1909	37,881,113.53	1919	101,123,031.51

CANADA AS A PRODUCER OF MOTOR CARS

THE INDUSTRY ASSUMES LARGE PROPORTIONS

ENTERPRISE REFLECTED AT OVERLAND FACTORIES

A resume of the progress of the motor car industry in Canada may fittingly find a place in the *Canadian Annual Review*. Those who are interested in Canadian industrial advancement may take special pride in the strides made by motor car manufacturers. In the United States no industry has grown with such leaps and bounds as that of the making of automobiles, and in Canada the same industry is showing like progress.

That the market in this country justifies the investment of millions of dollars in the motor car industry is evidenced by the fact that Canada has now reached second place among the world's motorized nations, having in use one automobile to every twenty-six persons. The tremendous possibilities in the industry are only realized when it is remembered that this condition has been attained in a comparatively few years. In 1909 there were only 4,711 motor cars registered in the Dominion: last year—just ten years later—the number had increased to 334,190. Last year's registrations were 64,437 more than the previous year's; and this year the number of new cars will doubtless pass the hundred-thousand mark.

In this market of unlimited potentialities, it is natural that the preponderance of demand is for light cars; and as the popularity and general utility of the automobile increases, the ratio of light cars to the more expensive styles will also increase. Recognizing this condition as having already arrived, at least one company in Canada has devoted its entire plant to the making of a light car. This is Willys-Overland Limited, of Toronto, whose factories are operating on a basis of quantity production.

In this connection, it is a matter of further gratification to know that a Canadian industry can accomplish, in so comparatively short a time, what has been done in the Overland factories in West Toronto. In the summer of 1919 this company started at zero, and within a year of the production of its first car it will have on the roads of Canada, scattered throughout every province, no less than 8,000 cars of this one model, while its production will have reached the rate of 15,000 a year.

It is a story of industrial progress unsurpassed in the annals of manufacturing in this country, if not in America. When the last issue of the *Canadian Annual Review* was compiled, Willys-Overland Limited were in the throes of transforming their plant from a war-time to a peace-time basis. During the war the factories had been devoted entirely to the manufacture of munitions and airplane engines. In the latter, the company is credited by the British authorities with having contributed more to the development of the Sunbeam Arab engine than any other concern in the Empire. When the war ended, this expert mechanical work also came to an end; but, with a promptness that reflects the business genius of Canadian industrial leaders, plans were executed whereby the factories were re-equipped for the manufacture of automobiles.

By September of 1919 the company was able to work into actual production, and the reception of the new light car known as the "Overland Four" was so favourable that an almost immediate demand was created far in excess of what the company could hope to supply in many months. With the coming of spring the cars were on roads everywhere, and the stories of the success of "Triplex" Springs in giving the new Overland a riding comfort that marked the greatest advancement in motor car manufacture since the introduction of pneumatic tires increased this demand. The result has been that the company's enterprise was so rewarded that a production of fifty cars a day was reached early in the summer. Only by employing 1,500 men, and utilizing the most modern manufacturing methods, this mass-production was made possible. With it all, the company exercised a most scrupulous care in the selection and inspection of raw materials, so as to ensure quality in the product.

Incidentally, it is interesting to note that the development of this splendid organization has resulted in the establishment of several new Canadian industries. For instance, prior to the Overland programme there had been no facilities in this country for the production of pressed steel, and the new stamping machines that turn out equipment for Overland cars have set a new standard in Canada. Other new industries contributory to the Overland product included plants at Welland, St. Catharines, Walkerville, Oshawa, Orillia and Toronto. It is quite within the bounds of reasonable expectation that an industry which has proved itself like that of Willys-Overland Limited will call for constant extensions, and will prove one of the big factors in the general industrial development of the Dominion.

Bird's Eye View of Willys-Overland Factories and Head Office at West Toronto

ADVERTISEMENTS

908

910

911

914

The National City Company
Limited

Bonds and Investment Securities

Canadian Headquarters
74 Notre Dame Street W., Montreal

10 King St. E., Toronto, Ont.   McCurdy Building, Halifax, N.S.

915

Canadian General Electric Co., Limited

Manufacturers and Distributors of

Electrical Apparatus, Supplies and Automotive Equipment

General Offices : King and Simcoe Streets, Toronto

FACTORIES:

Peterboro, Ontario   -   Toronto, Ontario

MAZDA and Carbon Lamp Works:

TORONTO   -   -   -   ONTARIO

Canadian Allis-Chalmers, Limited

Engineers, Iron and Brassfounders
Boilermakers, Shipbuilders

Designers and Builders of

MARINE ENGINES   CENTRIFUGAL PUMPS
LOCOMOTIVE   MARINE BOILERS
BILGE AND FEED PUMPS   STRUCTURAL STEEL
STEERING ENGINES   EDWARDS AIR PUMPS
FLOUR MILL MACHINERY

Architectural Bronze and Iron Work
Blast Furnaces and Heavy Machinery

FACTORIES:

Toronto, Ont.   Bridgeburg, Ont.
Montreal, Que.   Stratford, Ont.

Architectural Bronze and Iron Works:

TORONTO   -   -   -   ONTARIO

Prue Cottons

For all Industrial and Domestic Purposes

Dominion Textile Company, Limited

MONTREAL   TORONTO   WINNIPEG

920

The Life of Pasteur

By

A. Vallery-Radot

With an introduction by
Sir William Osler, Bart., M.D., F.R.S.

Louis Pasteur is known to the world for his epoch making scientific discoveries. His life story is among the most fascinating in the history of science. As a man he was one of the most beautiful personalities the world has ever known. It is in identifying the man and his work that makes this book an achievement and merits the dictum of the London TIMES that the book is "the greatest biography of our age."

Price $4.00 Postpaid

Life and Times of
Sir Alexander Tilloch Galt

By

Oscar Douglas Skelton

Few among the makers of Canada played so varied a part in her upbuilding as Alexander Tilloch Galt. Throughout the formative period of our national history, he played a part of lasting significance to the Canada and the Canadians of after days. The forces that shaped the life and the destiny of the Canada of the days before Confederation, and the new Canada of the first years after, are nowhere more fully displayed than in his manifold interests and achievements.

Price $4.00 Postpaid

S. B. GUNDY   TORONTO

Distinctive Canadian Books

FICTION

The Forging of the Pikes
By Anison North

The Prairie Mother
By Arthur Stringer

The Blower of Bubbles
By Arthur Beverley Baxter

The Touch of Abner
By H. A. Cody

Mist of Morning
By Isabel Ecclestone Mackay

Joan at Halfway
By Grace McLeod Rogers

Janet of Kootenay
By Evah McKowan

Golden Dicky
By Marshall Saunders

The Sky Pilot in No Man's Land
By Ralph Connor

Bulldog Carney
By W. A. Fraser

Sister Anne! Sister Anne!!
By Gertrude Arnold

In Orchard Glen
By Marian Keith

BIOGRAPHY

Reminiscences, Political and Personal
By Sir John Willison

The Grey Nuns in the Far North
By Father P. Duchaussois, O.M.I.

The Lady With the Other Lamp
The Story of Blanche Read Johnston as told to Mary Morgan Dean

Forty Years in Canada
By Major-General S. B. Steele

TRAVEL

Wild Life in Canada
By Capt. Angus Buchanan, M.C.

New Rivers of the North
By Hulbert Footner

The New North
By Agnes Dean Cameron

Among the Canadian Alps
By Lawrence J. Burpee, F.R.G.S.

POETRY

Canadian Singers and Their Songs
Edited by Edward S. Caswell

Canadian Poets
Edited by John W. Garvin

Canadian Poems of the Great War
Edited by John W. Garvin

A Canadian Twilight and Other Poems
By Bernard Freeman Trotter

Dr. Drummond's Complete Poems
Also individual volumes: The Habitant; Johnny Corteau; The Voyageur; Etc.

ESSAYS and MISCELLANEOUS

The Girl of the New Day
By Ellen M. Knox

Legends of Vancouver
By E. Pauline Johnson

Platform Sketches
By Jessie Alexander

Standard Canadian Reciter
Edited by Donald G. French

Optimism and Other Sermons
By Robert Law, D.D.

HISTORY and PIONEER LIFE

Confederation and Its Leaders
By M. O. Hammond

Old Days on the Farm
By A. C. Wood

Building the North
By J. B. MacDougall

McClelland & Stewart, Limited
Publishers   215-219 Victoria St.   Toronto, Canada

CPSIA information can be obtained
at www.ICGtesting.com
Printed in the USA
BVHW07*1000180918
527708BV00025B/207/P

9 780331 506396